The Animal Ethics Reader

The Animal Ethics Reader is an acclaimed anthology containing both classic and contemporary readings, making it ideal for anyone coming to the subject for the first time. It provides a thorough introduction to the central topics, controversies and ethical dilemmas surrounding the treatment of animals, covering a wide range of contemporary issues, such as animal activism, genetic engineering, and environmental ethics.

The extracts are arranged thematically under the following clear headings:

- Theories of Animal Ethics
- Animal Capacities: Pain, Emotion and Consciousness
- Primates and Cetaceans
- Animals for Food
- Animal Experimentation
- Animals and Biotechnology
- Ethics and Wildlife
- Zoos and Aquariums
- Animal Companions
- Animal Law and Animal Activism.

Readings from leading experts in the field including Peter Singer, Daniel C. Dennett and Bernard E. Rollin are featured, as well as selections from Donald Griffin, Marc Bekoff, Jane Goodall, Temple Grandin, Barbara Orlans, Tom Regan, and Baird Callicott. Classic extracts are well balanced with contemporary selections, helping to present the latest developments in the field.

This revised and updated second edition includes new readings on animal consciousness, anthropomorphism, farm animals, vegetarianism, biotechnology and cloning.

Featuring contextualizing introductions by the editors, study questions and further reading suggestions at the end of each chapter, this will be essential reading for any student taking a course in the subject.

With a foreword by Bernard E. Rollin.

Susan J. Armstrong is Professor Emerita and 2004 Outstanding Professor at Humboldt State University and has published widely on this and affiliated subjects.

Richard G. Botzler is Professor of Wildlife, also at Humboldt State University, and a leading published expert in the field. Together they have also edited *Environmental Ethics: Divergence and Convergence* (2004).

The Animal Ethics Reader

Second Edition

Edited by

Susan J. Armstrong and Richard G. Botzler

Routledge
Taylor & Francis Group

LONDON AND NEW YORK

Dedicated to:

my dear animal friends –
you know who you are

S.J.A.

Dedicated to my children:

Emilisa, Tin, Dorothy, Sarah, and Thomas,
with love and pride

R.G.B.

First published 2003
This edition published 2008
by Routledge
2 Park Square, Milton Park, Abingdon, Oxon OX14 4RN

Simultaneously published in the USA and Canada
by Routledge
711 Third Ave, New York, NY 10017

Routledge is an imprint of the Taylor & Francis Group, an informa business

© 2003, 2008 Selection and editorial material, Susan J. Armstrong and Richard G. Botzler; individual contributions, the authors

Typeset in Joanna and Bell Gothic by
RefineCatch Limited, Bungay, Suffolk

British Library Cataloguing in Publication Data
A catalogue record for this book is available from the British Library

Library of Congress Cataloging-in-Publication Data
The animal ethics reader / edited by Susan J. Armstrong and Richard G. Botzler. – 2nd ed.
    p. cm.
    Includes bibliographical references and index.
    1. Animal welfare – Moral and ethical aspects. 2. Animal rights. I. Armstrong, Susan J. (Susan Jean)
II. Botzler, Richard George, 1942–
    HV4708.A548 2008
    179′.3 – dc22   2007042197

ISBN-10: 0–415–77539–6
ISBN-13: 978–0–415–77539–7

Printed and bound in the United States of America by
Edwards Brothers Malloy on sustainably sourced paper

Contents

PART TWO
Animal Capacities: Pain, Emotion, Consciousness

Methods of Study

Anthropomorphism

Consciousness, Emotion, and Suffering

Foreword

Although I have been writing, lecturing, and otherwise actively working in the field of animal ethics since 1975, and had written in the 1970s that social interest in animal treatment would inevitably increase, I could not have anticipated the degree to which this issue would seize the popular imagination. A few examples can serve to underscore the impact of these concerns.

In the spring of 2002, the German Parliament included the protection of animals in the German Constitution. The amendment affirms that "the state takes responsibility for protecting the natural foundations of life and animals." There is a widespread belief among German scientists that this amendment will have major implications for animal research by making invasive research far more difficult. Equally impressive is the fact that most Western countries now have strong laws protecting research animals despite strong and vigorous opposition from the research community. In the United States, for example, in the 1980s, although research animal protection legislation was categorically rejected by those who speak for the research community, as potentially impeding human health, the U.S. public overwhelmingly supported its passage. And, in many countries, legislation requires that research animals suffering intractable pain *must* be immediately euthanized. (In the weaker U.S. law, they *may* be euthanized.)

In short, citizens have felt sufficiently strongly about the moral status of research animals (the overwhelming majority of which are rats and mice) to place significant constraints on medical research despite its patent advantage to humans.

According to both the U.S. National Cattlemen's Beef Association and the National Institutes of Health (the latter being the source of funding for the majority of biomedical research in the United States), both groups not inclined to exaggerate the influence of animal ethics, by the mid-1990s Congress had been consistently receiving more letters, phone calls, faxes, e-mails, and personal contacts on animal-related issues than on any other topic.

Whereas ten years ago one would have found no bills pending in the U.S. Congress relating to animal welfare, the last five to six years have witnessed 50–60 such bills annually, with even more proliferating at the state level. The federal bills range from attempts to prevent duplication in animal research, to saving marine mammals from becoming victims of tuna fishermen, to preventing importation of ivory, to curtailing the parrot trade. State laws passed in large numbers have increasingly prevented the use of live or dead pound animals for biomedical research and training and have focused on myriad other areas of animal welfare. Numerous states have abolished the steel-jawed leghold trap. When Colorado's politically appointed Wildlife Commission failed to act on a recommendation from the Division of Wildlife to abolish the spring bear-hunt (because hunters were liable to shoot lactating mothers, leaving their orphaned cubs to die of starvation), the general public ended the hunt through a popular referendum. Seventy percent of Colorado's population voted for that constitutional amendment. In Ontario, the environmental minister stopped a similar hunt by executive fiat in response to social ethical concern. California abolished the hunting of mountain lions, and state fishery management agencies have taken a hard look at catch-and-release programs on humane grounds.

In fact, wildlife managers have worried, in academic journals, about "management by referendum." According to the director of the American Quarter Horse Association, the number of state bills related to horse welfare filled a telephone-book-sized volume in 1998 alone. Public sentiment for equine welfare in California carried a bill through the state legislature making the slaughter of horses or shipping of horses for slaughter a felony in that state. Indeed, there is, as of 2007, no horse slaughter remaining in the U.S. Municipalities have passed ordinances ranging from the abolition of rodeos, circuses, and zoos to the protection of prairie dogs and, in the case of Cambridge, Massachusetts (a biomedical Mecca), the strictest laws in the world regulating research. Some thirty-five states have elevated animal cruelty from a misdemeanor to a felony.

Many animal uses seen as frivolous by the public have been abolished without legislation. Toxicological testing of cosmetics on animals has been truncated; companies such as the Body Shop have been wildly successful internationally by totally disavowing such testing, and free-range egg production is a growth industry across the world. Greyhound racing in the U.S. has declined, in part for animal welfare reasons, with the Indiana veterinary community spearheading the effort to prevent greyhound racing from coming into the state. Zoos that are little more than prisons for animals (the state of the art during my youth) have all but disappeared, and the very existence of zoos is being increasingly challenged, despite the public's unabashed love of seeing animals. And, as George Gaskell and his associates' work has revealed, genetic engineering has been rejected in Europe not, as commonly believed, for reasons of risk but for reasons of ethics; in part for reasons of animal ethics. Similar reasons (i.e., fear of harming cattle) have, in part, driven European rejection of bovine somatotropin (BST). Rodeos such as the Houston Livestock Show have, in essence, banned jerking of calves in roping, despite opposition from the Professional Rodeo Cowboys Association, who themselves never show the actual roping of a calf on national television.

Inevitably, agriculture has felt the force of social concern with animal treatment. Indeed, it is arguable that contemporary concern in society with the treatment of farm animals in modern production systems blazed the trail leading to a new ethic for animals. As early as 1965, British society took notice of what the public saw as an alarming tendency to industrialize animal agriculture by chartering the Brambell Commission, a group of scientists under the leadership of Sir Rogers Brambell, who affirmed that any agricultural system failing to meet the needs and natures of animals was morally unacceptable. Though the Brambell Commission recommendations enjoyed no regulatory status, they served as a moral lighthouse for European social thought. In 1988, the Swedish Parliament passed, virtually unopposed, what the *New York Times* called a "Bill of Rights" for farm animals, abolishing in Sweden, in a series of timed steps, the confinement systems currently dominating North American agriculture. Much of northern Europe has followed suit, and the European Union is moving in a similar direction.

Until very recently, U.S. society paid little attention to animal agriculture, largely, in my view, because of major public unfamiliarity with the change to industrialized agriculture—most urban people thought that farms were Old McDonalds' farm, as depicted in cartoons, an impression the industry did nothing to dispel. Public awareness has, however, been significantly elevated since the first edition of this book appeared. The success of retail markets like Whole Foods; purveyors of humane meat like Niman Ranch; restaurants like Chipotle; chefs like Wolfgang Puck; and caterers like Bon Appetit who buy humane animal products has helped to educate the public and make consumers more aware of practices in animal agriculture. Correlatively, people are increasingly voting with their dollars.

In addition, referenda in Florida and Arizona have abolished sow stalls ($2' \times 3' \times 6'$ cages in which breeding sows are kept for their entire productive life), as has state law in Oregon. The agriculture industry now believes that similar referenda would pass in every state. The National Commission on Industrial Farm Animal Production, better known as the Pew Commission, has raised public awareness about the problems of industrial agriculture, including issues of human health, animal welfare, environmental despoliation, and destruction of rural communities. The industry has begun to realize that change must occur.

Activist animal advocates have begun to realize what a powerful tool the law is. Eighty law schools teach courses in animal law, and many lawyers are using extant laws in novel ways to defend animals.

Although the Western social ethic has always, from Biblical times onward, contained provisions relating to animals, these have been very minimalistic, basically forbidding overt, deliberate, purposeless, sadistic cruelty and egregious neglect. Why have the last three decades witnessed the proliferation of concern about all areas of animal use and treatment and seen a correlative demand for a new ethic that goes well beyond cruelty?

There are, I believe, five reasons for this phenomenon. First, traditional animal use was largely husbandry agriculture, where producers did well if and only if animals did well. Thus producers put animals into optimal conditions for which the animals were biologically suited and supplemented their ability to survive with food during famine, water during drought, protection from predation, etc., so proper animal treatment followed from self-interest! Only the anti-cruelty ethic was needed to supplement self-interest by flagging sadists and psychopaths who hurt animals for no reason. The rise of industrialized agriculture and biomedical research after World War II made traditional moral categories for animals obsolete. For both of these pursuits were not husbandry, both caused animal suffering, yet were not initiated by motives of cruelty. Confinement agriculturalists sought cheap and plentiful food in the face of a rising population and shrinking agricultural land; researchers sought knowledge of disease. Yet both led to suffering on a scale far greater than cruelty, necessitating a new ethical vocabulary.

Second, the last fifty years have witnessed a major increase in ethical sensitivity toward disenfranchised humans—black people, third world people, women, the handicapped, children. This sentiment inevitably grew to include animals, with many leaders in the animal movement coming from other social movements.

Third, fewer and fewer people make their living directly from animals, with far less than 2 percent of the public engaged in animal production. Correlatively, the social paradigm for an animal has changed from a cow or horse (i.e., a work or food animal) to a companion animal. Most of the public professes to see their pets as "members of the family."

Fourth, an increasingly urban public has an endless fascination with animals and their behavior and treatment. Thus one finds animal stories occupying the greatest amount of television time during a week. "Animals sell papers," as one reporter said to me.

Finally, extremely bright and articulate people have sensed the need for a new ethic for animals, and attempted to provide one. Though largely philosophers, this group also includes scientists like Marc Bekoff and Jane Goodall. And, in a departure from usual philosophical practice, these philosophers have written books aimed not so much at other philosophers, as at the public. Such thinkers as Peter Singer, Tom Regan, Mary Midgley, David DeGrazia, Andrew Linzey, Steve Sapontzis, and Evelyn Pluhar have written persuasively and intelligently, articulating a new ethic, though with some family disagreements. Singer's *Animal Liberation* has been steadily in print since 1975; my *Animal Rights and Human Morality* since 1981.

This anthology is far and away the best, most comprehensive, and readable introduction to a full range of issues associated with the new thinking and concern about animal treatment. Drawing from the best writing by both philosophers and scientists, Professors Armstrong and Botzler have created a book that provides a firm conceptual basis for anyone interested in issues of animal treatment and animal ethics. Excellent and comprehensive as it is, this book should help create many new college and university courses in animal ethics by providing a wonderful assembly of relevant readings and suggestions for additional readings in an accessible format. In addition, it should be required reading for those people who use animals and wish to understand this powerful new social movement having a direct impact on their livelihood. This book is no slapdash assembly of obvious readings hurriedly gathered together to take advantage of an increasing market, but rather a true product of intensive scholarship and reflection. The second edition is greatly enhanced with new material, and I applaud the editors for undertaking this difficult and much needed project, and for achieving their goals in such a masterful way.

Bernard E. Rollin, University Distinguished Professor, Professor of Philosophy, Professor of Animal Sciences, Professor of Biomedical Sciences, University Bioethicist.

Colorado State University

List of Contributors

Ralph Acampora is Associate Professor of Philosophy at Hofstra University, Hempstead, N.Y. He is the author of *Corporal Compassion: Animal Ethics and Philosophy of Body* (2006).

Carol J. Adams has written over 100 articles and is the editor and co-editor of numerous books, including *Beyond Animal Rights, Ecofeminism and the Sacred*, and *Living Among Meat-Eaters*. She lives in the Dallas-Fort Worth area.

The Animal Agriculture Alliance was established in 2001. It is a non-profit organization which includes individuals, companies and organizations that have joined together to enhance consumer understanding of animal agriculture, to share animal well-being guidelines, and to protect America's excellent food supply. It is based in Arlington, Virginia.

Michael C. Appleby's publications include *Poultry Behaviour and Welfare* (2004). He is Trade Policy Manager with the World Society for the Protection of Animals, Eurogroup for Animal Welfare and the UK's RSPCA.

Jonathan Balcombe has been Associate Director for Education in the Animal Research Issues section of the Humane Society of the United States since 1993. He has degrees from York University and Carleton University, Toronto, and a doctoral degree in ethology from the University of Tennessee.

Marc Bekoff is Professor Emeritus in the Department of Ecology and Evolutionary Biology at the University of Colorado at Boulder. His most recent book is *The Emotional Lives of Animals* (New World, 2007).

Bob Bermond is a faculty member in the Department of Psychology, University of Amsterdam, the Netherlands. He has published regularly on animal consciousness and emotion, as well as alexithymia, the inability to verbalize emotions, in humans.

Lynda Birke has taught women's studies as well as courses in biology at Warwick University, Coventry, U.K. She was Senior Lecturer in the Centre for the Study of Women and Gender, but is now based in the Institute for Women's Studies at the University of Lancaster.

Bernice Bovenkerk is at the University of Melbourne. She is currently linked to the Ethics Institute at the University of Utrecht in the Netherlands.

Baruch A. Brody is the Leon Jaworski Professor of Biomedical Ethics and director of the Center for Medical Ethics and Health Policy at Baylor College of Medicine. He is also the Andrew Mellow Professor of Humanities in the Department of Philosophy at Rice University.

Jeffrey Burkhardt is part of the Ethics and Policy Program, Institute of Food and Agricultural Sciences, University of Florida, Gainesville. His expertise lies in ethics and policy in agriculture and natural resources, as well as in the history and philosophy of economics.

J. Baird Callicott is Professor in the Department of Philosophy and Religion Studies at the University of North Texas, Denton, Texas. He is a major contributor to the field of environmental ethics and has been a strong proponent of ecocentric perspectives, including those first developed by Aldo Leopold.

Paola Cavalieri is the editor of the international journal *Etica & Animali* and the author of *The Animal Question*. She co-edited (with Peter Singer) *The Great Ape Project* (St. Martin's 1994). She lives in Milan, Italy.

Grace Clement is an Associate Professor and Chair of the Philosophy Department at Salisbury University. She has written a book on feminist ethics, *Care, Autonomy and Justice: Feminism and the Ethic of Care* and is currently writing on the connections between feminist ethics and animal ethics.

Carl Cohen is Professor of Philosophy at the University of Michigan in Ann Arbor, Michigan. He is a vigorous civil libertarian and is co-editor of a widely used logic textbook. He is co-author of *The Animal Rights Debate* with Tom Regan (Rowman and Littlefield 2001).

Steven L. Davis is Professor Emeritus of Animal Science at Oregon State University.

Marian Stamp Dawkins is Professor of Animal Behaviour at the University of Oxford and a Fellow in Biological Sciences at Somerville College. She is the author of several books, including *Animal Suffering: The Science of Animal Welfare* (1980) and *Through Our Eyes Only? The Search for Animal Consciousness* (1993).

David DeGrazia is Professor of Philosophy at George Washington University. He is the author of a number of works, including *Human Identity and Bioethics, Animal Rights: A Very Short Introduction* (Oxford 2002), and *Taking Animals Seriously* (Cambridge 1996).

Daniel C. Dennett is a prominent American philosopher whose research centers on philosophy of mind and philosophy of science, particularly as those fields relate to evolutionary biology and cognitive science. He currently is the Director of the Center for Cognitive Studies as well as the Austin B. Fletcher Professor of Philosophy at Tufts University.

Chris DeRose heads the American organization Last Chance for Animals. He has been a Hollywood actor, a pilot, reporter, and a black belt in martial arts. He has spent time in jail for his activities in the animal liberation movement and continues to be a firm believer in direct action on behalf of animals.

Courtney L. Dillard is in the Department of Communication at Portland State University, Portland, Oregon.

Josephine Donovan is Emerita Professor at the University of Maine. She is co-editor of *Feminist Care Traditions in Animal Ethics* (2007) as well as numerous other works including *Animals and Women* (Duke 1995).

Kate Douglas is Lecturer in English at Flinders University in Adelaide, Australia.

Randall L. Eaton has written books on a wide variety of captive and wild animals, including marine mammals, cheetahs and leopards; he also edited a series on the world's cats and has written on environmental ethics.

Stephen T. Emlen is the Jacob Gould Schurman Professor of Behavioral Ecology at Cornell University. He is a world authority on the social behavior of animals, particularly birds. He is the author of over 100 scientific papers and has made pioneering contributions to our understanding of the diverse forms of animal societies.

Richard A. Epstein is James Parker Hall Distinguished Service Professor of Law at the University of Chicago Law School. His most recent book is *Antitrust Decrees in Theory and Practice: Why Less Is More* (AEI 2007).

Autumn Fiester, PhD, is the Director of Graduate Studies in the Department of Medical Ethics, University of Pennsylvania. She is also a Senior Fellow at the Center for Bioethics. Her research interests include animals and bioethics, clinical professionalism, and moral theory.

Martin Forward is Professor of Religious Studies and Executive Director of the Aurora University Center for Faith and Action at Aurora University in Aurora, Illinois. His most recent books are *Religion: A Beginner's Guide* (Oneworld 2001) and *Inter-religious Dialogue* (Oxford 2001).

R.G. Frey is Professor of Philosophy at Bowling Green State University in Ohio, and a Senior Resource Fellow of the Kennedy Institute of Ethics at Georgetown University. His recent books include, with Christopher Wellman, *The Companion to Applied Ethics* (Basil Blackwell 2003).

Rabbi Stephen Fuchs is Senior Rabbi of Congregation Beth Israel in West Hartford, Connecticut.

James Garbarino is Professor of Human Development at Cornell University, Ithaca, New York. Among his many publications are *Why Our Sons Turn Violent and How We Can Save Them* (2000) and *See Jane Hit* (2006).

Kathryn Paxton George is Emerita Professor of Philosophy at the University of Idaho. Her books include *Animal, Vegetable or Woman? A Feminist Critique of Ethical Vegetarianism* (SUNY 2000).

Juan Carlos Gómez is at the School of Psychology, University of St Andrews, Scotland. His publications include *Apes, Monkey, Children and the Growth of Mind* (Harvard 2004).

Jane Goodall is a world-renowned researcher on chimpanzees associated with the Gombe Stream Research Center, Kigoma, Tanzania, and the Jane Goodall Institute for Wildlife Research, Education, and Conservation, which has its headquarters in Arlington, Virginia. She is the author of over 70 scientific papers and more than 20 books.

Temple Grandin is Associate Professor of Animal Science at Colorado State University, Fort Collins, Colorado. She has designed one-third of all the livestock-handling facilities in the United States. She has authored or edited over ten books and over 300 articles in both scientific journals and livestock periodicals.

Donald R. Griffin (1915–2003) was a highly regarded scientist who followed his innovative work on echolocation in bats with ground-breaking work on the question of whether animals possess consciousness. He wrote several books, including *The Question of Animal Awareness*.

Alastair S. Gunn is Professor and Chair of the Department of Philosophy, University of Waikatao, Hamilton, New Zealand. He is a writer and teacher on the topic of environmental ethics and engineering, as well as on hunting, conservation, and ethics.

Ned Hettinger is Professor of Philosophy, College of Charleston, South Carolina. He teaches and writes on environmental philosophy courses, as well as aesthetics, ethics and the law.

Michael Hutchins was Director of Conservation and Science, American Zoo and Aquarium Association (AZA). He currently is the executive director for the Wildlife Society.

Dale Jamieson is Professor of Environmental Studies and Philosophy at New York University. His most recent book is *Morality's Progress: Essays on Humans, Other Animals, and the Rest of Nature* (2002).

Wesley V. Jamison is in the Interdisciplinary and Global Studies Division of Worcester Polytechnic University, Worcester, Massachusetts.

Frederike Kaldewaij is a doctoral student at Utrecht University working on the foundations of moral obligations to animals.

Marti Kheel has been in animal advocacy for over 20 years. In 1982 she co-founded Feminists for Animal Rights. She has worked to uncover the emotional basis and presuppositions of the decisions that we make regarding animals.

Diane Leigh and Marilee Geyer are former shelter workers. www.novoiceunheard.org

Aldo Leopold (1887–1948) began his professional career in 1909 when he joined the U.S. Forest Service. In 1924 he became Associate Director of the Forest Products Laboratory in Madison, Wisconsin, and in 1933 the University of Wisconsin created a chair of game management for him.

Donald G. Lindburg, Ph.D, is head of the behavior division for the Zoological Society of San Diego's Center for Reproduction of Endangered Species (CRES). Lindburg has written articles, chapters and books on a variety of zoological topics such as the relation of behavior and reproduction in endangered species.

Andrew Linzey is a member of the Faculty of Theology in the University of Oxford and holds the world's first post in Ethics, Theology and Animal Welfare. He is Director of the Oxford Centre for Animal Ethics and has written or edited 20 books and more than 100 articles.

Konrad Lorenz (1903–1989) was an Austrian ethologist who won the Nobel Prize in Medicine in 1973. His work laid the foundation of an evolutionary approach to mind and cognition.

Freya Mathews is Associate Professor of Philosophy at La Trobe University in Australia. Her recent books include *For the Love of Matter* (SUNY 2003) and *Reinhabiting Reality* (SUNY 2005).

Michael Mendl is in the Centre for Behavioural Biology of the Bristol University School of Medicine and has published extensively on the social structure and behavior, as well as social memory and social understanding, of pigs and other animals.

Anna Merz founded Ngare Sergoi Rhino Sanctuary in 1983 and directs the Lewa Wildlife Conservancy in Kenya.

Ben A. Minteer is an Assistant Professor at the School of Life Sciences, Arizona State University. He has written on environmental ethics and policy, ethics of ecological research and biodiversity management, as well as the history and philosophy of conservation.

Sandra D. Mitchell, Department of History and Philosophy of Science, University of Pittsburgh, Pennsylvania, has published a number of articles and books on epistemological and metaphysical issues in the philosophy of science, particularly on scientific explanations of complex behavior.

David Morton is Professor of Biomedical Science and Ethics, University of Birmingham, Edgbaston, Birmingham, UK.

F. Barbara Orlans is Research Assistant Professor, Kennedy Institute of Ethics, Georgetown University, Washington, D.C.

Clare Palmer is Associate Professor in Philosophy and Environmental Studies at Washington University in St. Louis. She is the author of *Environmental Ethics and Process Thinking* (1998) and is currently completing a book on wild animals and ethics.

Jaak Panksepp is Distinguished Research Professor Emeritus at Bowling Green State University. He is the author of *Affective Neuroscience: The Foundations of Human and Animal Emotions*.

Elizabeth S. Paul is in the Centre for Behavioural Biology and is interested in understanding the development of human attitudes to animal welfare and the use of animals in society.

Dale Peterson is Lecturer in English at Stanford University. Among his recent books is *Eating Apes* (University of California 2003).

Andrew J. Petto is an Associate Professor in the Division of Liberal Arts, University of the Arts, Philadelphia. His areas of interest include demography, life history, and education and he is particularly interested in work with primates such as prosimians and vervets.

Richard A. Posner is Senior Lecturer in Law at the University of Chicago Law School. He has written a number of books, most recently *Antitrust Law* (2nd ed. 2001). He was Chief Judge of the U.S. Court of Appeals for the Seventh Circuit from 1993 to 2000.

James Rachels (1941–2003) taught philosophy at the University of Alabama at Birmingham for twenty-five years. His writings include *Created from Animals: The Moral Implications of Darwinism* (1990) and *Problems for Philosophy* (2008).

Luke Rendell is EU Postdoctoral Research Fellow at the University of St Andrews. He has published several papers on behavior and acoustic communication of cetaceans.

Tom Regan is Emeritus Professor of Philosophy at North Carolina State University at Raleigh. He is the philosophical leader of the animal rights movement in the United States. Regan has written more than twenty books and numerous articles.

Jason Scott Robert is on the faculty staff in the Center for Biology and Society, School of Life Sciences, as well as the Consortium for Science, Policy and Outcomes, Arizona State University, Tempe, Arizona.

Bernard E. Rollin is University Distinguished Professor, Professor of Philosophy, Professor of Animal Sciences, Professor of Biomedical Sciences, and University Bioethicist at Colorado State University, Fort Collins, Colorado. He is the author of numerous books, including *An Introduction to Veterinary Medical Ethics* (Iowa State University Press 1999), *The Frankenstein Syndrome* (Cambridge 1995), and *Animal Rights and Human Morality* (Prometheus 1992).

Oliver A. Ryder is with the Center for Reproduction of Endangered Species, Zoological Society of San Diego, California, and also is an Adjunct Professor of Biology at the University of California, San Diego.

Sue Savage-Rumbaugh has been associated with the Department of Biology, Language Research Center, Georgia State University, Atlanta, Georgia. She has been studying ape language for more than two decades. Currently she is Lead Scientist at the Great Ape Trust of Iowa.

James Serpell is Marie A. Moore Professor of Humane Ethics and Animal Welfare and Director of the Center for the Interaction of Animals and Society, Department of Clinical Studies, School of Veterinary Medicine, University of Pennsylvania.

Paul Shepard (1925–1996) was a philosopher, essayist, and author of numerous books. In *Thinking Animals* (University of Georgia 1998) he argued that animals are indispensable to our being human.

Mark Peter Simmonds is International Director of Science for the Whale and Dolphin Conservation Society, Chippenham, UK. His books include *Whales and Dolphins of the World* (MIT Press 2004).

Peter Singer is DeCamp Professor of Bioethics in the University Center for Human Values at Princeton University. He is also Laureate Professor in the Centre for Applied Philosophy and Public Ethics at the University of Melbourne. His book *Animal Liberation* (1975) is widely credited with beginning the movement for animal rights.

Kevin R. Smith is a member of the Division of Molecular and Life Sciences at the University of Abertay, Dundee, Scotland.

Barbara Smuts is Professor of Psychology and Anthropology at the University of Michigan. She is editor of *Primate Societies* and author of *Sex and Friendship in Baboons*, as well as numerous scientific articles on social relationships in wild primates and dolphins.

Norman Solomon is retired from the Faculty of Oriental Studies at the University of Oxford, U.K. He recently published *The Historical Dictionary of Judaism* (Scarecrow Press 2006).

Robert Streiffer is an Associate Professor at the University of Wisconsin, Madison. He has a joint appointment in the Department of Medical History and Bioethics and the Philosophy Department.

Gary Varner is Associate Professor of Philosophy at Texas A&M University, College Station. He is the author of many journal articles and book chapters. His book *In Nature's Interests* was published by Oxford in 1998.

Chris Wemmer is a Research Associate at the National Zoological Park and the National Museum of Natural History, and a Fellow of the California Academy of Sciences.

Hal Whitehead is Killam Professor of Biology at Dalhousie University, and has authored over 100 papers on behavior, ecology, population biology, and conservation of whales; he also is co-editor of a book on cetacean societies.

Andrew Whiten is Professor of Evolutionary and Developmental Psychology at the University of St Andrews, Scotland. He is associated with the Scottish Primate Research Group, University of St Andrews, U.K.

Steven M. Wise, J.D., has taught Animal Rights Law at the Harvard, Vermont, and John Marshall Law Schools, and in the Masters Program in Animals and Public Policy at Tufts University School of Veterinary Medicine. He is President of the Center for the Expansion of Fundamental Rights, Inc., in Coral Springs, Florida.

Acknowledgments

Tom Regan, *The Case for Animal Rights*, Copyright © 2004, The Regents of the University of California Press. Reproduced with permission.

Carl Cohen, "Reply to Tom Regan" *The Animal Rights Debate*, C. Cohen and T. Regan (eds) 2001, reprinted by permission of Rowman & Littlefield Publishers, Inc.

Paola Cavalieri, "Are Human Rights Human?" *Logos: A Journal of Modern Society & Culture*, issue 4.2, 2005. Reprinted by kind permission of the author and journal.

Peter Singer, *Practical Ethics*, 2nd edn, 1993, Copyright © Cambridge University Press, reprinted with permission of the publisher and author.

Josephine Donovan, "Feminism and the Treatment of Animals: From Care to Dialogue" *Signs* vol. 31, no.2 © 2006 by The University of Chicago. All rights reserved. Reproduced with permission of The University of Chicago Press.

R.G. Frey, "Rights, Interests, Desires and Beliefs" *American Philosophical Quarterly* 16.3. © North American Philosphical Publications. Reprinted by permission of the publisher.

Frederike Kaldewaij, "Animals and the Harm of Death" in *Ethics and the politics of food Preprints of the 6th Congress of the European Society for Agricultural and Food Ethics*, edited by: Matthias Kaiser and Marianne Elisabeth Lien – Wageningen Academic Publishers, 2006, pp. 528–32. Reprinted by permission of the publisher.

M. Mendl and E.S. Paul, "Consciousness, Emotion and Animal Welfare: Insights from Cognitive Science", *Animal Welfare* 2004, 13: S17–25. Copyright © 2004 Universities Federation for Animal Welfare. Reprinted by kind permission of UFAW www.ufaw.org.uk.

Barbara Smuts, "Reflections" in Coetzee, J.M. *The Lives of Animals*. © 1999 Princeton University Press. Reprinted by permission of Princeton University Press.

Bob Bermond, "A neuropsychological and evolutionary approach to animal consciousness and animal suffering", *Animal Welfare* 2001, 10: S47–62. Copyright © 2001 Universities Federation for Animal Welfare. Reprinted by kind permission of UFAW www.ufaw.org.uk.

Dennett, Daniel C. 1995. "Animal conscousness: What matters and why" in *Humans and Other Animals*, Arien Mack (ed.)., Ohio State University Press. Reprinted by permission of the publisher.

Marian Stamp Dawkins, "Animal Minds and Animal Emotions" *Integrative and Comparative Biology* (formerly *American Zoologist*) 40(6): 883–8, 2000. Reprinted by kind permission of Oxford University Press and the author.

Donald R. Griffin and Gayle R. Speck, "New Evidence of Animal Consciousness", *Animal Cognition* (2004) 7: 5–18, Copyright © Springer-Verlag 2004 with kind permission from Springer Science and Business Media.

Bernard E. Rollin, "Animal Pain", in *The Unheeded Cry*, 1998. Reprinted by kind permission of the author and Blackwell Publishing Ltd.

Gary Varner, "How Facts Matter" reprinted from *Pain Forum* 8(2): 85–6. Copyright © 1999 Elsevier, reprinted with permission.

Sandra D. Mitchell, "Anthropomorphism and Cross-Species Modeling" *Thinking with Animals in Evolutionary Biology* eds Lorraine Daston and Gregg Mitman, Columbia University Press (March 30, 2005). Reprinted by permission of the publisher.

Marc Bekoff, "Deep Ethology, Animal Rights, and The Great Ape / Animal Project: Resisting Speciesism and Expanding the Community of Equals" *Journal of Agricultural and Environmental Ethics* 10: 269–96, © 1997 Kluwer Academic Publishers with kind permission from Springer Science and Business Media and the author.

Sue Savage-Rumbaugh, William M. Fields, and Jared Taglialatela, "Ape Consciousness—Human Consciousness: A Perspective Informed by Language and Culture" *Integrative and Comparative Biology* (formerly *American Zoologist*) 40(6): 910–21, 2000. Reprinted by kind permission of Oxford University Press and Sue Savage-Rumbaugh.

A. Whiten, J. Goodall, W.C. McGrew, T. Nishida, V. Reynolds, Y. Sugiyama, C.E.G. Tutin, R.W. Wrangham, and C. Boesch, "Cultures in Chimpanzees" reprinted by permission from Macmillan Publishers Ltd: *Nature* vol. 399: 682–5, Copyright © 1999.

Juan Carlos Gómez, "Are Apes Persons? The Case for Primate Intersubjectivity" in *Etica and Animali*. 1998, Copyright J.C. Gómez and Paola Cavalieri. Reprinted by kind permission of J.C. Gómez.

Jane Goodall, "Problems Faced by Wild and Captive Chimpanzees: Finding Solutions", pp. xiii–xxiv. Reprinted from *Great Apes and Humans: The Ethics of Coexistence* eited by B. B. Beck, T. S. Stoinski et al. (Washington, DC: Smithsonian Institution Press). Used by permission of the Smithsonian Institution. Copyright 2001.

Hal Whitehead, Luke Rendell, Richard W. Osborne, and Bernd Wursig, "Culture and Conservation of Non-Humans with Reference to Whales and Dolphins" reprinted from Biological Conservation 120: 431–441. Copyright © 2004 Elsevier, reprinted with permission.

Mark Peter Simmons, "Into the Brains of Whales" reprinted from *Applied Animal Behaviour Science*, Volume 100, Issues 1–2, October: 103–116. Copyright © 2006 Elsevier, reprinted with permission.

Paola Cavalieri, "Whales as Persons" in *Ethics and the politics of food*
Preprints of the 6th Congress of the European Society for Agricultural and Food Ethics, edited by: Matthias Kaiser and Marianne Elisabeth Lien – Wageningen Academic Publishers, 2006, pp. 28–35. Reprinted by permission of the publisher.

David DeGrazia, "Meat-Eating", in *Animal Rights: A Very Short Introduction*, 2002. Reprinted by kind permission of the author and Oxford University Press.

Temple Grandin, "Thinking like Animals" in *Intimate Nature: The Bond Between Women and Animals*, Linda Hogan, Deena Metzger, Brenda Petersen, eds, Fawcett Books, 1998, © Temple Grandin. Reproduced by kind permission of Temple Grandin.

Reprinted with permission from THE STATE OF THE ANIMALS: 2001, edited by Deborah J. Salem and Andrew N. Rowan (©2001 The Humane Society of the United States / Humane Society Press, Washington, D.C. 20037).

Michael C. Appleby, "Food Prices and Animal Welfare" in *Animal production and animal science worldwide* – WAAP book of the year 2005, Edited by A. Rosati, A. Tewolde and C. Mosconi (World Association for Animal Production), pp. 217–220, inc fig.1. Reprinted by permission of the publisher.

Animal Agriculture Alliance, *Animal Agriculture: Myths and Facts*, 1998. Reproduced by permission of Animal Agriculture Alliance.

Steven L. Davis, "The Least Harm Principle May Require that Humans Consume a Diet Containing Large Herbivores, not a Vegan Diet" *Journal of Agriculture and Environmental Ethics* 16: 387–394, © 2003 Kluwer Academic Publishers with kind permission from Springer Science and Business Media and the author.

Bernard E. Rollin, "The Ethical Imperative to Control Pain and Suffering in Farm Animals" in *The Well-Being of Farm Animals Challenges and Solutions*, G. John Benson and Bernard Rollin, 2004. Reprinted by permission of Blackwell Publishing Ltd.

James Rachels, "The Basic Argument for Vegetarianism" in *Food for Thought: The Debate over Eating Meat*, edited by Steve

F. Sapontzis (Amherst, NY: Prometheus Books, 2004), pp. 70–80. Copyright © 2004 by Steve F. Sapontzis. All rights reserved. Reprinted with permission of the publisher.

Carol J. Adams, "The Rape of Animals, the Butchering of Women" in *Sexual Politics of Meat: A Feminist-Vegetarian Critical Theory*, 1990. Reprinted by permission of The Continuum International Publishing Group.

Kathryn Paxton George, "A Paradox of Ethic Vegetarianism: Unfairness to Women and Children" in *Food for Thought: The Debate over Eating Meat*, edited by Steve F. Sapontzis (Amherst, NY: Prometheus Books, 2004), pp. 261–71. Copyright © 2004 by Steve F. Sapontzis. All rights reserved. Reprinted with permission of the publisher.

Norman Solomon, "Judaism" in from *Attitudes to Nature*, J. Holm ed., 1994, pp. 109–10. Reprinted by kind permission of Jean Holm.

Rabbi Stephen Fuchs, "Enhancing the Divine Image" adapted from *Rabbis and Vegetarianism: An Evolving Tradition*, Roberta Kalechofsky, ed., Micah Publications, 1996. Reprinted by kind permisson of Rabbi Stephen Fuchs and Micah Publications.

Andrew Linzey, "The Bible and Killing for Food" revised from Dan Cohn-Sherbok ed. *Using the bible today*, Bellew Publishing, 1991 and 2002, © Andrew Linzey. Reprinted by kind permission of the author.

Martin Forward and Mohamed Alam, "Islam" in *Attitudes to Nature*, J. Holm, 1994, ed. Reprinted by kind permission of Jean Holm and Martin Forward.

David DeGrazia, "The Ethics of Animal Research: What are the Prospects for Agreement?" *Cambridge Quarterly of Healthcare Ethics* (1999) 8: 23–34, 1999, Copyright © Cambridge University Press, reprinted with permission of the author and publisher.

Baruch A. Brody, "Defending Animal Research: An International Perspective" from Ellen Frankel Paul and Jeffrey Paul eds *Why Animal Experimentation Matters*, pp. 131–47. Copyright © 2001 by Transaction Publishers. Reprinted by permission of the publisher and author.

Lynda Birke, "Who—or What—are the Rats (and Mice) in the Laboratory?", *Society & Animals* 11:3, 2003. Reproduced by kind permission of Koninklijke Brill NV, www.brill.nl.

F. Barbara Orlans, "Ethical Themes of National Regulations Governing Animal Experiments: An International Perspective", pp. 131–147 from *Applied Ethics in Animal Research* edited by John P. Gluck, Tony DiPasquale and F. Barbara Orlans © 2002 Purdue University press. Reprinted with permission.

Jonathan Balcombe, "Summary of Recommendations". Reprinted with permission from *The Use of Animals in Higher Education* by Jonathan Balcombe, Ph.D., published by Humane Society Press, Washington, D.C.

Andrew J. Petto and Karla D. Russell, "Humane Education: The Role of Animal-based Learning" in (ed.) Francine L. Dolins, *Attitudes to Animals*, pp. 167–85, 1999, Copyright © Cambridge University Press, reprinted with permission of the author and publisher.

Ben A. Minteer and James P. Collins, "Ecological Ethics: Building a New Tool Kit for Ecologists and Biodiversity Managers", *Conservation Biology* 1803–1812 © 2005 Society for Conservation Biology, reprinted by permission of Blackwell Publishing Ltd.

Stephen T. Emlen, "Ethics and Experimentation: Hard Choices for the Field Ornithologist" *The Auk* 110, pp. 406–9. Reproduced by kind permission of the author and The Auk/American Ornithologists' Union.

David Morton, "Some Ethical Issues in Biotechnology Involving Animals", *Journal of Commercial Biotechnology*, Jan 2003: 9,2. Copyright © 2003 Palgrave Macmillan. Reprinted with kind permission of David Morton and Palgrave Macmillan.

Jason Scott Robert and Francoise Baylis, "Crossing Species Boundaries", *American Journal of Bioethics*, summer 2003, 3(3), reprinted by kind permission of the author and Taylor and Francis Group www.informaworld.com.

Robert Streiffer, "In Defense of the Moral Relevance of Species Boundaries", *American Journal of Bioethics,* summer 2003, 3(3), reprinted by kind permission of the author and Taylor and Francis Group www.informaworld.com.

Kevin R. Smith, "Animal Genetic Manipulation: A Utilitarian Response", *Bioethics* 16(1): 55–71, reprinted by permission of Blackwell Publishing Ltd.

Jeffrey Burkhardt, "The Inevitability of Animal Biotechnology? Ethics and the Scientific Attitude" in *Animal Biotechnology and Ethics*, A. Holland and A. Johnson eds, © 1998 Chapman & Hall, with kind permission from Springer Science and Business Media and the author.

Bernard E. Rollin, "On *Telos* and Genetic Engineering" from in *Animal Biotechnology and Ethics*, A. Holland and A. Johnson eds, © 1998 Chapman & Hall, with kind permission from Springer Science and Business Media and the author.

Bernice Bovenkerk, Frans W.A. Brom, and Babs J. van den Bergh, "Brave New Birds: The Use of 'Animal Integrity' in Animal Ethics", *Hastings Center Report* 32(1): 16–22. Reprinted by kind permission of Bernice Bovenkerk and The Hastings Center.

Oliver A. Ryder, "Cloning Advances and Challenges for Conservation" reprinted from *Trends in Biotechnology* 20: 231–3. Copyright © 2002 Elsevier, reprinted with permission.

Autumn Fiester, "Creating Fido's Twin: Can Pet Cloning be Ethical Justified?", *Hastings Center Report* 35. no. 4 (2005): 34–39. Reprinted by kind permission of the author and The Hastings Center.

J. Baird Callicott, "The Philosophical Value of Wildlife", in *Valuing Wildlife: Economic and Social Perspectives*, D.J. Decker and G.R. Goff, eds, Westview Press, 1987. Reprinted by kind permission of Dan Decker and J. Baird Callicott.

Grace Clement, "The Ethic of Care and the Problem of Wild Animals" from http://cla.calpoly.edu/~jlynch/clement.htm. Reprinted by kind permission of the author.

Aldo Leopold, "Game and Wildlife Conservation", *The Condor*, Vol. 34, No. 2 (Mar.–Apr., 1932), pp. 103–106, © Cooper Ornithological Society. Reprinted with permission.

Adapted with permission, from Marti Kheel, 1996, "The Killing Game: An Ecofeminist Critique of Hunting" *Journal of the Philosophy of Sport* 23(1):30–44.

Alastair S. Gunn, "Environmental Ethics and Trophy Hunting", *Ethics and the Environment* 6(1): 68–95, 2001, reprinted by permission of Indiana University Press.

Ned Hettinger, "Exotic Species, Naturalisation, and Biological Nativism", *Environmental Values* 10(2): 193–224, 2001. Reprinted by permission of The White Horse Press.

Dale Peterson, "To Eat the Laughing Animal", in Peter Singer (ed), *In Defense of Animals*, New York: Basil Blackwell, 2005, reprinted by permission of Blackwell Publishing Ltd.

Randall L. Eaton, "Orcas and Dolphins in Captivity", in *The Orca Project – A Meeting of Nations* 1998. © Randall Eaton. Reproduced by kind permission of the author.

Ralph Acampora, "Zoos and Eyes: Contesting Captivity and Seeking Successor Practices" *Society & Animals* 13:1, 2005. Reproduced by kind permission of Koninklijke Brill NV, www.brill.nl

Dale Jamieson, "Against Zoos", in Peter Singer (ed), *In Defense of Animals*, New York: Basil Blackwell, 2005, reprinted by permission of Blackwell Publishing Ltd.

Michael Hutchins, Brandie Smith and Ruth Allard," "In Defense of Zoos and Aquariums: the ethical basis for keeping wild animals in Captivity", *Journal of the American Veterinary Medical Association*, JAVMA, Vol. 223, No. 7, October 1, 2003.

Donald G. Lindburg, "Zoos and the Rights of Animals", *Zoo Biology*, 18, 1998. Copyright © Donald G. Lindburg, 1998. Reprinted with permission of John Wiley & Sons, Inc.

Chris Wemmer, "Opportunities Lost: Zoos and the Marsupial that Tried to be a Wolf", *Zoo Biology*, 21, 2002, Copyright © Chris Wemmer, 2002. Reprinted with permission of John Wiley & Sons, Inc.

"Affection's Claim", in Konrad Lorenz: *Man Meets Dog*. Published by Routledge, London and New York. © 1983 Deutscher Taschenbuch Verlag, Munich/Germany.

Bernard E Rollin and Michael D H Rollin, 'Dogmatisms and Catechisms: Ethics and Companion Animals', from *Anthrozoos, Volume14, Issue 1, pp. 4–11*. Reprinted by permission of the publisher. All rights reserved.

"The Pet World" from THE OTHERS by Paul Shepard. Copyright © 1996 by the author. Reproduced by permission of Island Press, Washington, D.C.

Anna Merz, "Hand-Raising a Rhino in the Wild", in *Intimate Nature: The Bond Between Women and Animals*, Linda Hogan, Deena Metzger, Brenda Petersen, eds, Fawcett Books, 1998, © Anna Merz. Reproduced by kind permission of Anna Merz.

Freya Mathews, "Living with Animals", *Animal Issues* 1(1): 1–18. Reprinted by permission of the author. See www.freyamathews.com for the full text of the article.

James Garbarino, "Protecting Children and Animals from Abuse: A Trans-Species Concept of Caring", pp. 9–15 from

Child Abuse, Domestic Violence, and Animal Abuse edited by Frank R. Ascione and Phil Arkow © 1999 Purdue University Press. Reprinted with permission.

James Serpell, Raymond Coppinger, and Aubrey H. Fine, "The Welfare of Assistance and Therapy Animals: An Ethical Comment", *Handbook on animal assisted therapy*, Aubrey H. Fine ed. 2000, Elsevier.

Clare Palmer, "Killing Animals in Animal Shelters" From *Killing Animals*. Copyright 2006 by Board of Trustees of the University of Illinois. Used with permission of the University of Illinois Press.

Diane Leigh and Marilee Geyer, "Miracle of Life" and "Afterword", *One at a Time: A Week in an American Animal Shelter*, No Voice Unheard; 4th edition (July, 2007). Reproduced by kind permission of the publisher, www.NoVoiceUnheard.org.

Steven M. Wise, "A Great Shout: Legal Rights for Great Apes" pp. 274–294. Reprinted from *Great Apes and Humans: The Ethics of Coexistence* eited by B. B. Beck, T. S. Stoinski et al. (Washington, DC: Smithsonian Institution Press). Used by permission of the Smithsonian Institution. Copyright 2001.

Richard A. Posner, "Book Review: *Rattling the Cage: Toward Legal Rights for Animals* by Steven M. Wise" *The Yale Law Journal* 110: 527–41. Reproduced by kind permission of the author.

Richard A. Epstein, "The Dangerous Claims of the Animal Rights Movement" in *The Responsive Community*, 2000. Reprinted by kind permission of the author.

Kate Douglas, "Just Like Us" New Scientist Magazine, 6/2/2007, Vol 194, Issue 2606, pp. 46–49. *Reproduced with permission.*

Wesley V. Jamison, Caspar Wenk, and James V. Parker, "Every Sparrow that Falls: Understanding Animal Rights Activism as Functional Religion" *Society & Animals* 8:3, 2000. Reproduced by kind permission of Koninklijke Brill NV, www.brill.nl

Tom Regan, "Understanding Animal Rights Violence" From *Defending Animal Rights*. Copyright 2001 by Board of Trustees of the University of Illinois. Used with permission of the University of Illinois Press.

Courtney L. Dillard, "Civil Disobedience: A Case Study in Factors of Effectiveness" *Society & Animals* 10:1, 2002. Reproduced by kind permission of Koninklijke Brill NV, www.brill.nl

Chris DeRose, *In Your Face: From Actor to Activist*, Duncan Publishing 1997. Reproduced by kind permission of the author.

Peter Singer, "Ten Ways to Make a Difference" from *Ethics into Action*, 2000, pp. 194–92. Reprinted by permission of Rowman and Littlefield Publishers, Inc. and the author.

Preface

This second edition includes 33 new articles in the various fields covered by this Reader. We hope the book will continue to be of value to undergraduate and graduate students, as well as to their instructors, and to the general reader. We appreciate the supportive comments we have received from students in courses which have used the book.

We also thank Prof. Erwin Lengauer of the University of Vienna. He has established the Reader as the key guide for lectures on animal ethics in Central Europe and has also provided guidance in the choice of new readings.

GENERAL INTRODUCTION

Animal Ethics: A Sketch of How It Developed and Where It Is Now

"All human communities have involved animals."
Mary Midgley, *Animals and Why They Matter* (1984: 112)

HISTORIANS ESTIMATE THAT the "hunter-gatherer" stage of human societies began around 500,000 years ago and lasted until about 11,000 years ago (Serpell 1999: 40). While there are problems with using living or recent hunter-gatherers as representatives of our pre-agricultural ancestors, a "remarkable degree of consistency" in attitudes and beliefs toward animals exists among present-day hunter-gatherer societies. Animals are perceived as being fully rational, sentient, and intelligent, with bodies animated by non-corporeal spirits or souls (Serpell 1999: 40). Hunted animals must therefore be treated with proper respect and consideration. Serpell locates the origin of contemporary hunting rules and rituals in these beliefs (Serpell 1999: 41). These respectful beliefs may have been fueled in pre-historic times by the fact that a number of carnivores were large enough to prey on stone-age humans. These carnivores includes some of the sabre-tooth cats, as well as the pre-historic wolves, hyenas, and bears. (Kruuk 2002: 103–14).

Agriculture and animal husbandry began roughly 11,000 years ago, producing a "dramatic shift in the balance of power between humans and the animals they depended on for food." At first animal guardian spirits were elevated to the status of "zoomorphic gods" (Serpell 1999: 43). For example, the first known written expression of prohibition to cruelty to animals is found in ancient Egypt, and this prohibition seems to be at least partly based on the belief that "all creatures were manifestations of the divine" (LaRue 1991: 3). Some gods assumed animal form. The list of sacred animals included "the vulture, hawks, swallows, turtles, scorpions, serpents" (LaRue 1991: 3). Chapter 125 of the Egyptian *Book of the Dead* prohibited mistreatment of animals (LaRue 1991: 34). While the ancient Egyptians ate animals, humans were expected to treat other creatures with respect and kindness, "for in the afterlife the treatment of animals would be included in actions to be judged" (LaRue 1991: 35). Cattle, particularly bulls, were the pre-eminent models for power and fertility. In Egypt, as well as other ancient civilizations, both dogs and snakes were strongly associated with death and healing. In early Mesopotamia, sheep began to fulfill an important surrogate religious role as substitute cattle (Schwabe 1994: 48–9).

This respectful relationship was not to last. As Serpell (1999: 43) points out, over time the connections between the gods and animals became more and more tenuous. The gods became increasingly associated with the agricultural cycle, and wholesale animal sacrifice was used as a way to please them. Religious belief systems became increasingly hierarchical.

This change was slow and complex, as can be seen in the intermittent history of vegetarianism (Dombrowski 1984: 1–2). Vegetarian communities may have existed as long as 8,000 years ago in the Mesolithic period.[1] Ryder affirms that by the time of the Middle Kingdom in Egypt, vegetarianism was common at least among priests, and neither pork nor beef were widely eaten (Ryder 1998: 6). The Greek poet Hesiod told of a Golden Age in which the first race of human beings were free from all sorrow, toil, grief, and evil. They were fed out of a boundless cornucopia of fruit. This Age of Cronus was followed by other less idyllic ages, but the nostalgia for earlier times remained into the time of the pre-Socratic philosopher Empedocles (495–435 BCE), who said that to kill an animal for food or sacrifice was "the greatest abomination among men" (Dombrowski 1984: 19–22).

The mathematical genius and mystic Pythagorus most probably lived in the sixth century BCE. In common with Hindu, Buddhist and many Aboriginal societies, Pythagoras taught the doctrine of the transmigration of souls between animals and humans. He seems to have based his vegetarianism on this religious belief, as well as on concerns for health and ethical concerns. These ethical concerns included the affirmation of moderation and care for animals. Though there is disagreement over the extent of his vegetarianism (Steiner 2005: 48–50), according to at least one ancient commentator even in moments of great mathematical achievements Pythagorus remained true to his vegetarian principles by sacrificing an ox made of dough (Dombrowski 1984: 38). Pythagorus' ethical concerns were founded on a principle of moderation. He believed that we have no right to cause unnecessary suffering. Animals have the same soul as we do; those who senselessly kill animals are murderers (Dombrowski 1984: 46).

While Socrates (470–399 BCE) was generally indifferent to what he ate (Dombrowski 1984: 55), Plato (428–347 BCE), strongly influenced by Pythagorus, affirmed both that those living in the age of Cronus were vegetarians and that philosophers should be vegetarians (Dombrowski 1984: 58ff). Animals share with humans the part of the soul which is mortal but not intrinsically irrational (Timaeus 69c–77c, 90e–92c). Nevertheless Plato does not condemn hunting, butchering, or raising livestock for consumption.

Aristotle (384–322 BCE) not only permitted meat-eating, but seemed to have been opposed to vegetarianism (Dombrowski 1984: 65–6). He affirmed that in each animal "there is something natural and beautiful" (*On the Parts of Animals* Bk. I, ch. 5), and taught that animals do possess sentient souls. However, because animals lacked reason for Aristotle they had no moral status (Steiner 2005: 57–92). Augustine and Thomas Aquinas both followed Aristotle in this view, thus greatly influencing the development of the Christian view of animals (Ryder 1998: 8). For example, Thomas Aquinas taught that "[the] life of animals . . . is preserved not for themselves, but for man" (*Summa Theologica*, Q64, 1, 1466.)

Beginning in the first century CE, Stoic philosophers believed that logos (reason) was both divine and a cosmic law, and that everything serves some purpose. Thus animals cannot be members of our moral community because they lack reason; nevertheless, their usefulness to human beings reflects divine intention (Boersema 2001: 202–3). While the Romans Seneca and Ovid advocated vegetarianism, animals simply did not count morally for most Romans (Dombrowski 1984: 85).

Plutarch (45–125 CE) was a Greek priest at Delphi. Dombrowski notes that he may have been the first to advocate vegetarianism on grounds of universal benevolence, rather than on the basis of transmigration of souls (Dombrowski 1984: 86–7). He strove to convince the Stoics that animals are indeed rational, arguing that sentience implies a reasoning mind through which to experience sentience (Preece 2005: 55). Plutarch was the only early thinker whose beliefs have had a demonstrable influence in later ages (Boersema 2001: 208). Plutarch suggested that sentiency is a matter of degree (Dombrowski 1984: 88). For Plutarch the difference between domesticated and wild (and harmful) animals is morally significant; we may not harm harmless animals. "Plutarch challenged his antagonists to use their teeth to rend a lamb asunder and consume it raw, as true carnivores do"

(Boersema 2001: 209). Overall, Plutarch exhibited a love of animals, "but never at the expense of the human race" (Boersema 2001: 210).

The great neo-Platonic philosopher Plotinus (204–270 CE) as well as his distinguished pupil Porphyry (232–c.305 CE) were vegetarians. Plotinus affirmed transmigration of souls and animals' capacity for suffering. But Porphyry went far beyond these affirmations. According to Dombrowski, he deserves recognition for having provided "the most comprehensive and subtly reasoned treatment of vegetarianism by an ancient philosopher" (Dombrowski 1984: 107). He not only offers the best possible reasons for vegetarianism but he collects the best reasons against it (Dombrowski 1984: 109–19). Nevertheless, despite the views of thinkers such as Plutarch and Porphyry, the attitude toward nature and animals in ancient cultures was largely dependent upon whether nature or the animals in question were perceived as helpful or harmful to human beings.

During medieval times, many were deeply ambivalent toward animals.[2] The importance of animals was taken for granted, and as a consequence animal symbolism was pervasive. But over the centuries there were changes in how animals were perceived. For early Christians animals were profoundly different from humans. But by the twelfth century thinkers began to share the Greco-Roman view of humans as existing on a continuum with animals. Despite these changes, lay culture continued to attribute human traits and feelings to animals throughout the medieval period (Cohen 1994: 68).

Salisbury notes that since saints were considered ideal humans, the stories of the interactions between saints and animals can illuminate the medieval understanding of what it means to be human. Many early Christian saints showed deep concern for animals, for example, in rescuing animals from hunters, talking with animals, sharing their food, and caring for sick or wounded animals. St Benedict (c. 480–547), the founder of the Benedictine order, stated that monks should not eat meat except when sick. (This rule was ignored, however, after the reinterpretation of Christianity by Thomas Aquinas in the thirteenth century.) In the early Middle Ages most inter-actions between saints and animals demonstrated the power of saints to suspend the bestial nature of animals. Some animals even acquired human qualities. Animals are grateful, kind, and bring food to saints. Because animals were so different from people, "any human-like behaviour on the part of the animal was considered miraculous in itself." (Salisbury 1994: 173). The prevalence of such medieval tales indicates that a mark of saintliness was the caring for our fellow creatures (Waddell 1970).

In the twelfth century, the early medieval paradigm began to break down. Saints continued to overturn beastly behavior, but now animals begin to show evidence of reason. St Francis of Assisi (c. 1181–1226) saw all creatures as mirrors of the creator. Legend tells of him prevailing upon a wolf to stop eating townspeople (Ryder 1989: 33). Saints even save animals' lives without expecting a human return. Thus animal lives had some intrinsic value. The Hermit of Eskedale was killed in 1159 after sabotaging a hunt (Ryder 1998: 34–5). An extreme example of a saint's cult that eliminated the lines between humans and animals is that of Saint Guinefort, a greyhound that was unjustly killed after rescuing a child. He was venerated as a saint that could be called upon to protect children (Salisbury 1994: 175). In the thirteenth century the Inquisition attempted to stamp out the veneration. Animals were kept as pets, considered to possess human virtues, and even tried by the courts and convicted of crimes. Masses were said for horses, and sick animals were shown the eucharistic bread to cure them (Ryder 1998: 14). Despite these medieval practices, it remains true that the Bible provides conflicting views of the human–animal relationship. Thus the larger question of whether traditional Christianity offers an ethic of compassion toward animals involves the question of whether Christianity is a "fixed set of canonical doctrines or a living phenomenon that can change with the times" (Steiner 2005: 113ff).

The sixteenth and seventeenth centuries in Europe were a time of great social change. The confluence of early capitalism, the beginnings of modern science, the dualistic thinking expressed by

René Descartes (1596–1650) and others, as well as the emergence of Protestantism, helped ensure that Christians ended any lingering deification of nature. Humans asserted their own importance, throwing off their medieval belief in the unity of creation and seeking to deny their own animal natures by emphasizing the boundaries between man and animals. Renaissance writers insisted on the uniqueness and importance of human beings. Nature, including animals, was no longer an organic whole but dead, soulless matter, indeed a machine, from which the minds and immortal souls of human beings were entirely distinct. All things were created principally for the benefit and pleasure of "man." According to Descartes and many others, human beings were distinguished from animals by the possession of speech, reason, the capacity for moral responsibility, and an immortal soul. Bestiality became a capital offense in 1534 and, except for a brief period, remained so until 1861 (Thomas 1983: 30). Cruel medieval practices such as bear-baiting, bull-baiting, and persecution of cats continued, to be joined by the dissection of living animals (vivisection) for scientific purposes.

Thomas asserts that "the most powerful argument for the Cartesian position was that it was the best possible rationalization for the way man actually treated animals" (1983: 34). The view that there was a total qualitative difference between humans and animals was "propounded in every pulpit" and underlay everyone's behavior (Thomas 1983: 35–6). Yet there were prominent dissenters throughout these centuries, including the vegetarian Leonardo da Vinci, who purchased birds in the marketplace to free them, the essayist Michel de Montaigne, who attacked cruelty in his essays of 1580, and William Shakespeare, who vividly depicted the suffering of animals. Martin Luther and John Calvin expressed concern for God's creatures. Sir Isaac Newton (1642–1727) invented cat flaps, and the great English philosopher John Locke (1632–1704) affirmed that children should be brought up to show kindness to animals. British Chief Justice Sir Matthew Hale wrote in 1661 that "I have ever thought that there was a certain degree of justice due from man to the creatures, as from man to man" (Ryder 1998: 13–14). And in 1683 Thomas Tyron, a Christian theologian, produced what may be the first printed use of the term "rights" in connection with animals (Munro 2000: 9).

Despite these examples of compassion for animals, in the seventeenth century the most common view held by intellectuals was that "beasts" had an inferior kind of reason which included sensibility, imagination, and memory but no power of reflection (Thomas 1983: 32–3). Thus, perhaps not surprisingly, the reform movements of the sixteenth and seventeenth centuries were based on the same ideology of human domination, as were the oppressions they sought to reform. Slavery was attacked because people were being treated like animals, but the slavery of animals was taken for granted. The main dispute during this period was thus between those who held that all humanity had dominion over the creatures, and those who believed that this dominion should be confined to a privileged group of humans (Thomas 1983: 48–9).

But at the same time there were social changes which worked against the idea of human dominion. For example, pet keeping had been fashionable among the well-to-do as well as among religious orders in the Middle Ages, but it was in the sixteenth and seventeenth centuries that pets seem to have established themselves as a normal feature of the middle-class household (Thomas 1983: 110). Pets included monkeys, tortoises, otters, rabbits, and squirrels, as well as hares, mice, hedgehogs, bats, and toads. Cage-birds were also common, including canaries as well as wild birds of every kind. Gradually, the idea that tamed animals were property was developed. Pets were distinguished by being allowed into the house and by going to church with their human companions, by being given individual personal names, and by never being eaten. The spread of pet-keeping created the psychological foundation for the view that some animals were entitled to moral consideration (Thomas 1983: 110–19).

In England, the growth of towns and the emergence of an industrial order in which animals became increasingly marginal to production were significant factors in the development of concern for animals' rights (Thomas 1983: 181). The reformist ideas were expressed either by well-to-do townspeople or by educated country clergymen (Thomas 1983: 182). The professional middle classes were unsympathetic to the warlike traditions of the aristocracy, which had valued hunting because it simulated warfare, and cock-fighting and bear-baiting because they represented private combat (Thomas 1983: 181). By the later seventeenth century the human-centered (anthropo-centric) tradition itself was being eroded. According to Thomas, this erosion is one of the great revolutions in modern Western thought, a revolution to which many factors contributed (Thomas 1983: 166).

Thomas cites factors such as the growth of natural history, which gradually resulted in classi-fications of animals according to the animals' structure alone, as well as a delight in the world's diversity at least somewhat independent of human standards. Second, people's actual experience of animals on the farms and in their houses conflicted with the theological orthodoxies of the time. Animals were everywhere and consequently were often thought of as individuals, since herds were small. Shepherds knew the faces of their sheep and some farmers could trace stolen cattle by distinguishing their hoof prints (Thomas 1983: 95). Anthropocentrism was still the prevailing out-look, but by the eighteenth century non-anthropocentric sensibilities became much more widely dispersed and were more explicitly supported by the religious and philosophical teaching of the time (Thomas 1983: 174–5). Cruelty to animals began to be regularly denounced. Ryder speculates that one reason for this moral awakening was the extreme cruelty which had been practiced in England for centuries (Ryder 1998: 16). English reformists targeted bull-baiting and bear-baiting, the treat-ment of horses, the treatment of cattle being driven to slaughter through the streets of London, and the traditional Shrove Tuesday sport of tying a cockerel to a stake and stoning him to death (Ryder 1998: 16). The campaign against cruelty to animals was enhanced by a new emphasis on sensation and feeling as the true basis of moral status (Thomas 1983: 180), as expounded in the utilitarianism of Jeremy Bentham. Once it had been accepted that animals had feelings and therefore should be treated with kindness, it seemed increasingly repugnant to kill them for meat (Thomas 1983: 288). From about 1790 there developed a highly articulate vegetarian movement (Thomas 1983: 295). An increasing number of people felt uneasy about killing animals for food, and so slaughterhouses were concealed from the public eye (Thomas 1983: 300).

By the later eighteenth century the most common view was that animals could indeed think and reason, though in an inferior way. A number of thinkers affirmed the kinship between man and "beast." Humphry Primatt published his dissertation on *The Duty of Mercy and the Sin of Cruelty to Brute Animals*, which presented almost all the arguments used in later centuries (Munro 2000: 10). There was an increasing tendency to credit animals with reason, intelligence, language, and almost every other human quality (Thomas 1983: 129). Perhaps most decisive was the revelation by comparative anatomy of the similarity between the structure of human and animal bodies (Thomas 1983: 129). The growing belief in the social evolution of humankind encouraged the view that humans were only animals who had managed to better themselves (Thomas 1983: 132).

Christians continued to be mixed in their attitude toward animals. In 1772 James Granger preached against cruelty to animals and received "almost universal disgust" at his daring to discuss dogs and cats from the pulpit (Passmore 1975: 200). On the other hand, a substantial number of biblical commentators took the view that animals would be eventually restored in heaven to the perfection they had enjoyed before the Fall (Thomas 1983: 139). The idea of animal immortality made more headway in England than anywhere else during this period (Thomas 1983: 140–1). In 1788 the vegetarian John Wesley, founder of the evangelical movement of Methodism, preached a famous sermon entitled "The Great Deliverance." In it Wesley proclaimed that the "whole brute creation" will be delivered into a far higher degree of vigor, strength, and swiftness than they had enjoyed on earth (Preece 2005: 163).

Courts in both Germany and Britain began to punish cruelty to animals on the basis that while animals themselves had no rights, maltreatment of animals violated the direct duty to God (Maehle 1994: 95–8). Eighteenth-century American writers Thomas Paine and Hermann Daggett affirmed the moral status of animals. British politicians introduced a bill to outlaw bullbaiting in 1800, but the bill was defeated. The Lord Chancellor Thomas Erskine, who had once physically attacked a man he found beating a horse, joined with Richard Martin to produce a successful bill in 1822 to make it an offense to wantonly beat, abuse, or ill-treat any horse, donkey, sheep, cow, or other cattle (unless it was the property of the offender). "Known as Martin's Act, this was the first national law against cruelty to animals enacted by full parliamentary process," according to Richard Ryder, though bull-baiting was not stopped until 1835 (1998: 19).

The organized animal welfare movement emerged at this time. One reason for the timing of this emergence was that after the Reformation in northern Europe "good works became increasingly secularized" (Ryder 1998: 25). Also the new general affluence of the period, teamed with increasing democracy, allowed compassionate people to institutionalize their concerns, whether it be opposed to the slave trade or to ill-treatment of animals. In addition, the Industrial Revolution was reducing the dependence on animals, particularly on horses and dogs (Boersema 2001: 237).

In 1824 a group of Members of Parliament as well as three churchmen met to establish two committees: one to publish literature to influence public opinion and the other to adopt measures for inspecting the treatment of animals. In its first year the Society for the Prevention of Cruelty to Animals (SPCA) brought "150 prosecutions for cruelty and engaged in campaigns against bullbaiting, dogfighting, the abuse of horses and cattle and the cruelties of the main London meat market at Smithfield" (Ryder 1998: 21). The society also condemned painful experiments on animals. Shortly thereafter societies were formed elsewhere in northern Europe. In 1840 Queen Victoria "granted the society the royal prefix," so that it became known as the "Royal Society for the Prevention of Cruelty to Animals" (RSPCA). Four of the society's founders were already well-known reformers who opposed slavery; two opposed the death penalty for minor offenses (Ryder 1998: 21–2). Kalechofsky (1992: 64) notes that throughout the nineteenth century there were "porous boundaries between the various reform causes, and those involved in anti-slavery, prison reform, and child abuse reform were often the same people involved in the women's movement, anti-vivisection, slum clearance, and the hygiene or sanitary movement." This observation works against the thesis argued by Turner (1980: 36–8), and still widely accepted, that concern for animals arose as a displaced compassion for human suffering. Finsen and Finsen (1994: 28ff) name Turner's view the "Displacement Thesis" and propose instead the "Extension Thesis": namely, that those who are concerned about one exploited group will often extend that concern to other groups.

The greatest campaign of the Victorian era in Britain was against the use of live animals in experiments. Such campaigns started as an outcry against demonstrations on cats and dogs by a French experimenter, and were augmented by reports of unanesthetized horses being tied down and slowly dissected by students. Protests were made to the French authorities. In England the Cruelty to Animals Act was passed in 1876, requiring licenses and certificates from the government. The bill was an inconvenience to researchers, though few prosecutions under the act were successful. After much public agitation, a Royal Commission recommended some improvements to the administration of the Act (Ryder 1998: 26–8).

Women were prominent in this antivivisection movement, beginning with Descartes' niece, Catherine, who famously rejected his doctrine of the "animal-machine" (Kalechofsky 1992: 61). To undermine women's effectiveness, nineteenth-century scientists viewed women as infantile, animal-like, and belonging to nature rather than to civilization. In contrast, the scientific "intellectual edifice" was identified as masculine, logical, and rational; anyone who opposed animal research was considered irrational, sentimental, and "womanly." These views were shown to be false by the many knowledgable and intellectually powerful women who combated the scientific cruelty of the time (Kalechofsky 1992: 70).

Finsen and Finsen point to the antivivisection movement as the ancestor of the animal rights movement, because the antivivisection movement, in contrast to the humane movement as represented by the RSPCA, "challenged an entire institution" (1994: 38). However, at the same time, the medical profession was attaining greater political power due to the successes in experimental medicine in the 1890s in connection with medical microbiology. The medical microbiology revolution required numerous forms of animal experimentation (Finsen and Finsen 1994: 39). For these and other reasons, as detailed by Finsen and Finsen, "the antivivisection movement ceased to be a vital and mass movement after the turn of the century," since it based its case not only on the immorality of vivisection but also on its scientific worthlessness (1994: 41). Complicating the assessment of vivisection is the presence of anthropomorphism within the laboratory as well as outside it: experimental animals were at times assimilated by the investigators to asylum inmates, infants, and patients in a hypnotic trance. The questions of which procedures are legitimate and who has the authority to intervene on behalf of the animal or human were and are entangled (White 2005).

While much of the U.S. concern for animals derives from British precedents, a body of laws protecting animals had in fact been approved by the Massachusetts Bay Colony in 1641. Anti-cruelty laws were passed early in the nineteenth century in several states, but organizations did not form until the 1866 birth of the American Society for the Prevention of Cruelty to Animals (ASPCA). Its founder, Henry Bergh, "rapidly became notorious for defending abused and overworked carriage horses in the streets of New York City." Bergh achieved many successful prosecutions, including those for cruel treatment of livestock, cock-fighting, and dog-fighting. George Angell founded the Massachusetts SPCA, with an emphasis on humane education. Societies modeled on Bergh's soon cropped up all over the country. Shortly thereafter the American Society for the Prevention of Cruelty to Children was formed. And, as was the case in England, many of the American animal welfare pioneers were active in the anti-slavery movement.

However, the American antivivisection movement was unsuccessful. It appears that proponents of animal research had learned from the British lesson, and formed an effective lobbying force for vivisection (Finsen and Finsen 1994: 48–9). Some vivisectors portrayed themselves as rational men of science whose work was being retarded by "middle-class, city-based female 'cranks' in humane societies" (Munro 2000: 18). Ryder speculates that the pioneering spirit of America may have welcomed the innovations of science more enthusiastically than did British culture. He notes also that American antivivisectionists lacked the equivalent of royal support (Ryder 1998: 28). During this same period, as Munro explains, the animal protection movement in Australia had begun with the 1873 formation of the Animal Protection Society of New South Wales. Due to circumstances peculiar to Australia, the animal protection movement developed in concert with the environmental movement, the first joint campaign being the elevation of the koala from vermin and commercial fur source to "national pet" (Munro 2000: 14).

Vegetarianism was adopted by some during this period in both Britain and America, the word itself being coined in 1847 at Ramsgate, England, from the Latin word "vegetare," meaning "to grow." By the end of the century vegetarianism was established among a "minority of the middle class," including Henry David Thoreau, George Bernard Shaw, Susan B. Anthony, Anna Kingsford, Howard Williams, and Henry Salt. The great Romantic poet Percy Bysshe Shelley urged, "Never take any substance into the stomach that once had life" (Kenyon-Jones 2001: 121). Mohandas Gandhi in the twentieth century attributed his commitment to vegetarianism to reading Henry Salt's *Plea for Vegetarianism* (1897) (Finsen and Finsen 1994: 25).

After World War I the animal welfare movement seemed to lose its mass appeal in both the U.S. and Britain. There were undoubtedly several reasons for this decline. It may be that incorporating meat into the diet during periods of disease and war was thought to be important for human health. Ryder comments that wars tend to revive the view that worrying about suffering is cowardly;

compassion is dismissed as weakness and effeminacy. In any case, those who called for bans on the exploitation of animals tended to be regarded as cranks or extremists (Ryder 1998: 28–9). Animal welfare organizations in Britain and America declined into charities for lost or abandoned dogs and cats, ignoring the "steady increase in the applied technology of cruelty in the laboratory, meat and wild-killing industries" (Ryder 1998: 29), Henry Salt (1851–1939) in Britain being an exception.[3] Although the National Antivivisection Society was founded in 1929, significant progress in the U.S. did not occur until the 1950s, when the Animal Welfare Institute and the Humane Society of the United States were founded. The Society for Animal Protective Legislation, founded in 1955, achieved the passage of the Humane Slaughter Act and the 1959 Wild Horses Act. During this period the International Society for Animal Rights and the Fund for Animals also came into being. In general, however, the postwar period in both Britain and the United States saw little progress in improving conditions for animals. Finsen and Finsen (1994: 3) assert that one reason for this lack of progress was that the humane movement had "promoted kindness and the elimination of cruelty without challenging the assumption of human superiority or the institutions that reflect that assumption," but they also note that the political climate was very conservative during this period.

Beginning with the 1960s in Britain, the humane concern for animals began to be transformed into the animal rights movement, which insists on justice and fairness in our treatment of animals. Guither (1998: 4–5) argues that the modern animal rights movement is "radically different" from the earlier antivivisection groups and the traditional humane societies. While this may be an over-statement, it is certainly true that many advocates of animal rights affirm the moral status of animals and oppose all ways in which animals are confined and used by human beings (1998: 4–5). One expression of this demand for justice was the formation of the Hunt Saboteurs in 1963. This British group "appears to be the first organization to speak openly and uncompromisingly of members as proponents of rights of animals in the modern sense" (Finsen and Finsen 1994: 55). The group employed confrontational tactics of direct action; it also represented a significant broadening of the animal movement to the working class. In 1964 Ruth Harrison published *Animal Machines*, a book which initiated much of the public concern for the welfare of farm animals. She is believed to have been the first to label confinement livestock and poultry production as "factory farming," calling attention to the fact that animal agriculture had come to be conducted behind closed doors (Ryder 1998: 30). In response to these concerns, the British Parliament set up an official committee of inquiry made up of scientists and concerned citizens, which issued the influential Brambell Report in 1965. The Report recommended certain mandatory standards and called for the government to establish regulations defining animal suffering; it set the stage for animal welfare reform in the United Kingdom and other northern European countries.

A powerful collection of essays titled *Animals, Men and Morals* was published in 1971 by a group of young philosophers and sociologists at Oxford, employing the new term "speciesism," coined by Richard Ryder. Peter Singer reviewed the book and was invited to expand his review into a book of his own. The resulting work was *Animal Liberation*, published in 1975, known as the first philosophic text to include recipes—vegetarian, of course. The book included clear and powerful argumentation together with well-documented descriptions of the conditions of animals in factory farms and research laboratories. Parliamentarian Douglas Houghton with others led the struggle to "put animals into politics," a campaign which issued in the (British) Animals (Scientific Procedures) Act of 1986 (Ryder 1998: 33).

Overall there was a marked increase in direct action, both legal and illegal, during the 1970s and 1980s. Ronnie Lee launched the Animal Liberation Front (ALF) in England in 1972, leading to raids on animal laboratories, factory farms, and abattoirs all over Europe and North America, and the International Fund for Animal Welfare broadened the move to include wildlife (Ryder 1998: 34). However, the climate of opinion changed in Britain during the years of Margaret Thatcher as Prime Minister, and the animal rights movement began to be looked at as a subversive threat to capitalism (Ryder 1998: 35). Acts of violence by groups such as the ALF led to a backlash within the animal rights movement as well as to long prison terms (Finsen and Finsen 1994: 101–2).

In the 1990s the British-led European movement again became active. Partly due to the effectiveness of the organization Compassion in World Farming, farm animals succeeded laboratory animals as the main focus among European animal welfarists in the 1990s. "Massive protests in British ports in 1994 against the exports of sheep and calves . . . escalated into self-sustaining grassroots local movements that continued for over a year" (Ryder 1998: 35). Prime Minister John Major invited animal welfarists to Downing Street, and the European Union Commission voted to phase out by 2006 the keeping of calves in crates in Europe. By 1995 4.5 percent of the British population was vegetarian (Ryder 1998: 37).

In the United States, Peter Singer and Tom Regan emerged as strong voices for animal liberation and animal rights, respectively, in the 1970s and 1980s. A number of organizations were formed, among them People for the Ethical Treatment of Animals (PETA), Trans-Species Unlimited, Farm Animal Reform Movement, Mobilization for Animals, and In Defense of Animals. The principal target of reform in the 1980s in the U.S. was the use of animals in laboratories. Two scandals in 1981 and 1984 helped lead to the upgrading of the oversight of research facilities and some reduction of pain and distress in procedures. Henry Spira led effective protests against the seizure of unwanted dogs from pounds for use in research laboratories.

The U.S. Animal Liberation Front (ALF) is a group of loosely knit cells which has conducted controversial direct action, using illegal tactics. In the United States the ALF has consistently held to a distinction between property damage and violence toward living beings. However, there have been ALF actions in which the methods used placed people in danger, and researchers who have been targeted claim psychological and professional harm (Finsen and Finsen 1994: 98–106). Finsen and Finsen point out that, whether or not one agrees with the tactics of the ALF, the information brought to light has in fact increased public awareness of what happens in some laboratories (1994: 106). Nevertheless, the cost is high, not only in property damage but in deaths among some released animals and, in a few cases, physical injury to humans.

Ryder observes (1998: 41) that disputes between those supporting animal rights versus those supporting animal welfare have sapped some of the movement's energies in the United States. Meanwhile, the factory-farming industry has rapidly expanded in both the United States and the world. Billions of farm animals are raised indoors in "conditions largely unknown to the general public" (Finsen and Finsen 1994: 5). Fortunately, not all of these changes in animal agriculture are negative for animal welfare, though many are (Fraser et al. 2001: 93–4). Overall, the U.S. animal welfare movement is a collection of national and local organizations that often do not work together due to concerns for organizational sovereignty and program purity. In the last few years, however, groups such as the Animals Voice and the Institute for Animals and Society have enabled the animal ethics movement to be more effective.[4]

Contemporary concerns and future directions

As noted in the Foreword by Bernard E. Rollin, since the mid-twentieth century animal agricultural practices have undergone major changes. Ryder (1998: 42) notes that those concerned with animals have come to see the fates of these animals as increasingly determined by the "moral blindness" found in the policies of many multinational corporations and international structures such as the World Trade Organization (Ryder 1998: 42). John Hodges, together with many others, identifies the focus on profit, reduced unit costs, and on the material prosperity of the individual as key contributors to global animal suffering, particularly in agriculture (Hodges and Han 2000: 260–1).

Fortunately there are many who seek to include environmental and human rights concerns into international trade. It is possible that animal welfare can be taken into account even under existing WTO rules: Article XX of the "General Agreement" says that measures necessary to protect public morals and human, animal, or plant health have priority over other agreements (Appleby 2003: 170).

In general, animal ethics is a subject marked with ambivalence. A 2001 study of meat livestock farmers and consumers in the Netherlands indicated that both groups show ambivalence as a result of discrepancies between perceptions and behaviour (Velde *et al.* 2002). Another study conducted in Scotland in 1998 found that while 76% of respondents stated that they were concerned about the possible mistreatment or suffering of farm animals, only 34% avoided certain food products on animal welfare grounds. It is estimated that only 10% of UK food consumers take an active interest in how their food is produced. (McEachern 2002). Complicating the assessment of animal agriculture is the frequent portrayal of the animal producer as wholly driven by the profit motive and hence as much worse than the medical researcher. According to Paul Thompson, this portrayal is inaccurate (Thompson 2004). Lund and Olsson argue that while many types of modern agriculture do have negative consequences for animal welfare and for the environment, sustainable agriculture can be beneficial for both (Lund and Olsson 2006).

Despite these obstacles to improvements in animal welfare, there are potentially hopeful factors. One important element is the view of the relationship between the divine and animal realms in the various world religions; new attitudes and scriptural interpretation are emerging. Many now believe that the Abrahamic traditions are properly understood not as being anthropocentric, but as theocentric: God, not man, is at the center as the ultimate source of meaning (Patton 2000: 408). Despite the fact that the Jewish and Christian traditions have affirmed that only human beings are created in God's image, numerous passages from the Hebrew and Islamic scriptures convey God's "fierce and tender devotion" to animals (Patton 2000: 409–13, 434). In Patton's felicitous phrase, animals display a "joyous devotion to the One who brought them into being" (Patton 2000: 434). Patton recounts the Russian Orthodox Father Thomas Hopko's affirmation of the "rabbithood of God": "there is an aspect of God's Self that at creation expressed itself as a rabbit, and nothing can better reveal that particular aspect of the divine nature than a real, living rabbit" (Patton 2000: 427). Novel reflections such as these may eventually prove to have a powerful effect on the treatment of animals.

In terms of philosophy, David DeGrazia (1999: 125–9) has identified several areas of "unrealized potential" for the future of animal ethics. One such area is found in the work of feminist theorists, who can contribute their powerful moral opposition to oppression as well as their incisive ability to analyze the ideology of speciesism and the various rationalizations for practices which harm animals. DeGrazia also affirms the value of a virtue ethics approach to animal ethics, developed at length so far only by Steve Sapontzis.[5] Virtue ethics emphasizes the importance of character and attitudes: our actions express what kind of people we are. For example, disrespectful treatment of animals may not always involve harm to an animal but rather may express our own growing willingness to exploit animals (DeGrazia 1999: 125–9). A recent example can be found in the creation in 2000 of a "transgenic artwork" in the form of a green fluorescent rabbit.[6] The artist, Eduardo Kac, a professor at the School of the Art Institute of Chicago, teamed up with French geneticists to produce the rabbit by injecting rabbit zygotes with a fluorescent protein gene derived from jellyfish. Such use of a living creature as a "new art form" seems to many to be disrespectful and sensationalist.

Finsen and Finsen (1994: 257) comment that the animal rights movement has had some impact to date, in the process "arousing intense opposition from [extremely powerful] industries with vested economic interests in the status quo." They join a number of other writers in identifying the reform/abolition split as the crucial distinction among members of the animal rights movement.

This split is often summarized in the question: should we work for larger cages or empty cages? The reformists usually want to work within the system to improve the conditions for animals, whereas the abolitionists work to eliminate all uses of animals that they see as causing pain and suffering (Guither 1998: 10). In the Foreword to this book, Bernard Rollin allies himself with reform, affirming that the animal ethics movement is dynamic, growing, and influential. A useful computer supported interactive learning tool has recently been developed for university and professional training which may aid interested persons to identify their own approach to animal ethics (www.aedilemma.net).

The reason for our treatment of animals has never been a mystery. As Ryder comments in his recent book *The Political Animal*, "the simple truth is that we exploit the other animals and cause them suffering because we are more powerful than they are" (1998: 51). The editors hope that this anthology will stimulate reflection on the misuse as well as the appropriate use of human power. Such reflection will both enrich the human relationship with the nonhuman world and contribute to better lives for animals.

Notes

1   Thomas points out that the tradition that humans were originally vegetarian is ancient and world-wide. He states that it "may reflect the actual practice of our remote ancestors, for apes are largely vegetarian" (1983: 288–9).
2   For articles discussing Christian, Jewish, and Islamic interpretations of scripture as it relates to animals, see Part Four of this volume. See also Paul Waudau's discussion of traditional Christian views in *The Specter of Speciesism: Buddhist and Christian Views of Animals* (2002), New York: Oxford University Press.
3   Both Peter Singer and Tom Regan have identified Henry Salt as an important influence on their thought.
4   The Institute for Animals and Society, www.animalsandsociety.org, is an independent research and educational organization, working to advance the status of animals in public policy and promote the study of human-animal relationships. The Animals Voice publishes the *Animals Voice Magazine* www.animalsvoice.com. A current annotated list of courses concerning animals and society is available at www.crle.org/prog_courses_main.asp.
5   S.F. Sapontzis (1987) *Morals, Reason and Animals*, Philadelphia: Temple University Press.
6   http://www.ekac.org/gfpbunny.html; Kac, Eduardo, "Transgenic Art," *Leonardo Electronic Almanac*, vol. 6, n. 11, December 1998. Republished in Gerfried Stock and Christine Schopf (eds) Ars Electronica '99-Life Science (Vienna, New York: Springer, 1999), pp. 289–96.

Bibliography

Appleby, Michael C. (2003) "The EU Ban on Battery Cages: History and Prospects." In Deborah J. Salem and Andrew N. Rowan (eds) *The State of the Animals II 2003*, Washington, D.C.: Humane Society Press.

Beers, Diane L. (2006) *For the Prevention of Cruelty: The History and Legacy of Animal Rights Activism in the United States*, Athens, Ohio: Ohio University Press.

Boersema, J.J. (2001) *The Torah and the Stoics on Humankind and Nature*, Leiden: Brill.

Cohen, E. (1994) "Animals in Medieval Perceptions: The Image of the Ubiquitous Other." In A. Manning and J. Serpell (eds) *Animals and Human Society:Changing Perspectives*, London and New York: Routledge, pp. 59–80.

DeGrazia, D. (1999) "Animal Ethics around the Turn of the Twenty-First Century." *Journal of Agricultural and Environmental Ethics* 11.2: 111–29.

Dombrowski, D.A. (1984) *The Philosophy of Vegetarianism,* Amherst: University of Massachusetts Press.

Finsen, L. and Finsen, S. (1994) *The Animal Rights Movement in America,* New York: Twayne Publishers.

Fraser, D., Mench, J. and Millman, S. (2001) "Farm Animals and Their Welfare." In D.M. Salem and A.N. Rowan (eds) *The State of the Animals 2001,* Washington, D.C.: Humane Society Press.

Guither, H.D. (1998) Animal *Rights: History and Scope of a Radical Social Movement,* Carbondale: So. Illinois University Press.

Hodges, John and Han I.K. (eds) (2000) *Livestock, Ethics and Quality of Life,* New York: CABI Publishing.

Jasper, J.M. and Nelkin, D. (1992) *The Animal Rights Crusade: The Growth of a Moral Protest,* New York: Macmillan.

Kalechofsky, R. (1992) "Dedicated to Descartes' Niece: The Women's Movement in the Nineteenth Century and Anti-Vivisection." *Between the Species* 8.2: 61–71.

Kenyon-Jones, Christine (2001) *Kindred Brutes: Animals in Romantic-period Writing,* Burlington, VT: Ashgate.

Kruuk, Hans (2002) *Hunter and Hunted: Relationships between Carnivores and People,* Cambridge, UK: Cambridge University Press.

LaRue, G.A. (1991) "Ancient Ethics." In P. Singer (ed.) *A Companion to Ethics,* Oxford: Blackwell.

Lund, Vonne and I. Anna S. Olsson (2006) "Animal Agriculture; Symbiosis, Culture or Ethical Conflict?" *Journal of Agricultural and Environmental Ethics*: 19: 47–56.

Maehle, A. (1994) "Cruelty and Kindness to the Brute Creation: Stability and Change in the Ethics of the Man–Animal Relationship, 1600–1850." In Manning and Serpell, pp. 81–105.

Manning, A. and Serpell, J. (eds) (1994) *Animals and Human Society: Changing Perspectives,* London and New York: Routledge.

McEachern, M.G. and M.J.A. Schroder (2002) "The Role of Livestock Production Ethics in Consumer Values Towards Meat," *Journal of Agricultural and Environmental Ethics* 15.2: 221–37.

Munro, L. (2000) *Compassionate Beasts: The Quest for Animal Rights,* Westport, CT: Praeger.

Passmore, John (1975) "The Treatment of Animals." *Journal of the History of Ideas* 36.2: 195–218.

Patton, K.C. (2000) "He Who Sits in the Heavens Laughs: Recovering Animal Theology in the Abrahamic Traditions." *Harvard Theological Review* 93.4: 401–34.

Preece, Rod (2005) *Brute Souls, Happy Beasts, and Evolution: The Historical Status of Animals,* Vancouver, Toronto: UBC Press.

Ritvo, H. (1994) "Animals in Nineteenth-century Britain: Complicated Attitudes and Competing Categories." In Manning and Serpell, pp. 106–26.

Rowlands, M. (1998) *Animal Rights: A Philosophical Defence,* New York: St. Martin's Press.

Ryder, R. (1989) *Animal Revolution: Changing Attitudes toward Speciesism,* Oxford: Basil Blackwell.

—— (1998) *The Political Animal: The Conquest of Speciesism,* Jefferson, NC: McFarland.

Salisbury, Joyce E. (1994) *The Beast within: Animals in the Middle Ages,* New York: Routledge.

Schwabe, C.W. (1994) "Animals in the Ancient World." In Manning and Serpell.

Serpell, J.A. (1999) "Working out the Beast: An Alternative History of Western Humaneness." In F.R. Ascione and P. Arkow (eds) *Child Abuse, Domestic Violence, and Animal Abuse,* West Lafayette, IN: Purdue University Press.

Serpell, J.A. and Manning, A. (1994) *Animals and Human Society: Changing Perspectives,* pp. 36–58. London and New York: Routledge.

Singer, P. (ed.) (1991) *A Companion to Ethics,* Oxford: Basil Blackwell.

Sorabji, R. (1993) *Animal Minds and Human Morals: The Origins of the Western Debate,* Ithaca, NY: Cornell University Press.

Steiner, Gary (2005) *Anthropocentrism and its Discontents: The Moral Status of Animals in the History of Western Philosophy,* Pittsburgh, PA: University of Pittsburgh Press.

Thomas, K. (1983) *Man and the Natural World: Changing Attitudes in England 1500–1800,* Magnolia: Peter Smith.

Thompson, Paul B. (2004) "Getting Pragmatic about Farm Animal Welfare." In Erin McKenna and Andrew Light (eds) *Animal Pragmatism*, Bloomington, IN: Indiana University Press.

Turner, J. (1980) *Reckoning with the Beast: Animals, Pain, and Humanity in the Victorian Mind*, Baltimore: Johns Hopkins University.

Velde, Hein Te, Noelle Aarts and Cees van Woerkum (2002) "Dealing with Ambivalence." *Journal of Agricultural and Environmental Ethics* 51.2: 203–19.

Waddell, Helen, trans. (1970) *Beasts and Saints*, London: Constable and Co., Ltd.

White, Paul S. (2005) "The Experimental Animal in Victorian Britain." In *Thinking with Animals: New Perspectives on Anthropomorphism*, New York: Columbia University Press.

Theories of animal ethics

INTRODUCTION TO PART ONE

ANIMAL ETHICS is involved with arguments over several key issues. The most basic issue concerns the basis of the moral value or moral status of animals. Why should animals count morally? This part includes excerpts from several influential theorists in the field of animal ethics.

Tom Regan's answer as well as that of Paola Cavalieri is based on the concepts of rights to which a being is entitled. Regan develops the concept of "subject-of-a-life" as an expansion of Immanuel Kant's focus on rational beings. Cavalieri uses the concept of "intentional beings" as an expansion of universal human rights theory. For Regan and Cavalieri animals have desires, intentions, feelings, and a psychological identity over time—there is "someone home" in an animal. Animals should be included in our moral community as beings with rights. Unlike Regan, Cavalieri grants the same value to the lives of all intentional beings. Carl Cohen rejects Regan's argument. While Cohen does not deny that animals have rudimentary desires and interests, he does deny that having interests is relevant to having moral rights.

Peter Singer rests his argument on the moral principle of the equal consideration of interests, the utilitarian principle which affirms that all sentient individuals, those capable of experiencing pleasure or pain, must be considered when we are contemplating an action. Singer advocates preference utilitarianism, a form of utilitarianism which takes into account what an individual wishes to do. He does not advocate equal treatment but rather equal consideration of animals' interests. Singer states that we have different obligations toward rational and self-conscious animals as contrasted with our obligations to animals lacking such capabilities.

Josephine Donovan critiques the over-reliance on reason by Regan and Singer. She maintains that feminist care theory, developed in order to emphasize the significance of emotional responses such as sympathy, empathy, and compassion, also acknowledges the importance of animal communications. She confronts some recent criticisms of care theory.

R.G. Frey critiques Regan and Singer from a different perspective. He maintains that animals, because they lack language, do not have interests in the sense of having desires; thus it is not necessary for scholars to address what relationship there might be between interests and rights.

In many theories of animal ethics, painless death is considered to be morally acceptable. Frederike Kaldewaij challenges this view. She argues that both humans and conscious animals are harmed by death because it deprives them of the goods that continued life would have brought them.

Chapter 1

Tom Regan

THE CASE FOR ANIMAL RIGHTS

This selection is from the influential *The Case for Animal Rights*, published in 1983. Regan explains his concept of "subject-of-a-life" as the basis for inherent value, the distinction between moral agents and moral patients, and two principles to be used in cases of unavoidable conflicts between subjects-of-a-life.

[. . .]

Moral agents and moral patients

A HELPFUL PLACE to begin is to distinguish between moral agents and moral patients [. . .]. Moral agents are individuals who have a variety of sophisticated abilities, including in particular the ability to bring impartial moral principles to bear on the determination of what, all considered, morally ought to be done and, having made this determination, to freely choose or fail to choose to act as morality, as they conceive it, requires. Because moral agents have these abilities, it is fair to hold them morally accountable for what they do, assuming that the circumstances of their acting as they do in a particular case do not dictate otherwise.

[. . .]

In contrast to moral agents, *moral patients* lack the prerequisites that would enable them to control their own behavior in ways that would make them morally accountable for what they do. A moral patient lacks the ability to formulate, let alone bring to bear, moral principles in deliberating about which one among a number of possible acts it would be right or proper to perform. Moral patients, in a word, cannot do what is right, nor can they do what is wrong. Granted, what they do may be detrimental to the welfare of others—they may, for example, bring about acute suffering or even death; and granted, it may be necessary, in any given case, for moral agents to use force or violence to prevent such harm being done, either in self-defense or in defense of others. But even when a moral patient causes significant harm to another, the moral patient has not done what is wrong. Only moral agents can do what is wrong. Human infants, young children, and the mentally deranged or enfeebled of all ages are paradigm cases of human moral patients. More controversial is whether human fetuses and future generations of human beings qualify as moral patients. It is enough for our purposes, however, that some humans are reasonably viewed in this way.

Individuals who are moral patients differ from one another in morally relevant ways. Of particular importance is the distinction between (a) those individuals who are conscious and sentient (i.e., can experience pleasure and pain) but who lack other mental abilities, and (b) those individuals who are conscious, sentient, and possess the other cognitive and volitional abilities discussed in previous chapters (e.g., belief and memory). Some animals, for reasons already advanced, belong in category (b); other animals quite probably belong in category (a).

[. . .]

Our primary interest, in this and in succeeding chapters, concerns the moral status of animals in category (b). When, therefore, the notion of a *moral patient* is appealed to in the discussions that follow, it should be understood as applying to *animals in category (b) and to those other moral patients like these animals in the relevant respects*—that is, those who have desires and beliefs, who perceive, remember, and can act intentionally, who have a sense of the future, including their own future (i.e., are self-aware or self-conscious), who have an emotional life, who have a psychophysical identity over time, who have a kind of autonomy (namely, preference-autonomy), and who have an experiential welfare. Some *human* moral patients satisfy these criteria—for example, young children and those humans who, though they suffer from a variety of mental handicaps and thus fail to qualify as moral agents, possess the abilities just enumerated. Where one draws the line between those humans who have these abilities and those who do not is a difficult question certainly, and it may be that no exact line can be drawn. But how we should approach the question in the case of human beings is the same as how we should approach it in the case of animals. Given any human being, what we shall want to know is whether his/her behavior can be accurately described and parsimoniously explained by making reference to the range of abilities that characterizes animals (desires, beliefs, preferences, etc.). To the extent that the case can be made for describing and explaining the behavior of a human being in these terms, to that extent, assuming that we have further reasons for denying that the human in question has the abilities necessary for moral agency, we have reason to regard that human as a moral patient on all fours, so to speak, with animals. As previously claimed, some human beings *are* moral patients in the relevant sense, and *it is only those individuals who are moral patients in this sense (who have, that is, the abilities previously enumerated), whether these individuals be human or nonhuman, who are being referred to, in this chapter and in the sequel, when reference is made to " 'moral patients.' "*

Moral patients cannot do what is right or wrong, we have said, and in this respect they differ fundamentally from moral agents. But moral patients can be on the receiving end of the right or wrong acts of moral agents, and so in this respect resemble moral agents. A brutal beating administered to a child, for example, is wrong, even if the child herself can do no wrong, just as attending to the basic biological needs of the senile is arguably right, even if a senile person can no longer do what is right. Unlike the case of the relationship that holds between moral agents, then, the relationship that holds between moral agents, on the one hand, and moral patients, on the other, is not reciprocal. Moral patients can do nothing right or wrong that affects or involves moral agents, but moral agents can do what is right or wrong in ways that affect or involve moral patients.

[. . .]

Individuals as equal in value

The interpretation of formal justice favored here, which will be referred to as *equality of individuals*, involves viewing certain individuals as having value in themselves. I shall refer to this kind of value as *inherent value* and begin the discussion of it by first concentrating on the inherent value attributed to moral agents.

The inherent value of individual moral agents is to be understood as being conceptually distinct from the intrinsic value that attaches to the experiences they have (e.g., their pleasures or preference satisfactions), as not being reducible to values of this latter kind, and as being incommensurate with these values. To say that inherent value is not reducible to the intrinsic values of an individual's experiences means that we cannot determine the inherent value of individual moral agents by totaling the intrinsic values of their experiences. Those who have a more pleasant or happier life do not therefore have greater inherent value than those whose lives are less pleasant or happy. Nor do those who have more "cultivated" preferences (say, for arts and letters) therefore have greater inherent value. To say that the inherent value of individual moral agents is incommensurate with the intrinsic value of their (or anyone else's) experiences means that the two kinds of value are not comparable and cannot be exchanged one for the other. Like proverbial apples and oranges, the two kinds of value do not fall within the same scale of comparison. One cannot ask, How much intrinsic value is the inherent value of this individual worth—how much is it equal to? The inherent value of any given moral agent isn't equal to any sum of intrinsic values, neither the intrinsic value of that individual's experiences nor the total of the intrinsic value of the experiences of all other moral agents. To view moral agents as having inherent value is thus to view them as something different from, and something more than, mere receptacles of what has intrinsic value. They have value in their own right, a value that is distinct from, not reducible to, and incommensurate with the values of those experiences which, as receptacles, they have or undergo.

The difference between the utilitarian-receptacle view of value regarding moral agents and the postulate of inherent value might be made clearer by recalling the cup analogy. On the receptacle view of value, it is *what goes into the cup* (the pleasures or preference-satisfactions, for example) that has value; what does not have value is the cup itself (i.e., the individual himself or herself). The postulate of inherent value offers an alternative. The cup (that is, the individual) has value *and* a kind that is not reducible to, and is incommensurate with, what goes into the cup (e.g., pleasure). The cup (the individual) does "contain" (experience) things that are valuable (e.g., pleasures), but the value of the cup (individual) is not the same as any one or any sum of the valuable things the cup contains. *Individual moral agents themselves have a distinctive kind of value*, according to the postulate of inherent value, but not according to the receptacle view to which utilitarians are committed. It's the cup, not just what goes into it, that is valuable.

[. . .]

All that is required to insure just treatment, on utilitarian grounds, is that the preferences (pleasures, etc.) of all affected by the outcome be considered and that equal preferences (pleasures, etc.) be counted equally. But if moral agents have a value that is *not* reducible to or commensurate with the value of their own or everyone else's valuable experiences, then how moral agents are to be treated, if they are to be treated justly, cannot be determined *merely* by considering the desires, and the like, of all involved, weighting them equitably, and then favoring that option that will bring about the optimal balance of goods over evils for all involved. To suppose otherwise is to assume that questions of just treatment can be answered by ignoring the value of the individual moral agent, which, if moral agents are viewed as equal in inherent value, simply is not true. Moreover, because all moral agents are viewed as equal in inherent value, if any have such value, what applies to how some may be justly treated applies to all, whatever their race, say, or sex. Given the postulate of inherent value, no harm done to *any* moral agent can possibly be justified merely on the grounds of its producing the best consequences for all affected by the outcome. Thus are we able to avoid the counterintuitive implications of act utilitarianism if we deny the receptacle view of moral agents and postulate their equal inherent value.

[. . .]

It might be suggested that *being-alive* is a *sufficient* condition of an individual's having inherent value. This position would avoid the problems indigenous to the view that being-alive is a necessary condition, but it stands in need of quite considerable analysis and argument if it is to win the day. It is not clear why we have, or how we reasonably could be said to have, direct duties to, say, individual blades of grass, potatoes, or cancer cells. Yet all are alive, and so all should be owed direct duties if all have inherent value. Nor is it clear why we have, or how we reasonably could be said to have, direct duties to collections of such individuals—to lawns, potato fields, or cancerous tumors. If, in reply to these difficulties, we are told that we have direct duties only to some, but not to all, living things, and that it is this subclass of living things whose members have inherent value, then not only will we stand in need of a way to distinguish those living things that have this value from those that do not but more importantly for present purposes, the view that being-alive is a sufficient condition of having such value will have to be abandoned. Because of the difficulties endemic both to the view that being-alive is a necessary condition of having inherent value and to the view that this is a sufficient condition, and granting that moral agents and moral patients share the important characteristic of being alive, it is extremely doubtful that the case could be made for viewing this similarity as the relevant similarity they share, by virtue of which all moral agents and patients have equal inherent value.

Inherent value and the subject-of-a-life criterion

An alternative to viewing being-alive as the relevant similarity is what will be termed *the subject-of-a-life criterion*. To be the subject-of-a-life, in the sense in which this expression will be used, involves more than merely being alive and more than merely being conscious. To be the subject-of-a-life is to be an individual whose life is characterized by those features explored in the opening chapters of the present work: that is, individuals are subjects-of-a-life if they have beliefs and desires; perception, memory, and a sense of the future, including their own future; an emotional life together with feelings of pleasure and pain; preference- and welfare-interests; the ability to initiate action in pursuit of their desires and goals; a psychophysical identity over time; and an individual welfare in the sense that their experiental life fares well or ill for them, logically independently of their utility for others and logically independently of their being the object of anyone else's interests. Those who satisfy the subject-of-a-life criterion themselves have a distinctive kind of value—inherent value—and are not to be viewed or treated as mere receptacles.

[. . .]

The subject-of-a-life criterion identifies a similarity that holds between moral agents and patients. Is this similarity a relevant similarity, one that makes viewing them as inherently valuable intelligible and nonarbitrary? The grounds for replying affirmatively are as follows: (1) A relevant similarity among all those who are postulated to have equal inherent value must mark a characteristic shared by all those moral agents and patients who are here viewed as having such value. The subject-of-a-life criterion satisfies this requirement. *All* moral agents and *all* those moral patients with whom we are concerned *are* subjects of a life that is better or worse for them, in the sense explained, logically independently of the utility they have for others and logically independently of their being the object of the interests of others. (2) Since inherent value is conceived to be a categorical value, admitting of no degrees, any supposed relevant similarity must itself be categorical. The subject-of-a-life criterion satisfies this requirement. This criterion does not assert or imply that those who meet it have the status of subject of a life to a greater or lesser degree, depending on the degree to which they have or lack some favored ability or virtue (e.g., the ability for higher mathematics or those virtues associated with artistic excellence). One either *is* a subject of a life, in the sense explained, or one *is not*. All those who are, are so equally. The subject-of-a-life criterion thus demarcates a categorical status shared by all moral agents and those moral patients with whom we are concerned. (3) A relevant similarity between moral agents and patients must go some way toward illuminating why we have direct duties to both and why we have less reason to believe that we have direct duties to individuals who are neither moral agents nor patients, even including those who, like moral agents and those patients we have in mind, are alive. This requirement also is satisfied by the subject-of-a-life criterion. Not all living things are subjects of a life, in the sense explained; thus not all living things are to be viewed as having the same moral status, given this criterion, and the differences concerning our confidence about having direct duties to some (those who are subjects) and our not having direct duties to others (those who are not subjects) can be at least partially illuminated because the former meet, while the latter fail to meet, the subject-of-a-life criterion. For these reasons, the subject-of-a-life criterion can be defended as citing a relevant similarity between moral agents and patients, one that makes the attribution of equal inherent value to them both intelligible and nonarbitrary.

[. . .]

Justice: the principle of respect for individuals

[. . .]

If individuals have equal inherent value, then any principle that declares what treatment is due them as a matter of justice must take their equal value into account. The following principle (*the respect principle*) does this: *We are to treat those individuals who have inherent value in ways that respect their inherent value*. Now, the respect principle sets forth an egalitarian, nonperfectionist interpretation of formal justice. The principle does not apply only to how we are to treat some individuals having inherent value (e.g., those with artistic or intellectual virtues). It enjoins us to treat *all* those individuals having inherent value in ways that respect their value, and thus it requires respectful treatment of all who satisfy the subject-of-a-life criterion. Whether they are moral agents or patients, we must treat them in ways that respect their equal inherent value.

[. . .]

It is not an act of kindness to treat animals respectfully. It is an act of justice. It is not "the sentimental interests" of moral agents that grounds our duties of justice to children, the retarded, the senile, or other moral patients, including animals. It is respect for their inherent value. The myth of the privileged moral status of moral agents has no clothes.

[. . .]

Comparable harm

[. . .]

A distinction [can be] drawn between those harms that are inflictions and those that are deprivations. Harms that are deprivations deny an individual opportunities for doing what will bring satisfaction, when it is in that individual's interest to do this. Harms that are inflictions diminish the quality of an individual's life, not just if or as they deprive that individual of opportunities for satisfaction, though they usually will do this, but because they detract directly from the individual's overall welfare.

[. . .]

[We can now] give content to the notion of comparable harm. Two harms are comparable when they detract equally from an individual's welfare, or from the welfare of two or more individuals. For example, separate episodes of suffering of a certain kind and intensity are comparable harms if they cause an equal diminution in the welfare of the same individual at different times, or in two different individuals at the same or different times. And death is a comparable harm if the loss of opportunities it marks are equal in any two cases.

[. . .]

The miniride principle

By making use of the notion of comparable harm, the rights view can formulate two principles that can be appealed to in order to make decisions in prevention cases. The first principle (*the minimize overriding principle*, or *the miniride principle*) states the following:

> Special considerations aside, when we must choose between overriding the rights of many who are innocent or the rights of few who are innocent, and when each affected individual will be harmed in a prima facie comparable way, then we ought to choose to override the rights of the few in preference to overriding the rights of the many.

This principle is derivable from the respect principle. This latter principle entails that all moral agents and patients are directly owed the prima facie duty not to be harmed and that all those who are owed this duty have an equally valid claim, and thus an equal prima facie moral right, against being harmed. Now, *precisely because* this right is equal, no one individual's right can count for any more than any other's, when the harm that might befall either is prima facie comparable. Thus, A's right cannot count for more than B's, or C's, or D's. However, when we are faced with choosing between options, one of which will harm A, the other of which will harm B, C, and D, and the third of which will harm them all, and when the foreseeable harm involved for each individual is prima facie comparable, then numbers count. *Precisely because* each is to count for one, no one for more than one, we cannot count choosing to override the rights of B, C, and D as neither better nor worse than choosing to override A's right alone. Three are more than one, and when the four individuals have an equal prima facie right not to be harmed, when the harm they face is prima facie comparable, and when there are no special considerations at hand, then showing equal respect for the equal rights of the individuals involved requires that we override the right of A (the few) rather than the rights of the many (B, C, D). To choose to override the rights of the many in this case would be to override an equal right three times (i.e., in the case of three different individuals) when we could choose to override such a right only once, and *that* cannot be consistent with showing equal respect for the equal rights of all the individuals involved.

To favor overriding the rights of the few in no way contravenes the requirement that each is to count for one, no one for more than one; on the contrary, special considerations apart, to choose to override the rights of the many rather than those of the few would be to count A's right for more than one—that is, as being equal to overriding the rights of three relevantly similar individuals. Accordingly, because we must not allow any one individual a greater voice in the determination of what ought to be done than any other relevantly similar individual, what we ought to do in prevention cases of the sort under consideration is choose to override the rights of the fewest innocents rather than override the rights of the many. And since this is precisely what the miniride principle enjoins, that principle is derivable from the respect principle.

[. . .]

The worse-off principle

[. . .]

Recall the earlier prevention case where we are called upon to choose between harming A quite radically (−125), or harming a thousand individuals modestly (−1 each), or doing nothing

[. . .]

The miniride principle, since it applies *only* in prevention cases where harms are prima facie comparable, cannot be relied on in cases, such as this one, where the harm all the innocents face is not prima facie comparable. The rights view thus requires a second principle, distinct from but consistent with the miniride principle, and one that is distinct from and not reducible to the minimize harm principle. The following principle (*the worse-off principle*) meets these requirements.

[. . .]

> Special considerations aside, when we must decide to override the rights of the many or the rights of the few who are innocent, and when the harm faced by the few would make them worse-off than any of the many would be if any other option were chosen, then we ought to override the rights of the many.

Unfinished business

Two issues deferred in earlier discussions may now be addressed. The first is the lifeboat case [. . .] There are five survivors: four normal adults and a dog. The boat has room enough only for four. Someone must go or else all will perish. Who should it be? Our initial belief is: the dog. Can the rights view illuminate and justify this prereflective intuition? The preceding discussion of prevention cases shows how it can. All on board have equal inherent value and an equal prima facie right not to be harmed. Now, the harm that death is, is a function of the opportunities for satisfaction it forecloses, and no reasonable person would deny that the death of any of the four humans would be a greater prima facie loss, and thus a greater prima facie harm, than would be true in the case of the dog. Death for the dog, in short, though a harm, is not comparable to the harm that death would be for any of the humans. To throw any one of the humans overboard, to face certain death, would be to make that individual worse-off (i.e., would cause *that* individual a greater harm) than the harm that would be done to the dog if the animal was thrown overboard. Our belief that it is the dog who should be killed is justified by appeal to the worse-off principle.

[. . .]

Thus has the case for animal rights been offered. If it is sound, then, like us, animals have certain basic moral rights, including in particular the fundamental right to be treated with the respect that, as possessors of inherent value, they are due as a matter of strict justice.

[. . .]

Chapter 2

Carl Cohen

REPLY TO TOM REGAN

In the following passage Carl Cohen analyzes Regan's use of "subject-of-a-life" and "inherent value" as the foundation for moral rights for animals. According to Cohen, Regan's fallacious logic can be clearly demonstrated.

Why "subjects-of-a-life"?

REGAN'S NEED IS to create some *link* between the imputed subjective experience of animals and the alleged rights of those animals. To this end a class of beings is marked off that Regan calls "subjects-of-a-life." These are the beings who are believed to have some subjective awareness of their own lives, and for whom, as a result, it may be said that things "fare well or badly." Of course we may not conclude, from the fact that things fare well or badly for an animal, that it can formulate the proposition expressing this, or can even grasp that notion in some sub-linguistic way. The judgment that "things are faring well *for me* these days" is not likely to be among the repertoire of chicken reflections. But some crude subjective experience there must be, since the chicken is drawn toward the food tray and runs away from the fox. This indicates, says Regan, that the chicken (like every "subject-of-a-life") has *interests*.

The strategy here is to devise some category into which both animal lives and human lives may be assimilated. Within this newfound category, since it is designed to include humans too, some of the lives led (the human ones) are plainly moral. From this he will go on to infer that *all* the lives in that class, lives so categorized by virtue of his definition, are moral. But this maneuver could succeed only if the criteria for admission to the newly invented category were themselves intrinsically moral—which of course they are not.

"Subjects-of-a-life" is a category of beings that Regan defines by his own stipulation; membership in that class requires only the crudest subjective experience. Having devised the category by fastening upon certain kinds of primitive experience that rats and humans do share, he goes on to assume that moral rights, possessed by humans, arise from just those interests. Some human interests (e.g., in food and sex) are no different in essence from those of rats, and since we all agree that humans do have rights, he infers that rats must have them, too.

In the sense that a sentient animal—even an octopus or a trout—seeks to avoid pain, it does indeed have interests; many animals obviously have interests in that sense. Were Regan to leap directly from the possession of interests to the claim that such interests establish moral rights, his argument—like [the] far-fetched claims of Bernard Rollin and Steven Sapontzis—would be a transparent failure.[1] To avoid this transparency Regan takes a more convoluted path.

A closer look at inherent value

The rights that are to be established flow, Regan contends, from the *"inherent value"* of rats and chickens, and their inherent value is held to be a consequence of their being "subjects-of-a-life." So he makes the passage from interests to rights *by way of* "subjects-of-a-life" and then "inherent value." Both these concepts, as in his 1983 book, are critical links for him: what has subjective experience must have inherent value, and what has inherent value must have rights.[2] This can explain, he argues, why moral respect is owed to rats and chickens.

Reasoning in this way supposes that the rights of rats and chickens are *derived* from the primitive capacities that give them interests. Like Rollin and Sapontzis, Regan is at bottom convinced that rights are the product of animal interests, that a being has rights because it has interests—and he cannot fathom how we could assert of humans, who surely do have interests, that their rights could flow from anything else.

But the conviction that human rights flow from human interests (a conviction shared expressly or tacitly by virtually all animal rights advocates) is one for which there is simply no foundation. The lives we humans lead are indeed moral lives, pervaded by duties and rights. But this moral character of our lives is not a byproduct of our subjective awareness. Our rights are not ours because we experience our lives as our own. Nonhuman creatures may have subjective interests like ours in survival and reproduction, and they may be supposed to have subjective experience of some sort. But from those interests moral rights cannot be inferred.

The plausibility of Regan's reasoning depends on the inference that animals have "inherent value" and then on what may be inferred from the possession of such value. The failure of the argument is a consequence of the fact that the "inherent value" that he infers from the reality of subjective experience is not the same "inherent value" from which rights are later derived. An academic shell game is afoot, in which readers are the marks. Having given our assent to what is plausible in one sense of the expression "inherent value," we are told that dramatic conclusions follow respecting rights. But these conclusions do *not* follow from the inherent value that we may have assented to in animals, although they may follow from inherent value in a very different sense of that term.

[. . .]

What is true of inherent value in the one sense is not true of inherent value in the other sense, and by slipping from one to the other meaning of the phrase Regan commits an egregious fallacy.

We earlier distinguished:

1   Inherent value in the very widely applicable sense that every unique life, not replaceable by other lives or things, has some worth in itself. In this sense every rat, and every octopus too, has inherent value. This value may be minimal; it certainly has no awesome moral content—but it is fair to say that, being irreplaceable and unique, even primitive living things ought not be destroyed for no reason whatever.

2   Inherent value in the far narrower sense arises from the possession of the capacity to make moral judgments, the value of beings with duties and the consciousness of duties. This is the rich philosophical sense of value made famous by Immanuel Kant and employed by many moral thinkers since; it is the sense of inherent worth flowing from the special *dignity* of those who have a moral will. The value of agents who have a moral will does indeed *inhere* in them and entitles them to be treated as ends, and never as means only. Beings with value in this sense—human beings, of course—have rights.

Now it is plain that most beings with inherent value in the first sense—live creatures in the wild, for example—although they may merit some protection, do not begin to possess inherent value in the second, moral sense. Trees and rats have value in the common sense, and we may plausibly call that value "inherent"—but that is no ground for ascribing/moral agency to them. The gap in the argument is here exposed: subjective experiences of rats and chickens lead us to conclude that they really do have interests, but subjective experiences cannot serve to justify the claim that they have rights.

[. . .]

Human beings, on the other hand, have inherent value in both senses. We have worth in that second, Kantian sense, to be sure, but value also in the simpler, common sense as well. [. . .] [The] slippage between these two senses of the same phrase [. . .] is obscured by reaching rights from subjectivity *through* the concept "subject-of-a-life." Within that category lie beings with inherent value in both senses (humans), and beings with inherent value in the first sense only (rats). The stage is set for slippage.

We humans are subjects of our own lives, of course, so we have inherent value in that simple first sense; and surely we do have moral rights. Regan then asks: if the rat is the subject of its own life, must it not also have the same "inherent value" that we have? In the first sense of inherent value it does. And if it does have inherent value as we do, does it not also have moral rights as we do? No, not at all! By moving *into* the concept of "inherent value" in the first sense (in which that value is shared), then drawing inferences *from* inherent value in the second sense (in which it is not shared), Regan pulls the rabbit from the hat, miraculously extending the realm of moral rights to include the rats and the chickens.

Underlying his equivocation is the tacit supposition that we humans have rights only as a *consequence* of our being "subject-of-a-life." But this is false, and we have not the slightest reason to think it true. Having assumed it true, Regan and his friends take themselves to have *amalgamated* the world of human moral experience with the world of rodent experience. That cannot be done with words, or with anything else.

The argument step by step

Here follow the steps of Regan's argument, essentially as he sets them forth, with brief comment on each. Close scrutiny will show that his critical steps rely on double meanings, his objectives reached by using whichever sense of the equivocal term is convenient for the purpose at hand.

1   Humans and rats are both "subjects-of-a-life."
     Comment: If all that is being said here is that other animals as well as humans have subjective interests and awareness, this premise is not in dispute. In having subjective interests "non-human animals are like us," Regan says. Yes, in the sense that they also have appetites, feel pain, and so on.
2   Beings that are "subjects-of-a-life" are beings having inherent value.
     Comment: This is the introduction of the central equivocal phrase. Animals with subjective experience do indeed have "inherent value" in the common sense that all living things, including humans, are unique and irreplaceable. But the vast majority of beings having subjective experiences do *not* have "inherent value" in the Kantian sense that would be needed to ground moral rights.
3   Since rats, like humans, have inherent value because they are "subjects-of-a-life," the inherent value that rats possess is essentially no different from the inherent value that humans possess.
     Comment: The distinction between the two very different senses of inherent value being here ignored or obscured, it seems plausible for Regan to assert here what is true (but innocuous) if the words are taken in one way, yet false (and very harmful) if taken in another. In the common sense both rats and humans do have inherent value. But this "inherent value" possessed by them both (sense 1) is profoundly different from the "inherent value" that is bound up with human moral agency (sense 2).

Regan writes, "The relevant similarity shared by humans who have inherent value is that we are subject-of-a-life" (p. 211). No, that similarity is not relevant to moral matters at all. On the contrary, we may say that the relevant *dissimilarity* between humans and rats is that, although both may have value as lives, only humans have inherent value in the sense from which rights may be inferred. Regan conflates the two very different senses of value, referring to both with the same words, and his argument depends upon this conflation.

5   The inherent value that we humans possess is what accounts for our moral rights. (In his words: "All those who possess inherent value possess the equal right to be treated with respect.")

    Comment: So long as we understand that it is Kantian inherent value (sense 2) here referred to, the claim that from it great moral consequences flow is not in dispute.

6   Since rats possess inherent value for the same reasons that humans do, rats must have moral rights just as humans do.

    Comment: Not at all! Here the switch is cashed out. Rats possess inherent value *in sense 1* for the same reason humans do, because they have subjective interests as humans also have. But from these primitive interests no moral rights can be inferred. Regan writes, "Relevantly similar cases should be judged similarly" (p. 212). But the circumstances of rats and humans are in the most essential matters *not* relevantly similar. Indeed, with regard to moral status they could hardly be more sharply dissimilar. The argument thrives on repeated equivocation.

7   Regan concludes, "It follows that all those human beings and all those animal beings who possess inherent value share the equal right to respectful treatment" (p. 212).

    Comment: Not on your life! The inherent value shared is value in the common sense, but what can entail respect for rights is *not* shared by rats. What is true of both rats and humans is the fact that they are living beings, the life of each unique, each having interests of its own. From this, nothing about moral rights may be validly inferred.

    Infected throughout by the equivocation between inherent value that "subjects-of-a-life" may possess and the entirely different sense of inherent value that may indeed ground human rights, the argument is worthless. The lives of rats and chickens are indeed like the lives of humans in some primitive ways, but it certainly does not follow from those likenesses that rats and chickens share membership in the community of moral beings. Repeatedly we encounter the same fallacious passage from the premise that animals have interests to the conclusion that animals have rights.

[. . .]

Notes

1   Rollin, B. (1992) *Animal Rights and Human Morality*, Amherst: Prometheus Books. Sapontzis, S.F. (1987) *Morals, Reason and Animals*, Philadelphia: Temple University Press.

2   Regan, T. (1983) *The Case for Animal Rights*, Berkeley: University of California Press.

Chapter 3

Paola Cavalieri

ARE HUMAN RIGHTS *HUMAN*?

Cavalieri offers a brief history of Western ethics, according to which animals have been completely excluded from the moral community. She evaluates more recent views in traditional morality according to which nonhuman beings are considered to be moral patients. Concluding that traditional morality is untenable, she bases her argument on the most widespread moral theory: the universal doctrine of human rights. Since the central criterion for the possession of human rights is intentionality, Cavalieri maintains that because animals are intentional beings, they should also be given the protection from institutional interference provided by shifting animals to being subjects of legal rights.

[. . .]

I

IMMANUEL KANT WRITES that "so far as animals are concerned, we have no direct duties. Animals are not self-conscious and are there merely as means to an end. That end is man. . . . Our duties towards animals are merely indirect duties towards humanity."[1]

In the idea that nonhumans are nothing but means one can perceive echoes of Aristotle: "the other animals [exist] for the good of man, the domestic species both for his service and for his food, and . . . most of the wild ones for the sake of his food and of his supplies of other kinds."[2] And the thesis of indirect duties betrays a reminiscence of Thomas Aquinas's remarks on the subject of biblical injunctions against cruelty to nonhumans: "this is . . . to remove man's thoughts from being cruel to other men, and lest through being cruel to animals one become cruel to human beings."[3]

Though other views appeared on the philosophical scene – consider for example the Cartesian idea that animals are mere *natural automata* with which we can do entirely as we wish, and on the opposite side the utilitarian ethical concern for all the beings endowed with the capacity for suffering and enjoyment – one might say that these short quotations contain in a nutshell the elements of the most enduring and pervasive thesis about the treatment of nonhumans in all Western culture. In short: animals, as mere means, have zero grade moral status – that is, they are excluded from the moral community. However, there are limits to what can be done to them. Such limits are dictated by the fact that our behavior towards animals can rebound upon our behavior towards the only true objects of moral concern, namely, other human beings.

We can recast such a view in more formal terms. At the center of ethics lies a set of norms to govern behavior towards (at least some) other entities. Asking which are the entities other than the agent that should have their interests protected, is tantamount to asking who is a *moral patient*. The moral patient is, i.e., a being whose *treatment* may be subject to direct moral evaluation.[4] It is apparent that not all entities necessarily belong to this category – for most ethical theories, to shatter a stone or to mow the meadow's grass are wholly irrelevant actions. What the view in question claims is that, just like stones and plants, nonhuman animals are not moral patients.

The boundaries of the class of moral patients have often changed in the course of history, and it also happened that many human beings were excluded from ethical consideration – Aristotle himself held that, like animals, human slaves too were mere means at their masters' disposal.[5] Today we can easily understand how unsatisfactory such an attitude was, because a long work of rational criticism has dismantled its justifications, revealing the true nature as an implicit appeal to prejudice of the high-sounding claims on behalf of the superiority of a sex to the other, or of one race to all the other races. But if we rightly regard such a critical process as a fundamental component of our moral evolution, a question spontaneously arises: if the justifications on behalf of intra-human discrimination turned out to be indefensible, isn't it possible that the same holds for the justifications put forward on behalf of the discrimination against other-than-human beings? We shall here put to the test this hypothesis.

II

How, then, can one defend the idea that human beings are ends, while nonhuman beings are means? Before tackling this issue, it is necessary to stress that when contemporary philosophers defend the ends/means doctrine, what they are usually referring to is not the traditional Kantian formulation, but instead a softened version of it. According to such version, nonhuman animals are no longer utterly excluded from the moral community – they are, that is, numbered among moral patients. Nonetheless, the moral community has a stratified, hierarchical structure, and the continued use of nonhuman beings for our benefit is allegedly justified by their being confined to second-class moral status with respect to human beings. Both the traditional and the more recent view are defended by the same arguments. Since it is not possible to offer here a complete survey of such arguments, we shall confine ourselves to considering the most representative ones.

While not being altogether overlooked by philosophers, the first argument is, owing to its simplicity, powerful and widespread mainly at the societal level. To the question of what may draw what we might call, following Bentham, the "insuperable line" between us and the other animals,[6] this argument replies: the fact that they are not human. On such a perspective, what makes the difference is simply the possession, or lack, of a genotype characteristic of the species *Homo sapiens*.

Is it an acceptable reply? One can doubt it. Those who appeal to species membership work in fact within the framework of the intra-human egalitarian paradigm. And yet, it is just the line of reasoning that has led to the defense of human equality which implies, by denying moral relevance to race and sex membership, the rejection of the idea that species membership *in itself* can mark a difference as far as moral status is concerned. If one claims that merely biological characteristics like race and sex cannot play a role in ethics, because ethics is a theoretical inquiry endowed with its own standards of justification, in which criteria imported from other domains cannot be directly relevant,[7] how can one attribute a role to another merely biological characteristic such as species? Ethical views that, while rejecting racism and sexism, accept *speciesism* – as was defined, with a neologism that alludes to the parallel intra-human prejudices, the view that grants to the members of our own species a privileged status with respect to all other creatures – are internally inconsistent. For speciesism and racism are twin doctrines.[8]

Compared to this hardly plausible way of construing the relationships between species and morality, there exist more sophisticated views, to which the theoretical defenders of traditional morality tend to turn. In particular, there are, at least among philosophers, two main ways of describing the alleged difference between humans and the other animals. The appeal to the possession of rationality is central to both of them. We can set aside for the sake of argument the (questionable) assumption that all and only human beings are endowed with this capacity, in order to focus on the importance that is attached to rationality from a moral point of view.

The first argument rests on the idea that rational beings are the existence condition of morality, and might be summarized more or less as follows. Ethical norms are addressed to a particular kind of beings –

moral agents. In brief, moral agents are those rational beings which can reflect morally on how to act, and whose behavior can be subject to moral evaluation. In this sense, if moral agents did not exist, there could be no ethical norms. As a consequence, ethics is an internal affair of moral agents.[9]

In spite of its apparent plausibility, the argument is based on a misunderstanding. Its conclusion is in fact reached only by the shift from the idea that only rational beings can be morally responsible to the idea that only what is done to rational beings has (full) moral weight. But the *how*, that is, the possibility of morality, is one thing; the *what*, that is, the object of morality, is another.[10] To acknowledge that moral agents make morality possible does not mean to make them the only (full) moral patients. That, on the other hand, we do not really hold this view is shown by the fact that we are far from withdrawing full moral protection from those members of our species who are unable to abide by ethical norms. Small children, or – if one wants to avoid the controversial question of potentiality – severely intellectually disabled individuals (the so-called marginal, or non-paradigmatic, humans),[11] are not on this ground relegated to the no-man's land surrounding the moral community.

A different role is played by rationality within the second argument which is usually advanced in defense of human superiority. Basically, what is ascribed to such a capacity is a particular kind of instrumental value. The core idea is that the introduction into the moral community can be justified by means of some sort of agreement. Since in order to abide by the agreement one must be rational, the agreement will include only rational beings, who will then turn out to be the only moral patients. In this light, moral norms would be the norms with which rational and self-interested individuals would agree to comply on condition that others undertook to do so as well. If the preceding argument can somehow point to the contemporary position of John Rawls, here is apparent the influence of the mutual advantage account of contractarianism of Hobbesian descent.[12]

It is not difficult to understand why not even this approach is acceptable. For, given that self-interested contractors gain no advantage from accepting principles that offer guarantees to individuals who are unable to give any guarantee in return, they can completely ignore the interests of those who are unable to reciprocate. But if the golden rule "treat others as you would have them treat you" is replaced by what we might call the silver rule, "treat others as they would treat you,"[13] mutual advantage has the devastating effect of driving ethical impartiality off the stage. Once more, current morality clearly grasps this point, insofar as it does not deprive of rights those human beings – again, children or the severely intellectually disabled – who cannot have duties.

But if none of the major arguments advanced in defense of the ends/means doctrine[14] – the appeal to the possession of a genotype *Homo sapiens*, the appeal to the possession of rationality as a precondition of morals, and the reference to this very same capacity as a means to intersubjective agreement – can justify maintaining nonhuman animals in their present inferior moral state, it seems plausible to conclude that traditional morality is untenable.

III

If one gives up the doctrine of human superiority, what kind of moral perspective should one adopt in its place? In which ways, and toward which beings, should traditional morality be reformed? In order to tackle this question, many among the authors who have dealt with the animal issue appeal to their own specific normative position – be it utilitarianism, deontologism, virtue ethics or any other. However, only an argument starting from premises that are, as far as possible, shared, can grant its conclusions the generality that is needed for moral reform. Because of this reason, we will directly start from what is today the most widespread and accepted among moral theories – the universal doctrine of human rights[15].

At the center of the theory of human rights lies the protection of the vital interests – in welfare, in freedom and in life – of some beings. Of which beings, exactly? Though the most common, and apparently tautological, answer is "of *human* beings," such a move is, as we have seen, precluded by the fact that discrimination based on species is analogous to those forms of discrimination that the very doctrine condemns in sexism and racism. Most of the philosophers who confront the issue seem to be somehow aware of this problem. When it is bestowed a role, in fact, reference to species is introduced in a hurried and oblique way.[16] What, then, plays in an effective, and not rhetorical, way the role of explaining the *why* of human rights – of illustrating, that is, what it is that, in the members of our species, justifies the equal attribution of the particular sort of moral claims lumped together under the label of "human rights"?

Among the solutions advanced for this problem, the most defensible, as well as the most theoretically fertile, is no doubt the one put forward by a line of argument that appeared at the beginning of the 1960s,[17] and culminating in the elaboration offered by the American philosopher Alan Gewirth. According to such a line, the criterion for the access to the protection that human rights warrant lies only in being an *agent*, that is, an intentional being that cares about its goals and wants to achieve them. All the beings that fulfill the requisite of intentionality are characterized by the capacity to enjoy freedom and welfare, as well as life which is a precondition for them, both directly and as prerequisites for action; and, for all these beings, the intrinsic value of their enjoyment is the same. To choose as a criterion, instead of intentionality, any other characteristic – be it rationality or any other among the cognitive skills traditionally seen as "superior" – would be arbitrary, since it would exclude from moral consideration interests which are relevantly similar in that they are equally vital for their bearers.[18]

Once articulated, such an answer – which has among other things the important effect of barring the way to discredited perfectionist worldviews – appears obvious. And yet, it involves a corollary which is not equally obvious: that, on the basis of the very doctrine that establishes them, human rights are not *human*. For not only does the more or less avowed acceptance of the idea that species membership is not morally relevant eliminate from the theory any structural reference to the possession of a genotype *Homo sapiens*, but the will to secure equal fundamental rights to all human beings, including the non-paradigmatic ones, implies that the criterion for the ascription of such rights must lie at a cognitive level accessible to a large number of non-human animals.

IV

If, in view of all this, we go back to our initial interrogative, it may be safely said that the current divergence in standards between humans and nonhumans is indefensible. All the more so: it is plausible to claim that, among those entitled to that minimum of equality and equity that allows one to live a life worth living – among, that is, those moral patients who deserve full moral status – there are many nonhuman beings. But what can it mean, in practice, to extend fundamental rights beyond the boundaries of our species? Confronted with this idea, some opponents tend to make recourse to various reductios, by evoking scenarios that are either concretely impossible, such as the obligation to bring our aid-commitment all the way to the deserts or the sea depths, or socially absurd, such as the revision to its foundations of our whole legal system.

None of this. In order to understand this point, it is worth defining more precisely that particular category of moral rights that we label as "human rights." Such category has in fact two significant peculiarities. Firstly, human rights do not cover the whole of morality, but concern the more limited theory of conduct which has been defined as "morality in the narrow sense," and which meets the special class of moral concerns which has to do with the basic protection of individuals from interference.[19] For in spite of the attempts to embody in the doctrine some *positive* rights, or rights to assistance, the ones which prevail are always *negative* rights, or rights to non-interference, that not only are more basic but – being less affected by conditions of scarcity – are less likely to be subject to exceptions.[20] Secondly, human rights clearly developed as an answer to those forms of institutionalized violence and discrimination which have marked the first half of the twentieth century. This implies, as it has been convincingly argued by the American philosopher Thomas Pogge, that the model both of their implementation and of their violation is based not on the interaction between individuals, but on the organization and the action of the state.[21]

Let's therefore reconsider the present situation in the light of these two aspects. Billions of nonhuman animals who meet the requisite of intentionality are tortured, confined and killed in the pursuit of the most varied human goals. But *codified* killing, confinement, mutilation and torture are just the opposite of that protection from *institutional interference* that human rights theory aims at granting. What, then, could an implementation at the social level of the conclusions so far reached mean in such a context? Far from involving impossible practical interventions and complicated legal alchemies, such implementation would merely require a legal change aimed at removing in the status of property the basic obstacle to the enjoyment of the denied rights. In other words, it would imply for these animals the shift from the condition of objects to that of subjects of legal rights,[22] and, as a consequence, the prohibition of all the practices that are today made possible by their current state, from raising for food to scientific experimentation to the most varied forms of commercial use and systematic extermination.

This is, I believe, the conclusion awaiting anyone who wants to seriously reflect on our current behavior toward nonhuman animals. Far from belonging in the different, and lesser, moral category in which they have till now been confined, (most) nonhumans confront us with all the force of a justified ethical demand. And this because it is the very logic of the doctrine that tried to overcome the most serious difficulties for intra-human cohabitation which forces us to extend basic rights beyond the boundaries of the species *Homo sapiens*, thus offering a plausible solution for the problems of a community broader than the human one.

Notes

1   Immanuel Kant, *Lectures on Ethics*, trans. Louis Infield (New York: Harper and Row, 1963), p. 239.

2   Aristotle, *Politics*, I, 3, 1256 b.

3   Thomas Aquinas, *Summa contra Gentiles*, book III, part II, chap. CXII.

4   We owe one of the first formulations of the concept to G. J. Warnock: cf. his *The Object of Morality* (London: Methuen, 1971), p. 148. See also Harlan B. Miller, "Science, Ethics, and Moral Status," *Between the Species* 10 (1994), p. 14.

5   See Aristotle, *Politics*, I, 2, 1253 b.

6   See Jeremy Bentham, *An Introduction to the Principles of Morals and Legislation* (New York: Hafner Press, 1948), chap. XVII, IV, note 1.

7   For the autonomy of ethics, see Thomas Nagel, "Ethics as an Autonomous Theoretical Subject," in *Morality as a Biological Phenomenon*, ed. Gunther S. Stent (Berkeley: University of California Press, 1978). For the moral irrelevance of biological characteristics, see e.g. Michael Tooley, "Speciesism and Basic Moral Principles," *Etica & Animali* 9 (1998), pp. 5–36.

8   Cfr. Peter Singer, *Animal Liberation*, 2nd edn. (New York: The New York Review of Books, 1990), p. 9.

9   Once again, we owe the paradigmatic formulation of this argument, which is particularly widespread in the continental philosophical tradition, to Immanuel Kant. See Immanuel Kant, *Foundations of the Metaphysics of Morals*, trans. Lewis W. Beck (Upper Saddle River, NJ: Prentice-Hall, 1997), p. 45.

10   See Steve F. Sapontzis, *Morals, Reason, and Animals* (Philadelphia: Temple University Press, 1987), pp. 146 ff.

11   A comprehensive survey of the discussion of the case of non-paradigmatic members of our species can be found in Daniel A. Dombrowski, *Babies and Beasts. The Argument from Marginal Cases* (Chicago: University of Illinois Press, 1997).

12   For the similarities and differences between Rawlsian impartial contractarian theory and Hobbesian mutual advantage approach, see Paola Cavalieri and Will Kymlicka. "Expanding the Social Contract," *Etica & Animali* 8 (1996), pp. 5–33.

13   I borrow the expression "silver rule" from Edward Johnson, *Species and Morality* (Ph.D. diss., Princeton University, July 1976 [University Microfilms International, Ann Arbor, MI]), p. 134.

14   For a concise critique of many minor arguments see Paola Cavalieri, *The Animal Question. Why Nonhuman Animals Deserve Human Rights* (New York: Oxford University Press, 2001), chapters III and IV.

15   For a more articulated version of the following argument see ibid., chapter VI.

16   Cf. for example. what Adam Bedau writes: "Are human rights to be thought of as possessed by all and only persons, human beings, or human persons? . . . [T]he last alternative . . . is the least controversial way to resolve the problem. The concept of human rights was not designed to embrace non-human persons, and it was clearly intended to exclude infra-human beings, such as animals." See Hugo Adam Bedau, "International Human Rights," in *And Justice for All*, eds. Tom Regan and Donald VanDeVeer (Totowa, NJ: Rowman & Allanheld, 1983), p. 298.

17   Its first seeds are to be found in Gregory Vlastos, "Justice and Equality," in *Social Justice*, ed. Richard B. Brandt (Englewood Cliffs, NJ: Prentice-Hall, 1962).

18   See Alan Gewirth, *Reason and Morality* (Chicago: University of Chicago Press, 1978). A summary of the argument can be found in Alan Gewirth, "The Basis and Content of Human Rights," in *Nomos XXIII: Human Rights*, eds. J. Roland Pennock and John W. Chapman (New York: New York University Press, 1981).

19   On the notion of narrow morality cf. in particular W. K. Frankena, "The Concept of Morality," *The Journal of Philosophy* 63 (1966); G. J. Warnock, *The Object of Morality* (London: Methuen, 1971), in particular chap. 2 and chap. 5; and J. L. Mackie, *Ethics. Inventing Right and Wrong* (London: Penguin, 1990), pp. 107–108.

20   In his "Human Rights, Old and New", in *Political Theory and the Rights of Man*, ed. D. D. Raphael (London: Macmillan, 1967), D. D. Raphael plausibly claims that *positive* rights, rather than as "human rights", are to be classified as "citizen's rights".

21   See Thomas Pogge, "How Should Human Rights Be Conceived?" *Jahrbuch für Recht und Ethik* 3 (1995), pp. 103–120.

22   For a discussion of this problem see e.g. Gary L. Francione, *Animals, Property, and the Law* (Philadelphia: Temple University Press, 1995).

Chapter 4

Peter Singer

PRACTICAL ETHICS

Peter Singer states that there is no moral justification for refusing to take animal suffering seriously. He calls for a boycott of the meat industry on the basis of equal consideration of interests. Singer affirms that experiments on animals should only be carried out if experimenters would be willing to also use human beings at an equal or lower level of consciousness. He then responds to common objections to his views. In a concluding section he presents a strong case against the killing of rational and self-conscious animals such as the great apes.

THE ARGUMENT FOR extending the principle of equality beyond our own species is simple, so simple that it amounts to no more than a clear understanding of the nature of the principle of equal consideration of interests.[1] We have seen that this principle implies that our concern for others ought not to depend on what they are like, or what abilities they possess (although precisely what this concern requires us to do may vary according to the characteristics of those affected by what we do). It is on this basis that we are able to say that the fact that some people are not members of our race does not entitle us to exploit them, and similarly the fact that some people are less intelligent than others does not mean that their interests may be disregarded. But the principle also implies that the fact that beings are not members of our species does not entitle us to exploit them, and similarly the fact that other animals are less intelligent than we are does not mean that their interests may be disregarded.

[. . .] [M]any philosophers have advocated equal consideration of interests, in some form or other, as a basic moral principle. Only a few have recognised that the principle has applications beyond our own species, one of the few being Jeremy Bentham, the founding father of modern utilitarianism. In a forward-looking passage, written at a time when African slaves in the British dominions were still being treated much as we now treat nonhuman animals, Bentham wrote:

> The day may come when the rest of the animal creation may acquire those rights which never could have been withholden from them but by the hand of tyranny. The French have already discovered that the blackness of the skin is no reason why a human being should be abandoned without redress to the caprice of a tormentor. It may one day come to be recognised that the number of the legs, the villosity of the skin, or the termination of the *os sacrum*, are reasons equally insufficient for abandoning a sensitive being to the same fate. What else is it that should trace the insuperable line? Is it the faculty of reason, or perhaps the faculty of discourse? But a fullgrown horse or dog is beyond comparison a more rational, as well as a more conversable animal, than an infant of a day, or a week, or even a month, old. But suppose they were otherwise, what would it avail? The question is not, Can they *reason*? nor Can they *talk*? but, *Can they suffer?*[2]

In this passage Bentham points to the capacity for suffering as the vital characteristic that entitles a being to equal consideration. The capacity for suffering – or more strictly, for suffering and/or enjoyment or happiness – is not just another characteristic like the capacity for language, or for higher mathematics. Bentham is not saying that those who try to mark 'the insuperable line' that determines whether the interests of a being should be considered happen to have selected the wrong characteristic. The capacity for suffering and enjoying things is a prerequisite for having interests at all, a condition that must be satisfied before we can speak of interests in any meaningful way. It would be nonsense to say that it was not in the interests of a stone to be kicked along the road by a schoolboy. A stone does not have interests because it cannot suffer. Nothing that we can do to it could possibly make any difference to its welfare. A mouse, on the other hand, does have an interest in not being tormented, because mice will suffer if they are treated in this way.

If a being suffers, there can be no moral justification for refusing to take that suffering into consideration. No matter what the nature of the being, the principle of equality requires that the suffering be counted equally with the like suffering – in so far as rough comparisons can be made – of any other being. If a being is not capable of suffering, or of experiencing enjoyment or happiness, there is nothing to be taken into account. This is why the limit of sentience (using the term as a convenient, if not strictly accurate, shorthand for the capacity to suffer or experience enjoyment or happiness) is the only defensible boundary of concern for the interests of others. To mark this boundary by some characteristic like intelligence or rationality would be to mark it in an arbitrary way. Why not choose some other characteristic, like skin colour?

Racists violate the principle of equality by giving greater weight to the interests of members of their own race when there is a clash between their interests and the interests of those of another race. Racists of European descent typically have not accepted that pain matters as much when it is felt by Africans, for example, as when it is felt by Europeans. Similarly those I would call 'speciesists' give greater weight to the interests of members of their own species when there is a clash between their interests and the interests of those of other species. Human speciesists do not accept that pain is as bad when it is felt by pigs or mice as when it is felt by humans.

That, then, is really the whole of the argument for extending the principle of equality to nonhuman animals; but there may be some doubts about what this equality amounts to in practice. In particular, the last sentence of the previous paragraph may prompt some people to reply: 'Surely pain felt by a mouse just is not as bad as pain felt by a human. Humans have much greater awareness of what is happening to them, and this makes their suffering worse. You can't equate the suffering of, say, a person dying slowly from cancer, and a laboratory mouse undergoing the same fate.'

I fully accept that in the case described the human cancer victim normally suffers more than the nonhuman cancer victim. This is no way undermines the extension of equal consideration of interests to nonhumans. It means, rather, that we must take care when we compare the interests of different species. In some situations a member of one species will suffer more than a member of another species. In this case we should still apply the principle of equal consideration of interests but the result of so doing is, of course, to give priority to relieving the greater suffering. A simpler case may help to make this clear.

If I give a horse a hard slap across its rump with my open hand, the horse may start, but it presumably feels little pain. Its skin is thick enough to protect it against a mere slap. If I slap a baby in the same way, however, the baby will cry and presumably does feel pain, for the baby's skin is more sensitive. So it is worse to slap a baby than a horse, if both slaps are administered with equal force. But there must be some kind of blow – I don't know exactly what it would be, but perhaps a blow with a heavy stick – that would cause the horse as much pain as we cause a baby by a simple slap. That is what I mean by 'the same amount of pain' and if we consider it wrong to inflict that much pain on a baby for no good reason then we must, unless we are speciesists, consider it equally wrong to inflict the same amount of pain on a horse for no good reason.

There are other differences between humans and animals that cause other complications. Normal adult human beings have mental capacities that will, in certain circumstances, lead them to suffer more than animals would in the same circumstances. If, for instance, we decided to perform extremely painful or lethal scientific experiments on normal adult humans, kidnapped at random from public parks for this purpose, adults who entered parks would become fearful that they would be kidnapped. The resultant terror would be a form of suffering additional to the pain of the experiment. The same experiments performed on nonhuman animals would cause less suffering since the animals would not have the anticipatory dread of being kidnapped and experimented upon. This does not mean, of course, that it would be *right* to perform the experiment on animals, but only that there is a reason, and one that is not speciesist, for preferring to use animals rather than normal adult humans, if the experiment is to be done at all. Note, however, that this same argument gives us a reason for preferring to use human infants – orphans perhaps – or severely intellectually disabled humans for experiments, rather than adults, since infants and severely intellectually disabled humans would also have no idea of what was going to happen to them. As far as this argument is concerned, nonhuman animals and infants and severely intellectually disabled humans are in the same category; and if we use this argument to justify experiments on nonhuman animals we have to ask ourselves whether we are also prepared to allow experiments on human infants and severely intellectually disabled adults. If we make a distinction between animals and these humans, how can we do it, other than on the basis of a morally indefensible preference for members of our own species?

There are many areas in which the superior mental powers of normal adult humans make a difference: anticipation, more detailed memory, greater knowledge of what is happening, and so on. These differences explain why a human dying from cancer is likely to suffer more than a mouse. It is the mental anguish that makes the human's position so much harder to bear. Yet these differences do not all point to greater suffering on the part of the normal human being. Sometimes animals may suffer more because of their more limited understanding. If, for instance, we are taking prisoners in wartime we can explain to them that while they must submit to capture, search, and confinement they will not otherwise be harmed and will be set free at the conclusion of hostilities. If we capture wild animals, however, we cannot explain that we are not threatening their lives. A wild animal cannot distinguish an attempt to overpower and confine from an attempt to kill; the one causes as much terror as the other.

It may be objected that comparisons of the sufferings of different species are impossible to make, and that for this reason when the interests of animals and humans clash, the principle of equality gives no guidance. It is true that comparisons of suffering between members of different species cannot be made precisely. Nor, for that matter, can comparisons of suffering between different human beings be made precisely. Precision is not essential. As we shall see shortly, even if we were to prevent the infliction of suffering on animals only when the interests of humans will not be affected to anything like the extent that animals are affected, we would be forced to make radical changes in our treatment of animals that would involve our diet, the farming methods we use, experimental procedures in many fields of science, our approach to wildlife and to hunting, trapping, and the wearing of furs, and areas of entertainment like circuses, rodeos, and zoos. As a result, the total quantity of suffering caused would be greatly reduced; so greatly that it is hard to imagine any other change of moral attitude that would cause so great a reduction in the total sum of suffering in the universe.

So far I have said a lot about the infliction of suffering on animals, but nothing about killing them. This omission has been deliberate. The application of the principle of equality to the infliction of suffering is, in theory at least, fairly straightforward. Pain and suffering are bad and should be prevented or minimised, irrespective of the race, sex, or species of the being that suffers. How bad a pain is depends on how intense it is and how long it lasts, but pains of the same intensity and duration are equally bad, whether felt by humans or animals. When we come to consider the value of life, we cannot say quite so confidently that a life is a life, and equally valuable, whether it is a human life or an animal life. It would not be speciesist to hold that the life of a self-aware being, capable of abstract thought, of planning for the future, of complex acts of communication, and so on, is more valuable than the life of a being without these capacities. (I am not saying whether this view is justifiable or not; only that it cannot simply be rejected as speciesist, because it is not on the basis of species itself that one life is held to be more valuable than another.) The value of life is a notoriously difficult ethical question, and we can only arrive at a reasoned conclusion about the comparative value of human and animal life after we have discussed the value of life in general. This is a topic for a separate chapter. Meanwhile there are important conclusions to be derived from the extension beyond our own species of the principle of equal consideration of interests, irrespective of our conclusions about the value of life.

Speciesism in practice

Animals as food

For most people in modern, urbanised societies, the principal form of contact with nonhuman animals is at meal times. The use of animals for food is probably the oldest and the most widespread form of animal use. There is also a sense in which it is the most basic form of animal use, the foundation stone on which rests the belief that animals exist for our pleasure and convenience.

If animals count in their own right, our use of animals for food becomes questionable – especially when animal flesh is a luxury rather than a necessity. Eskimos living in an environment where they must kill animals for food or starve might be justified in claiming that their interest in surviving overrides that of the animals they kill. Most of us cannot defend our diet in this way. Citizens of industrialised societies can easily obtain an adequate diet without the use of animal flesh. The overwhelming weight of medical evidence indicates that animal flesh is not necessary for good health or longevity. Nor is animal production in industrialised societies an efficient way of producing food, since most of the animals consumed have been fattened on grains and other foods that we could have eaten directly. When we feed these grains to animals, only about 10 per cent of the nutritional value remains as meat for human consumption. So, with the exception of animals raised entirely on grazing land unsuitable for crops, animals are eaten neither for health, nor to increase our food supply. Their flesh is a luxury, consumed because people like its taste.

In considering the ethics of the use of animal flesh for human food in industrialised societies, we are considering a situation in which a relatively minor human interest must be balanced against the lives and welfare of the animals involved. The principle of equal consideration of interests does not allow major interests to be sacrificed for minor interests.

The case against using animals for food is at its strongest when animals are made to lead miserable lives so that their flesh can be made available to humans at the lowest possible cost. Modern forms of intensive farming apply science and technology to the attitude that animals are objects for us to use. In order to have meat on the table at a price that people can afford, our society tolerates methods of meat production that confine sentient animals in cramped, unsuitable conditions for the entire duration of their lives. Animals are treated like machines that convert fodder into flesh, and any innovation that results in a higher 'conversion ratio' is liable to be adopted. As one authority on the subject has said, 'Cruelty is acknowledged only when profitability ceases.' To avoid speciesism we must stop these practices. Our custom is all the support that factory farmers need. The decision to cease giving them that support may be difficult, but it is less difficult than it would have been for a white Southerner to go against the traditions of his society and free his slaves; if we do not change our dietary habits, how can we censure those slaveholders who would not change their own way of living?

These arguments apply to animals who have been reared in factory farms – which means that we should not eat chicken, pork, or veal, unless we know that the meat we are eating was not produced by factory farm methods. The same is true of beef that has come from cattle kept in crowded feedlots (as most beef does in the United States). Eggs will come from hens kept in small wire cages, too small even to allow them to stretch their wings, unless the eggs are specifically sold as 'free range' (or unless one lives in a relatively enlightened country like Switzerland, which has prohibited the cage system of keeping hens).

These arguments do not take us all the way to a vegetarian diet, since some animals, for instance sheep, and in some countries cattle still graze freely outdoors. This could change. The American pattern of fattening cattle in crowded feedlots is spreading to other countries. Meanwhile, the lives of free-ranging animals are undoubtedly better than those of animals reared in factory farms. It is still doubtful if using them for food is compatible with equal consideration of interests. One problem is, of course, that using them as food involves killing them – but this is an issue to which, as I have said, we shall return when we have discussed the value of life in the next chapter. Apart from taking their lives there are also many other things done to animals in order to bring them cheaply to our dinner table. Castration, the separation of mother and young, the breaking up of herds, branding, transporting, and finally the moments of slaughter – all of these are likely to involve suffering and do not take the animals' interests into account. Perhaps animals could be reared on a small scale without suffering in these ways, but it does not seem economical or practical to do so on the scale required for feeding our large urban populations. In any case, the important question is not whether animal flesh *could* be produced without suffering, but whether the flesh we are considering buying was produced without suffering. Unless we can be confident that it was, the principle of equal consideration of interests implies that it was wrong to sacrifice important interests of the animal in order to satisfy less important interests of our own; consequently we should boycott the end result of this process.

For those of us living in cities where it is difficult to know how the animals we might eat have lived and died, this conclusion brings us close to a vegetarian way of life. I shall consider some objections to it in the final section of this chapter.

Experimenting on animals

Perhaps the area in which speciesism can most clearly be observed is the use of animals in experiments. Here the issue stands out starkly, because experimenters often seek to justify experimenting on animals by claiming that the experiments lead us to discoveries about humans; if this is so, the experimenter must agree that human and nonhuman animals are similar in crucial respects. For instance, if forcing a rat to choose between starving to death and crossing an electrified grid to obtain food tells us anything about the reactions of humans to stress, we must assume that the rat feels stress in this kind of situation.

People sometimes think that all animal experiments serve vital medical purposes, and can be justified on the grounds that they relieve more suffering than they cause. This comfortable belief is mistaken. Drug companies test new shampoos and cosmetics they are intending to market by dripping concentrated solutions of them into the eyes of rabbits, in a test known as the Draize test. (Pressure from the animal liberation movement has led several cosmetic companies to abandon this practice. An alternative test, not using animals, has now been found. Nevertheless, many companies, including some of the largest, still continue to perform the Draize test.) Food additives, including artificial colourings and preservatives, are tested by what is known as the LD50 – a test designed to find the 'lethal dose', or level of consumption that will make 50 per cent of a sample of animals die. In the process nearly all of the animals are made very sick before some finally die and others pull through. These tests are not necessary to prevent human suffering: even if there were no alternative to the use of animals to test the safety of the products, we already have enough shampoos and food colourings. There is no need to develop new ones that might be dangerous.

In many countries, the armed forces perform atrocious experiments on animals that rarely come to light. To give just one example: at the U.S. Armed Forces Radiobiology Institute, in Bethesda, Maryland, rhesus monkeys have been trained to run inside a large wheel. If they slow down too much, the wheel slows down, too, and the monkeys get an electric shock. Once the monkeys are trained to run for long periods, they are given lethal doses of radiation. Then, while sick and vomiting, they are forced to continue to run until they drop. This is supposed to provide information on the capacities of soldiers to continue to fight after a nuclear attack.

Nor can all university experiments be defended on the grounds that they relieve more suffering than they inflict. Three experimenters at Princeton University kept 256 young rats without food or water until they died. They concluded that young rats under conditions of fatal thirst and starvation are much more active than normal adult rats given food and water. In a well-known series of experiments that went on for more than fifteen years, H. F. Harlow of the Primate Research Center, Madison, Wisconsin, reared monkeys under conditions of maternal deprivation and total isolation. He found that in this way he could reduce the monkeys to a state in which, when placed among normal monkeys, they sat huddled in a corner in a condition of persistent depression and fear. Harlow also produced monkey mothers so neurotic that they smashed their infant's face into the floor and rubbed it back and forth. Although Harlow himself is no longer alive, some of his former students at other U.S. universities continue to perform variations on his experiments.

In these cases, and many others like them, the benefits to humans are either nonexistent or uncertain, while the losses to members of other species are certain and real. Hence the experiments indicate a failure to give equal consideration to the interests of all beings, irrespective of species.

In the past, argument about animal experimentation has often missed this point because it has been put in absolutist terms: would the opponent of experimentation be prepared to let thousands die from a terrible disease that could be cured by experimenting on one animal? This is a purely hypothetical question, since experiments do not have such dramatic results, but as long as its hypothetical nature is clear, I think the question should be answered affirmatively – in other words, if one, or even a dozen animals had to suffer experiments in order to save thousands, I would think it right and in accordance with equal consideration of interests that they should do so. This, at any rate, is the answer a utilitarian must give. Those who believe in absolute rights might hold that it is always wrong to sacrifice one being, whether human or animal, for the benefit of another. In that case the experiment should not be carried out, whatever the consequences.

To the hypothetical question about saving thousands of people through a single experiment on an animal, opponents of speciesism can reply with a hypothetical question of their own: would experimenters be prepared to perform their experiments on orphaned humans with severe and irreversible brain damage if that were the only way to save thousands? (I say 'orphaned' in order to avoid the complication of the feelings of the human parents.) If experimenters are not prepared to use orphaned humans with severe and irreversible brain damage, their readiness to use nonhuman animals seems to discriminate on the basis of species alone, since apes, monkeys, dogs, cats, and even mice and rats are more intelligent, more aware of what is happening to them, more sensitive to pain, and so on, than many severely braindamaged humans barely surviving in hospital wards and other institutions. There seems to be no morally relevant characteristic that such humans have that nonhuman animals lack. Experimenters, then, show bias in favour of their own species whenever they carry out experiments on nonhuman animals for purposes that they would not think justified them in using human beings at an equal or lower level of sentience, awareness, sensitivity, and so on. If this bias were eliminated, the number of experiments performed on animals would be greatly reduced.

Other forms of speciesism

I have concentrated on the use of animals as food and in research, since these are examples of large-scale, systematic speciesism. They are not, of course, the only areas in which the principle of equal consideration of interests, extended beyond the human species, has practical implications. There are many other areas that raise similar issues, including the fur trade, hunting in all its different forms, circuses, rodeos, zoos, and the pet business. Since the philosophical questions raised by these issues are not very different from those raised by the use of animals as food and in research, I shall leave it to the reader to apply the appropriate ethical principles to them.

Some objections

I first put forward the views outlined in this chapter in 1973. At that time there was no animal liberation or animal rights movement. Since then a movement has sprung up, and some of the worst abuses of animals, like the Draize and LD50 tests, are now less widespread, even though they have not been eliminated. The fur trade has come under attack, and as a result fur sales have declined dramatically in countries like Britain, the Netherlands, Australia, and the United States. Some countries are also starting to phase out the most confining forms of factory farming. As already mentioned, Switzerland has prohibited the cage system of keeping laying hens. Britain has outlawed the raising of calves in individual stalls, and is phasing out individual stalls for pigs. Sweden, as in other areas of social reform, is in the lead here, too: in 1988 the Swedish Parliament passed a law that will, over a ten-year period, lead to the elimination of all systems of factory farming that confine animals for long periods and prevent them carrying out their natural behaviour.

Despite this increasing acceptance of many aspects of the case for animal liberation, and the slow but tangible progress made on behalf of animals, a variety of objections have emerged, some straightforward and predictable, some more subtle and unexpected. In this final section of the chapter I shall attempt to answer the most important of these objections. I shall begin with the more straightforward ones.

How do we know that animals can feel pain?

We can never directly experience the pain of another being, whether that being is human or not. When I see my daughter fall and scrape her knee, I know that she feels pain because of the way she behaves – she cries, she tells me her knee hurts, she rubs the sore spot, and so on. I know that I myself behave in a somewhat similar – if more inhibited – way when I feel pain, and so I accept that my daughter feels something like what I feel when I scrape my knee.

The basis of my belief that animals can feel pain is similar to the basis of my belief that my daughter can feel pain. Animals in pain behave in much the same way as humans do, and their behaviour is sufficient justification for the belief that they feel pain. It is true that, with the exception of those apes who have been taught to communicate by sign language, they cannot actually say that they are feeling pain – but then when my daughter was very young she could not talk, either. She found other ways to make her inner states apparent, thereby demonstrating that we can be sure that a being is feeling pain even if the being cannot use language.

To back up our inference from animal behaviour, we can point to the fact that the nervous systems of all vertebrates, and especially of birds and mammals, are fundamentally similar. Those parts of the human nervous system that are concerned with feeling pain are relatively old, in evolutionary terms. Unlike the cerebral cortex, which developed fully only after our ancestors diverged from other mammals, the basic nervous system evolved in more distant ancestors common to ourselves and the other 'higher' animals. This anatomical parallel makes it likely that the capacity of animals to feel is similar to our own.

It is significant that none of the grounds we have for believing that animals feel pain hold for plants. We cannot observe behaviour suggesting pain – sensational claims to the contrary have not been substantiated – and plants do not have a centrally organised nervous system like ours.

Animals eat each other, so why shouldn't we eat them?

This might be called the Benjamin Franklin Objection. Franklin recounts in his *Autobiography* that he was for a time a vegetarian but his abstinence from animal flesh came to an end when he was watching some friends prepare to fry a fish they had just caught. When the fish was cut open, it was found to have a smaller fish in its stomach. 'Well', Franklin said to himself, 'if you eat one another, I don't see why we may not eat you' and he proceeded to do so.

Franklin was at least honest. In telling this story, he confesses that he convinced himself of the validity of the objection only after the fish was already in the frying pan and smelling 'admirably well'; and he remarks that one of the advantages of being a 'reasonable creature' is that one can find a reason for whatever one wants to do. The replies that can be made to this objection are so obvious that Franklin's acceptance of it does testify more to his love of fried fish than to his powers of reason.[3] For a start, most animals who kill for food would not be able to survive if they did not, whereas we have no need to eat animal flesh. Next, it is odd that humans, who normally think of the behaviour of animals as 'beastly' should, when it suits them, use an argument that implies that we ought to look to animals for moral guidance. The most decisive point, however, is that nonhuman animals are not capable of considering the alternatives open to them or of reflecting on the ethics of their diet. Hence it is impossible to hold the animals responsible for what they do, or to judge that because of their killing they 'deserve' to be treated in a similar way. Those who read these lines, on the other hand, must consider the justifiability of their dietary habits. You cannot evade responsibility by imitating beings who are incapable of making this choice.

Sometimes people point to the fact that animals eat each other in order to make a slightly different point. This fact suggests, they think, not that animals deserve to be eaten, but rather that there is a natural law according to which the stronger prey upon the weaker, a kind of Darwinian 'survival of the fittest' in which by eating animals we are merely playing our part.

This interpretation of the objection makes two basic mistakes, one a mistake of fact and the other an error of reasoning. The factual mistake lies in the assumption that our own consumption of animals is part of the natural evolutionary process. This might be true of a few primitive cultures that still hunt for food, but it has nothing to do with the mass production of domestic animals in factory farms.

Suppose that we did hunt for our food, though, and this was part of some natural evolutionary process. There would still be an error of reasoning in the assumption that because this process is natural it is right. It is, no doubt, 'natural' for women to produce an infant every year or two from puberty to menopause, but this does not mean that it is wrong to interfere with this process. We need to know the natural laws that affect us in order to estimate the consequences of what we do; but we do not have to assume that the natural way of doing something is incapable of improvement.

[. . .]

Ethics and reciprocity

[. . .]

[I]f the basis of ethics is that I refrain from doing nasty things to others as long as they don't do nasty things to me, I have no reason against doing nasty things to those who are incapable of appreciating my restraint and controlling their conduct towards me accordingly. Animals, by and large, are in this category. When I am surfing far out from shore and a shark attacks, my concern for animals will not help; I am as likely to be eaten as the next surfer, though he may spend every Sunday afternoon taking potshots at sharks from a boat. Since animals cannot reciprocate, they are, on this view, outside the limits of the ethical contract.

[. . .]

When we turn to the question of justification, we can see that contractual accounts of ethics have many problems. Clearly, such accounts exclude from the ethical sphere a lot more than nonhuman animals. Since severely intellectually disabled humans are equally incapable of reciprocating, they must also be excluded. The same goes for infants and very young children; but the problems of the contractual view are not limited to these special cases. The ultimate reason for entering into the ethical contract is, on this view, self-interest. Unless some additional universal element is brought in, one group of people has no reason to deal ethically with another if it is not in their interest to do so. If we take this seriously we shall have to revise our ethical judgments drastically. For instance, the white slave traders who transported African slaves to America had no self-interested reason for treating Africans any better than they did. The Africans had no way of retaliating. If they had only been contractualists, the slave traders could have rebutted the abolitionists by explaining to them that ethics stops at the boundaries of the community, and since Africans are not part of their community they have no duties to them.

Nor is it only past practices that would be affected by taking the contractual model seriously. Though people often speak of the world today as a single community, there is no doubt that the power of people in, say, Chad, to reciprocate either good or evil that is done to them by, say, citizens of the United States is limited. Hence it does not seem that the contract view provides for any obligations on the part of wealthy nations to poorer nations.

Most striking of all is the impact of the contract model on our attitude to future generations. 'Why should I do anything for posterity? What has posterity ever done for me?' would be the view we ought to take if only those who can reciprocate are within the bounds of ethics. There is no way in which those who will be alive in the year 2100 can do anything to make our lives better or worse. Hence if obligations only exist where there can be reciprocity, we need have no worries about problems like the disposal of nuclear waste. True, some nuclear wastes will still be deadly for a quarter of a million years; but as long as we put it in containers that will keep it away from us for 100 years, we have done all that ethics demands of us.

These examples should suffice to show that, whatever its origin, the ethics we have now does go beyond a tacit understanding between beings capable of reciprocity. The prospect of returning to such a basis will, I trust, not be appealing. Since no account of the origin of morality compels us to base our morality on reciprocity, and since no other arguments in favour of this conclusion have been offered, we should reject this view of ethics.

[. . .]

Conclusions

[T]here is no single answer to the question: 'Is it normally wrong to take the life of an animal?' The term 'animal' – even in the restricted sense of 'non-human animal' – covers too diverse a range of lives for one principle to apply to all of them.

Some non-human animals appear to be rational and self-conscious, conceiving themselves as distinct beings with a past and a future. When this is so, or to the best of our knowledge may be so, the case against killing is strong, as strong as the case against killing permanently intellectually disabled human beings at a similar mental level. (I have in mind here the direct reasons against killing; the effects on relatives of the intellectually disabled human will sometimes – but not always – constitute additional indirect reasons against killing the human.)

In the present state of our knowledge, this strong case against killing can be invoked most categorically against the slaughter of chimpanzees, gorillas, and orangutans. On the basis of what we now know about these near-relatives of ours, we should immediately extend to them the same full protection against being killed that we extend now to all human beings. A case can also be made, though with varying degrees of confidence, on behalf of whales, dolphins, monkeys, dogs, cats, pigs, seals, bears, cattle, sheep, and so on, perhaps even to the point at which it may include all mammals – much depends on how far we are prepared to go in extending the benefit of the doubt, where a doubt exists. Even if we stopped at the species I have named, however – excluding the remainder of the mammals – our discussion has raised a very large question mark over the justifiability of a great deal of killing of animals carried out by humans, even when this killing takes place painlessly and without causing suffering to other members of the animal community. (Most of this killing, of course, does not take place under such ideal conditions.)

When we come to animals who, as far as we can tell, are not rational and self-conscious beings, the case against killing is weaker. When we are not dealing with beings aware of themselves as distinct entities, the wrongness of painless killing derives from the loss of pleasure it involves. Where the life taken would not, on balance, have been pleasant, no direct wrong is done. Even when the animal killed would have lived pleasantly, it is at least arguable that no wrong is done if the animal killed will, as a result of the killing, be replaced by another animal living an equally pleasant life. Taking this view involves holding that a wrong done to an existing being can be made up for by a benefit conferred on an as yet non-existent being. Thus it is possible to regard non-self-conscious animals as interchangeable with each other in a way that self-conscious beings are not. This means that in some circumstances – when animals lead pleasant lives, are killed painlessly, their deaths do not cause suffering to other animals, and the killing of one animal makes possible its replacement by another who would not otherwise have lived – the killing of non-self-conscious animals may not be wrong.

Is it possible, along these lines, to justify raising chickens for their meat, not in factory farm conditions but roaming freely around a farmyard? Let us make the questionable assumption that chickens are not self-conscious. Assume also that the birds can be killed painlessly, and the survivors do not appear to be affected by the death of one of their numbers. Assume, finally, that for economic reasons we could not rear the birds if we did not eat them. Then the replaceability argument appears to justify killing the birds, because depriving them of the pleasures of their existence can be offset against the pleasures of chickens who do not yet exist, and will exist only if existing chickens are killed.

As a piece of critical moral reasoning, this argument may be sound. Even at that level, it is important to realise how limited it is in its application. It cannot justify factory farming, where animals do not have pleasant lives. Nor does it normally justify the killing of wild animals. A duck shot by a hunter (making the shaky assumption that ducks are not self-conscious, and the almost certainly false assumption that the shooter can be relied upon to kill the duck instantly) has probably had a pleasant life, but the shooting of a duck does not lead to its replacement by another. Unless the duck population is at the maximum that can be sustained by the available food supply, the killing of a duck ends a pleasant life without starting another, and is for that reason wrong on straightforward utilitarian grounds. So although there are situations in which it is not wrong to kill animals, these situations are special ones, and do not cover very many of the billions of premature deaths humans inflict, year after year, on animals.

In any case, at the level of practical moral principles, it would be better to reject altogether the killing of animals for food, unless one must do so to survive. Killing animals for food makes us think of them as objects that we can use as we please. Their lives then count for little when weighed against our mere wants. As long as we continue to use animals in this way, to change our attitudes to animals in the way that they should be changed will be an impossible task. How can we encourage people to respect animals, and have equal concern for their interests, if they continue to eat them for their mere enjoyment? To foster the right attitudes of consideration for animals, including non-self-conscious ones, it may be best to make it a simple principle to avoid killing them for food.

[. . .]

Notes

1   My views on animals first appeared in *The New York Review of Books*, 5 April 1973, under the title 'Animal Liberation'. This article was a review of R. and S. Godlovitch and J. Harris (eds), *Animals, Men and Morals* (London, 1972). A more complete statement was published as *Animal Liberation*, 2nd ed. (New York, 1990).

2   Bentham's defence of animals, quoted in the section 'Racism and Speciesism' is from his *Introduction to the*

Principles of Morals and Legislation, chap. 18, sec. 1, n.

3   The source for the anecdote about Benjamin Franklin is his *Autobiography* (New York, 1950), p. 41. The same objection has been more seriously considered by John Benson in 'Duty and the Beast', *Philosophy*, vol. 53 (1978): 545–7.

Chapter 5

Josephine Donovan

FEMINISM AND THE TREATMENT OF ANIMALS: FROM CARE TO DIALOGUE

In this essay Josephine Donovan discusses the development of feminist animal care theory from its beginnings in the early 1990s to the present. Feminist animal care theory developed in reaction against the animal rights theory developed by Tom Regan and the utilitarian theory enunciated by Peter Singer. She argues that these theories privilege reason or mathematical calculation. In addition, they are abstract theories which isolate the individual and obscure the particular circumstances of an ethical event. Donovan emphasizes the dialogical nature of care theory: listening to animals and caring about what they are telling us.

IN RECENT YEARS feminists have brought care theory to the philosophical debate over how humans should treat nonhuman animals. Care theory, an important branch of contemporary feminist theory, was originally articulated by Carol Gilligan (1982) and has been elaborated, refined, and criticized extensively since it was first formulated in the late 1970s. Since I and others applied care theory to the animal question in the early 1990s (see esp. Donovan and Adams 1996), it has established itself as a major vein of animal ethics theory (the others being liberal rights doctrine, utilitarianism, and deep ecology theory). It also has received close scrutiny from the philosophical community, which has yielded pertinent criticisms.

This article is an attempt to respond to these criticisms and thereby further refine and strengthen feminist animal care theory. Although focused on the issue of animal treatment, my analysis may have implications for care theory in general. As it is my conclusion that many of the critiques have misapprehended the original message of the feminist animal care theorists, I hope to reposition the discussion to emphasize the dialogical nature of care theory. It is not so much, I will argue, a matter of caring for animals as mothers (human and nonhuman) care for their infants as it is one of listening to animals, paying emotional attention, taking seriously—*caring about*—what they are telling us. As I state at the conclusion of "Animal Rights and Feminist Theory," "We should not kill, eat, torture, and exploit animals because they do not want to be so treated, and we know that" (Donovan 1990, 375). In other words, I am proposing in this article that we shift the epistemological source of theorizing about animals to the animals themselves. Could we not, I ask, extend feminist standpoint theory to animals, including their standpoint in our ethical deliberations?

Feminist animal care theory

Feminist animal care theory developed in reaction against the animal rights/utilitarian theory that had by the 1980s established itself as the dominant vein in animal ethics (Singer 1975; Regan 1983). Rooted in Enlightenment rationalism, liberal rights theory and utilitarianism, feminist care theorists argue, privilege reason (in the case of rights theory) or mathematical calculation (in the case of utilitarianism) epistemologically. Because of their abstract, universalizing pretenses, both rights theory and utilitarianism elide the particular circumstances of an ethical event, as well as its contextual and political contingencies. In addition, rights theory, following Kantian premises, tends to view individuals as autonomous isolates, thereby neglecting their social relationships. It also presumes a society of rational equals, a perspective that ignores the power differentials that obtain in any society but especially in one that includes both humans and animals. Finally, both rights and utilitarianism dispense with sympathy, empathy, and compassion as relevant ethical and epistemological sources for human treatment of nonhuman animals.

Feminist care theory attempted to restore these emotional responses to the philosophical debate and to validate them as authentic modes of knowledge. It also, following Gilligan, urged a narrative, contextually aware form of reasoning as opposed to the rigid rationalist abstractions of the "one-size-fits-all" rights and utilitarian approach, emphasizing instead that we heed the individual particularities of any given case and acknowledge the qualitative heterogeneity of life-forms.

Finally, implicit in feminist animal care theory—though perhaps not sufficiently theorized as such—is a dialogical mode of ethical reasoning, not unlike the dialectical method proposed in standpoint theory, wherein humans pay attention to—listen to—animal communications and construct a human ethic in conversation with the animals rather than imposing on them a rationalistic, calculative grid of humans' own monological construction.

Feminists—indeed most women—are acutely aware of what it feels like to have one's opinion ignored, trivialized, rendered unimportant. Perhaps this experience has awakened their sensitivity to the fact that other marginalized groups—including animals—have trouble getting their viewpoints heard. One of the main directions in feminist legal theory has insisted that legal codes drawn up based on male circumstances often do not fit the lives of women, whose differing realities and needs have not been recognized in the formulation of the law (West 1988, 61, 65; 1997; MacKinnon 1989, 224). Just, therefore, as feminism has called for incorporating the voices of women into public policy and ethical discourse, so feminist animal advocates must call for incorporating the voices of animals as well. Dialogical theory, therefore, means learning to see what human ideological constructions elide; to understand and comprehend what is not identified and recognized in these constructions; to, in short, attempt to reach out emotionally as well as intellectually to what is different from oneself rather than reshaping (in the case of animals) that difference to conform to one's own human-based preconceptions.

Response to criticisms and elaborations of feminist animal care theory

Before further developing the dialogical aspect of feminist animal care theory, I would like first to address recently proposed critiques and refinements of that theory. Such discussion will, I believe, help to elaborate the modifications in care theory I am proposing here.

I begin with the criticisms. A continuing criticism of care theory in general is that the individual experiences of caring on which it is based are not universalizable. Robert Garner, for example, labeled care theory "problematic" because, although he acknowledges that "contextualizing animal suffering in particular cases" (2003, 241) is enriching (citing in this regard Marti Kheel's proposal that all meat eaters should visit slaughterhouses to experience emotionally the circumstances that produce their food [Kheel (1985) 1996, 27]), such an individual experience cannot, he claims, be "universalize[d] to appeal to those who have not had that particular experience" (Garner 2003, 241).

Garner's criticism is a variation of Immanuel Kant's objections to care theory's eighteenth-century counterpart, sympathy theory (see Donovan 1996). Kant argued that sympathy is an unstable base for moral decision making because, first, the feeling is volatile; second, the capacity for sympathy is not evenly distributed in the population; and third, sympathy is therefore not universalizable (Kant 1957, 276–81). Instead, he proposed that one should act ethically out of a sense of duty and that one's sense of what is ethical be determined by imagining what would happen if one's actions were universalized. For example, if one were to universalize one's own lying as an ethical law, it would mean that everyone could lie, which would effect an adverse result, making one realize that lying is wrong. This is the so-called categorical imperative (302).

Kant therefore rooted the idea of universalizability in the individual decision maker—"the moral agent . . . in lonely cogitans" (Walker [1989] 1995, 143)—who attempts to imaginatively universalize his or her own ethical inclination in order to ascertain a moral imperative. Garner, however, seems to imagine an abstract arbiter (the philosopher perhaps) apart from the decision maker who does or does not universalize from the instance of a person revulsed by a slaughterhouse. While there seems to be some confusion among proponents of universalizability as to who is doing the universalizing (see Adler 1987, 219–20), the question is a crucial one for feminists, who have become suspicious of universalizing theories precisely because of who has traditionally done the universalizing and who has been left out. Indeed, many ethic-of-care theorists have dispensed with the universalizability criterion altogether, seeing it as incompatible with the particularistic focus of care (Benhabib 1987; Walker [1989] 1995). Margaret Urban Walker suggests in fact that a rigid application of universalized norms may result in "a sort of 'moral colonialism' (the 'subjects' of my moral decisions disappear behind uniform 'policies' I must impartially 'apply')" ([1989] 1995, 147).

Nevertheless, if generalizing is done from a feminist point of view, as in Kheel's argument—in other words, if we take seriously the perspective or standpoint of a marginalized individual as opposed to contending that such a perspective is invalid because not universalizable—I would argue that it is not illogical to contend that one might easily generalize from an individual ethical reaction, extending that reaction to others similarly situated, thus positing a general or universal precept. Thus, one might reason: if others could see the horrendous conditions in this slaughterhouse, they too would be revulsed and moved to take an ethical stand against such practices—for example, to condemn the slaughter of animals for food as morally wrong, to become vegetarians. Moreover, one can likewise generalize from the treatment of one cow in the slaughterhouse to contend that no cows should be treated in this way. Thus, through the use of the moral imagination one can easily extend one's care for immediate creatures to others who are not present. These remote others are not, however, the abstract disembodied "others of rational constructs and universal principles" envisaged by Kantian rights theorists but rather "particular flesh and blood . . . actual starving children in Africa," as care theorist Virginia Held pointed out with respect to remote suffering humans (1987, 118).

In other words, the injunction to care can be universalized even if all the particular details of an individual case cannot be so extrapolated.[1] The real question that is raised in applying care theory to animals then becomes who is to be included in the caring circle? Or, to put it in other terms, who is to be granted moral status? I will argue below that status should be granted to living creatures with whom one can communicate cognitively and emotionally as to their needs and wishes.[2] [. . .]

Garner offers a second criticism of care theory, namely, that it fails to provide a specific guide for action. He asks, for example, if it prohibits meat eating (2003, 241). It is hard to believe, given the volume of eco-feminist vegan/vegetarian theory that has emerged in the past decade, that anyone could doubt the answer to this question.[3] Garner wonders, however, if animals raised humanely (with care) and slaughtered humanely (but nevertheless slaughtered) would be acceptable under care theory (241), for the animals would be receiving compassionate treatment during their lives. Garner's question points to a misapprehension of care theory that I believe a dialogical theory will help to correct. From the point of view of a dialogical ethic of care, the answer to Garner's question would clearly be no, for if we care to take seriously in our ethical decision making the communicated desires of the animal, it is apparent that no animal would opt for the slaughterhouse. A Jain proverb states the obvious: "All beings are fond of life; they like pleasure and hate pain, shun destruction and like to live, they long to live. To all life is dear" (*Jaina Sûtras* [1884] 1973, I.2.3).[4] Humans know this, and a dialogical ethic must be constructed on the basis of this knowledge. Caring must therefore be extended to mean not just "caring about their welfare" but "caring about what they are telling us."

But what if, Garner continues, one encounters a situation in which there is a "conflict of caring, whose interests should we choose to uphold?" (2003, 241). In particular, he raises the issue of animal research, which may benefit humans and thus satisfy a caring ethic for humans if not for animals. Deborah Slicer, a major feminist animal care theorist, explored this issue thoroughly in her nuanced article, "Your Daughter or Your Dog?" (1991). Slicer makes the salient points in the feminist animal care argument: much of the research is, to be blunt, worthless (i.e., redundant and trivial), and, as is becoming increasingly evident (even more so since Slicer's article appeared), "animals often do not serve as reliable models for human beings and . . . it can be dangerous to extrapolate from results obtained from one species to another" (117).

One might argue that stressing the uselessness of the research evades the basic dilemma posed by Garner. I would counter, however, that a feminist animal care ethic insists that the political context of decision making is never irrelevant and that ethical decisions must include an assessment of that context (in this case, the questions of who benefits from the research economically and how reliable are the research results published by thusly interested parties). [. . .]

A dialogical ethic of care for the treatment of animals

Ludwig Wittgenstein once famously remarked that if a lion could speak we couldn't understand him (Wittgenstein 1963, 223e). In fact, as I have been proposing here, lions do speak, and it is not impossible to understand much of what they are saying. Several theorists have already urged that humans need to learn to read the languages of the natural world. Jonathan Bate has proposed that we learn the syntax of the land, not seeing it through our own "prison-house of language," in order to develop appropriate environmental understandings (1998, 65). Similarly, Patrick Murphy has called for an "ecofeminist dialogics" in which humans learn to read the dialects of animals. "Nonhuman others," he claims, "can be constituted as speaking subjects rather than merely objects of our speaking" (1991, 50).[5] Earlier, phenomenologist Max Scheler spoke similarly about the necessity for learning the "*universal grammar*" of creatural expression ([1926] 1970, 11). Indeed, over a century ago American writer Sarah Orne Jewett speculated about the possibility of learning the language of nonhumans, asking, "Who is going to be the linguist who learns the first word of an old crow's warning to his mate . . .? How long we shall have to go to school when people are expected to talk to the trees, and birds, and beasts in their own language! . . . It is not necessary to tame [creatures] before they can be familiar and responsive, we can meet them on their own ground" (1881, 4–5).

There are those, to be sure, who still raise the epistemological question of how one can know what an animal is feeling or thinking. The answer would seem to be that we use much the same mental and emotional activities in reading an animal as we do in reading a human.[6] Body language, eye movement, facial expression, tone of voice—all are important signs. It also helps to know about the species' habits and culture. And, as with humans, repeated experiences with one individual help one to understand that individual's unique needs and wishes. By paying attention to, by studying, what is signified, one comes to know, to care about, the signifier.[7] In this way, what Carol J. Adams (1990) famously termed the *absent referents* are restored to discourse, allowing their stories to be part of the narrative, opening, in short, the possibility of dialogue with them.

The underlying premise here is that one of the principal ways we know is by means of analogy based on homology. If that dog is yelping, whining, leaping about, licking an open cut, and since if I had an open wound I know I would similarly be (or feeling like) crying and moving about anxiously because of the pain, I therefore conclude that the animal is experiencing the same kind of pain as I would and is expressing distress about it. One imagines, in short, how the animal is feeling based on how one would feel in a similar situation.[8] In addition, repeated exhibitions of similar reactions in similar situations lead one inductively to a generic conclusion that dogs experience the pain of wounds as we do, that, in short, they feel pain and don't like it. The question, therefore, whether humans can understand animals is, in my opinion, a moot one. That they can has been abundantly proved, as Midgley points out, by their repeated success in doing so (1983, 113, 115, 133, 142).

Of course, as with humans, there is always the danger that one might misread the communication of the animal in question, that one might incorrectly assume homologous behavior when there is none. To be sure, all communication is imperfect, and there remain many mysteries in animal (as well as human) behavior. Feminist ethic-of-care theorists have explored some of the difficulties inherent in attempting to assess the needs of an incommunicative human and/or the risks of imposing one's own views or needs on her. But as Alison Jaggar summarizes, care theorists maintain that in general such "dangers may be avoided [or at least minimized, I would add] through improved practices of attentiveness, portraying attentiveness as a kind of discipline whose prerequisites include attitudes and aptitudes such as openness, receptivity, empathy, sensitivity, and imagination" (1995, 190).

Understanding that an animal is in pain or distress—even empathizing or sympathizing with him—doesn't ensure, however, that the human will act ethically toward the animal. Thus, the originary emotional empathetic response must be supplemented with an ethical and political perspective (acquired through training and education) that enables the human to analyze the situation critically so as to determine who is responsible for the animal suffering and how that suffering may best be alleviated. In her recent book *Regarding the Pain of Others* (2003), Susan Sontag warns that people do not automatically act ethically in response to pictures of other people's pain (she doesn't deal with images of animals). While she characterizes as a "moral monster" the person who through a failure "of imagination, of empathy" (8) does not respond compassionately, she nevertheless argues that various ideologies often interfere with the moral response. Too often, she claims, sympathy connotes superiority and privilege without self-reflection about how one is contributing to the suffering one is lamenting. She therefore urges that a heightened humanist political awareness must accompany the sympathetic response in order for truly ethical action to result. Photos of atrocity "cannot be more than an invitation to pay attention, to reflect" (117) on who is responsible for the suffering and similar questions.

Several of the contributors to the feminist animal care collection *Beyond Animal Rights* (Donovan and Adams 1996) argue in this vein for what Deane Curtin terms a "politicized ethic of caring for" ([1991] 1996, 65), one that recognizes the political context in which caring and sympathy take place. In my discussion of the celebrated Heinz hypothetical (in which Heinz has to decide whether to steal a drug, which he cannot obtain any other way, in order to save the life of his dying wife), I propose that "a political ethic-of-care response would include the larger dimension of looking to the political and economic context. . . . Thus the corporate-controlled health care system becomes the primary villain in the piece, and the incident should serve to motivate action to change the system" (Donovan 1996, 161). And, as Adams points out in "Caring about Suffering" (1996, 174), feminist animal care theory necessarily recognizes the "sex-species system" in which animal (and human) suffering is embedded.

In his much-cited article "Taming Ourselves or Going Feral?" (1995), Brian Luke reveals how a massive deployment of ideological conditioning forestalls what he sees as the natural empathetic response most people feel toward animals. Children have to be educated out of the early sympathy they feel for animals, he contends; ideological denial and justifications for animal exploitation and suffering are indoctrinated from an early age. Luke catalogs the ways in which such suffering is rationalized and legitimized by those who profit from it (303–11). To a great extent, therefore, getting people to see evil and to care about suffering is a matter of clearing away ideological rationalizations that legitimate animal exploitation and cruelty. Recognizing the egregious use of euphemism employed to disguise such behavior (copiously documented in Joan Dunayer's recent book, *Animal Equality* [2001]) would seem to be an important step in this direction.

But it is not just a matter of supplementing care with a political perspective; the experience of care can itself lead to political analysis, as Joan Tronto points out in her call for a "political ethic of care" (1993, 155): "Care becomes a tool for critical political analysis when we use this concept to reveal relationships of power" (172). In other words, although Tronto doesn't treat the animal question, if one feels sympathy toward a suffering animal, one is moved to ask the question, Why is this animal suffering? The answer can lead into a political analysis of the reasons for the animal's distress. Education in critical thinking, these thinkers emphasize, is therefore imperative if an ethic of care is to work.

We also need education, as Nel Noddings proposed (1984, 153), in the practices of care and empathy.[9] Years ago, in fact, Gregory Bateson and Mary Catherine Bateson contended that "empathy is a discipline" and therefore teachable (1987, 195). Many religions, they noted, use imaginative exercises in empathetic understanding as a spiritual discipline (195). Such exercises could be adapted for use in secular institutions like schools (including, especially, high school). Certainly a large purpose of such a discipline must be not just emotional identification but also intellectual understanding, learning to hear, to take seriously, to care about what animals are telling us, learning to read and attend to their language. The burgeoning field of animal ethology is providing important new information that will aid in such study.

In conclusion, therefore, a feminist animal care ethic must be political in its perspective and dialogical in its method. Rejecting the imperialist imperative of the scientific method, in which the "scientific subject's voice . . . speaks with general and abstract authority [and] the objects of inquiry 'speak' only in response to what scientists ask them" (as Sandra Harding [1986, 124] characterized the laboratory encounter), humans must cease imposing their voice on that of animals. No longer must our relationship with animals be that of the "conquest of an alien object," Rosemary Radford Ruether notes, but "the conversation of two subjects." We must recognize "that the 'other' has a 'nature' of her own that needs to be respected and with which one must enter into conversation" (1975, 195–96). On that basis and in reflecting upon the political context, a dialogical ethic for the treatment of animals may be established.[10]

Notes

I would like to thank Erling Skorpen, who stimulated my thinking in this direction years ago; Carol Adams for planting the idea of applying standpoint theory to animals; the *Signs* editors and readers for their suggestions; and my dogs Aurora and Sadie, with whom I dialogue daily.

1   Regarding Kant's other points, one might question whether a sense of moral duty and the capacity to reason are any more evenly distributed in the population than the capacity for sympathy. Indeed, care theorists, like most feminist theorists, believe that habits and practices are socially constructed, not innate (Kant's point about sympathy being unevenly distributed implies that only or mostly women have the capacity); thus, they are teachable. I would argue then, following Nel Noddings (1984, 153), that if compassion practice were taught systematically as a discipline in the schools, it would become a widely accepted socially sanctioned basis for moral decision making and therefore not dependent on the whim of various individual responses, thus replying to Kant's concern about subjective volatility.

2   By the term *cognitive* I do not mean restricted to rational discourse but rather including all communicative signs detectable by the human brain.

3   See, e.g., Adams 1995; Donovan 1995; Gaard and Gruen 1995; Lucas 2005.

4   As cited in Chapple 1986, 217. Jainism is an ancient Indian religion, a principal feature of whose practice is the vow of ahimsa (to do no harm to other living creatures). All Jains are thus vegetarians.

5   In the past few years a number of other literary theorists have begun exploring the possibility of a dialogical "animal-standpoint criticism." I have just completed an article (not yet published), "Animal Ethics and Literary Criticism," that further develops this concept.

6   This is to disagree somewhat with Thomas Nagel, who in "What Is It Like to Be a Bat?" (1974) argues that we humans cannot apprehend "bat phenomenology" (440); i.e., we can only imagine what it would be like for us to be bats, not what it is like for bats to be bats. To an extent Nagel is correct, of course; it is a truism of epistemology that we are limited by our mental apparatus. However, I believe more effort can be made to decipher animal communications and that while we may never fully understand what it feels like to be a bat, we can understand certain pertinent basics of his or her experience, sufficient for the formulation of an ethical response. For an alternative view to Nagel's, see Kenneth Shapiro's "Understanding Dogs" (1989), which

argues that we recognize the validity of interspecies "kinesthetic" communication. Although Val Plumwood proposes a "dialogical interspecies ethic" in her recent *Environmental Culture* (2002, 167–95) that would seem to be consistent with what I am proposing here, she inconsistently argues that it is ethically permissible to kill and eat nonhumans under this ethic: one can "conceive [them] both as communicative others and as food" (157). This would seem to defeat the purpose of a dialogical ethic, which is to respond ethically to what the "communicative other" is telling one, namely, and invariably, that he does not want to be killed and eaten.

7   Here I am modifying classical structuralist terminology.

8   In the locus classicus on the subject of knowing another's inner states, "Other Minds" ([1946] 1979), J. L. Austin insists that a primary prerequisite for such communication is that one must have had the feeling oneself (104). Austin, however, like Nagel, abjures the possibility of knowing "what it would feel like to be a cat or a cockroach" (105).

9   Noddings (1991) has, however, stipulated reservations about applying care theory to animals. See also my critique of Noddings's position (Donovan 1991).

10   Other theorists who have advocated and explored dialogical ethical theory include Martin Buber, Simone Weil, Iris Murdoch, and Mikhail Bakhtin. See further discussion in Donovan 1996.

References

Adams, Carol J. 1990. *The Sexual Politics of Meat: A Feminist-Vegetarian Critical Theory*. New York: Continuum.

———. 1995. "Comment on George's 'Should Feminists Be Vegetarian?'" *Signs: Journal of Women in Culture and Society* 21(1): 221–25.

Adler, Jonathan E. 1987. "Moral Development and the Personal Point of View." In *Women and Moral Theory*, ed. Eva Feder Kittay and Diana T. Meyers, 205–34. Totowa, NJ: Rowman & Littlefield.

Austin, J. L. (1946) 1979. "Other Minds." In his *Philosophical Papers*, 3rd ed., 76–116. Oxford: Oxford University Press.

Bateson, Gregory, and Mary Catherine Bateson. 1987. *Angels Fear: Towards an Epistemology of the Sacred*. New York: Bantam.

Benhabib, Seyla. 1987. "The Generalized and the Concrete Other: The Kohlberg-Gilligan Controversy and Moral Theory." In *Women and Moral Theory*, ed. Eva Feder Kittay and Diana T. Meyers, 154–76. Totowa, NJ: Rowman & Littlefield.

Chapple, Christopher. 1986. "Noninjury to Animals: Jania and Buddhist Perspectives." In *Animal Sacrifices: Religious Perspectives on the Use of Animals in Science*, ed. Tom Regan, 213–35. Philadelphia: Temple University Press.

Curtin, Deane. (1991) 1996. "Toward an Ecological Ethic of Care." In Donovan and Adams 1996, 60–76.

Donovan, Josephine. 1990. "Animal Rights and Feminist Theory." *Signs* 15(2): 350–75.

———. 1991. "Reply to Noddings." *Signs* 16(2):423–25.

———. 1996. "Attention to Suffering: Sympathy as a Basis for Ethical Treatment of Animals." In Donovan and Adams 1996, 147–69.

Donovan, Josephine, and Carol J. Adams, eds. 1996. *Beyond Animal Rights: A Feminist Caring Ethic for the Treatment of Animals*. New York: Continuum.

Dunayer, Joan. 2001. *Animal Equality: Language and Liberation*. Derwood, MD: Ryce.

Garner, Robert. 2003. "Political Ideologies and the Moral Status of Animals." *Journal of Political Ideologies* 8(2):233–46.

Gilligan, Carol. 1982. *In a Different Voice: Psychological Theory and Women's Development*. Cambridge, MA: Harvard University Press.

Harding, Sandra. 1986. *The Science Question in Feminism*. Ithaca, NY: Cornell University Press.

Held, Virginia. 1987. "Feminism and Moral Theory." In *Women and Moral Theory*, ed. Eva Feder Kittay and Diana T. Meyers, 111–28. Totowa, NJ: Rowman & Littlefield.

Jaggar, Alison M. 1995. "Caring as a Feminist Practice of Moral Reason." In *Justice and Care: Essential Readings in Feminist Ethics*, ed. Virginia Held, 179–202. Boulder, CO: Westview.

Jaina Sûtras. (1884) 1973. Trans. Hermann Jacobi. Delhi: Motilal Banarsidass.

Jewett, Sarah Orne. 1881. "River Driftwood." In her *Country By-Ways*, 1–33. Boston: Houghton Mifflin.

Kant, Immanuel. 1957. "Theory of Ethics." In his *Selections*, ed. Theodore Meyer-Green, 268–374. New York: Scribner's.

Kelch, Thomas G. 1999. "The Role of the Rational and the Emotive in a Theory of Animal Rights." *Boston College Environmental Affairs Law Review* 27(1): 1–41.

Kheel, Marti. (1985) 1996. "The Liberation of Nature: A Circular Affair." In Donovan and Adams 1996, 17–33.

——. 1995. "License to Kill: An Ecofeminist Critique of Hunters' Discourse." In *Animals and Women: Feminist Theoretical Explorations*, ed. Carol J. Adams and Josephine Donovan, 85–125. Durham, NC: Duke University Press.

Luke, Brian. 1995. "Taming Ourselves or Going Feral? Toward a Nonpatriarchal Metaethic of Animal Liberation." In *Animals and Women: Feminist Theoretical Explorations*, ed. Carol J. Adams and Josephine Donovan, 290–319. Durham, NC: Duke University Press.

MacKinnon, Catharine A. 1989. *Toward a Feminist Theory of the State*. Cambridge, MA: Harvard University Press.

Midgley, Mary. 1983. *Animals and Why They Matter*. Athens: University of Georgia Press.

Murphy, Patrick. 1991. "Prolegomenon for an Ecofeminist Dialogics." In *Feminism, Bakhtin, and the Dialogic*, ed. Dale M. Bauer and Susan Jaret McKinstry, 39–56. Albany: State University of New York Press.

Nagel, Thomas. 1974. "What Is It Like to Be a Bat?" *Philosophical Review* 83(4): 435–50.

Noddings, Nel. 1984. *Caring: A Feminine Approach to Ethics and Moral Education*. Berkeley: University of California Press.

——. 1991. "Comment on Donovan's 'Animal Rights and Feminist Theory.' " *Signs* 16(2):418–22.

Plumwood, Val. 2002. *Environmental Culture: The Ecological Crisis of Reason*. London: Routledge.

Regan, Tom. 1983. *The Case for Animal Rights*. Berkeley: University of California Press.

Ruether, Rosemary Radford. 1975. *New Woman/New Earth: Sexist Ideologies and Human Liberation*. New York: Seabury.

Scheler, Max. (1926) 1970. *The Nature of Sympathy*. Trans. Peter Heath. 3rd ed. Hamden, CT: Archon.

Shapiro, Kenneth J. 1989. "Understanding Dogs through Kinesthetic Empathy, Social Construction, and History." *Anthrozoös* 3(3):184–95.

Shiva, Vandana. 1994. *Close to Home: Women Reconnect Ecology, Health and Development Worldwide*. Philadelphia: New Society.

Singer, Peter. 1975. *Animal Liberation: A New Ethics for Our Treatment of Animals*. New York: Avon.

Slicer, Deborah. 1991. "Your Daughter or Your Dog?" *Hypatia* 6(1):108–24.

Sontag, Susan. 2003. *Regarding the Pain of Others*. New York: Farrar, Straus & Giroux.

Tronto, Joan C. 1993. *Moral Boundaries: A Political Argument for an Ethic of Care*. New York: Routledge.

Walker, Margaret Urban. (1989) 1995. "Moral Understandings: Alternative 'Epistemology' for a Feminist Ethics." In *Justice and Care: Essential Readings in Feminist Ethics*, ed. Virginia Held, 139–52. Boulder, CO: Westview.

West, Robin. 1988. "Jurisprudence and Gender." *University of Chicago Law Review* 55(1):1–71.

Wittgenstein, Ludwig. 1963. *Philosophical Investigations*. Trans. G. E. M. Anscombe. Oxford: Blackwell.

Chapter 6

R.G. Frey

RIGHTS, INTERESTS, DESIRES AND BELIEFS

R.G. Frey argues that the key question is whether animals are the kind of beings who can have rights. He distinguishes two senses of "interest" and maintains that animals have interests only in the sense that things can be good or bad for them, as oil is good or bad for a tractor. Animals do not have desires, because having desires requires the having of beliefs. Beliefs require that the creature be able to distinguish between true and false beliefs, and for this distinction language is required.

[. . .]

[T]HE QUESTION is not about *which* rights animals may or may not be thought to possess or about *whether* their alleged rights in a particular regard are on a par with the alleged rights of humans in this same regard but rather about the more fundamental issue of whether animals—or, in any event, the "higher" animals—are a kind of being which can be the logical subject of rights. It is this issue, and a particular position with respect to it, that I want critically to address here.

The position I have in mind is the widely influential one which links the possession of rights to the possession of interests. In his *System of Ethics*, Leonard Nelson is among the first, if not the first, to propound the view that all and only beings which have interests can have rights,[1] a view which has attracted an increasingly wide following ever since. [. . .] For Nelson, [. . .] it is because animals have interests that they can be the logical subject of rights, and his claim that animals *do have* interests forms the minor premiss, therefore, in an argument for the moral rights of animals: "All and only beings which (can) have interests (can) have moral rights; Animals as well as humans (can) have interests; Therefore, animals (can) have moral rights."

[. . .]

[I]t is apparent that the minor premiss is indeed the key to the whole matter. For given the truth of the major premiss, given, that is, that the possession of interests *is* a criterion for the possession of rights, it is nevertheless only the truth of the minor premiss that would result in the inclusion of creatures other than human beings within the class of right-holders. This premiss is doubtful, however, and the case against it a powerful one, or so I want to suggest.

[. . .]

To say that "Good health is in John's interests" is not at all the same thing as to say that "John has an interest in good health." The former is intimately bound up with having a good or well-being to which good health is conducive, so that we could just as easily have said "Good health is conducive to John's good or well-being," whereas the latter—"John has an interest in good health"—is intimately bound up with wanting, with John's wanting good health. That these two notions of "interest" are logically distinct is readily apparent: good health may well be in John's interests, in the sense of being conducive to his good or well-being, even if John does not want good health, indeed, even if he wants to continue taking hard drugs, with the result that his health is irreparably damaged; and John may have an interest in taking drugs, in the sense of wanting to take them, even if it is apparent to him that it is not conducive to his good or well-being to continue to do so. In other words, something can be *in* John's interests without John's *having* an interest in it, and John can *have* an interest in something without its being *in* his interests.

If this is right, and there are these two logically distinct senses of "interest," we can go on to ask whether animals can have interests in either of these senses; and if they do, then perhaps the minor premiss of Nelson's argument for the moral rights of animals can be sustained.

Do animals, therefore, have interests in the first sense, in the sense of having a good or well-being which can be harmed or benefited? The answer, I think, is that they certainly do have interests in this sense; after all, it is plainly not good for a dog to be fed certain types of food or to be deprived of a certain amount of exercise. This answer, however, is of little use to the Nelsonian cause; for it yields the counter-intuitive result that manmade/manufactured objects and even things have interests, and, therefore, on the interest thesis, have or at least are candidates for having moral rights. For example, just as it is not good for a dog to be deprived of a certain amount of exercise, so it is not good for prehistoric cave drawings to be exposed to excessive amounts of carbon dioxide or for Rembrandt paintings to be exposed to excessive amounts of sunlight.

[. . .]

Do animals, therefore, have interests in the second sense, in the sense of having wants which can be satisfied or left unsatisfied? In this sense of course, it appears that tractors do not have interests; for though being well-oiled may be conducive to tractors being good of their kind, tractors do not *have an interest* in being well-oiled, since they cannot *want* to be well-oiled, cannot, in fact, have any wants whatever. But farmers can have wants, and they certainly have an interest in their tractors being well-oiled.

What, then, about animals? Can they have wants? By "wants," I understand a term that encompasses both needs and desires, and it is these that I shall consider.

If to ask whether animals can have wants is to ask whether they can have needs, then certainly animals have wants. A dog can need water. But *this* cannot be the sense of "want" on which having interests will depend, since it does not exclude things from the class of want-holders. Just as dogs need water in order to function normally, so tractors need oil in order to function normally.

[. . .]

This, then, leaves desires, and the question of whether animals can have wants as desires. I may as well say at once that I do not think animals can have desires. My reasons for thinking this turn largely upon my doubts that animals can have beliefs, and my doubts in this regard turn partially, though in large part, upon the view that having beliefs is not compatible with the absence of language and linguistic ability. I realize that the claim that animals cannot have desires is a controversial one; but I think the case to be made in support of it, complex though it is, is persuasive.

[. . .]

Suppose I am a collector of rare books and desire to own a Gutenberg Bible: my desire to own this volume is *to be traced* to my belief that I do not now own such a work and that my rare book collection is deficient in this regard. By "to be traced" here, what I mean is this: if someone were to ask *how* my belief that my book collection lacks a Gutenberg Bible is connected with my desire to own such a Bible, what better or more direct reply could be given than that, without this belief, I would not have this desire? For if I believed that my rare book collection *did* contain a Gutenberg Bible and so was complete in this sense, then I would not desire a Gutenberg Bible in order to make up what I now believe to be a notable deficiency in my collection.

[. . .]

The difficulty in the case of animals should be apparent: if someone were to say, e.g., "The cat believes that the door is locked," then that person is holding, as I see it, that the cat holds the declarative sentence "The door is locked" to be true; and I can see no reason whatever for crediting the cat or any other creature which lacks language, including human infants, with entertaining declarative sentences and holding certain declarative sentences to be true.

[. . .]

If what is believed is that a certain declarative sentence is true, then no creature which lacks language can have beliefs; and without beliefs, a creature cannot have desires. And this is the case with animals, or so I suggest; and if I am right, not even in the sense, then, of wants as desires do animals have interests, which, to recall, is the minor premiss in the Nelsonian argument for the moral rights of animals.

But is what is believed that a certain declarative sentence is true? I think there are three arguments of sorts that shore up the claim that this *is* what is believed.

First, I do not see how a creature could have the concept of belief without being able to distinguish between true and false beliefs.

[. . .]

Second, if in order to have the concept of belief a creature must be possessed of the difference between true and false belief, then in order for a creature to be able to distinguish true from false beliefs that creature must—simply must, as I see it—have some awareness of, to put the matter in the most general terms, how language connects with, links up with the world; and I see no reason to credit cats with such an awareness.

[. . .]

Third, I do not see how a creature could have an awareness or grasp of how language connects with, links up with the world, to leave the matter at its most general, unless that creature was itself possessed of language; and cats are not possessed of language.

[. . .]

It may be suggested, of course, that there might possibly be a class of desires—let us call them simple desires—which do not involve the intervention of belief, in order to have them, and which do not require that we credit animals with language. Such simple desires, for example, might be for some object or other, and we as language-users might try to capture these simple desires in the case of a dog by describing its behavior in such terms as "The dog simply desires the bone".

[. . .]

Suppose, then, the dog simply desires the bone: is the dog aware that it has this simple desire or not? If it is alleged to have this desire but to be unaware that it has it, to want but to be unaware that it wants, then a problem arises. In the case of human beings, unconscious desire can be made sense of, but only because we first make sense of conscious desire; but where no desires are conscious ones, where the creature in question is alleged to have only unconscious desires, what cash value can the use of the term "desire" have in such a case?

[. . .]

There is nothing the dog can do which can express the difference between desiring the bone and being aware of desiring the bone. Yet, the dog would have to be capable of expressing this difference in its behavior, if one is going to hold, *on the basis of that behavior*, that the dog is aware that it has a simple desire for the bone, aware that it simply desires the bone.

Even, then, if we concede for the sake of argument that there are simple desires, desires which do not involve the intervention of belief in order to have them, the suggestion that we can credit animals with these desires, without also having to credit them with language, is at best problematic.

[. . .]

I conclude, then, that the Nelsonian position on the moral rights of animals is not a sound one: the truth of the minor premiss in his argument—that animals have interests—is doubtful at best, and animals must have interests if, in accordance with the interest thesis, they are to be a logical subject of such rights. For animals either have interests in a sense which allows objects and things to have interests, and so, on the interest thesis, to have or to be candidates for having moral rights or they do not have interests at all, and so, on the interest thesis, do not have and are not candidates for having moral rights. I have reached this conclusion, moreover, without querying the correctness of the interest thesis itself, without querying, that is, whether the possession of interests *really* is a criterion for the possession of moral rights.

Note

1   Leonard Nelson, *System of Ethics*, tr. by Norbert Guterman (New Haven, 1956), Part I, Section 2, Chapter 7, pp. 136–44.

Frederike Kaldewaij

ANIMALS AND THE HARM OF DEATH

Frederike Kaldewaij argues against the subjective value theory, maintained by Peter Singer among others, which identifies an individual's good with her own desires or values. According to such a theory animals are not harmed by death because they cannot have desires concerning their future existence. Kaldewaij argues that the subjective value theory is inadequate because it fails to acknowledge that life is instrumentally valuable. Human beings and conscious animals are harmed by death because they are deprived of goods they would have enjoyed had they not been killed. She concludes that conscious animals such as those killed in the food industry are seriously harmed by death.

I N W E S T E R N S O C I E T I E S, it is generally acknowledged that animals have an interest in not suffering. This is often considered to have ethical implications, one of which is that animal welfare should be a concern in animal agriculture. Whether painless death harms animals is a more controversial issue, and this is an important factor in determining the moral acceptability of the production and consumption of animal products like meat and dairy. (The dairy industry indirectly leads to killing of animals, for instance the male calves of dairy cows). In this paper, I will defend Thomas Nagel's view of the harm of death, which can be applied to conscious animals, against the view that animals are not harmed by death as they cannot have desires regarding their future existence. Next, I will consider different arguments that have been used to support the claim that animals are harmed much less by death than human beings. I will conclude that conscious animals such as those killed in the food industry are seriously harmed by death.

Can animals be harmed by death?

The question of whether death is harmful for human beings is a well-known philosophical problem. Epicurus (341–270 B.C.) points out that when we are alive, we are not yet harmed by death, and when we are dead, there is nobody to be harmed. If there is no (possibly unpleasant) afterlife, we need not fear death (Rosenbaum, 1993). However, death may not be a misfortune because it is (paradoxically) a bad state to be in, but rather because of what it takes away from us. Thomas Nagel's account of the harm of death has been called "the most popular anti-Epicurean view" (Feldman, 1993). Nagel (1993) argues that death is harmful because it deprives us of the goods that our future life would have contained.

There is an alternative view of the harm of death, according to which death is harmful because it thwarts an individual's desire to stay alive and other desires she may have for her future. Animals, according to this argument, are not harmed by death as they cannot have such desires, which involve sophisticated beliefs and concepts, such as the concept of one's own mortality. Two advocates of this view are Peter Singer and Ruth Cigman. Singer (1993) argues that only rational and self-conscious beings can have preferences regarding their future existence. Cigman (1981) argues that only beings who have the capacity of having "categorical desires" can be harmed by death. As Cigman explains it, while conditional desires (such as a desire to eat when one is hungry) presuppose being alive, categorical desires (e.g. to write a book or raise children), answer the question of whether one wants to remain alive.

Prudential value theory is concerned with the (nonmoral) good or interests of individuals. In subjective value theories, an individual's good is determined by reference to her own desires or values. Objective value theories, in contrast, claim that some things are valuable in themselves. Singer and Cigman's views imply a subjective value theory. An objective theory may be seen to be problematic, because it is unclear why certain things, such as accomplishment or knowledge, are in an individual's interest if she does not value them at all. Subjectivism especially seems to be a plausible theory within the context of animal ethics: it is usually said that a necessary condition for having interests is having feelings and desires (e.g. Feinberg, 1980; DeGrazia, 1996). While we do not say it is against a plant's interest if its leaves are pulled off, we do say that an animal is harmed when its leg is caught in a leg-trap: unlike the plant, it will suffer as a result of its injuries.

While an objective value theory may not be desirable, a theory that determines the subject's good solely in terms of the satisfaction of her actual desires is not either. Steve Sapontzis (1987) and Tom Regan (2004) have both, in the context of animals and the harm of death, pointed out that having an interest is not the same thing as taking an interest (in Sapontzis' terminology). In other words: your desires may not always reflect what is good for you. For example, children may not like eating vegetables, and addicts may crave cocaine. But how can we say that something can be in an individual's interest even if she does not desire it, without falling into the pitfalls of an objective value theory? This problem is often solved by appealing to the desires an individual would have, if she were fully informed and rational. A problem with this view with respect to the harm of death for animals is that animals are not *capable* of being rational and informed enough to understand that life is in their interest. Neither, for that matter, are very small children able to understand the health benefits of vegetables. But is this a reason to assume that these things are not in their interest?

Cigman argues that you must have the *capacity* to have categorical desires to be able to be harmed by death (she uses the term "misfortune" for "harm"). Even a suicidal person can be harmed by death: "X's misfortune must either be something which X did not want; or it must be something that X *should not* have wanted, because it so obviously conflicted with his interests" (1981, italics hers). According to Cigman, it can be unfortunate for human beings if they fail to have categorical desires, but animals cannot be pitied for not desiring something they cannot desire, i.e. life. However, Cigman does not, and cannot, explain *why* it "obviously" conflicts with human beings' interests to die, if they do not actually desire to live.

A good explanation for why something can be in our interest even if we do not desire it is that it is *instrumentally valuable* for something we do value. Vegetables are good for small children in the same way riboflavin is good for adults who have never heard of this vitamin, and eventually this can be explained in terms of their future well-being and desire-satisfaction. It is arbitrary to make a distinction between those who have the capacity to understand something is instrumentally valuable for them and those who do not. A fundamental aspect of Nagel's theory is that life has instrumental, not intrinsic value. As he notes, organic survival has no value for a permanently comatose patient (1993). Human beings and conscious animals are harmed by death because they are deprived of goods *that they would have valued, enjoyed, found desirable*. Nagel's theory of the harm of death is compatible with a subjective value theory, and offers an explanation of why people with reasonable prospects in life have an interest in life. We usually want to prevent people from committing suicide, because they may overcome their psychological problems and live many years filled with goods they will value.

An additional benefit of Nagel's theory is that it can explain the magnitude of the harm of death: death takes away the possibility of ever experiencing, doing or accomplishing anything you value again. According to Singer and Cigman, death is harmful because it thwarts the desires we have at the time of death. But is someone who just enjoys life as it comes harmed much less by death than someone who has his life completely planned out already? Cigman's example of the desire to eat when hungry as a conditional desire may seem compelling: you do not need to eat when you are dead. However, it is misleading: what about eating for pleasure as well as to avoid starvation, or valuing a meal shared with family and loved ones? Unlike writing a book, or raising children, we do not value such things as part of a "life plan". But not everybody may have such plans, while they may still enjoy the goods in their lives on a day-to-day basis. Animals do not only have desires like eating when they are hungry, desires to alleviate frustration. They actually like eating, grooming, rolling in the mud, playing, etc. Such desires give their life instrumental value, just like whatever we find valuable makes our lives worth living.

There is one way in which being rational and self-conscious is relevant to the harm involved in *some* deaths. Human beings who come to understand they will die soon, face a kind of psychological suffering that animals are probably not capable of. However, I am only concerned here with the *basic* harm of death, not with suffering related to death and dying. Even when you are killed suddenly, in your sleep, you can suffer this basic harm of death. For this harm, you need not have an abstract concept of your own mortality.

Is human life much more valuable than animal life?

Is the harm of animal death trivial compared to the harm that human beings suffer when they die? There have been two strategies to support this claim: according to the first, the goods associated with animal life are qualitatively less valuable than those involved in human life, and according to the second, animal lives contain fewer goods than human lives. I will discuss each of these arguments in turn.

Quality

The most well-known defense of the qualitative argument is Mill's claim that "[i]t is better to be Socrates dissatisfied than a fool satisfied, better to be a human being dissatisfied than a pig satisfied" (1957). According to Mill, someone acquainted with both "higher pleasures" (e.g. intellectual pleasures) and "lower pleasures", (e.g. sensual pleasures), will always give a preference to the "higher pleasures". Singer (1993) gives a similar argument, claiming that if one were in the position to be a horse, a human being, and in a third state, in which one could compare both, one would always choose the life of the most rational and self-conscious being. This kind of existence is "intersubjectively" more valuable.

This argument fails. To begin with, one can question whether people acquainted with both kinds of pleasure would always choose "higher pleasures". But the real problem is that the "being of higher faculties" is not competently acquainted with the life of someone with "lower faculties". It would be frustrating for Socrates to live a pig's life, but does that mean that a satisfied pig enjoys the goods involved in its life less than Socrates values the goods of his own life? The view that Socrates' life is better is made from our point of view, not from an intersubjective point of view. Saying, alternatively, that human goods are objectively better than a pig's is problematic, for what makes it objectively true that one individual's values and enjoyments are superior to another's?

Quantity

Regan seems to give a quantitative argument when he says that humans have "more sources of satisfaction" available to them than animals, such as aesthetic or scientific interests. But someone who has more sources of satisfaction may not lead a more satisfactory life. Someone may lead a simple life in the country, intensely enjoying a few goods, while another person in the city may mildly enjoy many goods. Both lives contain the same total amount of satisfaction. Is the second kind of life obviously better? Besides, as

Sapontzis (1987) points out, many animals have sources of goods we do not have, such as a dog's sense of smell or a bat's echolocation. We cannot claim that the goods associated with our capacities are better than theirs, this would be a qualitative claim.

But perhaps human lives always contain more goods in total than animal lives? As an empirical fact, it is true that human beings tend to live longer than other animals, with the exception of for instance certain varieties of turtles. Besides this, DeGrazia (1996) says we can perhaps assume that the mental lives of animals like trouts and alligators are pretty dim. If a cognitively very simple animal's behaviour can mainly be explained in terms of stimulus and response, this may be a reason for thinking it is not very conscious. But the animals we are mainly concerned with in animal agriculture are mammals and birds. Even fish turn out to have social intelligence (Leland, Brown and Krause, 2003), and healthy pigs are in fact curious, playful animals. These animals do not live their lives just going through the motions, it is most plausible to assume that they vividly experience their lives.

Conclusion and final remarks

Both human beings and conscious animals are harmed by death, because this deprives them of the goods that continued life would have brought them. Nagel's theory is compatible with a subjective value theory, because life is instrumentally valuable for those who enjoy and value the goods involved in their lives. There do not seem to be good reasons to assume that the harm that death causes animals that are kept for food production is much less serious than the human harm of death.

I have not yet argued what our moral obligations to animals are, or to what extent animal interests should be taken into account. For now, however, I can point out that increasingly, animal welfare is accepted as a legitimate moral concern. Implicit in this view is the idea that suffering is against the interests of animals. If we take animal interests seriously, we should, in the moral evaluation of the practice of raising and killing animals for food production, not only consider the welfare of animals during their lives, but also take into account the deprivation caused by premature death.

References

Cigman, R. (1981). Death, Misfortune and Species Inequality. *Philosophy and Public Affairs*, 10: 47–64.

DeGrazia, D. (1996). *Taking animals seriously. Mental life and moral status*. Cambridge, Cambridge University Press.

Feinberg, J. (1980). *Rights, Justice, and the Bonds of Liberty: Essays in Social Philosophy*. Princeton, Princeton University Press.

Feldman, F. (1993). Some Puzzles About the Evil of Death. In: *The Metaphysics of Death*. Fischer, J.M. (ed). Stanford, Stanford University Press. 305–326.

Leland, K.N., Brown, C. and Krause, J. (2003). Learning in fishes: from three second memory to culture. *Fish and fisheries*, 4: 199–202.

Mill, J.S. (1957). *Utilitarianism*. Priest, O. (ed). Indianapolis, The Bobbs-Merrill Company. (Original work published 1861).

Nagel, Th. (1993). Death. In: *The Metaphysics of Death*. Fischer, J.M. (ed). Stanford, Standford University Press. 59–69.

Regan, T. (2004). *The Case for Animal Rights* (2nd edition). Berkeley and Los Angeles, University of California Press.

Rosenbaum, S.E. (1993). How to Be Dead and Not Care: A Defense of Epicurus. In: *The Metaphysics of Death*. Fischer, J.M. (ed). Stanford, Stanford University Press. 117–134.

Sapontzis, S.F. (1987). *Morals, Reason, and Animals*. Philadelphia, Temple University Press.

Singer, P. (1993). *Practical Ethics* (2nd edition). Cambridge, Cambridge University Press.

FURTHER READING

Armstrong, S.J. (ed.) (2004) *Animal Ethics, Essays in Philosophy* 5.2 <www.humboldt.edu/~essays/archives.html>

Carruthers, P. (1992) *The Animals Issue*, Cambridge: Cambridge University Press.

DeGrazia, D. (1998) *Taking Animals Seriously: Mental Life and Moral Status*, Cambridge: Cambridge University Press.

Donovan, J. and C. Adams (eds.) (2007) *The Feminist Care Tradition in Animal Ethics: A Reader*, New York: Columbia University Press.

Jamieson, D. (ed.) (1999) *Singer and His Critics*, Oxford: Blackwell.

McKenna, E. and A. Light (eds.) (2004) *Animal Pragmatism: Rethinking Human-Nonhuman Relationships*. Bloomington, Ind.: Indiana University Press.

Midgley, M. (1998) *Animals and Why They Matter*, Athens, Ga.: University of Georgia Press.

Pluhar, E. (1995) *Beyond Prejudice: The Moral Significance of Human and Nonhuman Animals*, Durham, NC: Duke University Press.

Regan, T. (2004) *Empty Cages: Facing the Challenge of Animal Rights*, Lanham, MD: Rowman and Littlefield.

Rollin, B.E. (1992) *Animal Rights and Human Morality*, Amherst: Prometheus Books.

Sapontzis, S.F. (1987) *Morals, Reason and Animals*, Philadelphia, PA: Temple University Press.

Scully, M. (2002) *Dominion: The Power of Man, the Suffering of Animals, and the Call to Mercy*, New York: St. Martin's Press.

Singer, P. (ed.) (2006) *In Defense of Animals: The Second Wave*, Malden, MA: Blackwell.

Sunstein, C.R. and M.C. Nussbaum (eds.) (2004) *Animal Rights: Current Debates and New Directions*, New York: Oxford University Press.

Turner, Jacky and Joyce D'Silva (eds.) (2006) *Animals, Ethics and Trade: The Challenge of Animal Sentience*, London: Earthscan.

Warren, M.A. (1997) *Moral Status: Obligations to Persons and Other Living Things*, Oxford: Clarendon Press.

STUDY QUESTIONS

1 Tom Regan bases his argument on the concept of "subject-of-a-life." Do you agree that this concept identifies the crucial difference between a being with moral status and one without status? Explain your reasoning.

2 Carl Cohen identifies what he believes to be an equivocation in Regan's use of "inherent value." Do you agree with Cohen's point? Why or why not?

3 What might be some advantages for animal ethics of Cavalieri's emphasis on rights as protection from institutional interference?

4 Peter Singer uses the principle of equal consideration of interests to guide our practice concerning animals. Do you find this principle more or less convincing than Tom Regan's use of the equal inherent value of moral agents and moral patients? Explain your choice.

5 Do you agree with Donovan that Regan and Singer place too much emphasis on reason? What role should sympathy and compassion play in our treatment of nonhuman animals?

6 Frey argues that having desires requires having the capacity for language-based beliefs. Do you agree? Why or why not?

7 Kaldewaij argues that animals are harmed by premature death, whether it is painless or not. Do you find her reasoning persuasive?

8 In your view, which of the authors in this part presents the best approach to the moral status of animals? Are there significant modifications you would make to the view of the author you chose?

PART TWO

Animal capacities: pain, emotion, consciousness

INTRODUCTION TO PART TWO

T HE CAPACITY OF nonhuman animals to experience pain, to have a sense of consciousness embedded with cognitive abilities, and to have emotional lives is a challenging and controversial set of topics. On the one hand, a seemingly boundless set of examples of complex behaviors of these animals that correspond to sophisticated human behaviors are regularly reported by people with interest in and experience with individual animals, including pet owners, zoo personnel, farmers, and ranchers. On the other hand, scientists often have struggled to understand these topics in light of contemporary understandings of neurology, anatomy, biochemistry, physiology, ethology, and behavioral ecology of representatives of these various animal groups. Slowly some coherent pictures are emerging.

In the first two articles, Mendl and Paul, and Smuts, discuss some of the approaches used for gaining insights into animal capacities for experiencing sensations and emotions. Mendl and Paul look at parallels to cognitive science approaches used with humans to gain insights on nonhuman animals. Smuts found it essential to become immersed in the lives of the baboons she studied over a period of years, coming to know the animals on an individual basis. Mitchell evaluates the concept of anthropomorphism in relation to scientifically accessible information and moral insights.

Several authors address the notion of consciousness, emotion, and suffering in animals. Bermond takes the more conservative view that the essential anatomy to have these experiences is lacking in most animals, with the possible exception of apes.

Dennett argues that consciousness is not an all-or-nothing phenomenon that is present or absent, but a quality that may be present to varying degrees and not entirely a useful question in evolutionary perspectives; its application to mammals might be analogous to the question of whether birds are "wise" or reptiles have "gumption."

Griffin and Speck address the complex topics of animal cognition and consciousness. They argue that humans and other animals probably differ in both the content and the richness of their conscious experiences. They also recognize that animal communication is much richer than previously understood.

In contrast, Dawkins argues that consciousness and emotional awareness still are elusive ideas, but that if awareness of pleasure and pain reflect consciousness, then emotional awareness may be an evolutionarily old and common quality among animals. Rollin addresses what he believes to be the scientific incoherence of denying pain in animals and of denying moral consideration to them.

Varner briefly addresses the taxonomic distribution of pain capacity and concludes that all vertebrates, including fish, probably feel pain, whereas most invertebrates probably do not.

METHODS OF STUDY

Chapter 8

M. Mendl and E.S. Paul

CONSCIOUSNESS, EMOTION AND ANIMAL WELFARE: INSIGHTS FROM COGNITIVE SCIENCE

Mendl and Paul address the ability to understand nonhuman mental capacities through cognitive science. They argue that the theories and techniques from cognitive science offer promise in assessing the existence of conscious and nonconscious cognitive processing in nonhumans, and that some nonhumans have behaviors with functional parallels with human conscious cognitive processing. They also note that evidence for animal consciousness and emotion necessarily will be indirect.

Introduction

'CLEVER ANIMAL' STORIES fascinate the public. Amusement and quirkiness are probably the main selling points, but the stories are sometimes used to underpin arguments for or against particular forms of animal use. This is most noticeable for the great apes, where studies investigating 'higher' cognitive abilities such as self-concept, language, and theory of mind have been used as a significant part of the case for rights being extended to these species (Cavalieri & Singer 1993). It seems then that information about the intellectual abilities of other species can affect our attitudes to them (Davis & Cheeke 1998; Serpell 2004, pp 145–151). If so, research into the cognitive capacities of our common farm and laboratory animals could have a similar impact. But what if the research showed that they had quite limited cognitive capacities? Would this mean that we could use them with little regard for their welfare? Conversely, what if we discovered high levels of cognitive complexity? How should we treat them then?

To answer these questions we need to consider what exactly an understanding of the cognitive abilities of animals tells us about their capacity to suffer. Here we will focus on how knowledge of cognitive abilities, and how techniques and theory from cognitive science, may be able to offer new ways of investigating (i) animal consciousness and (ii) animal emotion – two areas of fundamental importance in animal welfare science. Given limited space, our aim is to provide a brief introduction to this area, and more detailed treatment of some of the issues that we discuss can be found in the review articles that we cite in this paper. Throughout, we refer to non-human animals as animals.

In the first part of the paper we consider what studies of animal cognition can tell us about animal consciousness. Cognition is to do with *information processing*, and we use a broad definition of cognition as referring to the range of processes involved in the acquisition, storage and manipulation of information (see

Shettleworth 1998). Consciousness, however, is usually defined in terms of the capacity to *be aware of feelings, sensations, thoughts and emotions*. This basic ability is often referred to as *phenomenal* or *feelings* consciousness (Block 1998; Macphail 1998), while the capacity to be subjectively aware of oneself as a unique thinking, feeling individual is referred to as *self-consciousness* (Macphail 1998; Damasio 2000). The simple cataloguing of complex cognitive capabilities as potential indicators of the presence of conscious experience in animals has rightly been criticised (eg Dawkins 2001), and we briefly discuss this approach. But this does not mean that the study of animal cognition offers no insight into the existence of consciousness in other species. In particular, we suggest that recent developments in the study of metacognition and blindsight may be especially illuminating.

In the second part of the paper we suggest ways in which studies of animal cognition can inform us about animal emotion. Most contemporary emotion researchers view emotions as multifaceted phenomena (eg Frijda 1988; Lang 1993; Lerner & Keltner 2000). That is, any emotional response can be regarded as comprising behavioural, physiological, cognitive, and conscious components. For example, 'fear' may involve fleeing behaviour, physiological stress responses, enhanced attention to threatening stimuli, and – what we would usually refer to as the emotion – a subjective feeling of terror or panic. There is debate as to whether this conscious component is present in non-human animals and, if so, in which species (see Damasio 2000; Berridge & Winkielman 2003). Although the cognitive science approaches that we describe here do not directly address this issue, they nevertheless provide powerful frameworks and methods for identifying the specific type or valence of an animal's emotion state.

Cognition and consciousness

For most of us, the conscious mental experiences of animals lie at the heart of our concern for animal welfare. We may also be concerned that animals should live natural lives, and that their biological functioning should be unimpeded (Duncan & Fraser 1997; Appleby & Sandøe 2002), but if we were really convinced that they could not suffer, we would probably be no more worried about their welfare than we are about that of plants. The problem is that most of us would also agree that we cannot know for sure whether and what another animal consciously experiences. If we accept this problem, and some argue that it is a constraint of a particular philosophical view of subjective experience (eg Wemelsfelder 1997) or that subjective experience is not the central determinant of animal welfare (eg McGlone 1993), then our research into animal welfare needs to be based on an *assumption* that the species we study are capable of conscious experience, particularly of negative states.

The need for this assumption is well recognised by animal welfare researchers (eg Dawkins 1990; Mason & Mendl 1993; Duncan & Fraser 1997), but the uncertainty of whether it is correct or not, and if so for which species, is an inherent weakness in animal welfare science (Sandøe *et al* 2004, pp 121–126), making the area vulnerable to those who simply do not believe it. Indeed, scientists and philosophers differ widely in their views. Some suggest that only humans and perhaps the great apes have conscious experiences, while others encourage us to consider the possibility that invertebrate species may also be sentient (eg Carruthers 1989; Griffin 1992, 1998; Kennedy 1992; Macphail 1998; Baars 2001; Bermond 2001; Sherwin 2001). Overall, we are sympathetic to the call that we should give animals the benefit of the doubt (Bradshaw 1998). However, we also argue that the gathering of evidence for or against the assumption should be one goal of animal welfare research because the assumption is so central to all that we do. Here we suggest that theory and techniques from cognitive science may be particularly useful in trying to tackle this difficult issue. However, we start by considering the limitations of a commonly held view about the links between cognition and consciousness.

Cognitive complexity and the emergence of consciousness: do clever animals suffer more?

A popular, and often implicit, assumption (or pitfall – see Dawkins 2001) is that the more 'cognitively complex' an animal is, the more likely it is to be conscious. However, this raises problems including how to define cognitive complexity, how to distinguish complex from 'simpler' processes, and why increasing complexity should necessarily be linked to the emergence of consciousness. We do not have the space to tackle these issues here, but they have been discussed at length by others (eg Gallup 1982; Griffin 1992, 1998; Bekoff 1994, 1998; Byrne 1995; Nicol 1996; Vauclair 1997; Macphail 1998; Bermond 2001; Dawkins 2001). Suffice to say that the thrust of this approach appears to be to grant potential 'consciousness status' to those species that demonstrate cognitive abilities which we view as key, perhaps even defining, attributes of humans (eg human-like language, theory of mind, sense of self). The research agenda is therefore to collect and catalogue examples of 'clever' behaviour. Notwithstanding the difficulties in ruling out 'simpler' associative learning explanations for behaviour that indicates the presence of these abilities (see Coussi-Korbel 1994; Nicol 1996; Heyes 1998; Held *et al* 2001a, 2002a), it is not clear why these abilities should necessarily indicate the capacity for conscious experience. Conversely, and importantly from an animal welfare perspective, it is also not clear that absence of these abilities indicates a lack of conscious experience – especially *feelings* consciousness (see below).

It seems logical to argue that if an animal can be demonstrated to possess a cognitive concept of self (eg in a mirror recognition test [Gallup 1970, 1982; de Veer & van den Bos 1999; for critiques see Heyes 1994; Macphail 1998]), then it has the potential for *self-consciousness* – subjective awareness of itself as a unique thinking, feeling individual. However, self-consciousness is usually viewed as a rather special form of conscious experience (Macphail 1998; Damasio 2000), in contrast to *feelings consciousness* – the basic awareness of feelings such as sensations and emotions (Block 1998; Macphail 1998). From an animal welfare perspective, it is feelings consciousness that is really important. Suffering may be equally great in a species that experiences "I feel pain" as in one that experiences "this is painful" (Bekoff 2002). Basic awareness of sensations or emotions *per se* is crucial, and it is difficult to see why this should depend on either self-consciousness or cognitive complexity (see also Dawkins 2001). Therefore, the presence or absence of a self-concept is of limited use in identifying which species can or cannot consciously experience feelings.

In humans, language is clearly associated with conscious experience. Some take the view that language, or at least a basic capacity for syntactic manipulation, may be important for conscious experience (Dennett 1996; Macphail 1998; Rolls 1999). This view is supported by evidence from split-brain patients who appear to lack conscious awareness of information presented solely to the non-linguistic (usually right) hemisphere (Gazzaniga 2000). But the fact that much conscious experience – touch, smell, joy, sorrow – feels so independent of language, and indeed appears to occur in people with catastrophic damage to their linguistic capabilities, leads others to the popular view that such feelings are likely to be common to linguistic and non-linguistic animals alike (eg Damasio 2000).

We therefore argue that the cataloguing of examples of 'cognitive complexity' – information processing abilities that may not be easily explained in terms of 'simpler' (eg associative) forms of learning – is of limited use in identifying the existence of feelings consciousness. However, if we were to make the assumption that a particular species did have feelings consciousness (ie to give them the 'benefit of the doubt' [see Bradshaw 1998]), knowledge of cognitive complexity could shed light on the types of situation in which suffering was or was not likely to occur (see Nicol 1996). For example, the possession of well-developed episodic memory and the ability to do anticipatory planning (eg Clayton & Dickinson 1998; Emery & Clayton 2001) could have a profound effect on the range of situations in which the animals might suffer, rendering them capable of brooding over past or potential future events (Byrne 1999; Lea 2001) but also able to pre-emptively avoid harmful situations. Individuals with the ability to perceive time and to learn that an aversive husbandry procedure has a limited duration would likely suffer less than those that treated each occurrence as the start of a potentially interminable ordeal (Duncan & Petherick 1991; Bekoff 1994). Therefore, assuming feelings consciousness to be present in the species under study, the search for cognitive complexity could help identify situations in which suffering is likely, and hence suggest ways of managing animals to avoid these (Held *et al* 2001b, 2002b; Mendl *et al* 2001). For example, it may be possible to signal the duration of aversive procedures to animals with well-developed time perception abilities (Spinka *et al* 1998; Taylor *et al* 2002), and thereby to increase predictability and reduce the perceived aversiveness of such procedures.

Metacognition and blindsight: conscious and non-conscious information processing in animals?

In contrast to gathering disparate examples of 'cognitive complexity' in animals, focused research on aspects of cognitive function that are known to be directly related to conscious information processing in humans may be a more fruitful approach to investigating animal consciousness. Here we discuss two research topics – metacognition and blindsight – that may be particularly informative.

Cognitive processes appear to be dissociable from conscious experience in humans. For example, memory processes may occur either 'explicitly', involving conscious recall, or 'implicitly', when people's behaviour or answers to questions are influenced without them being consciously aware of retrieving the relevant information (see discussions in Seger 1994; Shanks & St John 1994; Cleeremans *et al* 1998; Dienes & Perner 1999; Butler & Berry 2001; Curran 2001). The possibility is raised that animal cognition is primarily of this implicit, unconscious type. This has led cognitive scientists to develop ways of studying whether animals also demonstrate two levels of cognitive functioning similar to human implicit and explicit information processing.

Robert Hampton (2001) trained rhesus monkeys on a delayed-matching-to-sample task. An image (sample) was shown on a computer screen followed by a delay during which the screen was blank. In 33% of trials the monkey was then presented with four images, one of which was the original sample. Touching this image resulted in the delivery of a peanut – a preferred reward – but touching any of the other three images resulted in no reward. In 67% of trials the monkey was allowed to *choose* whether to take this test or not. If the test was declined the monkey received a primate pellet – a less preferred reward. If the test was taken the preferred peanut reward was only provided for a correct choice. Hampton reasoned that if monkeys could reflect on the quality of their memory for the task, they would choose to take the test only when their memory was good and their chances of getting the peanut were high. If they perceived their memory as poor, they should decline the test and go for the guaranteed but boring primate pellet. Overall, their performance on the test would therefore be better when they could choose whether to take it than when they were forced to take it, in which case their memory might be good on some occasions but poor on others. This is indeed what he found. He also found that with longer delays between presentation of the sample image and the option to choose whether to take the test, the monkeys tended to opt out more frequently, indicating that they perceived their memory for the sample to fade with time.

These findings suggest that monkeys can monitor the quality of their memory and use this information to moderate their behaviour in a memory task. They appear to have 'metacognition', ie to 'know what they know'. This represents a functional parallel with human explicit, conscious memory. Although the under-lying mechanisms remain to be elucidated, and definitive evidence that conscious processes are involved cannot be provided by this study (Hampton 2001), this research illustrates how ingenious but also quite simple experiments on animal cognition can start to investigate whether animals do have something like an explicit, conscious memory.

Other studies of metacognition have tested humans and animals in psychophysical discrimination tasks. For example, subjects are required to categorise a stimulus (eg an image of a box containing illuminated pixels [Smith *et al* 1997]) as being either 'dense' (2950 pixels) or 'sparse' (450–2949 pixels).

Correct responses are rewarded, but incorrect responses are penalised by a delay. An 'uncertain' response is available which allows a trial to be skipped and followed by a guaranteed but slightly delayed rewarded trial. The prediction is that if subjects are able to monitor their ability to solve the task, then they should choose the 'uncertain' response when the task is difficult (eg a box containing 2700 pixels). Humans, monkeys and dolphins use this response as predicted, and in a strikingly similar way, whereas rats and pigeons do not (Smith *et al* 1995, 1997, in press; Inman & Shettleworth 1999). Again, there are a number of interpretations for these findings, but one is that some species are able to refer to the quality of their knowledge, and to use this information to avoid making incorrect responses. This referral process involves conscious awareness in humans and may do so in other species. The failure of some species to show this behaviour may indicate that they possess a more limited form of metacognition (Smith *et al* in press).

A quite different paradigm involving the phenomenon of 'blindsight' has also been used to investigate the existence of conscious and non-conscious processing in animals. Humans with damage to the V1 area of the visual cortex report that they are blind in one part of their visual field, and yet they are able to detect and discriminate visual stimuli presented in this area (Weiskrantz 2001). It appears that there are conscious and non-conscious pathways mediating their behaviour in these visual tasks. Research has revealed parallels in rhesus monkeys. Cowey and Stoerig (1995) showed that monkeys with damage to the V1 area could be trained to detect and touch a visual stimulus on a computer screen when it was presented in both damaged and intact parts of their visual field. However, when trained to report the presence or absence of the stimulus by touching either a 'there' or 'not there' symbol, they reported that it was 'there' when presented in the intact part of the visual field, but 'not there' when presented in the damaged part. These findings once more indicate that two levels of cognitive processing appear to occur in monkeys.

We should emphasise that none of these studies can definitively answer the question of whether the animals involved are conscious or not. However, they do provide the best behavioural evidence to date that some animals may process information at two levels, one of which may be similar to human conscious information processing. One limitation of this approach is that the studies have so far focused on whether animals can report on their 'knowledge' state. It remains unclear whether an inability to do this, as may be the case in rats and pigeons, also reflects an inability to access and be aware of the subjective states most relevant for animal welfare – emotions and sensations (cf Dawkins 2000; Panksepp 2003). In the second part of this paper we consider how a knowledge of cognition–emotion relationships can be used to help develop better measures of animal emotion.

Cognition and emotion

As mentioned in the introduction, emotional responses can be regarded as comprising behavioural, physiological, cognitive and subjective components (eg Frijda 1988; Lang 1993; Lerner & Keltner 2000). Here we consider cognitive components of emotion. These have been investigated extensively in humans as detailed below, but have received little attention in animal studies.

In humans, initiation of an emotional response depends in part on 'cognitive inputs' – how the eliciting stimulus that gives rise to the emotion is 'appraised' by the subject (eg Scherer 1984; Ortony *et al* 1988; Lazarus 1991). Appraisal is the process by which the relevance of the stimulus is classified, for example either as threatening, in which case a fear response will occur, or as non-threatening, in which case there will be no fear response. Essentially a cognitive process – though not necessarily conscious (Öhman & Soares 1993; Gray 1999) – appraisal is influenced by innate 'automatic' responses that may have evolved over many generations (eg responses to a snake-like object), and also by learning and memory of previous encounters with stimuli during the individual's lifetime (LeDoux 1996).

Emotional events can also lead to changes in cognitive functioning such as an increased tendency to attend to threatening stimuli during fear, or an enhanced memory for unhappy events during sadness (eg Clark & Teasdale 1982; MacLeod *et al* 1986; Burke & Mathews 1992; Mogg *et al* 1992; Keogh *et al*

2001). These have been extensively studied in humans and are viewed as important functional 'cognitive outputs' that could well occur in other species.

Currently, measures of animal emotion focus primarily on the physiological and behavioural components of the emotional response (see Broom 1998 for examples). Escape behaviour, elevations in heart rate or 'stress hormones' such as cortisol, avoidance of moving to open arms in an elevated plus maze, and high levels of defecation are all examples of responses used as indicators of 'fear' or 'anxiety'. Although such measures are the bedrock of animal emotion assessment, they do have limitations. Standard measures of negative emotions far outweigh those of positive ones (although the approach of Wemelsfelder and colleagues [2001] emphasises positive as well as negative states). There is no a priori framework for interpreting different profiles of response. Is an animal showing high heart rate, low avoidance and moderate rises in cortisol exhibiting a different emotion from one showing another response profile? If so, which emotions map onto which responses? Finally, in humans at least, there is evidence for dissociations between physiological and behavioural responses and reported conscious experience of emotion. For example, some people appear unaware of subjective emotion despite showing behavioural and physiological emotional responses (Lane et al 1997a; Stone & Nielson 2001). Given that our ultimate goal in animal welfare research is to provide accurate estimates of conscious components of emotion, behavioural and physiological measures may be found wanting. We propose that approaches based on the measurement of cognition and information processing may help to address these problems and to develop new and better indicators of emotion (see Harding et al 2004).

Cognitive inputs: appraisal theories as frameworks for interpreting physiological and behavioural components of emotional responses

Much research on human emotion has focused on how cognitive appraisals of stimuli determine different felt emotions. For example, the work of Scherer (1999) has shown that if a stimulus is appraised as being unfamiliar, unpleasant, unpredictable, and occurring suddenly, an emotion of fear is usually reported. In contrast, a stimulus evaluated as being pleasant, of moderate predictability, and not sudden, triggers a happy emotion (in this case, familiarity appears to have little impact). Other appraisal characteristics are also important (see Scherer 1999), but the key point is that specific appraisal patterns appear to be linked to specific felt emotions. Recently, Dantzer (2002) and Desiré and colleagues (2002a) have proposed applying Scherer's theory to animals. They suggest designing stimuli that have properties that mimic appraisal criteria for different emotions. For example, by presenting a stimulus that is unpredictable, unfamiliar, unpleasant and sudden, the *profile* of behavioural and physiological responses that an animal shows to this stimulus could, a priori, be labelled as an expression of 'fear'. This approach offers the possibility of identifying the features of a variety of different emotions, thus establishing the range of emotions that a particular species can exhibit, without relying on a posteriori assessments of what kind of emotion a particular situation might be expected to induce. Limitations include the assumption that Scherer's theory of the link between human appraisal processes and emotions is correct – there are related theories (eg Ortony et al 1988; Lazarus 1991; Clore et al 1994; Smith & Kirby 2000) – and that it has validity in other species.

A similar approach can be taken using simpler frameworks for categorising emotions that may be more applicable to animals. For example, Rolls (1999) proposes that stimuli are appraised principally according to whether they are rewarding or punishing (see also Millenson 1967; Gray 1975). Emotional responses are determined by the intensity of reward or punishment and also by whether the stimuli are presented, omitted or terminated. Presentation of rewards leads to emotions such as happiness, while omission of rewards leads to frustration, anger or rage. The behavioural and physiological response profiles observed under these conditions could thus be used as indicators of putative animal emotions.

These approaches offer a priori frameworks for mapping behavioural and physiological responses to particular emotion states, including positive ones. Initial studies suggest that they can be used with farm animals. Sheep exhibit different response profiles to stimuli with different characteristics (Desiré *et al* 2002b). Further studies may reveal whether distinctive response profiles are reliably observed and can be used to assess the impact of real life husbandry conditions. It remains to be seen if such studies can contribute to an understanding of whether and how the felt component of emotions arises in animals.

Cognitive outputs: cognitive biases as indicators of emotions

Numerous cognitive changes occur in humans experiencing particular emotions or moods (Mathews & MacLeod 1994; Mineka *et al* 1998). For example, anxious people bias their attention towards threatening stimuli or information (eg Kindt & Van Den Hout 2001), tend to recall negative autobiographical memories (eg Williams *et al* 1997), and have negative expectations of future events — a pessimistic outlook (eg MacLeod & Byrne 1996). Opposite biases are observed in happy people (eg Wright & Bower 1992; Nygren *et al* 1996). Such cognitive biases have a survival function, increasing the likelihood that under threatening circumstances stimuli are appraised in a negative way, and actual dangers are identified more quickly (Bradley *et al* 1997). In cases of ongoing pathological anxiety or depression, however, such biases can become detrimental, perpetuating negative affective states and preventing recovery (MacLeod *et al* 1986).

Given that cognitive processes are so intimately and functionally involved in emotions in humans, it is conceivable that some animal species also exhibit cognitive emotional biases or 'outputs'. We are currently investigating whether this is indeed the case. In particular, we have been developing methods to determine whether animals are more likely to anticipate future events as being negative or positive, and whether any observed cognitive biases are affected by how stressed the animals are (Harding *et al* 2004). Such measures of cognitive bias may be especially informative as they indicate both the presence of current emotions, including positive ones, and a predisposition to future emotions. They may also be particularly useful for identifying ongoing, perhaps pathological, emotional states in captive animals that are no longer subject to direct stressors. Furthermore, human emotion theorists suggest that some cognitive biases associated with emotional states arise directly as a result of conscious emotional feelings being made use of as 'information' in processes of judgement and decision-making (Schwarz & Clore 1983, 1996; Bower & Forgas 2000). If this is correct, the possibility that certain cognitive components of emotion are directly indicative of the presence of conscious emotion, even in non-human animals, will need to be explored.

Cognitive techniques: using conditioning to investigate emotional states

Two other approaches to the measurement of animal emotion employ techniques from cognitive science. Similar to Harding and co-workers (2004), anticipatory behaviour has been identified as a potential indicator of emotion by Spruijt and colleagues (Spruijt *et al* 2001; van den Bos *et al* 2002; see Berridge 1996 for background to this approach). They suggest that animals experiencing an anhedonia-like state (decreased reward-sensitivity) attributable to stress or negative affect will show reduced anticipation of rewarding stimuli such as sweet foods. They propose that 'anticipatory behaviour' can be measured in a Pavlovian conditioning paradigm as the number of behavioural transitions occurring between the presentation of a conditioned stimulus predicting a sucrose reward and the arrival of that reward. Experimental studies have shown that rats exposed to social stress or isolation do indeed exhibit a reduced frequency of behavioural transitions (van den Berg *et al* 1999; von Frijtag *et al* 2000). Although the rationale behind their proposal is quite different from that developed by Harding and colleagues (2004), both approaches emphasise that measures of cognitive function such as anticipation can provide information about animal emotion.

A final approach uses operant conditioning techniques to reveal emotional states in animals. Carey and Fry (Carey *et al* 1992; Carey & Fry 1993, 1995) were able to train pigs to show one operant response when they were in a 'normal' state and a different response when they were in an 'anxious' state (dosed with an anxiogenic drug), indicating that the pigs could discriminate between these two states and alter their lever pressing behaviour accordingly. They also went on to show that undrugged pigs would make the response indicative of drug presence after having been exposed to a novel pen, a novel object, transportation or mixing with an unfamiliar pig (Carey & Fry 1995). The implication was that the pigs experienced a state similar to drug presence (or anxiety) following these treatments. These studies demonstrate another way in which cognitive techniques can be used to probe animal emotions.

Conclusions and animal welfare implications

Approaches to the measurement of welfare that sidestep the problem of animal consciousness have been highly successful in providing a pragmatic way forward (see Broom 1991; Duncan & Fraser 1997; Mendl 2001). But there should also be space in animal welfare science for attempts to further develop our understanding and measurement, however indirectly, of animal consciousness and the sensations and emotions that constitute suffering or happiness. Our aim in this paper has been to show that recent developments in cognitive science offer promising ways forward in this difficult endeavour.

The general tendency to search for examples of cognitive complexity to support arguments for the humane treatment of animals, or for the provision of rights, runs the risk of speciesism and the danger of ignoring those that may most need our protection (Burghardt 1997; Bekoff 1998). We and others (eg Dawkins 2001) argue that an individual's cognitive complexity, and this usually means its cognitive similarity to humans, tells us little about its capacity for feelings consciousness – the conscious awareness of sensations and emotions which lie at the heart of suffering. However, if we make the assumption that a particular species does have feelings consciousness, an understanding of its cognitive capacities may help identify those situations in which it is likely to suffer, and hence may suggest ways of changing management to eliminate or minimise these situations (Duncan & Petherick 1991; Bekoff 1994; Nicol 1996; Mendl 1999; Held *et al* 2001b, 2002b; Mendl *et al* 2001). More importantly, recent developments in cognitive science offer promising new ways of probing the possible conscious experiences of animals. Studies of metacognition and blindsight should yield fresh insight into the issue of whether animals process information consciously, and some of the techniques used (eg Smith *et al* 1997; Hampton 2001) could be adapted for common captive species.

Cognitive science also offers novel approaches to the measurement of animal emotion. Innovative use of traditional conditioning paradigms may provide new ways of assessing emotions. Knowledge of the links between cognition and emotion in humans can generate *a priori* frameworks for interpreting traditional physiological and behavioural indicators of animal emotion, can suggest new measures of positive and negative emotion such as cognitive bias, and may even identify cognitive components of emotion that might indicate the presence of subjective emotional states.

Could a programme of cognitive research provide evidence to confirm the assumption underpinning animal welfare research that the species we study are capable of conscious experience? On its own, we think this is unlikely. Nevertheless, we feel that it will provide important strands of evidence that, together with developments in philosophical approaches to the study of mind and brain, brain imaging studies and neuroscience research in humans and animals (eg Lane *et al* 1997; Gray 1999; Bush *et al* 2000; Chalmers 2000; Damasio *et al* 2000; O'Regan & Noe 2001; Crick & Koch 2003; Panksepp 2003), may take us closer to tackling the problem of whether we can ever know that another being is conscious.

Studies of animal cognition are of intrinsic interest to the general public. They are potentially powerful tools in changing attitudes and perceptions and hence the treatment of animals in society. They are also within the realm of study of animal welfare scientists, and represent a route by which we can contribute to an understanding of animal consciousness and emotion – critical issues in animal welfare science. The search for cognitive complexity has dominated thinking and research in this area. It is now time to take on board new ideas and methods from cognitive science that promise fresh advances in our understanding of animal consciousness, animal emotion, and animal welfare.

Acknowledgements

We are grateful to the Biotechnology and Biological Sciences Research Council (BBSRC) and the Universities Federation for Animal Welfare (UFAW) for supporting our work in this area.

References

Appleby M C and Sandøe P 2002 Philosophical debate on the nature of well-being: implications for animal welfare. *Animal Welfare 11*: 283–294

Baars B J 2001 There are no known differences in brain mechanisms of consciousness between humans and other mammals. *Animal Welfare 10*: S31–S40

Bekoff M 1994 Cognitive ethology and the treatment of non-human animals: how matters of mind inform matters of welfare. *Animal Welfare 3*: 75–96

Bekoff M 1998 Deep ethology, animal rights, and the great ape/animal project: resisting speciesism and expanding the community of equals. *Journal of Agricultural and Environmental Ethics 10*: 269–296

Bekoff M 2002 Animal reflections. *Nature 419*: 255

Bermond B 2001 A neuropsychological and evolutionary approach to animal consciousness and animal suffering. *Animal Welfare 10*: S47–S62

Berridge K C 1996 Food reward: brain substrates of wanting and liking. *Neuroscience and Biobehavioral Reviews 20*: 1–25

Berridge K C and Winkielman P 2003 What is an unconscious emotion? (The case for unconscious "liking"). *Cognition and Emotion 17*: 181–211

Block N 1998 How can we find the neural correlate of consciousness? *Trends in Neurosciences 19*: 456–459

Bower G H and Forgas J P 2000 Affect, memory and social cognition. In: Eich E, Kihlstrom J F, Bower G P, Forgas J P and Niedenthal P M (eds) *Cognition and Emotion* pp 87–168. Oxford University Press: Oxford, UK

Bradley B P, Mogg K and Lee S C 1997 Attentional biases for negative information in induced and naturally occurring dysphoria. *Behaviour Research and Therapy 35*: 911–927

Bradshaw R H 1998 Consciousness in non-human animals: adopting the precautionary principle. *Journal of Consciousness Studies 5*: 108–114

Broom D M 1991 Animal welfare – concepts and measurement. *Journal of Animal Science 69*: 4167–4175

Broom D M 1998 Welfare, stress and the evolution of feelings. *Advances in the Study of Behaviour 27*: 371–403

Burghardt G 1997 Review of the Great Ape Project (Cavalieri and Singer). *Society and Animals 5*: 83–86

Burke M and Mathews A M 1992 Autobiographical memory and clinical anxiety. *Cognition and Emotion 6*: 23–35

Bush G, Luu P and Posner M I 2000 Cognitive and emotional influences in anterior cingulate cortex. *Trends in Cognitive Sciences 4*: 215–222

Butler L T and Berry D C 2001 Implicit memory: intention and awareness revisited. *Trends in Cognitive Sciences 5*: 192–197

Byrne R 1995 *The Thinking Ape*. Oxford University Press: Oxford, UK

Byrne R W 1999 Primate cognition: evidence for the ethical treatment of primates. In: Dolins F L (ed) *Attitudes to Animals* pp 114–125. Cambridge University Press: Cambridge, UK

Carey M P and Fry J P 1993 A behavioural and pharmacological evaluation of the discriminative stimulus induced by pentylenetetrazole in the pig. *Psychopharmacology 111*: 244–250

Carey M P and Fry J P 1995 Evaluation of animal welfare by the self-expression of an anxiety state. *Laboratory Animals 29*: 370–379

Carey M P, Fry J P and White D G 1992 The detection of changes in psychological state using a novel pharmacological conditioning procedure. *Journal of Neuroscience Methods 43*: 69–76

Carruthers P 1989 Brute experience. *The Journal of Philosophy 89*: 258–269

Cavalieri P and Singer P 1993 *The Great Ape Project*. Fourth Estate: London, UK

Chalmers D J 2000 What is a neural correlate of consciousness? In: Metzinger T (ed) *Neural Correlates of Consciousness: Empirical and Conceptual Questions* pp 17–40. MIT Press: Cambridge, USA

Clark D M and Teasdale J D 1982 Diurnal variation in clinical depression and accessibility of memories of positive and negative experiences. *Journal of Abnormal Psychology 91*: 87–95

Clayton N S and Dickinson A D 1998 Episodic-like memory during cache recovery by scrub jays. *Nature 395*: 272–278

Cleeremans A, Destrebecqz A and Boyer M 1998 Implicit learning: news from the front. *Trends in Cognitive Sciences 2*: 406–416

Clore G L, Schwarz N and Conway M 1994 Affective causes and consequences of social information processing. In: Wyer R S and Srull T K (eds) *Handbook of Social Cognition, Volume 2, Second Edition* pp 323–417. Erlbaum: Hillsdale, New Jersey, USA

Coussi-Korbel S 1994 Learning to outwit a competitor in mangabeys, *Cerocebus t. torquatus*. *Journal of Comparative Psychology 108*: 164–171

Cowey A and Stoerig P 1995 Blindsight in monkeys. *Nature 373*: 247–249

Crick F and Koch C 2003 A framework for consciousness. *Nature Neuroscience 6*: 119–126

Curran T 2001 Implicit learning revealed by the method of opposition. *Trends in Cognitive Sciences 5*: 503–504

Damasio A 2000 *The Feeling of What Happens*. Vintage: London, UK

Damasio A R, Grabowski T J, Bechara A, Damasio H, Ponto L L B, Parvizi J and Hichwa R D 2000 Subcortical and cortical brain activity during the feeling of self-generated emotions. *Nature Neuroscience 3*: 1049–1056

Dantzer R 2002 Can farm animal welfare be understood without taking into account the issues of emotion and cognition? *Journal of Animal Science 80 (E Suppl I)*: E1–E9

Davis S L and Cheeke P R 1998 Do domestic animals have minds and the ability to think? A provisional sample of opinions on the question. *Journal of Animal Science 76*: 2022–2079

Dawkins M S 1990 From an animal's point of view: motivation, fitness and animal welfare. *Behavioral and Brain Sciences 13*: 1–61

Dawkins M S 2000 Animal minds and animal emotions. *American Zoologist 40*: 883–888

Dawkins M S 2001 Who needs consciousness? *Animal Welfare 10*: S19–S29

de Veer M W and van den Bos R 1999 A critical review of methodology and interpretation of mirror self-recognition research in non-human primates. *Animal Behaviour 58*: 459–468

Dennett D C 1996 *Kinds of Minds*. Weidenfeld and Nicolson: London, UK

Desiré L, Boissy A and Veissier I 2002a Emotions in farm animals: a new approach to animal welfare in applied ethology. *Behavioural Processes 60*: 165–180

Desiré L, Boissy A, Veissier I and Després G 2002b A cognitive approach to emotions: are the responses to suddenness and novelty different? In: Koene P and the Scientific Committee of the 36th Congress of the ISAE (eds) *Proceedings of the 36th International Congress of the International Society for Applied Ethology* p 139. Paul Koene: Wageningen, The Netherlands

Dienes Z and Perner J 1999 A theory of implicit and explicit knowledge. *Behavioral and Brain Sciences 22*: 735–808

Duncan I J H and Fraser D 1997 Understanding animal welfare. In: Appleby M C and Hughes B O (eds) *Animal Welfare* pp 19–31. CAB International: Wallingford, UK

Duncan I J H and Petherick J C 1991 The implications of cognitive processes for animal welfare. *Journal of Animal Science 69*: 5017–5022

Emery N J and Clayton N S 2001 Effects of experience and social context on prospective caching strategies by scrub jays. *Nature 414*: 443–446

Frijda N H 1988 The laws of emotion. *American Psychologist 43*: 349–358

Gallup G G 1970 Chimpanzees: self recognition. *Science 167*: 86–87

Gallup G G 1982 Self awareness and the emergence of mind in primates. *American Journal of Primatology 2*: 237–248

Gazzaniga M S 2000 Cerebral specialization and interhemispheric communication: does the corpus callosum enable the human condition? *Brain 123*: 1293–1326

Gray J A 1975 *Elements of a Two-Process Theory of Learning.* Academic Press: London, UK

Gray J A 1999 Cognition, emotion, conscious experience and the brain. In: Dalgleish T and Power M J (eds) *Handbook of Cognition and Emotion* pp 3–20. John Wiley and Sons: Chichester, UK

Griffin D R 1992 *Animal Minds.* University of Chicago Press: Chicago, USA

Griffin D R 1998 From cognition to consciousness. *Animal Cognition 1*: 3–16

Hampton R R 2001 Rhesus monkeys know when they remember. *Proceedings of the National Academy of Sciences 98*: 5359–5362

Harding E J, Paul E S and Mendl M 2004 Cognitive bias and affective state. *Nature 427*: 312.

Held S, Mendl M, Devereux C and Byrne R W 2001a Behaviour of domestic pigs in a visual perspective taking task. *Behaviour 138*: 1337–1354

Held S, Mendl M, Devereux C and Byrne R W 2001b Studies in social cognition: from primates to pigs. *Animal Welfare 10*: S209–S217

Held S, Mendl M, Devereux C and Byrne R W 2002a Foraging pigs alter their behaviour in response to exploitation. *Animal Behaviour 64*: 157–166

Held S, Mendl M, Laughlin K and Byrne R W 2002b Cognition studies with pigs: livestock cognition and its implication for production. *Journal of Animal Science 80 (E Suppl 1)*: E10–E17

Heyes C M 1994 Reflections on self-recognition in primates. *Animal Behaviour 47*: 909–919

Heyes C M 1998 Theory of mind in non-human primates. *Behavioral and Brain Sciences 21*: 101–114

Inman A and Shettleworth S J 1999 Detecting metamemory in nonverbal subjects: a test with pigeons. *Journal of Experimental Psychology: Animal Behaviour Processes 25*: 389–395

Kennedy J S 1992 *The New Anthropomorphism.* Cambridge University Press: Cambridge, UK

Keogh E, Dillon C, Georgiou G and Hunt C 2001 Selective attentional biases for physical threat in physical anxiety sensitivity. *Journal of Anxiety Disorders 15*: 299–315

Kindt M and Van Den Hout M 2001 Selective attention and anxiety: a perspective on developmental issues and the causal status. *Journal of Psychopathology and Behavioural Assessment 23*: 193–202

Lane R D, Ahern G L, Schwartz G E and Kasniak A W 1997a Is alexithymia the emotional equivalent of blindsight? *Biological Psychiatry 42*: 834–844

Lane R D, Fink G R, Chau P M L and Dolan R J 1997b Neural activation during selective attention to subjective emotional responses. *Neuroreport 8*: 3969–3972

Lang P J 1993 The three system approach to emotion. In: Birbaumer N and Öhman A (eds) *The Organization of Emotion* pp 18–30. Hogrefe-Huber: Toronto, Canada

Lazarus R S 1991 Cognition and motivation in emotion. *American Psychologist 46*: 352–367

Lea S E G 2001 Anticipation and memory as criteria for special welfare consideration. *Animal Welfare 10*: S195–S208

LeDoux J 1996 *The Emotional Brain.* Simon and Schuster: New York, USA

Lerner J S and Keltner D 2000 Beyond valence: toward a model of emotion-specific influences on judgement and choice. *Cognition and Emotion 14*: 473–493

MacLeod C and Byrne A 1996 Anxiety, depression, and the anticipation of future positive and negative experiences. *Journal of Abnormal Psychology 105*: 286–289

MacLeod C, Mathews A and Tata P 1986 Attentional bias in emotional disorders. *Journal of Abnormal Psychology 95*: 15–20

Macphail E M 1998 *The Evolution of Consciousness.* Oxford University Press: Oxford, UK

Mason G and Mendl M 1993 Why is there no simple way of measuring animal welfare? *Animal Welfare 2*: 301–319

Mathews A and MacLeod C 1994 Cognitive approaches to emotion and emotional disorders. *Annual Review of Psychology 45*: 25–50

McGlone J J 1993 What is animal welfare? *Journal of Agricultural and Environmental Ethics 6 (Suppl 2)*: 26–36

Mendl M 1999 Performing under pressure: stress and cognitive function. *Applied Animal Behaviour Science* 65: 221–244

Mendl M 2001 Assessing the welfare state. *Nature 410*: 31–32

Mendl M, Burman O, Laughlin K and Paul E 2001 Animal memory and animal welfare. *Animal Welfare 10*: S141–S159

Millenson J R 1967 *Principles of Behavioral Analysis*. Macmillan: New York, USA

Mineka S, Watson D and Clark A L 1998 Comorbidity of anxiety and unipolar mood disorders. *Annual Review of Psychology 49*: 377–412

Mogg K, Mathews A and Eysenck M 1992 Attentional bias to threat in clinical anxiety states. *Cognition and Emotion 6*: 149–159

Nicol C J 1996 Farm animal cognition. *Animal Science 62*: 375–391

Nygren T E, Isen A M, Taylor P J and Dulin J 1996 The influence of positive affect on the decision rule in risky situations. *Organizational Behaviour and Human Decision Processes 66*: 59–72

Öhman A and Soares J J 1993 On the automatic nature of phobic fear: conditioned electrodermal responses to masked, fear-relevant stimuli. *Journal of Abnormal Psychology 102*: 121–132

O'Regan J and Noe A 2001 A sensorimotor account of vision and visual consciousness. *Behavioural and Brain Sciences 24*: 939–1031

Ortony A, Clore G L and Collins A 1988 *The Cognitive Structure of Emotions*. Cambridge University Press: New York, USA

Panksepp J 2003 At the interface of the affective, behavioural, and cognitive neurosciences: decoding the emotional feelings of the brain. *Brain and Cognition 52*: 4–14

Rolls E T 1999 *The Brain and Emotion*. Oxford University Press: Oxford, UK

Sandøe P, Forkman B and Christiansen S B 2004 Scientific uncertainty – how should it be handled in relation to scientific advice regarding animal welfare issues? In: Kirkwood J K, Roberts E A and Vickery S (eds) *Proceedings of the UFAW International Symposium 'Science in the Service of Animal Welfare', Edinburgh, 2003. Animal Welfare 13*: S121–S126 (Suppl)

Scherer K R 1984 On the nature and function of emotion: a component process approach. In: Scherer K R and Ekman P (eds) *Approaches to Emotion* pp 293–317. Erlbaum: Hillsdale, New Jersey, USA

Scherer K R 1999. Appraisal theories. In: Dalgleish T and Power M (eds) *Handbook of Cognition and Emotion* pp 637–663. John Wiley and Sons: Chichester, UK

Schwarz N and Clore G L 1983 Mood, misattribution and judgements of well-being: informative and directive functions of affective states. *Journal of Personality and Social Psychology 45*: 513–523

Schwarz N and Clore G L 1996 Feelings and phenomenal experiences. In: Higgins T E and Kruglanski A (eds) *Social Psychology: a Handbook of Basic Principles* pp 433–465. Guilford Press: New York, USA

Seger C A 1994 Implicit learning. *Psychological Bulletin 115*: 163–196

Serpell J A 2004 Factors influencing human attitudes to animals and their welfare. In: Kirkwood J K, Roberts E A and Vickery S (eds) *Proceedings of the UFAW International Symposium 'Science in the Service of Animal Welfare', Edinburgh, 2003. Animal Welfare 13*: S145–S151 (Suppl)

Shanks D R and St John M F 1994 Characteristics of human dissociable learning systems. *Behavioral and Brain Sciences 17*: 367–447

Sherwin C M 2001 Can invertebrates suffer? Or how robust is argument from analogy? *Animal Welfare 10*: S103–S118

Shettleworth S J 1998 *Cognition, Evolution, and Behavior*. Oxford University Press: Oxford, UK

Smith C A and Kirby L D 2000 Consequences require antecedents: towards a process model of emotion elicitation. In: Forgas J P (ed) *Feeling and Thinking: the Role of Affect in Social Cognition* pp 83–106. Cambridge University Press: Cambridge UK

Smith J D, Schull J, Strote J, McGee K, Egnor R and Erb L 1995. The uncertain response in the bottlenosed dolphin *(Tursiops tursiops)*. *Journal of Experimental Psychology: General 124*: 391–408

Smith J D, Shields W E and Washburn D A The comparative psychology of uncertainty monitoring and metacognition. *Behavioral and Brain Sciences*: in press

Smith J D, Shields W E, Schull J and Washburn D A 1997 The uncertain response in humans and animals. *Cognition 62*: 75–97

Spinka M, Duncan I J H and Widowski T M 1998 Do domestic pigs prefer short-term to medium-term confinement? *Applied Animal Behaviour Science 58*: 221–232

Spruijt B M, van den Bos R and Pijlman F T A 2001 A concept of welfare based on reward evaluating mechanisms in the brain: anticipatory behaviour as an indicator for the state of reward systems. *Applied Animal Behaviour Science 75*: 145–171

Stone L A and Nielson K A 2001 Intact physiological response to arousal with impaired recognition in alexithymia. *Psychotherapy and Psychosomatics 70*: 92–102

Taylor P E, Haskell M J, Appleby M C and Waran N K 2002 Perception of time duration by domestic hens. *Applied Animal Behaviour Science 76*: 41–51

van den Berg C L, Pijlman F T A, Koning H A M, Diergaarde L, van Ree J M and Spruijt B M 1999 isolation changes the incentive value of sucrose and social behaviour in juvenile and adult rats. *Behavioural Brain Research 106*: 133–142

van den Bos R, Houx B B and Spruijt B M 2002 Cognition and emotion in concert in human and nonhuman animals. In: Bekoff M, Allen C and Burghardt G (eds) *The Cognitive Animal* pp 97–103. MIT Press: Cambridge, USA

Vauclair J 1997 Mental states in animals: cognitive ethology. *Trends in Cognitive Sciences 1*: 35–39

von Frijtag J C, Reijmers L G J E, van der Harst J E, Leus I E, van den Bos R and Spruijt B M 2000 Defeat followed by individual-housing results in long-term impaired reward- and cognition-related behaviours in rats. *Behavioural Brain Research 117*: 137–146

Weiskrantz L 2001 Commentary responses and conscious awareness in humans: the implications for awareness in non-human animals. *Animal Welfare 10*: S41–S46

Wemelsfelder F 1997 The scientific validity of subjective concepts in models of animal welfare. *Applied Animal Behaviour Science 53*: 75–88

Wemelsfelder F, Hunter T E A, Mendl M and Lawrence A B 2001 Assessing the 'whole animal': a free choice profiling approach. *Animal Behaviour 62*: 209–220

Williams J M G, Watts F, MacLeod C and Mathews A 1997 *Cognitive Psychology and Emotional Disorders, Second Edition*. John Wiley and Sons: Chichester, UK

Wright W F and Bower G H 1992 Mood effects on subjective probability assessments. *Organizational Behaviour and Human Decisions Processes 62*: 276–291

Chapter 9

Barbara Smuts

REFLECTIONS

Smuts reports on her studies with baboons, including the process of exploring the complex topic of human–baboon intersubjectivity. She came to know the 140 baboons in the troop as individuals, with characteristic things to communicate, favorite foods, favorite friends, and unique bad habits. She describes in elegant detail some of the personal relationships she experienced with this troop of baboons.

[. . .]

THE HEART, [. . .] IS "the seat of a faculty, *sympathy*, that allows us to share . . . the being of another." For the heart to truly share another's being, it must be an embodied heart, prepared to encounter directly the embodied heart of another. I have met the "other" in this way, not once or a few times, but over and over during years spent in the company of "persons" like you and me, who happen to be nonhuman.[1]

These nonhuman persons include gorillas at home in the perpetually wet, foggy mountaintops of central Africa, chimpanzees carousing in the hot, rugged hills of Western Tanzania, baboons lazily strolling across the golden grass plains of highland Kenya, and dolphins gliding languorously through the green, clear waters of Shark Bay.[2] In each case, I was lucky to be accepted by the animals as a mildly interesting, harmless companion, permitted to travel amongst them, eligible to be touched by hands and fins, although I refrained, most of the time, from touching in turn.

I mingled with these animals under the guise of scientific research, and, indeed, most of my activities while "in the field" were designed to gain objective, replicable information about the animals' lives. Doing good science, it turned out, consisted mostly of spending every possible moment with the animals, watching them with the utmost concentration, and documenting myriad aspects of their behavior. In this way, I learned much that I could confidently report as scientific findings. [. . .] When I first began working with baboons, my main problem was learning to keep up with them while remaining alert to poisonous snakes, irascible buffalo, aggressive bees, and leg-breaking pig-holes. Fortunately, these challenges eased over time, mainly because I was traveling in the company of expert guides—baboons who could spot a predator a mile away and seemed to possess a sixth sense for the proximity of snakes. Abandoning myself to their far superior knowledge, I moved as a humble disciple, learning from masters about being an African anthropoid.

Thus I became (or, rather, regained my ancestral right to be) an animal, moving instinctively through a world that felt (because it was) like my ancient home. Having begun to master this challenge, I faced another one equally daunting: to comprehend and behave according to a system of baboon etiquette bizarre and subtle enough to stop Emily Post in her tracks. This task was forced on me by the fact that the baboons stubbornly resisted my feeble but sincere attempts to convince them that I was nothing more than a detached observer, a neutral object they could ignore. Right from the start, they knew better, insisting that I was, like them, a social subject vulnerable to the demands and rewards of relationship. Since I was in their world, they determined the rules of the game, and I was thus compelled to explore the unknown terrain of human-baboon intersubjectivity. Through trial and embarrassing error, I gradually mastered at least the rudiments of baboon propriety. I learned much through observation, but the deepest lessons came when I found myself sharing the being of a baboon because other baboons were treating me like one. Thus I learned from personal experience that if I turned my face away but held my ground, a charging male with canines bared in threat would stop short of attack. I became familiar with the invisible line defining the personal space of each troop member, and then I discovered that the space expands and contracts depending on the circumstances. I developed the knack of sweetly but firmly turning my back on the playful advances of juveniles, conveying, as did the older females, that although I found them appealing, I had more important things to do. After many months of immersion in their society I stopped thinking so much about what to do and instead simply surrendered to instinct, not as mindless, reflexive action, but rather as action rooted in an ancient primate legacy of embodied knowledge.

Living in this way with baboons, I discovered what Elizabeth Costello means when she says that to be an animal is to "be full of being," full of "joy." Like the rest of us, baboons get grouchy, go hungry, feel fear and pain and loss. But during my times with them, the default state seemed to be a lighthearted appreciation of being a baboon body in baboon-land. Adolescent females concluded formal, grown-up-style greetings with somber adult males with a somersault flourish. Distinguished old ladies, unable to get a male's attention, stood on their heads and gazed up at the guy upside down. Grizzled males approached balls of wrestling infants and tickled them. Juveniles spent hours perfecting the technique of swinging from a vine to land precisely on the top of mom's head. And the voiceless, breathy chuckles of baboon play echoed through the forest from dawn to dusk.

During the cool, early morning hours, the baboons would work hard to fill their stomachs, but as the temperature rose, they became prone to taking long breaks in especially attractive locales. In a mossy glade or along the white-sanded beach of an inland lake, they would shamelessly indulge a passion for lying around in the shade on their backs with their feet in the air. Every now and then someone would emit a deep sigh of satisfaction. Off and on, they would concur about the agreeableness of the present situation by participating in a chorus of soft grunts that rippled through the troop like a gentle wave. In the early days of my fieldwork when I was still preoccupied with doing things right, I regarded these siestas as valuable opportunities to gather data on who rested near whom. But later, I began to lie around with them. Later still, I would sometimes lie around without them—that is, among them, but while they were still busy eating. Once I fell asleep surrounded by 100 munching baboons only to awaken half an hour later, alone, except for an adolescent male who had chosen to nap by my side (presumably inferring from my deep sleep that I'd found a particularly good resting spot). We blinked at one another in the light of the noonday sun and then casually sauntered several miles back to the rest of the troop, with him leading the way.

There were 140 baboons in the troop, and I came to know every one as a highly distinctive individual. Each one had a particular gait, which allowed me to know who was who, even from great distances when I couldn't see anyone's face. Every baboon had a characteristic voice and unique things to say with it; each had a face like no other, favorite foods, favorite friends, favorite bad habits. Dido, when chased by an unwelcome suitor, would dash behind some cover and then dive into a pig-hole, carefully peeking out every few moments to see if the male had given up the chase. Lysistrata liked to sneak up on an infant riding on its mother's back, knock it off (gently), and then pretend to be deeply preoccupied with eating some grass when mom turned to see the cause of her infant's distress. Apié, the alpha male, would carefully study the local fishermen from a great distance, wait for just the right moment to rush toward them, take a flying leap over their heads to land on the fish-drying rack, grab the largest fish, and disappear into the forest before anyone knew what was happening.

I also learned about baboon individuality directly, since each one approached his or her relationship with me in a slightly different way. Cicero, the outcast juvenile, often followed me and sat quietly a few feet away, seemingly deriving some small comfort from my proximity. Leda, the easygoing female, would walk so close to me I could feel her fur against my bare legs. Dakar, feisty adolescent male, would catch my eye and then march over to me, stand directly in front of me, and grab my kneecap while staring at my face intently (thanks to Dakar, I've become rather good at appearing calm when my heart is pounding). Clearly, the baboons also knew me as an individual. This knowledge was lasting, as I learned when I paid an unexpected visit to one of my study troops seven years after last being with them. They had been unstudied during the previous five years, so the adults had no recent experience with people coming close to them, and the youngsters had no such experience at all. I was traveling with a fellow scientist whom the baboons had never met, and, as we approached on foot from a distance, I anticipated considerable wariness toward both of us. When we got to within about one hundred yards, all of the youngsters fled, but the adults merely glanced at us and continued foraging. I asked my companion to remain where he was, and slowly I moved closer, expecting the remaining baboons to move away at any moment. To my utter amazement, they ignored me, except for an occasional glance, until I found myself walking among them exactly as I had done many years before. To make sure they were comfortable with me, as opposed to white people in general, I asked my friend to come closer. Immediately, the baboons moved away. It was I they recognized, and after a seven-year interval they clearly trusted me as much as they had on the day I left.

Trust, while an important component of friendship, does not, in and of itself, define it. Friendship requires some degree of mutuality, some give-and-take. Because it was important, scientifically, for me to minimize my interactions with the baboons, I had few opportunities to explore the possibilities of such give-and-take with them. But occasional events hinted that such relations might be possible, were I encountering them first and foremost as fellow social beings, rather than as subjects of scientific inquiry. For example, one day, as I rested my hand on a large rock, I suddenly felt the gentlest of touches on my fingertips. Turning around slowly, I came face-to-face with one of my favorite juveniles, a slight fellow named Damien. He looked intently into my eyes, as if to make sure that I was not disturbed by his touch, and then he proceeded to use his index finger to examine, in great detail, each one of my fingernails in turn. This exploration was made especially poignant by the fact that Damien was examining my fingers with one that looked very much the same, except that his was smaller and black. After touching each nail, and without removing his finger, Damien glanced up at me for a few seconds. Each time our gaze met, I wondered if he, like I, was contemplating the implications of the realization that our fingers and fingernails were so alike.

I experienced an even greater sense of intimacy when, in 1978, I had the exceptional privilege of spending a week with Dian Fossey and the mountain gorillas she had been studying for many years. One day, I was out with one of her groups, along with a male colleague unfamiliar to the gorillas and a young male researcher whom they knew well. Digit, one of the young adult males, was strutting about and beating his chest in an early challenge to the leading silverback male. My two male companions were fascinated by this tension, but after a while I had had enough of the macho energy, and I wandered off. About thirty meters away, I came upon a "nursery" group of mothers and infants who had perhaps moved off for the same reasons I had. I sat near them and watched the mothers eating and the babies playing for timeless, peaceful moments. Then my eyes met the warm gaze of an adolescent female, Pandora. I continued to look at her, silently sending friendliness her way. Unexpectedly, she stood and moved closer. Stopping right in front of me, with her face at eye level, she leaned forward and pushed her large, flat, wrinkled nose against mine. I know that she was right up against me, because I distinctly remember how her warm, sweet breath fogged up my glasses, blinding me. I felt no fear and continued to focus on the enormous affection and respect I felt for her. Perhaps she sensed my attitude, because in the next moment I felt her impossibly long ape arms wrap around me, and for precious seconds, she held me in her embrace. Then she released me, gazed once more into my eyes, and returned to munching on leaves.

[. . .]

Notes

1   The term *person* is commonly used in two different ways: first, as a synonym for human, and, second, to refer to a type of interaction or relationship of some degree of intimacy involving actors who are individually known to one another, as in "personal relationship," knowing someone "personally," or engaging with another "person to person." Here I use the word in the second sense, to refer to any animal, human, or nonhuman, who has the capacity to participate in personal relationships, with one another, with humans, or both. I return to the concept of animal "personhood" later in the essay.

2   Shark Bay is off the coast of Western Australia, the site of a research project on wild bottlenose dolphins.

ANTHROPOMORPHISM

Chapter 10

Sandra D. Mitchell

ANTHROPOMORPHISM AND CROSS-SPECIES MODELING

In this reading, Mitchell evaluates the concept of anthropomorphism, particularly as it relates to chimpanzees. She argues that broad arguments against anthropomorphism are not supported, but also that there is no easy application of human descriptive concepts to nonhumans. Rather, anthropomorphic models are specific claims of similarity between humans and nonhumans that are scientifically accessible and must be substantiated by evidence. In the moral sphere, she argues that rather than establishing the similarities and differences between humans and nonhumans, a more fundamental concern might be establishing what capacities in any creature might be the basis of moral consideration.

Introduction

"**ANTHROPOMORPHISM**" **HAS LONG** been considered a bad word in science.[1] It carries the stale dust of nineteenth-century anecdotal evidence for the continuity of humans with nonhuman animals. Darwin claims that "there can, I think, be no doubt that a dog feels shame . . . and something very like modesty when begging too often for food."[2] But anthropomorphism is neither prima facie bad or necessarily nonscientific. It can be both, but it need not be either.

[. . .]

There has been a recent resurgence of interest in anthropomorphism, attributable to two developments—the rise of cognitive ethology and the requirements of various forms of expanded, environmental ethics.

Some of the most interesting and relevant work in this area has been directed at explaining the behavior of chimpanzees. Since it is generally agreed that the chimp is our phylogenetically closest relative, it makes evolutionary sense that the features of that species are more likely to be similar to features of our species than those of species whose connection is more attenuated. Darwin's and our love of dogs notwithstanding, it is in primate research that the most plausible anthropomorphic theses are to be found. Or, as Daniel Povinelli claims in *Folk Physics for Apes*, "if the argument by analogy cannot be sustained when it comes to behaviors that we share in common with our nearest living relatives, it can hardly be expected to survive more general scrutiny."[3] Indeed, as I will report later, Povinelli argues just this—that a strong version of anthropomorphism cannot be sustained in explaining even some chimpanzee behaviors.

A strong version of anthropomorphism found in some advocates of cognitive ethology aims to explain behaviors of nonhumans by appeal to mental states similar to the ones we take to explain our own behavior. Of particular interest is the thesis that chimps have a "theory of mind," that is, beliefs about the beliefs of others. Such second-order beliefs are invoked to make sense of behavioral variation. For example, a human would respond differently to two actors on the basis of beliefs about what those actors could see. If one of them had a clear view of a source of food, while the other's view of the food was blocked by a barrier, then it would make sense to follow any indication of food given by the one whom you believe can see the food and hence will know where it is. Do chimps do the same thing? Do they do it for the same reasons? As I will discuss below, arguments from analogy and experimental results are brought to bear on answering this type of question.

The second source of interest in the similarities of humans and nonhuman animals arises from the animal rights and environmental ethics movements, which have sought to transform the criteria by which we determine what beings merit moral consideration. Animal welfare and animal rights ethical positions make the nature of nonhuman experience determinate of who and what we must count in judging the moral correctness of our actions. [. . .] Thus, the existence of feelings and cognitive states of nonhuman organisms is no longer just an academic question of whether or not the Rumbaugh's Kanzi has language[4] or dolphins can recognize themselves in a mirror[5] but is rather a set of facts about the world that we need to know to ethically decide what to eat and what to wear. Thus, the manner and degree to which nonhuman animals are similar to human beings becomes an even more pressing scientific problem in a context in which the very morality of our actions depends on the answer.

At its basis, anthropomorphism involves claims about the similarity of nonhuman objects or beings to humans and the centrality of human concepts and abilities to classify behaviors across ontological categories. Strong anthropomorphism asserts that some description of a feature of human beings applies in the same way to a feature of a nonhuman animal. Critics of anthropomorphism often attack the presumptive character of such claims, like Darwin's *lack of doubt* of the internal nature of a dog's experience. Observers have been too willing to characterize nonhumans using descriptive language that has humans as its primary referent. By describing a dog as feeling shame when it walks away with its tail between its legs, one is not gathering neutral data with which to test the myriad of theories about the nature of dogs but rather is assuming in that very description that dogs have mental or emotional states like human mental and emotional states. But what is at fault here? Is it the presumptiveness or the anthropomorphism?

After all, similarity between humans and nonhuman animals is just what we should expect on the basis of an evolutionary account of the origin and diversification of life on the planet—but not any willy-nilly similarity. As a scientific claim about the facts of the world, any specific similarity between human immune systems, say, and mouse immune systems, or between human beliefs and chimp beliefs, must be grounded in more than a general truth of the continuum of life and backed by more than an imposition of the same descriptive language.

In what follows I will evaluate the arguments and evidence for a range of stances toward anthropomorphism from global rejections to specific models. The bumper sticker version of this essay could be: Science made too easy is bound to be wrong. In the end I will argue that specific anthropomorphic theses are supported or not supported by the same rigorous experimental and logical reasoning as any other scientific model. However, even though anthropomorphic models can be treated as science as usual, unique problems for these models still will remain. These problems have to do with the way in which language descriptive of our experiences travels back and forth between scientific and social domains.

I will first consider some global objections to anthropomorphism. These attack the logical or conceptual transgressions that the act of describing nonhumans in human terms is supposed to commit. I will then look at empirical arguments for and against specific instances of the anthropomorphism ascribed to nonhuman primates. Finally I will consider some social contextual concerns that arise from the scientific anthropomorphic models.

Logical objections

A. Anthropomorphism entails a category mistake. To speak of dogs with feelings of shame is like referring to a Bach partita as being purple. This objection is easily dismissed as a relic of the view that humans are a separate and unique species, either created to be such or so far evolved that no predicates true of us could be true of other organisms. Surely the evolution of life on the planet tells against this being a logical claim. For a Cartesian who holds that animals are just complicated machines that lack the souls that make humans human, it might hold sway, but we are centuries beyond that.[6]

B. Anthropomorphism is defined as the *overestimation* of the similarity of humans and nonhumans and hence by definition could not yield accurate accounts.[7] But this is humpty-dumptyism. "When *I* use a word," Humpty Dumpty said, in rather a scornful tone, "it means just what I choose it to mean—neither more nor less."[8]

If we choose to let "anthropomorphism" be so defined, then we merely shift the question to be, *When* is it anthropomorphism, and *when* is it possibly a legitimate similarity? That is, when does a relevant similarity hold such that describing a cognitive state like "believing Sue cannot see the banana" could be equally true of an adult human, a human infant, and a chimpanzee? Such substantive questions cannot be reduced to mere matters of definition.

C. Anthropomorphism is *necessary* or *unavoidable*, since there is no amorphism or neutral language with which to describe behavior. If we do not use the predicates that describe our own human behavior, such as "believing X, wanting Y, deceiving Z" for describing nonhuman animals, then we have to use language appropriate for machines, like "moving toward the object, picking up the banana, looking toward the gate."

This position makes two mistakes. The first is that it presupposes a conceptual and linguistic impoverishment that is not justified. It underestimates our ability to discriminate and refer to multiple states of a system or many-valued parameters. As recent research has suggested, we may end up thinking that chimpanzees do not have the same kind of mental representations that we have but nevertheless think they have mental representations that mediate their behavior. They are not input-output machines but cogitating organisms. They just may not do it the way we do.[9] The second mistake is to confuse anthropocentrism with anthropomorphism. It is true that the descriptions we apply to anything are created *by* us, but they need not be *of* us. That is, we are the source of the terms and predicates, but they need not be terms and predicates that apply principally to our behaviors.

If anthropomorphism is not bad for *logical* reasons, then the extent of the acceptability of claims of similarity must be empirically grounded. This indeed is the conclusion that many recent commentators on anthropomorphism have reached.[10] Do chimpanzees have language, like us? Do they have beliefs about the beliefs of other chimps or of humans? Testing for the presence or absence of mental states, representations internal to the cognizing agent and presumably causally relevant to the behaviors we can observe is no easy matter. I will now turn to the two main types of observational evidence that are used to justify anthropomorphism; the argument by analogy and experimentation.

Empirical questions

Argument by analogy

An *argument by analogy* is invoked to support a claim about the unobserved features of one system—the "target" of the analogy—based on the presence of that feature in another system—the "model system." The relevant similarities between the two systems are what justify the inference. Traditional analyses of analogical arguments render them fairly weak.

Traditional account of analogical argument structure

> *Premise 1:*   System M is observed to have features a, b, c.
> *Premise 2:*   System T is observed to have features a, b, c.
> *Premise 3:*   System M is observed also to have feature d.
> *Conclusion:*   Therefore, system T must have feature d.

This inductive argument structure is supposed to capture everyday reasoning. For example, suppose two students in a class have the same study habits and the same grades on the midterm exam. I observe that student M gets an A on the final exam. Suppose student T has not yet taken the exam. On the basis of the observed similarities, I can infer that student T will also get an A. This is clearly not deductively valid, as student T might be ill or fail to study in the manner she studied in the past or might have lost her book or for any number of reasons not perform the way I expect on the basis of her similarity to student M. Thus there is no deductive guarantee that the conclusion, "Student T will get an A on the exam" is true. Nevertheless, the analogy permits inductive support for the inference. Certainly I would have more reason to believe student T would get an A than I would of other students who bear no similarities to student M.

The strength of an analogy is sometimes rendered in terms of the number of similarities between the two systems. The more features in common, the more likely the target system will have the ascribed unobserved feature. But quantifying over similarities is notoriously difficult and, quite frankly, beside the point. The sheer number of similar features does not immediately warrant the relevance of the similarities for the presence or absence of the feature of interest. Humans and mice have a large number of differences, and yet we are comfortable using the results of drug tests on mice to infer the consequences of those drugs on human biochemistry.

A more sophisticated rendering of the logic of analogical arguments, developed by Weitzenfeld[11] and related to structure-based accounts given in the cognitive sciences,[12] suggests that the inference of the presence of the unobserved feature in the target system is based on assumptions about the relations within each of the two analogous structures, rather than just their unstructured sets of properties. For example, according to Weitzenfeld's account, a claim that a human being will have an adverse reaction to saccharine based on experimental studies on mice is entailed by an assumption of the isomorphism obtaining between the causal structures governing mouse and human biochemistry. Thus, when using information about the model system to draw conclusions about the target system, for example, mice to human inferences or, as we shall see, human beliefs in anthropomorphic inferences to chimp beliefs, what establishes the relevant similarities will be the causal or determining structures in those two systems. If they have isomorphic structures, then the inference is sound. If not, then the conclusions are not supported.

There are two important components to this account of analogy. The first is that it is structural isomorphism between the model and target that deductively guarantees an inference from the observed feature of the model to the unobserved feature of the target. However, isomorphism is a rather weak relationship between two structures, since the reason the mapping works may be accidental. Think of the mapping from stellar constellations as seen from earth such as Orion or Ursa Major to the spatial configurations of hunters and bears. For analogical arguments to be informative, the reason the relations in the model structure—for example, mouse ingestion of large quantities of saccharine inducing mouse production of tumors—map onto the relations in the target structure—that is, human ingestion of saccharine in diet foods and subsequent cancers—must be nonaccidental, that is, governed by a rule or causal law. This is all rather abstract philosophy. The main point of the structural approach to analogical arguments is to focus attention on to the relationships between the variables in each system as well as the relationships between the two systems, rather than on simply the number of features shared by the two systems. Let's bring it back to the case at hand.

A clear reconstruction of the analogical argument for inferring that chimps are like us is provided by Povinelli:

P1:   I exhibit bodily behaviors of type B (i.e., those normally thought to be caused by second-order mental states).

P2:   Chimps exhibit bodily behaviors of type B.

P3:   My own bodily behaviors of type B are usually caused by my second-order mental states of type A.

C: Therefore bodily behaviors of type B exhibited by chimps are caused by their second-order mental states of type A, and so a fortiori chimps have second-order mental states of type A.

Povinelli, Folk Physics for Apes, 13.

In the traditional philosophical analysis of analogical arguments, the number of similarities between humans and chimpanzees would determine the strength of support for the conclusion. Phylogenetic proximity is brought to bear to suggest that we have more similarities with chimps than other species since we are historically closer to them. Divergence occurred more recently from chimpanzees than from other species and hence we expect them to be more like us than would be toads or amoebae. But notice how weak this support actually is. Divergence is presumed, and distinction is required for humans and chimps *not* to be the same species. Many features may be shared, but just the ones we are interested in, second-order mental states for example, may be the ones that constitute the break in the lineage. So evolutionary proximity may entail more similar features but not necessarily the relevant features.[13]

The more sophisticated analysis of analogical inference suggests a different understanding of the argument. Here, what makes human experience relevant to conclusions about chimp experience is not the number of similarities but the presence of isomorphic causal structures. What causes a human behavior B is, supposedly, a human second-order mental state A. But is this the same causal structure found in chimpanzees? If it is, then even though we cannot ask the chimp what belief motivated its behavior, we can be justified in thinking that if the human and chimp behaviors are the same or similar, then the beliefs that cause them are the same or similar. However, this shifts the question of the legitimacy of analogical reasoning to the determination of whether the causal structures generating behaviors in humans and in chimpanzees are isomorphic. That is the subject of the second type of empirical evidence that I will discuss below.

To summarize so far, anthropomorphic theses can be seen as instances of analogical inferences. We ascribe to other organisms the features we take to be true of us. Phylogenetic relatedness seems to render weak support for the conclusion of such inferences, so weak that they can only garner some modest plausibility for the conclusions. However, a stronger analogical inference is supported when there is justification for isomorphism of causal structures in the two systems generating the features we are interested in. On this account the analogy requires a different type of evidence than evolutionary history alone. Statistical and experimental data are required to support the premises that would entail the inference. So how can empirical evidence help?

Argument from experimental data

Advocates of cognitive ethology cry foul when their opponents reject the enterprise from the beginning just for being anthropomorphic. They would rather let the facts decide. But this is not as easy as it might sound. The controversial anthropomorphic theses ascribe to nonhumans just those sorts of features that are not directly accessible to observation. Allen and Hauser want to know whether apes have a concept of death.[14] Premack and Woodruff explore whether apes have a "theory of mind" that is invoked in generating behaviors that appear to be acts of deception.[15] It is obvious that we cannot just look at a chimpanzee, or another human being for that matter, and see its internal mental state. [. . .] We cannot ask a chimpanzee to report to us the content of its cognition. We have access experimentally and observationally only to the very behaviors we take as the effects of the ascribed mental causes. So how can observation and experiment help decide this issue?

It is worth nothing that the reason one suggests that concepts and second-order beliefs might be the causes of nonhuman behaviors is because we believe that they are the causes of our own behaviors. This view assumes there is a causal structure or mechanism that we can investigate that generates behaviors as the effect of beliefs.[16] When I think my husband is joking about where the car keys are, but a friend who is with us is telling the truth, then I do not walk in the direction of the place mentioned by my husband to find my keys. Rather I go to the location cited by my friend. I hear the utterances of each of them, and my behavior is caused not just by those utterances but also by my beliefs about the beliefs of the speakers.

[. . .]

How do I know this? It is introspection or personal self knowledge that gives me insight into the causal structure that underlies my actions.

If the evidence for beliefs being the cause of behavior is solely the subjective experience of the believer/actor, then I need to ascribe to other human beings the possession of an unobservable mental cause to explain their reasoned behaviors. This is the well-known philosophical problem of "other minds." But the ascription of unobservable mental causes to humans seems to be very much like the ascription to nonhuman beings. Why should it be sanctioned in the case of other humans and not sanctioned in the case of, say, honeybees? And where does that leave the inference when directed toward chimpanzee behavior?

There are two places to look for answers to these questions: background assumptions about the nature of intra- and interspecific similarity and behavioral experiments. I will first consider the background assumptions. There are good grounds to assume that basic causal structures or mechanisms are the same for different members of the same species of organism. Although different individual organisms are spatio-temporally distinct and harbor all sorts of variation in particular features, the basic biological mechanisms most directly connected to surviving and reproducing are most likely to be the same. The reason is that these are the features upon which evolution by natural selection will have been quickest and strongest to act. Variations that have relatively negative effects on survival and reproduction are not kept around. That is how evolution by natural selection works. Even with the caveat of recognizing the continual generation of variation within a species, it nevertheless is a safe assumption that there will be little variation in the basic functioning of organisms within a species. The species is the correct boundary for this degree of similarity because it is the potentially interbreeding population that is the receptacle for the consequences of natural selection.

[. . .]

Nevertheless, there are good, if fallible grounds for believing that other human beings have the same sort of second-order beliefs that are causally relevant to their actions since we have grounds for believing that the same causal mechanisms are at work in all members of the species.

What is the objection to extending this inference from humans to non-humans? First of all, we have fewer types of supporting evidence than in the case of human-to-human inference. There is no self-reporting to be acquired from the chimp about the reasons for its actions. There is no shared species membership from which to support causal isomorphism. However, we can look to the similarity or dissimilarity of neurophysiological structure, sensory apparatus, and so on. And, importantly, we can look to behavioral observations and experimentation (see table 10.1).

The experimental data on whether or not chimpanzees have second-order beliefs, unfortunately, permits of multiple interpretations. Povinelli's *Folk Physics for Apes* reports a number of experiments done on captive chimpanzees over a five-year period to investigate how they conceive of the physics that underlies their use of tools in particular or, more generally, to "elucidate the nature of the mental representations that guide this behavior" (1). In service to this goal, Povinelli provides evidence against the strong argument by analogy. A series of experiments were done to determine whether chimpanzees have the concept that others "see." This is a basic second-order belief. I look at another human being and have a visual experience of that person. I look at their eyes and notice that they are directed at the door. I form

Table 10.1 Grounds for attributing causal isomorphism

	Evolutionary relatedness	Self-reporting	Neurophysiological and other physical features	Behavioral statistics
Human-to-human inference	Strong support	Strong support	Strong support	Strong support
Human-to-chimpanzee inference	Weak support	N/a	Some support	Mixed support

a belief that the person sees the door, that is, a belief about her internal visual representation. I can then act on the basis of what I believe that she does or does not see. Povinelli's group studied whether chimpanzees engage in the same kind of cognitive process.

Povinelli dissects forming a belief that another organism sees a particular object into a number of components. The organism must notice the eyes of the other and then follow the gaze of the other toward the object under perception. Interest in eyes and gaze direction are present in a wide range of species, and these abilities may well have emerged as adaptations to predation and social interactions. But how much like humans are the internal states of other organisms that engage in these behaviors? Povinelli puts the point as follows:

> Some researchers interpret the mutual gaze that occurs between infants and adults, as well as among great apes during complex social interactions as *prima facie* evidence of an understanding of the attentional aspect of seeing. And admittedly, there is a certain allure to the idea that, because mutual gaze in adult humans is often attended by representations of the mental states of others, comparable behavior in human infants (or other species) is probably attended by similar representations. But is mutual gaze in apes (for example) really attended by the same psychological representations as in human adults, or is this just a projection of our own way of thinking onto other species? (22)

In short, is this just wishful anthropomorphism, or can we get evidence that apes have the same or similar cognitive state as humans?

The first step in Povinelli's study was to establish whether chimpanzees had the same behavioral abilities, that is, gaze following, as do human infants and human adults. For the analogical argument to work, the effects—behaviors in this case—expressed in the two systems have to be the same, and then one infers that the causes of these effects are also the same. Experiments show that chimps and one-and-one-half-year-old human infants similarly responded to head movement, eye movement, left/right specificity, gaze following outside of visual field, and so on. So he concluded that chimps and humans engage in similar responses to a series of eye movement stimuli presented to them. Behaviors are the same. But what more is going on?

Povinelli devised ingenious experiments to try to test if chimp's gaze-following behavior indicated the possession of second-order mental states. He entertained two possible explanations, a low-level and high-level account. The low-level account interprets the chimp's gaze-following behavior to express cognition about behavioral propensities of the person whose gaze they followed, where the high-level account claims chimps form concepts about the internal mental states of the person whose gaze they are following. That is, the low-level model is akin to what happens when a human visually follows the path of a billiard ball being hit by a cue ball. We see the ball being hit and its initial motion and develop expectations of its behavior at a subsequent time. It initially moves towards the corner pocket, hence it will continue to move in a straight line toward the pocket. The high-level model is akin to a human watching another human looking in the direction of the billiard ball. In this case the perceived eye motion induces beliefs about what the observer *sees*. The human's eyes move following the ball, hence the human sees the ball's motion. The Povinelli group hypothesized that the high- and low-level accounts would make different predictions in cases where the observed individual's gaze was obstructed by an opaque barrier. If the low-level account were right, the observing chimp would just scan a line from the eyes of the observed being until something was noticed. This is based on eyes looking right indicating something is right, and a barrier would be irrelevant. If the high-level account were right, the observing chimp would walk around the barrier to see what was being seen. This would be based on eyes looking right indicating there must be something that is seen that is on the other side of the barrier. The results of an opaque-barrier test were unambiguously in support of the high-level model. The chimps walked around the barrier to see what the person in the experiment was looking at. The conclusion naturally drawn was that chimps understand what it is for someone else to see or represent the world; hence they have second-order beliefs just like humans.

However, a dozen other experiments involving seeing supported the low-level model of cognition. In these experiments, the chimps were presented with two humans displaying different capacities to see them, and it was observed whether the chimps responded differently to the two humans. The test response was begging behavior, and the question was did the chimps beg significantly more to the human who did not have his gaze obstructed? The obstruction conditions of the humans in the test included being blindfolded, having a bucket over one's head, having hands over one's eyes, and facing backward in relation to the observing chimpanzee.

In three of the four conditions, the chimps were as likely to gesture to the person who could *not* see them as to the person who could. However, in the front-facing-versus-back-facing case they did beg more to the human with his front facing the chimp. So the low-level account captured three of the experimental conditions, whereas the high-level account was supported by one of the experimental conditions. To try to distinguish whether it was the seeing that mattered or the front position, Povinelli introduced a fifth experimental set up. This time, both humans had their backs to the observing chimp, but one was looking over her shoulder at the chimp, the other was not. "To our surprise and in full support of the low-level model, on the looking-over-the-shoulder trials the apes did not prefer to gesture to the person who could see them" (*Folk Physics*, 34).

Povinelli's group continued to introduce new seeing/not seeing experimental conditions to the chimps using screens and eyes-open/eyes-shut conditions to try to figure out what was going on. In the end, Povinelli rejected the high-level, second-order belief model and suggested that through trial and error the apes learned a set of procedural rules about successful gesturing (1. gesture to person whose front is facing forward; 2. if both fronts present or absent, gesture to person whose face is visible; and 3. if both faces visible or occluded, gesture to person whose eyes are visible). The chimpanzees do not appear to be using a concept of seeing to help them decide to whom to gesture. Instead, the chimpanzees after lots of trial and error behaved "as if" they had our concept of seeing. Important for Povinelli's conclusion is the fact that the behavior at the end of the study was different from the chimps' behavior at the beginning of the study. They learned something, namely, how to gesture to the person *we* would say could see them. In contrast, three-year-old human children compared in these experiments were shown to have the behaviors appropriate to understanding a concept of seeing from the beginning; no variation in behavior occurred for the humans.

Do these experiments tell us whether the similarity of chimp and human behavior indicates a similarity of internal mental cognition? Povinelli concludes that it is still open to interpretation. Indeed, he postulates three different ways to account for the behaviors of the chimps in the experiments. First, they could have entered the test without a concept of seeing but through the testing came to construct the concept. Second, they could have entered the test with a general conception of attention and constructed a notion of visual attention. And third, they could have neither entered nor exited the tests with an understanding of the mental state of visual attention (*Folk Physics*, 42). Rather, they constructed an "as-if" understanding of seeing-as-attention. The third option is like the familiar case of Clever Hans, the horse who appeared to be able to do arithmetic.[17]

An anomaly for Povinelli's preferred low-level interpretation is that the opaque-barrier tests did support the high-level model of cognition for the chimps. Povinelli takes the preponderance of evidence to suggest that the low-level model is much better supported and gives a reinterpretation of the opaque-barrier test that would account for this contrary bit of evidence. On the way, he points out that if we walk into the laboratory with an anthropomorphic attitude, we are much more likely to continually refine and retest experimental results that support the low-level model and accept on its face the results of tests like the opaque barrier test that support an anthropomorphic high-level model.

What conclusion should we draw from these experiments on chimpanzees? Does the fact that their behavior and our behavior are sometimes indistinguishable indicate that the causes of those behaviors in us and in them are also the same? Does the fact that their behavior and our behavior are sometimes different indicate that the cause of their behaviors are not the same as ours? The experimental results are, at best, ambiguous and, according to Povinelli, lean toward a rejection of strong anthropomorphism. Indeed, as you will recall, he said that if the similarity of human and non-human behaviors does not license the analogical inference to same causes for chimpanzees, then it can hardly be credible for other species. At least it should be clear how difficult it is to get unambiguous experimental results for anthropomorphic models. There is no consensus in the scientific community about the significance of the Povinelli experiments, with criticisms often focused on the possible crucial dissimilarity between captive chimps, the subjects of Povinelli's studies, and chimps in the wild.[18]

Conclusion

What is the fate of anthropomorphism in contemporary science? I have argued that the global arguments against anthropomorphism cannot be maintained in a post-Darwinian scientific world. Given that humans *are* biologically related to other species, the ascription of concepts whose natural home is in describing human features and behaviors may very well apply to nonhumans. That being said, there is also no global support for the cavalier exportation of human descriptive concepts to nonhumans. Rather, I have suggested that a piecemeal evaluation of the credibility of specific claims of similarity, based on a causal-isomorphism model of analogical reasoning, must be undertaken. There are a variety of types of evidential support for grounding specific anthropomorphic models, and so judgments of its legitimacy in different cases may well vary.

In short, anthropomorphic models are specific, scientifically accessible claims of similarity between humans and nonhumans. As such, they must be substantiated by evidence that there are similar causal mechanisms responsible for generating the apparently similar behaviors that are observed. If experimental and background theoretical support do provide that evidence, then there should be no objection to using the same descriptive language for both humans and nonhumans. If that evidence is not provided, then using the same predicate for a full-fledged human behavior to refer to an "as-if" nonhuman behavior will be misleading and inaccurate.

[. . .]

With respect to the issue of cognitive similarities, the current scientific debates indicate that it is difficult to get definitive evidence either way for even the simplest second-order belief that "A sees X." It would appear to get progressively more difficult when the descriptions carry not just casual assumptions but also social and moral baggage.

Not surprisingly, the most controversial and consequential claims about the similarity between humans and nonhuman animals are the most difficult to substantiate. And yet it is these claims that play a fundamental role in the growing field of cognitive ethology. Perhaps the most telling insights that will be gleaned from careful study of the nature of the cognitive similarity or dissimilarity between humans and nonhumans will be reflexive. That is, characterizing the ways in which nonhuman cognition differs from human cognition may force a reevaluation of our account of human cognition itself.

The same may be true for the advocates of expanding the domain of moral consideration to nonhumans. A deeper understanding of the lives of other animals may shift the focus from the anthropocentric question of whether other beings are sufficiently like humans to warrant the same moral rights as humans to a more generalized analysis of what capacities, whether found in humans or not, ought to be the basis of moral consideration.

Notes

This paper was presented at the Max Planck Society for the History of Science Conference on Thinking with Animals and the Pittsburgh–London Consortium in the Philosophy of Biology and Neuroscience. I wish to thank lively discussions at both those conferences and especially comments by Joel Smith, Lorraine Daston, Elliott Sober, and John Dupré.

1   See J. B. Kennedy, *The New Anthropomorphism* (Cambridge: Cambridge University Press, 1992), for an account of the behaviorist attack on anthropomorphism; Stewart Elliott Guthrie, "Anthropomorphism: A Definition and a Theory," in *Anthropomorphism, Anecdotes, and Animals: The Emperor's New Clothes?* ed. R. W. Mitchell, N. S. Thompson, and H. L. Miles (New York: SUNY Press, 1996), 501, cites criticisms of anthropomorphism back to Bacon, Spinoza, and Hume.

2   Charles Darwin, *The Descent of Man, and Selection in Relation to Sex* (1871; reprint, Princeton, N.J.: Princeton University Press, 1981), 42; quoted in Elizabeth Knoll, "Dogs, Darwinism, and English Sensibilities," in *Anthropomorphism, Anecdotes, and Animals: The Emperor's New Clothes?* ed. R. W. Mitchell, N. S. Thompson, and H. L. Miles (New York: SUNY Press, 1996), 14.

3   Daniel J. Povinelli, *Folk Physics for Apes* (Oxford: Oxford University Press, 2000), 9.

4   Sue Savage-Rumbaugh, Stuart G. Shanker and Talbot J. Taylor, *Apes, Language and the Human Mind* (New York: Oxford University Press, 1998). Kansi is a bonobo chimpanzee who can manipulate physical symbols in a way that looks very much like human language.

5   Mark Derr, "Brainy Dolphins Pass the Human 'Mirror' Test," *New York Times*, 1 May 2001.

6   See Emanuela Cenami Spada, "Amorphism, Mechanomorphism, and Anthropomorphism," in *Anthropomorphism, Anecdotes, and Animals: The Emperor's New Clothes?* ed. R. W. Mitchell, N. S. Thompson, and H. L. Miles (New York: SUNY Press, 1996), 37–50.

7   See Guthrie, "Anthropomorphism: A Definition," 53; and Hugh Lehman, "Anthropomorphism and Scientific Evidence for Animal Mental States," in *Anthropomorphism, Anecdotes, and Animals: The Emperor's New Clothes?* ed. R. W. Mitchell, N. S. Thompson, and H. L. Miles (New York: SUNY Press, 1996), 105.

8   Lewis Carroll, *Through the Looking Glass* (New York: Putnam, 1972), chapter 6.

9   See Povinelli, *Folk Physics*.

10   See Marc Beckoff, Colin Allen, and Gordon M. Burghardt, eds., *Cognitive Animal: Empirical and Theoretical Perspectives on Animal Cognition* (Cambridge, Mass.: MIT Press, 2002); and Povinelli, *Folk Physics*.

11   Julian S. Weitzenfeld, "Valid Reasoning by Analogy," *Philosophy of Science* 51 (1984): 137–49.

12   See J. R. Hayes and H. A. Simon, "Understanding Tasks Stated in Natural Language," in *Speech Recognition*, ed. D. R. Reddy. (New York: Academic Press, 1975); and M. L. Gick and K. J. Holyoak, "Schema Induction and Analogical Transfer," *Cognitive Psychology* 15 (1983): 1–38.

13   See Christopher Lang, Elliott Sober, and Karen Strier, "Are Human Beings Part of the Rest of Nature?" *Biology and Philosophy* 17 (2002): 661–71, for a detailed assessment of the import of phylogenetic proximity for casual similarity.

14   Colin Allen and Marc Hauser, "Concept Attribution in Nonhuman Animals: Theoretical and Methodological Problems in Ascribing Complex Mental Processes," *Philosophy of Science* 58 (1991): 221–40.

15   D. Premack and G. Woodruff, "Does the Chimpanzee Have a Theory of Mind?" *Behavioral Brain Sciences* 1 (1978): 515–26.

16   Of course, there is a debate on whether the folk notion of belief is a part of a scientific account of behavior; alternatives include epiphenomenalism with respect to beliefs as well as eliminativism in favor of physical neural structures. See Owen J. Flanagan, *Science of the Mind*, 2nd ed. (Cambridge, Mass.: MIT Press, 1991), for an overview of the various positions.

17   Clever Hans was a horse who lived in Berlin at the beginning of the twentieth century who allegedly could do arithmetic, indicating sums by the number of times he tapped his hoof to the ground. Of course, he failed to display this ability when his trainer, from whom he presumably was getting cues for foot tapping, was absent from the scene. See Oskar Pfungst, *Clever Hans (the Horse of Mr. Von Osten)* (Bristol, UK: Thoemmes Press, 1911).

18   See M. D. Hauser, "Elementary, My Dear Chimpanzee," *Science* 291 (2001): 440–41; A. Whiten, "Tool Tests Challenge Chimpanzees," *Nature* 409 (2001): 133; and Colin Allen, "A Skeptic's Progress," *Biology and Philosophy* 17 (2002): 695–702.

CONSCIOUSNESS, EMOTION, AND SUFFERING

Chapter 11

Bob Bermond

A NEUROPSYCHOLOGICAL AND EVOLUTIONARY APPROACH TO ANIMAL CONSCIOUSNESS AND ANIMAL SUFFERING

Bermond reviews the literature for evidence of whether an irreflexive animal consciousness, experienced only in the present and which adds no cognition to the experience, could experience suffering. He argues that irreflexive consciousness and suffering aren't linked because to experience suffering, a well developed prefrontal cortex is needed. Since the prefrontal cortex is phylogenetically the most recent structure, it is likely that most animals are unable to experience suffering. He concludes that emotional experiences of animals, and therefore suffering, may only be expected in anthropoid apes.

Introduction

AT **FIRST SIGHT** this contribution will be a bit weird for some readers. The reason for this is that the issues of consciousness and suffering both have a long tradition in psychology, therefore most arguments stem not from the field of ethology, but from the field of (neuro)psychology. It follows that, with regard to animals, the arguments presented are only valid if one assumes that, if there is animal consciousness or animal suffering, they should not be qualitatively different from human consciousness and human suffering. One could, of course, like Bateson (1991) assume that various animal species have their own type of consciousness, and that it may be totally different from human consciousness. There is nothing wrong with assumptions: science flourishes with assumptions. However, such flourishing is only possible if the assumption is specified (in this case by describing how the assumed animal consciousness deviates from the human consciousness), because only then is it possible to analyse the logical consequences of the assumption and only then is it a contribution to science. Since, with the exception of the idea of an irreflexive animal consciousness, I have never seen such specifications in the literature, I have chosen to present two approaches to the question of animal consciousness and animal suffering. Firstly, an analysis of the idea of an irreflexive consciousness, and secondly an analysis of the idea of an animal consciousness and animal suffering based upon the assumption that such an animal consciousness and animal suffering are not qualitatively different from the only consciousness and suffering we know anything about, human consciousness and human suffering. With this warning to the readers I can start with my contribution.

There is no generally accepted theory about consciousness (Lokhorst 1986; Wilkes 1988; de Vries 1991) and there is further serious doubt whether we will have such a theory in the near future (Chalmers

1996). Due to this deficiency, the door is wide open for all kinds of weird theories and assumptions and, if the argument is dominated by social aims, science will be reduced to politics. For instance, Verheijen *et al* (1993) wrote 'to decide whether or not to accept the analogy-postulate, the strength of arguments not only play a role, but also the consequences of acceptance versus rejection'. Dawkins is subtler – referring to 'welfare measurement' she wrote (1998 p 308): 'such gross welfare measures should be made at the level of the individual animal, not the farm unit'. If that were turned into practice then farm animals would have more social security than people and farming would become a troublesome business. Dawkins' statement is all the more surprising since in the same article she states that there are no correct welfare measurements at hand (Dawkins 1998 p 323):

> In a thoughtful and provocative essay entitled *The Myth of Animal Suffering*, Bermond (1997) correctly points out that none of the methods proposed so far for assessing 'suffering' in animals actually do so. 'Suffering', as applied to humans, means conscious experience of something very unpleasant. Strictly speaking, none of the measures of 'poor welfare' or 'stress' discussed so far demonstrates the presence of comparable states in nonhuman animals.

Several attempts have been made to substantiate the idea that most animals do have consciousness and are therefore capable of experiencing suffering. The following substantiating arguments for animal suffering are mentioned in the literature: i) physiological stress responses in animals; ii) conditioning of animals by negative reinforcers; iii) emotional behaviour in animals; iv) registration of behaviours indicating that some animals will overcome various barriers in order to flee from negative situations; v) information processing by animals on a rather high level; vi) Romanes' analogy postulate; vii) the assumption that there are species-specific types of consciousness; and, finally, viii) Pepperberg's talking parrot. Since I have argued before that all these arguments and assumptions are incorrect (Bermond 1997, 1998), I will not discuss them here and will merely refer to these earlier publications.

In this contribution 'suffering' is, in accordance with Dawkins (1998), defined as a conscious negative mental state, because suffering does not refer to behaviour but to an experience, and experiences are by definition conscious. Consciousness is, in this contribution, defined as 'knowing that you know'. An irreflexive consciousness is, within this definition, in principle possible. Further, this definition is less severe than that of, for instance, Carruthers (1989) who assumed that there is only consciousness if the knowing that you know results in further conscious cognitions.

An irreflexive animal consciousness?

An irreflexive consciousness is a consciousness with neither past nor future, and which does not add any cognition to the experience. For instance Lijmbach, who assumes such an irreflexive consciousness in animals, states (Lijmbach 1998 pp 5 & 149): 'I will emphasise this distinction and say that animal experience, unlike human experience, is impersonal, bodily bound, here-and-now experience', and: 'many ethologists see animal experiences as separated from animal behaviour, namely as causes of behaviour. I do not see them as separated from, and certainly not as causally related to, behaviour'. In other words, an irreflexive consciousness is a minimum, a pure phenomenological consciousness, containing only qualia without accompanying cognitions and without any function for behaviour.

Qualia refer to the quality of perceptions, in particular to those aspects of the perception which are represented in the physical world in a different way. For instance, in the physical world there are electro-magnetic waves with different wavelengths. However, we do not see wavelength, we see colours. Likewise, smells are, in the physical world, just certain molecules. The qualia (colours, taste, pain, emotional feelings, odours and sounds) exist, therefore, only in the mind of the conscious perceiver and not in the physical world. This is distinct from the cognitive aspects of a perception. When we see a yellow house, and we are not hallucinating, then there is a house in the outside world, but the yellow is only in our brain or mind.

This definition of qualia could easily lead to the false idea that correct animal motor responses to what humans experience as qualia are proof of animal consciousness. However, since it is known that most human reactions to stimuli are initiated before the stimulus is consciously perceived (see later in this contribution), it is possible that some species react to, for instance, different electromagnetic wavelengths without seeing anything. In fact, this has been described for some humans with lesions in the primary visual cortex. These persons are blind in the sense that they cannot see consciously any more, but they are still capable of giving correct motor responses to the 'unseen' stimuli (Weiskrantz et al 1974; Sacks 1995). This phenomenon has been named 'blindsight'. It has further been described that such people can, using this blindsight, also differentiate correctly between various colours, although they cannot experience the quale (singular of qualia) of the colours since they process visual stimuli only at a non-conscious level (Weiskrantz 1997).

The idea of a minimum consciousness has also been a subject in philosophy. Chalmers (1996), who separates qualia from cognition, assumes that such a consciousness could exist and, according to him, it is an epiphenomenon. He assumes that such a consciousness containing only qualia does not emanate from the brain, but that it is a basic natural phenomenon in itself which cannot be explained by physics: these ideas do not have many supporters.

Dennett (1996) and Searle (1997) have also speculated about such a minimum consciousness and both reject the idea. Dennett argues that such a minimum consciousness should not only have sensitivity, like a thermostat or photographic paper, but also something extra (X) in order to lift or turn the sensitivity into a conscious experience, and he asks himself (Dennett 1996 p 62):

> What does sentience amount to, above and beyond sensitivity? This is a question seldom asked and has never been properly answered. We shouldn't assume that there's a good answer. We shouldn't assume, in other words, that it's a good question.

According to Dennett, the real question is therefore what this X is, and since there has been no-one so far who could even suggest what this X may be, it is therefore better to reject this idea altogether.

Searle sets it aside because, according to him, the qualia and the accompanying cognitions cannot be separated from one another, since if they could there would be no consciousness left (Searle 1997). Likewise, Baars (1997 p 84) states: 'even animals with mainly sensory consciousness must be able to think about events outside the sensory field'. Baars' and Searle's ideas become clearer if we ask ourselves what an irreflexive consciousness could experience if the input was, for instance, a lemon. Certainly not a lemon, because that requires cognitive processing. In fact not even a yellow spot, since that is a cognitive interpretation also. What will be left is the experience of pure 'lemon yellow', whatever that may be. However, although we lack the imagination to conceive of such experiences, it is no proof that such experiences could not exist.

The emotional psychologist Frijda (1986) also makes a plea for an irreflexive consciousness and so a plea for animal consciousness. Frijda states (1986 p 188):

> Irreflexive emotional experience also, by its very nature, is 'projective': the properties are out there. These properties contain the relationship to the subject: emotional experience is perception of horrible objects, insupportable people, oppressive events. They contain that relationship implicitly: the 'to me' or 'for me' dissolves into the property.

This author has an ornate style, and is therefore sometimes hard to understand. What is meant here? Firstly, it is assumed that there is a relationship between the subject, the 'I', and the properties in the outside world which induces the emotional feeling. Secondly, it is assumed that this concept of 'I' or 'to me' or 'for me' dissolves into the properties of the outside world. One thing is clear: there is a contradiction – there is a concept of 'I', and at the same time this concept dissolves into thin air! The author does not explain how this dissolving takes place, he just states: 'the notion of irreflexive experience is that of awareness without awareness of itself' (Frijda 1986 p 188). However, we can still imagine something from Frijda's statement. During 'blind rage' or the '*crime passionnel*' we act like a machine, without any reflection; the reflection only comes afterwards, as does remorse. The 'I' concept does not dissolve: it is, during such an act, simply not there. The crucial question here, however, is whether we could become so angry without having ever registered that we are individuals among other individuals. If that were the case then it would have been impossible to blame someone else for our misfortune and it is this blaming which induces the feeling of anger. In other words, the emotional experience becomes, without the concept of 'I' or 'me', not only aimless but also without content.

Emotions are triggered by stimuli which are, for some reason, important to the perceiver (Frijda 1986). For this reason, conscious reflection is sometimes required since it is, sometimes, only after the reflection that the importance becomes clear. Further, we cannot imagine emotional experiences without accompanying conscious cognitions: for instance, the feeling of fear is unthinkable without thoughts like: 'How can I escape?', 'What should I do?', 'Should I defend myself or should I run?', etc. All these thoughts are part of our emotional experience. Finally, the emotional experience needs a subject. It is always an 'I' who is sad, afraid or happy. It is not, as Frijda assumes, projected onto the outside world. 'We' are irate if we are maltreated, but the world around us is not angry. The emotional feeling is part of us, not of the environment. The environment contains the emotion-inducing stimuli not the emotional feeling. However, the emotional behaviour does not require emotional feelings (Bermond 1997, 1998 and later in this contribution). If we add a fear-substance (a substance secreted by some types of fish after they are wounded) into an aquarium, then all other fish of that species will flee and hide, even if there is no predator around (Verheijen 1988; Bateson 1991). The fish's behaviour is induced by a stimulus response mechanism without any cognitive interpretation and, therefore, as we will see later, without any accompanying emotional feelings. In such cases, one could rightly say that the 'fear' is in the aquarium and not in the fish, which only show fear behaviour. However, if we speak about a fear experience then it is the subject who is loaded with emotions and not the environment. It is for this reason that LeDoux (1989) writes: 'emotional experiences, it is proposed, result when stimulus representations, affect representations, and self-representations coincide in working memory'. In other words, the emotional experience requires the concept of self, or self-consciousness.

Irreflexive consciousness and pain or suffering

Suffering is the experience of pain and negative emotions such as fear, sorrow and guilt. Although pain has already been defined by Aristotle and Plato as an emotion (Menges 1992), most people still think that the pain experience is just a sensorial experience. The fact that all sensorial experiences, except pain, can be induced by electrical stimulation of sensorial cortex (Libet 1982) indicates that pain is more than just a sensorial experience. There are two types of pain: i) pain as a sensorial registration which is experienced as neither negative nor positive; and ii) pain as a pain experience or pain emotion, which does induce suffering (Trigg 1970; Menges 1992). Likewise, Sherrington, who, early last century, observed pain behaviour in decorticated mammals, which he described as 'pseudo affective', drew a distinction between pain and 'nociception' (Bateson 1991). Furthermore, pain behaviour does not need a conscious pain experience, as is indicated by the pain behaviour of paraplegic patients (Jennett 1989). This observation also indicates that pain behaviour is already partly regulated at the spinal cord level.

The emotional experience, and thus the pain experience, disappears if our natural tendency to reflect upon the pain is blocked, as for instance after destruction of our evolutionarily most recent brain parts the prefrontal cortex (PFC; Trigg 1970; Damasio *et al* 1990). It was for this reason that, in the 40's and 50's, frontal lobotomy was used as a remedy to block chronic pain (Freeman & Watts 1950; Freeman 1971; Kucharski 1984; Kolb & Whishaw 1990). The pain before the operation was overwhelming and permanently the centre of attention, while after the operation patients lost any interest in their pain, although they claimed that the pain itself had not changed. After the operation the sensed pain did not annoy them any more; the pain left them literally cold (Trigg 1970). The important issue here is that such people can still experience pain as a pain stimulus, but they cannot experience it as a pain emotion, and thus they cannot experience pain suffering any more (Krystal & Raskin 1970; Trigg 1970).

The fact that pain suffering needs pain-related reflection explains why we can reduce our pain experience by directing our thinking to other issues, a trick used by many people when their molars are drilled out by a dentist. Further, since there are cultural differences in pain expectations, this also explains cultural differences in pain suffering, because the less pain we expect the less pain-related reflection, and thus the less pain we experience. Lerich, a front surgeon in the First World War, was told by Russian officers that the Cossacks did not need narcotics during operations. Limited in supplies, Lerich tried, although against his 'better' judgement, amputations on Cossacks without narcotics. To his surprise the 'poor victims' showed no signs of pain experience (Menges 1992).

It is interesting that after frontal lobotomy, when the emotional experience has fully disappeared, the frequency of emotional behaviours is increased, whereas the duration of emotional responses is decreased. At the same time, the emotional behaviour becomes, as it is in most animal species, stimulus-bound (Levine & Albert 1948; Freeman & Watts 1950; Jarvie 1954; Nemiah 1962; Trigg 1970; Kucharski 1984; Fuster 1989; Valenstein 1990; Damasio & Anderson 1993; Malloy & Duffy 1994). The behaviour of prefrontal patients is: 'captured by salient sensory cues that reflectively elicit strongly associated actions. They are unable to override these impulses' (Miller 2000 p 61). This not only demonstrates that there are different neural circuits for emotional behaviour and emotional feelings, but also that it is the emotional feeling which gives, by emotional rumination, the emotion duration until long after the external emotion-inducing stimuli have disappeared. Since the extended emotion steers our behaviour, it often results in maladapted behaviour. The psychological defence mechanism of displacement (you are angry at your boss, but you are not allowed to show that and therefore you yell, hours later, at your children or spouse) is an example of such maladapted behaviour. Such an extension of the emotional period is absent in most animal species. The lioness does not fall into a depression when her cubs are killed by the new alpha male: after a few days she comes into heat and mates with the killer. The foster parent birds do not hate the cuckoo chick which throws their own young out of the nest: they just keep on feeding the little bastard. It should be kept in mind that subjective feelings in humans require the PFC, and are therefore thought to be a relatively late evolutionary development (Plutchik 1994). As stated above, the extension of the emotional period due to the emotional feeling means that the emotion endures after all external emotion-inducing stimuli have disappeared, and that the emotion is kept alive with the aid of internal stimuli. Therefore, descriptions of animals which show long-term emotional behaviour while the inducing stimuli are still there cannot be used as an argument for animal consciousness. For instance, the primatologist Frans de Waal describes female monkeys which will often carry around their deceased baby for days, but if they lose the corpse, simply because it has fallen apart due to decay, then immediately all signs of grief disappear (de Waal 1996).

The experience of suffering requires reflection, imagination and understanding of 'duration', of past and future. Dennett writes (1996 pp 166–167):

> Many discussions seem to assume tacitly that suffering and pain are the same thing, on a different scale; that all pain is 'experienced pain'; and that the 'amount of suffering' is to be calculated ('in principle') just by adding up all the pains . . . What is wrong with this scenario is, of course, that you can't detach pain and suffering from their contexts. What is awful about losing your job, or your leg, or your reputation, or your loved one is not the suffering this event causes in you, but the suffering this event is.

Dennett's aim here is to indicate that the loss of, for instance, a child can only result in the experience of suffering if the context knowledge concerning that child (how life was when the child was still alive) can be retained, or if one can, much later, imagine how life now would be if the child was still around. Without knowledge of past and future, reflection and imagination, which are by definition absent in the irreflexive consciousness, there is no suffering.

In conclusion, we may say that if there is such a thing as an irreflexive consciousness then it will be free of pain experiences and suffering, although it remains possible that such a consciousness could still non-emotionally register pain stimuli which do not induce pain suffering.

Congenital pain indifference

Some people are born with pain indifference. They register pain, like frontal lobotomy patients, only as a stimulus and cannot experience pain as an emotion. They can therefore do all kinds of horrible things to themselves without being troubled by pain. Many of them could earn good money by performing 'pain' inducing theatre acts. One wanted to make a living by showing his own crucifixion. Special gold-plated wire nails were made, which were literally hammered through his hands and feet. Although he had planned several such performances, only one show was staged, since the audience fainted *en masse* during the first performance (Krystal & Raskin 1970). This is what remains of the pain experience if pain can only be registered as a stimulus and not experienced as a pain emotion. The suffering is in the observer, not in the 'self pain inducing' performer. Since we belong to a species which has, on average, a high capacity for empathy, we are inclined to project feelings of pain onto others if we get emotionally aroused by seeing that others are seriously hurt. That is why most of the public fainted while watching the crucifixion. For the same reason, it is almost impossible for us, because we become emotionally aroused if we see animals which are hurt or showing pain behaviour, to consider the possibility that these animals may not be suffering.

How did consciousness develop?

Consciousness as a natural 'emergent' property of increasing complexity

Some authors have argued that consciousness is an 'emergent' property of the increasing complexity of the brain, an idea which is now very popular in the field of artificial intelligence. However, Weiskrantz (1997) describes microscopically small lesions which do not make the human brain less complicated and which result in specific losses in consciousness. Weiskrantz therefore states (1997 p 82): 'it is obvious that the answer must lie in the way the nervous system is organised, not in complexity as such'. Further, since no-one can indicate which level of complexity should be the turning point, this assumption remains in the domain of belief and is thus not a part of science. How should the question be approached?

Three questions concerning consciousness and suffering

In order to approach the problem of animal consciousness and animal suffering we can pose ourselves three questions.

Firstly, we can ask ourselves which evolutionarily latest part of the human brain is a prerequisite for experiencing pain and suffering? Why the evolutionarily most recent brain part? Doesn't correct pain behaviour have an immense fitness value and should it not, for this reason, be assumed that it developed early in evolution? Yes, we should assume that! However, as argued before, pain behaviour is already regulated at the spinal cord level, while human pain emotion and the experience of suffering both need the PFC in order to occur. For these reasons, we have to assume that regulation of pain behaviour developed much earlier in evolution than the experience of pain suffering. Furthermore, brain parts are connected with one another. The longest distance between two neurones is only four synapses (Pöppel & Ruhnau 2000). Due to this high level of interconnection within the brain, inhibition or stimulation of a particular brain centre always results in inhibition or stimulation of other brain structures. This could easily result in wrong conclusions as, for instance, Baars (1997) who, firstly, correctly states that after bilateral destruction of a rather small nucleus in the brainstem humans lose consciousness and, secondly, that these nuclei are also present in all vertebrates. He then uses these two statements as an argument for the assumption of consciousness in all vertebrates. What is the described function of these brainstem nuclei? They regulate, through their connections with the nuclei reticularis thalami, the amount of sensorial information which is sent to the neocortex (Heilman *et al* 1993). Unilateral destruction of one of these brainstem nuclei induces such a severe reduction in the amount of sensorial information sent to one side of the neocortex that it results in unilateral neglect (stimuli in one side of the 'Umwelt' [environment], although processed correctly on a non-conscious level, cannot reach the consciousness level any more); bilateral destruction leads to neglect on both sides of the 'Umwelt' (Heilman *et al* 1993). No wonder that such patients lose consciousness: since the neocortex is deprived of information and since all sensorial information remains unconscious, there is nothing for their consciousness to react to. Baars' suggestion is like pulling the plug of the television set and then stating that the image-producing device is in the plug and not in the picture tube. Baars' (1997) suggestion is all the more dubious, since elsewhere in the same book he writes that conscious visual perceptions need area 17 of the neocortex.

The higher up one is in the brain, or the information stream, the fewer difficulties one has with the interpretation of the results. One could, of course, when a particular function disappears after lesioning the evolutionarily newest neural structure, assume that this function does emanate from an evolutionarily older structure, lower in the brain, which only needs pre-processed information of the newer structure in order to 'produce' the function being studied. However, if we make such a rather dubious assumption then it follows that the evolutionarily newer brain structure is still a prerequisite for that particular function to occur. It is for this reason that we have to look for the evolutionarily latest part of the human brain which is a prerequisite for the experience of pain as an emotion and suffering.

The line of reasoning presented here is, however, only correct if the functions of the evolutionarily older brain structures have, for the question being studied, not changed fundamentally. This assumption could very well be correct since evolution is 'ultraconservative' (Plutchik 1994), and the evolution of the vertebrate brain has mainly consisted of adding new functional elements to what was already there (MacLean 1990). This last argument implies that this approach is, in principle, only suitable within the sub-phylum of vertebrates. However, if we have specified the neural structures concerned we can describe them in functional neural architectural terms, and see whether these functional neural architectural interconnections have been described for non-vertebrate animals.

The second question is about which prerequisite cognitive capacities have to be there in order to give consciousness a fitness function. The assumption here is that consciousness is the result of an adaptive development. New developments never occur in isolation. Legs enabling organisms to move around quickly on solid ground are useless if these organisms still have gills instead of lungs. Likewise, consciousness and mental suffering are only useful if they occur in combination with other cognitive powers.

Finally, we can ask ourselves which human capacities are impossible without the interference of consciousness. The assumptions here are, again: i) that consciousness is not an epiphenomenon; ii) that it emanates from brain structures; iii) that evolution is economical, only developing new brain structures if they make something possible which could not be done before; and iv) that animal consciousness is not qualitatively different from human consciousness.

We start with the last question, because answering this question brings us naturally to the other two questions. It has been demonstrated that almost no human capacity needs consciousness, eg conditioning, acquisition of complex procedural knowledge, learning of natural and artificial grammars, breakthroughs in physics and mathematics, solving equations, and learning processes and decisions which steer our behaviour in daily situations (Nisbett & Wilson 1977a, b; van Heerden 1982; Lewicki 1985, 1986; Penrose 1989; Greenwald 1992; Carruthers 1996; Mook 1996). It has further been demonstrated that it takes 0.5s before a stimulus reaches consciousness, while our behavioural reaction to the stimulus takes only 0.25s (Libet 1982, 1993). It has also been demonstrated that the non-conscious 'brain decision' to act precedes our experience of 'free-will' to act by about 0.3s, and that 'free-will' can inhibit motor actions but not induce actions (Libet 1985, 1993; Näätänen 1985; Wegner & Wheatley 1999).

I know that the idea of a consciousness which lags behind real time is hard for most people to swallow. However, this lagging behind is to be expected, since only the end products of the neural analyses can reach consciousness (Nisbett & Wilson 1977a, b) and no matter how fast these neural processes are they still take time. Indeed, there are data which can only be explained by a consciousness with a time lag, like in the famous phenomenon which has been described by Dennett (1991), among others. In this experiment, two light spots are presented shortly after one other at different locations. The trick here is that the first light spot is green and the second red. This results in the perception of a moving light, which halfway along its route changes from green to red. Now we either have to assume that the perceived colour change is a paranormal preview of the near future or that the experience of the present is just a reconstruction of the recent past. Another example is presented by patients with unilateral neglect, induced by lesions in the pre-motor cortex. The one-sided neglect in these persons is not due to disturbances in the processing of sensory stimuli, but due to a disturbance in motor responses in the left side of the 'Umwelt'. It is remarkable that, therefore, the stimuli in the left visual field are also not perceived consciously any more. This indicates that the motor response to a stimulus adds up to the conscious perception of that stimulus, which in itself is only possible if consciousness lags behind in time. This assumption is confirmed if one presents the stimuli through a mirror device. The stimuli, although in the right part of the environment (where the motor response has to be made), are now seen as mirror reflections in the left visual field. Not only are these patients then able to give a correct motor response to the left visual field stimuli, but these stimuli are now also consciously perceived, whereas the stimuli in the right visual field (requiring a motor response to the left) are now not perceived consciously any more (Bisiach 1992). Bisiach describes more such examples, and concludes (1992 p 120):

> The division of preconscious labour among several processors with no sole gate-way to consciousness entails a relativity of the timing of consciousness as well as the possibility of ongoing rearrangement of what is being experienced.

The idea that consciousness does not induce behaviour was already assumed by early evolutionists like Huxley (Baars 1997), and this idea has recently been theoretically and experimentally confirmed by, for instance, Wegner and Wheatley (1999) and Gollwitzer (1999). It has further been demonstrated that human consciousness has no access to the unconscious brain modules that steer our behaviour (Nisbett & Wilson 1977a, b; Bargh & Chartrand 1999; Gollwitzer 1999; Wegner & Wheatley 1999). That consciousness fills the information gaps up with confabulations, and by doing so gives us false ideas about the reality around us, and the false impression that the behaviour is initiated by our consciousness or our 'free will' (Nisbett & Wilson 1977a, b; Gazzaniga & LeDoux 1978; van Heerden 1982; Farthing 1992; Mook 1996; Bargh & Chartrand 1999; Gollwitzer 1999; Wegner & Wheatley 1999). Furthermore, consciousness does not like loose ends. Information presented to it must make sense; it must fit into the cognitive knowledge which is already there and, if it does not fit, the information is reinterpreted until it does, which also results in confabulations. This tendency is so strong that Mook (1996) calls it 'a coherence motivation'. All these confabulations function as new input to our brains, and so steer our future behaviour (Bargh & Chartrand 1999). And, since these confabulations are by definition wrong descriptions of reality, they result in maladapted behaviour, making the question about the fitness value of consciousness all the more important.

It has also been demonstrated that the conscious working memory is far from perfect, since it can contain only between two and five elements (Bower & Hilgard 1981; Schwartz & Reisenberg 1991). It has further been demonstrated that people can easily experience exogenously induced behaviour as being produced by their own free will, and endogenously induced behaviour as being induced by others (Bargh & Chartrand 1999; Gollwitzer 1999; Wegner & Wheatley 1999). Finally, the linear conscious processes are extremely slow compared to the parallel-functioning non-conscious processes, and therefore may exceed the span of consciousness (Kihlstrom 1987). Altogether, these facts indicate that consciousness is an imperfect device and a recent development.

Conscious information processing always requires mental effort (Bargh & Chartrand 1999): we could therefore ask ourselves which cognitive processes cannot take place without mental effort. Long-term planning, especially the intention to act in the future differently than we are inclined to, and the inhibition of these pre-programmed behavioural intentions, always requires conscious mental effort (Bargh & Chartrand 1999). However, the execution of the planned behaviour itself does not require consciousness (Libet 1985; Bargh & Chartrand 1999). The intention to behave differently in the future requires, besides planning, initiative (Gollwitzer 1999). This brings us to the first question; for planning, inhibition of the behaviour we are inclined to, and initiative we need our most recent brain structure – the PFC. Further-more, the PFC is also required for the emotional experience and the tuning of our behaviour in accordance with the demands of the social situation (Trigg 1970; Valenstein 1990; Damasio & Anderson 1993; Damasio 1994; Malloy & Duffy 1994; Fuster 1997). We use our consciousness, of course, for far more functions: learning languages or complex motor responses, knowing who is a nice person and who is not, etc. However, the point here is, as argued above, that all these processes can also take place non-consciously.

Although a PFC can be identified in higher mammals, only anthropoid apes show a well-developed PFC (Kolb & Whishaw 1990; Kupfermann 1991) and some parts of the PFC are specific to humans (Luria 1980). The PFC is a higher order association area. Here, information which has already been processed in primary and secondary one-modality sensory neural projection areas, and also interpreted on high cognitive levels in multi-sensory modality-association areas, is once again reprocessed and reinterpreted. Further-more, the PFC has ample efferent connections to evolutionarily older neural structures and has thus a 'top down' control over these structures (Jones & Powell 1970; Kolb & Whishaw 1990; Miller 2000). Such extremely high neural step-by-step progress, neural processing systems with top down control, have not been described in animals without a PFC. This alone limits tremendously the number of species in which consciousness may be expected.

The fitness function of consciousness and suffering

Summarizing the literature concerning consciousness, Weiskrantz states (1992 p 8):

> One dominant theme is to attach its benefits to benefits of active thought itself – in allowing the initiation of predictive strategies, in detaching the observer from an immediate dependence on current inputs, by allowing current inputs to be linked, with or without imagery, to other events distant either in space or in time, and in allowing flexible rather than automatic processing

Likewise, Laird and Bresler (1992) reached the conclusion that a specific but very important aspect of consciousness, the emotional feelings, are not epiphenomena, but rather that they force us to reflect. Emotional experiences are, according to these authors, like other conscious contents, constructed from lower-order elements that are themselves not part of consciousness. When we feel an emotion, we are aware of information about the situation and how we are acting. This conscious information can then be processed like any other piece of conscious information. This processing may, by estimating the consequences and the long-term (social) demands of various alternative actions in advance, lead to conscious choices from alternative behaviour patterns. By means of an emotional experience, the stimulus-induced emotional behavioural tendencies can be inhibited so that the actual behaviour can be released from the obvious responses, and eventually a mode of behaviour more suitably matched to this or comparable future situations can be shown. The main functions of consciousness (see earlier in this contribution) and the emotional experience lie, therefore, not as generally assumed by laymen in the induction of (emotional) behaviour, but in the inhibition of the (emotional) behaviour to which we are inclined. The conscious free choice out of behavioural alternatives also enables the organism to manipulate others, by pretending behavioural tendencies or emotions.

The ability to deliberately (under volitional control) induce the wrong impression in others, at the right moment, has a great fitness value (Dennett 1996). It is for this reason that Leakey and Lewin assume that there was, in the early hominids, a selection pressure for the capacity to manipulate others (Leakey & Lewin 1992 p 294): 'the answer, I suggest, is the intense intellectual demands of primate social interactions, with the constant need to understand and outwit others in the drive for reproductive success'. Dennett (1996) comes to essentially the same conclusion, although by a totally different line of thinking (by asking himself how intelligence may have developed in evolution). He argues that higher cognitive powers, through which secret-keeping can emerge, and language (as a tool to take one element out of a cognitive network and place it freely in any other network) are prerequisites for consciousness. According to him, the fitness value of consciousness is given by the fact that it enables the organism to 'bluff' others.

All these ideas are derived from Nicholas Humphrey who argued, in the 70's, that the development of self-consciousness was a stratagem for developing and testing hypotheses about what is going through the minds of others. He suggested that one uses one's self-consciousness as a source of hypotheses about other-consciousness or, because when one gets into the habit of adopting the intentional stance toward others, one notices that one can usefully subject oneself to the same treatment (Dennett 1996). Leakey and Lewin state (1992 pp 296–297):

> The Inner Eye, as Nick Humphrey calls this mental model, must also generate a sense of self, the phenomenon we know as consciousness: the Inner 'I'. In evolutionary terms it must have been a major breakthrough . . . Imagine the biological benefits to the first of our ancestors who developed the ability to make realistic guesses about the inner life of his rivals; to be able to picture what another was thinking about and planning to do next; to be able to read the minds of others by reading his own.

Frans de Waal (1996), who reacts against the selfish gene idea of Richard Dawkins (1989), assumes that various animals could have moral ideas, and therefore morally guided behaviour. He assumes that non-cognitive or non-conscious moral behaviour could develop in groups in which the individuals are mutually dependent upon one another. Real altruism (helping others without benefiting yourself directly or indirectly) is a troublesome phenomenon for neo-Darwinism. De Waal therefore also writes that this moral behaviour could basically very well serve one's own interest. However, according to him, stressing this self-interest, as is done by the selfish gene idea, blocks our view of possible altruistic behavioural mechanisms which could develop on a basis of self-interest. Further, de Waal states that cognitive or conscious empathy is not widespread in the animal kingdom: according to him it is only seen in humans and, possibly, in anthropoid apes. It is a sobering thought, but we have no other option: the original function of consciousness was not social progress, but selfishness and deceit.

Summarizing, we can state that higher cognitive powers like language, the capacity to keep secrets, to have knowledge of the demands of the social environment, to judge the motives of others, and to evaluate the consequences of behavioural alternatives in advance are all prerequisites for consciousness in order to get positive fitness value. Due to the consciousness-induced extension of the emotional period and the consciousness-induced confabulations, consciousness would, without these higher cognitive powers, only have a negative fitness value.

Consciousness may therefore only be expected in animals which show these higher cognitive capacities in their behaviour. For the experience of emotional feelings, further knowledge of 'self' is required. Since these capacities have, up to now, only been recorded in the anthropoid apes (Plutchik 1994), they are the only species in which consciousness and suffering may be expected. Plutchik (1994 p 238) states:

> There is little existing evidence, other than anecdotal, for intentionality in animals, and there is even less evidence for self-consciousness . . . Investigators have replicated this phenomenon of self-recognition (and by implication, self awareness) in orangutangs as well as chimpanzees, but every attempt to replicate the phenomenon in lower primates – spider monkeys, capuchins, mandrill and hamadryas baboons, and gibbons – has failed.

De Waal (1996), referring to Gallup (1982), confirms these statements. According to de Waal, Gallup (1982) compared self recognition to higher cognitive capacities like language, knowing what is going on in the minds of others, deceit, reconciliation and empathy, and came to the conclusion that humans and anthropoid apes have cognitive powers which set them apart from other animals. De Waal further writes that no matter how much he wanted to record deceit in macaques, he was unable to see a single example of such behaviour.

However, even with the limitation of anthropoid apes only, we have to be careful in our conclusions. Firstly, although there are beautiful descriptions of planning and deceit in chimpanzees (*Pan troglodytes*; Dawkins 1993; de Waal 1996), formal experimental testing has indicated that this ability is limited: only one out of four showed deception of others in a situation in which such deceit paid off (Plutchik 1994). Secondly, the ability to plan also seems limited, in our close relatives, to the direct needs of the situation at hand. Christopher Wills (1989) correctly stated that a chimpanzee has never been observed to select a nice stick to be used for fishing for ants the next day. Thirdly, Dennett (1996) reminds us that the 'AHA Erlebnis' (sudden insight) of Köhler's apes was mainly based on trial and error learning, not on a sudden enlightening insight, and that some of Köhler's apes never saw the light.

Conclusions

Irreflexive consciousness and suffering don't go together. Suffering and pain which is experienced as unpleasant is an emotional experience, and reflection is a prerequisite for such experiences. However, pain perception as a pain stimulus, which does not induce suffering, could still be possible with an irreflexive consciousness.

Standard emotional behaviour is not induced by the emotional experience. On the contrary, the emotional experience derives its fitness function from the fact that it can inhibit the stimulus-bound emotional behaviour so that, by using imagination and information from the past and future, more adaptive behavioural responses can be imagined, planned and later executed.

The PFC, or comparable super higher order association area, is a prerequisite for spontaneous planning of this kind, and for the emotional experience, and thus for the experience of pain as an emotion, or suffering.

Consciousness confabulates, and conscious emotional feelings extend the emotion until long after the disappearance of the external inducing stimuli. Consciousness and emotional feelings are therefore sources of maladapted behaviour.

Higher cognitive powers like language and the capacity to keep secrets, to have knowledge of the demands of the social environment, to judge the motives of others, and to evaluate the consequences of behavioural alternatives in advance, are all prerequisites for consciousness and the experience of suffering in order to get positive fitness value. Consciousness may therefore only be expected in animals which show these capacities in their behaviour. Since these capacities have, up to now, only been recorded in the anthropoid apes, they are the only species in which consciousness may be assumed. And even then we have to be careful in our conclusions, since there are various indications that anthropoid apes show severe limitations in these capacities. However, as argued before, there is an important difference between the conscious registration of pain as a pain stimulus, which does not induce feelings of suffering, and the experience of pain as an emotion, which does induce suffering. According to the arguments presented in relation to the issue of an irreflexive consciousness, the conscious registration of non-emotion- and non-suffering-inducing pain stimuli could be possible in far more species than anthropoid apes alone.

I would therefore like to end with the following statement. Rejoice! Rejoice! For there is far less animal suffering than our anthropomorphic minds are inclined to believe.

References

Baars B J 1997 *In the Theater of Consciousness: the Workspace of Mind*. Oxford University Press: Oxford, UK

Bargh J A and Chartrand T L 1999 The unbearable automaticity of being. *American Psychologist 54*: 462–479

Bateson P 1991 Assesment of pain in animals. *Animal Behaviour 42*: 827–839

Bermond B 1997 The myth of animal suffering. In: Dol M, Kasanmoentalib S, Lijmbach S, Rivas E and Van den Bos R (eds) *Animal Consciousness and Animal Ethics. Perspectives from the Netherlands*. Van Gorcum: Assen, The Netherlands

Bermond B 1998 Consciousness or the art of foul play. *Journal of Agricultural and Environmental Ethics 10*: 227–247

Bisiach E 1992 Understanding consciousness: clues from unilateral neglect and related disorders. In: Milner A D and Rugg M D (eds) *The Neurophysiology of Consciousness* pp 113–137. Academic Press: London, UK

Bower G H and Hilgard E R 1981 *Theories of Learning, 5th edition*. Prentice-Hall Inc: Engelwood Cliffs, USA

Carruthers P 1989 Brute experience. *The Journal of Philosophy 89*: 258–296

Carruthers P 1996 *Language Thoughts and Consciousness*. Cambridge University Press: Cambridge, UK

Chalmers D J 1996 *The Conscious Mind: in Search of a Fundamental Theory*. Oxford University Press: New York, USA

Damasio A R 1994 *Descartes' Error*. Putnam's and Sons: New York, USA

Damasio A R and Anderson S W 1993 The frontal lobes. In: Heilman K and Valenstein E (eds) *Clinical Neuropsychology, 3rd edition*. Oxford University Press: New York, USA

Damasio A R, Tranel D and Damasio H 1990 Individuals with sociophatic behavior caused by frontal damage fail to respond autonomically to social stimuli. *Behavioral Brain Research 41*: 81–94

Dawkins M S 1993 *Through Our Eyes Only? The Search for Animal Consciousness*. Spektrum/Freeman: Oxford, UK

Dawkins M 1998 Evolution and animal welfare. *The Quarterly Review of Biology 73*: 305–328

Dawkins R 1989 *The Selfish Gene, new edition*. Oxford University Press: Oxford, UK

Dennett D C 1991 *Consciousness Explained*. Little, Brown and Co: USA

Dennett D C 1996 *Kinds of Minds*. Weidenfeld and Nicolson: London, UK

de Vries R 1991 Van wetenschap tot dierenleed: Wetenschapstheoretische opmerkingen over de plaats van het subjectieve in de natuur. *Antropologische Verkenningen 10*: 64–81

de Waal F 1996 *Van Nature Goed*. Conact: Amsterdam, The Netherlands (Dutch translation of *Good Natured*).

Farthing G W 1992 *The Psychology of Consciousness*. Prentice-Hall Inc: Englewood Cliffs, USA

Freeman W 1971 Frontal lobotomy in early schizophrenia. *British Journal of Psychiatry 119*: 621–624

Freeman W and Watts W 1950 *Psycho Surgery, 2nd edition*. Charles C Thomas: Springfield, USA

Frijda N H 1986 *The Emotions: Studies in Emotion and Social Interaction*. Cambridge University Press: Cambridge, UK

Fuster J M 1989 *The Prefrontal Cortex. Anatomy, Physiology and Neuropsychology of the Frontal Lobe*. Raven Press: New York, USA

Fuster J M 1997 *The Prefrontal Cortex. Anatomy, Physiology and Neuropsychology of the Frontal Lobe, 3rd edition*. Lippincott-Raven: Philadelphia, USA

Gallup G 1982 Self-awareness and the emergence of mind in primates. *American Journal of Primatology 2*: 37–248

Gazzaniga M and LeDoux J E 1978 *The Integrated Mind*. Plenum: New York, USA

Gollwitzer P M 1999 Implementation intentions. *American Psychologist 54*: 493–503

Greenwald A G 1992 Unconscious cognition reclaimed. *American Psychologist 47*: 766–779

Heilman K M, Watson R T and Valenstein E 1993 Neglect and related disorders. In: Heilman K M and Valenstein E (eds) *Clinical Neuropsychology, 3rd edition* pp 279–336. Oxford University Press: New York, USA

Jarvie H F 1954 Frontal lobe wounds causing disinhibition. *Journal of Neurology, Neurosurgery and Psychiatry 17*: 14–32

Jennett S 1989 *Human Physiology*. Churchill Livingstone: Edinburgh, UK

Jones E G and Powell T P S 1970 An anatomical study of converging sensory pathways within the cerebral cortex of the monkey. *Brain 93*: 793–820

Kihlstrom J F 1987 The cognitive unconscious. *Science 237*: 1445–1452

Kolb B and Whishaw I Q 1990 *Fundamentals of Human Neuropsychology, 3rd edition*. W H Freeman and Co: New York, USA

Krystal H and Raskin H A 1970 *Drug Dependence: Aspects of Ego Functions*. Wayne State University Press: Detroit, USA

Kucharski A 1984 History of frontal lobotomy in the US, 1935–1955. *Neurosurgery 14*: 765–772

Kupfermann I 1991 Localization of higher cognitive and affective functions: the association cortices. In: Kandel E R, Schwartz J H and Jessell T M (eds) *Principles of Neural Science, 3rd edition* pp 823–838. Elsevier: New York, USA

Laird J D and Bresler C 1992 The process of emotional experience: a self-perception theory. In: Clark M S (ed) *Emotion Review of Personality and Social Psychology, Volume 13* pp 213–234. Sage Publications: Newbury, UK

Leakey R and Lewin R 1992 *Origins Reconsidered: in Search of what Makes us Human*. Doubleday: New York, USA

LeDoux J E 1989 Cognitive-emotional interactions in the brain. *Cognition and Emotion 3*: 267–289

Levine J and Albert H 1948 Sexual behavior after lobotomy. *Society Proceedings of the Boston Society of Psychiatry and Neurology*. 18 November 1948 pp 166–168

Lewicki P 1985 Non conscious biasing effects of single instances on subsequent judgements. *Journal of Personality and Social Psychology 48*: 563–574

Lewicki P 1986 Information about covariation that cannot be articulated. *Journal of Experimental Psychology: Learning, Memory and Cognition 12*: 135–146

Libet B 1982 Brain stimulation in the study of neural functions for conscious sensory experience. *Human Neurobiology 1*: 235–242

Libet B 1985 Unconscious cerebral initiative and the role of conscious will in voluntary action. *Behavioural and Brain Sciences 8*: 529–566

Libet B 1993 The neural time factor in conscious and unconscious events. In: Nagel T (ed) *Experimental and Theoretical Studies of Consciousness. Ciba Foundation Symposium 174* pp 123–146. Wiley: Chichester, UK

Lijmbach S 1998 *Animal Subjectivity: a Study into Philosophy and Theory of Animal Experience*. PhD thesis, University of Wageningen, The Netherlands

Lokhorst G J C 1986 *Brein en Bewustzijn. De Geest-lichaam Theorieën van Moderne Hersenonderzoekers (1956–1986). Rotterdamse Filosofische Studies*. Erasmus Universiteit Rotterdam & Eburon: Delft, The Netherlands

Luria A R 1980 *Higher Cortical Functions in Man, 2nd edition*. Plenum Publishing Corporation: New York, USA

MacLean P D 1990 *The Triune Brain in Evolution: Role in Paleocerebral Functions*. Plenum Press: New York, USA

Malloy P and Duffy J 1994 The frontal lobes in neuropsychiatric disorders. In: Boller F and Graftman J (eds) *Handbook of Neuropsychology, Volume 9* pp 203–232. Elsevier: Amsterdam, The Netherlands

Menges L J 1992 *Over Pijn Gesproken*. Kok: Kampen, The Netherlands

Miller E K 2000 The prefrontal cortex and cognitive control. *Nature Reviews/Neuroscience 1*: 59–65

Mook D G 1996 *Motivation: the Organization of Action*. W W Norton and Co: New York, USA

Naätänen R 1985 Brain physiology and conscious initiation of movements. *Behavioral and Brain Sciences* 8: 549–550

Nemiah J C 1962 The effect of leucotomy on pain. *Psychosomatic Medicine 24*: 75–80

Nisbett R E and Wilson T D 1977a Telling more than we can know: verbal reports on mental processes. *Psychological Review 84*: 231–259

Nisbett R E and Wilson T D 1977b The halo effect: evidence for unconscious alteration of judgements. *Journal of Personality and Social Psychology 35*: 250–256

Penrose R 1989 *The Emperor's New Mind*. Oxford University Press: Oxford, UK

Plutchik R 1994 *The Psychology and Biology of Emotion*. Harper Collins College Publishers: New York, USA

Pöppel E and Ruhnau E 2000 Gehirn Bewustsein Zeit. In: *Materie Geist und Bewustsein* pp 85–89. Ibera Verlag: Vienna, Austria

Sacks O 1995 *An Anthropologist on Mars*. Picador: London, UK

Schwartz B and Reisenberg D 1991 *Learning and Memory*. Norton: New York, USA

Searle J R 1997 *The Mystery of Consciousness*. Granta Books: London, UK

Trigg R 1970 *Pain and Emotion*. Clarendon Press: Oxford, UK

Valenstein E S 1990 The prefrontal area and psychosurgery. *Progress in Brain Research 85*: 539–554

van Heerden J 1982 *De Zorgelijke Staat van het Onbewuste*. PhD thesis, University of Amsterdam, The Netherlands

Verheijen F J 1988 Pijn en angst bij een aan de haak geslagen vis. *Biovisie 68*: 166–172

Verheijen F J, de Cock Büning T, Flight W F G, Vorstenbosch J M G and Wendela-Bonga S E 1993 *Brief aan Ir S J Beukema, Ministerie van Landbouw, Natuurbeheer en Visserij* (Letter to the Dutch Ministry of Agriculture) 19 February 1993 obtainable from the Dutch Ministry of Agriculture

Wegner D M and Wheatley T 1999 Apparent mental causation, sources of the experience of will. *American Psychologist 54*: 480–492

Weiskrantz L 1992 Dissociated issues. In: Milner A D and Rugg M D (eds) *The Neuropsychology of Consciousness*. Academic Press: London, UK

Weiskrantz L 1997 *Consciousness Lost and Found*. Oxford University Press: Oxford, UK

Weiskrantz L, Wattington E K, Sanders M D and Marchal J 1974 Visual capacity in the hemianopic field following a restricted occipital oblation. *Brain 97*: 709–728

Wilkes K 1988 *Real People*. Clarendon Press: Oxford, UK

Wills C 1989 *The Wisdom of the Genes*. Basic Books Inc: New York, USA

Chapter 12

Daniel C. Dennett

ANIMAL CONSCIOUSNESS: WHAT MATTERS AND WHY

Dennett disagrees that nonhumans and even human newborns have consciousness; rather, he argues that, in order for a species to be conscious, it is necessary to have a certain informational organization that endows the organisms with a wide set of cognitive powers such as reflection and re-representation and that, with these abilities, consciousness emerges by immersion in human culture. He acknowledges that other species undoubtedly achieve some level of similar informational organization, but that the differences are so great that most speculative translations of imagination from humans to the other species make no sense.

ARE ANIMALS CONSCIOUS? The way we are? Which species, and why? *What is it like* to be a bat, a rat, a vulture, a whale?

[. . .]

Current thinking about animal consciousness is a mess. Hidden and not so hidden agendas distort discussion and impede research. A kind of comic relief can be found—if you go in for bitter irony—by turning to the "history of the history" of the controversies. I am not known for my spirited defenses of René Descartes, but I find I have to sympathize with an honest scientist who was apparently the first victim of the wild misrepresentations of the lunatic fringe of the animal rights movement. Animal rights activists such as Peter Singer and Mary Midgley have recently helped spread the myth that Descartes was a callous vivisector, completely indifferent to animal suffering *because of* his view that animals (unlike people) were mere automata. As Justin Leiber (1988) has pointed out, in an astringent re-examination of the supposed evidence for this, "There is simply not a line in Descartes to suggest that he thought we are free to smash animals at will or free to do so *because* their behavior can be explained mechanically." Moreover, the favorite authority of Descartes's accusors, Montaigne, on whom both Singer and Midgley also uncritically rely, was a gullible romantic of breathtaking ignorance, eager to take the most fanciful folktales of animal mentality at face value, and not at all interested in *finding out*, as Descartes himself was, how animals actually work!

[. . .]

Certain questions, it is said, are quite beyond science at this point (and perhaps forever). The cloaks of mystery fall conveniently over the very issues that promise (or threaten) to shed light on the *grounds* for our moral attitudes toward different animals. Again, a curious asymmetry can be observed. We do not require absolute, Cartesian certainty that our fellow human beings are conscious—what we require is what is aptly called *moral* certainty. Can we not have the same moral certainty about the experiences of animals? I have not yet seen an argument by a philosopher to the effect that we cannot, with the aid of science, establish facts about animal minds with the same degree of moral certainty that satisfies us in the case of our own species. So whether or not a case has been made for the "in principle" mystery of consciousness (I myself am utterly unpersuaded by the arguments offered to date), it is a red herring. We can learn enough about animal consciousness to settle the questions we have about our responsibilities. The moral agenda about animals is important, and for that very reason it must not be permitted to continue to deflect the research, both empirical and conceptual, on which an informed ethics could be based.

A striking example of one-sided use of evidence is Thomas Nagel's famous paper "What is it Like to be a Bat?" (1991). One of the rhetorical peculiarities of Nagel's paper is that he chose bats and went to the trouble to relate a *few* of the fascinating facts about bats and their echolocation, because, presumably, those hard-won, third-person-perspective scientific facts tell us *something* about bat consciousness. What? First and least, they support our conviction that bats *are* conscious. (He did not write a paper called "What is it Like to be a Brick?") Second, and more important, they support his contention that bat consciousness is very unlike ours. The rhetorical peculiarity—if not outright inconsistency—of his treatment of the issue can be captured by an obvious question: if a few such facts can establish *something* about bat consciousness, would more such facts not establish more? He has already relied on "objective, third-person" scientific investigation to establish (or at least render rationally credible) the hypothesis that bats are conscious, but not in just the way we are. Why wouldn't further such facts be able to tell us in exactly what ways bats' consciousness isn't like ours, thereby telling us what it *is* like to be a bat? What kind of fact is it that only works for one side of an empirical question?

The fact is that we all do rely, without hesitation, on "third-person" behavioral evidence to support or reject hypotheses about the consciousness of animals. What else, after all, could be the source of our "pretheoretical intuitions"? But these intuitions in themselves are an untrustworthy lot, much in need of reflective evaluation. For instance, do you see "sentience" or "mere discriminatory reactivity" in the Venus Fly Trap, or in the amoeba, or in the jellyfish? What more than mere discriminatory reactivity—the sort of competence many robots exhibit—are you *seeing* when you *see* sentience in a creature? It is, in fact, ridiculously easy to induce powerful intuitions of not just sentience but full-blown consciousness (ripe with malevolence or curiosity or friendship) by exposing people to quite simple robots *made to move in familiar mammalian ways at mammalian speeds.*

Cog, a delightfully humanoid robot being built at MIT, has eyes, hands, and arms that move the way yours do—swiftly, relaxedly, compliantly (Dennett, 1994). Even those of us working on the project, knowing full well that we have not even *begun* to program the high level processes that might arguably endow Cog with consciousness, get an almost overwhelming sense of being in the presence of another conscious observer when Cog's eyes still quite blindly and stupidly follow one's hand gestures. Once again, I plead for symmetry: when you acknowledge the power of such elegant, lifelike motions to charm you into an illusion, note that it ought to be an open question, still, whether you are also being charmed by your beloved dog or cat or the noble elephant. Feelings are too easy to provoke for them to count for much here.

If behavior, casually observed by the gullible or generous-hearted, is a treacherous benchmark, might composition—material and structure—provide some important leverage? History offers a useful perspective on this question. It was not so long ago—Descartes's day—when the hypothesis that a material brain by itself could sustain consciousness was deemed preposterous. Only immaterial souls could *conceivably* be conscious. What was inconceivable then is readily conceivable now. Today, we can readily conceive that a brain, without benefit of immaterial accompanists, can be a sufficient seat of consciousness, even if we wonder just how this could be. This is surely a *possibility* in almost everybody's eyes, and many of us think the evidence for its truth mounts close to certainty. For instance, few if any today would think that the "discovery" that, say, lefthanders don't have immaterial minds but just brains would show unmistakably that they are just zombies.

Unimpressed by this retreat, some people today baulk at the *very idea* of silicon consciousness or artifactual consciousness, but the reasons offered for these general claims are unimpressive to say the least. It looks more and more as if we will simply have to look at what entities—animals in this case, but also robots and other things made of nonstandard materials—*actually can do*, and use that as our best guide to whether animals are conscious and, if so, why and of what.

[. . .]

What I find insupportable is the coupling of blithe assertion of consciousness with the equally untroubled *lack of curiosity* about what this assertion might amount to, and how it might be investigated. Leiber (1988) provides a handy scorecard:

> Montaigne is ecumenical in this respect, claiming consciousness for spiders and ants, and even writing of our duties to trees and plants. Singer and Clarke agree in denying consciousness to sponges. Singer locates the distinction somewhere between the shrimp and the oyster. He, with rather considerable convenience for one who is thundering hard accusations at others, slides by the case of insects and spiders and bacteria; they, *pace* Montaigne, apparently and rather conveniently do not feel pain. The intrepid Midgley, on the other hand, seems willing to speculate about the subjective experience of tapeworms . . . Nagel . . . appears to draw the line at flounders and wasps, though more recently he speaks of the inner life of cockroaches.

The list could be extended. In a recent paper, Michael Lockwood (1993) supposes, as so many do, that Nagel's "what it is like to be" formula *fixes a sense of consciousness*. He then says: "Consciousness in this sense is presumably to be found in all mammals, and probably in all birds, reptiles and amphibians as well." It is the "presumably" and "probably" to which I want us to attend. Lockwood gives no hint as to how he would set out to replace these terms with something more definite. I am not asking for certainty. Birds aren't just *probably* warm-blooded, and amphibians aren't just *presumably* air-breathing. Nagel confessed at the outset not to know—or to have any recipe for discovering—where to draw the line as we descend the scale of complexity (or is it the cuddliness scale?). This embarrassment is standardly waved aside by those who find it just obvious that there is something it is like to be a bat or a dog, equally obvious that there is *not* something it is like to be a brick, and unhelpful *at this time* to dispute whether it is like anything to be a fish or a spider. What does it mean to say that it is or it isn't?

It has passed for good philosophical form to invoke mutual agreement here that we know what we're talking about even if we can't explain it yet. I want to challenge this. I claim that this standard methodological assumption has no *clear* pretheoretical meaning—in spite of its undeniable "intuitive" appeal—and that since this is so, it is ideally suited to play the deadly role of the "shared" intuition that conceals the solution from us. *Maybe* there really is a huge difference between us and all other species in this regard; *maybe* we should consider "radical" hypotheses. Lockwood says "probably" all birds are conscious, but *maybe* some of them—or even all of them—are rather like sleepwalkers! Or what about the idea that there could be unconscious pains (and that animal pain, though real, and—yes—morally important, was unconscious pain)? *Maybe* there is a certain amount of generous-minded delusion (which I once called the Beatrix Potter syndrome) in our bland mutual assurance that as Lockwood puts it, "*Pace* Descartes, consciousness, thus construed, isn't remotely, on this planet, the monopoly of human beings."

How, though, could we ever explore these "maybes"? We could do so in a constructive, anchored way by first devising a theory that concentrated exclusively on *human* consciousness—the one variety about which we will brook no "maybes" or "probablys"—and then *look and see* which features of that account apply to which animals, and why. There is plenty of work to do, which I will illustrate with a few examples—just warm-up exercises for the tasks to come.

In *Moby Dick*, Herman Melville asks some wonderful questions about what it is like to be a sperm whale. The whale's eyes are located on opposite sides of a huge bulk: "the front of the Sperm Whale's head," Melville memorably tells us, "is a dead, blind wall, without a single organ or tender prominence of any sort whatever" (Ch. 76). As Melville notes: "The whale, therefore, must see one distinct picture on this side, and another distinct picture on that side; while all between must be profound darkness and nothingness to him" (Ch. 74).

Nevertheless, any one's experience will teach him, that though he can take in an indiscriminating sweep of things at one glance, it is quite impossible for him, attentively, and completely, to examine any two things—however large or however small—at one and the same instant of time; never mind if they lie side by side and touch each other. But if you now come to separate these two objects, and surround each by a circle of profound darkness; then, in order to see one of them, in such a manner as to bring your mind to bear on it, the other will be utterly excluded from your contemporary consciousness. How is it, then, with the whale? . . . is his brain so much more comprehensive, combining, and subtle than man's, that he can at the same moment of time attentively examine two distinct prospects, one on one side of him, and the other in an exactly opposite direction?

Melville goes on to suggest that the "extraordinary vacillations of movement" exhibited by sperm whales when they are "beset by three or four boats" may proceed "from the helpless perplexity of volition, in which their divided and diametrically opposite powers of vision must involve them" (Ch. 74).

Might these "extraordinary vacillations" rather be the whale's attempt to keep visual track of the wheeling boats? Many birds, who also "suffer" from eyes on opposite sides of their heads, achieve a measure of "binocular" depth perception by bobbing their heads back and forth, giving their brains two slightly different views, and permitting the relative motion of parallax to give them approximately the same depth information we get all at once from our two eyes with their overlapping fields.

Melville assumes that whatever it is like to be a whale, it is similar to human consciousness in one regard: there is a single boss in charge, an "I" or "ego" that either superhumanly distributes its gaze over disparate scenarios, or humanly flicks back and forth between two rivals. But might there be even more radical discoveries in store? Whales are not the only animals whose eyes have visual fields with little or no overlap; rabbits are another. In rabbits there is no interocular transfer of learning! That is, if you train a rabbit that a particular shape is a source of danger by demonstrations carefully restricted to its *left* eye, the rabbit will exhibit no "knowledge" about that shape, no fear or flight behavior, when the menacing shape is presented to its *right* eye. When we ask what it is like to be that rabbit, it appears that at the very least we must put a subscript, *dexter* or *sinister*, on our question in order to make it well-formed.

[. . .]

I have argued at length, in *Consciousness Explained* (1991), that the sort of informational unification that is the most important prerequisite for *our* kind of consciousness is not anything we are born with, not part of our innate "hardwiring," but in surprisingly large measure an artifact of our immersion in human culture. What that early education produces in us is a sort of benign "user-illusion"—I call it the Cartesian Theater: the illusion that there is a place in our brains where the show goes on, towards which all perceptual "input" streams, and whence flow all "conscious intentions" to act and speak. I claim that other species—and human beings when they are newborn—simply *are not beset* by the illusion of the Cartesian Theater. Until the organization is formed, there is simply no user in there to be fooled. This is undoubtedly a radical suggestion, hard for many thinkers to take seriously, hard for them even to *entertain*. Let me repeat it, since many critics have ignored the possibility that I mean it—a misfiring of their generous allegiance to the principle of charity.

In order to be conscious—in order to be the sort of thing it is like something to be—it is necessary to have a certain sort of informational organization that endows that thing with a wide set of cognitive powers (such as the powers of reflection and re-representation). This sort of internal organization does not come automatically with so-called "sentience." It is not the birthright of mammals or warm-blooded creatures or vertebrates; it is not even the birthright of human beings. It is an organization that is swiftly achieved in one species, ours, and in no other. Other species no doubt achieve *somewhat similar* organizations, but the differences are so great that most of the speculative translations of imagination from our case to theirs *make no sense*.

My claim is not that other species lack our kind of *self*-consciousness, as Nagel (1991) and others have supposed. I am claiming that what must be added to mere responsivity, mere discrimination, to count as consciousness *at all* is an organization that is not ubiquitous among sentient organisms. This idea has been dismissed out of hand by most thinkers.[1] Nagel, for instance, finds it to be a "bizarre claim" that "implausibly implies that babies can't have conscious sensations before they learn to form judgments about themselves." Lockwood is equally emphatic: "Forget culture, forget language. The mystery begins with the lowliest organism which, when you stick a pin in it, say, doesn't merely react, but actually *feels* something."

Indeed, that is where the *mystery* begins if you insist on starting *there*, with the assumption that you know what you mean by the contrast between merely reacting and actually feeling. And the mystery will never stop, apparently, if that is where you start.

In an insightful essay on bats (and whether it is like anything to be a bat), Kathleen Akins (1993) pursues the sort of detailed investigation into functional neuroscience that Nagel eschews, and she shows that Nagel is at best ill-advised in simply *assuming* that a bat *must* have a point of view. Akins sketches a few of the many different stories that can be told from the vantage point of the various subsystems that go to making up a bat's nervous system. It is tempting, on learning these details, to ask ourselves "and where in the brain does the bat *itself* reside," but this is an even more dubious question in the case of the bat than it is in our own case. There are many parallel stories that could be told about what goes on in you and me. What gives one of those stories about *us* pride of place at any one time is *just this*: it is the story you or I will tell if asked (to put a complicated matter crudely).

When we consider a creature that isn't a teller—has no language—what happens to the supposition that one of *its* stories is privileged? The hypothesis that there is one such story that would tell us (if we could understand it) what it is actually like to be that creature dangles with no evident foundation or source of motivation—except dubious tradition. Bats, like us, have plenty of relatively peripheral neural machinery devoted to "low level processing" of the sorts that are routinely supposed to be entirely unconscious in us. And bats have no machinery analogous to our machinery for issuing public protocols regarding their current subjective circumstances, of course. Do they then have some *other* "high level" or "central" system that plays a privileged role? Perhaps they do and perhaps they don't. Perhaps there is no role for such a level to play, no room for any system to perform the dimly imagined task of elevating merely unconscious neural processes to consciousness. After all, Peter Singer has no difficulty supposing that an insect might keep its act together without the help of such a central system. It is an open empirical question, or rather, a currently unimagined and complex set of open empirical questions, what sorts of "high levels" are to be found in which species under which conditions.

Here, for instance, is one possibility to consider: the bat lacks the brain-equipment for *expressing* judgments (in language), but the bat may nevertheless have to *form* judgments (of some inarticulate sort), in order to organize and modulate its language-free activities. Wherever these inarticulate judgment-like things happen is where we should look for the bat's privileged vantage point. But this would involve just the sort of postulation about sophisticated judgments that Nagel found so implausible to attribute to a baby. If the distinction between conscious and unconscious has nothing to do with anything sophisticated like judgment, what else could it involve?

[. . .]

It turns out that we end up where we began: analyzing patterns of behavior (external and internal—but not "private"), and attempting to interpret them in the light of evolutionary hypotheses regarding their past or current functions.

The very idea of there being a dividing line between those creatures "it is like something to be" and those that are mere "automata" begins to look like an artifact of our traditional presumptions. I have offered (Dennett, 1991) a variety of reasons for concluding that in the case of adult human consciousness there is no principled way of distinguishing when or if the mythic light bulb of consciousness is turned on (and shone on this or that item). Consciousness, I claim, even in the case we understand best—our own—is not an all-or-nothing, on-or-off phenomenon. If this is right, then consciousness is not the sort of phenomenon it is assumed to be by most of the participants in the debates over animal consciousness. Wondering whether it is "probable" that all mammals have *it* thus begins to look like wondering whether or not any birds are *wise* or reptiles have *gumption*: a case of overworking a term from folk psychology that has losts its utility along with its hard edges.

Some thinkers are unmoved by this prospect. They are still unshakably sure that consciousness—"phenomenal" consciousness, in the terms of Ned Block (1992, 1993, 1995, forthcoming)—*is* a phenomenon that is either present or absent, rather as if some events in the brain glowed in the dark and the rest did not.[2] Of course, if you simply will not contemplate the hypothesis that consciousness might turn out *not* to be a property that thus sunders the universe in twain, you will be sure that I must have overlooked consciousness altogether. But then you should also recognize that you maintain the mystery of consciousness by simply refusing to consider the evidence for one of the most promising theories of it.

Postscript: pain, suffering, and morality

[. . .]

The phenomenon of pain is neither homogeneous across species nor simple. We can see this in ourselves, by noting how unobvious the answers are to some simple questions. Are the "pains" that usefully prevent us from allowing our limbs to assume awkward, joint-damaging positions while we sleep experiences that require a "subject" (McGinn, 1995), or might they be properly called unconscious pains? Do they have moral significance in any case? Such body-protecting states of the nervous system might be called "sentient" states without thereby implying that they were the experiences of any self, any ego, any subject. For such states to matter—whether or not we call them pains or conscious states or experiences—there must be an enduring, *complex* subject *to whom* they matter because they are a source of suffering. Snakes (or parts of snakes!) may feel pain—depending on how we choose to define that term—but the evidence mounts that snakes lack the sort of over-arching, long-term organization that leaves room for significant suffering. That does not mean that we ought to treat snakes the way we treat worn out tires, but just that concern for their suffering should be tempered by an appreciation of how modest their capacities for suffering are.

While the distinction between pain and suffering is, like most everyday, nonscientific distinctions, somewhat blurred at the edges, it is, nevertheless, a valuable and intuitively satisfying mark or measure of moral importance. When I step on your toe, causing a brief but definite (and definitely conscious) pain, I do you scant harm—typically none at all. The pain, though intense, is too brief to matter, and I have done no long-term damage to your foot. The idea that you "suffer" for a second or two is a risible misapplication of that important notion, and even when we grant that my causing you a few seconds pain may irritate you a few more seconds or even minutes—especially if you think I did it deliberately—the pain itself, as a brief, negatively-signed experience, is of vanishing moral significance. (If in stepping on your toe I have interrupted your singing of the aria, thereby ruining your operatic career, that is quite another matter.)

Many discussions seem to assume tacitly: (1) that suffering and pain are the same thing, on a different scale; (2) that all pain is "experienced pain"; and (3) that "amount of suffering" is to be calculated ("in principle") by just adding up all the pains (the awfulness of each of which is determined by duration-times-intensity). These assumptions, looked at dispassionately in the cold light of day—a difficult feat for some partisans—are ludicrous. A little exercise may help: would you exchange the sum total of the suffering you will experience during the next year for one five-minute blast of no doubt excruciating agony that summed up to the "same amount" of total pain-and-suffering? I certainly would. In fact, I would gladly take the bargain even if you "doubled" or "quadrupled" the total annual amount—just so long as it would be all over in five minutes. (We are assuming, of course, that this horrible episode does not kill me or render me insane—after the pain is over—or have other long-term effects that amount to or cause me further suffering; the deal was to pack all the suffering into one jolt.) I expect anybody would be happy to make such a deal. But it doesn't really make sense. It implies that the benefactor who provided such a service gratis to all, *ex hypothesi*, would be doubling or quadrupling the world's suffering—and the world would love him for it.

It seems obvious to me that something is radically wrong with the assumptions that permit us to sum and compare suffering in any such straightforward way. But some people think otherwise; one person's *reductio ad absurdum* is another's counter-intuitive discovery. We ought to be able to sort out these differences, calmly, even if the best resolution we can reasonably hope for is a recognition that some choices of perspective are cognitively impenetrable.

Notes

1   Two rare—and widely misunderstood—exceptions to this tradition are Julian Jaynes (1976) and Howard Margolis (1987), whose cautious observations survey the field of investigation I am proposing to open:

> A creature with a very large brain, capable of storing large numbers of complex patterns, and capable of carrying through elaborate sequences of internal representations, with this capability refined and elaborated to a very high degree, would be a creature like you and me. Somehow, as I have stressed, consciousness conspicuously enters the scheme at this point of highly elaborate dynamic internal representations. Correctly or not, most of us find it hard to imagine that an insect is conscious, at least conscious in anything approximating the sense in which humans are conscious. But it is hard to imagine that a dog is not conscious in at least something like the way an infant is conscious (Margolis, 1987, p. 55).

2   John Searle also holds fast to this myth. See, for example, Searle, 1992, and my review, 1993.

References

Akins, Kathleen, "What is it Like to be Boring and Myopic?" in Bo Dahlbom, ed., *Dennett and his Critics* (Oxford: Blackwells, 1993).

Block, Ned, "Begging the question against phenomenal consciousness" (commentary on Dennett and Kinsbourne), *Behavioral and Brain Sciences*, 15 (1992): 205–6.

Block, Ned, "Review of Daniel Dennett, *Consciousness Explained*," *Journal of Philosophy*, 90 (1993): 181–93.

Block, Ned, "On a Confusion about a Function of Consciousness," *Behavioral and Brain Sciences*, 18 (1995).

Block, Ned, "What is Dennett's Theory a Theory of?" in *Philosophical Topics*, Special issue on the work of Dennett, forthcoming.

Dennett, Daniel, *Consciousness Explained* (Boston: Little Brown, 1991).

Dennett, Daniel, "Review of John Searle, *The Rediscovery of Consciousness*," *Journal of Philosophy*, 90 (1993): 193–205.

Dennett, Daniel, "The practical requirements for making a conscious robot," *Phil. Trans. R. Soc. Lond.* A 349 (1994): 133–46.

Jaynes, Julian, *The Origins of Consciousness in the Breakdown of the Bicameral Mind* (Boston: Houghton Mifflin, 1976).

Leiber, Justin, " 'Cartesian Linguistics?' " *Philosophia*, 118 (1988): 309–46.

Lockwood, Michael, "Dennett's Mind," *Inquiry*, 36 (1993): 59–72.

Margolis, Howard, *Patterns, Thinking, and Cognition* (Chicago: University of Chicago Press, 1987).

McGinn, Colin, "Animal Minds, Animal Morality," *Social Research* 62:3 (1995).

Nagel, Thomas, "What we have in mind when we say we're thinking," (Review of *Consciousness Explained*), *Wall Street Journal* (November 7, 1991).

Searle, John, *The Rediscovery of Consciousness* (Cambridge, MA: MIT Press, 1992).

Chapter 13

Marian Stamp Dawkins

ANIMAL MINDS AND ANIMAL EMOTIONS

Dawkins notes that consciousness is still an elusive concept. She believes that many animals have a conscious awareness of pleasure and pain analogous to that experienced by humans. Alternatively, she acknowledges that consciousness emerges with the ability to form abstract concepts, plan for the future, or use language. She notes that if the first conscious experiences were awareness of pleasure and pain, then it implies that emotional awareness is evolutionarily very old and possibly very common among animals.

SYNOPSIS. The possibility of conscious experiences of emotions in non-human animals has been much less explored than that of conscious experiences associated with carrying out complex cognitive tasks. However, no great cognitive powers are needed to feel hunger or pain and it may be that the capacity to feel emotions is widespread in the animal kingdom. Since plants can show surprisingly sophisticated choice and "decision-making" mechanisms and yet we would not wish to imply that they are conscious, attribution of emotions to animals has to be done with care. Whether or not an animal possesses anticipatory mechanisms associated with positive and negative reinforcement learning may be a guide as to whether it has evolved emotions.

The search for animal consciousness is frequently seen as the search for higher and higher cognitive abilities in animals. Thus most theories of consciousness emphasise intellectual achievement – the ability to form abstract concepts, for example, to understand and to use language or to be able to plan ahead and work out what to do in novel situations. For this reason, the achievements of animals such as Alex the parrot (Pepperberg, 1999) and Kanzi the Bonobo (Savage-Rumbaugh and Lewin, 1994) are immensely significant. But although these achievements are impressive, too much emphasis on the cognitive and intellectual side of consciousness may lead us to overlook other aspects that are equally important. It does not take much intellectual effort to experience pain, fear or hunger. We can be conscious of a headache or afraid of flying without being able to put the experience into words or reason about it. We may in fact tell ourselves that flying is a relatively safe way of travelling – in other words, we try to dispel a basic emotion with cognitive reasoning.

Might it be, then, that our search for animal consciousness could fruitfully be extended to the realm of the emotions and therefore potentially to a much wider range of animals than just the ones that are outstandingly clever? Might it not be that the conscious experience of emotions is far older in evolutionary time than the ability to form concepts and certainly than that to use language? The purpose of this contribution is to see what the study of animal emotions can tell us about consciousness in animals.

My own interest in animal emotions arose from working for many years on animal welfare, where a central issue is whether and under what circumstances animals suffer – that is, experience strong or persistent negative emotions. These are questions of far more than just theoretical importance. If animals do experience fear and pain and if they experience frustration as a result of being unable to perform their natural behaviour patterns, then this has legal and ethical importance and in turn may have major economic consequences.

Indeed, the really important moral issues in animal welfare arise precisely because of the belief held by many people that animals do have conscious emotional experiences. An early advocate of this idea was Jeremy Bentham (1789) who wrote the often-quoted lines: "The question is not, Can they reason? nor, Can they talk? but Can they suffer?" And such views are echoed by more recent philosophers such as Bernard Rollin. It is thus very important that we have some way of studying suffering – the unpleasant emotions of animals.

There are basically two approaches that have been adopted to studying animal emotions – the functional and the mechanistic. The functional approach means examining the *role* of emotions in human behaviour and then asking whether the function is the same in humans and non-humans. In many cases it is possible to apply Darwinian ideas to emotions and ask how emotions (in us and in other species) contribute to an organism's fitness. Fear, for example, is adaptive and functions to increase fitness both through motivating an animal to remove itself from danger and also to avoid similar situations in the future.

A widely used framework for viewing emotions in a functional context is that described by Oatley and Jenkins (1998) who see emotions as having three stages: (i) *appraisal* in which there is a conscious or unconscious evaluation of an event as relevant to a particular goal. An emotion is positive when that goal is advanced and negative when it is impeded (ii) *action readiness* where the emotion gives priority to one or a few kinds of action and may give urgency to one so that it can interrupt or compete with others and (iii) *physiological changes, facial expression and then behavioural action*. The trouble with this formulation is that it is so general and unspecific that it encompasses almost all behaviour in the sense that almost everything that humans or other animals do would have to involve such stages. Building a robot to behave in an autonomous and useful way would almost certainly involve ensuring that it could evaluate its environment as either beneficial or harmful, give priority to one action that would be beneficial and then carry out the action. Worse, it even seems to apply to plants operating without nervous systems and using the simplest of mechanisms. For example, the parasitic plant, Dodder (*Cuscata europaea*) appears to "choose" which host plants to parasitise on the basis of an initial evaluation of a potential host's nutritional status. Kelly (1992) tied pieces of Dodder stem onto Hawthorn bushes which had been either fed extra nutrients or starved of nutrients. The transplanted growing shoots were more likely to coil on ("accept") host plants of high nutritional status and grow away from ("reject") hosts of poor quality and this acceptance or rejection occurred before any food had been taken from the host. It was thus based on an as yet unknown evaluation by the parasite of the host's potential food value and, within three hours, the growing tips could be seen either growing at right angles away from a rejected stem or coiling around one it would eventually feed from. By changing the time scale (hours rather than minutes) and the mechanism (growth rather than behaviour), we have an organism that shows appraisal, action readiness and action – the supposed functions of emotion without needing a nervous system at all. This suggests that merely defining emotions in a rather vague functional way of what they do in us and then asking whether there is evidence of similar functions in non-human animals is not going to be very fruitful. We need to look in more detail at how the functions are carried out.

The second possible approach to the study of animal emotions is therefore to look at the mechanisms underlying emotions and to see whether they are similar in ourselves and other species. Can we look at what changes both physiologically and behaviourally when we feel happy, sad, etc., and see whether similar changes take in place in non-human animals?

In humans, there are three systems underlying emotions (e.g., Oatley and Jenkins, 1998). These are (i) the cognitive/verbal. People can report on what they are feeling and indeed this is one of the main ways we have of knowing what other people are feeling. (ii) autonomic. These include changes in heart rate, temperature and hormone levels when we experience emotions (iii) behaviour/expressive. Different emotions give rise to different behaviour and different facial expressions.

Although of course we cannot use (i) for non-human species since they cannot tell us what they are feeling, it might be possible to use similarities in (ii) and (iii) to tell us what emotions they might be having. Unfortunately, there are problems since the three emotional systems do not necessarily correlate with each other, even in humans. Sometimes, for example, strong subjective emotions occur with no obvious autonomic changes, as when someone experiences a rapid switch from excitement to fear on a roller coaster. This does not mean that the change in emotional experience has no physiological basis. It just means that it is probably due to a subtle change in brain state rather than the obvious autonomic changes that most physiological methods pick up. At other times, the emotion we experience and report corresponds to several different kinds of autonomic change or one kind of autonomic change such as heart rate can be shown to accompany very different emotions (Wagner, 1989; Frijda, 1986; Cacioppo *et al.*, 1993).

This lack of correlation is not in fact, very surprising. Many of the physiological changes that occur in our bodies when we feel different emotions are related to the actions we are likely to take, such as running. As running occurs when we are afraid and are running away or excited and running towards (chasing) something we want, the same physiological preparations are appropriate for both situations and consequently a range of emotions.

Another reason why the different emotional systems may diverge is that we have 'multiple routes to action' in other words, the same actions can be prompted by instructions from different parts of the brain (Rolls, 1999). An obvious example is breathing. Most of the time we are not conscious of taking breath – it is done automatically. But if we are drowning or told to take deep breaths by a doctor, control shifts to a conscious route. The existence of multiple routes to action makes the comparison with other species particularly difficult, since non-humans could show similar behaviour to ourselves but have it controlled by a pathway that, in ourselves, is just one of the possible routes we can use. The fact that we can, when the occasion demands, become conscious of what we are doing does not, therefore, necessarily mean that other species have all the same circuits that we do. We may have evolved an additional conscious verbal route that is lacking in them. Indeed the evolution of the vertebrate brain has often involved overlaying existing pathways with new ones rather than eliminating existing ones (Panksepp, 1998).

But if neither similarities of function nor similarities of mechanisms between humans and non-humans can be reliably used to tell us about emotions in other species, what can we do? What is needed is a combination of functional and mechanistic approaches that is considerably more specific than the very general approaches I have outlined so far. Only by understanding the very specific mechanisms associated with emotions in ourselves can we hope to be able to know what to look for in other species. As we have already seen, by being too general (emotions are associated with appraisal and action readiness), we include plants and organisms and machines that operate on the very simplest of mechanisms. And by expecting emotions to be reflected in obvious autonomic measures (such as hormonal state and heart rate), we are unable to distinguish the subtleties of emotions even in ourselves.

Let us start with a more specific evolutionary argument. Animals are able to respond to challenges to their health and well-being in various ways and the mechanisms they use can be divided into those that repair damage to the organism's fitness when damage has already occurred and those that enable the organism to anticipate probable damage and take avoiding action so that the damage does not occur at all. The ability to fight off infection with the immune system and to heal wounds are examples of repair mechanisms, whereas most behaviour (drinking before dehydration occurs, hiding before a predator appears) falls into the category of anticipation and pre-emptive action. In fact, we can see the evolution of cognitive abilities in animals as the evolution of more and more sophisticated anticipatory mechanisms, reaching further and further back in time away from the danger itself, until in ourselves we may take out a health insurance policy many years before any damage is done.

The important point about these anticipatory mechanisms, however, is that many of them can be highly effective without the organism being in any way conscious. Where an aspect of the environment is highly predictable (such as the sun rising every day), very accurate anticipation can be achieved by endogenous rhythms or by simple kineses and taxes. The ability of Dodder plants to anticipate which hosts are likely to yield the most food before investing in the coiling and growth needed to extract any nutrients is a very good example of a simple anticipatory mechanism and should serve as an object lesson about the dangers of using words like 'choice' or 'appraisal' to imply similarity to the mechanisms we ourselves use. Just to emphasise this point, we should be equally cautious about the conclusions we draw from choice tests in animals, such as those that show that chickens prefer one kind of flooring to another (Hughes and Black, 1973) or will "work" (squeeze through gaps or push heavy weights) to get at something they like. Even plants will push up through concrete to get at light and air so both simple choice tests and those involving physical obstacles to allow animals to get what they 'want' could be nothing more than the operation of animals being evolved by natural selection to respond to certain sorts of stimuli and to keep on responding even when there are obstacles. Despite some of the claims that have been made (e.g., Dawkins, 1990), persistence in the face of physical difficulties does not imply that animals experience the same emotions that we have when we have to work harder to get what we want.

But some animals, including ourselves, have evolved anticipatory mechanisms that are quite different in kind from anything we find in plants, anticipatory mechanisms that cannot be explained by simple tropisms and taxes, anticipatory mechanisms that may necessitate emotions. The key is reinforcement learning or the ability to change behaviour as a result of experience so that behaviour is controlled by completely arbitrary stimuli, quite unlike anything that natural selection could have built into the organism. I am not speaking here of just any change that may occur as a result of experience. The immune system changes as a result of experience with certain pathogens but this can be done through a preprogrammed (if highly sophisticated) response. There is no need to invoke "emotions" in the way our immune systems change as a result of their experiences of different diseases. Similarly, if an organism (plant or animal) habituates or changes its response as a result of repeated experience, there is no reason to suppose that they have emotions because receptors can be linked (hard-wired) to response mechanisms in predictable ways.

But where an animal learns to perform an arbitrary response to approach or avoid a stimulus, natural selection cannot hard-wire connections between receptor and response mechanisms or evolve simple rules for how responses should change as a result of experience (Rolls, 1999). For example, suppose a rat learns that turning in a right-hand circle gives it food and turning in a left-hand circle gives it an electric shock and then, when the experimenter changes the rules of the experiment, learns to go left to get food and right to avoid a shock. Natural selection could not have led to the evolution of rats able to do this by any simple rules. Hard-wiring or innate response biases could not account for the completely arbitrary response (turning or anything else the irritating human chose to devise) nor for the ability of the animal to change and do something different.

The only way the rat could achieve such a feat would be by having a reward-punishment system which allowed it to associate any action [that] happened to make it "feel better" or "feel worse" and either repeat or avoid such actions in future (Rolls, 1999). Specific rules (such as always turn right or always turn towards red stimuli) would be very much less effective than more general rules (repeat what leads to feeling better or pleasure). General emotional states of pleasure and suffering would enable animals to exploit many more behavioural strategies to increase their fitness than specific stimulus-response links. The point is, however, that without emotions to guide it, an animal would have no way of knowing whether a behaviour never performed before by any of its ancestors should be repeated or not. By monitoring the consequences of its behaviour by whether it leads to "pleasure" or "suffering" it can build up a complex string of quite arbitrary responses. It can learn, for example, that pressing a lever leads to the appearance of a striped box which contains food. By finding the striped box "pleasurable" because it is associated with food and learning to press the lever to obtain this pleasure, the rat learns to obtain food through a route that is not open to an animal totally pre-programmed in its responses. Emotions are therefore necessary to reinforcement learning.

We have thus come full circle. If it is only animals that are clever enough to master certain cognitive tasks (those associated with reinforcement learning) that have emotions, then the apparent distinction between cognition and emotions is illusory. Only certain kinds of task require emotions. Others, including those achieved by plants, do not. At least this gives us a way of excluding plants from our discussion of consciousness and gives us a way of discriminating those organisms that are likely to have emotion from those that probably do not. We can at least do experiments to find out whether a given animal (an insect, say) does or does not have the capacity for arbitrary reinforcement learning.

But does this really solve the problem of the connection between emotion and consciousness? Of course it does not and I have to admit that I have so far blurred a distinction that is of great importance. I am guilty of using the word "emotion" in two quite different senses that must now be clearly distinguished (Dawkins, 1998). The first sense in which we might use the word "emotion" is to refer to strictly observable physiological and behavioural changes that occur under particular circumstances such as the appearance of a predator. But we might also use it in a second sense to refer to the subjective conscious experience (fear) that we know we experience under conditions of danger.

The problem with the word "emotion" is that it tempts us to slip from one meaning to the other, often without realising that we have done so. We start out describing what we can observe – the behaviour and physiology of the animals or people. I have indeed given an account of why emotional states may have evolved, with behavioural criteria for deciding whether they might exist in a given species. I carefully put scare quotes around words such as "pleasure" and "suffering" in describing positive and negative emotional states. But the problem is that issue of whether conscious experiences as we know them accompany these states in other species is a totally separate question. Given the ambiguous nature of the word "emotion", it may not be obvious that it is a separate question because it so easy to believe that once we have postulated a scale of positive to negative reinforcers, once, that is, we have a common currency in which different stimuli can be evaluated to how positive or negative they are on this emotional scale, then we have also [linked] into the conscious experience of pain and pleasure that we all know about from our human perspective. But this would be an error. It is quite possible (logically) for animals to have positive or negative emotional states without it *feeling like* anything. Stimuli could be evaluated as negative, in other words, but they wouldn't necessarily hurt.

Strictly speaking, therefore, consciousness still eludes us. It is my personal view that emotional states defined in the way I have described (using reinforcement value) does imply subjective experience – a conscious awareness of pleasure and pain that is not so very different from our own. But that should be taken for what it is: a personal statement of where I happen to stand, not a view that can be grounded in empirical fact. It is just as valid (and just as open to challenge) as the more widely held beliefs that consciousness "kicks in" with the ability to form abstract concepts or plan ahead or use a language (Rosenthal, 1993; Dennett, 1996).

If, however, consciousness is associated with reinforcement learning and the first conscious experiences that occurred on this planet were the basic ones of pain and pleasure, long before any concepts were thought of or any plans laid for the future, then this does have implications for the way we see other species. It implies that emotional awareness is evolutionarily very old and possibly very widespread in the animal kingdom. As Damasio (1999) and Rolls (1999) have, others have recently emphasised, emotion deserves much more attention than it has had so far.

References

Bentham, J. 1789. *Introduction to the principles of morals and legislation*. 1996 imprint. Clarendon Press, Oxford.

Cacioppo, J. T., D. J. Klein, and E. Hatfield, 1993. The psychophysiology of emotion. In G. C. Berntson, *Handbook of emotions* M. Lewis and J. M. Hatfield (eds), pp. 119–42. Guilford, New York.

Damasio, A. 1999. *The feeling of what happens: Body, emotion and the making of consciousness*. William Heinemann, London.

Dawkins, M. S. 1990. From an animal's point of view: Motivation, fitness and animal welfare. *Behavioral and Brain Sciences* 13:1–61.

Dawkins, M. S. 1998. Evolution and animal welfare. *Quart. Revi. Biol.* 73:305–28.

Dennett, D. C. 1996. *Kinds of minds: Towards and understanding of consciousness*. Weidenfeld & Nicolson, London.

Frijda, N. H. 1986. *The emotions*. Cambridge University Press.

Hughes, B. O. and A- J. Black. 1973. The preference of domestic hens for different types of battery cage floor. *British Poultry Science* 14:615–19.

Kelly, C. K. 1992. Resource choice in *Cuscuta europaea*. *Proc. Natl. Acad. Sci.* U.S.A. 89:12194–7.

Oatley, K. and J. M. Jenkins, 1998. *Understanding emotions*. Blackwell, Oxford.

Panksepp, J. 1998. *Affective neuroscience: The foundations of human and animal emotions*. Oxford University Press, Oxford.

Pepperberg, I. M. 1999. *The Alex studies: Cognitive and communicative abilities of grey parrots*. Harvard University Press, Cambridge, Mass.

Rollin, B. E. 1989. *The unheeded cry: Animal consciousness, animal pain and science*. Oxford University Press, Oxford.

Rolls, E. T. 1999. *The brain and emotion*. Oxford University Press, Oxford.

Rosenthal, D. 1993. Thinking that one thinks. In M. Davies and G. W. Humphreys (eds), *Consciousness*, pp. 197–223, Blackwell, Oxford.

Savage-Rumbaugh, S. and R. Lewin, 1994. *Kanzi: The ape at the brink of the human mind*. Doubleday, London.

Wagner, H. 1989. The peripheral physiology and differentiation of emotions. In H. Wagner and A. Mainstead (eds) *Handbook of social psychophysiology*, pp. 78–98. John Wiley, New York.

Chapter 14

Donald R. Griffin and Gayle B. Speck

NEW EVIDENCE OF ANIMAL CONSCIOUSNESS

Griffin and Speck propose that the search for neural correlates of consciousness has not found any consciousness-producing structure or process limited to humans. They also argue that appropriate responses to novel challenges for which nonhuman animals have not been prepared by genetic programming or previous experience provide suggestive evidence of animal consciousness. Finally they note that there are increasing numbers of cases of animal communication reporting subjective experiences.

Introduction

EXPERIMENTAL AND OBSERVATIONAL data about the complexity and versatility of animal cognition have been reported and discussed extensively since the subject was reviewed in the first issue of this journal (Griffin 1998). The term cognition is ordinarily taken to mean information processing in human and nonhuman central nervous systems that often leads to choices and decisions. But the possibility that nonhuman cognition is accompanied or influenced by consciousness has received relatively little attention, largely because many behavioral scientists have been extremely reluctant to consider nonhuman consciousness on the grounds that it is impossible to obtain objective evidence about subjective experiences. Yet much of the new evidence strengthens that case as well, and it is time to reconsider the longstanding aversion to scientific investigation of animal consciousness. In view of the confusions surrounding terms describing mental states, and despite the fact that some scientists feel that consciousness is a higher and more complex state than awareness, we will follow the common usage of aware and conscious as synonyms that describe subjective experiences. We will assume that these states or processes are produced by the functioning of living nervous systems and not something ethereal and different in kind from anything in the physical universe, as emphasized by Searle (2000, 2002) and Donald (2001).

[. . .]

Consciousness is the subjective state of feeling or thinking about objects and events. The word is often interpreted to mean full-blown human thinking, although of course no animal attains more than a trivial fraction of the scope and versatility of human conscious thinking. But many animals give evidence of what Natsoulas (1983, p. 29) defined as consciousness 3, "the state or facility of being mentally conscious or aware of anything." This has been called perceptual, primary or basic consciousness. However limited its content may be, such awareness is importantly different from unconscious cognition. Consciousness is often considered a complex and "higher" form of cognition; but as Dawkins (2000) has emphasized, the content of human consciousness ranges from very simple to enormously subtle and complex. Insofar as animals are conscious, the content of their awareness probably varies along a continuum from the simplest and crudest feelings to thinking about the challenges they face and alternative actions they might choose.

Computers process information, and robots can even simulate animal behavior; but they can only do what human designers have programmed them to do. It is very unlikely that they have subjective experiences without a living central nervous system. Although no single piece of evidence that an animal is conscious is totally conclusive, and alternate explanations not involving consciousness are always conceivable, suggestive evidence can serve as an entering wedge that stimulates further investigation leading to improved and more conclusive data. Following up on these possibilities provides opportunities and challenges for scientific investigation to evaluate the following hypothesis: Animals are sometimes aware of objects and events, including social relationships, memories, and simple short-term anticipation of likely happenings in the near future, and they make choices of actions they believe are likely to get what they want or avoid what they dislike or fear. Such basic consciousness may but need not include self-awareness or metacognition – thinking about one's thoughts or those of others – (Natsoulas' consciousness 4).

[. . .]

The central question about the consciousness of animals is whether they experience anything of the same general kind, and if so what is the content of their awareness. Whatever they feel and think must be important both to the animals concerned and to our understanding of them and their ways of life.

It is helpful to consider questions about the content of an animal's awareness in terms of the probability of awareness, pA. If we have complete certainty that a given animal has a particular conscious experience, then pA=1.0, and pA=0 means that we know with certainty that it does not. If we take literally the claim that it is impossible to learn anything about the so-called private experiences of other species, we are obliged to assume that pA is always 0.5. In practice, however, there has been a tendency to conclude from the impossibility of setting pA at 1.0 that it must be zero.

[. . .]

There are three general categories of evidence that show animals' pA is sometimes well above 0.5: (1) close similarity of basic central nervous system structure and function in a wide variety of animals, indicating that whatever processes lead to conscious experiences are not limited to human brains, (2) versatile adjustment of behavior in response to unpredictable challenges, and (3) animal communication, which often seems to inform receivers about the conscious experiences of the sender; and which can also provide information about them to eavesdropping cognitive ethologists. We rely heavily on both verbal and nonverbal communication to infer what our human companions are thinking and feeling, and the same basic approach can be applied to many other species. We will review these three areas in this paper.

Neural correlates of consciousness

As Crick and Koch (1998, p. 105) put it "The explanation of consciousness is one of the major unsolved problems of modern science. After several thousand years of speculation, it would be very gratifying to find an answer to it." It is theoretically conceivable that only the human nervous system has the capability of producing consciousness. If so, it is an important challenge for the neurosciences to discover the nature of this unique consciousness-producing ability. Some point to the size or the complexity of the human brain, or to specific areas, or else to language ability. But there is no clear evidence that any of these factors is necessary for consciousness. Another theoretical possibility is that simple conscious thinking is an important core function of living central nervous systems, and that in small brains it may therefore constitute a larger proportion of brain activity than in animals with very large brains.

Recognition of the importance of these questions has been part of the motivation for an extremely active and talented series of investigations that have recently attempted to identify the neural correlates of consciousness (NCC), as discussed by Crick and Koch (1998, 2000, 2003), Taylor (1999), Metzinger (2000), Searle (2000, 2002), and Baars (2002).

[. . .]

Baars (2002) has lucidly reviewed how modern methods of imaging brain function have provided objective evidence of neural activities correlated with consciousness. In many of these recent investigations of NCC, animals are used for better control of experiments or for invasive procedures, and it is simply taken for granted that they are conscious. Logothetis (1999, p. 70), in his investigations of binocular rivalry, notes that "monkey brains are organized like those of humans, and they respond to stimuli much as humans do. Consequently, we think the animals are conscious in somewhat the same way as humans are." Kanwisher (2001) concurs, stating "It seems reasonable to assume that when a monkey reports the presence of a particular stimulus, he is aware of the stimulus in something like the way that a human would be. Nevertheless it would be reassuring to find similar results in the human brain." She and her colleagues (Tong et al. 1998) do find similar results in a human experiment that was modeled after the monkey experiments of Logothetis. Engel and Singer (2001), after reviewing numerous studies, some of which involved monkeys and cats, implicitly assume that these animals were conscious. Seward and Seward (2000, p. 86) conclude that "in rodents and lower vertebrates, normal visual awareness is partly due to synchronized oscillatory activities in the optic tectum and partly due to similar activities in the visual cortex."

[. . .]

Blindsight is an intriguing phenomenon that has provided an opportunity to test whether a monkey is or is not conscious of particular visual stimuli. It was given this name by Weiskrantz et al. (1974) from studies of certain human patients who had lesions in the visual cortex that produced large blind areas in the visual field but who could nevertheless respond in limited ways to visual stimuli in their blind fields. If stimuli are presented in these blind areas and the patient is required to guess about them, he is as surprised as anyone that his guesses are far more accurate than expected from chance. [. . .]

Cowey and Stoerig (1995, 1997) and Stoerig et al. (2002) showed similar results in monkeys with large cortical lesions. The monkeys had been trained to touch a small bright square on a touch-sensitive computer screen to obtain food. With sufficient training they were able to do this even when the square fell in their blind field. These monkeys were then trained to touch a different visual pattern when no bright square was presented, and surprisingly they then touched this "no stimulus" pattern when the bright square was presented in their blind field – even though in other experiments they would touch the square to obtain food. It was thus possible to distinguish, under these experimental conditions, whether the monkey was or was not aware of particular stimuli.

Roth (2000) emphasizes brain size: "Among all features of vertebrate brains, the size of cortex or structures homologous to the mammalian cortex, as well as the number of neurons and synapses contained in these structures, correlate most clearly with the complexity of cognitive functions, including states of consciousness" (Roth 2000, p. 94). There is as yet no way to determine the minimum brain size necessary for the most basic level of consciousness, although several thousand neurons would seem adequate for the kinds of NCC that appear most plausible to contemporary neuroscientists. Roth is critical of the idea that language is required for consciousness. If we accepted that suggestion, he points out, "we would be forced to assume that animals are capable of unconsciously mastering cognitive tasks that in humans require highest concentration" (Roth 2000, p. 95).

Damasio (1999) emphasizes the importance of bodily emotions for consciousness. He allows that artifacts such as computers might be created that have the formal mechanisms of consciousness, but they would not be conscious in the full sense. "Feeling is, in effect, the barrier, because consciousness may require the existence of feelings. The "looks" of emotion can be simulated, but what feelings feel like cannot be duplicated in silicon" (Damasio 1999, p. 314). In Damasio (2000), he distinguishes what he calls "core consciousness," which "provides an organism with a sense of self about here and now . . . (but) . . . does not pertain to the future or the past," from "extended consciousness," which "provides the organism with an identity and a person, an elaborate sense of self, and places that self at a specific point in an individual historical time . . . (It) . . . offers awareness of the lived past and of the anticipated future, along with the objects in the here and now." Emphasizing that "consciousness depends most critically on evolutionarily old regions (of the vertebrate brain)," Damasio believes that core consciousness is not exclusively human, and that "simple levels of extended consciousness are present in some nonhumans" (Damasio 2000, pp. 112–118).

[. . .]

Crick and Koch (2003), propose a "framework" applicable to the visual system of primates, which they believe "knits all these ideas together, so that for the first time we have a coherent scheme for the NCC in philosophical, psychological and neural terms" (Crick and Koch 2003, p. 124). This framework emphasizes "competing coalitions" of neurons and two-way communication between coalitions in the back and front of the brain. They conclude that explicit representations and synchronized activity such as gamma frequency oscillations may be necessary, but not sufficient for consciousness. Reentrant pathways and back projections are widespread in central nervous systems, however, and if they constitute NCC there is no reason to rule out at least simple consciousness in many animals with central nervous systems.

Has this intensive search for NCC disclosed any structure or process necessary for consciousness that is found only in human brains? The short answer is no. But neither has this search identified any specific structure or process that we can yet be sure is both necessary and sufficient to generate human conscious experience. Thus it remains possible that if and when such an essential consciousness-generating neural mechanism is discovered, it might turn out to be something found only in human brains. [. . .]

Versatility

A type of versatility that is particularly relevant as evidence of consciousness is the departure from routine behavior patterns to cope with novel and unpredictable challenges in ways that suggest at least short-range planning of intended actions. Such versatility is helpful in allowing us to distinguish relatively inflexible preprogrammed behavior from being aware of the availability of alternative actions and choosing those the animal believes will have desired consequences. [. . .] Both natural selection and individual experience have doubtless contributed to the development of such versatile thinking and action; but the specific reactions to particular situations can scarcely have been pre-programmed if neither the animal nor its ancestors have previously encountered such situations.

[. . .]

Explicit learning and episodic memory

Students of human learning and memory often distinguish explicit from implicit learning and their resulting memories. The former can be both recalled and reported verbally; the latter entails changes in behavior resulting from prior exposure to stimuli that the subject cannot report because he is currently unaware of them. The concept of explicit memory is similar to declarative memory, which was so named because such memories could be reported or "declared" by human subjects. It is usually assumed that animals cannot have declarative memories because they lack (human) language. This widespread assumption is seriously undermined, however, by twentieth century discoveries about the versatility of animal communication, which can convey information based on memories by other means than human language, as reviewed by Griffin (2001). [. . .]

Memories of past events that include awareness of oneself perceiving the event on some remembered occasion are termed episodic; and Tulving (1972, 2002) and others have claimed that episodic memory is based on a uniquely human neural system. A strong challenge to the claim of human uniqueness comes from recent experiments by Clayton and Dickinson (1998) and Clayton et al. (2000, 2001, 2003). They first demonstrated that scrub jays (*Aphelocoma coerulescens*) can learn that a particular type of preferred food (wax-moth larvae) become unpalatable 5 days after the birds had stored them, but that peanuts, a less preferred food, remain edible. The jays were trained to cache these two types of food by burying them in sand in two different locations. When tested 4 days after caching, and after the sand had been replaced to prevent odor cues from affecting their choices, the jays were more likely to choose the location they knew contained larvae. But after 5 days they usually went where they had stored peanuts.

Clayton et al. (2001, p. 28) prefer to call this type of memory episodic-like rather than episodic because the latter term has been applied to human "autonoetic" memories, which are verbally reported to include a conscious experience of self. This they claim "has no obvious manifestation in nonlinguistic behaviour" (Griffiths et al. 1999). For this reason, "we regard the what-where-when memory for caching episodes as no more than an analogue of human episodic memory." [. . .] Emery and Clayton (2001, p. 443) discovered that scrub jays "with prior experience of pilfering another bird's caches subsequently re-cached food in new cache sites . . . but only when they had been observed caching. Jays without pilfering experience did not, even though they had observed other jays caching . . . Jays relate information about their previous experience as a pilferer to the possibility of future stealing by another bird, and modify their caching behavior accordingly." These birds appeared to have profited from traveling backwards and perhaps also forward in time. A similar example was provided by the dolphins Pryor et al. (1969) trained to perform on command a completely novel acrobatic action, since they had to remember their complete repertoires in order to create something new. Thus the claim that episodic memory in the full sense of the term is uniquely human rests largely on the assumption that nonhuman animals lack a conscious sense of self.

Knowing what one knows

Some scientists claim that although animals often know simple facts, they do not know *that* they know. This is a type of metamemory or memory about one's own recollection and would certainly be a higher level of awareness than is usually assumed for animals. With our human companions we assume they know that they know something because they can use human language to express this distinction. But how can we learn, for example, whether an animal not only knows that food is available at a certain time and place but also knows that she knows this? As with many such questions about nonhuman mentality, this one has seemed impossible to answer; but instead of recognizing our ignorance, it has been customary to leap to a negative conclusion.

Goal-directed desires and actions

Dickinson and Balleine (2000, p. 202) review experiments on goal evaluation by laboratory rats, which lead them to conclude that "Goal-directed actions of the rat are mediated by intentional representations of the causal relationship between action and outcome and of the value assigned to the outcome. The capacity for goal-directed action requires not only the evolution of intentional representations, but also the co-evolution of an interface between these representations and the animal's biological responses to the goal objects, events, or states. This interface, we suggest, is simple, nonreflexive consciousness in which the biological evaluation of a potential goal is manifested as an affective or hedonic response conjointly with an internal representation of the goal." By "simple, nonreflexive consciousness" Dickinson and Balleine appear to mean what we and others have called primary or perceptual consciousness. And if we understand them correctly, they are using the terms intention and intentional to include, though perhaps not be limited to, the customary sense of consciously intending to do something, and as one example of the broader philosophical usage of intentional to mean aboutness.

This suggestion by Dickinson and Balleine typifies the degree to which the antimentalistic taboos of behaviorism have been abandoned by leading investigators of animal learning. In addition to suggesting that rats experience simple consciousness, they believe that it plays a crucial role in producing adaptive behavior. Furthermore they propose that emotional feelings play an essential role in goal-directed intentions and the resulting goal-directed behavior. It is certainly reasonable to assume that the animals perceive their goals as desirable; and there is no reason why simple consciousness could not also accompany other forms of perception and influence other types of action.

Tools

The use and especially the making of tools require at least short-term planning and adaptation of behavior to specific and often unpredictable situations. Hart et al. (2001) describe how Asian elephants modify branches to make them useful for fly switching. Many aspects of tool use by chimpanzees are described in detail in Matsuzawa (2001). Sousa and Matsuzawa (2001) demonstrated that captive chimpanzees not only use tokens they have learned to exchange for desired food but also save the tokens for future use. Tonooka (2001) described how some chimpanzees fold leaves to hold drinking water.

New Caledonian crows (*Corvus moneduloides*) have provided perhaps the most surprising and significant new examples of tool use and manufacture, as described and analyzed in detail by Hunt (1996, 2000a, 2000b) and Hunt and Gray (2003). These crows probe for invertebrates in crevices and use different types to probe in different locations. The most complex tools are of two types: twigs stripped of leaves and often of bark and then cut so that a short projecting piece of a branch forms a hook, and long strips torn from pandanus leaves fashioned into tools by removing material from one end to form a hook. The crows then insert these hooks into cavities and drag out prey that would otherwise be difficult or impossible to dislodge. Although most hook tools are discarded after the prey has been obtained, they are sometimes carried about or later retrieved and reused. Young crows make clumsy efforts to obtain food in this way and sometimes try to probe with less effective pieces of vegetation.

[. . .]

Communication can report subjective experience

After reviewing evidence that visual imagery appears to be very similar in humans and monkeys, Frith et al. (1999, p. 107) conclude that "to discover what someone is conscious of we need them to give us some form of report about their subjective experience . . . however we do not need to use language to report our mental experiences. Gestures and movements can be made with a deliberate communicative intent . . . the same procedure can be used in studies of animals." This realization of the significance of communication as a source of evidence about conscious feelings and thoughts entails a simple transfer to animals of the basic methods by which we infer what our human companions are thinking or feeling, as discussed in detail by Griffin (1976, 1984, 1998, 2001).

There are three general kinds of animal communication that are useful as evidence of conscious experiences:

1   Systems derived from simple components of human language, such as manual gestures modified from the sign language of the deaf, as reviewed by Fouts (1997), the keyboard system used by apes at the Yerkes Laboratory, as reviewed by Savage-Rumbaugh et al. (1998) and the imitation of human words used meaningfully by African grey parrots, as reviewed by Pepperberg (1999). Fouts and Jensvold (2002) have video-recorded chimpanzees using manual gestures modeled on the sign language of the deaf to communicate with each other in the absence of any human observer. Savage-Rumbaugh et al. (1998) have added significantly to the already abundant evidence that chimpanzees and bonobos communicate a variety of conscious thoughts and emotional feelings by use of the Yerkes Laboratory keyboard system (which uses symbols for English words). These apes also

understand simple levels of human speech. Pepperberg (1999) has provided a coherent account of her extensive studies of how African grey parrots use their imitations of human words to express simple thoughts and answer moderately complex questions. Pepperberg and Lynn (2001) recognize that this type of communication is evidence of perceptual consciousness.

2   Experimental arrangements by which animals can communicate about their thoughts and feelings by responses to controlled stimulation designed for this purpose. For many years, animals have been used in experiments on visual perception, and their manual responses, such as pulling a lever or touching a spot on a computer screen, or making intentional eye movements, have been taken as reporting. In reference to binocular rivalry, for example, Rees et al. (2002, p. 263) remark: "Monkeys can be trained to report their percept during rivalry, and their behaviour is similar to that of humans." Herman (2002) has shown that captive dolphins can learn not only to understand gestural commands from human trainers but also that certain gestures represent body parts. Xitco et al. (2001) report that dolphins can also learn to point by orienting their bodies toward some object. They were observed to do this only when a human companion was present, and the pointing was sometimes related to the dolphin's receiving information about an object via an underwater keyboard of symbols modeled after the keyboards used with apes in the Yerkes Laboratory.

3   Natural communicative behavior of animals. Some of the most important new evidence about natural communication concerns alarm calls. Several new examples have been added to the classic experiments of Seyfarth et al. (1980) on the alarm calls of vervet monkeys (*Cercopithecus aethiops*) that designate which of three major predators has been sighted. [. . .] Manser (2001) has reported that in the social mongoose (*Suricata suricatta*) different call types are given in response to different predators, and that the urgency of the danger is also indicated by the noisiness of the call. From these and earlier studies it seems that some animals can communicate both urgency and level of arousal, and to a limited extent, the type of predator. Alarm calling is not a stereotyped reaction, for vervet monkeys occasionally withhold them, as discussed by Cheney and Seyfarth (1990, pp. 107–109).

Intriguing and puzzling data about the alarm calls of prairie dogs (*Cynomys gunnisoni*) have been reported in a review by Slobodchikoff (2002). These social rodents that live in a colonial burrow system were presented with real predators, models and human intruders, and the resulting alarm calls were then recorded. Responses of the prairie dogs to playbacks led Slobodchikoff to conclude that "A call can identify the category of predator, such as coyote, domestic dog, or red-tailed hawk . . . Each category of predator-specific calls elicits different escape responses . . . hawk and human alarm calls elicit running to the burrows and diving inside . . . Coyote and domestic dog alarm calls elicit either a running to the lip of the burrow and standing at the burrow entrance (coyote) or standing in place where the animal was feeding (domestic dog)" (Slobodchikoff 2002, p. 258). If confirmed, this level of semantic communication appears comparable to alarm calling by vervet monkeys and calls for further investigation.

[. . .]

Discussion

Although no single piece of evidence provides a "smoking gun" that proves with total certainty that pA, the probability of awareness, is 1.0, the cumulative impact of the data reviewed above, together with abundant evidence previously available, renders it far more likely than not that animal consciousness is real and significant. The basic nature of central nervous system function is much the same in all animals with central nervous systems, despite wide variation in gross anatomy and concentration of particular functions in specific areas of the brain. No uniquely human correlate of consciousness has been discovered.

[. . .]

References

Baars RJ (2002) The conscious access hypothesis: origins and recent evidence. Trends Cogn Sci 6:47–52

Cheney DL, Seyfarth RM (1990) How monkeys see the world, inside the mind of other species. University of Chicago Press, Chicago

Clayton NS, Dickinson A (1998) Episodic-like memory during cache recovery by scrub jays. Nature 398:272–74

Clayton NS, Griffiths DP, Dickinson A (2000) Declarative and episodic-like memory in animals: personal musings of a scrub jay. In: Heyes C, Huber L (eds) The evolution of cognition. MIT Press, Cambridge, Mass., pp 273–288

Clayton NS, Yu KS, Dickinson A (2001) Scrub jays (*Aphelocoma coerulescens*) form integrated memories of the multiple features of caching episodes. J Exp Psychol Anim Behav Process 27:17–29

Clayton NS, Yu KS, Dickinson A (2003) Interacting cache memories: evidence for flexible memory use by western scrub-jays (*Aphelocoma californica*). J Exp Psychol Anim Behav Process 29:14–22

Cowey A, Stoerig P (1995) Blindsight in monkeys. Nature 373: 247–249

Cowey A, Stoerig P (1997) Visual detection in monkeys with blindsight. Neuropsychologia 35:929–939

Crick F, Koch C (1998) Consciousness and neuroscience. Cereb Cortex 8:97–107

Crick F, Koch C (2000) The unconscious homunculus. In: Metzinger T (ed) Neural correlates of consciousness, empirical and conceptual questions. MIT Press, Cambridge, Mass., pp 103–110

Crick F, Koch C (2003) A framework for consciousness. Nat Neurosci 6:119–126

Damasio AR (1999) The feeling of what happens: body and emotion in the making of consciousness. Harcourt, Orlando, Fla.

Damasio AR (2000) A neurobiology for consciousness. In: Metzinger T (ed) Neural correlates of consciousness, empirical and conceptual questions. MIT Press, Cambridge, Mass., pp 111–120

Dawkins MS (2000) Animal mind and animal emotions. Am Zool 40:883–888

Dickinson A, Balleine BW (2000) Causal cognition and goal-directed action. In: Heyes C, Huber L (eds) The evolution of cognition. MIT Press, Cambridge, Mass., pp 185–204

Donald M (2001) A mind so rare, the evolution of human consciousness. Norton, New York

Emery NJ, Clayton NS (2001) Effects of experience and social context on prospective caching strategies by scrub jays. Nature 414:443–446

Engel AK, Singer W (2001) Temporal binding and the neural correlates of sensory awareness. Trends Cogn Sci 5:16–26

Fouts RS (1997) Next of kin: what chimpanzees have taught me about who we are. Morrow, New York

Fouts RS, Jensvold MLA (2002) Armchair dilusions versus empirical realities: a neurological model for the continuity of ape and human languaging. In: Goodman M, Moffat MLA (ed) Probing human origins. American Academy of Arts and Sciences, Cambridge, Mass., pp 87–101

Frith D, Perry R, Lumer E (1999) The neural correlates of conscious experience: an experimental framework. Trends Cogn Sci 3:105–114

Griffin DR (1976) The question of animal awareness. Rockefeller University Press, New York

Griffin DR (1984) Animal thinking. Harvard University Press, Cambridge, Mass.

Griffin DR (1998) From cognition to consciousness. Anim Cogn 1:3–16

Griffin DR (2001) Animal minds, beyond cognition to consciousness. University of Chicago Press, Chicago

Griffiths D, Dickinson A, Clayton NS (1999) Episodic memory: what can animals remember about their past? Trends Cogn Sci 3:74–80

Hart BL, Hart LA, McCoy M, Sarath CR (2001) Cognitive behaviour in Asian elephants; use and modification of branches for fly switching. Anim Behav 62:839–847

Herman LM (2002) Exploring the cognitive world of the bottlenose dolphin. In: Bekoff, M, Allen C, Burghardt GM (eds) The cognitive animal, empirical and theoretical perspectives. MIT Press, Cambridge, Mass., pp 275–283

Hunt GR (1996) Manufacture and use of hook-tools by New Caledonian crows (*Corvus moneduloides*). Nature 379:249–251

Hunt GR (2000a) Tool use by the New Caledonian crow (*Corvus moneduloides*) to obtain *Cerambycidae* from dead wood. Emu 100: 109–114

Hunt GR (2000b) Human-like, population-level specialization in the manufacture of pandanus tools by New Caledonian crows *Corvus moneduloides*. Proc R Soc Lond B 267:403–413

Hunt GR, Gray RD (2003) Diversification and cumulative evolution in New Caledonian crow tool manufacture. Proc R Soc Lond B 270:867–874

Kanwisher N (2001) Neural events and perceptual awareness. Cognition 79:89–113

Logothetis NK (1999) Vision: a window on consciousness. Sci Am Nov:69–75

Manser MB (2001) The acoustic structure of suricates' alarm calls varies with predator type and the level of response urgency. Proc R Soc Lond B Biol 268:2315–2324

Matsuzawa T (ed) (2001) Primate origins of human cognition and behavior. Springer, Berlin Heidelberg New York

Metzinger T (ed) (2000) Neural correlates of consciousness, empirical and conceptual questions. MIT Press, Cambridge, Mass.

Natsoulas TN (1983) Concepts of consciousness. J Mind Behav 4:13–59

Pepperberg IM (1999) The Alex studies, cognitive and communicative abilities of grey parrots. Harvard University Press, Cambridge, Mass.

Pepperberg IM, Lynn SK (2001) Possible levels of animal consciousness with reference to grey parrots (*Psittacus eritiacus*). Am Zool 40:893–901

Pryor, K, Haag R, O'Reilly J (1969) The creative porpoise: training for novel behavior. J Exp Anal Behav 12:653–661

Rees G, Kreiman G, Koch C (2002) Neural correlates of consciousness in humans. Nature Rev 3:261–270

Roth G (2000) The evolution and ontogeny of consciousness. In: Metzinger T (ed) Neural correlates of consciousness, empirical and conceptual questions. MIT Press, Cambridge, Mass., pp 77–97

Savage-Rumbaugh S, Shanker SG, Taylor TJ (1998) Apes, language, and the human mind. Oxford University Press, New York

Searle JR (2000) Consciousness. Annu Rev Neurosci 23:557–578

Searle JR (2002) Consciousness and language. Cambridge University Press, New York

Seward T, Seward MA (2000) Visual awareness due to neuronal activities in subcortical structures: a proposal. Conscious Cogn 9:86–116

Seyfarth D, Cheney D, Marler P (1980) Vervet monkey alarm calls: evidence for predator classification and semantic communication. Anim Behav 28:1070–1094

Slobodchikoff CN (2002) Cognition and communication in prairie dogs. In: Bekoff, M, Allen C, Burghardt GM (eds) The cognitive animal, empirical and theoretical perspectives. MIT Press, Cambridge, Mass., pp 257–264

Sousa C, Matsuzawa T (2001) The use of tokens as rewards and tools by chimpanzees (*Pan troglodytes*). Anim Cogn 4:213–221

Stoerig P, Zontanou A, Cowey A (2002) Aware or unaware: assessment of cortical blindness in four men and a monkey. Cereb Cortex 12:565–574

Taylor JG (1999) The race for consciousness. MIT Press, Cambridge, Mass.

Tong F, Nakayama K, Vaughan JT, Kanwisher N (1998) Binocular rivalry and visual awareness in human extrastriate cortex. Neuron 21:753–759

Tonooka R (2001) Leaf-folding behavior for drinking water by wild chimpanzees (*Pan troglodytes*) at Bossou, Guinea. Anim Cogn 4:325–334

Tulving E (1972) Episodic and semantic memory. In: Tulving E, Donaldson W (eds) Organization of memory. Academic, New York, pp 382–403

Tulving E (2002) Episodic memory: from brain to mind. Annu Rev Psychol 53:1–25

Weiskrantz L, Warrington EK, Sanders MD, Marshall J (1974) Visual capacity in the hemianopic field following a restricted cortical ablation. Brain 97:709–728

Xitco MJ Jr, Gory JD, Kuczaj SA II (2001) Spontaneous pointing by bottlenose dolphins (*Tursiops truncatus*). Anim Cogn 4: 115–123

Chapter 15

Bernard E. Rollin

ANIMAL PAIN

Rollin summarizes the rationale for asserting the scientific incoherence of denying pain in animals, the observability of mental states in animals, the common sense nature of mentation in animals, and the application of morality to animals in light of these understandings. He then points out how the human benefits derived from animals facilitated the rejection of ascribing moral worth to their treatment.

The scientific incoherence of denying pain in animals

[. . .]

[A]S DARWINIANS RECOGNISED, it is arbitrary and incoherent, given the theories and information current in science, to rule out mentation for animals, particularly such a basic, well-observed mental state as pain.

[. . .]

One can well believe that only by thinking of animal pain in terms of Cartesian, mechanical processes devoid of an experiential, morally relevant dimension could scientists have done the experimental work which has created the sophisticated neurophysiology we have today. But given that science, the neurophysiological analogies that have been discovered between humans and animals, certainly at least the vertebrates, are powerful arguments against the Cartesianism which made it possible. In a dialectical irony which would surely have pleased Hegel, Cartesianism has been its own undoing, by demonstrating more and more identical neurophysiological mechanisms in humans and animals, mechanisms which make it highly implausible that animals are merely machines if we are not.[1]

Pain and pleasure centres, like those found in humans, have been reported in the brains of birds, mammals, and fish; and the neural mechanisms responsible for pain behaviour are remarkably similar in all vertebrates. Anaesthetics and analgesics control what appears to be pain in all vertebrates and some invertebrates; and, perhaps most dramatically, the biological feedback mechanisms for controlling pain seem to be remarkably similar in all vertebrates, involving serotonin, endorphins and enkephalins, and substance P. (Endorphins have been found even in earthworms.) The very existence of endogenous opiates in animals is powerful evidence that they feel pain. Animals would hardly have neurochemicals and pain-inhibiting systems identical to ours and would hardly show the same diminution of pain signs as we do if their experiential pain was not being controlled by these mechanisms in the same way that ours is. In certain shock experiments, large doses of naloxone have been given to traumatized animals, reversing the effect of endogenous opiates, and it has been shown that animals so treated die as a direct result of uncontrolled pain.[2] In 1987, it was shown that bradykinin antagonists control pain in both humans and animals.

Denial of pain consciousness in animals is incompatible not only with neurophysiology, but with what can be extrapolated from evolutionary theory as well. There is reason to believe that evolution preserves and perpetuates successful biological systems. Given that the mechanisms of pain in vertebrates are the same, it strains credibility to suggest that the experience of pain suddenly emerges at the level of humans. Granted, it is growing increasingly popular, following theorists like Gould and Lewontin, to assume the existence of quantum leaps in evolution, rather than assume that all evolution proceeds incrementally by minute changes. But surely such a hypothesis is most applicable where there is evidence of a morphological trait which seems to suddenly appear in the fossil record. With regard to mental traits, this hypothesis might conceivably apply to the appearance of language in humans, if Chomsky and others are correct in their argument that human language differs in kind, as well as degree, from communication systems in other species. But in other areas of mentation – most areas apart from the most sophisticated intellectual abilities – and surely with regard to basic mental survival equipment like that connected with pain, such a hypothesis is both *ad hoc* and implausible. Human pain machinery is virtually the same as that in animals, and we know from experience with humans that the ability to *feel* pain is essential to survival; that people with a congenital or acquired inability to feel pain or with afflictions such as Hansen's disease (leprosy), which affects the ability to feel pain, are unlikely to do well or even survive without extraordinary, heroic attention. The same is true of animals, of course – witness the recent case of Taub's deafferented monkeys (monkeys in which the sensory nerves serving the limbs have been severed) who mutilated themselves horribly in the absence of the ability to feel. *Feeling* pain and the motivational influence of feeling it are essential to the survival of the system, and to suggest that the system is purely mechanical in animals but not in man is therefore highly implausible. If pain had worked well as a purely mechanical system in animals without a subjective dimension, why would it suddenly appear in man *with* such a dimension? (Unless, of course, one invokes some such theological notion as original sin and pain as divine punishment – hardly a legitimate scientific move!) And obviously, similar argument would hold for discomfort associated with hunger, thirst, and other so-called drives, as well as with pleasures such as that of sexual congress.

So not only does much scientific activity presuppose animal pain, as we have seen *vis-à-vis* pain research and psychological research, it fits better with neurophysiology and evolutionary theory to believe that animals have mental experiences than to deny it. Outside positivistic-behaviouristic ideology, there seems little reason to deny pain (or fear, anxiety, boredom – in short, all rudimentary forms of mentation) to animals on either factual or conceptual grounds. (Indeed, research indicates that all vertebrates have receptor sites for benzodiazepine, which, in turn, suggests that the physiological basis of anxiety exists in all vertebrates.)[3] One may cavil at attributing higher forms of reason to animals, as Lloyd Morgan did, but that is ultimately a debatable, and in large part empirically decidable, question.

The alleged unobservability of mental states

The one lingering doubt which positivism leaves us with concerns the ultimate unobservability of mental states in animals. After all, we cannot experience them, even in principle. Perhaps there is something fundamentally wrong with admitting such unobservable entities to scientific discourse, for would we not be opening a Pandora's box containing such undesirable notions as souls, demons, angels, entelechies, life forces, absolute space, and the rest? Would we not be giving up the hard-won ground by which we demarcate science from other forms of knowing, and opening ourselves to a dissolution of the line between science and metaphysics, science and speculation? Surely that consideration must far outweigh any benefit of admitting animal mentation into legitimate scientific discourse.

Since this is the key (official) reason behind the common sense of science's refusal to talk about animal mentation, it is worth examining in some detail. The first assumption behind this view is obviously that science is, or can be, and surely ought to be, totally empirical – in other words, that science ought to make no assumptions, postulate no entities, and countenance no terms which cannot be cashed empirically. This is, indeed, a mainstay of classical, hard-line positivism.

[. . .]

Mental states as a perceptual category

[T]here is no good 'scientific' reason for acquiescing to positivism's demand that only observables be permitted in science; first, because that demand cannot itself be observationally proved, and second, because it would exclude all sorts of basic things like other people and intersubjective physical objects in which science has much stake. Furthermore, it has become increasingly clear since Kant that there is no good reason for believing that facts can be gathered or even observations made independently of a theoretical base. Kant showed that sensory information must be 'boxed' before it becomes an object of experience, that even the notions of 'object' and 'event' are brought to sensation, rather than emerging from it. Indeed, examples demonstrating the role of theory in the broadest sense in perception are endless. To see a fracture or a lesion on a radiograph requires an enormous amount of theoretical equipment and a great deal of training, for which the radiologist is very well paid; though he gets the same sensations on his retina as you or I do, he doesn't see the same thing as we do. This is equally true of the woodland tracker, who spots a trail or some sign of an animal's passage; the artist, who sees dozens of colours in a person's face, whereas most of us see only 'flesh colour'; the horse *aficionado* who sees a thoroughbred, while we see only a horse. And what we see in the standard ambivalent figures like the one which can be seen as a vase or as two faces or the duck-rabbit or the young-old woman depends on what we are thinking about, expecting, hypothesizing, and the like.

Indeed, returning to our main concern, what we perceive or observe in science or consider worthy of calling a fact must be in large measure determined by our metaphysical commitments and their associated values. Aristotle saw the world as an array of facts of function and teleology. Galileo saw a mathematical machine. In so far as common sense has a metaphysics and an epistemology, it surely maintains that we perceive the mental states of others. Contrary to the stories that many philosophers have told in the twentieth century, and which we discussed earlier, I do not believe that common sense uses mental terms like 'happy', 'afraid', 'bored', and so on only to refer to overt behaviour in appropriate contexts. Nor do I believe that common sense simply *infers* mental states by analogy from overt behaviour. I think, rather, that common sense *perceives* mental states in others in exactly the way that it perceives physical states or objects.

[. . .]

On this view, perceiving in terms of mentation is one of the categories by which we commonsensically process reality, and mentation is a fundamental plank upon which our common-sense metaphysics is built. And the reason why this notion is so geographically and historically pervasive is because it works so well. Nothing can disconfirm our attribution of mentation to other humans *in general*, because mentation is a (if not *the*) fundamental cognitive category by which we map other humans.

[. . .]

When we use words attributing passion, rage, sadness, joy, depression, and the like to other people, we surely do not do so in the absence of behaviour relevant to and expressive of these mental states. On the other hand, we are not just talking about the behaviour; we are unavoidably referring to what the behaviour is directly and essentially tied to – namely, a feeling which, while perhaps somewhat unlike mine, serves the same function in the other person's life as the feeling in question does in mine.

[. . .]

Morality and the perception of mental states

There are doubtless a number of major reasons for our ubiquitous presumption of subjective experiences in others. Most obvious is the fact that without this presumption, we could not as readily predict or understand the actions of others. Second, in so far as we are taught moral concern for others, such concern is cogent only on the presumption that others have subjective experiences, that we can more or less know them, that their subjective states matter to them more or less as mine matter to me, and that my actions have major effects on what matters to them and on what they subjectively experience. If we genuinely didn't believe that others felt pain, pleasure, fear, joy, and so on, there would be little point to moral locutions or moral exhortations. Morality presupposes that the objects of our moral concern have feelings. And, what is logically equivalent, if there is no presumption of the possibility of feeling in an entity, there is little reason to speak of it 'in the moral tone of voice'.

Of course, the presumption of feeling is only a necessary condition for moral concern, not a sufficient one. One must also believe that the feelings of others warrant our attention. For most people, the mere realization that others experience negative feelings in the same way that they themselves do is enough to generate a stance of moral concern. . . .

[T]he attribution of mental states, especially those associated with pleasure and pain, joy and misery, is connected irrevocably with the possibility of morality. For this reason, only a science with blinders to the moral universe, and, most especially, only a *psychology* provided with such blinders could ever deny not only the legitimacy of talking about mental states, but their fundamental place in the world, which a genuine psychology must seek to explain.

[. . .]

Application of this theory to animals

But what of animals? Clearly, common sense and ordinary language have traditionally extended the presumption of mentation to animals. (In some cultures, this was explained by viewing animals as reincarnated humans.) Probably the major reason for doing so was that it works. By assuming that animals feel and have other subjective experiences, we can explain and predict their behaviour (and control it as well). Why beat a dog if it doesn't hurt him? Why does a lion hunt if it isn't hungry? Why does a dog drool and beg for scraps from the table if they don't taste good? Why does a cat in heat rub up against the furniture if it doesn't feel good? Why do animals scratch if they don't itch? Again, common sense continued to think in this way regardless of what scientific ideology dictated, and scientists continued to think in this way in their ordinary moments.

The moral reason for presuming consciousness and mental states in animals does not loom nearly so large. It is an interesting fact that although most cultures in most times and places have attributed mentation to animals, few have clearly set out moral rules for their treatment, and for many, animals do not enter the moral arena. For some philosophers, granting moral status to animals is highly problematic, which is why so many of them have been concerned, like Descartes, to prove that animals are really automata. For others, like Hume, who deem it absurd to deny the full range of mental experience to animals, and who are highly cognizant of the connection between morality and feeling, the question of moral treatment of animals nevertheless does not arise. For ordinary people, though their presumption of mentation in animals is strong, their application of moral notions to animals is minimal or non-existent. Only thus can one explain why for centuries animals were held morally and legally responsible for their actions, subject to trial, punishment, and death, yet at the same time had no legal protection whatever.[4]

Why is this the case? Why has common sense (and until recently the legal system as well) studiously avoided coming to grips with our moral obligations to other creatures?[5] For that matter, why has philosophy, which has notoriously concerned itself with all sorts of questions and which has explored all aspects of ethical theory, been virtually blind to questions concerning animals? (There are, of course, notable exceptions, such as the Pythagoreans; but here we must recall that their concern grew out of the doctrine of transmigration of human souls.) There is no certain answer to this question. Perhaps part of an answer lies in the influence of our theological traditions, most especially the Christian tradition, which has stressed that the proper study of man is man. More plausibly perhaps, a key part of the answer lies in a remark made to me by one of my veterinary students at the end of an ethics course in which I put great stress on moral questions pertaining to animals. 'If I take your teaching seriously', she said,

> no part of my life is untouched, and all parts are severely shaken. For if I ascribe moral status to animals, I must worry about the food I eat, the clothes I wear, the cosmetics I use, the drugs I take, the pets I keep, the horses I ride, the dogs I castrate and euthanize, and the research I do. The price of morality is too high – I'd rather ignore the issue.

Perhaps in a culture which has no choice but to exploit animals in order to survive, one cannot even begin to think about these questions, or even see them as moral choices rather than pragmatic necessities. Or perhaps because the use of animals for our purposes without consideration of their interests is so pervasive and our dependence upon it so great, it becomes invisible to us, in much the same way that exploitation of women and minorities was invisible for too long. Indeed, it is interesting that moral interest in these long-neglected areas arose at virtually the same historical time and place, a point to which we will return.

If I am at all correct, the traditional common-sense view of animals went something like this. On the one hand, common sense took it for granted that animals were conscious and experienced pain, fear, sadness, joy, and a whole range of mental states. Indeed, at times common sense probably gave too much credit to the mental lives of many animals, falling into a mischievous anthropomorphism. Yet in the same breath, common sense consistently ignored the obvious moral problems growing out of attributing thought and feeling to animals, since it had an unavoidable stake in using them in manners which inevitably caused them pain, suffering, and death, and thus, ordinary common sense had its own compartmentalization in this area. Indeed, such animal use was often directed not only at satisfying basic needs such as food and clothing, but more frivolous ones, such as entertainment, as in bear- and bull-baiting, fox-hunting, falconry, bull-fighting, cock-fighting, dog-fighting, gladiatorial contests, and indiscriminate bird shoots. (If the moral issue *was* ever raised, the 'Nature is red in tooth and claw anyway' and 'Animals kill each other' responses quickly dismissed it.)

In this way, though common sense and Darwinism reinforced one another, in general, neither felt the need to draw out the obvious moral implications of its position (allowing, of course, for a few exceptions like M. P. Evans and Henry Salt).[6] And when what we have called the ideology or common sense of science arose, at about the same time that animal experimentation became a crucial part of scientific activity, it had both an ideological and a vested interest in perpetuating blindness to moral issues. Hence, though it violated both common sense and the evolutionary theory which it continued to accept by its denial of animal consciousness, positivistic-behaviouristic ideology, with its denial of the legitimacy of asking moral questions in and about science, buttressed, reinforced, and even to some extent justified and grounded common sense and Darwinism's systematic disregard of moral issues surrounding animal use and exploitation. Though common sense might balk at science's denial of consciousness to animals, it had no problem at all with science's rejection of moral concern for animals, since scientific use of animals was, after all, like agricultural and other uses of animals, one more area of human benefit. Even lurid, periodic newspaper accounts of 'vivisection' aroused in most people not so much moral indignation as aesthetic revulsion – 'I don't want to know about that.' (Most people still react that way to slaughterhouses and packing plants.) Thus, for a long time, there was little social moral opposition to scientific denial or ignoring of animal pain, suffering, and mentation, even as common sense might have objected to the strangeness of quantum theory, but certainly had no moral qualms about it. So for science, convenience and ideology went hand in hand, and both were unchecked by common sense, which mostly didn't care much about what scientists did. Though it thought their activities odd, it certainly didn't worry about them morally, most especially in biomedical areas, which promised – and delivered – many glittering advances of direct benefit to all of us. And, as we have seen, common sense's tolerant attitude towards biomedical research was not limited to animal subjects; it extended for a long time to human subjects as well, especially when the subjects were not 'us', but 'them' – prisoners, indigents, primitives, lunatics, retarded persons, and the like.

Notes

1   Stephen Walker's recent book *Animal Thought* elegantly documents the neurophysiological similarity between humans and animals.

2   M. Fettman *et al.*, 'Naloxone therapy in awake endotoxemic Yucatan minipigs'.

3   J. A. Gray, *The Neuropsychology of Anxiety*.

4   M. P. Evans, *Criminal Prosecution and Capital Punishment of Animals*.

5   See Rollin, *Animal Rights*, pt. 2.

6   M. P. Evans, *Evolutionary Ethics and Animal Psychology*; H. S. Salt, *Animals' Rights Considered in Relation to Social Progress*.

Chapter 16

Gary Varner

HOW FACTS MATTER

Varner addresses the question of which animals can feel pain. Based on a literature review, he concludes that all vertebrates, including cold-blooded vertebrates such as fish and herpetofauna, probably feel pain whereas most invertebrates do not; however, cephalopods such as octopi and squid may be invertebrates that can experience pain.

[. . .]

Reference of the term "animals"

A LMOST EVERYONE BELIEVES that *some* animals are conscious, but even with protozoa removed, the animal kingdom as understood today includes such simple organisms as corals, sponges, and *Trichoplax adhaerens*. The lattermost, although composed of a few thousand cells, has no specialized systems devoted to sensation, digestion, or even reproduction [4], let alone nociceptors or a central nervous system. There are reasons to doubt that even more complex organisms like flatworms, insects, and crustaceans are conscious of pain. Therefore, it cannot be said flatly that it is absurd to deny that "animals" feel pain.

How could we decide, in a principled way, which kinds of animals are and are not capable of feeling pain? This is surely a complex and difficult question, but the most detailed treatments I have seen (Smith and Boyd [6], Rose and Adams [5], DeGrazia and Rowan [2], and Bateson [1]) have all reached the same conclusion: Probably all vertebrates are capable of feeling pain, but probably not invertebrates (with the likely exception of cephalopods). These studies compared normal adult humans to various vertebrate and invertebrate animals on behavioral and neurophysiological criteria, such as whether the animals in question have a highly developed central nervous system, whether nociceptors are known to be present and connected to it, whether endogenous opiates are present, whether their responses to what would be painful stimuli for us are similar to ours, and whether these responses are modified by analgesia. It is not true that vertebrates score positively on each and every one of these comparisons and invertebrates score negatively. For instance, despite a disciplined search for them, nociceptors have not been isolated in fish or herpetofauna, and endogenous opiates have been found in earthworms and insects. As the working party of the British Institute of Medical Ethics put it, "the most obvious divide is between the vertebrates and the invertebrates" [6] because the comparisons are almost all positive on the former side of the line and almost all negative on the latter side. The case for thinking that all vertebrates can feel pain is thus very strong, while the case for thinking that invertebrates can feel pain is extremely weak by comparison (with the possible exception of cephalopods like octopus and squid, which have stunning learning abilities [3,8], but about whom little is known regarding nociception, endogenous opiates, and responses to analgesics). (On the points made in this paragraph, see generally Varner [7], pp. 51–4.)

If we have such relatively weak evidence for saying that most invertebrates can feel pain, then it is not absurd to deny that *those* animals feel pain. By the same token, if we have relatively strong evidence for saying that all vertebrates can feel pain, then exclusion of the cold-blooded vertebrates from protection under an animal welfare act is unjustifiable. If pain is a bad thing for the individual who suffers it, and we are committed as a society to reducing unnecessary pain, then whether an animal is cold-blooded or scaly, rather than furred or feathered, should not matter. A careful examination of *which* animals can feel pain can give us good reason to think that not every species in the animal kingdom should be of concern to the animal welfarist, but it also suggests that the U.S. Animal Welfare Act should be amended to protect cold-blooded vertebrates, including fish and herpetofauna.

References

1. Bateson P.: Assessment of pain in animals. *Animal Behav.* 42:827–39, 1991.
2. DeGrazia D., Rowan A.: Pain, suffering, and anxiety in animals and humans. *Theoretical Med* 12:193–211, 1991.
3. Fiorito G., Scotto P.: Observational learning in *Octopus vulgaris*. *Science* 256:545–7, 1992.
4. Margulis L., Schwartz K.V.: *Five kingdoms: An illustrated guide to the phyla of life on earth*, 3rd ed. W.H. Freeman and Company, New York, 1998.
5. Rose M., Adams D.: Evidence for pain and suffering in other animals. pp. 42–71. In Gill Langley (ed): *Animal experimentation: The consensus changes*. Chapman and Hall, New York, 1989.
6. Smith J.A., Boyd K.M. (eds): *Lives in the balance: The ethics of using animals in biomedical research*. Oxford University Press, Oxford, 1991.
7. Varner G.: *In nature's interests? Interests, animal rights and environmental ethics*. Oxford University Press, Oxford, 1998.
8. Wells M.J.: *Octopus: Physiology and behavior of an advanced invertebrate*. Chapman and Hall, London, 1978.

FURTHER READING

Baker, Steve (2001) *Picturing the Beast: Animals, Identity, and Representation*. Urbana: University of Illinois.

Barresi, J. and Moore, C. (1996) "Intentional relations and social understanding." *Behavioral and Brain Sciences* 19: 107–154.

Bekoff, Marc (2002) *Minding Animals: Awareness, Emotions, and Heart*, New York: Oxford University Press.

Bekoff, Marc, Allen, Colin, and Burghardt, Gordon M. (2002) *The Cognitive Animal: Empirical and Theoretical Perspectives on Animal Cognition*, Cambridge, MA: The MIT Press.

Blumberg, Mark S. and Greta Sokoloff (2003) "Hard heads and open minds: A reply to Panksepp (2003)." *Psychological Review* 110: 389–394.

Bradshaw, R. H. (1998) "Consciousness in non-human animals: Adopting the precautionary principle." *Journal of Consciousness Studies* 5: 108–114.

Butler, Ann B., Paul R. Manger, B. I. B. Lindahl, and Peter Arhem (2005) "Evolution of the neural basis of consciousness: a bird—mammal comparison." *BioEssays* 27: 923–936.

Carruthers, Peter (2005) "Why the question of animal consciousness might not matter very much. *Philosophical Psychology* 18: 83–102.

Cartmill, Matt (2000) "Animal consciousness: Some philosophical, methodological, and evolutionary problems." *American Zoologist* 40: 835–846.

Crick, Francis and Christof Koch (2003). "A framework for consciousness." *Nature Neuroscience* 6: 119–126.

Dennett, Daniel C. (2001). "Are we explaining consciousness yet?" *Cognition* 79: 221–237.

Dennett, Daniel C. (2002) "How could I be wrong? How wrong could I be?" *Journal of Consciousness Studies* 9: 13–16.

Dixon, Beth (2001) "Animal emotions." *Ethics & the Environment* 6(2): 23–30.

Dol, M. *et al* (eds.) (1997) *Animal Consciousness and Animal Ethics: Perspectives from the Netherlands*, Van Gorcum.

Frijda, Nico H. (1995) "Emotions in robots." Chapter 20, pp. 501–516. In: *Comparative Approaches to Cognitive Science*, Herbert L. Roitblat and Jean-Arcady Meyer (eds.) Cambridge, MA: The MIT Press.

Griffin, Donald (2001) *Animal Minds: Beyond Cognition to Consciousness*, Chicago: University of Chicago Press.

Heinrich, Bernd (2002) "Raven consciousness." Chapter 7, pp. 47–52. In: *Cognitive Animal*, M. Bekoff, C. Allen, and G. M. Burghardt (eds.), Cambridge, MA: The MIT Press.

Kimler, William C. (2000) "Reading Morgan's Canon: Reduction and unification in the foraging of a science of the mind." *American Zoologist* 40: 853–861.

Kistler, John M. (2000) *Animal Rights: A Subject Guide, Bibliography, and Internet Companion*, Westport, CT: Greenwood Press.

Langford, D. J., S. E. Crager, Z. Shehzad, S. B. Smith, S. G. Sotocinal, J. S. Levenstadt, M. L. Chanda, D. J. Levitin, and J. S. Mogil (2006) "Social modulation of pain as evidence for empathy in mice." *Science* 312: 1967–1970.

Macer, Daryl (1998) "Animal consciousness and ethics in Asia and the Pacific." *Journal of Agricultural and Environmental Ethics* 10: 249–267.

McFarland, David (1995) "Opportunity versus goals in robots, animals and people." In *Comparative Approaches to Cognitive Science*, Herbert L. Roitblat and Jean-Arcady Meyer (eds.). Cambridge, MA: The MIT Press.

Macphail, Euan M. (1998) *The Evolution of Consciousness*, New York: Oxford University Press.

Mather, Jennifer A. (1995) "Cognition in cephalopods." *Advances in the Study of Behavior* 24: 317–353.

Mitchell, Robert W., Thompson, Nicholas S., and Miles, H. Lyn (eds.) (1997) *Anthropomorphism, Anecdotes, and Animals*, Albany, NY: State University of New York Press.

Netting, J. (2000) "U.S. Dispute over definition of animal distress." *Nature* 406: 668. (see also www.aphis.usda.gov/ppd)

Panksepp, J. (1998) *Affective Neuroscience: The Foundations of Human and Animal Emotions*, New York: Oxford University Press.

Ritvo, Harriet (2000) "Animal consciousness: Some historical perspective." *American Zoologist* 40: 847–852.

Rollin, Bernard E. (1998) *The Unheeded Cry: Animal Consciousness, Animal Pain and Science*, Ames, IA: Iowa State University Press.

Rollin, Bernard E. (1999) "Some conceptual and ethical concerns about current views of pain." *Pain Forum* 8(2):78–83.

Rutherford, K.M.D. (2002) "Assessing pain in animals" *Animal Welfare* 11: 31–53.

Shusterman, Ronald J., Reichmuth Kastak, Colleen, and Kastak, David (2002) "The cognitive sea lion: Meaning and memory in the laboratory and in nature." Chapter 28, pp. 217–228. In: *The Cognitive Animal: Empirical and Theoretical Perspectives on Animal Cognition*, M. Bekoff, C. Allen, and G. M. Burghardt (eds.), Cambridge MA: The MIT Press.

Staddon, J. E. R. (2000) "Consciousness and theoretical behaviorism." *American Zoologist* 40: 874–882.

Thompson, Roger K. (1995) "Natural and relational concepts in animals." Pp. 175–224. In: *Comparative Approaches to Cognitive Science*, Herbert L. Roitblat and Jean-Arcady Meyer (eds), Cambridge, MA: MIT Press.

Wall, Patrick D. (~1991) "Defining 'pain in animals'." Chapter 3, pp. 63–79. In: *Animal Pain*, Charles E. Short and Alan van Poznak (eds.) New York: Churchill Livingstone.

Weiskranz, L. (ed.) (1991) *Thought without Language*, Oxford: Clarendon Press.

STUDY QUESTIONS

1. Based on Mendl and Paul's article on consciousness and emotion, how well do you believe it is likely that cognitive science studies can give a relatively clear answer on the level of consciousness and emotional experience in nonhuman animals?

2. To what degree do you believe that Smuts' objectivity for describing baboons' lives might be affected by her interpersonal relations with them? Justify your thinking.

3. Based on Mitchell's presentation, what do you think is the fate of anthropomorphism in contemporary science, as it relates to nonhuman primates? To other mammals? To other vertebrates?

4. To what degree are Bermond's and Rollin's position on animal experience of pain compatible, and incompatible? Clarify your reasons.

5. How would you compare the perspectives of Bermond, Dennett? What are the key points that Bermond and Dennett might hold in common? On what score do they differ?

6. Compare Griffin and Speck to Dennett. What points would you expect that they could agree upon? Give two or three of their most outstanding differences.

7. Compare the perspectives on the emotional lives of animals described by Dawkins with that of your own. What themes do they share and how do they differ? How would you respond to Dawkins on the points where you seem to differ?

8. Based on Varner's position that cephalopods can feel pain, how do you believe that cephalopods should be treated differently from other invertebrates, if at all? Explain your reasoning.

Primates and cetaceans

INTRODUCTION TO PART THREE

THIS PART HIGHLIGHTS SOME OF the issues involved with the great apes and cetaceans. One issue is whether study should be laboratory-based or should be observation of great apes and cetaceans in the wild. A second issue is whether our focus should be on species or on individual animals. And a third issue is whether the moral status of an animal should be related to its cognitive abilities.

The great apes exhibit such extraordinary capacities that a number of thinkers, such as Steven Wise (ch. 79), have proposed that they be given basic legal rights. In his essay Marc Bekoff argues against line-drawing between animal species; we should avoid "primatocentrism" and focus not on animal cognitive abilities but simply on animal pain and suffering. Individuals count, whatever their species. The linguistic capacities and self-awareness of great apes is discussed by Sue Savage-Rumbaugh and her co-authors in their essay. Their pioneering work with chimpanzees and bonobos has been conducted in a laboratory setting, allowing for carefully controlled observations. Andrew Whiten and his co-workers discuss their findings from their observations of chimpanzees in the wild. They present their evidence for cultural variations between chimpanzee communities—a feature previously thought to be unique to human communities.

Juan Carlos Gómez addresses the specific question of whether or not apes are persons. He rejects definitions of personhood such as that of Daniel Dennett dependent upon that persons exhibited levels of cognitive complexity which require linguistic communication. Based on his studies of great apes, Gómez emphasizes the importance of the second-person, of mutual relationships in person-hood. Accordingly, we as human beings attain our personhood before we know how to speak. Apes are persons also, though not the same as human persons.

Jane Goodall discusses problems faced by chimpanzees both in their natural habitats and in captivity. Her comments are based on over thirty years of observations of wild chimpanzees. She states that it is because of knowing chimpanzees who are "wild and free and in control of their own lives" that she is concerned not only with chimpanzees as a species but also with individual chimpanzees in whatever circumstances they find themselves.

Hal Whitehead and his co-authors address the importance of culture as a determinant of behavior in whales and dolphins. They urge that nonhuman culture be integrated into conservation biology. Mark Simmonds provides evidence for cetacean intelligence and self-awareness and suggests that this intelligence may have developed in response to the unpredictable prey resources and cognitive demands of living in complex social groups. Paola Cavalieri discusses the gradual emergence of the idea that whales are entitled to life. She argues that recent evidence supports the attribution of "person" to whales.

PRIMATES

Chapter 17

Marc Bekoff

DEEP ETHOLOGY, ANIMAL RIGHTS, AND THE GREAT APE/ANIMAL PROJECT: RESISTING SPECIESISM AND EXPANDING THE COMMUNITY OF EQUALS

Bekoff advocates expanding The Great Ape Project to The Great Ape/Animal Project and acknowledging that all individual animals count and should be admitted into a Community of Equals based on ascribing moral status and rights to them. He argues that limiting this moral status to primates is speciesist. He argues that at least some past animal research and other activities violating their rights must not continue, and that the burden to justify animal research lies on those who wish to conduct it.

[. . .]

IN 1993, *The Great Ape Project: Equality Beyond Humanity* (Cavalieri and Singer 1993) was published. This important and seminal project has become known widely as the GAP. I was a proud contributor to the GAP (Bekoff 1993), and strongly supported its ambitious and major goal, namely that of admitting Great Apes (including all humans) to the Community of Equals in which the following basic moral principles or rights, enforceable at law, are granted: (i) the right to life, (ii) the protection of individual liberty, and (iii) the prohibition of torture. [. . .] I believe that the time really has come to expand the GAP to The Great Ape/Animal Project, or the GA/AP, and to expand the Community of Equals. [. . .]

Narrow-minded primatocentrism must be resisted in our studies of animal cognition and animal protection and rights. [. . .] I and others have previously argued that it is *individuals* who are important (see Rachels 1990 for a discussion of species-neutral *moral individualism* and also Bekoff and Gruen 1993 and Frey 1996 for further discussion). Thus, careful attention must be paid to *within* species individual variations in behavior.

We must not think that monkeys are smarter than dogs for each can do things the other cannot. *Smart* and *intelligent* are loaded words and often are misused: dogs do what they need to do to be dogs—they are dog-smart in their own ways—and monkeys do what they need to do to be monkeys—they are monkey-smart in their own ways—*and neither is smarter than one another.*

[. . .]

[W]hen we are unsure about an individual's ability to reason or to think, then we should assume that they can in their own ways—and certainly when we are uncertain about an individual's ability to experience pain and to suffer, then we must assume that they can. *We must err on the side of the animals.*

[. . .]

People often ask whether "lower" nonhuman animals such as fish or dogs perform sophisticated patterns of behavior that are usually associated with "higher" nonhuman primates. [. . .] In my view, these are misguided questions [. . .] because animals have to be able to do what they need to do in order to live in their own worlds. This type of speciesist cognitivism also can be bad news for many animals. If an answer to this question means that there are consequences in terms of the sorts of treatment to which an individual is subjected, then we really have to analyze the question in great detail (for discussion with respect to fish, see Dionys de Leeuw 1996 and Verheijen and Flight 1997). It is important to accept that while there are species differences in behavior, behavioral differences in and of themselves may mean little for arguments about the rights of animals.

I want to reemphasize that the use of the words "higher" and "lower" and activities such as line-drawing to place different groups of animals "above" and "below" others are extremely misleading and fail to take into account the lives and the worlds of the animals themselves. These lives and worlds are becoming increasingly accessible as the field of cognitive ethology matures. Irresponsible use of these words can also be harmful for many animals. It is disappointing that a recent essay on animal use in a widely read magazine, *Scientific American* (Mukerjee 1997, p. 86), perpetuates this myth—this ladder view of evolution—by referring to animals "lower on the phylogenetic tree." (For discussion see Crisp 1990, Bekoff 1992, Sober 1998, and Verheijen and Flight 1997; in the same issue of *Scientific American* we are told that "In my opinion, the arguments for banning experiments on animals—that there are empirically and morally superior alternatives—are unpersuasive" (Rennie, 1997, p. 4).) There are a number of objections to hierarchical ladder views of evolution, two of which are: (i) a single "ladder view" of evolution does not take into account animals with uncommon ancestries (Crisp 1990); (ii) there are serious problems deciding which criteria for moral relevance should be used and how evaluations of these criteria are to be made, even if one was able to argue convincingly for the use of a single scale (Bekoff 1992). To be sure, ladder views are speciesist.

As I noted above, some primatologists write as if only some nonhuman primates along with human primates have theories of mind. To dismiss the possibility that at least some nonprimates are capable of having a theory of mind many more data need to be collected and existing data about intentionality in nonprimates need to be considered. Furthermore, primatocentric claims are based on very few comparative data derived from tests on very small numbers of nonhuman primates who might not be entirely representative of their species. The range of tests that have been used to obtain evidence of intentional attributions is also extremely small, and such tests are often biased towards activities that may favor apes over monkeys or members of other nonprimate species. However, there is evidence that mice can outperform apes on some imitation tasks (Whiten and Ham 1992). These data do not make mice "special," and I am sure few would claim that these data should be used to spare mice and exploit monkeys. Rather, these results show that it is important to investigate the abilities of various organisms with respect to their normal living conditions. Accepting that there are species differences in behavior, and that behavioral differences in and of themselves may mean little to arguments about the rights of animals, is important, for speciesist cognitivism can be bad news for many animals.

[. . .]

It is important to talk to the animals and let them talk to us; these reciprocal conversations should allow us to *see* the animals for whom they are. To this end, [. . .] Gluck (1997), in stressing the importance of considering what we do to animals from the perspective of the animal, emphasizes the need to go beyond science and to see animals as who they are. Our respect for animals must be motivated by who they are and not by who we want them to be in our anthropocentric scheme of things. As Taylor (1986, p. 313) notes, a switch away from anthropocentrism to biocentrism, in which human superiority comes under critical scrutiny, "may require a profound moral reorientation." So be it.

We are still a long way from having an adequate data-base from which stipulative claims about the taxonomic distribution of various cognitive skills or about the having of a theory of mind can be put forth with any degree of certainty. Furthermore, we still have little idea about the phylogenetic distribution of pain and suffering in animals. We can only hope that adequate funding will be available so that these important studies can be pursued rigorously.

With respect to possible links between the study of animal cognition and the protection of innocent nonconsenting animals, I believe that a "deep reflective ethology" is needed to make people more aware of what they do to nonhumans and to make them aware of their moral and ethical obligations to animals. We must enter into intimate and reciprocal relationships with all beings in this more-than-human world (Abram 1996). In many circles it simply is too easy to abuse animals. I use the term "deep reflective ethology" to convey some of the same general ideas that underlie the "deep ecology" movement, in which it is asked that people recognize that they not only are an integral part of nature, but also that they have unique responsibilities to nature. Most people who think deeply about the troubling issues surrounding animal welfare would agree that the use of animals in research, education, for amusement, or for food needs to be severely restricted, and in some cases simply stopped. Those who appeal to the "brutality of nature" to justify some humans' brutal treatment of nonhumans fail to see that animals are not moral agents and cannot be held responsible for their actions as being "right" or "wrong" or "good" or "bad" (Bekoff and Hettinger 1994). If animals were to be viewed as moral agents (rather than as moral patients), there are a number of cognitive abilities that are correlated with the ability to make moral judgments, the possession of which would make animal abuse even more objectionable. It is essential to accept that most individual nonhuman animals experience pain and do suffer, even if it is not the same sort of pain and suffering that is experienced by humans, or even other nonhumans, including members of the same species. Furthermore, when all individuals are admitted to the Community of Equals, their rights must be vigorously protected regardless of their cognitive skills or of their capacities to experience pain and to suffer.

Deepening ethology also means we need to bond with the animals we study and even name them (Davis and Balfour 1992). Many individual animals come to trust us and we should not breach this trust.

[. . .]

Let me emphasize once again that studying nonhuman animals is a privilege that must not be abused. We must take this privilege seriously. Although some believe that naming animals is a bad idea because named animals will be treated differently—usually less objectively—than numbered animals, others believe just the opposite, that naming animals is permissible and even expected when working closely with at least certain species, especially with the same individuals over long periods of time. Manes (1997, p. 155) notes:

> If the world of our meaningful relationships is measured by the things we call by name, then our universe of meaning is rapidly shrinking. No culture has dispersed personal names as parsimoniously as ours . . . officially limiting personality to humans . . . [and] animals have become increasingly nameless. Some*thing* not some*body*.

It is interesting to note that early in her career, the well-known primatologist, Jane Goodall, had trouble convincing reviewers of one of her early papers that naming the chimpanzees she studied should be allowed. Professor Goodall refused to make the changes they suggested, including dropping names and referring to the animals as "it" rather than "he" or "she," or "which" rather than "who," but her paper was published. It seems noteworthy that researchers working with nonhuman primates and some cetaceans usually name the animals they study; we read about Kanzi, Austin, Sherman, Koko, Phoenix, and

Akeakamai and often see pictures of them with their proud human companions. We also read about Alex, an African gray parrot who Irene Pepperberg has studied extensively. Yet most people do not seem to find naming these individuals to be objectionable. Is it because the animals who are named have been shown to have highly developed cognitive skills? Not necessarily, for these and other animals are often named *before* they are studied intensively. Or, in the case of most nonhuman primates, is naming permissible because these individuals are more similar to humans than are members of other species? Why is naming a rat or a lizard or a spider more off-putting than naming a primate or a dolphin or a parrot? We need to know more about why this is so.

The context in which animals are used can also inform attitudes that people have even to individuals of the same species. For example, scientists also show different attitudes toward animals of the same species depending on whether they are encountered in the laboratory or at home; many scientists who name and praise the cognitive abilities of the companion animals with whom they share their home are likely to leave this sort of "baggage" at home when they enter their laboratories to do research with members of the same species. Based on a series of interviews with practicing scientists, Phillips (1994, p. 119) reported that many of them construct a "distinct category of animal, the 'laboratory animal,' that contrasts with namable animals (e.g., pets) across every salient dimension . . . the cat or dog in the laboratory is perceived by researchers as ontologically different from the pet dog or cat at home."

We must also pay attention to the oftentimes limited use, success, and even knowledge of animal models (see Lafollette and Shanks 1996 and Shapiro 1997 for detailed discussions) and to the many successes of using non-animal alternatives. (It seems a safe bet that most people would not venture to go to work if they had as little chance of reaching their destination as some models have of helping humans along.) And we must not be afraid of what those successes might mean in the future—the reduction and then the abolition of animal use as models based on computer simulations or work on humans emerge superior.

Everyone must be concerned with the treatment of nonhuman animals, not only the rich and those with idle time on their hands. [. . .] We must not only think of the animals when it is convenient for us to do so. Although the issues are at once difficult, frightening, and challenging, this does not mean they are impossible with which to deal. *Certainly we cannot let the animals suffer because of our inability to come to terms with difficult issues.*

We need to teach our children well for they are the custodians of the future. They will live and work in a world in which increasingly science will not be seen as a self-justifying activity, but as another human institution whose claims on the public treasury must be defended. It is more important than ever for students to understand that to question science is not to be anti-science or anti-intellectual, and that to ask how humans should interact with animals is not in itself to demand that humans never use animals. Questioning science will make for better, more responsible science, and questioning the ways in which humans use animals will make for more informed decisions about animal use. By making such decisions in an informed and responsible way, we can help to insure that in the future we will not repeat the mistakes of the past, and that we will move towards a world in which humans and other animals may be able to share peaceably the resources of a finite planet.

We and the animals who we use should be viewed as partners in a joint venture. We must broaden our taxonomic concerns and funding must be made available for those who choose not to work on nonhuman primates. We must not be afraid of what broadening our taxonomic interests may bring concerning animal cognitive abilities and their ability to feel pain and to suffer. As Savage-Rumbaugh (1997, p. 68) stressed: "I believe it is time to change course. It is time to open our eyes, our ears, our minds, our hearts. It is time to *look* with a new and deeper vision, to *listen* with new and more sensitive ears. It is time to *learn* what animals are really saying to us and to each other" (my emphases). These three L's should be used to motivate us to act on behalf of all animals. Humans can no longer be at war with the rest of the world, and no one can be an island in this intimately connected universe. Nobel laureate, Barbara McClintock, claimed that we must have a feeling for the organisms with whom we are privileged to work. Thus, bonding with animals and calling animals by name are right-minded steps. It seems unnatural for humans to continue to resist developing bonds with the animals who they study. By bonding with animals, one should not fear that the animals' points of view will be dismissed. In fact, bonding will result in a deeper examination and understanding of the animals' points of view, and this knowledge will inform further studies on the nature of human–animal interactions.

What I fear the most is that if we stall in our efforts to take animal use and abuse more seriously and fail to adopt extremely restrictive guidelines and laws, even more insurmountable and irreversible damage will result. Our collective regrets about what we failed to do for protecting animals' rights in the past will be moot. One way to begin is to expand the GAP and implement the GA/AP and admit all animals into the Community of Equals. It should be presupposed that at least some animal research and other activities that violate the rights of animals must not continue—the burden is on those who want to engage in these activities even if in the past they were acceptable.

My overall conclusion remains unchanged from that which I wrote a few years ago (Bekoff 1997). Specifically, if we forget that humans and other animals are all part of the same world—the more-than-human world—and if we forget that humans and animals are deeply connected at many levels of inter-action, when things go amiss in our interactions with animals, as they surely will, and animals are set apart from and inevitably below humans, I feel certain that we will miss the animals more than the animal survivors will miss us. The interconnectivity and spirit of the world will be lost forever and these losses will make for a severely impoverished universe.

[. . .]

References

Abram, D., *The Spell of the Sensuous: Perception and Language in a More-than-Human World* (New York: Pantheon Books, 1996).

Bekoff, M., "What is a 'Scale of Life?'," *Environmental Values* 1 (1992), 253–6.

Bekoff, M., "Common Sense, Cognitive Ethology and Evolution," in P. Cavaleri and P. Singer (eds), *The Great Ape Project: Equality Beyond Humanity* (London: Fourth Estate, 1993), pp. 102–8.

Bekoff, M., "Tierliebe in der Wissenschaft," in M. Tobias and K. Solisti (eds), *Ich spürte die Seele der Tiere* (Stuttgart: Kosmos, 1997).

Bekoff, M., and L. Gruen, "Animal Welfare and Individual Characteristics: A Conversation Against Speciesism," *Ethics and Behavior* 3 (1993), 163–75.

Bekoff, M., and N. Hettinger, "Animals, Nature, and Ethics," *Journal of Mammalogy* 75 (1994), 219–23.

Cavalieri, P., and Singer, P., *The Great Ape Project: Equality Beyond Humanity* (London: Fourth Estate, 1993).

Crisp, R., "Evolution and Psychological Unity," in M. Bekoff and D. Jamieson (eds), *Interpretation and Explanation in the Study of Animal Behavior, Volume II: Explanation, evolution, and adaptation* (Boulder, Colorado: Westview Press, 1990), pp. 394–413.

Davis, H., and D. Balfour (eds), *The Inevitable Bond: Examining Scientist-Animal Interactions* (New York: Cambridge University Press, 1992).

Dionys de Leeuw, A., "Contemplating the Interests of Fish," *Environmental Ethics* 18 (1996), 373–90.

Frey, R. G., "Medicine, Animal Experimentation, and the Moral Problem of Unfortunate Humans," in E. F. Paul, F. D. Miller, Jr., and J. Paul (eds), *Scientific Innovation, Philosophy, and Public Policy* (New York: Cambridge University Press, 1996), pp. 181–211.

Gluck, J. P., "Learning to see the animals again," in H. LaFollette (ed.), *Ethics in Practice: An Anthology* (Cambridge, Massachusetts: Blackwell Publishers, 1997), pp. 160–7.

LaFollette, H., and N. Shanks, *Brute Science: Dilemmas of Animal Experimentation* (New York: Routledge, 1996).

Manes, C., *Other Creations: Rediscovering the Spirituality of Animals* (New York: Doubleday, 1997).

Mukerjee, M., "Trends in Animal Research," *Scientific American* 276 (1997), 86–93.

Phillips, M. T., "Proper Names and the Social Construction of Biography: The Negative Case of Laboratory Animals," *Qualitative Sociology* 17 (1994), 119–42.

Rachels, J., *Created from Animals: The Moral Implications of Darwinism* (New York: Oxford University Press, 1990).

Rennie, J., "The Animal Question," *Scientific American* 276 (1997), 4.

Savage-Rumbaugh. E. S., "Why are We Afraid of Apes with Language?," in A. B. Scheibel and J. W. Schopf (eds), *Origin and Evolution of Intelligence* (Sudbury, Massachusetts: Jones and Bartlett, 1997), pp. 43–69.

Shapiro, K. J., *Animal Models of Human Psychology: Critique of Science, Ethics, and Policy* (Kirkland, Washington: Hogrefe and Huber, 1997).

Sober, E. "Morgan's Canon," in D. Cummins and C. Allen (eds), *The Evolution of Mind* (New York: Oxford University Press, 1998).

Taylor, P. W., *Respect for Nature: A Theory of Environmental Ethics* (Princeton, New Jersey: Princeton University Press, 1986).

Verheijen, F. J., and W. F. G. Flight., "Decapitation and Brining: Experimental Tests Show That After These Commercial Methods for Slaughtering Eel, *Anguilla Anguilla* (L.), Death is not Instantaneous," *Aquaculture Research* 28 (1997), 361–6.

Whiten, A., and R. Ham., "On the Nature and Evolution of Imitation in the Animal Kingdom: Reappraisal of a Century of Research," *Advances in the Study of Behavior* 21 (1992), 239–83.

Chapter 18

Sue Savage-Rumbaugh, William M. Fields, and Jared Taglialatela

APE CONSCIOUSNESS–HUMAN CONSCIOUSNESS: A PERSPECTIVE INFORMED BY LANGUAGE AND CULTURE[1]

Savage-Rumbaugh and her co-workers summarize recent findings that provide insights on the occurrence of consciousness in nonhuman animals. They view consciousness as a fundamental property of the universe, much like space, time, mass, etc. In particular they present the evidence for consciousness in bonobos and the findings that they are capable of comprehending human speech and employing a lexical communication system. They find that bonobos have first "person" accounts to offer of their lives. They affirm the significant power of culture on biology and as a force in evolution.

What is consciousness?

[. . .]

According to John Searle,

> consciousness refers to the state of sentience or awareness that typically begins when we wake from a dreamless sleep and then continues through the day until we fall asleep again, die, go into a coma, or otherwise become unconscious. Dreams are also a form of consciousness, though in many respects they are quite unlike normal waking states
>
> (Searle, 1998)

We accept Searle's description of consciousness and agree with the view that subjective experience must be taken seriously as an object of study. Moreover, we would observe that "consciousness cannot be understood unless it is accurately described and that reductive approaches are inherently inappropriate to this descriptive task" (Velmans, 1998). For the time being, we believe that it is useful to assume that "consciousness may be an irreducible fundamental property of the universe in the same category as space and time or mass and electric charge. [. . .] Our position is a simple assumption: consciousness is a property (Searle, 1992) which the brain manipulates in ways we might conceive of as bending, folding, focusing, or magnifying. Such contouring of consciousness is a function of the brain's typology, which we assert has been fashioned by culture. We suggest that reality is a construction of consciousness molded by forces of the brain shaped by culture.

We use the term culture in the anthropological sense, a variation of Leslie White's famous definition of culture. That is, culture is a force that has emerged which allows adaptation by the species to the environment at a rate which biology alone would not allow. We further argue that culture, language, and tools ride upon a common neural substrate. As forces, language and tools are subsets of culture.

We suggest that consciousness is quite general among animal species. The differences in what we as humans might interpret as degrees of consciousness are dependent upon the power (size) of the neural substrate to fold or bend consciousness into the appropriate reality. Thus, culture and consciousness co-construct the driving force in the evolutionary mechanism acting upon the highly plastic matter of biological life. [. . .]

Given this co-interactive framework, it is only reasonable to suspect that the culture in which an ape is reared will significantly affect the form of consciousness it develops, as well as its communicative expression of that consciousness. If reared in a human culture, ape consciousness will be molded according to a form that human beings can recognize more easily as similar to their own and thus understandable by them. Such cross-cultural rearing studies can be understood as experiments in the grafting of cultural consciousness across biological platforms. Moreover, the expectations of the human participants in such studies will, unwittingly, affect the outcome. This is because the extent to which they extend their activities of "humanness" to permit the incorporation of alternative biological platforms into their group cultural consciousness, will affect the capacity of the developing organism. Thus studies of ape competence on "human tasks" can never be pure measures of ape capacity. The expectancies and culture of the measurer will inevitably affect them. Nonetheless, they inform us with regard to ourselves, the role of our expectancies and the plasticity of apes.

Ape language: insights into human bias and cultural expectation

[. . .]

When the "Lana Project" began, the chimpanzee Washoe had learned some signs, and serious questions were beginning to surface regarding the amount of imitation that underlay her actions (Terrace *et al.*, 1979). Moreover, her signs were often inarticulate and difficult to decipher for all but those who lived and interacted with her on a daily basis. [. . .] The lexical keyboard system proposed by Duane Rumbaugh, provided a potential means of propelling apes beyond the limitations posed by these other methodologies. In addition, it offered a more accurate means of data collection as it was linked to a computer, which recorded all utterances of experimenter and ape. [. . .] The first studies left no doubt that Lana could discriminate lexigrams visually, and that she could learn the simple ordering rules sufficiently well to apply them to novel sequences. Lana could also associate different symbols with various real world people, places, and things (Rumbaugh, 1977) and the computer-collected data demonstrated that imitation was not the basis of her performance.

Like many other novel findings in science, the work with Lana raised more questions than it answered. It was not clear that Lana *always* understood what was said to her through lexigrams, particularly if the requests were somewhat unusual. It was also not clear why she sometimes made what seemed to be incomprehensible errors and formed nonsensical strings. [. . .] Lana's errors were more appropriately characterized as "puzzling" and it was often difficult to figure out what Lana was trying to say.

[. . .]

The second generation of language studies with the lexical-keyboard system attempted to compensate for some of the perceived inadequacies in Lana's semantic performance. Her errors had revealed that while she grasped the combinatorial rules of her syntax, she often did not consistently apply semantic content.

[. . .]

Consequently the ensuing effort, with two young male chimpanzees (Sherman and Austin) was directed toward the careful inculcation of single words and a more objective analysis of both semantic and pragmatic word functions as contrasted with lexical "assignment." The "meaning" of words came under intense focus, and *receptive understanding*, along with object labeling became an important component of the linguistic instruction. The social aspect of language and culture was also enriched far beyond what had been the case for Lana. And lastly, in place of working with a single subject, efforts were concentrated upon communications between two co-reared apes, Austin and Sherman (Savage-Rumbaugh, 1986).

This simple change had profound theoretical implications that are still not widely understood. *It meant that, for the first time in the field of animal language, the experimenter was removed as half of every subject-experimenter interaction.* Such a change fundamentally altered the traditional experimental psychological paradigm in which every action of an animal subject is both preceded by a structured event, (usually termed the "stimulus") and followed by a structured event (usually termed the "reinforcer").

Previous animal work with apes, dolphins, and parrots followed the experimental control paradigm. These paradigms are insufficient for either the inculcation or analysis of functional linguistic phenomena. *Linguistic communication necessarily takes place between individuals in a multiplicity of exchanges that cannot be controlled from the outside either by intentionally setting the stage of the preceding stimulus or effecting a particular reinforcing event.* If there can be said to be a "reinforcing event" for the speaker during normal conversation, it can only be that of the comprehension of the listener. If there can be said to be a stimulus event that prompts the verbal selections of the speaker, it can only be the prior utterances of the listener, which are themselves a reflection of the listener's prior comprehension.

In attempting to analyze linguistic exchanges, one inevitably comes to focus upon the exchange of meaning between participants, in a situation where "meaning" is not controlled either at the level of input, output or reward by any experimentally manipulatable variable. Consequently, as one moves from the experimenter–subject paradigm to the study of communications between two or more participants, the boundaries of the traditional approach to the study of animal behavior are pressed beyond normal limits. Finally, once the exchange of meaning is the focus of investigation, it quickly becomes apparent that what we call "meaning" cannot exist outside of a socio-cultural context. What one party's utterances "mean" to another can only be determined within a socio-culture framework that permits utterances to assume certain inter-individual expectancies and obligations. This leap into the social dynamics of language took the work beyond the "can they talk" phase into something far more complex, and began to open up the issue of what talking is all about as well as how it is that social contracts are constructed. It required new skills on the part of Sherman and Austin, skills that had been missing in Lana, and for which little, if any, behavioral evidence existed.

The work with Sherman and Austin revealed that symbolic communication of a high level, with the use of an abstract code and with mutual understanding and cooperation, was possible between non-human creatures [. . .]. It also revealed that the semantic processing of the symbolic components of the communicative system was not just lexically based and dependent upon stimulus-response associative phenomena. It was instead, semantically grounded and functionally abstract. Finally, it illustrated, for the first time in the field of animal language, the critical components of listener comprehension and listener co-operation.

[. . .]

The next phase of work pressed the boundaries of scientific method in a different way. The findings with Sherman and Austin brought forth a sensitivity to the process of comprehension as an invisible phenomenon, in the process of language acquisition. Consequently, when research efforts with Kanzi, a young bonobo, began, the emphasis was not on production but comprehension. There is no way to reward comprehension, because, in its initial stages, there is no overt behavioral indication of what is taking place. This made it essential to move away from any type of training.

[. . .]

The bonobo's capacity to acquire high level linguistic skills in essentially the same manner as a child, albeit more slowly, revealed that the burden of linguistic development was carried by comprehension not production (Savage-Rumbaugh *et al.*, 1986). It is especially important that comprehension emerged in contextually meaningful situations, with many variables, not in repetitive training sessions with only a few variables characteristic.

Language competency appeared in Kanzi through an osmotic process in which caretakers passed on their linguistic culture without awareness or intent. These findings raised, for the first time, the serious possibility that bonobos possessed a sentience similar in kind, if not degree, to our own. It also followed logically that this sentience had gone unrecognized in field studies simply because we could not easily grasp the highly abstract and symbolic nature of their communications in the wild (Savage-Rumbaugh *et al.*, 1996b).

Because Kanzi's mode of acquisition was very different from that of other linguistically tutored animals, his linguistic output was dramatically changed as well. Analysis of his utterance corpus revealed a basic comprehension of syntactical ordering rules as well as a comprehension of grammatical classes (Greenfield and Savage-Rumbaugh 1991). But more than this, his understanding encompassed all manner of novel events and even of metaphor. His understanding of language informed his interpretation of real world events and his broadened capacity to interpret and appropriately classify real world events informed his linguistic comprehension in a boot strapping effect. An example of this was the ease with which Kanzi learned to flake stone tools given a modicum of both visual and verbal instruction. Similar attempts by other apes required long and arduous conditioning and shaping regimens (Toth *et al.*, 1993).

Because Kanzi's achievements went far beyond the accomplishments of Lana, Sherman and Austin, it became essential to determine the degree to which these remarkable capacities were a function of Kanzi's species versus a function of the unique rearing circumstances surrounding his development. Kanzi's rearing had taken place in a free-form captive environment modeled upon the type of existence a young bonobo might experience in the wild. This contrasted with the formal training regimens encountered by Sherman, Austin and Lana. Kanzi's linguistic accomplishments raised two possibilities. The first was that bonobos and human beings somehow shared a peculiar and unique genetic heritage for linguistic competency, and that studies of wild bonobos had simply failed to reveal the true abstract nature of their communication system. The other possibility was that something about the unstructured socio-cultural approach—with its absence of training and its focus upon comprehension—facilitated language in a manner that classical learning approaches did not and could not.

Kanzi's culture was characterized by many objects and by a variety of participants, including human beings who served as caretakers, but also by many others. There were repairmen who cleaned the lab, fixed the cages, and repaired the bridges in the field. [. . .] But Kanzi's world was not solely a human one; it was also "peopled" by Matata who was raised as a wild bonobo in the Congo. Across time, as Matata produced more offspring, Kanzi's world grew to include many nonlinguistically competent siblings who multiplied in number and began to form a bonobo community.

Kanzi thus developed as a being within a *Pan paniscus/Homo sapiens* socio-cultural world. That is, as a bicultural entity who learned multiple of ways of relating to and communicating with others in both his bonobo and human cultures. His linguistic acts were fully, intimately and irrevocably embedded within both these cultures. Moreover, his behavior indicated an awareness that his biological mother could not fully relate to, or trust, many of his human caretakers. The same was true of the majority of his human caretakers; they could not completely understand or adequately relate to the culture and ways of his bonobo mother. Kanzi served, and continues to serve, as something of a liaison between these two cultures in ways that remain to be adequately documented. He will, for example, often employ the keyboard to request food for his mother and siblings who do not know the lexigrams.

Because Kanzi's language development was enmeshed within a culture, his life and communications evidenced a richness and depth that transcended the symbolic communications of Sherman, Austin and Lana. Kanzi became able to "mean" in a variety of ways. He also appeared to understand that symbolic meaning is something that can be constructed between individuals in the act of social engagement. He seemed to recognize as well that the "meanings" constructed through joint action develop a history, expectancies and even a certain necessity of being, once undertaken in a legitimate fashion. But Kanzi's very existence made it necessary to determine the relative effects that biology and environment had played in his development.

Consequently, the ensuing research project sought to separate the species variable from the environmental variable by co-rearing a bonobo (Panbanisha) and a chimpanzee (Panzee) in an environment that was essentially the same as that encountered by Kanzi. However, unlike Kanzi, these two apes were always together and therefore always inevitably exerting some indeterminable degree of influence over the development of the other. By introducing two additional apes to the environment built around Kanzi, the cultural aspects of the work expanded greatly. In addition, Kanzi himself provided a model for the behavioral and linguistic development that was very different from the one that Matata had provided for him. He could use the keyboard—she could not. Thus it was not really possible to precisely replicate Kanzi's experiences with additional apes. What we did do was to attempt to avoid the structured training, the emphasis upon production and the failure to ground the language within a rich socio-cultural environment that had characterized earlier work with Lana, Sherman and Austin. We concentrated upon comprehension in cultural context, we continued to make natural spoken English the main route of linguistic input and we spent as much time as possible in the natural forest setting.

Like Kanzi, Panbanisha and Panzee experienced a social environment within which keyboard usage was a daily affair by human caretakers. Because Kanzi was already lexically competent, the keyboard, which had begun with only 1 lexigram in his case, had grown to a board of 256 symbols. Thus the keyboard could not grow with Panbanisha and Panzee, as it did with Kanzi. If Kanzi was to be a part of their linguistic world, his 256 symbols had to be present as well. Consequently, Panbanisha and Panzee were exposed to 256 lexigrams utilized in complex communications from the first week of life. Perhaps for this reason, their acquisition of these symbols was much more rapid than Kanzi's. Similarly, their combinations appeared far earlier and Panbanisha composed more complex utterances of greater duration than Kanzi, although Panzee did not. [. . .] Nonetheless, in mapping onto all the major capacities that were observed in Kanzi, but previously absent in Lana, Sherman and Austin, Panzee clearly demonstrated that Kanzi's skill was not limited to bonobos. Instead, it was a function of his early exposure to the bicultural social environment.

The process by which Kanzi, Panbanisha and Panzee acquired their lexicons include components of rapid mapping of sound to referent, similar to those utilized by human children (Lyn and Savage-Rumbaugh, 2000; Lyn et al., 1998). In addition, it has been found that no interaction with the ape itself is required, it is sufficient to speak to other individuals about a novel object in front of the ape. New words are learned and understood even when the apes appear to be disinterested in the conversation (Lyn and Savage-Rumbaugh, in press; Lyn et al., 1998). The cognitive and social processes that were found in Kanzi's proto grammatical utterances also characterized those of Panbanisha and Panzee, suggesting that there exist, within the genus Pan, basic cognitive processes that permit language acquisition in a human culture (Greenfield et al., in press). Work with wild bonobos supports this position through the finding that bonobos employ intentional alteration of vegetation in a symbolic fashion to communicate to other bonobos who are following them (Savage-Rumbaugh et al., 1996a). These findings are the first to indicate learned non-human intra-species symbolic communication across the domain of time.

Like Kanzi, Panbanisha and Panzee also attempted to produce human-like vocal sounds. Panzee gained far more voluntary motor control over the ability to produce low frequency sounds than either Kanzi or Panbanisha, suggesting that something about the vocal tract of Pan troglodytes is more amenable to the lower registrar than the bonobo vocal tract. Recent work has shown that Panbanisha has the ability to decode some sounds produced by Kanzi and to translate them to us.

It was not only the linguistic aspects of the Pan paniscus/Homo sapiens culture that were passed on to Panbanisha and Panzee. They acquired many tool-use skills as well. For example, Panbanisha acquired the capacity to flake stone by observing Kanzi. But unlike Kanzi she began, with precision, to employ the technique of bimanual percussion. Even though Kanzi had observed his human models demonstrate this technique, and even though he had attempted to emulate the bimanual technique, he did not become proficient in that skill without passing through a number of phases. [. . .] Whereas Kanzi developed this skill over a two-year period, Panbanisha's bimanual technique was oriented toward the edges of the stone almost from the beginning. It may be that observation of a bonobo model provided the needed input to permit Panbanisha to propel rapidly into direct aimed bimanual percussion.

[. . .]

The fact that a competent bonobo model existed for many aspects of Panbanisha's development, coupled with the observation that in nearly every aspect of language and tool use Panbanisha made more rapid progress than Kanzi, may be attributable to the modeling he provided. However, it should be noted, that Panbanisha did not appear to be motivated to watch Kanzi or to attempt to do things she observed him do in any sort of imitative manner. She preferred to spend her time with human female caretakers and with her bonobo mother Matata and seemed more prone to actively observe and emulate their actions. [. . .] All three apes that are linguistically competent (Kanzi, Panbanisha, and Panzee) have also been shown to exhibit complex skills in planning travel routes (Menzel, in preparation).

PET scans done to compare Lana's linguistic capacity with that of Panzee revealed that Panzee's information processing skills were more highly elaborated and much more human-like than those of Lana. These findings regarding cortical function correspond tightly to the rearing and behavioral differences encountered between Lana and Panzee. They also reveal that the question of "do apes have language" is far too simple. Both Lana and Panzee "have" language to a certain degree, but their functional competencies vary greatly, as does the neurological processing of verbal material.

In sum, the work with Panzee and Panbanisha demonstrated that the powerful variable was that of rearing, not species. In an environment that did not require training, Panzee learned language faster than Sherman, Austin or Lana. She also comprehended spoken English while they did not. She produced more novel combinations and far more spontaneous utterances. Unlike them, she learned lexigrams independently of keyboard position.

The issue is no longer one of data, the adequacy of data, of potential cueing or experimenter effects, or of conditioning. In addition the issue is no longer that of "apes" in the general sense, but rather that one that must take into account, in detail, the socio-cultural experience of *each* ape, in determining how its performance on the continuum of linguistic competency is to be evaluated. The paradigms of the past, in which animal cognition is viewed as riding upon a different substrate than human cognition, are breaking down and the research at LRC has been a component of this change (Tomasello and Call, 1997).

[. . .]

The importance of the research to date is not only that it offers the basic outline of a new paradigm for understanding the mind of the other, but also in addition it provides techniques and data to support the approach.

The long standing philosophical issue of how meaning emerges has been significantly informed by work with apes, in a manner that could never have occurred, if all language studies were limited to *Homo sapiens* (Savage-Rumbaugh, 1990, 1991; Savage-Rumbaugh *et al.*, 1993). This work has clarified the Quinean problem and laid open the road for new insights into that which we give the name of "language." It is beginning to reveal that "meaning" can be packed into any gesture, glance, lexicon, or printed symbol. The packing of "meaning" requires inter-subjectivity—the mutual attribution of intentionality and a joint history, informed by mutually shared affective experiences. These components of communication are not limited to *Homo sapiens*, nor are they a peculiarity of the human capacity for reason.

[. . .]

Consciousness in other minds

Detecting consciousness: We agree with Searle's principle of connection between consciousness and the intrinsic intentionality that underpins linguistic meaning. The time has come to break away from views which hold that meaning, reference, and intentionality are not measurable phenomena and hence are closed to scientific investigation. Intentionality is systematically observable. While we do not ignore needs, wants, and desires as matters of intentionality, our current research with great apes emphasizes first the

> measurable sequence[s] of complex monitoring responses in which the [person]: (a) checks to see that a listener is present before emitting a communicative signal, (b) engages the attention of the listener before emitting this signal, (c) emits a signal that requires a specific behavioral or verbal response on the part of the listener. [and] (d) monitors the listener's response visually and auditorially . . .
>
> (Savage-Rumbaugh, 1986)

More importantly, we recognize that intentionality has a dynamic quality when intentional processes emerge between speaker and listener. With respect to our research, we do engage dialogs, i.e., intentional processes between listeners and speakers in which both are human and nonhuman primates.

[. . .]

Regarding the concept of "degree of consciousness" as stated, we reject this notion. We believe that the metaphors of bending and folding that we have applied to consciousness are a process that the neural substrate performs in the creation of reality. We reiterate our introductory remark, culture controls the topology of the neural substrate and therefore we believe culture is driving speciation. If we are correct, the brain of a nonhuman primate like Kanzi, reared in a *Pan/Homo* culture, capable of understanding spoken English and uttering lexical English counterparts, should possess a brain which is morphologically different than a brain of a feral bonobo or a bonobo reared without human language, culture and tools.

Our experience with great apes convinces us that they in fact possess consciousness, for they have first "person" accounts to offer of their lives. As a matter critical to the survival of scientific methodology, "We accept the[se] first person accounts and . . . the irreducible nature of experience, while at the same time refusing both a dualistic concession and a pessimistic surrender" to the debate regarding consciousness issues (Varela, 1998) or animal language research. We emphasize the power of cultural forces upon the neural substrate of biology and the significant role of culture as a force in evolution.

[. . .]

Note

1   From the Symposium *Animal Consciousness: Historical, Theoretical, and Empirical Perspectives* presented at the Annual Meeting of the Society for Integrative and Comparative Biology, 6–10 January 1999, at Denver, Colorado.

References

Greenfield, P., H. Lyn, and E. S. Savage-Rumbaugh. (In press). Semiotic Combinations in Pan: A cross-species comparison of communication in a chimpanzee and a bonobo.

Greenfield, P. M., and E. S. Savage-Rumbaugh. 1991. Imitation, grammatical development and the invention of protogrammar by an ape. In N. Krasnegor, D. M. Rumbaugh, M. Studdert-Kennedy, and R. L. Schiefelbusch (eds.), *Biological and behavioral determinants of language development*, pp. 235–58 Lawrence Erlbaum Associates, Inc, Hillsdale, NJ.

Lyn, H. and E. S. Savage-Rumbaugh, 2000. Observational Word Learning by Two Bonobos. *Language and Communication* 20:255–73.

Lyn, H., E. S. Savage-Rumbaugh, and D. Rumbaugh. 1998. Observational word learning in bonobos (*Pan paniscus*). *American Journal of Primatology*, 45:193 (Abstract).

Rumbaugh, D. M. 1977 *Language learning by a chimpanzee: The Lana project.* Academic Press, NY.

Savage-Rumbaugh, E. S. 1986. *Ape language: From conditioned response to symbol.* Columbia University Press, NY.

Savage-Rumbaugh, E. S. 1990. Language acquisition in a nonhuman species: Implications for the innateness debate. Special Issue: The idea of innateness: Effects on language and communication research. *Developmental Psychobiology* 23(7): 599–620.

Savage-Rumbaugh, E. S. 1991. Language learning in the bonobo: How and why they learn. In Norman A. Krasnegor (ed.), *Biological and behavioral determinants of language development*, pp. 209–33: Lawrence Erlbaum Associates, Inc., Hillsdale, NJ.

Savage-Rumbaugh, E. S., K. McDonald, R. A. Sevcik, W. D. Hopkins, and E. Rubert. 1986. Spontaneous symbol acquisition and communicative use by pygmy chimpanzees (*Pan paniscus*). *J Exp Psychol.* (General), 115(3):211–35.

Savage-Rumbaugh, E. S., J. Murphy, R. A. Sevcik, D. M. Rumbaugh, K. E. Brakke, and S. Williams. 1993. Language comprehension in ape and child. Monographs of the Society for Research in Child Development, 58(233):1–242.

Savage-Rumbaugh, E. S., S. L. Williams, T. Furuichi, and T. Kano. 1996a. Language perceived: Paniscus branches out. In B. McGrew, L. Marchant, and T. Nishida (eds.), *Great ape societies*, pp. 173–84. Cambridge University Press, London.

Savage-Rumbaugh, E. S., S. L. Williams, T. Furuichi, and T. Kano. 1996b. Language perceived: Paniscus branches out. In W. C. McGrew, L. F. Marchant, and T. Nishida (eds.), *Great ape societies*, pp. 173–84. Cambridge University Press, NY.

Searle, J. 1992. *The rediscovery of the mind.* MIT Press, Cambridge, MA.

Searle, J. 1998. How to study consciousness scientifically. In S. R. Hammeroff, A. W. Kaszniak, and A. C. Scott (eds.). *Toward a science of consciousness II: The second Tucson discussions and debates*, pp. 14–29. MIT Press, Cambridge, MA.

Terrace, H. S., L. A. Petitto, R. J. Sanders, and T. G. Bever, 1979. Can an ape create a sentence? *Science,* 206(4421):891–902.

Tomasello, M. and J. Call. 1997. *Primate cognition.* Oxford University Press, NY.

Toth, N., *et al.* 1993. Pan the tool-maker: Investigations into the stone tool-making and tool-using capabilities of a bonobo (*Pan Paniscus*). *Journal of Archeological Science.* 20:81–91.

Velmans, M. 1998. Goodbye to reductionism. In S. R. Hammeroff, A. W. Kaszniak, and A. C. Scott (eds.). *Toward a science of consciousness II: The second Tucson discussions and debates*, pp. 44–52. MIT Press, Cambridge, MA.

Chapter 19

A. Whiten, J. Goodall, W.C. McGrew, T. Nishida, V. Reynolds, Y. Sugiyama, C.E.G. Tutin, R.W. Wrangham, and C. Boesch

CULTURES IN CHIMPANZEES

Whiten and co-workers summarize numerous years of research on chimpanzee culture. They found that 39 different behavior patterns, including tool use, grooming and courtship, were customary in some communities but absent in others; ecological explanations could be discounted. They noted that the combined repertoire of these behavior patterns was a highly distinctive feature found in human cultures, but previously not observed in nonhuman species.

A S AN INCREASING number of field studies of chimpanzees (*Pan troglodytes*) have achieved long-term status across Africa, differences in the behavioural repertoires described have become apparent that suggest there is significant cultural variation[1-7]. Here we present a systematic synthesis of this information from the seven most long-term studies, which together have accumulated 151 years of chimpanzee observation. This comprehensive analysis reveals patterns of variation that are far more extensive than have previously been documented for any animal species except human.[8-11] We find that 39 different behaviour patterns, including tool usage, grooming and courtship behaviours, are customary or habitual in some communities but are absent in others where ecological explanations have been discounted. Among mammalian and avian species, cultural variation has previously been identified only for single behaviour patterns, such as the local dialects of song-birds.[12,13] The extensive, multiple variations now documented for chimpanzees are thus without parallel. Moreover, the combined repertoire of these behaviour patterns in each chimpanzee community is itself highly distinctive, a phenomenon characteristic of human cultures[14] but previously unrecognized in non-human species.

Culture is defined in very different ways in different academic disciplines.[15] At one extreme, some cultural anthropologists insist on linguistic mediation, so that culture is constrained to be a uniquely human phenomenon.[16] In the biological sciences, a more inclusive definition is accepted, in which the significance of cultural transmission is recognized as one of only two important processes that can generate evolutionary change: inter-generation transmission of behaviour may occur either genetically or through social learning, with processes of variation and selection shaping biological evolution in the first case and cultural evolution in the second. From this perspective, a cultural behaviour is one that is transmitted repeatedly through social or observational learning to become a population-level characteristic.[17] By this definition, cultural differences (often known as 'traditions' in ethology) are well established phenomena in the animal kingdom and are maintained through a variety of social transmission mechanisms.[18] Well documented examples include dialects in song-birds,[12,13] sweet-potato washing by Japanese macaques (*Macaca fuscata*) at Koshima,[19] and stone handling by Japanese macaques at Arashiyama.[20] However, each case refers to variation in only a single behaviour pattern.

Tabulations of population differences amongst chimpanzees have indicated that multiple behavioural variants may exist.[2-7] However, these tabulations have been based on published reports, which, although they record the presence of behaviours, remain problematic in three respects: they are incomplete; they frequently do not clarify the extent to which each behaviour pattern is habitual in the community; and they do not systematically document the absence of behaviour patterns present elsewhere. We therefore adopted a different strategy in our attempt to provide a definitive assessment of what is now known of chimpanzee cultural variation.

Phase 1 of the study established a comprehensive list of candidate cultural variants, which are behaviours suspected by research workers to be specific to particular chimpanzee populations. Beginning with a list drawn from literature review by A.W. and C.B., the research directors of the major chimpanzee field projects . . . added and defined unpublished candidate patterns. The patterns were then split and lumped as appropriate. This complex, collaborative and iterative process produced a listing of candidate cultural variants that were fully and consensually defined. . . . The scope of this list, differentiating 65 categories of behaviour, represents a unique record of the inventiveness of wild chimpanzees.

In phase 2, the research directors assigned to each of these behaviour categories one of the following six codes, as applicable at their site: (1) customary, for which the behaviour occurs in all or most able-bodied members of at least one age-sex class (such as adult males); (2) habitual, for which the behaviour is not customary but has occurred repeatedly in several individuals, consistent with some degree of social transmission; (3) present, for which the behaviour is neither customary nor habitual but is clearly identi-fied; (4) absent, for which the behaviour has not been recorded and no ecological explanation is apparent; (5) ecological explanation, for which absence is explicable because of a local ecological feature; and (6) unknown, for which the behaviour has not been recorded, but this may be due to inadequacy of relevant observational opportunities. These codings were cross-checked and confirmed by senior colleagues at each site. Our results are for the seven chimpanzee groups with the most long-term observation record, so the 'unknown' code was seldom applicable. These studies bring together a total of 151 years of direct observation (range 8–38 years), so our data summarize the enormous increase in our knowledge of chimpanzee behaviour achieved in the latter half of this century.

[. . .]

The profile of codings of particular interest with respect to cultural variation is that in which behaviours are recorded as customary or habitual in some communities, yet absent at others. Three other classes of profile need to be recognized and discriminated from this.

First, seven behaviours proposed as potential cultural variants in phase 1 were shown instead to be either customary or habitual in all communities. Second, 16 patterns failed to achieve habitual status in any community. The third class includes profiles in which all cases of absence are explicable by local conditions; just three cases were identified. Absence of algae-fishing can be explained by the rarity of algae, and any absence of ground night-nesting by high predator risk. Use of an additional stone to balance an anvil (anvil-prop) occurs only at Bossou, but it is not expected elsewhere because stone anvils are either not used or (at Taï) are embedded in the ground.

The remaining behaviours are absent at some sites but are customary or habitual at others. We have found 39 such behavioural variants, significantly more than previously suspected for chimpanzees.[1-6] We know of no comparable variation in other non-human species, although no systematic study of this kind appears to have been attempted.

We arrive at a similar comparative conclusion when we examine the overall profiles of cultural variants in the different communities. Some customary and habitual patterns are unique to certain com-munities, but others are shared between two or more communities, so the clusters of variants that characterize each community are not mutually exclusive. Nevertheless, the profiles of each community are distinctively different, each with a pattern comprising many behavioural variants. These patterns vary as much between sites associated with the same subspecies [. . .] as between subspecies themselves. The only major difference between the western and eastern populations is that nut-cracking occurs only in the west, although the fact that this behaviour terminates abruptly at the Sassandra-N'Zo river within the range of the *verus* subspecies shows that it is culturally, rather than genetically, transmitted.[21] The patterns can thus be seen to resemble those in human societies, in which differences between cultures are constituted by a multiplicity of variations in technology and social customs.[14] It remains to be shown whether chimpanzees are unique in this respect, or whether any other animal species, if studied in the same way, would reveal qualitatively similar patterns.

Other comparisons between human and non-human animal cultures have focused on the cognitive processes involved, arguing that if processes of human cultural transmission, such as imitative learning and teaching, are not found in animals, then culture in animals is merely an analogue of that in humans, rather than homologous with it.[22,23] Our data agree with experimental studies that have shown that chimpanzees copy the methods used by others to manipulate and open artificial 'fruits' designed as analogues of wild foods.[24,25] These experimental designs show differential copying of each of two quite different methods used to process the foods. Similarly, some of the differences between communities described here represent not only the contrast between habitual versus absent, but also the contrast between different versions of an otherwise similar pattern. Examples include cases of tool use, such as two different methods of ant-dip; in the first of these, a long wand is held in one hand and a ball of ants is wiped off with the other, whereas in the second method a short stick is held in one hand and used to collect a smaller number of ants, which are transferred directly to the mouth. Other examples occur in social behaviour, such as the variants used to deal with ectoparasites discovered during grooming, with leaf-squash, leaf-inspect and index-hit occurring in different communities. It is difficult to see how such behaviour patterns could be perpetuated by social learning processes simpler than imitation, the most commonly suggested alternative to which is stimulus enhancement, in which the attention of an observer is merely drawn to a relevant item such as a stick.[26] But this does not mean that imitation is the only mechanism at work. Experimental studies on the acquisition of tool-use and food-processing skills by both children and captive chimpanzees indicate that there is a complex mix of imitation, other forms of social learning, and individual learning.[24,25,27-30]

Our results show that chimpanzees, our closest sister-species, have rich behavioural complexity. However, although this study represents the definitive state of knowledge at present, we must expect that more extended study will elaborate on this picture. Every long-term study of wild chimpanzees has identified new behavioural variants.

Notes

1   McGrew, W. C. and Tutin, C. E. G. Evidence for a social custom in wild chimpanzees? *Man* 13, 234–51 (1978).

2   Goodall, J. *The Chimpanzees of Gombe: Patterns of Behavior* (Harvard Univ. Press, Cambridge. Massachusetts, 1986).

3   Nishida, T. *The Chimpanzees of the Mahale Mountains: Sexual and Life History Strategies* (Tokyo Univ. Press, Tokyo, 1990).

4   McGrew, W. C. *Chimpanzee Material Culture Implications for Human Evolution* (Cambridge Univ. Press, Cambridge, 1992).

5   Sugiyama, Y. in *The Use of Tools by Human and Non-human Primates* (eds Berthelet, A. and Chavaillon, J.) 175–87 (Clarendon, Oxford, 1993).

6   Wrangham, R. W., McGrew, W. C., de Waal, E. B. M. and Heiltne, P. G. (eds) *Chimpanzee Cultures* (Harvard Univ. Press, Cambridge, Massachusetts, 1994).

7   Boesch, C. The emergence of cultures among wild chimpanzees. *Proc. Br. Acad.* 88, 251–68 (1996).

8   Bonner, J. T. *The Evolution of Culture in Animals* (Princeton Univ. Press, New Jersey, 1980).

9   Mundinger, P. C. Animal cultures and a general theory of cultural evolution. *Ethol. Sociobiol.* 1, 183–223 (1980).

10   Lefebvre, L. and Palamets, B. in *Social Learning: Psychological and Biological Perspectives* (eds Zentail, T. and Galef, B. G. Jr) 141–64 (Erlbaum, Hillsdale, New Jersey, 1988).

11   McGrew, W. C. Culture in non-human primates? *Annu. Rev. Anthropol.* 27, 301–28 (1998).

12   Marler, P. and Tamura, M. Song 'dialects' in three populations of white-crowned sparrows. *Science* 146, 1483–86 (1964).

13   Catchpole, C. K. and Slater, P. J. B. *Bird Song: Themes and Variations* (Cambridge Univ. Press, Cambridge, 1995).

14   Murdock, G. P. *Ethnographic Atlas* (Univ. Pittsburgh Press, Pittsburgh, 1967).

15   Kroeber, A. L. and Kluckhohn, C. *Culture: A Critical Review of Concepts and Definitions* (Random House, New York, 1963).

16   Bloch, M. Language, anthropology and cognitive science. *Man* 26, 183–98 (1991).

17   Nishida, T. in *Primate Societies* (eds Smuts, B. B., Cheney, D. L., Seyfarth, R. M., Wrangham, R. W. and Struhsaker, T. T.) 462–74 (Univ. Chicago Press, Chicago, 1987).

18   Whiten, A. and Ham, R. On the nature of imitation in the animal kingdom: reappraisal of a century of research. *Adv. Study Behav.* 21, 239–83 (1992).

19   Imanishi, K. Identification: A process of enculturation in the subhuman society of *Macaca fuscata. Primates* 1, 1–29 (1957).

20   Huffman, M. in *Social Learning in Animals: The Roots of Culture* (eds Heyes, C. M. and Galef, B. G.) 267–89 (Academic Press, London, 1996).

21   Boesch, C., Marchesi, P., Marchesi, N., Fruth, B. and Joulian, F., Is nut cracking in wild chimpanzees a cultural behaviour? *J. Hum. Evol.* 26, 325–38 (1994).

22   Galef, B. G. Jr. The question of animal culture. *Hum. Nature* 3, 157–78 (1992).

23   Tomasello, M., Kruger, A. C. and Ratner, H. H. Cultural learning. *Behav. Brain Sci.* 16, 495–552 (1993).

24   Whiten, A., Custance, D. M., Gotner, J.-C., Teixidor, F. and Bard, K. A. Imitative learning of artificial fruit-processing in children (*Homo sapiens*) and chimpanzees (*Pan troglodytes*). *J. Comp. Psychol.* 110, 3–14 (1996).

25   Whiten, A. Imitation of the sequential structure of actions by chimpanzees (*Pan troglodytes*). *J. Comp. Psychol.* 112, 270–81 (1998).

26   Spence, K. W. Experimental studies of learning and the mental processes in infra-human primates. *Psychol. Bull.* 34, 306–50 (1957).

27   Sumita, K., Kitahara-Frisch, J. and Norikoshi, K. The acquisition of stone tool use in captive chimpanzees. *Primates* 26, 168–81 (1985).

28   Tomasello, M., Davis, Dasilva, M., Camak, L. and Bard, K. Observational learning of tool-use by young chimpanzees. *Hum. Evol.* 2, 175–83 (1997).

29   Paquett, D. Discovering and learning tool-use for fishing honey by captive chimpanzees. *Hum. Evol.* 7, 17–30 (1992).

30   Nagell, K., Olguin, K. and Tomasello, M. Processes of social learning in the tool use of chimpanzees (*Pan troglodytes*) and children (*Homo sapiens*). *J. Comp. Psychol.* 107, 174–86 (1993).

Chapter 20

Juan Carlos Gómez

ARE APES PERSONS? THE CASE FOR PRIMATE INTERSUBJECTIVITY

Gómez argues that apes can perceive others as having intentions (third-person modality) and also can perceive themselves in relationships with others involving mutual intentions (second-person modality). Second-person modality is a feature Gómez believes qualifies apes to be characterized as "persons." He does not argue that apes possess a metarepresentational ability to be aware of their own personhood, but rather possess a special kind of mutual-awareness. They are persons who do not describe themselves as persons, but may act and feel as persons and can recognize themselves and others as individual subjects capable of feeling and behaving intersubjectively.

[. . .]

THE PHILOSOPHER Daniel Dennett (1976) suggests a set of Hcriteria to distinguish persons. His "conditions of personhood" can be summarized into two clusters of cognitive features that are characteristic of persons: a first cluster amounts to being an intentional agent, and a second cluster involves the ability to understand that others are intentional agents as well. Persons are, first of all, *intentional agents*, that is to say, creatures whose behavior is governed, not by external stimuli and blindly learned contingencies of reinforcement or punishment, but by internal representations that allow them to follow *goals* with alternative *means* and generate *expectations* about events, and react to these expectations before the actual events have happened. Apes seem to fare reasonably well in relation to these criteria.

But in Dennett's account, persons must also be capable of understanding that other creatures are intentional agents like themselves; that is to say, a person's representations of the external world should include representations of other creatures' representations; or, in other words, a person should understand that the external world is made, among other things, of the *internal worlds* better known as "minds" of other creatures. This ability of representing representations has come to be known as having a *metarepresentational* ability.

Furthermore, and again following Dennett's detailed discussion, persons should also understand that the representations entertained by their fellow creatures may include representations of other creatures' representations, i.e., that others have a metarepresentational ability too.

[. . .]

Intersubjectivity versus "theory of mind"

Dennett's analysis tries to capture an essential feature of persons: their ability to reciprocally recognize each other's intentionality (or, what is the same, each other's mental states). For him, "recognizing" seems to be synonymous with "representing explicitly" each other's mental states. But would it not be possible to engage in this mutual recognition without explicitly representing the intentions of others as internal mental states? Several authors have tried to explore this possibility and have referred to this form of interpersonal mutuality as *intersubjectivity* (Trevarthen, 1979, 1980; Hobson, 1993). The idea is that subjects (intentional agents, in Dennett's terminology) can coordinate their "subjectivities" (i.e., their mental states) with other creatures' subjectivities (i.e., other creatures' mental states) without having recourse to metarepresentations or any other sort of explicit representation of mental states as internal properties of subjects. For example, Trevarthen (1979, 1980) asserts that during their first year of life human infants achieve inter-subjectivity with their caregivers through emotional/expressive interactions that do not require any representations of their underlying mental states. Infants *feel* the subjectivity of others in the emotional and expressive behaviors displayed in their face-to-face interactions with adults. Hobson (1990, 1993) developed a similar view to oppose the "distorting cognitivist frame" advanced by the theory-of-mind approach to intersubjectivity and personhood. In his view, human infants "find themselves relating to people in ways that are special to people" long before they are capable of any metarepresentational ability. Indeed, the metarepresentational understanding of others as persons is built upon the solid foundations provided by this more primitive ability to *relate with* others as persons.

In summary, these authors assert that there is an emotional, expressive, pre-reflective intersubjectivity that precedes the "intellectual", metarepresentational intersubjectivity of Dennett and other students of "theory of mind" abilities (see Gómez, 1999, for a more detailed comparison of approaches). The problem for this approach is to offer a more precise characterization of the mechanisms and features of this earlier form of intersubjectivity. Let me offer you my own version of how this can be achieved in relation to the problem of nonhuman primate intersubjectivity.

As I understand it, this expressive intersubjectivity is not based upon a distinction between external behaviors and internal mental states. For example, an expression of fear is not understood by the young infant as being an index of an internal emotion that causes its external manifestation. Similarly, an expression of attention (e.g., gazing to a target) need not be represented as an indication of an internal mental state that causes that gazing behavior. Fear and attention are experienced as properties of behaviors that are inseparable from those behaviors. They are like colors that are not conceived of as internal essences of objects, but just as properties (dynamic properties, in the case of emotional and cognitive expressions) that may appear or not in the other creatures.

An important characteristic of this intersubjectivity is that it typically appears in face to face inter-actions. The subjectivity of the other is not understood in an abstract, third-person way, but in a concrete, second-person mode. Others are not understood as persons because we infer from their behaviors that they must have intentions and ideas about other people's intentions, but because we are capable of engaging with them in specific patterns of intersubjective interaction that include emotional and expressive behaviors. What matters is that we are capable not only of engaging with them in intersubjective inter-actions, but also of representing and understanding them as capable of engaging in these interactions. Persons are capable of representing others as "second persons", i.e., as creatures capable of engaging in intersubjective encounters. Let me clarify what I mean with an example involving apes.

Understanding mental states without metarepresentations

In Gómez (1990) I presented a study in which I claimed to provide an analysis of the emergence of "attention understanding" in a hand-reared gorilla who, in her interactions with human people, developed the skill to look at the eyes of the person at crucial moments of the interaction. There I made it clear that the kind of "understanding of attention" I was attributing to the gorilla was a *practical* one, equivalent to what Piaget (1936) termed "sensorimotor intelligence" in his explanation of early object manipulation and tool use in human infants. This practical understanding of attention implied the gorilla's ability to *see* the expressions of attention of others as causal links that connect her behavior with their behavior. I attributed to the gorilla the possession of a "sensorimotor concept of subjects" not only as entities that are capable of acting by themselves (what some authors call "animacy"), but also as creatures whose executive behavior is causally connected with their perceptual states, as expressed, in this case, in their gaze behavior. Specifically, I proposed that, in the same way that apes seem to understand (in a practical or sensorimotor way) that when using a stick to retrieve an object they must establish physical contact between the tool and the object and apply certain forces to them, they also understand (in a similarly practical or sensorimotor way) that to exert an influence upon other organisms by means of gestures, first they must establish "attention contact" with them and then produce gestures and expressions addressed to their attention. There need be no understanding of the attention of the other as an internal mental state, no understanding of the internal cognitive effects provoked by perception, no abstract conception of intentions and internal mental experiences: all they need is a definite differentiation between physical objects and social subjects, that incorporates not only the understanding of them as animate and goal-directed (cf. Tomasello and Call, 1997), but also as *subjective* entities.

[. . .]

For example, attention is a mental state. It has, however, the interesting property of being indissociable from the behavior of looking. It is impossible that I am visually attending to an object if I am not physically looking at it[1] Visual attention is, therefore, a mental state that closely corresponds to external behaviors. In contrast, knowledge and beliefs can never be directly perceived. There is therefore the possibility that an organism without metarepresentational abilities can nonetheless understand and represent attention as an externally expressed subjective state. Such an organism could generate representations of other organisms attending to particular targets, i.e., being in particular *subjective* relations to a target. Apes may see, remember, represent others intending things and attending to things. This would be equivalent to seeing other creatures as intentional agents. This non-metarepresentational way of perceiving and representing others would capture the most basic property of intentionality: being *about* something. Apes would be perceiving others' actions and attentional and expressive displays as being about objects and targets in general. The intentionality is attributed to, seen in, the actions and bodily attitudes of others, not their minds—those mysterious immaterial entities we humans are used to postulate in our dealings with each other.[2]

This view of what it is like to attribute intentionality without metarepresentation could open the doors of personhood *à la* Dennett to apes—and any other animal that demonstrates the ability to perceive others as subjects in the above sense.

However, there is still an obstacle. According to Dennett, what counts for being a person is not only to be able to see others as intentional agents (or subjects, in my own terminology), but also to see others as capable of adopting the intentional stance in mutual relation to oneself. It is the entry into this recursive circle of mutual intentional attributions that singles out real persons from non-persons. Could creatures endowed exclusively with the sort of non-metarepresentational attribution of intentionality that I have suggested cross the doors of mutual recursive intentionality?

Intersubjectivity in the second person

Let's return to the case of visual attention. In other types of attention (e.g., auditory or olfactive), the act of someone attending to something can only be perceived in a modality that is different from the one in which the organism is displaying its attention: for example, I cannot hear you listening to me. However, the act of attending visually is visually perceivable itself. Thus when we attend to the visual attention of someone, this very act reveals *ipso facto* our own attention; or conversely, when someone attends to our visual attention, his/her own visual attention is overtly displayed for the benefit of any beholder . . . including whoever is his/her current target of attention. Indeed when two organisms happen to be attending to each other's direction of attention, a peculiar pattern is generated in which their respective gazes meet; this pattern is known as *eye contact*.

[. . .]

Evolutionarily, many animals seem to have developed a special sensitivity to eye-contact-like patterns. Curiously enough, usually this sensitivity is expressed in the activation of escape and defensive responses, as if the most adaptive way of responding to being the target of attention of another organism is to fly away (Baron-Cohen, 1995). Nonhuman primates clearly show this sensitivity to eye contact: in many species of monkeys, prolonged eye contact is used as an important component of aggressive displays, and may be quite effective as a threat on its own. But something interesting happens in apes in relation to eye contact: instead of reacting to it in a single, predominantly aggressive/defensive way, they seem to make a more generalized use of it as a pivotal component of different kinds of social interactions. For example, for chimpanzees eye contact is not only a component of aggressive displays, but also of their very opposite: reconciliation behaviors. Captive apes have been also reported to use eye contact as part of their inter-actions with humans (to request food, objects, play bouts, etc.; Gómez, 1991, 1996) and to produce gestures among themselves when the recipients are at least bodily oriented to them (Tomasello *et al.*, 1985).

Of course, the crucial point is not whether apes do or do not make use of eye contact, but how they *understand* eye contact. Do they understand the recursive intentionality embodied in this pattern? I suggest that the answer to this question is "Yes" and "No", depending on what kind of understanding we are asking about. If we are asking about a metarepresentational understanding *à la* Dennett, the answer is probably No; not only for the apes, but also probably for adult humans, who do not seem to understand attention contact in metarepresentational terms either (unless they are cognitive scientists engaging in propositional redescriptions with scientific purposes). However, if we are asking about the ability to perceive and represent eye contact as attention contact in a non-metarepresentational way, the answer is most likely Yes: I suggest that the special use of eye contact made by apes reflects an adaptation to the detection and elicitation of "attention contact" (Gómez, 1996). Apes, and perhaps to some degree other primates, may have discovered and exploited the potentialities of mutual visual attention, as expressed in eye contact, for intersubjective interaction.

[. . .]

Second persons: apes and humans

I suggest that we have evidence in apes of a non-metarepresentational system of intersubjectivity built upon distinctive adaptations to the emotional and cognitive expressions of others when they are experienced in both a third- and a second-person modality. The third-person modality allows the perception (and repre-sentation) of the behavior of others as oriented to targets in the environment (i.e., as *intentional* in the fundamental sense of this word); the second-person modality allows the perception (and representation) of others as intersubjective beings (i.e., as *mutually intentional*). It is this second modality of perception and representation that allows apes to engage in the sort of mutually intentional exchanges that characterize persons.

[. . .]

In this view, apes are intentional agents (subjects) endowed with brain mechanisms specialized in perceiving and treating others as intentional agents (subjects). In a Dennettian mood, we could still ask: but do they understand all this? Are they aware that they are perceiving others as persons and that they themselves are persons? If by "understand" we mean: "Are they capable of elaborating metarepresentations of themselves holding representations of others as subjects?", then the answer is most likely "No", because to begin with, they probably never hold metarepresentations. But this objection would be beside the point. Being aware of being a person is a different phenomenon from being a person. Dennett states that what is crucial for personhood is to possess a special kind of self-awareness. I would rather suggest that what is crucial for personhood is to possess a special kind of *mutual-awareness*. Apes seem indeed to possess such a special kind of mutual-awareness—one that is expressed in the mutuality of attention-contact situations (cf. Gómez, 1994).

Apes are capable of adopting a second-person attitude that is devoid of all the metarepresentional noise of human first- and third-person attitudes. Certainly, in humans, metarepresentations may add a new resonance to the basic psychological processes that make us persons, like the masks of the ancient Greek and Roman actors—the *personae*—could add resonance to their voices. But these additional artefacts cannot create persons on their own. The keys of human personhood will never be found in our metarepresentational fireworks. Apes are not "cheap" versions of persons evolutionarily overcome by the high-tech, metarepresentational minds of humans who are capable of achieving much more sophisticated versions of consciousness and personhood. Our metarepresentional *personae* are mounted upon the solid intersubjective foundations that evolution planted before the advent of *Homo sapiens*. Second-person perceptions and representations are essential parts of ourselves, capable of achieving feats that are not within the reach of third-person representations, that would need to engage in hopeless metarepresentational spirals in a vain attempt to try to imitate what a second-person system achieves in an immediate and direct way (Gómez, 1994, 1996).

In the personhood of apes we may find some of the keys to escape our stubborn persistence in reducing to first- or third-person terms what belongs to the realm of the second-person. I am not a person in so far that I think I am a person; I am not a person in so far as another thinks of me as a person. I am a person in so far as I and another perceive and treat each other as persons.

But we must, on the other hand, avoid the error of "humanizing" the apes. Their mentality, including their mentalizing abilities, are related, but not identical to ours. They are persons that do not describe themselves as persons neither perhaps think of themselves as persons: they, however, may act and feel as persons in the most essential sense of the word, which I take to be the ability to recognize others and themselves as individual subjects capable of feeling and behaving intersubjectively. We are not persons because we can claim we are so. Before speaking we already are human persons. Apes, without speaking, perhaps without thinking in the same sense as we do, also are ape persons. We are lucky enough to have a different evolutionary version of persons. Perhaps we, human persons, will be wise enough to preserve and respect these other ape persons.

Notes

1   Some degree of dissociation can be, however, achieved within the scene we are looking at: I may be mentally attending to an object that is in my peripheral vision instead of to the object in front of my eyes, but my visual attention is still constrained by the presence of the object in my visual field. It could be argued that visual attention is, in fact, a combination of two different mental activities: seeing (which would be the one subject to the behavioral constraint of looking) and attending (which could be purely mental and dissociable from external manifestations). The sort of attentiveness I am exploring in the text is the one that remains indifferentiated from the behavior of looking.

2   Cf. Hobson 1993 for a similar account of early infant intersubjectivity.

References

Baron-Cohen, S. (1995), *Mindblindness: an Essay on Autism and Theory of Mind*, MIT Press, Cambridge, MA.

Dennett, D.C. (1976), "Conditions of personhood", in A.O. Rorty (ed.), *The Identities of Persons*, University of California Press, Berkeley. [Reprinted in D.C. Dennett (1978), *Brainstorms*, Penguin, London.]

Gómez, J.C. (1990), "The emergence of intentional communication as a problem-solving strategy in the gorilla", in S.T. Parker and K.R. Gibson (eds), *"Language" and Intelligence in Monkeys and Apes: Comparative Developmental Perspectives*, Cambridge University Press, Cambridge, pp. 333–55.

Gómez, J.C. (1991), "Visual behavior as a window for reading the minds of others in primates", in A. Whiten (ed.), *Natural Theories of Mind: Evolution, Development and Simulation of everyday Mindreading*, Blackwell, Oxford, pp. 195–207.

Gómez, J.C. (1994), "Mutual awareness in primate communication: a Gricean approach", in S.T. Parker, M. Boccia, and R. Mitchell (eds), *Self-recognition and Awareness in Apes, Monkeys and Children*, Cambridge University Press, Cambridge, pp. 61–80.

Gómez, J.C. (1996), "Ostensive behavior in the great apes: the role of eye contact", in A. Russon, S.T. Parker, and K. Bard (eds), *Reaching into Thought: the Minds of the Great Apes*, Cambridge University Press, Cambridge, pp. 131–151.

Gómez, J.C. (1999), "Do concepts of intersubjectivity apply to non-human primates?", in S. Braten (ed.), *Intersubjective Communication and Emotion in Ontogeny: a Source Book*, Cambridge University Press, Cambridge.

Hobson, P. (1990), "On acquiring knowledge about people and the capacity to pretend: responses to Leslie (1987)", *Psychological Review* 1, 97, pp. 114–21.

Hobson, P. (1993), *Autism and the Development of Mind*, LEA, Hove.

Praget, J. (1936), *La naissance de l'intelligence chez l'enfant*, Delachaux et Niestlée, Neuchatel.

Tomasello, M. and Call, J. (1997), *Primate Cognition*, Oxford University Press, Oxford.

Tomasello, M., George, B., Kruger, A., Farrar, J. and Evans, E. (1985), 'The development of gestural communication in young chimpanzees", *Journal of Human Evolution* 14, pp. 175–86.

Trevarthen, C. (1979), "Communication and cooperation in early infancy", in M. Bullowa (ed.), *Before Speech: The Beginnings of Human Communication*, Cambridge University Press, Cambridge, pp. 321–47.

Trevarthen, C. (1980), "The foundations of intersubjectivity: development of interpersonal and cooperative understanding in infants", in D.R. Olson (ed.), *The Social Foundations of Language and Thought*, Norton, New York, pp. 316–42.

Chapter 21

Jane Goodall

PROBLEMS FACED BY WILD AND CAPTIVE CHIMPANZEES: FINDING SOLUTIONS

Goodall provides a brief summary of her work and experiences with chimpanzees, and offers her perspectives on problems faced by these primates in their natural habitats, sanctuaries established by the Jane Goodall Institute to allow orphaned chimpanzees to be raised, the role of zoos, chimpanzees as pets, chimpanzees in circuses or used for entertainment, medical research, and bringing just solutions to "surplus" chimpanzees. She ends with a call to work together to give these animals a good chance to survive and have the best possible quality of life.

IN 1960 I began a study of the chimpanzees living in the Gombe National Park in Tanzania. Today I am seldom able to visit more than three or four times a year, for two weeks at a time, but the work continues. Data are collected daily by a team of researchers, making the Gombe project the longest unbroken study of any group of wild animals. Information from this research and from other chimpanzee study sites has provided a wealth of data about these apes. Rich data have also accumulated from studies of gorillas and bonobos in Africa and orangutans in Asia. This information, together with behavioral, psychological, and physiological data from a variety of studies of captive great apes around the world, has served to emphasize their close evolutionary relationship to ourselves. How shocking, then, to learn that these amazing beings are vanishing in the wild and being subjected to abuse in many captive situations.

[. . .]

Chimpanzees show intellectual abilities once thought unique to our own species. They have excellent memories, and they can plan for the immediate future. They are capable of cross-modal transfer of information, generalization and abstraction, and simple problem solving. They are aware of themselves as individuals, and they can interpret the moods and identify the wants and needs of others. They have demonstrated a sense of humor. Moreover, although harder to prove, they undoubtedly feel and express emotions similar to those that we label happiness, sadness, rage, irritation, fear, despair, and mental as well as physical suffering. None of this should surprise us in view of the remarkable similarity between the anatomy of the brain and central nervous system of chimpanzee and human. All of this helps to blur the line, once perceived as so sharp, between humans and the rest of the animal kingdom. Once science admits that it is not, after all, only humans who have personalities, are capable of rational thought, and know emotions similar to happiness, sadness, anger, despair, this should lead to a new respect for other animals with whom we share the planet, especially for the great apes, our closest living relatives. In fact that respect is seldom apparent.

[. . .]

Problems faced by chimpanzees in the wild

There are still some chimpanzees living in utterly remote wilderness areas who seldom if ever encounter humans—for example, those in the Ndoke National Park area in the People's Republic of Congo (Brazzaville). There are a number of areas, spread across the range of the chimpanzee, that have been given protected status to preserve wildlife. In some countries (e.g., Tanzania and Uganda) efforts are made by wildlife authorities to patrol such areas. Protection is also afforded by wildlife research teams working within these forests. Too often, though, poachers with guns, snares, or spears have easy access, and there are many illegal logging operations with pit saws and illegal mining.

[. . .]

The most severe threat to the Gombe chimpanzees is human population growth in the areas around the tiny 30-square-mile national park. The 120 or so chimpanzees, in three different communities, are isolated, cut off from other conspecifics by cultivated hillsides on three sides, the lake on the fourth. Even 15 years ago chimpanzee habitats stretched far along the eastern shore of Lake Tanganyika. Today the trees have gone as more and more desperate people, including large numbers of refugees from Burundi and Congo, try to grow food on the very steep slopes. In the rainy season the precious thin layer of topsoil is washed down into the lake. In some places the shoreline looks like rocky desert, and the fish breeding grounds have become silted up.

How can we hope to save the forest jewel that is the Gombe National Park, and its famous chimpanzees, when the local people are facing starvation? There are now more people living there than the land can support, there is almost nowhere for them to move to, and they mostly cannot afford to buy food from other areas. In many places the women have to dig up the roots of previously cut trees to get wood to cook their food.

The Jane Goodall Institute has initiated a project in the Kigoma region to try to address this problem. Tree nurseries have been established in 33 villages around Gombe and along the lakeshore. Fruit trees and fast growing trees for building poles, firewood, and charcoal are nurtured as seedlings, then planted in the villages. George Strunden, project manager, has picked a team of qualified Tanzanians who introduce the program into the villages. He has also trained women who demonstrate appropriate tree growing methods. Farming methods that help control and prevent soil erosion are introduced. And there is a strong conservation education element that includes taking small groups of secondary school students to Gombe. There is a big push to increase the self-esteem of women, teaching them skills that will enable them to earn money for themselves. A number of scholarships are offered annually to enable girls from primary schools to benefit from further education. A small microcredit program has been introduced based on the Grameen Bank system. By working with the local medical authorities, TACARE (Lake Tanganika Catchment Reforestation and Education Project) is able to bring primary health care to the village women, along with family planning and AIDS education. Most recently we have formed a partnership with UNICEF that will enable us to bring hygenic latrines and freshwater wells to 33 villages in the area. It should be stressed that the villagers are consulted about their needs, and only projects that have their absolute support are introduced.

Only if we work with the villagers, helping to improve the standard of living of some of the poorest people in Tanzania, do we have a chance to protect the Gombe chimpanzees. Without the goodwill of the local people, the last forests within the park itself, and the tiny remnant forests outside, would surely disappear. A significant factor in our battle to save the Gombe chimpanzees is our employing field staff from communities around the park since 1988. These men follow the chimpanzees, make detailed reports, use 8-mm video cameras, and are proud of their work. They talk about it to family and friends. They care about the chimpanzees as individuals. I believe this is why, until the recent influx of refugees from eastern Congo (people who traditionally eat the meat of monkeys and apes), we had only one case of poaching at Gombe.

Across Africa the great apes face problems caused by the relentless growth of human populations, habitat destruction, and fragmentation of populations. Peasants clear-cut forests to create fields for crops and grazing. They cut down hundreds of trees for the charcoal industry. The forest soils are fragile and soon become infertile and barren when the tree cover is destroyed. So the desert spreads.

In some parts of Africa apes are hunted for the live animal trade and for food. In addition they may be caught in the snares set by village hunters for antelopes and bush pigs. They can usually break the wire, but the tightened noose causes great pain and typically results in gangrene and the loss of the affected hand or foot and sometimes ends in death. Between 40 and 50 percent of all adult chimpanzees in the study communities at Budongo and in the Tai Forest have lost a hand or foot in this way.

Wildlife is sometimes endangered as a result of the ethnic violence so tragically prevalent in many parts of the chimpanzees' range. These conflicts may displace hundreds of refugees who flee their homes, as in Liberia, the Democratic Republic of Congo, Sierra Leone, and Rwanda. Typically they are starving and forced to hunt wild animals for food. Those chimpanzees remaining in Cabinda are endangered by the land mines that have been placed throughout the forests in northwest Angola.

The great apes are also threatened by the live animal trade, when dealers pay hunters to shoot females simply to steal their infants for export. This trade is by no means as extensive as it was in the days before the Convention on International Trade in Endangered Species of Wild Fauna and Flora (CITES), but there is still brisk business in some parts of the world, such as the United Arab Emirates, various countries in South America, and parts of eastern Europe. For every infant that arrives at its final destination alive, about ten chimpanzees are estimated to have died in Africa: mothers who escaped only to die later of their wounds, along with their infants; infants killed during capture; other individuals who tried to protect the victims; and captured infants who die of wounds, dehydration, malnutrition, or shock and depression.

Chimpanzees and other wildlife in remote unprotected forests are seriously and increasingly threatened by commercial activities, particularly logging. Even companies that practice sustainable logging have a highly adverse effect on much animal life. Roads made for transportation of logs open up the forests for settlements. People then cut down trees to grow crops, for firewood, for building poles. They set snares to catch antelopes and other animals for food. And they carry human diseases into areas where they have never been before, and the great apes are susceptible to almost all of our infectious diseases. Most serious of all, the roads provide easy access to previously inaccessible areas for commercial hunters who ride the logging trucks. The roads and trucks provide, for the first time, the means for meat, dried or even fresh, to be transported from the heart of the forest to towns far away. Subsistence hunting permitted indigenous people to live in harmony with the forests for hundreds of years. It is the new commercial hunting that threatens the animals of many of the remaining forests. This is the infamous bushmeat trade, exposed by Karl Ammann.

Thus it is clear that wild chimpanzees, gorillas, and bonobos are, only too often, persecuted by their closest relatives, the human apes. The chimpanzee population, that must have numbered more than one million at the beginning of the twentieth century, has been reduced to 200,000 at the very most, spread through 21 countries. It is the rate of decrease of all the great apes that is so alarming. If nothing is done to halt the bushmeat trade, it is estimated that almost no great apes will remain in the Congo Basin in 10 to 15 years. Many organizations have joined The Bushmeat Crisis Task Force in the United States and the Ape Alliance in Europe, which are working on developing methods to slow down and ultimately eliminate this trade.

Sanctuaries

There is not much meat on an infant chimpanzee. Orphans, whose mothers have been shot and sold for meat, are sometimes offered for sale in native or tourist markets. In some areas mothers are shot only so that their infants can be stolen for sale. These pathetic orphans are sometimes bought as pets, to attract customers to a hotel or other place of business, or simply because people feel sorry for them. Paying money for any wild animal for sale serves only to perpetuate a cruel trade. Yet it is hard to turn away from a small infant who looks at you with eyes filled with pain and hopelessness. A solution to this moral dilemma is to persuade government officials to confiscate these victims, because in most African countries there is a law prohibiting the hunting and sale of endangered species, such as the great apes, without a license.

After confiscation, the orphan must be cared for. The Jane Goodall Institute has established sanctuaries in a number of locations. The biggest is in Congo (Brazzaville), where Graziella Cotman cares for 80 at the time of writing (October 2000). The Tchimpounga sanctuary, north of Pointe-Noire on the coast, was built by the petroleum company Conoco, in 1991. It was designed for 25 chimpanzees at most. It has become urgent to add additional enclosures, but we have been delayed by civil war.

In this area, as at Gombe, we employ individuals from the surrounding villages to care for the chimpanzees (and other animals) and as support staff. We also buy fruit and vegetables locally, and this boosts the economy. In addition, we use these orphans as the focus of an environmental education program. The local people are amazed and fascinated when they see the chimpanzees close up. We are trying to establish a wildlife reserve to protect the remaining forest—savanna mosaic in the area. Most of the savanna has been destroyed by eucalyptus plantations, a project of Shell Oil working with a Congolese company, but there is a beautiful unspoiled area around our sanctuary. With permission from the central government we are working with local government officials and also employing ecoguards from each of the seven nearby villages. There are more wild chimpanzees in the area than we believed. When the fighting stops it may be possible to attract tourists and thus bring foreign exchange into the country. Although the building and maintenance of chimpanzee sanctuaries is very expensive, we are not only caring for abandoned orphans but raising awareness through conservation education, and trying to protect the wild chimpanzees.

[. . .]

Zoos

There are approximately 250 chimpanzees living in zoos accredited by the American Zoo and Aquarium Association (AZA) and participating in the chimpanzee Species Survival Plan. There are about 1,700 in all zoos worldwide. There is much controversy regarding zoos, with many animal rights activists believing that they should be closed. Of course, chimpanzees belong in the wild, and if they are lucky enough to live in a protected area, or one remote from people, that is the best life. That life cannot be replicated in captive situations. In the forest they have a great deal of freedom of choice. They can choose whether to travel on their own, in a small group, or to join large excitable gatherings. They can usually choose which individuals to associate with. Females can wander off, with their dependent young, and stay feeding peacefully and grooming together for hours, or even days. Close companions meet often, others may avoid each other. They know the excitement of participating in hunts or boundary patrols, and even aggressive, almost war-like encounters with individuals of neighboring social groups. To survive they must spend much time searching for and sometimes preparing their food—they are occupying their brains, using their skills. They are free. Nevertheless, when compared with the life of chimpanzees living in danger zones in Africa, it sometimes seems to me that those in the really good zoos—those in which there are large enclosures, rich social groups, and an enriched environment—may in fact be better off.

On the other hand, there are still many zoos that should be closed—zoos where chimpanzees are forced to live alone or in pairs in tiny cement-floored, iron-barred, old-fashioned cages. There they suffer terribly from boredom. In African zoos, where sometimes even the keepers can only eat one meal a day, if that, conditions are often appalling for all the animals, and there is much suffering. Lack of water is often a major problem, because there may be no running water and water is delivered very sporadically by keepers who are in the business simply for a job.

[. . .]

The medical research lab

Many ex-pet and ex-entertainment chimpanzees end their days in medical research. It is hard for me to visit the laboratories to see chimpanzees, who have committed no crime, locked into 5 ft × 5 ft × 7 ft high prison cages. They are there because their biology and physiology is so like ours that they can be infected with almost all human diseases. Hundreds have been used in hepatitis and AIDS research. Admittedly some laboratories are improving, developing programs to enrich their prisoners' lives, giving them more space. But there are still hundreds in the United States and other parts of the world in such cells.

Surplus chimpanzees

A major problem today is the so-called "surplus" chimpanzee population. [. . .] The following stories of three chimpanzees, two born in the wild and one in captivity, serve to remind us that, when we talk of the "surplus" problem we are actually talking of the fate of individuals, each with his or her own personality, each having been exploited by humans.

Gregoire was born in the wild, in the northern forests of Congo (Brazzaville). When I met him he was alone in a dark cage, one in a row of similarly caged, solitary primates at the Brazzaville Zoo. Gregoire had been given to the zoo when his owners left the country, and he had been there since about 1949, some 40 years. He was almost hairless, and I could see nearly every bone in his body. Most of the animals at that zoo were starving; it was cheaper to replace animals who died of malnutrition than to buy an adequate diet. I knew I had to help Gregoire even though he had, somehow, survived without help for so long. A small group of people got together and agreed to save up food and deliver it to the zoo. The Jane Goodall Institute employed its own keeper to care for Gregoire and the other primates. Gregoire put on weight and his hair began to grow. Then the Brigitte Bardot Foundation gave us a small grant (after she saw a video of Gregoire), and we were able to build a small "patio" for him. By this time Graziella Cotman was living in Brazzaville, and she was able to introduce three small orphans to the old male. One was a 2-year-old female, whom I named Cherie. A wonderful relationship, a bit like a grandfather and granddaughter, developed between this little girl and old Gregoire. Things were going well, until civil war broke out again. The zoo, near the airport, was in the middle of the war zone. Fortunately Gregoire, his young companions, and the two adult chimpanzees could be airlifted to the Tchimpounga Sanctuary (along with a group of young gorillas and bonobos). When Gregoire arrived his back was raw, apparently because he had rushed under his low bed shelf whenever the shelling got too close. But once again this old man adapted, and his hair grew back. Today he is in a group with two adult females and three youngsters.

Sebastian was brought to Kenya (where there are no wild chimpanzees) from West Africa. He ended up in the orphanage run by the Kenya Wildlife Service. There he lived for more than 20 years, becoming the star attraction. When I met him his quarters consisted of a small indoor and private cage that led into a circular mesh enclosure. He lived alone because he had seriously hurt females who had been introduced to him. He was very gentle with humans whom he liked, and loved to manicure my nails with a piece of twig. But when crowds of visitors arrived, especially when these were children who would make faces and tease him, he would display wildly, back and forth in the enclosure, throwing anything he could find. Yet when he was put in a newly built enclosure that prevented the public from approaching closely, he became seriously depressed and refused to eat. Eventually he was returned to his original home where he quickly recovered. Several years later he again became depressed when the orphanage was temporarily closed for reconstruction. Not until it was again opened to the public, and the daily teasing and displaying sessions resumed, did he recover. Clearly, the crowds provided stimulation and entertainment.

Lucy was born in captivity. As a tiny baby she was adopted by Jane and Maurice Temerlins, a psychoanalyst and his zoologist wife. Lucy was brought up like a human child, clothes and all. The original plan was to find out whether a chimpanzee brought up with love and affection would be able to nurture her first baby despite having no experience of other chimpanzees. But as she reached adolescence the Temerlins decided that their lives had been ruled by Lucy for too long. After considering all options, they decided, with the best of intentions, to give her her freedom, to send her to Africa. Although she went with a trusted human, all that she had learned in her "human" days had to be forgotten. She had learned sign language, but her signs were ignored by the only person she knew, the person with whom, until the nightmare began, she had communicated in sign language. Lucy was introduced to two rambunctious young wild-born chimpanzees. She wanted nothing to do with them. She fell into deep depression. Although she eventually began to behave more like a chimpanzee, I personally believe the exercise was very cruel. Lucy died, years after arriving in Africa and ultimately being released on an island. Her body was found on the island with hands and feet removed. The whole exercise can be compared with taking a middle-class American girl of about 14 years old to live with a group of indigenous people in some far off part of the world. She would leave behind all her clothes, all her comforts, and all her culture. And her American companion would pretend not to understand a word she said.

These three chimpanzees had unnatural life styles to which they adapted. Humans created those situations. We have no right to try to effect change from our arrogant human perspective of "we know what is best." Rather we should try to get inside the mind of the individual chimpanzees and move slowly, a step at a time, toward a solution that is *best for them*.

Conclusions

Clearly chimpanzees today face many problems, both in the wild and in captivity. These problems are all different and need their own unique solutions that take into account all the variables; the country, the different people involved, the resources available, especially financial, and the personalities of the chimpanzees themselves. We cannot draw sweeping conclusions about the correct procedure in all zoos, in all sanctuaries, and in all situations.

Those trying to help the great apes have their own perspectives. There are many differences of opinion. But so long as we all have the same goals—the improvement of conditions for the great apes, in the world and in captivity—we should be able to work together.

[. . .]

I have encountered criticism for starting sanctuaries (they have been called a waste of money to help a few individuals when precious funds are needed to save the species), but for me there was no option. I simply could not look into the eyes of a pathetic orphan and leave it to its fate, because, for so many years, I have been able to look into the eyes of chimpanzees who are wild and free and in control of their own lives.

Let us move forward, united toward our goal of conserving the great apes in the wild, striving for the best treatment for all captive apes, and eliminating them from invasive medical research. Whether we care about the apes as species or as individuals, we all want solutions that will give them a chance to survive and to enjoy the best possible quality of life.

CETACEANS

Chapter 22

Hal Whitehead, Luke Rendell, Richard W. Osborne, and Bernd Würsig

CULTURE AND CONSERVATION OF NON-HUMANS WITH REFERENCE TO WHALES AND DOLPHINS: REVIEW AND NEW DIRECTIONS

Whitehead and co-authors address the increasing evidence that culture is an important determinant of behavior in apes and cetaceans (whales and dolphins). They note that culture transmitted within generations ("horizontal" culture) may assist animals deal with anthropogenic changes. In contrast, culture transmitted principally between generations ("vertical" culture) may impede adaptation to environmental change. The authors argue that non-human culture should be integrated in conservation biology when addressing species with these characteristics.

Introduction

"CONSERVATION", WHEN APPLIED to humans, almost always refers to valued cultural attributes: to art forms, architecture, languages or "ways of life". For instance, the organization Cultural Survival (2002) declares "The diversity of cultures around the world is increasingly endangered. This diversity constitutes the wealth of all humanity. We have more than a moral obligation to respect and promote cultural diversity – it is in our interest."

For all other forms of life conservation has been tightly focused on genetic diversity. We are going to suggest that in some circumstances, for some species, culture should be integrated into conservation biology. We will take most of our examples from cetaceans. However, many of our arguments apply to other non-human species for which culture seems important (see Sutherland, 1998). For instance, culture has begun to be considered in the conservation of chimpanzees, *Pan troglodytes* (Goodall, 1994; McGrew, 2003), and elephants, *Elephantidae* (McComb et al., 2001).

Culture has been defined in many varied ways (e.g., Mundinger, 1980). The definition that we prefer is "information or behavior – shared by a population or subpopulation – which is acquired from conspecifics through some form of social learning" (Rendell and Whitehead, 2001a). Here, "population" could include the whole species, and "subpopulation" any subdivision of a population which contains at least a few individuals in each set. This definition has four important elements: that culture affects behavior and thus phenotypes; that it is a group phenomenon; that it is transmitted from individual to individual and so, like genes, is an inheritance system (Boyd and Richerson, 1985); and that the transmission is through some form of social learning (see Whiten and Ham, 1992 for definitions of social learning). Our definition is similar to that used by most of those who study culture in other non-humans (e.g., Slater, 2001; Laland and Hoppitt, 2003; McGrew, 2003), cultural theorists (e.g., Boyd and Richerson, 1996), and some social scientists (Cronk, 1999). However, some psychologists restrict culture to transmission only through imitation and teaching (Galef, 1992), a restriction that we and others contest (Whiten and Ham, 1992; Boesch, 2001; Rendell and Whitehead, 2001a; Laland and Hoppitt, 2003), and there are anthropologists and other social scientists who use completely different definitions including elements such as "shared values" (e.g., Ingold, 2001), which cannot currently be applied to non-humans.

Culture, as conceived by us and many others, has some similarities with genetic inheritance. It can mutate and evolve, is subject to the natural selection of both cultural variants and culture-bearers, and often leads to adaptive behavior. However, there are some important differences (see Boyd and Richerson, 1985): individuals can receive culture from a range of donors in addition to their parents; they can choose which culture to adopt; and their own experiences and behavior can influence the form of culture that is transmitted to other individuals, so acquired characters can be inherited. A consequence is that culture can affect behavioral and population biology, and thus conservation issues, in ways that are importantly different from those traditionally expected from a model that only includes genetic inheritance.

Culture is very varied, and this variation has implications for its interactions with conservation. For instance, contrasts have often been drawn between "horizontal" cultures, where transmission is between members of the same generation, and "vertical" or "oblique" cultures where animals learn behavior from parents or other members of previous generations (Cavalli-Sforza et al., 1982). Horizontal cultural transmission can be highly effective in quickly changing population behavior in adaptive ways, an example being the rapid decrease in the use of certain chemicals by humans once they are shown to be toxic. Conversely, vertical cultures, like some religions, can be highly conservative and can constrain adaptive responses to environmental change.

Using our definition of culture, or any similar one, culture is quite common among animals, especially those that are more cognitively advanced (Boyd and Richerson, 1996). However, in most of the species possessing recognized cultural capacities, only a small proportion of behavior seems to be determined by social learning, and much of this may be functionally neutral, as has been argued for songbirds (Slater, 1986; although see Grant and Grant, 1996). Generally, in these cases, it seems unlikely that culture will be an important factor in population biology or conservation. In contrast, among the great apes and cetaceans, and perhaps in a few other groups (other primates, elephants, bats and parrots are good candidates; see de Waal and Tyack, 2003), social learning likely determines a large proportion of behavior, including functionally important behavior such as foraging (McGrew, 1992; Whiten et al., 1999; Rendell and Whitehead, 2001b; van Schaik et al., 2003). In these species, culture can affect fitness and population biology in important ways, and so, we argue, have a potential bearing on conservation biology. This is especially the case when the form that culture takes leads to discrete, behaviorally differentiated population segments that can possess quite distinct ecological roles. Luck et al. (2003) argue that population diversity, especially in terms of the range of ecosystem services provided, should be an important element of population and conservation biology. Culture can provide such population diversity.

We will primarily use the cetaceans, whales and dolphins, to make our case. Cetaceans have been studied less thoroughly than the great apes, and less is known of their behavior. However, primatologists have acknowledged that cetaceans have behavior, social learning skills and cultural capacities which appear at least as advanced as those of the non-human great apes (Dunbar, 2001; Whiten, 2001). Furthermore, the cetacean culture that is emerging from current studies includes a feature that is not known among non-human great apes and that has particular significance for conservation: stable, sympatric, culturally determined groups within populations.

We will briefly summarize the evidence for culture in whales and dolphins, and then show how different forms of culture can have consequences for conservation biology. We provide few solid prescriptions for dealing with these consequences but rather seek to highlight issues that may require further consideration in cultural species.

Cetacean culture

[. . .]

Despite difficulties in studying the behavior of the whales and dolphins, and, compared to primates and songbirds, a lack of knowledge on behavior, communication and social structure, there is strong evidence for cetacean cultures in the four best studied species (Rendell and Whitehead, 2001b), and some most interesting speculations for some of the others (for instance on spinner dolphins, *Stenella longirostris*, Norris, 1994). Sophisticated social learning abilities exist, at least in bottlenose dolphins and orcas (Boran and Heimlich, 1999). Of the several types of social learning which have been recognized (e.g., Whiten and Ham, 1992), imitation is often singled out as being particularly significant for the promulgation of culture (e.g., Galef, 1992; Boyd and Richerson, 1996 but see Laland and Hoppitt, 2003). The bottlenose dolphin can imitate both vocally and non-vocally and has been shown to understand the broad concept of imitation (Herman and Pack, 2001). Some consider it the most sophisticated non-human imitator (e.g., Whiten, 2001).

This social learning seems to have led to culture, of various types. Among the baleen whales (suborder Mysticeti), there are several known cases of horizontally transmitted cultures (Rendell and Whitehead, 2001b). The best understood horizontal culture of cetaceans is the mating song of the male humpback whale. At any time during the winter breeding season, all the males in any ocean sing more or less the same elaborate song, but this communal song evolves over months and years (Payne, 1999). Songs in different oceans at any time are different but follow the same general syntactical and evolutionary rules.

Horizontal cultures are also found in the suborder Odontoceti, the toothed whales and dolphins. An example is the "dead-salmon carrying" fad of the well-studied "southern resident", fish-eating, orcas of the Puget Sound area of the northeast Pacific. It began with a female in K-Pod carrying around a dead salmon in 1987, spread to the other two pods in the southern resident community over a 5–6 week period and then stopped (R. Osborne, personal observation). It was noted a few times the following summer, and then never again.

Probably more significant from the conservation perspective are vertically or obliquely transmitted cultures. Populations of all the well-studied odontocetes are culturally structured and subpopulations with distinct cultural trait groups are often sympatric. Among the bottlenose dolphins of Shark Bay, Western Australia, there are at least four distinctive foraging specializations, at least some of which are likely transmitted vertically from mother to daughter (Connor, 2001; Mann, 2001; Mann and Sargeant, 2003). Similar population structure by foraging specializations is found in other dolphin communities, for instance in cases of human–dolphin fishing co-operatives. In Brazil there are at least two cases where some, but not all, bottlenose dolphins in a community have a long-standing and complex cooperative relationship with local fishers which is almost certainly vertically transmitted between generations of both dolphins and fishers (Simões-Lopes et al., 1998).

The population of orcas off the west coast of Canada is clearly structured at a number of hierarchical levels, and much of this structuring seems to be cultural. At the highest level, different "types" of orca ("residents" and "transients") are sympatric, but show sufficient differences in feeding behavior, vocalizations, social systems, morphology, and genetics that they may be incipient species (Baird, 2000). It has been suggested that this division was originally cultural (Baird, 2000). At lower levels, "communities", "clans" and "pods" of orcas may differ in vocalizations, foraging behavior and social behavior, but often have overlapping ranges (Ford et al., 1999). The complex, stable and sympatric vocal and behavioral cultures of orca groups have no known parallel outside humans (Rendell and Whitehead, 2001b). The closest analog is with the sperm whale, whose society is also arranged into a multi-level hierarchy, at least two levels of which may support cultural differences among sympatric groups: the approximately 10-member "social units" and ocean-wide "clans" with thousands of members each (Rendell and Whitehead, 2003; Whitehead, 2003).

Some of the attributions of culture to behavioral differences between segments of cetacean populations which are mentioned in this paper are not fully proven and have been contested (see commentaries on Rendell and Whitehead, 2001b). For instance, there is a segment of the scientific community which is unwilling to ascribe culture to a species without experimental proof of social learning (e.g., Galef, 1992). Among cetaceans this is impossible for the larger whales, only exists for the bottlenose dolphin (see above), and, even here, the apparently cultural characteristics of wild populations of this species have not been experimentally tested in the laboratory. However, there are many reasons for questioning such a restriction for culture, including the observation that transmission mechanisms for most human culture have not been experimentally tested in the laboratory (Boesch, 2001; Rendell and Whitehead, 2001a). In all the cases of cetacean behavioral differences cited below, we believe that the evidence strongly points to culture rather than alternative genetic, environmental or ontogenetic causes (Rendell and Whitehead, 2001a).

The emerging picture, then, is that whale and dolphin behavior is strongly affected by culture. The culture comes in a range of forms, from high-turnover horizontal cultures of the baleen whales to the stable vertical cultures that structure odontocete populations. Cetacean cultural behavior includes vocalizations, foraging and ranging behavior, and social norms, but, in contrast to chimpanzees and orangutans, *Pongo* spp., there is little evidence of material cultures (Rendell and Whitehead, 2001b).

Horizontal cultures and conservation

It has been suggested several times that a principal adaptive advantage of culture in humans is to navigate environmental change (e.g., Boyd and Richerson, 1985; Laland et al., 1996): if animals can learn from each other they can adapt to changing environments more quickly than if each individual must learn the optimal behavior independently, and much more quickly than is possible with natural selection of genetically determined behavior. Thus species with cultural capacities possess a potential advantage when environments change, even if they themselves are the agents of the change.

[. . .]

In several areas of the world, cetaceans have learned to remove fish from fishing gear, and given the rapid spread of the behavior within populations, there is little doubt that social learning is responsible for at least some of the recruitment to the population of fish-stealers. Examples include orcas and/ or sperm whales taking fish from long-lines in the fisheries for Patagonian tooth-fish, *Dissostichus eleginoides*, off the southern parts of South America, bluenose, *Hyperoglyphe antarchia*, off New Zealand, halibut, *Hippoglossus stenolepis*, and sablefish, *Anoplopoma fimbria*, near Alaska (e.g., Yano and Dahlheim, 1995; Ashford et al., 1996; National Marine Fisheries Service, 1998; Nolan et al., 2000).

[. . .]

In many of these cases of crop-raiding by elephants and fish-stealing by whales the animals suffer hostile repercussions from angry farmers and fishers including shooting and calls for culls. If elephants and cetaceans did not learn so well from other elephants and cetaceans, it seems highly likely that these problems would be much less severe.

Vertical, and oblique, cultures and conservation

Vertical, and oblique, cultures are passed between generations and can be stable over many generations, particularly if enhanced by conformity, the imperative "to do the done thing" (Richerson and Boyd, 1998). Vertical cultures can influence genetic evolution (Laland, 1992; Grant and Grant, 1996; Whitehead, 1999) and may structure populations (e.g., Nettle, 1999; Rendell and Whitehead, 2003).

Cultural conservatism

While rapidly evolving horizontal cultures may make a species more able to adapt to environmental change, stable vertical cultures can have the opposite effect. They may inhibit the adaptive responses that stimulus-response behavior, individual learning and innovation would normally produce (although to a lesser extent than overriding genetic determination). For example, if, due to cultural traditions, orcas continued to use areas of their habitat despite excessive vessel traffic, sewage, or underwater noise, their adherence to tradition could potentially over-ride what would otherwise be avoidance of noxious environmental conditions (Osborne, 1999).

For cetaceans perhaps the most important aspect of this cultural conservatism relates to the reestablishment of a species in an ecological niche following extirpation due to whaling. Most large whale populations were enormously reduced by commercial whaling which began hundreds of years ago but reached its peak during the 1960s (Clapham et al., 1999). These populations are now virtually protected from whaling so that recovery is expected, and in some cases apparent. However, while reasonable, and sometimes growing, population densities are found in some areas, other traditionally important habitat remains deserted. [. . .] While we can document the end of traditional use of a habitat, whaling probably removed other cultural knowledge from populations, and this loss likely inhibits their recovery.

Maladaptive behavior

More fundamentally, cultural evolution has a greater potential to lead to maladaptive behavior than genetic evolution or individual learning (Boyd and Richerson, 1985). This is particularly the case for conformist cultures in which individuals actively adopt the most common cultural variants in their experience. Conformist cultures can be particularly stable, and lead to strong group identification and cultural group selection (Richerson and Boyd, 1998). This process is a leading candidate for explaining genetically maladaptive behavior by humans (Boyd and Richerson, 1985), such as religiously prescribed fertility limitations, or the eating of dead relatives' brains. Conformist cultural evolution can also potentially result in maladaptive behavior in non-humans. This can lead to the appearance of conservation problems, where no anthropogenic threat is actually operating.

[. . .] We have suggested that mass strandings of cetaceans may be linked to conformist cultures (Rendell and Whitehead, 2001b). In this scenario, healthy animals run up on the beaches and die at least partially because the culturally transmitted imperative to remain with the group holds sway over the individual's survival instinct. Although culture has not been studied in pilot whales, they seem to have social structures with similar general attributes to orcas and sperm whales (Heimlich-Boran, 1993; Ottensmeyer and Whitehead, 2003), the types that seem to promote conformist cultures.

The implications is that for cetaceans, like humans, strange, and apparently maladaptive, behavior may be a product of cultural evolution and not a result of anthropogenic changes to their environment, especially it if is a group phenomenon. Thus not all weird behavior indicates a conservation problem, although some, such as mass strandings of several whale species simultaneously, does (Balcomb and Claridge, 2001; Jepson et al., 2003).

Reintroduction and translocation

Culture interacts with conservation in the introduction of captive animals into the wild and the forced movement of animals between areas (Sutherland, 1998). Reintroductions and translocations are important conservation tools in some circumstances, and culture will affect their success. The principal issues are whether the animals possess the knowledge to survive and breed in their new habitat.

Cultural aspects undoubtedly affect the success of cetacean reintroductions (see, e.g., Wells et al., 1998), but reintroduction is not generally considered an important tool in cetacean conservation (e.g., Reeves and Mead, 1999). Translocations from the highly impacted Yangtze River to a protected oxbow have been attempted in attempts to save the critically endangered baiji (*Lipotes vexillifer*), but these were not successful (Zhang et al., 2003). Cultural aspects may have had a role in this. Translocations of finless porpoises (*Neophocaena phocaenoides*) between the same two habitats have been successful (Ding et al., 2000). This contrast may partially result from differences in the role of cultural knowledge in the two species.

Sympatric cultural variants

Conservation biology is complicated by population subdivisions. Anthropogenic threats may affect the different segments in different ways leading to multiple responses. The situation is particularly complex when the population segments are sympatric. [. . .]

In the ocean territoriality is much less prevalent than on land, leaving more opportunities for sympatric socially learned behavioral variants within species. A well-studied example is the sea otter, *Enhydra lutris*, in which individuals that share habitat have distinctive foraging styles, which are learned from their mothers, and so may possess distinctive ecological roles (Estes et al., 2003). Among cetaceans, sympatric groups often have distinctive behavioral repertoires resulting from vertical cultural transmission and apparently rendered stable by conformism, a situation which has a range of conservation ramifications. Culturally discrete sub-populations in the same habitat may face different conservation threats, or may respond to the same threat in different ways.

In Moreton Bay, Australia, bottlenose dolphins regularly feed from trawler discards (Chilvers and Corkeron, 2001). Among the several hundred dolphins that use Moreton Bay, two sympatric communities have been recognized, one of which generally feeds with trawlers, and the other of which never does (Chilvers and Corkeron, 2001). Although they live in the same area, dolphins from the two communities rarely interact socially, except possibly for some mating (Chilvers and Corkeron, 2001). It may become necessary to restrict trawling to safeguard the resources, peneaid prawns. How will this affect the trawler dolphins? Other impacts, such as the effect of pollutants run-off into sea-grass beds, may primarily affect the non-trawler dolphins (Chilvers and Corkeron, 2001), so the conservation issues are difficult.

Similar conundrums are emerging for other species. For instance, dusky dolphins (*Lagenorhynchus obscurus*) near the Kaikoura Canyon, New Zealand, feed at night on mesopelagic fishes and squid (Würsig et al., 1989). A subset of those animals, and habitually the same every year, travel about 160 km north to the Marlborough Sounds in winter and there feed in the day on near-surface schooling fishes (K.J. Benoit-Bird, B. Würsig and C.J. McFadden, submitted). Traveling to Marlborough Sounds is thought to be culturally transmitted (B. Würsig, pers. comm.). The Marlborough Sounds users are now facing increasingly choked bays due to extensive mussel farm development in the Marlborough Sounds area, and the dolphins do not use areas with mussel farms (Markowitz et al., 2004).

[. . .]

In orcas, too, sympatric culturally distinguished groupings face different conservation threats. For instance, off southern Vancouver Island, fish-eating "residents" are found in the same waters as mammal-eating "transients". The residents are threatened by declines in salmon stocks and by rampant whale-watching (Osborne, 1999; Trites and Barrett-Lennard, 2001; Erbe, 2002; NOAA, 2002), while for transients extreme concentrations of pollutants linked to their high trophic level (Ross et al., 2000) are probably the major concern.

Sympatric cultural variants and evolutionarily significant units

These situations, in which sympatric culturally distinct populations have characteristic conservation issues, or may respond differently to threats, indicate the importance of preserving both genetic and cultural diversity (Sutherland, 1998). [. . .]

Conservation is often believed to be promoted through considering the status of populations below the sub-species level, sometimes called "evolutionarily significant units" (ESUs). A consensus definition of ESU has yet to be achieved, and the practice of assigning them is very much under development. We can now add a further twist to this difficult issue: should culture be considered in the determination of ESUs?

Geographically distinct cultures could be used as part of the process of dividing populations, so that, for example, chimpanzee populations in different parts of Africa might be assigned to different ESUs based upon cultural similarity (Whiten et al., 2001) as well as geographic and genetic proximity. The situation becomes more difficult when population segments overlap geographically and genetically, but are clearly distinguishable based upon culturally transmitted behavior.

A controversial case that contains strong cultural undercurrents is that of the "southern resident" orcas. The southern resident community contains about 80 fish-eating orcas whose range straddles the US–Canadian border. The population has been declining since 1995, but the reasons for this are unclear (NOAA, 2002). The southern residents are sympatric with the mammal-eating "transient" orcas, and share some of their range with the "northern resident community" which also eat fish. There are about 200 northern residents, and although they seem less threatened than the southern residents, their population has also started to decline recently (Trites and Barrett-Lennard, 2001). There is little mating between the northern and southern residents, and they are genetically distinct (Barrett-Lennard, 2000). However, genetic divergence is small, just one base pair in the control region of the mitochondrial genome and $F_{ST} = 0.144$ using 11 microsatellite loci (Barrett-Lennard, 2000). The principal, and probably fundamental, differences between the communities are cultural. The Committee on the Status of Endangered Wildlife in Canada (COSEWIC) reviewed orca status in 2001, and divided the orcas into "nationally significant populations" assigning a status of "Endangered" (the highest risk category available for an extant population) to the southern residents, "Threatened" to the northern residents, and "Threatened" to the transients (www.cosewic.gc.ca). In contrast, the US National Marine Fisheries Service (NMFS) in 2002 refused a petition to declare the southern residents "Endangered", listing them only as "Depleted" as they were not considered a "distinct population segment" but were "part of the general killer whale population in the North Pacific, which is considered healthy" (NOAA, 2002; NOAA Press release 02–076; http://www.nwr.noaa.gov/mmammals/whales/srkwnews.pdf). Supporting this decision, NMFS noted that the northern and southern residents use similar habitat types, that loss of the southern residents would not necessarily result in a gap in the species' range, and that the genetic differences between the northern and southern residents is small (NOAA, 2002). NMFS also considered "pod-specific traits, such as acoustic repertoire, that have been described by some biologists as 'cultural'" but concluded "that there was insufficient evidence to indicate whether these 'cultural' traits were inherited or learned, and thus whether they truly signify an evolutionarily important trait" (NOAA, 2002). This reasoning is confused, as cultural traits must be learned and may or may not also be inherited between generations. However, the implication seems to be that traits acquired through learning are not evolutionarily important, and, thus, in apparent contrast to the Canadian listing agency (COSEWIC), NMFS specifically appears to disregard culture in this listing decision.

Where do these practices stand in the light of the evolving theory of ESUs? There have been many approaches to defining ESUs (Fraser and Bernatchez, 2001), but the focus is on genetic separation, not cultural differences. In the definitions of Dizon et al. (1992), Moritz (1994) and Fraser and Bernatchez (2001), ESUs are delineated entirely on the basis of information and inferences about gene flow and differences in allele distributions. There are some broader approaches which do not specifically mention genes in the basic definition. Waples (1991) and O'Brien and Mayr (1991), extending the biological species concept, consider ESUs as population subsets that are substantially reproductively isolated. However, "reproduction" is of genes not cultural variants. One definition of ESU that, on the surface, appears to allow cultural entities to be listed *per se*, comes from the cladistic approach of Vogler and DeSalle (1994) in which ESUs are discriminated using characters which cluster individuals or populations to the exclusion of other such clusters. Such characters must be heritable, which admits many culturally determined attributes. However characters must also "define phylogenetic (i.e., genetically separated) lineages" (Vogler and DeSalle, 1994), and so we are back to genes again.

The emphasis on genetic patterns and processes, or restrictions to reproductively isolated population segments, would probably rule out ESU designation for most known instances of the culturally determined segregation of a sympatric population, such as the Moreton Bay bottlenose dolphins and sperm whale clans. In contrast, the "types" and communities of orcas are largely reproductively isolated, and show genetic differences (Barrett-Lennard, 2000), allowing potential discrimination into ESUs under several of the criteria.

Fundamentally we are trying to conserve biodiversity, which may be defined as the "full variety of life on Earth" (Takacs, 1996). A large part of this variety is heritable phenotypic variation. The mechanism by which information is transferred between generations is of secondary significance. There are several mechanisms by which information which determines phenotypes may be transferred between generations, of which genetics is much the most significant, and culture the clear runner up (Maynard Smith, 1989). Definitions of the ESU which are neutral as to transmission mechanisms could easily be derived from current proposals. For instance, Fraser and Bernatchez's (2001) "lineage demonstrating highly restricted gene flow from other such lineages within the higher organizational level (lineage) of the species" could become a "lineage demonstrating highly restricted flow of information that determines phenotypes from other such lineages within the higher organizational level (lineage) of the species".

Such an approach would lead to "cultural ESU's" only very rarely: both a large and functionally important part of the behavior of animals would have to be due to social learning, and there would need to be little cultural exchange between population segments, despite the segments sharing geographical ranges and most functionally important genes. In most species cultural variants are either geographically or genetically discrete or of little functional importance, but orcas would probably qualify, and maybe sperm whales and elephants. We believe that preserving significant cultural variants in such species is an important part of conserving the species itself.

Conclusion

We have heard arguments that if we are at the stage of conserving non-human cultures, then the real conservation battles have already been won. We disagree. For a range of non-human animals, culture is a vital determinant of phenotype, and so how the animals interact with humans and our cultural artifacts. Thus, culture should be an integral element of the conservation biology of these species.

Cultural organisms do not behave like those for which culture has little significance. Clearly maladaptive behavior is often taken as a sign of a threat to individuals or populations, but genetically maladaptive behavior is to be expected in conformist cultures. In cultural societies, individuals with important cultural knowledge may have population significance far in excess of their reproductive capacities (McComb et al., 2001), and populations may be structured in significant ways by cultural knowledge and cultural habit. As we hope we have shown, these mean that conservation takes on an additional dimension. This is manifestly recognized for humans, but we should also consider culture in the conservation of other species – in individual cases by noting how cultural diversity interacts with anthropogenic threats, as well as perhaps more systematically by adding the potential for culture to our concepts of ESUs and other staples of conservation biology.

It has been suggested that the recognition of culture in other animals should affect our perception of them (Fox, 2001). Cultural Survival (2002) believes that there is a "moral obligation" to conserve human cultural diversity. So, in addition to considering culture as a part of the mix of biological attributes that affects how organisms interact with anthropogenic threats, perhaps culture should also be inserted into the roots of our conservation biology: why we wish to conserve organisms, and what we wish to conserve about them. These questions are difficult, and perhaps beyond the scope of most practicing conservation biologists. However, this does not mean that the implications of non-human cultures should just be left to the ethicists: non-human culture is not just "chimpanzees/dolphins/elephants reading poetry", it is the source of survival skills fundamental to the daily lives of these animals.

Acknowledgments

Thanks to Bill McGrew for his perspective on the relationship between culture and conservation in chimpanzees, to Marilyn Dahlheim for information about the development of fish-stealing among Alaskan orcas, and to two anonymous reviewers for encouragement and comments.

References

Ashford, J.R., Rubilar, P.S., Martin, A.R., 1996. Interactions between cetaceans and longline fishery operations around South Georgia. Marine Mammal Science 12, 452–456.

Baird, R.W., 2000. The killer whale – foraging specializations and group hunting. In: Mann, J., Connor, R.C., Tyack, P., Whitehead, H. (Eds.), Cetacean Societies. University of Chicago Press, Chicago, pp. 127–153.

Balcomb, K.C., Claridge, D.E., 2001. A mass stranding of cetaceans caused by naval sonar in the Bahamas. Bahamas Journal of Science 5, 2–12.

Barrett-Lennard, L., 2000. Population structure and mating patterns of killer whales (Orcinus orca) as revealed by DNA analysis. Ph.D. Dissertation, University of British Columbia, Vancouver.

Boesch, C., 2001. Sacrileges are welcome in science! Opening a discussion about culture in animals. Behavioral and Brain Sciences 24, 327–328.

Boran, J.R., Heimlich, S.L., 1999. Social learning in Cetaceans: hunting, hearing and hierarchies. Symposia of the Zoological Society, London 73, 282–307.

Boyd, R., Richerson, P.J., 1996. Why culture is common, but cultural evolution is rare. Proceedings of the British Academy 88, 77–93.

Boyd, R., Richerson, P., 1985. Culture and the Evolutionary Process. Chicago University Press, Chicago.

Cavalli-Sforza, L.L., Feldman, M.W., Chen, K.H., Dornbusch, S.M., 1982. Theory and observation in cultural transmission. Science 218, 19–27.

Chilvers, B.L., Corkeron, P.J., 2001. Trawling and bottlenose dolphins' social structure. Proceedings of the Royal Society of London B268, 1901–1905.

Clapham, P.J., Young, S.B., Brownell, R.L.J., 1999. Baleen whales: conservation issues and the status of the most endangered populations. Mammal Review 29, 35–60.

Connor, R.C., 2001. Individual foraging specializations in marine mammals: culture and ecology. Behavioral and Brain Sciences 24, 329–330.

Cronk, L., 1999. That complex whole: culture and the evolution of human behavior. Westview Press, Boulder, CO.

Cultural Survival, 2002. Annual Report 2001–2002. Celebrating 30 years of Cultural Survival, Cultural Survival. Cambridge, MA.

de Waal, F.B.M., Tyack, P.L., 2003. Animal social complexity; intelligence, culture, and individualized societies. Harvard University Press, Cambridge, MA.

Ding, W., Renjun, L., Zhang, X., Jian, Y., Wei, Z., Zhao, Q., Wang, X., 2000. Status and conservation of the Yangtze finless porpoise. In: Reeves, R.R., Smith, B.D., Kasuya, T. (Eds.), Biology and Conservation of Freshwater Cetaceans in Asia. IUCN Species Survival Commission, Gland, Switzerland, pp. 81–85.

Dizon, A.E., Lockyer, C., Perrin, W.F., Demaster, D.P., Sisson, J., 1992. Rethinking the stock concept. Conservation Biology 6, 24–36.

Dunbar, R.I.M., 2001. Do how *do* they do it? Behavioral and Brain Sciences 24, 332–333.

Erbe, C., 2002. Underwater noise of whale-watching boats and potential effects on killer whales (*Orcinus orca*), based on an acoustic impact model. Marine Mammal Science 18, 394–418.

Estes, J.A., Riedman, M.L., Staedler, M.M., Tinker, M.T., Lyon, B.E., 2003. Individual variation in prey selection by sea otters: patterns, causes and implications. Journal of Animal Ecology 72, 144–155.

Ford, J.K.B., Ellis, G.M., Barrett-Lennard, L.G., Morton, A.B., Palm, R.S., Balcomb, K.C., 1999. Dietary specialization in two sympatric populations of killer whales (*Orcinus orca*) in coastal British Columbia and adjacent waters. Canadian Journal of Zoology 76, 1456–1471.

Fox, M.A., 2001. Cetacean culture: philosophical implications. Behavioral and Brain Sciences 24, 333–334.

Fraser, D.J., Bernatchez, L., 2001. Adaptive evolutionary conservation: towards a unified concept for defining conservation units. Molecular Ecology 10, 2741–2752.

Galef, B.G., 1992. The question of animal culture. Human Nature 3, 157–178.

Goodall, J., 1994. Postcript – conservation and the future of chimpanzee and bonobo research in Africa. In: Wrangham, R.W., McGrew, W.C., de Waal, F.B.M., Heltne, P.G. (Eds.), Chimpanzee Cultures. Harvard University Press, Cambridge, MA, pp. 397–404.

Grant, B.R., Grant, P.R. 1996. Cultural inheritance of song and its role in the evolution of Darwin's finches. Evolution 50, 2471–2487.

Heimlich-Boran, J.R., 1993. Social organization of the short-finned pilot whale *Globicephala macrorhynchus*, with special reference to the comparative social ecology of delphinids. Ph.D. Dissertation, Cambridge University, Cambridge, UK.

Herman, L.M., Pack, A.A., 2001. Laboratory evidence for cultural transmission mechanisms. Behavioral and Brain Sciences 24, 335–336.

Ingold, T., 2001. The use and abuse of ethnography. Behavioral and Brain Sciences 24, 337.

Jepson, P.D., Arbelo, M., Deaville, R., Patterson, I.A., Castro, P., Degollada, E., Ross, H.M., Herráez, P., Pocknell, A.M., Rodriguez, F., Howiell, F.E., Espinosa, A., Reid, R.J., Jaber, J.R., Martin, V., Cunningham, A.A., Fernández, A., 2003. Gas bubble lesions in stranded cetaceans. Nature 425, 575–576.

Laland, K.N., 1992. A theoretical investigation of the role of social transmission in evolution. Ethology and Sociobiology 13, 87–113.

Laland, K.N., Hoppitt, W., 2003. Do animals have culture? Evolutionary Anthropology 12, 150–159.

Laland, K.N., Richerson, P.J., Boyd, R., 1996. Developing a theory of animal social learning. In: Heyes, C.M., Galef, B.G.J. (Eds.), Social Learning in Animals: The Roots of Culture. Academic Press, San Diego, CA, pp. 129–154.

Luck, G.W., Daily, G.C., Ehrlich, P.R., 2003. Population diversity and ecosystem services. Trends in Ecology and Evolution 18, 331–336.

Mann, J., 2001. Cetacean culture: definitions and evidence. Behavioral and Brain Sciences 24, 343.

Mann, J., Sargeant, B., 2003. Like mother, like calf: the ontogeny of foraging traditions in wild Indian ocean bottlenose dolphins (*Tursiops* sp.). In: Fragaszy, D.M., Perry, S. (Eds.), The biology of traditions: models and evidence. Cambridge University Press, Cambridge, UK, pp. 236–266.

Markowitz, T.M., Harlin, A.D., Würsig, B., McFadden, C.J., 2004. Dusky dolphin foraging habitat: overlap with aquaculture in New Zealand. Aquatic Conservation: Marine and Freshwater Ecosystems 14, 133–149.

Maynard Smith, J., 1989. Evolutionary Genetics. Oxford University Press, Oxford, UK.

McComb, K., Moss, C., Durant, S.M., Baker, L., Sayialel, S., 2001. Matriarchs as repositories of social knowledge in African elephants. Science 292, 491–494.

McGrew, W.C., 2003. Ten dispatches from the chimpanzee culture wars. Intelligence, culture, and individualized societies. In: de Waal, F.B.M., Tyack, P.L. (Eds.), Animal Social Complexity. Harvard University Press, Cambridge, MA.

McGrew, W.C., 1992. Chimpanzee material culture: implications for human evolution. Cambridge University Press, Cambridge, UK.

Moritz, C., 1994. Defining 'evolutionary significant units' for conservation. Trends in Ecology and Evolution 9, 373–375.

Mundinger, P.C., 1980. Animal cultures and a general theory of cultural evolution. Ethology and Sociobiology 1, 183–223.

National Marine Fisheries Service, 1998. Sperm whale (Physeter macrocephalus): North Pacific stock, Stock Assessment Report, pp. 111–114.

Nettle, D., 1999. Language variation and the evolution of societies. In: Dunbar, R.I.M., Knight, C., Power, C. (Eds.), The Evolution of Culture. Rutgers University Press, Piscataway, NJ, pp. 214–227.

NOAA, 2002. Status Review under the Endangered Species Act: Southern Resident Killer Whales (Orcinus orca), NOAA Technical Memorandum NMFS-NWAFSC-54, Seattle, WA.

Nolan, C.P., Liddle, G.M., Elliot, J., 2000. Interactions between killer whales (Orcinus orca) and sperm whales (Physeter macrocephalus) with a longline fishing vessel. Marine Mammal Science 16, 658–664.

Norris, K.S., 1994. Comparative view of cetacean social ecology, culture, and evolution. In: Norris, K.S., Würsig, B., Wells, R.S., Würsig, M. (Eds.), The Hawaiian Spinner Dolphin. University of California Press, Berkeley, CA, pp. 301–344.

O'Brien, S.J., Mayr, E., 1991. Species hybridization and protection of endangered animals. Science 253, 251–252.

Osborne, R.W., 1999. A historical ecology of Salish Sea resident killer whales (Orcinus orca): with implications for management. Ph.D. Dissertation, University of Victoria, Victoria, British Columbia.

Ottensmeyer, C.A., Whitehead, H., 2003. Behavioural evidence for social units in long-finned pilot whales. Canadian Journal of Zoology 81, 1327–1338.

Payne, K., 1999. The progressively changing songs of humpback whales: a window on the creative process in a wild animal. In: Wallin, N.L., Merker, B., Brown, S. (Eds.), The Origins of Music. MIT Press, Cambridge, MA, pp. 135–150.

Reeves, R.R., Mead, J.G., 1999. Marine mammals in captivity. In: Twiss, J.R., Reeves, R.R. (Eds.), Conservation and Management of Marine Mammals. Smithsonian Institution Press, Washington, DC, pp. 412–436.

Rendell, L., Whitehead, H., 2003. Vocal clans in sperm whales (Physeter macrocephalus). Proceedings of the Royal Society of London B270, 225–231.

Rendell, L., Whitehead, H., 2001a. Cetacean culture: still afloat after the first naval engagement of the culture wars. Behavioral and Brain Sciences 24, 360–373.

Rendell, L., Whitehead, H., 2001b. Culture in whales and dolphins. Behavioral and Brain Sciences 24, 309–324.

Richerson, P.J., Boyd, R., 1998. The evolution of human ultrasociality. In: Eibl-Eibesfeldt, I., Salter, F.K. (Eds.), Indoctrinability, Ideology and Warfare. Berghahn Books, London, pp. 71–95.

Ross, P.S., Ellis, G.M., Ikonomou, M.G., Barrett-Lennard, L.G., Addison, R.F., 2000. High PCB concentrations in free-ranging Pacific killer whales (Orcinus orca): effects of age, sex and dietary preference. Marine Pollution Bulletin 40, 504–515.

Simões-Lopes, P.C., Fabián, M.E., Menegheti, J.O., 1998. Dolphin interactions with the mullet artisanal fishing on southern Brazil: a qualitative and quantitative approach. Revista Brasileira de Zoologia 15, 709–726.

Slater, P.J.B., 2001. There's CULTURE and Culture. Behavioral and Brain Sciences 24, 356–357.

Slater, P.J.B., 1986. The cultural transmission of bird song. Trends in Ecology and Evolution 1, 94–97.

Sutherland, W.J., 1998. The importance of behavioural studies in conservation biology. Animal Behaviour 56, 801–809.

Takacs, D., 1996. The Idea of Biodiversity: Philosophies of Paradise. Johns Hopkins University Press, Baltimore, MD.

Trites, A.W., Barrett-Lennard, L.G., 2001. COSEWIC status report on killer whales (*Orcinus orca*), Committee on the Status of Endangred Wildlife in Canada, Ottawa.

van Schaik, C.P., Ancrenaz, M., Borgen, G., Galdikas, B., Knott, C.D., Singleton, I., Suzuki, A., Utami, S.S., Merrill, M., 2003. Orangutan cultures and the evolution of material culture. Science 299, 102–105.

Vogler, A.P., DeSalle, R., 1994. Diagnosing units of conservation management. Conservation Biology 8, 354–363.

Waples, R.S., 1991. Pacific salmon, *Oncorhynchus* spp. and the definition of 'species' under the Endangered Species Act. Marine Fisheries Review 53, 11–22.

Wells, R.S., Bassos-Hull, K., Norris, K.S., 1998. Experimental return to the wild of two bottlenose dolphins. Marine Mammal Science 14, 51–71.

Whitehead, H., 2003. Sperm Whales: Social Evolution in the Ocean. University of Chicago Press, Chicago, IL.

Whitehead, H., 1999. Culture and genetic evolution in whales. Science 284, 2055a.

Whiten, A., 2001. Imitation and cultural transmission in apes and cetaceans. Behavioral and Brain Sciences 24, 359–360.

Whiten, A., Ham, R., 1992. On the nature and evolution of imitation in the animal kingdom: reappraisal of a century of research. Advances in the Study of Behavior 21, 239–283.

Whiten, A., Goodall, J., McGrew, W.C., Nishida, T., Reynolds, V., Sugiyama, Y., Tutin, C.E.G., Wrangham, R.W., Boesch, C., 2001. Charting cultural variation in chimpanzees. Behaviour 138, 1481–1516.

Whiten, A., Goodall, J., McGrew, W.C., Nishida, T., Reynolds, V., Sugiyama, Y., Tutin, C.E.G., Wrangham, R.W., Boesch, C., 1999. Cultures in chimpanzees. Nature 399, 682–685.

Würsig, B., Würsig, M., Cipriano, F., 1989. Dolphins in different worlds. Oceanus 32, 71–75.

Yano, K., Dahlheim, M.E., 1995. Killer whale, *Orcinus orca*, depredation on long-line catches of bottomfish in the southeastern Bering Sea and adjacent waters. Fishery Bulletin US 93, 355–372.

Zhang, X., Wang, D., Liu, R., Wei, Z., Hua, Y., Wang, Y., Chen, Z., Wang, L., 2003. The Yangtze river dolphin or baiji (*Lipotes vexillifer*): population status and conservation issues in the Yangtze River, China. Aquatic Conservation: Marine and Freshwater Ecosystems 13, 51–64.

Chapter 23

Mark Peter Simmonds

INTO THE BRAINS OF WHALES

Simmonds argues that various complex behaviors and social structures earlier found for a few cetacean species seem to be broadly applicable to cetaceans generally, and are particularly well developed for some odontocete species. He argues that, because of this high intelligence, the potential impacts of whale removals, including whaling, may be far greater than previously believed and that new approaches to the conservation of these species are required that address their intelligence, societies, cultures, and potential to suffer.

1. Introduction

THE MAMMALIAN ORDER Cetacea includes over 80 known species of whales, dolphins and porpoises and is popularly believed to contain some of the most intelligent animals. Although research on cetacean social systems lags some three decades behind equivalent work on primates (Connor et al., 1998), new research and expert analyses of research and behaviour (e.g. Whitehead, 2003, Mann et al., 2000 and Connor et al., 1998) mean that, whilst acknowledging the limitations of our present understanding, we can now engage in a well informed consideration of cetacean intelligence, society and culture and attempt to relate our conclusions to urgent conservation and welfare issues.

However, there are a number of significant methodological difficulties involved in evaluating cetacean intelligence. Lusseau and Newman (2004) noted that "animal social networks are substantially harder to study than networks of human beings because they do not give interviews or fill out questionnaires . . ." Consequently, information must be gained by direct observation of individuals and their interactions with conspecifics. However, when studying marine mammals, the practical difficulties and expense involved in observational work are considerable, including the fact that individuals tend to be wide-ranging, fast moving and, in the case of several species, also very deep-diving. This has led to the development of stringent photo-identification techniques which in recent years have provided an important insight into cetacean social networks. A further complication is the degree to which the cetacean behaviour observable at the sea surface reflects their activities more generally. This is especially true of the deep divers such as the beaked whales of the family Ziiphidae or the cachalots (or sperm whales), *Physeter macrocephalus*, which spend so much of their time in the depths. In the case of the latter in particular, studies at the surface are now being combined with sophisticated acoustic techniques which enable the animals to be monitored underwater, including monitoring particular individuals (Whitehead, 2003).

Another tier of complexity is provided by the likelihood that physically proximate individuals, apparently operating as a distinct group, may actually be in acoustic contact with other more distant animals creating a larger, dispersed social unit that is far more difficult to study. Janik (2000a) recently calculated that wild common bottlenose dolphin, *Tursiops truncatus*, whistles in the Moray Firth, Scotland, could be discernible 20–25 km away (in water of 10 m depth and with a sea state of zero). The larger, louder whales may be in contact across entire ocean basins. In fact, cetaceans predominantly perceive their world using sound and remarkable hearing abilities; a distinction that makes comparison with primates difficult.

Another methodological issue is the anatomical differences between cetaceans and primates. Goold and Goold in *The Animal Mind* (1994) commented ". . . privately many primatologists (and publicly a few) concede that they assume that their subjects are to some degree self aware. In part this may arise not because primates are so much smarter than others species, but because it is easier for humans to read primate gestures and emotional expressions than the equivalents in, say, beavers or dolphins. It is also easier for us to empathize with behavioural responses to situations that could touch our own lives." Thus they highlight the possibility that our interpretation of cetacean behaviour might be hampered by a lack of empathy which could also have significant implications for conservation priorities and welfare issues.

In terms of behavioural interpretation, the physical differences between primates and cetaceans are significant. For example, whilst the arrangement of bones in the cetacean forelimb is similar to our own, the phalanges are encased within a flipper, which acts as an aqua-foil for lift and steering. Thus they lack the manipulative abilities of primates and cannot gesture or point with the same facility. Similarly, the musculature of their heads prohibits facial expressions, although a few species such as the beluga, *Delphinapterus leucas*, have some 'facial' mobility.

From their work on primates, Russon and Bard (1996) identified the following signs of intelligence: problem solving by insight; tool use/manufacture; imitation; sense of self; pedagogy and culture. This paper reviews the recent key literature and results concerning relevant cetacean attributes in these key areas and, additionally, considers some evidence that suggests emotional responses in cetaceans. It is also worth commenting at the outset that two evolutionary pressures on cetaceans are likely to have resulted in the development of high cognitive functioning: firstly the patchy unpredictable prey resources that they tend to exploit (Rendall and Whitehead, 2001) and, secondly, the cognitive demands of living in complexly bonded social groups (Dunbar, 2003).

2. Brain development and cetacean senses

The size and complexity of the brain has long been used as a basic indicator of intelligence. The only animal group that rivals the primates in this regard is the cetaceans (Marino et al., 2004). In fact, amongst the odontocetes (the toothed cetaceans), some relative brain sizes challenge the hominid mammalian line and arise from a substantial increase in encephalisation apparent during the Oligocene (Marino, 2002). The relative cerebellum size is greater in some dolphins than in any of the primates, including humans (Marino et al., 2000). The larger whales have large bodies as an adaptation to their ecological niches – including some organs such as the acoustic lens in the head of cachalots and their thick layer of blubber that require little nervous control – and this may explain why they fare less well if brain size is compared to body size (Parsons et al., 2004).

Brain development in cetaceans has been related to acoustic signal 'processing needs'. Most cetaceans are active 'echolocators', producing high frequency clicks to investigate the world around them (Simmonds et al., 2004), these and the non-echolocators may also use ambient sounds to help them navigate (Clark cited in Carey, 2005). The full alacrity of cetacean hearing across the entire order is still not clear but some notion of their high sensitivity has been known since the early 1950s when it was shown that dolphins would respond with sound signals to a single BB shot (air rifle pellet) dropped into their pool (Benjamin and Bruce, 1982). In open waters, bottlenose dolphins can detect the presence of a water-filled sphere of diameter 7.6 cm over distances of up to 110 m (Au and Snyder, 1980).

Modern cetaceans have been evolving separately from their closest living relatives for at least 52 million years and from the primates for 92 million years. Marino et al. (2004) challenge the notion that the single remaining human lineage pruned down from a "bushier tree" of relatives means that several species of highly encephalised animals cannot co-exist. In fact, their review of the fossil record and extant species shows that multiple highly encephalised delphinoids coexist today and have done so for at least 15 million years.

3. Examples of intelligent behaviours

Brain size and comparative development is, at best, only an indicator of intelligence and a better way to assess intelligence may be to look at behaviour, including communication skills. Captive cetaceans, especially bottlenose dolphins and orcas, *Orcinus orca*, have successfully been taught to repeat a wide range of actions. In fact, bottlenose dolphins modify taught behaviours and invent new ones (Norris, 2002). They appear to make their play more complex and difficult over time, arguably a 'hallmark of intelligence' and innovative play is also known in wild dolphins.

The bottlenose dolphin can imitate both vocally and non-vocally and is considered by some to be the most sophisticated non-human imitator (e.g. Whitten, 2001). Herman (cited in Norris, 2002) suggests that the extensive vocal and behavioural mimicry of the dolphins is "a seemingly unique combination of abilities among non-human animals" and notes that dolphins can copy behaviours and sounds without extensive repetition or training. Behavioural fads have also been seen to spread spontaneously among captives.

Bottlenose dolphins have also shown that they can learn and generalise a variety of reporting tasks. This includes reporting on named objects in their environment; reporting on the behaviour of others (including other dolphins, humans and seals) by mimicry; reporting their own behaviour (Mercado et al., 1998). From their experiments, Mercado et al. (1998) suggest that dolphins can 'flexibly access memories of their recent actions' that are of sufficient detail for re-enactment. For example, bottlenose dolphins will 'point' at objects to guide humans to them. They do this by stopping their forward progress, often less than 2 m from an object, aligning their anterior–posterior axis for a few seconds and then alternating head direction between the object and the trainer (Xitco et al., 2004). These pointing behaviours are affected by the degree of attentiveness of the experimenters, and do not occur with humans absent.

Despite their lack of fingers and thumbs, both wild and captive dolphins may spontaneously manipulate objects. There is one well-documented use of tools in a wild Indo-Pacific bottlenose dolphin, *Tursiops aduncus*, population which occurs in Shark Bay, Australia. The animals (almost exclusively females) are often seen carrying sponges on the ends of their beaks probably to protect them whilst they forage in the sediments on the seafloor where spiny sea urchins might otherwise cause puncture wounds (Smolker et al., 1997).

Another example of manipulation involves the bubbles that dolphins produce underwater. Breathing is a voluntary activity in cetaceans and the bubbles may be released in streams, clouds or as single bubble-rings. Although the physics that create these doughnut-shaped bubble formations are well understood (a bubble bigger than two centres in diameter tends to become a ring because of pressure differences between the top and bottom), the production of stable rings probably requires practice, expertise and forethought (McCowan et al., 2000). Dolphins manipulate their bubble-rings by forming vortices around them, causing them to flip, turn vertically or fuse. McCowan et al. (2000) concluded that this form of manipulation was consistent with at least 'low level planning' prior to bubble production, again implying self-monitoring. They also report anecdotal evidence that young dolphins learn to produce rings from their mothers.

4. Self-awareness

Hart and Karmel (1996) identify the following behaviours as evidence of self-awareness: linguistic markers such as recalling personal memories; linguistic self-referencing (rare but known in language-trained apes); cognitive behavioural markers, particularly mirror self referencing based on marks on face (shown by apes); imitation; emotional markers–divided into self conscious emotions (e.g. guilt, shame, embarrassment or pride) and empathy (e.g. helping a wounded individual).

Until recently, only humans and great apes had shown convincing evidence of mirror-self recognition but similar tests have also been applied to bottlenose dolphins with unequivocal results (Reiss and Marino, 2001). Two captive animals exposed to reflective surfaces used them to investigate marks placed on various parts of their bodies by orientating themselves appropriately at the reflective surfaces. The dolphins did not display any attempts at social behaviour towards their mirror images and spent more time at the mirrors when marked than when sham-marked (where the marking process was repeated but without leaving a mark). One dolphin, when marked for the first and only time on the tongue, swam straight to a mirror and engaged in a mouth opening and closing sequence never before exhibited by this individual. Interestingly, and unlike chimpanzees, they showed no interest in the artificial marks placed on each other. Reiss and Marino (2001) suggest that this may be because dolphins, unlike primates, do not groom. The previous apparent confinement of self-recognition to man and apes has naturally generated interest in its relationship to higher levels of abstract psychological self-awareness. In humans, the ability to recognise oneself does not emerge reliably until about 18–24 months of age. This dolphin study now indicates that this ability is not limited to the primate line of evolution.

Emotional responses may be an indicator of higher cognitive functions. However, Frohoff (2000) warns of the significant interspecies communication problems in interpreting cetacean emotions. For example, she reports that she has often seen captive dolphins exhibiting what were to her blatant indications of stress or aggression while interacting with human visitors, but that these signals are usually misunderstood or ignored. Nonetheless, various emotions (in addition to stress and aggression) have been attributed to cetacean behaviour. For example, two male orcas appeared to exhibit grief after the body of an older female was found dead. The circumstances giving rise to this observation are extremely rare as cetacean corpses are typically lost at sea. In life, the female was always accompanied by two younger males, believed to be her sons. These animals had been monitored since the 1970s and, uniquely, for a day or two after the dead body was found, in mid-November 1990, the two sons swam together but without contact with any other orcas, visiting again and again the places that their mother had passed in the last few days of her life. Rose (2000a), an experienced orca researcher, who reported this event, commented that their steady swimming retracing the mother's movements seemed expressive of grief. Both orcas are still alive, still swimming side by side and whilst now they do occasionally socialise with others, they are still often seen alone.

Other emotions proposed for cetaceans include parental love, as exhibited by orcas (Rose, 2000b), and prolonged grieving following the loss of a calf (Herzing, 2000a). Herzing (2000b), a renowned field biologist, also identifies 'joy' in the long term subjects of her work, the Atlantic spotted dolphins, *Stenella frontalis*, living off the Bahamas. Whilst these accounts of emotions might be dismissed because they are anecdotal or unproven they are provided by experienced field scientists who have studied these animals for many years.

Frohoff (2000) reports that the altruistic behaviour sometimes shown to people by dolphins (for example, saving swimmers from drowning) is actually inconsistent; for example, whilst she has witnessed a small group of wild spotted dolphins deliberately go to help a nearby swimmer in distress (an action that has also been reported by others (Simmonds, 2004)), on another occasion she was 'abandoned' by a group of wild dolphins and left in the presence of a 12-foot bull shark. Frohoff comments that such inconsistency indicates that "the emotional life of dolphins is probably as multifaceted and colourful as our own, and our appreciation of them needs to encompass their full range of emotional expression – not just the parts that we find attractive".

One interesting example of an angry response from a dolphin is recounted by Schusterman (2000) and relates to the efforts to teach captive bottlenose dolphins artificial language in Hawaii. A female dolphin had just been given a series of gestural signals. When she did not respond correctly she was given 'negative feedback' and a moment later responded by grabbing a large plastic pipe floating nearby and hurling it at the trainer, missing the young lady's head by inches. Cartilidge (pers commun.) reports a similar event when an 'angry' dolphin deliberately threw the spiny-part of a fish which injured its trainer's hand when he instinctively grabbed the missile. In fact, from his experience, Cartilidge (pers. commun.) reports that in his experience captive cetaceans often behaved in an emotional (frustrated or angry) manner when given negative feedback.

5. Language

Cetaceans are certainly amongst the most vocal of animals. However, the question of whether they have language has proved vexing. It was probably John Lilly in the 1960s who first speculated in favour of a dolphin language, although most biologists remain sceptical (Norris, 2002). Nevertheless, various lines of research support this notion, including attempts to teach dolphins artificial languages, thereby indicating that their mental capacities are adequate to such a task. Such studies, at the University of Hawaii, have shown that dolphins can acquire an artificial language including concepts of grammar and syntax (Norris, 2002). Goold and Goold (1994) commented that whilst the vocabulary taught to dolphins is relatively small (about three dozen words), their ability to decode 5-word sentences is "remarkable".

Several authors have proposed that bottlenose dolphins have distinctive 'signature whistles' that are specific to individuals and which also provide evidence of the significance of vocal mimicry in the wild. In a study of wild Scottish common bottlenose dolphins, Janik (2000b) found that these signals were copied and repeated by conspecifics that were out of visual contact, suggesting that they address each other individually, using learned sound patterns. Other researchers have challenged such a straight-forward signature whistle hypothesis (McCowan and Reiss, 2001) but there is agreement that bottlenose dolphins have a large whistle repertoire that changes substantially during the animals' development and that sequences of whistles could contain considerable information. McCowan and Reiss (2001) also noted that infant dolphins babble sequences of whistles that become more organised as they mature.

Research into cetacean communication may have been hampered by an exclusive focus on those calls that are most easily audible to humans, rather than their full range of vocalisations. This approach ignores the potential of their higher frequency 'clicks' to convey information (as well as primarily being a tool for echolocation) (Simmonds, 2004). Secondly, the captive conditions where most studies have been made may affect their communications by creating an inappropriate acoustic environment or not offering contact with conspecifics with common 'language'. There is also a general lack of adequate appreciation of both non-verbal signals and of the context of communications.

Wild cetaceans also have many dramatic natural behaviours that have no obvious purpose, such as breaching and tail-slapping, but which may have a communicatory function. Certainly the noise of a tail-slap or breach would be a more significant sound source underwater. Bubblestreams have also recently been suggested as having a role in communication (Fripp, 2005).

As with human languages, a particular emitted sound could have one meaning in one context – say during a co-ordinated feeding activity – and another during a different one, such as breeding behaviour. The meaning of the sound might also be further modified by posture of the emitter (or even the intended recipient) or the order of events during which it is created.

In the wild, in addition to the studies on bottlenose dolphin whistles, wild orca communications have also been studied in some detail. In British Columbia, matrilineal groups of resident orcas have 7–17 identified call types that vary amongst pods and the pods all have distinctive features in their call repertoires, creating 'dialects' (Ford, 2002).

Until we can monitor all possible sources of signals and the context in which they are made – which will require some very sophisticated underwater research – the issue of language will probably remain unproven. However, it is clear that many cetaceans live in co-operative societies in which they co-ordinate many of their activities, including predation, and their calls (which at the very least have the potential to convey considerable information) and other signals are important in this.

6. Group living

"During the summer of 1977, 30 false killer whales (*Pseudorca crassidens*) floated in the shallows of the dry Tortugas for 3 days . . . A large male in the centre of the group lay on his side, bleeding from his right ear. When a shark swam by, the whales flailed their tails. Individuals became agitated when people separated the whales to return them to deeper water but became calm once back in physical contact with other whales. Despite the risk of stranding and growing blisters from exposure to the sun, the group stayed together and did not leave until the male died on the third day" (Connor, 2000). Connor (2000) used this incident to illustrate the remarkably strong dependence of cetaceans on group living. This ranges from orcas which are regarded as living in the "most stable groups known among mammals" (Connor, 2000) to individuals, which whilst not appearing to live in stable groups, regularly join with others for particular activities, such as feeding (e.g. humpback whales, *Megaptera novaeangliae*) or migration (e.g. gray whales, *Eschrichtius robustus*). In between these strategies lie the flexible 'fission–fusion' societies of the bottlenose dolphins, in which individuals associate in small groups which change composition on a regular basis (sometimes daily or even hourly).

Connor (2000) emphasises that no other group of mammals has evolved in an environment so devoid of refuges from predators. Consequently, many species, especially the smaller open ocean dwellers, have "nothing to hide behind but each other". Not only will this factor have significantly shaped the societies of cetaceans but it will undoubtedly have bearing on the nature of their intelligence. Connor et al. (1998) report that two contrasting results emerge from comparisons of the better known odontocetes with terrestrial mammals, both convergent and divergent strategies. There are remarkable convergences between the social systems of cachalots and bottlenose dolphins and terrestrial species–particularly elephants and chimpanzees, respectively. However, studies on orcas and Baird's beaked whales, *Berardius bairdii*, reveal novel social solutions related to aquatic living. For example, the fact that neither male nor female orcas disperse from the groups that they were born into in some populations does not seem to have a terrestrial equivalent. Connor et al. (1998) suggest that it is the low cost of travel at sea for these superbly streamlined animals that allows them to range widely enough to ensure that different orca pods meet adequately often to allow breeding to occur effectively. In fact bottlenose dolphins and orcas represent two ends of a spectrum of cetacean social strategies: the first living in highly flexible 'fission–fusion societies' and the second exhibiting stable relationships that last years and sometimes life-times.

Whilst the mating system of bottlenose dolphins has been ridiculously sensationalised by some in the media as 'gang rape', male competition is a common component of many mammal mating systems. It is taken to a particularly sophisticated level in some (but not all) bottlenose dolphin populations, where males form 'nested' levels of allegiances to sequester females in reproductive condition (Krutzen et al., 2004). Allegiances within social groups are comparatively rare in mammals. In fact, bottlenose dolphins are the only species other than humans wherein the males have been shown to form two levels of nested alliance formation within a social group. They also have two strategies in this regard: the first consists of small long-term alliances (the longest lasting of which was observed for 17 years). These pairs or trios of males control access to individual females in reproductive condition. Teams of two or more of these first-order alliances may co-operate to attack other allegiances or defend such attacks themselves.

The second strategy is where the first-order alliances are more labile and exist within a stable second-order alliance or 'super-alliance' within which the males frequently switch their alliance partners. Connor et al. (2001) found that whilst the shifting make-up of alliances invited the hypothesis that members treated each other as interchangeable resources, there are strong preferences and avoidances at play. In addition, Krutzen et al. (2004) have shown that the animals following the first strategy tend to be more closely related than by chance and, in the second strategy, the males in the group are not closely related. From a recent study of paternity conducted on the well-researched bottlenose dolphins of Shark Bay, Western Australia, it appears that these co-operative strategies are successful, although calves are also fathered by males without alliance partners (Krutzen et al., 2004).

Another form of co-operative behaviour was recently reported for common bottlenose dolphins in Cedar Key, Florida (Gazda et al., 2004). Dolphins hunting in a group have two types of specialisations: the 'driver dolphins' (which are consistently the same individuals in the two groups studied) herd fish towards the 'barrier dolphins'. Group hunting with a division of role and individual specialisation is very rare and Gazda et al. (2004) report that it has only been previously recorded from a study of co-ordinated group hunts in lions, *Panthera leo*.

Lusseau and Newman (2004) recently applied a new tool to the study of dolphin populations revealing further complexity. They applied techniques developed for the analysis of human social networks to the well-studied social network of the 62 Indo-Pacific bottlenose dolphins, *T. aduncus*, of Doubtful Sound, New Zealand. In addition to identifying various sub-groupings within the population, this technique identified what they termed 'broker dolphins' that acted as links between sub-communities. These 'brokers' played a crucial role in the social cohesion of the community as a whole.

There have been few studies of the societies of baleen whales. The humpback whale is the best studied baleen species but research has to a significant extent focused on male mating strategies (prompted by the whales' complex calls), foraging ecology and life history (Clapham, 2000). Connor (2000) comments that "although baleen whales appear to lack the stable social groups that are common among odontocetes, several observations suggest that long-term bonds might be more common than is commonly thought to be the case." Alongside other factors he notes the potential for long distance communication in these species.

In the case of the minke whales (the commercial whalers currently favoured target species) very little is known of their behaviour. However, there is one place where one population of minke whales on the Great Barrier Reef in Australia is proving tractable to long-term study, including recognition and monitoring of individuals. This population of dwarf minke whales – regarded as an undescribed sub-species of the northern minke whale (i.e. *Balaenoptera acutorostrata* sp.) – is being studied with the help of local whale watching operations (Birtles and Arnold, 2002 and Birtles et al., 2002). Known adult females return on an annual basis to within metres of where they were previously seen. Known individuals have also been regularly seen together in a style that at least emulates the fission—fusion society of some dolphins. Overall, these 6 tonne animals are reported to be remarkably inquisitive and sociable, and a range of repeated behaviours have been identified for them: bubble streaming and blasting; rolling over in the water, white belly up; jaw gapping and jaw clapping (Birtles and Arnold, 2002). Moreover, whilst these minke whales, like all the other baleen species, lack the system of air sacs in the forehead region used by toothed whales to produce sounds, they are far from mute. Their sounds probably come from the larynx region (although they also lack vocal cords) and are in the 10–9400 Hz range (so for the most part audible to us) including a mechanical sounding call that has three rapid pulses and a longer trailing note. They also produce sounds that are described as grunts, moans and belches. [. . .]

7. Conclusions

The issue of cetacean intelligence has been very controversial in the last few decades and the enthusiasm of some popular authors for promoting cetaceans as highly intelligent in the 1960s arguably caused a counter-productive back-lash (Samuels and Tyack, 2000); with sceptics highlighting lack of rigorous scientific proof, reliance on anecdotal information and failure to separate instinct from intelligence. Gaskin underpinned his very thoughtful – and still widely cited – criticism by asking two basic questions:

"1   Is there any real social structure in cetacean populations?
2   Do cetaceans have highly developed social behaviour?" (Gaskin, 1982).

We now have the benefit of more than two decades of further and increasingly sophisticated research which has shown relationships and behaviours that were hinted at in Gaskin's day. I therefore propose

Table 23.1 A summary of evidence for higher cognitive functioning in cetaceans

i.	High level of encephalisation, including very well developed cerebellum in many species
ii.	Long lives and long periods of parental care (evidence of post-reproductive care-givers)—exploiters of typically patchy and unpredictable prey
iii.	Ability to learn complex behaviours and solve problems
iv.	Ability to improvise/innovate
v.	Tool use (but not tool manufacture)
vi.	Vocal and behavioural imitation
vii.	Ability to learn artificial languages (limited vocabulary but understand grammar and syntax)
viii.	Many species exhibit closely co-ordinated behaviours
ix.	Many species have complex social interactions
x.	Evidence of self awareness, awareness of others, including emotional responses
xi.	Cultural transmission of information

that the answer to Gaskin's two primary questions is now, for some species at least, an unequivocal 'yes'.

The emerging body of evidence for the advanced cognitive abilities of some cetaceans is outlined in Table 23.1 and, if we accept this perspective, the next question is how should this knowledge affect our interactions with these animals? [T]o this can be added some statistics, for example:

- It has been estimated that some 200,000 cetaceans are killed annually in fishing nets (Read et al., 2003).
- The last available data for Japanese whaling reveal that only 40.2% of animals die 'instant-aneously' (Brakes and Fisher, 2004)—similar statistics from other hunts are presented in Table 23.2.

There is not room here to fully explore the relationship between the intelligence of these animals and the conservation and welfare matters that affect them, but it is clear that deaths in hunts and fishing nets may often be prolonged and painful and also significantly affect more members of the population than just the animals killed. It is also clear that we are having a widespread impact on their environment. Our relationship with these animals therefore needs to move to a new paradigm. What were previously regarded as 'living marine resources' – and typically widespread species distributed across an inexhaust-ible sea – should now be recognised as unique individuals, communities, societies and cultures and valued as such.

[. . .]

Table 23.2 Examples of recent whaling data based on information provided to the international Whaling Commission (from Brakes and Fisher, 2004)

Nation concerned/species	Year	Number killed	Died immediately (%)	Average TTD	Max TTD (min)	Number struck but lost
Norwegian, Minke whales	2001	552	79.7	145 s	90	10
	2002	634	80.7	141 s	90	1
Japan, Minke whales	2001/2002	440	33.0	203 s	No data	No data
	2002/2003	440	40.2	157 s	No data	No data
Russian Federation, Gray whales	2002	131	–	32 min	56	–
Russian Federation, Bowhead whales	2002	2	–	41 min	53	1
US (Alaskan Innuit hunt) Bowheads	2002	39	–	–	–	11
Greenland (West), Minke whales	2002	131	5.3	16 min	300	5
Greenland (East), Minke whales	2002	10	0	21 min	90	0
Greenland, Fin whales	2002	13	7.7	9 min	25	0

TTD: time to death.
* "A blue whale, which lives 100 years, that was born in 1940, today has had his acoustic bubble shrunken from 1000 to 100 miles because of noise pollution" (Clark in Carey, 2005).

References

Au and Snyder, 1980 Au, W.W.L., Snyder, K.J., 1980. Long-range target detection in open waters by an echolocating Atlantic Bottlenose dolphin (*Tursiops truncatus*). *J. Acoust. Soc. Am.* 68, 1077–1084.

Benjamin and Bruce, 1982 Benjamin, L.T., Bruce, D. 1982. From a bottle-fed chimp to a bottlenose dolphin: a contemporary appraisal of Winthrop, *Kellog. Psychol. Record* 32, 461–482.

Birtles and Arnold, 2002 Birtles, A., Arnold, P. 2002. Dwarf minke whales in the Great Barrier Reef— current state of knowledge. CRC Reef Brochure. CRC Research Centre Ltd., Townsville Australia. Available at: http://www.reef.crc.org.au/publications/brochures/index.html.

Birtles et al., 2002 R.A. Birtles, P.W. Arnold and A. Dunstan, Commercial swim programmes with dwarf minke whales of the Northern Great Barrier Reef, Australia: Some characteristics of encounters with management implications, *Aust. Mammal.* 24 (2002), pp. 23–38.

Brakes and Fisher, 2004 Brakes P., Fisher, S. 2004. Commercial and Aboriginal Subsistence Whaling. Chapter 6 in Brakes, P., Butterworth, A., Simmonds, M. and Lymbery, P. (Eds.), Troubled Waters – a review of the welfare implications of modern whaling activities. World Society for the Protection of Animals, London. Available at http://www.wspa-international.org.

Carey, 2005 Carey, B. 2005. Noise pollution disrupts whale communication. MSNBC news 20/2/2005. At: http://www.msnbc.msn.com/id/7003587/.

Clapham, 2000 P.J. Clapham, The Humpback Whale—seasonal feeding and breeding in a baleen whale. In: J. Mann, R.C. Connor, P.L. Tyack and H. Whitehead, Editors, *Cetacean Societies: Field Studies of Dolphins and Whales*, The University of Chicago Press, Chicago, USA (2000), pp. 173–196.

Connor, 2000 R.C. Connor, Group living in whales and dolphins. In: J. Mann, R.C. Connor, P.L. Tyack and H. Whitehead, Editors, *Cetacean Societies: Field Studies of Dolphins and Whales*, The University of Chicago Press, Chicago, USA (2000), pp. 199–218.

Connor et al., 1998 R.C. Connor, J. Mann, P.L. Tyack and H. Whitehead, Social evolution in toothed whales, *Trends Ecol. Evol.* **13** (1998), pp. 228–232. SummaryPlus | **Full Text + Links** | PDF (96 K) | View Record in Scopus | Cited By in Scopus

Connor et al., 2001 R.C. Connor, M.R. Heithaus and L.M. Barre, Complex social structure, alliance, stability and mating access in a bottlenose dolphin 'super-alliance', *Proc. R. Soc., Lond. B* **268** (2001), pp. 263–267. View Record in Scopus | Cited By in Scopus

Dunbar, 2003 R.I.M. Dunbar, The Social Brain: mind language and society in evolutionary perspective, *Annu. Rev. Anthropol.* **32** (2003), pp. 163–181. **Full Text** via CrossRef | View Record in Scopus | Cited By in Scopus

Ford, 2002 J.K.B. Ford, Dialects. In: J. Mann, R.C. Connor, P.L. Tyack and H. Whitehead, Editors, *Cetacean Societies: field studies of dolphins and whales*, The University of Chicago Press, Chicago, USA (2002).

Fripp, 2005 D. Fripp, Bubblestream whistles are not representative of a bottlenose dolphin's vocal repertoire, *Marine Mammal Sci.* **21** (2005), pp. 29–44. **Full Text** via CrossRef | View Record in Scopus | Cited By in Scopus

Frohoff, 2000 T. Frohoff, The dolphin's smile. In: M. Berkoff, Editor, *The Smile of the Dolphin*, Discovery Books, London (2000).

Gaskin, 1982 D.E. Gaskin, *The Ecology of Whales and Dolphins*, Heinemann, London and Exeter (1982).

Gazda et al., 2004 S.K. Gazda, R.C. Connor, R.K. Edgar and F. Cox, A division with role specialization in group-hunting bottlenose dolphins (*Tursiops truncatus*) off Cedar Key, Florida, *Proc. R. Soc. B* **272** (2004) (1559), pp. 135–140.

Goold and Goold, 1994 J.L. Goold and C.G. Goold, The Animal Mind, Scientific American Library, New York (1994).

Hart and Karmel, 1996 D. Hart and M.P. Karmel, Self awareness and self-knowledge in humans, apes and monkeys. In: A.E. Russon, K.A. Bard and S.T. Parker, Editors, *Reaching into the Thought—The Minds of Great Apes*, Cambridge University Press (1996).

Herzing, 2000a D.L. Herzing, A trail of grief. In: M. Berkoff, Editor, *The Smile of the Dolphin*, Discovery Books, London (2000).

Herzing, 2000b D.L. Herzing, The pleasure of their company. In: M. Berkoff, Editor, *The Smile of the Dolphin*, Discovery Books, London (2000).

Janik, 2000a V. Janik, Source levels and the estimated active space of bottlenose dolphin (*Tursiops truncatus*) whistles in the Moray Firth, Scotland, *J. Comp. Physiol. A* **186** (2000), pp. 673–680. **Full Text** via CrossRef | View Record in Scopus | Cited By in Scopus

Janik, 2000b V. Janik, Whistle matching in wild bottlenose dolphins, *Science* **289** (2000), pp. 1355–1357. **Full Text** via CrossRef | View Record in Scopus | Cited By in Scopus

Krutzen et al., 2004 M. Krutzen, L.M. Barre, R.C. Connor, J. Mann and W.B. Sherwin, Oh father: where art thou?—paternity assessment in an open fission–fusion society of wild bottlenose dolphins (*Tursiops* sp.) in Shark Bay, Western Australia, *Mol. Ecol.* **13** (2004), pp. 1975–1990. **Full Text** via CrossRef | View Record in Scopus | Cited By in Scopus

Krutzen et al., 2005 M. Krutzen, J. Mann, M.R. Heithaus, R.C. Connor, L. Bejder and W.B. Sherwin, Cultural transmission of tool use in bottlenose dolphins, *PNAS* **102** (2005), pp. 8939–8943. **Full Text** via CrossRef | View Record in Scopus | Cited By in Scopus

Lusseau and Newman, 2004 D. Lusseau and M.E.J. Newman, Identifying the role that animals play in their social networks, *Proc. R. Soc., Lond. B. (Suppl.)* **271** (2004), pp. S477–S481. **Full Text** via CrossRef | View Record in Scopus | Cited By in Scopus

Mann et al., 2000 J. Mann, R.C. Connor, P. Tyack and H. Whitehead, Cetacean Societies—Field Studies of Dolphins and Whales, The University of Chicago Press, Chicago and London (2000).

Marino, 2002 L. Marino, Brain size evolution. In: W.F. Perrin, B. Würsig and J.G.M. Thewissen, Editors, *Encyclopedia of Marine Mammals*, Academic Press, San Diego, USA (2002), pp. 158–162.

Marino et al., 2000 L. Marino, J.K. Rilling, S.K. Lin and S.H. Ridgway, Relative volume of the cerebellum in dolphins and comparison with anthropoid primates, *Brains Behav. Evol.* **56** (2000) (4), pp. 204–211. **Full Text** via CrossRef | View Record in Scopus | Cited By in Scopus

Marino et al., 2004 L. Marino, D.W. McShea and M.D. Uhen, Origin and evolution large brains in toothed whales, *Anatom. Rec. Part A* **81A** (2004), pp. 1–9.

McCowan and Reiss, 2001 B. McCowan and D. Reiss, The fallacy of 'signature whistles' in bottlenose dolphins: a comparative perspective of 'signature information' in animal vocalisations, *Anim. Behav.* **62** (2001), pp. 1151–1162. Abstract | **Abstract + References** | PDF (638 K) | View Record in Scopus | Cited By in Scopus

McCowan et al., 2000 B. McCowan, L. Marino, E. Vanve, L. Walke and D. Reiss, Bubble ring play of bottlenose dolphins (*Tursiops truncatus*): implications for cognition, *J. Comp. Psychol.* **114** (2000), pp. 98–106. Abstract | **Full Text** via CrossRef | View Record in Scopus | Cited By in Scopus

Mercado et al., 1998 E. Mercado III, S.O. Murray, R.K. Uyeyama, A.A. Pack and L.M. Herman, Memory for recent actions in the bottlenose dolphin (*Tursiops truncatus*): repetition of arbitrary behaviours using an abstract rule, *Anim. Learn. Behav.* **26** (1998) (2), pp. 210–218. View Record in Scopus | Cited By in Scopus

Norris, 2002 S. Norris, Creatures of culture? Making the case for cultural systems in whales and dolphins, *Bioscience* **52** (2002), pp. 9–14. **Full Text** via CrossRef | View Record in Scopus | Cited By in Scopus

Parsons et al., 2004 Parsons, E.C.M., Rose, N.A., Simmonds, M.P., 2004. Whales—individuals, societies and cultures, Chapter 4. In: Brakes, P., Butterworth, A., Simmonds, M., Lymbery, P. (Eds.). Troubled Waters – A Review of the Welfare Implications of Modern Whaling Activities. World Society for the Protection of Animals, London. Available at www.wspa-international.org.

Read et al., 2003 Read, A.J., Drinker, P., Northridge, S., 2003. By-catches of marine mammals in US fisheries and a first attempt to estimate the magnitude of global marine mammal by-catch. Paper submitted to the Scientific Committee of the International Whaling Commission SC/55/BC. 12 pages.

Reiss and Marino, 2001 D. Reiss and L. Marino, Mirror self-recognition in the bottlenose dolphin: a case of cognitive convergence, *PNAS* **98** (2001), pp. 5937–5942. **Full Text** via CrossRef | View Record in Scopus | Cited By in Scopus

Rendall and Whitehead, 2001 L. Rendall and H. Whitehead, Culture in whales and dolphins, *Behav. Brain Sci.* **24** (2001), pp. 309–324.

Rose, 2000a N.A. Rose, A death in the family. In: M. Berkoff, Editor, *The Smile of the Dolphin*, Discovery Books, London (2000).

Rose, 2000b N.A. Rose, Giving a little latitude. In: M. Berkoff, Editor, *The Smile of the Dolphin*, Discovery Books, London (2000).

Russon and Bard, 1996 A.E. Russon and K.A. Bard, Exploring the minds of great apes: issues and controversies. In: A.E. Russon, K.A. Bard and S.T. Parker, Editors, *Reaching into the Thought – The Minds of Great Apes*, Cambridge University Press (1996).

Samuels and Tyack, 2000 A. Samuels and P. Tyack, Flukeprints – a history of studying cetacean societies. In: J. Mann, R.C. Connor, P. Tyack and H. Whitehead, Editors, *Cetacean Societies—Field Studies of Dolphins and Whales*, The University of Chicago Press, Chicago and London (2000).

Schusterman, 2000 R.J. Schusterman, Pitching a fit. In: M. Berkoff, Editor, *The Smile of the Dolphin*, Discovery Books, London (2000).

Simmonds, 2004 M.P. Simmonds, *Whales and Dolphins of the World*, New Holland Publishers Ltd., London, UK (2004).

Simmonds et al., 2004 Simmonds, M.P., Dolman, S.D., Weilgart, L. 2004. Oceans of Noise 2004. Whale and Dolphin Conservation Society, Chippenham, UK. Available at: http://www.wdcs.org/dan/publishing.nsf/allweb/48A0C8D9C559FA0680256D2B004027D4.

Smolker et al., 1997 R. Smolker, A. Richards, R. Connor, J. Mann and P. Berggren, Sponge-carrying by dolphins (Delphinidae, *Tursiops* sp.)—a foraging specialisation involving tool use, *Ethology* **103** (1997), pp. 454–465. View Record in Scopus | Cited By in Scopus

Whitehead, 2002 H. Whitehead, Culture in whales and dolphins. In: W.F. Perrin, B. Würsig and J.G.M. Thewissen, Editors, *Encyclopaedia of Marine Mammals*, Academic Press, San Diego, USA (2002).

Whitehead, 2003 H. Whitehead, *Sperm Whales: Social Evolution in the Ocean*, University of Chicago Press, Chicago, USA (2003).

Whitten, 2001 A. Whitten, Imitation and cultural transmission in apes and cetaceans, *Behav. Brain Sci.* **24** (2001), pp. 359–360.

Xitco et al., 2004 M.J. Xitco, J.D. Gory and S.A. Kuczaj II, Dolphin pointing is linked to the attentional behaviour of a receiver, *Anim. Cogn.* **7** (2004), pp. 231–238. **Full Text** via CrossRef | View Record in Scopus | Cited By in Scopus.

Chapter 24

Paola Cavalieri

WHALES AS PERSONS

Cavalieri argues that, based on the neurological complexity of whales, as well as their elaborate communication skills, whales have a rich inner life and a capacity for self-consciousness that is deemed necessary for personhood. Such a quality fully requires a right to life for them. She further argues that the personhood of whales calls on the international community to enforce the protection of whales both globally and nationally.

I

IN THE MORNING of a Sunday of December 2005, in the open water east of the Farallones Islands, about 18 miles off the coast of San Francisco, a female humpback whale on her usual migratory route between the Northern California coast and Baja California became entangled in the nylon ropes that link crab pots. The whale, estimated to weigh 50 tons, was spotted by a person at 8:30 a.m. The combined weight was pulling the whale downward, forcing her to struggle mightily to keep her blow-hole out of the water. Soon, an environmental group was radioed for help. By 2:30 p.m., the rescuers had reached the whale and evaluated the situation. Team members realized the only way to save the endangered leviathan was to dive into the water and cut the ropes. It was a very risky maneuver, because the mere flip of a humpback's massive tail can kill a human being.

"My heart sank when I saw all the lines wrapped around her" the first diver in the water said, "I really didn't think we were going to be able to save her." At least 12 crab traps, weighing 90 pounds each, hung off the whale. Rope was wrapped at least four times around the tail, the back and the left front flipper, and there was a line in the whale's mouth. The crab pot lines were cinched so tight that the rope was digging into the whale's blubber and leaving visible cuts. Four divers spent about an hour cutting the ropes with a special curved knife. The whale floated passively in the water the whole time, they said, giving off a strange kind of vibration. "When I was cutting the line going through the mouth, her eye was there winking at me, watching me, following me the whole time" one rescuer said. "It was an epic moment of my life – I will never be the same".

When the whale realized she was free, she began swimming around in joyous circles. She then came back to each and every diver, one at a time, and nudged them, pushed them gently around and flapped. "It felt to us like she was thanking us, knowing that she was free and that we had helped her", the rescue divers said, "it was the most incredibly beautiful experience of their lives"[1].

In recent centuries, whales have been savagely hunted to near extinction. Even today, despite decades of international restrictions, they are killed by the thousand every year. But, at present, most nations in the world are opposed to whale hunting, millions of people regard the killing of whales as inconsistent with current moral ideals, and a multifarious group of committed individuals wages a continuing war against whale hunters from a small number of countries. Is this new perspective justified?

II

A few years ago, legal scholars Anthony D'Amato and Sudhir Chopra dealt with this question in a dense essay, in which they argued that it is time to extend to whales the most fundamental of all human rights – the right to life[2]. In support they advanced a juridical argument connected with the broadening international consciousness which manifests itself in the history of the policies of the international institutions concerned with "whaling" – as, with an unpleasant locution, whale hunt has come to be defined. Claiming that these policies moved through five stages – free resource, regulation, conservation, protection and preservation – and are now pointing to a sixth, entitlement, D'Amato and Chopra discuss the six stages employing purposive as well as descriptive materials, a reflection of the fact that customary international law is a synthesis of qualitative and quantitative elements. [. . .]

The idea of entitlement clearly implies a major theoretical change: to claim that whales are "entitled" to life means to recognize this right as belonging to the whales themselves. But, though involving a radical philosophica shift, the entitlement stage actually represents simply an incremental advance in the series of the progressive stages in question. Set within the framework of international jurisprudence is that trend in the component of customary international law which is called *opinio juris*. The development of international custom is a dynamic process: the seeds of a future conflict-resolving synthesis are present in the clash of thesis and antithesis constituting the claim conflicts among states. Thus, to anticipate a customary trend is to argue that, in a sense, it already exists. In the case of whales, the practice of states has moved through several stages that are best characterized as increases in international breadth of consciousness – and such combination of practice and consciousness is just what formally constitutes the material and psychological elements of general custom. Since what states do becomes what they legally ought to do, by virtue of a growing sense that what they do is right, proper and natural, the dawning sense of duty to the whales is evidence of a sense of obligation that constitutes the *opinio juris* component of binding customary international law. In this light, the attainment of the final stage – the entitlement of whales to life – in its inevitability has already been anticipated in the law.

The idea of having an entitlement includes a notion of a moral right that can inform existing law or push it in a certain direction. In a legal context, when a court accepts the moral claim of right and recognizes it as somehow subsisting in the law all along, though legal precedent was to the contrary, it is said that the court "articulates" the preexisting right. Along these lines, an international court could articulate a right to life of whales arising from the customary law practice of their preservation. This because whales' entitlement is already implicit in international law as resulting from progression through the previous stages, and from a sense that further development is morally legitimate.

III

Thus, according to D'Amato and Chopra's argument, the new perspective regarding whales is legally justified. But is the sense that such further development is *morally legitimate* warranted? In other words, is the new perspective also ethically sound? Should we grant whales a right to life? In concluding the presentation of the argument from *opinio juris*, D'Amato and Chopra notice that history has seen the continuous widening of the circle of rights holders, with a progression in ascribing fundamental rights to women, children, the mentally enfeebled and racial minorities. Such ascription, it should be added, has usually occurred through the inclusion in the number of "persons". And it is just the notion of person which can offer a clue to moral enquiry within this context.

Roughly speaking, ethics has as its object two sorts of theory of conduct. Morality in the broad sense is an all-inclusive theory of conduct, which includes precepts about the character traits to be fostered and the values to be pursued. Morality in the narrow sense, or social morality, consists instead of a system of constraints on conduct, usually expressed in terms of negative duties, whose task is to prevent harm to others – first and foremost, in the two main forms of the infliction of suffering and the taking of life[3]. In our philosophical landscape, the notion of person, usually contrasted with the notion of thing, has always played an important role with reference to the protection from such harms[4]. For, while "person" is defined so that it is a descriptive term, whose determinative conditions of application have to do with the presence or absence of certain factual characteristics – most prominently rationality and self-consciousness – the assignment of descriptive content is guided by moral considerations[5]. And if, traditionally, to say of some being that it was a person meant to ascribe it a particular moral status, such as to prevent its use as a mere means to others' ends, the notion has gradually come to be especially tied to the question of the wrongness of killing. Accordingly, in present debates, to say of some being that it is a person is not only, as we have suggested, to ascribe it some rights, but most prominently, to grant it the right to life[6].

Is the concept of person coextensive with the concept of "member of the species *Homo sapiens*"? Arguably not. On the one hand, the notion of person being a creature of ethical theories, it may be pointed out that, historically, its theological use in connection with God has prevented it from simply becoming another term for human being. On the other, and more theoretically, in recent years an *ad hominem* argument directed at the paradigm of human equality has drawn philosophical attention to the inconsistency of denying a moral role to biological characteristics like race or sex while at the same time attributing a moral role to another biological characteristic such as species[7]. Against this background, an important strand of thinking in contemporary moral philosophy, arguing that the facts which are morally relevant *in themselves* are not biological facts, but rather psychological facts, has claimed that the concept of a person is the concept, not of a being belonging to a certain species, but of a being endowed with certain mental traits[8].

In particular, elaborating on Locke's basic idea that a person is a being that can consider itself as itself in different times and places,[9] many authors have argued that the mental trait which is central to personhood is not so much rationality, as rather the property of being aware of oneself as a distinct entity, existing in time and endowed with a past and a future – in other words, self-consciousness[10]. It is evident that what is at play here is the connection between personhood and the prohibition of killing. For if a being is aware of oneself as a distinct entity, existing in time and endowed with a past and a future, it clearly has the possibility of conceiving of one's death as the discontinuance of one's existence, and of dreading, and being harmed by, this discontinuance; and if the function of rights is to protect interests, the interest of such being in its continued existence ought to be protected by a right to life. In this context, then, our initial question becomes: Are whales self-conscious?

In spite of the difficulty of deciphering the minds of beings as evolutionarily distant from us as whales – suffice it to think of how alien the acoustic-aquatic cetacean cognitive environment is for beings like us, whose natural environment is visual-terrestrial – it can hardly be doubted that whale brains are impressive pieces of biological hardware, supporting a sophisticated type of awareness. Cognitive scientists, emphasizing the psychological mechanism of knowing one's self through interaction, argue that the brain creates the self through relationship. Over million of years, whale brains evolved through a similar process as those of humans – the need for complex societies and relationships. In the first-ever comprehensive analysis of its kind, a study guided by psychologist Lori Marino used computed tomography to investigate the pattern of encephalization in some fossil cetacean species in the past 47 million years, and analyzed these data along with those for some modern species[11]. Marino's conclusion is that the highly expanded brain size of cetaceans is, in a sense, convergently shared with humans, and that, while evolving along quite different paths, the brains of primates and cetaceans arrived at the same cognitive space.

Despite the fact that logistical problems with observing giant cetaceans in their removed habitats make it difficult to obtain in their case the same detailed evidence – regarding e.g. the capacity for mirror self-recognition or for verbal language apprehension – which is now available for their smaller relatives, the dolphins,[12] conclusions analogous to those stemming from Marino's study have recently been reached by scientists studying whale behavioral patterns. For example, according to biologist Hal Whitehead from the

Cetacean Science Center at Dalhousie University, whales learn and live in ways that previously have only been identified as "human"[13].

If culture can be defined as behavior or information affecting behavior that is transmitted between individuals by non-genetic means – namely, social learning – there is ample evidence for culture and cultural transmission in whales. This holds in particular, though by no means exclusively, with reference to the specific patterns of communicative vocalization better known as whale songs, that are emitted at a much greater wavelength than human-produced sounds and whose transmission speed in the water is four times faster than the transmission speed in the air. Taking an ethnographic, as contrasted with an experimental, approach, biologists found evidence both for horizontal – or within generation – and for vertical – or parent-offspring – cultural processes. Innovations spread rapidly in social units, with many members of the group abandoning traditional feeding habits in favor of new habits introduced by creative individuals, and whale mothers create with their children close bonds which can stretch over decades, devoting time and energy to rearing them[14]. We have now a number of scientific descriptions of imitation and teaching, as well as of complex and stable vocal and behavioural cultures in many groups of whales – cultures which, representing an effect of genes affecting culture, or culture affecting genes, have no parallel outside humans and had previously only been suggested for our species[15]. Indeed, cultural transmission is so crucial that menopause, previously thought a unique human characteristic, has now been detected in several whale species, arguably in connection with the importance of increasing the life span of older females who are the main source of information for the group.

Learning has a strong role in the development of vocal patterns, and cetacean vocalisation is an important aspect of their underlying social structure. Male humpback whales produce at any given time nearly identical songs which change yearly, while unknown means of learning enable them to keep singing in unison; and it can happen that, when some humpback whales migrate, they teach humpbacks in their new neighbourhood to start singing differently[16]. Female sperm whales display dialects – groups emit typical "codas" of several clicks partially overlapping, and individuals from different vocal clans jointly modify their codas into identical patterns, in a friendly vocal duet[17]. Since dialects will survive for several generations, and since whales in groups with different dialects tend to interact with each other quite often, cetaceans can be said to offer the only nonhuman example of multicultural societies where each individual has its own culture but is also interacting with individuals in a different culture[18].

Finally, various instances of whale behaviors directly testify to the presence of the backward, present, and forward looking attitudes forming the foundation upon which awareness of oneself as a distinct entity existing in time is mounted. A relevant backward looking attitude is revealed e.g. when hordes of whales returning to their original territory after long-distance trips first sing the old songs of the previous year, and then the new songs. The existence of a conscious self in the present, with the attendant ability to attribute mental states to others, is apparent for example in cases of gray whales doing acrobatic maneuvers to warn approaching vessels of their presence so as to avoid risks of serious damage. And undoubtedly, female killer whales' tutoring of their offspring in the dangerous activity of shallow water hunting offers evidence of the requisite forward- looking attitude in the form of a capacity for formulating and carrying out plans[19].

All considered, then, it can be claimed that the neurological and behavioral complexity of whales, as well as their elaborate communication skills, suggest that cetacean brains can produce not only a rich inner life, but also that capacity for self-consciousness that is deemed necessary for personhood[20]. If so, a consistent application of our moral standards would validate the present *opinio juris*, thus corroborating the reform at which it points – that is, the extension of the right to life to whales.

IV

In the light of all this, it seems plausible to conclude that in any conflict between whales and whalers the latter lack any moral entitlement to kill the whales, and that the international community is bound to enforce the protection of the whales both globally and nationally. Before reaching this conclusion, however, an objection must be met. It is a distinctively legal, as contrasted with ethical, objection. For it might be claimed that, since the moment when D'Amato and Chopra's essay was published, in 1991, the trend regarding whaling has slightly changed. Though the great majority of states have responded enthusiastically to the anti-whaling movement, with the United States emerging at the forefront of the controversy as a supporter of the moratorium and unilaterally enacting pieces of legislation intended to augment the enforcement power of the IWC, a pro-whaling bloc not only keeps existing, but is becoming more vocal. [. . .]

Does all this have an adverse impact on the argument from *opinio juris*, with the consequence of relegating the ethical case for whales' personhood and right to life to the abstract level of a merely theoretical aspiration? Arguably not. For it is not really unusual that ethically justified principles or rights backed by that sense of obligation that constitutes the *opinio juris* component of customary international law are not accepted by all nations. The conventions that are today collectively known as the "1949 Geneva Conventions" on the treatment of prisoners of war and of civilians in war, for example, have been subscribed to only by about 150 countries out of 192; and when the Universal Declaration of Human Rights was ratified through a proclamation by the U.N. General Assembly in 1948, eight nations abstained – including countries as different as Czechoslovakia, Saudi Arabia, South Africa and USSR[21]. But – quite apart from the fact that countries can, and often do, expand their moral consciousness – such lack of consensus, however regrettable, did not, and does not, prevent the involved nations from seeing the principles or rights they agreed to not only as ethically sound but also as binding customary international law, and from endeavouring to enforce them by various means, such as political pressures and economic sanctions. This holds in particular in a moment when the nation-state appears in the process of losing many of its prerogatives in favor of a globalized community[22]. Due to this process, which is clearly testified by the international recognition of the legitimacy of some forms of humanitarian intervention to stop genocides or to impose the respect of human rights within the boundaries of independent countries, the various stances and policies of the individual nation-states, far from being seen as the unchangeable outcomes of wholly autonomous entities, tend now to be considered as the proper objects of international moral censure and correction. In view both of the past record in the field of international jurisprudence and of the ongoing process of globalization, it can be argued that the fact that countries like Japan, Norway or Iceland keep opposing any granting of an entitlement to life to whales is a regrettable reality which cannot – and should not – jeopardize the emerging basic international consensus regarding the whales' status.

If this is so, then the overall argument so far developed stands. But if the new perspective regarding whales is justified, an important change is in order. We have mentioned that when the U.N. demand for a ten-year moratorium of commercial whaling was rejected by the IWC's Scientific Committee, questions were raised about the IWC role, and proposals were made calling for the U.N. to assume jurisdiction. This idea has become more relevant today. It seems plausible that, now that consciousness about whales has broadened, an institution which was initially created with the goal of regulating whales' exploitation can no longer be seen as the best organization to deal with their protection. As humanity as a whole comes to recognize the moral standing of whales, the time is ripe to remove human/cetacean relations from the hands of the former whaling nations. It would be fully in line with the present trend towards greater global governance in a variety of areas – trade and the environment, as well as peace and the protection of human rights – to create a new, *ad hoc* U.N. institution with the task of internationally declaring, and then elaborating in a series of covenants, the whales' right to life.

Among other things, the creation of such an institution would have the important side-effect of neutralizing the threat of withdrawal which the pro-whaling nations constantly use as a sort of blackmail towards the IWC. Admittedly, the problem of how to induce compliance would still remain. But this problem – which is common to all fields of international law – would not be altered for the worse in this new scenery. As it was in the past, when pro-whaling nations were prone to base their concrete decisions on their assessment of U.S. intentions, it will still be up to the anti-whaling countries to lead the battle, and to provide with their policies of suasion, pressure and sanctions the required enforcement mechanisms for whales' right to life.

Notes

1   Peter Fimrite, "Daring rescue of whale off Farallones", *San Francisco Chronicle*, December 14, 2005, http://sfgate.com/cgi-bin/article.cgi?file = /c/a/2005/12/14/HUMPY.TMP

2   Anthony D'Amato and Sudhir K. Chopra, "Whales: Their Emerging Right to Life", *American Journal of International Law* 85 (1), 1991.

3   Geoffrey J. Warnock, *The Object of Morality*, Methuen, London, 1971, p. 148; Peter F. Strawson, "Social Morality and Individual Ideal", *Philosophy: The Journal of the Royal Institute of Philosophy* 36 (Jan. 1968).

4   Adolf Trendelenburg, "A Contribution to the History of the Word Person", *Monist*, July 1910. The best-known formulation of the person/thing dichotomy can be found in Kant's moral philosophy; see Immanuel Kant, *Foundations of the Metaphysics of Morals*, trans. Lewis W. Beck, Upper Saddle River, N.J.: Prentice-Hall, 1997, p. 45.

5   On this, see generally the special issue of *Etica & Animali* devoted to "Nonhuman Personhood" (vol. 9, 1998).

6   Joel Feinberg, "Abortion", in Tom Regan, ed., *Matters of Life and Death*, 2nd ed., New York: Random House, 1986.

7   Peter Singer, *Animal Liberation*, 2nd edn, New York: The New York Review of Books, 1990, p. 9.

8   Paola Cavalieri, *The Animal Question*, Oxford University Press, New York 2001, pp. 117 ff.

9   John Locke, *An Essay Concerning Human Understanding*, Cleveland: World Publishing Co., 1964, book 2, chap. 9, part 29, p. 211.

10   Such perspective, though grown in the English-speaking world and detailedly developed in the context of contemporary bioethical discussions of the morality of abortion and euthanasia, has antecedents in continental philosophy as well. Leibniz, for example, connects personhood with consciousness of self and recollection of a former state (Gottfried Wilhelm Leibniz, *Epistula ad Wagnerum de vi activa corporis, de anima, de anima brutorum*, 1710), and even Kant, in spite of all his insistence on rationality, claims that it is the fact of being able to represent to themselves their own selves that elevates persons above all living beings (Immanuel Kant, *Anthropology from a Pragmatic point of View*, trans. Victor Lyle Dowdell, Southern Illinois University Press, Carbondale, Ill. 1978, book I, part I).

11   Lori Marino, Mark D. Uhen, Nicholas D. Pyenson and Bruno Frohlich, "Reconstructing cetacean brain evolution using computed tomography", *Anatomical Record (The New Anatomist)* 272B, 2003.

12   Denise L. Herzing and Thomas I. White, "Dolphins and the Question of Personhood", *Etica & Animali*, Special issue: "Nonhuman Personhood" 9, 1998; Thomas I. White, *The Sea Peoples*, Oxford: Blackwell, forthcoming.

13   Jonathan Dieli Colburn, "Listening to whales", interview with Hal Whitehead, *San Francisco Chronicle*, January 9, 2003, http://www.sfgate.com/cgi-bin/article.cgi?f=/chronicle/a/2003/01/09/MN184029.DTL

14   Luke Rendell and Hal Whitehead, "Culture in whales and dolphins", *Behavioral and Brain Sciences*, 24 (2), 2001; M. T. Weinrich, M. R. Schilling and C. R. Belt, "Evidence for acquisition of a novel feeding behaviour: lobtail feeding in humpback whales, *Megaptera novaeangliae*", *Animal behaviour* 44, 1992; Whitehead, H., "Cultural Selection and Genetic Diversity in Matrilineal Whales", *Science*, 282, 1998.

15   Luke Rendell and Hal Whitehead, "Culture in whales and dolphins", cit.

16   Michael J. Noad, Douglas H. Cato, and M. M. Bryden, "Cultural Displacement and Replacement in the Songs of Australian Humpback Whales", *Nature* 408, 537, 2000.

17   L. S. Weilgart, "Vocalizations of the sperm whale (*Physeter macrocephalus*) off the Galapagos Islands as related to behavioral and circumstantial variables", Doctoral dissertation Dalhousie University, Halifax, Nova Scotia, Canada, 1990.

18   Jonathan Dieli Colburn, "Listening to whales", interview with Hal Whitehead, cit.

19   "Secrets Of Whales' Long-Distance Songs Unveiled", interview with Christopher Clark from Cornell University, March 24, 2005, *Spacedaily*, http://www.spacedaily.com/news/life-05t.html; "Gray Whale Migration Update", February 25, 1998, report by Etai Timna, Channel Islands National Marine Sanctuary, http://www.learner.org/jnorth/spring1998/critters/gwhale/Update022598.html; C. Guinet and J. Bouvier, "Development of intentional stranding hunting techniques in killer whale (*Orcinus orca*) calves at Crozet Archipelago", *Canadian Journal of Zoology*, 73, 1995.

20   This is a conclusion which is also suggested, though in lesser detail, by other authors such e.g. Michael Tooley (*Abortion and Infanticide*, Oxford University Press, Oxford 1983, pp. 412), Peter Singer (*Practical Ethics*, 2nd, ed., Cambridge University Press, Cambridge 1993, pp. 117–119), Harlan B. Miller ("Science, Ethics, and Moral Status", *Between the Species*, Vol. 10, n. 1–2 (1994 etc.)

21   University of Minnesota, Human Rights Library, "Human Rights Education", http://www1.umn.edu/humanrts/education/4thR-F97/EleanorRoosevelt.htm

22   Peter Singer, *One World: The Ethics of Globalization*, Yale University Press, New Haven 2002.

FURTHER READING

Beck, B.B., Stoinski, T.S., Hutchins, M., Maple, T.L., Norton, B., Rowan, A., Stevens, E.F., and Arluk, A. (eds.) (2001) *Great Apes and Humans: The Ethics of Coexistence*, Washington, D.C., Smithsonian Institution Press. Important, well-written articles.

Bickerton, D. (2000) "Resolving discontinuity: A minimalist distinction between human and non-human minds," *American Zoologist* 40: 862–873.

Blum, D. (1995) *The Monkey Wars*, New York: Oxford University Press. Exploration of the controversial use of primates in research based on Blum's 1992 Pulitzer Prize winning newspaper articles.

Bofysen, S.T. and Hallberg, K.I. (2000) "Primate numerical competence: Contributions toward understanding nonhuman cognition," *Cognitive Science* 24(3): 423–443. An historical overview of primate numerical studies, illustrating complex cognitive skills including a concept of number.

Cavalieri, P. and Singer, P. (eds.) (1994) *The Great Ape Project: Equality Beyond Humanity*, New York: St. Martin's Press. This book launched the Great Ape Project (GAP) as an international movement.

Cavalieri, P. and Singer, P. (eds.) (1996) "The Great Ape Project," *Etica & Animali* 8: 1–178. An issue dedicated to developing the view that nonhuman great apes should have the same basic rights as human beings.

Coetzee, J.M. (1999) *The Lives of Animals*, Princeton, N.J.: Princeton University Press. A literary, postmodern approach to the question of animal lives.

De Waal, F. (1995) "Bonobo sex and society," *Scientific American* 274: 82–8. Well-written account by a prominent researcher.

De Waal, F. (1996) *Good Natured*, Cambridge, MA: Harvard University Press. The beginnings of morality are found in nonhuman primate societies.

De Waal, F. (2001) *The Ape and the Sushi Master: Cultural Reflections by a Primatologist*, New York: Basic Books. Enjoyable book for the general reader by a central figure in the study of chimpanzees and bonobos.

Fouts, R. (with Mills, S.T.) (1997) *Next of Kin: What Chimpanzees Have Taught Me About Who We Are*, New York: William Morrow. Fouts taught American Sign Language to Washoe, the first chimpanzee to communicate with humans by this means.

Galdikas, B.M.F. and Shapiro, G.L. (1996) "Orangutan ethics," *Etica & Animalia* 8: 50–67. Fascinating account of wild orangutans.

Hauser, M.D., Kralik, J., Botto-Manan, C., Garrett, M., and Oser, J. (1995) "Self-recognition in primates:

Phylogeny and the salience of species-typical features," *Proceedings of the National Academy of Science, USA* 92: 10811–14.

Kalin, Ned H. (2002) "The Neurobiology of Fear," *Scientific American Special* 12: 77–81. Researchers are identifying the neurochemical mechanisms that give rise to various fears in monkeys.

Matsuzawa, T. (ed.) (2001) *Primate Origins of Human Cognition and Behavior*, Tokyo, Japan: Spring. A Japanese view of primates, primate culture, primate science, and the cognitive capacities of chimpanzees and macaques.

Matsuzawa, T. (2002) "Chimpanzee Ai and her son Ayumu: An episode of education by master-apprenticeship." In: *The Cognitive Animal: Empirical and Theoretical Perspectives on Animal Cognition*, M. Bekoff, C. Allen, and G.M. Burghardt (eds.), Cambridge, MA: The MIT Press.

National Research Council (1997) *Chimpanzees in Research: Strategies for Their Ethical Care, Management, and Use*, Washington, D.C.: National Academy Press. Recommendations include a 5-yr breeding moratorium, not endorsing euthanasia for population control, and assuring lifetime support for the core population of chimpanzees.

National Research Council (1998) *The Psychological Well-being of Nonhuman Primates*, Washington, D.C.: National Academy of Sciences.

New Zealand Animal Welfare Act (1999) <http://rangi.knowledge-basket.co.nz/gpacts/public/text/1999/an/142.html> (accessed 12 October 2002). First act to give specific legal protection for nonhuman great apes.

Povinelli, D.J., Bering J.M., and Giambrone, S. (2000) "Toward a science of other minds: Escaping the argument by analogy," *Cognitive Science* 24(3): 509–41. Chimpanzees do not reason about seeing or about other mental states.

Savage-Rumbaugh, S. and Brakke, Karen E. (1996) "Animal language: Methodological and interpretive issues." Chapter 18, pp. 269–288. In: *Readings in Animal Cognition*, M. Bekoff and D. Jamieson (eds.) Cambridge, MA: The MIT Press. Language in 11 apes of the Language Research Center at George State and Yerkes Primate Research Center of Emory University.

Savage-Rumbaugh, S., Fields, W.M. and Taglialatela, J.P. (2001) "Language, speech, tools and writing," *Journal of Consciousness Studies* 8(5–7): 273–92.

Schueller, G.H. (2000) "Hey! Good looking," *New Scientist* 17 June 30–34. Discussion of mirror studies as evidence of self-awareness.

Seyfarth, R.M. and Cheney, D.L. (2000) "Social awareness in monkeys," *American Zoologist* 40: 902–909.

Shumaker, R.W. and Swartz, K.B. (2002) "When traditional methodologies fail: cognitive studies of great apes." In: *The Cognitive Animal: Empirical and Theoretical Perspectives on Animal Cognition*, M. Bekoff, C. Allen, and G.M. Burghardt (eds.), Cambridge, MA: The MIT Press.

Tomasello, M. (2000) "Primate cognition: introduction to the issue," *Cognitive Science* 24(3): 351–61. Argues that human cognition is unique due to its collective nature.

Tyack, P.L. (2000) "Dolphins whistle a signature tune," *Science* 289 1310–11.

Whiten, A. (2000) "Primate culture and social learning," *Cognitive Science* 24(3): 455–508. Focus on imitation and emulation.

Whiten, A. and Boesch, C. (2001) "The cultures of chimpanzees," *Scientific American* 280(1): 60–7. Useful summary.

Chimpanzee cultures website: http://chimp.st-and.ac.uk/cultures/ (accessed 12 October 2002).

Wild Chimpanzee Foundation website: http://www.wildchimps.org (accessed 12 October 2002).

Great Ape Project website: http://www.greatapeproject.org (accessed 12 October 2002).

STUDY QUESTIONS

1   In your view, is it more important to study animals at the species level or on an individual basis? Explain the reasons for your answer.
2   Do you agree with Marc Bekoff that we should not base our moral treatment of animals on their cognitive abilities?
3   In your view, are apes or dolphins persons? What definition of "person" are you using? Explain why your definition should be adopted.
4   Is the information concerning culture in chimpanzees and in whales and dolphins important for your view of the moral status of these animals? Explain your answer.
5   Should the information concerning consciousness and self-awareness in bonobos presented by Savage-Rumbaugh and her co-workers be taken into account in our treatment of bonobos? If so, in what ways?

Animals for food

INTRODUCTION TO PART FOUR

THE USE OF ANIMALS FOR food is a highly charged topic for many people. For some the emotional lives of animals are reason enough not to eat them. For those who do eat animals, accurate information on how animals for food are raised and slaughtered is important for an informed moral judgment. David DeGrazia describes the conditions of pigs, chickens, and cattle in modern factory farms, which now supply most of the meat and dairy products in the U.S., Great Britain, and most other industrial countries. He argues that factory farming causes more harm to animals than any other human practice.

Temple Grandin has designed 30 percent of the livestock-handling facilities in the U.S. She affirms that we owe animals a decent life and a painless death. Her essay "Thinking like Animals" explains how her life as a person with autism has enabled her to better understand animal emotions. She has found that cattle are sensitive to the same things that disturb people with autism, and has designed restraint chutes for holding cattle for slaughter with the emotional needs of cattle in mind. In "A Major Change" she describes the improvements made in the handling and stunning of animals between 1997 and 1999, the importance of proper transport of cattle and pigs, and the promotion of better stockmanship.

In "Animal Agriculture: Myths and Facts" the Animal Agriculture Alliance presents the view of food producers. The Alliance points out that a very high percentage of U.S. farms are family-owned and operated. The proper housing of animals protects their health and welfare and is scientifically designed for the specific needs of the animal. The Alliance states that all forms of restraint are designed for the welfare of the animal as well as efficiency of production.

Bernard E. Rollin delineates how confinement agriculture, which began after WWII, is based on forcing animals to serve the twin goals of profitability and productivity. He describes the emergence of a new ethic which values farm animal welfare and which requires "husbandry-smart" people. One obstacle to the development of such an ethic is "scientific ideology," a set of inaccurate assumptions. Rollin describes approaches which allow farm animals to live lives free from pain and suffering.

Michael Appleby explains some of the factors in the relationship between animal welfare and production costs. He argues that improvements in farm animal welfare could be achieved with only minor increases in the price paid for food by consumers.

Two of the authors in this Part argue for vegetarianism. James Rachels provides what he calls the "basic argument," based on the principle that it is wrong to cause pain unless there is a "good enough reason" for such pain. In "The Rape of Animals, the Butchering of Women," Carol J. Adams argues that both women and animals are "absent referents," made absent through language and metaphor, and also, in the case of animals, through death. Patriarchal culture transforms women and animals into commodities to be used and consumed.

Several articles argue against vegetarianism. Kathryn Paxton George presents a critique of ethical vegetarianism in which she points out that the arguments provided by Regan, Singer, and Adams are discriminatory, applying only to most men and some women aged 20–50 in industrialized countries. This assumption of the "male norm" is mistaken. George advocates "semivegetarianism" and attention to common-sense duties to animals and humans. Steven L. Davis argues that Regan's Least Harm Principle directs us to consume a diet containing both plants and some animal products.

The final four essays in this Part concern the doctrines of some of the world religions with regard to the slaughter and eating of animals. Norman Solomon explains the Jewish tradition. While the Torah does not require vegetarianism, it does demand that one not practice cruelty to animals. Also, the Torah places restraints on which animals may be eaten and on the method of slaughter. In "Enhancing the Divine Image" Rabbi Fuchs explains how his decision to become a vegetarian was based on his understanding of the early chapters of Genesis. The Rev. Andrew Linzey argues for vegetarianism from a Christian perspective, based on his reading of Genesis as well as other books of the Bible. Martin Forward and Mohamed Alam explain the Islamic view of animals. Few Muslims are vegetarians, but certain animals are forbidden to Muslims, and all creatures used for food must be killed in a prescribed manner.

ANIMALS FOR FOOD

Chapter 25

David DeGrazia

MEAT-EATING

David DeGrazia describes the conditions endured by chickens, pigs, and cows during their lives and deaths as part of the factory farming system in the U.S., Great Britain, and most other industrialized countries. American farm animals have virtually no legal protection. DeGrazia argues that consumers are morally obliged to make a reasonable effort to not provide financial support to institutions that cause extensive unnecessary suffering.

HEN X BEGINS life in a crowded incubator. She is taken to a 'battery' cage made entirely of wire—and quite unlike the outdoor conditions that are natural for her—where she will live her life. (Having no commercial value, male chicks are gassed, ground up alive, or suffocated.) Hen X's cage is so crowded that she cannot fully stretch her wings. Although her beak is important for feeding, exploring, and preening, part of it has been cut off, through sensitive tissue, in order to limit the damage caused by pecking cage mates—a behaviour induced by overcrowding. For hours before laying an egg, Hen X paces anxiously among the crowd, instinctively seeking a nest that she will not find. At egg-laying time, she stands on a sloped, uncomfortable wire floor that precludes such instinctual behaviours as pecking for food, dust bathing, and scratching. Lack of exercise, unnatural conditions, and demands for extreme productivity— she will lay 250 eggs this year—cause bone weakness. (Unlike many hens, Hen X is not subjected to forced moulting, in which water is withheld for one to three days and food for up to two weeks in order to extend hens' productive lives.) When considered spent at age two, she is jammed into a crate and transported in a truck—without food, water, or protection from the elements—to a slaughterhouse; rough handling causes several weak bones to break. At her destination, Hen X is shackled upside down on a conveyor belt before an automated knife slices her throat. Because the (US) Humane Slaughter Act does not apply to poultry, she is fully conscious throughout this process. Her body, which was extensively damaged during her lifetime, is suitable only for pot pies, soup, and the like.

After weaning at four weeks of age, Hog Y is taken to a very crowded, stacked nursery cage. Due to poor ventilation, he breathes in powerful fumes from urine and faeces. Upon reaching a weight of 50 pounds, he is taken to a tiny 'finishing' pen. It is slatted and has a concrete floor with no straw bedding or sources of amusement. Despite being a member of a highly intelligent and social species, Hog Y is separated from other hogs by iron bars and has nothing to do except get up, lie down, eat, and sleep. He sometimes amuses himself by biting a tail in the next crate—until all the hogs' tails are 'docked' (cut off). Both this procedure and castration are performed without anaesthesia. When he is deemed ready for slaughter, Hog Y is roughly herded into a truck with thirty other hogs. The two-day journey is not pleasant for Hog Y, who gets in fights with other hogs while receiving no food, water, rest, or protection from the summer heat. At the slaughterhouse, Hog Y smells blood and resists prodding from the human handlers.

They respond by kicking him and smashing him repeatedly from behind with an iron pipe until he is on the restraining conveyor belt that carries him to the stunner. Hog Y is fortunate in so far as the electric stunning procedure is successful, killing him before his body is dropped in scalding water and dismembered. (Although the Humane Slaughter Act requires that animals other than poultry be rendered unconscious with a single application of an effective stunning device before being shackled, hoisted upside down, and dismembered, many slaughterhouse employees state that violations occur regularly. Fearing that a higher voltage might cause 'bloodsplash' in some carcasses, many slaughterhouse supervisors apparently encourage use of a voltage that is much too low to ensure unconsciousness. Moreover, in numerous slaughterhouses stunners have to stun an animal every few seconds and face extreme pressure not to stop the line of animals.)

Although it is natural for cows and their calves to bond strongly, Cow (then Calf) Z is taken from her mother shortly after birth to begin life as a dairy cow. She never receives colostrum—her mother's milk— which would help her fight disease. She lives in a very crowded 'drylot', which is devoid of grass, and her tail is docked without anaesthesia. In order to produce twenty times more milk than a calf would need, she receives a diet heavy in grain—not the roughage that cows have evolved to digest easily—causing metabolic disorders and painful lameness. And like many dairy cows, she often has mastitis, a painful udder inflammation, despite receiving antibiotics between lactations. To maintain continuous milk production, Cow Z is induced to bear one calf each year. To stimulate additional growth and productivity, she receives daily injections of bovine growth hormone. Her natural life span is twenty or more years, but at age 4 she can no longer maintain production levels and is deemed 'spent'. During transport and handling, Cow Z is fortunate: although deprived of food, water, and rest for over two days, and frightened when prodded, she is not beaten; at the slaughterhouse her instincts—unlike hogs'—allow her to walk easily in a single-file chute. Unfortunately, the poorly trained stun operator has difficulty with the air-powered knocking gun. Although he stuns Cow Z four times, she stands up and bellows. The line does not stop, however, so she is hoisted up on the overhead rail and transported to the 'sticker', who cuts her throat to bleed her out. She remains conscious as she bleeds and experiences some of the dismemberment and skinning process alive. (The federal inspector cannot see what is happening where he is stationed; besides, he's frenetically checking carcasses that whiz by, for obvious signs of contamination.) Cow Z's body will be used for processed beef or hamburger.

The institution of factory farming

The animals portrayed above offer examples of life in modern factory farms, which now supply most of our meat and dairy products in the USA, Great Britain, and most other industrial countries. Since the Second World War, factory farms—which try to raise as many animals as possible in very limited space in order to maximize profits—have driven three million American family farms out of business; over the same time period, Great Britain and other nations have witnessed similar transformations in their agricultural sectors. Scientific developments that have fuelled the emergence of factory farming include the artificial provision of vitamin D (which otherwise requires sunlight for its synthesis), the success of antibiotics in minimizing the spread of certain diseases, and advanced methods of genetic selection for production traits. Since the driving force behind this institution is economic efficiency, factory farming treats animals simply as means to this end—as mere objects with no independent moral importance, or moral status, whatever.

Considering both numbers of animals involved and the extent to which they are harmed, *factory farming causes more harm to animals than does any other human institution or practice*. In the USA alone, this institution kills over 100 million mammals and five billion birds annually. American farm animals have virtually no legal protections. The most important applicable federal legislation is the Humane Slaughter Act, which does not cover poultry—most of the animals consumed—and has no bearing on living conditions, transport, or handling. Moreover, as Gail Eisnitz and others have extensively documented, the

Act is rarely enforced. Apparently, the US Department of Agriculture supports the major goal of agribusiness: absolute maximization of profit without hindrance. This is not surprising when one considers that, since the 1980s, most top officials at USDA either have been agribusiness leaders themselves or have had close political and financial ties to the industry.

By contrast, European nations have curbed some of the excesses typified by American factory farming. For example, Great Britain has banned veal crates and limits to fifteen hours the amount of time animals can go without food and water during transport. The European Community and the Council of Europe have developed requirements for the well-being of farm animals that are translated into law in different member nations. These requirements generally provide animals with more space, greater freedom to engage in species-typical behaviours, and more humane living conditions than those of farm animals in the USA. Despite the more humane conditions that are typical in Europe, however, most European animal husbandry remains sufficiently intensive to merit the term 'factory farming'.

So far this discussion has provided a descriptive sense of factory farms primarily through three cases. Therefore it might be objected that the situations of Hen X, Hog Y, and Cow Z do not represent universal features of factory farming. That is correct. But the experiences of these three animals, the evidence suggests, are not atypical—at least in the USA. Still, while a thorough description of factory farms is impossible here, it may be helpful to add a few general remarks about other types of farm animals. The following generalizations are meant to describe the American situation, although some of them accurately describe the experiences of animals in many other countries as well.

Cattle raised specifically for beef are generally better off than the other animals described here. Many have the opportunity to roam outdoors for about six months. After that, they are transported long distances to feedlots, where they are fed grain rather than grass. Major sources of pain or distress include constant exposure to the elements, branding, dehorning, unanaesthetized castration, the cutting of ears for identification purposes, and a sterile, unchanging environment. We may add, of course, the harms associated with transportation to the slaughterhouse and what takes place therein.

Broiler chickens spend their lives in enclosed sheds that become increasingly crowded as tens of thousands of birds grow at an abnormally fast rate. Besides extreme crowding, major sources of concern include cannibalism, suffocation due to panic-driven piling on top of one another, debeaking, and very unhealthful breathing conditions produced by never-cleaned droppings and poor ventilation. Veal calves' deprivations are similar to many of those that hogs experience. Formula-fed veal calves in particular live in solitary crates too small to permit them to turn around or sleep in a natural position. Denied water and solid food, they drink a liquid milk replacer deficient in iron—making possible the gourmet white flesh and resulting in anaemia. This diet and solitary confinement lead to numerous health problems and neurotic behaviours.

Let us now consider the overall picture: *factory farming routinely causes animals massive harm in the form of suffering, confinement, and death*. Regarding suffering—or experiential harm in general—all evidence suggests that factory farm animals, in the course of their lives, typically experience considerable pain, discomfort, boredom, fear, anxiety, and possibly other unpleasant feelings. Furthermore, factory farms by their very nature *confine* animals in our stipulated sense of the term; that is, they impose external constraints on movement that significantly interfere with living well. (For at least part of their lives, cattle raised specifically for beef are not confined in this sense.) And, of course, factory farming ultimately kills animals raised for meat, adding the harm of death—assuming (. . .) that death harms such beings as cows, pigs, and chickens. Then again, death counts as a harm here only if we consider the sorts of lives these animals *could* have under humane treatment. Given animals' current treatment, death would seem to be a blessing, except possibly in the case of beef cattle. In any event, the general thesis that factory farms cause massive harm to animals is undeniable.

Moral evaluation

If the first crucial insight in a moral evaluation of factory farms is that they cause massive harm to animals, the second crucial insight is this: *consumers do not need the products of factory farms*. We cannot plausibly regard any of the harms caused to these animals as *necessary*. Unusual circumstances aside—say, where one is starving and lacks alternatives—we do not need to eat meat to survive or even to be healthy. The chief benefits of meat-eating to consumers are *pleasure*, since meat tastes especially good to many people, and *convenience*, since switching to and maintaining a vegetarian diet requires some effort. Putting the two key insights together brings us to the conclusion that *factory farms cause massive unnecessary harm*. Since causing massive unnecessary harm is wrong if *anything* is wrong, the judgement that factory farming is an indefensible institution seems inescapable.

Note that this condemnation of factory farming does not depend on the controversial assumption that animals deserve equal consideration. Even if one accepts a sliding-scale model of moral status, which justifies less-than-equal consideration for animals, one cannot plausibly defend the causing of massive unnecessary harm. Thus, it appears that if one takes animals at all seriously—regarding them as beings with at least some moral status—one must find factory farming indefensible.

But what about the consumer? She isn't harming animals; she's just eating the products of factory farming. Well, imagine someone who says, 'I'm not kicking dogs to death. I'm just paying someone else to do it.' We would judge this person to act wrongly for encouraging and commissioning acts of cruelty. Similarly, while meat-eaters may typically feel distant from meat production, and may never even think about what goes on in factory farms and slaughterhouses, the purchase of factory-farmed meat directly encourages and makes possible the associated cruelties—so the consumer is significantly responsible. In general, the following moral rule, although somewhat vague, is defensible: *make every reasonable effort not to provide financial support to institutions that cause extensive unnecessary harm*.

By financially supporting massive unnecessary harm, the purchase of factory-farmed meat violates this principle and is therefore, I argue, morally indefensible. Interestingly, we reached this important conclusion without commitment to any specific ethical theory such as utilitarianism or a strong animal-rights view. In any event, while our case against factory farming and buying its products has so far cited considerations of animal welfare, it is further strengthened by considerations of human welfare. How so?

First, animal products—which are high in fat and protein and contain cholesterol—are associated with higher levels of heart disease, obesity, stroke, osteoporosis, diabetes, and certain cancers. Medical authorities now recommend much less meat and more grains, fruits, and vegetables than Americans, for example, typically consume. Second, American factory farming has driven three million family farms out of business since the Second World War, as huge agribusinesses, enjoying billions of dollars in annual government subsidies, have increasingly dominated; while American consumers frequently hear that factory farming lowers meat prices at the cash register, they are rarely reminded of the hidden cost of tax subsidies. In Britain and many other countries, relatively few large agribusinesses have similarly come to dominate, putting many smaller farms out of business. Third, factory farming is devastating for the environment. It excessively consumes energy, soil, and water while causing erosion of topsoil, destruction of wildlife habitat, deforestation, and water pollution from manure, pesticides, and other chemicals. Fourth, factory farming has a perverse effect on the distribution of food to humans. For example, it takes about 8 pounds of protein in hog feed to generate 1 pound of pork for humans and 21 pounds of protein in calf feed to yield 1 pound of beef. Consequently, most US-produced grain, for example, goes to livestock. Unfortunately, wealthy countries' demand for meat makes plant proteins too costly for the masses in the poorest countries. Poor communities often abandon sustainable farming practices to export cash crops and meat, but profits are short-lived as marginal lands erode, causing poverty and malnutrition. There is, in fact, easily enough grain protein, if used sensibly, to feed every human on Earth. Fifth, perhaps especially in the USA, factory farming is cruel to its employees. It subjects them to extreme work pressures—as seen in a worker who cuts up to ninety chickens per minute, or urinates on the workline for fear of leaving it—and to some of the worst health hazards faced by any American workers (for example, skin diseases, respiratory problems, crippling hand and arm injuries, injury from wild, improperly stunned animals)—all for low pay. Finally, deregulation of the American meat industry since the 1980s, combined with extremely fast production lines, have made it virtually impossible to ensure safe meat. . . .

Thus, receiving further support from considerations of human welfare, the case for boycotting factory farm products is extremely powerful. But let us not ignore the following important objection. One might argue that the continuation of factory farming is economically necessary. Putting this industry out of business—say, through a successful boycott—would obviously be devastating for agribusiness owners, but would also eliminate many jobs and possibly harm local economies. These consequences, the argument continues, are unacceptable. Thus, just as factory farming is necessary, so is the extensive harm it inevitably causes to animals—contrary to my charge of massive *unnecessary* harm.

In reply, we may accept the factual assumption about likely consequences while rejecting the claim that they are unacceptable. First, as Peter Singer notes, the negative costs of ending factory farming would have to be borne only once, whereas perpetuating this institution entails that the costs to animals continue indefinitely. Also, considering how badly factory farm employees are treated, it is hard to believe they would be seriously harmed by having to seek alternative employment, as innumerable 'burnt out' employees do anyway. More generally, the various threats to human well-being posed by factory farming—health risks, environmental destruction, inefficient use and perverse distribution of grain proteins, etc.—could be avoided if this industry is eliminated (assuming it is not simply replaced by less intensive animal husbandry, which would perpetuate some of these problems). Avoiding these risks and harms, not once but indefinitely, would seem to counterbalance any short-term economic harm. Finally, I submit that *there are moral limits to what we may do to others in the pursuit of profit or employment—and causing sentient beings massive harm in pursuing these goals oversteps those bounds.* (Cases in which people are forced into prostitution, pornography, or slavery vividly exemplify the violation of such limits.) If that is correct, then factory farming cannot be considered necessary. In conclusion, I suggest that these rebuttals, taken together, undercut the argument from economic necessity.

Traditional family farming

This chapter has focused on factory farms because most of the animal products we consume come from this source. But people also eat animals from other sources, including traditional family farms.

Because they involve far less intensive rearing conditions, family farms cause much less suffering to animals than factory farms do. Family farms may not even confine animals in our sense of imposing constraints on movement that significantly interfere with living well. But, . . . farm animals cannot fully escape harm because they are ultimately killed, entailing the harm of death.

Causing much less harm to animals, and avoiding at least some threats that factory farming poses to human well-being (for example, water pollution, extremely hazardous working conditions), family farming is much more defensible than its dominant competitor. Still, there is a strong moral case against family farming and the practice of buying its products. For one thing, this institution does impose some significant suffering through certain practices: branding and dehorning cattle; castrating cattle and hogs; separating mothers from offspring, which may well cause distress even to birds; and treating animals roughly in transport, handling, and slaughter. And, again, all the animals die. Since meat-eating is—unusual circumstances aside—unnecessary, these harms are unnecessary. It is difficult to defend the routine imposition of unnecessary harm.

A few possible replies, however, may strengthen the case for some forms of family farming. For example, chickens and turkeys can escape most of the harms just described. If a chicken or turkey is able to live a pleasant life—say, with family intact—and is never abused, the only relevant harm would be death.

[. . .]

Alternatively, if one (unlike the present author) accepts the sliding-scale model of moral status, one would grant unequal moral weight to the interests—including the avoidance of suffering—of different beings depending on their cognitive, emotional, and social complexity. Perhaps proponents of this ethical framework would defend practices of family farming that keep the admittedly unnecessary suffering to a minimum. They might argue that it is not always wrong to cause *minimal* unnecessary harm, even to mammals, especially if there are some significant benefits such as employment for farmers. Then again, one would need to consider negative effects on human welfare, such as extremely inefficient use of grain protein, in assessing the plausibility of this line of argument.

Seafood

Much of the meat we consume comes from the sea. Beginning with fish and cephalopods (octopuses and squid), we concluded [in an earlier chapter] that these creatures are sentient, subject to pain and distress; we left somewhat more open whether they can experience suffering in the specific sense: a highly unpleasant emotional state associated with more-than-minimal pain or distress. Now catching fish and cephalopods requires hooking or netting them and causing them to suffocate. Clearly, they experience unpleasant feelings in the process. While traditional fishing methods do not involve confinement—since the animals are at liberty in their natural environment—death is obviously unavoidable. Death harms such creatures to *some degree* on the opportunities-based account of the harm of death, but not on the desire-based view.

There are several ways in which one might argue that fish and cephalopods are harmed only minimally: by claiming that any suffering is very brief; by denying that they suffer at all; or by arguing that the harm of death in their case is negligible to non-existent. Then one might argue that this minimal harm is adequately counterbalanced by certain benefits to humans: pleasure, convenience, rounding out a healthful diet, and employment for fishers. (One who believes that animals have rights in the strongest, utility-trumping sense would reject such reasoning, however.) Naturally, a proponent of the sliding-scale model of moral status will find the production and consumption of seafood easier to defend, since fish and cephalopods would be relatively low in the moral hierarchy.

One complicating factor in our analysis is that many fish today are raised in fish farms. These are so crowded that they amount to confinement and increase the unpleasantness of the fishes' lives. When fish are raised in this way, the case for boycotting these products is stronger.

What about lobsters, crabs, shrimp, and other invertebrates other than cephalopods? Available evidence leaves open the issue of their possible sentience. If they are not sentient, our actions cannot harm them. People might reasonably disagree about whether, in this state of uncertainty, we should give them the benefit of the doubt and assume they are sentient.

As we think about the issue of eating seafood, we must not ignore any harms caused to creatures other than those consumed. For example, suppose you buy tuna fish from a company whose nets often ensnare and kill dolphins—whose cognitive, emotional, and social complexity rivals that of Great Apes. The harms thereby caused to dolphins might make the purchase of tuna from this company as serious a moral matter as buying meat from factory farms.

Chapter 26

Temple Grandin

THINKING LIKE ANIMALS

Temple Grandin describes the similarities between autistic emotion and animal emotion, and explains how she has designed chute systems for handling cattle in slaughter plants to keep cattle calm. She also discusses how important the attitude of the handler is and the growing role of women in slaughter plants. Grandin affirms that life and death are inseparable, and that it is important to accept our own mortality.

LANGUAGE-BASED THOUGHT is foreign to me. All my thoughts are full-color motion pictures, running like a videotape in my imagination. It was always obvious to me that cattle and other animals also think in pictures. I have learned that there are some people who mainly think in words and I have observed that these verbal thinkers are more likely to deny animals' thought; they are unable to imagine thought without words. Using my visual thinking skills, it is easy for me to imagine myself in an animal's body and see things from their perspective. It is the ultimate virtual reality system. I can imagine looking through their eyes or walking with four legs.

My life as a person with autism is like being another species: part human and part animal. Autistic emotion may be more like an animal's. Fear is the dominant emotion in both autistic people and animals such as deer, cattle, and horses. My emotions are simple and straightforward like an animal's, my emotions are not deep-seated. They may be intense while I am experiencing them but they will subside like an afternoon thunderstorm.

For the last fifteen years I have designed chute systems for handling cattle in slaughter plants. The conveyorized restraint system I designed is used in slaughtering one third of all the cattle in the United States.

Cattle are not afraid of the same things that people fear. The problem is that many people cannot observe this because they allow their own emotions to get in the way. To design a humane system I had to imagine what it would be like if I were the animal. I had to become that animal and not just be a person in a cow costume.

Cattle and people are upset by different things. People are repulsed by the sight of blood, but blood does not bother cattle. They are wary of the things that spell danger in the wild, such as high-pitched noise, disturbances of the dirt, and sudden jerky movements. A high-pitched noise may be a distress cry, and dirt or grass that is displaced may mean that there has been a struggle to avoid being eaten. Abrupt motion may be associated with a predator leaping onto its prey. These are all danger signals.

Many times I have observed cattle balking and refusing to move through a chute at a slaughter plant. They may balk at a jiggling gate, a shadow, a shiny reflection, or anything that appears to be out of place. A coffee cup dropped on the floor can make the cattle stop and turn back. But cattle will walk quietly into a slaughterhouse if the things they are afraid of are eliminated. Solid sides on chutes prevent them from seeing people up ahead and muffling devices lessen the shrill sounds that alarm them.

Cattle are sensitive to the same things that disturb people with autism. Immature development in the lower brain systems causes some people with autism to have a heightened sense of hearing, and an intense fear is triggered when anything in their environment is out of place. A curled-up rug, or a book that is crooked on the shelf, causes the same fear as being stalked by a predator. The autistic brain is acutely aware of details that most other people ignore. Sudden high-pitched sounds in the middle of the night cause my heart to race as if a lion was going to pounce.

Like a wild animal, I recoil when people touch me. A light touch sets off a flight reaction and my oversensitive nerve endings do not tolerate hugging. I want the soothing feeling of being held, but the sensations can be too overwhelming, so I pull away. My need for touch started my interest in cattle.

Puberty began the onslaught of hormones that sensitized my nervous system and started the constant fear and anxiety. I was desperate for relief. At my aunt's ranch I observed that when cattle were placed in a squeeze chute for their vaccinations, the pressure from the side panels squeezing against their bodies relaxed them. Pressure over wide areas of the body has a calming effect on many animals. Pressure applied to the sides of a piglet will cause it to fall asleep. Firm touch has a calming effect, while a light tickle touch is likely to set off a flight reaction.

Many parents of autistic children have observed that their child will seek pressure by getting under sofa cushions or a mattress. Therapists often use deep pressure to calm autistic children. I decided to try the squeeze chute and discovered that the intense pressure temporarily made my anxiety go away. When I returned home from the ranch I built a squeezing machine. Early versions pressed against my body with hard wood. When I first started using the machine I flinched and pulled away from it like a wild animal. As I adjusted to being held I used less intense pressure and I remodeled the side panels with foam rubber padding to make the machine more comfortable.

As I became able to tolerate being held I became more interested in figuring out how the cattle felt when they were handled and held in squeeze chutes at the feed yards. Many of the animals were scared because people were rough with them. They chased them, yelled at them, and prodded them. I found that I could coax most cattle to walk through a chute to be vaccinated by moving them quietly, at a slow walk. When an animal was calm I could observe the things that would catch his eye, like shadows or people leaning over the top of the chute. The leader would look at the things that concerned him. He would stop and stare at a coffee cup on the floor or move his head back and forth in time with a small chain that was swinging in the chute. Before moving forward he had to carefully scrutinize the things that attracted his attention. If the handlers tried to force him to move before he had determined that the chain was harmless, he and all the other cattle would panic. Cattle moved quietly and quickly through the chutes as soon as the swinging chain was removed.

I found that the animals were less likely to resist being held by the squeeze chute if pressure was applied slowly. An animal would panic if suddenly bumped. I also discovered the concept of optimum pressure. The chute must apply sufficient pressure to provide the feeling of being held but not cause pain. Many people make the mistake of mashing an animal too tight when it struggles. And the chute always needs solid sides, so that the cattle do not see people deep inside their flight zone. The flight zone is the animal's safety zone. They become anxious and want to get away when people get too close.

Years later, when I designed a restraint chute for holding cattle for slaughter, I was amazed that the animals would stand still and seldom resist the chute. I found that I could just ease their head and body into position by adjusting the chute. When I got really skilled at operating the hydraulic controls, the apparatus became an extension of my arms and hands. It was as if I could reach through the machine and hold each animal very gently. It was my job to hold the animal gently while the rabbi performed the final deed.

During the last ten years, more and more women have been hired to handle cattle and operate chutes in both feed yards and slaughter plants. At first the men were skeptical that women could do the work, but today progressive managers have found that women are gentler and work well with the animals. Some feed yards now hire only women to doctor sick cattle and vaccinate the new arrivals. In slaughter plants, two of the best operators of kosher restraining chutes are women. They were attracted to the job because they couldn't stand to see the guys abusing cattle.

When I first started designing equipment I thought that all the problems of the rough treatment of animals in slaughter plants could be solved with engineering. But engineering is only part of the equation. The most important thing is the attitude of management. A strong manager acts as the conscience of the employees in the trenches. To be most effective in maintaining high standards of animal treatment the manager has to be involved enough to care, but not so much that he or she overdoses on the constant death. The managers who are most likely to care and enforce humane handling are most likely to have close associations with animals, or are close to the land.

I am often asked how I can care about animals and be involved in their slaughter. People forget that nature can be harsh. Death at the slaughter plant is quicker and less painful than death in the wild. Lions dining on the guts of a live animal is much worse in my opinion. The animals we raise for food would have never lived at all if we had not raised them. I feel that our relationship with animals must be symbiotic. In nature there are many examples of symbiosis. For example, ants raise aphids and use them as "dairy cows." The ants feed the aphids and in return they provide a sugar substance. It is important that our relationship with farm animals is reciprocal. We owe animals a decent life and a painless death.

I have observed that the people who are completely out of touch with nature are the most afraid of death, and places such as slaughter houses. I was moved by Birute Galdikas's book on her research on orangutans. The people in the Borneo rain forests live as a part of nature and have a totally different view of life and death. To the native people, "death is not separate from life." In the jungle they see death every day. Birute states, "For me, as for most middle-class North Americans death was just a tremor far down, far away at the end of a very long road, not something to be lived with every hour of every single day."

Many people attempt to deny the reality of their own mortality. When I designed my first system I had to look my own mortality straight in the eye. I live each day as if I could die tomorrow. I want to make the most of each day and do things to make the world a better place.

Chapter 27

Temple Grandin

A MAJOR CHANGE

In this article Temple Grandin notes that progress has been made in both handling and stunning from 1997 to 1999, largely through the decision of two fast-food companies to audit U.S. plants to make sure they complied with industry guidelines. Grandin describes the animal welfare problems with transporting sick or weak animals. The increase in the numbers of such animals indicates to Grandin that producers may be pushing animals beyond their biological limits. She stresses the importance of continually monitoring animal welfare, using vocalization as an objective measure.

I HAVE WORKED as a consultant to the meat industry since the early 1970s. I've been in more than 300 slaughter plants in the United States, Canada, Mexico, Europe, Australia, New Zealand, and South America. During the course of my career. I've seen many changes take place, but I'm going to focus in this paper on my work to improve conditions for the slaughter of cattle and calves and later address transport and other animal-handling issues.

[. . .]

I saw more improvement in both handling and stunning from 1997 to 1999 than I had seen previously in my entire career. Two fast-food companies started auditing U.S. plants during 1999 to make sure they complied with the American Meat Institute Guidelines (Grandin 1997c). Both federally inspected beef and pork plants were scored objectively. Many plants now have better stunner maintenance, and electric prod usage has been greatly reduced. One company audited forty-one beef plants in 1999; I was present at about half of the audits. By the end of 1999, 90 percent of beef plants were stunning 95 percent of the cattle they processed with one shot: 37 percent were stunning 99 percent to 100 percent with one shot (Grandin 2000b). If the first shot missed, the animal was immediately restunned. (This was a big improvement over performance noted in the 1996 USDA survey [Grandin 1997a,b].) Large flags were being used to move pigs, and a piece of plastic on a stick was being used to move cattle. These devices had replaced many electric prods.

In beef production, plants were scored on percentage of cattle stunned with one shot, insensibility on the bleed rail, and vocalization during handling. Vocalization (moos and bellows) is a sensitive indicator of welfare-related problems such as excessive electric prod use, slipping and falling, missed stunner shots, and excessive pressure from a restraint device (Grandin 1998a,b).

Researchers have found that vocalization in both cattle and pigs is correlated with physiological indicators of stress (Dunn 1990; Warriss et al. 1994; White et al. 1995). Vocalization is also correlated with pain (Watts and Stookey 1998; Weary 1998). Vocalization scoring can pinpoint handling problems. Beef plants with good handling practices will have 3 percent or less of their cattle vocalizing during handling in the stunning chute (Grandin 1998b). (To keep scoring simple, vocalization is scored on a "yes" and "no" basis—a cow either vocalizes or it does not. Vocalization in the yards where cattle are standing undisturbed is not scored.) In 1999 74 percent of forty-two U.S. beef plants had vocalization scores of 3 percent or less for cattle. In 1996 only 43 percent of the plants had a vocalization score of 3 percent or less. Excessive electric prod use, due to cattle balking, had raised vocalization scores to as high as 17 percent at some plants.

Vocalization scoring can be used to chart handling improvement within a plant. It also works well on feedlots and ranches. Vocalization scores will often be higher than 3 percent when animals are ear-tagged on ranches or feedlots. In contrast, it is easy to have a 0 percent vocalization rate for animals moving through the chutes, being restrained in the squeeze chute, and being vaccinated.

The presence of distractions, which makes cattle balk, makes a 3 percent or less vocalization score almost impossible. The movement of a small chain hanging in a chute, for example, will make an approaching animal stop and impede the flow of the other animals. Lighting a dark restrainer entrance will often improve animal movement. (Information on debugging systems and removing distractions can be found in Grandin 1998c, 1996.)

People manage the things that they measure. Bad practices become "normal" if there is no standard to which they can be compared. Vocalization scoring can be used to chart progress as a plant improves its equipment and practices.

[. . .]

Dairy and pig industry problems

The number-one transport problem in the 1970s—and the number-one transport problem today—is loading onto a truck animals who are not fit for transport. The dairy industry has some of the worst such problems. Baby dairy calves, who are too young to walk, are not fit for transport. Emaciated or lame dairy cows are not fit for transport. Downer dairy cows, those who are unable to walk, are more prevalent now than in 1994. Numbers of beef cattle downers have decreased slightly (Smith *et al.* 1994, 1995; Roeber 2001). The 1999 audit by Smith *et al.* indicated that 1.5 percent of all culled dairy cows arrived at a slaughter plant down and unable to walk. In the beef industry, 0.77 percent of the cows were downers.

In the past thirty years, although the handling of beef cattle on ranches and feedlots has improved, welfare problems in the transport of old, culled dairy cows have worsened. Genetics is partly to blame. Selection of individuals for milk production has increased the incidence of lameness. John Webster at Bristol University in the United Kingdom states that the typical cow's foot can no longer support its weight. A dairy veterinarian in Florida told me that the incidence and aspects of lameness in dairy cows are horrendous. Leg conformation is heritable, and good conformation will help prevent lameness (Boettcher *et al.* 1998; Van Dorp *et al.* 1998). Slaughter plant managers and truck drivers have reported that dairies that use bovine somatrophin (BST), bovine growth hormone, in their dairy herds sometimes have more thin, weak cows. Administration of BST reduced body condition score (Jordan *et al.* 1991; and West *et al.* 1990). Unless the cow is fed very well, it may lose body condition. The degree of body condition reduction is related to the dose of BST.

Single-trait selection of pigs for rapid growth and leanness has created pigs who are more fragile and likely to die during transport. I have observed that death losses during transport have tripled in the 1990s compared to the 1980s. Some hybrid pigs are very excitable, which makes handling them more difficult (Grandin 2000a). These pigs act as though they have high sympathetic nervous system arousal. A tap on the rump will make them squeal. Normal pigs are much less likely to startle. Pigs who are selected solely for productivity may have a loss of disease resistance. Genetic factors affect susceptibility to disease.

One of my biggest concerns is the possibility that producers are pushing animals beyond their biological limits. The pig industry, for example, has repeated most of the mistakes that the broiler-chicken industry made. Genetic traits are linked in unexpected ways. Some pigs grow so fast that they have very weak bones. These pigs have large bulging muscles but are so fragile that livestock insurance companies will not sell transport insurance to producers to cover them. Fortunately, some breeders are now selecting far more "moderate" pigs, which will have fewer problems. [. . .]

Conclusions

Promoting better stockmanship is essential to improving animal welfare. Large meat-buying customers such as fast-food restaurants in the United States and supermarket chains in the United Kingdom can motivate great change by insisting that suppliers uphold better animal welfare standards, The greatest advances of the last thirty years have been the result of company audits. To maintain such progress, handling and stunning must be continually audited, measured, and managed. Handlers tend to revert to rough handling unless they are monitored and managed. An objective scoring system provides a standard that can be upheld. An overworked employee cannot do a good job of taking care of animals. Good stockmanship requires adequate staffing levels. More efforts are also needed to address problems of faulty stunning equipment, ever-increasing line speed, and enforcement of the Humane Slaughter Act when violations occur.

Attitudes can be changed, and that change can improve both animal welfare and productivity.

References

Boettcher, P.J., J.C. Dekkers, L.O. Warnick, and S.J. Wells. 1998. Genetic analysis of lameness in cattle. *Journal of Dairy Science* 81: 1148–56.

Dunn, C.S. 1990. Stress reactions of cattle undergoing ritual slaughter using two methods of restraint. *Veterinary Record* 126: 522–5.

Grandin, T. 1996. Factors that impede animal movement at slaughter plants. *Journal of the American Veterinary Medical Association* 209: 757–9.

—— 1997a. Assessment of stress during handling and transport. *Journal of Animal Science* 75: 249–57.

—— 1997b. Survey of handling and stunning in federally inspected beef, pork, veal, and sheep slaughter plants. *ARS Research Project No. 3602–32000–002–08G*. Washington, D.C.: U.S. Department of Agriculture.

—— 1997c. *Good management practices for animal handling and stunning*. Washington, D.C.: American Meat Institute.

—— 1998a. Objective scoring of animal handling and stunning practices in slaughter plants. *Journal of the American Veterinary Medical Association* 212: 36–93.

—— 1998b. The feasibility of using vocalization scoring as an indicator of poor welfare during slaughter. *Applied Animal Behavior Science* 56: 121–8.

—— 1998c. Solving livestock handling problems in slaughter plants. In *Animal welfare and meat science*, ed. N.G. Gregory. Wallingford, U.K.: CAB International.

—— 2000a. *Livestock handling and transport*. Second Edition. Wallingford. U.K.: CAB International.

—— 2000b. 1999 Audits of stunning and handling in federally inspected beef and pork plants. Paper presented. American Meat Institute 2000 Conference on Handling and Stunning, Kansas City, Mo.

Jordan, D.C., A.A. Aquilar, J.D. Olson, C. Bailey, G.F. Hartnell, and K.S. Madsen, 1991. Effects of recombinant methionyl bovine somatrophic (sometribove) in high-producing cow's milk three times a day. *Journal of Dairy Science* 74: 220–6.

Roeber, D.L., P.D. Mies, C.D. Smith, K.E. Belk, T.G. Field, J.D. Tatum, J.A. Scanga, and G.C. Smith. 2001. National market cow and bull beef quality audit: 1999: A survey of producer-related defects in market cows and bulls. *Journal of Animal Science* 79: 658–65.

Smith, G.C., J.B. Morgan, J.D. Tatum, C.C. Kukay, M.T. Smith, T.D. Schnell, and G.G. Hilton. 1994. Improving the consistency and competitiveness of non-fed beef: and improving the salvage value of cull cows and bulls. The final report of the National Cattlemen's Beef Association. Fort Collins: Colorado State University.

Smith, G.C., *et al.* 1995. Improving the quality, consistency, competitiveness, and market share of beef: A blueprint for total quality management in the beef industry. The final report of the National Beef Quality Audit. Fort Collins: Colorado State University.

Warriss, P.D., S.N. Brown, and S.J.M. Adams. 1994. Relationship between subjective and objective assessment of stress at slaughter and meat quality in pigs. *Meat Science* 38: 329–40.

Watts, J.M., and J.M. Stookey. 1998. Effects of restraint and branding on rates and acoustic parameters of vocalization in beef cattle. *Applied Animal Behavior Science* 62: 125–35.

Weary, D.M., L.A. Braithwaite, and D. Fraser. 1998. Vocal response to pain in piglets. *Applied Animal Behavior Science* 56: 161–72.

West, J.W., K. Bondair, and J.C. Johnson. 1990. Effect of bovine somatotropin on milk yield and composition, body weight, and condition score of Holstein and Jersey cows. *Journal of Dairy Science* 73: 1062–8.

White, R.G., J.A. DeShazer, C.J. Tressler, G.M. Borcher, S. Davey, A. Waninge, A.M. Parkhurst, M.J. Milanuk, and E.T. Clems. 1995. Vocalizations and physiological response of pigs during castration with and without anesthetic. *Journal of Animal Science* 73: 381–6.

Van Dorp, T.E., J.C.M. Dekkers, S.W. Martin, and J.P., Noordhuizen, T.M. 1998. Genetic parameters of health disorders and relationships with 305-day milk yield and information traits in registered dairy cows. *Journal of Dairy Science* 81: 2264–70.

Chapter 28

Michael C. Appleby

FOOD PRICES AND ANIMAL WELFARE

Michael Appleby points out that while economic efficiency in animal food production was initiated by public policies during and after WWII, it subsequently became market driven, with competition between producers and retailers predominant. Consumers do not drive the market: very little of the consumers' money reaches farmers. Thus improvements in farm animal welfare could be achieved with only minor increases in the price paid for food by consumers.

Introduction

THE PROPORTION OF income spent on food has been in steady decline. It was typical in the years after World War II for people in developed countries to spend between one quarter and one third of their income on food but now about 10% is usual. In practical terms the increase in economic efficiency of agriculture has been spectacular. Broiler production provides probably the strongest example: in the post-war period a meat chicken took over 13 weeks to grow to 2 kg and cost the equivalent of what is now about $50. Nowadays, because of genetic selection and changes in management, it takes less than 6 weeks and costs under $3. Dairy production is another extraordinary demonstration of this effect. Production of milk involves maintenance of cows and many other complex processes with impacts on staff, the local community, and the environment. Yet in supermarkets in many countries, milk is cheaper than water.

Most people could readily pay more for food. Indeed, most consumers already pay more than necessary, by buying specialist products, convenience foods or ready-cooked meals. However, there are costs associated with cheap food produced from animals that reach well beyond the dollars paid by citizens at the checkout register of a supermarket or fast food restaurant. A morally significant effect of pressure for cheap food production has been modifications to production methods that have impacts on animal welfare.

Animal welfare and production costs

The relationship between animal welfare and production costs is complex, partly because welfare is itself complex. It is recognized that people vary in their attitude to welfare, emphasizing physical aspects, mental aspects, naturalness, or a combination of these (Fraser et al., 1997). The three approaches can also be identified in the Five Freedoms (FAWC, 1997), which include freedom from physical problems such as disease and mental problems such as hunger, as well as freedom to perform normal or natural behavior.

There are many instances where improvement of welfare will reduce the costs incurred by farmers, for example when measures are taken to reduce disease and mortality. However, there are others where improving welfare would raise costs, for example if larger space allowances are provided for livestock.

Sometimes increased costs can be offset by increased income, by obtaining price premiums for products, such as free range eggs, that are perceived to be associated with high welfare or with other benefits like food quality.

Some of these complexities have been modeled by Bennett (1997) and McInerney (1998): see Figure 28.1. Imagine that humans are starting to exploit animals, at point A. This model assumes that up to point B, animals and humans derive mutual benefit from their association. B marks maximum welfare for animals with some benefits for humans. However, maximum output of animal products for human benefit would be achieved at point E, at a cost to animal welfare; exploitation beyond this point would reduce production. The decision for society is where on the curve from B to E should we be? Society may decide that anything beyond D constitutes cruelty. However, it may also be that if we really knew society's preferences, then we should rather be at point C (i.e. achieving a lower level of production but with higher welfare) (Bennett, 1997).

One example of a reduction in welfare arising from increased production, represented by the part of the curve between B and E, is that selection of pigs for higher growth rate in piglets has meant that pregnant sows cannot be fed ad libitum or they would become obese. On the restricted food allowances that they are given commercially, sows are continuously hungry (Lawrence *et al.*, 1988) and, when they are kept in housing that prevents foraging behavior, develop stereotypic (repetitive) behavior indicative of frustration (Appleby and Lawrence, 1987).

Pressure for reduced costs

The pressure for lower production costs is not simply attributable to individual farmers. It is sometimes described – including by the animal production industry – as a consumer demand for cheap food. It is not surprising, indeed it is reasonable, that offered two otherwise similar products most shoppers will buy the cheaper. However, this is not actually the main pressure for economic efficiency. This was initiated by public policies – before, during and after World War II – in favor of more abundant, cheaper food (Williams, 1960). It subsequently became market driven, with competition between producers and between retailers to sell food as cheaply as possible, and thereby acquired its own momentum.

The fact that consumer behavior is not the main driving force behind on-farm efficiency is demonstrated by the fact that little of the consumer's money actually reaches farmers. For example in the USA it

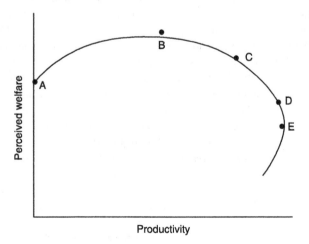

Figure 28.1   A model of the relationship between productivity of farm animals and perceptions of their welfare; after Bennett (1997) and McInerney (1998). For explanation, see text.

is estimated that only 19c of each dollar spent on food by the consumer goes to the farmer, the rest being accounted for by packaging, transport, marketing etc. (Economic Research Service, 2004). The increasing extent to which this is true adds to the decline in food prices to produce an even sharper decline in farm incomes: in the 1950s about 8% of household finances went to farmers but now only about 2%.

This point was emphasized by the editor of the industry paper Watt Poultry USA who wrote an article called "Efficiency: What has it gotten us?" and said that. "the problem is that all the efficiencies of production have not really led to increased margins over the years" (Olentine, 2003).

Improving welfare

The corollary, though, is that improvements in farm animal welfare could be achieved with only minor increases in the price paid for food by consumers. As one illustration, the capital costs of animal production (housing and so on) typically account for about 10% of production costs. Suppose we double the space and facilities provided for the animals, increasing production costs by 10%. When a consumer buys a meal in a supermarket or restaurant, the cost of animal products in that meal accounts for only about 5% of its purchase price. So increasing the cost of production by 10% need only add 0.5% to the price of the meal. Most consumers would not even notice such a change and would probably support it if asked.

A real example is provided by the UK ban on stalls and tethers for pregnant sows, for welfare reasons, which took effect in January 1999. McInerney (1998) estimated that this would increase pork production costs by 5%, but retail prices by only 1%. Householders might buy slightly less pork than hitherto, so their expenditure on food would stay level or very slightly decrease (by perhaps 0.03%). Meanwhile it should be possible for the farmers to maintain their profits, offsetting increased costs with increased selling prices.

An obstacle to such change, however, is what may be called economic inertia. Producers tend to resist legislation – or pressure from intermediary buyers – to improve conditions for animals because in existing price structures buyers continue to expect low prices. Any increased cost of production would therefore be borne by producers and they would suffer losses or reduced profits, at least short-term. If these short-term effects can be avoided, though, by making changes gradually or deploying public subsidy, a new situation with increased costs and increased income from increased food prices need not be disadvantageous to producers. This is the expectation behind legislation in the European Union over recent years to protect animal welfare: that by creating a "level playing field" for all livestock producers, this legislation will not cause a significant disadvantage to any individual producers. A major consideration, of course, is protection against imports of food products from countries without similar legislation. Such protection, taking into account animal welfare standards, is being sought by the European Union (supported by welfare groups) in negotiations at the World Trading Organization. It is also a possible outcome of development by the World Organization for Animal Health of guidelines for welfare of farm animals (OIE, 2004).

In other countries such as the USA there has been much less change in relevant legislation. However, despite economic inertia, there have been some initiatives to improve farm animal welfare in the USA in recent years, led by retailers and others. These vary from decisions by some retailers that their customers expect them to safeguard the welfare of animals that supply their products, to development of niche markets such as that for organic food (Mench, 2003; Appleby, 2004). These niche markets depend on the fact that many different concerns are expressed over the impact of conventional production methods: on animal welfare, on the environment and on other priorities such as food safety and developing countries. As such, some people are willing to seek out and pay more for food produced by alternative methods that take these concerns into account. There have always been some producers who use such methods and obtain higher selling prices to offset higher production costs. They do this either because they share the concerns, or for business reasons, or both. Despite having only a small share of the market, such farmers offer a vision for the future of agriculture (Appleby, 2005). These farmers, and the consumers who buy their products, are having a disproportionate effect on legislation in some countries (particularly Europe) and on the retail sector in others (such as the USA): they are affecting more of animal production than just the proportion directly covered by their own sales. Sale of products like organic and free range has always been a minority, but has led the way for legislation in Europe affecting all farm animals.

Conclusions

- The most important effects on farm animal welfare are not exerted by food prices as such, but by the cost of food production. Major improvements in farm animal welfare would result in small increases in food prices. It would be appropriate to investigate mechanisms to achieve this.
- Society does not need cheaper food production. On the contrary, from the viewpoint of doing what is appropriate for animal welfare and the environment, free market competition should no longer be the main determinant of farm practices and food prices.
- Animal scientists can serve the long-term interests of animal agriculture by combining efforts to do the right thing for welfare of animals with more traditional goals.

References

Appleby, M.C. 2004. Alternatives to conventional livestock production methods. Pages 339–350 in *The Well-Being of Farm Animals: Challenges and Solutions*, Benson, G.J., & B.E. Rollin, (Eds). Blackwell, Ames, USA.

Appleby, M.C. 2005. Sustainable agriculture is humane, humane agriculture is sustainable. *J. Agric. & Envir. Ethics* 18.

Appleby, M.C. & A.B. Lawrence. 1987. Food restriction as a cause of stereotypic behaviour in tethered gilts. *Anim. Prod.* 45: 103–110.

Bennett, R.M. 1997. Economics. Pages 235–248 in *Animal Welfare*, Appleby, M.C., & B.O. Hughes, (Eds). CAB International, Wallingford, UK.

Economic Research Service. 2004. Calculating the food marketing bill. Amber Waves, February.

FAWC (Farm Animal Welfare Council). 1997. *Report on the Welfare of Laying Hens*. FAWC, Tolworth, UK.

Fraser, D., D.M. Weary, E.A. Pajor, & B.N. Milligan. 1997. A scientific conception of animal welfare that reflects ethical concerns. *Anim. Welf.* 6: 187–205.

Lawrence, A.B., M.C. Appleby, & H.A. MacLeod. 1988. Measuring hunger in the pig using operant conditioning: the effect of food restriction. *Anim. Prod.* 47: 131–137.

McInerney, J.P. 1998. The economics of welfare. Pages 115–132 in *Ethics, Welfare, Law and Market Forces: The Veterinary Interface*, Michell, A.R., & R. Ewbank, (Eds). Universities Federation for Animal Welfare, Wheathampstead, UK.

Mench, J.A. 2003. Assessing animal welfare at the farm and group level: a United States perspective. *Anim. Welf.* 12: 493–503.

OIE (World Organization for Animal Health). 2004. Global conference on animal welfare: an OIE initiative. OIE, Paris.

Olentine, C. 2003. Efficiency: What has it gotten us? *Watt Poultry USA*, February, p. 12.

Williams, H.T. 1960. *Principles for British Agricultural Policy*. Oxford University Press, Oxford, UK.

Chapter 29

Animal Agriculture Alliance

ANIMAL AGRICULTURE: MYTHS AND FACTS

The Animal Agriculture Alliance argues that the general population accepts the human right to use animals. Further, farmers and ranchers constantly attend to their animals' welfare, because healthy animals provide a greater return on their investment. Most of the farms in the U.S. are owned by an individual or a married couple. The Alliance goes on to explain the treatment of pigs, dairy cows, laying hens, and veal calves, addressing questions of animal welfare and the use of antibiotics in food animals.

Myths	Facts
Farm animals deserve the same rights as you or I. All creatures deserve to share the planet equally with man.	To believe that man and all other animals exist with the same rights is anthropomorphism, or the "humanizing" of animals. This is a belief held by some vegetarians and animal rights extremists, and is not accepted by the general population. There are theological, scientific and philosophical arguments for why man cares for animals so they may serve him. Certainly, man has the moral obligation to avoid cruelty in dealing with all animals in all situations.
Farmers care less for their animals than they do for the money animals bring them. Agribusiness corporations mislead farmers into using production systems and drugs that mean profits at the cost of animal welfare.	Farmers and ranchers are neither cruel nor naive. One of the main reasons someone goes into farming or ranching is a desire to work with animals. A farmer would compromise his or her own welfare if animals were mistreated. Agriculture is very competitive in the U.S., a career which pays the farmer a slim profit on the animals he cares for. It is in the farmer's own best interest to see the animals in his charge treated humanely, guaranteeing him a healthy, high quality animal, a greater return on his investment, and a wholesome food product. No advertising campaign or salesman can convince a farmer to use a system or product that would harm an animal. Farmers are always looking for ways to improve their farms to ensure animal welfare and the economics of production.

Myths	Facts
	We must also understand the difference between what an animal may want and what it needs. It is not generally in the best interest of the animal to be left untended. An animal may eat poisonous plants if in the open, or fall prey to predators. An animal may "want" to do these things, but does it "need" to?
Farming in the U.S. is controlled by large corporations which care about profits and not about animal welfare.	Of the 2.2 million farms in the U.S., 87 percent are owned by an individual or a married couple responsible for operating the farm. If partnerships— typically a parent and one or more children or other close relatives—are added to this total, 97 percent of U.S. farms are family-owned and operated, according to the U.S. Department of Agriculture's "1987 Fact Book of U.S. Agriculture." Even those farms which are legally corporations are generally family controlled, with USDA reporting only 7,000 non-family controlled corporate farms in the U.S.
Farm animals are routinely raised on "factory farms," confined in "crowded, unventilated cages and sheds."	Animals are generally kept in barns and similar housing, with the exception of beef cattle, to protect the health and welfare of the animal. Housing protects animals from predators, disease, and bad weather or extreme climate. Housing also makes breeding and birth less stressful, protects young animals, and makes it easier for farmers to care for both healthy and sick animals. Modern animal housing is well ventilated, warm, well-lit, clean and scientifically designed for the specific needs of the animal, such as the regular availability of fresh water and a nutritionally balanced feed. For instance, a hog barn wouldn't be used for cows, any more than an adult would sleep in a child's crib. Housing is designed to allow the farmer to provide the best animal care and control costs.
Not only are all animals confined, most are held in crates and cages and not allowed to move at all.	Animal behavior is as varied as human behavior. In some cases, animals are restrained to avoid injuring themselves, other animals or the farmer. All forms of restraint are designed for the welfare of the animal as well as efficiency of production. Breeding sows are helped during breeding so they are not injured by the larger, heavier boar. When a sow is ready to farrow or give birth, she is placed typically for 3–4 weeks in a stall to make her delivery easier, help with veterinary care if necessary ensure she does not step on or roll over and crush

Myths	Facts

her litter, while allowing her piglets to be near her. Pigs are naturally aggressive and curious, and what has been described as "manic" or abnormal behavior during this protective restraint is currently under study by swine specialists.

Dairy cows are milked in stalls, usually twice a day. This is so farmers can use modern milking equipment, and to protect the cow and the farmer. Placing the cows in these stalls during milking also facilitates medical treatment of an animal weighing more than 1,200 lbs. At other times, most dairy farmers will turn cows out into pasture or into large pens.

Laying hens are kept in cages to ensure adequate feed and water reaches every bird every day and to facilitate egg collection. It allows the farmer to care for more birds efficiently and produce the millions of eggs consumers value each year. Sorting the birds into small groups helps control naturally aggressive behavior, such as pecking and cannibalism, while allowing the birds to interact with their penmates. It takes greater amounts of land, labor and money to raise laying hens in open flocks because of exposure to bad weather, disease, predators, etc. Today, one egg farm may house 50,000–100,000 hens. If layers were not raised in a controlled environment, feeding, cleaning, preventing disease, treating sick birds, and locating where 50,000 birds laid thousands of eggs each day would greatly increase the cost of eggs, and price a valuable food out of the diet of many consumers.

Veal calves may be raised in stalls, hutches, pens or in small groups. The system used by an individual farmer varies by region and climate, type of calf, farmer preference and size of farm. One system cannot arbitrarily be said to be better than another in all situations. Studies comparing these various housing systems are on-going.

Veal calves are generally kept in individual stalls to provide individual attention, improve general health, separate aggressive young bulls from each other, minimize or eliminate injury to the animals and the farmer, and to aid in feeding efficiency and veterinary care.

In modern stall systems, calves can stand, lie down, see, touch and react to other calves in well-lit, sanitary barns. It is not true that veal calves are kept in "boxes" or perpetual darkness. Veal feed is a liquid

Myths	Facts
	milk "replacer" product that is specially formulated for baby calves. It is a fortified formula containing minerals, vitamins, and animal health products, including minimum recommended amounts of iron to ensure calf health. The farmer would be compromising his own economic welfare if calves weren't kept healthy.
	Beef cattle in large herds or feedlots are restrained generally when being given veterinary care. In cow/calf operations, housing allows for protection from predators and the elements, disease control and ease of handling.
Farm animals are routinely "mutilated" by beak trimming, tail docking, branding, dehorning, castration, and other practices to make it easier for the farmer.	To the inexperienced viewer, some routine farm animal handling practices necessary to the welfare and health of the animal and the insurance of quality food may appear brutal, just as some life-saving human surgical and medical practices may seem brutal to the casual observer. All of these practices are done in a professional manner to ensure the welfare of the animal.
	Egg laying hens may have their beaks trimmed— not removed—to avoid injury to each other as a result of the bird's natural cannibalistic tendencies. Claws may be trimmed to avoid injury during mating.
	With hogs, piglets may have their needle teeth trimmed shortly after birth to avoid injury to the nursing sow and to litter mates. Tails may be docked or shortened to end a natural tendency toward tail biting that occurs in some swine herds.
	Beef cattle, sheep and some dairy cattle may be dehorned when young to avoid injury to each other and to the rancher; castration, or neutering, may be necessary to help control aggressive behaviors in young animals, and to insure the quality meat consumers demand. In sheep, tails may be docked to improve hygiene and prevent fly and parasite infestation.
	Permanently identifying animals by earmarking, tattooing, branding and other means is necessary to maintain accurate health records to prevent the spread of disease to animals and man. It also helps during marketing.
	All of these practices are under regular review and new research is done to ensure their necessity and effectiveness, and to ensure the required results are achieved in the most humane, efficient manner.

Myths

A vegetarian diet is healthier than a diet that includes meat, milk and eggs.

Facts

Both the federal government and the American Heart Association contend a diet containing meat, milk and eggs is appropriate to both groups' dietary guidelines. The Washington Post, reporting on the First International Congress on Vegetarian Nutrition held in Washington in March, 1987, had this to say: "The Congress didn't uncover any earth-shattering findings or recommend that everyone take up bean sprouts full time," the Post reported. Health benefits can be derived by nonvegetarians who follow a prudent diet that is low in fat, sodium, sugar and alcohol. Just as there are nonvegetarian diets that are unhealthy, so too there are poorly planned vegetarian diets. The approach to healthful eating should be common sense.

Farm animals in "confinement" are prone to disease, forcing farmers to routinely use antibiotics, hormones and drugs to keep them alive. This jeopardizes animal and human health.

Animal scientists, veterinarians and on-farm experience show animals kept in housing are no more likely to get sick than animals kept in the open. In fact, they're generally healthier because they are protected. However, farm animals do sometimes get sick. To prevent illness and to ensure that an animal remains healthy all of its life, farmers will take preventive measures, including the use of animal health products. These products are generally given to the animal in a scientifically formulated feed best suited to the animal's needs. This is the simplest way to make sure each animal gets the care indicated.

Animal health products include animal drugs and vaccines, in addition to vitamins, minerals and other nutrients the animal needs in a balanced diet. Not all animals are given the same treatment in all situations.

Animal drugs include antibiotics to prevent and treat animal disease, and most are not used in human medicine. There are antibiotics used in humans that are also used in animals. There is now an unresolved scientific debate over these uses. Since there is no conclusive scientific proof that the use of human antibiotics in animals—a practice going back 35 years—is a risk to human health, these products are used to prevent and treat illness in some animals, in addition to aiding growth.

Grain fed to livestock and poultry could be used to feed the hungry overseas.

Grain fed to livestock and poultry is generally referred to as "feed grade." It is not usually intended for human consumption and is not generally the same quality and nutrient value as grain used in human

Myths	Facts
	food production. Animals, in fact, are the most efficient converters of this lower-quality grain and other grasses and forages into high-quality protein.
The average U.S. farm animal is fed whatever the farmer happens to have available, without regard to what the animal needs for good health.	The average U.S. farm animal, from the standpoint of nutrition, eats better than the average U.S. citizen. There are more than a thousand professional livestock and poultry nutritionists in the U.S.—many are Ph.Ds—who spend much of their professional time determining the needs of each animal for each phase of the animal's life cycle for about 40 basic nutrients. When nutritional research indicates how much of a given nutrient is needed in a given ration, both the feed manufacturer and the farmer who owns the livestock or poultry, have an economic incentive to provide animals with exactly the indicated amount of necessary nutrients for animal health. The result is a healthier animal. While most people don't know how many calories they consume in a day, feed manufacturers and farmers see that each farm animal receives almost precisely the correct amount of such vital nutrients as minerals, vitamins, amino acids, etc.

Many of the ingredients used in animal rations are agricultural by-products of other industries, such as cotton, rice, flour milling, meat packing and alcohol production. Many of these ingredients—high in animal nutrition value—would have little or no value to man were they not used to feed animals. Some of these products would create significant disposal problems were they not used as animal feed ingredients and had to be dumped.

Medical and social benefits of livestock production

Most of us are not aware that the farmer provides us with more than just a healthy, inexpensive diet. Animals raised for food are also invaluable in human medical treatments and in our everyday lives, by providing us with materials which make our lives easier and safer. Listed below by contributing animal category, are just a few of myriad medical and social benefits provided to us by livestock production:

Cattle:

Medical contributions:

Adrenal glands:

Epinephrine is used to relieve some symptoms of hay fever, asthma and some allergies.

It is also used as a heart stimulant in some crisis situations, and by dentists to prolong the effect of local anesthetics.

Blood:

Thrombin from cattle blood helps blood clotting, and is valuable in treating wounds to inaccessible parts of the body. It is also used in skin grafting.

Liver:

Liver extract is sometimes combined with folic acid and injected to treat various types of anemia.

Pancreas:

Perhaps the best known contribution, insulin derived from cattle pancreas is used to treat diabetes. Glucagon helps counteract insulin-shock.

Medical benefits derived from cattle by-products include rennet, epinephrine, thrombin, insulin, heparin, TSH, ACTH, cholesterol, estrogen, thyroid extract.

Product contributions using cattle by-products:

Tires	*Buttons*
Antifreeze	*China*
Upholstery	*Photographic film*
Leather	*Musical instrument*
Sports equipment	*components such*
Surgical sutures	*as strings*
Soaps	*Brushes*
Cosmetics	*Explosives*

Chapter 30

Steven L. Davis

THE LEAST HARM PRINCIPLE MAY REQUIRE THAT HUMANS CONSUME A DIET CONTAINING LARGE HERBIVORES, NOT A VEGAN DIET

Steven L. Davis examines Tom Regan's conclusion that being a vegan is morally required by the animal rights view. Davis points out the large number of animals of the field being killed annually in the production of corn, beans, rice, etc. If pastures were instead used for forage, fewer passages through the field with farm equipment would be necessary. He estimates that significantly fewer animals would die if half of the U.S. land was used for plants for human consumption and half for pasture for cattle.

ALTHOUGH THE DEBATE over moral vegetarianism has been going on for millennia (Shapiro, 2000), there has been a resurgence of interest in this issue in the last part of the 20th century. One of the foundational philosophical works on this subject is *The Case for Animal Rights* (1983). This paper will not critique Regan's (1983) theory on animal rights. Rather, for the moment, suppose he is right; animals are subjects-of-a-life with interests of their own that matter as much to them as similar interests matter to humans. Therefore, animals have the right to live their lives without interference from humans. His conclusion follows, therefore, that animal agriculture interferes in the lives of millions of animals annually, so humans are morally obligated to consume a vegan or vegetarian diet. The purpose of this paper is to examine the moral vegan conclusion of Regan's animal rights theory, rather than the rights theory itself. It is also the objective of this paper to examine alternative conclusions. In other words, might there be alternatives to the moral vegetarian conclusion drawn from animal rights theory?

The concept of least harm

As I was thinking about the vegan conclusion, I remembered my childhood on the farm and where our food comes from and how it is produced. Specifically, I remembered riding on farm equipment and seeing mice, gophers, and pheasants in the field that were injured or killed every time we worked the fields. Therefore, I realized that animals of the field are killed in large numbers annually to produce food for humans. Kingsolver (2001) describes these killings very effectively. "I've watched enough harvests to know that cutting a wheat field amounts to more decapitated bunnies under the combine than you would believe." "She stopped speaking when her memory lodged on an old vision from childhood: A raccoon she found just after the hay mower ran it over. She could still see the matted grey fur, the gleaming jaw bone and shock of scattered teeth. . . ." Consequently, a vegan diet doesn't necessarily mean a diet that doesn't interfere in the lives of animals. In fact, production of corn, beans, rice, etc. kills many animals, as this paper will document. So, in 1999, I sent an email to Regan, pointing this out to him. Then I asked him, "What is the morally relevant difference between the animals of the field and those of the farm that makes it acceptable to kill some of them (field mice, etc.) so that humans may eat, but not acceptable to kill others (pigs, etc.) so we may eat?" His reply (Regan, 1999, personal communication) was that we must choose the method of food production that causes the least harm to animals. (I will refer to this concept as The Least Harm Principle or LHP.) In his book, Regan (1983) calls this the "minimize harm principle" and he describes it in the following way:

> Whenever we find ourselves in a situation where all the options at hand will produce some harm to those who are innocent, we must choose that option that will result in the least total sum of harm.

It seems that Regan is saying that least harm would be done to animals in the production of a plant-based diet, because then at least you wouldn't be killing both the animals of the farm and those of the field, thus supporting the conclusion that humans are morally obligated to consume a vegan diet. But is that conclusion the one that best satisfies the LHP? Are there other ways of accomplishing least harm?

I find Regan's vegan conclusion to be problematic because he seems to think that there are no other alternatives. There is an old adage to the effect, "There is more than one way to skin a cat." Do alternative food production systems exist that may cause even less harm to animals?

How many animals of the field would die if a vegan diet were adopted?

Animals living in and around agricultural fields are killed during field activities and the greater the number of field activities, the greater the number of field animals that die. A partial list of animals of the field in the USA include opossum, rock dove, house sparrow, European starling, black rat, Norway rat, house mouse, Chukar, gray partridge, ring-necked pheasant, wild turkey, cottontail rabbit, gray-tailed vole, and numerous species of amphibians (Edge, 2000). In addition, Edge (2000) says, "production of most crops requires multiple field operations that may include plowing, disking, harrowing, planting, cultivating, applying herbicides and pesticides as well as harvesting." These practices have negative effects on the populations of the animals living in the fields. For example, just one operation, the "mowing of alfalfa caused a 50% decline in gray-tailed vole population" (Edge, 2000). Although these examples represent crop production systems in the USA, the concept is also valid for intensive crop production in any country. Other studies have also examined the effect of agricultural tillage practices on field animal populations (Johnson et al., 1991; Pollard and Relton, 1970; Tew et al., 1992).

Although accurate estimates of the total number of animals killed by different agronomic practices from plowing to harvesting are not available, some studies show that the numbers are quite large. Kerasote (1993) describes it as follows: "When I inquired about the lives lost on a mechanized farm, I realized what costs we pay at the supermarket. One Oregon farmer told me that half of the cottontail rabbits went into his combine when he cut a wheat field, that virtually all of the small mammals, ground birds, and reptiles were killed when he harvested his crops. Because most of these animals have been seen as expendable, or not seen at all, few scientific studies have been done measuring agriculture's effects on their populations." In a study that has been done to examine the effect of harvesting grain crops, Tew and Macdonald (1993) reported that mouse population density dropped from 25/ha preharvest to less than 5/ha postharvest. This decrease was attributed to both migration out of the field and to mortality. They estimated the mortality rate to be 52%. In another study, Nass et al. (1971) reported that the mortality rate of Polynesian rats was 77% during the harvest of sugar cane in Hawaii. These are the estimated mortality rates for only a single species, and for only a single operation (i.e., harvesting). Therefore, an estimate somewhere between 52 and 77% (say 60%) for animals of all kinds killed during the production year would be reasonable. If we multiply the population density shown in Tew and Macdonald's (1993) paper (25/ha) times a 60% mortality rate, that equals a mortality of 15 animals/ha each year.

If that is true, how many animals would die annually in the production of a vegan diet? There are 120 million ha of cropland harvested in the USA (USDA, 1997) each year. If all of that land was used to produce crops to support a vegan diet, and if 15 animals of the field are killed per ha per year, then 15 × 120 million = 1800 million or 1.8 billion animals would be killed annually to produce a vegan diet for the USA.

Would a pasture/ruminant model kill fewer animals?

Production of forages, such as pasture-based forages, would cause less harm to field animals (kill fewer) than intensive crop production systems typically used to produce food for a vegan diet. This is because pasture forage production requires fewer passages through the field with tractors and other farm equipment. The killing of animals of the field would be further reduced if herbivorous animals (ruminants like cattle) were used to harvest the forage and convert it into meat and dairy products. Would such production systems cause less harm to the field animals? Again, accurate numbers aren't available comparing the number of animals of the field that are killed with these different cropping systems, but, "The predominant feeling among wildlife ecologists is that no-till agriculture will have broadly positive effects on mammalian wildlife" populations (Wooley et al., 1984). Pasture-forage production, with herbivores harvesting the forage, would be the ultimate in "no-till" agriculture. Because of the low numbers of times that equipment would be needed to grow and harvest pasture forages it would be reasonable to estimate that the pasture-forage model may reduce animal deaths. In other words, perhaps only 7.5 animals of the field per ha would die to produce pasture forages, as compared to the intensive cropping system (15/ha) used to produce a vegan diet.

If half of the total harvested land in the US was used to produce plant products for human consumption and half was used for pasture-forage production, how many animals would die annually so that humans may eat?

> 60 million ha, plant production × 15 animals/ha = 0.9 billion
> 60 million ha, forage production × 7.5 animals/ha = 0.45 billion
> Total: 1.35 billion animals

According to this model then, fewer animals (1.35 billion) would die than in the vegan model (1.8 billion). As a result, if we apply the LHP as Regan did for his vegan conclusion, it would seem that humans are morally obligated to consume a diet of vegetables and ruminant animal products.

But what of the ruminant animals that would need to die to feed people in the pasture-forage model? According to USDA numbers quoted by Francione (2000), of the 8.4 billion farm animals killed each year for food in the US, approximately 8 billion of those are poultry and only 37 million are ruminants (cows, calves); the remainder includes pigs and other species. Even if the numbers of cows and calves killed for food each year was doubled to 74 million to replace the 8 billion poultry, the total number of animals that would need to be killed under this alternative method would still be only 1.424 billion, still clearly less than in the vegan model.

Other alternatives

The pasture/ruminant model would have other advantages. For one, it would provide habitat for many species of animals and insects, helping them to survive. In addition, ruminants are capable of surviving and producing on diets containing only forages, which humans cannot digest. This is beneficial in two ways. First, crops such as corn and soybeans could all be fed to humans instead of to animals. Second, pasture forage can be produced on lands that are too rough to be usable to produce crops for human consumption. Grasses are currently grown and harvested by cows in many countries on lands that are too hilly, and/or rocky, and/or dry to be usable for production of crops like corn and soybeans.

Are there other alternatives that would cause "Least Harm"? As I have discussed this analysis with others, additional alternatives have been suggested. These include the following: [. . .]

1   Another alternative, suggested by Peter Cheeke (personal communication), would be to eliminate intensive agriculture altogether and have everyone produce their own vegan diet on small plots of land using no-till production systems to reduce killing/harm to animals of the field. I believe that this system would also be unpractical and not viable. The human populations are too large, land is concentrated in the hands of the few rather than many, and social systems would need to revert to those of primitive cultures.

2   But if herbivores are used, wouldn't it cause least harm if we used the fewest possible, therefore, the largest herbivores? Elephants might be used, but in practical terms, I believe that the majority of people would object to eating elephants. Large draft horse breeds developed previously as working horses, may be up to twice the size of a cow. Perhaps they could be used to harvest or convert forages into meat and dairy products. Again, I don't believe many humans would support this option; otherwise there would already be more people willing to consume horsemeat.

3   Kerasote (1993) proposed that least harm would be done if humans were to hunt locally, particularly large animals like elk for their own food. But his least harm concept appears to be related as much to least harm to the environment (less fossil fuel consumption) as least harm to animals. Furthermore, this doesn't seem to be a practical idea, because there are too few animals and there would be too many hunters. As Taylor (1999) said, one "issue that arises from Kerasote's argument is whether hunting for one's food is practical on a large scale."

Intended vs. unintended deaths

Taylor (1999) says that another issue arises from Karasote's argument, and that is the matter of intentional infliction of harm versus harm that is the unintentional, but a foreseeable side effect of one's actions. The animals of the field die not intentionally, but incidentally as a consequence of producing food for humans. On the other hand, farm animals (chickens, pigs, cows, and sheep) are killed intentionally to provide food for humans. Perhaps I don't fully understand the nuances or moral significance of this difference, but it seems to me that the harm done to the animal is the same – dead is dead. Furthermore, many farmers do intentionally kill some animals of the field because their presence causes reduced yields. Taylor (1999) says about the questions of intent, "A utilitarian is likely to see no moral difference between the two, since utilitarianism holds that it is consequences that count and not intentions."

Conclusion

1   Vegan diets are not bloodless diets. Millions of animals of the field die every year to provide products used in vegan diets.

2   Several alternative food production models exist that may kill fewer animals than the vegan model.

3   More research is needed to obtain accurate estimations of the number of field animals killed in different crop production systems.

4   Humans may be morally obligated to consume a diet from plant based plus pasture-forage-ruminant systems.

References

Comstock, G., *Is There a Moral Obligation to Save the Family Farm?* (Iowa State University Press, Ames, IA, 1987), p. 400.

Edge, W.D., "Wildlife of Agriculture, Pastures, and Mixed Environs," in D.H. Johnson and T. A. O'Neill (eds.) *Wildlife-Habitat Relationships in Oregon and Washington* (Oregon State University Press, Corvallis, OR, 2000), pp. 342–360.

Francione, G. L., *Introduction to Animal Rights: Your Child or the Dog?* (Temple University Press, Philadelphia, PA, 2000), p. xx.

Johnson, I. P., J. R. Flowerdew, and R. Hare, "Effects of Broadcasting and Drilling Methiocarb Molluscicide Pellets on Field Populations of Wood Mice, *Apodemus sylvaticus,*" *Bull. Environ. Contam. and Toxicol.* 46 (1991), 84–91.

Kerasote, T., *Bloodties: Nature, Culture, and the Hunt* (Random House, NY, 1993), pp. 232, 233, and 254, 255.

Kingsolver, B., *Prodigal Summer* (Harper Collins, NY, 2001), pp. 322–323.

Nass, R. D., G. A. Hood, and G. D. Lindsey, "Fate of Polynesian Rats in Hawaiian Sugar Cane Fields During Harvest," *J. Wildlife Management* 35 (1971), 353–356.

Pollard, E. and T. Relton, "A study of Small Mammals in Hedges and Cultivated Fields," *J. of Applied Ecol.* 7 (1970), 549–557.

Regan, T., *The Case for Animal Rights* (University of California Press, Berkeley, CA, 1983), pp. 266–329.

Shapiro, L. S., *Applied Animal Ethics* (Delmar Press, Albany, NY, 2000), pp. 25–36.

Taylor, A., *Magpies, Monkeys, and Morals: What Philosophers say about Animal Liberation* (Broadview Press, Ontario, Canada, 1999), p. 87.

Tew, T. E. and D. W. Macdonald. "The Effects of Harvest on Arable Wood Mice," *Biological Conservation* 65 (1993), 279–283.

Tew, T. E., D. W. Macdonald, and M. R. W. Rands, "Herbicide Application Affects Microhabitat Use by Arable Wood Mice *Apodemus sylvaticus,*" *J. of Appl. Ecol.* 29 (1992), 352–359.

USDA, www.nass.usda.gov/Census/Census97/highlights, accessed 2000.

Wooley, Jr., J. B., L. B. Best, and W. R. Clark, "Impacts of No-Till Row Cropping on Upland Wildlife," *Trans. N. Amer. Wildlife and Natur. Resources Conf.* 50 (1984), 157–168.

Chapter 31

Bernard E. Rollin

THE ETHICAL IMPERATIVE TO CONTROL
PAIN AND SUFFERING IN FARM ANIMALS

Bernard E. Rollin points out that protection for farm animals has not kept pace with society's concern for laboratory animals, animals in zoos, and so forth. He identifies public ignorance, particularly in the United States, as the cause. Rollin argues that agriculture must get in step with the emerging social ethic for animals by overcoming the obstacle of scientific ideology in agricultural sciences.

[. . .]

IT SHOULD BE patent to anyone who even superficially examines ethical concerns across Western societies that moral concern for animals – how they are treated – and concern for their pain and suffering have been emerging as major issues during the past 30 years. According to both the National Cattlemen's Association and the National Institutes of Health, Congress received more letters, faxes, telephone calls, and so on dealing with animal welfare between 1980 and 1995 than any other issue. In 1991, a poll conducted by *Parents* magazine found that 85 percent of its readers affirmed that animals had rights (*Parents*, 1989).

Whereas, 25 years ago, the U.S. Congress saw no bills dealing with animal welfare, the last few years have witnessed legislative proposals numbering in the scores. According to an official of the American Quarter Horse Association, the largest equine association in the United States, the organization's largest expense in the late 1990s was hiring a research firm to monitor state and local legislation pertaining to equine welfare. In California, a law has been passed making shipping horses to slaughter a felony, as is knowingly selling a horse to someone who will so ship it. Animal cruelty has been made a felony in over 30 states, and some two dozen law schools now include courses in animal law, with numerous legal scholars working to raise the status of animals from property to quasi-personhood. Activist cities like San Francisco and Boulder, Colorado, have floated ordinances declaring that people who have pets are not owners of these animals, but guardians.

Europe has witnessed a steady increase in concern for farm animal welfare in recent years, largely due to careful scrutiny of intensive, industrialized confinement agriculture. Americans are generally surprised at the degree to which factory farming has captured public concern in Europe. Sweden passed a law in 1988 phasing out the high-confinement agriculture we take for granted in North America, which the *New York Times* called a "Bill of Rights for Farm Animals" (*New York Times*, 1988). Britain and the European Union have followed suit, with the latter announcing the elimination of sow stalls within a decade.

No area of animal use has failed to feel the effects of moral concern for animals. Animal circuses have lost the support of the public, with Cirque de Soleil, a show that does not use animals, the most popular in America. The American public's disaffection with wildlife authorities' management of wildlife populations for hunters, spring bear hunts that can lead to the death of a lactating mother bear and the consequent death by dehydration of her cubs, steel-jawed traps, lethal control of predators and pests, and mountain lion hunts have all resulted in what one authority called "management by referendum," with the public, by right of referendum, usurping the job of wildlife managers. Funds for "pest control" are ever-increasingly directed toward contraception and other nonlethal methods. Somewhat surprisingly, PETA and other groups have found the public generally sympathetic when they target the welfare of aquatic animals, even fish. The fish importing industry was sufficiently concerned with this issue to invite me to lecture to two international meetings two years in a row. Sale of lobsters in Great Britain dropped precipitously until the industry developed a "lobster stunner" so that housewives did not have to drop a live, conscious animal into boiling water. The sale of live fish has precipitated major protests in San Francisco's Chinatown. Disavowal of animal testing for toxicity of cosmetics has propelled the Body Shop into a billion-dollar industry. As early as 1978, the readership of *Glamour Magazine*, when polled, affirmed that a new cosmetic does not justify the animal suffering required to develop it.

Most surprising, perhaps, was the virtually worldwide development of laws protecting laboratory animals, mostly rats and mice. In Switzerland, a law was promulgated by referendum banning animal research, which would have passed, according to polls, had the pharmaceutical industry not spent large sums of money at the last minute defending animal research. Laws in virtually all Western countries now mandate researcher control of animal distress. In many countries (e.g., Britain), an animal suffering intractable pain that cannot be controlled must be killed. (In the United States, the animals *may be* killed at the discretion of the Animal Care and Use Committee at a research institution.) In America, these laws address not only physical pain but also "distress," and they mandate exercise for dogs and environments for nonhuman primates that "enhance their psychological well-being." The National Institutes of Health *Guide to the Care and Use of Laboratory Animals* strongly urges enriching the captive environment for all laboratory animals, and trade journals regularly cover these issues. Zoos, also, have been forced by public concern into taking cognizance of animals' behavioral needs. In Germany, a constitutional amendment passed in the spring of 2002 protects animals from all but the most exigent reasons for inflicting pain.

One could list examples endlessly, but the point has been made. Society is concerned about the pain, suffering, and distress of all animals used for its benefit. The extent of such concern may be gleaned from the dramatic story of U.S. laboratory animal legislation. The research and medical communities were dead set against these laws, as were such ancillary groups as the American Associations of Medical Colleges, Veterinary Colleges, Land Grant Universities, and the pharmaceutical industry. In cleverly orchestrated campaigns, these powerful groups threatened the public with danger to human health if laws protecting research animals passed. Most extraordinary was a film entitled "Will I Be All Right, Doctor?" which said in essence that children's health was threatened by protection of laboratory animals. The public simply did not believe these preposterous claims, and in 1985 two laws were passed to that end.

Why, one may ask, have we not seen a similar furor regarding the protection of farm animals? The answer is simple – public ignorance. For reasons unclear to me, there seems to be a media blackout on issues of farm animal welfare. Even when the swine industry was being examined for environmental despoliations, no allusion was made to the related animal welfare issues. According to reporters I spoke to at the time, editors tend to see animal welfare as "fringe." Neither mass media nor the agricultural press cover these issues, and the ignorance of U.S. farmers and agricultural scientists as well as the general public on these issues in Europe is appalling.

The result is, as Paul Thompson has remarked, that the U.S. public still thinks that farms are Old McDonald's Farm—mixed, extensive, family-run small businesses (Thompson, 1991). For many years, high-confinement poultry producer Frank Perdue helped to perpetuate this misperception by running advertisements showing chickens pecking in a barnyard, complete with red barn and rising red sun, while a voiceover declared, "At Perdue, we raise happy chickens." In short, the public is largely clueless about how food animals are produced, though when the media did cover severe confinement of veal calves, the confinement veal industry was virtually destroyed.

The agriculture industry's response to all of this is curious. Rather than admitting that confinement agriculture raises welfare problems, spokesmen for the industry (but not farmers themselves) tend to fall back on the non sequitur that the public needs to know where its food comes from. "People think bacon and eggs come from the supermarket," I often hear. "We need to show them where it comes from." Needless to say, I have serious doubts about this claim. If people were to tour confinement egg production facilities and see the hens in small cages, debeaked, one sometimes walking and defecating on top of the other in an effort by the industry to get more production per cage; or if people could view confinement swine facilities, with a 600 pound sow forced into a "crate" that measures two and a half feet high by seven feet long by three feet wide (sometimes two feet wide in an effort to force more crates into a barn), where she can't lie down straight, much less turn around, they would not be happy. If they saw newborn baby pigs castrated and tattooed, with teeth clipped all without anesthesia, then saw them raised in pens that get more and more tight as they grow, never seeing daylight and breathing air that sometimes requires that employees wear respirators, they would be even less happy. If they saw pig and chicken shipping and slaughter, I doubt it would make them appreciate the industry more than they do now! What public ignorance entails is a grace period for the confinement industries to clean up their own acts, with Europe for a model. What the emerging ethic for animals demands for farm animals is pretty clear from the examples of Europe and Britain. Before exploring this in depth, however, it behooves us to examine why animal issues have suddenly come into focus internationally.

II

There are several reasons why animal issues have seized the public imagination during the last three decades. Most obvious, perhaps, is demographic change. Although a century ago over half the population made a living producing food, this has dramatically changed. Today, barely 1.7 percent of the population works in production agriculture, with perhaps half of that group or less in animal agriculture. Furthermore, few members of the population have relatives on farms either. As a result, concepts of animals have changed. A hundred years ago, if one ran a word association test on the rural or urban population asking what the word *animal* evokes, people would likely say *horse, cow, work, food*. As late as the 1960s, over 80 percent of veterinarians were employed by agriculture. Now, such veterinarians constitute less than 8 percent of veterinarians, most of whom work in the area of companion animals who are, in fact, the new paradigm for animals in society. (One rancher friend of mine was shocked when, upon bringing a range cow into our veterinary hospital, he was asked by the female and urban students, "What is her name?") Companion animals dominate the social mind, with almost 100 percent of the public claiming to view their pets as "members of the family." Such a paradigm is considerably jarred by farm animals in confinement.

Second, since we are largely removed from animals and animal life, we yearn for closer proximity, interaction, and knowledge. This is supplied by the mass media, who are quite cognizant, as one reporter told me, that "animals sell papers." My cable system has two 24-hour-a-day Animal Planet stations, and many other channels endlessly cover animal stories. (One large-city TV news producer told me that he routinely will begin the news with an animal story teaser and not finish the story until the end of the newscast, to hold viewers.) Recall that when two whales were trapped in an ice floe, they were freed by Soviet icebreakers! Was this an overflowing of Soviet compassion (surely an oxymoron for those who gave us pogroms, Stalin, and the Gulag)? It was rather that someone in the Kremlin was smart enough to realize that releasing the whales was a cheap way to win kudos from the U.S. public. If the U.S. public had been unaware of these whales, the Russians would probably have sent whaling boats, not icebreakers!

Third, the U.S. (and world) public has had 50 years of ethical sensitivity priming. The last 50 years have seen the rise of civil rights for minorities, women's rights, gay rights, children's rights, student rights, patients' rights, the rights of indigenous populations, environmentalism, and the rights of the disabled. Concern about the weakest and most disenfranchised part of human society, animals, was inevitable. Indeed, leaders of activist animal groups often come from other social movements such as civil rights, labor, the women's movement, the gay movement, and so on. These people take seriously the dictum that the morality of a society is best judged by how it treats its least enfranchised. Exploitation of animals is definitely politically incorrect.

Fourth, the nature of animal use changed quickly and dramatically at mid-twentieth century. Historically, the major use of animals in society was agriculture—food, fiber, locomotion, and power. The key to agricultural success was animal husbandry, from the old Norse word *hus/bond*—bonded to one's household. Animal husbandry betokened an ancient and symbiotic contract between humans and domestic animals, perhaps best expressed by western American cattle ranchers, the last large group of husbandmen in the United States, when they intone, "we take care of the animals and they take care of us." One of my colleagues, a rancher and beef specialist, has declared that the worst thing that ever happened to his department was betokened by the name change from Department of Animal Husbandry to Department of Animal Science. Animal husbandry was about putting square pegs into square holes, round pegs into round holes, and creating as little friction as possible while doing so. Animal science is about efficiency and productivity. The husbandman put the animal into optimal conditions of the sort the animal was evolved for, and then augmented the animal's natural ability to survive and thrive by providing the animal with food during famine, water during drought, medical attention, help in birthing, help during natural disasters, and so on. The animals gave us their products, their toil, and sometimes their lives; we gave them better, more comfortable lives. Not only was husbandry reinforced by practicality, it was also taught as an articulated ethic. So powerful was this ethic, that when the psalmist wished to create a metaphor for God's ideal relationship to people, he chose the image of the shepherd in the Twenty-third Psalm: "The lord is my shepherd; I shall not want. He maketh me to lie down in green pastures; he leadeth me beside the still waters. He restoreth my soul." We want no more from God than the shepherd gives his sheep!

This lovely ethic can still be seen among western ranchers, for whom husbandry is as much a way of life as it is a way of making a living. Cowboys routinely spend more on a sick calf than is economically justified; most ranchers and ranch wives will sit up all night with a sick or marginal calf in their kitchen. If this were a matter of economics alone, they would value their labor and sleep time at pennies an hour. Beyond economics, there is generally a strong love for the animals and a strong sense of duty. I know one cowboy who unhesitatingly plunged into a frozen pond to save a calf who had fallen through the ice, and who afterward incurred devastating lung problems. "And I would do it again," he wheezed.

Confinement agriculture sprang up in mid-twentieth century, when values of efficiency and productivity—business values—prevailed over values of husbandry and way of life. Intensification was born of fear that people were forsaking agriculture after the Dust Bowl and the depression. It was born of fear of loss of agricultural workers to better-paying urban jobs. It was born of fear that burgeoning population would encroach on agricultural land and make feeding that population by traditional means untenable. The issue of animal welfare, if considered at all, was erroneously thought to be assured by animal productivity. Alas! This was only true for husbandry agriculture, which, as we said earlier, was about putting square pegs into square holes and creating as little friction as possible. The producer did well if and only if the animal did well. This is not to say that there was no animal pain in husbandry agriculture—that claim is belied by knife castration, branding, and dehorning. But these were short-term insults seen as inevitable and as ones from which the animals recovered rapidly. Confinement agriculture was based on a brand new model, that of using technological sanders to help force square pegs into round holes. Whereas a nineteenth-century attempt to raise a hundred thousand chickens in one building would have ended abruptly with the deaths of the animals, technology gave us antibiotics, vaccines, bacterins, and air-handling systems, which allowed the animals to survive and produce, while still experiencing severely truncated welfare. Such compromised welfare was irrelevant to profitability and productivity of the operation as a whole.

Confinement swine producers do not jump into ponds to save animals. In fact, they don't even treat sick animals; rather they knock them in the head, since the value of each animal is too small to bother with. Although each animal may be miserable, the operation as a whole is economically solvent. No wonder that cowboys hate factory farms! As the president of the Colorado Cattlemen's Association once said at an agricultural meeting, "If I had to raise animals like the veal people do, I'd get the hell out of the business."

The Western world became aware that Old McDonald's Farm had become Old McDonald's Factory in the mid-1960s when journalist Ruth Harrison (Harrison, 1964) published her *Animal Machines* (significantly prefaced by Rachel Carson). Harrison's writings, buttressed by other journalists such as Elspeth Huxley, caused a furor among the British public, whose strong negative reaction led the British government to charter a commission of inquiry, the Brambell Committee (Brambell, 1965), headed by Sir Rogers Brambell. Though having no political authority, the Brambell Committee report immediately became a moral beacon for Britain and Europe when it stated that any agricultural system that failed to allow animals to perform the behaviors dictated by their biological natures was morally unacceptable, morally foreshadowing the Swedish law of 1988, and laying the basis for the conservative (rather than radical!) demand for husbandry we have called the emerging social ethic for animals.

III

The nature of the new ethic that would emerge in response to the new agriculture, as well as to the vastly increased mid-twentieth-century use of animals for research and toxicity testing (a use that violated the fair bargain found in husbandry agriculture, since we burned, poisoned, wounded, and inflicted disease upon animals for our benefit or for the benefit of other animals with no compensatory benefit to the research animals themselves) was quite rational and predictable. I did indeed foresee its development in my writings of the late 1970s and early 80s (Rollin, 1981). The traditional social ethic for animals—embodied in anticruelty laws—presupposed husbandry and thus could not replace it. The anticruelty ethic existed to deal with those (mainly sadists and psychopaths) who were not motivated by self-interest. These laws were directed against sadistic, deviant, intentional, and willful infliction of pain and suffering on an animal for fun or out of perverted desires, not normal social use or consumption of animals. For this reason, these laws could not be shaped to cover research or factory farming or steel-jawed traps. However, if one considers a pie chart representing all the suffering animals currently experience at human hands, one will quickly realize that only a tiny fraction of that chart—1 percent or less, my audiences typically estimate—is the result of deliberate, sadistic cruelty. Most comes, in fact, from the new approaches to agriculture and research enumerated above. It is estimated that U.S. confined broiler chickens go to slaughter with 80 percent of the eight billion produced bruised or fractured. If this is true, we have in that industry about 6.4 billion cases of suffering. Thank heavens, there is probably nothing like that number of acts of deliberate cruelty in the whole world. Thus, a new ethic is needed to replace the connected ethics of husbandry and anticruelty.

It was clear to me, as Plato taught, that new ethics doesn't come from nowhere, but builds on established ethics. It was thus also obvious to me that society would turn to our established ethic for humans to serve as the basis for our newly sought animal ethic. And our human ethic had indeed addressed the fundamental conflict of the good of the majority group of humans against the benefit of the minority. This is a perennial problem in human ethics that recurs in every society. If it benefits society as a whole (i.e., the majority) to tax the wealthy, is it morally acceptable? If the entire society is upset by my verbal message, may I ethically be silenced? If a disease needs to be studied and no one volunteers to be a research subject, is it ethically acceptable to force someone to serve? And so on. In absolutistic, totalitarian societies, there is no issue—sacrifice the minority. But in democratic societies like ours we endeavor to do minimum damage even to small minorities, a stance growing out of our making the individual the primary focus of moral concern. Pursuant to this goal, we build protective fences around key aspects of an individual human to protect his or her nature, or fundamental interests, from being submerged even for the general welfare. These fundamental protections for the individual from being submerged for the sake of the majority are called "rights." Those interests guarded by rights are the ones seen as fundamental to human life and human nature—not being tortured, being allowed to express oneself, holding on to one's property, being able to behave religiously (or not believe) as one chooses, being allowed to form associations by choice, and so on—and are fundamental human interests encoded in the Bill of Rights. This is, in essence, a theory of human nature. Other rights may be deduced from these and from more vague rights, such as "due process," as social conditions change.

Clearly, as the Brambell Committee noted, animals have natures, the thwarting of which matters to them as much as the thwarting of our interests matters to us. Under husbandry, protection of these interests was not an issue. Failure to nurture those interests led to diminished productivity. But now that husbandry has been replaced by industry, these "rights" are no longer naturally protected. Thus, the society would eventually demand that these rights be artificially imposed (i.e., protected in the legal system). This is why the *New York Times*, as we saw, designated the 1988 Swedish law as "a bill of rights for farm animals."

A nice example of what we are discussing can be found in a 1985 legal case brought by the Animal Legal Defense Fund (formerly Attorneys for Animals Rights) against the New York State Department of Environmental Conservation, which administers public land use in New York State. The lawyers attempted to argue that the department was guilty of violating the cruelty laws by failing to stipulate time requirements for those using the steel-jawed trap on public lands to check their traps. Lack of such a stipulation meant that an animal could be trapped with no food or water or medical attention if injured for an indefinite amount of time, which was alleged to count as neglect, given the anticruelty laws (Animal Legal Defense Fund, 1985). The judge's reason was fascinating. While condemning the traps, he affirmed that the society had not spoken against it, and thus it was a socially acceptable instrument. If people wished to ban the trap, he opined, they should go to the legislature, not the judiciary, to create new protections (i.e., rights) for animals to protect the needs flowing from their nature (or *telos*, as I have called it following Aristotle). This, as we saw earlier, is exactly what society has been doing! It is interesting support of our theory that the chief administrators from NIH and USDA responsible for enforcing the laboratory laws of 1985 asserted that these laws created new rights for animals, that is, their right to have the pain caused by research manipulations controlled!

IV

Thus agriculture must accord with the emerging social ethic for animals or risk losing its autonomy and being legislated as research was. As difficult as it was to legislate for science without destroying the creativity, freedom, and spontaneity essential to it, it would be considerably more difficult to legislate for agriculture in a manner that would be enforceable without being prohibitively expensive. Such legislation would need to cover the extensive management practices that cause pain to animals—castration, branding, and dehorning—as well as eliminate the aspects of confinement agriculture causing pain, suffering, and distress. It would be far wiser for producers to preempt legislation and to soften systems injurious to animal welfare. Much of the work necessary to effect such change has been done in Europe—for example, in Sweden and Britain. U.S. knowledge of such research is extremely limited. One thing the animal welfare movement could do that would help this situation is establish exchange programs between the United States and Europe so that American agriculture can learn how Europe has softened confinement systems. It is extremely unlikely that confinement can be fully reversed, but we can vector animals' welfare into the design of these systems and modify them to fit animals' needs and natures.

Indeed, even if we were to return to fully extensive agriculture, we could not be sure that our managing of the animals was optimal for assuring their well-being. Although extensive systems require general satisfaction of the animals' needs and natures, no one to my knowledge had ascertained that the system in question was the best it could be vis-à-vis animal welfare and profitability. For example, although beef cattle production on western rangeland is the best of all current systems, from a welfare point of view, it could probably be better. Certainly, the management practices mentioned earlier—hot-iron branding, dehorning, and castration—could be improved or replaced. No one has done the research, but it may well be that the use of minimally expensive local anesthesia for castration not only decreases "shrink" (stress-induced weight loss) but also reduces disease susceptibility due to stress. And transportation of beef cattle has been known for a century to cause both welfare problems for the animals and losses for producers via shipping fever, bruising, and immunosuppression. As another example, it may be economically advantageous, as well as welfare advantageous, for ranchers using open range in hot climates to provide shade, cutting down on heat stress. In fact, in extensive systems, the more welfare is increased, the more likely is increased productivity.

One can argue that systems that are at the extreme end of extensive, such as turning cattle loose on enormous, harsh acreage like desert Australia where they cannot be at all under human surveillance, are deleterious to welfare because human husbandry assistance is rendered impossible, for example, in finding water. Similarly, the "survival of the fittest" approach, which has characterized sheep management in New Zealand, though extensive, clearly does not maximize animal welfare. For example, help is intentionally not given to animals in birthing, even under inclement conditions, since it is believed that one will thereby produce hardier animals. This may be the case, but it produces major welfare costs to individual animals. In short, we must recall that husbandry involves both putting the animals into conditions as close as possible to the ideal conditions they are evolved for *and* helping them when they need help.

The lesson is that merely managing animals extensively is no guarantee of welfare. Relationships with humans are also important [. . .]. The problem is that in current confinement systems *neither* conditions for which they have evolved nor human "animal-smart" attention (cf. the good shepherd) are provided to them. Any "intelligence" is built into the system, making it inflexible and devoid of husbandry. Hence, we see the contrast between western cattle ranchers, who sometimes spend more in money or time than the animal is worth (e.g., on sick or marginal calves) as compared with confinement swine operations that treat disease by knocking the animals in the head!

One can, in fact, agree that the optimal production system, like the old small family dairy farm, is a balance between the extremes of extensive and intensive. In cold areas, barns were provided, which the animals voluntarily entered in inclement weather, even though pasture was available. At the same time, dairymen often gave each animal a name and knew their individual variations, with good and gentle treatment and herdsman personality assuring maximum milk production. In such operations, cows and owners bonded, and the animals lived for ten or more lactations. Today, with breeding cattle for maximal productivity *and*, in many cases, adding exogenous BST or BGH (bovine somatotropin or bovine growth hormone, which partitions nutrients into milk production), the animals last two lactations and "burn out," requiring replacement, which may not be economically sound and is certainly not welfare friendly.

Thus, contrary to industry caricature, welfare-friendly agriculture does not mean turning the animals loose on land we don't have. It does mean having husbandry-smart people to work with them. A friend of mine who grew morally sick of raising sows in total confinement moved to a system employing large sow pens and Quonset huts for the animals. His revenue remained the same and even grew some because his pork was more appealing to Japanese markets. One can find in agricultural magazines and newspapers ads requesting "pasture pork—top dollar paid." My friend was able to do this, and confinement factories could not, he said, because he employed three generations of Iowa "pig-smart" people—a grandfather, father, and son. Total confinement operations employ minimum-wage, [. . .] ignorant labor that does not know—or care about—animal needs.

At a time when social concern for animal welfare is high, and people flee the cities, it might well behoove society to provide husbandry training to a new generation of young people. As Tim Blackwell and Dave Linton in Ontario have shown (Blackwell et al., 2002), pig-smart husbandmen can create and manage welfare-friendly barns, which are cheaper to capitalize and run and thus create more profit for the producer. In Colorado, for example, where corporate swine factories have been banished for environmental reasons, the lacuna created by their absence could help generate a renaissance in small husbandry-based swine operations, which could in turn revivify small communities turned into ghost towns by confinement operations, and restore the 80 percent of small producers displaced since the early 1970s by the large operators. (Small, partially extensive operations utilize manure as pasture fertilizer, turning what is an insoluble problem for huge confinement operations into an asset.)

V

In order to create welfare-compatible systems, we must overcome a number of barriers. Most formidable, perhaps, is the virtually universal acceptance among scientists, particularly in agricultural sciences, of what I have elsewhere called *scientific ideology*, the set of assumptions taught to nascent scientists along with the facts and theories relevant to their respective disciplines. All fields of human activity must begin with a set of assumptions because, as Aristotle pointed out, if we attempt to prove everything, we are led to an infinite regress, proving our assumptions on the basis of other assumptions, which are proven on the basis of other assumptions, and so on. Thus, as in the paradigm case of geometry, we just take certain assumptions for granted! That, however, does not mean that the assumptions cannot be challenged, examined, and discarded for good reasons, as Einstein ushered in contemporary physics by challenging Newton's assumptions about the existence of absolute space and time.

Sometimes, however, one's assumptions include the assumption that one's assumptions are not subject to questioning or criticism. Such a hardening creates an ideology where the assumptions are insulated from examination. [. . .]

Two features of scientific ideology germane to our discussion must be noted. One is the claim that science is "value-free," that is, does not make value judgments in general nor ethical judgments in particular. One can find this view directly announced in science textbooks, and in pronouncements by leading scientists such as James Wyngaarden, then director of NIH, who announced in 1989 that though new areas of science such as genetic engineering are always controversial, science should "never be hindered by ethical considerations" (Michigan State *News*, 1989). When society questioned the morality of research animal use in the 1970s and 1980s, one often heard from researchers that animal use was not a moral issue but a "scientific necessity," as if that ended the issue. One heard similar defenses of research on humans that society found morally wrong, such as the Tuskegee syphilis experiments or the Willowbrook hepatitis studies. Such ideology was commonly used as a defense by researchers who worked on the atomic bomb and was also indirectly taught to science students by teachers, journals, and conferences failing to discuss or even raise ethical issues naturally growing out of science. Resistance by students to performing invasive experiments on animals was enough to cause a student to fail a class, or elicit threats to the effect that the student did not belong in science, or veterinary medicine, or human medicine. One associate dean of a medical school actually said in my presence in reference to a required hemorrhagic shock lab exercise on a dog that "our faculty does not believe you can be a good doctor unless you first kill a dog."

The second element of scientific ideology relevant to our discussion is the claim that one cannot know or study consciousness or states of awareness such as pain, fear, anxiety, boredom, or loneliness in animals or in people. This, in turn, led to a science that did not acknowledge felt pain in animals even in the study of anesthesia! The first textbook of veterinary anesthesia published in the United States in 1973 does not even *mention* control of felt pain as a reason for anesthesia (Lumb and Jones, 1973), and animal analgesia was essentially unknown until scientific attention was focused on it by federal legal mandate in 1985 to control pain in research animals.

The reason behind scientific ideology was laudable—to provide a clear criterion of demarcation between what is scientifically legitimate to talk about and what isn't. That criterion became observability, testability, and measurability in the early twentieth century. It was used to banish, as we saw, absolute space and time and aether from physics, and "life force" from biology. Since, as Wittgenstein once remarked, if we take an inventory of all the facts in the universe, we won't find it a fact that killing is wrong, science must also be value free. Since we cannot study states of consciousness or feelings objectively, they too must be banished from scientific discourse.

A moment's reflection reveals that scientific ideology must be wrong. Science makes value judgments such as, "double-blind studies are better sources of knowledge than are anecdotes," and ethical judgments when it affirms that the value of an invasive experiment on animals outweighs the pain and suffering or death of the animal. Further, not everything in science can be proven—neither the Big Bang nor the reality of an external world existing independently of our perceptions can be tested. Further, we cannot dismiss private experience from science, because our only approach to the "objective world" is by way of our subjective perceptions!

The ways in which these ideological components impact on farm animal welfare issues is clear. In the first place, the concept of welfare in animals cannot be evaluated without reference to value judgments. Consider: science can give us facts relevant to animal welfare—it can tell us whether the animal is or is not gaining weight, has or doesn't have a salmonella infection, has or doesn't have intestinal parasites, behaves in repetitive stereotypical ways or not, etc. However, to say the animal is "well-off" or "not well-off" requires a value judgment on what counts as well-off! (This is true of humans as well.) Historically, under confinement agriculture, agricultural scientists assumed that if an animal was well fed, free of infection, and gaining weight, it must be well-off. The Brambell Committee, on the other hand, affirmed that a social animal must be with others of its own kind to be well-off. The U.S. Congress, in framing the 1985 laboratory laws, affirmed that a dog could not be well-off without exercise, nor could a primate without an "enriched environment to enhance its psychological well-being"! So clearly, what constitutes welfare is going to be in part valuational; which values drive what facts are relevant to an animal's having positive welfare!

This, in turn, leads to the way in which denial of consciousness in science hindered research into—and even understanding of—animal welfare. For ordinary common sense, part of—indeed the main part of—a person's or an animal's being in a state of positive welfare is whether it is happy (i.e., is in part defined by reference to the being in question's subjective state). We all know people with all the observable trappings of health, wealth, and success who are nonetheless miserable, and we would not say of such people that they enjoyed positive well-being. (For example, this state is depicted in *Richard Cory* by poet E. A. Robinson.) Similarly with an animal. Common sense says of the sow in confinement that exhibits compulsive, repetitive stereotypical behaviors such as bar-biting, that the animal cannot be well-off or happy, because it is "bored," or "driven crazy by the austere environment," or "has no one to play with." In my ethical writings, I have argued that in reference to animal welfare, how the animal feels subjectively, what it experiences, is the key feature of welfare or well-being. An irreducible component of being well-off is feeling well and not having enduring negative subjective experiences. But except for Marian Dawkins and Ian Duncan, most scientists working in this area have dismissed animal subjective experience in accord with the second component of scientific ideology articulated above.

This scientific ideology has in effect blocked agricultural scientists from viewing welfare as ordinary common sense (i.e., the general public) views it. Instead of thinking through the value judgments constituting welfare, the agricultural scientists have tended to assume that the productive animal is well-off or that having food and water and shelter suffices to guarantee animal welfare. Instead of looking at subjective states of happiness and unhappiness, the agricultural community has tended to lump all forms of subjective misery under the *psychological* rubric of "stress" as measured by cortisol, and to equate misery with levels of stress hormones. But it is plain that having certain levels of stress hormones such as cortisol is neither necessary nor sufficient to prove misery. Copulation and play, surely pleasant activities in animals and in humans, generate elevated stress hormones. Lack of such hormones does not prove that the animal is not miserable, as when animals achieve "learned helplessness."

Indeed, the traditional animal science/agriculture view of stress until about 1990 was that the psychological stress response was either on or off, like a light switch. This was dogma, despite the fact that scientists like Jay Weiss (1972) in psychology and John Mason (1971) in psychiatry had clearly shown that this allegedly nonspecific response view of stress—that it was all or nothing—was false. These researchers showed that animal psychological stress responses were variable given the same stressor, depending on the animal's *subjective cognitive state regarding the stressor*. Mason showed that if an animal could anticipate a stressor (elevated ambient temperature), it showed far less of a physiological stress response than when it was unable to anticipate the change. Similarly, Weiss showed that if an animal felt it could control a noxious stimulus (an electric shock), it showed far less of a physiological stress response to it than if it had no control over the stressor. Further augmenting the importance of an inherent psychological dimension of stress over its physical manifestations is the fact, long ago reported by Kilgour, that, for cattle, exposure to a new environment itself causes a greater stress than does an electric shock (Kilgour, 1978)! This is again potentiated by research showing that how an animal is treated by caretakers can create a huge difference in an animal's reproductive success (Hemsworth, 1998), as well as in its response to disease agents (e.g., a 2 percent cholesterol diet in rabbits, who developed far less atherosclerosis when treated with TLC [Nerein et al., 1980]).

In short, whoever designs new systems with the intention of increasing animal welfare of farm animals must proceed in accordance with society's definition of animal welfare that can be reconstructed as something like this: Assuming that an animal has adequate welfare requires that it be in a position to actualize the needs and interests dictated by its biological and psychological nature or *telos*—the "cowness" of the cow, the "pigness" of the pig—and that, experientially, it does not experience prolonged noxious mental states, such as, fear, anxiety, boredom, loneliness, social isolation, and so on.

Though traditional scientific ideology scoffs at attributing such states to animals as at worst mystical and at least mindless anthropomorphism, those who live and work with animals cannot avoid such psychologistic locutions. In a classic study of zookeepers, psychologist David Hebb showed that they were unable to do their jobs if forbidden to use such mentalistic attributions (Hebb, 1946). My students who work with cattle have told me the same thing. The fact is that before the U.S. federal laboratory animal laws mandated the control of pain in laboratory animals, the scientific community complained that it could not even identify painful states in animals, much less control them (there were virtually no articles available on laboratory animal analgesia). Fifteen years later, articles on pain and treatment modalities for it have proliferated, as have useful pain classifications and the realization that, if we can study pain in animals as models for human pain, then what we know of human pain can be reciprocally employed to help understand animal pain!

Further, creative scientists have given us operational discussions and definitions of noxious mental states in animals. Wemelsfelder, for example, has discussed at great length the recognition, understanding and nature of boredom in farm animals and laboratory animals (Wemelsfelder, 1989). And the entire field of behavioral enrichment, as pioneered by ethologists like Hal Markowitz (1982), has pointed us in the direction of how to alleviate the noxious state of boredom. Others have studied play in animals, once thought to be a uniquely human phenomenon (Huizinga, 1950). Both NIH and USDA, in interpreting federal laws and regulations pertaining to the welfare of laboratory animals, are placing ever-increasing emphasis on the concepts of "distress" and "suffering," catchall phrases used at a time when essentially no one was recognizing subjective states as legitimately studiable in animals. We can be morally certain that, if someone were to offer 50 million dollars in research money to study loneliness or fear or anxiety in animals (or all of those), the money would not go "a-begging."

The U.S. public firmly believes in animal mental states and has a voracious appetite for knowing more about such states. Books like the *Horse Whisperer, The Secret Life of Dogs, When Elephants Weep*, Darwin's classic *The Expression of Emotion in Man and Animals*, and others eloquently attest to this belief, as do the endless television programs dealing with animal emotion and cognition. Thus, the U.S. public will simply not accept scientific agnosticism about the animal mind, particularly as far as the mental states pertaining to animal welfare are concerned. Those who believe that they understand the emotions of their pets, and that their own emotions are reciprocally understood—and empathized with—by these animals, will not accept a huge bifurcation between pets and farm animals. A society that believes, as polls show, that an animal's life matters to it as much as, and in the same way as, a human life matters to a human will not buy scientific agnosticism about morally relevant mental states.

VI

What all of this tells us is the direction that future agriculture must go. If animals are going to be raised for food, they must live, in balance, happy lives, or at least lives free from pain and suffering. New systems should combine the best of traditional extensive agriculture, particularly husbandry, with technological advances that allow us to satisfy an animal's basic interests, constitutive of its *telos*. Many models for this exist in the areas of "enhancing primate psychological well-being" or meeting animals' basic behavioral/psychological needs in the zoo. Hal Markowitz has described satisfying the serval's inborn interest in predating low-flying birds by shooting their rations across their enclosures at random with cannons (Markowitz and Line, 1989). Further long-term ethological studies should be conducted on farm species to determine their natural behavioral needs. Wood-Gush and Stolba's work with pigs in a small, naturalistic environment (a "pig park") over 25 years stands as a model (Wood-Gush and Stolba, 1981), as do the ethological studies done by Duncan, Hughes, Mench and others on behavior of great importance to laying hens. Housing should be designed in accordance with this knowledge. The handling of livestock should move beyond macho posturing to knowledge-based gentle science. People like Temple Grandin and Bud Williams have blazed trails in this area. Equipment for handling and transporting animals, be it squeeze chutes or trucks, should again be based on ethological knowledge—cattle defecating on other cattle in double-decker trucks is not morally acceptable, and probably never was. Again, Temple Grandin's work is an exemplar in this area. Systems of slaughter, too, should be accountable first to animal well-being and only second to efficiency. No animal should die in pain or terror. Kosher slaughter or halal slaughter should be held to the same high standards. Being a Jew who studied the Talmud, I believe it is clear that kosher slaughter as currently practiced is largely incompatible with the humane moral imperatives that inspired kosher slaughter in antiquity. Temple Grandin (1991) has again done an incomparable job in studying the Talmud and showing this incompatibility, even to the satisfaction of *Kashrut*, a magazine devoted to kosher living, whose editors endorsed her recommendations.

In summary, as the Bible indicated, if we are to use animals for our benefit, it is morally incumbent upon us to make sure that they benefit as well, by at least living decent lives, not lives of misery, fear, and pain. To expect any less is not only immoral, it is dishonorable. It is, as I hope we have shown, ethically timely to use our science and technology for the benefit of the animals we use, not merely for their exploitation.

References

Animal Legal Defense Fund vs. The Department of Environment Conservation of the State of New York, 1985. Index a6670/85.
Blackwell, T., et al. 2002. *Alternative Housing for Gestating Sows* (a film). OMAFRA, Fergus, Ontario.
Brambell, F. W. R. 1965. Report of the Technical Committee to Enquire into the Welfare of Animals Kept Under Intensive Livestock Husbandry Systems. HMSO, London.
Grandin, T. 1991. Humane restraint equipment for kosher slaughter. *Kashrus* 11 (5): 18–21.
Harrison, R. 1964. *Animal Machines*. Vincent Stuart, London.
Hebb, D. O. 1946. Emotion in man and animals. *Psychology Review* 53: 88–106.
Hemsworth, P. 1998. *Human Livestock Interaction: The Stockperson and the Productivity and Welfare of Intensively Farmed Animals*. CAB International, New York.
Huizinga, J. 1950. *Homo Ludens: A Study of Play in Culture*. Beacon Press, Boston.
Kilgour, R. 1978. The application of animal behavior and the humane care of farm animals. *Journal of Animal Science* 46: 1478ff.
Lumb, W. V., and E. W. Jones. 1973. *Veterinary Anesthesia*. Lea and Febiger, Philadelphia.
Markowitz, H. 1982. *Behavioral Enrichment in the Zoo*. Van Nostrand Reinhold, New York.

Markowitz, H., and S. Line. 1989. The need for responsive environments. In: Rollin, B., and M. Kesel, The *Experimental Animal in Biomedical Research*, Volume 1. CRC Press, Boca-Raton, FL.

Mason, J. W. 1971. A re-evaluation of the concept of "non-specificity" in stress theory. *Journal of Psychiatry Research* 8:323–333.

Michigan State *News*. February 27, 1989, p. 8.

Nerein, R. M., et al. 1980. Social environment as a factor in diet-induced atherosclerosis. *Science* 208:1475–1476.

New York Times. October 25, 1988.

Parents. 1989. Parents poll on animals rights, attractiveness, television and abortion (survey by Kane and Parsons, New York).

Rollin, B. E. 1981. *Animals Rights and Human Morality*. Prometheus Books, Buffalo, NY.

Thompson, P. 1991. Unpublished paper read at USDA conference on animal welfare.

Weiss, J. 1972. Psychological factors in stress and disease. *Scientific American* 226 (March 1972): 101–113.

Wemelsfelder, F. 1989. Boredom and laboratory animal welfare. In Rollin, B., and M. Kesel. *The Experimental Animals in Biomedical Research*, Volume 1. CRC Press, Boca Raton, FL.

Wood-Gush, D., and A. Stolba. 1981. Behavior of pigs and the design of a new housing system. *Applied Animal Ethology* 8: 583–585.

Chapter 32

James Rachels

THE BASIC ARGUMENT FOR
VEGETARIANISM

James Rachels identifies Peter Singer's argument that it is wrong to cause pain unless there is a good enough reason as the argument which convinced him to become a vegetarian. Rachels describes some of facts involved in the meat-production industry and maintains that such facts are a vital part of the argument. Since the facts are well-established, how can we account for so many people being unmoved by these facts? According to Rachels, there is a difference between how scientists and animal-rights advocates think about the cognitive abilities of non-humans. But for Rachels the important issue is animal pain.

I

IN 1973 Peter Singer, who was then a young, little-known philosopher from Australia, published an article called "Animal Liberation" in the *New York Review of Books*.[1] The title suggested that there was a parallel between our treatment of animals and the unjust treatment of blacks and women. At first, it was hard to take the comparison seriously. Many proponents of "black liberation" and "women's liberation," as those movements were then known, found the comparison insulting, and most philosophers thought the topic was hardly worth discussing. But Singer kept at it, writing more articles and a now-famous book. It is now commonly said that the modern animal-rights movement grew out of those works. Thanks to Singer, many people, including me, became convinced that a fundamental change in our attitude toward animals was necessary. The indispensable first step was becoming a vegetarian.

The argument that persuaded me to become a vegetarian was so simple that it needs only a little elaboration. It begins with the principle that it is wrong to cause pain unless there is a good enough reason. The qualification is important, because causing pain is not always wrong. My dentist causes me pain, but there's a good reason for it, and besides, I consent. My children's doctor caused them pain when he gave them their shots, and they did not consent, but that was all right, too. However, as the principle says, causing pain is acceptable only when there is a good enough reason for it. Justification is required.

The second step in the argument is to notice that in the modern meat-production business, animals are made to suffer terribly. There is a reason for this suffering, too. We eat the meat, and it helps to nourish us. But there is a catch: we could just as easily nourish ourselves in other ways. Vegetarian meals are also good. Nonetheless, most people prefer a diet that includes meat because they like the way it tastes. The question, then, is whether our enjoyment of the way meat tastes is a good enough reason to justify the amount of suffering that the animals are made to endure. It seems obvious that it is not. Therefore, we should stop eating the products of this business. We should be vegetarians instead.

I will call this the basic argument. It has a limited application. It says nothing about animals raised on old-fashioned family farms or animals killed in hunter-gatherer societies. It addresses only the situation of people like us, in modern industrial countries. But it does point out, in a simple and compelling way, why those of us in the industrial countries should not support the meat-production business as it now exists.

When I emphasize the argument's simplicity, I mean that it does not depend on any controversial claims about health or on any religiously tinged notions of the value of life. Nor does it invoke any disputable ideas about "rights." Further claims of these kinds might strengthen the case for vegetarianism, but the basic argument does not depend on them. Nor does it rest on any contentious philosophical theory about the nature of morality. Philosophers sometimes misunderstand this when they think it is a merely utilitarian argument and that it can be refuted by refuting utilitarianism. But the basic argument is not tied to any particular theory about the nature of ethics. Instead, it appeals to a simple principle that every decent person already accepts, regardless of his or her stand on other issues. The most striking thing about the argument is that it derives such a remarkable conclusion from such a sober, conservative starting point.

The basic argument, then, is common ground for people of various moral and political persuasions. Matthew Scully is in most respects the antithesis of Peter Singer. Scully, a former speechwriter for various Republicans including President George W. Bush, recently surprised his conservative friends by writing a book, *Dominion: The Power of Man, the Suffering of Animals, and the Call to Mercy*,[2] in which he detailed the cruelties of the modern factory farm – cruelties that are, in his words, "hard to contemplate."[3] Scully reports:

> Four companies now produce 81 percent of cows brought to market, 73 percent of sheep, half our chickens, and some 60 percent of hogs. From these latter, the 355,000 pigs slaughtered every day in America, even the smallest of mercies have been withdrawn. In 1967 there were more than a million hog farms in the country; today there are about 114,000, all of them producing more, more, more to meet market demand. About 80 million of the 95 million hogs slaughtered each year in America, according to the National Pork Producers Council, are intensively reared in mass-confinement farms, never once in their time on earth feeling soil or sunshine. Genetically engineered by machines, inseminated by machines, monitored, herded, electrocuted, stabbed, cleaned, cut, and packaged by machines – themselves treated as machines "from birth to bacon" – these creatures, when eaten, have hardly ever been touched by human hands.[4]

Scully visited some of these automated pig farms in North Carolina, and his report is chilling. Sows have been engineered to weigh five hundred pounds each. Pigs are crowded twenty each in pens only seven-and-a-half feet square. The close confinement creates problems in managing the animals. Pigs are intelligent and social animals who normally build nests and keep them clean. They will not urinate or defecate in their nests, as they must do in the pens. They form bonds with other animals. They want to suck and chew, but in the pens, being deprived of a normal environment in which they can do these things, they begin to chew on the tails of the animals in front of them. In such close quarters, the victims cannot escape. The chewing causes infection, and sick pigs are no good. The solution is "tail docking," a procedure recommended by the U.S. Food and Drug Administration, in which the pigs' tails are snipped (without anesthetic) by pliers. The point is to make the tails more sensitive to pain, so that the animals will make a greater effort to avoid their neighbors' attacks. Surveying the whole setup, the operator of one such "farm" observes: "It's science driven. We're not raising pets."[5]

When critics of the meat-production industry report such facts, their accounts are often dismissed as "emotional appeals." But that is a mistake. It may be true that such descriptions engage our emotions. However, emotionalism is not the point. The point is to fill in the details of the basic argument. The basic argument says that causing pain is not justified unless there is a sufficiently good reason for it. In order to apply this principle to the case of factory farming, we need to know how much pain is involved. If only a little pain were being caused, a fairly insubstantial reason (such as our gustatory pleasure) might be sufficient. But if there is extensive suffering, that reason is not enough. Thus, these facts are a vital part of the argument, and it is necessary to keep them in mind when considering whether the argument is sound. For those of us who have no firsthand knowledge of the subject, reports by such relatively impartial observers as Matthew Scully are indispensable.

Another report recently appeared in the *New York Times Magazine*.[6] The author, Michael Pollan, went to a great deal of trouble to find out what happens to cattle who are raised and slaughtered for beef. "Forgetting, or willed ignorance, is the preferred strategy of many beef-eaters,"[7] he says, but Pollan wanted to see for himself the conditions in which the animals live and die. So he bought a steer – "No. 534" – at the Blair Brothers Ranch in South Dakota, and followed its progress to the slaughterhouse. No. 534 spent the first six months of his life in pastures alongside his mother. Then, having been weaned and castrated, he was shipped to Poky Feeders, a feedlot operation in Garden City, Kansas.

"A cattle feedlot," says Pollan, "is a kind of city, populated by as many as 100,000 animals. It is very much a premodern city, however – crowded, filthy and stinking, with open sewers, unpaved roads and choking air."[8] Fecal dust floats in the air, causing irritation to the eyes and lungs. Searching for No. 534, Pollan found his animal standing in a "deep pile of manure."[9] Dried manure caked on the animals is a problem later, in the slaughterhouse, where steps must be taken to ensure that the meat does not become contaminated. In the feedlot itself, disease would kill the animals were it not for massive doses of antibiotics.

At the Blair Brothers Ranch, No. 534 ate grass and was given corn and alfalfa hay to fatten him up. In his last six weeks at the ranch, he put on 148 pounds. After being shipped to Poky Feeders, he would never eat grass again. His diet would be mostly corn and protein supplement, "a sticky brown goop consisting of molasses and urea."[10] Corn is cheap, and it produces "marbled" beef, although it is not what the animals naturally desire. In a grisly sort of forced cannibalism, the animals are also fed rendered cow parts. The animals could not live on this diet for long – it would "blow out their livers," said one of the feedlot operators. But they are slaughtered before this can happen. The diet is effective, however: the animals weigh more than 1,200 pounds when taken to the slaughterhouse.

No. 534 was slaughtered at the National Beef Plant in Liberal, Kansas, a hundred miles down the road from Poky Feeders. This is where Pollan's personal observations come to a stop. He was not allowed to watch the stunning, bleeding, and evisceration process; nor was he permitted to take pictures or talk to the employees.

Opposing cruelty should not be seen as a specifically liberal or conservative cause. Scully, the conservative Republican, emphasizes that one should oppose it "even if one does not accept [the animal rights advocates'] whole vision of the world." He makes a point of distancing himself from Peter Singer, who champions various left-wing causes. Singer is wrong about the other issues, says Scully, but he is right about the animals.[11]

II

The basic argument seems to me obviously correct. But its very obviousness suggests a problem: if it is so simple and obvious, why doesn't everyone accept it? Why doesn't everyone who has this argument explained to them become a vegetarian? Of course, many people do, but most do not. Part of the explanation may be that it is natural for people to resist arguments that require them to do things they don't want to do. If you want to go on eating meat, you may pay no attention to arguments that say otherwise. Moreover, people generally do not respond to ethical appeals unless they see others around them also responding. If all your friends are eating meat, you are unlikely to be moved by a mere argument. It is like an appeal for money to provide vaccinations for third-world children. The argument that the vaccinations are more important than your going to a movie may be irrefutable, considered just as an argument. But when no one around you is contributing, and your friends are all going to the movie, you are likely to ignore the charitable appeal and spend the money on popcorn instead. It is easy to put the children out of mind.

All this may be true. But there is a more pressing problem about the basic argument—at least, a more pressing problem for me, as a philosopher. Many of my professional colleagues are unmoved by this argument, and I am not sure why. Those who study ethics, especially from a nonreligious point of view, often find the argument compelling. But others do not. This is puzzling because professional philosophers—those who teach in colleges and universities—study arguments dispassionately, and while they often disagree, they disagree about arguments only when the issues are tricky or obscure. But there is nothing tricky or obscure about the basic argument. Thus I would expect that, on so simple a matter, there would be widespread agreement. Instead, many philosophers shrug the argument off.

The same is true of other academics who study cognitive science, psychology, and biology. They are at least as smart as I am, if not smarter, and they are morally decent people. Yet, while I think the basic argument is compelling, many of them do not. It is not that they think the argument makes a good point, even though they are unwilling to act on it. Rather, they find the argument itself unconvincing. How can this be?

Sometimes philosophers explain that the argument is unconvincing because it contains a logical gap. We are all opposed to cruelty, they say, but it does not follow that we must become vegetarians. It only follows that we should favor less cruel methods of meat production. This objection is so feeble that it is hard to believe it explains resistance to the basic argument. It is true enough that, if you are opposed to cruelty, you should prefer that the meat-production business be made less brutal. But it is also true that, if you are opposed to cruelty, you have reason not to participate in social practices that are brutal as they stand. As it stands, meat producers and consumers cooperate to maintain the unnecessary system of pig farms, feedlots, and slaughterhouses. Anyone who finds this system objectionable has reason not to help keep it going. The point would be quickly conceded if the victims were people. If a product—curtains, let's say—were being produced by a process that involved torturing humans, no one would dream of saying: "Of course I oppose using those methods, but that's no reason not to buy the product. After all, the curtains are very nice."

Many in the animal-rights movement believe that scientists are blinded by the need to justify their own practices. The scientists are personally committed to animal experimentation. Their careers, or the careers of their colleagues, are based on it, and they would have to stop this research if they conceded that animals have moral claims on us. Naturally they do not want to do this. Thus they are so biased in favor of current practices that they cannot see the evil in them. This explains why they cannot see the truth even in something so simple as the basic argument.

Perhaps there is something to this, but I do not want to pursue it. On the whole it is a condescending explanation that insults the scientists, cuts off communication with them, and prevents us from learning what they have to teach us. It should be noted, however, that the basic argument about vegetarianism is independent of any arguments about animal experimentation. Indeed, the case against meat eating is much stronger than the case against the use of animals in research. The researchers can at least point out that, in many instances, their work has a serious purpose that can benefit humankind. Nothing comparable can be said in defense of meat eating. Thus, even if some research using animals was justified, meat eating would still be wrong.

I believe a better explanation is in terms of the overall difference between how scientists and animal-rights advocates think about the nature of nonhumans. Defenders of animal rights tend to see the differences between humans and nonhumans as slight. They frequently emphasize how much the animals are like us, in order to argue that our ethical responsibilities to the animals are similar to our responsibilities to one another. Animals are pictured as intelligent and sociable creatures who love their children, who experience fear and delight, who sulk, play, mourn their dead, and much more. So how can it be denied that they have rights, just as we do? I have argued in this way myself, more than once.

Many scientists, however, see this as naive. They believe the differences between humans and other animals are vast—so vast, in fact, that putting humans in a separate moral category is entirely justified. Moreover, they feel they have some authority on this score. After all, the scientific study of animals is their professional concern. In light of this, how should we expect them to react when they are confronted by belligerent amateurs who insist they know better? It is only natural that the scientists should disregard the amateurs' arguments.

A case in point is the anthropologist Jonathan Marks, who teaches at the University of North Carolina at Charlotte. In 1993, Peter Singer and Paola Cavalieri, an Italian writer on animal issues, initiated a campaign known as "the Great Ape Project," an effort to secure basic rights for our closest relatives, the chimpanzees, gorillas, and orangutans.[12] The rights being demanded were life, liberty, and freedom from torture. Marks was invited to participate in a debate about these demands, and he recorded his thoughts in an engaging book, *What It Means to Be 98% Chimpanzee.*[13] "Since their brains are closely related to our brains," Marks says, "it should come as no surprise that the apes can approach humans in their cognitive functions."[14] Despite this, "Apes are often objectified by callous and cynical entrepreneurs, who neither regard them nor treat them as the sentient, emotionally complex creatures they are."[15] Marks does not think this is acceptable. "Apes deserve protection," he says, "even rights."[16]

Reading these words, one would expect Marks to be an ally of Singer and Cavalieri. But he is not. The Great Ape Project, he thinks, is completely wrongheaded. Why? Marks's attempt at philosophical argument is unimpressive—he says the critical issues are that chimps, gorillas, and orangutans aren't human, and that in any case we are politically powerless to guarantee such rights even for humans. Of course, these arguments get us nowhere. Everyone knows the animals aren't human; the point is that they are sufficiently like humans to deserve the same basic protections. And the fact that we cannot ensure rights for humans does not mean that we should stop thinking humans ought to have them.

The underlying reason for Marks's scorn of the animal-rights ideology becomes clear when he turns to the scientific study of animal behavior. The similarities between humans and other great apes, he intimates, are only superficial: "Where clever, controlled experimentation has been possible, it has tended strongly to show that in specific ways, ape minds work quite differently from human minds."[17] For support, he cites the work of the psychologist Daniel J. Povinelli, who argues that chimpanzees' conceptions of physical interactions (as, for example, when a hook is used to manipulate an object) are very different from human understanding.[18] Marks does not say how this fits with his earlier assertion that "Apes deserve protection, even rights," but clearly, in his view, the latter thought trumps the former.

We find this pattern repeated again and again: The scientists concede that the animal rights advocates have a bit of a point, but then the scientists want to talk about the facts. They think we do not know nearly enough about the details of how animal minds work to justify any firm moral conclusions. Moreover, such knowledge as we do have suggests caution: the animals are more different from us than it seems. The advocates of animal rights, on the other hand, think the facts are well enough established that we can proceed without further ado to the ethical conclusions. Anyone who suggests otherwise is viewed as dragging their feet, perhaps to avoid the unpleasant truth about the injustice of our behavior toward the animals.

III

What are we to make of all this? One obvious idea is that we should take seriously what the scientists tell us about what animals are like and adjust our moral conceptions accordingly. This would be an ongoing project. It would take volumes even to begin, by considering what is currently known. But those volumes would be out of date by the time they were completed, because new discoveries are being made all the time.

However, where the basic argument is concerned, the only relevant part of this project would be what science can tell us about the capacity of animals to experience pain. Jeremy Bentham famously said, "The question is not, Can they *reason?* nor Can they *talk?* but *Can they suffer?*"[19] To this we might add that, contrary to Jonathan Marks, it is irrelevant whether chimps have a different understanding of physical interactions. It is irrelevant, that is, if we are considering whether it is acceptable to treat them in ways that cause them pain.

This point is easily misunderstood, so it is worth elaborating just a bit. Of course, the facts about an individual are important in determining how that individual should be treated. (This is true of humans as well as non-humans.) How an animal should be treated depends on what the animal is like—its nature, its abilities, and its needs. Different creatures have different characteristics, and these must be taken into account when we frame our ethical conceptions. The scientific study of animals gives us the factual information we need. But not every fact about an individual is relevant to every form of treatment. *What facts are relevant* depends on *what sorts of treatment* we are considering. To take a simple example, whether an animal can read is relevant if we are considering whether to admit him to university classes. But the ability to read is irrelevant in deciding whether it is wrong to operate on the animal without anesthesia. Thus, if we are considering whether it is wrong to treat pigs and cattle in the ways we have described, the critical issue is not whether their minds work in various sophisticated ways. The critical issue is, as Bentham said, whether they can suffer.

What does science tell us about this? The mechanisms that enable us to feel pain are not fully understood, but we do know a good bit about them. In humans, nocioceptors—neurons specialized for sensing noxious stimuli—are connected to a central nervous system, and the resulting signals are processed in the brain. Until recently it was believed that the brain's work was divided into two distinct parts: a sensory system operating in the somatosensory cortex, resulting in our conscious experiences of pain, and an affective-motivational system associated with the frontal lobes, responsible for our behavioral reactions. Now, however, this picture has been called into question, and it may be that the best we can say is that the brain's system for processing the information from the nocioceptors seems to be spread over multiple regions. At any rate, the human nociceptive system also includes endogenous opioids, or endorphins, which provide the brain with its natural pain-killing ability.

The question of which other animals feel pain is a real and important issue, not to be settled by appeals to "common sense." Only a completed scientific understanding of pain, which we do not yet have, could tell us all that we need to know. In the meantime, however, we do have a rough idea of what to look for. If we want to know whether it is reasonable to believe that a particular kind of animal is capable of feeling pain, we may ask: Are there nocioceptors present? Are they connected to a central nervous system? What happens in that nervous system to the signals from the nocioceptors? And are there endogenous opioids? In our present state of understanding, this sort of information, together with the obvious behavioral signs of distress, is the best evidence we can have that an animal is capable of feeling pain.

Relying on such evidence, some writers, such as Gary Varner, have tentatively suggested that the line between animals that feel pain and those who do not is (approximately) the line between vertebrates and invertebrates.[20] However, research constantly moves forward, and the tendency of research is to extend the number of animals that might be able to suffer, not decrease it. Nocioception appears to be one of the most primitive animal systems. Nocioceptors have now been identified in a remarkable number of species, including leeches and snails.

The presence of a perceptual system does not, however, settle the question of whether the organism has conscious experiences connected with its operation. We know, for example, that humans have perceptual systems that do not involve conscious experience. Recent research has shown that the human vomeronasal system, which works through receptors in the nose, responds to pheromones and affects behavior even though the person is unaware of it. (It was long believed that this system was vestigial in humans, but it turns out that it is still working.) The receptors for "vomerolfaction" are in the nostrils, alongside the receptors for the sense of smell; yet the operation of one is accompanied by conscious experience, while the operation of the other is not.[21] We do not know why this is so. But this suggests at least the possibility that in some species there may be nocioceptive systems that do not involve conscious experiences. In that case, those animals might not actually feel pain, even though various indications are present. Is this true of leeches and snails? of snakes? of hummingbirds? We may have strong hunches, but we don't really know.

Clearly, then, we still have a great deal to learn about the phenomenon of pain in the animal world, and the scientists who work in this area are right to caution us against quick-and-easy opinions. The ongoing study of animal pain is a fascinating subject in itself, and it has enormous importance for ethics. But should this make us less confident of the basic argument? If the issue were our treatment of snails and leeches, perhaps it should. But pigs and cattle are another matter. There is every reason to believe they feel pain—the facts about their nervous systems, their brains, their behavior, and their evolutionary kinship to human beings, all point to the same conclusion as common sense: our treatment of them on factory farms and in the slaughterhouses is one of the world's great causes of misery. If further investigation were to prove otherwise, it would be one of the most astonishing discoveries in the history of science.

Strict vegetarians may want more than the basic argument can provide, because the basic argument does not support sweeping prohibitions. If opposition to cruelty is our motive, we will have to consider the things we eat one at a time. Of course we should not eat beef and pork produced in the ways I have described, and we ought also to avoid factory-farm poultry, eggs, and milk. But free-range eggs and humanely produced milk are all right. Eating shrimp may also turn out to be acceptable. Moreover, from this point of view, not all vegetarian issues are equally pressing: eating fish may be questionable, but it is not nearly as bad as eating beef. This means that becoming a vegetarian need not be regarded as an all-or-nothing proposition. From a practical standpoint, it makes sense to focus first on the things that cause the most misery. As Matthew Scully says, whatever one's "whole vision of the world" may be, the pig farms, feedlots, and slaughterhouses are unacceptable.[22]

Notes

1   Peter Singer, "Animal Liberation," *New York Review of Books*, April 5, 1973.

2   Matthew Scully, *Dominion: The Power of Man, the Suffering of Animals, and the Call to Mercy* (New York: St. Martin's Press, 2002).

3   Ibid., p. x.

4   Ibid., p. 29.

5   Ibid., p. 279.

6   Michael Pollan, "This Steer's Life," *New York Times Magazine*, March 31, 2002, pp. 44–51, 68, 71–72, 76–77.

7   Ibid., p. 48.

8   Ibid., p. 50.

9   Ibid., p. 68.

10   Ibid., p. 50

11   Scully, *Dominion*, pp. 326–38.

12   Peter Singer and Paola Cavalieri, *The Great Ape Project: Equality and Beyond* (London: Fourth Estate, 1993).

13   Jonathan Marks, *What It Means to Be 98% Chimpanzee: Apes, People, and Their Genes* (Berkeley: University of California Press, 2002).

14   Ibid., p. 189.

15   Ibid., p. 185.

16   Ibid., p. 188.

17   Ibid., p. 195.

18   Daniel J. Povinelli, *Folk Physics for Apes: The Chimpanzee's Theory of How the World Works* (Oxford: Oxford University Press, 2000).

19   Jeremy Bentham, *The Principles of Morals and Legislation* (New York: Hafner, 1948; originally published in 1789), p. 311.

20   Gary Varner, *In Nature's Interests? Interests, Animals Rights, and Environmental Ethics* (New York: Oxford University Press, 1998).

21   L. Monti-Bloch, C. Jennings-White, and D. L. Berliner, "The Human Vomeronasal Organ: A Review," *Annals of the New York Academy of Sciences* 855 (1998): 373–89.

22   I have learned a great deal from Colin Allen's essay, "Animal Pain," [*NOUS* 2004 – ed. note] It is the best discussion of the question of animal pain known to me.

Chapter 33

Carol J. Adams

THE RAPE OF ANIMALS, THE
BUTCHERING OF WOMEN

In her powerful essay, Carol J. Adams uses the concept of "absent referent" to describe the erasure of both women and animals used for food. Patriarchal culture strengthens oppression by "always recalling other oppressed groups." She points out how patriarchal culture violently transforms living animals to dead consumable ones both literally and conceptually through words of objectification such as "food-producing unit" to refer to a living animal.

The absent referent

THROUGH BUTCHERING, animals become absent referents. Animals in name and body are made absent *as animals* for meat to exist. Animals' lives precede and enable the existence of meat. If animals are alive they cannot be meat. Thus a dead body replaces the live animal. Without animals there would be no meat eating, yet they are absent from the act of eating meat because they have been transformed into food.

Animals are made absent through language that renames dead bodies before consumers participate in eating them. Our culture further mystifies the term "meat" with gastronomic language, so we do not conjure dead, butchered animals, but cuisine. Language thus contributes even further to animals' absences. While the cultural meanings of meat and meat eating shift historically, one essential part of meat's meaning is static: One does not eat meat without the death of an animal. Live animals are thus the absent referents in the concept of meat. The absent referent permits us to forget about the animal as an independent entity; it also enables us to resist efforts to make animals present.

There are actually three ways by which animals become absent referents. One is literally: as I have just argued, through meat eating they are literally absent because they are dead. Another is definitional: when we eat animals we change the way we talk about them, for instance, we no longer talk about baby animals but about veal or meat: the word *meat* has an absent referent, the dead animals. [. . .] The third way is metaphorical. Animals become metaphors for describing people's experiences. In this metaphorical sense, the meaning of the absent referent derives from its application or reference to something else.

As the absent referent becomes metaphor, its meaning is lifted to a "higher" or more imaginative function than its own existence might merit or reveal. An example of this is when rape victims or battered women say, "I felt like a piece of meat." In this example, meat's meaning does not refer to itself but to how a woman victimized by male violence felt. That meat is functioning as an absent referent is evident when we push the meaning of the metaphor: one cannot truly *feel* like a piece of meat. Teresa de Lauretis comments: "No one can really *see* oneself as an inert object or a sightless body,"[1] and no one can really feel like a piece of meat because meat by definition is something violently deprived of all feeling. The use of the phrase "feeling like a piece of meat" occurs within a metaphoric system of language.

The animals have become absent referents, whose fate is transmuted into a metaphor for someone else's existence or fate. Metaphorically, the absent referent can be anything whose original meaning is undercut as it is absorbed into a different hierarchy of meaning; in this case the original meaning of animals' fates is absorbed into a human-centered hierarchy. Specifically in regard to rape victims and battered women, the death experience of animals acts to illustrate the lived experience of women.

The absent referent is both there and not there. It is there through inference, but its meaningfulness reflects only upon what it refers to because the originating, literal experience that contributes the meaning is not there.[2] We fail to accord this absent referent its own existence.

Women and animals: overlapping but absent referents

This chapter posits that a structure of overlapping but absent referents links violence against women and animals. Through the structure of the absent referent, patriarchal values become institutionalized. Just as dead bodies are absent from our language about meat, in descriptions of cultural violence women are also often the absent referent. Rape, in particular, carries such potent imagery that the term is transferred from the literal experience of women and applied metaphorically to other instances of violent devastation, such as the "rape" of the earth in ecological writings of the early 1970s. The experience of women thus becomes a vehicle for describing other oppressions. Women, upon whose bodies actual rape is most often committed, become the absent referent when the language of sexual violence is used metaphorically. These terms recall women's experiences but not women.

When I use the term "the rape of animals," the experience of women becomes a vehicle for explicating another being's oppression. Some terms are so powerfully specific to one group's oppression that their appropriation to others is potentially exploitative: for instance, using the "holocaust" for anything but the extermination of Jewish people, or "slavery" for anything but the forced enslavement of black people. Yet, feminists, among others, appropriate the metaphor of butchering without acknowledging the originating oppression of animals that generates the power of the metaphor. Through the function of the absent referent, Western culture constantly renders the material reality of violence into controlled and controllable metaphors.

Sexual violence and meat eating, which appear to be discrete forms of violence, find a point of intersection in the absent referent. Cultural images of sexual violence, and actual sexual violence, often rely on our knowledge of how animals are butchered and eaten. For example, Kathy Barry tells us of "*maisons d'abattage* (literal translation: houses of slaughter)" where six or seven girls each serve 80 to 120 customers a night.[3] In addition, the bondage equipment of pornography—chains, cattle prods, nooses, dog collars, and ropes—suggests the control of animals. Thus, when women are victims of violence, the treatment of animals is recalled.

Similarly, in images of animal slaughter, erotic overtones suggest that women are the absent referent. If animals are the absent referent in the phrase "the butchering of women," women are the absent referent in the phrase "the rape of animals." The impact of a seductive pig relies on an absent but imaginable, seductive, fleshy woman. Ursula Hamdress is both metaphor and joke; her jarring (or jocular) effect is based on the fact that we are all accustomed to seeing women depicted in such a way. Ursula's image refers to something that is absent: the human female body. The structure of the absent referent in patriarchal culture strengthens individual oppressions by always recalling other oppressed groups.

Because the structure of overlapping absent referents is so deeply rooted in Western culture, it inevitably implicates individuals. Our participation evolves as part of our general socialization to cultural patterns and viewpoints, thus we fail to see anything disturbing in the violence and domination that are an inextricable part of this structure. Consequently, women eat meat, work in slaughterhouses, at times treat other women as "meat," and men at times are victims of sexual violence. Moreover, because women as well as men participate in and benefit from the structure of the absent referent by eating meat, neither achieve the personal distance to perceive their implication in the structure, nor the originating oppression of animals that establishes the potency of the metaphor of butchering.

The interaction between physical oppression and the dependence on metaphors that rely on the absent referent indicates that we distance ourselves from whatever is different by equating it with something we have already objectified. For instance, the demarcation between animals and people was invoked during the early modern period to emphasize social distancing. According to Keith Thomas, infants, youth, the poor, blacks, Irish, insane people, and women were considered beastlike: "Once perceived as beasts, people were liable to be treated accordingly. The ethic of human domination removed animals from the sphere of human concern. But it also legitimized the ill-treatment of those humans who were in a supposedly animal condition."[4]

Racism and the absent referent

Through the structure of the absent referent, a dialectic of absence and presence of oppressed groups occurs. What is absent refers back to one oppressed group while defining another. This has theoretical implications for class and race as well as violence against women and animals. Whereas I want to focus on the overlapping oppressions of women and animals, further exploration of the function of the absent referent is needed, such as found in Marjorie Spiegel's *The Dreaded Comparison: Human and Animal Slavery*. Spiegel discusses the connection between racial oppression and animal oppression and in doing so demonstrates their overlapping relationship.[5]

The structure of the absent referent requires assistants who achieve the elimination of the animal, a form of alienated labor. Living, whole animals are the absent referents not only in meat eating but also in the fur trade. Of interest then is the connection between the oppression of animals through the fur trade and the oppression of blacks as slaves rather than Native Americans. Black historians suggest that one of the reasons black people rather than Native Americans were oppressed through the white Americans' institution of slavery is because of the slaughter of fur-bearing animals. As Vincent Harding describes it in *There Is a River: The Black Struggle for Freedom in America*: "One important early source of income for the Europeans in North America was the fur trade with the Indians, which enslavement of the latter would endanger."[6] While the factors that caused the oppression of Native Americans and blacks is not reducible to this example, we do see in it the undergirding of interactive oppressions by the absent referent. We also see that in analyzing the oppression of human beings, the oppression of animals ought not to be ignored. However, the absent referent, because of its absence, prevents our experiencing connections between oppressed groups.

When one becomes alert to the function of the absent referent and refuses to eat animals, the use of metaphors relying on animals' oppression can simultaneously criticize both that which the metaphor points to and that from which it is derived. For instance, when vegetarian and Civil Rights activist Dick Gregory compares the ghetto to the slaughterhouse he does so condemning both and suggesting the functioning of the absent referent in erasing responsibility for the horrors of each:

> Animals and humans suffer and die alike. If you had to kill your own hog before you ate it, most likely you would not be able to do it. To hear the hog scream, to see the blood spill, to see the baby being taken away from its momma, and to see the look of death in the animal's eye would turn your stomach. So you get the man at the packing house to do the killing for you. In like manner, if the wealthy aristocrats who are perpetrating conditions in the ghetto actually heard the screams of ghetto suffering, or saw the slow death of hungry little kids, or witnessed the strangulation of manhood and dignity, they could not continue the killing. But the wealthy are protected from such horror. . . . If you can justify killing to eat meat, you can justify the conditions of the ghetto. I cannot justify either one.[7]

Sexual violence and meat eating

To rejoin the issue of the intertwined oppressions with which this chapter is primarily concerned, sexual violence and meat eating, and their point of intersection in the absent referent, it is instructive to consider incidents of male violence. Men's descriptions of their own violence suggest the structure of overlapping but absent referents. In defense of the "Bunny Bop"—in which rabbits are killed by clubs, feet, stones and so on—sponsored by a North Carolina American Legion post, one organizer explained, "What would all these rabbit hunters be doing if they weren't letting off all this steam? I'll tell you what they'd be doing. They'd be drinking and carousing and beating their wives."[8]

One common form of domestic violence is the killing of a family's pet. Here the absent referent is clearly in operation: the threatened woman or child is the absent referent in pet murders. Within the symbolic order the fragmented referent no longer recalls itself but something else.[9] Though this pattern of killing pets as a warning to an abused woman or child is derived from recent case studies of domestic violence, the story of a man's killing his wife's pet instead of his wife can be found in an early twentieth-century short story. Susan Glaspell's "A Jury of Her Peers" exposes this function of the absent referent and the fact that a woman's peers, i.e., other women, recognize this function.[10]

Generally, however, the absent referent, because of its absence, prevents our experiencing connections between oppressed groups. Cultural images of butchering and sexual violence are so interpenetrated that animals act as the absent referent in radical feminist discourse. In this sense, radical feminist theory participates in the same set of representational structures it seeks to expose. We uphold the patriarchal structure of absent referents, appropriating the experience of animals to interpret our own violation. For instance, we learn of a woman who went to her doctor after being battered. The doctor told her her leg "was like a raw piece of meat hanging up in a butcher's window."[11] Feminists translate this literal description into a metaphor for women's oppression. Andrea Dworkin states that pornography depicts woman as a "female piece of meat" and Gena Corea observes that "women in brothels can be used like animals in cages."[12] Linda Lovelace claims that when presented to Xaviera Hollander for inspection, "Xaviera looked me over like a butcher inspecting a side of beef."[13] When one film actress committed suicide, another described the dilemma she and other actresses encounter: "They treat us like meat." Of this statement Susan Griffin writes: "She means that men who hire them treat them as less than human, as matter without spirit."[14] In each of these examples, feminists have used violence against animals as metaphor, literalizing *and* feminizing the metaphor. Thus, Mary Daly appropriates the word "butcher" to describe lobotomists, since the majority of lobotomies have been performed on women.[15]

Because of this dependence on the *imagery* of butchering, radical feminist discourse has failed to integrate the *literal* oppression of animals into our analysis of patriarchal culture or to acknowledge the strong historical alliance between feminism and vegetarianism. Whereas women may feel like pieces of meat, and be treated like pieces of meat—emotionally butchered and physically battered—animals actually are made into pieces of meat. In radical feminist theory, the use of these metaphors alternates between a positive figurative activity and a negative activity of occlusion, negation, and omission in which the literal fate of the animal is elided. Could metaphor itself be the undergarment to the garb of oppression?

The cycle of objectification, fragmentation, and consumption

What we require is a theory that traces parallel trajectories: the common oppressions of women and animals, and the problems of metaphor and the absent referent. I propose a cycle of objectification, fragmentation, and consumption, which links butchering and sexual violence in our culture. Objectification permits an oppressor to view another being as an object. The oppressor then violates this being by object-like treatment: e.g., the rape of women that denies women freedom to say no, or the butchering of animals that converts animals from living breathing beings into dead objects. This process allows fragmentation, or brutal dismemberment, and finally consumption. While the occasional man may literally eat women, we all consume visual images of women all the time.[16] Consumption is the fulfillment of oppression, the annihilation of will, of separate identity. So too with language: a subject first is viewed, or objectified, through metaphor. Through fragmentation the object is severed from its ontological meaning. Finally, consumed, it exists only through what it represents. The consumption of the referent reiterates its annihilation as a subject of importance in itself.

Since this chapter addresses how patriarchal culture treats animals as well as women, the image of meat is an appropriate one to illustrate this trajectory of objectification, fragmentation, and consumption. The literal process of violently transforming living animals to dead consumable ones is emblematic of the conceptual process by which the referent point of meat eating is changed. Industrialized meat-eating cultures such as the United States and Great Britain exemplify the process by which live animals are removed from the idea of meat. The physical process of butchering an animal is recapitulated on a verbal level through words of objectification and fragmentation.

Animals are rendered being-less not only by technology, but by innocuous phrases such as "food-producing unit," "protein harvester," "converting machine," "crops," and "biomachines." The meat-producing industry views an animal as consisting of "edible" and "inedible" parts, which must be separated so that the latter do not contaminate the former. An animal proceeds down a "disassembly line," losing body parts at every stop. This fragmentation not only dismembers the animal, it changes the way in which we conceptualize animals. In *The American Heritage Dictionary* the definition of "lamb" is illustrated not by an image of Mary's little one but by an edible body divided into ribs, loin, shank, and leg.[17]

After being butchered, fragmented body parts must be renamed to obscure the fact that these were once animals. After death, cows become roast beef, steak, hamburger; pigs become pork, bacon, sausage. Since objects are possessions they cannot have possessions; thus, we say "leg of lamb" not a "lamb's leg." We opt for less disquieting referent points not only by changing names from animals to meat, but also by cooking, seasoning, and covering the animals with sauces, disguising their original nature.

Only then can consumption occur: actual consumption of the animal, now dead, and metaphorical consumption of the term "meat," so that it refers to food products alone rather than to the dead animal. In patriarchal culture, meat is without its referent point. This is the way we want it, as William Hazlitt honestly admitted in 1826:

> Animals that are made use of as food should either be so small as to be imperceptible, or else we should . . . not leave the form standing to reproach us with our gluttony and cruelty. I hate to see a rabbit trussed, or a hare brought to the table in the form which it occupied while living.[18]

The dead animal is the point beyond the culturally presumed referent of meat.

Notes

1   Teresa de Lauretis, *Alice Doesn't: Feminism, Semiotics, Cinema* (Bloomington: University of Indiana Press, 1984), p. 141.

2   I am indebted to Margaret Homans' discussion of the absent referent in literature for this expanded explanation of the cultural function of the absent referent. See her *Bearing the Word: Language and Female Experience in Nineteenth-Century Women's Writing* (Chicago: University of Chicago Press, 1986), p. 4.

3   Kathy Barry, *Female Sexual Slavery* (Englewood Cliffs, NJ: Prentice Hall, 1979), p. 3.

4   Keith Thomas, *Man and the Natural World: A History of the Modern Sensibility* (New York: Pantheon, 1983), p. 44.

5   Marjorie Spiegel, *The Dreaded Comparison: Human and Animal Slavery* (Philadelphia, PA: New Society Publishers, 1988).

6   Vincent Harding, *There Is a River: The Black Struggle for Freedom in America* (New York: Harcourt Brace Jovanovich, 1981, New York: Vintage Books, 1983), p. 7. Harding's source is Peter H. Wood's *Black Majority: Negroes in Colonial South Carolina from 1670 through the Stono Rebellion* (New York: Alfred A. Knopf, 1974). Wood discusses the reasons that the Proprietors of the Carolina colony protested the enslavement of Indians. They did so not only because they feared "prompting hostilities with local tribes" but also because "they were anxious to protect their peaceful trade in deerskins, which provided the colony's first source of direct revenue to England. With the opening up of this lucrative Indian trade to more people in the 1690s, the European settlers themselves became increasingly willing to curtail their limited reliance upon native American labor." *Black Majority*, p. 39.

7   Dick Gregory, *The Shadow That Scares Me*, ed. James R. McGraw (Garden City, NY: Doubleday & Co., Inc., 1968), pp. 69–70.

8   Commander Pierce Van Hoy quoted in Cleveland Amory, *Man Kind? Our Incredible War on Wildlife* (New York: Harper & Row, 1974), p. 14.

9   Another example of this can be found in the case of Arthur Gary Bishop, a child molester and murderer of five boys, who relived his first murder by buying and killing as many as twenty puppies.

10   Susan Glaspell, *A Jury of Her Peers* (London: Ernest Benn, Ltd., 1927).

11   R. Emerson Dobash and Russell Dobash, *Violence Against Wives: A Case Against the Patriarchy* (New York: The Free Press, Macmillan, 1979), p. 110.

12   Andrea Dworkin, *Pornography: Men Possessing Women* (New York: Perigee Books, 1981), p. 209; Gena Corea, *The Hidden Malpractice: How American Medicine Mistreats Women* (New York: William Morrow and Co., 1977, New York: Jove-Harcourt Brace Jovanovich Books, 1978), p. 129.

13   Linda Lovelace with Mike McGrady, *Ordeal* (New York: Citadel Press, 1980, Berkley Books, 1981), p. 96. Note that this is one woman looking at another as "meat."

14   Susan Griffin, *Rape: The Power of Consciousness* (San Francisco: Harper & Row, 1979), p. 39.

15   Daly defines "butcher" as "a bloody operator, esp. one who receives professional recognition and prestige for his 'successes.' " (*Websters' First New Intergalactic Wickedary of the English Language* [Boston: Beacon Press, 1987], p. 188.) Her failure to include animals in this definition is all the more notable because her book discusses hunting and vivisection, argues for our ability to communicate with animals, and is dedicated to the late Andrée Collard who had written on violence against animals. (See Andrée Collard with Joyce Contrucci, *Rape of the Wild: Man's Violence against Animals and the Earth* [London: The Women's Press, 1988].)

16   Annette Kuhn remarks: "Representations are productive: photographs, far from merely reproducing a pre-existing world, constitute a highly coded discourse which, among other things, constructs whatever is in the image as object of consumption—consumption by looking, as well as often quite literally by purchase. It is no coincidence, therefore, that in many highly socially visible (and profitable) forms of photography women dominate the image. Where photography takes women as its subject matter, it also constructs 'woman' as a set of meanings which then enter cultural and economic circulation on their own account." (*The power of the image: Essays on representation and sexuality* [London: Routledge and Kegan Paul, 1985], p. 19.) Also see Kaja Silverman, *The Subject of Semiotics* (New York: Oxford University Press, 1983), especially her chapter on "Suture," pp. 194–236.

17   William Morris, ed., *The American Heritage Dictionary of the English Language* (Boston: American Heritage Publishing Co., Inc., and Houghton Mifflin Co., 1969), p. 734.

18   William Hazlitt, *The Plain Speaker* (EL, n.d.), 173, quoted in Keith Thomas, *Man and the Natural World*, p. 300.

Chapter 34

Kathryn Paxton George

A PARADOX OF ETHICAL VEGETARIANISM: UNFAIRNESS TO WOMEN AND CHILDREN

Kathryn Paxton George argues that the "Regan-Singer arguments" assume the adult male body to be normative. Because their arguments ignore the nutritional needs of women, children, the elderly, and persons in "developing societies," the arguments violate the principle of equality. George maintains that no one has a moral requirement to be a vegetarian, though each of us should attend to common-sense duties to animals and humans.

VEGETARIANISM[1] HAS BEEN promoted by a variety of authorities as both humanitarian and healthful. Not only should people avoid harming animals by eating them, but we can also avoid the harmful effects of high-fat diets by avoiding meat, eggs, and dairy products. The claim that vegetarian diets are healthful is separate from the claim that such diets are morally required, but these ideas do influence one another. I argue here that the apparent safety and benefits of vegetarian diets for adult males between the ages of twenty and fifty have led some philosophers, especially Peter Singer, Tom Regan, and some feminists, to assume—probably unwittingly—that the male body is considered the normal *human* body. Then, assuming facts about this male human norm and using the Principle of Equality, they derive a general moral rule demanding ethical vegetarianism for everyone regardless of age, sex, or environment. I will refer to these arguments as the "Regan-Singer arguments."[2] I will show that their assumption about the male norm is mistaken and their call for ethical vegetarianism results in ageism, sexism, and classism. The Regan-Singer arguments rely on the Principle of Equality, but if all animals are equal, women and children become "less equal" than men. This paradoxical outcome will show that these arguments are incoherent and fail. Finally, the standard against which risk is presumed to be measured is arbitrarily assumed to be the adult male body.[3]

First, let's review the moral claims of the Regan-Singer arguments. The general claim is that we may not kill animals for food. According to Singer, we may not use their products unless we could be sure that these products are obtained under painless conditions. Singer's utilitarian position would permit some people to eat animals or use their products if they have a strong welfare interest (say, for reasons of ill health), but these would be *exceptional cases*. Singer's reasons are similar to those offered by Tom Regan, whose rights position allows certain people to consume meat as an exception based on what he calls the *Liberty Principle*:

> Provided that all those involved are treated with respect, and assuming that no special considerations obtain, any innocent individual has the right to act to avoid being made worse-off even if doing so harms other innocents.[4]

Being made to starve or suffer a significant decline in health and vigor would make a person worse-off, and Regan concedes that if some humans have a strong welfare-interest in consuming meat or animal products, this would excuse them from a duty to be vegetarians. But Regan clearly thinks that most people do not fall into such a category. He briefly discusses protein complementation and then dismisses the argument from nutrition: "Certain amino acids are essential for our health. Meat isn't. We cannot, therefore, defend meat eating on the grounds that we will ruin our health if we don't eat it or even that we will run a very serious risk of doing so if we abstain."[5]

Traditional moral theories used by Regan and Singer assume the moral equality of persons regardless of age, sex, race, and so forth. This assumption is called the *Principle of Equality*. Without the Principle of Equality, Regan and Singer cannot begin to make their arguments for the rights and welfare of animals. Rights-holders deserve equal treatment, and the rules generated by the moral system should be impartial and nondiscriminatory concerning facts about the rights-holders that they cannot change by choice. No particular group of people should bear a very much greater burden than others in attempting to keep the moral rule. That can mean that society should eliminate moral, social, or legal constraints that will cause people to suffer an increased burden in their attempts to function in society, at least as far as possible. For example, the Principle of Equality gives us the underlying reason to provide ramps and elevators for those who cannot use stairs. Because we subscribe to the Principle of Equality, we think it wrong to punish criminal offenders of one race more harshly than those of another. Nondiscrimination is the attempt by fair-minded people to affirm the equal worth of each member of the moral community. No single group can simply assume that its own practices are the only right ones, or even the best ones. If the rule prescribing ethical vegetarian diets is truly impartial, it should not require greater or very much greater burdens for some groups because of facts about themselves that they cannot change by choice and that are thought to be neutral to the interests served by the rule.

Having set out a brief exposition of the foundations for ethical vegetarianism, I will now present a critical examination of this proposed moral rule. My claim is that the rule is partial to adult males and that no one has noticed that the rule systematically imposes greater burdens on women, children, and the elderly. In addition, the rule unfairly penalizes people who live in certain kinds of economic and environmental circumstances. My critique has three parts:

(1) Regan and Singer assume that females, children, and the elderly have no significant differences in nutritional needs from those of adult males. To make their moral arguments, these scholars rely on conclusions drawn from nutritional studies done largely on adult males in industrialized countries. In addition, they do not consider studies citing the limitations of such diets for other age groups and for many women. Instead, the adult male body is assumed to be the norm for all. Women, children, and others are referred to in the scientific literature as "nutritionally vulnerable" with respect to certain vitamins and minerals such as iron, calcium, vitamin D, and zinc. All current arguments for ethical vegetarianism treat such nutritional vulnerability as an *exception* rather than as a norm. But, the very fact that the majority is regarded as a mere exception suggests that the ideal is skewed to favor a group in power.

(2) The requirement of ethical vegetarianism is also inconsistent and classist because it presupposes a society largely structured on wealth generated from unsustainable environmental, agricultural, and industrial practices. But most people in the world live in ethnic, cultural, economic, and environmental circumstances where this supposed ethical ideal poses much more serious health risks than it does for people in the United States, Europe, and other wealthy countries.

(3) Attempts to correct inequities by requiring supplementation for women and children exacerbate rather than resolve the problem of unfairness.

The first criticism will show that the Regan-Singer arguments become incoherent because they cannot consistently apply the Principle of Equality. Neither Singer nor Regan considers the different nutritional needs of adults versus infants and children and men versus women, although these differences are well documented in the medical and nutritional literature.[6] Infants and young children have higher energy, vitamin, and mineral needs than adults do because they are continuously growing and adding new tissue to their bodies. Nationally recognized nutrition authority, Dr. Johanna T. Dwyer, of Tufts University's School of Medicine and Nutrition, writes: "Vegetarianism in children deserves special attention because diets that sustain adults in good health are not necessarily appropriate for infants, young children, or adolescents."[7] Phyllis B. Acosta, of Florida State University's Department of Nutrition and Food Science, states her concerns in stronger terms: "Eating practices that promote health in the adult may have detrimental effects on growth and health status of the infant and young child."[8] Adolescents also need diets that are dense in nutrients per kilocalorie because they undergo the pubertal growth spurt. "Sex differences in nutrient needs become especially pronounced during adolescence."[9] The onset of menstrutation in females increases their iron needs, and the need for protein in adolescence increases because the body size is increasing rapidly. Because bone mass is being accumulated, calcium needs remain higher in both sexes until about age twenty-five. The recommended daily allowances (RDAs) are "considerably higher for adolescents than they are for younger children or adults, especially if they are expressed on a nutrients-per-calorie basis."[10] Pregnant adult women have greater protein, calcium, iron, vitamin C, vitamin D, vitamin E, thiamin, riboflavin, niacin, vitamin B_6, folate, vitamin B_{12}, phosphorus, magnesium, zinc, selenium, and iodide needs than adult males, and breast-feeding women have requirements that are higher still for almost all of these nutrients. People over age fifty have different requirements for several nutrients as reflected in the RDAs.

In pregnant women, "certain dietary practices that restrict or prohibit the consumption of an important source of nutrients, such as avoidance of all animal foods or of vitamin D-fortified milk, increase the risk of inadequate nutrient intake."[11] Pregnant vegan women may be at greater nutritional risk for "inadequate weight gain, low protein intake, inadequate iron intake with resulting anemias, low calcium, zinc, and vitamin B_{12} intakes, and in some instances low vitamin D, zinc, and iodide intakes."[12] Because the health of the fetus depends on the health of the individual woman carrying it, these factors may pose a fetal risk as well. In some cases, nutritional deficiency in a woman at the time of conception can seriously impair fetal development or the health of a breast-feeing child (e.g., folic acid deficiency, vitamin B_{12} deficiency).

Women and children are more likely to suffer iron deficiency than adult males even in industrialized societies, but iron deficiency is less severe in countries where food intake is adequate and includes meat. Only a few years ago, marginal iron levels in women were not regarded with much alarm by physicians and nutritionists. Recently, however, scientists have found that iron plays a vital role in childhood development and maintenance of the central nervous system, organ function, and immune function. Researchers usually categorize their test subjects as "normal," "iron deficient," or "iron deficient anemic," where iron deficiency is a state preceding anemia. In a review of forty-five studies on children, Hercberg and Galan note that iron deficiency has

> effects on skeletal muscle, cardiac muscle, brain tissue, liver tissue, gastrointestinal tractus [sic], body temperature relation, [and] DNA synthesis [because] iron participates in a wide variety of biochemical processes. . . . The key liabilities of tissue iron deficiency, even at a mild degree relate to decrease in intellectual performance, and in physical capacity during exercise, alteration of temperature regulation, [and] immune function.[13]

Moreover, the effects of diets without adequate available sources of iron in infancy and young childhood cannot be compensated for by later improvements or later supplementation, and "maternal mortality, prenatal, and perinatal infant death and prematurety are significantly increased" for iron deficiency in pregnancy.[14]

Women are particularly sensitive to iron deficiency because of periodic blood loss at menses and during pregnancy. Because iron carries oxygen to body cells, anemia causes reduction in capacity to perform work, reduction in mental acuity, greater vulnerability to other kinds of illnesses, and a variety of other symptoms. A significant number of women become iron deficient during pregnancy. "Although pregnant vegan women [in the U.S.] can meet increased needs for most nutrients during pregnancy by diet alone . . . iron needs rise so much after the second trimester that supplements are usually needed since plant sources of iron are less bioavailable than heme iron."[15] Supplements are commonly available in industrialized environments but are often not available to women in countries where food supplies are marginal. So both vegans and vegetarians are at risk for iron deficiency on unsupplemented diets, and women and children are at significantly greater risk than adult males.

Calcium adequacy is a risk for vegans, and again women, children, and the elderly are at greater risk on vegan diets than are adult males. Vegans reject dairy products, significantly reducing their dietary sources of calcium. Most concern about calcium centers on bone health. Continued inadequacy of calcium, especially in childhood and adolescence, is a major contributing factor to osteoporosis. Milk is regarded as the best source of calcium because of its bioavailability. Osteoporosis is a major concern for post-menopausal women because it causes bone loss and fractures, particularly of the hip, forearm, and vertebrae. Women are at much greater risk for this disease than are men, although males are affected in later old age. The generally denser skeletons and testosterone levels in males prevent its occurrence until quite late in life.

The time to prevent osteoporosis appears to be in childhood and adolescence. Peak bone mass is built at that age, and the better bone is built the more there will be. When bone loss begins, the time to reach a stage of severe depletion is longer. Young women have already built almost all of their bone by age seventeen, with some new bone formation perhaps continuing into the twenties. By age thirty, many women begin to lose bone. In women, "over the first several years after menopause, the skeleton undergoes a period of accelerated mineral loss in the process of adapting to declining concentrations of estrogen. After this period of adjustment, the rate of bone loss declines and remains fairly constant."[16]

The nutritional evidence suggests that the best candidates for vegetarianism and veganism are young, adult, healthy males living in industrialized cultures. Males have generally larger skeletons, maintain bone health due to higher levels of testosterone, and so have a lower risk of osteoporosis in late middle and old age. Adult males have higher iron levels than females and are at much less risk of anemia in adolescence and adulthood because they do not have periodic blood loss with menstruation and childbirth. They do not have protein, vitamin, or mineral stresses from feeding a rapidly growing fetus or a nursing infant, nor are they unduly stressed by their own growth requirements, as most of their growth is accomplished.

Do these facts mean that women and children in the United States cannot be healthy vegetarians? No, they do not. All risks for vegans in the United States can be overcome with a well-planned and well-supplemented diet. What does "well-planned" mean? Here is Johanna Dwyer's answer.

> For those who wish to progress to a vegan diet that includes no animal foods whatsoever, additional care in dietary planning is needed. In addition to iron and zinc, unplanned vegan diets are often low in kilocalories, calcium, and are always low in vitamin B_{12} and vitamin D unless supplementary sources of these vitamins are provided, since plant foods contain no known sources of these vitamins. The assistance of a registered dietitian is helpful, since a good deal of skill in planning and familiarity with unconventional food sources is needed by omnivores who wish to alter their dietary intakes in this way. *Certainly, if the individual in question is an infant, child, pregnant or lactating woman, over 65 years of age, recovering from an illness, or a chronic sufferer of a disease, dietetic consultation is highly advisable in order to incorporate these additional considerations into dietary planning and to avoid or circumvent adverse nutritional consequences.* Several good articles are available to guide counseling efforts for vulnerable groups.[17]

Moralists like Regan and Singer claim that anyone can be an ethical vegetarian with no extra special burden, but as shown above, that is not true. If the risk of harm can be overcome only by imposing significantly greater burdens on the groups highlighted above, while adult males gain health benefits, then the standard against which the risk is measured must surely be unfair.

Those defending vegetarianism with Regan-Singer arguments and feminist moral theories would say that anyone who needs to eat eggs, meat, or milk should not be required to abstain.[18] But they assume or argue that these people will be *exceptional cases* falling outside of the norm. This assumption is false.

Here is the core of my objection: Who are these others that traditionalists like Regan and Singer think may be excused? They are the vast majority of the *world's* population. And, if women, infants, children, adolescents, the elderly, and people who live almost everywhere else besides Western societies are *routinely* excused for doing what would normally be considered wrong, this relegates them to a *moral underclass* of beings who, because of their natures or cultures, are not capable of being fully moral. They are *physiologically* barred from doing the right thing because they are not the right *kind* of thing. The structure of this ethical thinking degrades the reality and human worth of these groups of people who do not fit.

Second, the Regan-Singer arguments assume a social standard structured largely on wealth generated from unsustainable environmental, agricultural, and industrial practices. These arguments also require women, children, and people who live in poorer cultures and environments to conform their ethical behavior as if they have the same kind of bodies as adult males living in wealthy cultures or be granted an exception.

From the perspective of a white middle-class college professor, American or Western society may appear quite homogeneous. The education level is high, food is plentiful, fortified, and available in great variety; the unemployed have food stamps; supplements seem readily available. These are conditions of great wealth by world standards, and they make vegetarianism reasonably safe. But, even in the United States, many people in poor economic circumstances do not have access to adequate food or to nutritional information. For example, many inner-city residents cannot buy vegetables—there is no supermarket nearby. Shall we simply excuse them then? But there really is something quite arrogant about excusing all of these people from attaining the ideal; it supposes the richer are better. They are not. They are just luckier.

Now I wish to discuss and reply to two possible counterarguments to my critique of ethical vegetarianism: (1) if these vulnerable groups use supplements, concerns about inequity vanish; and (2) improved medical care, education, and sanitation will make ethical vegetarianism globally equitable.

The first claim is that if women, children, and other nutritionally vulnerable groups use dietary supplements, then their risk is minimized. Therefore, these people should take supplements. This counterargument is flawed for two reasons. First, even if risks for vegetarians were equalized, burdens would not be. Western adult male vegetarians have many fewer burdens to bear, while women and child vegetarians must work harder to be "equal" simply because of their age or sex. Adult males rarely suffer anemia; they do not lose iron through periodic menstruation; they do not carry fetuses in their bodies or nurse infants; their growth is completed, and they almost always have larger skeletons than females and so have a much lower incidence of osteoporosis. Supplements are expensive; some are best prescribed by a physician to avoid overdose; they are usually not covered by insurance; and they may increase a vegetarian woman's personal and psychological worries. Second, the arbitrary adult male norm remains. Even if it is not too risky for a middle-class infant, child, adolescent, pregnant, lactating, perimenopausal, postmenopausal female, or elderly person to be an ethical vegetarian, that judgement will surely be made from a biased perspective—one that assesses the risk from the standpoint of the supposed male norm. Women, children, and seniors are being told to fix, mend, or correct their imperfect bodies as necessary (by supplementation, fortified foods, or eating in special ways) to meet a vegetarian ideal that is much less burdensome for adult males.

Now for the second counterargument: many nutritionists point out that people in "developing" countries are vegans not by choice but by circumstance of having no meat or dairy products available. Such people have a poor health status attributable to "environmental factors (such as lack of medical care, vaccination, education, and sanitation) rather than solely to diet."[19] Morally, we should improve these background conditions to a level similar to that of the United States. Then, supplemented vegan diets would constitute little risk in those places, too. We might conclude that the risks would then be equalized (although burdens would not be equalized) among the sexes and ages, at least in theory. Not only would the fundamental problem of bias remain, but such a program would come at a cost to humans and to animals. Vegan and vegetarian diets are lower in risk in Western nations when individuals have access to education, medical care, and sufficient resources to buy proper foods and supplements. Most importantly, these diets pose less risk in our culture largely because much of our food is fortified. We tend to think of our food as "naturally" protecting us. And it does! A diet consisting of the worst junk food is unlikely to result in pellagra or beriberi in the United States because virtually all flours are vitamin B fortified. Vitamin D is added to milk and is perhaps the single most important factor in the near eradication of rickets in children and osteomalacia in women and adolescents.

In many other parts of the world, beriberi, pellagra, rickets, scurvy, kwashikor, megaloblastic anemia, and iron deficient anemia are still endemic, although the incidence has declined in the twentieth century and the severity of the affected is usually less marked. Our food system protects us against these diseases, but that protection depends on an industrialized and unsustainable network of mono-cropping, food preservation, transportation, fortification, variety, and plenty—a system that is often inconsistent with environmental goals. In our culture, fortification and food processing require a complex industrialized food system with research biochemistry laboratories, food processing plants, mines to produce supplements, quality control bureaucracies, food-preservation techniques including spraying and refrigeration, trucking and other petroleum-consuming industries, and perhaps even chemical-dependent agriculture. A sophisticated scientific research and industrial complex with vitamin and mineral factories able to synthesize supplements without using animal products would be needed. For that, research biochemistry and chemistry labs are necessary, mines for extraction of raw materials, a network of universities to train scientists, and so forth. All of these aspects of our food systems have environmental consequences, many or most of which are at odds with environmental goals such as the preservation of habitat and reduction of pollution. Exporting safe vegan or vegetarian diets to the rest of the developing world would export these food systems and their environmental consequences, too. A strict moral censure of meat eating will be hard-pressed to escape the exploitation of the earth, of non-industrialized cultures, and of the animals it seeks to spare. Such censures are more likely to preserve class distinctions and discrimination than to dissipate them.

While we should, of course, encourage the worldwide availability of health care and good nutrition, the concomitant requirement of ethical vegetarianism may defeat environmental sustainability and would sustain a false norm in nutrition. The best course seems to be a middle ground such as semivegetarianism with moderate continued food fortification and preservation. Individuals should choose whether or not they wish to be vegetarians for reasons of health or personal taste. But I argue no one has a *moral* requirement to adopt this diet, even though we do have duties not to overconsume. People commonly eat together in families and among friends. We influence each other profoundly about diet and the acceptability of certain foods. Thus, each of us must consider his or her individual context and balance common-sense duties to animals and humans. Should we admire the strict moral vegetarian as going "above and beyond the call of duty"?[20] While this is a tempting tack to take, I must answer, "no." Semivegetarianism provides balanced diets and can be tolerated by almost everyone, and so the practice is good. But because there is no duty of strict ethical vegetarianism, we have no basis to admire the vegetarian on moral grounds. And, such admiration may even be pernicious to equality and human rights due to the inherent bias that lies within the assumption of the adult male norm.

Notes

1   Lacto-ovo vegetarians include plant foods, milk, eggs, and dairy products in their diets, but they exclude all meat, fish, and poultry. Semivegetarian diets include plant foods, milk and dairy products, eggs, and some fish and poultry. Vegans omit all meat, fish, and animal products. When I use the term "vegetarians," I will generally be referring to lacto-ovo vegetarians, whereas the term "strict vegetarians" refers to vegans.

2   Singer's arguments are developed in his *Animal Liberation*, 2d ed. (New York: Random House, 1990); Regan's in his *The Case for Animal Rights* (Berkeley: University of California Press, 1983). These arguments and the feminist

arguments are discussed in detail in my book, *Animal, Vegetable or Woman? A Feminist Critique of Ethical Vegetarianism* (Albany: State University of New York Press, 2000).

3   "Adult male body" shall always refer, in this essay, to men aged twenty to fifty living in industrialized societies.

4   Regan, *The Case for Animal Rights*, p. 333.

5   Ibid., p. 337.

6   For recent examples, in addition to the studies quoted in this essay, see: A. W. Root, "Bone Strength and the Adolescent," *Adolescent Medicine* 13, no. 1 (2002): 53–72; M. K. Javaid and C. Cooper, "Prenatal and Childhood Influences of Osteoporosis," *Best Practice and Research, Clinical Endocrinology and Metabolism* 16, no. 2 (2002): 349–67; E. Seeman, "Pathogenesis of Bone Fragility in Women and Men," *Lancet* 359, no. 9320 (2002): 1841–50; North American Menopause Society, "The Role of Calcium in Peri- and Postmenopausal Women," *Consensus Opinion of the North American Menopause Society* 8, no. 2 (2001): 84–95; E. M. Lau and J. Woo, "Nutrition and Osteoporosis," *Current Opinion in Rheumatology* 10, no. 4 (1998): 368–72; and A. Hackett, I. Nathan, and I. Burgess, "Is a Vegetarian Diet Adequate for Children?" *Nutrition and Health* 12, no. 3 (1998): 189–95.

7   Johanna T. Dwyer, "Vegetarianism in Children," in *Handbook of Pediatric Nutrition*, ed. Patricia M. Queen and Carol E. Lang (Gaithersburg, MD: Aspen Publishers, 1993), p. 171.

8   Phyllis B. Acosta, "Availability of Essential Amino Acids and Nitrogen in Vegan Diets," *American Journal of Clinical Nutrition* 48 (1988): 872.

9   Johanna T. Dwyer, "Nutrition and the Adolescent," in *Textbook of Pediatric Nutrition*, 2nd ed., ed. Robert M. Suskind and Leslie Lewinter-Suskind (New York: Raven Press, 1993), p. 258.

10 Ibid., p. 257.

11 Institute of Medicine, Subcommittee on Nutritional Status and Weight Gain during Pregnancy, Subcommittee on Dietary Intakes and Nutrient Supplements during Pregnancy, Committee on Nutritional Status during Pregnancy and Lactation, Food and Nutrition Board, National Academy of Sciences, "Nutrition during Pregnancy" (Washington, DC: National Academy Press, 1990), p. 18.

12 Johanna T. Dwyer, "Nutritional Consequences of Vegetarianism," *Annual Reviews in Nutrition* 11 (1991): 75–76.

13 Serge Hercberg and Pilar Galan, "Biochemical Effects of Iron Deprivation," *Acta Paediatrica Scandinavica* 361 (1989 supplement): 63–70.

14 Nevin S. Scrimshaw, "Iron Deficiency," *Scientific American* (October 1991): 50.

15 Johanna T. Dwyer and Franklin M. Loew, "Nutritional Risks of Vegan Diets to Women and Children: Are They Preventable?" *Journal of Agricultural and Environmental Ethics* 7, no. 1 (1994): 91.

16 Bess Dawson-Hughes, "Calcium Supplementation and Bone Loss: A Review of Controlled Clinical Trials," *American Journal of Clinical Nutrition* 54 (1991 supplement): 274S–80S.

17 Dwyer, "Nutritional Consequences of Vegetarianism," pp. 82–83 (emphasis added).

18 Singer's view is less strict than Regan's since Singer is a utilitarian. If it could be shown that more aggregate harm would result from universal vegan diets, then he could admit some use of animal products and even some meat eating. But his view still fails on the same assumptions as Regan's, as I will show.

19 Dwyer and Loew, "Nutritional Risks of Vegan Diets to Women and Children," p. 88.

20 My thanks to Andrea Veltman of the University of Wisconsin-Madison for this possible resolution.

RELIGIOUS PERSPECTIVES

Chapter 35

Norman Solomon

JUDAISM

Norman Solomon points out that while Judaism prohibits cruelty to animals, human life is valued above animal life. Harm to animals must be evaluated in the context of what alternatives exist. The passage contains a brief description of the required method of slaughter.

[. . .]

THE TORAH DOES not enjoin vegetarianism, though Adam and Eve were vegetarian [And God said, "Behold, I have given you every plant yielding seed which is upon the face of all the earth, and every tree with seed in its fruit; you shall have them for food"] (Gen. 1:29 RSV). Restrictions on meat eating perhaps indicate that it is a concession to human weakness; among the mediaeval Jewish philosophers of the Iberian peninsula, Joseph Albo (1380–1435) wrote that the first people were forbidden to eat meat because of the cruelty involved in killing animals (*Sefer Ha-Iqqarim* 3: 15). Isaac Abravanel (1437–1508) endorsed this in his commentary on Isaiah, Ch. 11 and also taught in his commentary on Genesis, Ch. 2, that when the Messiah comes we would return to the ideal, vegetarian state. Today the popular trend to vegetarianism has won many Jewish adherents though little official backing from religious leaders.

Although the Torah does not insist on vegetarianism, it places considerable restraints on the eating of meat; only the meat of certain animals may be eaten, certain parts may not be eaten at all, the blood must be drained, and there are regulations as to how the animals should be slaughtered. *Shehitah*, the method of slaughter, is by a single sharp cut across the trachaea and oesophagus; this may be performed only by a qualified religious expert, and nowadays there are special pens and procedures to ensure that the animal suffers the minimum of psychological distress as well as the minimum pain. Since in any case the animal very swiftly loses consciousness, generally before the onset of pain from the sharp cut, this is a relatively humane process.

From time to time voices are heard suggesting that *shehitah* is cruel to animals, but the criticisms often concern inessential aspects of *shehitah*, such as the form of casting-pen used, rather than *shehitah* itself. Nevertheless, there is at least a theoretical problem for Jews of what to do should it be demonstrated that the *shehitah* process is to some extent cruel; there would be a contradiction between two equally clear demands of the Torah, that meat not be eaten unless *shehitah* has been correctly performed, and that one should not practise cruelty to animals. Since the only cruelty which could conceivably be demonstrated would be minor, it is probable that the decision reached would be that *shehitah* be continued, and the procedures improved as far as possible; otherwise, orthodox Jews would be forced to be vegetarians. Judaism does not recognise cruelty to animals as an absolute value. Human life is consistently valued above animal life, so that any prima facie instance of harm to animals must be evaluated as to its seriousness and then balanced against alternatives.

[. . .]

Chapter 36

Rabbi Stephen Fuchs

ENHANCING THE DIVINE IMAGE (REVISED)

Rabbi Stephen Fuchs explains his vegetarianism as based on the creation story in Genesis, as "exquisite religious poem." Genesis details God's goal, which is to create a caring, compassionate society. Being vegetarian is a way to take our place as a partner with God.

MOST PEOPLE READ the Bible in one of two ways. For Fundamentalists the Bible is the scientifically and historically true immutable "Word of God." "The Bible says it, I believe it, and that settles it," reads a bumper sticker that subscribes to this viewpoint. In contrast many dismiss the Bible as merely a set of antiquated laws and cute fairy tales. I reject both perspectives. For me the "truth" of Scripture lies not in its historicity or scientific veracity but in the answer to the question, "What does it teach me?"

In 1988 I became a lacto ovo vegetarian for spiritual reasons. I "graduated" to becoming a vegan in 2000 for health reasons. My decision to become a vegetarian rests on the lessons of Genesis' earliest stories, in particular its magnificent creation poem.

In his book, *In the Beginning*, the late prolific author Isaac Asimov fell into the trap of viewing the creation story as an obsolete scientific thesis when he wrote: "The biblical writers did the best they could with the scientific material available to them. If they had written those earlier chapters of Genesis knowing what we know today, we can be certain they would have written it completely differently."[1]

No, Mr. Asimov, the biblical authors were not concerned with making a scientific statement any more than Mozart was concerned with writing "Rock 'n' Roll" music. Genesis' creation story does not attempt to teach us HOW the world was created. Its purpose is to offer invaluable religious perspective on WHY.

The story's main lesson is that we human beings – created in God's image – are in charge of and responsible for this world. We can protect and preserve it or pollute it. We have awesome powers that God wants us to use with caring and compassion. Hopefully, our dominion over the other creatures on earth will impel us to care for and nurture them, not wantonly slaughter them to slake our appetites.

Among the many rabbinic comments on the opening chapter of Genesis is the one which notes that the first word of the Torah, *Bereshit*, begins with the letter *Beth* (as opposed to *Aleph*, the first letter). *Beth* is the first letter of the Hebrew word *Bracha* which means "blessing." Creation begins with *Beth* to remind us that each person has the potential by her or his actions to make life a blessing for ourselves, for those around us, for the other creatures God created and for future generations.[2]

Chapters two through eleven in Genesis, the chapters which follow the story of creation tell, as I interpret them, of three attempts on God's part to create what has been from the beginning God's highest goal: a just, caring and compassionate society. Each of those societies has ground rules.[3]

Eden, the first society was a place of no birth, no death, no sexuality (in my view, although this point is debated vigorously by biblical commentators) and no need to work hard. It was a place in which God permitted the first couple to eat their fill but only of fruits and vegetables.

The second society, which I call "Post Eden-Pre Flood", was the opposite of Eden. People were born, died, had sex, and had to work hard for a living. It too was a vegetarian society. God ended that society with the flood because humanity constantly chose corruption and cruelty over caring and compassion.

After the flood God established three new ground rules. First, God promised never to destroy the earth again (Genesis 8:22). Second, we humans must punish wrongdoers. Now, the responsibility to punish cruelty and create a world of justice and righteousness shifts from God to human beings (Genesis 9:6). Finally, and most pertinent to our discussion, for the first time after the flood humanity receives permission to eat meat (Genesis 9:3)

The Torah presents God as making adjustments from society to society. Perhaps the permission humanity received to eat meat at the start of the third, "Post Flood" society was a concession to human nature. Veganism was the original ideal, but God was willing to make allowances for human weakness.

Still the third society did not work out any better than the first two. In a fourth attempt to have humanity establish a righteous and just society God makes a Covenant with Abraham, Sarah and their descendants.

The permission we received to eat meat is still in force, but subsequent Jewish tradition curtailed that privilege by reminding us through the elaborate rituals of *Kashrut* of the magnitude of what we do each time we kill a living being.

For me, the laws of *Kashrut* are insufficient. I have not been able to shake the notion that if we really wanted to do God's will, we would abstain from meat altogether.

So in 1988, even though I always loved a good steak, a delicious roast or a juicy hamburger, I became a vegetarian. I decided that I did not want animals to die so that I could eat.

I reached a point where I had to take seriously and personally the creation story's teaching that we humans are in charge of and responsible for this planet and the other creatures with whom we share it. The impact of that realization forces me to balance my lusty enjoyment of meat with the responsibility of living up to the Divine Image in which God created us.

Another major teaching of the creation story is that life is no accident; it has purpose and meaning. We are not puppets and God is not a puppeteer. That means we have free will. We can choose to be kind or cruel.

The horrific cruelty of the meat slaughtering and packing industry has been well researched and documented. Several books, magazines and web sites graphically and accurately depict the pain and suffering of animals raised for slaughter and subsequent human consumption.

God does not make the choice of kindness or cruelty for us, but urges us as Scripture says:

> I call heaven and earth to witness against you this day: I have put before you life and death, the blessing and the curse. Therefore choose life that may live by loving the Lord your God, following his commands and clinging to him.
>
> (Deuteronomy 30:19–20, my translation)

In the year 2000 my understanding of "Therefore choose life," took on a deeper dimension. Through the lectures of Dr. Frank Sabatino of the Regency House Spa in Hallandale Beach, Florida, it became clear to me that I could enjoy greater health vitality, and, I hope, longevity by avoiding dairy and eggs, and so I became a vegan. I lost a significant amount of weight, my acid reflux condition disappeared, my serum cholesterol level lowered, and my regular headaches decreased in frequency and intensity. In short I feel much better.

I also feel better about myself and more wholehearted in my quest to take my place as a worthy covenantal partner with God. When I refrain from eating meat, fish, dairy and eggs I feel I am doing a better job of fulfilling the covenantal charge God first uttered to Abraham 4000 years ago: "Be a blessing!" Genesis 12:2). It is the very blessing God had in mind in deciding to use the letter *Beth* to begin the story of creation.

Notes

1   Isaac Asimov, *In the Beginning* (New York: Crown Publishers, 1981), 3
2   *Bereshit Rabbah* 1:10
3   For a fuller discussion of these ground rules, see my doctoral thesis, *Standing at Sinai: Looking Backward, Looking Forward* (Nashville, Tennessee: Vanderbilt University, 1992), 28–54

Chapter 37

Andrew Linzey

THE BIBLE AND KILLING FOR FOOD

Andrew Linzey discusses the contradiction between the divine command of vegetarianism in Genesis 1 and the reversal of this command in Genesis 9. He states that Biblical vegetarians should not claim that it has never been justifiable to kill animals, but rather that it is not now necessary, and that a vegetarian life is closer to the biblical ideal of peace. Similarly, Linzey argues that while Jesus ate fish in the context of first-century Palestine, the question for us is what we eat now.

> And God said, 'Behold, I have given you every plant yielding seed which is upon the face of all the earth, and every tree with seed in its fruit; you shall have them for food. And to every beast of the earth, and to every bird of the air, and to everything that creeps on the earth, everything that has the breath of life, I have given every green plant for food.'
>
> (Gen. 1:29–30; RSV)

> And God blessed Noah and his sons, and said to them '. . . Every moving thing that lives shall be food for you; as I gave you the green plants, I give you everything.'
>
> (Gen. 9:1–4; RSV)

AT FIRST GLANCE, these two passages may be taken as epitomizing the difficulty of appealing to scripture in the contemporary debate about animal rights. The sheer contradictoriness of these statements presses itself upon us. Genesis 1 clearly depicts vegetarianism as divine command. Indeed 'everything' that has the breath of life in it, is given 'green plant for food'. Genesis 9, however, reverses this command quite specifically. '(A)s I gave you the green plants, I give you everything' (9:3). In the light of this, the question might not unreasonably be posed: cannot both vegetarians and carnivores appeal to scripture for justification and both with *equal* support?

Food of paradise

In order to unravel this conundrum we have first of all to appreciate that those who made up the community whose spokesperson wrote Genesis 1 were not themselves vegetarians. Few appreciate that Genesis 1 and 2 are themselves the products of much later reflection by the biblical writers themselves. How is it then that the very people who were not themselves vegetarian imagined a beginning of time when all who lived were vegetarian (herbivore to be precise) by divine command?

To appreciate this perspective we need to recall the major elements of the first creation saga. God creates a world of great diversity and fertility. Every living creature is given life and space (Gen. 1:9–10; 24–5). Earth to live on and blessing to enable life itself (1:22). Living creatures are pronounced good (1:25). Humans are made in God's image (1:27) given dominion (1:26–9), and then prescribed a vegetarian diet (1:29–30). God then pronounces that everything was 'very good' (1:31). Together the whole creation rests on the sabbath with God (2:2–3). When examined in this way, we should see immediately that Genesis 1 describes a state of paradisal existence. There is no hint of violence between or among different species. Dominion, so often interpreted as justifying killing, actually precedes the command to be vegetarian. Herb-eating dominion is hardly a licence for tyranny. The answer seems to be then that even though the early Hebrews were neither pacifists nor vegetarians, they were deeply convinced of the view that violence between humans and animals, and indeed between animal species themselves, was not God's original will for creation.

But if this is true, how are we to reconcile Genesis 1 with Genesis 9, the vision of original peacefulness with the apparent legitimacy of killing for food? The answer seems to be that as the Hebrews began to construct the story of early human beginnings, they were struck by the prevalence and enormity of human wickedness. The stories of Adam and Eve, Cain and Abel, Noah and his descendants are testimonies to the inability of humankind to fulfil the providential purposes of God in creation. The issue is made explicit in the story of Noah:

> Now the earth was corrupt in God's sight, and the earth was filled with violence. And God saw the earth, and behold, it was corrupt; for all flesh had corrupted their way upon the earth. And God said to Noah, 'I have determined to make an end of all flesh; for the earth is filled with violence through them.'
>
> (Gen. 6:11–14; RSV)

The radical message of the Noah story (so often overlooked by commentators) is that God would rather not have us be at all if we must be violent. It is violence itself within every part of creation that is the pre-eminent mark of corruption and sinfulness. It is not for nothing that God concludes: 'I am sorry that I have made them' (Gen. 6:7).

Ambiguous permission

It is in *this* context—subsequent to the Fall and the Flood—that we need to understand the permission to kill for food in Genesis 9. It reflects entirely the situation of the biblical writers at the time they were writing. Killing—of both humans as well as animals—was simply inevitable given the world as it is and human nature as it is. Corruption and wickedness had made a mess of God's highest hopes for creation. There just had to be some accommodation to human sinfulness. 'Every moving thing shall be food for you; and as I gave you the green plants, I give you everything' (Gen. 9:3). For many students of the Bible this seems to have settled the matter of whether humans can be justified in killing animals for food. In the end, it has been thought, God allows it. And there can be no doubt that throughout the centuries this view has prevailed. Meat eating has become the norm. Vegetarians, especially Christian vegetarians, have survived from century to century to find themselves a rather beleaguered minority. The majority view can be summed up in this beautifully prosaic line of Calvin:

> For it is an insupportable tyranny, when God, the Creator of all things, has laid open to us the earth and the air, in order that we may thence take food as from his storehouse, for these to be shut up from us by mortal man, who is not able to create even a snail or a fly.[1]

What Calvin appears to overlook, however, as has most of the Christian tradition, is that the permission to kill for food in Genesis 9 is far from unconditional or absolute:

> Only you shall not eat flesh with its life, that is, its blood. For your lifeblood I will surely require a reckoning; of every beast I will require it and of man. . . .
>
> (Gen. 9:4–5; RSV)

Understanding these lines is far from straightforward. At first sight these qualificatory lines might be seen as obliterating the permission itself. After all, who can take animal life without the shedding of blood? Who can kill without the taking of blood, that is, the life itself? In asking these questions we move to the heart of the problem. For the early Hebrews life was symbolized by, even constituted by, blood itself. To kill *was* to take blood. And yet it is precisely *this* permission which is denied.

It is not surprising then that commentators have simply passed over these verses, suggesting that some ritual, symbolic significance was here entertained but one which in no way substantially affected the divine allowance to kill. But this, I suggest, is to minimize the significance of these verses. Rereading these verses in the light of their original context should go rather like this: The world in which you live has been corrupted. And yet God has not given up on you. God has signified a new relationship—a covenant with you—despite all your violence and unworthiness. Part of this covenant involves a new regulation concerning diet. What was previously forbidden can now—in the present circumstances—be allowed. You may kill for food. But you may kill only on the understanding that you remember that the life you kill is not your own—it belongs to God. You must not misappropriate what is not your own. As you kill what is not your own—either animal or human life—so you need to remember that for every life you kill you are personally accountable to God.[2]

If this reading is correct, and I believe few scholars would now dissent from this interpretation, it will be seen immediately that Genesis 9 does not grant humankind some absolute right to kill animals for food. Indeed, properly speaking, there is no *right* to kill. God allows it only under the conditions of necessity. A recent statement by the Union of Liberal and Progressive Synagogues expresses it this way: 'Only after the Flood (contends Genesis 9:3) was human consumption of animals permitted and that was later understood as a concession, both to human weakness and to the supposed scarcity of edible vegetation.'[3]

To give a more complete account of biblical themes requires us to move on from Genesis 1 and 2, to Isaiah 11. We need to appreciate that while killing was sometimes thought to be justifiable in the present time, biblical writers were also insistent that there would come another time when such killing was unnecessary. This is the time variously known as the 'future hope of Israel' or the 'Messianic Age'. Isaiah speaks of the one who will establish justice and equity and universal peace. One of the characteristics of this future age is the return to the existence envisaged by Genesis 1 before the Fall and the Flood:

> The wolf shall dwell with the lamb, and the leopard shall lie down with the kid, and the calf and the lion and the fatling together, and a little child shall lead them. The cow and the bear shall feed; their young shall lie down together; and the lion shall eat straw like the ox. The sucking child shall play over the hole of the asp, and the weaned child shall put his hand on the adder's den. They shall not hurt or destroy in all my holy mountain; for the earth shall be full of the knowledge of the Lord as the waters cover the sea.
>
> (Isa. 11:6–9; RSV)

It seems therefore that while the early Hebrews were neither vegetarians nor pacifists, the ideal of the peaceable kingdom was never lost sight of. In the end, it was believed, the world would one day be restored according to God's original will for all creation. Note, for example, how the vision of peaceable living also extends to relations between animals themselves. Not only, it seems, are humans to live peaceably with animals, but also formerly aggressive animals are to live peaceably with other animals.

We may sum up the main elements of the biblical approach as follows: killing for food appears essential in the world as we now know it, influenced as it is by corruption and wickedness. But such a state of affairs is not as God originally willed it. Even when we kill under situations of necessity we have to remember that the lives we kill do not belong to us and that we are accountable to God. Moreover, God's ultimate will for creation shall prevail. Whatever the present circumstances, one day all creation, human and animal, shall live in peace.

Living without violence

It should now be seen that far from being confused and contradictory, the biblical perspectives on killing for food have not only internal integrity but also enormous relevance to the contemporary debate about animal rights and vegetarianism. There are three ethical challenges in particular that we should grapple with.

The first thing that should be noted is that the Bible does not minimize the gravity of the act of killing animals. So often in our heavily industrialized societies we think of animals, especially farm animals, as merely food machines or commodities that are to be bought or sold for human consumption. This can never be the biblical view. Genesis 1 specifically speaks of animal life as that which 'has the breath of life' (1:30). This life is a gift from God. It does not belong to human beings. It may be used only with the greatest reserve and in remembrance of the One from whose creative hands it comes. Those who wish to use animals frivolously or with no regard for their God-given worth cannot claim the Bible for their support.

[. . .]

The second challenge is that we have no biblical warrant for claiming killing as God's will. God's will is for peace. We need to remember that even though Genesis 9 gives permission to kill for food it does so only on the basis that we do not misappropriate God-given life. Genesis 9 posits divine reckoning for the life of every beast taken even under this new dispensation (9:5). The question may not unnaturally be asked: how long can this divine permission last?

[. . .]

In this respect it is interesting that one highly regarded Talmudic scholar, Abraham Isaac Kook, maintains that the most spiritually satisfying way of reading the practical biblical injunctions concerning killing is in terms of preparation for a new dawn of justice for animals. 'The free movement of the moral impulse to establish justice for animals generally and the claim for their rights from mankind,' he argues, 'are hidden in a natural psychic sensibility in the deeper layers of the Torah.' Given the corruption of humankind, it was natural and inevitable that moral attention had first to be paid to the regulation of human conduct towards other humans. But in Kook's view the various injunctions concerning the selection and preparation of meat (in, for example, Lev. 17:13; Ezek. 16:63; Lev. 22:28 and Deut. 22: 26–7) were commandments 'to regulate the eating of meat, in steps that will take us to the higher purpose'. And what is this higher purpose? None other it seems than universal peace and justice. Kook maintains that just as the embracing of democratic ideals came late within religious thinking 'so will the hidden yearning to act justly towards animals emerge at the proper time'.[4]

The third challenge to be grasped is that those who wish now to adopt a vegetarian or vegan lifestyle have solid biblical support. Biblical vegetarians will not say, 'It has *never been* justifiable to kill animals,' rather they should say, 'It is *not now* necessary to kill for food as it was once thought necessary.' The biblical case for vegetarianism does not rest on the view that killing may never be allowable in the eyes of God, rather on the view that killing is always a grave matter. When we have to kill to live we may do so, but when we do not, we should live otherwise. It is vital to appreciate the force of this argument. In past ages many—including undoubtedly the biblical writers themselves—have thought that killing for food was essential in order to live. We now know that—at least for those now living in the rich West—it is perfectly possible to sustain a healthy diet without any recourse to flesh products. This may not have always been true in the past. Conventional wisdom was always that meat was essential to live and to live well. Only during the past 200 years has vegetarianism become a publicly known and acceptable option.

Those individuals who opt for vegetarianism can do so in the knowledge that they are living closer to the biblical ideal of peaceableness than their carnivorous contemporaries. The point should not be minimized. In many ways it is difficult to know how we can live more peaceably in a world driven by violence and greed and consumerism. Individuals often feel powerless in the face of great social forces beyond even democratic control. To opt for a vegetarian lifestyle is to take one practical step towards living in peace with the rest of creation. It has been estimated that over 500 million animals are slaughtered for food in the UK every year. In the US the numbers are 6–9 billion annually. To become vegetarian is to take a practical step to reduce the rate of institutionalized killing in the world today. One fewer chicken eaten is one fewer chicken killed.

Nevertheless, we do well to appreciate the biblical perspective that we do not live in an ideal world. The truth is that even if we adopt a vegetarian or vegan lifestyle, we are still not free of killing either directly or indirectly. Even if we eat only beans and nuts and lentils, we have to reckon with the fact that competing animals are killed because of the crops we want to eat. Even if we decide not to wear dead animal skins, we have to face the fact that alternative substances have been tested for their toxicity on laboratory animals. Even if we eat only soya beans we do well to remember that these have been force fed to animals in painful experiments. As I have written elsewhere, there is no pure land.[5] If we embark on vegetarianism, as I think we should, we must do so on the understanding that for all its compelling logic, it is only *one* small step towards the vision of a peaceful world.

Prince of peace

Before I conclude, there is one major—and some would say conclusive—objection to my pro-vegetarian thesis that should be considered. It is this: Jesus was no vegan and possibly no vegetarian. There are no recorded examples of Jesus eating meat in the Gospels. The only possible exception is the Passover itself, but it is not clear, to say the least, that Jesus ate the traditional Passover meal. Jesus did, however, eat fish if the Gospel narratives are to be believed. How are we to reconcile this to the established Christian view of Jesus as the Prince of Peace? There are four possible answers to this question.

The first is that the canonical Gospels are mistaken and Jesus was actually a vegetarian. However implausible this view may appear, among those who are pro-animals there have always been a significant number who have never believed that Jesus ate the flesh of other living creatures.[6] Those who take this view argue that 'fish' in the New Testament did not actually mean fish as we know it today. Moreover it is sometimes argued that Jesus was really a member of the Essene sect who were, it seems, strict vegetarians. Indeed there are various 'Essene gospels' in which Jesus is depicted as a committed vegetarian.[7] On the face of it, it does seem highly unlikely that such a convenient view is true and the Essene gospels strike me as of rather doubtful antiquity. Nevertheless, I would like to keep an open mind. It is just conceivable that some of these gospels do somehow contain genuine historical reminiscences (we know so little about the historical Jesus in any case) but I think it is a rather remote possibility.

The second possible answer is that Jesus was not perfect in every conceivable way. Jews and Muslims would, of course, have no difficulty with this proposition but orthodox Christians would surely find this idea difficult. After all traditional Christian belief has always been that Jesus Christ was truly God and truly man. Most Christians would hold that being sinless was an essential part of being God incarnate. Those who argue that Jesus was not wholly perfect, however, are not, of course, wholly without biblical support. The question of Jesus: 'Why do you call me good?' And his answer: 'No one is good but God alone,' is recorded in all three synoptic Gospels (Luke 18:19; Matthew 19:17; Mark 10:18). Moreover, it is not inconceivable that Jesus could have been *both* God incarnate and less than morally perfect in every way. Some scholars, such as John Robinson, have maintained this.[8] Perhaps it could be argued that while Jesus committed no sin of commission (deliberate wrongdoing), it could be argued that of necessity every human being commits some sin of omission (things left undone). However, such a view certainly falls short of traditional Christian doctrine and biblical texts such as Hebrews 4:15 which argues that Jesus 'was tempted as we are, yet without sin'.

The third answer is that the killing of fish is not a morally significant matter or, at least, not as significant as the killing of mammals. There is something to be said for this view. Even those who argue rigorously for animal rights sometimes do so on the basis that animals as God's creatures are 'subjects of a life'—that is they have sensitivity and consciousness and the ability to suffer—but it is not clear that all fish do actually possess all these characteristics. In many cases we simply do not know. This must mean, I think, that their moral status is somewhat different from those animals where self-consciousness and sentience can reasonably be taken for granted. Nevertheless, do not fish merit some benefit of the doubt? Are they not also fellow creatures with some God-given life and individuality which means that wherever possible their lives should be respected?

The fourth answer is that sometimes it can be justifiable to kill fish for food in situations of necessity. Such a situation, we may assume, was present in first-century Palestine where geographical factors alone seem to have suggested a scarcity of protein. Such a view would on the whole be more consistent with the biblical perspective that we may kill but only in circumstances of real need. Hence we may have to face the possibility that Jesus did indeed participate in the killing of some life forms in order to live. Indeed we may say that part of his being a human being at a particular stage and time in history necessitated that response in order to have lived at all.

Of all the four possible responses, I find this last one the most convincing. As I have indicated before, the biblical view is not that killing can never be justified and ought to be avoided at all costs. There are times, for example, when euthanasia may well be the most compassionate response to an individual undergoing unrelievable suffering. But even if we accept that killing for food may be justified in those situations of real necessity for human survival, such as may be argued in the case of Jesus himself, this in no way exonerates us from the burden of justifying what we now do to animals in circumstances substantially different. This last point is centrally important and must not be obscured. There may have been times in the past, or even now in the present, where we have difficulty imagining a life without killing for food. But *where we do have the moral freedom* to live without killing, without recourse to violence, there is a *prima facie* case that we should do so. To kill without the strict conditions of necessity is to live a life with insufficient generosity.

It would be wrong, however, to give the impression that the life and teaching of Jesus is a disappointment as far as the enlightened treatment of animals is concerned. While it is true that there is a great deal we do not know about Jesus's precise attitudes to animals, there is a powerful strand in his ethical teaching about the primacy of mercy to the weak, the powerless and the oppressed. Without misappropriation, it is legitimate to ask: who is more deserving of this special compassion than the animals commonly exploited in our world today? Moreover, it is often overlooked that in the canonical Gospels Jesus is frequently presented as identifying himself with the world of animals. As I have written elsewhere:

> His birth, if tradition is to be believed, takes place in the home of sheep and oxen. His ministry begins, according to Mark, in the wilderness 'with the wild beasts' (1:13). His triumphal entry into Jerusalem involves riding on a 'humble ass' (see Matthew 21:4–5). According to Jesus it is lawful to 'do good' on the Sabbath, which includes the rescuing of an animal fallen into a pit (see Matthew 12:10–12). Even the sparrows, literally sold for a few pennies in his day, are not 'forgotten before God' (Luke 12:6). God's providence extends to the entire created order, and the glory of Solomon and all his works cannot be compared to that of the lilies of the field (Luke 12:27). God so cares for his creation that even 'foxes have holes, and birds of the air have nests; but the Son of Man has nowhere to lay his head'.
>
> (Luke 9:58)[9]

The significance of these and other verses may be much more than had previously been thought. One small example must suffice. Mark describes Jesus's ministry as taking place first within the context of wild animals (1:13). Richard Bauckham has recently argued that the context in which this verse should be understood is messianic in orientation. Jesus is shown to be in continuity with the Isaianic tradition in seeing the messianic age as bringing about a reconciliation between nature and humanity.[10] If this is true, it may be that Mark is seeking to demonstrate how the Gospel of Jesus has implications for the whole of the created world, and for harmony within the animal world in particular. Those who follow Jesus might argue that in seeking to realize what can now be realized in our own time and space of the messianic age is to live now in conformity with the Spirit of Jesus itself.

In conclusion, reference has already been made to how vegetarians have formed a rather beleaguered minority in times past. But it is worth recalling that not a few of the great figures in Christendom have adopted a vegetarian diet. Among these should not go unnoticed the countless saints who have expressed a particular regard for animals and opposed their destruction. 'Poor innocent little creatures,' exclaimed St Richard of Chichester when confronted with animals bound for slaughter. 'If you were reasoning beings and could speak you would curse us. For we are the cause of your death, and what have you done to deserve it?'[11] There has always been an ascetical strand within Christianity which has insisted that humans should live gently on the earth and avoid luxury food. The rule of life penned by St Benedict for his religious community, for example, expressly forbade the eating of meat. 'Except the sick who are very weak, let all abstain entirely from the flesh of four-footed animals.'[12] Moreover, it often comes as a surprise for Christians to realize that the modern vegetarian movement was strongly biblical in origin. Inspired by the original command in Genesis 1, an Anglican priest, William Cowherd, founded the Bible Christian Church in 1809 and made vegetarianism compulsory among its members. The founding of this Church in the United Kingdom and its sister Church in the United States by William Metcalfe, effectively heralded the beginning of the modern vegetarian movement.[13]

The subsequent, if rather slow, growth of vegetarianism from 1809 to 1970, and its rapid and astonishing growth from 1970 to the present day is testimony that Cowherd may have been right in his view that mainstream biblical theology had overlooked something of importance in Genesis 1. It may be that when the history of twentieth-century cuisine is finally written, the radical changes in diet which we are currently experiencing will be found to be due more to the rediscovery of two biblical verses (Gen. 1:29–30) than anything else. These two verses, we may recall, came into existence by people imagining possibilities in the light of their belief in God the Creator. By rekindling the same vision in our own time, we may be enabled to realize—at least in part—those possibilities which our forebears could only imagine. Forwards, we may say, not backwards to Genesis.

Notes

1   John Calvin, *Commentaries on the First Book of Moses*, vol. 1, ET by John King (Edinburgh: Calvin Translation Society, 1847), pp. 291 f. Extract in Andrew Linzey and Tom Regan (eds) *Animals and Christianity: A Book of Readings* (London: SPCK and New York: Crossroad, 1989), pp. 199–200.

2   This argument is developed at length in Andrew Linzey, *Christianity and the Rights of Animals* (London: SPCK and New York: Crossroad, 1987), especially pp. 141–9.

3   *Where We Stand on Animal Welfare* (London: Rabbinic Conference of the Union of Liberal and Progressive Synagogues, May 1990), p. 1.

4   Abraham Isaac Kook, *The Lights of Penitence, The Moral Principles, Lights of Holiness, Essays, Letters, and Poems*, ET by B. Z. Bokser, preface by J. Agus and R. Schatz, *The Classics of Western Spirituality* (London: SPCK, 1979), pp. 317–23. I am grateful to Jonathan Sacks for this reference.

5   See inter alia *Christianity and the Rights of Animals, ibid,* p. 148.

6   See, e.g., Geoffrey L. Rudd, *Why Kill for Food?* (Cheshire: The Vegetarian Society, 1970), pp. 78–90, and Steven Rosen, *Food for the Spirit: Vegetarianism and the World Religions* (New York: Bala Books, 1987), pp. 33–9.

7   For example, *The Gospel of the Holy Twelve* and *The Essene Humane Gospel of Jesus*, cited and discussed in Rosen, *ibid.*

8   J. A. T. Robinson, "Need Jesus have been Perfect?" in S. W. Sykes and J. P. Clayton (eds) *Christ, Faith and History*, Cambridge Studies in Christology (Cambridge: CUP, 1972), pp. 39–52.

9   "Introduction" to Andrew Linzey and Tom Regan (eds) *Compassion for Animals: Readings and Prayers* (London: SPCK, 1989), p. xv.

10   I am grateful to Richard Bauckham for his recent lecture at Essex University on this theme and for bringing to my attention the significance of this verse. I understand that his work will shortly be published as *Jesus and the Greening of Christianity*.

11   St Richard of Chichester, cited in Butler's *Lives of the Saints*, also extract in *Compassion for Animals: Readings and Prayers, ibid*, p. 66.

12   *The Rule of St Benedict*, ET by Justin McCann, Spiritual Masters Series (London: Sheed and Ward, 1976) chp. 39, p. 46.

13   See Richard D. Ryder, *Animal Revolution: Changing Attitudes Towards Speciesism* (Oxford: Blackwells, 1989), p. 96. For a history of the Church in America see *The History of the Philadelphia Bible-Christian Church, 1817–1917* (Philadelphia: J. B. Lippincott Company, 1922). I am grateful to Bernard Unti for this last reference.

Chapter 38

Martin Forward and Mohamed Alam

ISLAM

Martin Forward and Mohamed Alam explain the Muslim view of the animal-human relationship. Animals are not to be treated as valueless by human beings, but by God's permission human beings have power over the animals and are entitled to use animals for human purposes. Forward and Alam explain the restrictions under which animals may be eaten and the required ritual method of slaughter.

[. . .]

A CCORDING TO THE Qur'ān, 'there is not an animal on earth, nor a bird that flies on its wings — but they are communities like you . . . and they shall all be gathered to their Lord in the end' (6: 38). This means that they fulfil the plan which God has allotted to them in his purpose. They are not to be treated as valueless by human beings. It has not usually been taken by commentators of the Qur'ān or jurists to mean that animals share in the bliss (or torment) of life after death. Human beings are distinguished from animals by their capacity to make moral judgements. Only they, of all species of life, can choose to obey or disobey God, and so earn paradise or hell.

Islam is not a sentimental religion. By God's permission, human beings have power over the animals, as over all creation, and they can be used for various purposes.

[. . .]

Islam forbids the keeping of some animals for domestic purposes. Most Muslims do not have dogs as pets. [. . .] Muhammad did not like dogs. [. . .] However, he did not mean that dogs could be mistreated. A prostitute who saw a thirsty dog hanging around a well one day, gave it water to drink. For this act of kindness, the Prophet pardoned all her sins.

[. . .]

Other traditions of the Prophet forbid treating animals cruelly. They are not to be caged, or beaten unnecessarily, or branded on the face, or allowed to fight each other for human entertainment. They must not be mutilated while they are alive, which forbids vivisection. Muslims are opposed to battery farming, the slaughter of calves for veal, and all other forms of animal-husbandry which are cruel to creatures or which needlessly kill them. These interdicts arise out of the Islamic emphasis that human beings have a moral obligation towards animals.

[. . .]

A very important function of animals is to provide human beings with food. Few Muslims are vegetarians. But certain animals are forbidden to Muslims, and all creatures used for food need to be killed in a prescribed manner.

Islamic law declares certain things permissible (*111alāl*) for human beings, and other things harmful (*111arām*). This division covers all aspects of life, including what Muslims can eat. Muslims regard all things as *111alāl* unless God has commanded otherwise. There are four forbidden categories of food, which are derived from the Qur'ān (5: 4):

1   meat of dead animals
2   blood
3   pigs' flesh
4   meat over which another name than God's has been invoked.

The meat of dead animals is taken to mean a beast or fowl which dies of natural causes, without being slaughtered or hunted by humans. The qur'ānic verse offers five classifications of dead animals:

1   the strangled
2   those beaten to death
3   those fallen from a height
4   those gored by other animals
5   those partly eaten by wild animals.

Scholars have elaborated a number of reasons for this prohibition. The animal might have died of some disease. Muslims should intend to kill an animal for food, offering it to God, and not thoughtlessly make use of a deceased creature. By this ban, God makes food available to other animals and birds.

Islamic law has exempted fish, whales and other sea-creatures from the category of dead animals. The Qur'ān says: 'The game of the sea is permitted to you and so is its food' (5: 99). Traditions relate that the Prophet allowed dead food that comes from the sea to be eaten. One story tells of a group of Muslims sent by Muhammad to ambush his enemies. They became very hungry, until the sea threw out a huge, dead whale. They ate its meat, rubbed their bodies with its fat, and, when one of its ribs was fixed over the ground, a rider passed beneath it (Bukhari, in Khan 1984, vol. 7: 293 f.). Many jurists have amplified this permission so that all marine creatures, those which live in the sea and cannot survive outside it, are *111alāl*. It does not matter whether they are taken from the water dead or living, whole or in bits, whether they are caught by a Muslim or someone else.

The interdict on blood is interpreted to mean flowing blood, which was felt by jurists to be repugnant and injurious to health. The law does not forbid eating blood that remains in the animal after the flow has ceased.

Pork is outlawed on a number of grounds. It is dangerous to eat in hot climates, where it quickly goes off. It is regarded as an unclean animal, eating filth and offal, and so its meat is repugnant to decent people. Some scholars have claimed that it incites those who eat it to shameful and lustful thoughts.

Finally, God's name must be invoked when the animal is slaughtered. The man who slits its throat says: *bi-smillāhi, allāhu akbar*, 'in the name of God, God is most great'. It is not acceptable to invoke the name of an idol, as Arab polytheists at the time of Muhammad did. Nor is it all right to say nothing. Killing an animal for food is a devotional act. God gave humans control over all the earth, subjecting animals to them, and allowing them to take an animal's life for food. Pronouncing God's name while killing the creature is a reminder of God's permission and ultimate control over all things.

Other than these four categories, all food can be eaten and enjoyed (2: 172; 6: 119). Indeed, the emphasis in Islam is upon what can be eaten and enjoyed, rather than on what is forbidden. Only a few things are forbidden. There is no virtue in exceedingly strict food laws.

[. . .]

Nowadays, the ritual killing of animals is condemned by many non-Muslim individuals and groups. The bottom line for Muslims is that it is commanded by God, and this order counts for more than the opinions of others. Muslims are not mawkish about such matters. Islam began on the fringes of the desert, where staying alive was the pre-eminent concern of many people, and meat was regarded by them as a necessity, not a luxury. Most Muslims today live in relatively poor countries, where survival counts for more than middle-class values, which can seem excessively indulgent. Islam gives human beings power over, and responsibility for, animals, which should be treated with kindness and consideration, but which, by God's permission, provide food, clothing and transport.

[. . .]

Bibliography

Khalid, F. with O'Brien, J. (eds) (1992) *Islam and Ecology*, London, Cassell.

Khan, M.M. (ed.) (1984) *Sahah Al-Bukhari*, vols 1–9, Delhi, Kitab Bhavan.

Nasr, S.H. (1976) *Islamic Science: an illustrated study*, London, Thames and Hudson.

Robson, J.R. (1970 edn) *Mishkat al-Masibih*, vols 1–2, Lahore, Muhammad Ashraf.

Siddiqi, A.H. (ed.) (1977) *Sahih Muslim*, vols 1–4, Delhi, Kitab Bhavan.

Yusuf Ali, A. (1975 edn) *The Holy Qu'rān: Text, Translation and Commentary*, Leicester, Islamic Foundation.

FURTHER READING

Benson, G. John and Rollin, Bernard E. (eds.) (2004) *The Well-Being of Farm Animals: Challenges and Solutions,* Ames, IA: Blackwell.

Gregory, N.G. with a chapter by Grandin, T. (1998) *Animal Welfare and Meat Science,* New York: CABI Publishing.

Kaiser, Matthias and Lien, Marianne Elisabeth (eds.) (2006) *Ethics and the Politics of Food: Preprints of the 6th Congress of the European Society for Agricultural and Food Ethics,* The Netherlands: Wageningen.

Kalechofsky, R. (ed.) (1992) *Judaism and Animal Rights: Classical and Contemporary Responses,* Marblehead, MA: Micah.

Kunkel, H.O. (2000) *Human Issues in Animal Agriculture,* College Station, Texas: Texas A & M University Press.

Masri, A.B.A. (1989) *Animals in Islam,* Hants, England: The Athene Trust.

Rosati, A., Tewolde, A. and Mosconi, C. (eds.) (2005) *Animal Production and Animal Science Worldwide,* The Netherlands: Wageningen.

Sapontzis, S.F. (ed.) (2004) *Food for Thought: The Debate over Eating Meat,* New York: Prometheus.

Scully, Matthew (2002) *Dominion: The Power of Man, the Suffering of Animals, and the Call to Mercy,* New York: St. Martin's Griffin.

Turner, Jacky and D'Silva, Joyce (eds.) (2006) *Animals, Ethics and Trade: The Challenge of Animal Sentience,* London: Earthscan.

Walters, K.S. and Portmess, L. (eds.) (1999) *Ethical Vegetarianism: From Pythagorus to Peter Singer,* Albany: SUNY.

Webster, John (2005) *Animal Welfare: Limping Towards Eden: A Practical Approach to Redressing the Problem of our Dominion over the Animals,* Oxford, UK: Blackwell.

STUDY QUESTIONS

1   Do you agree with George that vegetarianism is an aesthetic or personal health choice rather than a moral duty? Explain your reasoning. In your view, does George satisfactorily address the issues raised by Adams?

2   Rachels provides an argument for vegetarianism and concludes that it is not an all-or-nothing proposition. Do you agree that we should "focus on the things that cause the most misery"? In your view, what are these things?

3   The passages by Solomon and Forward represent the use of a sacred text as prescribing moral behavior toward animals. The passages by Fuchs and Linzey represent a reformist approach toward sacred texts. In your view, what is the proper relationship between a sacred text such as the Bible or the Koran and contemporary moral practice?

4   Do you agree with DeGrazia's evaluation of the harm caused to human beings by factory farming? How might this harm be diminished?

5   Based on DeGrazia's discussion of family farming and your own views, what sort of animal food production (if any) is morally acceptable?

6   Is it morally acceptable to eat fish or other seafood? Why or why not?

7   Evaluate the points made by the Animal Agriculture Alliance and by Davis. How does this information affect your current view on the morality of meat-eating?

8   Rollin and Appleby address the current issues in agricultural animal welfare. They point to economic and ideological reasons for the general inattention to these issues. Which reasons do you believe to be most important?

9   Which diet(s) do you believe to be morally acceptable: that of an omnivore, a vegan, or a vegetarian? What special circumstances might affect your answer?

Animal experimentation

INTRODUCTION TO PART FIVE

I N THIS PART, we focus on some ethical issues in the context of using nonhuman animals as research subjects in laboratory and fieldwork, and as teaching subjects in educational institutions. Collectively the authors address a wide range of ethical issues on these topics.

In addressing traditional use of animals in laboratory studies, Tom Regan clearly articulates why no animals should be used in harmful experiments. In particular, reducing their value to human utility does not afford them the respect they deserve. David DeGrazia explores areas in which those opposing ("animal advocates") and those favoring ("biomedicine") use of animals in scientific research might find common ground; he also identifies several topics on which agreement appears unlikely. Responding to DeGrazia's description of the biomedicine perspective, Baruch A. Brody articulates a position supporting animal research based on the special obligations humans have to each other, including members of their families, communities, and species.

Lynda Birke addresses the conflicting metaphors associated with laboratory rodents, ranging from potent icons of scientific research to "not quite animals." Barbara Orlans assesses the range of legal protection governing animal-based research and briefly summarizes the international variation in levels of animal protection. She also addresses the role of ethical criteria, including animal-harm scales as a means to assess animal research.

On the issue of using animals for educational purposes, Jonathan Balcombe summarizes twenty-eight recommendations advocated by the Humane Society of the United States to reduce both the numbers of animals used in schools, as well as the suffering experienced by these animals. Andrew Petto and Karla Russell explore an innovative strategy of fully involving students in making ethical decisions about using animals in their classrooms, including what work can be conducted appropriately as well as the sources, care, and disposal of all animals used.

Ben Minteer and James Collins call for bringing ethicists, scientists, and biodiversity managers together for ethical analysis and problem-solving in ecological field studies. Stephen T. Emlen provides a case study of some of the issues involved with field work as he responds to criticisms of an earlier study; in his defense he also raises some broader ethical issues associated with ecological field work.

LABORATORY STUDIES

Chapter 39

Tom Regan

THE CASE FOR ANIMAL RIGHTS

In *The Case for Animal Rights,* Regan makes a case for total elimination of harmful use of animals in research. He argues that animals have a value that cannot be reduced to their utility to others and that their use in research fails to treat them with the respect they are due.

[. . .]

ROUTINE USE OF animals in research assumes that their value is reducible to their possible utility relative to the interests of others. The rights view rejects this view of animals and their value, as it rejects the justice of institutions that treat them as renewable resources. They, like us, have a value of their own, logically independently of their utility for others and of their being the object of anyone else's interests. To treat them in ways that respect their value, therefore, requires that we *not* sanction practices that institutionalize treating them as if their value was reducible to their possible utility relative to our interests. Scientific research, when it involves routinely harming animals in the name of possible "human and humane benefits," violates this requirement of respectful treatment. Animals are not to be treated as mere receptacles or as renewable resources. Thus does the practice of scientific research on animals violate their rights. Thus ought it to cease, according to the rights view. It is not enough first conscientiously to look for nonanimal alternatives and then, having failed to find any, to resort to using animals.[1] Though that approach is laudable as far as it goes, and though taking it would mark significant progress, it does not go far enough. It assumes that it is all right to allow practices that use animals as if their value were reducible to their possible utility relative to the interests of others, provided that we have done our best not to do so. The rights view's position would have us go further in terms of "doing our best." *The best we can do in terms of not using animals is not to use them.* Their inherent value does not disappear just because we have failed to find a way to avoid harming them in pursuit of our chosen goals. Their value is independent of these goals and their possible utility in achieving them.

[. . .]

The rights view does not oppose using what is learned from conscientious efforts to treat a sick animal (or human) to facilitate and improve the treatment tendered other animals (or humans). In *this* respect, the rights view raises no objection to the "many human and humane benefits" that flow from medical science and the research with which it is allied. What the rights view opposes are practices that cause intentional harm to laboratory animals (for example, by means of burns, shock, amputation, poisoning, surgery, starvation, and sensory deprivation) preparatory to "looking for something that just might yield some human or humane benefit." Whatever benefits happen to accrue from such a practice are irrelevant to assessing its tragic injustice. Lab animals are not our tasters; we are not their kings.

The tired charge of being antiscientific is likely to fill the air once more. It is a moral smokescreen. The rights view is not against research on animals, if this research does not harm these animals or put them at risk of harm. It is apt to remark, however, that this objective will not be accomplished merely by ensuring that test animals are anesthetized, or given postoperative drugs to ease their suffering, or kept in clean cages with ample food and water, and so forth. For it is not only the pain and suffering that matters—though they certainly matter—but it is the *harm* done to the animals, including the diminished welfare opportunities they endure as a result of the deprivations caused by the surgery, *and* their untimely death. It is unclear whether a *benign* use of animals in research is possible or, if possible, whether scientists could be persuaded to practice it. That being so, and given the serious risks run by relying on a steady supply of human volunteers, research should take the direction away from the use of any moral agent or patient. If nonanimal alternatives are available, they should be used; if they are not available, they should be sought. That is the moral challenge to research, given the rights view, and it is those scientists who protest that this "can't be done," in advance of the scientific commitment to try—not those who call for the exploration—who exhibit a lack of commitment to, and belief in, the scientific enterprise—who are, that is, antiscientific at the deepest level.

[. . .]

The rights view, then, is far from being antiscientific. On the contrary, as is true in the case of toxicity tests, so also in the case of research: it calls upon scientists *to do science* as they redirect the traditional practice of their several disciplines away from reliance on "animal models" toward the development and use of nonanimal alternatives. All that the rights view prohibits is science that violates individual rights. If that means that there are some things we cannot learn, then so be it. There are also some things we cannot learn by using humans, if we respect their rights. The rights view merely requires moral consistency in this regard.

The rights view's position regarding the use of animals in research cannot be fairly criticized on the grounds that it is antihumanity. The implications of this view in this regard are those that a rational human being should expect, especially when we recall that nature neither respects nor violates our rights. Only moral agents do; indeed, only moral agents *can*. And nature is not a moral agent. We have, then, no basic right against nature not to be harmed by those natural diseases we are heir to. And neither do we have any basic right against humanity in this regard. What we do have, at this point in time at least, is a right to fair treatment on the part of those who have voluntarily decided to offer treatment for these maladies, a right that will not tolerate the preferential treatment of some (e.g., Caucasians) to the detriment of others (e.g., Native Americans). The right to fair treatment of our naturally caused maladies (and the same applies to mental and physical illnesses brought on by human causes e.g. pollutants) is an *acquired right* we have against those moral agents who acquire the duty to offer fair treatment because they voluntarily assume a role within the medical profession. But those in this profession, as well as those who do research in the hope that they might improve health care, are not morally authorized to override the *basic rights* of others in the process—rights others have, that is, independently of their place in any institutional arrangement and independently of any voluntary act on the part of anyone. And yet that is what is annually done to literally millions of animals whose services, so to speak, are enlisted in the name of scientific research, including that research allied with medical science. For this research treats these animals as if their value is reducible to their possible utility relative to the interests of others. Thus does it routinely violate their basic right to respectful treatment. Though those of us who today are to be counted among the beneficiaries of the human benefits obtained from this research in the past might stand to lose some future benefits, at least in the short run, if this research is stopped, the rights view will not be satisfied with anything less than its total abolition. Even granting that we face greater prima facie harm than laboratory animals presently endure if future harmful research on these animals is stopped, and even granting that the number of humans and other animals who stand to benefit from allowing this practice to continue exceeds the number of animals used in it, this practice remains wrong because unjust.

[. . .]

A final objection urges that the rights view cannot have any principled objection to using mammalian animals for scientific purposes generally, or in research in particular, before these animals attain the degree of physical maturity that makes it reasonable to view them as subjects-of-a-life, in the sense that is central to the rights view. For example, use of newly born mammalian animals must stand outside the scope of the proscriptions issued by the rights view.

This objection is half right. *If certain conditions are met*, the rights view could sanction the scientific use of mammalian animals at certain stages of their physical development. As has been remarked on more than one occasion in the preceding, however, where one draws the line, both as regards what species of animals contain members who are subjects-of-a-life and as regards when a given animal acquires the abilities necessary for being such a subject, is controversial. We simply do not know, with anything approaching certainty, exactly where to draw the line in either case. Precisely because we are so palpably ignorant about a matter so fraught with moral significance, we ought to err on the side of caution, not only in the case of humans but also in the case of animals. Though during the earliest stages of development it is most implausible to regard a fetal mammalian animal as conscious, sentient, and so on, it becomes increasingly less implausible as the animal matures physically, acquiring the physical basis that underlies consciousness, perception, sentience, and the like. Although throughout the present work attention has been for the most part confined to normal mammalian animals, aged one or more, it does not follow that animals less than one year of age may be treated in just any way we please. Because we do not know exactly where to draw the line, it is better to give the benefit of the doubt to mammalian animals less than one year of age who have acquired the physical characteristics that underlie one's being a subject-of-a-life. The rights view's position concerning those animals, then, is against their use for scientific purposes.

There are Kantian-like grounds that strengthen the case against using newborn and soon-to-be born mammalian animals in science. To allow the routine use of these animals for scientific purposes would most likely foster the attitude that animals are just "models," just "tools," just "resources." Better to root out at the source, than to allow to take root, attitudes that are inimical to fostering respect for the rights of animals. Just as in the analogous areas of abortion and infanticide in the case of humans, therefore, the rights view favors policies that foster respect for the rights of the individual animal, even if the creation of these attitudes requires that we treat some animals who may not have rights as if they have them.

Finally, even in the case of mammalian animals in the earliest stages of fetal development, the rights view does not issue a blank check for their use in science. For though, on the rights view, we do not owe a duty of justice to these fetuses, we do owe justice to those animals who would be enlisted to produce them in the number researchers are likely to desire. Were mature animals used as "fetal machines" and, as a result, were they housed in circumstances conducive to their reproducing at the desired rate, it is most unlikely that the rights of these mature animals would be respected. For example, it is very unlikely that *these* animals would be provided with a physical environment conducive to the exercise of their preference autonomy, or one that was hospitable to their social needs; and it is equally unlikely that they would avoid having their life brought to an untimely end, well in advance of their having reached a condition where killing them could be defended on grounds of preference-respecting or paternalistic euthanasia. Once they had stopped reproducing, they would likely be killed. To the extent that we have reason to believe that these mature mammals would be treated as if they had value only relative to human purposes, to that extent the rights view would oppose the scientific use of fetal mammalian animals, not because these latter have rights that would be violated, but because this would be true in the case of the mature animals used as breeders. Those who would use mammalian animals in the earliest stages of their fetal development, then, may do so, according to the rights view, but only if they ensure *both* that (1) the lab animals used to produce the fetuses are treated with the respect they are due *and* that (2) reliance on mammalian fetuses does not foster beliefs and attitudes that encourage scientists to use mature mammalian animals for scientific purposes, including research. It is unclear that science could institute policies that satisfied the first condition. It is clear that a policy could be introduced that satisfied the second. This would be for science to cease using mammalian animals who are subjects-of-a-life in ways that harm them directly, or that put them at risk of harm, or that foster an environment in which their harm is allowed. That is a policy the rights view could allow,[2] but one science has yet to adopt.

[. . .]

The use of animals in science was the final area for which the major implications of the rights view were set forth. For a variety of reasons, the rights view takes a principled stand against the use of animals in educational contexts, in toxicity testing of new products and drugs, and in research. Dissection of living mammalian animals in high school and university lab sections is to be condemned, all the more so since the relevant knowledge obtained by this practice can be secured without engaging in it. To anesthetize these animals will not avoid the rights view's condemnation, since it is the animals' untimely death, not merely their pain or suffering, that is morally relevant. To the objection that most animals used in high school and university labs are not mammals and so do not fall within the scope of the principles advocated by the rights view, it was noted that (1) where we draw the line between those animals that are, and those that are not, subjects-of-a-life is far from certain, so that we ought to err on the side of caution, giving animals the benefit of the doubt in many cases, including the present one, and that (2) routine use of even non-mammalian animals fosters beliefs and attitudes that contribute to acceptance of acts and institutions that fail to show respect for, and thus violate the rights of, mammalian animals. Both reasons provide compelling grounds for discontinuing standard lab sections in high school and university courses in the life sciences.

[. . .]

The same call is made by the rights view when it comes to the use of animals in research. To harm animals on the chance that something beneficial for others might be discovered is to treat these animals as if their value were reducible to their possible utility relative to the interests of others, and to do this, not to a few, but to many millions of animals is to treat the affected animals as if they were a renewable resource— renewable because replaceable without any wrong having been done, and a resource because their value is assumed to be a function of their possible utility relative to the interests of others. *The rights view abhors the harmful use of animals in research and calls for its total elimination.* Because animals have a kind of value that is not the same as, is not reducible to, and is incommensurate with their having utility relative to the interests of others, because they are owed treatment respectful of their value as a matter of strict justice, and because the routine use of laboratory animals in research fails to treat these animals with the respect they are due, their use in research is wrong because unjust. The laudatory achievements of science, including the many genuine benefits obtained for both humans and animals, do not justify the unjust means used to secure them. As in other cases, so in the present one, the rights view does not call for the cessation of scientific research. Such research should go on—but not at the expense of laboratory animals. The overarching challenge of scientific research is the same as the similar challenge for toxicology and all other facets of the scientific enterprise: to do science without violating anyone's rights, be they human or animal.

The rights view does not deny in principle that use of mammalian embryos in science, including research, might be justified. Fetuses in the early stages of their development can be used, according to the rights view, if we have good reason to believe that allowing their use will not foster beliefs and attitudes that sanction treatment violative of the rights of those animals who have rights, in particular the rights of those animals used as breeders. Though it is not clear that this challenge can be met, it is clear that it cannot be met if scientists themselves continue to use *both* mammalian embryos *and* mature animals. An essential part of the evidence necessary to justify use of mammalian embryos, therefore, consists in scientists not using mature mammalian animals (or other mammalian animals who, though less than one year old, ought to be given the benefit of the doubt). As such, the rights view will take seriously a defense of the use of mammalian embryos only when scientists themselves cease using mammals at later stages of their life. But not until then. The onus of proof is where it belongs.[3]

Notes

1   This is the view recommended in Jamieson and Regan, "On the Ethics of the Use of Animals in Science" (see chap. 8, n. 23). In disassociating myself from this earlier view, I speak only for myself. I am in no position to speak for Professor Jamieson.

2   Note that replies analogous to those given in the last three paragraphs could be given in response to the view that it is all right to eat farm animals or to hunt or trap wild animals less than one year old, including those who are newly born and soon-to-be-born. Concerning farm animals first, since (1) we do not know with anything approaching certainty that these young animals are not subjects-of-a-life; since (2) whether they are or not, we want to encourage the development of beliefs and attitudes that lead to the respectful treatment of those animals who are subjects-of-a-life; and (3) since the adult animals who would be used as "fetal machines" in agriculture would in all likelihood not be treated with the respect they are due, the rights view opposes this defense of meat eating. Points (1) and (2) apply to hunting and trapping newly born wild animals and are the principal (but not the only) sorts of reason the rights view gives against the slaughter of newly born seals, for example. The rights view offers reasons of the same kind in support of its condemnation of killing nonmammalian animals (e.g., birds and fish of all kinds) in the name of sport or in pursuit of a profit. Even assuming birds and fish are not subjects-of-a-life, to allow their recreational or economic exploitation is to encourage the formation of habits and practices that lead to the violation of the rights of animals who are subjects-of-a-life.

3   Comments by Henry Shapiro, professor of psychology at Bates College, helped me see the relevance and importance of the idea of risk-taking in assessing the morality of our treatment of animals. Helpful discussions about rights with my colleague Donald Van De Veer inched me forward to a better understanding of what rights are.

Chapter 40

David DeGrazia

THE ETHICS OF ANIMAL RESEARCH: WHAT ARE THE PROSPECTS FOR AGREEMENT?

DeGrazia assesses the perspectives of those favoring, and those opposed to, animal research. He identifies ten principles where he believes these two perspectives can agree, and at least four additional issues he believes will serve as continuing points of difference. He then makes ten suggestions for continuing to build on the various points of agreement.

FEW HUMAN USES of nonhuman animals (hereafter simply "animals") have incited as much controversy as the use of animals in biomedical research. [. . .] However, a healthy number of individuals within these two communities offer the possibility of a more illuminating discussion of the ethics of animal research.

One such individual is Henry Spira. Spira almost single-handedly convinced Avon, Revlon, and other major cosmetics companies to invest in the search for alternatives to animal testing. Largely due to his tactful but persistent engagement with these companies – and to their willingness to change – many consumers today look for such labels as "not tested on animals" and "cruelty free" on cosmetics they would like to buy.

Inspired by Spira, this paper seeks common ground between the positions of biomedicine and animal advocates. (The term "biomedicine" here refers to everyone who works in medicine or the life sciences, not just those conducting animal research. "Animal advocates" and "animal protection community" refer to those individuals who take a major interest in protecting the interests of animals and who believe that much current usage of animals is morally unjustified. The terms are not restricted to animal activists, because some individuals meet this definition without being politically active in seeking changes.) The paper begins with some background on the political and ethical debate over animal research. It then identifies important points of potential agreement between biomedicine and animal advocates; much of this common ground can be missed due to distraction by the fireworks of the current political exchange. Next, the paper enumerates issues on which continuing disagreement is likely. Finally, it concludes with concrete suggestions for building positively on the common ground.

Background on the debate over animal research

What is the current state of the debate over the ethics of animal research? Let us begin with the viewpoint of biomedicine. It seems fair to say that biomedicine has a "party line" on the ethics of animal research, conformity to which may feel like a political litmus test for full acceptability within the professional community. According to this party line, animal research is clearly justified because it is necessary for medical progress and therefore human health – and those who disagree are irrational, antiscience, misanthropic "extremists" whose views do not deserve serious attention. (Needless to say, despite considerable conformity, not everyone in biomedicine accepts this position.)

In at least some countries, biomedicine's leadership apparently values conformity to this party line more than freedom of thought and expression on the animal research issue. (In this paragraph, I will refer to the American situation to illustrate the point.) Hence the unwillingness of major medical journals, such as *JAMA* and *The New England Journal of Medicine*, to publish articles that are highly critical of animal research. Hence also the extraordinary similarity I have noticed in pro-research lectures by representatives of biomedicine. I used to be puzzled about why these lectures sounded so similar and why, for example, they consistently made some of the same philosophical and conceptual errors (such as dichotomizing animal welfare and animal rights, and taking the latter concept to imply identical rights for humans and animals). But that was before I learned of the "AMA [American Medical Association] Animal Research Action Plan" and the AMA's "White Paper." Promoting an aggressive pro-research campaign, these documents encourage AMA members to say and do certain things for public relations purposes, including the following: "Identify animal rights activists as anti-science and against medical progress"; "Combat emotion with emotion (e.g [sic], 'fuzzy' animals contrasted with 'healing' children)"; and "Position the biomedical community as moderate – centrist – in the controversy, not as a polar opposite."[1]

It is a reasonable conjecture that biomedicine's party line was developed largely in reaction to fear – both of the most intimidating actions of some especially zealous animal advocates, such as telephoned threats and destruction of property, and of growing societal concern about animals. Unfortunately, biomedicine's reaction has created a political culture in which many or most animal researchers and their supporters do not engage in sustained, critical thinking about the moral status of animals and the basic justification (or lack thereof) for animal research. Few seem to recognize that there is significant merit to the opposing position, fewer have had any rigorous training in ethical reasoning, and hardly any have read much of the leading literature on animal ethics. The stultifying effect of this cultural phenomenon hit home with me at a small meeting of representatives of biomedicine, in which I had been invited to explain "the animal rights philosophy" (the invitation itself being exceptional and encouraging). After the talk, in which I presented ideas familiar to all who really know the literature and issues of animal ethics, several attendees pumped my hand and said something to this effect: "This is the first time I have heard such rational and lucid arguments for the other side. I didn't know there were any."

As for the animal protection community, there does not seem to be a shared viewpoint except at a very general level: significant interest in animal welfare and the belief that much current animal usage is unjustified. Beyond that, differences abound. For example, the Humane Society of the United States opposes factory farming but not humane forms of animal husbandry, rejects current levels of animal use in research but not animal research itself, and condemns most zoo exhibits but not those that adequately meet animals' needs and approximate their natural habitats.[2] Meanwhile, the Animal Liberation Front, a clandestine British organization, apparently opposes all animal husbandry, animal research, and the keeping of zoo animals.[3] Although there are extensive differences within the animal protection community, as far as our paper topic goes, it seems fair to say that almost everyone in this group opposes current levels of animal research.

That's brief sketch of the perspectives of biomedicine and animal advocates on the issue of animal research. What about the state of animal ethics itself? The leading book-length works in this field exhibit a near consensus that the status quo of animal usage is ethically indefensible and that at least significant reductions in animal research are justified. Let me elaborate.

Defending strong animal rights positions in different ways, Tom Regan and Evelyn Pluhar advocate abolition of all research that involves harming animals.[4] Ray Frey and Peter Singer, by contrast, hold the use of animals to the very stringent utilitarian standard – accepting only those experiments whose benefits (factoring in the likelihood of achieving them) are expected to outweigh the harms and costs involved –

where the interests of animal subjects (e.g., to avoid suffering) are given the same moral weight that we give comparable human interests.[5]

Without commiting either to a strong animal rights view or to utilitarianism, my own view shares with these theories the framework of equal consideration for animals: the principle that we must give equal moral weight to comparable interests, no matter who has those interests.[6] But unlike the aforementioned philosophers, I believe that the arguments for and against equal consideration are nearly equal in strength. I therefore have respect for progressive views that attribute moral standing to animals without giving them fully equal consideration. The unequal consideration view that I find most plausible gives moral weight to animals' comparable interests in accordance with the animals' cognitive, affective, and social complexity – a progressive, "sliding scale" view. Since I acknowledge that I might be mistaken about equal consideration, my approach tracks the practical implications both of equal consideration and of the alternative just described.

Arguing from pluralistic frameworks, which are developed in different ways, Steve Sapontzis, Rosemary Rodd, and Bernard Rollin support relatively little animal research in comparison with current levels.[7] Drawing significantly from feminist insights, Mary Midgley presents a view whose implications seem somewhat more accepting of the status quo of animal research but still fairly progressive.[8] Of the leading contributors to animal ethics, the only one who embraces the status quo of animal research and does not attribute significant moral status to animals is Peter Carruthers.[9] (It is ironic that while biomedicine characterizes those who are critical of animal research as irrational "extremists," nearly all of the most in-depth, scholarly, and respected work in animal ethics supports such a critical standpoint at a general level.)

In discussing the prospects for agreement between biomedicine and animal advocates, I will ignore political posturing and consider only serious ethical reflection. In considering the two sides of this debate, I will assume that the discussants are morally serious, intellectually honest, reflective, and well informed both about the facts of animal research and about the range of arguments that come into play in animal ethics. I will not have in mind, then, the researcher who urges audiences to dismiss "the animal rights view" or the animal activist who tolerates no dissent from an abolitionist position. The two representative interlocutors I will imagine differ on the issue of animal research, but their views result from honest, disciplined, well-informed ethical reflection. Clearly, their voices are worth hearing.

Points on which the biomedical and animal protection communities can agree

The optimistic thesis of this paper is that the biomedical and animal protection communities can agree on a fair number of important points, and that much can be done to build upon this common ground. I will number and highlight (in bold) each potential point of agreement and then justify its inclusion by explaining how both sides can agree to it, without abandoning their basic positions, and why they should.

1. The use of animals in biomedical research raises ethical issues. Today very few people would disagree with this modest claim, and any who would are clearly in the wrong.[10] Most animal research involves harming animal subjects, provoking ethical concerns, and the leading goal of animal research, promotion of human health, is itself ethically important; even the expenditure of taxpayers' money on government-funded animal research raises ethical issues about the best use of such money. Although a very modest assertion, this point of agreement is important because it legitimates a process that is sometimes resisted: *discussing* the ethics of animal research.

[. . .]

2. Sentient animals, a class that probably includes at least the vertebrates, deserve moral protection. Whether because they have moral status or because needlessly harming them strongly offends many people's sensibilities, sentient animals deserve some measure of moral protection. By way of definition, sentient animals are animals endowed with any sorts of feelings: (conscious) sensations such as pain or emotional states such as fear or suffering. [. . .] Lately, strong support has emerged for the proposition that at least vertebrate animals are very likely sentient.[11] This proposition is implicitly endorsed by major statements of principles regarding the humane use of research animals, which often mention that they apply to vertebrates.[12] (Hereafter, the unqualified term "animals" will refer to sentient animals in particular.)

3. Many animals (at the very least, mammals) are capable of having a wide variety of aversive mental states, including pain, distress (whose forms include discomfort, boredom, and fear), and suffering. In biomedical circles, there has been some resistance to attributing suffering to animals, so government documents concerned with humane use of animals have often mentioned only pain, distress, and discomfort.[13] Because "suffering" refers to a *highly* unpleasant mental state (whereas pain, distress, and discomfort can be mild and transient), the attribution of suffering to animals is morally significant.

[. . .]

4. Animals experiential well-being (quality of life) deserves protection. If the use of animals raises ethical issues, meaning that their interests matter morally, we confront the question of what interests animals have.

[. . .]

Another difficult issue is whether animal well-being can be understood *entirely* in terms of experiential well-being – quality of life in the familiar sense in which (other things equal) pleasure is better than pain, enjoyment better than suffering, satisfaction better than frustration. Or does the exercise of an animal's natural capacities count positively toward well-being, even if quality of life is not enhanced?

[. . .]

Whatever the answers to these and other issues connected with animal well-being, what is not controversial is that animals have an interest in experiential well-being, a good quality of life. That is why animal researchers are normally expected to use anesthesia or analgesia where these agents can reduce or eliminate animal subjects' pain, distress, or suffering.

5. Humane care of highly social animals requires extensive access to conspecifics. It is increasingly appreciated that animals have different needs based on what sorts of creatures they are. Highly social animals, such as apes, monkeys, and wolves, need social interactions with conspecifics (members of their own species). Under normal circumstances, they will develop social structures, such as hierarchies and alliances, and maintain long-term relationships with conspecifics. Because they have a strong instinct to seek such interactions and relationships, depriving them of the opportunity to gratify this instinct harms these animals.

[. . .]

6. Some animals deserve very strong protections (as, for example, chimpanzees deserve not to be killed for the purpose of population control). Biomedicine and animal advocates are likely to disagree on many details of ethically justified uses of animals in research, as we will see in the next section. Still, discussants can agree that there is an obligation to protect not just the experiential well-being, but also the lives, of at least some animals. This claim might be supported by the (controversial) thesis that such animals have life interests. On the other hand, it might be supported by the goal of species preservation (in the case of an endangered species), or by the recognition that routine killing of such animals when they are no longer useful for research would seriously disturb many people.[14]

[. . .]

7. Alternatives should now be used whenever possible and research on alternatives should expand. Those who are most strongly opposed to animal research hold that alternatives such as mathematical models, computer simulations, and in vitro biological systems should replace nearly all use of animals in research. (I say "nearly all" because, as discussed below, few would condemn animal research that does not harm its subjects.) Even for those who see the animal research enterprise more favorably, there are good reasons to take an active interest in alternatives. Sometimes an alternative method is the most valid way to approach a particular scientific question; often alternatives are cheaper.[15] Their potential for reducing animal pain, distress, and suffering is, of course, another good reason. Finally, biomedicine may enjoy stronger public support if it responds to growing social concern about animal welfare with a very serious investment in nonanimal methods. This means not just using alternatives wherever they are currently feasible, but also aggressively researching the possibilities for expanding the use of such methods.

8. Promoting human health is an extremely important biomedical goal. No morally serious person would deny the great importance of human health, so its status as a worthy goal seems beyond question. What is sometimes forgotten, however, is that a worthy goal does not automatically justify all the means thereto. Surely it would be unethical to force large numbers of humans to serve as subjects in highly painful, eventually lethal research, even if its goal were to promote human health. The controversy over animal research focuses not on the worthiness of its principal goal – promoting human health – but rather on the means, involving animal subjects, taken in pursuit of that goal.

9. There are some morally significant differences between humans and other animals. [. . .] First, the principle of respect for autonomy applies to competent adult human beings, but to very few if any animals. This principle respects the self-regarding decisions of individuals who are capable of autonomous decisionmaking and action. Conversely, it opposes paternalism toward such individuals, who have the capacity to decide for themselves what is in their interests. Now, many sentient beings, including human children and at least most nonhuman animals, are not autonomous in the relevant sense and so are not covered by this principle.[16] Thus it is often appropriate to limit their liberty in ways that promote their best interests, say, preventing the human child from drinking alcohol, or forcing a pet dog to undergo a vaccination. We might say that where there is no autonomy to respect, the principles of beneficence (promoting best interests) and respect for autonomy cannot conflict; where there is autonomy to respect, paternalism becomes morally problematic.

Second, even if sentient animals have an interest, other things [being] equal, in staying alive (as I believe), the moral presumption against taking human life is stronger than the presumption against killing at least some animals. [. . .] Leaders in animal ethics consistently support – though in interestingly different ways – the idea that, ordinarily, killing humans is worse than killing at least some animals who have moral status.

[. . .]

10. Some animal research is justified. [. . .] Let me explain by responding to the three likeliest reasons some animal advocates might take exception to the claim.

First, one might oppose all uses of animals that involve *harming them for the benefit of others* (even other animals) – as a matter of absolute principle – and overlook the fact that some animal research does not harm animal subjects at all. Although such nonharmful research represents a tiny sliver of the animal research enterprise, it exists. Examples are certain observational studies of animals in their natural habitats, some ape language studies, and possibly certain behavioral studies of other species that take place in laboratories but do not cause pain, distress, or suffering to the subjects. And if nonsentient animals cannot be harmed (in any morally relevant sense), as I would argue, then any research involving such animals falls under the penumbra of nonharming research.

Moreover, there is arguably no good reason to oppose research that imposes only *minimal* risk or harm on its animal subjects. After all, minimal risk research on certain human subjects who, like animals, cannot consent (namely, children) is permitted in many countries; in my view, this policy is justified. Such research might involve a minuscule likelihood of significant harm or the certainty of a slight, transient harm, such as the discomfort of having a blood sample taken.

Second, one might oppose all animal research because one believes that none of it actually benefits human beings. Due to physical differences between species, the argument goes, what happens to animal subjects when they undergo some biomedical intervention does not justify inferences about what will happen to humans who undergo that intervention. Furthermore, new drugs, therapies, and techniques must always be tried on human subjects before they can be accepted for clinical practice. Rather than tormenting animals in research, the argument continues, we should drop the useless animal models and proceed straight to human trials (with appropriate protections for human subjects, including requirements for informed or proxy consent).

Although I believe a considerable amount of current animal research has almost no chance of benefitting humans, I find it very hard to believe that no animal research does.[17] While it is true that human subjects must eventually be experimented on, evidence suggests that animal models sometimes furnish data relevant to human health.[18] If so, then the use of animal subjects can often decrease the risk to human subjects who are eventually involved in experiments that advance biomedicine, by helping to weed out harmful interventions. This by itself does not justify animal research, only the claim that it sometimes benefits humans (at the very least human subjects themselves and arguably the beneficiaries of biomedical advances as well).

Note that even if animal research never benefited humans, it would presumably sometimes benefit conspecifics of the animals tested, in sound veterinary research.[19] It can't be seriously argued that animal models provide no useful information about animals! Moreover, in successful *therapeutic* research (which aims to benefit the subjects themselves), certain animals benefit directly from research and are not simply used to benefit other animals. For that reason, blanket opposition to animal research, including the most promising therapeutic research in veterinary medicine, strikes me as almost unintelligible.

Almost unintelligible, but not quite, bringing us to the third possible reason for opposing all animal research. It might be argued that, whether or not it harms its subjects, all animal research involves *using animals (without their consent) for others' benefit*, since – qua research – it seeks *generalizable knowledge*. But to use animals in this way reduces them to *tools* (objects to be used), thereby *disrespecting* the animals.

Now the idea that we may never use nonconsenting individuals, even in benign ways, solely for the benefit of others strikes me as an implausibly strict ethical principle. But never mind. The fact that some veterinary research is intended to benefit the subjects themselves (as well as other animals or humans down the road) where no other way to help them is known shows that such research, on any reasonable view, is *not* disrespectful toward its subjects. Indeed, in such cases, the animals *would* consent to taking part, if they could, because taking part is in their interests. I fully grant that therapeutic veterinary research represents a minuscule portion of the animal research conducted today. But my arguments are put forward in the service of a goal that I think I have now achieved: demonstrating, beyond a shadow of a doubt, that some animal research is justified.

[. . .]

Points on which agreement between the two sides is unlikely

Even if biomedicine and the animal protection community approach the animal research issue in good faith, become properly informed about animal ethics and the facts of research, and so forth, they are still likely to disagree on certain important issues. After all, their basic views differ. It may be worthwhile to enumerate several likely points of difference.

First, disagreement is likely on the issue of *the moral status of animals in comparison with humans*. While representatives of biomedicine may attribute moral status to animals, they hold that animals may justifiably be used in many experiments (most of which are nontherapeutic and harm the subjects) whose primary goal is to promote human health. But for animal advocates, it is not at all obvious that much animal research is justified. This suggests that animal advocates ascribe higher moral status to animals than biomedicine does.[20]

Second, disagreement is likely to continue on the issue of *the specific circumstances in which the worthy goal of promoting human health justifies harming animals*. Biomedicine generally tries to protect the status quo of animal research. Animal advocates generally treat not using animals in research as a presumption, any departures from which would require careful justification. Clearly, animal advocates will have many disagreements with biomedicine over when it is appropriate to conduct animal research.

Third, in a similar vein, continuing disagreement is likely on the issue of *whether current protections for research animals are more or less adequate*. Biomedicine would probably answer affirmatively, with relatively minor internal disagreements over specific issues (e.g., whether apes should ever be exposed to diseases in order to test vaccines). Animal advocates will tend to be much more critical of current protections for research animals. They will argue, for example, that animals are far too often made to suffer in pursuit of less than compelling objectives, such as learning about behavioral responses to stress or trauma.

In the United States, critics will argue that the basic principles that are supposed to guide the care and use of animals in federally funded research ultimately provide very weak protection for research animals. That is because the tenth and final principle begins with implicit permission to make exceptions to the previous nine: "Where exceptions are required in relation to the provisions of these Principles, . . ."[21] Since no limits are placed on permissible exceptions, this final principle precludes any absolute restraints on the harm that may be inflicted on research animals – an indefensible lack of safeguards from the perspective of animal advocates. (Although similar in several ways to these American principles, including some ways animal advocates would criticize, the *International Guiding Principles for Biomedical Research Involving Animals* avoids this pitfall of a global loophole. One of its relatively strong protections is Principle V: "Investigators and other personnel should never fail to treat animals as sentient, and should regard their proper care and use and the avoidance or minimization of discomfort, distress, or pain as ethical imperatives."[22])

Although protections of research animals are commonly thought of in terms of preventing unnecessary pain, distress, and suffering, they may also be thought of in terms of protecting animal life. A fourth likely area of disagreement concerns *whether animal life is morally protectable*. Return to a question raised earlier: whether a contented animal in good health is harmed by being painlessly killed in her sleep. Since government documents for the care and use of research animals generally require justification for causing pain or distress to animal subjects, but no justification for painless killing, it seems fair to infer that biomedicine generally does not attribute life interests to animals. Although I lack concrete evidence, I would guess that most animal advocates would see the matter quite differently, and would regard the killing of animals as a serious moral matter even if it is justified in some circumstances.

The four issues identified here as probable continuing points of difference are not intended to comprise an exhaustive list. But they show that despite the fact that the biomedical and animal protection communities can agree on an impressive range of major points, given their basic orientations they cannot be expected to agree on every fundamental question. Few will find this assertion surprising. But I also suggest, less obviously, that even if both sides cannot be entirely right in their positions, differences that remain after positions are refined through honest, open-minded, fully educated inquiry can be reasonable differences.

What can be done now to build upon the points of agreement

Let me close with a series of suggestions offered in the constructive yet critical-minded spirit of Henry Spira's work for how to build on the points of agreement identified above. For reasons of space, these suggestions will be stated somewhat tersely and without elaboration.

First, biomedical organizations and leaders in the profession can do the following: openly acknowledge that ethical issues involving animals are complex and important; educate themselves or acquire education about the ethical issues; tolerate views departing from the current party line; open up journals to more than one basic viewpoint; and stop disseminating one-sided propoganda.

Second, the more "militant" animal advocates can acknowledge that there can be reasonable disagreement on some of the relevant issues and stop intimidating people with whom they disagree.

Third, biomedicine can openly acknowledge, as NASA recently did in its principles, that animals can suffer and invite more serious consideration of animal suffering.

Fourth, the animal protection community can give credit to biomedicine where credit is due – for example, for efforts to minimize pain and distress, to improve housing conditions, and to refrain from killing old chimpanzees who are no longer useful for research but are expensive to maintain.

Fifth, animal researchers and members of animal protection organizations can be required by their organizations to take courses in ethical theory or animal ethics to promote knowledgeable, skilled, broad-minded discussion and reflection.

Sixth, the animal protection community can openly acknowledge that some animal research is justified (perhaps giving examples to reduce the potential for misunderstanding).

Seventh, more animal research ethics committees can bring aboard at least one dedicated animal advocate who (unlike mainstream American veterinarians) seriously questions the value of most animal research.

Eighth, conditions of housing for research animals can be improved – for example, with greater enrichment and, for social animals, more access to conspecifics.

Ninth, all parties can endorse and support the goal of finding ways to *eliminate* animal subjects' pain, distress, and suffering.[23]

Tenth, and finally, governments can invest much more than they have to date in the development and use of alternatives to animal research, and all parties can give strong public support to the pursuit of alternatives.

Notes

1   American Medical Association. Animal Research Action Plan. (June 1989), p. 6. See also American Medical Association. White Paper (1988).

2   See the Humane Society of the United States (HSUS). *Farm Animals and Intensive Confinement*. Washington, D.C.: HSUS, 1994; *Animals in Biomedical Research*. Washington, D.C.: HSUS, revised 1989; and *Zoos: Information Packet*. Washington, D.C.: HSUS, 1995.

3   Animal Liberation Front. Animal Liberation Frontline Information Service: the A.L.F. Primer. (website)

4   Regan T. *The Case for Animal Rights*. Berkeley: University of California Press, 1983; Pluhar E. *Beyond Prejudice*. Durham, North Carolina: Duke University Press, 1995.

5   Frey R. G. *Interests and Rights*. Oxford: Clarendon, 1980; Singer P. *Animal Liberation*, 2nd ed. New York: New York Review of Books, 1990.

6   DeGrazia D. *Taking Animals Seriously*. Cambridge: Cambridge University Press, 1996.

7   Sapontzis S. F. *Morals, Reason, and Animals*. Philadelphia: Temple University Press, 1987; Rodd R. *Biology, Ethics, and Animals*. Oxford: Clarendon, 1990; and Rollin B. E. *Animal Rights and Human Morality*, 2nd ed. Buffalo, New York: Prometheus, 1992.

8   Midgley M. *Animals and Why They Matter*. Athens, Georgia: University of Georgia Press, 1983.

9   Carruthers P. *The Animals Issue*. Cambridge: Cambridge University Press, 1992.

10   In a letter to the editor, Robert White, a neurosurgeon well known for transplanting monkeys' heads, asserted that "[a]nimal usage is not a moral or ethical issue . . ." (White R. Animal ethics? [letter]. *Hastings Center Report* 1990;20(6):43). For a rebuttal to White, see my letter, *Hastings Center Report* 1991;21(5):45.

11   See Rose M., Adams D. Evidence for pain and suffering in other animals. In: Langley G., ed. *Animal Experimenta-*

tion. New York: Chapman and Hall, 1989; 42–71; Smith J. A., Boyd K. M. *Lives in the Balance*. Oxford: Oxford University Press, 1991: ch. 4. See also note 7 Rodd 1990: ch. 3; and DeGrazia D., Rowan A. Pain, suffering, and anxiety in animals and humans. *Theoretical Medicine* 1991;12:193–211.

12   See, e.g., U.S. Government Principles for the Utilization and Care of Vertebrate Animals Used in Testing, Research, and Training. In: National Research Council. *Guide for the Care and Use of Laboratory Animals*. Washington, D.C.: National Academy Press, 1996: 117–8; National Aeronautics and Space Administration. *Principles for the Ethical Care and Use of Animals*. NASA Policy Directive 8910.1, effective 23 March 1998; and Council for International Organizations of Medical Sciences. *International Guiding Principles for Biomedical Research Involving Animals*. Geneva: CIOMS, 1985:18.

13   See note 12, National Research Council 1996; CIOMS 1985.

14   Note that the term "euthanasia," which means a death that is good for the one who dies, is inappropriate when animals are killed because they are costly to maintain or for similarly human-regarding reasons.

15   See note 11, Smith, Boyd 1991: 334.

16   See note 6, DeGrazia 1996: 204–10.

17   That is, except those humans who benefit directly from the conduct of research, such as researchers and people who sell animals and laboratory equipment.

18   See, e.g., note 11, Smith, Boyd 1991: ch. 3.

19   Peter Singer reminded me of this important point.

20   The idea of differences of moral status can be left intuitive here. Any effort to make it more precise will invite controversy. (See note 6, DeGrazia 1996: 256–7.)

21   See note 12, National Research Council 1996: 118.

22   See note 12, CIOMS 1985: 18.

23   This is the stated goal of a new initiative of the Humane Society of the United States, which expects the initiative to expand to Humane Society International.

Chapter 41

Baruch A. Brody

DEFENDING ANIMAL RESEARCH: AN INTERNATIONAL PERSPECTIVE

Brody compares and contrasts legal and attitudinal differences towards the use of experimental animals between the U.S. and Europe. He believes that as humans we have special obligations to ourselves, our family members, our friends, and our fellow citizens, that go beyond our obligations to members of other species. Those special obligations lend support to human use of animals in research.

Introduction

I N A RECENT article, "The Ethics of Animal Research," philosopher David DeGrazia asks the very important question of whether or not there is room for at least some agreement between "biomedicine" and "animal advocates" on the issue of animal research.[1] This is an important question, but one on which we are unlikely to make any progress until the contents of both positions are clearly understood. This essay is devoted to better articulating the position which supports animal research, the position that DeGrazia labels the "biomedicine" position; I leave the analysis of the animal-advocacy position for other occasions.

My reason for adopting this strategy is as follows: There has been in recent years an extensive philosophical discussion of various versions of the animal-advocacy position, and the variations on this position have been analyzed by several authors.[2] Much less attention has been paid to development of the pro-research position. DeGrazia himself describes the articulation of that position in negative terms:

> It seems fair to say that biomedicine has a "party line" on the ethics of animal research, conformity to which may feel like a political litmus test for full acceptability within the professional community. According to this party line, animal research is clearly justified because it is necessary for medical progress and therefore human health. . . . [M]any or most animal researchers and their supporters do not engage in sustained, critical thinking about the moral status of animals and the basic justification (or lack thereof) for animal research.[3]

Whether or not this is fully accurate, this perception of the status of the pro-research position seems to be widespread. It therefore seems important to attempt a better articulation and defense of a reasonable version of that position.

What do I mean by a reasonable pro-research position on animal research, the type of position that I wish to defend? I understand such a position to be committed to at least the following propositions:

1   Animals have interests (at least the interest in not suffering, and perhaps others as well), which may be adversely affected either by research performed on them or by the conditions under which they live before, during, and after the research.

2 The adverse effect on animals' interests is morally relevant, and must be taken into account when deciding whether or not a particular program of animal research is justified or must be modified or abandoned.

3 The justification for conducting a research program on animals that would adversely affect them is the benefits that human beings would receive from the research in question.

4 In deciding whether or not the research in question is justified, human interests should be given greater significance than animal interests.

Some preliminary observations about these propositions are in order. Propositions (1) and (2) commit the reasonable pro-research position to a belief that animal interests are morally relevant, and that the adverse impact of animal research on these interests should not be disregarded. This distinguishes the position I am trying to articulate from positions (such as the classical Cartesian position) that maintain that animals have no interests or that those interests do not count morally.[4] In light of their ability to experience pleasures and pains, it is implausible to deny animals interests or to give those interests no moral significance at all. Propositions (3) and (4) distinguish the pro-research position from the animal-advocacy position by insisting that it is permissible for animals to be adversely affected by legitimate research—they do not have a trumping right not to be used adversely for human benefit.[5] Toward this end, proposition (4) asserts that human benefits have greater significance than harms to animals in determining the legitimacy of the research, as animals have less moral significance than humans.[6]

What is the nature of humans' greater significance? [. . .] The reasonable pro-research position is actually a family of positions that differ both theoretically (on their conceptions of the nature of the priority of human interests) and practically (on the resulting types of justified research). What is needed first is a full examination of this family of positions, an examination that explores the plausibility of different views on the priority of human interests. Once we can identify the more plausible of these views, we can begin the attempt to justify one of them.

[. . .]

The U.S. and European positions

The best statement of the U.S. policy on animal research is found in a 1986 document from the Public Health Service entitled "U.S. Government Principles for the Utilization and Care of Vertebrate Animals Used in Testing, Research, and Training."[7] [. . .] I want to highlight what is and is not present in the U.S. principles; they call upon researchers to:

- use the "minimum number [of animals] required to obtain valid results"
- consider alternatives such as "mathematical models, computer simulation, and in vitro biological systems"
- practice the "avoidance or minimization of discomfort, distress, or pain when consistent with sound scientific practices"
- use "appropriate sedation, analgesia, or anesthesia"
- kill animals painlessly after experiments when the animals "would otherwise suffer severe or chronic pain or distress that cannot be relieved"
- provide living conditions that are "appropriate for their species and contribute to their health and comfort."[8]

All of these principles are compatible with the familiar program, developed by W. M. S. Russell and R. L. Burch in 1959, which has come to be called the 3R program.[9] This program calls for the *replacement* of animal experimentation with other research methods where possible; this is why the U.S. principles request the consideration of alternative research techniques. The program also calls for the *reduction* of the number of animals used; hence, the U.S. principles state a commitment to minimizing the number of animals used as much as is consistent with obtaining scientifically valid results. Finally, the 3R program calls for *refining* both the conduct of the research and the environment in which the research animals live; the aim is to minimize the animals' pain and suffering. This is why the U.S. principles talk about pain relief, euthanasia when necessary, and species-appropriate living conditions.

[. . .]

All of this is very much in the spirit of propositions (1) and (2) of my account of the responsible pro-research position on animal research. It is because animals have interests that may be adversely affected by the research—interests that count morally—that we are called upon to replace, reduce, and refine the use of animals in research. Proposition (3) is also explicitly part of the U.S. principles, which assert that "procedures involving animals should be designed and performed with due consideration of their relevance to human or animal health, the advancement of knowledge, or the good of society."[10] But what about proposition (4)? What sort of greater significance are human interests given over animal interests in the U.S. regulations?

In fact, that question is never directly addressed. This stands in sharp contrast to the U.S. regulations on human subjects in research. These regulations require the minimization of risks, but they also require that the minimized risks be "reasonable in relation to anticipated benefits, if any, to subjects, and the importance of the knowledge that may reasonably be expected to result."[11] Nothing like these strictures occurs in the U.S. principles and regulations governing animal research.

Something else can be inferred from the wording of the U.S. principles on animal research. Discomfort, distress, or pain of the animals should be minimized "when consistent with sound scientific practices." The number of animals used should be minimized to "the number required to obtain valid results." Unrelieved pain necessary to conduct the research is acceptable so long as the animal is euthanized after or during the procedure.[12] What this amounts to in the end is that whatever is required for the research is morally acceptable; the 3R principles are to be applied only as long as they are compatible with maintaining scientifically valid research. There is never the suggestion that the suffering of the animal might be so great—even when it is minimized as much as possible while still maintaining scientific validity—that its suffering might outweigh the benefits from the research. Even when these benefits are modest, the U.S. principles never morally require the abandonment of a research project.

This is a position that gives very strong priority to human interests over animal interests, especially to the human interests that are promoted by scientific research using animals as subjects. Given the wide variety of such animal research projects, which range from developing and testing new life-saving surgical techniques to developing and testing new cosmetics, the human interests that are given this strong priority over animal interests are very diverse.

[. . .]

The European approach to these issues is quite different. [. . .] [T]he Europeans find these principles incomplete and augment them with additional principles that give greater significance to animal interests by disallowing some research because the costs to the animal subjects are too great.

The 1986 Directive from the Council of the European Communities (now called the European Community) [. . .] stipulates that the relevant authority "shall take appropriate judicial or administrative action if it is not satisfied that the experiment is of sufficient importance for meeting the essential needs of man or animal."[13] This is a limited provision, as it involves animal interests outweighing human interests only in the case of severe and prolonged pain. The provision does not clearly specify what the "appropriate" actions in such cases are, and it implies that even severe and prolonged pain is acceptable if the research is of "sufficient importance." Nevertheless, it goes beyond anything in the U.S. principles and regulations by giving somewhat greater significance to animal interests.

This approach is developed in national legislation in several European countries. [. . .] While these national provisions are both broader in application and more explicit in their implications than is the E.C. directive, they still leave a crucial question unanswered.

Consider a whole continuum of positions, ranging from the claim that animal interests and human interests count equally (the *equal-significance position*) to the claim that even though one may attend to animal interests, human interests always take precedence (the *human-priority position*). In moving from the first position to the second, the significance of animal interests in comparison to human interests is gradually discounted. The intermediate positions move from those that discount animal interests modestly (and are therefore increasingly close to the equal-significance position) to those that discount them significantly (and are therefore increasingly close to the human-priority position). The U.S. position is the human-priority end of this continuum, and the animal rights movement's rejection of proposition (4) of the pro-research position puts that movement at the other end. The European positions are somewhere in-between, but there is no way to tell from their regulations where they are on the continuum.

[. . .]

[P]roposition (4) of the pro-research position, the principle of giving greater significance to human interests than to animal interests, is understood very differently in the United States and in Europe. For the United States, the proposition means that human interests in conducting research always take lexical priority over animal interests. This lexical priority is not characteristic of the European positions, which allow for some balancing of interests. But there is no evidence that the Europeans have rejected proposition (4) and adopted the equal-significance position that is characteristic of the animal-advocacy position. They seem, instead, to have adopted some discounting of animal interests in comparison to human interests, with the crucial discount rate being undetermined.

Are there any reasons for supposing that a lexical-priority approach is a more plausible articulation of proposition (4) than is a discounting approach (or vice versa)? This is the question I will examine in the next section of this essay.

Lexical priority versus discounting

There are two arguments I will consider in this section. The first argument, in favor of a lexical-priority approach to proposition (4), argues that the cross-species comparison of interests that is presupposed by the discounting approach is meaningless, and that the discounting approach must, therefore, be rejected in favor of a lexical-priority approach. The second argument, in favor of the discounting approach, asserts that lexical priority is incompatible with significant components of the 3R program, and that pro-research adherents of that program must, therefore, adopt the discounting approach.

[. . .]

The challenge of the first argument . . . has two components. The first component is the claim that there is no basis for placing animal pain and pleasure (if one defines 'interests' hedonistically) or the satisfaction of animal preferences (if one defines 'interests' in terms of preference-satisfaction) on a common metric with human pain and pleasure or human preference-satisfaction. I will refer to this first component of the challenge as the *incommensurability claim*. The second component is the claim that even if there were such a basis, we do not know enough about the sensations or preferences of animals to make such comparisons; I will call this component the *cross-species ignorance claim*.

[. . .]

[E]ven if one accepts this two-pronged challenge, it does not necessarily follow from this that we should adopt the lexical-priority approach to proposition (4). Those who oppose the lexical-priority approach on the intuitive grounds that it does not give sufficient significance to animal interests can simply conclude that some other approach, one which captures those intuitions, must be developed. All that does follow from the first argument's two-pronged challenge is that the lexical-priority approach to proposition (4) is more plausible than is the discounting approach (which, if the incommensurability claim is correct, has no plausibility at all).

But should we grant the challenge's components? I see no reason to accept the incommensurability claim. Human pain and pleasure is quantified on the basis of dimensions such as duration and intensity; animal pain and pleasure can also be quantified on those dimensions. Duration is certainly not conceptually different for different species, and no reason has been offered for why we should treat intensity as differing conceptually for different species. Thus, there is a basis for a common metric for hedonistic comparisons of the impact of research on human and animal interests. I think that the same is true for preference-satisfaction comparisons of the impact of research on human and animal interests, but it is hard to say that with the same degree of confidence, since we still have little understanding of the dimensions on which we quantify preference-satisfaction.

[. . .]

The cross-species ignorance claim is more serious. [. . .] This issue has been faced most directly by a working party of the British Institute of Medical Ethics (an unofficial but respected interdisciplinary group of scholars) in a report published in 1991.[14] The working party's members took note of the fact that the quantification of interests on a common metric seems to be required by the British Animals Act, and that there are doubts as to whether this can be done. In response to these concerns, they make two observations, which seem to me to be the beginning of a good answer to these concerns. First, they note that not every reliable judgment must be based upon a mathematically quantifiable balancing of values: it is often sufficient to have confidence in "the procedures which have been used to arrive at that judgment, . . . upon whether [researchers] have taken into account all the known morally relevant factors, and whether they have shown themselves responsive to all the relevant moral interests."[15] Second, the working party claims that it is possible to identify the moral factors relevant to the assessment of animal research and the degree to which they are present in a given case; this knowledge would allow for reliable judgments about the moral acceptability of proposed protocols for animal research. In fact, the working party goes on to create such a scheme and to show by examples how it might work in a reliable fashion.[16]

[. . .]

This brings me to the second argument of this section. There are, this second argument suggests, reasons for doubting that the lexical-priority approach is compatible with even the 3R approach to the reasonable pro-research position. Satisfying the 3R principles, even if done in a way that allows the proposed research to proceed, involves considerable costs. These costs mean that other human interests, in research or otherwise, will not be satisfied. If human interests truly take precedence over animal interests, this seems inappropriate. A lexical-priority approach, then, cannot support even the now widely accepted 3R approach to protecting animal interests; this, it seems to me, makes the lexical-priority interpretation of proposition (4) an implausible version of the pro-research position.

Consider, for example, that aspect of the 3R program's refinement plank that calls for modifications in the environment in which research animals live in order to make those environments species-appropriate and not a source of distress or discomfort. Those modifications, now widely required throughout the world, are often quite costly, and these costs are passed on to the researchers as a cost of doing research. Some poorly funded research never takes place because these extra costs cannot be absorbed. Other, better funded, research projects go on, but require extra funding. This extra funding may mean that other research projects are not funded, or that the funded research will not be as complete as originally envisioned. To avoid these outcomes, extra funding would have to be provided to research efforts in general, but this would compromise funding for other human interests. In these ways and others, the adoption of this aspect of the 3R program is not compatible with maintaining the full research effort and/ or with meeting other human interests. Hence, human interests are not being given full priority, contrary to the basic premise of the lexical-priority position.

None of this, of course, is a problem for the discounting approach unless the discounting of animal interests is so significant that it approaches the lexical-priority position. If the discounting is not this extensive—if animal interests count a lot, even if not as much as the interests of humans—then it seems reasonable to suppose that the interests of the animals in living in a species-appropriate environment are sufficiently great to justify imposing these burdens on the research effort.

In short, then, those who want a reasonable pro-research position to incorporate the widely adopted 3R program should find the discounting approach more plausible than the lexical-priority approach. But what could possibly justify such a discounting of animal interests? We turn to that question in the next section.

The rationale for discounting

Before attempting to develop an approach to justifying discounting, it is important to be clear as to exactly what is claimed by discounting. [. . .] Discounting [. . .] is the claim that the same unit of pain counts less, morally, if it is experienced by an animal than it would if it is experienced by a human being, not because of the human's associated experiences but simply because of the species of the experiencer. Discounting directly denies the equal consideration of interests across species.

I am emphasizing this point to make it clear that *discounting* of animal interests is radically different than the *preference* for human interests that even animal advocates such as Peter Singer accept.

[. . .]

But for Singer and other supporters of the equal-significance position, all that follows from this is that humans may suffer more and that this quantitative difference in the amount of suffering is morally relevant. What discounting affirms, and what they deny, is that even when there is no quantitative difference in the amount of suffering, the human suffering counts more morally.

With this understanding of the claim of discounting, we can easily understand why many would find its claims ethically unacceptable. Why should the moral significance of the same amount of suffering differ according to the species of the sufferer if there are no associated additional differences?

[. . .]

I see no reasonable alternative for the adherent of the discounting position except to challenge the whole idea that we are, in general, morally committed to an equal consideration of interests. This is a plausible move, since equal consideration of interests has come under much challenge in contemporary moral philosophy, totally independently of the debate over the moral significance of the interests of animals. I would trace the beginning of the idea that we should not accept equal consideration of interests to W. D. Ross's contention, as early as 1930, that we have special obligations to ourselves, our family members, our friends, our fellow citizens, etc.[17] Recognizing these special obligations means, of course, giving higher priority to the interests of some (those to whom we have special obligations) than to the interests of others (those to whom we do not). Equally important is the emphasis in the 1980s on the idea that we have a morally permissible prerogative to pay special attention to our own interests in the fulfillment of some of our central projects.[18] Recognizing this prerogative means giving a higher priority to at least some of our interests over the interests of others. Each of these ideas, in separate ways, presupposes a denial of equal consideration of interests, and both are best understood as forms of the discounting of certain interests.

How should we understand the special obligations that we have? One good way of understanding them is that we have special obligations to some people to give a higher priority to their interests than we do to those of others. This may call upon us to promote their interests even at the cost of not promoting the greater interests of strangers. Note, by the way, that it is implausible to see this as a form of lexical priority favoring the interests of those people to whom we have special obligations. When their interests at stake are modest, and when the conflicting interests of strangers are great, we are not obliged to put the interests of those to whom we are specially obligated first; we may not even be permitted to do so. It would appear, then, that special obligations might well be understood as involving a requirement that we discount the interests of strangers when they compete with the interests of those to whom we have special obligations.

The same approach sheds much light upon our prerogative to pursue personal goals even at the cost of not aiding others (or even hindering them) in the pursuit of their interests. This is, once again, hardly a lexical priority. No matter how important a goal may be to me, I may be morally required to put it aside if the competing interests of others are especially great. Our prerogative may best be understood as involving only a permission to discount the interests of strangers when they compete with our interests in attaining our goals.

Note, by the way, that this means that we really have a whole family of theories about special obligations and about personal prerogatives. Different theories will differ on the acceptable discount rate.

Looked at from this perspective, the discounting approach to the animal research position no longer seems anomalous. Rather than involving a peculiar discounting of the interests of animals, in violation of the fundamental moral requirement of the equal consideration of interests, the approach represents one more example of the discounting of the interests of strangers, a feature that is pervasive in morality.

We can see another way of developing this point if we consider the difference between the following two questions:

1A   Why should the interests of my children count more than do those of others?
1B   Why should the interests of my children count more for me than do those of others?

The former question, asked from an impersonal perspective, is unanswerable. The latter question, which is asked from the personal perspective, is answerable. The same needs to be said about the following pair of questions:

2A   Why should the interests of humans count more than do those of animals?
2B   Why should the interests of humans count more for human beings than do those of animals?

As with the previous pair of questions, what is unanswerable from one perspective may be very answerable from the other perspective.

There is, of course, an important difference between special obligations, even to oneself, and personal prerogatives. The former *require* you to give certain interests priority, while the latter just *permit* you to do so. This difference is helpful in explaining a certain ambiguity in the reasonable pro-research position. While its adherents often seem to be attempting to justify only the permissibility of animal research, they sometimes talk as though they are arguing that such research is required. Consider, for example, the standard Food and Drug Administration requirement that new drugs be tested on animals before they are tested on humans. I would suggest the following: when adherents justify the permissibility of animal research, they are invoking the analogy to prerogatives, but when they want to require this research, they are invoking the analogy to special obligations. On the latter view, we have an obligation to human beings, as part of our special obligations to members of our species, to discount animal interests in comparison to human interests by testing new drugs on animals first.

This defense of animal research on the ground of species solidarity has been developed elsewhere by the British philosopher Mary Midgley, although her emphasis seems to me to be more on psychological bonds and less on the logical structure of the consideration of interests in moral thought.[19]

[. . .]

Further issues

[. . .]

There remain, of course, several aspects of the discounting approach that require fuller development. An appropriate discount rate is yet to be determined; the process of cross-species comparisons of gains and losses in interests must be refined; and the conditions under which discounting is merely permissible as opposed to when it is mandatory need to be defined.

In addition to these necessary developments, there is a fundamental challenge that still needs to be confronted. It is a variation on the issue of equal consideration of interests, and it requires much further theoretical reflection. [. . .] Discounting the interests of members of other races or of the other gender seems to be part of the wrong of racism and sexism. Might one not argue that discounting the interests of the members of other species is equally wrong? That is the wrong of "speciesism."

This point can also be put as follows: The charge of speciesism might just be the charge that discounting animal interests is wrong because it violates the principle of equal consideration of interests. This charge is severely weakened by the challenge to the legitimacy of the equal-consideration principle. But the charge might be the very different claim that discounting animal interests is wrong because it is a *discriminatory* version of discounting; this charge is not challenged by the general challenge to the principle of the equal consideration of interests. This version of the charge is articulated by DeGrazia in a critique of Midgley:

> Can appeals to social bondedness in justifying partiality towards humans be convincingly likened
> to family-based preferences but contrasted with bigotry? Why are racism and sexism unjustified,
> if species-based partiality is justified?[20]

It is of interest and importance to note that the examples DeGrazia invokes are of partiality toward family members, on the one hand, and toward members of our race or gender, on the other hand. Left out are partiality toward fellow citizens, fellow believers, and fellow members of an ethnic group. All of these seem, *as long as they are not excessive*, to be within the bounds of acceptable partiality toward our fellows and of acceptable discounting of the interests of others. This is why it is appropriate that so much charitable giving is organized by religions and national groups. This is, also, why it is appropriate that nearly all redistribution is done at the individual-country level rather than at the international level. These examples are important in reminding us that the rejection of the equal consideration of interests principle in common morality is very broad, and covers large-scale groups that are more analogous to species than to family members. Of course, this by itself is not a refutation of the discrimination charge leveled against the pro-research position. It does, however, place the position in the company of partialities and discountings that are widely accepted in moral theory and in public policy.

What my arguments foreshadow is the need for further ethical reflection on these controversial issues. We have seen that morality can legitimately involve the discounting of even other people's interests when one acts from a prerogative or a special obligation. A question that requires much more exploration is what differentiates legitimate discounting from discrimination? Only an answer to this question can fully justify the discounting-based, reasonable pro-research position that I have articulated in this essay.

Notes

1   David DeGrazia, "The Ethics of Animal Research," *Cambridge Quarterly of Healthcare Ethics* 8, no. 1 (Winter 1999): 23–34.

2   For summaries of the extensive literature, see, for example, Tom Beauchamp, "The Moral Standing of Animals in Medical Research," *Law, Medicine, and Health Care* 20, nos. 1–2 (Spring/Summer 1992): 7–16; and David DeGrazia, "The Moral Status of Animals and Their Use in Research: A Philosophical Review," *Kennedy Institute of Ethics Journal* 1, no. 1 (March 1991): 48–70.

3   DeGrazia, "The Ethics of Animal Research," 23–4.

4   For a discussion of Descartes's position on these issues, see F. Barbara Orlans, *In the Name of Science: Issues in Responsible Animal Experimentation* (New York: Oxford University Press, 1993), 3–4.

5   This is in opposition to the position articulated in Tom Regan, *The Case for Animal Rights* (Berkeley: University of California Press, 1983).

6   This is in opposition to the position articulated in Peter Singer, *Practical Ethics*, 2nd ed. (New York: Cambridge University Press, 1993).

7   National Institutes of Health—Office for Protection from Research Risks (NIH-OPRR), *Public Health Service Policy on Humane Care and Use of Laboratory Animals* (Bethesda, MD: NIH-OPRR, 1986).

8   NIH-OPRR, *Policy on Humane Care and Use of Laboratory Animals*, i.

9   W. M. S. Russell and R. L. Burch, *The Principles of Humane Experimental Technique* (London: Methuen, 1959).

10   NIH-OPRR, *Policy on Humane Care and Use of Laboratory Animals*, principle 2, p. i.

11   45 C.F.R. sec. 46.111 (1999).

12   NIH-OPRR, *Policy on Humane Care and Use of Laboratory Animals*, principles 3, 4, and 6, p. i.

13   Council Directive of November 24, 1986, art. 12, sec. 2, reprinted in Baruch Brody, *The Ethics of Biomedical Research: An International Perspective* (New York: Oxford University Press, 1998), 237–40.

14   Jane A. Smith and Kenneth M. Boyd (eds), *Lives in the Balance: The Ethics of Using Animals in Biomedical Research— The Report of a Working Party of the Institute of Medical Ethics* (Oxford: Oxford University Press, 1991).

15   Ibid., 141.

16   Ibid., 141–6.

17   W. D. Ross, *The Right and the Good* (Oxford: Oxford University Press, 1930), chap. 2.

18   Samuel Scheffler, *The Rejection of Consequentialism* (Oxford: Oxford University Press, 1982), chap. 3.

19   Mary Midgley, *Animals and Why They Matter* (Harmondsworth, Middlesex: Penguin Books, 1983).

20   David DeGrazia, *Taking Animals Seriously: Mental Life and Moral Status* (New York: Cambridge University Press, 1996), 64.

Chapter 42

Lynda Birke

WHO—OR WHAT—ARE THE RATS (AND MICE) IN THE LABORATORY?

Birke traces two intertwined strands of metaphors associated with laboratory rodents. The first focuses on the idea of medical/scientific progress; in this context she views the metaphor of laboratory rodents epitomizing medical triumph or serving as helpers or saviors. In the second strand she addresses the ambiguous status of laboratory rodents who simultaneously are animals and not animals (data). She argues that because of these ambiguous meanings, rodent laboratories are doubly "othered" – first in the way that animals so often are made other to humans and then other in the relationship of the laboratory animal to other animals.

[. . .]

IN THIS PAPER, drawing on representations from various sources, I want to explore some of the meanings of "the laboratory rat" or "laboratory rodent." I start with the rats, partly because I am particularly familiar with them in laboratories. However, much of the argument applies also to mice, and I draw also on representations of more generalized rodents. At times, these two different kinds of rodent may be practically interchangeable in their use in scientific research and their histories as specifically bred animals in the laboratory.

I will begin by sketching how wild rats, harbingers of disease, came to be bred specifically for scientific research (alongside mice); in doing so, they took on new significance. Now, the image of a laboratory rodent conveys a great deal—not so much about the animal who, in many ways, remains a mystery—but about the processes and values of scientific research. The rodent has become a potent icon. So, my main concern here is to examine some of the referents of this icon in order to ask, what does the laboratory rodent signify for us? What does this rodent tell us about the practices of science? And what can we learn from these meanings about human relationships to animals?

Creating the rodent in the laboratory

Even when they are white, laboratory rats—the animals bred by the million for various kinds of experimental purposes—are derived from brown rats (Rattus norvegicus). [. . .]

There were, then, two stages in the development of laboratory rodents as we know them. The first was the process of bringing them from the wild into the labs, via the fanciers' breeding rooms. This entailed a transformation from wild to tame and from animals exemplifying certain species (such as brown Norway rats) to multitudes of different types, colors, and strains. It also, of course, required a transformation from being an animal that routinely elicited reactions of disgust and horror from people to becoming an animal that would represent medical progress. The second stage was what might be called a process of greater industrialization, in which lab animals become standardized and increasingly became a production process and part of the apparatus of science (Logan, 2001; Shapiro, 2002). Although many of these generalizations apply also to other species, it was rodents who became particularly standardized and who now exemplify "laboratory work".

Rodents were chosen for early experimental studies for several reasons. They bred quickly, so facilitating studies of inheritance; they were altricial (i.e. they are born immature), so facilitating studies of early development; and rats particularly were thought to have strong sex drives, important to early twentieth century studies of reproduction and sexual behavior (Burian, 1993; Logan, 2001). By the 1930s, rats had become "a kind of generic standard in research on physiology and behavior", so displacing earlier emphases on species diversity in physiological studies (Logan, p. 287). On the contrary, just as studies increasingly came to focus on only one species, more and more subdivisions within that species emerge—a new, but more controlled, form of diversity. [. . .]

Changing meanings

We may shun the sewer rat or try to exterminate rats and mice from our houses and farms, but, in the laboratory, rats mean a great deal to us. I want now to explore some of these meanings, in two broad, overlapping areas. First, how we understand the laboratory rat today draws on widespread cultural metaphors of medical triumph and the conquest of disease. Laboratory rats may be represented in ways that signify not only successes in conquering diseases but also the triumph of specifically scientific (Western) medicine. Global science relies on a global production of standardized rodents. Yet, rodents in such iconography often seem to become our saviors, standing in for us in their suffering. These metaphors in turn structure how we think about both scientific laboratories and rodents.

Secondly, the transformation into "the" laboratory rat has entailed a loss of the rat understood as an animal or as exemplar of a species. Rather, the laboratory rat has become transformed from what most of us would commonly call an animal into something that stands in for data and scientific analysis. I will explore each of these in turn.

Global conquest: the triumphant rodent

Mapping metaphors in biology are now ubiquitous. We can map the genome of mouse or human, although we have long been mapping the body of rodents through dissection guides and other reference books (there are various "Atlases of the Rat Brain"). We can also map the distribution of hormone receptors, say, within that brain.

It is not, of course, only rodents who are thus "mapped"; indeed, much of the impetus for genome mapping comes from the efforts to sequence the DNA in the human genome. In practice, however, there are very few organisms around whose genomes there is such intensive mapping effort; among these select few are laboratory rats and mice. The significance of their genomes does not lie in understanding them as exemplars of their species but on their role as stand-ins for human disease. Mice and rats attain a particular status thereby; their chromosomes can be compared directly to maps of human ones in relation to the genetics of specific diseases.[1]

Mapping metaphors can be added to Arluke's (1994) classification of three types of images used in advertising laboratory animals: the "classy chemical;" consumer goods (both of which construct the lab animal as analogous to a chemical reagent) or the "team player" in which, typically, cartoon animals are portrayed as "helping" in the service of medicine. Inevitably, the huge interest now in genome mapping is mirrored in advertising. In several advertisements for laboratory rats and mice,[2] the rodent's image appears either juxtaposed to images of gel electrophoresis (the typical "bars" of DNA analysis), or next to a map. In one advertisement,[3] one-half of the (white) rat is shown photographically, but the image merges and its hindquarters appear as diagrammatic isoclines—the mapped rat body.

The mapping metaphor is, as Haraway (1997) has pointed out, a highly pervasive—and persuasive—one, drawing on imagery and rhetoric of global conquest and triumph. Haraway analyzes an image used by New England Biolabs, depicting a young white woman superimposed on a map of Africa, noting the connotations of gender and race. A rat image nearby a world map similarly advertises Charles River Laboratories' (1997) advertisement for the International Genetic Standard CD Rat. This rat is not morphing into the map, as the woman/Africa image does but stands nearby, the image representing the availability of "total uniformity" for the "global research community." This, then, is the globalized research tool, and the lab rodent thus comes to symbolize the victory of Western science and medicine, not only over disease (the claim that is explicitly made) but also—more implicitly—over other knowledge and forms of medicine.

While scientific medicine becomes triumphant in advertising images and associated narratives, the laboratory animal becomes a willing participant. Arluke (1994) noted the theme of lab animals as "helpers" or "team players" in advertising. This may take the form of jokey, cartoon, characters, such as the cartoon mouse dressed as a corporate executive (or perhaps a desk scientist) that was used to advertise GenPharm's transgenic mice. Or, it may portray the animal as victor, as in one of the advertisements Arluke analyzed. [. . .]

The image of laboratory rodents as saviors is a powerful one and figures in many images. One review (Paigen, 1995) of "mouse models" began with a heading: "A Miracle Enough: the Power of Mice," going on to outline ways in which mice are the ideal animals for genomic research, potential saviors who will lead to new therapies and means of preventing human disease. It is the creature, the text claims, to whom we turn experimentally because it is "so important in reaching an understanding of ourselves."

This kind of rhetoric draws partly on the arguments put forward by proponents of animal-based research, who usually emphasize a view of medicine as progress, a progress that has *depended* on the use of animals (Quimby, 1994; Paton, 1993). So, lab animals become constructed as necessary to the creation of all medical advances, thus facilitating their images as our helpers.

In many ways, laboratory rats and mice have been created to bear our diseases—from animals selectively bred to have little or no functional immune system to those who have been genetically engineered with human genes. They have been transformed from bearers of highly contagious diseases such as plague to become benign assistants in the medical fight against infections. In that sense, they become symbols of Christian salvation stories, suggests Haraway (1997). The history of science itself draws heavily on an iconography of salvation (Midgley, 1992), so it perhaps is not surprising that laboratory animals become such symbols. [. . .]

The intertwined metaphors of mapping and of rodents as helpers/saviors signify beliefs in conquest, the triumph of medicine over disease. However problematic the idea of medical triumph and progress may be, laboratory rats and mice are potent icons. Although all kinds of lab animals may be represented as part of the fight against disease, rodents particularly symbolize that fight—not least because of their strong cultural association with disease. It is no accident that advertisements for lab animals so frequently juxtapose statements about fighting disease with images of rodents, for rodent strains are created as bearers of specific diseases. In a sense, the place of rodents as key players in our salvation from illness symbolizes the ultimate triumph of good over evil—a process in which the rodents themselves are transformed from evil, disease-full vermin into sanitized, germ-free angels of mercy.

Not quite an animal

To become our saviors in the struggle against ill health, rats and mice also must become something other than the rodent-as-animal: These, after all, are animals we generally loathe. Scientists today use millions of laboratory rats and mice. Rodents are not only medical models for this massive industry (Paton, 1993), but are also beings defined as "not quite" animals. The United States Animal Welfare Act has controversially excluded rats, mice, and birds from the definition of "animals" coming under its protection. Legislation in Britain covers all vertebrate animals; information published annually by the Home Office about animal use under current legislation (The Animals [Scientific Procedures] Act, 1986), however, always emphasizes the large percentage of animals who are rodents (approximately 80%). Organizations defending the use of animals in biomedical research make similar arguments, taking the line that most research is for potential medical benefit and most research involves rodents. Somehow, this emphasis implies that it is more acceptable to use animals in research if they are rats or mice.

And to many people, indeed it is. Public opinion is more likely to support painful experiments on rats and mice than on monkeys,[4] while many scientists who would accept using rats or mice in research might draw the line at certain other species (Arluke, 1988; Michael & Birke, 1994). That it is generally more acceptable to cause suffering to rodents reflects the negative view most people have of these animals: Public acceptance is greater just because they are animals we abhor (and this in turn is heeded by antivivisectionist organizations, which rarely use rats or mice in their illustrations).

That scientists, too, draw a line perhaps reflects a need to establish distance from rats or mice as animals in the lab (Arluke, 1988). Accordingly, most laboratory animals (especially rodents) are not named but given only numbers, while references to the naturally behaving animal tend not to enter laboratory reports, even though they may pepper scientists' speech. This schism is particularly noticeable if the animal in question belongs to a species widely accepted as sentient, such as chimpanzees, who typically are given individual names in the laboratory, though not reported as such in subsequent papers (Wieder, 1980).

Rats, however, rarely gain such status as a name. They are more likely to be numbered lots, hidden away in their racked cages, not exposed to view—they no longer have individual histories (Shapiro, 2002). Indeed, in an interview with a technician in one of my own studies, she recounted that the scientists in that lab insisted that she put the rats in opaque cages. They did not like having rats in clear cages because the "animals could look at you." They become a little too like real animals outside the lab when they do that.

Yet at the same time, scientific understanding of the animal and the animal's husbandry relies ultimately on a conception of the animal as an animal. Among other things, the animal might curl around and bite the experimenter. But these features of animalness must not enter written reports, which simplify and mathematicize. It is extremely rare to find a scientific report based on work with rats that refers to the animals in any other way.

Concepts of lab rats as barely animate tools for the job coexist with an (often tacit) understanding of them as being emotional and capable of being influenced by the affect of the researcher (Dror, 1999; Dewsbury, 1992). Partly, this reflects the way in which lab reports are written and by whom. Knowledge of the rat as an animal is explicitly excluded from reports;[5] moreover, it is the animal caretakers rather than the scientists who will have most of this tacit knowledge about everyday rat behavior. Rats have a highly ambiguous status in the laboratory, reflecting in part the ambivalence of the scientists who use them. Meriting special treatment, rats always are both faceless objects of scientific experiment and candidates for simultaneously becoming pets (Herzog, 1988; Arluke, 1988).

In the laboratory, lab animals symbolically must become something other than animals, just as cows and pigs must become something other than animals in order to become food. In his ethnographic study of laboratory neuroscientists, Lynch (1988) described how they sometimes use contrasting models of what is meant by "the animal." The "naturalistic animal" is the animal of common sense, the kind we are familiar with outside the laboratory. But, in order to use them experimentally, animals must be made into "analytic animals"; that is, they must become data.

The transformation into analytic animal begins even before the rat enters the laboratory. Sprague-Dawley rats were used in the lab Lynch (1988) studied because of their

> appropriate size, docile disposition, ability to survive stressful operations, and uniformity of
> brain dimension from one individual to another. . . . The selection and breeding of rats was thus

done with an orientation to a generalized 'mathematical' space transcending the brain of any given animal.

(p. 273)

From the beginning, these transformations have been part and parcel of the breeding programs of laboratory strains of rats and mice; rodents have, in a sense, been created to fit their own mathematization.

Rodents are both handy models of human disease and originate in a despised animal; these two aspects of how we see them make it easier to perceive rodents in particular as merely data. Latour (1987), a sociologist of science, has described the ways in which "facts" are created in the course of laboratory work. Latour argues that through processes of persuasion and agreement and reliance on output from accepted devices to produce graphical output, scientists construct stories that become accepted—through repetition and rhetoric—as facts. An initial suggestion that, say, a mammalian brain produces a particular molecule that may be a neurotransmitter can quickly become codified and accepted as evidence that there is such a transmitter (Latour). These transitions begin with an animal. That set of moves, however, from animal to data to inference to established facts, is easier if the first move is foreshortened—if the animal already is not quite an animal.

So, in the production of results from the laboratory, the animals who ate, slept, and played with their friends—hidden from human eyes—disappear. Indeed, for scientists to do their work, the animals must disappear. The lab rat has been metamorphosed from a rat, with particular characteristics of species-typical behavior, to a "laboratory animal" representing numbers. However many millions of rats and mice are used annually in the service of science, we know remarkably little about their characteristics as species.[6] Rather, lab rats—unlike many other kinds of animals studied in the laboratory—no longer stand as exemplars of their species. Looking through back issues of the journal *Animal Behaviour*, I was struck by the difference in how certain animals are described. Most papers refer to studies with a specific species, identified by the Latin binomial and some reference to the habitat in which the animal is found in the wild. Occasionally, studies use rats: Few of these studies are concerned with the Norway rat as such but may use rats to study some specific biological mechanism. In striking contrast to references to other species ("the white-footed mouse," identified in English as a member of a particular species), the studies using rats significantly refer to the animal only as "the laboratory rat." It is as though "the laboratory rat" becomes the species name.[7]

Furthermore, if rats and mice are perceived in the first place as models for human physiology, then their own ratness or mouseness is irrelevant; they already are part way to becoming de-naturalized analytic animals precisely because they are perceived as (and reduced to) "models" (Shapiro, 2002). Models are abstractions. A model of a physiological system in textbooks might mean an abstract diagram or graphical representation of a set of processes. The reader is not meant to think of a living animal while scrutinizing these graphs.

Yet, advertising for laboratory rodents may bring out the "animalness" by using images of the lab rat or mouse without a context. The image in such advertisements (aimed at users of lab animals) may well include representations of data (some emblem of DNA or graphs) but rarely portrays the animal actually in a cage or laboratory or even with a scientist in evidence. Most advertisements, rather, include a photograph of a white rodent, lit from above, casting a shadow and standing over the shadow, so distinguishing the image from the white page. In these images, the animal's eyes are often oriented to the viewer, so becoming, paradoxically, more like a naturalistic animal.

One aspect of being a model for human physiology is that toxicological studies use millions of rodents to test drugs and other chemicals to which we are exposed. Alongside these routine tests, scientists can gain information about chemical exposures from epidemiological studies of our own species as well as "sentinel" species of wildlife or companion animals whose physiological responses to chemicals in the environment can be monitored. The ideal species for such surveys would be one that shares our environment and is equally exposed to our diet—hence, the use of data obtained from companion animals (National Research Council, 1991). The animals who most closely fit these criteria are, of course, the rodents who live so commensally with us in and around our habitations. But we cannot use them as sentinels outside the laboratory for the simple reason that we also are trying to poison them by putting down rodenticides. As indicators of toxicity, laboratory rodents really are a breed apart.

One set of meanings attached to the label "the laboratory rat" is that this rat is, and is not, an animal. This rat's animal status is ambiguous, mirroring the ambivalence of our human relationship to the rat. This rat, when representing animality, may bite or gaze at nervous experimenters. This rat must stand, with shining fur, as though on a plinth, but never appear caged. When not standing for animality, these rats must become part of the equipment of science, fitting literally (cages or stereotaxic equipment to hold heads in place must fit the animals; but so too must the animals be selected to fit the equipment) or metaphorically by narratives that move them into the realm of data or as models for "man." In these meanings, the rat is not so much an animal as a device for producing an output.[8]

Shapechangers: (laboratory) rats and other animals

There are, then, a multitude of overlapping and contradictory meanings attached to "the laboratory rat": The rat neither is quite in nature (having been brought into the lab), nor outside of nature. Like other animals, this rat is "other" to ourselves. Such others include animals we like as well as those we dislike. But what seems to be happening in the story of the laboratory rat is a double othering, whereby first the rat as an animal is other, and then is made other to other kinds of animals in transference to the laboratory. Both moves strip the rat of subject status, of rat persona. And both moves contribute to a double-sidedness, an either/or status.

All lab animals are doubly othered ethically, because things may be done to them in the lab that are not readily permitted outside the lab. Rats and mice may be killed in large number, just as they are in laboratories. However, there is a clear distinction in the way that invasive and sometimes painful procedures may be carried out in labs and in labs alone. Lab rodents in this sense are made, through law and ethics, into others within the others.

Yet, in practice, too, the lab rodent has been doubly othered. These rats are made other to other kinds of animals first in the literal transfer to the laboratory through breeding programs and taming that serve to separate them from the wild *Rattus* or *Mus* counterparts; they are further differentiated from other animals[9] in how they are sequestered in specialized animal houses (from which, of course, wild, naturalistic rodents are scrupulously excluded). They also are made other, symbolically, in the transition from those naturalistic animals. Laboratory animals are, in some senses, already partly not-naturalistic animals. Even in their cages in the animal house, their hiddenness and numbering ensure that they are not quite real animals.

In the processes both of breeding for specific traits of use to scientific experiments and in the processes of representation as a "model," laboratory rodents are reduced to something else—particular gene effects or physiological responses. This perhaps makes it easier for us to forget their history and associations with disease and to forget that whatever changes domestication has brought, these laboratory rodents remain living animals. Yet, ironically, they also are represented as our helpers. It is as though, by portraying them as altruistic, we can—metaphorically at least—return to them at least some of their status as animal subjects, even if in practice they have none in laboratories.

Shapiro (2002), writing about the role of the laboratory rat in the history of psychology, notes how, in the process, the animals have been de-individuated and de-animalized as well as de-speciated (in the sense that they no longer represent their original species). This, he notes, very effectively plays down their sentience and consciousness. Yet, alongside the recent development of techniques such as the creation of transgenic organisms, which further reduce laboratory animals to laboratory apparatus, there is renewed interest in the cognitive abilities and awareness of animals.[10] Increasingly, scientists are faced with evidence that not only do laboratory rats and mice have considerable intelligence but that they undoubtedly do suffer a great deal in many (or most) laboratory procedures. This shift of focus begins a process of "re-minding" the laboratory rodent, which might return these rodents to their animal status and so promote the animals' welfare.

The rat, Burt and Ellman (2002) write, is an icon of modernization as well as of the plagues of the past, as rats spread themselves through the networks of modern culture and habitation. The modernized rat is the standardized rat of laboratory breeding. Yet, rats, they note, also can be multiplicities[11] representing post-modernity. That is, what the rat means to us is many things at once—just as the animals can be many things at once in their considerable success at colonizing the world in our wake. The rat and mouse, like the coyote, are shape-changers: They can be much-loved pet and hated adversary; they can be dirt personified, and they can symbolize the eradication of disease. In the laboratory, they are both animals and not quite animals; they are vermin in the pipework under the lab but a useful piece of equipment in the lab; they are equipment, yet we can be mindful of their minds; they are bearers of disease while promising to liberate us from disease. These are contradictory, multiple, and elusive meanings indeed: It seems we can never know who is the laboratory rat.

Notes

1   For example, the JAX website allows one to compare the mouse genome directly to either human or rat, via the Mouse and Human (or rat) Orthology Map. Interestingly, the website directs the viewer toward a genomics dictionary (or atlas) of standardized nomenclature for embyonic stages. The mapping metaphor yields to the language of DNA as a dictionary of life.

2   In journals such as *Science*, *Laboratory Animals* or *Nature Genetics* or on websites for companies producing laboratory animals, I have examined a range of advertisements for laboratory animals from these journals and websites, which I summarize here. Like Arluke (1994), rats and mice were by far the most commonly portrayed lab animals in the advertisements I analyzed. One significant change since Arluke's study, however, has been the enormous research effort in genome mapping; this is reflected in advertisements, which increasingly make reference to genomes and genome expression.

3   For GeneSpring, www.sigenetics.com; advertisement in *Science*, 292, 2001.

4   A poll for *New Scientist* indicated that, for example, 49% of people polled would disapprove of testing a new drug that might cause pain if the subjects were mice, compared to 61% if the subjects were monkeys.

5   Lederer (1992) has noted how the style of written texts in scientific journals may reflect editorial policies, stemming from fear of antivivisectionist activity.

6   An exception is the ethological studies of Barnett (2001). For a discussion of this point in relation to the history of the use of rats in psychology, see Shapiro (2002).

7   The JAX website, however, notes that the origins of laboratory mice are more multiple, deriving primarily from two subspecies of *Mus musculus*. However, some more recent types may derive also from *M. spretus*. Because of the complex histories, the website advocates that mice "should not be referred to by species name, but rather as laboratory mice or by use of a specific strain or stock" (http://www. informatics.jax.org, 12th Jan, 2003).

8   Latour (1987) argues that the practices of science prioritize the output of "inscription devices"—apparatuses which generate numbers and graphs. Scientific results can only become truth, suggests Latour, when they are generated by such inscription devices.

9   Some of this applies, to be sure, to other animals bred in laboratories. But, I would argue, lab rodents are the most extreme case in their long history of breeding highly specialized multiple strains for specific purposes.

10   It is ironic that the creature whose own abilities are downplayed in the reductionistic process of creating "models", has to stand as a model in psychology for our much-vaunted human intelligence.

11   Citing the notion of multiplicities in Deleuze and Guattari's concept of becoming (1987).

References

Arluke, A. (1988). Sacrificial symbolism in animal experimentation: Object or pet? *Anthrozoös*, 2, 97–116.

Arluke, A. (1994). We build a better beagle: Fantastic creatures in lab animal ads. *Qualitative Sociology*, *17*, 143–158.

Burian, R.M. (1993). How the choice of experimental organism matters: Epistemological reflections on an aspect of biological practice. *Journal of the History of Biology*, 26, 351–367.

Burt, J., & Ellman, M. (2002). *Rat*. Unpublished essay.

Deleuze, G., & Guattari, F. (1987). *A thousand plateaus*. London: Athlone Press.

Dewsbury, D. A. (1992). Studies of rodent-human interactions in animal psychology. In: H. Davis & D. Balfour (Eds.), *The inevitable bond: Examining Scientist-Animal Interactions* (pp. 27–43). Cambridge: Cambridge University Press.

Dror, O. (1999). The affect of experiment: The turn to emotions in Anglo-American physiology, 1900–1940. *Isis*, *90*, 205–237.

Haraway, D. (1997). *Modest_witness@second millennium: Female Man Meets OncoMouse*. London: Routledge.

Herzog, H. A. (1988). The moral status of mice. *American Psychologist*, *43*, 473–474.

Latour, B. (1987). *Science in action*. Buckingham: Open University Press.

Lederer, S. (1992). Political animals: The shaping of biomedical research literature in twentieth-century America. *Isis*, *83*, 61–79.

Logan, C. A. (2001). 'Are Norway rats . . . things?': Diversity versus generality in the use of albino rats in experiments on development and sexuality. *Journal of the History of Biology*, *34*, 287–314.

Lynch, M. (1988). Sacrifice and the transformation of the animal into a scientific object: Laboratory culture and ritual practice in the neurosciences. *Social Studies of Science*, *18*, 265–289.

Michael, M., & Birke, L. (1994). Science and morality in animal experiments: Demarcating the core set. *Social Studies of Science 24*, 81–95.

Midgley, M. (1992). *Science as: A modern myth and its meaning*. London: Routledge.

National Research Council (1991). *Animals as sentinels of environmental health hazards*. Washington, DC: National Academy Press.

Paigen, K. (1995). A miracle enough: The power of mice. *Nature Medicine*, 1, 215–217.

Paton, W. (1993). *Man and mouse: Animals in medical research*. Oxford: Oxford University Press.

Quimby, F. W. (1994). Twenty-five years of progress in laboratory animal science. *Laboratory Animals*, *28*, 158–171.

Shapiro, K. (2002). A rodent for your thoughts: The social construction of animal models. In: Mary Henninger-Voss (Ed.), *Animals in human histories* (pp. 439–469) Rochester: University of Rochester Press.

Wieder, D. L. (1980). Behavioristic operationalism and the life-world: Chimpanzees and the chimpanzee researchers in face-to-face interaction. *Sociological Inquiry*, 50, 75–103.

REGULATING ANIMAL EXPERIMENTATION

Chapter 43

F. Barbara Orlans

ETHICAL THEMES OF NATIONAL REGULATIONS GOVERNING ANIMAL EXPERIMENTS: AN INTERNATIONAL PERSPECTIVE

Among laws governing use of experimental animals, Orlans identifies eight regulatory dimensions ranging from minimal to extensive protections to laboratory animals; she also reviews and compares the international distribution of animal research laws. Orlans argues that public concerns have led to more stringent protections in recent years. She also believes that this increased regulation has stemmed both from animal rights activities and scientific insights on the intellectual and emotional capabilities of animals.

THIS ESSAY REPORTS on worldwide progress in the enactment of national laws governing the humane use of laboratory animals in biomedical research, testing, and education. During the last one hundred years, national laws to improve the welfare of laboratory animals have become enacted in at least twenty-three countries. I identify here eight ethical themes for discussion: (1) simple provision of basic husbandry requirements and inspection of facilities; (2) control of animal pain and suffering; (3) critical review of proposed experimental protocols; (4) specification of investigator competency; (5) bans on certain invasive procedures, sources of animals, or use of certain species; (6) application of the Three R alternatives—to refine procedures, reduce animal use, or replace animal procedures with nonanimal use where possible; (7) use of ethical criteria for decision making; and (8) mandatory use of animal-harm scales that rank degrees of increasing ethical cost to the animal. Countries in which all eight themes are addressed have the highest standards of animal care and use.

[. . .]

Countries with and without animal protection laws

By 2000 at least twenty-three countries worldwide had enacted laws requiring certain humane standards for experimenting on animals. [. . .] In 1985 the World Health Organization promulgated *Guiding Principles for Biomedical Research involving Animals*, guidelines designed to provide a framework within which specific legislative or regulatory systems could be built in any country, including less-developed countries. Voluntary acceptance of these modest standards is better than having no provisions at all.

Ethical issues in current laws

The eight issues I have previously listed can be used for comparison among the nations. Within the sequence of this listing is a loose, overall historical pattern. The first enactment of laws in any country typically deals only with the first two topics, basic husbandry requirements and inspection of facilities and control of animal pain and suffering. Only later (in amendments to the law) are refinements addressed that illustrate the next four topics—critical review of protocols, specification of investigator competency, bans on certain activities, and the use of the Three R alternatives. The last two topics, which address the complicated issue of how to justify each specific protocol, represent the cutting edge of new legislation. As yet, they are only found in laws of the most progressive countries concerned with animal welfare.

Husbandry standards, inspections, and record keeping

Husbandry and inspections

A basic ethical concern requires that captive animals be housed and cared for humanely. Official government inspection of research facilities maintains standards of sanitation, provision of food and water, space allocation by species' needs, daily care, and other basic requirements. Usually only minimum husbandry standards are mandated, and the tendency has been for animal facilities to conform to the lowest acceptable standards rather than providing optimal housing.

Inspections by government officials are needed to establish compliance. The frequency and adequacy of inspections vary from country to country, as do the standards required. In the United States, inspections are carried out once per year at each of the approximately 1,500 facilities registered with the controlling governing agency. In some countries, inspections are so infrequent and inadequate that the law exists on paper alone.

Historically, standards for housing space have been inadequate. [. . .] However, housing standards for captive animals have been gradually improving in some countries. Reform has been sparked not only by more sympathetic public attitudes to animals but by research demonstrating that poor housing conditions cause stress to the animal, which can confound the experimental results obtained. Also, research has demonstrated that abnormal, stereotypic behaviors (such as pacing, cage biting, etc.) of laboratory, zoo, and farm animals do not occur if the animals are housed in enriched environments—ones as close as possible to those conditions experienced by free-living animals.

In the United States, Congress enacted an amendment to the Animal Welfare Act in 1985 that requires promotion of the "psychological well-being" of primates. This legal provision sparked new funding for environmental enrichment studies and has been profoundly effective in improving the housing conditions of primates. There is a trend toward increased space allocation, group-housing animals of similar species, and the addition of branches, toys, and exercise apparatus to the cages where appropriate. European countries and Australia have been in the forefront of enriching the housing of many common laboratory species, not only primates but also dogs, cats, rabbits, guinea pigs, and rats.

Record keeping

Public reporting of the numbers and species of animals used is a basic requirement of effective oversight and accountability of animal experiments. The rationale is that the public has a right to know what is happening in this socially controversial area of harming animals for human good. [. . .] Worldwide, estimates of the total number of animals used range as high as fifty to a hundred million annually, since many animals are uncounted.

It is unclear whether the total number of animals used worldwide is declining, as animal advocates hope, or increasing. A few countries, including the Netherlands, have reported a decline. In the United States, very probably the largest user of animals worldwide, inadequate data make trends impossible to assess.

[. . .]

Controls on animal pain and suffering

National laws also require that every effort be made to reduce or eliminate pain and suffering that result from an experimental procedure. Anesthetics, analgesics, and postoperative care should be used wherever needed, and animals in extreme pain should be put to death. It is generally considered a matter of plain humanity that the degree of animal pain and suffering be minimized. Indeed, it is a moral imperative.

But such provisions have not necessarily come with the first enactment of a national law. For instance, in the United States, animal pain was not addressed in 1966 when the law was first passed. Indeed, at that time, whether animals actually perceived pain was widely doubted. Not until 1976 was the Animal Welfare Act, the federal law governing laboratory animals, amended to require for the first time the use of anesthetics and analgesics. As a result, research on animal pain and its alleviation accelerated. Textbooks devoted to the physiology and relief of animal pain were published, new anesthetics and analgesics were developed, and postsurgical care became an important topic. Great progress has been made, and by now it is well recognized in national policies throughout the world that vertebrate animals do indeed feel pain.

Methods of killing of animals represent another aspect of control of pain. In the 1980s, the American Veterinary Medical Association established standards for recommended euthanasia practices to ensure that methods used are as rapid and painless as possible. These standards, which are now law in the United States, have been repeatedly updated, and other countries have adopted similar standards.

Critical review of protocols

Not all countries include legal provisions for review of investigators' proposed protocols. Sometimes investigators are subjected to either no formal procedure for protocol review or review only by their peers within their own discipline (for instance, in departmental review at a university or pharmaceutical company).

Nonetheless, there has been considerable growth in the establishment of oversight review committees that function as gatekeepers for approval of proposed experiments. These committees are variously called Animal Care and Use Committees (ACUCs) or Ethical Committees.

[. . .]

The ethical rationale behind such review is that investigators should be accountable in what they do, not only to their peers but also to the public. These committees may be institutional or regional.

They typically operate with considerable autonomy, being only loosely regulated by national bodies. The resulting framework is often characterized as "enforced self-regulation."

The composition of these committees varies among countries, but most include representation of several viewpoints. Committee membership typically includes animal researchers, veterinarians, and lay (nonscientist) members of the public. Representatives from the animal-protection movement should be included because this is the constituency most concerned about humane standards. Experience has shown that to avoid rubber stamping, committee membership should not be dominated by animal researchers, and the chair should be an independent person and not an animal researcher.

The value of public representation on these committees is well established, and most committees would benefit with increased public representation.

[. . .]

The purpose of oversight committee review is to ensure compliance with established standards of care and use by modifying (to improve the animal's welfare) or disapproving proposed projects. This does not necessarily mean that ethical debate that questions the fundamental justification of a project occurs. Indeed, most commonly there is an assumption of fundamental justification of a project. Thus there is room for considerable improvement in the level of debate within most of these oversight committees. I discuss this further in the section "Ethical Criteria for Decision Making."

Specification of investigator competency

The question concerning investigator competency is "What training is required before a person is allowed to conduct *any* animal experiment?" Untrained persons are likely to inflict greater harm on an animal than trained persons attempting the same procedure and furthermore are unlikely to produce experimental results that are of scientific value. So the benefits are less and the harms greater. Establishment of competency standards is important, yet only a few countries have adequately addressed these issues.

[. . .]

In addition to controls over qualifications for persons working in animal-research facilities, several countries place controls over what is permitted by beginning biology students in early stages of their education. [. . .] Historically, a real problem existed in U.S. junior and senior high schools in the 1960s to early 1980s. Youths from age eleven to seventeen sought to impress judges of science-fair competitions by attempting highly invasive experiments on live animals. Often the students conducted these experiments in their homes, and supervision was absent or cursory. Extreme animal suffering occurred. Typical were high school student projects of attempted mammalian surgery, blinding, injection of lethal substances, and starving animals to death. Because the public protested strongly about these abuses, improvements have been made. But still today there is inadequate control over the use of animals in junior and senior high school education in the United States, as well as insufficient encouragement to use nonharmful alternatives. Federal laws do not exist. Unsatisfactory 1995 guidelines (which are voluntary and unenforceable) of the National Association of Biology Teachers include no provisions to ban the infliction of animal pain or suffering on sentient creatures and encourage dissection. Further reforms are still urgently needed.

As for the use of animals in U.S. colleges, there has been limited progress. The 1985 amendment to the Animal Welfare Act required for the first time that oversight committees review the use of animals in undergraduate college courses at some (but by no means all) tertiary educational institutions. [. . .] Rats, mice, and birds, the species most used in college classes, are not covered under the Animal Welfare Act. Thus, a number of colleges fall outside the law, so that much of the use of animals in U.S. biology classes is unregulated.

There are a number of ethical rationales for prohibiting students from harming or killing animals: (1) nonpainful, nonharmful animal projects, nonharmful human studies, and other projects that carry no ethical burden are readily available that are equally or more instructive; (2) because projects at this educational level are primarily demonstrations of known facts, they lack the major ethical justification for harming animals that is based on the reasonable likelihood of obtaining significant, original knowledge; (3) unskilled students are likely to inflict greater harm than trained researchers; and (4) allowing emotionally immature youth to harm animals under the guise of education desensitizes students' feeling of empathy with animals. It can be argued that these points apply not only to primary and secondary school students but also to undergraduate college-level students. It is usually not until graduate school that a student makes a serious career commitment, and even then, not all careers in the biological sciences require expertise in animal experimentation techniques.

Bans on certain activities

Experimental procedures that cause intense and prolonged animal suffering have been the focus of the greatest public protest and demands for prohibition. Even if useful scientific results might be obtained, the lack of justification holds.

Some success in banning such activities has been achieved. A 1986 amendment to a German law, the Animal Protection Act, forbids experimentation on animals for development and testing of weapons, as well as the testing of tobacco products, washing powders, and cosmetics. The Netherlands and the United Kingdom also ban the use of animals for cosmetic testing. Recently, the British government announced its commitment to stop licensing any further testing of tobacco or alcohol products on animals. Indeed, in the whole field of animal testing, with the bans on the notorious LD50 test (the lethal dose that painfully kills 50 percent of the animals) and the Draize eye irritancy test (which can cause blindness in rabbits), considerable progress has been made.

Recently, three European countries (the Netherlands, Switzerland, and the United Kingdom) have banned the use of the ascites method of monoclonal antibody production. This procedure, used on mice, causes considerable suffering, including respiratory distress, circulatory shock, difficulty walking, anorexia, and other disabilities. It is estimated that in the United States up to one million animals a year are killed using this experimental method, but efforts to ban it in the United States have failed.

[. . .]

Another issue, apart from the experimental procedure, is the source of the subject animal. There are three potential sources: former animal pets, either stolen for research or abandoned by their owners; free-living wild animals; or purpose-bred animals (those specifically raised by commercial breeders for research). All sources have come under criticism (antivivisectionists object to every source), but most criticism has focused on the use of one-time companion animals and on the capture of wild animals, especially nonhuman primates.

Of the three possible sources, the use of purpose-bred animals is preferred. The ethical reasoning is that purpose-bred animals are likely to suffer less; they do not have to make a stressful transition from a free life to a life in captivity. Purpose-bred animals know no other life than living in confined quarters; they have been singly caged all their lives with little or no opportunity to make decisions for themselves over what exercise they take, what they eat, whom they spend time with, and so on. But former pets and free-living wild animals are different; they have usually lived rich social lives where they were accustomed to expressing their own free will. To lose this freedom can be traumatic. The period of transition can cause considerable suffering, including the stresses that come with transportation (sometimes for thousands of miles, as with some nonhuman primates, and which can result in death), close confinement, and social and other forms of deprivation.

In addition, the experimental results from purpose-bred animals are more reliable because, unlike former pets and wild animals, their genetic and health backgrounds are known. This reduces the number of variables that can confound experimental results.

[. . .]

Three R alternatives

The Three R principles (refine, reduce, replace), first enunciated by Russell and Burch in 1959, state that experimental procedures should be refined to lessen the degree of pain or distress, that the numbers of animals used should be reduced consistent with sound methodological design, and where possible, that nonanimal methods should be used in preference to those that do use animals. Legal mandates requiring the Three Rs facilitate the acceptance of these concepts by investigators and oversight reviewers. The countries that specifically address all Three Rs in their legislation include the United States, the Netherlands, Sweden, Switzerland, and New Zealand.

The Three R principles are increasingly becoming accepted worldwide by both the humane and scientific communities. Although antivivisectionists focus on replacement alternatives exclusively, others believe that incremental improvements in laboratory animal welfare are best achieved at this time by pursuing all Three Rs.

Promising advancements can be made in refining experimental methods by improving anesthetic and other pain-relieving regimens, using humane experimental end points, and employing only rapid and painless methods of euthanasia. To a lesser extent, reductions in numbers are feasible through the better use of statistics in methodological design. Replacement alternatives may not be applicable, but increasingly, nonanimal alternatives are being developed, especially in animal testing and in teaching biology to students.

[. . .]

Although the concept of the Three Rs is now fairly well accepted on a universal basis as an ideal, it has proved very difficult to persuade regulatory bodies to stop requiring safety tests that involve use of whole animals before a new product can be approved. Although validated nonanimal tests are available in many cases, the regulatory bodies continue to mandate whole-animal testing. The nonanimal tests are thereby unreasonably being held to a much higher standard of validation than animal tests.

The evaluation of progress in implementing the Three Rs is a new topic and is in its infancy; most countries do not have adequate data for analysis. However, the Netherlands provides a unique model. Analysis of official data shows a significant decline in the percentage of total experiments that involve severe animal pain, from 29.3 percent in 1984 to 18.8 percent in 1997 (Orlans 2000). In addition, over the same period, the number of animals used has dropped by about half: in 1984 the total was 1,242,285 and in 1997 it was 618,432 (Orlans 2000).

[. . .]

Ethical criteria for decision making

In general, existing laws do not address the fundamental ethical question, "Should this particular animal experiment be done at all?" The usual presumption of the law is that animal experimentation is justified and that proposed projects should be approved so long as the individual investigator believes that useful scientific knowledge might be gained. Indeed, oversight committees tend to approve almost everything that investigators propose, even highly invasive procedures on primates. Although some projects are modified (typically by application of a refinement), rarely is any proposal totally disapproved. It is thus a step forward when national policies specifically acknowledge that ethical decisions are involved in assessing the justification of an animal experiment, giving credence to the possibility that a proposed work is not justified.

Several countries have taken the lead in requiring a cost-benefit analysis that links animal pain (and other harms) to the scientific worthiness and social significance of the experiment's purpose. [. . .] The concept of making a cost-benefit analysis sounds reasonable but is difficult to apply because the costs and benefits are incommensurable. Almost all the harms fall on the animals and all the benefits on humans. Nevertheless, the cost-benefit view has gained considerable acceptance as a tool for clarifying ethical choices.

[. . .]

Use of animal-harm scales

An important issue on the cutting edge of new reforms in national laws is the requirement to assess and rank the sum total of animal harms for any particular procedure. The ranking systems are variously called severity banding, invasiveness, or more colloquially and inaccurately, pain scales. First mandated in the Netherlands in 1979, such systems are now found in other countries (in chronological order, the United Kingdom, Finland, Canada, Switzerland, and New Zealand). This spread attests to the usefulness of these schemes. Pressure exists in the United States and other countries to adopt similar systems.

According to these systems, the degree of pain or distress is ranked according to a severity banding of either minor, moderate, or severe. For example, in the minor category are such procedures as biopsies or cannulating blood vessels; in the moderate category are major surgical procedures under general anesthesia and application of noxious stimuli from which the animal cannot escape; in the severe category are trauma infliction on conscious animals and cancer experiments with death as an end point. At some point (according to one's point of view), procedures become unethical because of the severity of animal pain.

Mandatory use of these ranking systems forces laboratory personnel to think carefully about the condition of the animal and its state of well-being or adversity throughout the experiment. It also encourages laboratory personnel to learn how to identify clinical signs of well-being and adversity.

In recent years, adoption of harm scales by various countries has acted as a significant stimulus to clinical investigations of animals in assessing signs of well-being and adverse states. A notable contribution that has attracted worldwide attention is that of Mellor and Reid (1994). Their categorization system, which represents a major step forward in assessing the condition of animals, has been adopted with minor modification as national policy in New Zealand and is the gold standard by which other harm rankings should be measured.

Summary

Laboratory animals are much benefited by enforcement of legally established standards for humane care and use. Nonetheless, an absence of laws in many countries where animal experimentation takes place needs to be corrected. New provisions along the lines of the topics discussed here are also needed, as is enforcement of many existing laws. It takes a great deal of effort to enact legal protections for animals, but the value of such laws has been indisputably established, as evidenced by the vast improvements that have come about in the standards of animal care and use found in today's laboratories compared with those of previous years. I also believe that improved conditions that serve to support the welfare of animals serve also to improve immeasurably the quality of the resulting science.

References

Australian Government Publishing Service. 1990. *Australian code of practice for the care and use of animals for scientific purposes*. Canberra: Australian Government Publishing Service.

Mellor, D.J., and C.S.W. Reid, 1994. Concepts of animal well-being and predicting the impact of procedures on experimental animals. In *Improving the well-being of animals in the research environment*, 3–18. Glen Osmond, South Australia: Australian and New Zealand Council for the Care of Animals in Research and Teaching.

National Animal Ethics Advisory Committee. 1988. *Guidelines for institutional animal ethics committees*. September 16–17. Wellington, New Zealand: National Animal Ethics Advisory Committee.

Orlans, F.B. 2000. Public policies on assessing and reporting degrees of animal harm: International perspectives. In *Progress in the reduction, refinement, and replacement of animal experimentation*, edited by M. Balls, A.-M. van Zeller, and M.F. Halder, 1075–82. Amsterdam: Elsevier Science.

Russell, W.M.S., and R.L. Burch. 1959. *The principles of humane experimental technique*. London: Methuen. Reprinted 1992 by Universities Federation for Animal Welfare, 8 Hamilton Close, South Mimms, Potters Bar, Herts, UK ENG 3QD.

World Health Organization, 1985. *Guiding principles for biomedical research involving animals*. Geneva: Council for International Organizations of Medical Sciences.

ANIMALS IN EDUCATION

Chapter 44

Jonathan Balcombe

SUMMARY OF RECOMMENDATIONS

Balcombe provides twenty-eight recommendations on the use of animals for classroom educational purposes. The recommendations are designed to facilitate use of fewer animals in the classroom, reduction in the range of activities for which animals are used, and reduction of suffering among individual animals.

1   Biology teachers should emphasize active, inquiry-based learning and engage their students in the doing of science.

2   Hands-on exercises should be pursued, but not at the expense of animal lives; countless ways exist for achieving exciting, engaging, hands-on exercises for students (e.g., having students study themselves, and outdoor studies of animals and plants).

3   The time required to perform good-quality dissections should be used instead to make room for more pressing life science topics such as cell biology, molecular genetics, evolution, biochemistry, environmental science, and animal behavior.

4   Teacher training should be reformed so that exposure to alternatives is included and dissection of animals is not a training prerequisite for obtaining a science teaching license.

5   Students should be fully involved in ethical decision making in the classroom.

6   Conscientious objection should not be seen as rebelliousness aimed at disrupting a teacher's efforts to teach, but rather, respected as evidence of concern and reflection.

7   Concern for animals should not be labeled as "squeamishness" but should be acknowledged as a legitimate manifestation of empathy for others. "Squeamish" students ought not be pressured or humiliated into participation in exercises they find distasteful.

8   Teachers and students should be made more aware of the connexion between cruelty to animals and interpersonal violence; though mutilation of dissected specimens may only reflect a temporary desensitization, it should not be ignored as a possible sign that a student is prone to antisocial behavior.

9   Ethics should be part of the education of all children, and dissections should not be conducted in the absence of ethical discussion about the origins of the animals and the moral implications of using them.

10 Animal dissection should be eliminated from the precollege curriculum.

11 All procurement of animals for dissection should be from ethical sources, such as animal shelters, veterinary clinics, and wildlife rehabilitation facilities. Guardian-consent programs should be established so that cats (and other companion animals) who have died or been euthanized for medical or humane reasons can be donated from shelters or veterinary clinics to schools for educational use. These cadavers should replace the supply of cats from random sources, fetal pigs from slaughter-houses, frogs from wetlands, etc.

12   The United States Department of Agriculture (USDA), which is responsible for inspecting biological supply companies (classified by the USDA as "Class B Dealers"), should begin requiring biological supply companies to provide annual reports. These reports should include the numbers and species of animals killed and sold to schools for educational use, and the methods of capturing, transporting, handling, and killing the animals.

13   Biological supply companies should be required to conduct environmental impact assessments prior to collecting from wild animal populations.

14   Students should be informed of the specifics regarding the sources of animals used in the classroom, including methods used for capturing, transporting, handling, and killing the animals.

15   Dissection of species whose populations are known to be overexploited and/or in decline (e.g., leopard frogs, bullfrogs, spiny dogfish sharks) should be discontinued.

16   Students involved in dissections should be provided with gloves, masks, and safety instruction to minimize the hazards of exposure to formaldehyde.

17   Science teacher training should, without exception, include training in the use of computer simulations and other alternatives resources, including alternative databases and loan programs.

18   School exercises that involve killing, undernourishing, or otherwise harming live animals should be replaced with humane alternatives, such as computer simulations, observational and behavioral field study, and benign investigations of the students themselves.

19   The traditional frog- and turtle-pithing exercises should be terminated and replaced with computer packages, which have been shown to save time and money without compromising educational value. Studies that involve the students as investigators and subjects should be more widely adopted.

20   Medical schools still using live terminal dog labs should follow the lead of other schools that have replaced these procedures with humane alternatives.

21   Veterinary schools should accelerate the current trend towards replacement of purpose-bred and/or healthy animals with clinical cases for surgical training, including spay/neuter of shelter animals.

22   Recognizing that perioperative experience, including handling live tissue, is a critical part of a veterinary education, student participation in actual clinical cases coupled with primary surgical experience performing procedures of benefit to the animal (e.g., spay/neuter of shelter animals) should wholly replace traditional "survival" surgeries.

23   For common surgeries that are not medically required by an individual animal, only two options should exist: (1) terminal surgery on anesthetized terminally ill animals with guardian consent, or (2) cadaver surgery where cadavers are ethically obtained.

24   All science fairs should abide by a policy against inflicting deliberate harm on sentient animals.

25   Laws should be implemented that require a certain level of competency before a person is allowed to conduct animal experiments.

26   All students should have a legally mandated right to use humane alternatives to dissection and other classroom exercises harmful to animals. Currently, fewer than one in five American states have statewide laws or policies mandating student choice in dissection. The result is that some students are granted rights denied to others. States still lacking such laws should make their enactment a high priority.

27   Dissection choice laws should apply to students at all levels of education; currently, such laws apply only to precollege students and exclude post-secondary students even though the validity of conscientious objection is independent of learning level.

28   IACUCs should apply more stringent restrictions on proposals for animal use in instruction and should always look for ways to piggyback teaching exercises that involve animals into ongoing research at the institution.

Chapter 45

Andrew J. Petto and Karla D. Russell

HUMANE EDUCATION: THE ROLE
OF ANIMAL-BASED LEARNING

Petto and Russell address the complex issue of incorporating animal use in education, and outline a process for involving students as well as teachers in making humane decisions about animal studies in the curriculum. Issues addressed by students would include decisions on whether and how animals ought to be introduced into the curriculum, as well as various practical issues such as acquisition, classroom care and use, and disposition of animals at completion of the studies. While oriented toward secondary and early levels of education, many of their suggestions are also applicable to university levels.

[. . .]

Concept of the 'humane'

'**HUMANE' IS A COGNITIVE** concept for humans and subject to the same constraints as other cognitive concepts held by humans (Atran, 1990). It is universal in the sense that all cultures seem to have a concept that some actions and attitudes toward animals (and toward other humans) are desirable and others are unacceptable. However, often the set of acceptable and proscribed actions towards non-human animals differs greatly from one culture to another, and, even within a culture, attitudes toward treatment of animals can vary by class or socio-economic status (Driscoll, 1992; Löfgren, 1985).

[. . .]

The challenge for anyone trying to describe a process through which one learns about animals and with animals as 'humane education', then, is to focus not only on the final rules for behaviours toward animals, but also to examine the pathways to those rules. There are two main goals of this examination. The first is to find opportunities in the learning process to understand better both the 'natural' and the 'cultural' animal (sensu Lévi-Strauss, 1965) and to discover what we can learn from all the different ways in which our culture and others know these animals. The second is to reline the pedagogical process so that we develop in our students a humane attitude that includes appreciation of the animal's natural life, role in the environment, and the costs (to animals and humans) of its capture and study.

The process of considering these issues for animals in education has three stages. The first stage focuses on pedagogical issues and is generally the domain of the teacher. The main issues in this stage relate to the objectives of the lesson, integration of the animal-based activities with other aspects of the curriculum, the design and presentation of the materials, actions and reactions of the learners, and an evaluation of the learning by each individual as well as of the lesson or activity as a whole. The second stage focuses on the impact on the animals themselves. The main issues in this stage relate to the acquisition, care and use, and disposition of the animals being used for education. Finally, the third stage focuses on the wider social impact. The main issues in this stage relate to the outcome(s) of the process on the educational climate in the schools, the community, and in society in general.

We do not believe that this approach will or must lead to an abolition of animals in the classroom nor that it should do so. Rather, we hold that humane education is embodied in the process of considering a variety of issues including the nature of the lesson to be taught, the opportunities for multiple approaches to that knowledge, the active consideration of the life (sensu Regan, 1993) of the animal subject as an important issue, the conservation of resources, and the outcome of the exercise for the teacher, the student, and the animal.

Our use of the term 'active consideration' throughout this chapter is meant to convey a sense that each choice to use animals in education is explored and investigated by the teachers and students as appropriate to the students' experience and abilities; that this exploration is not merely a perfunctory checklist of health, safety, and physical comfort issues, but an integral part of the educational experience; that the conclusions and choices to be made are not a foregone conclusion before the process begins; and that executing this exploration requires a set of learning activities that may take the student beyond the immediate lesson and classroom environment to do background research, to check sources of information, to document past educational uses and their outcomes, etc. If successful, the members of the learning community – teachers and students – have turned the hit-or-miss experiences of the classroom 'pet' into an integrated, multi-disciplinary exploration of the biology, psychology, economics, and anthropology of educational use of non-human animals.

The experience of this process is the essence of humane education. The absence of real experience with non-human animals in the context of a humane educational setting eliminates an important opportunity to develop the concept of 'humane' in our students. Unless all members of the learning community are actively engaged in learning how information about animals is obtained and used in the classroom, we cannot fully demonstrate to the community in practice how to foster an environment of respect for those animals. We illustrate the values of humane education by accepting the responsibility to think clearly and responsibly about the role(s) that animals may play in our planned educational activities and the impact of those activities on the lives of animals.

Issues in teaching and learning

There are many ways in which animals may appear in an educational setting, but we will be concerned with just two subject areas – biological and behavioural sciences. [. . .] [M]ost of the examples that we will use and most of the discussion will centre on secondary and introductory level university students. We believe that the approach and concepts apply through a lifelong education, but our examples drawn from our own teaching and learning experiences draw us to this more restricted phase in our student's formal education.

The first step in a humane approach to animals in education is for the teacher to identify the best pathway to meet the lesson's objectives. The teacher must take into account the learners' stage of cognitive development, prior or collateral knowledge that the learners bring to the lesson, resources available to plan and execute the lesson, plans for evaluating the success of the lesson and the learners, the internal environment of the classroom, and the external environment imposed by systemic or other standard for mastery of life sciences content and concepts at this and subsequent stages of education (see Table 45.1).

[. . .]

If the lesson or any learning activity will include the use of live animals or animal products, the teacher first should be able to provide a compelling and significant pedagogical justification for such use. That means that the use of animals in the classroom provides an added component to the learning that is non-trivial and unique or unattainable in other ways and that there is substantive evidence to support this assertion.

Table 45.1 Issues in teaching and learning with animals

Learning styles (intelligence)

Does the proposed activity allow or encourage acquisition and construction of knowledge by learners in a variety of ways?

Does this proposed activity engage the learner actively in the process of discovery, learning, evaluation, and assimilation of knowledge?

(Cognitive) developmental stage / age / level

Is the proposed activity appropriate to the abilities of the learners to understand and assimilate the main points of the lesson?

Is the proposed activity better performed at an earlier or later developmental stage?

Has the prior preparation for the proposed activity been adequate and appropriate to both the developmental stage of the learners and to the expected learning outcomes or culminations?

Lesson objectives

When the lesson objectives and goals are clearly formulated, how does the proposed activity support their attainment? What skills or knowledge are being developed, and how and when are they necessary for future learning?

What other pathways to the objective might be used and how would they affect the educational outcome of the activities?

Will the proposed activity be a superficial, one-time event or will it reflect and support the main theme throughout a curriculum unit or longer-term educational effort?

Career stage

How does the development of specific skills and knowledge translate into a potential for future study or career choices for learners?

Conversely, how would lack of specific skills inhibit the student's future plans and expectations?

What are the best ways to learn these skills and to what depth at this stage in the learner's academic career?

[. . .]

Most educational uses of live animals or animal tissues are based on the demonstrated value of a practical or 'hands-on' component to the lesson. The power of adding visual and 'bodily-kinaesthetic' components to what Gardner (1993:8) called the 'linguistic' and 'logical-mathematical' biases of nineteenth and twentieth-century education is illustrated in many disciplines. This approach has been most appreciated, perhaps not surprisingly, in arts education (e.g. Petto, 1994; Lowenfeld and Brittain, 1970; Arnheim, 1969). In these disciplines, both learning and its evaluation take into account a rich array of interactions among the teacher, the learner, and the subject matter, including sensory, emotional, spatial, interpersonal, and kinaesthetic.

There is no question that what educators call active learning throughout multiple modalities makes learning better in at least two ways. First, students learn more when they confront learning problems that engage them in inquiry, problem posing, problem solving, and defence of their ideas before their classmates (Peterson and Jungck, 1988; Jungck, 1985). In most cases, teachers are referring to their personal experiences as well as a reflection on their intuitive (emotional or interpersonal, sensu Gardner, 1993, 9) sense that hands-on laboratory activities with animals add significantly to learning biology (e.g. Offner, 1993; Keiser and Hamm, 1991; Mayer and Hinton, 1990). This is not merely a matter of developing manual dexterity or hand–eye co-ordination or facility and self-confidence with some laboratory technique, as some have described it (e.g. Kinzie *et al.*, 1993; Quentin-Baxter and Dewhurst, 1992). Rather, these practical or hands-on lessons provide non-linguistic ways of learning, and for some students the movement, proprioception, and emotional reaction to the learning and to other learners cannot be replaced by linguistic, visual, or symbolic (i.e. logical-mathematical) representations of the problem.

Secondly, this approach to learning engages more students in the process (e.g. Petto, 1994; Gardner, 1993; Markova and Powell, 1992). Such a wider engagement allows more students to participate in, and contribute to, the learning experience and may give them more of a sense of control or self-direction in constructing their own learning. In addition, Petto (1994) reports that the personalization of the learning activity through the incorporation of the emotional response to the activity, materials, and even the other learners is a key factor in both the retention of learned material and the ability of students to relate that material or lesson to other knowledge or life experience. Furthermore, the perspectives of those students whose learning is not primarily linguistic or logical-mathematical contribute insights into the learning that may be overlooked by fellow learners, including the teacher. Even the learners who prefer expository teaching and declarative evaluation of their learning, learn more and better when using multiple modalities, as illustrated in a recent study on reinforcing the lessons learned through dissection by using prior preparation with an interactive video demonstration (Kinzie *et al.*, 1993).

[. . .]

Finally, the main issue in humane education with animals is that biology is the study of the living (Lock, 1994; Orlans, 1991). In teaching and learning about living animals, one might consider, for example, their way of life, social and environmental needs (in nature and in captivity), feeding strategies and nutritional needs, and their role in the ecosystem. [. . .] This approach raises a paradox for the learning community, since almost any proposed educational use of animals will disrupt the animals' lives to varying extents.

One solution to this apparent paradox was proposed by Donnelley and colleagues (1990) under the term 'moral ecology'. Considering the moral ecology of the proposed use of an animal in education (or research) includes asking about the life that the animals (would) lead outside the educational context and how any proposed use would contribute to the educational objectives of the lesson. This is where the educational use of animals becomes humane. First, the teachers and students examine what needs to be learned and how an animal might contribute to that learning. Next, they review the needs of the animals and the impact on that animal of the proposed learning activity, considering, perhaps, alternatives that include using the animals in a different way, using different animals, or using non-animal resources. Then they should discuss the source of the animals, their acquisition, and their disposition after the educational activity.

[. . .]

Such a process places a heavy responsibility, however, on science teachers who may not have had any formal training in bioethics, particularly in exploring complex ethical issues with children (Downie, 1993; Downie and Alexander, 1989). Lock (1993, 114), in particular, points out the responsibility of the teacher to demonstrate 'a caring and humane approach in all their work with living things'. The responsibility for the teacher, then, is to be sure that the students have accurate, up-to-date information from a variety of sources about the animals they propose to study, including information relevant to the moral ecology of the use of particular animals in specific learning activities and projects.

In summary, the justification of any educational use of animals must have a strong pedagogical basis. This justification must include consideration of the choice of species, the type of learning activity, the developmental readiness and scholastic abilities of the students, the necessity for adequate foundations for future study, and advanced preparation and study by the students and teachers. A part of this justification is to balance the needs of, and outcomes for, the learners against the impact of the proposed educational usages on the animals.

Effects on animals

After careful consideration of the pedagogical issues, if the teacher concludes that there is an appropriate educational role for animals in the lesson, then s/he must determine whether there are any animals suitable for the lesson and the classroom environment. The main issues pertain to the acquisition, care and use, and disposition of the animals used in the lesson.

[. . .]

Moral ecology may be viewed as an attempt at operationalization of the 'subject-of-a-life' criterion proposed by Regan (1993). It presents a set of principles against which we might explore by what criteria we may judge the subjective lives of animals and the impact on their 'individual experiential welfare' (Regan, 1993, 203) of various uses of these animals by humans. Moral ecologists recognize that the life's experience and the expectations for future life differ greatly among individuals of the same species (e.g. Sapontzis, 1987; Rodd, 1990). Therefore, the impact upon their individual experiential welfare of their interactions with humans in an educational setting may also be different.

[. . .]

[A] humane approach requires that everyone involved in the educational use of animals explores explicitly the effects of the proposed use on the animal subjects. Indeed, such background research before any classroom activity is a hallmark of the proposed standards for life sciences education from the US National Research Council (NRC, 1994).

[. . .]

The issues in Table 45.2 expand the sphere of inquiry of the effects of educational use on the animals beyond whether the subject animals will live or die. This process includes learning about their lives before the animals come to the classroom (in nature or in any other environment), how the animals will be cared for and by whom, how the proposed use will affect the animals and the learners, and what the effects of this activity might be on the animal's future life once the project is over. It also requires us to identify and evaluate the sources of this information and to determine what message each of these is bringing to the lesson at hand.

Although no such list can ever include all the issues that could be raised, we believe that the process of considering explicitly the impact of educational usage on the animals themselves is vital to the development of a humane ethic in education. The desire to add other items to the list is a healthy expression of a learning community that takes seriously the need for such a development. Perhaps most importantly, this list is applicable to all animals and to any proposed use in education from behavioural observations of free-ranging animals in the schoolyard to dissection of mammalian species.

(Human) social issues

An important question in the use of animals in education that is often overlooked is the effect on human society and on the learners that experience it. Both the lore of scientific training and the criticisms from the animal rights literature point out the distancing, the deadening of emotion, the objectification of the animals, and the desensitization to suffering and death that educational uses of animals can have on the people who use them (e.g. Davis and Balfour, 1992; Shapiro, 1990, 1991). These emotional 'adaptations' are expected for all uses of animals, but are particularly pronounced when the animal use results in death or dismemberment or involves suffering. These studies argue that being forced to partake in these activities may require a psychological adjustment by the learners that degrades or devalues animal life. Similar

Table 45.2 Inventory of issues for use of animals in education

---

Acquisition

How are the acquisition and use of the animals to be introduced to the students?

How and from where will the animals be acquired?

Can they be studied in their natural habitats, or must they be introduced to the classroom?

Can they be acquired and placed in an appropriate classroom habitat without harm to the animals?

Does the acquisition pose any harm to the students?

Care and use

Habitat

Is the classroom habitat safe for the animal? Are temperature, humidity, appropriate?

Is proposed classroom activity appropriate to activity cycle?

Are materials appropriate for digging, nesting, foraging, tunnelling, etc.?

Does the habitat provide appropriate options for movement, rest?

Social life

Is habitat appropriate to the type, frequency, intensity of social contact typical of this species?

If there is more than one individual in an enclosure, how should they be matched or mixed by age, sex, size, or other important variables?

Is there adequate opportunity for access to food, water, hiding places for all individuals in a social group?

Life cycle needs

Is there adequate opportunity for physical growth and development or social maturation?

Can normal life cycle functions such as reproduction and birth/hatching be carried out?

If reproduction is successful, can the offspring survive and thrive in the classroom habitat?

How and up to what point will this population growth be sustained?

Disposition

What will happen to the animals after the completion of the lesson(s)?

Can they return to their natural habitat?

Is any sort of preparation, training, or rehabilitation required before the animal can return to nature or its previous way of life? Is so, how will this be carried out and by whom?

How will the disposition of the animal(s) be introduced to and discussed with the students?

---

reactions to the plight of human subjects in scientific research has been well documented for decades (e.g. Milgram, 1974). Under social pressure from peers and authority figures. experimental assistants new to the project were rather easily convinced to administer what they believed were painful procedures to unseen subjects for the sake of the experimental protocol.

However, the contributors to the volume by Davis and Balfour (1992) demonstrate that this outcome is not unavoidable. Furthermore, researchers and research technicians are frequent contributors to the journal *Humane Innovations and Alternatives* (Petto *et al.*, 1992; Cohen and Block, 1991; O'Neill, 1987). In recent years some winners of the journal's annual recognition award have also been on the research staff in biomedical research facilities (Anon., 1992, 1993).

Furthermore, one may argue that confronting the animal subject of our learning 'face-to-face' can be the basis of a sensitizing process in which the students learn about the real needs of non-human animals and the animals' observable reactions to handling, care, and educational activities of various sorts. The presence of living animals in the classroom can be a valuable way to increase the appreciation of learners for the real animal and its experience of life.

[. . .]

Rather than desensitizing the students to the animals that will enrich their education, this process requires the students to confront the real needs that living animals have in their environments. Direct, personal interactions with living animals provide the best opportunity for the bonding and empathetic responding between student and non-human animal that is universally acknowledged from Davis and Balfour (1992) to Shapiro (1990, 1991) to Weatherill (1993) and Ascione (1992). Because there are real and observable consequences in such a situation for making poorly informed choices about learning activities, habitat construction, or even choice of appropriate animal subject, students and teachers must confront and accept the consequences of their actions through interactions with living animals. Davis and Balfour (1992) argue that these interactions also bring benefits to human scientific and educational activities.

Another consequence of educational animals use is the development of an industry that serves the needs of thousands of schools that will use animals in some way. This is an important issue in Hepner's (1994) examination of the role of animals in education. The sheer volume of animals that must be killed, skeletonized, and/or preserved in some form every year in North America alone would probably surprise most educators. It is not only a matter of volume, but a matter of the effect on our expectations of the educational experience with animals.

[. . .]

If the process to acquire each of the animals supplied from these sources took an approach similar to the one we propose here, then the existence of large, centralized supply houses that kill and preserve millions of animals annually might be somewhat less worrisome. However, the sheer volume of this industry's output should be enough to make us reconsider how our choices to use animals in education relates to this phenomenon. The realities of the animal supply business must be a part of the process of choosing to use animals in education.

If there is a determined need for animals or animal tissues in the classroom, the humane educational process is enhanced by the explicit discussion by teachers and learners of the questions of source and supply. Is it better to use purpose-bred animals, or specimens from slaughter-houses, or body parts from hunters or taxidermists? And, what social, economic, and moral implications does each of these choices have? How should, or could, we decide among them and on what basis?

The process of recognizing the social implications of animal use beyond the classroom adds another important dimension to humane education. The whole learning community makes an informed and conscious choice for specific learning activities in which at least one component is animal based. It is vitally important that the learning community take this discussion beyond the blanket prescription or proscription of animal use.

Conclusions

What we have proposed here is an outline for making the choice to include animals in the curriculum a humane learning activity. All members of the learning community should be actively engaged in the process of constructing the humane ethic that will govern the choice to use animals in the classroom and the decisions on how they will be used. It must be clear from the start that there is a choice to be made. We wish to avoid the phenomenon described by McGinnis (1992) of beginning with the conclusion that animal use in education is automatically either 'noa' or 'taboo' – prescribed or forbidden. When the outcome of this consideration is not a foregone conclusion, the process of making these choices adds a valuable dimension to the educational process for all members of the learning community.

For the whole learning community, this process of considering the various practical issues of acquisition, classroom care and use, and disposition of animals used in educational activities is the essence of humane education, because it requires the students to confront these issues explicitly. In so doing, it shows that the teacher and the school value the animals as entities in themselves worthy of such consideration and not only as a means to an end.

In the end, taking this process seriously may mean, perhaps, that some activities using animals in the classroom will not be done at particular times and places – even when they clearly have pedagogical value. It may mean that there will be several learning activities and that not all students will participate in each of them. It may mean that the curricular activities involving animals will be developed around different choices. However, none of what we have described as the process of humane education means that these learning activities will never be done. In the end 'humane' education is a process that increases, not decreases sensitivity of all the members of the learning community to the impact of their learning. This, we believe, can be accomplished through a process of active consideration of these impacts in the various dimensions that are affected by these choices.

References

Anon. (1992). PSYeta's *Human Innovations and Alternatives* Annual Award, 1992. Viktor Reinhardt. *Humane Innovations and Alternatives*, 6, 317.

Anon. (1993). PSYeta's *Human Innovations and Alternatives* Annual Award, 1993. Peggy O'Neill Wagner. *Humane Innovations and Alternatives*, 7, 423.

Arnheim, V. (1969). *Visual Thinking*. Berkeley: University of California Press.

Ascione, F. R. (1992). Enhancing children's attitudes about the humane treatment of animals: generalization to human-directed empathy. *Anthrozoös*, 5, 176–91.

Atran, S. (1990). *Cognitive Foundations of Natural History: Towards an Anthropology of Science*. New York: Cambridge University Press.

Cohen, P. S. and Block, M. (1991). Replacement of laboratory animals in an introductory-level psychology laboratory. *Humane Innovations and Alternatives*, 5, 221–5.

Davis, H. and Balfour, D. (1992). *The Inevitable Bond: Examining Scientist-Animal Interactions*. New York: Cambridge University Press.

Donnelley, S. (with Dresser, R., Kleinig, J. and Singleton, R.). (1990). Animals in science: the justification issue. In *Animals, Science, and Ethics*, ed. S. Donnelley and K. Nolan, Hastings Center Report, Suppl. 20(3), 8–13.

Downie, R. (1993). The teaching of bioethics in the higher education of biologists. *Journal of Biological Education*, 27(1), 34–8.

Downie, R. and Alexander, L. (1989). The use of animals in biology teaching in higher education. *Journal of Biological Education*, 23(2), 103–11.

Driscoll, J. W. (1992). Attitudes toward animal use. *Anthrozoös*, 5(1), 32–9.

Gardner, H. (1993). *Multiple Intelligences: The Theory in Practice*. New York: Basic Books.

Hepner, L. A. (1994). *Animals in Education: The Facts, Issues, and Implications*. Alberquerque, NM: Richmond Publishers.

Keiser, T. D. and Hamm, R. W. (1991). Forum: dissection: the case for. *The Science Teacher*, 58(1), 13, 15.

Kinzie, M. B., Strauss, R. and Foss, J. (1993). The effects of interactive dissection simulation on the performance of high school biology students. *Journal of Research in Science Teaching*, 30(8), 989–1000.

Jungck, J. R. (1985). A problem-posing approach to biology education. *The American Biology Teacher*, 47(5), 264–6.

Lévi-Strauss, C. (1965). *Le Totémisme Aujourd'hui*. Paris: Presses Universitaires de France.

Lock, R. (1993). Animals and the teaching of biology/science in secondary schools. *Journal of Biological Education*, 27(2), 112–14.

Lock, R. (1994). Biology – the study of living things? *Journal of Biological Education*, 28(2), 79–80.

Löfgren, O. (1985). Our friends in nature: class and animal symbolism. *Ethnos*, 50(3–4), 184–213.

Lowenfeld, V. and Brittain, W. L. (1970). *Creative and Mental Growth*, 5th edn. New York: Macmillan.

Markova, D. and Powell, A. R. (1992). *How Your Child is Smart: A Life-changing Approach to Learning*. Berkeley, CA: Conari Press.

Mayer, V. I. and Hinton, N. K. (1990). Animals in the classroom: considering the options. *The Science Teacher*, 57(3), 27–30.

McGinnis, J. R. (1992). The taboo and the 'noa' of teaching science-technology-society (STS): a constructivist approach to understanding the rules of conduct teachers live by. Paper presented at the annual meeting of the Southeastern Association for the Education of Teachers of Science, Wakulla Springs FL. Feb 14–15.

Milgram, S. (1974). *Obedience to Authority*. NY: Harper and Row.

National Research Council, National Committee on Science Education Standards and Assessment. (1994). *National Science Education Standards*. Washington, DC: National Academy Press.

Offner, S. (1993). The importance of dissection in biology teaching. *The American Biology Teacher*, 55(3), 147–9.

O Neill, P. L. (1987). Enriching the lives of primates in captivity. *Humane Innovations and Alternatives*, 1, 1–5.

Orlans, F. B. (1991). Forum: dissection: the case against. *The Science Teacher*, 58(1), 12, 14.

Peterson, N. S. and Jungck, J. R. (1988). Problem posing, problem solving, and persuasion in biology education. *Academic Computing*, 2(6), 14–17, 48–50.

Petto, A. J., Russell, K. D., Watson, L. M. and LaReau-Alves, M. L. (1992). Sheep in wolves' clothing: Promoting psychological well-being in a biomedical research facility. *Humane Innovations and Alternatives*, 6, 366–70.

Petto, S. G. (1994). Time and time again: holistic learning through a multimodal approach to art history. MFA Thesis. Boston University.

Quentin-Baxter, M. and Dewhurst, D. (1992). An interactive computer-based alternative to performing rat dissection in the classroom. *Journal of Biological Education*, 26(1), 27–33.

Regan, T. (1993). Ill-gotten gains. In *The Great Ape Project: Equality beyond Humanity*. ed. P. Cavalieri and P. Singer. New York: St Martin's Press.

Rodd, R. M. (1990). *Biology, Ethics, and Animals*. Oxford: Oxford University Press.

Sapontzis, S. F. (1987). *Morals, Reason, and Animals*. Philadelphia: Temple University Press.

Shapiro, K. (1990). The pedagogy of learning and unlearning empathy. *Phenomenology and Pedagogy*, 8, 43–8.

Shapiro, K. (1991). The psychology of dissection. *The Animals' Agenda*, pp. 20–1.

Weatherill, A. (1993). Pets at school: Child animal bond sparks learning and caring. *Inter Actions*, 11(1), 7–9.

ECOLOGICAL STUDIES

Chapter 46

Ben A. Minteer and James P. Collins

ECOLOGICAL ETHICS: BUILDING A NEW TOOL KIT FOR ECOLOGISTS AND BIODIVERSITY MANAGERS

Ben A. Minteer and James P. Collins argue that the ethical questions that develop in areas of ecological research and biodiversity management call for bringing ethicists, scientists, and biodiversity managers together in a collaborative effort to study and inform the methods of ethical analysis and problem solving in these fields. They present some cases to illustrate the kinds of ethical questions generated by practicing scientists and managers and call for an extensive case database and a new ethical framework they call "ecological ethics."

[. . .]

Introduction

WHEN THEY CONFRONT difficult ethical questions in their work, biomedical scientists and clinicians can turn to bioethics, a recognized field within applied philosophy with a rich literature, for scholarly insight and practical guidance. Bioethics has a strong institutional presence in hospitals and research centers; scientists and clinicians often can and sometimes must consult directly with ethics committees or qualified bioethical personnel in their home institutions. Bioethics is embedded within these research and clinical communities, providing a recognized forum for the discussion of ethical issues, an established scholarly area of research yielding new research findings, and a support network to assist researchers and clinicians in making practical ethical decisions.

There is, however, no analogous subfield of applied or practical ethics devoted expressly to investigating the special kind of ethical issues raised within ecological research and biodiversity management contexts. Environmental ethics comes closest to filling this need, but it has not developed any special focus on the design and conduct of ecological field and laboratory experiments or (with a few notable exceptions) paid sufficient attention to the ethical dilemmas that often plague decision making in biodiversity management (including natural areas, botanical gardens, zoos, and aquaria). There is a need for a novel approach within practical ethics that cannot be met by simply stretching the current disciplinary boundaries of bioethics or environmental ethics as some have argued (e.g., Ehrlich 2003).

Experimental ecologists and biodiversity managers need a network and an ethical support system analogous to the one linking bioethics with biomedical scientists and clinicians. In recent years there have been increasing pleas for scientists to play a more active role in environmental policy discussions and to be more responsive to citizens' interests in maintaining biologically diverse, healthy, and productive ecosystems (e.g., Lélé & Norgaard 1996; Lubchenco 1998; Wilson 2002). These arguments are not entirely new, but their increasing frequency and moral seriousness suggest that more than ever ecologists are being asked to provide citizens and policy makers with the knowledge and tools for conserving biological resources and planning for sustainable development. In attempting to meet their end of this "social contract," ecological researchers confront an expanding set of ethical challenges that are in part a function of their field's growing technical acumen and increasing, though by no means complete or infallible, predictive power. Indeed, designing and conducting ecological research and managing biological resources often raise ethical considerations relating not only to an ecologist's responsibilities to public welfare and the scientific community but also to his or her obligations to wild animals, species, and ecosystems.

Consider the following case (recently documented in *Science*). Six of the Channel Islands of California have endemic subspecies of the island fox (*Urocyon littoralis*), an endangered species, and feral pig (*Sus scrofa*) populations. Golden Eagles (*Aquila chrysaetos*), a federally protected species, recently colonized the islands and drove two fox subspecies to extinction and reduced a third species to < 100 animals (Courchamp et al. 2003). Eradicating pigs was planned for early 2004, but population models demonstrate that eagles will then feed more heavily on foxes and trigger their extinction. Translocation alone will not eradicate the eagles, so lethal removal is suggested as the way to save the fox. What values should guide the decision regarding the appropriate conservation target in this case? Should both species be saved at any cost? If not, why does one species deserve to be saved and not the other? Is there a principled way to resolve these questions?

We believe that ecological scientists, biodiversity managers, and practical ethicists have for the most part devoted little systematic effort to exploring these sorts of issues. Exceptions include a handful of researchers who have investigated the social roles and ethical responsibilities of conservation biologists, including their obligations to ecological systems (e.g., Shrader-Frechette & McCoy 1999; Potvin et al. 2001; Lodge & Shrader-Frechette 2003) and related discussions regarding the ethical context of ecological restoration (e.g., Light & Higgs 1996; Gobster & Hull 2000). Still others have considered some of the animal and environmental ethical questions raised by zoo conservation strategies and techniques (Norton et al. 1995), the conceptual and moral considerations surrounding in situ and ex situ conservation of plants (Rolston 2004), and the ethical obligations of scientists who study wildlife in the field (Bekoff & Jamieson 1996; Monamy & Gott 2001; Swart 2004).

[. . .]

Although we can point to these and related attempts to focus more intently on the moral dimensions of ecological research and management, this work has not been coordinated in such a manner that it forms a self-conscious intellectual community with an explicit research agenda. Consequently, there needs to be a more concerted attempt to organize and integrate the discussion across the sciences, humanities, and conservation professions. Writing in these pages some years ago, Farnsworth and Rosovsky (1993) advocated a multidisciplinary dialog among field biologists and philosophers that would address some of the ethical questions we have identified. Our reading and experience, however, suggest this dialog has still not happened (Marsh & Kenchington 2004).

[. . .]

Scientists, managers, and ethicists can all learn by studying jointly the ethical issues confronting practicing ecologists and biodiversity managers. Doing so will help ecologists respond more effectively to the ethical challenges encountered in their research and help them lead discussions of proper research design and management rather than waiting for more slow-moving, ambiguous, and often unwieldy legal guidelines and prohibitions to point the way (Angulo & Cooke 2002). In short, we need a new approach in practical ethics, one we term "ecological ethics."

We offer a few exemplary cases in ecological research and biodiversity management and discuss some of the specific ethical considerations they raise for scientists and managers. We also outline the relevant literatures in theoretical and applied ethics that speak to the duties and responsibilities of these same communities. We end with a call for the collaborative development of a pluralistic ethical framework for making decisions, one that will be a heuristic and analytical instrument informed by multiple domains within theoretical and applied ethics.

Ethical dilemmas in ecology and conservation biology

[. . .]

Using genetically modified organisms to conserve and control species

European wild rabbits (*Oryctolagus cuniculus*) from southwestern Europe are widely introduced into other countries worldwide and can be pests. Angulo and Cooke (2002) summarize a case with complexities that extend beyond those usually associated with deliberate release of genetically modified organisms (GMOs). Rabbits native to Europe support predators, including endangered Imperial Eagle (*Aquila adalberti*) and Iberian lynx (*Lynx pardinus*) populations. In the last 50 years rabbit populations have declined mainly because of the viral myxomatosis and rabbit hemorrhagic diseases. One solution being pursued is releasing a genetically modified virus based on an attenuated myxoma (MV) strain that protects against both viruses. Only a few rabbits must be vaccinated to immunize the larger population because the strain can be transmitted horizontally among rabbits in the field. The same rabbit species is an Australian pest. A control strategy being considered is releasing a genetically modified MV that reduces rabbit fertility through transmissible (virally vectored) immunocontraception; in other words, an introduced contagious virus would disseminate a contraceptive agent through the exotic populations of rabbits. This is not a solitary case. Opossums, foxes, cats, and rodents are also candidates for control by virally vectored immunocontraception (Angulo & Cooke 2002).

Some regulations focus on research and release of genetically modified organisms, but few agreements specifically address safe research, handling, and release of these organisms internationally (Angulo & Cooke 2002). What are the human, animal, and ecological consequences of releasing genetically modified MV? Is it wise to genetically modify viruses for conservation and pest control? Tyndale-Briscoe (1994) considers some of the ethical implications of this practice, but in general what are we to make of an applied research program for rabbit management with opposing goals: conserving a declining species in Europe and killing the same species in Australia?

[. . .]

Choosing between protected and endangered species

The declining desert bighorn sheep (*Ovis canadensis*) population in New Mexico prompted the state's game commission to pass a new regulation in 2002 allowing hunters to kill its primary predator, the mountain lion (*Puma concolor*) during the hunting season. Both animals are rare: The sheep are federally listed as an endangered species, and the mountain lion is a state-protected species. Critics of the lion management plan (including animal protective associations) argue that the kill quotas are too high and that hunting threatens the long-term survival of the population. Others argue that evidence of predation on the endangered sheep does not warrant the increased hunting quotas (West 2002).

Is it right to favor protection of the sheep over the lions in this case, or does this decision reflect an inappropriate and longstanding prejudice against predators? How much influence should stakeholders (e.g., hunters, animal protection associations, environmentalists) have in the decision-making processes of the New Mexico Department of Game and Fish compared with that of the department's (and non-departmental) scientists? What should be the evidentiary standards for concluding that lion predation on sheep requires active management intervention? Should managers be compelled to pursue nonlethal lion population controls even if these are more costly and difficult to administer?

Ethical tools for ecological problem solving

Ecological researchers and biodiversity managers need to be able to seek appropriate guidance in answering questions such as those we posed here. In particular, they need to be able to identify and use relevant ethical principles and related considerations in problematic situations. Following the pragmatic insights of philosopher John Dewey, we hold the view that moral principles are best understood as tools for practical problem solving. The various expressions of value, duty, and obligation in these areas of ethical theory, that is, will prove useful in revealing the moral responsibilities in specific decision contexts and may be used as deliberative resources in the process of determining what should be done in concrete research and management situations (Dewey 1982, 1989; Minteer 2001; Minteer et al. 2004). This pragmatic approach places much greater emphasis on the process of moral reasoning and moral deliberation—the experimental rehearsal, testing, and revision of principles and decision scenarios in the imagination and public debate—than it does on the adherence to any single principle that might be thought of as uniquely authoritative or privileged in moral reflection.

Four primary domains of theoretical and applied ethics are the most relevant to the ethical questions raised by work in ecology and biodiversity management [. . .] (traditional) normative ethical theory, research ethics, animal ethics, and environmental ethics. Each domain and its constituent principles may contribute to our understanding of the moral responsibilities of the ecological researcher and biodiversity manager to the public good, the scientific and professional community, and to individual plants, animals, and ecosystems. In our view, however, each tradition is limited to the extent that it typically highlights only a particular dimension of the moral situation.

For example, the discussion in environmental ethics focuses largely on establishing the moral standing of parts or processes of nature (e.g., nonhuman individuals, species, and ecosystems). Although this may help identify general obligations and responsibilities to natural parts and wholes in ecological research and biodiversity management, scientific researchers and biodiversity managers also have significant obligations beyond the duties that they may be said to owe to species and ecosystems. These include obligations to uphold scientific integrity and avoid conflicts of interest and responsibilities to the greater public good or welfare. These latter obligations may entail both "negative" duties such as refraining from any activities that may produce social harms and "positive" duties such as the protection and promotion of biological diversity and environmental quality for an array of human cultural values. In addition to traditional environmental ethical considerations, then, these other responsibilities may also figure prominently in the deliberations in reaching an ethical judgment about what should be done in a particular research or management context.

We believe a pluralistic ethical framework is therefore the best and most effective way to conceive of the moral resources required by practicing researchers and managers (Norton 1991; Minteer & Manning 1999). The primary task of creating this pluralistic framework lies with the identification and organization of practical ethical principles across the theoretical and applied ethics literatures in ways that will help ecologists and biodiversity managers delineate the moral aspects of specific research and management dilemmas. The framework would distill from this work multiple sets of moral principles—rendered in the form of clear prescriptive statements—relevant to ecological research and biodiversity management in the laboratory and field. Such statements should include both traditional normative ethical principles speaking to ecologists' and biodiversity managers' duties to avoid social harms and promote the general public good (now and in the future), principles relating to their obligations to the scientific or professional community, and ethical principles speaking to their responsibilities to organisms, species, and ecosystems.

The best way to go about creating this framework is to form and cultivate a "deliberative community" of academic researchers and managers that can give shape to this new conceptual and practical tool kit. This community should be interdisciplinary and include ethicists, social scientists, research ecologists, and biodiversity managers tasked with exploring and debating the ethical dimensions of ecological research and biological conservation practices. The group would perform the creative functions of identifying and assembling a comprehensive ethical framework relevant to ecological research and biodiversity management and fulfill the critical role of providing peer review of this framework as a tool to aid moral deliberation and practical problem solving.

The resulting ecological ethics framework we envision will not produce absolute and definitive answers to the specific moral quandaries encountered in environmental research and management settings, but it would provide an important service by offering an instrument for clarifying and reasoning through the relevant principles and values that bear on problematic research and management situations. Still, one of the great difficulties that haunts any pluralistic model of ethics is the challenge of developing a method of integrating multiple principles, or, alternatively, of articulating one or more rules to direct the selection and application of one or more principles in particular situations. Along these lines, there have been some important attempts by other interdisciplinary teams of scholars to identify and integrate, on largely a conceptual level, various environmental and social values and duties in conservation contexts. Two of the more notable examples are Shrader-Frechette and McCoy's (1999) "two-tier" method of moral decision making in conservation biology (incorporating both general utilitarian and deontological principles) and Mumford and Callicott's (2003) conceptual assimilation of multiscalar environmental and community values, an analysis based on their study of stakeholders in the Great Lakes region.

Our own preference (keeping with our pragmatist leanings) is to emphasize the contextual and situational dimension of ethical integration and decision making within problematic research and management situations rather than the more conceptual aspects of this process. Ethical integration is not only a theoretical or intellectual activity (i.e., the philosophical assimilation of multiple values, duties, and interests) but also a form of practical reasoning, one performed by conflicted moral agents in complex and often morally and empirically ambiguous situations. We believe the most important "integrative" tasks in any sound model of ethical analysis are therefore action oriented and methodological in nature: improving individuals' sensitivity to the ethical context of specific practices (and their awareness of the relevant moral principles that bear on these practices) and facilitating the sharpening of individuals' imaginative and analytical skills so that they may learn to take a more reflective, creative, and systematic approach to moral problems.

This more pragmatic and "particularist" approach to ethics does not deny the role of general principles in ethical problem solving so much as it attempts to place them within a larger experimental process of moral deliberation and inquiry, a process that can also lead to the transformation of values as inquirers rehearse potential courses of action and share information and trade arguments with others over what should be done in specific environmental research and management contexts (Dewey 1982, 1989; Wallace 1996; Minteer et al. 2004).

Of course, such pluralistic and dynamic moral models are notoriously messy; principles can and do often come into significant conflict despite our best attempts to achieve either conceptual or pragmatic integration. In such cases, hard decisions will undoubtedly have to be made. At the same time, however, we should remember that there are often opportunities for moral deliberation to settle on practical actions and decisions that reflect the convergence rather than the divergence of different interests and values (Norton 1991; Minteer & Manning 2000). On this point there may be much to learn from established dispute resolution and "negotiated agreement" approaches (e.g., Fisher & Ury 1983; Susskind & Cruikshank 1987). Especially relevant to the vision of practical ethics we have outlined here are these methods' emphasis on the search for shared interests and mutual gain and their focus on the development of novel tactics and solutions to complex problems through organized negotiation and consensus-building activities (Minteer 2004).

Finally, in addition to creating a pluralistic ecological ethics framework, our proposed project leads to the preparation of a wide-ranging set of case studies in ecological research and biodiversity management (such as more developed versions of the kinds of cases presented above) that would become a useful database for scientists, managers, and students interested in learning how ethical questions emerge in the course of field and laboratory practices and about the moral claims that may be placed on them in a given situation (e.g., Dubycha & Geedey 2003). As we have witnessed with the rapid growth of the field of bioethics, such a case database can be an important educational and analytical tool, sharpening our understanding of ethical issues, our critical thinking, and our problem-solving skills (e.g., Crigger 1998; Murphy 2004; Pence 2004).

The development of a similarly detailed and organized case literature in ecological ethics would allow scientists, managers, and students to compare a variety of ethical, research, and managerial issues across experiential and value contexts, and would provide them with an opportunity to learn from the specific differences and similarities of the issues and cases. Such cases, developed as full educational modules complete with discussion questions, background readings, and supporting materials, could then be housed on a Web site that would serve as an integrative focus for interdisciplinary work and dialog in this new area of practical ethics. Through these kinds of activities we hope to facilitate the interdisciplinary conversation and preparation of the ecological ethics "tool kit" for environmental researchers and managers.

Conclusion

We call for a new approach in practical ethics—"ecological ethics"—and a new conceptual and analytical tool kit for ecologists and biodiversity managers that will help them deal with the moral questions raised by their work. These questions have to date not been addressed in a systematic fashion within the established areas of applied ethics. A comprehensive ethical framework and case study database is therefore needed to help research scientists and biodiversity managers better understand and respond to the ethical issues they face in their research and conservation activities. These tools not only will provide critical assistance to researchers and managers as they deliberate within specific decision-making contexts but also will ultimately help create a larger and necessary forum for discussion of the complex ethical dimensions of ecological research and conservation practices.

Literature cited

Angulo, E., and B. Cooke. 2002. First synthesize new viruses then regulate their release? The case of the wild rabbit. Molecular Ecology 11:2703–2709.

Bekoff, M., and D. Jamieson, 1996. Ethics and the study of carnivores: doing science while respecting animals. Pages 15–45 in J. L. Gittleman, editor. Carnivore behavior, ecology, and evolution. Cornell University Press, Ithaca, New York.

Courchamp, F., R. Woodroffe, and G. Roemer, 2003. Removing protected populations to save endangered species. Science 302:1532.

Crigger, B. J. 1998. Cases in bioethics: selections from the Hastings Center Report. St. Martin's Press, Boston.

Dewey, J. 1982 (orig. 1920). Reconstruction in philosophy. Collected in volume 12 of J. A. Boydston, editor. John Dewey: the middle works. Southern Illinois University Press, Carbondale.

Dewey, J. 1989 (orig. 1932). Ethics. Collected in volume 7 of J. A. Boydston, editor. John Dewey: the later works. Southern Illinois University Press, Carbondale.

Dubycha, J. L., and C. K. Geedey. 2003. Adventures of the mad scientist: fostering science ethics in ecology with case studies. Frontiers in Ecology and the Environment 1:330–333.

Ehrlich, P. R. 2003. Bioethics: are our priorities right? BioScience 53:1207–1216.

Farnsworth, E. J., and J. Rosovsky. 1993. The ethics of ecological field experimentation. Conservation Biology 7:463–472.

Fisher, R., and W. Ury. 1983. Getting to yes. Penguin Books, New York.

Gobster, P. H., and R. B. Hull, editors. 2000. Restoring nature: perspectives from the social sciences and the humanities. Island Press, Washington, D.C.

Lélé, S., and R. B. Norgaard, 1996. Sustainability and the scientist's burden. Conservation Biology 10:354–365.

Light, A., and E. Higgs. 1996. The politics of ecological restoration. Environmental Ethics 18:227–247.

Lodge, D. M., and K. Shrader-Frechette. 2003. Nonindigenous species: ecological explanation, environmental ethics, and public policy. Conservation Biology 17:31–37.

Lubchenco, J. 1998. Entering the century of the environment: a new social contract for science. Science 279:491–497.

Marsh, H., and R. Kenchington. 2004. The role of ethics in experimental marine biology and ecology. Journal of Experimental Marine Biology and Ecology 300:5–14.

Minteer, B. A. 2001. Intrinsic value for pragmatists? Environmental Ethics 23:57–75.

Minteer, B. A. 2004. Beyond considerability: a Deweyan view of the animal rights-environmental ethics debate. Pages 97–118 in E. McKenna and A. Light, editors. Animal pragmatism: rethinking human-nonhuman relationships. Indiana University Press, Bloomington.

Minteer, B. A., and R. E. Manning. 1999. Pragmatism in environmental ethics: democracy, pluralism, and the management of nature. Environmental Ethics 21:191–207.

Minteer, B. A., and R. E. Manning. 2000. Convergence in environmental values: an empirical and conceptual defense. Ethics, Place, and Environment 3:47–60.

Minteer, B. A., E. A. Corley, and R. E. Manning. 2004. Environmental ethics beyond principle? The case for a pragmatic contextualism. Journal of Agricultural & Environmental Ethics 17:131–156.

Monamy, V., and M. Gott. 2001. Practical and ethical considerations for students conducting ecological research involving wildlife. Austral Ecology 26:293–300.

Mumford, K., and J. B. Callicott. 2003. A hierarchical theory of value applied to the Great Lakes and their fishes. Pages 50–74 in D. G. Dallmeyer, editor. Values at sea: ethics for the marine environment. University of Georgia Press, Athens.

Murphy, T. F. 2004. Case studies in biomedical research ethics. MIT Press, Cambridge, Massachusetts.

Norton, B. G. 1991. Toward unity among environmentalists. Oxford University Press, New York.

Norton, B. G., M. Hutchins, E. F. Stevens, and T. L. Maple, editors. 1995. Ethics on the ark: zoos, animals welfare, and wildlife conservation. Smithsonian Institution Press, Washington, D.C.

Pence, G.E. 2004. Classic cases in medical ethics: accounts of cases that have shaped medical ethics, with philosophical, legal, and historical backgrounds. 4th edition. McGraw-Hill, New York.

Potvin, C. J., M. Kraenzel, and G. Seutin, editors. 2001. Protecting biological diversity: roles and responsibilities. McGill-Queen's University Press, Montreal.

Rolston, H., III. 2004. In situ and ex situ conservation: philosophical and ethical concerns. Pages 21–39 in E. O. Guerrant Jr., K. Havens, and M. Maunder, editors. Ex situ plant conservation: supporting species in the wild. Island Press, Washington, D.C.

Shrader-Frechette, K., and E. D. McCoy. 1999. Molecular systematics, ethics, and biological decision making under uncertainty. Conservation Biology 13:1008–1012.

Susskind, L., and J. Cruikshank. 1987. Breaking the impasse. Basic Books, New York.

Swart, J. A. A. 2004. The wild animal as a research animal. Journal of Agricultural & Environmental Ethics 17:181–197.

Tyndale-Briscoe, C. H. 1994. Virus-vectored immunocontraception of feral mammals. Reproduction, Fertility and Development 6:281–287.

Wallace, J. D. 1996. Ethical norms, particular cases. Cornell University Press, Ithaca, New York.

West, K. 2002. Lion vs. lamb. Scientific American 286(5):20–21.

Wilson, E. O. 2002. The future of life. Alfred A. Knopf (distributed by Random House), New York.

Chapter 47

Stephen T. Emlen

ETHICS AND EXPERIMENTATION: HARD CHOICES FOR THE FIELD ORNITHOLOGIST

In responding to a critique of an earlier study, Emlen defends his earlier work and also addresses the broader issue of ethical trade-offs in experimental science. He agrees that animal pain and suffering should be minimized in animal research whenever possible and that scientists have a responsibility to carefully compare the value of their research against the harm their work causes. He further argues that some animal experimentation is needed—not just for human interests, but as a benefit to the natural world, and ultimately to minimize pain and suffering among nonhuman species.

EVERY SCIENTIST MUST make difficult ethical decisions when designing experiments, whether such experiments are conducted in the laboratory or in the field. Typically, these decisions require weighing the likely scientific gain (in terms of new information to be learned) against the animal cost (in terms of suffering of the individuals involved). The question of when the pursuit of knowledge justifies the imposition of suffering on animal subjects is one that should be honestly confronted and constantly reassessed. Most scientific societies have published guidelines to help individual scientists formulate their answers (e.g. Oring *et al.* 1988, Dawkins and Gosling 1992. Anonymous 1987, 1992). However, even with such guidelines, there is no magic "threshold" of agreement. Rather, there is a broad gray area within which different opinions are vehemently expressed. Peer feedback is useful in defining these gray areas and in stimulating discussion about them. It is in this light that I welcome the opportunity to reply to the commentary of Bekoff (1993).

Bekoff (1993) criticized our study (Emlen *et al.* 1989) of experimentally induced infanticide in jacanas on ethical grounds and chastised the American Ornithologists' Union for publishing our article in the *Auk*. As the senior author of the challenged paper, I wish to justify our specific experiments, as well as address the broader issue of ethical trade-offs in experimental science.

If asked, everyone would agree that unnecessary and unnatural pain and suffering in animals should be minimized wherever possible, but there exists a spectrum of opinions on when and whether intervention and experimentation are appropriate. At one end, few would disagree that many birds are kept in captivity under sufficiently inhumane conditions that no degree of scientific justification can excuse their poor care. At the other, field ornithologists routinely witness nestlings suffering from predation and starvation, yet few would advocate intervention to eliminate predators or to provide supplemental food to under-nourished chicks. In between these extremes the answers are less clear-cut.

How then should scientists balance the trade-off of knowledge gained versus suffering caused (or permitted, by nonintervention)? Bateson (1986) and Driscoll and Bateson (1988) offered a useful "model" in the form of a decision cube with three dimensions: the certainty of benefit (knowledge gained), the quality of the research, and the amount of animal suffering. In relative terms, animal suffering is justified only when the research is of high quality and has a high certainty of benefit.

But what qualifies as "benefit"? Bateson (1986) and Driscoll and Bateson (1988) couched benefit largely in terms of knowledge that has obvious potential benefit to humans. In his original paper, Bateson used "certainty of *medical* benefit" as his first dimension (emphasis mine). I strongly disagree. In this era of diminishing biodiversity it is imperative that we increase our knowledge of organisms that can serve as general models for larger categories of species. Whether we wish it or not, we are becoming stewards for increasing numbers of threatened species on this planet. To be effective stewards, we must have better knowledge of a wide array of species representing different phylogenetic, ecological, physiological, and behavioral types. Gaining such knowledge frequently requires experimental testing of specific hypotheses.

I suggest that "scientific value" replace Bateson's "certainty of medical benefit" as a critical criterion in the decision of when, and whether, animal suffering can be justified. I further suggest two specific criteria as useful guidelines for assessing the scientific value of any study: (1) the conceptual importance of the question being asked; and (2) the degree to which the results will be generalizable to other species (so that, ultimately, fewer experiments will need to be conducted on other species). These considerations were critical factors in our decision to conduct an experimental test of infanticide in jacanas.

The question of the possible adaptive significance of the infanticidal killing of conspecific young is, in my view, one of considerable conceptual importance. Such behavior occurs commonly in a wide variety of species, including our own (Hrdy 1979, Hausfater and Hrdy 1984). When infanticide was found to be widespread among primates, it aroused considerable scientific interest among both evolutionary biologists and anthropologists. Hrdy (1974, 1977) offered a comprehensive adaptive hypothesis for one form of infanticide, that which occurs when a new male in a harem polygynous primate species displaces a male breeder and "takes-over" the breeder's assemblage of females. Such incoming males frequently kill young that are still dependent upon the female(s). Hrdy (1974, 1977) speculated that such behavior was adaptive to the infanticidal male because the removal of dependent young caused females to come into estrous and to reproduce with the new male much more rapidly than would otherwise be the case. This sexually selected infanticide hypothesis proposed specific benefits (enhanced reproductive success) for the perpetrator and predicted the conditions (following takeovers by new mates) under which it was expected to occur.

Alternative hypotheses were rapidly advanced, including several that considered infanticidal killing to be a nonadaptive behavior, aberrantly expressed under conditions of artificially high population density or excessive human disturbance (Curtin and Dolhinow 1978, 1979, Boggess 1979, Sommer 1987). One of the difficulties in differentiating among these hypotheses has been the scarcity of direct observations of the behavior. Infanticide is usually inferred. And even when infanticide is observed, we are left with descriptive and correlational data only; cause and effect can only be tested experimentally. Although a growing body of data are consistent with Hrdy's predictions (e.g. Hausfater and Hrdy 1984, Sommer 1987), we have only weak inference tests of the hypothesis.

Because of their behavioral role-reversal, jacanas offered a unique opportunity to examine the hypothesis of sexually selected infanticide. Jacanas provide a mirror image of the polygynous mating systems in which infanticide has been reported in mammals. In jacanas it is females that hold "harems" of males and that compete intensively for mates. Jenni and Collier (1972) reported that males frequently change "ownership" during their lifetime. Stephens (1982, 1984) concurred and speculated that infanticide might occur.

By inducing infanticide experimentally, we were able to confirm the specific predictions of the Hrdy hypothesis with a rigor not possible from descriptive observations alone. Further, by our choice of jacanas as the model species, we were able to extend the applicability of the hypothesis (1) across taxa (to birds as well as mammals) and (2) across sexes (since females, as predicted by theory, are the infanticidal sex under conditions of role reversal). Our results thus provided an unusually robust test of the hypothesis. An adaptive explanation for infanticide was strongly supported, and the generality of the Hrdy hypothesis was greatly extended.

What of Bekoff's specific criticisms? In the experiment, we removed two polyandrously breeding female jacanas and then observed the behavior of the incoming females that competed to take-over the residents' territories and the males that occupied them. Bekoff (1993) questioned: (1) the methods used to remove the two breeding females; and (2) the allowing of the "maiming and killing of seven of their chicks." He also challenged (3) the review process that allowed publication of a paper that he believes violated AOU guidelines. Below I address each of these criticisms.

(1) The females were collected by shooting. According to the AOU guidelines, shooting is the most humane method of collection because individuals are killed outright. Our observations were part of a pilot study to determine the feasibility of a more intensive project on the social behavior and breeding biology of this species. The collected individuals served an additional purpose. Blood and tissue samples from these specimens confirmed the suitability of the molecular method of DNA fingerprinting (Jeffries *et al.* 1985, Westneat 1990) for assignment of paternity in jacanas. We determined that blood samples would be sufficient for later studies of promiscuity and paternity, eliminating any need for collection of additional individuals for tissue samples.

(2) Following the removal of each resident female, neighboring females rapidly expended their territories to encompass the vacated areas (and the resident males they contained). These replacement females actively sought out and attacked the chicks of the former female. The males attempted to defend their young, but were unsuccessful. The behavior was dramatic; it provided clear answers to Hrdy's predictions. It also caused the death of five chicks.

After removal of the second female, I called off further experiments. Our sample sizes were extremely small (three of three incoming females infanticidal; four of four broods attacked; five of nine chicks killed and two evicted); however, the results were sufficiently clear that I did not wish to induce further suffering. By terminating the experiment at two female removals, we were unable statistically to confirm that incoming females are infanticidal (a sample of three females or four broods is too small to achieve significance with a Fisher exact test). Ironically, this trade-off "cost" us the opportunity of publishing the results in an interdisciplinary journal of wider circulation because one reviewer felt that the sample sizes were insufficient.

(3) Did this research violate AOU guidelines? The guidelines state that researchers must "avoid or minimize distress and pain to the animals, consistent with sound research design." The design of this experiment, however, was to test whether infanticidal behavior would be induced under specific conditions. One cannot easily control behavior in field situations. Bekoff questioned why we did not intervene to recapture the injured chicks, nursing them back to health or, if fatally injured, killing them humanely. This was not logistically possible. The remaining way of minimizing suffering is to limit the number of individuals attacked. We did this by terminating the experiment after only two removals.

I have no disagreement with Bekoff that animal pain and suffering are sometimes caused by scientific research, that such pain and suffering should be minimized whenever possible, and that scientists have a moral and ethical obligation to weigh carefully the scientific value of their research against the magnitude of suffering that it might cause. However, he and I differ on how such trade-offs should be decided, and on where the line of justification lies. Medical researchers argue that animal experimentation is required if we are to combat human diseases and avoid pain and suffering in our own species. I would expand their argument to encompass the need for selective animal experimentation to enhance our general knowledge of the behavior and ecology of representative species, knowledge that is required if we are to protect and conserve the diversity of life and, ultimately, to minimize pain and suffering in nonhuman species.

I thank Natalie J. Demong and Douglas J. Emlen for their comments.

Literature cited

Anonymous. 1987. Acceptable field methods in mammalogy: Preliminary guidelines approved by the American Society of Mammalogists. *J. Mammal.* 68(4, suppl):1–18.

Anonymous. 1992. Sigma Xi statement on the use of animals in research. *Am. Sci.* 80:73–6.

Bateson, P. 1986. When to experiment on animals. *New Scientist* 109(1496):30–2.

Bekoff, M. 1993. Experimentally induced infanticide: The removal of birds and its ramifications. *Auk* 110:404–6.

Boggess, J. 1979. Infant killing and male reproductive strategies in langurs (*Presbytis entellus*). Pages 283–310 in *Infanticide: Comparative and evolutionary perspectives* (G. Hausfater and S. Hrdy, eds). Aldine, New York.

Curtin, R. A., and P. Dolhinow. 1978. Primate social behavior in a changing world. *Am. Sci.* 66:468–75.

——— 1979. Infanticide among langurs—A solution to overcrowding? *Science Today* 13:35–41.

Dawkins, M. S., and M. Gosling. 1992. *Ethics in research on animal behavior: Readings from Animal Behavior.* Academic Press, London. Pages 1–64.

Driscoll, J. W., and P. Bateson. 1988. Animals in behavioural research. *Anim. Behav.* 36:1569–1574.

Emlen, S. T., N. J. Demong, and D. J. Emlen. 1989. Experimental induction of infanticide in female Wattled Jacanas. *Auk* 106:1–7.

Hausfater, G., and S. B. Hrdy. 1984. *Infanticide: Comparative and evolutionary perspectives.* Aldine, New York.

Hrdy, S. B. 1974. Male-male competition and infanticide among the langurs (*Presbytis entellus*) of Abu, Rajasthan. *Folia Primatol.* 22:19–58.

——— 1977. Infanticide as a primate reproductive strategy. *Am. Sci.* 65:40–9.

——— 1979. Infanticide among animals: A review, classification, and examination of the implications for the reproductive strategies of females. *Ethol. and Sociobiol.* 1:13–40.

Jeffries, A. J., V. Wilson, and S. L. Thein. 1985. Hypervariable 'minisatellite' regions in human DNA. *Nature* 314:411–20.

Jenni, D. A., and G. Collier. 1972. Polyandry in the American Jacana (*Jacana spinosa*). *Auk* 89:743–65.

Oring, L. W., K. P. Able, D. W. Anderson, L. F. Baptista, J. C. Barlow, A. S. Gaunt, F. B. Gill, and J. C. Wingfield. 1988. Guidelines for the use of wild birds in ornithological research. *Auk* 105(suppl):1a–41a.

Sommer, V. 1987. Infanticide among free-ranging langurs (*Presbytis entellus*) at Jodhpur (Rajasthan/India): Recent observations and a reconsideration of hypotheses. *Primates* 28:163–97.

Stephens, M. L. 1982. Mate takeover and possible infanticide by a female Northern Jacana, *Jacana spinosa*. *Anim. Behav.* 30:1253–4.

——— 1984. Maternal care and polyandry in the Northern Jacana, *Jacana spinosa*. Ph.D. thesis, Univ. Chicago, Chicago.

Westnext, D. F. 1990. Genetic parentage in the Indigo Bunting: A study using DNA fingerprinting. *Behav. Ecol. Sociobiol.* 27:67–76.

FURTHER READING

American Association for Laboratory Animal Science (AALAS), Institutional Animal Care and Use Committees: A comprehensive online resource at: http://www.iacuc.org.

Balcombe, J.P., Barnard, N.D., and C. Sandusky (2004) "Laboratory routines cause animal stress," *Contemporary Topics in Laboratory Animal Science* 43: 42–51.

Baumans, V. (2004) "Use of animals in experimental research: An ethical dilemma?" *Gene Therapy* 11: S64–S66.

Bishop, Laura Jane, and Nolen, Anita Lonnes (2001) "Animals in research and education: Ethical issues," Scope Note 40. *Kennedy Institute of Ethics Journal* 11: 91–112.

Dich, T., Hansen, T., Algers, A., Hanlon, A., Loor, H., and P. Sandoe (2006) "Animal Ethics Dilemma/: A computer supported learning tool." In *Ethics and the Politics of Food*, M. Kaiser and M. E. Lien (eds.), The Netherlands: Wageningen Academic Publishers, www.aedilemma.net.

Frey, Raymond. G. (2002) "Ethics, animals and scientific inquiry." Pp. 13–24, in *Applied Ethics in Animal Research: Philosophy, Regulation, and Laboratory Applications*, J. P. Gluck, T. DiPasquale, and F. B. Orlans (eds.), West Lafayette, IN: Purdue University Press.

Gluck, J.P., DiPasquale, T., and Orlans, F.B. (eds.) (2002) *Applied Ethics in Animal Research: Philosophy, Regulation, and Laboratory Applications*. West Lafayette, IN: Purdue University Press.

Hagelin, J., Hau, J., and H.-E. Carlsson (2002) "The refining influence of ethics committees on animal experimentation in Sweden," *Laboratory Animals* 37: 10–18.

Humane Society of the United States (n.d.) *Animals & Society: A List of Courses (Animal Ethics, Animal Rights, Animal Welfare)*. Online at http://www.hsus.org/programs/research/animals_education.html.

Langford, D.J., Crager, S.E., Shehzad, Z., Smith, S.B., Sotocinal, S.G., Levenstadt, J.S., Chanda, M.L., Levitin, D.J., and Mogil, J.S. (2006) "Social modulation of pain as evidence for empathy in mice," *Science* 312: 1967–1970.

Mangan, Katherine S. (2000) "Can vet schools teach without killing animals?" *The Chronicle of Higher Education* 46 (issue of 4 Feb. 2000): 2 pp.

Morrison, A.R. (2001) "A scientist's perspective on the ethics of using animals in behavioral research." In *Animal Research and Human Health*, M. Carroll and J.B. Overmier (eds.), Washington, D.C.: American Psychological Association.

New England Anti-Vivisection Society Ethical Science and Education Coalition (n.d.) Online at http://www.neavs.org/esec.html and http://www.neavs.org.

Nuffield Council on Bioethics (2006) "The ethics of research involving animals," www. nuffieldbioethics.org.

Shanks, H., and Green, K. (2004) "Evolution and the ethics of animal research," *Essays in Philosophy* 5: 21 pp.

STUDY QUESTIONS

1 Select one of the four issues DeGrazia believes will continue to serve as a point of difference between proponents and opponents of animal use, and explain how you might move the two sides closer together on that issue.

2 How might Brody respond to Regan's claim that animals have a value that cannot be reduced to human utility?

3 In light of Orlan's discussion, what additional laws regulating animal use, if any, do you believe should be adopted by the U.S.?

4 What constraints do you believe are appropriate for the use of live animals in elementary school education? Clarify your reasoning.

5 Based on Minteer and Collins' recommendations for a new field in ecological ethics, give three traits of this ethic you would propose to initiate fruitful discussions.

6 Emlen asserts that animal experimentation is needed to benefit the natural world, including minimizing suffering in nonhuman animals. To what extent do you agree and disagree with his assertion?

Animals and biotechnology

INTRODUCTION TO PART SIX

AUTHORS OF THIS PART GRAPPLE with some of the very difficult issues associated with biotechnology. David Morton argues that protection of animals and the environment matters most and, if humans have the right motivation and intention, right actions will follow. Some of the moral issues associated with genetic engineering are addressed in the next four papers. Robert and Baylis, and Streiffer, present some opposing views on whether human-to-animal embryonic chimeras would introduce inexorable moral confusion in our existing relationships with nonhumans. Arguing from a utilitarian perspective, Kevin Smith believes that there is no clear moral mandate against genetic sequence alteration; likewise he argues that within the concept of "replaceability," killing of transgenic animals is acceptable for animals not identified with "personhood." Smith does advocate a general prohibition on studies that entail significant suffering for animals. Finally, Jeffrey Burkhardt argues that most of the arguments raised in opposition to biotechnology lack ethical force because most scientists and science policy makers lack the moral education necessary to fully understand the significance of the arguments made. Burkhardt calls for ethical training to become an established part of the training and thinking of scientists and science policy makers.

Using the Maxim to Respect *Telos*, Bernard E. Rollin agrees with Kevin Smith that there is no clear justification to preclude genetic engineering of animals; he notes that genetic modifications should be assessed in relation to the Principle of Conservation of Welfare. Bernice Bovenkirk, Frans Brom and Babs van den Bergh respond to Rollin's perspective by introducing the notion of integrity as a set of characteristics of an animal humans believe important to preserve; they call for moral discussion to identify these features and note that, even if there is not full agreement on what constitutes integrity for an animal, the discussions can provide a basis for evaluating existing practices.

Oliver Ryder notes that cloning techniques with animals might be particularly valuable in work with endangered species, and raises the possibility of resurrecting extinct animals. He calls for increased research, careful targeting of technology, and an increase in banking cells for possible future application. Autumn Fiester argues that even pet cloning may be defensible under certain circumstances.

Chapter 48

David Morton

SOME ETHICAL ISSUES IN BIOTECHNOLOGY INVOLVING ANIMALS

Morton argues that biotechnological discoveries have given rise to ethical issues, particularly concerning the welfare of animals and the protection of the environment with regard to other animal species. He argues that protection of animals and the environment should have the highest concern and, further, that if humans have good motivation and intentions, then appropriate good actions will follow.

Introduction

THIS PAPER PROVIDES a personal view of some of the ethical issues that have arisen in the light of some biotechnological discoveries or ideas, particularly concerning the welfare of animals and the protection of the environment with regard to other animal species. It does not address broader and important legal and consumer concerns. [. . .] In this paper it is argued that protection of animals and the environment matter most, and that given the right motivation and intention of human beings then the right actions will follow. It is hoped that this essay will generate some discussion that will enable readers to question their own views and attitudes.

Benefits of genetic manipulation

Recent advances in our understanding of how cells work at the molecular level have sparked a plethora of ideas as to how to harness this knowledge to our (human) advantage. Adding genes to animals from the same or other species (transgenesis), removing other genes through knock-out technology, and cloning animals using embryonic and somatic cells have been fundamentally important advances, and some of these advances have led, or may lead, to significant improvements in the health and welfare of both humans and animals. For example, the genetic modification of farm animals to be resistant to zoonotic diseases such as *Salmonella* and spongiform encephalopathy (eg bovine SE or new variant CJD, scrapie) would improve both human and animal welfare. (Note that if animals are sick their welfare is compromised, and so health is one important welfare measure.)

Changing the sentience of animals through gene deletion so that they suffer less stress during their lives could be seen, on the one hand, as a desirable outcome and another aspect of domestication. On the other hand, it might be seen as an undesirable outcome and inherently objectionable as it goes against the very essence of what an animal is.[1] Genetically engineering animals to produce leaner meat, to grow faster and to utilise feed more efficiently would be good for both consumers and farmers, but would it be good for animal welfare? The production and isolation of therapeutic proteins from the milk of sheep carrying and expressing human genes (eg human essential clotting factors, alpha-1-anti-trypsin) would help those with haemophilia and emphysema, and possibly those with cystic fibrosis, to have a better quality of life with little impact on the welfare of the sheep.

Genetically manipulating (GM) pigs to provide a supply of organs and tissues for those waiting for a human transplant would save lives, and would probably involve little more harm to the animals other than killing it humanely. Note that it is not only mammals that are being utilised in this way. GM salmon that grow six times faster than ordinary salmon have been created, and if they escape (and some GM fish have), theoretically they could make the native salmon population extinct in 40 generations. Similarly, adding cold resistant genes could help create tropical fish for food in other than their natural waters and 'pet' fish (as well as other animals) could be manipulated for size, shape, colour, etc. for the amusement of their owners.

Finally, in this medley of potential benefits, the 'ultimate' goal of making new organs, tissues and cells from somatic stem cells taken from the diseased patient herself, thus avoiding the need for immuno-suppression, would be a significant advance. These advances in stem cell technology, together with a better understanding of cell differentiation, cell signalling and cellular integration in whole organs, provide for exciting prospects for the development of even more ingenious therapeutic modalities.

Ethical issues

However, all of these developments have ethical dimensions that should make us think twice before rushing headlong into what seems to be such worthwhile efforts. The persuasive power of the dollar, euro, etc., in our society tends sometimes to conflict with ethical concerns, as making money can appear to be the primary, rather than a secondary, goal at the expense of the sick humans or the welfare of animals. The motivation and intentions of those carrying out these genetic manipulations, or implicated in other ways, such as funding and giving ethical approval, has also to be questioned. There surely needs to be a strong element of good intention if we are to indirectly affect the welfare of animals or disturb the environment in a serious way before the work starts. Even if finance was not directly involved, there are perhaps some things that we should not do to humans or animals, like altering their sentience (ie ability to experience pain and pleasure) or their gross shape [. . .]. Our current predominantly anthropocentric view of life (putting human interests first) in our ecosystem with respect to the environment and animals is increasingly being challenged so that the possible outcomes of our actions should also be fully considered before going ahead. This is not a Luddite statement but rather that we should be giving careful and serious thought to what we do before we do it.[1-4] The fact that we 'can' do something does not mean we 'ought' to do it.

The ethical issues revolve around what we might do to other humans, to animals and to the environment, and this short paper focuses on animals. Before that it is worth a comment on ethics in science. Scientists often claim that science is ethically neutral; they provide facts and the ethical issues are really about how those facts are used, and not linked to their discovery. But there are ethical considerations to be taken into account before certain lines of investigation are followed. We should consider how that scientific information might be used before carrying out experiments, or the direct impact of an experiment on the animals or environment (or on the scientists themselves). Scientists, just as other moral agents, are responsible for their actions and, apart from lines of investigation, it is important that scientific research is conducted in an ethical manner. The following examples illustrate this point.

The very act of transferring a piece of human DNA into animals has been questioned on religious grounds as some believe that it is unethical to do so because being 'human' denotes something God-given and, therefore, special and not to be tampered with. On the other hand, humans have many gene sequences in common with bananas, rats and chimpanzees (nearly 99 per cent), and so the claim that human genes are unique cannot be sustained. However, there may be some unique human genes, for example for self-awareness: would it be right to transfer these into animals?

With shared genes, considerable benefits could accrue from transgenic technology, for example the production of therapeutic proteins in animals – so-called gene pharming. This 'artificial' production of proteins that can be given to humans and animals deficient in them would produce considerable benefits. An example is the production of human insulin in yeast for the treatment of diabetes (an increasingly common disease in the developed countries). More recently, the production and purification of human proteins from the milk of transgenic sheep is being trialled to treat humans with emphysema, and other proteins being researched include those involved in the clotting process in order to treat people with haemophilia.[5]

There are also considerable advantages in gene pharming as yields are higher than conventional methods (purification from human plasma) since the resultant products are free from potential human infections such as HIV and hepatitis. So in the instance of therapeutic proteins one might argue that the benefits for humans far outweigh the harms done to the sheep (and maybe cattle) that produce the milk and it is reasonable to do so. But it should not be forgotten that there are hidden costs to this approach. These are in the *development* of the transgenic animal lines that produce these proteins, and include superovulation and death of the donor animals, embryo transfer into a recipient, sometimes Caesarean sections for the dam, and even then some neonates die or are abnormal at birth. However, those animals born alive and that survive to a reproductive age may well go on to found the production line. These founder animals and their offspring are likely to have a good quality of life and, almost certainly, a longer life compared with their cohorts that are slaughtered for food, simply because of their economic and scientific value.

Cloning is also being used to generate animals from the transgenic line and although recently there has been some evidence that they have a higher rate of abnormal and overweight lambs than normal animals, and that they may age quicker (by no means unequivocal), these adverse effects may be overcome in the longer term. In terms of what 'society' regards as acceptable for animals, it is relevant to note that these harms are far fewer overall (both in type, intensity and duration) than those caused to millions of intensively farmed animals such as chickens and pigs.

Some companies are writing codes of ethics for their employees to follow. For example, the Genetic Savings & Clone (GSC) company – a biotechnology company which markets genetic services to the public via the Internet – has a Code of Ethics for all its employees. All GSC employees are contractually bound to follow this code which governs the treatment of all the animals involved in the development of their technology and also the future application of their technology.[6]

[. . .]

In the UK, the law controlling animal research (the Animals (Scientific Procedures) Act 1986) uses a utilitarian approach when considering whether to grant a project licence for a programme of research work. In the present context, an application for a project licence would have to detail the consequences of developing a transgenic line with descriptions of how it is to be done including any uncertainties, and the anticipated benefits. Both these statements of benefits and harms are, of course, predictions at this stage, and under the 1986 Act the scientist, the local ethics committee (or ethical review process) and the Home Office Inspectorate have then to decide whether the work should go ahead. The Inspector is the final arbiter (although there is an appeal process) and if s/he agrees with the submission then a licence is granted, although often with amendments concerning experimental design and refinement of the scientific protocol.

[. . .]

Another conundrum that some philosophers have raised (notably Singer[7]) when opposing the use of animals in science is whether humans have the right to carry out research on animals that would not be carried out on humans. The question is phrased somewhat differently: 'What are the morally relevant differences between animals and humans that make it acceptable to carry out research on animals but not on humans?' To condone current practice, the answer has to place all humans in one 'box' and all non-human animals in another. One answer might be that we are human beings and not animals, but this really gets us no further forward, for what is it about being a human being that separates us from all the other species? Indeed the very reason for using animals as models for ourselves is our close genetic, physiological and anatomical similarities. Some might argue that we use animals in this way simply because it is custom and practice, so why should any change be necessary? But the fact is that all human cultures continually evolve and had this answer been accepted in the past, then we would still have slavery, women would not have the right to vote, and so on. The fact that something happens at present, does not make it right. Perhaps animal research can be justified because humans are stronger than animals, in which case should women be used as research subjects? Or if the criterion is intelligence, then perhaps men! But seriously, our ability to reflect on these questions potentially sets us apart as a species, but is this a *morally relevant* difference? Would it protect mentally retarded children for example? Perhaps we should protect the vulnerable and give as much consideration to chimpanzees as to mentally retarded children (who may even be less intelligent than the chimpanzee) and so do research on neither. But do we know where to draw the line between the species – at primates, pigs, dogs, mammals, parrots, chickens, reptiles, amphibians, fish, octopus, etc.? The evidence is lacking for our present legal position, but it errs on the side of caution over physical pain and distress.

Another proposition is that 'suffering' is the key objection to animal research and humans would suffer mentally more than animals, eg we can think about the future as well as experience pain, distress and so on. But are we sure that only humans have this ability? As it happens there is increasing evidence that many non-human primates, and even non-primate species, have some limited degree of self-awareness and can anticipate the future.[8,9] But to what degree and to what end (their death?) we can only ascertain indirectly and in a very limited way. The recent debate over stag and fox hunting in the UK illustrates this point well. Descartes (1596–1650) was sure that using animals was acceptable on the basis that they could not speak and were irrational, and so they could not suffer; whereas Jeremy Bentham (1748–1832) asked, 'Surely the question is not whether they can talk, or whether they can reason, but whether they can suffer?'

Do religious beliefs help here, even though many people do not have a faith? Religions differ widely on this matter.[10] Compare Buddhists who believe in not harming any living creature as well as in reincarnation, with the Hindus who protect cows, with the traditional Judeo-Christian belief that animals are put on this earth for us and we have dominion over them. (Linzey disputes this interpretation of 'dominion'; see, eg, Linzey and Turner[11] and Linzey.[12]) Overall, there seems to be no universal agreement that can be gained from religion on this matter.

To summarise then, the use of animals in research when we would not use humans has been termed *speciesism*[13] and has been likened to racism, sexism and ageism. It is simply a prejudice, and not a justifiable position. We should either use both animals and humans in the same way[14] or we should use neither. There are other philosophical arguments against the use of animals in research and utilitarians argue that the benefits of the research should outweigh the harms. Where this is not the case, or the anticipated benefit is so unlikely, or the predicted harm is so great, then the work should not proceed. Some research indeed may have no benefit but simply help us understand better how the body works, but that in itself is a benefit, even if less predictable.[15] Whatever animal research is carried out for the direct or indirect prevention of human and animal suffering it will always require careful justification.

Going further with the utilitarian line of thought it can be understood that balancing harms against benefits can still be subject to certain ethical rules in order to minimise the harms and maximise the benefits. Indeed, these rules would be seen as good things to do in themselves. Animal welfarists believe it is wrong to cause animals to suffer or to take their lives but their caveat is that it is only permissible when it is unavoidable, ie least harm is caused, and is done for a good reason. In other words it has to be backed by good reasons.

Before deciding whether a particular experiment is acceptable or not, utilitarians might draw on other ethical considerations and ask questions to help them decide. For example, is the work worth doing? Is it going to answer a scientifically valuable question? Could the scientific objective be achieved without using animals, or by using animals that are not likely to suffer such as bacteria, or invertebrates, or lower forms of vertebrates with a less well-developed neuro-physiological sensitivity? Could cell cultures or computer modelling be used instead, that is could the use of sentient animals be *replaced* in some way? Has the number of animals to be used been *reduced* to the minimum for the work, and has good statistical advice been taken? Is the level of suffering to be caused to the animals the minimum required to achieve the scientific objective, for example through the use of good anaesthetic and analgesic regimes, through good experimental design?[16]

This *refinement* of experiments to cause only that degree of animal suffering which is necessary is key to a humane and responsible scientific process (and is part of scientific ethics and a scientist's integrity). The application of these three Rs, as Replacement, Reduction and Refinement are known, were first described by Russell and Burch as long ago as 1959[17] and are part of the scientific licensing process in the UK under the 1986 Act.[18] But it should be appreciated that applying the three Rs is not the end of the matter, as the 'basic' question still remains, should the work proceed even though there are no replacements, the number of animals has been reduced to the minimum, and there is no avoidable suffering? A weighing of the predicted harms against the anticipated benefits has then to be carried out to try to ensure that the harms done to the animals are in proportion to the benefits, but it is like comparing chalk with cheese: animal suffering versus human benefit. How can it be carried out in practice? This is the subject of current debate and is the meat of ethical discussion that would normally involve scientists, veterinarians, medics, lay members, even an ethicist(!). There is some general agreement that the greater the scientific benefit, such as developing a vaccine against AIDS or cancer, or making new replacement organs, might merit a higher degree of animal suffering than say for a gain in fundamental knowledge with no anticipated medical benefit.[19] [. . .]

The future

However, let us return to some of our earlier futuristic biotechnological considerations. The prospect of improved and novel therapeutic approaches through gene pharming almost certainly will be welcomed by most as the balance of good over harm would seem to be significantly greater even though during the developmental phase a relatively high price had been paid. Similarly most would welcome the manipulation of animals to promote a genetically determined disease resistance, but how about increased agricultural efficiency and meat quality at the expense of animal well-being or animal integrity? How would you react if lumps of chicken or sheep flesh or steaks were grown in test tubes or plates in a laboratory to contain different flavours or have varying degrees of tenderness? What if chicken eggs were produced by isolated ovaries cultured in test tubes? Many of these 'advances' would certainly be more welfare-friendly than all current farming practices and avoid the pain, fear and distress and other adverse effects that are presently caused. But should we do it? Is there not something rather unnatural about these means of food production? What about making animals that removed something unwanted, such as meat with no gristle, leading to animals that could not walk but feel no pain, and that made no noise. This might mean that those animals could only feed, even be force-fed by machine (like foie gras) and if they did not feel pain in a controlled and protected environment, then would it matter?

Interfering with the integrity of animals for such commercial purposes is not new; after all, humans have deliberately bred through genetic selection farm and companion animals in this way for centuries. The new technologies may speed this up, or may enable us to produce food in the different ways described above. Perhaps they are 'a step too far' and would cause a public outcry – at the present. 'At the present' as new developments tend to go ahead of public opinion but with time, public opinion changes and a practice becomes acceptable as has already happened with kidney transplantation, freezing semen, IVF, cloning animals, gene therapy. [. . .] The question is, should we do it? Or even start to research it? And what does it say about us as human beings if we do?

References

1 Rollin, B. E. (1995), 'The Frankenstein Syndrome: Ethical and Social Issues in the Genetic Engineering of Animals', Cambridge University Press, New York.
2 Bryant, J., La velle, L. B. and Searle, J. (2002), 'Bioethics for Scientists', John Wiley & Sons Ltd, Chichester.
3 Benson, J. (2000), 'Environmental Ethics: An introduction with readings', based on the Open University coursebook, Routledge, London.
4 Rollin, B. E. (2001), 'Livestock production and emerging social ethics for animals', in 'Eursafe 2001: Proceedings of the Third Congress of the European Society for Agricultural and Food Ethics', Florence, 3–5 October, pp. 79–85.
5 Walsh, G. (2000), 'Biopharmaceutical benchmarks', *Nature Biotechnol.*, Vol. 18(8), pp. 831–833.
6 URL: http://www.savingsandclone.com/ethics_codeofethics.cfm?div/
7 Singer, P. (1975) 'Animal Liberation', Jonathan Cape/Thorsons Ltd., Wellingborough; 2nd edn (1990) HarperCollins, London.
8 Morton, D. B. (2000), 'Self-consciousness and animal suffering', *The Biologist*, Vol. 47, pp. 77–80.
9 Dawkins, M. S. (1993), 'Through Our Eyes Only. The Search for Animal Consciousness'. W.H. Freeman, Spektrum, Oxford.
10 Kraus, A. L. and Renquist, D. (eds) (2000), 'Bioethics and the Use of Laboratory Animals: Ethics in Theory and Practice', Gregory C. Benoit Publishing, Dubuque, for the American College of Laboratory Animal Medicine.
11 Linzey, A. and Turner, J. (1998), 'Bioethics: Making animals matter', *Biologist*, Vol. 45, pp. 209–211.
12 Linzey, A. (1994), 'Animal Theology', SCM Press Ltd., London.
13 Ryder, R. D. (1975), 'Victims of Science – The Use of Animals in Research', National Anti-vivisection Society, Davis-Pointer Ltd., London.
14 Frey, R. G. (1988), 'Moral standing, the value of lives and speciesism', *Between the Species*, Vol. 4, pp. 191–201.
15 LaFollette, H. and Shanks, N. (1996), 'Brute Science: Dilemma of Animal Experimentation', Routledge, London.
16 Morton, D. B. (1998), 'The importance of non-statistical design in refining animal experimentation'. ANZCCART Facts Sheet, *ANZCCART News*, Vol. 11(2), June, insert.
17 Russell, W. M. S. and Burch, R. L. (1959), 'The principles of humane experimental technique', Special Edition (1992), Wheathampstead.
18 HMSO (2000), Home Office Guidance on the Operation of the Animals (Scientific Procedures) Act 1986, The Stationery Office, London, HC 321.
19 Home Office (2001), Guidance on the Operation of the Animals (Scientific Procedures) Act 1986 HMSO HC 321.

ISSUES IN GENETIC ENGINEERING

Chapter 49

Jason Scott Robert and Françoise Baylis

CROSSING SPECIES BOUNDARIES

Robert and Baylis evaluate the biology of species identity and the morality of crossing species boundaries in the context of emerging research that involves combining human and nonhuman animals at the genetic or cellular level. They review biological and philosophical problems of defining species as well as earlier attempts to forbid crossing species boundaries. While not attempting to establish the immorality of crossing species boundaries, they suggest that such crosses will result in important moral concerns and confusion about social and ethical obligations to novel interspecies beings.

Introduction

CROSSING SPECIES BOUNDARIES in weird and wondrous ways has long interested the scientific community but has only recently captured the popular imagination beyond the realm of science fiction. [. . .] As part of the project of harnessing the therapeutic potential of human stem cell research, researchers are now involved in creating novel interspecies whole organisms that are unique cellular and genetic admixtures (Dewitt 2002). A human-to-animal embryonic chimera is a being produced through the addition of human cellular material (such as pluripotent or restricted stem cells) to a nonhuman blastocyst or embryo. To give but four examples of relevant works in progress, Snyder and colleagues at Harvard have transplanted human neural stem cells into the forebrain of a developing bonnet monkey in order to assess stem cell function in development (Ourednik et al. 2001); human embryonic stem cells have been inserted into young chick embryos by Benvenisty and colleagues at the Hebrew University of Jerusalem (Goldstein et al. 2002); and most recently it has been reported that human genetic material has been transferred into rabbit eggs by Sheng (Dennis 2002), while Weissman and colleagues at Stanford University and StemCells, Inc., have created a mouse with a significant proportion of human stem cells in its brain (Krieger 2002).

Human-to-animal embryonic chimeras are only one sort of novel creature currently being produced or contemplated. Others include: *human-to-animal fetal or adult chimeras* created by grafting human cellular material to late-stage nonhuman fetuses or to postnatal nonhuman creatures; *human-to-human embryonic, fetal, or adult chimeras* created by inserting or grafting exogenous human cellular material to human embryos, fetuses, or adults (e.g., the human recipient of a human organ transplant, or human stem cell therapy); *animal-to-human embryonic, fetal, or adult chimeras* created by inserting or grafting nonhuman cellular material to human embryos, fetuses, or adults (e.g., the recipient of a xenotransplant); *animal-to-animal embryonic, fetal, or adult chimeras* generated from nonhuman cellular material whether within or between species (excepting human beings); *nuclear-cytoplasmic hybrids*, the offspring of two animals of different species, created by inserting a nucleus into an enucleated ovum (these might be intraspecies, such as sheep–sheep; or interspecies, such as sheep–goat; and, if interspecies, might be created with human or nonhuman material); *interspecies hybrids* created by fertilizing an ovum from an animal of one species with a sperm from an animal of another (e.g., a mule, the offspring of a he-ass and a mare); and *transgenic organisms* created by otherwise combining genetic material across species boundaries.

For this paper, in which we elucidate and explore the concept of species identity and the ethics of crossing species boundaries, we focus narrowly on the creation of interspecies chimeras involving human cellular material—the most recent of the transgressive interspecies creations. Our primary focus is on human-to-animal *embryonic* chimeras, about which there is scant ethical literature, though the scientific literature is burgeoning.

Is there anything ethically wrong with research that involves the creation of human-to-animal embryonic chimeras? A number of scientists answer this question with a resounding "no." They argue, plausibly, that human stem cell proliferation, (trans)differentiation, and tumorigenicity must be studied in early embryonic environments. For obvious ethical reasons, such research cannot be carried out in human embryos. Thus, assuming the research must be done, it must be done in nonhuman embryos—thereby creating human-to-animal embryonic chimeras. Other scientists are less sanguine about the merits of such research. Along with numerous commentators, they are quite sensitive to the ethical conundrum posed by the creation of certain novel beings from human cellular material, and their reaction to such research tends to be ethically and emotionally charged. But what grounds this response to the creation of certain kinds of part-human beings? In this paper we make a first pass at answering this question. We critically examine what we take to be the underlying worries about crossing species boundaries by referring to the creation of certain kinds of novel beings involving human cellular or genetic material. In turn, we highlight the limitations of each of these arguments. We then briefly hint at an alternative objection to the creation of certain novel beings that presumes a strong desire to avoid introducing moral confusion as regards the moral status of the novel being. In particular we explore the strong interest in avoiding any practice that would lead us to doubt the claim that humanness is a necessary (if not sufficient) condition for full moral standing.

Species identity

Despite significant scientific unease with the notion of *species identity*, commonplace among biologists and commentators are the assumption that species have particular identities and the belief that the boundaries between species are fixed rather than fluid, established by nature rather than by social negotiation. Witness the ease with which biologists claim that a genome sequence of some organism—yeast, worm, human—represents the identity of that species, its blueprint or, alternatively, instruction set. As we argue below, such claims mask deep conceptual difficulties regarding the relationship between these putatively representative species-specific genomes and the individual members of a species.

The ideas that natural barriers exist between divergent species and that scientists might some day be able to cross such boundaries experimentally fuelled debates in the 1960s and 1970s about the use of recombinant DNA technology (e.g., Krimsky 1982). There were those who anticipated the possibility of research involving the crossing of species boundaries and who considered this a laudable scientific goal. They tried to show that fixed species identities and fixed boundaries between species are illusory. In contrast, those most critical of crossing species boundaries argued that there were fixed natural boundaries between species that should not be breached.

At present the prevailing view appears to be that species identity is fixed and that species boundaries are inappropriate objects of human transgression. The idea of fixed species identities and boundaries is an odd one, though, inasmuch as the creation of plant-to-plant[1] and animal-to-animal hybrids, either artificially or in nature, does not foster such a vehement response as the prospective creation of interspecies combinations involving human beings—no one sees rhododendrons or mules (or for that matter goat-sheep, or geep) as particularly monstrous (Dixon 1984). This suggests that the only species whose identity is generally deemed genuinely "fixed" is the human species. But, what is a *species* such that protecting its identity should be perceived by some to be a scientific, political, or moral imperative? This and similar questions about the nature of species and of species identities are important to address in the context of genetics and genomics research (Ereshefsky 1992; Claridge, Dawah, and Wilson 1997; Wilson 1999b).

Human beings (and perhaps other creatures) intuitively recognize species in the world, and cross-cultural comparative research suggests that people around the globe tend to carve up the natural world in significantly similar ways (Atran 1999). There is, however, no one authoritative definition of species. Biologists typically make do with a plurality of species concepts, invoking one or the other depending on the particular explanatory or investigative context.

One stock conception, propounded by Dobzhansky (1950) and Mayr (1940), among others, is the *biological species concept* according to which species are defined in terms of reproductive isolation, or lack of genetic exchange. On this view, if two populations of creatures do not successfully interbreed, then they belong to different species. But the apparent elegance and simplicity of this definition masks some important constraints: for instance, it applies only to those species that reproduce sexually (a tiny fraction of all species); moreover, its exclusive emphasis on interbreeding generates counterintuitive results, such as the suggestion that morphologically indistinguishable individuals who happen to live in neighboring regions but also happen never to interbreed should be deemed members of different species. (Imagine viewing populations of human beings "reproductively isolated" by religious intolerance as members of different species, and the biological species concept fails to pick out *Homo sapiens* as a discrete species comprising all human beings.)

Such results can be avoided by invoking other definitions of species, such as the *evolutionary species concept* advanced by G. G. Simpson and E. O. Wiley, which emphasizes continuity of populations over geological time: "a species is a single lineage of ancestral descendant populations of organisms which maintains its identity from other such lineages and which has its own evolutionary tendencies and historical fate" (Wiley 1978, 18; see also Simpson 1961). Unlike the biological species concept, this definition of species applies to both sexually and asexually reproducing creatures and also underscores shared ancestry and historical fate—and not merely capacity to interbreed—as what unifies a group of creatures as a species. The evolutionary species concept is by no means unproblematic, however, mainly because it is considerably more vague than the biological species concept, and so also considerably more difficult to operationalize.

A third approach to defining species has lately received considerable attention among philosophers of biology. This approach is known as the *homeostatic property cluster* view of species, advocated in different ways by Boyd (1999), Griffiths (1999), and Wilson (1999a). Following Wilson (1999a, 197–99) in particular, the homeostatic property cluster view of species is properly understood as a thesis about natural kinds, of which a species is an instance. The basic idea is that a species is characterized by a cluster of properties (traits, say) no one of which, and no specific set of which, must be exhibited by any individual member of that species, but some set of which must be possessed by all individual members of that species. To say that these property clusters are "homeostatic" is to say that their clustering together is a systematic function of some causal mechanism or process; that an individual possesses any one of the properties in the property cluster significantly increases the probability that this individual will also possess other properties in the cluster. So the list of distinguishing traits is a property cluster, wherein the properties cluster as a function of the causal structure of the biological world. Of course, an outstanding problem remains, namely that of establishing the list of traits that differentiate species one from the other. Presumably this would be achieved by focusing on reproductive, morphological, genealogical, genetic, behavioral, and ecological features, no one of which is necessarily a universal property of the species and no set of which constitutes a species essence. We return below to the homeostatic property cluster view of species when we consider how best to characterize *Homo sapiens*.

To these definitions of species many more can be added: at present, there are somewhere between nine and twenty-two definitions of species in the biological literature.[2] Of these, there is no one species concept that is universally compelling. Accordingly, rather than asking the generic question, "How is 'species' defined?" it might be useful to focus instead on the narrower question "How is a species defined?" In response to the latter question Williams (1992) proposes that a species be characterized by a description comprising a set of traits differentiating that species from all others. It is no small task, however, to devise a satisfactory species description for any particular group of beings. Take, for example, *Homo sapiens*. Significantly, not even a complete sequence of *the* human genome can tell us what particular set of traits of *Homo sapiens* distinguishes human beings from all other species.

[. . .]

Although human beings might share 99.9% commonality at the genetic level, there is nothing as yet identifiable as *absolutely* common to all human beings. According to current biology, there is no genetic lowest common denominator, no genetic essence, "no single, standard, "normal" DNA sequence that we all share" (Lewontin 1992, 36). [. . .]

What is *Homo sapiens*?

What, then, is *Homo sapiens*? Though clearly there is no one authoritative definition of species, notions of "species essences" and "universal properties of species" persist, always in spirit if not always in name, in discussions about breaching species boundaries. For this reason, on occasion, attempts to define *Homo sapiens* are reduced to attempts to define *human nature*. This is a problem, however, insofar as the literature exhibits a wide range of opinion on the nature of *human nature*; indeed, many of the competing conceptions of *human nature* are incommensurable (for a historical sampling of views, see Trigg 1988). On one view the claim that there is such a thing as human nature is meant to be interpreted as the claim that all members of *Homo sapiens* are essentially the same. But since everything about evolution points toward variability and not essential sameness, this would appear to be an inherently problematic claim about human nature (Hull 1986). One way of avoiding this result is to insist that talk of human nature is not about essential sameness but rather about universality and then to explain universality in terms of distinct biological attributes—a functional human nervous system, a human anatomical structure and physiological function, or a human genome (Campbell, Glass, and Charland 1998). A classic example of the latter strategy, explaining universality genetically, appears in an article on human nature by Eisenberg (1972), who writes that "one trait common to man everywhere is language; in the sense that only the human species displays it, the capacity to acquire language must be genetic" [. . .]. In this brief passage Eisenberg moves from the claim that language is a human universal, to the claim that the ability to have a language is unique and species specific, to the claim that this capacity is genetic (Hull 1986). But, of course, language is not a human universal—some human beings neither speak nor write a language, and some are born with no capacity whatsoever for language acquisition. Yet, in a contemporary context, no one would argue that these people, simply by virtue of being nonverbal and/or illiterate, are not members of the same species as the rest of us.

And therein lies the rub. We all know a human when we see one, but, really, that is all that is known about our identity as a species. Of course we all know that human beings are intelligent, sentient, emotionally-complex creatures. We all know the same of dolphins, though. And, of course, not all human beings are intelligent, sentient, or emotionally complex (for instance, those who are comatose); nevertheless, most among us would still consider them human.

The homeostatic property cluster approach to species avoids the problem of universality but at the possible expense of retaining an element of essentialism. Recall that, according to the homeostatic property cluster view, membership in a species is not determined by possession of *any particular* individual homeostatically clustered property (or *any particular sets* of them) but rather by possession of *some* set of homeo-statically clustered properties. Nevertheless, although possession of property *x* (or of property set *x-y-z*) is not *necessary* for species membership, possession of *all* the identified homeostatically clustered properties is *sufficient* for membership, which suggests that a hint of essentialism persists (Wilson 1999a).

[. . .]

Moral unrest with crossing species boundaries

[. . .]

Scientifically, there might be no such thing as fixed species identities or boundaries. Morally, however, we rely on the notion of fixed species identities and boundaries in the way we live our lives and treat other creatures, whether in decisions about what we eat or what we patent. Interestingly, there is dramatically little appreciation of this tension in the literature, leading us to suspect that (secular) concern over breaching species boundaries is in fact concern about something else, something that has been mistakenly characterized in the essentialist terms surveyed above. But, in a sense, this is to be expected. While a major impact of the human genome project has been to show us quite clearly how similar we human beings are to each other and to other species, the fact remains that human beings are much more than DNA and moreover, as we have witnessed throughout the ages, membership within the human community depends on more than DNA. [. . .]

Although in our recent history we have been able to broaden our understanding of what counts as human, it would appear that the possible permeability of species boundaries is not open to public debate insofar as novel part-human beings are concerned. Indeed, the standard public-policy response to any possible breach of human species boundaries is to reflexively introduce moratoriums and prohibitions.[3]

But why should this be so? Indeed, why should there be *any* ethical debate about the prospect of crossing species boundaries between human and nonhuman animals? After all, hybrids occur naturally, and there is a significant amount of gene flow between species in nature.[4] Moreover, there is as yet no adequate biological (or moral) account of the distinctiveness of the species *Homo sapiens* serving to capture all and only those creatures of human beings born. As we have seen, neither essentialism (essential sameness, genetic or otherwise) nor universality can function as appropriate guides in establishing the unique identity of *Homo sapiens*. Consequently, no extant species concept justifies the erection of the fixed boundaries between human beings and nonhumans that are required to make breaching those boundaries morally problematic. Despite this, belief in a fixed, unique, human species identity persists, as do moral objections to any attempt to cross the human species boundary—whatever that might be.

[. . .]

[Some] maintain that combining human genes or cells with those of nonhuman animals is [. . .] inherently unnatural, perverse, and so offensive. Here the underlying philosophy is one of repugnance. [. . .] For many, the mainstay of the argument against transgressing species "boundaries" is a widely felt reaction of "instinctive hostility" (Harris 1998, 177) commonly known as the "yuck factor." [. . .]

A robust explanation for the instinctive and intense revulsion at the creation of human-to-animal beings (and perhaps some animal-to-human beings) can be drawn from Douglas's work on taboos (1966). Douglas suggests that taboos stem from conceptual boundaries. Human beings attach considerable symbolic importance to classificatory systems and actively shun anomalous practices that threaten cherished conceptual boundaries. This explains the existence of well-entrenched taboos, in a number of domains, against mixing things from distinct categories or having objects/actions fall outside any established classification system. Classic examples include the Western response to bi-sexuality (you can't be both heterosexual and homosexual) and intersexuality. Intersexuality falls outside the "legitimate" (and exclusive) categories of male and female, and for this reason intersex persons have been carved to fit into the existing categories (Dreger 2000). Human-to-animal chimeras, for instance, are neither clearly animal nor clearly human. They obscure the classification system (and concomitant social structure) in such a way as to constitute an unacceptable threat to valuable and valued conceptual, social, and moral boundaries that set human beings apart from all other creatures. Following Stout, who follows Douglas, we might thus consider human-to-animal chimeras to be an abomination. They are anomalous in that they "combine characteristics uniquely identified with separate kinds of things, or at least fail to fall unambiguously into any recognized class." Moreover, the anomaly is loaded with social significance in that interspecies hybrids and chimeras made with human materials "straddle the line between *us* and *them*" (Stout 2001, 148). As such, these beings threaten our social identity, our unambiguous status as human beings.

But what makes for unambiguous humanness? Where is the sharp line that makes for the transgression, the abomination? According to Stout, the line must be both sharp and socially significant if trespassing across it is to generate a sense of abomination: "An abomination, then, is anomalous or ambiguous with respect to some system of concepts. And the repugnance it causes depends on such factors as the presence, sharpness, and social significance of conceptual distinctions" (Stout 2001, 148). As we have seen, though, there is no biological sharp line: we have no biological account of unambiguous humanness, whether in terms of necessary and sufficient conditions or of homeostatic property clusters. Thus it would appear that in this instance abomination is a social and moral construct.

Transformative technologies, such as those involved in creating interspecies beings from human material, threaten to break down the social dividing line between human beings and nonhumans. Any offspring generated through the pairing of two human beings is by natural necessity—reproductive, genetic, and developmental necessity—a human. But biology now offers the prospect of generating offspring through less usual means; for instance, by transferring nuclear DNA from one cell into an enucleated egg. Where the nuclear DNA and the enucleated egg (with its mitochondrial DNA) derive from organisms of different species, the potential emerges to create an interspecies nuclear-cytoplasmic hybrid.

In 1998 the American firm Advanced Cell Technology (ACT) disclosed that it had created a hybrid embryo by fusing human nuclei with enucleated cow oocytes. The goal of the research was to create and isolate human embryonic stem cells. But if the technology actually works (and there is some doubt about this) there would be the potential to create animal–human hybrids (ACT 1998; Marshall 1998; Wade 1998). Any being created in this way would have DNA 99% identical with that of the adult from whom the human nucleus was taken; the remaining 1% of DNA (i.e., mitochondrial DNA) would come from the enucleated animal oocyte. Is the hybrid thus created simply part-human and part-nonhuman animal? Or is it unequivocally human or unequivocally animal (see Loike and Tendler 2002)? These are neither spurious nor trivial questions. [. . .]

It has recently been suggested that human stem cells should be injected into mice embryos (blastocysts) to test their pluripotency (Dewitt 2002). If the cells were to survive and were indeed pluripotent, they could contribute to the formation of every tissue. Any animal born following this research would be a chimera—a being with a mixture of (at least) two kinds of cells. Or, according to others, it would be just a mouse with a few human cells. But what if those cells are in the brain, or the gonads (Weissman 2002)? What if the chimeric mouse has human sperm? And what if that mouse were to mate with a chimeric mouse with human eggs?

All of this to say that when faced with the prospect of not knowing whether a creature before us is human and therefore entitled to all of the rights typically conferred on human beings, we are, as a people, baffled.

One could argue further that we are not only baffled but indeed fearful. Hybrids and chimeras made from human beings represent a metaphysical threat to our self-image. [. . .] Hybrids and chimeras made from human materials blur the fragile boundary between human beings and "unreasoning animals," particularly when one considers the possibility of creating "reasoning" nonhuman animals (Krieger 2002). But is protecting one's privileged place in the world solid grounds on which to claim that hybrid- or chimera-making is intrinsically or even instrumentally unethical?

Moral confusion

Taking into consideration the conceptual morass of species-talk, the lack of consensus about the existence of God and His role in Creation, healthy skepticism about the "yuck" response, and confusion and fear about obscuring, blurring, or breaching boundaries, the question remains as to why there should be any ethical debate over crossing species boundaries. We offer the following musings as the beginnings of a plausible answer, the moral weight of which is yet to be assessed.

All things considered, the engineering of creatures that are part human and part nonhuman animal is objectionable because the existence of such beings would introduce inexorable moral confusion in our existing relationships with nonhuman animals and in our future relationships with part-human hybrids and chimeras. The moral status of nonhuman animals, unlike that of human beings, invariably depends in part on features other than species membership, such as the intention with which the animal came into being. With human beings the intention with which one is created is irrelevant to one's moral status. In principle it does not matter whether one is created as an heir, a future companion to an aging parent, a sibling for an only child, or a possible tissue donor for a family member. In the case of human beings, moral status is categorical insofar as humanness is generally considered a necessary condition for moral standing. In the case of nonhuman animals, though, moral status is contingent on the will of regnant human beings. There are different moral obligations, dependent on social convention, that govern our behavior toward individual nonhuman animals depending upon whether they are bred or captured for food (e.g., cattle), for labor (e.g., oxen for subsistence farming), for research (e.g., lab animals), for sport (e.g., hunting), for companionship (e.g., pets), for investment (e.g., breeding and racing), for education (e.g., zoo animals), or whether they are simply cohabitants of this planet. In addition, further moral distinctions are sometimes drawn between "higher" and "lower" animals, cute and ugly animals, useful animals and pests, all of which add to the complexity of human relationships with nonhuman animals.

These two frameworks for attributing moral status are clearly incommensurable. One framework relies almost exclusively on species membership in *Homo sapiens* as such, while the other relies primarily on the will and intention of powerful "others" who claim and exercise the right to confer moral status on themselves and other creatures. For example, though some (including ourselves) will argue that the biological term *human* should not be conflated with the moral term *person*, others will insist that all human beings have an inviolable moral right to life simply by virtue of being human. In sharp contrast, a nonhuman animal's "right to life" depends entirely upon the will of some or many human beings, and this determination typically will be informed by myriad considerations.

It follows that hybrids and chimeras made from human materials are threatening insofar as there is no clear way of understanding (or even imagining) our moral obligations to these beings—which is hardly surprising given that we are still debating our moral obligations to some among us who are undeniably biologically human, as well as our moral obligations to a range of nonhuman animals. If we breach the clear (but fragile) *moral* demarcation line between human and nonhuman animals, the ramifications are considerable, not only in terms of sorting out our obligations to these new beings but also in terms of having to revisit some of our current patterns of behavior toward certain human and nonhuman animals.[5] As others have observed (e.g., Thomas 1983), the separateness of humanity is precarious and easily lost; hence the need for tightly guarded boundaries.

Indeed, asking—let alone answering—a question about the moral status of part-human interspecies hybrids and chimeras threatens the social fabric in untold ways; countless social institutions, structures, and practices depend upon the moral distinction drawn between human and nonhuman animals. Therefore, to protect the privileged place of human animals in the hierarchy of being, it is of value to embrace (folk) essentialism about species identities and thus effectively trump scientific quibbles over species and over the species status of novel beings. The notion that species identity can be a fluid construct is rejected, and instead a belief in fixed species boundaries that ought not to be transgressed is advocated.

[. . .]

Our point is not that the creation of interspecies hybrids and chimeras adds a huge increment of moral confusion, nor that there has never been confusion about the moral status of particular kinds of beings, but rather that the creation of novel beings that are part human and part nonhuman animal is sufficiently threatening to the social order that for many this is sufficient reason to prohibit any crossing of species boundaries involving human beings. To do otherwise is to have to confront the possibility that humanness is neither necessary nor sufficient for personhood (the term typically used to denote a being with full moral standing, for which many—if not most—believe that humanness is at least a necessary condition).

In the debate about the ethics of crossing species boundaries the pivotal question is: Do we shore up or challenge our current social and moral categories? Moreover, do we entertain or preclude the possibility that humanness is not a necessary condition for being granted full moral rights? How we resolve these questions will be important not only in determining the moral status and social identity of those beings with whom we currently coexist (about whom there is still confusion and debate), but also for those beings we are on the cusp of creating. Given the social significance of the transgression we contemplate embracing, it behooves us to do this conceptual work now, not when the issue is even more complex—that is, once novel part-human beings walk among us.

Conclusion

To this point we have not argued that the creation of interspecies hybrids or chimeras from human materials should be forbidden or embraced. We have taken no stance at all on this particular issue. Rather, we have sketched the complexity and indeterminacy of the moral and scientific terrain, and we have highlighted the fact that despite scientists' and philosophers' inability to precisely define *species*, and thereby to demarcate species identities and boundaries, the putative fixity of putative species boundaries remains firmly lodged in popular consciousness and informs the view that there is an obligation to protect and preserve the integrity of human beings and *the* human genome. We have also shown that the arguments against crossing species boundaries and creating novel part-human beings (including interspecies hybrids or chimeras from human materials), though many and varied, are largely unsatisfactory. Our own hypothesis is that the issue at the heart of the matter is the threat of inexorable moral confusion.

With all this said and done, in closing we offer the following more general critique of the debate about transgressing species boundaries in creating part-human beings. The argument, insofar as there is one, runs something like this: species identities are fixed, not fluid; but just in case, prohibiting the transgression of species boundaries is a scientific, political, and moral imperative. The scientific imperative is prudential, is recognition of the inability to anticipate the possibly dire consequences for the species *Homo sapiens* of building these novel beings. The political imperative is also prudential, but here the concern is to preserve and protect valued social institutions that presume pragmatically clear boundaries between human and nonhuman animals. The moral imperative stems from a prior obligation to better delineate moral commitments to both human beings and animals before undertaking the creation of new creatures for whom there is no apparent a priori moral status.

As we have attempted to show, this argument against transgressing species boundaries is flawed. The first premise is not categorically true—there is every reason to doubt the view that species identity is fixed. Further, the scientific, political, and moral objections sketched above require substantial elaboration. In our view the most plausible objection to the creation of novel interspecies creatures rests on the notion of moral confusion—about which considerably more remains to be said.

Notes

1   A possible exception is the creation of genetically modified crops. But here the arguments are based on human health and safety concerns, as well as on political opposition to monopolistic business practices, rather than on concern for the essential identity of plant species.

2   Kitcher (1984) and Hull (1999) each discuss nine concepts. Mayden (1997) discusses twenty-two.

3   See, for example, s6(2)(b) Infertility (Medical Procedures) Act 1984 (Victoria, Australia); s3(2)(a)–(b) and s3(3)(b) Human Fertilisation and Embryology Act 1990 (United Kingdom); and Article 25 Bill containing rules relating to the use of gametes and embryos (Embryo Bill), September 2000 (the Netherlands). See also Annas, Andrews, and Isasi (2002).

4   A particularly well-documented example of gene flow between species is Darwin's finches in the Galapagos Islands. For a recent account, see Grant and Grant (2002).

5   Animal-rights advocates might object to the creation of part-human hybrids on the grounds that this constitutes inappropriate treatment of animals solely to further human interests. Obviously, proponents of such a perspective will not typically have a prior commitment to the uniqueness and "dignity" of human beings. For this reason we do not pursue this narrative here.

References

Advanced Cell Technology. 1998. Advanced Cell Technology announces use of nuclear replacement technology for successful generation of human embryonic stem cells. Press release, 12 November. Available from: http://www.advancedcell.com/pr_11–12–1998.html.

Annas, G. J., L. B. Andrews, and R. M. Isasi. 2002. Protecting the endangered human: Toward an international treaty prohibiting cloning and inheritable alterations. *American Journal of Law & Medicine* 28:151–78.

Atran, S. 1999. The universal primacy of generic species in folkbiological taxonomy: Implications for human biological, cultural, and scientific evolution. In *Species: New interdisciplinary essays*, ed. R. A. Wilson, 231–61. Cambridge: MIT Press.

Boyd, R. 1999. Homeostasis, species, and higher taxa. In *Species: New interdisciplinary essays*, ed. R. A. Wilson, 141–85. Cambridge: MIT Press.

Campbell, A., K. G. Glass, and L. C. Charland. 1998. Describing our "humanness": Can genetic science alter what it means to be "human"? *Science and Engineering Ethics* 4:413–26.

Claridge, M. F., H. A. Dawah, and M. R. Wilson, eds. 1997. *Species: The units of biodiversity*. London: Chapman and Hall.

Dennis, C. 2002. China: Stem cells rise in the East. *Nature* 419:334–36.

Dewitt, N. 2002. Biologists divided over proposal to create human–mouse embryos. *Nature* 420:255.

Dixon, B. 1984. Engineering chimeras for Noah's ark. *Hastings Center Report* 10:10–12.

Dobzhansky, T. 1950. Mendelian populations and their evolution. *American Naturalist* 84:401–18.

Douglas, M. 1966. *Purity and danger*. London: Routledge and Kegan Paul.

Dreger, A. D. 2000. *Hermaphrodites and the medical invention of sex*. Cambridge: Harvard University Press.

Eisenberg, L. 1972. The *human* nature of human nature. *Science* 176:123–28.

Ereshefsky, M., ed. 1992. *The units of evolution: Essays on the nature of species*. Cambridge: MIT Press.

Goldstein, R. S., M. Drukker, B. E. Reubinoff, and N. Benvenisty. 2002. Integration and differentiation of human embryonic stem cells transplanted to the chick embryo. *Developmental Dynamics* 225:80–86.

Grant, P. R., and B. R. Grant. 2002. Unpredictable evolution in a 30-year study of Darwin's finches. *Science* 296:633–35.

Griffiths, P. 1999. Squaring the circle: Natural kinds with historical essences. In *Species: New interdisciplinary essays*, ed. R. A. Wilson, 209–28. Cambridge: MIT Press.

Harris, J. 1998. *Clones, genes, and immortality: Ethics and the genetic revolution*. New York: Oxford University Press.

Hull, D. L. 1986. On human nature. *Proceedings of the Biennial Meeting of the Philosophy of Science Association* 2:3–13.

———. 1999. On the plurality of species: Questioning the party line. In *Species: New Interdisciplinary essays*, ed. R. A. Wilson, 23–48. Cambridge: MIT Press.

Kitcher, P. 1984. Species. *Philosophy of Science* 51:308–33.

Krieger, L. M. 2002. Scientists put a bit of man into a mouse. *Mercury News*, 8 December. Available from: http://www.bayarea.com/mld/mercurynews/4698610.htm.

Krimsky, S. 1982. *Genetic alchemy: The social history of the recombinant DNA controversy*. Cambridge: MIT Press.

Lewontin, R. C. 1992. The dream of the human genome. *New York Review of Books*, 28 May, pp. 31–40.

Loike, J. D., and M. D. Tendler. 2002. Revisiting the definition of *Homo sapiens. Kennedy Institute of Ethics Journal* 12:343–50.

Marshall, E. 1998. Claim of human–cow embryo greeted with skepticism. *Science* 282:1390–91.

Mayden, R.L. 1997. A hierarchy of species concepts: The denoument in the saga of the species problem. In *Species: The units of biodiversity*, ed. M. F. Claridge, H. A. Dawan, and M. R. Wilson, 381–424. London: Chapman and Hall.

Mayr, E. 1940. Speciation phenomena in birds. *American Naturalist* 74:249–78.

Ourednik, V., J. Ourednik, J. D. Flax et al. 2001. Segregation of human neural stem cells in the developing primate forebrain. *Science* 293:1820–24.

Simpson, G. G. 1961. *Principles of animal taxonomy*. New York: Columbia University Press.

Stout, J. 2001. *Ethics after Babel: The languages of morals and their discontents*. Boston: Beacon Books, 1988. Reprint, in expanded form and with a new postscript, Princeton: Princeton University Press.

Thomas, K. 1983. *Man and the natural world: Changing attitudes in England, 1500–1800*. London: Allen Lane.

Trigg, R. 1988. *Ideas of human nature: An historical introduction*. Oxford, U.K.: Basil Blackwell.

Wade, N. 1998. Researchers claim embryonic cell mix of human and cow. *New York Times*, 12 November, p. A1. Available from: http://query.nytimes .com / search / article-page.html?res = 9C04E3D71731F931A25752C1A96E 958260.

Weissman, I. 2002. Stem cells: Scientific, medical, and prolitical issues. *New England Journal of Medicine* 346:1576–79.

Wiley, E. O. 1978. The evolutionary species concept reconsidered. *Systematic Zoology* 27:17–26.

Williams, M. B. 1992. Species: Current usages. In *Keywords in evolutionary biology*, ed. E. F. Keller and E. A. Lloyd, 318–23. Cambridge: Harvard University Press.

Wilson, R. A. 1999a. Realism, essence, and kind: Resuscitating species essentialism? In *Species: New Interdisciplinary essays*, ed. R. A. Wilson, 187–207. Cambridge: MIT Press.

——— . 1999b. *Species: New Interdisciplinary essays*. Cambridge: MIT Press.

Chapter 50

Robert Streiffer

IN DEFENSE OF THE MORAL RELEVANCE
OF SPECIES BOUNDARIES

Streiffer argues that it is premature to conclude, as Robert and Baylis do, that the arguments against crossing species boundaries have been shown to be largely unsatisfactory. He notes that there continues to be considerable disagreement about the propriety of crossing species boundaries, but acknowledges that there still are no satisfactory principles that provide oversight on the matter.

Public opinion and biotechnology

JASON SCOTT ROBERT and Françoise Baylis (2003) hypothesize that what explains public worries about human-to-animal embryonic chimeras (henceforth, "chimeras") is the concern that "the existence of such beings would introduce inexorable moral confusion in our existing relationships with nonhuman animals and in our future relationships with part-human hybrids and chimaeras." Thus, what worries people is a consequentialist concern, namely, that the creation of chimeras will undermine the usefulness of perceived, even if fictitious, boundaries.

Robert and Baylis offer no empirical evidence to support this claim, and there is substantial evidence against it. The U.S. Office of Technology Assessment's (OTA) report on public perceptions of biotechnology, which remains the most comprehensive study of its kind, found that consequentialist concerns were cited by only a meager 1% (for environmental concerns) to 8% (for unforeseen consequences) of the respondents who believed that creating cross-species plants or animals was morally wrong (OTA 1987). Concerns about playing God and tampering with nature were much more prevalent, and the concern Robert and Baylis hypothesize apparently didn't even merit reporting by the OTA.

At any rate, it would be both surprising and disappointing if oversight bodies gave weight to the concern about moral confusion that Robert and Baylis say is at the heart of the public controversy. To prevent scientific research on the grounds that it would force people to reexamine a particular moral view by demonstrating the falsity of its underlying factual assumptions would be to prevent not only scientific progress but moral progress as well.

Crossing species boundaries

Public opinion aside, what about Robert and Baylis's substantive criticisms of the argument that creating chimeras is wrong because it involves crossing species boundaries? Their first criticism arises from their claim that there are intractable disagreements surrounding how to define "the species *Homo sapiens*." Their second criticism arises from their claim that species boundaries are fluid, not fixed.

Conceding both claims, if only for the sake of argument, it still remains that Robert and Baylis provide little explanation as to how those claims provide reasons against the idea that crossing species boundaries is morally problematic. Indeed, I doubt that these claims actually do provide any such reasons.

There are, after all, intractable disagreements about how to delineate many key concepts relevant to ethics: killing and letting die, life and death, consciousness, rationality, equality, respect, rights, goodness. This does not imply that these concepts are morally irrelevant. The presence of those intractable disagreements will tempt some to moral relativism, but my view, which I won't argue for here, is the opposite: intractable disagreement typically means that there is an objective fact of the matter (Streiffer 2003).

Nor does the moral relevance of species boundaries require "the erection of fixed boundaries" between species. It is clear, for example, that the groups constituting one's family and one's fellow citizens change over time (and, it might be added, are subject to numerous indeterminacies and controversies), and yet the boundaries of those groups retain robust moral significance. Thus, fixed boundaries are not necessary for moral relevance.

Robert and Baylis make a third criticism: "Indeed, why should there be *any* ethical debate about the prospect of crossing species boundaries between human and nonhuman animals? After all, hybrids occur naturally, and there is a significant amount of gene flow between species in nature" (emphasis in original). The unstated assumption is that if something happens in nature, then there is nothing wrong with our doing it. Clearly this is false.

Perhaps the following is a more charitable interpretation of their remarks: Some people object to crossing species boundaries on the grounds that it is unnatural. But given that horizontal gene flow between species occurs in nature, it isn't unnatural.

But naturalness is relative to the agent who is performing the action. It can be natural for fish to live underwater without its being natural for human beings to live underwater. Similarly, it can be natural for bacteria to move genes across species boundaries without it being natural for human beings to do so.

The yuck factor

Even though Robert and Baylis's criticisms of the unnaturalness objection fail, there are difficulties in providing a positive defense of the objection as well, both in defining "unnatural" and in defending the alleged relationship between something's being unnatural and its being morally problematic. Robert and Baylis note that no one objects to mules even though they are unnatural. These difficulties have led some to reject the unnaturalness objection as muddled thinking.

But we should be wary of dismissing the objection too quickly. I have already noted the difficulties in arguing that if a concept is hard to delineate, it is morally irrelevant. And there seem to be clear examples of wrong actions where the only explanation of their wrongness appears to be that they are unnatural. Bestiality and pedophilia are wrong even when they cause no physical or psychological harm. Merely pointing to the lack of valid consent certainly won't explain their wrongness: children and animals cannot give valid consent to *anything* done to them.

At this stage in the dialectic, the unnaturalness objection can be supplemented by considerations of the "yuck factor." Proponents of the yuck factor argue that the revulsion some people experience in contemplating certain activities sometimes suffices for knowing that the activity is wrong, even in the absence of satisfactory justification for the revulsion. So proponents of the unnaturalness objection can insist that in spite of the above difficulties, they still know that crossing species boundaries is wrong.

Some think that the yuck factor has been discredited because it has been used to rationalize discrimination (Thompson 2000). Racists claimed to "know simply by looking" that interracial marriages were wrong. But the fact that an argument has been used inappropriately in some areas does not mean that it is inappropriate in other areas. Paternalistic arguments were used to rationalize unjust treatment of women, but that doesn't mean that they are inappropriate when applied to children.

Even opponents of the yuck factor must concede that, sometimes, we know that an action is wrong merely on the basis of our reaction to it, even if we cannot satisfactorily justify that reaction. We know it is wrong to kill a healthy person so that his organs can be used to save five lives, even though we presently lack any theoretically satisfactory way of distinguishing that case from the various trolley cases prominent in the killing/letting-die literature. Robert and Baylis's epistemological claim that intuitions must be justified if they are to "have any moral force" is mistaken.

Should the repugnance some feel at the crossing of species boundaries be dismissed (as the reaction of a racist should be), or does it constitute yet another intuition in a long line of intuitions where our difficulties in providing satisfactory theoretical explanations merely indicate theoretical inadequacy? Given the poor state of the arguments on both sides of this debate, it is too early to tell.

Conclusion

It therefore seems premature to conclude, as Robert and Baylis do, that the arguments against crossing species boundaries have been "shown" to be "largely unsatisfactory." This issue deserves continued investigation to provide guidance to those conducting, overseeing, and funding the relevant research. Two examples illustrate this need.

First, at a recent conference to discuss standards for human embryonic stem (HES) cell research, scientists failed to reach a consensus because of disagreement about how to handle chimeras (Dewitt 2002).

Second, during our deliberations in the University of Wisconsin (UW) Bioethics Advisory Committee (2001), we flagged research involving the introduction of HES cells into animals early in fetal development as requiring "special review." But we have yet to satisfactorily articulate the principles that should govern that review. Because of the Wisconsin Alumni Research Foundation's patents on HES cell lines and because UW's HES cell lines are considered the gold standard, UW's policy will constrain HES cell researchers worldwide. Thus, it is obviously important that progress be made on this issue.

Acknowledgments

Thanks to Alan Rubel for helpful discussion. This material is based upon work supported by the Cooperative State Research, Education, and Extension Service, U.S. Department of Agriculture, under Agreement No. 00–52100–9617. Any opinions, findings, conclusions, or recommendations expressed in this publication are those of the author and do not necessarily reflect the views of the U.S. Department of Agriculture.

References

Dewitt, N. 2002. Stem-cell proposal stirs debate. *Wall Street Journal*, 22 November, p. A7, European edition.
Office of Technology Assessment. 1987. *New developments in biotechnology. Background paper: Public perceptions of biotechnology*. OTA-BP-BA–45. Washington: GPO.
Robert, J. S., and F. Baylis. 2003. Crossing species boundaries. *The American Journal of Bioethics* 3(3): 1–13.
Streiffer, R. 2003. *Moral relativism and reasons for action*. New York: Routledge.
Thompson, P. 2000. *Food and agricultural biotechnology: Incorporating ethical considerations*. Ottawa: Canadian Biotechnology Advisory Committee.
University of Wisconsin. Bioethics Advisory Committee. 2001. Second Report of the Bioethics Advisory Committee on Human Embryonic Stem Cell Research at the University of Wisconsin-Madison. Madison: University of Wisconsin.

Chapter 51

Kevin R. Smith

ANIMAL GENETIC MANIPULATION:
A UTILITARIAN RESPONSE

Smith considers several objections to genetically manipulating animals. He rejects the belief that deliberate genetic sequence change is intrinsically wrong, and the belief that such knowledge will inevitably lead to human genetic manipulation. Smith proposes that the concept of replaceability can justify the killing of transgenic animals, but supports a general prohibition on transgenic studies that entail significant suffering of animals.

IS IT MORALLY acceptable to genetically manipulate animals? I shall address this question by outlining the process and outcomes of animal genetic manipulation with reference to its morally salient features, followed by a discussion of various objections to the genetic manipulation of animals.

Background to animal genetic manipulation

[. . .]

Biologists view transgenic animals as essential research tools. This is particularly so for research into complex systems, involving interactions between different cells or organs. Transgenic animals are especially valued for their medical use as models of human disease. Such animal models are valued as means for the exploration of abnormal functioning and as testbeds for new therapies.

The agricultural biotechnology industry uses transgenic research in pursuit of quantitative and qualitative changes in animal products. Potential quantitative changes include more milk, more meat and more wool, while potential qualitative changes include altered milk composition (for example, to make cow's milk more suitable for human babies), leaner meat and pest-resistant wool.

Truly novel uses of transgenic animals are also under development. For example, transgenic animals as 'bioreactors' are able to produce human proteins. Such proteins, produced in the milk, have potential medical uses. Another example is research aimed at producing transgenic animals with human-compatible organs for human transplantation ('xenotransplantation').

A final point concerns the types of animals used for transgenesis. Although transgenesis has been successfully carried out on a very wide range of animals, ranging from insects to primates, more than 99 per cent of transgenic animals currently produced are laboratory mice.

The process of transgenesis

Consideration of the morality of animal genetic manipulation requires an understanding of the actual steps involved in transgenesis. This section aims to furnish such an understanding. Aspects that have moral salience are emphasised, and technical (scientific) language is minimised as far as possible.

General features of transgenesis

Foreign DNA molecules (termed 'transgenes') are introduced to a host embryo such that the resident genetic sequence (the 'genome') of the embryo – and hence that of the resulting animal – is altered by the incoming transgene genetic sequences. In most forms of transgenesis (see below), host embryos must be removed from the reproductive tracts of 'donor' females. Donor females are prepared for embryo collection by a course of hormone injections. Embryos may be collected from large agricultural animals by the relatively non-invasive procedure of 'flushing' the upper portions of the reproductive tract via the vagina. For smaller animals, surgery is used or, as is the case with mice, donor females are killed to allow efficient embryo collection. Genetically manipulated embryos are transferred to the reproductive tract of a 'recipient' female. Recipients must be in a 'pseudopregnant' state; this is induced by hormone injections and/or by mating the recipients with vasectomised males. In most animal types, including mice, embryo transfer requires surgery under general anaesthesia. When the potentially transgenic offspring are born, tissue samples (typically blood or skin) must be taken to enable laboratory determination of transgeneity. Most methods of transgenesis are less than 100 per cent efficient: the majority of potentially transgenic offspring test negative for transgene genetic sequences. Such animals are routinely killed. Finally, depending on the degree of precision of genetic manipulation associated with each method of transgenesis, further killing occurs when transgenic animals do not satisfy desired criteria.

Specific methods of transgenesis

There are several available methods for the genetic manipulation of animals. [. . .] See below for a tabulation of transgenic methods and their associated *prima facie* morally salient features (Table 51.1).

Outcomes of transgenesis

The outcomes of genetic manipulation, comparing transgenic animals with their non-manipulated counterparts fall into three main categories: 1. No physiological changes expected; 2. Physiological changes that do not cause suffering; 3. Physiological changes that are likely to cause suffering.

Some transgenic experiments do not aim to alter physiology. An example would be attempts to direct a transgene to a particular non-essential part of the genome, as part of fundamental studies of gene targeting.

[. . .]

Transgene-induced physiological changes need not necessarily cause suffering to the host animals. For example, human proteins produced in the milk of transgenic ewes have no detrimental effects on the lactating animals. [. . .] There are many more examples of such transgene-induced physiological changes, in which suffering is not entailed. Utilitarians have no clear grounds for objecting to such outcomes of transgenesis.

[. . .]

Table 51.1 Transgenic Methods and Associated *Prima Facie* Morally Salient Features

Method of Transgenesis	Donor Females as Egg/ embryo Source?	Physical Manipulation of Host Embryos?	Pseudo-pregnant Females as Recipients?	Killing of Non-Transgenic Offspring?	Wastage through lack of in vitro selection?
Retroviral Transfer	Yes, 8-cell embryos	Not usually required	Yes	Yes, only ca. 30% transgenic	Yes
Pronuclear Microinjection	Yes. one-cell embryos	Yes, by injection into one-cell embryos	Yes	Yes, only ca. 25% transgenic	Yes
ESCs* Transgenesis	Yes, early embryos (and as original source of ESCs)	Yes, by addition of ESCs to embryos	Yes	Yes, only ca. 40% germline transgenic	No
Nuclear Transfer Transgenesis	Yes, unfertil-ised eggs	Yes, transfer of cell nuclei into enucleated eggs	Yes	No, all selected embryos transgenic	No
Sperm- Mediated Transgenesis	Only for non-AI* methods	Only for ICSI* methods	Only for non-AI methods	Yes, not all animals expected to be transgenic	Yes

* ESCs = Embryonic stem cells; AI = Artificial insemination; ICSI = intra cytoplasmic sperm injection

Certain transgene-induced physiological changes may cause animal suffering as an incidental effect of the purpose of the experimentation. [. . .] Suffering is more certain in animals manipulated to develop a specific disease that, in humans, has pain as a central feature. Many such transgenic disease 'models' have been created. For example, transgenic mice have been produced which reliably develop certain cancers. The induction of pain, such as that resulting from invasive tumours, is only justifiable to utilitarians if outweighed by the avoidance of a greater amount of suffering elsewhere. Of course, a central defence of transgenic disease models is that 'the end justifies the means', in that animal suffering is claimed to be outweighed by alleviation of suffering from cancer arising from experiments on transgenic models. I shall take up this issue later.

[. . .]

Moral objections to transgenesis

I am not persuaded by arguments from pro-animal absolutism, and this discussion of objections to transgenesis will start from the assumption, shared by most forms of utilitarianism, that *some* research with animals is morally permissible.

I will consider the following claims:

1   Transgenesis is objectionable because it is intrinsically wrong to deliberately alter genetic sequences;
2   Transgenesis is objectionable because it may lead to the genetic manipulation of humans;
3   Transgenesis is objectionable because it necessitates the killing of animals;
4   Transgenesis is objectionable because it involves the infliction of suffering on animals.

Intrinsic wrongness of deliberate sequence alteration

Genetic manipulation entails the deliberate alteration of genetic sequences within the genome. The same fundamental process of sequence alteration occurs as a result of genetic selection, both natural (as with evolution) and artificial (as with selective breeding of domesticated plants and animals). In terms of sequence alteration, the only significant difference between genetic manipulation and genetic selection is that the former process is very much faster than the latter. Thus, an assault on the ethics of transgenesis based on a notion of the intrinsic wrongness of sequence manipulation would be sustainable only as a subset of a much broader assault on all forms of *deliberate sequence alteration* (DSA). A coherent anti-DSA argument would entail the approval or acceptance of sequence alterations occurring naturally (from evolution) and the rejection of deliberate forms of alteration (breeding and genetic manipulation). Thus, to assume an ethical stance against DSA would be to subscribe to an unsubtle 'naturalistic fallacy'. Further, it is difficult to see how any form of utilitarian argument could be made against DSA in respect of its actual historical consequences, considering the vast expansion of thriving humanity that would not have been possible without centuries of selective breeding of domesticated plants and animals.

[. . .]

Thus, I hold that genetic sequence alteration *per se* is ethically neutral. [. . .] Assuming genetic sequence alteration *per se* to be ethically acceptable, it follows that the genetic sequence alteration inherent in animal transgenesis must also be considered ethically acceptable.

Risks of genetic manipulation being applied to humans

Some people object to transgenic research because they take the view that such work represents the 'thin end of a wedge' towards human genetic manipulation. Without doubt, the spectre of human genetic manipulation raises a plethora of moral questions. However, the fact is that most current transgenic techniques could (in principle) be readily applied to humans. Therefore, if the 'wedge' argument represents a valid objection to transgenesis, time has rendered such an objection passé.

However, the following variant of the 'wedge' objection avoids the charge of outmodedness: If transgenesis is allowed to proceed, it will increasingly be applied to 'higher' animals including primates, until the 'highest' primates—humans—become the next easy step. [. . .] The first premise for this objection is difficult to contest: higher animals *will* undoubtedly be used with increasing frequency, assuming continued progress in transgenic science. In addition, there may well be moral grounds for objecting to (at least some aspects of) transgenesis when particular non-human animals are concerned, where such animals have attributes of 'persons'.

However, the preceding 'wedge' argument depends crucially upon a claimed 'easy step' from non-human to human transgenesis. Is this notion of an 'easy step' valid? It is difficult to make a coherent case in its favour. Peoples of all cultures appear well able to discern a firm human/non-human line in terms of what is deemed permissible within each category.

I conclude that, if transgenesis really is the 'thin end of a wedge' on the way to human genetic manipulation, the onus must rest with the proponents of such a position to come forward with persuasive arguments.

Wrongness from killing

The production of transgenics undoubtedly necessitates the *killing* of many animals (such as animals that either fail to become transgenic or fail to express the transgene appropriately). The argument may be advanced that, since it is wrong *prima facie* to kill, it is wrong to produce transgenics. However, this position is opposed by the 'replaceability argument', which holds that it is not wrong to kill if a death is 'balanced' by the bringing into existence of another (equally happy) life. This situation is generally the case with transgenic science, where animals killed are replaced by breeding.

Assuming that significant suffering is not inflicted from an instance of killing (whether directly to the individual being killed or to others as a 'side-effect'[1]), it is difficult for utilitarians to argue against the replaceability argument. One objection to replaceability runs as follows: replaceability does not apply to humans, therefore to invoke the replaceability argument in the case of non-human animals is speciesist. A more sophisticated variant of this objection is the appeal to 'personhood', which starts by dividing sentient life into 'self-conscious' *vs.* 'non-self-conscious' beings.[2] The designation 'self-consciousness' denotes entities that are aware of themselves as distinct entities with a past and a future—entities that we may readily describe as 'persons'. Human beings (except for those with severe neurological deficits) are undoubtedly self-conscious, while very simple life forms (e.g. insects, assuming these to be sentient) are probably non-self-conscious. Proponents of this approach hold that replaceability may be applied to non-self-conscious entities but not to self-conscious entities—those with personhood. This personhood approach is plausible, but it contains at least two major weaknesses. Firstly, it is difficult to give strong reasons for viewing self-conscious entities as non-replaceable. Possibly the least flawed reason is the 'life as a journey' metaphor, where a self-conscious life is held to be inherently non-replaceable, because to end such a life would be to interrupt a coherent life narrative (complete with plans and hopes for the futures) prior to its completion. However, it is not clear why one such 'journey' may not be potentially replaceable by another, equally enjoyable 'journey', or why one large 'journey' may not be replaced by several smaller 'journeys'.

A second weakness of the personhood approach is the very real problem of attributing personhood. [. . .] [A]t the present time, it is impossible to say with confidence which, if any, of the animals commonly used for transgenesis (i.e. mice, sheep, pigs) merit the designation 'persons'.

Thus, the debate on killing and replaceability has not been resolved. [. . .] [A]n 'intermediate position' is highly desirable, in which a *provisional* line is drawn between animals deemed 'persons' and others not so designated, pending ongoing research into personhood. This provisional division would need to be based on (a) the (few) specific research findings presently available, and (b) on general observations of animal behaviour. On this approach, my own tentative preference would be to attribute personhood to (for example) pigs, rats and all higher primates, and withhold it from (for example) mice, sheep and chickens. However, such preferences are inevitably highly subjective. There is no perfect way to avoid such subjectivity, but a 'jury' approach, in which a group of 'disinterested' people is asked to provisionally attribute/withhold personhood, may be the best way forward.

I conclude that, categorisation difficulties notwithstanding, if the moral validity of personhood is accepted, transgenesis (in so far as killing is concerned) ought to be restricted to non-self-conscious animals.

Wrongness from suffering

I suggest that animal suffering gives the strongest grounds for objection to transgenesis. Specifically, I propose that *prohibition* should be considered in cases where either of the following negative consequences are entailed:

A   Significant suffering arising in any animals used in the process of transgenesis.

B   Significant suffering arising in transgenics from the development of a pathological condition engineered into the animals' genetic makeup.

I use the term '*significant suffering*' to exclude suffering likely to occur to an animal in a non-experimental situation. [. . .] If the extent of suffering unavoidably entailed by a particular transgenic approach is clearly less than that likely to occur inevitably in the life of the animal, utilitarians have no clear grounds for objection.

Other occurrences of suffering may be associated with transgenesis, such as suffering arising from failures in basic welfare provision (unsuitable animal accommodation, lack of veterinary care, etc.), and suffering arising from subsequent experimentation on transgenics (invasive surgery, stressful procedures, etc.). These occurrences of suffering have clear moral content. Moreover, the stringency of steps necessary to genuinely ensure adequate welfare may be formidable. For example, the happiness of some higher primates depends *inter alia* on the existence of environmental features such as extensive climbing opportunities, and on the freedom to engage in social groupings, all of which ought (morally) to be provided for such animals, as a prerequisite for any experimentation. Even laboratory mice require extensive welfare provision, such as adequately large cages with features to allow exploration. However, because such welfare issues are not the special reserve of *transgenic* animal science, I will not consider them in this discussion.

Although I propose that prohibition should be considered for negative consequences A and B (above), this should not be taken to mean transgenic cases entailing A or B ought automatically to be prevented. Rather, it is necessary, at least in principle, to weigh costs (significant suffering) against potential benefits (for example, a contribution to the development of a new anticancer drug).

Conclusion

Although conceptually simple, the calculus described above is notoriously difficult to conduct in practice. In the following sections, I shall consider the methods and outcomes of transgenesis from the perspective of significant suffering. I shall argue that there ought to be a strong presumption in favour of prohibition, in transgenic cases involving significant suffering where the extent, value or likelihood of realisation of a potential benefit is uncertain.

Methods of transgenesis

From the perspective of suffering, there are two key morally salient features of genetic manipulation that can lead to negative mental states, such as pain and fear. These features are (i) invasive procedures to recover and transfer embryos, and (ii) killing of animals involved in or arising from transgenesis.[3]

The first question should be: Can the degree of suffering arising from (i) and (ii) be *reduced*, without jeopardising the scientific purposes of transgenic experiments? An affirmative answer is possible for cases in which one method of transgenesis could be substituted for another. The various methods of transgenesis are not all equal in respect of features (i) and (ii). From Table 1 (above), it is apparent that both the 'traditional' methods of transgenesis (pronuclear microinjection and ESCs) entail features (i) and (ii). This is in contrast with the more 'novel' methods (nuclear transfer and sperm-mediated transgenesis). Given that nuclear transfer transgenesis allows the pre-selection of transgene-positive embryos, this method should largely avoid the need to kill non-transgenic offspring. However, invasive procedures (for the recovery and transfer of embryos) are still necessitated by nuclear transfer transgenesis. Conversely, sperm-mediated transgenesis, coupled with artificial insemination, retains the need for killing while avoiding the need for invasive procedures. Thus, substitution of a 'novel' method of transgenesis for one of the 'traditional' methods may permit a reduction in suffering. If such a substitution can be made without undermining experimental objectives, then it follows that such substitutions ought to be made wherever possible. However, it is important to emphasise that, as discussed previously, nuclear transfer transgenesis is in its infancy and sperm-mediated transgenesis is very far from being established as a viable method. Therefore, reducing suffering by choice of transgenesis method should be seen as a future possibility rather than as a practical proposition at present.

Thus, it seems undeniable that the process of transgenesis inevitably entails *some* (significant) suffering. The question now becomes: is this suffering outweighed by good consequences? I suggest that—assuming impeccable welfare provisions—an affirmative answer should be given. The 'good consequences' arising from transgenesis may be summarised under the heading of 'scientific progress'. As discussed previously, the scientific value of transgenesis can be in no doubt. Most forms of utilitarianism view scientific progress (in terms of an increased understanding of nature, and of the possible beneficial uses from such understanding) as morally desirable. Thus, prevention of transgenic research *per se* would only be justifiable on the grounds of major negative consequences. I contend that the inevitable significant suffering entailed by transgenesis is insufficiently large to outweigh the benefits to society arising from the contribution of transgenesis to scientific progress. The amount of significant suffering implicit in transgenesis cannot be quantified. However, the suffering actually entailed by the invasive procedures and killing used in transgenesis ought to be relatively minimal. Typically, donor and recipient animals are used only once in their lifetimes: this is in marked contrast to the many protracted experiments that 'ordinary' laboratory animals endure. Moreover, the procedures themselves are not of a severe nature: at worst (but under proper welfare conditions), embryo collection or transfer is akin to the sterilisation operations commonly used with household pet animals. Similarly, euthanasia is the most frequent fate of pet animals.

In summary: although all possible steps ought to be taken to reduce the amount of suffering entailed in the process of transgenesis, it would be wrong to prohibit animal genetic manipulation *per se*.

Outcomes of transgenesis

As discussed previously, the outcomes of transgenesis that have relevance here are those that are likely to cause suffering. Taking this category of transgenic outcomes in general, the consequences are of the same type as those for transgenesis *per se*, scientific progress is the benefit; and suffering is the cost. However, the degree of suffering implicit in this category of outcomes is greater than is the case for the process of transgenesis. On *prima facie* grounds, I contend that transgenic outcomes that cause significant suffering are contenders for prohibition. I suggest that utilitarians take a 'default' position in which experimentation entailing such negative transgenic outcomes is deemed unacceptable, unless (on a case-by-case basis) a watertight argument has been made to the effect that suffering is clearly outweighed by good consequences. For example, the generation of transgenics that develop an analogue of a painful human cancer ought to be permissible only if the experimenters could clearly demonstrate a major, tangible, high probability payoff in terms of a specific advance in cancer treatment. The difficulties in practice of convincingly demonstrating such benefits should not be underestimated: the majority of research using transgenic disease models is *not* expected to yield discernible immediate medical benefits. Moreover, there are many forms of transgenic experimentation for which a cost-benefit justification is *impossible*: for example, pain research may well fall into this category.

What I am suggesting is that, in the case of protracted or acute significant suffering arising in transgenic animals, the general 'scientific progress' benefit (although undeniable) is simply too nebulous to justify such experimentation. By contrast, there are circumstances in which one might envisage very direct benefits to humans that are both highly probable and highly proximate. In such exceptional cases, where it can be firmly demonstrated that the significant suffering of transgenic animals would be outweighed by the prevention of such suffering in humans (or by the saving of many human lives that would otherwise be lost), the prohibition ought to be lifted.

This 'default prohibition' position has radical implications because its application would entail the proscription of many transgenic experiments. However, unless the misconceived equation of utilitarianism with the notion 'the end always justifies the means' is accepted, or speciesism is resorted to, default prohibition appears to be the only coherent position compatible with utilitarianism. The alternative is that we would have to accept the doctrine of 'anything goes' in the name of scientific progress: I assume it axiomatic that no utilitarian would accept such a doctrine.

Notes

1   For example, other animals might become terrified as a consequence of their awareness of a nearby killing.
2   See P. Singer. 1993. *Practical Ethics*, 2nd ed. Cambridge, Cambridge University Press: 110–31.
3   Although killing may in principle be free of suffering, I suggest that this is so difficult to achieve in practice that the safest option is to assume *some* suffering, even under the most humane conditions.

Chapter 52

Jeffrey Burkhardt

THE INEVITABILITY OF ANIMAL BIOTECHNOLOGY? ETHICS AND THE SCIENTIFIC ATTITUDE

Burkhardt believes that a moral or ethical re-education of scientists and science policy makers is essential if ethical thinking is to enter the scientific establishment. He further believes that fundamental changes in the scientific attitude would be necessary for any ethical arguments to have force and that there probably will be considerable resistance to inclusion of ethical matters in scientific training. He argues that only when ethics becomes an established part of scientific thinking can the issues of the morality of using animals or the propriety of biotechnology be understood by scientists.

Introduction

MOST OBSERVERS OF biotechnology are aware that the main standard critiques of animal biotechnology are based on either animal rights/welfare arguments, ecological-oriented arguments, or socioeconomic consequences arguments. In this chapter, I want to suggest that despite the logic or seeming appropriateness of many of these critiques, they lack *ethical force*. By this I mean that the arguments (and the arguers) are unlikely to actually change the minds of those engaged in biotechnology practices and policy-making (Stevenson, 1944; Olshevsky, 1983). This is because of the orientation or attitude of those entrusted with doing and overseeing biotechnological work with non-human animal species. I will argue that this orientation must change before ethical arguments concerning animal biotechnology, indeed ethics generally (in the philosophical sense as opposed to legalistic or professional courtesy senses), mean anything to the scientific community. [. . .]

There are philosophical reasons, but more important, practical reasons for the proposal in this chapter. Philosophically, while some of the ethical objections to animal biotechnology or to particular biotechnology practices may be justifiable, behind many of them is a misplaced Platonic assumption that the problem with those engaged in animal biotechnology is that they do not know 'the good'. That is, if the scientists or policy makers knew or understood the philosophical objections, then they would stop doing what they are doing. The problem with this assumption is that scientists would have to accept the fundamental criteria for justifiability or reasonableness upon which philosophical argument rests before they would even fathom these criticisms as reasonable ones. This relates to my practical concern.

Practically, the rights/welfare, environment/ecology, and socioeconomic approaches are usually bound to fall on deaf ears. Arguments concerning 'ethics and animal biotechnology' are generally irrelevant, at best, to the actual members of the bioscience community or 'Science Establishment'. Scientists and policy makers may fathom some ethical concerns when their scientific or policy-making 'hats' are off. But to scientists and science-oriented policy makers *qua* scientists and science-oriented policy makers, proponents of animal rights/welfare arguments, environmental/ecological ethics arguments, or social justice arguments, can easily be relegated to the role of 'philosophers crying in the wind' (or howling at the moon). Ethical arguments which do not first assume the *a priori* legitimacy of whatever the scientific enterprise has decided to pursue are bound to be 'external' and 'externalized'. [. . .] My belief is that we should accept the inevitability of continued animal biotechnology research and development, and hope that the legalistic-type controls now in place in many nations continue to work or work even better. In the meantime, we should also 'sympathetically' impress on scientists the value of ethical reflection on their work.

Why the standard ethical critiques fail

Animal welfare, rights, and natural kinds arguments

Animal rights or animal welfare arguments regarding animal biotechnology arise because in all of these biotechnology activities, non-human animals are *involved*. The strongest argument objects to the use of animals *per se*. The rights argument, articulated so forcefully initially by Regan (1985), maintains that individuality and 'subject-of-a-life'-hood of non-human animals (in particular larger mammals) ethically demands their being treated in a quasi-Kantian manner: as ends in themselves, with appropriate stakes in life, liberty and self-actualization. Genetically altering an individual non-human animal, either before or after conception, *ipso facto* intrudes upon the autonomy of the being.

[. . .]

The philosophical underpinnings to the rights objection to animal biotechnology are easily countered by the scientific community. Most direct genetic engineering of animals (i.e. altering an animal's genetic structure) is performed either so early in the fetal developmental process that a distinct individual animal (in terms of moral autonomy) is indiscernible, or, more often, occurs even before conception takes place. Under any or all of Regan's criterion of the animal's having some rudimentary consciousness, or Singer's criterion of sentience, or Fox's criterion of 'telos-possession' (Fox, 1990), there is no 'subject of a life' (Rachels, 1990) whose inherent value or rights or unique purpose are disrespected through the engineering process.

[. . .]

Rights or welfare arguments may be appropriate to an appraisal of some biotechnology techniques, nonetheless. In particular, the use of biotechnologically produced hormones, pharmaceuticals and other agents may be seen as in some way disrespecting animals' rights or may cause a decrease in welfare. Using a chemical which artificially increases milk production in dairy cows, but which also increases incidences of disease (mastitis) and shortens an individual cow's productive life (and by implication, its life), may be bad for the cow in both rights and welfare terms. The issue here is, however, less an animal biotechnology matter than a simple matter of people using cows in dairy production systems.

[. . .]

One final point on the rights/welfare approaches: if any ethical concession is to be made to the fact that animals are used by humans, then some animal biotechnology may in fact be more ethical than some other research and production practices currently employed. If, as various humane societies have argued, better treatment of non-human animals ought to be our goal, biotechnology might be precisely the means to achieve that goal. This would, of course, depend on exactly what is being done with or to the animals, individually or by species (see, for example, NABC, 1992).

The natural kinds argument is the other main kind of animal-based objection to genetic engineering. Rifkin (1983) argued that the very ideology of genetic engineering—'algeny'—challenged the naturalness of those species which were either created by God or evolved through natural selection. Independent of the potentially disastrous ecological consequences of tampering with these longstanding kinds, there is a fundamentally immoral audacity in those people who would 'play God' and change the natural order for whatever purposes they intended.

[. . .]

Again, there are science-based replies to natural kinds arguments. Simply stated, humans have used animals for millennia, and in many respects, the very animal species which they used now exist only because of their use.

[. . .]

In terms of ethical force, the appropriate ethical critiques of animal biotechnology are not, at least as animal biotechnology is currently practised, either the animal rights/welfare sorts of argument, or the natural kinds approach advanced by Rifkin. These kinds of criticisms, which I refer to as 'intrinsic' critiques, can generally be met with reasonable points about either the nature of the practices performed on animals, or the extent to which they produce suffering, or the extent to which they are no different in principle from any other animal-using scientific practice. I suggest that other, 'extrinsic' or consequentialist critiques may be more appropriate and forceful challenges to biotechnology, to the extent that there is science-based (and hence, 'reasonable') evidence to support their claims. I will argue, nevertheless, that these criticisms can also fail because they miss major points about what biotechnology, and animal biotechnology in particular, can potentially do.

Consequentialist critiques and irreversibility arguments

Consequentialist-type arguments regarding animal biotechnology usually focus on ecological or socio-economic cultural ills associated with biotechnology in general, and animal biotechnology in particular. One common theme among these arguments, and, perhaps, underlying fear among their proponents, is that these consequences are or may tend to be irreversible: that is, once the technology or its products have been developed, adopted, or widely used or released into the world, severe negative effects will obtain which will be difficult or impossible to stop or reverse (Comstock, 1990).

The ecological arguments are most straightforward, though most originally were advanced with respect to microorganisms and plant species with little thought given to (larger) animal implications. According to this line of argument, a genetically altered individual or species of organism is necessarily different from its natural or wild counterpart. In fact, the reason behind genetic engineering is to design plants, animals or organisms with traits which would allow the organism to cope with the environment in ways different from the non-engineered kin, for instance withstand different and hostile climatic conditions, resist pests, better absorb nutrients from the environment. [. . .] These creatures of bio-engineering were intended to perform in their environments in ways to be preferred to those of their natural relatives.

The prime concern of the ecological-ethical critique is that bioengineered organisms, once outside controlled laboratory conditions, might behave in ecologically inappropriate ways. For instance, the engineered species might out-compete its natural relatives to the point of the extinction of the latter; or new predator species might evolve in response to the changes in the original species; or the new species just might grow out of control; or the new species might simply upset the 'biotic community' (Holland, 1990). [. . .] Note that it is again not bioengineering *per se* that is at issue. Rather, it is the *results* of bioengineering.

[. . .]

There may be sound moral premises behind this critique, such as, 'We morally should not risk ecosystemic disruption because of risks to present or future people or to the ecosystem itself'. Once we have allowed these organisms into the environment, we cannot get them back. Even so, there is again a reasonable reply in this case. We risk ecosystemic disruption all the time, and in fact *cause* ecosystemic disruption through many things much more dangerous than genetically engineered animals or animal products. So, unless the point is that we should leave the ecosystem alone, a practical impossibility, these potential ecosystemic disruptions are not necessarily immoral. [. . .] Because we know the genetic makeup of the engineered species even better than that of the non-engineered ones, we are in fact in a better position to control the new species or even eradicate those individuals who begin to get out of control.

[. . .]

Risk and irreversibility are also behind the economic and social consequentialist arguments vis-à-vis biotechnology. The argument here is that, unlike ecosystemic behaviour, we have clear precedents with respect to how new technologies affect social or economic behaviour, relationships, or structures (Burkhardt, 1988). On this basis, it is argued that animal biotechnology is potentially socially disastrous, and hence likely to be immoral in that regard.

[. . .]

Despite the force of ethical precedents, the reply to socioeconomic criticisms is straightforward. [. . .] The objection to biotechnology's socioeconomic consequences is really an objection to technology in general, or perhaps to capitalist socioeconomic arrangements. [. . .] [A]ny [. . .] particular product or process might change socioeconomic relations, but that is not the fault of the technology, only the system into which it is introduced (Burkhardt, 1991).

[. . .]

There is one further consequentialist argument to attend to here. This might be called the 'cultural consequence' argument. [. . .] [W]idespread diffusion of biotechnological products (from altered animals and plants to bioengineered chemicals and food products) might open the door for general public acceptance of the ethical appropriateness of engineering *people*. [. . .] As more biotechnology becomes the norm, a whole culture might come to accept whatever is bioengineered as even morally preferable to the non-engineered. Given *real* slippery slopes in attitudes, and *real* risks to longstanding human values such as freedom of choice and perhaps diversity among people, biotechnology accordingly is a cultural threat.

Like the potential ecological consequences critique, this last concern plays up the element of uncertainty. Unlike the environmental/ecological position, however, it is less a matter of how bioengineered organisms or ecosystems will behave or be affected than a matter of how people will act and react toward biotechnology. The question is whether there are any reasons for the public or policy makers to be concerned about the standard science-based reply to this position, namely, it will not happen. I will argue in the next section that the answer is predicated on whether there is indeed any reason for us to be concerned that biotechnology will continue to be employed without prior or at least concomitant ethical reflection. There may be little reason to fear biotechnology progressing, but only if biotechnology is either regulated and monitored, or ethics becomes an intrinsic part of the scientific attitude—the fundamental ideological/epistemological basis for science.

The biotechnology culture and the scientific attitude

[. . .]

A realistic appraisal of biotechnology, in general, has to begin with this fact: something in the biotechnology area has occurred, and likely will continue to occur. Philosophers and social analysts have long pointed to the power that science has in modern society. This notion was given contemporary expression and force by Rosenberg (1976) in his notion of 'Scientism'—the ideology of science solving all human problems. Scientism, it is argued, has become another dominant '-ism' of our day.

[. . .]

The extent to which Scientism undergirds both the biotechnology enterprise as practised as well as public policy regarding biotechnology is astounding. It is this fact which lends credibility to the cultural critique described above.

[. . .]

In the public policy arena, moreover, we have witnessed a gradual but steady strengthening of the power of biotechnology or bioscience in general (Busch et al., 1991). Even as funding for some specific kinds of basic research (e.g. AIDS) has been questioned by members of the United States' Congress, the general level of support for biotechnology has grown. In addition, much of the regulatory oversight which grew up in the early years of biotechnology—the late 1970s and early 1980s—has gradually devolved (NABC, 1994). Public policy priorities have shifted from concerns about the potential negative effects of biotechnological research to concerns that the advances in bioscience and especially bioengineered products are not coming fast enough. [. . .] [T]here is little reason to believe that anything short of an environmental catastrophe caused by a bioengineered product or experiment gone awry could actually cause a reduction in the enthusiasm with which biotechnology has been embraced at nearly all levels of research management, oversight or policy making.

[. . .]

There are a number of reasons or causes to which the biotechnology craze might be attributed. One might simply be the excitement or enchantment that members of the scientific establishment experience when, as I mentioned above, what was conceivable becomes possible, or what was possible becomes actual.

[. . .]

There are other, perhaps less noble, reasons for the degree of excitement and commitment to biotechnology in general and agricultural (plant and animal) biotechnology in particular. [. . .] The motivation also appears to have been the time element involved: whereas a new plant variety or pharmaceutical product might take several years or even decades to develop under older research methods, the new biotechnologies offered hope for quicker new products and processes. Again, in an increasingly competitive environment, the quicker the better.

Whatever the reason for the interest in and excitement about biotechnology, there is one additional glaring fact about the scientific attitude concerning biotechnology: ethical considerations such as those discussed above matter little, if at all. This orientation has permeated the science establishment. This lack of concern for deeper ethical matters, as opposed to legalities or professional courtesies, may permeate all society as well (save theologians and philosophers trying to conserve older ways of thinking about what is or is not moral). So long as science continues to deliver or at least forecast new promises—for corporations, for policy makers, and ultimately for the general public—ethics is irrelevant.

The scientific attitude

Biologist Frederick Grinnell, in *The Scientific Attitude* (1987), described what I take to be the underlying reason why 'ethics and science' or 'ethics and biotechnology' have been seen as beyond the pale in terms of attitudes and practices of members of the scientific community. [. . . Grinnell] hits on the idea that science must become, for scientists, a 'way of seeing' and a 'way of being'.

By 'way of seeing', Grinnell means that the material with which much physical and biological science operates (though perhaps true of social sciences such as economics as well) is only visible once one has come to appreciate and accept the appropriate theoretical or ideological foundation.

[. . .]

The 'way of being' of the scientist is of more direct and critical concern. For, as Grinnell suggests, this means adopting 'the scientific attitude', which in essence is to come to believe in Scientism: Rosenberg's (1976) book was aptly titled *No Other Gods*. And believing in Scientism means always being willing to act on making what is conceivable possible, and what is possible actual. In other words, to *be* a scientist (in this ideal typology), one must accept the *doctrine* that science defines what is real. Those who do not accept either that reality or its technological ramifications (the tools employed or the products created) are wrong at best, *irrational* at worst. This becomes the crux of the matter.

That this sort of attitude might engender a degree of arrogance or self-righteousness is clear (Feyerabend, 1978). However, not all individual scientists, or even most, need to or do display those personality traits. It is enough that the science establishment—research administrators, policy setters, leading scientific spokespersons—has the power to define what is or is not real, reasonable or rational. This is power in sociologist Stephen Lukes' (1986) sense of a 'third dimension' of power (the first two being physical force and persuasive ability)—the ability to define the terms in which rational discourse takes place. The work, perceptions, and professional communications of members of the scientific community all take as a given the reality and importance of scientific rationality, and whatever emanates from rational scientific work.

Scientists, including biotechnologists, may in fact be quite humble in the face of new problems, new theories, new frontiers. Nevertheless, there is a sort of moral imperative in the widely shared attitude that 'the work (of science) *must go on*' (J. Burkhardt, L. Busch and W. Lacy, personal interview, 1988). Moreover, significantly, whatever appears to impede or constrain the work of science must be based on some irrational or non-scientific force. As such, lack of funding (to the extent that some of this work lacks funding) is unreasonable. Even more unreasonable, and immoral by this doctrine, are rules, regulations, oversight committees, and reporting requirements. [. . .] In a word, constraints are unreasonable.

This characterization of the scientific attitude and Scientism undoubtedly overstates the case, and may even be questioned for grossly caricaturing science and the scientist. However, the ease with which the science establishment, and many individual scientists, can dismiss criticism or the kinds of objections to biotechnology discussed above is telling. There is not only nothing wrong with biotechnology (that is not wrong with any part of science), but to suggest otherwise is to either fail to understand science or simply be irrational. This refers back to my earlier point: any criticism or ethical concern which does not *a priori* assume the legitimacy of the scientific enterprise and the necessity of using science (including biotechnology) to solve problems must be ignored or, better, rendered impotent. One way to emasculate those criticisms is to fall back on the power that the science establishment has long had in Western society: change the terms of the discourse.

The culture of biotechnology

The case of bovine somatotrophin, one of the first commercial animal-affecting products to emerge from the biotechnology enterprise, is a telling example of the power of the bioscience community to actually change the terms of discourse—to the advantage of the biotechnology enterprise, of course. Bovine somatotrophin is a naturally occurring compound, produced in the pituitary glands of cows, which regulates growth and indirectly affects milk production. [. . .] Scientists at a number of United States universities, under grants or contracts with Dow Chemical and Monsanto corporations, became able in the early 1980s to produce the compound using recombinant DNA methods. The product could now be produced in greater quantities, and much more cheaply and efficiently.

Bovine somatotrophin was originally named 'bovine growth hormone' (BGH) when scientists and company representatives began touting the chemical for its potential use in animal agriculture. Quite soon afterwards, however, representatives of the bioscience establishment began to be met with resistance from consumer advocacy groups, and eventually lawsuits were even filed to prevent the US Food and Drug Administration from permitting the use of BGH in agriculture. Emphasis was placed on the nature of this compound as a *hormone*, despite scientists' and the industry's assurances that it was a non-steroidal-type hormone, and would not in any adverse way affect consumers of milk from BGH-treated cows. About the same time, however, the term 'BGH' disappeared from scientific publications and company promotions. Bovine somatotrophin became known by its real abbreviation, 'BST'. The resistance and criticisms of the substance did not disappear overnight, but the bioscience establishment managed to diffuse a significant amount of consumer activists' policy-affecting power by simply redirecting the concern away from a 'hormone' to just another productivity-increasing 'treatment' (Browne, 1987).

The whole BGH/BST story is much more complicated and drawn out (Burkhardt, 1992), but just this name change element in the story is sufficient to suggest my point. With nothing more than a semantic sleight of hand, the bioscience establishment was able to effectively control the public forum as well as public policy agenda. There are undoubtedly many, and more glaring cases of science winning a public relations battle or war. The only times the science establishment does not win hands down, it seems, is when it faces an equally formidable foe, for example the tobacco industry in the US, or organized religion, especially the Roman Catholic Church.

[. . .]

Critics of the agricultural research establishment have for a number of years pointed to a 'circle the wagons' mentality among people in the science establishment (Busch and Lacy, 1983). Always mindful of potential criticisms—from environmentalists, animal-rightists and animal welfarists, and small-farm and labour activists—the establishment (it was claimed) sought to dismiss or ignore the reasonableness of criticisms. In the case of the new generation of the bioscience/biotechnology community, the strategy seems more intended to pre-empt or co-opt criticisms than to ignore or dismiss them. The result is, nevertheless, that critics become marginalized, unless, again, there is significant political or social power behind them. Given the inherent (and self-defined) 'reasonableness' of the views, activities, and arguments of the scientific community, even formidable social challenges are likely to fail.

These points may suggest nothing more than that the bioscience community, including practitioners of animal biotechnology, probably have little or no reason to fear that their activities will be fundamentally challenged in the actual public arena. Moreover, to the extent that the scientific establishment is becoming more sophisticated about 'science education', the likelihood of even a powerful challenge diminishes greatly. Science writers, science popularizers, and spokespersons for universities and corporations are out in force, promoting the legitimacy and safety of biotechnology. Surveys suggest that as the public becomes more 'informed' and 'educated' about science, concern diminishes significantly. Further, as policy makers become more informed and educated as to the relative benefits and risks of biotechnology (as defined by scientists themselves), strong legislative action is unlikely. Indeed, as mentioned above, the result of all this information and education may well be simply greater levels of funding for the biotechnology enterprise. The only conclusion to be reached is that 'the beast will go on'. The spectre of a broader, social 'culture of biotechnology', with attendant human genetic engineering, is real.

Conclusion: ethics by regulation, committee, or (re-)education

In the early 1970s, a gathering of concerned scientists was held in Asilomar, California, to discuss the risks and benefits of genetic engineering. What emerged from those meetings was a set of biosafety guidelines concerning biotechnology. Many of those guidelines made their way into federal regulations and general governmental oversight. Though fairly stringent at the time, the guidelines and subsequent rules have been gradually weakened. Scientists argue that, as their knowledge about bioengineering has grown, what were reasonable concerns are now known to be unfounded fears. Recall that the USDA abolished its biotechnology oversight committee. Apparently it was thought to be an unnecessary public expenditure. Most universities have in-house biosafety committees, and corporations, it has been argued, exercise extreme caution because of the risk of lawsuits or prosecution under environmental or human safety regulations.

[. . .]

The scientific establishment continues to engage in genetic engineering practices involving animals. And, technologies will continue to have impacts, some of them negative, on particular socioeconomic groups in society. Barring some sort of major catastrophe, or major gestalt shift, animal biotechnology, biotechnology in general, and even more generally, technological research and development will undoubtedly continue. If ethical considerations are to fit anywhere in this scientific enterprise, it would seem that it would have to be through the current system of oversight and control, or through the force of higher levels of government action. Given the power of science and Scientism, the latter is unlikely, though not impossible.

One conclusion that can be reached is this: if ethics in a substantive sense is to make its way into the scientific establishment, and the bioscience community in particular, it will have to be at least in part if not exclusively through the moral or ethical re-education of scientists and science policy makers. And the moral or ethical education of young scientists and students would also be a key. Indeed, the ethical force of particular kinds of arguments pertaining to animal biotechnology is dependent on *any* ethical argument having force. And for any ethical argument to have force, fundamental changes in the scientific attitude would be necessary. As Grinnell noted, the way of seeing and way of being of science are *learned* orientations. *Seeing* ethical considerations as inherently part of the scientific enterprise, as well as *being* an ethically aware scientist or policy maker, must also be learned.

Just as there is considerable resistance on the part of the science establishment to external control— to the point of pre-empting *rational* discussion of criticisms—there may also be considerable resistance to the inclusion of ethics as part of the indoctrination into the scientific attitude. Nevertheless, there are enough scientists who do engage in ethical reflection when their scientific 'hats are off' that there is at least some promise for ethics to be a part of the scientific mind-set. Already, there are college and university courses, colloquia, and informal discussion among members of the bioscience community about 'science ethics'. With considerable effort on the part of theologians, philosophers, and social scientists—duly respectful of the ability of science to define the terms of rational discussion—more such inclusion of ethics might continue.

Only when ethics becomes a legitimate—and rational—part of the scientific attitude will concerns about particular aspects of animal biotechnology be taken seriously, or taken at all. Only when ethics is a routine concern among scientists will considerations of whether we should be using animals, or engaging in biotechnology, even be fathomed. I do not believe that we will stop using animals in research (or for food purposes) in the near future. Nor do I believe that the scientific establishment will stop engaging in biotechnology any time soon, if at all. I do believe, however, that any critique which does not first address the need for including discussion of ethics in the very process of 'doing science' is doomed to failure. It does little practical or political good to challenge science from the outside. Rather, rational, informed, science-based discussion of ethical considerations has to be the key to whether continued biotechnological research and development, whether in the animal, plant, or human domains, will simply be inevitable.

Note

A considerable amount of the 'evidence' for the theses in this chapter is based on 'research' performed by the author, a professional philosopher, but whose appointment is in the agricultural science college at a major state university in the US. Although the author wishes to indict no particular scientists or administrators for espousing 'the scientific attitude', or especially indict them for 'ethical insensitivity', both orientations have been found to be extant (though the former far more prevalent) among the physical and biological scientists with whom the author interacts on a daily basis.

References

Browne, W. (1987) Bovine Growth Hormone and the Politics of Uncertainty: Fear and Loathing in a Transitional Agriculture. *Agriculture and Human Values*, **4** (1).

Burkhardt, J. (1988) Biotechnology, Ethics, and the Structure of Agriculture. *Agriculture and Human Values*, **4** (2).

Burkhardt, J. (1991) The Value Measure in Public Agricultural Research, in *Beyond the Large Farm* (eds P. Thompson and W. Stout), Westview Press, Boulder, CO.

—— (1992) On the Ethics of Technical Change: The Case of bST. *Technology and Society*, **14**.

Busch, L. and Lacy, W. (1983) *Science, Agriculture, and the Politics of Research*, Westview Press, Boulder, CO.

Busch, L., Lacy, W., Burkhardt, J and Lacy, L. (1991) *Plants, Power and Profit*. Blackwell, Oxford.

Comstock, G. (1990) The Case against bGH, in *Agricultural Bioethics* (eds S. Gendel, A. Kline, D. Warren and F. Yates), Iowa State University Press, Ames.

Feyerabend, P. (1978) *Science in a Free Society*, NLB, London.

Fox, M. (1990) Transgenic Animals: Ethical and Animal Welfare Concerns, in *The Bio-Revolution*, (eds P. Wheale and R. McNally), Pluto Press, London.

Grinnell, F. (1987) *The Scientific Attitude*. Westview Press, Boulder, CO.

Holland, A. (1990) The Biotic Community: A Philosophical Critique of Genetic Engineering, in *The Bio-Revolution* (eds P. Wheale and R. McNally), Pluto Press, London.

Lukes, S. (1986) *Power*, New York University Press, New York.

NABC (National Agricultural Biotechnology Council, USA) (1992) *Animal Biotechnology: Opportunities and Challenges*, NABC Report 4, Ithaca, NY.

—— (1994) *Agricultural Biotechnology and the Public Good*, NABC Report 6, Ithaca, NY.

Olshevsky, T. (1983) *Good Reasons and Persuasive Force*, University Presses of America, New York.

Rachels, J. (1990) *Created from Animals*, Oxford University Press, Oxford.

Regan, T. (1985) *The Case for Animal Rights*, University of California Press, Berkeley, CA.

Rifkin, J. (1983) *Algeny*, Viking Press, New York.

Rosenberg, C.E. (1976) *No Other Gods*, Johns Hopkins University Press, Baltimore, MD.

Stevenson, C. (1944) *Ethics and Language*, Yale University Press, New Haven, CT.

TELOS AS AN INFLUENCE ON ETHICAL ISSUES

Chapter 53

Bernard E. Rollin

ON *TELOS* AND GENETIC ENGINEERING

Rollin addresses the notion of *telos,* the essence and purpose of a creature, and proposes that there is no direct reasoning to argue that the notion of *telos* in animals and the Maxim to Respect *Telos* should preclude genetic engineering of animals. He notes that for domestic animals, each proposed modification should be assessed in relation to the Principle of Conservation of Welfare. For non-domestic animals, he believes that such modifications also may be valuable. He exercises proceeding cautiously so as to avoid possible ecological impacts or affecting other animals adversely.

Telos

ARISTOTLE'S CONCEPT OF *telos* lies at the heart of what is very likely the greatest conceptual synthesis ever accomplished, unifying common sense, science, and philosophy. By using this notion as the basis for his analysis of the nature of things, Aristotle was able to reconcile the patent fact of a changing world with the possibility of its systematic knowability. [. . .] Though individual robins come and go, 'robin-ness' endures, making possible the knowledge that humans, in virtue of their own *telos* as knowers, abstract from their encounters with the world. Common sense tells us that only individual existent things are real; reflective deliberation, on the other hand, tells us that only what is repeatable and universal in these things is knowable.

[. . .]

For Aristotle, as for common sense, the fact that animals had *tele* was self-evident—the task of the knower was to systematically characterize each relevant *telos.* [. . .] [T]he notion of *telos* has in fact been refined and deepened by the advent of molecular genetics, as a tool for understanding the genetic basis of animals' physical traits and behavioural possibilities. At the same time, the classical notion of *telos* is seen as threatened by genetic engineering, the operational offspring of molecular genetics. For we may now see *telos* neither as eternally fixed, as did Aristotle, nor as a stop action snapshot of a permanently dynamic process, as did Darwin, but rather as something infinitely malleable by human hands.

Contemporary agriculture

Despite the fact that the concept of *telos* has lost its scientific centrality, there are two major and conceptually connected vectors currently thrusting the notion of *telos* into renewed philosophical prominence, both of which are moral in nature. These vectors are social concern about the treatment of animals, and the advent of practicable biotechnology. The former concern reflects our recently acquired ability to use animals without respecting the full range of their *telos*; the latter concern reflects our in-principle ability to drastically modify animal *telos* in unprecedented ways. There obtain significant conceptual connections between the two concerns, but before these are dealt with one must understand the social conditions militating in favour of a revival of the concept of *telos*.

[. . .]

The overwhelmingly preponderant use of animals in society since the dawn of civilization has unquestionably been agricultural—animals were kept for food, fibre, locomotion and power. Presupposed by such use was the concept of husbandry; placing the animals in environments congenial to their *telos*—the Biblical image of the shepherd leading his animals to green pastures is a paradigm case—and augmenting their natural abilities by provision of protection from predators, food and water in times of famine and drought, medical and nursing attention, etc. In this ancient contract, humans fared well if and only if their animals fared well, and thus proper treatment of animals was guaranteed by the strongest possible motive—the producer's self-interest. Any attempt to act against the animals' interests as determined by their natures resulted in damage to the producers' interests as well. In this contract, both sides benefited— the animals' ability to live a good life was augmented by human help; humans benefited by 'harvesting' the animals' products, power or lives. One could not selectively accommodate some of the animals' interests to the exclusion of others, but was obliged to respect the *telos* as a whole.

[. . .]

All of this changed drastically in the mid-twentieth century with the advent of high-technology agriculture, significantly portended as university departments of animal husbandry underwent a change in nomenclature to departments of 'animal science'. In this new approach to animal agriculture, one no longer needed to accommodate the animal's entire *telos* to be successful. [. . .] Technology has allowed animal producers to divorce productivity from total or near-total satisfaction of *telos*.

High-technology agriculture was not the only mid-twentieth century force significantly deforming the ancient contract with animals. Large-scale animal use in biomedical research and toxicology is, like intensive agriculture, a creature of the mid-twentieth century. Like confinement agriculture, too, successful use of animals in biomedicine does not necessitate accommodating the animals' *tele*.

[. . .]

Thus, both the advent of industrialized agriculture and large-scale animal use in science created an unprecedented situation in the mid-twentieth century by inflicting significant suffering on animals which was nonetheless not a matter of sadism or cruelty. Agriculturalists were trying to produce cheap and plentiful food in a society where only a tiny fraction of the population was engaged in agricultural production; scientists were attempting to cure disease, advance knowledge and protect society from toxic substances. As society became aware of these new animal uses neither bound by the ancient contract nor conceptually captured by the anti-cruelty ethic, and concerned about the suffering they engendered, it necessarily required an augmentation in its moral vocabulary for dealing with animal treatment.

[. . .]

It is th[e] notion of rights, based on plausible reading of the human *telos*, which has figured prominently in mid-century concerns about women, minorities, the handicapped and others who were hitherto excluded from full moral concern. It is therefore inevitable that this notion would be exported, *mutatis mutandis*, to the new uses of animals. In essence, society is demanding that if animals are used for human benefits, there must be constraints on that use, equivalent to the natural constraints inherent in husbandry agriculture. These constraints are based in giving moral inviolability to those animal interests which are constitutive of the animals' *telos*. If we are to use animals for food, they should live reasonably happy lives, i.e. lives where they are allowed to fulfil the interests dictated by their *telos*. [. . .] For the baboon used in biomedicine, this means creating a housing system which, in the words of US law, enhances the animals' 'psychological well-being', i.e. social non-austere containment for these animals that accommodates 'species-specific behaviour' (Rollin, 1989, pp. 177–81). For the zoo animals, it means creating living conditions which allow the animals to express the powers and meet the interests constitutive of its *telos* (Markowitz and Line, 1989).

Thus, *telos* has emerged as a moral norm to guide animal use in the face of technological changes which allow for animal use that does not automatically meet the animals' requirements flowing from their natures. In this way, one can see that the social context for the re-emergence of the notion of *telos* is a pre-eminently moral one: *telos* provides the conceptual underpinnings for articulating social moral concern about new forms of animal suffering. From this moral source emerge epistemological consequences which somewhat work against and mitigate the reductionistic tendencies in science alluded to earlier. For example, it is moral concern for *telos* which is sparking a return of science to studying animal conscious-ness, animal pain and animal behaviour, areas which had been reduced out of existence by the mechanistic tendencies of the twentieth-century science that affords pride of place to physicochemistry (Rollin, 1989). In an interesting dialectical shift, moral concern for animals helps revive the notion of *telos* as a fundamental scientific concept, in something of a neo-Aristotelian turn.

Genetic engineering

If our analysis of the moral concerns leading to the resurrection of the notion of *telos* is correct, we can proceed to rationally reconstruct the concept and then assess its relevance to the genetic engineering of animals. By rationally reconstruct, I mean first of all provide an articulated account of *telos* which fills the moral role society expects of it. Second, I mean to protect it from fallacious accretions which logically do not fit that role but which have attached, or are likely to attach to it for purely emotional, aesthetic or other morally irrelevant reasons. A simple example of such a conceptual barnacle might be those who would restore the notion of 'Divine purpose' to the concept of *telos*, and then argue that any genetic engineering is wrong simply because it violates that Divine purpose.

What sense can we make out of the notion of *telos* we have offered? In that sense, the *telos* of an animal means 'the set of needs and interests which are genetically based, and environmentally expressed, and which collectively constitute or define the "form of life" or way of living exhibited by that animal, and whose fulfilment or thwarting matter to the animal'. The fulfilment of *telos* matters in a positive way, and leads to well-being or happiness; the thwarting matters in a negative way and leads to suffering (see Rollin, 1992, Part I). Both happiness and suffering in this sense are more adequate notions than merely pleasure and pain, as they implicitly acknowledge qualitative differences among both positive and negative experiences. The negative experience associated with isolating a social animal is quite different from the experience associated with being frightened or physically hurt or deprived of water. Since, as many (but not all) biologists have argued, we tend to see animals in terms of categories roughly equivalent to species, the *telos* of an animal will tend to be a characterization of the basic nature of a species. On the other hand, increased attention to refining the needs and interests of animals may cause us to further refine the notion of *telos* so that it takes cognisance of differences in the needs and interests of animals at the level of sub-species or races, or breeds, as well as of unique variations found in individual animals, though, strictly speaking, as Aristotle points out, individuals do not have natures, even as proper names do not have meaning.

Thus, we may attempt to characterize the general *telos* of the dog as a pack animal requiring social contact, a carnivore requiring a certain sort of diet, etc. At this level we should also characterize gender- and age-specific needs, such as nest-building for sows, or extensive play for puppies and piglets.

[. . .]

This is perfectly analogous to moral notions we use vis-à-vis humans. Our *ur*-concern is that basic human interests as determined by human nature are globally protected—hence the emphasis on general human rights. We may also concern ourselves with refinement of those interests regarding subgroups of humans, although these subgroups are as much cultural as genetic.

[. . .]

Thus, *telos* is a metaphysical (or categorial) concept, serving a moral and thus value-laden function, and is fleshed out in different contexts by both our degree of empirical knowledge of a particular kind of animal and by our specificity and degree of moral concern about the animals in question. For example, the earliest stages of moral concern about the *telos* of laboratory animals focused only on very basic needs: food, ambient temperature, water, etc. As our moral concern grew, it focused on the less obvious aspects of the animals' natures, such as social needs, exercise, etc. As it grew still more, it focused on even less evident aspects.

[. . .]

Thus, the notion of *telos* as it is currently operative is going to be a dynamic and dialectical one, not in the Darwinian sense that animal natures evolve but, more interestingly, in the following sense: as moral concern for animals (and for more kinds of animals) increases in society, this will drive the quest for greater knowledge of the animals' natures and interests, which knowledge can in turn drive greater moral concern for and attention to these animals.

It is not difficult to find this notion of *telos* operative internationally in current society. Increasing numbers of people are seeking enriched environments for laboratory animals, and this is even discussed regularly in trade journals for the research community. Indeed, one top official in the US research community has suggested that animals in research probably suffer more from the way we keep them (i.e. not accommodating their natures) than from the invasive research manipulations we perform. The major thrust of international concern about farm animals devolves around the failure of the environments they are raised in to meet their needs and natures, physical and psychological.

[. . .]

Respect for *telos* and the conservation of well-being

This, then, is a sketch of the concept of *telos* that has re-emerged in society today. Though it is partially metaphysical (in defining a way of looking at the world), and partially empirical (in that it can and will be deepened and refined by increasing empirical knowledge), it is at root a moral notion, both because it is morally motivated and because it contains the notion of what about an animal we *ought* at least to try to respect and accommodate.

What, then, is the relationship between *telos* and genetic engineering? One widespread suggestion that has surfaced is quite seductive (Fox, 1986). The argument proceeds as follows. Given that the social ethic is asserting that our use of animals should respect and not violate the animals' *telos*, it follows that we should not alter the animals' *telos*. Since genetic engineering is precisely the deliberate changing of animal *telos*, it is *ipso facto* morally wrong.

[. . .]

Seductive though this move may be, I do not believe it will stand up to rational scrutiny, for I believe it rests upon a logical error. What the moral imperative about *telos* says is this:

Maxim to Respect *Telos*:

If an animal has a set of needs and interests which are constitutive of its nature, then, in our dealings with that animal, we are obliged to not violate and to attempt to accommodate those interests, for violation of and failure to accommodate those interests matters to the animal.

However, it does not follow from that statement that we cannot change the *telos*. The reason we respect *telos*, as we saw, is that the interests comprising the *telos* are plausibly what matters most to the animals. If we alter the *telos* in such a way that different things matter to the animal, or in a way that is irrelevant to the animal, we have not violated the above maxim. In essence, the maxim says that, given a *telos*, we should respect the interests which flow from it. This principle does not logically entail that we cannot modify the *telos* and thereby generate different or alternative interests.

The only way one could deduce an injunction that it is wrong to change *telos* from the Maxim to Respect *Telos* is to make the ancillary Panglossian assumption that an animal's *telos* is the best it can possibly be vis-à-vis the animal's well-being, and that any modification of *telos* will inevitably result in even greater violation of the animal's nature and consequently lead to greater suffering. This ancillary assumption is neither *a priori* true nor empirically true, and can indeed readily be seen to be false.

Consider domestic animals. One can argue that humans have, through artificial selection, changed (or genetically engineered) the *telos* of at least some such animals from their parent stock so that they are more congenial to our husbandry than are the parent stock. I doubt that anyone would argue that, given our decision to have domestic animals, it is better to have left the *telos* alone, and to have created animals for whom domestication involves a state of constant violation of their *telos*.

By the same token, consider the current situation of farm animals mentioned earlier, wherein we keep animals under conditions which patently violate their *telos*, so that they suffer in a variety of modalities yet are kept alive and productive by technological fixes. As a specific example, consider the chickens kept in battery cages for efficient, high-yield, egg production. It is now recognized that such a production system frustrates numerous significant aspects of chicken behaviour under natural conditions, including nesting behaviour (i.e. violates the *telos*), and that frustration of this basic need or drive results in a mode of suffering for the animals (Mench, 1992). Let us suppose that we have identified the gene or genes that code for the drive to nest. In addition, suppose we can ablate that gene or substitute a gene (probably *per impossibile*) that creates a new kind of chicken, one that achieves satisfaction by laying an egg in a cage. Would that be wrong in terms of the ethic I have described?

If we identify an animal's *telos* as being genetically based and environmentally expressed, we have now changed the chicken's *telos* so that the animal that is forced by us to live in a battery cage is satisfying more of its nature than is the animal that still has the gene coding for nesting. Have we done something morally wrong?

I would argue that we have not. Recall that a key feature, perhaps *the* key feature, of the new ethic for animals I have described is concern for preventing animal suffering and augmenting animal happiness, which I have argued involves satisfaction of *telos*. I have also implicitly argued that the primary, pressing concern is the former, the mitigating of suffering at human hands, given the proliferation of suffering that has occurred in the twentieth century. I have also argued that suffering can be occasioned in many ways, from infliction of physical pain to prevention of satisfying basic drives. So, when we engineer the new kind of chicken that prefers laying in a cage and we eliminate the nesting urge, we have removed a source of suffering. Given the animal's changed *telos*, the new chicken is now suffering less than its predecessor and is thus closer to being happy, that is, satisfying the dictates of its nature.

This account may appear to be open to a possible objection that is well known in human ethics. As John Stuart Mill queried in his *Utilitarianism*, is it better to be a satisfied pig or a dissatisfied Socrates? His response, famously inconsistent with his emphasis on pleasure and pain as the only morally relevant dimensions of human life, is that it is better to be a dissatisfied Socrates. In other words, we intuitively consider the solution to human suffering offered, for example, in *Brave New World*, where people do not suffer under bad conditions, in part because they are high on drugs, to be morally reprehensible, even though people feel happy and do not experience suffering. Why then, would we consider genetic manipulation of animals to eliminate the need that is being violated by the conditions under which we keep them to be morally acceptable?

[. . .]

In the case of animals, [. . .] there are no ur-values like freedom and reason lurking in the background. We furthermore have a historical tradition as old as domestication for changing (primarily agricultural) animal *telos* (through artificial selection) to fit animals into human society to serve human needs. We selected for non-aggressive animals, animals that depend on us not only on themselves, animals disinclined or unable to leave our protection, and so on. Our operative concern has always been to fit animals to us with as little friction as possible—as discussed, this assured both success for farmers and good lives for the animals.

If we now consider it essential to raise animals under conditions like battery cages, it is not morally jarring to consider changing their *telos* to fit those conditions in the same way that it jars us to consider changing humans.

Why then does it appear to some people to be *prima facie* somewhat morally problematic to suggest tampering with the animal's *telos* to remove suffering? In large part, I believe, because people are not convinced that we cannot change the conditions rather than the animal.

[. . .]

On the other hand, suppose the industry manages to convince the public that we cannot possibly change the conditions under which the animals are raised or that such changes would be outrageously costly to the consumer. And let us further suppose, as is very likely, that people still want animal products, rather than choosing a vegetarian lifestyle. There is no reason to believe that people will ignore the suffering of the animals. If changing the animals by genetic engineering is the only way to assure that they do not suffer (the chief concern of the new ethic), people will surely accept that strategy, though doubtless with some reluctance.

From whence would stem such reluctance, and would it be a morally justified reluctance? Some of the reluctance would probably stem from slippery slope concerns—what next? Is the world changing too quickly, slipping out of our grasp? This is a normal human reflexive response to change—people reacted that way to the automobile. The relevant moral dimension is consequentialist; might not such change have results that will cause problems later? Might this not signal other major changes we are not expecting?

Closely related to that is a queasiness that is, at root, aesthetic. The chicken sitting in a nest is a powerful aesthetic image, analogous to cows grazing in green fields. A chicken without that urge jars us. But when people realize that the choice is between a new variety of chicken, one *without* the urge to nest and denied the opportunity to build a nest by how it is raised, and a traditional chicken *with* the urge to nest that is denied the opportunity to build a nest, and the latter is suffering while the former is not, they will accept the removal of the urge, though they are likelier to be reinforced in their demand for changing the system of rearing and, perhaps, in their willingness to pay for reform of battery cages. This leads directly to my final point.

The most significant justified moral reluctance would probably come from a virtue ethic component of morality. Genetically engineering chickens to no longer want to nest could well evoke the following sort of musings: 'Is this the sort of solution we are nurturing in society in our emphasis on economic growth, productivity and efficiency? Are we so unwilling to pay more for things that we do not hesitate to change animals that we have successfully been in a contractual relationship with since the dawn of civilization? Do we really want to encourage a mind-set willing to change venerable and tested aspects of nature at the drop of a hat for the sake of a few pennies? Is tradition of no value?' In the face of this sort of component to moral thought, I suspect that society might well resist the changing of *telos*. But at the same time, people will be forced to take welfare concerns more seriously and to decide whether they are willing to pay for tradition and amelioration of animal suffering, or whether they will accept the 'quick fix' of *telos* alteration. Again, I suspect that such musings will lead to changes in husbandry, rather than changes in chickens.

We have thus argued that it does not follow from the Maxim to Respect *Telos* that we cannot change *telos* (at least in domestic animals) to make for happier animals, though such a prospect is undoubtedly jarring. A similar point can be made in principle about non-domestic animals as well. Insofar as we encroach upon and transgress against the environments of all animals by depositing toxins, limiting forage, etc. and do so too quickly for them to adjust by natural selection, it would surely be better to modify the animals to cope with this new situation so they can be happy and thrive rather than allow them to sicken, suffer, starve and die, though surely, for reasons of uncertainty on how effective we can be alone as well as aesthetic reasons, it is far better to preserve and purify their environment.

In sum, the Maxim to Respect *Telos* does not entail that we cannot change *telos*. What it does entail is that, if we do change *telos* by genetic engineering, we must be clear that the animals will be no worse off than they would have been without the change, and ideally will be better off. Such an unequivocally positive *telos* change from the perspective of the animal can occur when, for example, we eliminate genetic disease or susceptibility to other diseases by genetic engineering, since disease entails suffering. The foregoing maxim which does follow from the Maxim to Respect *Telos*, we may call the Principle of Conservation of Well-being. This principle does of course exclude much of the genetic engineering currently in progress, where the *telos* is changed to benefit humans (e.g. by creating larger meat animals) without regard to its effect on the animal. A major concern in this area which I have discussed elsewhere is the creation of genetically engineered animals to 'model' human genetic disease (Rollin, 1995b, Chapter 3).

There is one final caveat about genetic engineering of animals which is indirectly related to the Maxim to Respect *Telos*, and which has been discussed, albeit in a different context, by biologists. Let us recall that a *telos* is not only genetically based, but is environmentally expressed. Thus, we can modify an animal's *telos* in such a way as to improve the animal's *telos* and quality of life, but at the expense of other animals enmeshed in the ecological/environmental web with the animal in question. For example, suppose we could genetically engineer the members of a prey species to be impervious to predators. While their *telos* would certainly be improved, other animals would very likely be harmed. While these animals would thrive, those who predate them could starve, and other animals who compete with the modified species could be choked out. Thus, we would, in essence, be robbing Peter to pay Paul. Furthermore, while the animals in question would surely be better off in the short run, their descendants may well not be—they might, for example, exceed the available food supply and may also starve, something which would not have occurred but for the putatively beneficial change in the *telos* we undertook. Thus, the price of improving one *telos* of animals in nature may well be to degrade the efficacy of others. In this consequential and environmental sense, we would be wise to be extremely circumspect and conservative in our genetic engineering of non-domestic animals, as the environmental consequences of such modifications are too complex to be even roughly predictable (Rollin, 1995a, Chapter 2).

Conclusion

In conclusion, there is no direct reason to argue that the emerging ethical/metaphysical notion of *telos* and the Maxim to Respect *Telos* logically forbid genetic engineering of animals. In the case of domestic animals solidly under our control, one must look at each proposed genetic modification in terms of the Principle of Conservation of Welfare. In the case of non-domestic animals, there is again no logical corollary of the maxim of respect for *telos* which forestalls genetically modifying their *telos*, and, on occasion, such modification could be salubrious. Given our ignorance, however, of the systemic effects of such modifications, it would be prudent to proceed carefully, as we could initiate ecological catastrophe and indirectly affect the functionality of many other animals' *tele*.

References

Fox, M.W. (1986) On the genetic engineering of animals: a response to Evelyn Pluhar. *Between the Species*, **2** (1), 51–2.

Markowitz, H. and Line, S. (1989) The need for responsive environments, in *The Experimental Animal in Biomedical Research*, vol. I (eds B.E. Rollin and M.L. Kesel), CRC Press, Boca Raton, Florida, pp. 153–73.

Mench, J.A. (1992) The welfare of poultry in modern production systems. *Critical Reviews in Poultry Biology*, **4**, 107–28.

Rollin, B.E. (1989) *The Unheeded Cry: Animal Consciousness, Animal Pain and Science*, Oxford University Press, Oxford.

Rollin, B.E. (1992) *Animal Rights and Human Morality*, Prometheus Books, Buffalo, NY.

Rollin, B.E. (1995a) *Farm Animal Welfare: Ethical, Social, and Research Issues*, Iowa State University Press, Ames, Iowa.

Rollin, B.E. (1995b) *The Frankenstein Syndrome: Ethical and Social Issues in the Genetic Engineering of Animals*, Cambridge University Press, New York.

Chapter 54

Bernice Bovenkerk, Frans W.A. Brom, and Babs J. van den Bergh

BRAVE NEW BIRDS: THE USE OF ANIMAL INTEGRITY IN ANIMAL ETHICS

Bovenkirk, Brom, and van den Bergh use the terms "integrity" and "naturalness" to address the notions of bioengineering and *telos* raised by Rollin. They note that the concept of integrity refers to a set of characteristics of a species humans define and believe is important to preserve, and that the identity of such characteristics can be elucidated by moral discussion. Even in the absence of full agreement, such discussions can help clarify the issues and evaluate existing practices.

BESIDES PROVIDING US with new biological knowledge and opening up some intriguing possibilities in medicine and agriculture, genetic engineering provides philosophers with some interesting thought experiments. Inspired by Bernard Rollin's remark in *The Frankenstein Syndrome*[1] about the creation of wingless, legless, and featherless chickens, Gary Comstock urges us to imagine just that: the transition of chickens into living egg machines.[2]

[. . .]

What if we could make these animals adjust better to their environment and genetically engineer them into senseless humps of flesh, solely directed at transforming grain and water into eggs. [. . .] Intuitively, treating an animal in this way—or rather creating an animal for these purposes—is morally problematic. This intuition is also prompted by uses of biotechnology that are already feasible and indeed are already in use, but the "brave new birds" provide a paradigmatic case.

In public debate in The Netherlands, these sorts of cases evoke appeals to such notions as integrity and naturalness.[3] In the case of the egg machines, for example, we might say that the chickens' integrity has been violated because we have interfered with their physical makeup, not for their own good, but for ours. We have tampered with the characteristics that make a chicken a chicken.

Why animal integrity?

This intuition that changing chickens into senseless, living egg machines is problematic and cannot be elaborated solely with the help of traditional moral concepts such as animal interests or animal rights.

"Welfarists," like Rollin, take animals to have interests because, and only insofar as, they are sentient. In other words, Rollin holds that animals have interests by virtue of their sentience, and therefore that only welfare matters from a moral point of view.

[. . .]

Since the chickens are senseless, Rollin cannot raise any objection to the use of genetic engineering to turn these animals into machines. But even though Rollin asserts that he "sees no moral problem if animals could be made happier by changing their natures," elsewhere he seems to acknowledge that creating living egg machines is not a desirable course of action. Rather, it is the lesser of two evils "while it is certainly a poor alternative to alter animals to fit questionable environments, rather than alter the environments to suit the animals, few would deny that an animal that does mesh with a poor environment is better off than one that does not." This assertion seems to acknowledge the moral intuition that changing an animal's nature is objectionable, while holding that the circumstances may make it necessary. Clearly, however, suffering is not the main issue here. In other words, Rollin's concept of interest is too narrow to analyze our moral intuition.[4]

Animal rights proponents, such as Tom Regan, argue that raising animals for food is wrong not primarily because it causes animal suffering, but because it is wrong in principle. This is because animals, like humans, are valuable in themselves and not only by virtue of their value to others. In other words, they possess inherent value and therefore have moral standing.[5] According to Regan, the basis for this inherent value is that animals are "subjects-of-a-life."[6] Regan regards mammals that possess a certain amount of awareness as paradigmatic subjects-of-a-life. If so, the senseless egg machines in our example are probably not subjects-of-a-life, and it is probably not wrong in principle to change chickens into them.

[. . .]

Animal ethicists in The Netherlands have proposed the notion of animal integrity precisely because of the inability of interests and rights to accommodate the moral intuition that we should adjust the farm environment to the animal and not vice versa. Integrity has been described by Bart Rutgers as the "wholeness and intactness of the animal and its species-specific balance, as well as the capacity to sustain itself in an environment suitable to the species."[7]

Some objections

'Integrity' seems to be helpful because it has an objective, biological aspect. It implies that the animal is intact or whole, which is an attribute of the animal itself, not just some value we have placed on it. Integrity therefore could play an important role in elaborating moral concerns not only about genetic engineering but also about other interventions in animal life, like cross-breeding or intensive animal husbandry.

It is important to note that we would not speak of the violation of integrity in all cases in which an animal's intactness is violated. Rutgers holds that docking a dog's tail for aesthetic reasons constitutes a violation of the dog's integrity, but when the dog's tail must be docked for medical reasons, he claims that its integrity has not been violated. In effect, docking a dog's tail for these two reasons could be regarded as two different actions, depending on the intention with which the action is carried out.

But this raises a problem. If the physiological result of the two different kinds of docking is the same, then it seems that integrity is not a biological aspect of the animal itself after all. The concept then loses its objective, biological character and becomes a moral rather than an empirical notion. It does not refer to a notion of factual intactness or wholeness so much as to a *perceived* intactness. It refers to how we feel an animal *should* be.[8] That leaves us wondering how objective the notion of integrity really is.

A second difficulty with the notion of integrity is the problem of "gradation." If we are to judge the acceptability of, say, a certain scientific experiment on animal subjects, then we need to be able to weigh the moral good against the moral wrong.[9] Only when we can deem one type of experiment more acceptable than another will 'integrity' have meaning in the context of ethical deliberation. If gradation were impossible, then every intervention constituting a violation of integrity would have to be dealt with similarly: either they would all have to be condemned, no matter how trivial the purpose, or none of them could be condemned, no matter how severe the consequences.

Gradation could be achieved in three different ways. First, violations of integrity could be graded based on the good that the violation aims at. The problem with this first position is that all the work has to be done by weighing goals and not by grading the moral wrongs. Integrity itself is not graded at all.

Second, one could consider respect for integrity as a prima facie duty that must be weighed against other prima facie duties. The problem with this strategy is that we must know more about integrity to do the weighing, which leads us back to the question about integrity's content.

The third way would be to describe different kinds of violations of integrity, some more severe than others. The problem with the third way is that, unlike the notions of well-being and health, integrity—conceived of as intactness or wholeness—seems to be an absolute notion.[10] A body is either intact or not, and so either has integrity or not. It's like being pregnant: a woman is either pregnant or she is not; she cannot be more or less pregnant. The *violation* of integrity is not necessarily this absolute. Docking a dog's tail, for instance, does not seem to be as harsh a violation of its integrity as, say, the removal of one of its legs. The question is what basis we have for judging the weight of a violation of integrity. What criteria can we use to establish which of two violations is worse? And what criteria can be used to argue that the violation is bad enough to reject the possible good it constitutes (as in the case of scientific experiments)? We need grounds to make this kind of gradation possible. In other words: how can we measure integrity?

Human integrity

Thus the notion of integrity is problematic. It carries a false pretense of objectivity, of being "empirically determinable," and it is not clear how it can be of practical use, as this would entail criteria to measure it. Do these problems render the concept of animal integrity useless? To answer this question, it is helpful to look at two parallel discussions in which integrity plays a role: human integrity and ecosystem integrity.

A widely shared moral intuition exists that no matter what the benefits, every human being has the right not to be physically violated without his or her consent. The concept of human integrity is often employed to give voice to this intuition.

Physical and mental integrity concerns the inviolability or intactness of a person's body and mind. Historically, the concept originates in the debate about the relationship between the state and its citizens. The most important human right is the right not to be imprisoned arbitrarily or to have the integrity of one's person or body violated in any other way. This right has now been extended to the medical sphere, where it plays a central role in defining the relationship between physicians and their patients, obliging doctors to request the patient's informed consent before carrying out an invasive action.[11] More precisely, informed consent is based on two complexly interrelated pillars—autonomy over and integrity of one's mind and body. Sometimes, but not always, they support each other. Protection from invasive action cannot be lifted without the permission of the patient. However, permission is not always a sufficient condition for integrity not to be violated. The concept of integrity provides some restraint on self-determination: some violations might be objectionable even if the person wants them.

If a patient is not able to give permission for whatever reason, others have to see to the protection of her body from invasive action. This is where integrity becomes most important; it establishes the inviolability of the bodies of people who cannot dispose of their bodies themselves, including children, prisoners, and those who are mentally handicapped or comatose. The same intuition plays a role in decisions about people who out of sheer poverty feel forced to "donate" their organs. Socioeconomic circumstances prevent these people from exercising their autonomy. When we want to argue against allowing them to sell their organs, we could appeal to their physical integrity.

[. . .]

It is important to note that the law not only concerns violations of the body resulting in suffering or in adverse health conditions, but that it also deals with infringements on the body without such detrimental effects. In fact, as with animals, it is this dimension of inviolability that is best expressed by the notion of integrity. Even though the person with Down syndrome who receives a contraceptive injection can hardly be said to suffer a great deal of pain or illness as a result of the injection, the notion of integrity allows one to argue that she has been violated and that the administration of contraceptive injection is—at the very least—morally problematic and in need of justification.

Plainly the concept of integrity is well established in the field of medical ethics as a way of structuring discussions. Yet here, too, it is not free of problems. The problems can be illustrated by considering the implications of Article 11 of the Dutch Constitution, which states that every person has the right, apart from limitations imposed by law, to the inviolability of her body. The clause is part of the right to protection of personal privacy and contains two elements: (1) the right to be protected from harm of and infringement upon the body by a third party, and (2) the right to self-determination of the body. Thus in its explanation of what 'integrity' involves, the law makes a distinction between a person and her body and allows a person to dispose of her body freely.

This distinction is controversial in philosophy, but it is undeniably useful for understanding and regulating the doctor-patient relationship. If the distinction is admitted, however, then protecting the integrity of a *person* can lead to a violation of the integrity of the person's *body*. The right to physical integrity contends that every person has the right to remain free from infringements upon the body by others, but it also states that every person has a right to determine the disposition of one's body.

If the body has integrity of its own that could be violated, then a trans-sexual who undergoes a sex-change may very well be violating her own physical integrity. If we do not want to draw this conclusion, then we must hold that an intervention into the body is not a violation when it is approved of by the person. We could say that as the operation seems to bring the person more in harmony with her body, in the overall picture the person's integrity has not been violated.[12] Integrity as a moral notion can therefore be diametrically opposed to integrity as an empirical notion. Here, as with animal integrity, we see that an intervention constitutes a violation of integrity only if it is *perceived* as such. Clearly the problem of objectivity is present in the domain of human integrity as well as in that of animal integrity.

Ecosystem integrity

The notion of integrity has also been applied within the science of ecology in order to help protect environmental resources. Aldo Leopold employed the concept in relation to ecosystems. In what must be the most quoted passage in ecological ethics, he asserted that "A thing is right when it tends to preserve the integrity, stability, and beauty of the biotic community. It is wrong when it tends to do otherwise."[13]

Ecological integrity refers to the wholeness, unity, or completeness of an ecosystem. Immediately, of course, the question arises what we are to make of the stability and wholeness of an ecosystem when it is a central feature of ecosystems that they change continuously. Parts of an ecosystem can be destroyed while the ecosystem as a whole seems to flourish. There is an uninterrupted movement through life cycles; some individuals die and others are born, but the ecosystem as a whole remains. How can we determine whether or not the integrity of an evolving ecosystem has been violated?

James Kay's definition of ecosystem integrity takes this dynamic character into account and calls attention to certain processes found within ecosystems. According to Kay, constitutive elements of ecosystem integrity are the ability of ecosystems to maintain optimum operations, to cope with environmental stress, and to self-organize.[14] Laura Westra adds a human element to this definition; she asserts that an ecosystem must be able to maintain its "conditions as free as possible from human intervention" and to withstand anthropocentric stresses upon the environment.[15] Westra also distinguishes ecosystem integrity from ecosystem health. An ecosystem can be healthy even when it is intensively managed by people, but it possesses integrity only "when it is wild, that is, free as much as possible today from human intervention, when it is an "unmanaged" ecosystem, although not a necessarily pristine one."[16]

When the first European settlers came to Australia in 1788, they encountered a more or less harmonious ecosystem, characterized by native flora and fauna that were well adapted to their environment. Delicate relations between the land and its vegetation and between different kinds of plants and animals kept all in balance. Understandably, however, the settlers felt homesick in this alien land. Also, it did not at first sight seem to offer very many food crops. Thus the settlers thought it would be a good idea to bring some of their own native plants and animals to Australia, in order both to sustain themselves and to remind them of their homeland. Little did they know what havoc they were to cause by this introduction of exotic species.

[. . .]

Biodiversity was lost, and the ecosystem can no longer be said to be free and unmanaged in Westra's sense. The native vegetation has been overgrown, and animals that fed on the native plants have lost a food source. In effect, an altogether new ecosystem has evolved. The initial ecosystem could not respond well.

Several attempts have been made to put the concept of ecological integrity to practical use. This has proven to be difficult, but it is also very important, as it could help guide policy. For instance, managers of different national parks adhere to different approaches about whether or not to prevent naturally occurring fires. Westra's account of ecosystem integrity gives us some criteria to employ in thinking about this problem. Her account suggests that while the health of a forest might be damaged by naturally occurring fires, its integrity cannot be said to be violated because the effects are not the result of human action.

The problems that beset the concept of ecosystem integrity include those of both objectivity and gradation. There is no easy way of establishing objectively whether or not a violation of an ecosystem has occurred. All that seems clear is that ecosystems' integrity is violated when we destroy the whole world, for then it is quite clear that the ecosystem has not been able to cope with anthropocentric stress. As John Lemons notes, "it could be said that any ecosystem that can maintain itself without collapsing has integrity. . . . There is no scientific reason why a changed ecosystem necessarily has less ability to maintain optimum operations under normal environmental conditions, cope with changes in environmental conditions less effectively, or be limited in its ability to continue the process of self-organisation on an ongoing basis."[17] Thus ecological integrity does not allow us to demarcate precisely which intervention does and which does not violate the integrity of an ecosystem.

Moreover, as with animal integrity, it is difficult to find criteria to determine how severely the ecosystem's integrity has been violated. How, for example, can we determine the severity of the damage caused by blackberries in Australia? A new balance was found between different plants and animals within the ecosystem, and in a sense, optimum operations were restored. It is because we find the change undesirable that we say the ecosystem's integrity has been violated. In short, whether or not an ecosystem's integrity has been violated "must be based on human judgement regarding the acceptability of a particular change."[18]

As we saw before in the case of animal integrity, whether or not such a change is rendered acceptable largely depends on the purpose for which the intervention is carried out. The example of the forest destroyed by naturally occurring fire makes clear that integrity is primarily a moral term, referring to human action. Only when the fire has been lit by humans do we speak of a violation of the forest's integrity. Moreover, setting the forest on fire could actually benefit it,[19] and in that case, even a human-induced fire would probably not be counted as a violation of integrity. It is the ends an act serves that makes us judge it favorably or not.

Flawed but workable

As we have seen, arguments about "integrity" are problematic not only in the animal domain but in parallel discussions as well. The concept refers not to a state of affairs that can be assessed empirically, but rather to our own ideals for a human, an animal, or an ecosystem. Violations of integrity cannot be objectively proven, nor can their severity be established.

Yet despite these problems, "integrity" is used in the ecological and human domains to structure discussions and to reach agreements. In these domains, it serves a useful critical function. It has proven especially valuable in the field of medicine, and at least in continental Europe seems to be widely accepted, alongside the concepts of autonomy and dignity.[20] These other concepts are also rather obscure, but nevertheless they have been translated into principles whose usefulness is widely accepted, despite disputes about their exact meaning.

In the field of environmental policy, too, "integrity" seems to be a sound notion. Appeals to integrity frequently pop up in the management of national parks. Even though it is sometimes hard to establish whether or not a policy will amount to a violation of an ecosystem's integrity, the concept hands policymakers and park managers a tool to structure and clarify their discussion. Here, as in the case of medical interventions, an appeal to integrity gives us the opportunity to criticize certain proposed actions that have repercussions for an ecosystem's functioning. Again, the concept of integrity generates no knock-down arguments, but it nonetheless appears to be quite workable in a practical context. It gives us a way to communicate moral reservations we might have about environmental policies.

When we envision a future in which we buy eggs from a warehouse housing hundreds of rows of flesh-colored humps created from what we once knew as chickens, a feeling of discomfort comes over us. We—or many of us, anyway—have a moral intuition that changing chickens into living egg machines is wrong. The moral notion that gives voice to this intuition is "integrity." Integrity goes beyond considerations of an animal's health and welfare, and it applies not only to present but also to future animals. An animal's integrity is violated when through human intervention it is no longer whole or intact, if its species-specific balance is changed, or if it no longer has the capacity to sustain itself in an environment suitable to its species. However, when the intervention is directed toward the animal's own good, we do not speak of a violation of its integrity.

One of the main appeals of the use of integrity seems to be its objective, biological aspect. As we have shown, however, integrity is not as objective a notion as it appears at first sight. Should we therefore do away with the concept of animal integrity? Not necessarily, or rather, necessarily not. The concept has been introduced to fill a gap between moral theory and moral experience. It is important to do justice to this moral experience, and not to reject the concept too swiftly because of difficulties in setting out precisely what it involves. In the light of ongoing technological developments we are confronted ever more frequently with moral dilemmas that traditional moral concepts cannot deal with, and we have a responsibility to try to refine our moral thinking and to develop criteria that help us act in a morally justifiable way.

So let's take a closer look at the problems with the concept of integrity. We argued that the purpose of potential violation of integrity is crucial for judging whether or not the action actually constitutes a violation of integrity. When we dock a dog's tail, for example, our reason for docking it is decisive in deciding whether the dog's integrity has been violated. The concept of integrity thus does not refer to an objective state of affairs, but one that *we* feel is important to preserve.

Yet we need not regard the concept as completely subjective, either. While it does not refer to empirically ascertainable biological facts, we can still establish intersubjective criteria for its application. Through moral discussion, we can reach agreement about which sorts of actions do and do not lead to violations of integrity. And even if we could not reach this agreement, the notion of integrity still has an important function, namely to clarify the moral debate and criticize existing practices. Integrity can give opponents of Rollin's thought experiment a way to voice their criticism of the creation of living egg machines without having to appeal to traditional moral concepts like welfare, interests, or rights, none of which seem to capture what is important in Rollin's scenario. "Integrity" should therefore remain a part of our moral discussion. Its content can be continually refined through an ongoing learning process.

References

1 B.E. Rollin, *The Frankenstein Syndrome: Ethical and Social Issues in the Genetic Engineering of Animals* (New York: Cambridge University Press, 1995).

2 G. Comstock, *What Obligations Have Scientists to Transgenic Animals?*, discussion paper by the Center for Biotechnology, Policy and Ethics, 8, College Station, Tex.: Texas A&M University, 1992.

3 In this article we will limit ourselves to a discussion of the former. F.W.A. Brom, J.M.G. Vorstenbosch, and E. Schroten, "Public Policy and Transgenic Animals: Case-by-Case Assessment as a Moral Learning Process," in *The Social Management of Genetic Engineering*, ed. P. Wheale, R. von Schomberg, and P. Glasner (Aldershot: Asgate, 1998), 249–64.

4 Other welfarists, such as Nils Holtug, object to changing animals into senseless machines by arguing that attention to welfare should not be limited to the prevention of suffering, but should also be directed to the promotion of positive experiences. By making animals senseless we would deny animals the possibility to enjoy positive experiences. See N. Holtug, "Is Welfare All that Matters in our Moral Obligations to Animals?" *Acta Agriculturae Scandinavica* Sect. A, Animal Science Supplement 27 (1996): 16–21. However, welfarists need to invoke an extra premise, not reducible to mere sentience, to explain why positive experiences matter to the animal. See F.W.A. Brom, "Animal Welfare, Public Policy and Ethics," in *Animal Consciousness and Animal Ethics: Perspectives from the Netherlands*, ed. M. Dol *et al.* (Assen: Van Gorcum, 1997), 208–22.

5 T. Regan, *The Case for Animal Rights* (London: Routledge and Kegan Paul, 1983).

6 To be a "subject-of-a-life" is to "have beliefs and desires; perception, memory, and a sense of the future, including their own future; an emotional life together with feelings of pleasure and pain; preference and welfare-interests; the ability to initiate action in pursuit of their desires and goals; a psychophysical identity over time; and an individual welfare in the sense that their experiential life fares well or ill for them, independently of their utility to others." See Regan, *The Case for Animal Rights*, 243.

7 L.J.E. Rutgers, F.J. Grommers, and J.M. Wijsmuller, "Welzijn-Intrinsieke waarde-Integriteit," *in Tijd-schrift voor Diergeneeskunde* (1995): 490–4; and L.J.E. Rutgers and F.R. Heeger "Inherent Worth and Respect for Animal Integrity," in *Recognizing the Intrinsic Value of Animals: Beyond Animal Welfare*, ed. M. Dol *et al.* (Assen: Van Gorcum, 1999).

8 F.W.A. Brom, "Animal Welfare," and F.W.A. Brom, "The Good Life of Creatures with Dignity," *Journal for Agricultural and Environmental Ethics* 13, nos. 1–2 (2000): 53–63.

9 We intentionally do not use the terms "benefits" and "advantages" because they imply a utilitarian framework, whereas our discussion depends on a deontological one.

10 J.M.G. Vorstenbosch, "The Concept of Integrity: Its Significance for the Ethical Discussion on Bio-technology and Animals," *Livestock Production Science* 36 (1993): 109–12.

11 T.L. Beauchamp and J.F. Childress, *Principles of Biomedical Ethics*, 4th ed. (New York: Oxford University Press, 1994), 128.

12 On the other hand, as integrity is not an absolute notion, it might well be that it is a violation that is justified, because the appeal to integrity is in this case overruled by an appeal to autonomy. However, we doubt that transsexuals even experience their bodies' integrity as being violated by the sex change.

13 A. Leopold, *A Sand County Almanac* (Oxford: Oxford University Press, 1949), 224–5.

14 J. Kay (1992), quoted in J. Lemons, "Ecological Integrity and National Parks," in *Perspectives on Ecological Integrity*, ed. L. Westra and J. Lemons (Dordrecht: Kluwer Academic Publishers, 1995).

15 Lemons, "Ecological Integrity," 180.

16 L. Westra, "Ecosystem Integrity and Sustainability: The Foundational Value of the Wild," in *Perspectives on Ecological Integrity*, ed. L. Westra and J. Lemons (Dotdrecht: Kluwer Academic Publishers, 1995), 12.

17 Lemons, "Ecological Integrity."

18 Lemons, "Ecological Integrity."

19 This is the case with fire-prone and fire-resistant trees, such as gum trees in Australia, that need fire in order to regenerate. Moreover, if regular burning is not conducted in some Australian forests, a fuel buildup on the forest floor will lead to unintended raging bush fires. See on this subject A.M. Gill, R.H. Groves, and I.R. Noble, eds.; *Fire and the Australian Biota* (Canberra: Australian Academy of Science, 1981).

20 Beauchamp and Childress, *Principles of Biomedical Ethics*.

ISSUES IN CLONING

Chapter 55

Oliver A. Ryder

CLONING ADVANCES AND CHALLENGES FOR CONSERVATION

Ryder points out that recent successes in cloning animals raise the possibility that cloning technology can assist with the management of endangered species. He acknowledges that the reduced fitness of some cloned animals is still problematic, but believes this technique can contribute to conservation efforts. He calls for increased research, targeted application of the technology, and an expanded effort to bank cells to allow for the future success of cloning technology.

Although controversy surrounds cloning efforts, the cloning of animals to assist efforts to preserve genetic variation in support of endangered species conservation efforts has attracted serious interest. A recent report by Loi *et al.* describing the cloning of a mouflon (a species of wild sheep) in a domestic sheep surrogate points to potential conservation opportunities and additional challenges in the evaluation of appropriate technologies for present and future efforts to conserve gene pools of endangered species.

Published online: 10 April 2002

EACH MAJOR REPORT about cloning involving somatic nuclei brings new insights and new debates. As the controversy around human cloning expands [1,2] there is a diversity of opinion regarding the potential of cloning for the conservation of endangered species [3–5]. It is important to evaluate separately the issues surrounding human cloning and those of animal cloning.

With respect to predictions for loss of species, technologies for assisted reproduction, such as artificial insemination, embryo transfer and cloning from somatic cells, have been advocated as technologies that could contribute to conservation of biological diversity [6].

Successful cloning of an endangered sheep

Discussion of the application of cloning technology to conservation efforts for endangered species [3] was an immediate result from Ian Wilmut's 1997 report of the cloning of Dolly [7]. Although reports of embryo development [8,9] and newborn animals have appeared as a result of cloning technology, the recent report of surprising success in cloning mouflon (a species of wild sheep) [10] is notable for several reasons. The success rate was much greater than when the domestic sheep, Dolly, was cloned. A higher proportion of embryos (constructed by nuclear transfer to enucleated domestic sheep ova) developed *in vitro* to blastocysts and, subsequently, to pregnancies and live birth in surrogate dams than previously reported [7,11]. It is also noteworthy that the donor nuclei were obtained from dead donor mouflon. These rather unexpected findings might serve as the basis for additional studies to help identify factors contributing to the rate of success. Studies of telomere length were not reported and future work in this area will be of interest.

From a theoretical perspective, there is reason to believe that cloning can assist in the preservation of genetic diversity in precariously small populations. The cloned animals, as individuals, might serve as conduits for the retention of genetic variation otherwise lost. There are many vulnerable and endangered forms of sheep (including forms of argali, urial, desert bighorn and Marco Polo and snow sheep) for which this technology could be considered in defined programs of gene pool preservation.

Objections to the use of cloning technology for conservation focus on inefficiencies of the current process, impracticalities involved in applying these techniques to non-domestic ova donors and surrogate dams, and the lack of fitness for survival of cloned animals in the natural environment. Fitness concerns are heightened owing to the use of domestic surrogates that fail to impart appropriate behavioral attributes for cloned offspring that will interact with others of their species raised by conspecific mothers (i.e. mothers of the same species).

Defects in cloned animals

Abnormal morphology and lack of developmental success in cloned mice is associated with abnormal regulation of imprinted genes [12]. Thus, imprinted genes in successfully (and unsuccessfully) cloned animals have been investigated in detail [13]. As the specific loci subject to imprinting have been modified in the course of mammalian evolution [14,15], further studies of the evolution of imprinting and imprinted genes in mammals might also provide useful insights. Active management of deprogramming differentiated nuclei and epigenetic effects is an area of active investigation that might eventually increase the fitness of cloned animals.

As discussions of the fitness of clones continue, the question is not so much whether Dolly has arthritis as whether her descendants have a reduction in their fitness associated with the deprogramming of her genome that facilitated her development from the nucleus of a differentiated cell. Also, apparently normal cattle have resulted from cloning [16]. The over-arching concern for the genetic continuity of a species rather than for the fitness of a single individual is a crucial difference between application of cloning technologies to endangered animals in comparison to humans.

Cloning as a tool for assisting in conservation of gene pools

When considering the potential role of cloning to help the conservation of endangered species, a crucial point is whether cloning represents a functional technology suitable to the management of gene pools. The changes in gene pools of vulnerable populations becoming endangered will limit viability of some populations with grave prospects for recovery. The potential to modulate loss of genetic variation in small populations undergoing sexual reproduction by incorporating genetic variation from unrelated individuals or individuals of known genotype or phenotype from preserved cell nuclei offers a form of intervention previously unimaginable in the animal breeding or conservation breeding context. Although we would prefer to envision that, if intervention is required, some limited form of management will be sufficient to ensure the viability of populations in protected areas and, indeed, all suitable habitats, we can by no means say that this is assured.

Allelic diversity is lost owing to drift and, in small populations, the persistence of rare alleles becomes vulnerable to chance events. Practical intervention will probably consist of managing retention of genetic variation, including heritable attributes that are most likely yet to be identified. Deleterious loci might need to be detected and their frequencies managed in the population. Haplotype diversity might also be desirable to manage, and evidence for selection for some haplotypes might become apparent as a result of population studies.

Alteration in allele frequencies that could accumulate over generations as a result of differential selection and drift in a captive environment might be mitigated if founder and early generation individuals could be used for breeding to provide individuals for reintroduction and augmentation programs.

Cell banking and research should top the current agenda

We are probably not at the stage where cloning technology is ready to be applied to maintain population viability or conserve species for which the technology is available and, in any case, cloning is no panacea. However, in the struggle to maintain self-sustaining populations cloning might have a future role more significant than present technology suggests. Looking to the future, there will probably be instances in which cloning technology can make a crucial difference for some species. Although it might be decades from now that answers become clear, it is apparent that access to declining levels of genetic diversity is more readily available now than in the future. Additional research should be welcomed and evaluated in the context of conservation.

Anticipation of potential benefits to be derived from the strategic use of cloning technology will require a broad understanding of its limitations in the context of specific conservation goals. For which species might cloning technology be considered? Where might the most significant benefit be derived from initial efforts? Surely, cells that might be later used for a variety of purposes, including cloning, should be collected as opportunity allows—for many species in peril this needs to be done sooner rather than later. We will not be able to explore the potential of cloning without additional studies, which could be focused on development of a strategic tool for conservation management of small populations. Such studies will require access to cells that have been previously banked from species for which loss of genetic variation is considered to be detrimental to the maintenance of a self-sustaining population. There are few sources of such cells because, with a few exceptions, banking cells from small populations of endangered animals has not been undertaken. These exceptional collections offer much in the way of resources that might be used in evaluating the circumstances in which cloning technology might offer practical conservation benefits. Delaying such experimentation will forestall the collection of information crucial to the evaluation of cloning technology for targeted management of small populations for conservation.

Planning for the future

Certainly, a concerted effort involving collaborations of field biologists familiar with the status of threatened and endangered species with reproductive scientists, geneticists and others with expertise and resource banking should be undertaken to match conservation and technological opportunities. Identification of the taxa at risk and the systematic collection of samples as opportunities arise, consistent with the conservation management of threatened and endangered species, offer increased opportunities for preventing extinction and for the preservation of gene pools.

In the future, even if efforts to establish banks of cells from endangered species are viewed as a needlessly pessimistic strategy, these cell banks will be of great use for a variety of biological studies that will increase the understanding of the natural world and its evolution. It has been suggested that an abrogating effect of the effort to bank cells is the establishment of unrealistic and unattainable programs for effective conservation and insufficient diligence to ensure preservation of sufficient natural habitat for conservation of biodiversity. However, an effort in genetic resource banking for endangered species serves the interests of future generations irrespective of the application of cloning technology. Furthermore, cell-banking efforts are not envisaged as efforts *in lieu* of *in situ* conservation but as supporting efficiencies and informed decision making capabilities that assist *in situ* conservation efforts.

Summary

The successful cloning of a mouflon from cells of an animal found dead in the field again raises the possibility that cloning technology can assist with the management of endangered species. Although the fitness of cloned animals remains a subject of controversy, the potential of cloned individuals to contribute to the retention of genetic variation in small populations provides an opportunity for this technology to contribute to conservation efforts. Increased research, targeted application of the technology and an expanded effort to bank cells are indispensable before this technology will make a significant impact on small population management for conservation.

References

1 Jaenisch, R. and Wilmut, I. (2001) Developmental biology – Don't clone humans. *Science* 291, 2552

2 Solter, D. (2000) Mammalian cloning: Advances and limitations. *Nat. Rev. Genet.* 1, 199–207

3 Ryder, O.A. and Benirschke, K. (1997) The potential use of 'Cloning' in the conservation effort. *Zoo Biology* 16, 295–300

4 Loskutoff, N.M. Role of embryo technologies in genetic management and conservation of wildlife. *Symposium on Reproduction and Integrated Conservation Science.* Zoological Society of London. (In press)

5 Critser, J.K. *et al.* Application of nuclear transfer technology to wildlife species. *Symposium on Reproduction and Integrated Conservation Science.* Zoological Society of London. (In press)

6 Lanza, R.P. *et al.* (2000) Cloning Noah's ark. *Sci. Am.* 283, 84–9

7 Wilmut, I. *et al.* (1997) Viable offspring derived from fetal and adult mammalian cells. *Nature* 385, 810–13

8 White, K.L. *et al.* (1999) Establishment of pregnancy after the transfer of nuclear transfer embryos produced from the fusion of argali (*Ovis ammon*) nuclei into domestic sheep (*Ovis aries*) enucleated oocytes. *Cloning* 1, 47–54

9 Chen, D.Y. *et al.* (1999) The giant panda (*Ailuropoda melanoleuca*) somatic nucleus can dedifferentiate in rabbit ooplasm and support early development of the reconstructed egg. *Science in China Series C-Life Sciences* 42, 346–53

10 Loi, P. *et al.* (2001) Genetic rescue of an endangered mammal by cross-species nuclear transfer using post-mortem somatic cells. *Nat. Biotechnol.* 19, 962–4

11 Galli, C. *et al.* (1999). Mammalian leukocytes contain all the genetic information necessary for the development of a new individual. *Cloning* 1, 161–70

12 Rideout, W.M. *et al.* (2001) Nuclear cloning and epigenetic reprogramming of the genome. *Science* 293, 1093–8

13 Humpherys, D. *et al.* (2001) Epigenetic instability in ES cells and cloned mice. *Science* 293, 95–7

14 Killiam, J.K. (2001a) Monotresse IGF2 expression and ancestral origin of genomic imprinting. *J. Exp. Zool.* 291, 205–12

15 Killam, J.K. (2001b) Divergent evolution in M6P/IGFZR imprinting from the Jurassic to the Quaternary. *Hom. Mol. Genet.* 10, 1721–8

16 Lanza, R.P. *et al.* (2001) Cloned cattle can be healthy and normal. *Science* 294, 1893–4

Chapter 56

Autumn Fiester

CREATING FIDO'S TWIN: CAN PET CLONING BE ETHICALLY JUSTIFIED?

Fiester acknowledges that pet cloning may appear to be a frivolous practice, costly to both the cloned pet's health and human financial investment. She notes critics' arguments that it can be misguided and unhealthy, and a way of exploiting grief to the detriment of the animal, its owner, and perhaps even animal welfare in general. However, she argues that the practice might be defensible if it becomes more broadly recognized that the willingness to engage in such difficult and expensive work will raise the status of companion animals in the public perspective.

C OMMERCIAL PET CLONING—currently cats only—is now available from the firm Genetic Savings and Clone for the small price of $30,000. In December 2004, a nine-week-old cat clone was delivered to its owner, the first of six customers waiting for the identical twin of a beloved pet.[1] "Little Nicky," as he's known, has stirred up a great deal of ethical controversy, with more to come as the firm expands to dog cloning sometime in 2005.

For many, the cloning of companion animals seems morally suspect in a way that the cloning of animals for agricultural purposes or for biomedical research does not. In judging the ethics of cloning animals that will be healthier to eat or will advance science or medicine, there is a natural argument to be made that the technique will serve the greater human good. But in the case of pet cloning, there is really no analogous argument, however wonderful the original "Missy," the mixed-breed dog whose owner funded the now-famous Missyplicity Project at Texas A&M to make pet cloning possible. Cloned companion animals will not significantly enhance general human well-being. In balancing the cost to animals against the possible benefit to humans, the ethics of pet cloning seems to be a simple equation: a concern for animal welfare equals an anticloning stance.

But what if there were benefits to animals, and what if these benefits outweighed the pain and suffering they endure from cloning research and procedures? Then there would be an argument in favor of pet cloning at least as strong as those offered for cloning conducted for agriculture or medical research. The idea of animals suffering for *animal* benefit makes a tidy moral case that just might justify the practice.

Of course, making this case will be a challenge given the serious anticloning objections raised by animal advocacy organizations and cloning critics. But the benefit to animals that I will consider is this: the practice of pet cloning—like advanced veterinary care such as transplants, neurosurgery, orthopedics, and psychopharmaceuticals—might improve the public's perception of the moral status of companion animals because it puts animals in the category of being worthy of a very high level of expense and concern. Something that warrants this level of commitment and investment seems valuable intrinsically, not merely instrumentally, and this change in the public's perception could have far-reaching benefits for all animals.

Of course, even if this controversial claim is true—that pet cloning might contribute to an increase in the public's esteem for companion animals—it can justify pet cloning only for those who already find some forms of animal cloning morally acceptable. My case rests on the premise that some types of cloning are morally justified by the benefits that will result from them. People opposed in principle to all forms of animal cloning—for example, because this type of biotechnology is "playing God" or because animals should never be used in research—will not accept this consequentialist starting point. The most straightforward way to make the point is this: we can talk about justifying pet cloning only on the assumption that animal cloning for clearly important ends—like medical or pharmaceutical advances—is morally permissible. If one rejects those types of cloning, the argument about pet cloning cannot get off the ground.

The anti-cloning case

Critics of pet cloning typically offer three objections: (1) the cloning process causes animals to suffer; (2) widely available pet cloning could have bad consequences for the overwhelming numbers of unwanted companion animals; and, (3) companies that offer pet cloning are deceiving and exploiting grieving pet owners.

Animal suffering

Animal welfare advocates have been quick to point out the cost of animal cloning to the animals involved in the procedures.[2] A large body of literature documents high rates of miscarriage, stillbirth, early death, genetic abnormalities, and chronic diseases among the first cloned animals. These problems occur against a backdrop of what in cloning science is called "efficiency," the percentage of live offspring from the number of transferred embryos. The efficiency of animal cloning has typically been about 1 to 2 percent, meaning that of every one hundred embryos implanted in surrogate animals, ninety-eight or ninety-nine fail to produce live offspring.[3] Given the invasive techniques used to implant the embryos in the surrogate, these numbers represent a certain amount of suffering on the part of the donor animals: for every one or two live animals, one hundred eggs must be harvested and one hundred embryos implanted. In the experiments conducted to clone "CC" the calico cat, one hundred and eighty-eight eggs were harvested, eighty-seven cloned embryos were transferred into eight female cats, two of the females became pregnant, and one live kitten was born.[4]

Further, of the live clones born, many have experienced compromised health status or early death. In one study of cloned pigs, researchers reported a 50% mortality rate for the live offspring, with five out of ten dying between three and one hundred and thirty days of age from ailments including chronic diarrhea, congestive heart failure, and decreased growth rate.[5] A study published last year showed that cloned mice experience early death due to liver failure and lung problems.[6] Another study showed that cloned mice had a high tendency to morbid obesity.[7]

Cloning scientists respond that both efficiency rates and health outcomes are radically improving, and that we can reasonably expect in the very near future to see fewer animals involved in the cloning process and better health status for the clones that are born.[8] Although the process that produced "CC" was inefficient, there were no kittens born with compromised health status. Research on cloned cattle published last year showed that once the animals survived infancy, they had no health problems when compared with non-clones.[9] Genetics Savings and Clone claims that it has pioneered a new cloning technique that not only improves the health status of clones but greatly increases cloning efficiency, achieving pregnancy loss rates on a par with those of breeders.[10] Although information is limited, the company claims that six healthy kittens have been born with no deformities. If this proves to be true, then the animal suffering caused by the process is limited to that of the surrogate mothers. There aren't even any donor animals involved, since the company uses eggs harvested from ovaries purchased from spay clinics. And the suffering of the surrogates is surely not greater than that of cats who "donate" kidneys for feline kidney transplants, a practice that has not received widespread criticism on grounds of inordinate feline suffering.[11]

Unwanted pets

A second objection to pet cloning is that there are millions of unwanted pets in the United States. How can we justify the creation of designer companion animals when so many wonderful animals languish in shelters? This is the main argument behind the Humane Society's anticloning position. Says Senior Vice President Wayne Pacelle, "The Humane Society of the United States opposes pet cloning because it is dangerous for the animals involved, it serves no compelling social purpose, and it threatens to add to the pet overpopulation problem. It doesn't sit well with us to create animals through such extreme and experimental means when there are so many animals desperate for homes."[12] To be sure, the data on the number of companion animals euthanized in American shelters are sobering. The 2001 Humane Society report on the state of animals in the United States found that four to six million dogs and cats were euthanized in shelters in 2001.[13] These figures do not include the millions of stray animals in the country: the ASPCA estimates that 70 million stray dogs and cats live in the United States.[14]

But what is the connection between the sorry state of unwanted companion animals in this country and the anti-pet-cloning stance? Surely one cannot hold that no new animals ought to be intentionally created until all shelter animals are adopted. Anticloners would then have bigger fish to fry than pet cloning—namely, the breeders and puppy farms that produce millions of dogs and cats each year. By comparison, pet cloning, even if it becomes a viable industry, will produce only trivial numbers of animals.

[. . .]

Exploitation and deception

But what about the concern that pet owners are being tricked into believing that they are getting Fido back, when in truth, Fido and the clone could be as different as any identical twins? There are two separate charges here: one is about false advertising or exploitation on the part of the cloning firm; the other is about the pet owner's self-deception.

Take the cloning firm first. Opponents argue that grieving pet owners are deceived by companies like Genetic Savings and Clone into believing that cloning is a way of resurrecting a deceased and beloved pet. [. . .] But whatever policies need to be put in place to make sure the owner has realistic expectations, how cloning firms market pet cloning and educate potential customers does not bear on the moral legitimacy of pet cloning itself. There is a clear need to regulate this emerging industry to ensure truth in advertising, but that could be achieved without eliminating the product.

As for the self-deception of the pet owner, this is a psychological, not an ethical, concern. [. . .] If the customers don't feel betrayed or deceived (and indeed, they do not) and are satisfied with their investment and comforted by the clone's existence, then it is hard to get this psychological concern going. The bereft pet owner might know full well that the clone will be nothing more than a genetic twin, and the decision to clone might be merely an attempt to preserve something important from the original animal, rather than *resurrect* it.

Pet cloning and "rising status"

Now consider an argument in favor of pet cloning: pet cloning may change common views of what in philosophy is called the "moral status" of animals. The fact that companion animals are deemed worthy recipients of this level of effort and expense might encourage people to view animals as having intrinsic value and uniqueness.

The public's perception of the value of animals is not fixed. In fact, the public's estimation of animals' status is arguably rising fast. Getting at perceptions of animal status is difficult, but consider some of the following facts: a 2001 ABC News poll found that 41 percent of Americans believe that animals go to heaven,[15] and a May 2003 Gallup poll found that a full 33 percent of Americans are at least somewhat supportive of an all-out ban on medical research involving laboratory animals.[16] Attitudes among pet owners are even more interesting. For example, a 1999 survey by the American Animal Hospital Association found that 84 percent of pet owners refer to themselves as their pet's "mommy" or "daddy," 63 percent celebrate the pet's birthday, and 72 percent of married respondents greet their pet first when they return home.[17] There are also more pet owners now than ever before; 62 percent of households in the United States own pets in 2005,[18] up from 50 percent in 1975.[19]

The dramatic shift in the status of American pets can also be seen in the resources devoted to them. Americans spent over $30 billion on small animal companions in 2003,[20] a 10 percent increase over 2002 spending,[21] and two and a half times the spending levels of 1978 (in adjusted dollars, Americans spent $11 billion in 1978 vs. $30 billion today).[22] [. . .]

The argument I want to advance is that the treatment of companion animals by their caretakers alters what the public in general thinks about them. Attitudes toward companion animals are heavily influenced by the dominant view and mainstream practice (indeed it is the majority of Americans who currently have pets).

More specifically, I want to offer a hypothesis about one mechanism by which this kind of cultural change takes place, namely, that the routinization of certain practices and expenses on the part of pet owners normalizes that behavior, which affects the general view of what care animals deserve; and this in turn enhances the public's estimation of the value of companion animals because it encourages the public to view animals as entities worthy enough to merit this attention and care. One of the most significant influences on the public's perceptions is the effort expended to improve the health and extend the lives of companion animals. Pet cloning is just the extreme form of pet owners' attempts to extend the life (in this case, in the form of the genome) of a beloved animal.

Advanced veterinary care is the paradigm case. Veterinary services are the fastest-growing segment of the companion animal industry, increasing at an annual rate of 4.7 percent, with current expenditures pegged at close to $8 billion.[23] [. . .]

As each new procedure or service is incorporated into veterinary care, pet owners' acceptance of the new standard of care alters the overall public's attitude toward those procedures. No longer seen as a bizarre or exorbitant waste of money and resources, the new procedure starts to seem entirely warranted. Think of the public's attitude toward now commonplace treatments, such as daily shots of insulin, arthritis medicines, corrective surgery for orthopedic problems, or antianxiety medicines. These expenses easily exceed the original price of the animal, but few people would now tell a pet owner to cut her losses and buy a new pet. What is happening to the public's attitude toward companion animals if these advance treatments seem like reasonable measures and expenses to protect animal lives and well-being? At a minimum, the normalization of advanced veterinary care indicates the public's recognition of the "irreplaceability" for the pet owner of one animal with some other. We no longer think of companion animals as disposable or interchangeable, despite the ready supply of homeless animals.

Of course, this argument may suffer from the classic "chicken or the egg" question: is the attention given to animals raising public perceptions of animals' status, or is the perception of animals' status rising independently of the actions of pet owners? In fact, it can go both ways. To the pet owner, the intrinsic value of the companion animal is already recognized, which is why she expends the resources and energy to treat the animal. To someone observing that practice, the effect is to affirm or alter the perception of value that companion animals have—or ought to have. [. . .]

Pet cloning makes the statement that one's companion animal is so important that it is worth trying to come as close as possible to preserving it by investing in a genetic twin. The hypothesis is that when pet cloning is seen as a rational, justifiable activity for pet owners as a response to the (impending) death of an animal, the societal effect—as with advanced veterinary care—will be to enhance the companion animal's position on the moral map through the public's recognition that these entities have high value.

One possible rejoinder is that the dignity and uniqueness of the original pet is degraded by an attempt to obtain a clone. Believing that we can replace a companion animal with its clone demonstrates that animals are, in fact, mere objects, not at all like children, and the effect of widespread use of pet cloning will be to downgrade animals' status, not raise it. But whether pet cloning will have this effect will depend on how society interprets it. A pet-cloning-as-mass-production view will undoubtedly reinforce the idea that companion animals are replaceable consumer goods, and this will have a deleterious effect on perceptions of their status. In the cloning-as-solace view as I have described above, however, companion animal cloning will be seen as a tribute to the value of the original animal. There are parents who desperately want to clone their lost children.[24] Pet owners, mirroring their feelings, are making a statement about both the animal's immeasurable value and the level of loss and grief they feel at its death. Whatever one thinks of human cloning, no one argues that the parents who request it don't assign the highest possible worth to the deceased child; the sentiment to clone is a testimony to the parents' belief in the infinite value of that unique person. If this becomes widely understood, the cloning-as-solace interpretation may indeed win out.

If pet cloning bolsters even slightly a perception that companion animals have intrinsic value, then the positive consequences for companion animals will far outweigh the minimal suffering the animals undergo through the cloning process. The rising status of companion animals has already begun to translate into laws that offer more protection for them, including changes in the designation of pet owners to "animal guardians" in some areas.[25] If companion animals' status continues to rise, and if pet cloning contributes at all to that trend, then there is an argument for the moral legitimacy of pet cloning.

References

1 P. Fimrite, "Cat Has 10 Lives, Thanks to $50,000 Cloning," *San Francisco Chronicle*, December 23, 2004.

2 See H. Bok, "Cloning Animals Is Wrong," *Journal of Applied Animal Welfare Science 5*, no. 3 (2002), 233–38.

3 A. Coleman, "Somatic Cell Nuclear Transfer in Mammals: Progress and Application," *Cloning* 1 (1999), 185–200. See also L. Paterson, "Somatic Cell Nuclear Transfer (Cloning) Efficiency," available at: http:// www.roslin. ac.uk/ public/webtables-GR.pdf.

4 T. Shin et al., "Cell Biology: A Cat Cloned by Nuclear Transplantation," *Nature* 415 (2002): 859.

5 A.B. Carter, "Phenotyping of Transgenic Cloned Pigs," *Cloning and Stem Cells* 4(2002): 131–45.

6 N. Ogonuki et al., "Early Death of Mice Cloned from Somatic Cells," *Nature Genetics* 30 (2002): 253–54.

7 K. Tamashiro, "Cloned Mice Have an Obese Phenotype Not Transmitted to Their Offspring," *Nature Genetics* 8 (2002): 262–67.

8 *Nature Biotechnology* recently published a metareview of the health status of clones from prior studies, and it reports that 77 percent of cloned animals showed no developmental abnormalities throughout the period of follow-up, although the percentage of healthy clones ranged from 20 percent to 100 percent across the studies. J.B. Cibelli et al. "The Health Profile of Cloned Animals," *Nature Biotechnology* 20 (2002), 13–14.

9 C. Yang, X.C. Tian, and X. Yang, "Serial Bull Cloning by Somatic Cell Nuclear Transfer," *Nature Bio-technology* 22 (2004), 693–94.

10 M. Fox, "Company Says It Cloned Copy Cats," Reuters, August 5, 2004; Fimrite, "Cat Has 10 Lives."

11 Of course, the obvious objection to this comparison is that the kidneys are harvested to save the life of another cat, whereas the animals who suffer through egg harvesting and embryo implantation are not saving an existing cat but creating an entirely new (unneeded) one. But what is in question here is the amount of suffering—not the justification for it.

12 Humane Society of the United States, "Cat Cloning Is Wrong-Headed," February 14, 2002; available at: http://hsus.org/ace/13214.

13 P.G. Irwin, "Overview: The State of Animals in 2001," in *The State of Animals 2001*, ed. D.J. Salem and A.N. Rowan, (Washington, D.C.: Humane Society Press, 2001).

14 American Society for the Prevention of Cruelty to Animals, "Annual Shelter Statistics,"; available at http://www.aspca.org.

15 The Roper Center For Public Opinion Research, "Do You Think Animals Go to Heaven When They Die or Only People Go to Heaven?" ABC News/BeliefNet Poll (June 2001); available at http:/sol;roperweb. ropercenter. uconn.edu:80/cgi-bin/ hsrun.exe/Roperweb/iPOLL/StateID/CXw GMIyhSS673RN-NenOz5_uZT_uw-VbGn/ HAHApage/SelectedQs_Link.

16 The Roper Center For Public Opinion Research, "Banning All Medical Research on Laboratory Animals," Gallup Poll (May, 2003); available at http://roperweb.ropercenter.uconn.edu:80/cgi-bin/hsrun.exe/ Roperweb/iPOLL/StateId/C20XmmyYwFM72ocWchjh2obiYPb8—UeHc/HAHTpage/ Study_Link? stdy_id=26427.

17 American Animal Hospital Association, Pet Owner Survey, 1999; available at: http:// www.healthypet.com.

18 American Pet Products Manufacturers Association, "APPMA Survey Finds Pet Ownership Continues Growth Trend in U.S."; available at http://www.appma.org/press/press_releases/2001/nr_05–02– 02.asp.

19 C.W. Schwabe et al., *Veterinary Medicine and Human Health*, third ed. (Baltimore, Md.: Williams & Wilkins Co, 1976).

20 *DVM News Magazine*, "Pet Spending to Top $37 Billion by '08"; available at: http:// www.dvmnewsmagazine.com/dvm/content/pringContentPopup.jsp?id=85154.

21 S. Aschoff, "Pet RX," *Floridian*, June 10, 2003.

22 Schwabe et al., *Veterinary Medicine and Human Health*.

23 *DVM News Magazine*, "Pet Spending to Top $37 Billion by '08"; available at http:// www.dvmnewsmagazine.com/dvm/content/pringContentPopup.jsp?id=85154.

24 Offering a pro-pet cloning argument in no way commits me to a pro-human cloning argument, although I can understand the powerful sentiments that would drive a parent to desire the ability to clone a beloved child. The difference is that we can accept a sacrifice in animal lives (we euthanize them, we experiment on them, and we eat them) that we cannot accept in human lives. But if human cloning could be guaranteed never to result in a birth defect, stillbirth, or compromised health status of a child, the debate about human cloning would be quite different.

25 *CBS Evening News*, "Legal Relationship Between Pets and Their Owners," CBS News Transcripts, Aug. 7, 2000; B. Pool, "In West Hollywood, Pets are Part of the Family," *Los Angeles Times*, February 22, 2001; "Pet Owners in San Francisco become 'Pet Guardians,'" *The San Diego Union Tribune*, March 1, 2001; and "Students Make History by Helping to Draft & Pass Animal Rights Legislation," *New from General Assembly*, September 26, 2001; available at http://www.rilin.state.ri.us/leg_press/2001/september/ Denniganpercent20pets.htm (last visited Oct. 16, 2003).

FURTHER READING

Best, S. and Kellner, D. (2002) "Biotechnology, ethics and the politics of cloning," *Democracy and Nature* 8: 439–465.

Christiansen, S. B. and Sandoe, P. (2000) "Bioethics: Limits to the interference with life," *Animal Reproduction Science* 60–61: 15–29.

DeSalle, R. and Amato, G. (2004) "The expansion of conservation genetics," *Nature Reviews (Genetics)* 5: 702–712.

De Vries, R. (2006) "Genetic engineering and the integrity of animals," *Journal of Agricultural and Environmental Ethics* 19: 469–493.

Gjerris, M. and Sandoe, P. (2005) "Farm animal cloning: The role of the concept of animal integrity in debating and regulating the technology," pp. 320–324 in *Animal Production and Animal Science Worldwide*, A. Rosati, A. Tewolde, and C. Mosconi (eds.), Wageningen Academic Publishers, The Netherlands.

Holt, W. V., Pickard, A. R., and Prather, R. S. (2004) "Wildlife conservation and reproductive cloning." *Reproduction* 127: 317–324.

Kaiser, Jocelyn (2002) "Cloned pigs may help overcome rejection," *Science* 295: 25–7.

Loi, Pasqualino, Barboni, Barbara, and Ptak, Grazyna (2002) "Cloning advances and challenges for conservation," *Trends in Biotechnology* 20(6): 233.

Munro, Lyle (2001) "Future animals: Environmental and animal welfare perspectives on the genetic engineering of animals," *Cambridge Quarterly of Healthcare Ethics* 10: 314–324

Rojas, M., Venegas, F., Montiel, E., Servely, J. L., Vignon, X., and Guillomot, M. (2005) "Attempts at applying cloning to the conservation of species in danger of extinction," *International Journal of Morphology* 23: 329–336.

Tsunoda, Y. and Kato, Y. (2002) "Recent progress and problems in animals cloning," *Differentiation* 69: 158–161.

Weidensaul, Scott (2002) "Raising the dead," *Audubon* 94: 58–66.

STUDY QUESTIONS

1   Do you believe that increased knowledge of genetic engineering will inevitably lead to increased human genetic manipulation? Justify your response.

2   What is your view on developing genetically engineered animal strains with a telos that would make them well adapted to the conditions associated with intensive farming and production?

3   What role do you believe is appropriate for cloning technology in the management of endangered species?

4   In light of Burkhardt's discussion, do you agree that ethical preparation is lacking in scientific education? If so, what approach do you propose for best incorporating ethical training into science education? If not, clarify your reasons.

5   How do you respond to Fiester's assertion about the potential benefits of pet cloning?

Ethics and wildlife

INTRODUCTION TO PART SEVEN

IN THIS PART, THE AUTHORS focus on issues affecting the human relationship to wildlife. J. Baird Callicott compares instrumental values, in which wildlife is used to fulfill human wants and needs, such as subsistence and economic values, with inherent (intrinsic) values, in which wildlife is valued for its own sake. Callicott advocates the ecocentric perspective. Grace Clements focuses on intrinsic values and advocates going beyond arguments of justice, and incorporating an ethic of care in our relations to nonhuman animals.

Three authors assess moral issues related to the hunting of wild animals. Aldo Leopold calls for a greater cooperative spirit among protectionists and sportsmen toward common concerns for wildlife, and argues that hunting plays an important role in the economics and management of wildlife well-being. Marti Kheel challenges the morality of sport hunting and offers a number of thoughtful responses to the justifications given for hunting, including psychological, ecological, and spiritual benefits. Using feminist psychoanalytic theory, she offers a more deep-seated basis for the propensity of men to seek to kill animals as part of the hunting ritual. Alastair S. Gunn addresses the morality of hunting generally, and then delves more deeply into the issue of trophy hunting and its role in the economy and culture of poorer countries. Despite reservations that he and many feel about trophy hunting, he proposes that it ultimately may be an important strategy to protect the interests of both wildlife and people.

Two authors deal with special wildlife-related issues. Ned Hettinger addresses the arguments surrounding introduction of exotic species to new habitats. He also counters the argument that opposition to exotic species may be comparable to a xenophobic response to various cultural and ethnic groups among humans and concludes that the loss of biological purity and the greater homogenization of the earth's biodiversity are compelling reasons to oppose introduction of exotic species. Dale Peterson addresses the problem of bushmeat in developing countries, especially as it relates to primates, and develops key reasons for conserving primate biodiversity by reducing the use of apes for food.

VALUING WILDLIFE

Chapter 57

J. Baird Callicott

THE PHILOSOPHICAL VALUE OF WILDLIFE

Callicott distinguishes the notions of instrumental and inherent value as applied to wildlife and then explores the various philosophical foundations for ascribing inherent value to wildlife. He recognizes the contributions of utilitarian philosophy and theocentric sources of inherent value, but also finds these foundations outmoded and lacking in persuasiveness. Callicott goes on to affirm that Aldo Leopold's ecocentric perspectives best articulate ecologically informed understandings about wildlife, subordinating individual animals to the values of populations, species, and communities.

I N "THE LAND ETHIC" of *A Sand County Almanac*, Aldo Leopold wrote: "It is inconceivable to me that an ethical relation to land can exist without love, respect, and admiration for land, and a high regard for its value. By value, I of course mean something far broader than mere economic value; I mean value in the philosophical sense" (1966:261). By land, of course, Leopold (1966:189) also meant something far broader than mere real estate; he meant "all of the things on, over, or in the earth"—which would, and certainly did for Leopold, prominently include wildlife.

We have a fairly clear, if general, idea of the economic value of wildlife. The economic value is the expected answer to the question, What good is it? According to Leopold (1966:190), asking this question about an animal or plant is "the last word in ignorance." But what could the value of wildlife in "the philosophical sense" possibly be?

Instrumental and intrinsic value

Philosophers like myself are not accustomed to dealing with value questions in these terms—economic versus philosophical value; rather, philosophers more often oppose instrumental and intrinsic value (Callicott 1986a). The instrumental value of something is its utility as a means to some end. The intrinsic value of something is its inherent worth as an end in itself.

Though nothing is universally accepted in philosophy, in the prevailing traditions of Western moral thought human beings or their states of consciousness (like pleasure or happiness or more recently "preference satisfaction") are generally agreed to be the intrinsically valuable things and everything else to be the instrumentally valuable things (Callicott 1984). Gifford Pinchot is supposed to have said that there are two kinds of beings in this world: people and their resources. This statement perfectly captures the kinds of values recognized in Western philosophy and the places where they reside.

The Biblical proverb, "man does not live by bread alone," reminds us that we human beings have spiritual as well as material needs. And wildlife and nature generally have served as spiritual as well as material resources. Indeed, one major historical conflict in U.S. resource management may be understood as a conflict between the spiritual and material utility of natural resources (Nash 1973). Wild things may be fed, eaten, worn, made into implements, built with, and so on, and/or they may be listened to, watched, studied, worshipped, enjoyed, and so on. In other words, the question "what good is a woodcock?" can be answered equally appropriately by saying that its "sky dance" enchants a spring evening and satisfies a deep need for visual variety, grace, and beauty as by saying that a woodcock may "serve as a target and pose gracefully on a slice of toast" (Leopold 1966:36). Those for whom wildlife and other natural resources satisfy primarily spiritual needs usually regard such uses as "better" or "higher" than material ones (Nash 1973). But my point is that from the prevailing perspective of modern Western philosophy, wildlife and other natural resources remain only instrumentally valuable—whether as a means to satisfy the widest possible range of human spiritual needs or the most narrow range of human material needs.

Economic valuation, ideally conceived, is one clear way—though perhaps not the only or even the best way—to compare and adjudicate conflicts between the different utilities that wildlife and other natural resources represent (Daly 1980). It is ideally possible in economics, though perhaps difficult and uncertain in practice, to compare, say, the real dollar value of redwood trees converted into picnic tables and tomato stakes with the shadow-priced dollar value of uncut redwood trees as objects of beauty, awe, and inspiration.

However, since real-world economics rarely takes into account the dollar value of the nonconsumptive/nonmaterial utilities of trees on the stump, birds on the wing, ungulates on the hoof, soil in conservancy (to say nothing of pollinators, decomposers, nitrogen fixers, and other members of nature's service industry), the nonmaterial utilities of wildlife and other natural resources are usually excluded by the term *economic value. Economic value*, in other words, often connotes just material, instrumental value and often not even the full range of that type. Leopold, therefore, could have meant by the term *philosophical value* as opposed to *economic value* the more subtle and spiritual, as opposed to the more immediate and material, kinds of instrumental values of land; but the context indicates that he did not.

In general, Leopold recommended a wholly unprecedented ethical relationship between people and land—a relationship between ends and ends, not ends and means. And more particularly, he mentioned in the same breath with philosophical value, love, respect, admiration, and high regard—attitudes we reserve for intrinsically valuable beings, not for instrumentally valuable things however noble and ethereal their uses. From the higher utilitarian point of view, we may be delighted by the song of a mockingbird, awed by the size and age of a redwood, arrested by the stoop of a Peregrine falcon, overcome by the sight of a grizzly bear, but we can only love and respect a being whose worth transcends the positive experiences it affords us and other human beings.

So by the philosophical value of wildlife, if we may take Aldo Leopold as our guide and inspiration, we should understand what philosophers themselves would more technically call *intrinsic* or *inherent value*. The burden of this chapter may thus be transposed into the following question: How may we ground or justify Leopold's ethical proposition that in addition to the full spectrum of instrumental values, spiritual as well as material, wildlife possesses intrinsic value?

The conceptual foundations of intrinsic value

Animal liberation

The most visible and vocal contemporary defense of the intrinsic value of wildlife has ironically evolved out of classic utilitarianism (Callicott 1980). According to Jeremy Bentham (1823), founding father of utilitarianism, pleasure is good and pain is evil; and an ethical person should attempt, in choosing courses of action, to maximize the one and minimize the other, no matter whose pain or pleasure may be involved. Utilitarians conventionally limited the impartial weighing of pleasures and pains to human beings.

However, though entirely clear even in Bentham's day, the combined evidence of comparative anatomy, physiology, neurology, ethology, and paleontology, now overwhelmingly confirms that many animals—all vertebrates most certainly—are also conscious beings that experience pleasure and pain (Midgley 1983). Hence, by the same principle of impartiality, we ought to give equal consideration to the pleasure and pain of other animals, no less than of other human beings, in choosing our courses of action (Singer 1975).

This grounding of the intrinsic value of some nonhuman animals—sentient animals—is popularly known as animal liberation and has been recently and most notably espoused by Peter Singer (1975). I have been a resolute philosophical opponent of animal liberation as a serviceable environmental ethic because it provides for no discrimination between wild and domestic animals, or between overabundant and rare animals, or between native and exotic animals (Callicott 1980). A Holstein steer, a specimen of an overabundant, domestic, exotic species, is equally sentient and therefore is entitled to as much moral consideration as a Dall ram, a specimen of a rare, wild, indigenous species.

On a deeper level, animal liberation is concerned exclusively with the welfare of individual animals, so much so that should the welfare of individuals conflict with that of a population of them—as is often the case with cervids—animal liberation unhesitatingly gives uncompromising priority to the welfare of individuals, more holistic considerations be damned (Singer 1979).

Most disturbingly, a ruthlessly consistent deduction of the consequences of animal liberation would be a universal predator eradication program as a policy of wildlife management (Callicott 1986b)! Why? Because predators obviously inflict pain and death on their prey. If we should stop humans from hunting, as animal liberationists advocate, then by parity of reasoning, we should also stop other animals from hunting. The result, of course, would be an ecological nightmare.

This consideration reveals a moral repugnance for wild nature at the core of animal liberation. Death and often pain are at the heart of nature's economy. To the extent that animal liberation morally condemns pain and death, it is irreconcilably at odds with the ecological facts of wild life. Thus we shall have to look elsewhere for a theory of the intrinsic value of wildlife consistent with the ecological facts of wild life.

Theocentrism

One of wildlife's greatest champions, John Muir, stressed the spiritual utility of wild nature: "Mountain parks and reservations are useful not only as fountains of timber and irrigating rivers but as fountains of life" (1901:1). In a more intimate journal, prepared posthumously for publication by William Frederick Badé, Muir (1916), for the first time that I am aware of in U.S. conservation literature, gave expression to the distinctly philosophical value of wildlife.

Muir's argument for the intrinsic value of wildlife was primarily theological. According to the Bible, God created other forms of life as well as human life, and He declared them all to be "good" (May and Metzger 1966:2). More technically expressed, God created all life forms and either at that time or by a subsequent fiat conferred intrinsic value upon them. In Muir's words, "From the dust of the earth, from the common elementary fund, the Creator has made *Homo sapiens*. From the same material he has made every other creature, however noxious and insignificant to us . . . They dwell happily . . . unfallen, undepraved, and cared for with the same species of tenderness and love as is bestowed on angels in heaven or saints on earth" (1916:98, 139). In Muir's view this Biblical truth—if it is a truth—constitutes the grounds for "the rights of all the rest of the creation" (1916:98).

Muir's theological theory of the intrinsic value of wildlife provides a conceptual context more congenial to an ecologically informed program of wildlife conservation than does Singer's theory. Its intractably individualistic value orientation is the main problem with the animal liberation ethic, from the viewpoint of wildlife conservation (Callicott 1980). On the other hand, Genesis clearly implies that in His acts of creation God established and conferred value upon species primarily, whereas individual specimens are understood to come and go. Nor is there any overriding obligation placed upon us in Genesis or elsewhere in the Bible to try to prevent animals from experiencing pain (though gratuitous cruelty is proscribed). Hence, Muir's theory of the intrinsic value of wildlife is not in direct conflict (as Singer's is) with the more holistic value orientation of wildlife ecology and management.

The main problem with Muir's theocentric axiology is not that its practical implications are inconsistent with an ecologically informed program of wildlife conservation but that its theoretical premises are inconsistent with the scientific foundations of wildlife ecology and conservation. According to science, wildlife species were not created as we find them today; they evolved into their present form. Nature is regarded as autochthonous and autonomous. To the extent that we believe that science gives us a true understanding of nature, a theocentric grounding of the intrinsic value of wildlife simply rests upon false beliefs about the natural world. This deep theoretical inconsistency is rendered more acute and vitiating when we reflect that our appreciation and respect for wildlife are deepened the more science discloses about the origins and interactions of wild things. As Leopold observed, "wild things . . . had little [philosophical] value until . . . science disclosed the drama of where they came from [evolution] and how they live [ecology]" (1966:xvii).

Biophilia

Leopold accordingly grounds the intrinsic value of wild things in evolutionary and ecological biology. A theory of the intrinsic value of wildlife grounded exclusively in a scientific world view seems immediately implausible, however. According to the metaphysical foundations of modern science, the natural world, from atoms to galaxies—including the middle-sized organic world—is value free, value neutral. Values, from a general scientific point of view, are subjective: They originate in consciousness and are projected onto objects. If all consciousness were eradicated, there would be no value anywhere in nature; there would remain only brute facts (Callicott 1985).

Leopold appears to respect this objective-fact/subjective-value dichotomy of modern science (Callicott 1984, 1986). Values remain subjective, consciousness dependent in his land ethic. But a closer scrutiny of human values reveals that, though subjective, all values are not subject oriented, that is, selfish (Callicott 1982, 1984, 1985, 1986a, 1986b). We value ourselves and/or certain of our own experiences, but we are also capable of valuing other things equally with ourselves or even more than ourselves (Callicott 1984, 1985, 1986a, b). In other words, although the value of objective things depends upon some conscious subject valuing them, a conscious subject, at least a human conscious subject, can value them for themselves as well as for what they may do for him or her. Most people, for example, value their children and other loved ones in this way.

For human beings and other social animals, this other-oriented valuational capacity is a product of natural selection. In his second great work Darwin (1871) argued that what he called the "moral sentiments," following David Hume and Adam Smith, were naturally selected as a means to social integration and evolution. In short, social membership increases the inclusive fitness of the individuals of some species. But social membership is impossible without "limitations on freedom of action [in regard to proximate individuals of the same species] in the struggle for existence" (Leopold 1966:238). Among social mammals these requisite limitations have taken the form of other-oriented sentiments—love, respect, admiration, fellow-feeling, sympathy, and high regard. In the final analysis, intrinsic value—the value of something as an end in itself—is a philosophical abstraction from these primitive moral sentiments (Callicott 1985).

Since the moral sentiments and the philosophical value that is ultimately erected upon them originally evolved in conjunction with the evolution of mammalian societies, there is a close correlation among community, perceived social membership, and intrinsic value. In the past only our own clan or tribe and our fellow tribespeople were regarded as ends in themselves, and all other human beings and human groups were treated as mere means (Nash 1977). More recently, for many a sense of community has come to embrace all humankind (Nash 1977). Accordingly, modern humanism affirms the intrinsic value of all human beings regardless of race, creed, or national origin and of all humankind. Aldo Leopold observed that today ecology represents both human beings and wild things as members of "one humming community," the biotic community (Leopold 1966:193). Because we now perceive wild creatures as belonging to this expanded ecological society, we are naturally impelled to extend to the biotic community itself and to wild things as members in good standing the same value—philosophical or intrinsic value—once more restrictively reserved for more narrowly defined classes.

In my opinion, therefore, Aldo Leopold's account of the philosophical value of wildlife is the most persuasive of the three alternatives reviewed here. It best articulates our ecologically informed intuitions about the transutilitarian value of wildlife. It subordinates the value of specimens to populations, species, and biocenoses. And it is based neither on an outmoded moral philosophy (utilitarianism) or on an outmoded theology (Judeo-Christian theism), but squarely on modern science.

References

Bentham, J. 1823. An introduction to the principles of morals and legislation. Vol. 1. W. Pickering, London. 381 pp.

Callicott, J. B. 1980. Animal liberation: a triangular affair. Environ. Ethics 2(4):311–338.

——. 1982. Hume's is/ought dichotomy and the relation of ecology to Leopold's land ethic. Environ. Ethics 4(2):163–174.

——. 1984. Non-anthropocentric value theory and environmental ethics. Am. Philos. Q. 21(4):299–309.

——. 1985. Intrinsic value, quantum theory, and environmental ethics. Environ. Ethics 7(2):257–275.

——. 1986a. On the intrinsic value of non-human species. Pages 138–172 in B. Norton, ed. The preservation of species. Princeton Univ. Press, Princeton, N.J.

——. 1986b. The search for an environmental ethic. Pages 381–424 in T. Regan, ed. Matters of life and death. 2nd ed. Random House, New York.

Daly, H. 1980. Economics, ecology, ethics. W. H. Freeman and Co., San Francisco. 372pp.

Darwin, C. 1871. The descent of man and selection in relation to sex. 2nd ed. J. A. Hill and Co., New York. 314pp.

Leopold, A. 1966. A sand county almanac. Ballatine Books, New York. 226pp.

May, H. G., and G. M. Metzger, editors. 1966. Genesis. Pages 1–66 in The holy bible: revised standard version containing the old and new testaments. Oxford Univ. Press, New York.

Midgley, M. 1983. Animals and why they matter. Univ. Georgia Press, Athens, Ga. 158pp.

Muir, J. 1901. Our national parks. Houghton-Mifflin and Co., New York. 370pp.

——. 1916. A thousand mile walk to the gulf. Houghton-Mifflin and Co., New York. 220pp.

Nash, R. 1973. Wilderness and the American mind. Yale Univ. Press, New Haven, Conn. 300pp.

——. 1977. Do rocks have rights? Cent. Mag. 10(6):2–12.

Singer P. 1975. Animal liberation: a new ethics for our treatment of animals. New York Rev., New York. 297pp.

——. 1979. Not for humans only. Pages 191–206 in K. E. Goodpaster and K. M. Sayer, eds. Ethics and problems of the 21st century. Univ. Notre Dame Press, Notre Dame, Indiana.

Chapter 58

Grace Clement

THE ETHIC OF CARE AND THE PROBLEM
OF WILD ANIMALS

Clement addresses traditional reasons for extending moral concern to animals and argues that these arguments are beneficial, but incomplete and inadequate. She challenges the arguments of animal defense theories made by Peter Singer and Tom Regan and argues in favor of extending an ethic of care to human relations with nonhuman animals. Clement addresses potential arguments on why a theory of care may be more pertinent to domestic than wild animals, but concludes that an ethic of care and an ethic of justice are appropriate for both wild and domestic animals.

RECENTLY, A NUMBER of feminists concerned with the welfare of nonhuman animals have challenged the prevailing approaches to animal defense theory. A collection of essays, *Beyond Animal Rights: A Feminist Caring Ethic for the Treatment of Animals*, challenges the "rights" or "justice" approaches usually taken by animal defense theories, most notably those of Peter Singer and Tom Regan, and argues in favor of an ethic of care for our relations to nonhuman animals. This work arises out of feminist discussions over the past fifteen years of the "feminine" ethic of care and its relationship to the "masculine" ethic of justice. Those writing in *Beyond Animal Rights* have extended this discussion by recognizing that the care–justice debate is important not only for relationships among humans but for human relationships to nonhumans as well. [. . .]

In this essay, I will examine the claim that an ethic of care is preferable to an ethic of justice for our relationships with nonhuman animals. To limit my discussion, I will focus on our obligations to animals, even though there are obviously important questions about our obligations to nonanimal members of the biotic community, and I will focus on the morality of eating animals, even though this is only one of many important moral questions about our treatment of nonhuman animals. While I regard the care proposal as promising, I will argue that the distinction between domestic and wild animals raises an important problem for it: while the ethic of care seems to fit our interactions with domestic animals well, it is at best unclear how it might guide our interactions with wild animals. I will consider three different alternative moral approaches to wild animals: a holistic environmentalist approach, an individualistic justice approach, and a justice approach in interaction with and influenced by a care approach. By drawing on the lessons of the recent care/justice debate regarding human-to-human relations, I will show that the third of these alternatives works best. Because I do not regard care and justice as dichotomous, I see this not as a rejection of the thesis of *Beyond Animal Rights* but as a sympathetic extension of it. The "Introduction" to *Beyond Animal Rights* provides four reasons for thinking that an ethic of care is more appropriate for our relationships to nonhuman animals than an ethic of justice (or, what is generally considered the same thing, a rights theory).

First, an ethic of justice "envisages a society of rational, autonomous, independent agents whose property is entitled to protection from external agents" (Donovan and Adams 1996, 14), and thus uses rationality as a test of moral considerability, a test which nonhumans are likely to fail. On the other hand, the ethic of care focuses on relationships *between* individuals rather than on separate individual identities, and thus requires no such test of rationality for moral considerability. Second, an ethic of justice "presumes a society of equal autonomous agents, who require little support from others, who need only that their space be protected from others' intrusions" (Donovan and Adams 1996, 15). But humans and animals are in most ways *unequals*, and thus better fit into the care model which assumes an inherent inequality between carer and cared-for. Third, an ethic of justice is a rationalistic approach, prioritizing reason and suppressing emotion-based appeals for animal welfare. However, feelings play a central role in human relationships to animals, and the ethic of care regards feelings as morally relevant and informative. Finally, an ethic of justice tends to be abstract and formalistic, focusing on universal rules of morality, while our complex relationships with nonhuman animals seem better accounted for by the ethic of care's contextual approach focusing on the particulars of given situations.

These objections to exclusively justice-oriented approaches are valuable. The extent to which prevailing approaches to animal welfare are *exclusively* justice-oriented and thus problematic is evident in Singer's and Regan's insistence that moral arguments must not appeal to our feelings about animals. [. . .] Our feelings may not provide infallible moral guidance, but sometimes they are all we have to appeal to. Perhaps, then, we ought to proceed not by banishing feelings from our moral considerations on the grounds that they are unreliable, but by paying *more* attention both to our feelings *and* to the mechanisms by which they are and can be socially manipulated (Luke 1995 & 1996). As the authors of *Beyond Animal Rights* point out, this is an approach that the ethic of care is much more attuned to than the ethic of justice.

While the ethic of care is certainly a promising approach to our relationships with nonhuman animals in this and other ways detailed in *Beyond Animal Rights*, there is a difficulty with this approach left largely unaddressed by these authors. That is, the arguments in this book make domestic animals the paradigm, and it seems at least possible that they work *only* for domestic animals. We can see this by returning to the four arguments offered in the book's "Introduction."

First, the ethic of justice is said to be inappropriate for our dealings with nonhuman animals because it "envisages a society of rational, autonomous, independent agents whose territory or property is entitled to protection from external agents" (Donovan and Adams 1996, 14). Without addressing the difficult issue of the rationality of nonhuman animals, the autonomy and independence of at least wild animals can be and has been defended. In fact, environmental ethicists have long emphasized the difference between wild and domestic animals along these lines: Aldo Leopold wrote that the essence of environmental ethics was "reappraising things unnatural, tame, and confined in terms of things natural, wild, and free" (Callicott 1992, 67). According to environmental ethicist J. Baird Callicott, wild animals are autonomous and independent, while domestic animals are human creations which are *metaphysically* unfree. By this Callicott means that domestic animals are nothing but what we have selectively bred them to be, such that it is as meaningless to speak of *setting free* domestic animals as it would be to speak of setting free a chair. Callicott and other environmental ethicists may be speaking of autonomy in a different sense than the rational autonomy used as a criterion by those defending an ethic of justice, but in any case it seems at least somewhat appropriate to think of human relationships with *wild* animals in terms of a society of independent agents whose territory is entitled to protection from others. The second argument against the justice approach to nonhuman animals likewise seems to apply to domestic rather than to wild animals. Again, the ethic of justice "presumes a society of equal autonomous agents, who require little support from others, who need only that their space be protected from others' intrusions." The editors of *Beyond Animal Rights* continue: "But domestic animals, in particular, are dependent for survival upon humans. We therefore have a situation of unequals, and need to develop an ethic that recognizes this fact" (Donovan and Adams 1996, 15). Clearly, in this argument domestic animals are taken as paradigmatic, for wild animals are certainly not dependent for survival upon humans, at least not upon human *support*. Instead, they are dependent upon humans' putting an end to destruction of natural habitats, or on humans' *restraint*. In fact, just as the ethic of justice would say, it seems that they *do* need only that their space be protected from others' intrusions. While domestic animals depend upon human support, wild animals would most benefit from the disappearance of humans entirely.

Even the argument about the role of emotion in moral argument seems to work better in domestic than in wild contexts. This is evident in "The Caring Sleuth: Portrait of an Animal Rights Activist," in which Kenneth Shapiro discusses the crucial role of sympathy in moral considerations about animals. He quotes Helen Jones, founder of the International Society for Animal Rights, who wrote that:

> My first awareness of animal suffering was at the age of four or five. My mother took me to a zoo. As we entered we saw a large white rabbit, transfixed with fear, in a cage with a snake. Within a second or two the snake began swallowing the rabbit . . . My mother never again entered a zoo. I did, many years later, only to collect evidence for a legal case.
>
> (Shapiro 1996, 130)

Jones experienced a sympathy for the rabbit that many of us share. But in a certain sense this sympathy is odd. After all, snakes *do* eat rabbits, however upsetting it is for us to see a rabbit be eaten, and we certainly cannot legitimately condemn snakes for this behavior, nor can we hope to protect rabbits from this fate. Or, we can only protect rabbits from this fate in places like zoos, when they are rabbits we take into our protection. But it does not seem that our sympathetic reaction to the rabbit in this situation is dependent on the fact that this rabbit is in a zoo. That is, it seems as if the sympathies to which the ethic of care appeals might be more relevant for domestic than for wild animals. As Callicott puts it, in the wild, the fundamental fact of life is eating *and being eaten*, but our sympathies would seem to be out of line with this fact, such that there are good reasons *not* to act on our sympathies for wild animals. This suggests that the fourth argument cited above also works better for domestic animals than for wild animals: at least when it comes to wild animals, a *contextual* approach focusing on particular situations seems less appropriate than an *abstract* approach focusing on the general facts of environmental biology. From these considerations, it seems possible that the claims on behalf of the ethic of care in *Beyond Animal Rights* apply to domestic but not to wild animals. [. . .]

I will first address an objection to this proposal that would be raised by environmental ethicists. Environmentalists would begin by pointing out that the focus on domestic animals I have identified is present not only in the care approach to animal defense theory, but in standard (or "justice") approaches as well, and that *neither* approach works for wild animals. For instance, Mark Sagoff asks, "If the suffering of animals creates human obligation to mitigate it, is there not as much an obligation to prevent a cat from killing a mouse as to prevent a hunter from killing a deer?" (Sagoff 1993, 88). Similarly, if nonhuman animals are said to have certain rights, such as a right to life, then we have a corresponding obligation to protect those rights. While it might be appropriate to endeavor to protect domestic animals' rights to life, it would be absurd, not to mention ecologically disastrous, to endeavor to protect wild animals' right to life (Sagoff 1993, 88–89).

Environmental ethicists would argue that animal defense theories, whether of the justice or care variety, fail in the context of wild animals because they are individualistic in the sense that it is *individual* beings that are considered morally important. What is needed, they would say, is an approach which is holistic in its focus, in that it is *wholes* such as biotic communities and species that are considered morally important. As Aldo Leopold put it, "a thing is right when it tends to preserve the integrity, stability, and beauty of the biotic community. It is wrong when it tends otherwise" (Leopold 1995, 152). [. . .]

According to environmental ethicists, in the context of wild animals, advocates of the ethic of care and advocates of the ethic of justice are *equally* mistaken in their moral attention to individual beings. These considerations suggest that perhaps within the realm of domestic animals, it is appropriate to focus on individual animals, while outside that realm, it is appropriate to think more holistically. In fact, Callicott defends a version of this view in his most recent account of the relationship between animal liberation and environmental ethics (Callicott 1995). He develops an account of "nested communities" that reflect our degree of relationship to various beings and thereby provide the basis for our moral obligations. According to Callicott, we have the greatest moral obligations to those closest to us—to our immediate family—and gradually lesser obligations to those in our more distant communities—such as to neighbors, to citizens, to human beings in general, and to animals in general. One of the ways this account differs from traditional hierarchies which place nonhuman animals last in our moral consideration is by incorporating Mary Midgley's argument that domestic animals are and have always been members of one of our more intimate communities, the "mixed community" (Midgley, 1995). For Callicott, humans' close relationships with domestic animals means that domestic animals have a corresponding moral priority.

I will have something to say about Callicott's position on domestic animals shortly, but first I will challenge the claim that, in relation to wild animals at least, humans are morally bound only by holistic concerns about the health of the ecosystem. This would mean that in relation to members of well-populated species, there would be no moral problem with, say, torturing an animal for the fun of it. Environmentalists do not make a point of this, and, in fact, when the environmentalist Holmes Rolston defends meat eating, he says that "when eating [humans] ought to minimize animal suffering" (Rolston 1993, 140). Such a claim is uncontroversial enough that we might not notice that he doesn't say *why* humans ought to minimize animal suffering. In fact, he *can't* provide a reason for this claim within a system that only takes holistic concerns into account. That is, a "moral" approach that focuses *exclusively* on holistic concerns such that suffering becomes morally irrelevant violates some of our most basic moral convictions. [. . .] Since Callicott's environmental ethic for human-wild animal relations is too holistic to allow for some of our basic moral convictions, it might seem to follow that human-wild animal relations should be understood in terms of the individualism of the ethic of justice. That is, it might be argued that while we share with wild animals a *biotic* community, we do not share with them a *moral* community of a kind that would be necessary to ground the claim that we have positive responsibilities to them. While environmental critics of justice ethics point out the absurdity of extending the right to life to wild animals, an ethic of justice need not affirm that wild animals have a right to life. Instead, it can affirm that our primary obligation to wild animals is *noninterference.*

While there is something right about this view, I want to show that it also oversimplifies and distorts matters in important ways. Difficulties with this view are revealed by recent discussions among feminist ethicists of the analogous view that the "private sphere" of family and friends ought to be governed by the ethic of care, while the "public sphere" of government and business ought to be governed by the ethic of justice. According to this view, the partialist ethic of care should be confined to the private sphere, and the rights-oriented ethic of justice should be confined to the public sphere. One reason to be wary of this view is that the public/private dichotomy is strongly gender-coded—the private sphere is regarded as feminine and the public sphere as masculine—and serves to reinforce gender divisions. Moreover, the boundary between public and private spheres is itself at issue, as the private and public sphere are not as different from one another as is commonly assumed. For instance, power relations, which are usually considered the distinguishing feature of the political, are also present in personal relations, as evidenced by widespread domestic violence. Also, dependence and vulnerability, which are usually considered distinctive of personal relations, are also present in public relations. Such overlapping features suggest that the private sphere should be not only caring but just, and that the public sphere should be not only just but caring. In fact, when the two ethics are dichotomized, they tend to take on distorted and damaging forms. For instance, an ethic of care which does not value autonomy tends to result in forms of "caring" which are oppressive to either the caregiver or the recipient of care. Likewise, an ethic of justice which does not value caring tends to result in forms of "justice" that are indifferent to individual suffering (Clement 1996).

These conclusions have clear implications for the present discussion. First, just as the public/private dichotomy is gender-coded, so too is the wild/domestic animal dichotomy. Karen Davis has shown that the wild/domestic animal dichotomy is analogous to the public/private dichotomy, such that these dichotomies serve in similar ways to justify the devaluation of women and domestic animals. [. . .] It might be thought that Callicott does not fit this model because his view of nested communities claims to give domestic animals a higher moral priority than wild animals. However, he clearly does not regard domestic animals with the respect he has for wild animals. Above all, Callicott prizes the natural and the wild, and his deepest moral conviction seems to be that humans ought to overcome their alienation from nature and become more wild.

This leads to a second difficulty revealed by the feminist discussion of the public/private dichotomy. Like that dichotomy, the distinction between domestic and wild animals is not as clear as it is often made out to be. [. . .]

If wild and domestic animals are not completely different, this suggests that our moral stances toward them should not be completely separate, and that when they are, they will tend to be distorted. We can see that this is the case in Callicott's discussion of our obligations toward domestic animals. With his discussion of the mixed community and the trust established between humans and domestic animals, Callicott defends something like an ethic of care toward domestic animals. Yet this ethic is consistent with raising farm animals to kill and eat them, on the grounds that, as a result of selective breeding, farm animals are nonautonomous beings who exist only for this purpose. To the extent that this claim is true, the introduction of justice considerations is important because it reveals that this is a distorted version of the ethic of care. Just as there is a moral problem with caring for persons in a way that undermines their autonomy, there is a moral problem with caring for animals in a way that undermines their autonomy (to whatever extent they can be autonomous). In this way the ethic of justice and its emphasis on autonomy plays an important role in evaluating the ethic of care toward domestic animals.

Just as the ethic of justice has a role to play in an ethic of care toward domestic animals, the ethic of care should play a role in an ethic of justice toward wild animals. First, even if an ethic of justice does not affirm that wild animals have a right to life, there are clearly problems with the individualism of the ethic of justice in the context of wild animals. For instance, for such an ethic, moral claims are based exclusively on characteristics of individual beings, such that environmental concerns about the stability and integrity of the biotic community become morally irrelevant. For instance, an individual member of a well-populated or even overpopulated species is no less valuable than an individual member of an endangered species, or even the *last* members of an endangered species. Taken to this extreme, such individualism seems to threaten the environmental considerations that are essential to the continuance of the individual lives protected. Thus, like the extreme holism of environmental ethics, the extreme individualism of the ethic of justice is morally problematic.

While environmental holists and individualist justice theorists debate whether individuals or wholes should be prioritized, the ethic of care reveals a third possibility. The ethic of care is individualistic in one sense: its moral attention is to *individuals* in virtue of their particular needs. However, it is holistic in another sense: it understands the basic reality to be relationships *between* individuals rather than individuals with their own separate characteristics. Thus, relationships, rather than individuals' characteristics, define the moral realm, but the particularities of individuals dictate the appropriate moral response.

One way in which this middle ground between holism and individualism affects an ethic of justice toward wild animals is the following. In general, we ought to adopt an ethic of noninterference with regard to wild animals because we are unaware of the negative effects our attempts to help animals might have on the natural environment. However, to understand our relationship with wild animals *exclusively* in terms of noninterference suggests that humans are *unnatural* beings who should not in any way be involved in the natural world. The ethic of care helps us avoid this moral distortion by understanding human moral responsiveness to individual animals as arising from the relationship between humans and nonhumans, namely our shared participation in nature. Consider a situation in which an individual encounters a wild animal who is suffering. Should one refuse to alleviate the animal's suffering on the grounds that doing so would be interfering with natural processes that we cannot understand? To do so, I think, would be contrary to one of our most basic moral convictions. This is not to claim that there ought to be public policy devoted to the alleviation of wild animal's suffering, only that when an *individual* human being is confronted by the suffering of an *individual* animal, it would be morally unacceptable to say that we have a moral obligation *not* to relieve that suffering.

[. . .]

There are good reasons to believe that the sympathy we feel toward a suffering animal is at least as natural as, or in fact *more natural than* the hunting "instinct" championed by environmentalists (Luke 1995, 309). For instance, children's sympathies for animals often lead them to refuse to eat meat when they learn that it comes from slaughtered animals, at least until they are given "good" reasons not to act on these sympathies. More generally, the naturalness of our sympathies for animals is supported by the fact that elaborate social mechanisms are necessary to distance us from or to deny the reality of the animal suffering we cause, even, significantly, the suffering that hunting causes (Luke 1995).

Animal welfare advocates who operate from an exclusively justice approach share environmentalists' distrust of our sympathies for animals. However, contrary to Callicott's view that we need to abandon our sympathies and become more "natural," Singer and Regan in effect seek to "tame" us through appeals to reason. Again, the ethic of care reveals a third possibility, in which we recognize the moral importance of our *natural* sympathies toward animals, valuing, like Callicott, participation in nature, but disagreeing with Callicott's account of what is natural and what is artificial. As Luke puts it, instead of "taming ourselves," this involves "going feral" (Luke 1995). I have suggested that, in general, our moral obligations toward wild animals can be understood in terms of noninterference. However, such an approach can easily lead to the morally distorted view that we ought not be involved in nature at all, or that we are unnatural beings, and the ethic of care is necessary as a check against such a distortion. In this essay I have considered a problem raised by the suggestion that the ethic of care, rather than the ethic of justice, is the appropriate ethic for our interactions with nonhuman animals. The problem is that this suggestion seems to make more sense for domestic than for wild animals, and that in fact, for the most part, the ethic of justice *does* seem to make sense for wild animals. That is, the ethic of care seems to "fit" our relations to domestic animals, while the ethic of justice seems to "fit" our relations with wild animals. However, I have shown that these "fits" are only approximate, and that to develop a moral approach to both domestic and wild animals that does justice to our most basic moral convictions, we need to understand the two ethics not dichotomously, but as working together. This means that while the ethic of care will not work as the exclusive or predominant moral approach to wild animals, a satisfactory moral approach to wild animals must include the ethic of care.

Bibliography

Callicott, J. Baird. 1992. Animal Liberation: A Triangular Affair. In *The Animal Rights/Environmental Ethics Debate: The Environmental Perspective*, ed. Eugene C. Hargrove, 37–69. Albany: State University of New York Press.

Callicott, J. Baird. 1995. Animal Liberation and Environment Ethics: Back Together Again. In *Earth Ethics*, ed. James P. Sterba, 190–198. Englewood Cliffs, New Jersey: Prentice Hall.

Clement, Grace. 1996. *Care, Autonomy, and Justice: Feminism and the Ethic of Care*. Boulder: Westview.

Donovan, Josephine and Carol J. Adams, ed. 1996. *Beyond Animal Rights: A Feminist Caring Ethic for the Treatment of Animals*. New York: Continuum.

Leopold, Aldo. 1995. The Land Ethic; Conservation as a Moral Issue, Thinking Like a Mountain. In *Earth Ethics*, ed. James P. Sterba, 147–156. Englewood Cliffs, New Jersey: Prentice Hall.

Luke, Brian. 1995. Taming Ourselves or Going Feral? Toward a Nonpatriarchal Metaethic of Animal Liberation. In *Animals and Women: Feminist Theoretical Explorations*, ed. Carol J. Adams and Josephine Donovan, 290–319. Durham: Duke University Press.

Luke, Brian. 1996. Justice, Caring, and Animal Liberation. In *Beyond Animal Rights: A Feminist Caring Ethic for the Treatment of Animals*, ed. Josephine Donovan and Carol J. Adams, 77–102. New York: Continuum.

Midgley, Mary. 1995. The Mixed Community. In *Earth Ethics*, ed. James P. Sterba, 80–90. Englewood Cliffs, New Jersey: Prentice Hall.

Regan, Tom. 1983. *The Case for Animal Rights*. Berkeley: University of California.

Rolston, Holmes III. 1993. Challenges in Environmental Ethics. In *Environmental Philosophy: From Animal Rights to Radical Ecology*, ed. Michael Zimmerman et al., 135–157. Englewood Cliffs, New Jersey: Prentice Hall.

Sagoff, Mark. 1993. Animal Liberation, Environmental Ethics: Bad Marriage, Quick Divorce. In *Environmental Philosophy: From Animal Rights to Radical Ecology*, ed. Michael Zimmerman et al., 84–94. Englewood Cliffs, New Jersey: Prentice Hall.

Shapiro, Kenneth. 1996. The Caring Sleuth: Portrait of an Animal Rights Activist. In *Beyond Animal Rights: A Feminist Caring Ethic for the Treatment of Animals*, ed. Josephine Donovan and Carol J. Adams, 126–146. New York: Continuum.

Singer, Peter. 1992. *Animal Liberation: A New Ethics for Our Treatment of Animals*. New York: Avon Books.

HUNTING CONTROVERSIES

Chapter 59

Aldo Leopold

GAME AND WILD LIFE CONSERVATION [1932]

Leopold emphasizes the importance of both preservationist and sportsperson perspectives in the struggle to enhance the well-being of wildlife; he further calls for more cooperative efforts between these factions. He also affirms the importance of hunting as an important connection between humans and nature as well as an essential economic foundation for managing wildlife.

T**HIS IS A** reply to Mr. T. T. McCabe's well written and persuasive *exposé* of two recent manifestations of the sportsman's movement: my *Game Survey of the North Central States*, and the several publications issued by More Game Birds in America. Both are, I take it, inclusively condemned as "a framework of pernicious doctrines, too often speciously glossed over."

Mr. McCabe's attitude raises what seems to me a fundamental issue. I hope that it may provoke some badly needed cerebration among both protectionists and sportsmen, and especially among those inter-grades like myself, who share the aspirations of both.

There are many sportsmen who laugh at any attempt to embody the protectionist point-of-view in any game program. "Whatever you do the protectionists will be against it." Mr. McCabe's paper furnishes scant comfort to those of us who have been holding out against this attitude, because we see in it the indefinite continuation of the present deadlock, from which the sharpest pens gain much glory, but the game gains nothing except a further chance to disappear.

[. . .]

I realize that every time I turn on an electric light, or ride on a Pullman, or pocket the unearned increment on a stock, or a bond, or a piece of real estate, I am "selling out" to the enemies of conservation. When I submit these thoughts to a printing press, I am helping cut down the woods. When I pour cream in my coffee, I am helping to drain a marsh for cows to graze, and to exterminate the birds of Brazil. When I go birding or hunting in my Ford, I am devastating an oil field, and re-electing an imperialist to get me rubber. Nay more: when I father more than two children I am creating an insatiable need for more printing presses, more cows, more coffee, more oil, and more rubber, to supply which more birds, more trees, and more flowers will either be killed, or what is just as destructive, evicted from their several environments.

What to do? I see only two courses open to the likes of us. One is to go live on locusts in the wilderness, if there is any wilderness left. The other is surreptitiously to set up within the economic Juggernaut certain new cogs and wheels whereby the residual love of nature, inherent even in Rotarians, may be made to recreate at least a fraction of those values which their love of "progress" is destroying.

A briefer way to put it is: if we want Mr. Babbitt to rebuild outdoor America, we must let him use the same tools wherewith he destroyed it. He knows no other.

I by no means imply that Mr. McCabe should agree with this view. I do imply that to accept the economic order which is destroying wild life disqualifies us from rejecting any and all economic tools for its restoration, on the grounds that such tools are impure and unholy.

With what other than economic tools, for instance, can we cope with progressive eviction of game (and most other wild life) from our rich agricultural lands by clean farming and drainage? Does anyone still believe that restrictive game laws alone will halt the wave of destruction which sweeps majestically across the continent, regardless of closed seasons, paper refuges, bird-books-for-school-children, game farms, Izaak Walton Leagues, Audubon Societies, or the other feeble palliatives which we protectionists and sportsmen, jointly or separately, have so far erected as barriers in its path? Does Mr. McCabe know a way to induce the average farmer to leave the birds some food and cover without paying him for it? To raise the fund for such payment without in some way taxing sportsmen?

I have tried to build a mechanism whereby the sportsmen and the Ammunition Industry could contribute financially to the solution of this problem, without dictating the answer themselves. The mechanism consists of a series of game fellowships, set up in the agricultural colleges, to examine the question of whether slick-and-clean agriculture is really economic, and if not, to advise farmers how they can, by leaving a little cover and food, raise a game crop, and market the surplus by sale of shooting privileges to sportsmen. This mechanism is, I take it, specious. Have the protectionists a better one to offer?

Another mechanism which I have tried to build is the committee of sportsmen and protectionists charged with setting forth a new wild life policy. Has Mr. McCabe read it?

These things I have done, and I make no apology for them. Even if they should ultimately succeed, they will not restore the good old days of free hunting of wholly natural wild life (which I loved as well as Mr. McCabe), but they may restore something. That something will be more native to America, and available on more democratic terms, than More Game Birds pheasants, even though it be less so than Mr. McCabe's dreams of days gone by.

Let me admit that my cogs and wheels are designed to perpetuate wild life to shoot, as well as wild life to look at. This is because I believe that hunting takes rank with agriculture and nature study as one of three fundamentally valuable human contacts with the soil. Secondly, because hunting revenue offers the only available "coin of the realm" for buying from Mr. Babbitt the environmental modifications necessary to offset the inroads of industry.

I admit the possibility that I am wrong about hunting. The total cessation of it would certainly conserve some forms of wild life in some places. Any ecologist must, however, admit that the resulting distribution and assortment of species would be very irregular and arbitrary, and quite unrelated to human needs. The richest lands would be totally devoid of game because of the lack of cover, and the poorer lands nearly so because of the lack of food. The intermediate zones might have a great deal of game. Each species would shrink to those localities where economic accident offered the requisite assortment of environmental requirements. That same condition—namely the fortuitous (as distinguished from purposeful) make-up of wild life environments—shares, with overshooting, the credit for our present deplorable situation.

The protectionists will, at this point, remind me of the possibilities of inviolate sanctuaries, publicly owned, in which habitable environments are perpetuated at public expense. Let us by all means have as many as possible. But will Mr. Babbitt vote the necessary funds for the huge expansion in sanctuaries which we need? He hasn't so far. It is "blood money" which has bought a large part of what we have. Moreover, sanctuaries propose to salvage only a few samples of wild life. I, for one, demand more. I demand of Mr. Babbitt that game and wild life be one of the normal products of every farm, and the enjoyment of it a part of the normal environment of every boy, whether he live next door to a public sanctuary or elsewhere.

Mr. McCabe taxes me with omitting any mention of game production on public lands, where the one-gallus hunter will have free access to it. I can only infer that he has not read the American Game Policy. Has any group ever proposed a larger public land program, and called for more wild life production thereon? The Policy admits, to be sure, the unpleasant fact that lands must be cheap in order to be public. It advocates the paid-hunting system only for those lands too expensive for the public to own.

Finally Mr. McCabe taxes me with too much interest in exotics. Modesty forbids me to refute this charge in detail. I have persuaded two states to go out of the pheasant business, and several others to limit it to half their area. I devised the "glaciation hypothesis" which seems to exclude pheasants from about a third of the United States. On the other hand, I have recommended the continuation of pheasants and Hungarians in certain regions where economic changes have so radically altered the environment as to make the restoration of native game prohibitive in cost. Just what native species would Mr. McCabe recommend for east-central Wisconsin, or for northern Iowa, or for farm land in Massachusetts?

Let it by no chance be inferred that because I speak as a sportsman I defend the whole history of the sportman's movement. Hindsight shows that history contains any number of blunders, much bad ecology, and not a few actions which must be construed as either stubbornness or hypocrisy. For every one of these, one could point out a counterpart in the history of the protectionists, only there has been no "Emergency Committee" with either the means or the desire to compile and advertise them. Fifteen years ago, for instance, the protectionists closed the prairie chicken in Iowa, and then sat calmly by while plow and cow pushed the species almost to the brink of oblivion. Was this a blunder? Yes—but what of it? Is there any human aspiration which ever scored a victory without losing to some extent its capacity for self-criticism? The worthiness of any cause is not measured by its clean record, but by its readiness to see the blots when they are pointed out, and to change its mind. Is there not some way in which our two factions can point out each other's sophistries and blunders without losing sight of our common love for what Mr. Babbitt is trampling under foot? Must the past mistakes of each group automatically condemn every future effort of either to correct them?

To me, the most hopeful sign in the sportsman's movement is that several little groups have publicly avowed that the old program is a failure. Each is struggling to devise a new formula. I am conceited enough to believe that the formula my little group is trying to put together comes as near meeting the ugly realities of economics on the one hand, and the ideals of the protectionists on the other, as any yet devised. [. . .]

In short, I beg for a little selectivity in weighing the new departures proposed by the other fellow. I also pray for the day when some little group of protectionists will publicly avow that their old formula of restriction is not the whole Alpha-to-Omega of conservation. With both sides in doubt as to the infallibility of their own past dogmas, we might actually hang together long enough to save some wild life. At present, we are getting good and ready to hang separately.

Chapter 60

Marti Kheel

THE KILLING GAME: AN ECOFEMINIST CRITIQUE OF HUNTING

Kheel addresses the morality of sport hunting and concludes that it lacks justification as a moral activity. She goes on to address the flaws she finds in the various justifications of hunting often cited, including the psychological, moral, and social benefits; ecological benefits; and spiritual benefits. Using feminist psychoanalytic theory, Kheel then proposes that the killing of animals allows the hunter to ritually enact the death of his longing for a return to a primordial female/animal world through death of the animal.

HUNTING IS AN act of violence. And for some, it is a sport. Increasingly, these two facts present hunters with a major public relations problem. While at the turn of the century hunting was considered a praiseworthy activity, today 63 percent of the American public disapproves of hunting for recreation or sport (9).

[. . .]

Hunters have responded to the new public climate by taking refuge in a discourse designed to present what they do as morally laudable. Using a confused amalgam of arguments, they have represented hunting simultaneously as a cultural and spiritual asset, a biological drive, a management tool, and a return to the natural world.

[. . .]

A note about terminology is in order. A growing number of hunters eschew the word "sport hunting," claiming that they hunt for "ecological" or "spiritual" reasons, not merely for "sport." Although I make distinctions among types of hunters based on their self-professed motives for hunting, I hope to demonstrate that these differences are not as pronounced as many hunters would have us believe. Because, in addition, I challenge the validity of the very notion of hunting as a "sport," generally I use the term *hunting* without the qualifying word *sport*. My use of the word *hunter*, however, does not encompass subsistence hunters. Although I do not rule out the possibility that subsistence hunters share some of the characteristics of the hunters in this study, the more complicated nature of their motives places subsistence hunters beyond the scope of this article. This study examines those who hunt out of desire.

Is hunting a sport?

[. . .]

The distinction between sport and play is generally thought to reside in the greater complexity of sport. According to Thomas, "Sport has elements of play but goes beyond the characteristics of play in its rule structure, organization, and criteria for the evaluation of success" (29: p. 18). In addition, although sport is thought to have its basis in play, according to Thomas it has a second distinguishing feature, that is, its agonistic quality. Play, by contrast, is viewed as an inherently "co-operative interaction that has no explicit goal, no end point, and no winners" (11: p. 481).

Caillois (3: pp. 3–10) developed a framework listing six features common to play: (a) Its outcome is uncertain; (b) it is an activity that is freely engaged in; (c) it is unproductive; (d) it is regulated; (e) it takes place in a separate area; and (f) it is make-believe. Although these features are not universally agreed upon, they provide a helpful starting point for evaluating whether hunting conforms to common conceptions of play and sport.

The first of Caillois's features, the notion that play must not have a predetermined outcome, is inherent in the very nature of hunting as an activity. According to Cartmill, hunting is, by definition, "the deliberate, violent killing of unrestrained, wild animals" (4: p. 30).

[. . .]

The notion of competing with an animal, however, raises a moral problem. Because the animal has not consented to the competition, the game lacks symmetry of structure. [. . .] As Schmitz points out, hunting is more like a contest in which there is only one contestant (i.e., the hunter) (25: p. 30). The morality of a sport in which there is only one participant, however, is highly problematic. The animal's experience is obliterated, subsumed under the rules of a game that require the animal's death.

This relates to the second feature of play (i.e., that it is freely engaged in). Sport hunting is, by definition, an activity that is freely engaged in by hunters. The sport hunter typically is contrasted with the subsistence hunter, who hunts out of need, not out of "desire." [. . .] Yet, there is a major logical flaw in the notion of sport hunting as a voluntary activity, in that only one of the "participants" has chosen to compete.

[. . .]

The notion of hunting as a voluntary activity is also closely allied with the third of Caillois's features, that is, the notion of play as unproductive. Sport hunting, like play or sport in general, is an activity that is thought to be its own reward. Unlike work, it is not undertaken for any external reason.

[. . .]

Although this notion may accurately portray the attitude of many hunters (i.e., they may hunt more for the experience of pursuing the animal than for the moment of the kill), there is a moral problem entailed in the idea of pursuing the death of another living being for the opportunity it affords one to engage in an enjoyable experience.

Hunters frequently invoke the fourth of Caillois's features of play (i.e., that hunting has rules, to defend their "sport" from the charge of cruelty). Hunters, it is said, do not hunt indiscriminately: they conform to rules of good conduct (i.e., limitations on the number of animals killed, the season, and the weapons used). Such rules are said to give the animal a "fair chance." [. . .] [A]ccording to Leopold, the ethical value of hunting resides in the fact that hunters are bound not only to the laws about hunting but to their conscience as well (10: p. 212).

The fifth feature of play, that it takes place in a separate area, clearly applies to sport hunting. [. . .] [H]unting must occur outside and, traditionally, in an area that is considered "wild."

The last feature of Caillois's framework, the make-believe aspect of play, interestingly applies to hunting. For many hunters, sport hunting imaginatively recaptures a time when it is believed that men had to hunt for reasons of survival. In their attempt to lure their prey, hunters often describe an imaginary experience in which they feel as though they have become the animal they intend to kill.

[. . .]

The moral problem with the make-believe aspect of hunting is glaring, for the goal of the hunter's "game" is deadly serious. While hunters may play a "game" in which they imaginatively seek to understand another animal, this game has irrevocable consequences that extend beyond the world of make believe. The hunter does not pretend to kill the animal; the death of the animal is quite real.

Whereas the competitive, goal-oriented nature of hunting fits the notion of a sport, the nonvoluntary conscription of the animal into this "game" casts doubt on the validity of this idea. Both the willingness to "play" and the amusement derived from the activity are one sided. Although hunters may *experience* the activity of hunting as a sport, the skewed symmetry of the "game" renders this notion unintelligible. Hunters thus face a conceptual problem. On the one hand, hunting can exist as a sport only by conferring subjective identity on the animal. On the other hand, hunters can only pursue the death of an animal as playful activity by denying the animal's subjective experience and focusing exclusively on their own experience.

Most hunters ignore the question of the animal's subjective experience, defending their actions by reference to the purity of their own motives and desires, and, in particular, by presenting their *desire* to hunt as a *need*. Hunters have used several strategies to justify hunting, which I have categorized by means of a tripartite typology that distinguishes hunters according to the particular need they argue hunting fulfills: the "happy hunter" hunts for the purpose of enjoyment and pleasure, as well as character development (psychological need); the "holist hunter" hunts for the purpose of maintaining the balance of nature (ecological need); and the "holy hunter" hunts in order to attain a spiritual state (religious need). Whereas the happy hunter once gained status by calling hunting a sport, today's holist and holy hunters seek to distance themselves from the notion of sport. What unites the three types of hunters is their claim that hunting provides some redeeming social, moral, or personal value that is not just desirable but necessary.

The happy hunter: psychological need

The happy hunter is an unabashed sport hunter who freely admits to the pleasure that he derives from this "sport." Significantly, the animal is literally called "game." As one hunter proclaimed, "I hunt because it is something I like to do" (cited in 17: p. 20). Or, as another states, "The adrenalin flows. It's a good feeling" (cited in 17: p. 34). And, in Ernest Hemingway's inimitable words, "I think they (birds) were made to be shot and some of us were made to shoot them and if that is not so well, never say we did not tell you that we like it" (8: p. 152). In the United States, the conception of hunting as a pleasurable, recreational activity emerged in the middle of the nineteenth century in response to increased urbanization and leisure time. Like other forms of recreation, sport hunting was also thought to confer particular moral and social benefits. This notion of hunting as a beneficial activity stood in stark contrast to the ideas of the colonial period in New England, where hunting was considered a frivolous pastime of irresponsible young men, permissible only insofar as it was necessary for livelihood.

[. . .]

In the late 1800s, happy hunters helped to institutionalize "rules of fair play" in the form of laws designed to stop the decimation of wildlife by commercial and sport hunters. These laws, which included limitations on time, place, and type of weaponry, were seen as necessary not to preserve the animals in and of themselves, but rather to preserve their "sport."

The early conservationist hunters saw hunting as useful in building character, that is, male character. They argued that hunting was a necessary corrective for men who had become overly feminized by the encroaches of civilization. Theodore Roosevelt represents this view (22: p. 1236). [. . .] Messner explains this turn to competitive sports: "With no frontier to conquer, with physical strength becoming less relevant in work, and with urban boys being raised and taught by women, it was feared that males were becoming 'soft,' that society itself was becoming 'feminized' " (15: p. 14). Thus, sport hunting came to be seen as a necessary release for "man's" instinctual and aggressive drives. The point, however, was not for men to be reduced to the level of the animal world. By complying with the rules of "fair play," sport hunters felt they were able to express their "animal instincts," while also demonstrating their superiority to the animal world.

The notion that hunting is a psychologically beneficial release for man's aggression has persisted into this century. Aldo Leopold claimed that hunting is an instinctual urge, in contrast to golf (10: p. 227). [. . .] The value of hunting, for Leopold, resides in the exercise of this aggressive impulse as well as in its control. Leopold's concern is not the preservation of individual animals, but, rather, the "inalienable right" to hunt and kill them (p. 227). Leopold derives this right from a "fact" of nature, which modern hunting is intended to preserve, namely, the Darwinian notion of conflict or survival of the fittest. As Leopold states, "Physical combat between men and beasts was [once] an economic fact, now preserved as hunting and fishing for sport" (10: p. 269). According to Leopold, "An individual's instincts prompt him to compete for his place in the community, but his ethics prompt him also to cooperate (*perhaps in order that there may be a place to compete for*)" [emphasis added] (10: p. 239).

[. . .]

Happy hunters claim hunting provides a variety of additional psychological benefits. According to Leopold, it stimulates an awareness of history. That is, the hunter is "reenacting the romance of the fur trade." And it promotes a sense of "our dependency on the soil-plant-animal-man food chain, and of the fundamental organization of the biota" (10: p. 212). Another sportsman claims that hunting "renews the traditional kinship between men, wild things, and the land" (13: p. 71). All of these purported benefits have in common the claim that sport hunting helps men to become morally mature.

The holist hunter: ecological need

Whereas the happy hunter is unabashedly anthropocentric, extolling hunting for its psychological benefits for human beings (and in particular for men), the holist hunter claims more altruistic motives. Although hunting journals still openly extol the pleasures of the hunt, increasing numbers of hunters feel compelled to cite less self-serving reasons for hunting. Holist hunters claim that without their services, the animals they kill would die from starvation. Hence, they are performing a laudable ecological role.

Relinquishing the realm of recreation and pleasure, holist hunters have entered the world of business management and science. Using terms such as "population density," "sustainable yield," and the necessity of "culling" or "harvesting" the "excess" animals that would otherwise starve, holist hunters claim the title of "managers" for the biotic community. Their management partners in this undertaking are the federal and state fish and wildlife agencies, which manage both the animals and the hunters themselves. While hunters claim to be responding to nature's unfortunate excesses, the game management journals reveal another story. For example, according to an article in the *Journal of Wildlife Management*. "The primary management plan has been the one directed at increasing the productivity of the whitetail deer through habitat manipulation and harvest regulation . . . to produce optimum sustained deer yields . . . and hunter satisfaction" (16: p. 92). In short, holist hunters are intent on "managing" animals so that sufficient numbers will remain for them to kill.

For holist hunters, it is not the hunter who is the agent of death, but rather nature or ecology. The hunter is merely carrying out nature's inexorable directives, a participant in a "drama" not of his own making. The violence that hunting inflicts merely expresses the reality of violence in the natural world and thus is beyond ethical reproach. The holist hunter believes that not only should hunting not be shunned, but that it should be embraced.

Holist hunters, however, overlook the vast differences between human predation and natural predation. Whereas natural predators prey on the old, the weak, and the sick, human hunters typically select the biggest and healthiest animals to kill. As a consequence, hunters promote what Teale has called a kind of "evolution in reverse" (28: p. 161). Moreover, sport hunters overlook the extent to which their own actions have produced the problems that they claim to resolve. Sport hunters have pursued a deliberate policy of eliminating natural predators in numerous areas throughout the country, precisely so that they can claim the status of predators for themselves.

The alliance between hunting and the science of ecology has been a fortuitous partnership for modern hunters. Responding to a modern public that rejects the conjunction of pleasure and violence, happy hunters have found in the world of science and business a convenient refuge from attack. Armed with the claim that their mental state has been purified of the taint of pleasure, holist hunters contend that their motives are beyond rebuke. Although their official trade journals continue to enumerate the multiple pleasures to be found in the hunt, increasing numbers of happy hunters assume the camouflage of the holist hunt.

The holy hunter: spiritual need

For the holy hunter, hunting is not a means of recreation, nor is it a form of work. For the holy hunter, hunting is a religious or spiritual experience. As James Swan has stated, for many it is their religion (27: p. 35). Holy hunters contrast their spiritual attitude of reverence and respect with the crass and superficial mentality of the typical sportsman or happy hunter. Although they too emphasize the notion of emotional self-restraint, they see it as a by-product of a transformed world view. Hunting is akin to a religious rite. In the words of Holmes Rolston, "Hunting is not *sport*: it is a *sacrament* of the fundamental, mandatory seeking and taking possession of value that characterizes an ecosystem and from which no culture ever escapes" (21: p. 91).

The spiritual nature of the hunt is thought to derive from a particular type of awareness, often described as a meditative state. As Richard Nelson states, "Hunting for me can be almost hypnotic. It's like a walking meditation" (18: p. 89). And for Ortega y Gassett, "The hunter is the alert man" who achieves a "universal attention, which does not inscribe itself on any point and tries to be on all points" (19: p. 91). [. . .] And according to Ortega y Gassett, hunting entails a "mystical union with the animal" (19: p. 124).

[. . .]

Like the holist hunters, holy hunters draw on the science of ecology not for a management policy, but for the spiritual lessons that it is thought to inspire. As Young explains, "What is religious about hunting is that it leads us to remember and accept the violent nature of our condition, that every animal that eats will in turn one day be eaten" (32: p. 139). Holy hunters claim a humble and submissive attitude, seeking not to conquer nature, but rather to "submit to ecology" (21: p. 92). Once again, desire and necessity are elided. Hunting is seen not as manifestly the desire to kill, but rather as an ecological necessity.

Holy hunters frequently draw on the spiritual traditions of native cultures to bolster the notion of the holy hunt. James Swan cites the "wisdom of native peoples" that claims that "under the right conditions, the success of the hunter is not just a reflection of skill but the choice of the animal" (27: p. 21). [. . .] The association of hunting with spirituality does, in fact, have a long history among subsistence hunters in native cultures. Some, but by no means all, of these cultures promoted the notion of saying a prayer before killing an animal, as well as the idea that the animal "gives" her or his life as a gift to the hunter. However, there are a number of ethical problems with invoking the traditions of native cultures.

First, the spiritual teachings of diverse native cultures cannot accurately be treated as a monolithic model from which to draw on for our own interactions with animals. Second, it is ethically questionable to extirpate a narrative from one cultural context and to graft it onto another. To the extent that native cultures hunted for subsistence reasons, their experience cannot be applied to a culture where this is no longer the case.

[. . .]

In place of the notion of an inherently aggressive drive that must be contained through adherence to a code of conduct, the holy hunter claims to restrain his aggression to the point of nonexistence at least within the holy hunter's mind. Holy hunters do not "kill" animals according to this world view: rather, animals "give" their lives. Nor do holy hunters perpetrate violence; instead they are passive participants in nature's cycles.

The hunt for psychosexual identity

It is time to ask if there are common underlying themes in all three categories of hunters. The association between hunting and masculine self-identity has been a recurring theme throughout history. Many cultures require a young boy to hunt and kill an animal as a symbolic rite of passage into manhood. Significantly, the young boy is frequently sequestered from the world of women as well. Although hunting is not an exclusively male activity, the vast majority of hunting has been performed by men.

[. . .]

The connection between hunting and masculinity is also commonly expressed in the notion that hunting provides an outlet for men's sexual energy. Thus, according to the holy hunter proponent Dudley Young, there is "an almost erotic connection between hunter and hunted," with the emotion-filled kill being analagous to "sexual ecstasy" (32: pp. 138, 134). And, for the holist environmental writer Holmes Rolston, hunting is viewed as a safety valve for sexual energy. In his words, "the sport hunt sublimates the drive for conquest, a drive without which humans could not have survived, without which we cannot be civilized." He concludes that "perhaps the hunting drive, like the sexual urge, is dangerous to suppress and must be reckoned with" (21: p. 91). For these writers, hunting is not simply a desire, but a biological need.

Hunting is also frequently conceptualized as having a narrative structure that resembles a sexual encounter. There is the initial build up of tension in the course of the chase, leading ultimately to the climax of the kill. Hunters can no more eliminate the kill from the narrative structure of the hunt than it would seem that many men can eliminate orgasm as the goal of sex.

[. . .]

Hunters, however, do not typically depict their sport as the crass expression of a sexual drive. More frequently, hunting is portrayed as an urge to achieve intimacy with nature and as the quintessential act of connection. The priest Theodore Vitali argues that "hunting is a direct participation in nature and has the potential of deepening the spiritual and moral bonds between human and subhuman communities" (30: p. 210). Vitali contrasts hunting with activities such as nature photography and hiking, which he considers "virtually voyeuristic" in that they "lack the intimacy with nature that hunting achieves" (p. 211).

[. . .]

The ingestion of the flesh of the conquered animal is also described by a number of writers as an erotic act. According to Shepard, whereas the "ecstatic consummation of love is killing," the "formal consummation is eating" (26: p. 173). Similarly. Nelson states that "I get a great deal of pleasure from knowing that my body is made in no small measure from deer. I am passionately in love with deer but I also kill them. I appreciate the fact that I am made out of the animal I love" (18: p. 92).

[. . .]

The analogy with sex is instructive, however. Sex is both a biological urge and a socially constructed activity. A man who rapes a woman cannot credibly defend his actions by saying he was simply following his "animal instincts." Nor can he claim that the rape provided a much needed outlet for his sexual energy, nor that it builds (male) character, nor that the rape was performed according to rules of good conduct. Rape is wrong because it is a violation of another living being. Significantly, the literature on rape argues that rapists are not motivated by the urge to fulfill a sexual drive, nor are they out of control. On the contrary, rape is designed to establish men's dominance and control (1). Similarly, hunting may be seen as a symbolic attempt to assert mastery and control over the natural world.

[. . .]

Feminist psychoanalytic theory has sought to explain men's greater propensity for violence. According to object relations theorists, the development of identity in boy children is established through a process of negative identification. Unlike girls, who are able to continue the initial, primary identification with the mother figure, boys must not only disidentify with the mother figure, but they must deny all that is female within themselves, as well as their involvement with the female world (5: p. 167). As a consequence, according to Chodorow, "girls emerge from this period with a basis for 'empathy' built into their primary definition of self in a way that boys do not" (p. 167).

Dorothy Dinnerstein extends this analysis to all of nature. As she argues, boys not only establish their identity in opposition to women, but to all of the natural world (6). Having established a second and alienated nature, it appears that men then face a lifelong urge to return to the original state of oneness that they left behind. The return to an original undifferentiated state, however, is precisely what must be avoided because such a return would constitute an annihilation of the masculine self.

The conflict between these two drives may shed light on the hunter's urge to achieve intimacy in death. The pursuit of the animal expresses the hunter's yearning to repossess his lost female and animal nature. The death of the animal ensures that this oneness with nature is not genuinely attained. Violence becomes the only way in which the hunter can experience this sense of oneness while asserting his masculine self-identity as an autonomous human being. By killing the animal, the hunter ritually enacts the death of his longing for a return to a primordial female/animal world.

Beyond the killing game: toward a life-giving play/sport

Psychologists and philosophers note that one of the functions of play is to facilitate the maturation process and the development of self-identity. Significantly, hunters claim this is characteristic of hunting. They argue that hunting helps humans (mostly men) to attain full status as human beings. Like play in general, hunting is thought to be particularly useful for young (male) children, aiding them to attain skills that will help them as adults. According to Shepard, the "play" activity of hunting prepares the young boy for future religious experience (26: p. 200).

Another function of children's games often discussed in the literature is their role in developing feelings of empathy for others. According to George Herbert Mead (14) and Jean Piaget (20), games provide children with a means by which to learn to take the role of the other and to come to see themselves through another's eyes.

Interesting differences appear at a young age between the play of boys and girls, which may shed light on men's propensity to hunt. Building on Piaget's studies on rules of the game, Lever found that boys tended to play far more competitively than girls and were more likely to play at structured games, which accorded importance to being proclaimed the winner (11: p. 479). By contrast, girls tended to "keep their play loosely structured [and played] until they [were] bored" (p. 479). Lever's study also found that girls' games were "mostly spontaneous, imaginative, and free of structure or rules. Turn-taking activities like jump rope may be played without setting explicit goals" (p. 481). In addition, "disputes are not likely to occur" and when they do, the game tends to be stopped (p. 479). Playing in smaller, more intimate groups, Lever found that girls' play tended to foster the development of empathy and sensitivity necessary for taking the role of "the particular other," and pointed toward knowing the other as different from the self.

Hunters claim that in the course of stalking their prey, they imaginatively enter into the life of the animal. But whereas hunters claim that this exercise in imagination helps them develop feelings of empathy for the animal, it is their inability to understand the experience of nonhuman animals that is a prerequisite of their hunt. As we have seen, hunters also emphasize the keen sense of alertness and attention that characterizes their state of mind. It is apparent, however, that if hunters were truly attending to nature, instead of to their own amorphous feelings of "love" and "connection," they would feel the terror and fright of the animal they seek to kill.

[. . .]

Ecofeminist philosophy recognizes a crucial distinction that hunters overlook: it is one thing to accept the reality and necessity of death, and quite another to deliberately kill a living being.

The notion of "attentive love," first used by Simone Weil (31), has been employed by a number of feminist philosophers as a central idea in the development of caring interactions toward others. For Weil, attentive love was a certain form of pure, receptive perceiving, as contrasted to egoistic perception, whereby one asks of the other, "What are you going through?" As Ruddick develops this idea, even the notion of empathy is not devoid of egoistic perception. As she explains, "The idea of empathy, as it is popularly understood, underestimates the importance of knowing another *without* finding yourself in her" (23: p. 121). By contrast, "attention lets difference emerge without searching for comforting common-alities, dwells upon the *other* and lets otherness be (23: p. 122).

The ability to achieve this form of attention entails a kind of playful leap of imagination into another's world. Maria Lugones develops this idea in her notion of an imaginative, playful world traveling, in which we can learn to "travel" into different worlds and realities, identifying with others so that "we can understand what it is to be them and what it is to be ourselves in their eyes" (12: p. 17). Sara Ebenreck has suggested that "awareness of imaginative activity may be especially important for environmental ethics, in which the guidelines for action have to do with response to others who are not human, for whom respectful attention may require of us the probing work of imaginative perception" (7: p. 5).

According to Burke, play is "an activity which is free, complete in itself, and artificial or unrealistic" (2: p. 38). As he elaborates, play's "true significance" lies in the fact that it develops our "creative, imaginative ability," enabling us to "live not only in the 'real' world but also in countless symbolic worlds of [our] own making" (2: p. 42). A problem arises, however, when living beings are forcibly conscripted into an artificial world to play the role of symbols themselves. All too often, women and animals have been relegated to the status of symbols, objects, or props for the construction of masculine self-identity. It is one thing to transcend the reality of the mundane world, and quite another to transcend the experience of other living beings.

Modern Western culture has achieved an unprecedented alienation from nature. For many, the urge to reconnect with nature is, in fact, experienced as a deep spiritual or psychological need. Killing is not the best way, however, to fulfill this need, and certainly not the most compassionate. The cooperative play of young girls would appear to provide a more mature and compassionate model for attaining intimacy with nature than hunting. The Council of All Beings workshops developed by John Seed and Joanna Macy (24) provide an example of a playful and imaginative connection with animals that conforms to the cooperative nature of girls' play. In these councils, participants are asked to imaginatively enter into the world of another species and to then bring their experience back to the group. People express profound feelings of empathy, grief, and rage when they realize the impact of deforestation, factory farming, and hunting on nonhuman animals. Through the expression and sharing of such feelings, people become motivated for a larger context of action.

The root of the word *sport* is "to leap joyously." Perhaps, through playful leaps of imagination such as these, we can learn to engage in a play/sport that affirms with love and compassion a genuine connection to all of life.

Bibliography

1   Brownmiller, Susan. *Against Our Will: Men, Women and Rape*. New York: Simon and Schuster, 1975.
2   Burke, Richard. "Work and Play." *Ethics*, 88 (1971), 33–47.
3   Caillois, Roger. *Man, Play, and Games*. Translated by Meyer Barash. New York: The Free Press of Glencoe, 1961.
4   Cartmill, Matt. *A View to a Death in the Morning: Hunting and Nature Through History*. Cambridge and London: Harvard University Press, 1993.
5   Chodorow, Nancy. *The Reproduction of Mothering*. Berkeley: University of California Press, 1978.
6   Dinnerstein, Dorothy. *The Mermaid and the Minotaur: Sexual Arrangements and Human Malaise*. New York: Harper, 1967.
7   Ebenreck, Sara. "Opening Pandora's Box: The Role of Imagination in Environmental Ethics." *Environmental Ethics*, 18:1 (1996), 3–18.
8   Hemingway, Ernest. "Remembering Shooting-Flying." *Esquire* (February 1935).
9   Kellert, Stephen. *The Value of Life: Biological Diversity and Human Society*. Washington, DC: Island Press, 1996.
10 Leopold, Aldo. *A Sand County Almanac: With Essays on Conservation from Round River*. Oxford: Oxford University Press, 1966.
11 Lever, Janet. "Sex Differences in the Complexity of Children's Play and Games." *American Sociological Review*, 43 (1978), 471–83.
12 Lugones, Maria. "Playfulness, 'World-Traveling' and Loving Perception." *Hypatia* 2 (1987), 3–19.
13 Madson, Chris. "State Wildlife Agencies and the Future of Hunting." *Second Annual Governor's Symposium*. Pierre, SD. August 24–6, (1993), pp. 64–71.
14 Mead, George Herbert. *Mind, Self, and Society*. Chicago: University of Chicago Press, 1934.
15 Messner, Michael A. *Power at Play: Sports and the Problem of Masculinity*. Boston: Beacon, 1992.
16 Mirarchi, Ralfe, Scanloni, Patrick, and Kirkpatrick, Roy L. "Annual Changes in Spermatozoan Production and Associated Organs of White-Tailed Deer." *Journal of Wild-life Management*, 41:1 (1977), 92–9.
17 Mitchell, John G. *The Hunt*. Harmondsworth, England: Penguin, 1981.
18 Nelson, Richard. "Life Ways of the Hunter." In *Talking on the Water: Conversations about Nature and Creativity*. Edited by Jonathan White. San Francisco: Sierra Club Books, 1994, pp. 79–97.
19 Ortega y Gasset, José. *Meditations on Hunting*. Translated by Howard B. Wescott, with a forward by Paul Shepard. New York: Scribner's, 1985.
20 Piaget, Jean. *The Moral Judgement of the Child*. New York: The Free Press, 1968.
21 Rolston, Holmes, III. *Environmental Ethics: Duties to and Values in the Natural World*. Philadelphia: Temple University Press, 1988.
22 Roosevelt, Theodore. "The Value of an Athletic Training." *Harper's Weekly* 37 (23 December, 1893), p. 1236.
23 Ruddick, Sara. *Maternal Thinking: Toward a Politics of Peace*. New York: Ballantine, 1989.
24 Seed, John, Macy, Joanna, Flemming, Pat, and Naess, Arne. *Thinking Like a Mountain: Toward a Council of All Beings*. Philadelphia: New Society Publishers, 1988.
25 Schmitz, Kenneth L. "Sport and Play: Suspension of the Ordinary." In *Sport and the Body: A Philosophical Symposium*. Edited by Ellen W. Gerber. Philadelphia: Lea & Febiger, 1972, pp. 25–32.
26 Shepard, Paul. *The Tender Carnivore and the Sacred Game*. New York: Scribner's, 1973.
27 Swan, James A. *In Defense of Hunting*. San Francisco: HarperCollins, 1995.
28 Teale, Edwin Way. *Wandering Through Winter*. New York: Dodd, Mead and Company, 1966.
29 Thomas, Carolyn E. *Sport in a Philosophic Context*. Philadelphia: Lea & Febiger, 1983.
30 Vitali, Theodore R. "The Dialectical Foundation of the Land Ethic." *Proceedings, Governor's Symposium on North America's Hunting Heritage*, Montana State University. Bozeman, July 16–18, (1992), pp. 203–14.

31 Weil, Simone. "Reflections on the Right Use of School Studies with a View to the Love of God." *Waiting for God*. Translated by E. Craufurd. New York: Harper, 1951.
32 Young, Dudley. *Origins of the Sacred: The Ecstasies of Love and War*. New York: St. Martin's Press, 1991.

Chapter 61

Alastair S. Gunn

ENVIRONMENTAL ETHICS AND TROPHY HUNTING

Gunn addresses the morality of hunting, including trophy hunting, in relation to animal death, animal suffering, hunting ethics, biodiversity and ecosystems, and human needs. Despite sharing with many sport hunters a distaste for trophy hunting, he argues that from broad-based economic and human survival values, trophy hunting is justified. Using Zimbabwe as a case study, he argues that trophy hunting successfully integrates both conservation and development and may be the only feasible strategy to protect the interests of both wildlife and people.

Introduction

THE PUBLICATION IN 1980 of J. Baird Callicott's "Animal Liberation: A Triangular Affair" introduced the conflict for environmental management and policy between animal liberation and environmental ethics. Hunting provides a prime example of this still unresolved controversy.

I have found no published source that condemns hunting per se. There is a spectrum in the environmental literature. At one end is the view that hunting is justified only for self protection and for food, where no other reasonable alternative is available. Most writers also agree that hunting is sometimes justified in order to protect endangered species and threatened ecosystems where destructive species have been introduced or natural predators have been exterminated. Others accept hunting as part of cultural tradition or for the psychological well being of the hunter, sometimes extended to include recreational hunting when practiced according to "sporting" rules. Nowhere in the literature, so far as I am aware, is hunting for fun, for the enjoyment of killing, or for the acquisition of trophies defended. However, as I argue towards the end of this paper, trophy hunting is essential in parts of Africa for the survival of both people and wildlife.

Throughout this paper, I assume that animals have interests, and that we have an obligation to take some account of those interests: roughly, that we are entitled to kill animals only in order to promote or protect some nontrivial human interest and where no reasonable alternative strategy is available. This position is roughly that presented by Donald VanDeVeer (1979). Versions of it are widely defended in the literature, though there are different views about *which* human interests are sufficiently significant to justify killing. I restrict my discussion to cases where the interest in question cannot reasonably be achieved without killing animals.

[. . .]

Wildlife management: the conventional Western view

[. . .]

Anti-hunting organizations present a number of arguments against both hunting in general and specifically the hunting of marine mammals, elephants, large carnivores, great apes, rhinos, and other large ungulates. In this paper, I concentrate particularly on elephants.

Some common arguments against hunting include the following, each of which is discussed in more detail later.

- Hunting wrongfully deprives animals of something that is valuable to them — their lives (Regan 1983, Taylor 1996). Killing, and not merely successful stalking, is recognized by both supporters and opponents as a central feature of hunting. As Roger King (1991) notes, for proponents of hunting such as José Ortega y Gasset (1972) and Paul Shepherd (1973), the central meaning of hunting is killing, and killing is essential to "Participation in the life cycle of nature" (King 1991, 80). Ann Causey says, "The one element that stands out as truly essential to the authentic hunting experience is the kill" (Causey 1989, 332). Some ecofeminists believe that hunting is a prime example of patriarchal oppression of nature: in Mary Daly's terms, of a "necrophiliac" culture (Daly 1978).
- Hunting causes suffering. [. . .] A high proportion of land mammals and ducks are injured rather than being killed instantly; these "cripples" may suffer for days before either recovering or dying.
- Great apes, elephants, whales, and dolphins are special animals. They are highly intelligent; many species have developed elaborate social systems; they exhibit altruistic behavior toward each other and apparently suffer grief at the death of group members; members of some species including the great apes, orca, and some dolphins are sociable towards humans and are even recorded as having saved human lives; some (humpbacked whales) compose and perform music.
- Hunting is unworthy of civilized beings: "The hunter . . . as a "redneck," bloodthirsty villain storming the woods each fall with a massive arsenal . . . hunting [as] a disgusting sport that recalls and rehearses the worst in human behavior" (Vitali 1990, 69).
- Hunting is a threat to biodiversity. It threatens the existence of target species, many of which are already rare, threatened, or endangered. Sport hunting also degrades the gene pool of ungulate species because the most valued targets, dominant males, are the individuals "most fit to pass on the best genes" (Loftin 1984, 69).
- Hunting is not necessary for the fulfillment of important human interests; these interests can be satisfied by other means that do not require killing. Hunting is not economically necessary nor even particularly useful. There are substitutes for all marine and most land mammal products and because whaling, in particular, is probably not a sustainable industry, it cannot make a long-term contribution to the economy (Clark 1973).

Animal deaths

[. . .] The question for sport hunting advocates to address, if it is admitted that the life of an animal is valuable to it and that animals have an interest in continued life, is whether this interest may justly be overridden. The most obviously persuasive argument is that sustainable hunting kills only animals that would die anyway—or more precisely, since we don't know which animals will die from "natural causes," a proportion of the population will die each year, usually much more slowly and painfully through predation. starvation, or disease.

[. . .]

Animal suffering

It is inevitable that some animals that are hunted will suffer. [. . .] Where the target is animals whose numbers are widely agreed to be in need of control, supporters of hunting claim that it causes less suffering than alternative methods. Causey believes that "The genuine sport hunter, due to his earnest regard for his prey, is usually highly sensitive to the animal's pain and suffering, and makes every effort to minimize both. Proper weaponry and hunter training can minimize both" (Causey 1989, 335).

[. . .]

Special status of major target species

The mammals which Western environmentalists especially wish to protect from hunting, and trophy hunters especially wish to bag, are often referred to as "charismatic megafauna." Large land and marine mammals certainly have an appeal to many people, because of their sheer size and presence and in some cases because of special qualities they are said to have.

[. . .]

Claims of intelligence, social structure, altruism, and artistic ability that are comparable to humans, must however be met with some skepticism. Decades of research on humans have failed to obtain widespread agreement on the nature of human intelligence or even on whether there is such a thing as "general intelligence," let alone on how to test it.

[. . .]

Perhaps a case could be made (though not consistently with animal liberation) for giving special protection to species that are particularly intelligent or social or altruistic or which meet a particular standard of aesthetics, but it would need to be a consistent one. Since many species of "lower" mammals, birds, reptiles, fish, and invertebrates meet one or more of these criteria, it follows that we should oppose killing them too.

Hunting as uncivilized

[. . .] "Shooters" who kill for an extrinsic goal are not necessarily blameworthy. They may, for instance, kill pests or overabundant animals in order to protect ecosystems or endangered species, or to feed their families, and this may be morally justifiable or even a duty. From the idealized hunting perspective shooters do not exhibit the virtues promoted by Ortega y Gasset (1972), Shepherd (1973), and Vitali (1990), but this does not make them vicious. Trophy hunters, however, who kill purely for the sake of acquiring prestigious evidence that they have killed an animal, surely act immorally, because they achieve a trivial benefit for themselves at the expense of the life of an animal. Unlike professional cullers, they may also be considered to exhibit serious character defects. They want to control, to have power, to reduce animals to easy targets, to kill, and to brag about it.

[. . .]

Biodiversity and ecosystems

It is certainly true that many hunters seek to kill trophy animals which are precisely the animals that the species can least afford to lose: the "genetically prime animals," as Vitali (1990) puts it. However, he believes that most hunters are "opportunistic . . . They take what they can get, and oftentimes this amounts to the young, the weak, and the disabled," as do stalking animal predators. He also points out that opportunistic predators such as lions kill a large number of prime animals "precisely because of the opportunities the animals themselves provide"—for instance, prime male wildebeest are usually alone and, "during the rut . . . tend to be incautious and thus vulnerable to attack" (Vitali 1990, 70). In any case, controlled trophy hunting that is part of an ecologically sound wildlife management program will not unduly affect the gene pool. This is in contrast to the uncontrolled hunting of the past, which in the case of elephants has led to an alarming increase in tusklessness in many parts of Africa.

[. . .]

Hunting in general is not a major threat to biodiversity. In the past, a number of species have become extinct due to hunting pressure—palaeolithic hunters contributed to the extermination of many species of megafauna (Uetz and Johnson 1974; Martin and Klein 1984), while in recent centuries species such as the great auk appear to have died out entirely due to hunting (Halliday 1980). But the millions of species around the world that are currently at risk are threatened not by hunting but by habitat destruction and pollution, loss of food sources, and human disturbance. Opposition to hunting, on its own, will do little to protect biodiversity. The comparatively few species that are commercially hunted—mostly large mammals—can be sustainably managed. Nor is hunting necessarily a threat to ecosystems. In most of Europe and the United States, for instance, humans have exterminated large predators, but are able to control the populations of ungulates by culling and sustainable hunting. We should not allow opposition to hunting to deflect us from the much greater threat to biodiversity posed by habitat loss and degradation.

[. . .]

Protecting existing wilderness may not require any killing, but the restoration of degraded environments is very different. Conservation agencies in New Zealand have killed literally millions of introduced pests, including rodents, goats, deer, possums, and predators in order to restore damaged environments on both the mainland and off-shore islands.

[. . .]

Gary Varner (1994) has argued that what he calls therapeutic hunting ("hunting motivated by and designed to secure the aggregate welfare of the target species and/or the integrity of its ecosystem") is justified in the case of an obligatory management species ("one that has a fairly regular tendency to overshoot the carrying capacity of its range, to the detriment of future generations of it and other species"). Therapeutic hunting is not merely consistent with animal liberation; it is morally required under certain circumstances, where fewer animals would die "than if natural attrition is allowed to take place" (Varner 1994, 257–8). Animal liberationists, obviously, prefer non-lethal methods of control, but "Wildlife requires management, and hunting is at this time the most efficient means to do it" (Vitali 1990, 70).

Opponents of hunting (and trapping) as methods of pest control often advocate contraception. However, at the time of writing, no such methods exist except for a few species on a small scale. Even if effective methods did exist, the costs would be phenomenal and for years to come the contracepted animals would continue to destroy vegetation and to compete with and prey on other animals.

[. . .]

In many areas that were colonized by Europeans, native animals have suffered from predation, competition, and habitat destruction by feral introduced animals. [. . .] *In these and many other cases the conflict between animal liberation and environmental protection is quite inescapable*: Foxes and lyrebirds, feral dogs and kiwis, mallards and their close relatives absolutely cannot coexist, so whatever we do, we will be responsible for some animals living and others dying. The "do-nothing" option is effectively a choice to allow the introduced animals to kill, directly or indirectly, the native animals, as well as upsetting ecological equilibrium.

[. . .]

I conclude that it is legitimate to kill introduced animals that threaten the livelihood of native species, and that sport hunting, where it is an effective means of control (at no cost to society) is legitimate. More controversially, perhaps. I also believe that trophy hunting is also legitimate in these circumstances, even though I also share sports hunters' low opinion of trophy hunting.

Hunting and human needs

Writers who identify or sympathize with animal liberation (Varner 1994 and 1998 is an exception) usually accept killing only in situations where human survival is at stake. In this view, hunting is regrettable because it causes major harm to animals, or violates their rights, or fails to respect them for their intrinsic or inherent value or intrinsic worth, or deprives them of something (life) that is valuable to them (e.g., Regan 1983; Singer 1975; Taylor 1986). But, as Paul Taylor notes, to insist that even subsistence hunting is wrong is to expect people to sacrifice "their lives for the sake of animals, and no requirement to do that is imposed by respect for nature" (Taylor 1986, 294).

Self-defense is established as a full justification for killing a human attacker, typically by appeal to rights. [. . .] Wild elephants killed 358 people in Kenya between 1990 and 1995 and 53 people in one area of Sri Lanka in 1995; the killing of 43 elephants by the local people in the same year is regrettable, and regretted by the villagers themselves, but hardly blameworthy (Sugg 1996). I take it that this case is uncontroversial.

The self-defense justification is very narrowly conceived where the attacker is human. In contrast, almost everyone would accept the killing of a less direct threat from an animal such as a plague-infected rat or a swarm of locusts, but not an equally infectious human plague sufferer or a crop devastating polluter, which suggests that we don't consider animals' interests to be equal to the like interests of humans. Following Donald VanDeVeer (1979), we might accept that hunting animals (but not humans) to protect one's livelihood is also justified. Laura Westra (1989), who advocates an ethic of respect for animals, accepts that we may kill animals if it is necessary for our survival—it is by restricting our utilization to the meeting of needs that we show respect for both animals and ecosystems. Traditional subsistence hunters are commonly said to show respect for their prey, for instance by refraining from killing totem animals even when food is scarce, explaining to animals why the hunter needs to kill them, asking for their forgiveness, and even mourning their deaths, and are praised for their complete usage of every part of the animal (e.g., Mails 1972).

[. . .]

Conservation: rich and poor nations

The remainder of this paper is concerned with broadly economic issues: I argue that economic consider-ations (at the extreme, the survival of thousands of people) justify commercial trophy hunting.

First, however, I wish to draw attention to the global economic context in which wildlife management must be discussed. Calls from the North to preserve rainforests, set up national parks, and save endangered species might be more effective if local communities within nations of the South were agreed to have property rights over their fauna and flora (Gunn 1994). Typically, however, genetic resources are appropriated by multinational companies and countries that can afford to research their potential to develop food and industrial and pharmaceutical products. Thus there is little incentive for poor countries to forego the advantages of immediate exploitation (Tietenberg 1990).

[. . .]

Conventional preservation measures will not help poor countries to deal with pressing problems such as malnutrition, poverty, disease, and overcrowding. Indeed, protecting large areas from human encroachment often exacerbates social and economic problems. Nowhere is this more evident than in Africa.

[. . .]

The social and economic costs of preservation are often allocated quite unfairly. For instance, India's "Project Tiger" has possibly—just possibly—saved the species, but according to one report (Chippindale 1984), on average about one person per week is killed by tigers in India. The Amboseli National Park, in Southern Kenya, illustrates the injustice (and also the ineffectiveness) of viewing national parks as "biological islands" which must be preserved from all human use except scientific study and limited tourism. The nomadic Maasai who had traditionally used this region were excluded from it for the benefit of others.

[. . .]

Over the next few decades, wildlife numbers in the "protected" park actually declined, mainly due to illegal hunting. However, a change in land use philosophy in Amboseli NP in the mid 1970s improved both the numbers of wildlife and the economic position of the Maasai. Revenue sharing was introduced, the central government absorbed developmental and recurrent costs of the park, local Maasai were granted title to land outside the Park, to be owned cooperatively as group ranches, and cash compensation was paid for loss of grazing, to cover livestock losses from wildlife migrating outside the Park borders. The Maasai became less dependent on cattle because of these measures and, more importantly, because of the revenue they received from tourist campsites and employment in the Park, with which they were able to build community facilities. Reduction in livestock numbers meant less competition with wildlife, and because the Maasai were now part of the enterprise, illegal hunting greatly declined. As a result, within ten years wildlife numbers had greatly increased (Western 1984).

The economics of hunting

Commercial and sport hunting are economically significant activities in many developed countries. For instance, according to the BFSS (n.d.) 33,000 jobs in the United Kingdom depend on hunting. [. . .] However, the economies of rich countries do not depend significantly on hunting and if it was banned, recreational hunters would simply switch their discretionary spending, thus creating jobs in other sectors of the economy.

The situation is quite different in poorer countries, where wildlife has always been used as a resource and "Use or non-use is not the issue; sustainable use is" (Makombe 1993, 17). The colonial powers, after reducing many species to rarity or extinction, generally adopted policies of strict preservation of wildlife. This was done without regard to the needs of local people who were regarded as poachers even when they engaged in traditional subsistence hunting (Makombe 1993, 18).

Poor countries gain considerable revenue from trophy hunting. The impoverished Mongolian government charges $10,000 for a permit to shoot a snow leopard and a 16-day hunt with one snow leopard costs $25,000 per person; any wolves shot along the way are thrown in for $600. Bulgarian dealers sell falcons in the West for $10,000. Orangutan were sold in Taiwan in the 1980s at $30,000 each, though the local traders in Indonesia received less than $200 each for them—still a very considerable sum by local standards (information from Ghazi 1994, Anon. 1993 and 1994). None of these cases is part of a sustainable management program, but other countries which manage their wildlife effectively have achieved substantial revenues from trophy hunting while maintaining or increasing their wildlife populations.

Zimbabwe: a case study

Wild resources are vital to the survival of millions of Africans. One study estimated that wild resources contributed over $120 million to the Tanzanian economy in 1988 (Kiss 1990); hunting licenses alone yielded $4.5 million in 1990. [. . .] Before Kenya imposed a ban on hunting, the total revenue from sport hunting contributed about 6.5 percent to the total foreign exchange from tourism (Makombe 1993, 28). [. . .] In some countries, a large proportion of household income is derived from wildlife based enterprises—in Malawi, for instance, rural communities derive 2.5 times more cash from wildlife than the market value of their subsistence agricultural products (Makombe 1993, 22). In Zimbabwe, local people are allowed to hunt sustainably both for their own families and to take to market, and a limited number of trophy hunting permits are sold. Zimbabwe—12.7 percent of whose area is devoted to national parks and reserves—also has some of the toughest anti-poaching (in the sense of illegal hunting) units in Africa and spends 0.60 percent of its budget on wildlife (whereas the United States spends only 0.15 percent). This is a substantial commitment in a country which cannot afford to provide adequate health care and education for much of its population and in which 50 percent of the population is unemployed.

[. . .]

Rich countries such as the United States, Australia, and New Zealand which oppose hunting of large animals including whales, and especially trophy hunting, have a very bad reputation in Zimbabwean conservation circles such as Africa Resources Trust (ART) and Zimbabwe Trust (ZIMTRUST). These private organizations strongly support the government CAMPFIRE Association (an acronym for Communal Areas Management Programme for Indigenous Resources) which was set up by the Zimbabwean Department of National Parks and Wildlife Management in 1986, with the support of the Worldwide Fund for Nature, the Office of USAID, Harare, and the Centre for Applied Social Sciences (CASS) at the University of Zimbabwe. The objectives of CAMPFIRE, "based on the rationale that communities will invest in environmental conservation if they can use their resources on a sustainable basis," are:

- to initiate a programme for the long-term development, management and sustainable utilisation of the natural resources in the communal areas;
- to achieve management of resources by placing their custody and responsibility with the resident communities;
- to allow communities to benefit directly from the exploitation of natural resources within the communal areas; and
- to establish the administrative and institutional structures necessary to make the programme work. (ZIMTRUST 1993)

The communal areas are the marginal and submarginal lands which were created early in the twentieth century when the British colonists "took over the most fertile lands and forced much of the indigenous population into arid and semi-arid areas" which are unsuitable for agriculture because they have insufficient or unreliable rainfall. However, they make excellent wildlife habitat" (Anon 1996). The 1975 Parks and Wildlife Act gave ownership of wildlife (including hunting rights) to all property owners, and in 1982 this was extended to the communal areas through their Rural District Councils (Murphree 1991, 8). Over five million people—almost half the population—live in communal areas, which make up 42 per- cent of the country. Communities may decide to participate in CAMPFIRE, which around half had done in August 1996.

In 1995, CAMPFIRE generated $2.5 million, a substantial sum given that game wardens are paid as little as $80 per month (CAMPFIRE News 1996). This revenue is gained from hunting safaris, tourism such as photographic safaris, sales of products such as animal products and crocodile eggs (for sale to crocodile farmers), and rafting licenses (ZIMTrust 1993; CAMPFIRE News 1996). Around 90 percent of the revenue is generated from the sale of big game hunting licenses, and 64 percent of this is derived from elephant trophy hunting licenses which in March 1996 cost $9,000 (CAMPFIRE News 1996). Over the period 1989–93, 22 percent of revenue was reinvested in wildlife management and 54 percent devolved to the participating communities on the communal lands. Communities spent their shares on infrastructure development such as water supply, clinic and school development, farm fencing (to keep out crop-destroying elephants, hippos, buffalo, and kudu) and roading, income generating projects, and cash distributions to families for their own use. In some areas, this income amounts to 50 percent of a household's annual income and enables families to pay for items such as school fees (CAMPFIRE News 1996). Masoka Ward, a formerly impoverished area, earned $100,000 in 1994 from a safari hunting concession organized through CAMPFIRE. The ward used the money to build a health clinic, pay game guards, and fund a football team, and each of the 140 households also received more than four times their annual income for drought relief, either in cash or maize (CAMPFIRE News 1996). This revenue, of course, would not be available without the sale of hunting licences. It would be even greater were it not for the ban on international trade in elephant products under the Convention on International Trade in Endangered Species and Their Products (CITES) since 1990.

Zimbabwe's policies are a conservation success. Whereas the total population of African elephants fell by half between 1975 and 1990 (from 160,000 to 16,000 in Kenya), Zimbabwe's elephants have increased steadily—32,000 in 1960, 52,000 in 1989, and over 70,000 in 1993 (Ricciutti 1993). The national trophy off-take is restricted to no more than 0.7 percent per year, which is clearly sustainable. For instance, the elephant population density of the Omay Communal Land, a CAMPFIRE participant, is the same as that in the adjacent Matusadona NP, where hunting is strictly prohibited, and the Omay population grew at 3–4 percent per year from 1982 to 1992, even though, counting "problem" elephants shot by villagers, the average annual off-take was 1.03 percent (Taylor n.d.).

Because they have a stake in sustaining populations of economically valuable game animals, Zimbabweans have a commitment to conservation. As a result, species such as elephants which are rare or extinct in many other countries are thriving in Zimbabwe, along with populations of other animals which benefit from protection of big game habitat. It is sadly ironic that governments of the same European nations that reduced Zimbabwe's elephants to around 4,000 in 1900 (Thomas n.d.) are now highly critical of Zimbabwe's effective and socially equitable sustainable management policies.

It may be claimed that economic benefits could be obtained without the deaths of big game animals, by encouraging wilderness tourism and big game viewing. Norman Myers, who has played an important role in protecting East African wildlife, has argued that animals such as lions are actually much more valuable, economically, than dead ones. He notes (Myers 1981) that a trophy hunter will pay $8,500 to shoot a lion in Kenya, whereas the same animal will generate $7 3/4 million over its lifetime from people such as myself who wish to view and photograph wildlife, not to kill it. But this is unsound economics, for several reasons. First, each lion is substitutable by another lion. Wildlife tourists want to see lions, not any particular lion. So long as there is a reasonably good chance of seeing lions, people will continue to visit parks. Second, the viability of lions as a species, or of a given population, is not threatened by the carefully controlled issue of permits to trophy hunters. Lions reproduce rapidly and the revenue that would have been generated by Myers's hypothetical lion over its lifetime will continue to be generated by other lions. Third, and most importantly, the number of lions—which the tourists want to view and the trophy hunters want to kill—is limited by the carrying capacity of the environment. The available environment is restricted to National Parks and other protected wildlife areas, such as private game lands. When the human population of Africa (and other areas where lions used to live) was small, lions and humans coexisted, if not necessarily happily on the part of either. With rising human populations, and different expectations, it is utterly impossible that lions will ever again exist in any numbers outside protected areas. Therefore, lion numbers will have to be regulated, and if this can be done for the economic benefit of impoverished local people by the issuing of game licenses, why not?

Conclusion

As Africa's population continues to grow, and habitat shrinks, pressure on wildlife will increase. Africans, like Western environmentalists, are entitled to a materially adequate standard of life. They cannot and should not be expected to protect wildlife if it is against their interests to do so. The only feasible strategy to protect the interests of both wildlife and people is one that integrates conservation and development, as in Zimbabwe. Whatever we may think of trophy hunting—and I share the distaste of serious sports hunters for it—at present it is a necessary part of wildlife conservation in Southern Africa.

References

Africa Resources Trust website, www.art.org.uk.

Anon. 1996. *Zimbabwe's CAMPFIRE: Empowering Rural Communities for Conservation and Development*. Harare: Africa Resources Trust and CAMPFIRE Association.

——. 1994. "Cash Quest Could Mean End of Snow Leopard." *New Zealand Herald*, October 10.

——. 1993. "Back to Nature's Bosom." *New Zealand Herald*. September 22.

British Field Sports Society. n.d. "Hunting: The Facts." Website www.countryside-alliance/org/country/foxhunting.html.

Callicott, J. Baird. 1980. "Animal Liberation: A Triangular Affair." *Environmental Ethics* 2: 311–38.

CAMPFIRE News. 1996. Issue 12. Harare: CAMPFIRE Association.

Care for the Wild website: www.cftw@fastnet.co.uk

Causey, Anne S. 1989. "On the Morality of Hunting." *Environmental Ethics* 11: 327–43.

Chippindale, Peter. 1984. "Tigers Too Safe Now." *New Zealand Herald*, March 24.

Clark, Collin W. 1973. "Profit Maximization and the Extinction of Animal Species." *Journal of Political Economy* 81: 950–61.

Daly, Mary. 1978. *Gyn/Ecology: The MetaEthics of Radical Feminism*. Boston: Beacon Press.

Ghazi, Polly. 1994. "Illegal Help at Circuses." *New Zealand Herald*, December 28.

Gunn, Alastair S. 1994. "Environmental Ethics and Tropical Rainforests: Should Greens Have Standing?" *Environmental Ethics* 16: 21–40.

Halliday, Tim. 1980. *Vanishing Birds*. Harmondsworth: Penguin Books.

King, Roger J.H. 1991. "Environmental Ethics and the Case for Hunting." *Environmental Ethics* 13: 59–85.

Kiss, A., 1990. "Living with Wildlife: Wildlife Resource Management with Local Participation in Africa." Washington, DC: World Bank Technical Paper No. 130, Africa Technical Department Series.

Loftin, Robert F. 1984. "The Morality of Hunting." *Environmental Ethics* 6: 241–50.

Mails, T. E. 1972. *The Mystical Warriors of the Plains*. Garden City, NY: Doubleday.

Makombe, Kudzai (ed.) 1993. "Sharing the Land: Wildlife, People and Development in Africa," IUCN/ROSA Environmental Series No. 1. Harare, IUCN/ROSA, and Washington DC, IUCN/SUWP.

Martin, Paul and R.G. Klein (eds) 1984. *Quaternary Extinctions: A Prehistoric Revolution*. Tucson: University of Arizona Press.

Murphree, M.W. 1991. "Communities as Institutions for Resource Management." *Harare: Occasional Paper Series*, Centre for Applied Social Studies, University of Zimbabwe, 1991.

Myers, Norman. 1981. "The Exhausted Earth." *Foreign Policy* **42**: 141–55.

Ortega y Gasset, José. 1972. *Meditations on Hunting*. New York: Charles Scribner's Sons.

Regan, Tom. 1983. *The Case for Animal Rights*. Berkeley: University of California Press.

Ricciuti, Edward. 1993. "The Elephant Wars." *Wildlife Conservation* March/April.

Shepherd, Paul. 1973. *The Tender Carnivore and the Sacred Game*. New York: Charles Scribner's Sons.

Singer, Peter. 1975. *Animal Liberation*. New York: New York Review.

Sugg, Ike G. 1996. "Selling Hunting Rights Saves Animals." *Wall Street Journal*, July 24.

Taylor, Paul. 1986. *Respect for Nature*. Princeton: Princeton University Books.

Taylor, Russell. n.d. "From Liability to Asset: Wildlife in the Omay Communal Land of Zimbabwe." Wildlife and Development Series booklet No. 8, published by the International Institute for Environment and Development and CAMPFIRE Collaborative Group for Africa Resources Trust and available on the ART website.

Thomas, Stephen, n.d. "The Legacy of Dualism in Decision-making Within." CAMPFIRE. *Wildlife and Development Series booklet No. 4*, published by the International Institute for Environment and Development and CAMPFIRE Collaborative Group for Africa Resources Trust and available on the ART website.

Tietenberg, T.N. 1990. "The Poverty Connection to Environmental Policy." *Challenge*, Sept/Oct: 26–32.

Uetz, G. and D.L. Johnson. 1974. "Breaking the Web." *Environment* 16: 31–9.

VanDeVeer, Donald. 1979. "Interspecific Justice." *Inquiry* 22: 55–70.

Varner, Gary E. 1998. *In Nature's Interests? Interests, Animal Rights, and Environmental Ethics*. New York: Oxford University Press.

——. 1994. "Can Animal Rights Activists be Environmentalists?" In Christine Pierce and Donald VanDeVeer (eds) *People, Penguins, and Plastic Trees*. Belmont, CA: Wadsworth, 2nd ed: 254–73.

Vitali, Theodore. 1990. "Sport Hunting: Moral or Immoral?, *Environmental Ethics* 12: 69–82.

Western, David. 1984. "Amboseli National Park: Human Values and the Conservation of a Savanna Eco-system" in Jeffrey A. McNeely and Kenton R. Miller (eds), National Parks, Conservation, and Development: the Role of Protected Areas in Sustaining Society: proceedings of the World Congress on National Parks, Bali, Indonesia, 11–22 October 1982. Washington, D.C.: Smithsonian Institution Press: 93–9.

Westra, Laura. 1989. "Ecology and Ethics: Is There a Joint Ethic of Respect?" *Environmental Ethics* 11: 215–30.

ZIMTRUST. 1993. "Historical Overview and Background to CAMPFIRE." Unpublished report. Harare: Zimbabwe Trust.

SPECIAL PROBLEMS

Chapter 62

Ned Hettinger

EXOTIC SPECIES, NATURALISATION, AND BIOLOGICAL NATIVISM

Hettinger addresses arguments both in favor of and in opposition to the continued introduction of exotic species to many habitats. He concludes that there are good reasons for opposing their introduction; even the presence of species that are naturally dispersing and nondamaging leads to a loss of biological purity and to a greater global homogenization of plants and animals.

IT IS WELL-KNOWN that the spread of exotic species has caused—and continues to cause—significant environmental degradation, including extinction of native species and massive human influence on natural systems. What is less clear, however, is how we are to conceptualise exotic species. Consider, for example, [. . .] wild pigs (*Sus scrofa*) in the Hawaiian rainforest, whose ancestors were brought to Hawaii by Polynesians perhaps 1500 years ago. Are they still an exotic species or have they 'naturalised' despite constituting an ongoing threat to the native biota in this extinction capital of the world? One commentator put his finger on the problem of understanding exotic species when he said, 'The terms "exotic" and "native" . . . are . . . about as ambiguous as any in our conservation lexicon (except perhaps "natural")' (Noss 1990: 242).

This essay sifts through the mix of biological theorising and philosophical evaluation that constitutes this controversy over understanding, evaluating, and responding to exotic species. I propose a precising definition of exotics as any species significantly foreign to an ecological assemblage, whether or not the species causes damage, is human introduced, or arrives from some other geographical location. My hope is to keep separate the distinct strands typically woven into this concept while still capturing most of our fundamental intuitions about exotics.

[. . .]

What is an exotic species?

[. . .]

The fundamental idea underlying the concept of an exotic species is a species that is alien or foreign. Such a species is foreign in the sense that it has not significantly adapted with the local species and to local abiotic environment. [. . .] Geographical considerations are typically taken as what distinguishes natives from exotics. [. . .] On this account, exotics are species that originally evolved in some other place. Woods and Moriarty (2001) call this the 'evolutionary criterion'.

Specifying the natives of a region as those that originally evolved there is both too stringent a requirement and perhaps overly broad. Too stringent because, by this criterion, humans would be native only to Africa. But all species move around. Species evolve in one locale, then migrate or expand their range to other places, and thrive for thousands of years perfectly at home in these new regions. Few species in a region would be natives if we accepted this evolutionary origin criterion of native species.

[. . .]

I do not think we should require that natives fit an ecosystem, much less be good fits. There might be 'native misfits' as well as 'exotic fits'. [. . .] Consider that the Asian long-horned beetle (*Anoplophora glabripennis*) recently discovered devouring trees in Chicago is also an important threat to trees in its native range (Corn *et al.* 1999). Barnacles are an example of species that proliferate wildly in their native ranges. [. . .] Unless one accepts an idyllic conception of perfectly-harmonious natural systems, one must admit that native species can wreak havoc in their native ranges.

Similarly, we should not assume that natives are well-integrated into 'balanced' and 'self-regulating communities'. [. . .] Presupposing a tightly integrated and balanced, community conception of natural systems is highly controversial given the recent emphasis in ecology on disequilibrium, instability, disturbance, and heterogeneous patchy landscapes (Hettinger and Throop 1999).

[. . .]

Native species will have significantly adapted with resident species and the local abiotic environment, not in the sense that they necessarily have become good fits or are controlled by others, but in the sense that native species will have 'forged ecological links' (Vermeij 1996: 4) with some other natives. Natives will have 'responded to each other ecologically' and frequently evolutionary (Vermeij 1996: 5). Natives are established species (i.e., more or less permanent residents) tied to some other residents via predation, parasitism, mutualism, commensalism, and so on. Often native species will have affected the abundance of other native individuals, perhaps altering the frequencies of alleles in the gene pool of native populations and thus exerting selective pressure on other natives. A native species will also likely have adapted to the abiotic features of the local environment.

Let me stress again that by 'adapted' I do not mean 'positively fit in'. A species has adapted when it has changed its behaviour, capacities, or gene frequencies in response to other species or local abiota. Aggressively competing is as much adapting as is establishing symbiotic relationships. By adapted, I also do not mean fit or well-suited to survive in an environment. Species that have historically adapted in my sense may go extinct and species that have never actually adapted to a local assemblage may nonetheless be suited to survive there.

In contrast with native species, an exotic species is one that is foreign to an ecosystem in the sense that it has not significantly adapted to the resident species and/or abiotic elements that characterise this system and, perhaps more importantly, the system's resident species have not significantly adapted to it. On the account defended here, species that are introduced to new geographical locations by humans, or that migrate or expand their ranges without such assistance, may or may not be exotics in these new regions. Species are exotic in new locations only when the species movement is ecological and not merely geographical. That is, if a species moves into a type of ecological assemblage that is already present in its home range(s), then the immigrant species is not exotic (foreign) in this new locale: It will already have adapted with the species and types of abiotic features there. If, on the other hand, the species movement results in its presence in a type of ecological assemblage with which it has not previously adapted, then the species is an exotic in this new location.

[. . .]

When the first finches appeared on the Galapagos Islands, they were exotics because they had not adapted with the local species and to the local environment (Woods and Moriarty 2001). [. . .] In contrast, when bison (*Bison bison*) expand their range north or west out of Yellowstone National Park into the surrounding grasslands, they are not exotics because they enter a habitat with species with which they have adapted. [. . .] What counts is ecological difference, not geographical distance.

Whether a species is exotic to an assemblage is a matter of degree. The greater the differences between the species, the abiota, and their interrelationships in the old and new habitats, the more exotic an immigrant will be. After passing a certain threshold of difference, we can be quite comfortable with judgements about a species being exotic. [. . .] But there will be borderline cases where neither the designation exotic nor nonexotic is clearly appropriate. For example, the mountain goats that are moving into Yellowstone Park from the north would be neither clearly exotic nor nonexotic to the Yellowstone assemblages they join, if the flora, fauna, and abiota in their native habitat is somewhat but not all that similar to those they encounter in Yellowstone.

By requiring that a native species has actually adapted to (some of) the other natives in an ecological assemblage, we allow for the possibility of 'exotic fits'; that is, aliens that arrive in new ecosystems but are well-suited to them. Westman (1990: 254) calls this phenomenon 'preadaptation' and says it is possible because different species can play functionally similar roles. For example, even if Asian snow leopards (*Panthera uncia*) could play the same ecological roles that the restored grey wolves (*Canis lupus*) play in the Yellowstone assemblage, this would not make them native.

[. . .]

Exotics and human-introduced species

Although exotics are often defined as human-introduced species, the examples of cattle egrets moving to South America and the Galapagos' first finches show that exotic species need not be introduced by humans. Nor need human-introduced species be exotics. Species that humans place into an assemblage as part of a restoration project are often not exotics. For example, the restoration of grey wolves to Yellowstone Park is not exotic introduction, even though humans captured wolves from Canada and released them in regions (Wyoming and Montana) hundreds of miles south of their home. Despite the fact that the individual organisms involved were not previously in the recipient assemblages and despite the fact that they were put there by humans, on the account given here, the released wolves are not an exotic species.

[. . .]

Even human introduction of species to locations where they have never previously existed need not count as exotic introduction. As long as the resident species have adapted with the introduced species, the immigrant will not be exotic. Consider [. . .] introducing a fish species into a high mountain lake previously devoid of that species of fish because a waterfall blocks its dispersal pathway. This need not count as exotic introduction, if the life forms in the lake had adapted with that species of fish and if that species had adapted to abiotic conditions like those in the lake.

[. . .]

Disvaluing human-introduced exotics and U.S. park service policy

Although exotics need not be human introduced, recently many—likely most—are introduced by humans, including those that are the most exotic in their new habitats. Modern humans regularly transport exotics distances, with speeds, and between ecological assemblages that do not frequently occur (or are impossible) with naturally-dispersing exotics. When an exotic species is introduced by humans, whether directly or indirectly, intentionally or nonintentionally, this provides one reason for the negative appraisal commonly levelled at such species. This negative evaluation is justified independently of whether the human-introduced exotic causes damage. Negatively evaluating human-assisted immigrant species—and not those arriving on their own—is a controversial value judgement. It is supported by a number of reasons, briefly outlined below.

Massive human alteration of the earth is ongoing (Vitousek 1997). Perhaps half of the planet's surface is significantly disturbed by humans, and half of that is human dominated (Hannah *et al.* 1993). Humans are increasingly influencing, altering, and controlling the planet's natural systems. The result is a radical diminution in the sphere of wild nature on earth. An important reason to value natural areas and entities is because they are relatively free of human influence.

[. . .]

The presence of human-introduced species diminishes the wildness of natural systems and thus provides a reason for disvaluing exotic species when they are human introduced.

[. . .]

Some charge that there is misanthropy behind such a distinction in value between human-introduced and naturally-dispersed exotics (Scherer 1994: 185). But valuing humans, even loving humanity, is quite compatible with not wanting humans or their works everywhere, especially in National Parks and wilderness areas.

One of the mandates of U.S. National Parks like Yellowstone is to let nature take its course. [. . .] As a natural area where human influences should be minimised, the negative evaluation of human-introduced exotics is especially compelling and Yellowstone has a strong reason to remove human-introduced exotics. For closely related reasons, the Park has a strong rationale for welcoming naturally-dispersing aliens. The presence of such exotics is a manifestation of wild nature, a world that made us rather than one we have made. Removing naturally-dispersing exotics would (typically) increase human control and manipulation over natural systems.

[. . .]

[H]owever, [i]f naturally-dispersing exotics cause sufficient damage, they may warrant control. The policy of letting nature take its course is not absolute. Respect for wild natural processes can be outweighed by concern for certain outcomes in nature. For example, the protozoan parasite (*Myxobolus cerebralis*) that causes whirling disease (an affliction that cripples some fish species) is a recent European immigrant to Yellowstone's ecosystems. If this species somehow travelled from Europe into Yellowstone without the aid of humans, the Park would be hard pressed to justify welcoming such a naturally-dispersing exotic. If the parasite threatened to destroy the entire Yellowstone cutthroat population, the Park would have strong reasons not to let nature take its course.

Exotics and damaging species

Some define exotic species as those that damage the new regions they occupy (Scherer 1994: 185). Indeed, exotics have caused massive amounts of damage, both ecologically and economically. [. . .] Pimentel *et al.* (1999) estimate that there are about 50,000 species of non-U.S. origin in the country, a fifteenth of the estimated total of 750,000 species. [. . .] According to Pimentel *et al.*, the yearly quantifiable damage these species cause is at least $138 billion.

[. . .]

Exotics have caused the extinction of native species. [. . .] Approximately 40 percent of threatened or endangered species on the U.S. Endangered Species lists are at risk primarily because of exotic species (Pimentel *et al.* 1999).

Despite the massive ongoing harm such species cause, we should not identify exotics with damaging species. We have already noted that some native species also cause damage. Furthermore, not all immigrants to new ecosystems are harmful. Most get extirpated before they become established. [. . .] According to the 'tens rule', 10 percent of exotics that are introduced into an area succeed in establishing breeding populations and 10 percent of those will become highly invasive (Bright 1998: 25). Even if only 1 percent of exotics typically cause serious problems, this is of little comfort, for as Bright argues, 'since the global economy is continually showering exotics over the Earth's surface, there is little consolation in the fact that 90 percent of these impacts are "duds" and only 1 percent of them really detonate. The bombardment is continual, and so are the detonations' (1998: 24).

[. . .]

Exotics can even be beneficial in the new habitats they occupy. Vermeij speaks of the 'potentially crucial role invasions and invaders have played in stimulating evolution' and says that 'in the absence of invasions, communities and species and interactions comprising them may stagnate, especially if the economic base of energy and nutrients remains fixed' (1996: 7). Exotics sometimes provide habitat for native species. A species of *Eucalyptus* tree introduced into California from Australia over 120 years ago benefits Monarch butterflies (*Danaus plexippus*) who rely on them during annual migrations (Woods and Moriarty 2001). Eucalyptus also benefits native birds and salamanders (Westman 1990: 255). There are also examples of exotics benefiting endangered species: grizzly bears consume substantial amounts of nonnative clover in Yellowstone Park (Reinhart, *et al.* 1999) and, in some locations in the U.S., nutria (*Myocastor coypus*) (a South American relative of the beaver) are a principal food source for the endangered red wolf (*Canis niger*).

[. . .]

Still, there are good reasons for being suspicious of the disruptive potential of exotic species. Exotics often arrive without the predators, parasites, diseases, or competitors that are likely to limit their pro-liferation in their native habitat. Local prey, hosts, and competitors of exotics have not had a chance to evolve defensive strategies. Past experience, [. . .] is another reason for suspicion. Nevertheless, as with the connection between human introduction and exotics, one ought not to move from an empirical correlation between the presence of exotics and damaging results to a conceptual connection between exotic species and those that cause damage.

When an exotic species causes serious damage or harm, we have a reason for a negative appraisal of this exotic. When exotics cause harm to human interests, the ground for a negative evaluation of these exotics is fairly straightforward. [. . .] When exotic species harm or impoverish nonhuman nature, the justification for a negative evaluation is less straightforward. Many worry about whether it makes sense to harm natural systems and they challenge us to provide a principled distinction between harming a natural system and changing it (Throop 2000). (For example, in what sense did the chestnut blight harm or damage eastern U.S. forests as opposed to merely changing them?) But when an exotic species invades a diverse native community and changes it into a virtually uniform stand of a single species vastly diminished in suitability for wildlife habitat or forage (e.g., *Phragmites* in eastern U.S. wetlands, *Melaleuca* in Florida), a negative appraisal on nonanthropocentric grounds seems straightforward. Such an appraisal is also clearly called for when an exotic species, plentiful in its native habitat and present as an alien around the world, causes large numbers of extinctions of other species (e.g., brown tree snakes). The damage to humans and to nonhuman nature that some exotic species have caused is a significant reason to be worried about exotic species.

Naturalisation of exotics

[. . .]

I suggest that the process of naturalising and becoming native is neither arbitrary nor purely scientific. [. . .] To become native, an exotic species must not only naturalise ecologically (i.e., adapt with local species and to the local environment), but it must also naturalise evaluatively. This means that for an exotic to become a native, human influence, if any, in the exotic's presence in an assemblage must have sufficiently washed away for us to judge that species to be a natural member of that assemblage.

Ecological naturalisation

An exotic species naturalises in an ecological sense when it persists in its new habitat and significantly adapts with the resident species and to the local abiota. This is a matter of degree and typically increases over time. Immigrant species will immediately casually interact with elements of the local ecological assemblage, but significant adaptation between the immigrant and residents and between the immigrant and the local abiota takes time and increases over time. Exertion of evolutionary pressure between the immigrant, the residents, and the abiota will also not be immediate.

Determining what is to count as significant adaptation requires context sensitive judgement. Adaptation can continue indefinitely. Whether adaptation is sufficient for ecological naturalisation may depend on the adaptive potential of a particular species/ecosystem complex. If a great deal of adaptation is going to take place (perhaps including co-evolution of the exotic and several resident species), then until this occurs, we likely would not judge the exotic to have ecologically naturalised. On the other hand, if the exotic tends to employ resources and modes of living that were not previously exploited in the recipient habitat, then perhaps not much adaptation need take place before we judge the species to have ecologically naturalised. In highly individualistic and loose assemblages, where few ecological or evolutionary links exist between members and where many species have wide-ranging tolerances to a diversity of abiotic factors (and so are unlikely to have adapted much to local conditions), a newcomer may be no more exotic (that is, unadapted to the local species and abiotic conditions) than are the resident species. Perhaps very little adaptation is sufficient to ecologically naturalise to such an assemblage. Ecological naturalisation can also occur in assemblages where the vast majority of species are human-introduced exotics (e.g., Hawaiian forests, or cities and suburbs where people have eradicated the natives and planted exotics). Over a sufficient time period, a large group of exotics would ecologically naturalise with each other and the surviving natives would also adapt with the new assemblage.

[. . .]

Evaluative naturalisation

Should ecological naturalisation be all that is required before an exotic species is to be considered native? I think not. Many immigrant species have been in their new habitats long enough to ecologically naturalise (i.e., significantly adapt with local species) and yet we justifiably hesitate to consider them natives. Consider [. . .] Holmes Rolston's claim that mustangs on the western range are not natives even though they (and the ecological assemblages with which they interact) have had several hundred years to adapt. Many still consider Hawaiian feral pigs nonnative even after some 1500 years. It is hard to believe that significant ecological naturalisation has not occurred during that time span. The judgements that these species are not yet natives—despite having significantly adapted with resident species and to local abiota—

can be explained by treating judgements about naturalisation and the resultant nativity as involving an evaluative component in addition to the ecological one.

Onetime exotic species that are judged to have naturalised and become full-fledged natives are ones that we take to be 'natural' members of their ecological assemblages. For this to be the case, we must judge their presence in these assemblages as not representing significant, ongoing human influence. [. . .] This is true even if the immigrant species has significantly ecologically naturalised and is thus no longer exotic.

We do not prevent human-introduced exotics from becoming native when we require that they not only significantly adapt but also become natural members of their new assemblages. For exotics can evaluatively naturalise as well as ecologically naturalise. Human influence on natural systems and species 'washes out' over time, like bootprints in the spring snow. Natural processes can once again take control, as when old mining roads erode and vegetation overgrows them. This washing away of human influence over time constitutes evaluative naturalisation and it allows human-introduced exotics that have ecologically naturalised to become full-fledged natives.

A number of factors affect the washing away of human influence and the resultant evaluative natural-isation (Hettinger and Throop 1999: 20–21). First, the greater the human influence, the longer it takes to wash out. Perhaps this is why we are reluctant to think of feral animals as capable of naturalising and becoming natives even over long time-periods. Domestication of animals constitutes significant human influence over them, and so even after several hundred years we might think that feral horses, for example, are still not native (fully naturalised) on the American range, despite having significantly ecologically naturalised. Withholding the judgement that they have evaluatively naturalised reflects the view that the human influence on those species is of ongoing significance.

[. . .]

Increasing temporal distance from human influence is another factor that contributes to the washing away of such influence. For an exotic species to naturalise ecologically, it must significantly adapt with other natives and the local abiota, and this ensures that it will have some temporal longevity in an assemblage. This longevity may—but need not—be sufficient to ensure evaluative naturalisation.

[. . .]

A third factor affecting the washout of human influence is the extent to which a natural system becomes similar to what it would have been absent that influence. [. . .] Mountain goats would be in Yellowstone if humans had not influenced natural systems. In contrast, [. . .] it is likely that Hawaiian nature would have remained without pigs virtually forever but for human intervention. Thus it is reasonable to view pigs on Hawaii as representing continuing human influence in this respect.

A fourth factor affecting washout of human influence is the extent to which natural forces have reworked a human-influenced system (independently of whether the result is similar to what it would have been absent human intervention). For example, if humans introduce coyotes into an area with significant wolf presence, human influence on the assemblage resulting from coyote introduction would be lessened quickly because wolves significantly dominate coyotes. When a human-introduced exotic has naturalised in the ecological sense, natural forces have reworked the affects of human action to some degree. Thus ecological naturalisation contributes to evaluative naturalisation in this dimension as well, though again there is no reason to think that it is sufficient for it.

[. . .]

Let me summarise the implications of my account of naturalisation for the distinction between exotics and natives. Exotics are species that have not significantly adapted with the local ecological assemblage. Once a species has significantly adapted (ecologically naturalised), it is no longer exotic. But such a species might still not be native. If it was human introduced and if its presence in the assemblage represents significant and ongoing human influence, then it is not a natural member of this assemblage and so is not native. Perhaps kudzu, western mustangs, and Hawaiian pigs are such examples of species that are no longer exotic (because they have ecologically naturalised), but are not yet natives either (because the human influence on their presence is still significant).

Although human introduction is not part of my account of exotics, it is a factor in my account of native species. Are the problems I identified with the human-introduced account of exotics applicable to my account of natives? Although I need not count the restored Yellowstone wolves as exotics (as must the human-introduced account of exotics), it might seem that I cannot say that they are natives either, given the significant human involvement in their return to Yellowstone. But because this is return of a species that humans had previously eradicated, the restoration of wolves to Yellowstone is, in one important respect, a lessening of human influence over both Yellowstone and the wolf as a species. Yellowstone with wolves is now like it would be had humans never eradicated them. Similarly, by returning the wolf to its former range, humans are, in one respect, lessening their overall impact on wolves. Thus, in these respects, wolves are natural and hence native members of Yellowstone, despite being restored by humans.

Xenophobia, biodiversity, and disvaluing exotics as exotics

Nativists are those who favour native inhabitants over immigrants and/or want to preserve indigenous cultures. Biological nativists favour native flora and fauna, and they combat the introduction and spread of exotic species in order to preserve native assemblages.

[. . .]

Such an opposition to exotic species has been compared to a xenophobic prejudice toward immigrant peoples. [. . .] Jonah Peretti argues that 'nativist trends in Conservation Biology have made environmentalists biased against alien species', and he wants to 'protect modern environmentalists from reproducing the xenophobic and racist attitudes that have plagued nativist biology in the past' (1998: 183, 191).

In contrast, David Ehrenfeld thinks that comparing the antagonism toward exotics with real biases such as racial profiling of African-Americans and Hispanics 'deserves ridicule'. [. . .] After noting some exceptions, Ehrenfeld concludes, 'There are more than enough cases in which exotic species have been extremely harmful to justify using the stereotype' (1999: 11).

Ehrenfeld is on shaky ground if the 'ten's rule' is accurate. If only one in one hundred exotics cause serious problems, then stereotypes about the damaging nature of exotic species may be no more statistically grounded than are some of the morally-obnoxious, racial, and sexual stereotypes about humans.

[. . .]

When exotics are also distinguished from human-introduced species (as I have done), what justification for a negative evaluation of exotics remains? Those who oppose naturally dispersing, nondamaging exotics seem to be doing so because these species are alien, and negatively evaluating a species simply because it is foreign does suggest a xenophobic attitude and a troubling nativist desire to keep locals pure from foreign contamination.

[. . .]

Biological nativists' opposition to exotic species can be defended by distinguishing between types of nativism and purism and the reasons for them. While nativisms based on irrational fear, hatred, or feelings of superiority are morally objectionable, I will argue that some versions of both cultural nativism and biological nativism are rational and even praise- worthy. For example, I believe the protection and preservation of indigenous peoples and cultures is desirable. This may involve favouritism for local peoples and opposition to the dilution of local cultures (a kind of purism), but it is based on an admirable attempt to protect the diversity of human culture. Similarly, biological nativism is laudatory because it supports a kind of valuable biodiversity that is increasingly disappearing.

It might seem strange to oppose exotic species on grounds of biodiversity, for the presence of alien species seems to enhance a region's biodiversity, not decrease it. [. . .] But this argument takes too narrow a view of biodiversity. Since the breakup of the supercontinent Pangaea some 180 million years ago, the earth has developed into isolated continents with spectacularly diverse ecological regions. Biological nativists value and want to preserve this diversity of ecological assemblages. This diversity is in jeopardy due to modern humans' wanton mixing of species from around the globe. The objection biological nativists can have to exotic species as exotics—at least in the current context—is that although they immediately add to the species count of the local assemblage and increase biodiversity in that way, the widespread movement of exotic species impoverishes global and regional biodiversity by decreasing the diversity between types of ecological assemblages on the planet. For example, adding a dandelion (*Taraxacum officinale*) to a wilderness area where it previously was absent diminishes the biodiversity of the planet by making this place more like everyplace else. Adding a mimosa tree to Sullivan's Island makes the Low-country of South Carolina more like some Asian assemblages. When this is done repeatedly, as humans are now doing and at an ever increasing rate, the trend is toward a globalisation of flora and fauna that threatens to homogenise the world's ecological assemblages into one giant mongrel ecology. Bright calls the spread of exotics 'evolution in reverse' (1998: 17) as the branches of the evolutionary bush are brought back together creating biosimilarity instead of biodiversity.

The loss of biodiversity resultant from the presence of exotics is greatly exacerbated by damaging exotics that invade, extirpate endemic species, or turn diverse native assemblages into near monocultures of themselves. But such causal diminishment in diversity is distinct from the conceptual diminution identified here: the mere presence of massive numbers of exotics in a great number of assemblages diminishes the diversity between ecological assemblages independently of whether they physically replace or diminish natives. Note that opposition to exotics on these conceptual grounds avoids the unfair stereo-typing charge that must be addressed by those who oppose exotics because they are likely to cause damage.

It might be objected that presence of exotic species can enhance inter-assemblage biodiversity in certain respects, as well as decreasing it in others, and thus that the spread of exotics may not be a threat to overall biodiversity. For example, the movement of Asian snow leopards into Yellowstone Park would not only increase Yellowstone's species count but it would also make Yellowstone's assemblages differ from those of the Absoroka-Beartooth wilderness to the north in a way they previously did not: now they diverge in the types of mammals present. While snow leopards in Yellowstone would make Yellowstone's assemblages more like some Asian assemblages, it would also increase differences between Yellowstone and the wilderness areas to the north.

It is true that the presence of exotics can increase inter-assemblage biodiversity in the way suggested. More generally, species movement into new assemblages need not be a threat to overall biodiversity. In evolutionary history, such movement has frequently enriched ecosystems, brought on speciation, and enhanced global biodiversity. Careful planned and monitored human introduction of exotics into selected assemblages might be able to enhance biodiversity as well. But this is no defence for the blind and large-scale human introduction of exotics that is taking place on the planet today. In today's world, the increase in inter-assemblage diversity due to snow leopards' presence in Yellowstone would not last. Snow leopards would quickly find their way (or be introduced) into the Absoroka-Beartooth wilderness, and the increase in regional biodiversity would be lost. If we focus on individual cases of exotic introduction—without considering the cumulative impact of massive numbers of exotic introductions over time—we may be able to convince ourselves that the presence of exotics is benign (or even beneficial) in terms of biodiversity. But in the context of the current flood of exotics, such a focus is myopic. The logical end point of the ongoing, massive spread of exotics is that ecological assemblages in similar climatic and abiotic regions around the world will be composed of the same species. This is a clear case of biotic impoverishment.

[. . .]

In addition to this tragic loss in biodiversity, the spread of exotics also helps to undermine an important feature of human community. Globalisation of flora and fauna contributes to the loss of a human sense of place. As Mark Sagoff perceptively argues, native species 'share a long and fascinating natural history with neighbouring human communities. . . . Many of us feel bound to particular places because of their unique characteristics, especially their flora and fauna. By coming to appreciate, care about, and conserve flora and fauna, we, too, become native to a place' (1999: 22). Using knowledge of—and love for—local native species to help ground a sense of place will no longer make sense in a world where most of these species are cosmopolitan.

Just as the spread of exotic species threatens to homogenise the biosphere and to intensify the loss of a human sense of place, so too economic globalisation and the cosmopolitanisation of humans threaten to impoverish the diversity of the earth's human cultures and to undermine people's senses of community.

[. . .]

[T]he mass importation of exotics does significantly threaten biodiversity and biological nativists typically do not believe in the superiority of the species native to their lands. The charge that biological nativists are xenophobic ignores their admiration of foreign flora and fauna in their native habitats. Although biological nativists favour native biotic purity, they do so in the name of global biodiversity, the preservation of the spectacular diversity between Earth's ecological assemblages. Ironically, it is those who favour the cosmopolitanisation of plants and animals that support purity of an invidious sort: in that direction lies a world with the same mix of species virtually everywhere.

Opposition to exotics as exotic can thus be both rational and praiseworthy. Being a foreign species is a disvalue when humans are flooding the earth's ecological assemblages with exotics. Given the significant and ongoing homogenisation and cosmopolitanisation of the biosphere by humans, we may justifiably oppose exotic species even if they have arrived under their own power and cause no physical damage.

Conclusion

Exotic species are best characterised as species that are foreign to an ecological assemblage in the sense that they have not significantly adapted with the biota and abiota constituting that assemblage. Contrary to frequent characterisations, exotics need not cause damage, be introduced by humans, or be geographically remote. Exotic species become natives when they have ecologically naturalised and when human influence over their presence in ecological assemblages (if any) has washed away. Although the damaging nature and anthropogenic origin of many exotic species provide good reasons for a negative evaluation of such exotics, in today's context, even naturally-dispersing, nondamaging exotics warrant opposition. Biological nativists' antagonism toward exotics need not be xenophobic nor involve unfair stereotyping, and it can be justified as a way of preserving the diversity of ecological assemblages from the homogenising forces of globalisation.

References

Bright, Christopher 1998. *Life Out of Bounds: Bioinvasion in a Borderless World*. New York: W. W. Norton & Co.

Corn, M.L., Buck E.H., Rawson J., Fischer, E. 1999. *Harmful Non-Native Species: Issues for Congress*. Washington, DC: Congressional Research Service. Library of Congress. Available at http//www.cnie.org/nle/biodv26.html.

Ehrenfeld, David 1999. 'Andalusian Bog Hounds'. *Orion* Autumn: 9–11.

Hannah, Lee, Lohse, David, Hutchinson, Charles, Carr, John L., and Lankerani, Ali 1993. 'A Preliminary Inventory of Human Disturbances of World Ecosystems', *Ambio* **23**: 246–50.

Hettinger, Ned and Throop, Bill 1999. 'Refocusing Ecocentrism: De-emphasizing Stability and Defending Wildness', *Environmental Ethics* **21**: 3–21.

Noss, Reed 1990. 'Can We Maintain Our Biological and Ecological Integrity?' *Conservation Biology* **4**: 241–3.

Peretti, Jonah H. 1998. 'Nativism and Nature: Rethinking Biological Invasion', *Environmental Values* **7**: 183–92.

Pimentel, D., Lach, L., Zuniga R., and Morrison D. 1999. *Environmental and Economic Costs Associated with Non-indigenous Species in the United States.* Presentation at American Association for the Advancement of Science, Anaheim, CA, January 1999. For text, see http://www.news.cornell.edu/releasesljan99/species_costs.html.

Reinhart, D., Haroldson, M., Mattson, D., and Gunther, K. 1999. 'The Effect of Exotic Species on Yellowstone's Grizzly Bears'. Paper delivered at the *Yellowstone National Park Conference on Exotic Organisms in Greater Yellowstone: Native Biodiversity under Siege.* Mammoth Hot Springs. October 11–13.

Sagoff, Mark 1999. 'What's Wrong with Exotic Species?' *Report from the Institute for Philosophy and Public Policy* **19** (Fall): 16–23.

Scherer, Donald 1994. 'Between Theory and Practice: Some Thoughts on Motivations Behind Restoration', *Restoration and Management Notes* **12**: 184–8.

Throop, William 2000. 'Eradicating the Aliens', in William Throop (ed.) *Environmental Restoration: Ethics, Theory, and Practice*, pp. 179–91. Amherst, NY: Humanity Books.

Vermeij, Geerat 1996. 'An Agenda for Invasion Biology', *Biological Conservation* **7**: 83–9.

Vitousek, Peter 1997. 'Human Domination of Earth's Ecosystems', *Science* **277**: 494–9.

Westman, Walter 1990. 'Park Management of Exotic Species: Problems and Issues'. *Conservation Biology* **4**: 251–60.

Woods, Mark and Moriarty, Paul 2001. 'Strangers in a Strange Land: The Problem of Exotic Species', *Environmental Values* **10**: 163–91.

Chapter 63

Dale Peterson

TO EAT THE LAUGHING ANIMAL

Dale Peterson addresses the problem of bushmeat in developing countries, especially as it relates to primates and calls for conserving primate biodiversity by reducing the use of apes for food. He acknowledges the importance bushmeat plays in subsistence diets but also points out how bushmeat hunting has developed a strong commercial component in some areas, and its severe impact on some primates and other species. He develops a number of arguments that can be made to reduce the use of primates for food.

I **FIRST HEARD** an ape laugh while following a large group of wild chimpanzees in the great Tai Forest of Côte d'Ivoire, West Africa, as they moved on their daily circuit, a complex progression from food to food to food, from obscure fruits to tender herbs to hard nuts.

These West African chimpanzees are well known for their stone- and hardwood-tool-using culture, and at two or three moments during the day I paused to watch a large number of the nomadic apes assemble in a glade of African walnut trees (*Coula edulis*), pick up the stone and wood hammers they had previously left lying about on the ground, place individual ripe walnuts on top of stone and wood anvils, and then methodically crack open the hard walnut shells to get at the meat inside. That whole procedure was astonishing, particularly since the hammers seemed indistinguishable from rough human artifacts and also since the apes themselves (looking about, picking up walnuts in their hands, walking upright to carry them over to the tools, and squatting intently while they hammered away) seemed to me then hardly distinguishable from people. But my biggest shock that day came from watching a couple of juvenile chimps wrestling, teasing each other, tumbling and chasing – and laughing, laughing their heads off. It was not an action that simply *reminded* me of human laughter or merely *seemed* like human laughter. It was without question genuine laughter, virtually identical to human laughter minus some of the vocalized overlay (producing a gasping, panting, frenetic sort of wood-sawing sound).

Since then, I have observed chimpanzee laughter at other times, in other places. I have also seen wild-born bonobos and gorillas laugh, again apparently as a frantic expression of delight and mirth. And I have been told by experts that orangutans, too, sometimes laugh.

Animal play is not surprising, and one can easily believe that neurologically complex animals experience complex pleasure, something akin to "mirth" or, perhaps, an irresistible sensation of emotional lightness. But laughter? The laughter of apes is entirely different from any mere facial upturn of pleasure: a dog's smile, for instance. And it is another thing altogether from the high-pitched hyena vocalizations, sometimes described as "laughter" but completely unassociated with play or pleasure. Laughter may be among the most fragile and fleeting of vocal utterances. What does it mean? That apes laugh is undeniable. That their laughter means anything significant is a matter of opinion. Still, the laughter of apes provokes us to consider the possibility of an underlying complexity of cognition and intellect, to wonder about the existence of an ape mind.

The great apes – the three species commonly known as chimpanzees, bonobos, and gorillas in Africa, and orangutans in Southeast Asia – are special animals because they are so close to human.

[. . .]

The four nonhuman apes, our closest relatives, mirror our faces and bodies, our hands and fingers, our fingernails and fingerprints. They make and use tools, are capable of long-term planning and deliberate deception. They seem to share our perceptual world. They appear to express something very much like the human repertoire of emotions. They look into a mirror and act as if they recognize themselves as individuals, are manifestly capable of learning symbolic language, share with us several recognizable expressions and gestures – and they laugh in situations that might cause us to laugh too.

So people living in the Western tradition have recently come to accept, to a significant degree, a special bridge of kinship between apes and humans (or to understand that from the professional biologist's point of view humans are actually a fifth member of the ape group). Perhaps it is because of this recent cultural perception that Westerners are sometimes particularly surprised to learn that the three African apes – chimpanzees, bonobos, and gorillas – have long been a food source for many people living in Central Africa's Congo Basin (a largely forested region claimed by the nations of Cameroon, Central African Republic, Congo, Democratic Republic of Congo, Equatorial Guinea, and Gabon).

The fact, however, should surprise no one. Around the globe, people living in or on the edges of the world's great forests have traditionally taken the protein offered by wild animals: as true in Asia, Europe, and the Americas as it is in Africa. Moreover, the exploitation of wild forest animals for food is really no different from the widespread reliance on seafood, commonly accepted around the world.

But the African tropical forests are particularly rich in variety and have provided Central Africans with a very diverse wealth of game species – collectively known as *bushmeat* – consumed within a very complex milieu of traditions, tastes, habits, and cultural preferences and prohibitions. Some religious prohibitions (notably, the Muslim prohibition against eating primate meat) and a number of village or tribal traditions have kept apes off the menu in a scattered patchwork across the continent. [. . .]

And yet the very quality – human resemblance – that places apes on the prohibited list for some traditions actually lands them on the preferred list in others. Apes look like humans but possess a superhuman strength. The combination of human resemblance and superhuman strength may help explain why apes are, in some places, culturally valued as a food for ambitious men who would like to acquire the strength, and perhaps also the supposed virility, of an ape. [. . .]

These food preferences, based partly upon symbolic value, blend into the preferential logic expressed by symbolic medicine. Symbolic (or "fetish") medicine is a thriving business in the big cities of Central Africa; my own experience suggests that a person can rather easily locate ape parts in the city fetish markets. In Brazzaville, Congo's capital, I once looked over gorilla heads and hands. The hands, so the fetish dealer explained, are used especially by athletes who would like to be stronger. They boil pieces of the flesh until the water is all gone. Then they grind the remnants at the bottom of the pot down to a powder and press the powder into a cut in the skin, thus magically absorbing great strength from the great ape. Likewise, according to Mbongo George, an active commercial meat hunter in southeastern Cameroon, rubbing pulverized gorilla flesh into your back will cure a backache, and chimp bones tied to the hips of a pregnant young girl will ease the process of labor when her own hips are narrow.

Yes, there are many domestic alternatives to bushmeat in Central Africa, particularly in the urban areas. City markets offer domestic meat, both imported and home-grown – and indeed at least some of the bushmeat sold in the city markets is more expensive than some domestic meats. I am persuaded this is true for chimpanzee and elephant meat compared to beef and pork, at least, because I once asked an ordinary citizen in Cameroon's capital city of Yaoundé to buy – bargaining as he would in ordinary circumstances – equivalent-by-weight amounts of chimpanzee, elephant, beef, and pork. In that way, I acquired a strange collection of flesh in my hotel room (severed hand of chimp, slice of elephant trunk, cube of cow, etc.), which I weighed and otherwise compared, and concluded that city people were paying approximately twice as much for chimpanzee and elephant as for beef and pork. Why would anyone pay more for chimp and elephant? Taste is clearly an important but not the only factor in people's food preferences. Many Central Africans still prefer the taste of bushmeat, in all its prolific variety, but millions of recent urbanites also value bushmeat as a reminder of their cultural identity and roots in traditional villages.

In the rural areas where people are in many cases still living in a style close to traditional village life, the market cost hierarchy is reversed, with domestic meats more and bushmeat less expensive. For many rural Africans, then, bushmeat is also attractive simply because it's cheaper.

The standard dynamics of supply and demand mean that this pattern of consumption is about to hit a wall. While Africa is by far the most impoverished continent on the planet, it is also (and not coincidentally) the fastest growing. A natural rate of increase of 3.1 percent per year for Middle Africa indicates that human numbers are doubling every twenty-three years in this part of the world. If food consumption habits continue, in short, demand for bushmeat as a source of dietary protein will double in little more than two decades.

While the demand increases so rapidly, the supply is simply collapsing as a result of at least three factors. First, traditional hunting technologies are being replaced by ever more efficient modern ones, including wire snares, shotguns, and military hardware, and as a direct consequence animals across the Basin are being very efficiently *mined*, rather than *harvested*, out of the forests. Wire snares are particularly devastating because they kill indiscriminately; and, since snare lines are only periodically checked, they allow for considerable waste from rot. Wire snares tend to maim rather than kill bigger animals like the apes, but modern shotguns loaded with large-ball *chevrotine* cartridges enable many of today's hunters to target such larger and more dangerous species with impunity. Apes, who would have been unapproachably dangerous quarry for many (though certainly not all) hunters even a few years ago, are now attractive targets offering a very good deal in hunting economics: ratio of meat to cartridge.

Second, a $1 billion per year commercial logging industry, run primarily by European and Asian firms to supply 10 million cubic meters per year of construction, marine, and finish hardwoods primarily for the pleasure and benefit of European and Asian consumers, has during the last two decades cast a vast network of roads and tracks and trails into profoundly ancient and previously remote forests across the Congo Basin. Loggers degrade these forests, haul in large numbers of workers and families, and often hire hunters to supply the bushmeat to feed the workers and their dependents. Most seriously, though, for the first time in history (and the ecological history of these great forests takes us back to the era of the dinosaurs), the loggers' roads and tracks and trails allow hunters in and meat out. Vast areas of forest that even a decade ago were protected by their remoteness are no longer protected at all.

Third, as a result of the new hunting technologies and the new opportunity offered by all those roads and tracks and trails cut by the European and Asian loggers, a small army of African entrepreneurs has found new economic opportunity in the bushmeat trade, which has quite suddenly become efficient and utterly commercialized. Bushmeat is now big business. It is no longer merely feeding the people in small rural villages and other subsistence communities but instead reaching very deeply into the forests and then stretching very broadly out to the towns and big cities throughout Central Africa. In Gabon alone, the trade currently amounts to a $50 million per year exchange. Altogether, this commerce today draws out of Central Africa's Congo Basin forests an estimated and astonishing 5 million metric tons of animal meat per year. That amount is absolutely unsustainable. The depletion of the supply of wild animals and their meat is not even remotely balanced by the replenishment offered via natural reproduction in a stable ecosystem.

A generally accepted estimate holds that around 1 percent of the total bushmeat trade involves the meat of the great apes: chimpanzees, bonobos, and gorillas. A blind and drunk optimist might imagine that 1 percent of 5 million metric tons is a somewhat tolerable amount. It is not, of course. And even in the best of circumstances, where apes happen to inhabit legally protected forests (that is, national parks and reserves), a recent survey based on responses from professional fieldworkers tells us that chimpanzees are hunted in 50 percent of their protected areas, bonobos in 88 percent, and gorillas in 56 percent.

The impact of the current explosion in market hunting across the Congo Basin is threatening the existence of several wild animal species – but it disproportionately devastates the great apes. Biologists theoretically examining the sustainability of hunting consider, among other things, the ability of a species to replenish itself. A species with a quick rate of replenishment can likely, other factors being equal, withstand a high rate of depletion from hunting. Thinking about the impact hunting has on the survival of any particular species, in other words, requires us to examine that species' reproduction rates; and the great apes are unfortunately very slow reproducers. Perhaps because they are intelligent animals requiring extended periods of immature dependency while the young learn from their elders, apes wean late, reach independence and puberty late, and produce surprisingly few offspring. Altogether, the apes show about one quarter the reproduction rate of most other mammals.

Given such a slow reproduction rate, biologists calculate that chimpanzees and bonobos can theoretically withstand a loss of only about 2 percent of their numbers per year and still maintain a steady population. Gorillas may be able to tolerate losses of 4 percent per year. Monkeys have about the same low tolerance for loss, ranging from 1 to 4 percent, depending on the species. Ungulates, depending on the species, should be able to withstand yearly losses ranging most typically around 25 percent; and rodents can do just fine with losses from 13 percent to 80 percent per year, again depending on the species. In an ideal world, hunters would be equipped with pocket calculators to keep track on how sustainable their hunting is. In the real world, commercial hunters usually shoot whatever happens to wander in front of their guns. As a result, active hunting in a forest tends to deplete the fauna in a predictable progression. Apes and monkeys go first. Ungulates next. Rodents last. Indeed, it ought to be possible to measure the faunal disintegration of a forest by comparing the ratio of monkeys to rats sold in local markets.

[. . .]

Based on the "informed consensus of experts," the commercial hunting of apes for meat is "out of control and unsustainable," and it continues "to spread and accelerate" (Buytinksi 2001: 27). With the current levels and patterns of demand for apes as food, how long can they last?

One measure of how fast commercial hunting can reduce an ape population has been provided by the recent history of eastern Democratic Republic of Congo's Kahuzi-Biega National Park, supposedly protected as a UNESCO World Heritage Site but not protected well enough to keep out the professional hunters. In only three years during the last decade, hunters in Kahuzi-Biega earned a living by transforming into meat ("if our worst fears prove founded," so one investigator writes cautiously – Redmond 2001: 3) some 80 to 90 percent of the 17,000 individuals who until then comprised the subspecies *Gorilla gorilla grauerai*.

In sum, conserving biodiversity – saving the apes from extinction – amounts to one argument against using apes as a human food. A second argument has to do with public health. [. . .]

In fact, apes are susceptible to an enormous variety of diseases that will also infect humans, including bacterial meningitis, chicken pox, diphtheria, Epstein—Barr virus, hepatitis A and B, influenza, measles, mumps, pneumonia, rubella, smallpox, whooping cough, and so on. Far more serious, however, is the possible scenario of a person already infected with HIV 1 or HIV 2 coming into intimate contact (through butchering, for instance) with one of several related viruses, the several SIVs endemic among several monkey species, thereby producing a successful cross, a recombinant virus that could become HIV 3. The government of Cameroon recently sponsored an extended study on primate viruses where researchers tested the blood of 788 monkeys kept as pets or sold as meat and discovered that around one-fifth of those samples were infected with numerous varieties of SIV, including five previously unknown types. So the potential for new epidemics based on recombinants should be taken very seriously.

The public health threat is not, of course, limited to Central Africa. Rather, it is a global threat that still tends to be vastly underappreciated by those in the West who are most capable of doing something about it – even as the threat grows with ever-expanding human numbers, international migration, and commerce. In the year 2003, for example, an estimated 11,600 tons of bushment (from antelopes, camels, monkeys, snails, snakes, as well as chimpanzees and gorillas) was illegally smuggled into Great Britain.

The final argument against apes as food is perhaps the one many people think of first but often have trouble describing fully or convincingly, and that is the ethical one: the special case against eating the animal who laughs. Many ethical vegetarians refuse to eat animals capable of suffering, thus drawing a distinction between plants and, at least, vertebrate animals, while possibly giving some invertebrates the benefit of the doubt. Indeed, I believe that most thoughtful people maintain an examined or unexamined hierarchy of value in their vision of the natural world that includes distinctions within the vertebrates – recognizing humans, for example, as among the most complex of the vertebrates with the most compelling capacity for suffering, a perception that possibly accounts for our common and particular horror at the idea of nutritional cannibalism. To the degree that we now see humans as surprisingly closely related to apes, or as belonging taxonomically within the larger group of apes, that makes eating the laughing animal also worthy of our special concern.

References

Buytinski, Tom (2001) "Africa's Great Apes," in Benjamin B. Beck, Tara S. Stoinksi, Michael Hutchins, Terry L. Maple, Bryan Norton, Andrew Rowan, Elizabeth F. Stevens, and Arnold Arluke (eds), Great Apes: The Ethics of Coexistence, Washington, D.C.: Smithsonian Institution Press, pp. 3–56.

Redmond, Ian (2001) Coltan Boom, Gorilla Bust: The Impact of Coltan Mining on Gorillas and Other Wildlife in Eastern D. R. Congo. Private report sponsored by the Dian Fossey Gorilla Fund and the Born Free Foundation.

FURTHER READING

Bader, H.R. and Finstad, G. (2001) "Conflicts between livestock and wildlife: An analysis of legal liabilities arising from reindeer and caribou competition on the Seward Peninsula of western Alaska," *Environmental Law* 31(3): 549–580.

Cohn, Priscilla (ed.) (1999) *Ethics and Wildlife*, Lewiston, New York: Edwin Mellen Press.

Conover, Michael (2002) *Resolving Human–Wildlife Conflicts*, Lewis Publishers (A CRC Company) Boca Raton, FL: CRC Press.

Curnutt, J. (1996) "How to argue for and against sport hunting," *Journal of Social Philosophy* 27(2): 65–89.

Curtis, John A. (2002) "Ethics in wildlife management: What price?" *Environmental Values* 11: 145–61.

Everett, Jennifer (2001) "Environmental ethics, animal welfarism, and the problem of predation: A Bambi lover's respect for nature," *Ethics & The Environment* 6(1): 42–66.

Francione, Gary L. (1999) "Wildlife and animal rights," Chapter II (pp. 65–81). In: *Ethics and Wildlife*, Priscilla Cohn (ed.), Lewiston, NY: The Edwin Mellen Press.

Houston, P. (1995) *Women on Hunting*, Ecco Press, Hopewell, New Jersey.

Kerasote, T. (1993) *Bloodties: Nature, Culture, and the Hunt*, Kodansha, New York.

Leopold, A. (1966) *A Sand County Almanac with Essays from Round River*, Oxford: Oxford University Press.

List, C.J. (1997) "Is hunting a right thing?" *Environmental Ethics* 19: 405–416.

Lombard, A.T., Johnson, C.F., Cowling, R.M., and Pressey, R.L. (2001) "Protecting plants from elephants: Botanical reserve scenarios within the Addo Elephant National Park, South Africa," *Biological Conservation* 102 (no. ER2): 191–203

Luke, B. (1997) "A critical analysis of hunters' ethics," *Environmental Ethics* 19: 25–44.

Michelfelder. (2003) "Valuing wildlife populations in urban environments," *Journal of Social Philosophy* 34: 79–90.

Moriarty, P.V. and Woods, M. (1997) "Hunting =/= Predation," *Environmental Ethics* 19: 391–404.

Palmer, C. (2003) "Placing animals in urban environmental ethics," *Journal of Social Philosophy* 34: 64–78.

Sagoff, Mark (1999) *What's Wrong with Exotic Species?*, Institute for Philosophy and Public Policy. www.puaf.umd.edu//IPPP/fall1999/exotic_species.htm. Defends non-native species.

Scruton, Roger (1997) "From a view to a death: Culture, nature and the huntsman's art," *Environmental Values* 6(4): 471–82.

Shafer, Craig L. (2000) "The northern Yellowstone elk debate: Policy, hypothesis, and implications," *Natural Areas Journal* 20(4): 342–359.

Shah, N.J. (2000) "Eradication of alien predators in the Seychelles: An example of conservation action on tropical islands," *Biodiversity and Conservation* 10(7): 1219–1220.

Stearns, Beverly Peterson and Stearns, Stephen C. (1999) *Watching from the Edge of Extinction*, New Haven, CT: Yale University Press.

STUDY QUESTIONS

1 Do you agree with Callicott that utilitarian and theocentric sources of inherent values for wildlife are outmoded? How would you support or contest these two as sources of inherent value?

2 Give two conditions under which you believe that sport hunting might be morally acceptable and two conditions where you believe it might not. Give your reasoning.

3 Do you agree with Gunn's assertion that trophy hunting is justified in Zimbabwe under the conditions he describes? Give your reasoning.

4 Based on Hettinger's discussion, do you agree with the notion of opposing exotic species, including those that are naturally dispersing and nondamaging? Explain your perspective.

5 What is your response to the tension between the role of bushmeat among some subsistence communities and the severe impact hunting has on some primate populations. Is it feasible for both concerns to be addressed? If so, how might that be approached?

Zoos and aquariums

INTRODUCTION TO PART EIGHT

I N THIS PART, the authors address some of the important moral issues associated with the long history of use of animals for purposes of human entertainment. In particular, there is a focus on zoos (Regan, Hutchins *et al.*, Lindburg, Wemmer) and marine mammal aquaria (Eaton), with references to a few others.

Randall L. Eaton finds that animals in aquaria often are not well cared for and that the aquaria themselves are often under poor management. Ralph Acampora finds that zoos have a decided analogy to pornography and should be replaced by more respectful forms of human–nonhuman spectatorship and relationship. Dale Jamieson assesses both the strengths and weaknesses of zoos, and makes the argument that the overall balance is tipped against zoos. Michael Hutchins *et al.* and Donald G. Lindburg note that the entertainment value of zoos for the public is just one part of a larger set of values, including the scientific research conducted by zoos to gain greater knowledge of nature that is essential to wildlife conservation, particularly to endangered species management. Zoo animals are important as ambassadors for their species, securing public support for wildlife and their habitats. Zoos also help educate the public about wildlife and help generate greater public interest in and support for wildlife conservation. Chris Wemmer goes on to assess the responsibilities and directions of zoos and aquariums in light of the global diversity crisis, and calls for a greater emphasis among zoo professionals on science and conservation efforts.

Chapter 64

Randall L. Eaton

ORCAS AND DOLPHINS IN CAPTIVITY

Eaton assesses public aquariums and finds them often affected by poor management, lack of imagination and creativity, politics, lack of openness to scientific research, waste, and inefficiency, among other problems. He provides a number of suggestions on how these aquaria can improve their care of marine mammals.

THE EXHIBITION OF delphinids in captivity has done more to raise concern for cetaceans than everything else put together. [. . .] There are millions upon millions of people in North America, Europe, Japan, South Africa and Australia who visit aquariums and become turned on by dolphins and orcas.

[. . .]

More people in North America go to zoos and aquariums than take in all the college and professional athletic events combined. That says much of importance about man's desire to recover his soul. The animal is central to man's psyche, his origins, and his affections; thus, the zoo is much more than anyone has ever conceived. It is where we humans reconnect with our earthly kin, and where we share the common lament for another time and place. We visit the zoo to be inspired by the beauty, intelligence and wonder of nature. We also go there to know why we feel wistful about being caged with the animals in civilization, which, try as we may to deny it, is destroying us. The caged animal tells us that there is something fundamentally wrong with the way we and they live. So in this virtually religious homage that hundreds of millions of people annually make to the zoo the animal is not only an ambassador of good will for his still wild brethren, he speaks for their dubious condition, for ours, and also for the communal fact of all life.

Aquariums are significantly different than zoos for two reasons: a) the human's perception of the aquatic environment; and b) the nature of the creatures in the aquariums and what, as a consequence, they communicate to humans. When we humans, who are adapted by evolution and culture to live on land visit an aquarium, we perceive it to be a sizable body of water, what might constitute a very large swimming pool for us. If we saw two orca-sized land animals, say elephants, confined to an area the size of a typical aquarium pool used by orcas we might think that these behemoths have very little space. And if we had seen elephants in the wild or read that they often move over hundreds or thousands of square miles in a year then we would certainly wonder how extreme confinement might influence their behavior and needs. [. . .] Any reasonably thoughtful or empathetic person could easily wonder about a lot of the undesirable circumstances for elephants at the zoo, but few aquarium visitors ever see dolphins or orcas exhibiting what is the equivalent of pacing in a zoo animal.

An orca is adapted to move through huge expanses of water on a regular basis. Like elephants they have immense social tendencies and needs, as much, from all indications, as humans. In degree, each of these species has had to cope with the basic problems of all complex societies—finding food, cooperative foraging, protection of infants against predators, competition for limiting resources, balancing conflicts of interest, which exist for societies based on kinship, competition among polygamous males for females and the specter of violent warfare, and so on. An orca spends incredible portions of time and energy to locate, assess and capture food, and to do so they visit different environments which present different kinds of obstacles and demand variable strategies and solutions. Their feeding space is not only more variable in terms of factors like cover, prey species, and the like, it is three-dimensional, fluid and often dark, demanding the use of systematically more complex perceptual and communication faculties.

Contrast what altogether constitutes the most complicated niche occupied by any organism in the world with its life in what is for it something less than a bathtub. Compare living in a society of a hundred dolphins of every sex and age coordinating its cooperative feeding, defense, child-rearing, government, mating life and health in a dynamic, fluid ocean with living in a round, shallow tank with the company of three or four dolphins with nothing to do but make humans happy by repeating the same thing over and over, day in and day out, year after year. No catching of fish, no swimming at top speed or cavorting or playing at will through unlimited aquatic space, no diving deep or harassing sea lions or taking human children for tows in friendly harbors, no interaction with other groups of your kind, no cooperative anti-predator tactics, just the same old, easy-to-master job of jumping together through hoops for the enjoyment of enthusiastic onlookers. For the most curious, exploratory, mobile, playful creature on the planet, an aquarium must be very boring indeed.

All the evidence says so. Poor even by zoo standards, the dolphins and orcas have miserable records in captivity: lousy breeding success; much shorter life than in the wild; and, poor health in captivity—a lot of "brain disease." The stress engendered by boredom and lack of emotional needs being met should be nothing foreign to human consciousness in this day and age. [. . .]

That elephants don't attack humans far more often is actually a credit to their intelligence, and I mean that literally, besides which it should be mentioned that they are among the very large-brained creatures, right behind the toothed whales and man. That orcas don't attack humans in captivity is all the more remarkable considering their even greater ability to do so, their predatory nature, and their comparatively worse condition.

In 1979, we conducted a survey of the world's aquariums and learned that most aquariums had no more than a single orca. Here we have a large delphinid, with a tremendous repertoire of social expressions and, by inference, needs, being deprived of any social life save that with humans. Many aquariums do not let their personnel enter the water with orcas, which must make matters all the worse for the orcas, who, like the dolphins, seem to do their utmost to interact with humans as social surrogates. I wasn't surprised a few years ago when the male orca in San Diego's Sea World aquarium grabbed hold of the young woman's leg as she was trying to leave the pool after having made a commercial. She had been swimming with the orca for several minutes, and when she started to leave, he placed his jaws over her thigh. When she struggled, he wounded her. Flesh wounds only, the woman required stitches to mend. That the orca wanted her to stay and play with him seems likely; that he wanted to bite and hurt her seems unlikely. After all, had he intended to harm her, she would have had her leg snapped off, or worse. If anything he bit her very lightly; by orca standards, his may have been a love bite, intended perhaps to communicate affection.

Under captive conditions where dolphins are greatly loved, respected and admired, humans relate to them as persons, and enter the water to swim and play with them. In such circumstances the relationship between dolphins and humans is nothing less than beautiful and awe-inspiring, if not entirely incredible. There the humans have no doubt about the fact that they are dealing with creatures very like humans in some ways. And, I think it must be quite natural in these situations for deep, intimate affection to emerge between species, as has been described to me by experts with first-hand knowledge.

[. . .]

Orcas have survived about ten years on average in aquariums, no matter how old they are when captured. For reasons I discuss elsewhere, we know that one orca died in the wild at an age of at least 140 years, then by accident. Some estimates run 70 years for males, 100 for females in the wild. That they succumb to disease is not definite. Despite their authoritarian utterings, cetacean medicine men don't know much about whales or their maladies. Disease may result from stress, boredom and loneliness. (One must keep in mind that aquariums are not eager to retain marine mammal veterinarians who point to the conditions of captive life as the cause of whale disease, poor breeding and short life. Neither would most of these specialists want to admit it publicly.)

Breeding success is an indicator of how well a species tolerates captivity. In all the aquariums in all the years that sexually mature pairs of orcas have resided, only four births occurred before 1986, three of these to the same parents, all dead within a month.

[. . .]

Many public zoos and aquariums suffer from everything that any public facility does—poor management, lack of imagination and creativity, the horrible influence of politics, lack of spirit among employees, and all the rest of it, including waste and inefficiency. On the other hand are the majority of private zoos and aquariums which, despite claims and appearances to the contrary, are after profits. I say this knowing quite well that there are exemplary exceptions on both sides of the coin. Private aquariums may not be expected to sacrifice profits except for the sake of public relations. Their much publicized research programs or financial assistance to projects outside the aquarium itself are geared toward promotion, which is profitable for them, or for knowledge which may help protect their sizeable investment in expensive, hard to acquire animals such as orcas.

Fortunately, I also took considerable effort to communicate [. . .] how [. . .] to improve conditions for orcas, add to their longevity in captivity, propagate them successfully and curtail disease. I emphasized why all this would be profitable. At the time I was in the midst of orca studies in Puget Sound which had been associated with tremendous public disapproval of capturing orcas and placing them in captivity, and I argued that before long it might be impossible to capture additional orcas for aquariums, in which case, their big money maker would be lost, and their profits would plummet accordingly. Even if they could capture orcas in other places than Puget Sound, which they did for a while in Iceland after Puget Sound was declared off limits to them, they had to see the writing on the wall. Sooner or later the public would demand that all orcas, possibly all dolphins, be left in the sea. (I predict that this will happen unless we ruin the seas.)

I meticulously outlined the social needs of orcas—keeping a group of at least two males and three or four females from wild-living pods. Animals from the same region are already socialized to one another and most apt to interact well in captivity, and if adults, already could have bred. Such a group would provide each orca with "social security," fulfillment of social needs. And they would have to be kept in a pool or series of pools much larger than anything yet constructed in the world, though I urged them to consider developing a naturalistic aquarium.

It would be cheap to net off a bay or cove compared to building a concrete pool with all its expensive support facilities which include filtering systems, and such a setting would offer many of the sources of stimulation normally encountered by orcas in the wild, but not in captivity. Fish would swim into the cove or could be released there for orcas to catch their own food, or some of it anyway. Many tourists could be accommodated at numerous locales in easy access to major cities or travel routes on the east or west coast. Orcas would not have to perform for their dinner, and I am confident that the paying visitors would find a naturalistic situation more rewarding. Imagine walking on a floating boardwalk over a large cove by the sea watching a group of orcas with their young behaving naturally, compared with seeing an orca leap out of a small pool surrounded by concrete.

People prefer driving through a naturalistic wildlife park rather than seeing the same animals in a zoo because of the reversal of the role of animal and human. [. . .] Likewise, people would relish a sense of non-obtrusive intimacy with seemingly free, untamed orcas. No doubt the orcas would befriend people, but no matter how they would interact with human onlookers, the sight and sound of orcas themselves would be highly profitable. Why a counterpart to a drive-through wildlife park does not exist among seaquariums is a mystery; one with orcas, dolphins, and other sea mammals would be a gold mine.

[. . .]

In 1985 an orca was born. Able to feed from its mother in the largest aquarium in the world, it was the first to survive in captivity. Months later, the TV program 20–20 aired the events including the coaching by human wetnurses, the actual birth and the infant's behavior. [. . .] With proper care and wise management, that baby orca may become an ambassador for the orca nation, and more. Hopefully, its birth indicates the cessation of orca captures on the one hand, and the building of an intimate bridge between them and us on the other. Orcas are the world's leading attraction, and she became the most popular of orcas.

I wish [aquariums] would feed the orcas live fish so as to let them exercise in the proper manner as predators, a level of stimulation they may need. When we meet the natural needs of orcas we not only improve their health, we also make them more interesting to the public. From a research point of view, observations of orcas using communication to catch fish would be illuminating.

Imagine what the consequences would be if someone began to talk to an orca? What if, for example the orca said it wanted to return to the sea, to be free? That could be the end of profits, which brings us full circle back to the problem of self-interests: if the salvation of wild orcas, dolphins and other whales, possibly even the sea, were enhanced by deciphering orcanese, and humans could talk to them, the profiteers would perceive such a revolutionary breakthrough as a threat to their wealth. Profits and enlightenment don't mix when the latter must be given up for the former.

[. . .]

[John] Lilly and I agree on the short-sightedness of commercial aquariums regarding openness to scientific research. They fear poor publicity that could result from public knowledge of the abominable conditions and care received by most cetaceans in captivity. Basically the same could be said of most commercial zoos. Overall, scientists could immeasurably improve aquarium conditions and operations in ways beneficial to the commercial interests of the aquariums, the visitors and the whales. Zoo standards have improved dramatically in the past twenty years due to a combination of increasing public interest in animal life and welfare, and increasing behavioral research in zoos.

My experience in aquariums indicated that the major obstacle is ignorance of the behavioral adaptations and needs of captive cetaceans, and too great an emphasis and trust in veterinary medicine, which, being so ignorant of cetacean biology and behavior, may kill more creatures than it aids. The real progress made in the health and medical treatment of wild animals in captivity has not come through advances in the traditional veterinary sciences such as anatomy, physiology or treatment but in behavioral understanding, which includes nutrition. I made these same criticisms of zoos, and though that meant ostracism by some of the old guard zoo directors, time has proved me right: the leading wild animal medicine specialists would agree that prevention of disease from accommodating behavioral needs of organisms has meant the most progress in zoos, and the same is possible for aquariums if they or the public expect the much needed improvements.

Chapter 65

Ralph Acampora

ZOOS AND EYES: CONTESTING CAPTIVITY AND SEEKING SUCCESSOR PRACTICES

Acampora argues that zoos are similar to the phenomenon of pornography. He points out that zoos make the nature of their subjects disappear by overexposing them and asserts that the animals are degraded or marginalized through the marketing and consumption of their visibility. He criticizes the presumption of preservation and argues that zoos be phased out in favor of richer and less oppressive modes of encountering other forms of life. He explores and assesses some alternative approaches to nonhuman animal spectatorship and cross-species relationship.

THROUGHOUT ITS PAST, the zoo has demonstrated a relational dynamic of mastery. Originally, in its days as a private garden, the zoo was a powerful symbol of dominion: It projected an imperial image of man-the-monarch—ruler of nature, lord of the wild. Eventually, the zoo was converted into a public menagerie and became a ritual of entertainment, projecting almost trickster imagery of man-the-magician—tamer of brutes, conjurer of captives. The contemporary zoo has become a scientific park and aesthetic site. Its meaning is redemptive; it stands as an emblem of conservation policy, projecting a religious image of man-the-messiah—the new Noah: savior of species, the beasts' benign despot. From empire to circus to museum or ark, the zoo has been organized according to anthropocentrist and, arguably, androcentrist hierarchies and designs (Mullan & Marvin, 1987).

Historically marked by patterns of paternalism and traces of patriarchy, zoological institutions now are justified by appeal to their allegedly saving graces. Zoos are legitimized as havens of wildlife protection, vessels for the rescue of a nonhuman animal kingdom under attack by industrial civilization. Following Berger (1977), I argue that this self-promotion is an ideology caught in contradiction—for the very exposition established by zoos erases the most manifestly "natural" traits of what once were wild beings, namely, their capacities either to elude or engage others freely. Such an erasure occurs even if one eschews a classical doctrine of natural kinds.

The modern zoo

My argument depends not on immutable essences of species as such but on received meanings of wildness for any animal at all. The modern zoo promises its visitors a brush with the wild, and the premium of this entertainment value is evident in the current effort increasingly to display animals in mock-ups of their natural habitats. However, sheer placement in a recreated habitat cannot provide the experience that zoo visitors seek. For the experience to approximate an encounter in the wild—as an experience of the "wildness" of the animal—the visitor must have some purchase in a transactional relationship with the animals' acting normally in their regular environment and with the spectator engaged in some way as a participant. However, as one might easily recognize, the behavior of animals not in captivity generally does not include close relationships with human beings. This is true not only because of fear the animal might experience but also because of lack of interest, nocturnal patterns of activity, territorial range, and mode of locomotion. The activities of animals in their natural habitats are not organized in terms of human conveniences. Yet, it is precisely animals as they would be if the spectator were not there that is the object of visive interest and desire. Thus, the zoo's exhibitionism extinguishes for us the existential reality of its animal presentations even as it proclaims to preserve their biological existence.

Even the astute zoo apologist Hahn (1967) admits, "the wild animal in conditions of captivity . . . is bound to alter in nature and cease being the creature we want to see" (p. 16). The situation, however, involves more than just making animals ill at ease or failing to replicate the conditions for them to behave as they would were they actually in their respective, natural environments. The very structure of the human-animal encounter is disrupted, and the interaction that is sought—encountering the animals—becomes impossibility as the "real" animals disappear and the conditions for seeing are undermined. Not only can we as spectators not truly see the animals; but we cannot be seen by them. We are just as invisible—at least in terms of being encountered and approached as the animals we are—as the animals we expect to see (but cannot find) in the zoo.

Berger (1977) elaborates this irony thus: Despite the ostensible purpose of the place, ". . . nowhere in a zoo can a stranger encounter the look of an animal. At most the animal's gaze flickers and passes on. They look sideways. They look blindly beyond. They scan mechanically" (p. 26). Hence "the zoo to which people go to meet animals, to observe them, to see them, is, in fact, a monument to the impossibility of such encounters" (Berger, p. 19).[1] In this respect then, insofar as it effectively forces its show-items into an overexposure that degrades their real nature, the zoo can be seen to partake in the paradoxical form of pornography defined as visive violence. Ordinarily, this form of pornography obviously is not about sex; much as feminist analyses of human pornography have detailed, however, it does engage a destructive desire in relation to the object of inspection. [. . .]

The zoo and pornography analogy

[. . .]

A useful comparison and persuasive justifications

The broad analogy between zoos and pornography is useful because, if it holds true in the relevant respects (as I argue it does), the comparison casts a new and decidedly critical light on the debate over keeping and breeding animals in the wild in captivity (as well as shifting the balance of concern to include effects on human spectators). As an illustration, consider the controversy over pornography. There are several conceivable defenses of the institution, but imagine for a moment an apologist's taking the position that we should permit—indeed promote—the practice because it excites or inspires us (particularly the young) to esteem the subjects displayed, because it "educates" us to look out for the welfare of those so exposed. [. . .]

The centerfold, in other words, would be seen as an icon of sympathy or respect!

Yet few of us, even among those who wish to defend pornography, find such justifications persuasive. Why is it that a similar form of reasoning is accepted readily in the case of zoological exhibition? One explanation might be that zoos instruct their visitors about biology and ecology. But this alleged difference does not hold up under scrutiny. There are tough questions that such a defender would need to answer. Shepard (1996) writes, "The zoo presents itself as a place of education. But to what end? To give people a respect for wildness, a sense of human limitations and of biological community, a world of mutual dependency?" (p. 233).

Certainly not, we must reply, for there is strong evidence that zoos teach poorly or, worse, leave their visitors to formulate distorted and even quite detrimental impressions of animals and their relationships to human beings. One environmental researcher found, "zoo-goers [are] much less knowledgeable about animals than backpackers, hunters, fishermen, and others who claim an interest in animals, and only slightly more knowledgeable than those who claim no interest in animals at all" (Kellert, 1979). Nearly 20 years later, his verdict still is dismal: "[T]he typical visitor appears only marginally more appreciative, better informed, or engaged in the natural world following the experience"; in effective response to Shepard's question, Kellert (1997) finds that "many visitors leave the zoo more convinced than ever of human superiority over the natural world" (p. 99).

Message and mission

Why do zoos fail to educate? Several unsurprising reasons are apparent: The public is largely indifferent to zoo education efforts (few stop even to look at, let alone read, explanatory placards); animals are viewed briefly and in rapid succession; and people tend to concentrate on so-called babies and beggars—their cute countenances and funny antics capture audience attention (Ludwig, 1981). People come to zoos with an expectation of entertainment, not education. For the viewing public, amusement is at the heart of what a zoo is (scientific ideologies of self-promotion notwithstanding).

Consequently, and insidiously, what visits to the zoo instruct and reinforce over and over again is the not-so-subliminal message that nonhuman animals exist, at least in their placement in the zoo, specifically to entertain us humans. Even when, during our deluded moments of enlightenment, we insist they are present to edify—even then their presence still essentially is managed around a human viewing audience. That is to say, even in the less common moments in which we approach the zoological display for educational purposes, the very structure of that encounter is organized in accordance with human interests and the demands that follow from how humans are able best to inspect, observe, witness, and scrutinize their objects of investigation.

The educational mission of the zoo requires that humans encounter animate beings other than their fellow humans. It promises the cultivation of an appreciation for other forms of life. The phenomenological grammar of their appearance, however, diminishes the manifestation of otherness (autopoietic activity at variance with a given identity). This is what it means to put, and keep, a live body on display: A structural inauthenticity is engendered that remains despite even the best intentions of humanitarian or ecological pedagogy.

If this description sounds too pornographic, perhaps we can purge the association by discovering the relevant disanalogy elsewhere. Undoubtedly, it will appear to some that the similarity I allege is strained because of the obvious difference in attraction. We might call this a difference between *erotic* and *biotic* entertainment. Indeed, I do not suggest that the average zoo visitor is motivated by sexual attraction to the animal inhabitants, but I am suggesting that there is a certain economy of desire operative that has structural similarities in these cases. The aesthetics of the zoo are not, I believe, far removed from that of pornography. We find in both cases fetishes of the exotic, underlying fear of nature, fantasies of illicit or impossible encounter, and a powerful presumption of mastery and control (Griffin, 1981). Given these similarities, I do not think it at all unbelievable to claim that zoo inhabitants and porn participants are very much alike in this respect: They are visual objects whose meaning is shaped predominantly by the perversions of a patriarchal gaze (Adams, 1994, pp. 23–84).[2] [. . .]

Reconstruction: toward transformation of animal encounter

[. . .]

Possible reforms and changes

Is the zoo really beyond rehabilitation? Can no reforms provide opportunities that would be genuinely educational and fulfill the need described above? [. . .]

To open the possibility for genuine encounters with animal others, it is necessary first to strip the zoo of its exoticism. The Belize Tropical Education Center keeps only native animals and usually only those who have been injured or orphaned (Coc, Marsh, & Platt, 1998, p. 389). A second step would involve abridgment or abandonment of the notion and practice of keeping. At Phillip Island on the south-east edge of Australia's mainland, a site has been established for the protection and viewing of Blue (Fairy) penguins who retain access both to the sea and their regular roosting burrows. In this case, it is the viewers who are corralled and whose actions and activities are regulated and restricted (no flash photography, no eating or drinking, little sonic interference, and presence only within the perimeter established by the wildlife center). [. . .]

Comparisons and contrasts

[. . .]

The ecotourist encounter of the kind described above also rests upon an element of chance: The penguins simply might not return to the beach on a particular day, the weather might be inhospitable for human viewing. The organization of interests, again, is driven largely by accommodating the needs of the animals. [. . .]

To achieve a situation more favorable to [. . .] human desires would undermine precisely the interests and activities of the animals. The animals prefer dusk so as to elude preying animals who might be close to the shore. Their concern is to locate their young in the nests in the rocks to feed them the fish they have caught during their day out at sea. They locate their young by making distinctive cries and barks and listen for a reply. Noise from human voices and mechanical vehicles interferes with this process and creates a hostile environment, and so it is strictly monitored.

Again, the very organization of these sighting opportunities establishes a set of relationships in which the interest in genuinely understanding something about the animal not only is possible but also desirable. Even those who come only to see the penguins cannot help learning something about their natural habitat and their patterns of relations with each other and other nonhuman animals in their ordinary lives. One cannot help becoming better educated, even when one is disappointed by the perceived quality of the spectacle. It seems to me that whatever else one may say about such ecotourism one of its cardinal virtues is that it allows the animals to engage in, or break off, any encounter with human visitors. Observance of this elemental kind of "etiquette" (Weston, 1994) marks a distinctive departure from the patterns of pornography and carcerality I have criticized above.

Transforming zoöscopic practices

Yet, this is not all that needs to be changed. I wish to investigate further the possibilities for transforming zoöscopic practices by examining and weighing relevant phenomenologies and hermeneutics of vision as set forth by provocative and productive thinkers such as Frye (1983) and Lingis (1983). The first of these, a theorist of feminist critique, should help us to recapitulate my diagnosis and then aid in characterizing alternatives. Frye speaks of "arrogant eyes which organize everything seen with reference to themselves and their own interests" (p. 67); she has in mind the controlling gaze of patriarchy and its effects on women, but her analysis in several respects is quite capable of extrapolation to the gaze of anthropocentrism and its effects on nonhuman animals. [. . .]

A salient alternative

If this is a sort of spectatorship to be avoided, what might a kind to be fostered literally look like? Frye (1983) calls a salient alternative, "the loving eye." Negative descriptions give us some idea of what she means when she writes, "the loving perceiver can see without the presupposition that the other poses a constant threat or that the other exists for the seer's service," [. . .]. Frye's positive characterization is open-ended; for her, the loving eye lavishes a creative type of attention since "[i]t knows the complexity of the other as something which will forever present new things to be known" (p. 76).[3] [. . .]

Conclusion

[. . .] Distinct from erotogenic or romantic models of fusion, the loving eye—as Frye (1983) portrays it—maintains the distance of vision itself. One who employs it does not dissolve into the other: "There are boundaries between them [seer and seen]; she and the other are two; their interests are not identical; they are not blended in vital parasitic or symbiotic relations" (p. 75). Elsewhere, I have underscored the ethical significance of a jointly held form of bodily consciousness called "symphysis" (Acampora, 1995); here we see a complementary apprehension of separation, which is necessary to engage periodically so as to keep in play an ontological and moral dialectic of difference and similarity. In Frye's (1983) words, ". . . it is a matter of being able to tell one's own interests from those of others and of knowing where one's self leaves off and another begins" (p. 75).

This power of discrimination is a necessary condition for relationships to be conducted along an axis of optimal freedom, whereby the spell of captivity cast by the arrogant eye is broken and encounter becomes volitional rather than compulsory. The advantage of such a transformation is palpable: "It is one mark of a voluntary association that the one person can survive displeasing the other, defying the other, dissociating from the other" (Frye, p. 73). All too often, of course, just the opposite holds in the lives (and deaths) of zoo and circus animals, companion and working animals, and even wildlife who get too, "in the face of" civilization.

Thus, changing over from the vision of arrogance to that of love could produce remarkably beneficial results not only for interpersonal but also for interspecies relationships. Finally, in the twilight of the zoo, it will be up to biologists, animal advocates, and concerned citizens to look ahead with new eyes, devise novel and better modes of cross-species encounter, and see them through to implementation and inevitable revision.

Notes

1   Here, possible parallels with gender analyses of the pornographic may be intimated poignantly by substituting "strip-bar . . . men . . . women" for "zoo . . . people . . . animals" (Kappeler, 1986, p. 75).
2   For more on this connection, see the discussion below on the "arrogant eye."
3   Cf. Yi-Fu Tuan's conception of love in *Dominance and affection: The making of pets*, p. x.

References

Acampora, R. (1995, Winter/Spring). The problematic situation of post-humanism and the task of recreating a symphysical ethos. *Between the Species: A Journal of Ethics*, 11 (1–2), 25–32.
Adams, C. (1994). *Neither man nor beast: Feminism and the defense of animals*. New York: Continuum.

Berger, J. (1977). Why look at animals? In J. Berger (Ed.), *About looking* (pp. 1–26). New York: Pantheon, (1980).

Coc, R., Marsh, L., & Platt, E. (1998). The Belize zoo: Grassroots efforts in education and outreach. In R. B. Primack, D. B. Bray, H. A. Galletti, & I. Ponciano (Eds.), *Timber, tourists, and temples: Conservation and development in the Maya forest of Belize, Guatemala, and Mexico* (pp. 389–395). Washington, DC: Island Press.

Frye, M. (1983). In and out of harm's way. In M. Frye (Ed.), *The Politics of Reality* (pp. 52–83). Trumanburg, NY: Crossing Press.

Hahn, E. (1967). *Animal gardens*. Garden City: Doubleday.

Kellert, S. (1979). Zoological parks in American society. Address given at the meeting of American Association of Zoological Parks and Aquaria, St. Louis, MO.

—— (1997). *Kinship to mastery: Biophilia in human evolution and development*. Washington, DC: Island Press.

Ludwig, E. G. (1981). People at zoos: A sociological approach. *International Journal for the Study of Animal Problems*, 2 (6), 310–316.

Mullan Robert and Garry Marvin (1987) *Zoo Culture* London: Weidenfeld & Nicolson.

Shepard, P. (1996). *The others: How animals made us human*. Washington, DC: Island Press.

Weston, A. (1994). *Back to Nature: Tomorrow's Environmentalism*. Philadelphia: Temple University Press.

Chapter 66

Dale Jamieson

AGAINST ZOOS

Jamieson reviews a number of the arguments for and against zoos. He points out that while there are a number of arguments made in favor of zoos such as preservation, research, amusement, and education, these often are not compatible interests and thus only some benefits can occur in any one zoo. Further he addresses the moral problems of keeping wild animals in captivity, the detrimental impacts of captivity, and the implicit message of a false sense of the human place in the natural order.

W E C A N S T A R T with a rough-and-ready definition of zoos: they are public parks which display animals, primarily for the purposes of recreation or education. Although large collections of animals were maintained in antiquity, they were not zoos in this sense. Typically these ancient collections were not exhibited in public parks, or they were maintained for purposes other than recreation or education.

[. . .]

Today in the United States alone there are hundreds of zoos, and they are visited by millions of people every year. They range from roadside menageries run by hucksters, to elaborate zoological parks staffed by trained scientists.

[. . .]

Animals and liberty

Before we consider the reasons that are usually given for the survival of zoos, we should see that there is a moral presumption against keeping wild animals in captivity. What this involves, after all, is taking animals out of their native habitats, transporting them great distances, and keeping them in alien environments in which their liberty is severely restricted. It is surely true that in being taken from the wild and confined in zoos, animals are deprived of a great many goods. For the most part they are prevented from gathering their own food, developing their own social orders, and generally behaving in ways that are natural to them. These activities all require significantly more liberty than most animals are permitted in zoos. If we are justified in keeping animals in zoos, it must be because there are some important benefits that can be obtained only by doing so.

Against this it might be said that most mammals and birds added to zoo collections in recent years are captive-bred. Since these animals have never known freedom, it might be claimed that they are denied nothing by captivity. But this argument is far from compelling. A chained puppy prevented from playing or a restrained bird not allowed to fly still have interests in engaging in these activities. Imagine this argument applied to humans. It would be absurd to suggest that those who are born into slavery have no interest in freedom since they have never experienced it. Indeed, we might think that the tragedy of captivity is all the greater for those creatures who have never known liberty.

The idea that there is a presumption against keeping wild animals in captivity is not the property of some particular moral theory; it follows from most reasonable moral theories. Either we have duties to animals or we do not. If we do have duties to animals, surely they include respecting those interests which are most important to them, so long as this does not conflict with other, more stringent duties that we may have. Since an interest in liberty is central for most animals, it follows that if everything else is equal, we should respect this interest.

[. . .]

Arguments for zoos

What might [. . .] important benefits be? Four are commonly cited: amusement, education, opportunities for scientific research, and help in preserving species.

Amusement was certainly an important reason for the establishment of the early zoos, and it remains an important function of contemporary zoos as well. Most people visit zoos in order to be entertained, and any zoo that wishes to remain financially sound must cater to this desire. Even highly regarded zoos have their share of dancing bears and trained birds of prey. But although providing amusement for people is viewed by the general public as a very important function of zoos, it is hard to see how providing such amusement could possibly justify keeping wild animals in captivity.

Most curators and administrators reject the idea that the primary purpose of zoos is to provide entertainment. Indeed, many agree that the pleasure we take in viewing wild animals is not in itself a good enough reason to keep them in captivity. Some curators see baby elephant walks, for example, as a necessary evil, or defend such amusements because of their role in educating people, especially children, about animals. It is sometimes said that people must be interested in what they are seeing if they are to be educated about it, and entertainments keep people interested, thus making education possible.

This brings us to a second reason for having zoos: their role in education. This reason has been cited as long as zoos have existed. For example, in its 1898 annual report, the New York Zoological Society resolved to take "measures to inform the public of the great decrease in animal life, to stimulate sentiment in favor of better protection, and to cooperate with other scientific bodies . . . [in] efforts calculated to secure the perpetual preservation of our higher vertebrates." Despite the pious platitudes that are often uttered about the educational efforts of zoos, there is little evidence that zoos are very successful in educating people about animals. Indeed, a literature review commissioned by the American Zoo and Aquarium Association (available on their website) concludes that "[l]ittle to no systematic research has been conducted on the impact of visits to zoos and aquariums on visitor conservation knowledge, awareness, affect, or behavior." The research that is available is not encouraging. Stephen Kellert has found that zoo-goers display the same prejudices about animals as the general public. [. . .] One reason why some zoos have not done a better job in educating people is that many of them make no real effort at education. In the case of others the problem is an apathetic and unappreciative public.

Edward G. Ludwig's (1981) study of the zoo in Buffalo, New York, revealed a surprising amount of dissatisfaction on the part of young, scientifically inclined zoo employees. Much of this dissatisfaction stemmed from the almost complete indifference of the public to the zoo's educational efforts. Ludwig's study indicated that most animals are viewed only briefly as people move quickly past cages. The typical zoo-goer stops only to watch baby animals or those who are begging, feeding, or making sounds. [. . .]

Of course, it is undeniable that some education occurs in some zoos. But this very fact raises other issues. What is it that we want people to learn from visiting zoos? Facts about the physiology and behavior of various animals? Attitudes towards the survival of endangered species? Compassion for the fate of all animals? To what degree does education require keeping wild animals in captivity? Couldn't most of the educational benefits of zoos be obtained through videos, lectures, and computer simulations? Indeed, couldn't most of the important educational objectives better be achieved by exhibiting empty cages with explanations of why they are empty?

A third reason for having zoos is that they support scientific research. This, too, is a benefit that was pointed out long ago. [. . .] Zoos support scientific research in at least three ways: they fund field research by scientists not affiliated with zoos; they employ other scientists as members of zoo staffs; and they make otherwise inaccessible animals available for study.

We should note first that very few zoos support any real scientific research. Fewer still have staff scientists with full-time research appointments. Among those that do, it is common for their scientists to study animals in the wild rather than those in zoo collections. Much of this research, as well as other field research that is supported by zoos, could just as well be funded in a different way – say, by a government agency. The question of whether there should be zoos does not turn on the funding for field research which zoos currently provide. The significance of the research that is actually conducted in zoos is a more important consideration.

Research that is conducted in zoos can be divided into two broad categories: studies in behavior and studies in anatomy and pathology.

Behavioral research conducted on zoo animals is controversial. Some have argued that nothing can be learned by studying animals that are kept in the unnatural conditions that obtain in most zoos. Others have argued that captive animals are more interesting research subjects than are wild animals: since captive animals are free from predation, they exhibit a wider range of physical and behavioral traits than do animals in the wild, thus permitting researchers to view the full range of their genetic possibilities. Both of these positions are surely extreme. Conditions in some zoos are natural enough to permit some interesting research possibilities. But the claim that captive animals are more interesting research subjects than those in the wild is not very plausible. Environments trigger behaviors. No doubt a predation-free environment triggers behaviors different from those of an animal's natural habitat, but there is no reason to believe that better, fuller, or more accurate data can be obtained in predation-free environments than in natural habitats.

Studies in anatomy and pathology have three main purposes: to improve zoo conditions so that captive animals will live longer, be happier, and breed more frequently; to contribute to human health by providing animal models for human ailments; and to increase our knowledge of wild animals for its own sake.

The first of these aims is surely laudable, if we concede that there should be zoos in the first place. But the fact that zoo research contributes to improving conditions in zoos is not a reason for having them. If there were no zoos, there would be no need to improve them.

The second aim, to contribute to human health by providing animal models for human ailments, appears to justify zoos to some extent, but in practice this consideration is not as important as one might think. There are very severe constraints on the experiments that may be conducted on zoo animals. [. . .]

Finally, there is the goal of obtaining knowledge about animals for its own sake. Knowledge is certainly something which is good and, everything being equal, we should encourage people to seek it for its own sake. But everything is not equal in this case. There is a moral presumption against keeping animals in captivity. This presumption can be overcome only by demonstrating that there are important benefits that must be obtained in this way if they are to be obtained at all. It is clear that this is not the case with knowledge for its own sake. There are other channels for our intellectual curiosity, ones that do not exact such a high moral price. Although our quest for knowledge for its own sake is important, it is not important enough to overcome the moral presumption against keeping animals in captivity.

In assessing the significance of research as a reason for having zoos, it is important to remember that very few zoos do any research at all. Whatever benefits result from zoo research could just as well be obtained by having a few zoos instead of the hundreds which now exist. The most this argument could establish is that we are justified in having a few very good zoos. It does not provide a defense of the vast majority of zoos which now exist.

A fourth reason for having zoos is that they preserve species that would otherwise become extinct. As the destruction of habitat accelerates and as breeding programs become increasingly successful, this rationale for zoos gains in popularity. There is some reason for questioning the commitment of zoos to species preservation: it can be argued that they continue to remove more animals from the wild than they return. In the minds of some skeptics, captive breeding programs are more about the preservation of zoos than the preservation of endangered species. Still, without such programs, the Pere David Deer, the Mongolian Wild Horse, and the California Condor would all now be extinct.

Even the best of such programs face difficulties, however. A classic study by Katherine Ralls, Kristin Brugger, and Jonathan Ballou (1979) convincingly argues that lack of genetic diversity among captive animals is a serious problem for zoo breeding programs. In some species the infant mortality rate among inbred animals is six or seven times that among noninbred animals. In other species the infant mortality rate among inbred animals is 100 percent.

Moreover, captivity substitutes selection pressures imposed by humans for those of an animal's natural habitat. After a few years in captivity, animals can begin to diverge both behaviorally and genetically from their relatives in the wild. After a century or more it is not clear that they would be the same animals, in any meaningful sense, that we set out to preserve.

There is also a dark side to zoo breeding programmes: they create many unwanted animals. In some species (lions, tigers, and zebras, for example) a few males can service an entire herd. Extra males are unnecessary to the program and are a financial burden. Some of these animals are sold and end up in the hands of individuals and institutions which lack proper facilities. Others are shot and killed by Great White Hunters in private hunting camps. [. . .] In order to avoid the "surplus" problem, some zoos have considered proposals to "recycle" excess animals: a euphemism for killing them and feeding their bodies to other zoo animals.

The ostensible purpose of zoo breeding programs is to reintroduce animals into the wild. In this regard the California Condor is often portrayed as a major success story. From a low of 22 individuals in 1982, the population has rebounded to 219, through captive breeding. Since 1992 condors have been reintroduced, but most have not survived and only six eggs have been produced in the wild. Most eggs have failed to hatch, and only one chick has fledged. Wolf reintroductions have also had only limited success. Wolves, even when they have learned how to hunt, have often not learned to avoid people. Familiarity with humans and ignorance about their own cultures have devastated reintroduced populations of big cats, great apes, bears, rhinos, and hippos. According to the philosopher Bryan Norton, putting a captive-bred animal in the wild is "equivalent to dropping a contemporary human being in a remote area in the 18th or 19th century and saying, 'Let's see if you can make it' " (quoted in Derr 1999). In a 1995 review, Ben Beck, Associate Director of the National Zoological Park in Washington, found that of 145 documented reintroductions involving 115 species, only 16 succeeded in producing self-sustaining wild populations, and only half of these were endangered species.

Even if breeding programs were run in the best possible way, there are limits to what can be done to save endangered species in this way. At most, several hundred species could be preserved in the world's zoos, and then at very great expense. For many of these animals the zoo is likely to be the last stop on the way to extinction. Zoo professionals like to say that they are the Noahs of the modern world and that zoos are their arks, but Noah found a place to land his animals where they could thrive and multiply. If zoos are like arks, then rare animals are like passengers on a voyage of the damned, never to find a port that will let them dock or a land in which they can live in peace. The real solution, of course, is to preserve the wild nature that created these animals and has the power to sustain them. But if it is really true that we are inevitably moving towards a world in which mountain gorillas can survive only in zoos, then we must ask whether it is really better for them to live in artificial environments of our design than not to be born at all.

Even if all these questions and difficulties are overlooked, the importance of preserving endangered species does not provide much support for the existing system of zoos. Most zoos do very little breeding or breed only species which are not endangered. Many of the major breeding programs are run in special facilities which have been established for that purpose. They are often located in remote places, far from the attention of zoo-goers. (For example, the Wildlife Conservation Society [formerly the New York Zoological Society] operates its Wildlife Survival Center on St Catherine's Island off the coast of Georgia, and the National Zoo runs its Conservation and Research Center in the Shenandoah Valley of Virginia.) If our main concern is to do what we can to preserve endangered species at any cost and in any way, then we should support such large-scale breeding centers rather than conventional zoos, most of which have neither the staff nor the facilities to run successful breeding programs.

The four reasons for having zoos which I have surveyed carry some weight. But different reasons provide support for different kinds of zoo. Preservation and perhaps research are better carried out in large-scale animal preserves, but these provide few opportunities for amusement and education. Amusement and perhaps education are better provided in urban zoos, but they offer few opportunities for research and preservation. Moreover, whatever benefits are obtained from any kind of zoo, we must confront the moral presumption against keeping wild animals in captivity. Which way do the scales tip? There are two further considerations which, in my view, tip the scales against zoos.

First, captivity does not just deny animals liberty but is often detrimental to them in other respects as well. The history of chimpanzees in the zoos of Europe and America is a good example.

Chimpanzees first entered the zoo world in about 1640 when a Dutch prince, Frederick Henry of Nassau, obtained one for his castle menagerie. The chimpanzee didn't last very long. In 1835 the London Zoo obtained its first chimpanzee; he died immediately. Another was obtained in 1845; she lived six months. All through the nineteenth and early twentieth centuries zoos obtained chimpanzees who promptly died within nine months. It wasn't until the 1930s that it was discovered that chimpanzees are extremely vulnerable to human respiratory diseases, and that special steps must be taken to protect them. But for nearly a century zoos removed them from the wild and subjected them to almost certain death. Even today there are chimpanzees and other great apes living in deplorable conditions in zoos around the world.

Chimpanzees are not the only animals to suffer in zoos. It is well known that animals such as polar bears, lions, tigers, and cheetahs fare particularly badly in zoos. A recent (2003) report in *Nature* by Ros Clubb and Georgia Mason shows that repetitive stereotypic behavior and high infant mortality rates in zoos are directly related to an animal's natural home range size. For example, polar bears, whose home range in the wild is about a million times the size of its typical zoo enclosure, spend 25 percent of their days in stereotypic pacing and suffer from a 65% infant mortality rate. These results suggest that zoos simply cannot provide the necessary conditions for a decent life for many animals. Indeed, the Detroit Zoo has announced that, for ethical reasons, it will no longer keep elephants in captivity. The San Francisco Zoo has followed suit.

Many animals suffer in zoos quite unnecessarily. In 1974 Peter Batten, former director of the San Jose Zoological Gardens, undertook an exhaustive study of two hundred American zoos. In his book *Living Trophies* he documented large numbers of neurotic, overweight animals kept in cramped, cold cells and fed unpalatable synthetic food. Many had deformed feet and appendages caused by unsuitable floor surfaces. Almost every zoo studied had excessive mortality rates, resulting from preventable factors ranging from vandalism to inadequate husbandry practices. Batten's conclusion was: "The majority of American zoos are badly run, their direction incompetent, and animal husbandry inept and in some cases non-existent" (1976: ix).

Many of these same conditions are documented in Lynn Griner's (1983) review of necropsies conducted at the San Diego Zoo over a fourteen-year period. This zoo may well be the best in the country, and its staff are clearly well trained and well intentioned. Yet this study documents widespread malnutrition among zoo animals; high mortality rates from the use of anesthetics and tranquilizers; serious injuries and deaths sustained in transport; and frequent occurrences of cannibalism, infanticide, and fighting almost certainly caused by overcrowded conditions.

The Director of the National Zoo in Washington resigned in 2004 when an independent review panel commissioned by the National Academy of Sciences found severe deficiencies at the zoo in animal care, pest control, record keeping, and management that contributed to the deaths of twenty-three animals between 1998 and 2003, including, most spectacularly, the loss of two pandas to rat poison. Despite the best efforts of its well-paid public relations firm, it is difficult to trust an institution that cannot avoid killing its most charismatic and valuable animals in such a stupid and unnecessary way.

The second consideration which tips the scales against zoos is more difficult to articulate but is, to my mind, even more important. Zoos teach us a false sense of our place in the natural order. The means of confinement mark a difference between humans and other animals. They are there at our pleasure, to be used for our purposes. Morality and perhaps our very survival require that we learn to live as one species among many rather than as one species over many. To do this, we must forget what we learn at zoos. Because what zoos teach us is false and dangerous, both humans and other animals will be better off when they are abolished.

References

Batten, P. (1976) *Living Trophies*, New York: Thomas Y. Crowell Co.

Beck, B. (1995) "Reintroduction, Zoos, Conservation, and Animal Welfare," in B. Norton, M. Hutchins, E. F. Stevens, and T. L. Maple (eds), *Ethics on the Ark: Zoos, Animal Welfare, and Wildlife Conservation*, Washington, D.C.: Smithsonian Institution Press, pp. 155–63.

Clubb, R., and Mason, G. (2003) "Animal Welfare: Captivity Effects on Wide-Ranging Carnivores," *Nature*, October 2; 425(6957), 473–4.

Derr, M. (1999) "A Rescue Plan for Threatened Species," *New York Times*, January 19.

Griner, L. (1983) *Pathology of Zoo Animals*, San Diego: Zoological Society of San Diego.

Ludwig, E. G. (1981) "People at Zoos: A Sociological Approach," *International Journal for the Study of Animal Problems* 2(6), 310–16.

Ralls, K., Brugger, K., and Ballou, J. (1979) "Inbreeding and Juvenile Mortality in Small Populations of Ungulates," *Science* 206, 1101–3.

Chapter 67

Michael Hutchins, Brandie Smith, and Ruth Allard

IN DEFENSE OF ZOOS AND AQUARIUMS: THE ETHICAL BASIS FOR KEEPING WILD ANIMALS IN CAPTIVITY

Hutchins and his coauthors argue that a strong commitment to wildlife conservation and animal welfare provide powerful ethical justifications for accredited zoos and aquariums. They note that zoo animals play an increasingly important role as ambassadors for their species in securing a future for wildlife and their habitats. They note the strong financial contribution of zoos to conservation efforts and have been effective at increasing quality of life for captive animals through exhibit design, scientifically based animal programs, and policy. They argue that the benefits of exhibiting animals in zoos are greater than the costs in individual animal welfare.

AMERICA'S ZOOS AND aquariums have been the focus of recent criticism by some animal rights and welfare advocates and in print and electronic media.[1–7] These critics have characterized zoos and aquariums as animal prisons or, even worse, as exploiters and traffickers of wildlife. These accusations have fueled growing public and governmental concern about the welfare of zoo and aquarium animals and the appropriate use of these animals by public institutions.

Critics often generalize their claims to include all zoologic facilities, regardless of their quality or accomplishments. It is important to understand that there are 2 different kinds of wildlife facilities in the United States: those that are accredited by the American Zoo and Aquarium Association (AZA) and those that are not. The AZA is the only zoo and aquarium association in the world with an effective accreditation program that helps ensure quality animal care, a code of professional ethics that helps guide and regulate its members' actions, and a dedicated conservation vision.[8–10] Of the more than 2,300 animal exhibitors licensed by the USDA's Animal and Plant Health Inspection Service (APHIS), fewer than 10% are qualified to be AZA members. Our comments are restricted to zoos and aquariums accredited by the AZA.

Although critics of zoos and aquariums tend to receive plenty of media attention, their generalizations about public perceptions of accredited zoologic facilities are not supported by the facts: more than 135 million people visit AZA-accredited institutions annually,[11] more than 58,000 people volunteer more than 5 million hours annually at AZA facilities,[12] a 1992 Roper poll identified zoos and aquariums as the third most trusted messenger on wildlife conservation and environmental issues (trailing only National Geographic and Jacques Cousteau),[13] and reputable print and electronic media outlets produce numerous positive reports about the conservation, scientific, and educational efforts of AZA institutions.[14–17] Given these often disparate perspectives, how should ethically mature, caring people view accredited zoos and aquariums today? Are accredited zoos and aquariums justifiable? If so, under what conditions are they justifiable?

Some zoo and aquarium opponents are more extreme in their criticism than others. For example, some animal rights advocates are vehemently opposed to all forms of captivity, arguing that individual sentient animals have an intrinsic right to liberty.[2] For some people, even domestic pets are subjugated by their human owners; in their view, animals should interact with humans only as voluntary companions. It is highly unlikely that arguments presented here will change the minds of those who currently believe that zoos and aquariums are inherently wrong and should be eliminated.

More mainstream animal welfare advocates are not intrinsically opposed to zoos and aquariums; instead, they contend that the welfare of wild animals is diminished under human care and that it is impossible for zoos and aquariums to provide the richness of experience, freedom of movement, and quality of life animals would experience if left in nature.[1] They have also challenged zoos' and aquariums' reasons for existence, contending that, by itself, recreation is not a sufficient justification for maintaining captive wild animals, especially endangered species. The basis of the argument is that zoos and aquariums and their captive breeding programs do little to support wildlife and habitat conservation. Being conservationists and animal welfare advocates, we believe these arguments provide the most valid and difficult ethical challenges to zoos and aquariums today and, as such, they will be the focus of this report.

It is not our intent to provide a final answer to these complex questions. One cannot resolve moral questions for others, as different people have different opinions, depending on their own experiences, attitudes, and vantage points. Our intent is to contribute to the continual process of critical discussion and deliberation by providing an ethical justification for the existence of accredited zoos and aquariums at the beginning of the 21st century.

[. . .]

Conservation role of zoos and aquariums

Zoos and aquariums that value biological diversity have a clear moral obligation to support wildlife and habitat conservation efforts worldwide. The missions of professionally managed zoos and aquariums are complex, but generally include conservation, education, research, and recreation.[18] Although providing wholesome recreational opportunities for the public is important, most people would likely agree that recreation (entertainment) alone is not sufficient justification for the existence of zoos and aquariums or for holding wild animals in captivity.[19] In fact, many animals held by zoos and aquariums are endangered in the wild, and their commercial use exclusively for entertainment purposes would be distasteful, if not illegal. Entertainment is an even less convincing justification if one assumes that the welfare of individual animals may be compromised to some degree as a result of captivity.[1,2]

Conservation, education, and research are other matters. If zoos and aquariums demonstrate an ability to study, manage, preserve, and restore wild animals and their habitats in nature, it would provide a powerful ethical justification for their continued existence.[20–22] This is particularly true given the many serious and pervasive threats facing wildlife and nature today. Wild animals in zoos and aquariums are ambassadors for their species, helping to raise public awareness and funds to support education, research, on-the-ground conservation activities in range countries, and a host of other relevant activities.[20–22] Zoos and aquariums must display and sustainably breed some animals to meet their conservation goals.

The following is a brief overview of some of the numerous conservation activities in which AZA and its members are currently engaged. In 1999 and 2000, AZA and its member institutions supported more than 1,400 field conservation and related scientific research and educational initiatives in more than 80 countries worldwide.[23]

Reintroduction

Zoos and aquariums of the 1980s and early 1990s viewed and described themselves as modern Noah's Arks and organized cooperative breeding programs to sustain populations of endangered species until they could be reintroduced to nature.[24] During the past several years, zoo and aquarium professionals have begun to question this notion, adopting a much broader definition of zoo- and aquarium-based conservation. Central to this concept is the assumption that zoos and aquariums must do more to support in situ conservation in range countries.[20–22, 25, 26] There are far too many endangered species and not nearly enough space to breed them all in captivity and, in many cases, far too little habitat remaining in which to reintroduce them. In addition, reintroduction programs are difficult and expensive, and they amount to treating the symptoms of species loss rather than the causes.[27–29] Though this shift in focus has been well documented,[21–23] critics imply that zoos and aquariums are not active conservation organizations, because they are not releasing a steady stream of animals into the wild. This argument reflects an ignorance of the breadth, scope, and goals of conservation itself.

[. . .]

Endangered species recovery

In nature, living organisms are interconnected, and ecosystems cannot function unless they retain most of their essential parts. Endangered species must persist until essential habitat can be restored, better protected, or expanded. Because there are so many species in need of help, zoo and aquarium efforts are often focused on flagship species (those that have the ability to capture the public's attention and help preserve habitat and other taxa). Examples of the many zoo-and aquarium-sponsored efforts to recover endangered species include the Toledo Zoos for the Mona/Virgin Islands boa[30]; Atlanta, National, and San Diego Zoos for the giant panda in China[31]; Fort Worth Zoos for the Jamaican iguana[32]; and Minnesota Zoos for the Sumatran tiger.[33]

Habitat restoration

Many of the world's natural habitats have been fragmented, altered, or lost because of human activity, with devastating effects on wildlife. In some cases, attempts to conserve biological diversity can be aided through habitat restoration. Restoration activities by zoos and aquariums have, among other things, involved the reestablishment of native vegetation and elimination or control of invasive exotic species.[34]

[. . .]

Scientific research

Scientific research is critical to wildlife conservation and for improving zoo and aquarium animal management. In situ and ex situ conservation efforts cannot succeed in the absence of knowledge.[35] Unfortunately, our knowledge of most wild animals and their habitats is far from complete. Contemporary zoos and aquariums are investing enormous resources in research, estimated at $50 million annually.[12] Zoos and aquariums offer unique opportunities to study animal behavior, physiology, reproduction, growth, and development of a wide variety of taxa under semicontrolled conditions. Many of these studies would be difficult, if not impossible, to conduct in nature, because of practical or ethical limitations. For example, much of what we know about the biology of arboreal, fossorial, and wide-ranging aquatic species has come from studies[35] of captive animals.

Development of relevant technologies

Many technologies developed or tested by zoo and aquarium biologists are relevant to field conservation, a largely unrecognized benefit of maintaining collections of wild animals.[21] As remaining wildlife habitats become progressively smaller and more isolated, the need for active management of wildlife and their habitats grows. Consequently, technologies developed by zoos and aquariums, including those for small population management, ecologic restoration, contraception, and veterinary care, are becoming increasingly relevant to the conservation of wildlife and their habitats.[20–21]

[. . .]

Support of protected areas

Habitat loss and lack of law enforcement in and around protected areas are major factors contributing to species endangerment around the world, especially in developing countries.[36] Consequently, there is a recognized need for North American zoos and aquariums to increase their support for conservation on a landscape level.[20–22,29] The AZA and its member institutions are moving in this direction, both individually and collectively.

[. . .]

Conservation education

Raising public awareness about endangered species and other environmental issues is an important aspect of conservation. If conservation efforts are to be successful, people must be interested in nature and be made aware of the problems and potential solutions facing wildlife and their habitats. With 135 million visitors each year, accredited zoos and aquariums are unique among conservation organizations, because they have a direct connection to the public.

The educational efforts of AZA members are numerous, and accredited zoos and aquariums are continually striving to evaluate their impact on visitors behavior. Evidence indicates that zoo and aquarium educational programs are effective, at least in the short term, in building public appreciation and understanding of wildlife and wildlife conservation issues.[37] The AZA Conservation Education Committee (CEC) has initiated a major study[38] to assess the impact of zoo- and aquarium-based educational efforts on public knowledge, attitudes, and perceptions, with the goal of ensuring that critical conservation messages and concepts are reaching visitors in the most effective way.

Fundraising to support conservation

For conservation to succeed, it is critical that it be put on a solid financial base. The AZA and its member institutions are developing improved mechanisms to support conservation and the related scientific and educational activities of its members and collaborators. In this regard, the AZA was the first zoologic association to establish a fund dedicated to supporting wildlife and nature conservation.[39] During the past decade, the AZA Conservation Endowment Fund has provided over $2.5 million to support 164 projects in more than 30 countries. Furthermore, 14 accredited zoos and aquariums have developed their own grant programs to support local and global conservation.

Conservation planning and coalition building

The AZA and its member institutions are becoming increasingly active in conservation planning and coalition building, which are the first steps in effective conservation. Partnerships can greatly enhance organizations' abilities to take action, because expertise and expenses can be shared.

The AZA and its members have been involved in creating 2 major conservation coalitions: the Bushmeat Crisis Task Force (BCTF) and the Butterfly Conservation Initiative (BFCI). The BCTF is a coalition of 34 conservation and animal protection organizations and accredited zoos committed to curbing illegal commercial trade of wild animals for meat in Africa.[40] The coalition was created as the result of a 1998 meeting organized by the AZA. In just over 2 short years, BCTF's accomplishments have been substantial and too numerous to list here. To learn more about this project, please visit the BCTF website at www.bushmeat.org.

[. . .]

Animal welfare—the critical caveat

The evidence presented here illustrates that zoo and aquarium contributions to wildlife and habitat conservation are substantial. However, the crux of the debate over zoos and aquariums comes down to a question of focus. Animal rights advocates believe in the intrinsic rights of individual animals, whereas conservationists focus their attention on populations, species, and ecosystems.[41] While we believe that individual animals are morally considerable, we also believe that conservation must be our highest priority. The irreversible loss of populations, species, or ecosystems will not only result in the untold suffering of many individual animals (including humans), it will also result in the loss of millions of future lives. We acknowledge that this broader perspective might appear callous to those who are strict adherents to animal rights philosophy, but zoos' and aquariums' commitment to conservation is matched by an equally strong commitment to animal welfare.[22,42–44] This increased focus on animal welfare helps ensure that the collective benefits derived from wildlife conservation outweigh the costs to individual animals. No reputable zoo or aquarium professional would defend an institution that contributed to conservation, but abused or provided substandard care for its animals. A conservation-oriented mission and staunch commitment to maintaining the highest standards of animal care are the core values of accredited zoos and aquariums.[43,44]

One of the founding fathers of animal rights, Tom Regan, refers to any attempt to usurp the rights of individual sentient animals (be they endangered or common) to preserve populations, species, or ecosystems as "environmental fascism."[45] Several prominent environmental ethicists and conservationists have challenged this view. For example, Warren[46] writes, "It is less important to maintain that other animals have moral rights than to maintain that we have moral obligations to them," and Norton[47] argues, on ethical grounds, that we must balance our obligations to individual animals with our obligations to perpetuate and conserve natural processes. Because there is often a conflict between what is good for individual animals and what is good for populations, species, or ecosystems, this will sometimes mean compromising the welfare of some individuals for the greater good.[47,48]

The following are some examples of how accredited zoos and aquariums are addressing ethical issues related to animal care and propagation.

Providing appropriate environments

One of the biggest criticisms from zoo and aquarium detractors is that animal welfare is diminished in captivity, simply because the wild can never be duplicated exactly. This is true. However, zoos and aquariums make up for these inadequacies by creating an environment that offers some of the accouterments of the wild while providing shelter from some of the stresses, such as predation and starvation.[44] Some accredited zoos and aquariums have been criticized for having older, inadequate facilities and care programs for specific taxa.

The comparatively new science of environmental enrichment has been embraced by accredited zoos and aquariums and provides numerous techniques for improving the lives of captive animals.[49] Enrichment is the species-appropriate enhancement of the physical and social environment. Accreditation by the AZA now requires that all member institutions develop and implement an environmental enrichment plan that improves the quality of life of captive animals by providing novel experiences and a variety of stimuli that encourage a range of natural behaviors.[43] These programs demonstrate accredited zoos' and aquariums' commitment to continually improving the welfare of animals in their care.

Ensuring quality animal care

Animal care is being improved and standardized through creation and distribution of husbandry manuals and thorough, scientifically based animal care standards that define appropriate management practices. The AZA Board of Directors approved management and care standards for elephants in 2001,[50] and the AZA Animal Welfare Committee is formulating standards for all remaining mammals.[43] Experts on reptile, amphibian, bird, and invertebrate husbandry have been called on to develop resources for captive management of these taxa as well. Ultimately, standards will be developed for all major taxa in AZA institutions' collections.

[. . .]

Training and use of animals in public education

Training and the use of animals in education pose some difficult animal care issues for zoos and aquariums. When does training compromise or enhance animal welfare? [. . .] The zoo and aquarium community is continually assessing the impact of professional practices on the animals under our care, and these questions are the subject of considerable debate among the members of the AZA and its Animal Welfare Committee. The Committee is currently working on a draft policy on animals in entertainment to be considered by the AZA Board. If they are to be justified, animal shows, training programs, and exhibit design must contribute to the overall conservation and education goals of the association and not diminish animal welfare.

Surplus animals

The zoo and aquarium profession uses the term surplus to refer to animals that are not needed to meet the population management or conservation goals of an institution or program. It is not that these animals are unwanted or neglected, and despite the penchant of certain critics for misinterpreting the word, surplus does not mean superfluous. All AZA facilities dedicate themselves to providing quality care to all animals in their custody for as long as necessary. Zoos and aquariums make known the availability of their surplus animals in case they can be of conservation or education value to another institution. The AZA also requires that all accredited facilities complete an institutional collection plan to ensure that populations stay within the captive carrying capacity (ie, the available holding space). Institutional collection plans also help zoos and aquariums define the conservation goals for all of the species in their collections.[51]

[. . .]

Beyond AZA

Discussions of zoo and aquarium relevance in today's world often come down to issues of individual animal welfare versus overall species and ecosystem conservation. While we believe that conservation must be the primary mission of modern zoos and aquariums, we also contend that to be morally defensible, zoos and aquariums must demonstrate an equally unwavering commitment to maintaining high standards of animal welfare.

Conclusions

In this report, we have argued that a strong commitment to wildlife conservation and animal welfare provides a powerful ethical justification for accredited zoos and aquariums. As true ambassadors for their species, zoo and aquarium animals play an increasingly important role in securing a future for wild animals and their habitats in nature. This is particularly true given the current global context. The future of wildlife and the ecosystems on which it depends is in grave and immediate danger, and as we have documented in this report, zoos and aquariums contribute to conservation efforts in a wide variety of ways.

One question that must be resolved is how much conservation is enough, and how can these contributions be measured? What is a reasonable investment in conservation: 1, 5, or 10% or more of zoos' and aquariums' budgets? Even a 1% investment in conservation out of an estimated combined budget of over $1 billion would mean that accredited zoos and aquariums contribute $10 million per year to conservation. However, factoring in personnel time, facility costs, and all funds currently being spent on projects, the cumulative investment in conservation, research, and education by accredited zoos and aquariums would easily exceed that amount.[12] Regardless of their financial contribution, how do we measure the quality and impact of zoo- and aquarium-based conservation efforts? We must be committed to evaluating proposed and ongoing projects if zoos and aquariums are to spend their limited conservation resources wisely.

Also, how much should zoos and aquariums be required to improve animal welfare, short of completely replicating the wild? Zoos and aquariums are in a position to greatly increase quality of life for captive animals through improvements in exhibit design, scientifically based animal care programs, and policy. As we expand our accomplishments in these areas, the benefits of exhibiting animals in zoos and aquariums are increasingly likely to vastly outweigh the costs, as measured in terms of individual animal welfare. There will always be a gray area where costs and benefits are arguably equal, and it is here that ethical considerations should be carefully weighed when deciding whether a captive program is necessary. This is similar to the ethical considerations used by biomedical researchers when weighing the benefits of the research against the costs to individual animal welfare,[52] but in those cases, the cost to the animals is weighed against the benefit to humans and other animals. In this case, the cost to the individual animals is weighed against the benefit of the very survival of their species and the habitats on which they depend.

Like evolutionary change in any profession, the complex transformation of accredited zoos and aquariums into conservation and animal welfare organizations is being fueled in part by self-preservation, need, changing societal expectations, our increasing knowledge, and internal pressures. While external critics have certainly played a role in this process, much recent change has been generated from within. There has been a vast influx of talented, extremely well-educated people into accredited zoos and aquariums during the past decade. Some have come directly out of graduate school and others from responsible positions in academia, business, government, or the military. They have come to the zoologic profession with a love for animals and nature and a strong commitment to conservation and animal welfare. One consequence of this recent migration of new, highly trained personnel has been a growing professionalism, which has also led to an abundance of critical thinking and self-evaluation, including useful debate on the ethical basis for keeping wild animals in captivity.[53] We hope this report will continue the growth process by spurring additional discussion and debate throughout and beyond the zoologic community.

References

1 Jamieson D. Zoos revisited. In: Norton BG, Hutchins M, Stevens EF, et al, eds. *Ethics on the Ark: zoos, animal welfare and wildlife conservation*. Washington, DC: Smithsonian Institution Press, 1995;52–66.
2 Regan T. Are zoos morally defensible? In: Norton BG; Hutchins M, Stevens EF, et al, eds. *Ethics on the Ark: zoos, animal welfare and wildlife conservation*. Washington, DC: Smithsonian Institution Press, 1995;38–51.

3   Malamud R. *Reading zoos: representations of animals and captivity.* Washington Square, NY: New York University Press, 2000.

4   Goldston L. Animals to go. *San Jose Mercury News* 1999;Feb:7–10.

5   Farinato R. Another view of zoos. In: *The state of the animals 2001.* Washington, DC: Humane Society of the United States, 2001;145–147.

6   Satchell M. Investigative report: cruel and usual. *US News and World Report* 2001;133:26–33.

7   Green A. *Animal underworld: inside America's black market for rare and exotic species.* New York: Center for Public Integrity, 1999.

8   *Guide to certification and standardized guidelines.* Silver Spring, Md: American Zoo and Aquarium Association, 2001.

9   Taylor S. Why accreditation? in *Proceedings.* Annu Conf Am Zoo Aquar Assoc 2000;7–12.

10   *AZA long-range plan 2001–2006.* Silver Spring, Md: American Zoo and Aquarium Association, 2001.

11   Ballentine J, ed. *The 2003 AZA membership directory.* Silver Spring, Md: American Zoo and Aquarium Association, 2003.

12   *The collective impact of America's zoos and aquariums.* Silver Spring, Md: American Zoo and Aquarium Association, 1999.

13   *Public attitudes towards aquariums, theme parks and zoos.* Storrs, Conn: The Roper Center for Public Opinion Research, 1992.

14   Tarpy C. New zoos: taking down the bars. *National Geographic* 1993;Jul:2–37.

15   Sundquist F. End of the Ark? Captive breeding is out; conservation in the wild is in. *Int Wildl* 1995;Nov/Dec:22–29.

16   Cohn JP. Working outside the box. Zoos and aquariums are shifting their conservation focus to the wild. *Bioscience* 2002;50: 564–569.

17   Ebersole, RS. The new zoo. *Audubon* 2001;Nov/Dec:64–70.

18   Croke V. *The modern Ark: the story of zoos: past, present and future.* New York: Scribner, 1997.

19   Hancocks D. *A different nature: the paradoxical world of zoos and their uncertain future.* Berkeley, Calif: University of California Press, 2001.

20   Conway W, Hutchins M. Introduction. In: Conway WG, Hutchins M, Souza M, et al, eds. *AZA field conservation resource guide.* Atlanta, Ga: Zoo Atlanta and Wildlife Conservation Society, 2001;1–7.

21   Hutchins M, Conway WG. Beyond Noah's Ark: the evolving role of modern zoological parks and aquariums in field conservation. *Int Zoo Yearbook* 1995;34:117–130.

22   Hutchins M, Smith B. Characteristics of a world class zoo or aquarium in the twenty-first century. *Int Zoo Yearbook* 2003;38:130–141.

23   Lankard J, ed. *Annual report on conservation and science, 1999–2000.* Silver Spring, Md: American Zoo and Aquarium Association, 2000.

24   Foose TJ. Riders of the last Ark: the role of captive breeding in conservation strategies. In: Kaufman L, Mallory K, eds. *The last extinction.* Cambridge, Mass: The MIT Press, 1986;141–165.

25   Wiese R, Willis K, Hutchins M. Is genetic and demographic management conservation? *Zoo Biol* 1994;13:297–299.

26   Smith B, Hutchins M. The value of captive breeding programmes to field conservation: elephants as an example. *Pachyderm* 2000;28:101–109.

27   Hutchins M, Willis K, Wiese R. Author's response. *Zoo Biol* 1995;14:67–80.

28   Hutchins M, Wiese R, Willis K. Why we need captive breeding, in *Proceedings.* Reg Conf Am Zoo Aquar Assoc 1996;77–86.

29   Synder NFR, Derrickson SR, Bessinger SR, et al. Limitations of captive breeding in endangered species recovery. *Conserv Biol* 1996;10:338–348.

30   Tolson P. The Mona/Virgin Islands boa SSP, the US Fish and Wildlife Service and the Departmento de Recursos Naturales de Pureto Rico. In: Conway WG, Hutchins M, Souza M, et al, eds. *AZA field conservation resource guide.* Atlanta, Ga: Zoo Atlanta and Wildlife Conservation Society, 2001;177–180.

31   Hudson R. The Jamaican iguana recovery story: rediscovery to recovery, 1990–1998. In: Conway WG, Hutchins M, Souza M, et al, eds. *AZA field conservation resource guide.* Atlanta: Zoo Atlanta and Wildlife Conservation Society, 2001;42–48.

32   Maple TL. *Saving the giant panda.* Atlanta, Ga: Longstreet Press, 2000.

33 Tilson R, Franklin N, Bastoni P, et al. In situ conservation of the Sumatran tiger (*Panthera tigris sumatrae*) in Indonesia. *Int Zoo News* 1996;43:71–79.

34 Tolson P. Partnering to restore biodiversity: a vision for AZA institutions. *AZA Communique* 2002:Jan:7–8.

35 Hutchins M. Research. In: Bell CE, ed. *Encyclopedia of the world's zoos*. Vol 3. Chicago: Fitzroy Dearborn, 2001;1076–1080.

36 Wilson EO. *The future of life*. Cambridge, Mass: Harvard University Press, 2001.

37 Stoinski YT, Ogden J, Gold KC, et al. Captive apes and zoo education. In: Beck BB, Stoinski TS, Hutchins M, et al, eds. *Great apes and humans: the ethics of coexistence*. Washington, DC: Smithsonian Institution Press, 2001;113–132.

38 Ogden J. Measuring our impact: what MIRP can mean to you. *AZA Communique* 2002;Sep:23–24.

39 Hutchins M, Souza M. AZA Conservation Endowment Fund: zoos and aquariums supporting conservation action. In: Conway WG. Hutchins M, Souza M, et al, eds. *AZA field conservation resource guide*. Atlanta: Zoo Atlanta and Wildlife Conservation Society; 2001;281–297.

40 Eves H, Hutchins M. The Bushmeat Crisis Task Force: cooperative efforts to curb the illegal commercial bushmeat trade in Africa. In: Conway WG, Hutchins M, Souza M, et al, eds. *AZA field conservation resource guide*. Atlanta: Zoo Atlanta and Wildlife Conservation Society, 2001:181–186.

41 Vrijenhook R. Natural processes, individuals, and units of conservation. In: Norton BG, Hutchins M, Stevens EF, et al, eds. *Ethics on the Ark: zoos, animal welfare and wildlife conservation*. Washington, DC: Smithsonian Institution Press, 1995;74–92.

42 Hutchins M. Zoo and aquarium animal management and conservation: current trends and future challenges. *Int. Zoo Yearbook* 2003;38:14–28.

43 Hutchins M. What is AZA doing to enhance the welfare of captive animals? in *Proceedings*. Annu Conf Am Zoo Aquar Assoc 2001;117–129.

44 Maple TL, McManamon R, Stevens E. Defining the good zoo: animal care, maintenance and welfare: In: Norton BG, Hutchins M, Stevens EF, et al, eds. *Ethics on the Ark: zoos, animal welfare and wildlife conservation*. Washington, DC: Smithsonian Institution Press, 1995;219–234.

45 Regan T. *The case for animal rights*. Berkeley, Calif; University of California Press, 1988.

46 Warren MA. The moral status of great apes. In: Beck BB, Stoinski T, Hutchins M, et al, eds. *Great apes and humans: ethics of coexistence*. Washington, DC: Smithsonian Institution Press, 2002;313–328.

47 Norton B. Caring for nature: a broader look at animal stewardship. In: Norton BG, Hutchins M, Stevens EF, et al, eds. *Ethics on the Ark: zoos, animal welfare and wildlife conservation*. Washington, DC: Smithsonian Institution Press, 1995; 102–121.

48 Hutchins M, Wemmer C. Wildlife conservation and animal rights: are they compatible? In: Fox MW, Mickley LD; eds. *Advances in animal welfare science* 1986/87. Boston: Martinus Nijhoff Publishing, 1987;111–137.

49 Shepherdson D, Mellen J, Hutchins M, eds. *Second nature: environmental enrichment for captive animals*. Washington, DC: Smithsonian Institution Press, 1999.

50 *AZA standards for elephant management and care*. Silver Spring, Md: American Zoo and Aquarium Association, 2001.

51 Thompson SD, Bell KJ. Institutional collection planning. *Zoo Biol* 1998;17: 55–57.

52 Orlans B, Beauchamp TL, Dresser R, et al, eds. *The human use of animals: case studies in ethical choice*. New York: Oxford University Press, 1998.

53 Norton B, Hutchins M, Stevens EF, et al, eds. *Ethics on the Ark: zoos, animal welfare and wildlife conservation*. Washington, DC: Smithsonian Institution Press, 1995.

Chapter 68

Donald G. Lindburg

ZOOS AND THE RIGHTS OF ANIMALS

Lindburg explores the need for zoo and aquarium professionals to respect both the needs of individual animals and the need of species to survive over evolutionary time, and how these needs might be integrated. He notes that zoo professionals are more strongly committed to animal welfare than animal rights and that when individual welfare conflicts with species preservation, zoo professionals normally give higher priority to species preservation.

Introduction

MANY IN OUR profession may harken back to a time when the welfare of their charges rested largely on their individual sensitivities. Concerns for humane treatment and quality of life within zoological institutions reflected the attitudes of society toward human–animal relationships at the time and were only modestly regulated by a professional code of ethics, largely unwritten. During the past three decades, however, we have witnessed the rise of philosophically driven activism that has profoundly altered the way society views these relationships. Where once such activities as feeding live prey or shipping a gorilla to another zoo fell largely within the purview of the profession, the reality of today is that the entire spectrum of zoo and aquarium activities is repeatedly held up to public scrutiny and judgment (Hutchins and Fascione, 1991).

[. . .]

It is widely recognized that the original objectives of zoos in maintaining collections of wild animals can no longer be condoned. Modern-day zoos, therefore, have redefined their missions in light of questions about the right to hold animals captive and the relevance and humaneness of this practice. They have done so by aligning themselves with conservationist objectives, a process that has entailed the investment of substantial resources in education, improved training of staff, modernization of exhibits, breeding, and, in some cases, reintroductions, and research designed to improve health, welfare, and propagation efforts. The modern zoo also takes note of the world-wide decline in populations and their habitats and increasingly envisions a time when at least some species will exist only within their confines (Soulé et al., 1986). For the vast majority of those who labor in the profession, therefore, pride of achievement and a personal sense of fulfillment are commonly found. Indeed, for most it is a pursuit to be nobly and passionately held.

What, then, does the rights movement have to offer the zoo/aquarium community other than its condemnation? Can any agreement on principle be found? Can respect for different viewpoints be engendered, such that joint action on shared objectives may be realized? The need for improved welfare for animals within our institutions gets no argument (Fox, 1986; Gibbons et al., 1995; Hutchins et al., 1995; Mapie et al., 1995; Shepherdson et al., 1998), but more problematic for zoos and aquariums are the moral concerns flowing from the proposition that animals indeed have certain basic rights (Singer and Regan, 1976; Regan, 1983).

Taking as their major premise that animals do not exist to serve the interests of humans, true adherents to the animal-rights view oppose the use of animals for food, clothing, companionship, entertainment, sport, and experimentation of any kind. Actions that cause animals any measure of suffering, including research designed to benefit either humans or the animals themselves, are uniformly opposed.

[. . .]

It would be inaccurate to assert that all who are concerned with the humane treatment (welfare) of animals, including many who subscribe to vegetarianism, hold to the rights view. Nor would it be accurate to assume that all opposition to the keeping of wild animals in captivity arises only from this quarter. In an article entitled "Against Zoos," animal liberationist Dale Jamieson [1985] stressed human domination of animals and their loss of freedom during confinement in zoos, rather than a rights ethic, as presumptively wrong. He, and many others who are deeply committed to conservation, does not see zoos as offering viable alternatives to in situ efforts. Although critical of inhumane conditions, many animal welfare advocates nevertheless recognize a role for zoos (e.g., Grandy, 1989; Bekoff, 1995). In addition, some conservationists working in in situ contexts see zoos as anachronistic and inhumane (see Eudey, 1995; Loftin, 1995 for examples of critiques of captive breeding programs). However, because of their activist tactics, the zoo/aquarium profession is more concerned about animal rightists than about opposition from welfarists and conservationists.

Hutchins and Wemmer (1987), in reviewing areas in which animal rightists and conservationists (including zoo/aquarium professionals) are in substantial disagreement, also conclude that "the two views are not completely antithetical" (p. 131). They, and others (e.g., Ehrenfeld, 1991) called for united efforts between the two where there is common ground (see also Varner, 1994, and Jamieson, 1998). Although the intent of this commentary is to lay out some of the more salient issues in a non-advocative manner, my bias is that of the conservationist. There are zoo and aquarium professionals who believe animals have rights who also believe they should be conserved, and there are zoo and aquarium professionals who place a high value on animal welfare, yet hold rights advocates in utmost contempt. Despite deeply held positions for which no reconciliation is likely to occur, my objective is to increase understanding of the rights view and the zoo view in hopes of enhancing both welfare and conservationist prospects for endangered wildlife. To that end, I discuss animal rights as a political movement and as a belief system for that movement, and the implications of these views for zoo-based conservation efforts.

Animal rights as a political movement

Although many individuals in our society subscribe to the view that animals have rights, it is equally clear that this stance means different things to different people. For a majority, the intent in bequeathing rights on animals is to assert that they deserve humane, respectful treatment. Rowan (1992) states that this is the more common view held by the general public, 80 percent of whom believe that animals have rights. At the other extreme are those who reject the notion that only humans among living creatures can have rights. The basis for this view is variable, depending in some instances on animals' advanced social or rational capacities or on having the quality of sentience (the ability to experience pain and to suffer). Rightists stress the *similarities* between humans and animals, and granting rights to animals is but a logical extension of the struggle by humans to achieve social equality between races, classes, and genders as society becomes increasingly sensitized to its unprincipled biases against minorities.

However divergent the views of its adherents might be, the impact of the rights movement on how society interacts with both domestic and wild animals is far reaching. [. . .] In U.S. college newspapers, researchers using animals in experiments have seen themselves featured as "vivisector of the month," and in the aftermath of the destruction of a research laboratory at Texas Tech in 1989, university officials received over 10,000 letters opposing the work of the scientist in question (Herzog, 1993). Closer to home for zoos, in 1993 citizens of the city of Vancouver, British Columbia, Canada, voted by a 54 percent majority to close down its Stanley Park Zoo, founded in 1893. Although not listed in recent issues of the American Zoo Association (AZA) Directory of accredited institutions, and perhaps deserving of its fate, the important point is that the winning campaign was led by animal rights advocates whose principal argument was that wild animals ought not to be publicly displayed for the entertainment of people (Los Angeles *Times*, Oct. 6, 1995).

Unquestionably, the most significant indicator of the power of the animal rights movement in the United States is amendment of the Animal Welfare Act of 1985, requiring improved treatment of animals in laboratories and such other factors as the reduction of duplication in research and the consideration of alternative research methods to the use of animals. Although portions of the Act, such as improving the psychological health of captives, were initially resisted as undefinable and as requiring a huge outlay of money to implement, many labs were remodeled, and enrichment efforts on the part of laboratory staff are now routinely encouraged.

[. . .]

[T]he animal rights movement has significantly altered the views of society on human–animal relationships and on the ways in which scientists, doctors, veterinarians, zoo and aquarium managers, circus personnel, wildlife managers, agriculturists, pet owners, many corporate executives, and even hunters and fishers interact with members of the animal kingdom. There is no denying that much good has resulted from this effort. Although there are many among the ranks of scientists, for example, who have shown a lifetime of sensitivity to animal welfare, it took the passion of the animal rights movement to bring about widespread change in the ethical culture of the research laboratory. Few can deny, furthermore, that zoos and aquariums have made great strides in effecting more humane exhibitry and management, based at least in part on the impact of the rights movement on public sentiments (for further discussion of these points, see Geist, 1992; Herzog, 1993; Morrison, 1994; Norton *et al.*, 1995). The zoo/aquarium profession, nevertheless, finds itself at cross purposes with rightists on a wide range of issues from euthanasia policy to the validity of its educational, scientific, and conservation missions.

Animal rights as a belief system

[. . .]

Here, I examine the two main philosophies espoused by the movement, *utilitarianism* and *deontology* (also known as "the rights view"). [. . .] The utilitarian view justifies an action only if its good consequences outweigh its harmful ones. In identifying pain and suffering as harmful, Singer (1975) calculates that because the harm to animals used in research, for example, outweighs any resulting good, most animal-based research is immoral. This formula is applicable only to animals capable of experiencing pain or mental anguish, i.e., those described as sentient, and is today commonly used to deny the use of animals or their products for food, clothing, shelter, entertainment, and various other benefits to humans.

[. . .]

Although agreeing with his sentiments, Tom Regan [1983, 1995], a deontologist [. . .] rejects Singer's criteria for ethical treatment of animals since, under the utilitarian view, the benefits or harm to those humans interacting with them at the time must also be considered in deciding the morality of an action. [. . .] To Regan and his followers in the rights movement, exploitation of animals is wrong independently of the interests of their exploiters.

Alternatively, Regan believes it is the *sort* of individual, not the consequences of any act toward it, that defines morally acceptable behavior. In certain fundamental ways, some animals have the same qualities as human beings, i.e., they have interests, expectations, desires, perceptions, memories, a sense of the future, an emotional life together, and numerous other qualities that Regan (1983) terms "*the subject-of-a-life criterion*" that entitles an animal to the same respect we would extend to a fellow human. Stated another way, individuals meeting this criterion have *inherent* value, independently of the valuing agent.

[. . .]

This philosophy works only if one provides an "out" for animals that do things that, in human terms, would be immoral. A human who kills another human commits murder, whereas the lion that kills the zebra for food does not. Only humans can be *moral agents*. In contrast, animals are likened to "marginal" humans, i.e., infants or the mentally retarded who cannot be held accountable for their acts. They are, by contrast, *moral patients*. Animals, then, according to the rights view, have rights but not responsibilities. One can immediately perceive a certain inconsistency in the logic, namely, that it is their *likeness* to humans that enjoins our respect, but a profound *difference* from humans in terms of moral accountability that gives them special standing.

This point is further illustrated in rightists' approach to euthanasia, a procedure that, it is held, should be limited to circumstances in which it complies with the wishes of the animal in question. Animals suffering acute pain in the final stages of a fatal disease, accordingly, allow us to "do for them what they cannot do for themselves" (Regan, 1983, p. 114). By ending their misery, we are *complying with their will* and engaging in "preference-respecting" euthanasia.

[. . .]

Regan's "subject-of-a-life criterion" lies at the root of a recent proposal to bring the three great apes (orangutans, chimpanzees, and gorillas) into the human community as moral equals (The Great Ape Project (see Cavalieri and Singer, 1993)). In support of this proposal, a distinguished roster of scientists and philosophers wrote of the strong similarities between humans and apes in social, emotional, rational, and even incipiently moral capabilities, and used these to argue for an end to human dominion over the great apes, particularly those held in captive situations. Despite the obviously high level of sentience in these taxa and deeply felt concerns for their welfare, this case aptly demonstrates the difficulties encountered in finding a neat formula for action in moral philosophies that are based on arguments that "likes" ought to be treated alike (see discussion of "moral monism" by Norton, 1995). By wanting to do for apes what they cannot do for themselves, it must be asked if we can logically stress their continuity with humans in making the case for preferential treatment without at the same time highlighting their differential standing as moral patients. Put another way, it is a *discontinuity* between humans and apes that enables us to respect them for their *continuities*. In striving to increase respect for the apes, care must be taken not to draw oversimplistic depictions such as their having the elements of a social system that is socially transmitted across the generations (Noske, 1993), a "finding" that will come as no shock to any reputable zoologist. There are many welfare advocates on the other side of this issue who worry that such well-intentioned eagerness leaves us but a short step removed from a Disney-esque world of talking animals coming together to discuss the rules of the jungle. As Zak (1989) stressed, it is the unlikes between humans and animals and an infinite combination of likes and unlikes among non-human creatures that often leaves us on uncertain moral ground.

[. . .]

Animal rights and conservation

Many zoos and aquariums have had first-hand experience with members of the animal rights community. Perhaps the most common of these is some form of organized demonstration against a particular action, usually with advance notification to the television and print media. Representatives of zoos and aquariums have at times had to respond to media questions about charges emanating from these dissents. Among the issues that may be raised are

- the conditions under which animals are kept, often precipitated by some unusual event such as an escape or an accidental death, and commonly expanded into a challenge of the legitimacy of holding any animals captive
- euthanasia generally, but particularly as relates to the disposal of genetic surplus or highly sentient individuals
- the feeding of live prey and, in some cases, whole animal carcasses
- transfers of individuals between zoos, particularly when social relationships that are believed to have attributes in common with those of humans are ruptured as a result
- the use of animals in entertainment, especially performing animals
- bringing new animals in from the wild to augment captive holdings or to start new breeding programs
- the employment of invasive technologies such as embryo manipulation or exogenous hormonal stimulation in breeding efforts
- all research involving animals, even when it is the health and longevity of animals that stand to benefit.

We should be quick to acknowledge that protest is in many cases warranted. Dissent is among our most cherished constitutional prerogatives, and it often forces zoo personnel to examine the ramifications of their actions in ways that otherwise might not occur. There is, furthermore, a difference in views within the zoo community itself regarding the wisdom or legitimacy of a particular course of action, leading in some instances to staff having at least guarded sympathy with the positions of animal rightists. Far from wanting to stifle dissent, we are required to acknowledge that it often has a beneficial effect. Opposition to dissent arises, however, when there are sharp philosophical differences between positions taken by the institution and the dissenting group. It is therefore useful to consider how the philosophies driving the animal rights movement may differ from those underlying the conservation efforts of the zoo/aquarium profession, and how these may have a temporizing effect on certain of the latter's activities.

Attributes common to both Singer's utilitarianism and Regan's notion of inherent value are 1) a disavowal of moral anthropocentrism, 2) granting highest priority to the welfare of individuals, and 3) dependence on a single, fundamental principle such as sentience or self-awareness in granting animals equivalent moral standing with humans.

[. . .]

Although they as a rule give utmost respect to individuals, members of the zoo community are less inclined to grant them rights (Koontz, 1995) and side with holist philosophers in placing greater value on communities of individuals (see chapters in Norton et al., 1995).

[. . .]

As noted in an earlier quote from Regan, once inherent value is granted, there is little ground for making distinctions between individuals. This applies to the distinction between animals that are rare or endangered versus those that are more common. According to the rights view, a rare individual has no higher moral standing than one that is common, since all share equally the basis on which they are granted inherent value. Regan (1983), in an oft quoted comment, states "That an individual animal is among the last remaining members of a species confers no further right to that animal, and its right not to be harmed must be weighed equitably with the rights of any others who have this right" (p. 359). Taken to its logical conclusion, this view allows for no special treatment in protecting threatened ecosystems by culling of unwanted animals (see Hutchins and Wemmer, 1987, for an extended discussion of this point), nor can it condone invasive technologies and the attendant suffering of individuals that are intended to secure their future as a taxon on grounds of rareness (Varner and Monroe, 1991, but see rejoinder by Hutchins and Wemmer, 1991). Animal rights philosophers do not oppose efforts to save endangered species, but neither do they single them out for special treatment. According to Regan (1983), "the general policy recommended by the rights view is: *let them be!*" (p. 361, original italics). In contrast, the zoo biologist or the park manager will usually opt in favor of steps that insure the survival of species over survival of its individual members (see, e.g., Lacy, 1991, 1995).

[. . .]

Norton (1995) points out that humans tacitly acknowledge differential obligations to animals according to context, and uses an example from interactions with wild versus domestic animals. One might chase off a house cat stalking a songbird in the back yard, for example, but would find it unthinkable to interfere with a wild cat's foraging activities. It is the *context* of the encounter that defines value and shapes the morally appropriate response. Furthermore, as this example shows, animals elicit different levels of responsibility from us, with emphasis on the individual when it comes to the community of domesticated animals but on populations, species, and generative processes in experiences of those in a wild state.

This contextual valuation may have particular relevance for the zoo profession. The animal taken into captivity, ostensibly to ensure its future survival, incurs increased obligations from the human community commensurate with its dependence on humans for food, shelter, psychological and physical health, etc. These obligations arise from valuing individuals as individuals, and in recognizing the moral requirement to treat them with respect. Left unsolved by the agreement that, as captives, animals should be granted heightened value, is the morality of taking them into captivity in the first instance. Here, a different value, operating on a different time scale, and at the level of the individual as member of a species or other collective comes into play. Norton suggests that all life forms are engaged in a struggle to survive—an individual striving—but are also engaged in a correlative striving to perpetuate their kind. This striving to perpetuate may fail, and the species is in danger of becoming extinct. At this point, because we value the taxon above the individual, we do for it what it cannot do for itself (notice the similarity in phrasing to the rightist's approach to euthanasia) and take the extraordinary measure of bringing it into the human community. A recent, widely publicized example of an apparent successful intervention illustrating this point is that of the California condor, whose last wild survivors were brought into captivity for protected breeding in 1987 (Toone and Wallace, 1994), and whose descendants are now being returned to the wild.

Although for their benefit, confining wild animals to a captive environment may be said to harm them (Jamieson, 1985, 1995). At this point, the concept of animal altruism is invoked, to wit, the wild animal taken captive sacrifices its freedom and sometimes its life for the good of its kind. By analogy, the soldier who gives his life for his country goes into the breech willingly so that others might live and is regarded as a hero. A difficulty with this analogy is the absence of volunteerism on the part of animals taken into captivity. Lacking the capacity to evaluate and to decide for themselves, their sacrifice on behalf of an abstract principle is without their consent. However, as noted by Norton (1995), an ethic that bases all moral decisions on a single criterion such as Regan's subject-of-a-life is "likely to conclude that sacrifice of individuals for species survival is always wrong because the individuals cannot fulfill the key requirement of voluntary acceptance of risk" (p. 113). This, he points out, is to define altruism in anthropomorphic terms, thereby disqualifying animals from ever acting altruistically in a cause implicit in their struggle to perpetuate their genes.

But, perhaps a slight modification of the analogy, not dependent on the element of volunteerism, is applicable. All-volunteer armies are probably fairly rare, and at least in recent history we have been made painfully aware of the process of conscripting soldiers to defend societies. Far from becoming voluntarily engaged, many conscripts would rather be at home with family than in a fox hole but heed the call when duty demands it. It would be inaccurate to say that acts of heroism are performed only by those who come into harm's way voluntarily. The conscript risking loss of life in battle would surely be severely punished if he/she deserted at that moment. But, self sacrifice would seem to be infrequently coerced by fear of the consequences of desertion. Though not in the situation voluntarily, the conscript accepts the obligation to stay and fight, even against his/her will. And we would see their self-sacrificing acts as no less heroic than those of the volunteer soldier. Following this analogy, the captive exotic is conscripted to sacrifice its freedom in the struggle to perpetuate its kind.

Defending one's country entails a context in which the usual rules of the game are suspended, and values undergo a change commensurate with the needs of society at the time. This, incidentally, may be one context in which having equal inherent value as envisioned by rights advocates does not hold. A rigid rank order, a chain-of-command, and a remarkable difference in rights and privileges are characteristic of all defensive entities, are sanctioned by society in the name of the discipline needed to mount protective actions, and are not to be measured in the same currency as differences in race, gender, and social class. Similarly, defending species from the finality of extinction may be said to have elements of a desperate struggle in which non-voluntary compliance with an extraordinary set of rules comes into play for certain individuals in the community under threat. Assuming captive animal "conscripts" are truly used to help save their kind in a significant way, the deprivation of freedom that is a major concern of rightists/liberationists (see Bostock, 1993, and Jamieson, 1995, for thoughtful discussions of this issue) may to some extent be ameliorated.

Conclusion

To summarize, the pluralistic ethic as set forth by Norton embraces a shifting value, depending on whether the animal is in the wild context, in which case we have a greater duty to collectives than to individuals, or in the community of domesticated animals, where individual welfare takes precedence. The community of zoo animals is, by contrast, a *mixed* community in which both the striving for life and for perpetuation over evolutionary time creates obligations to combine respect for individuals with respect for the process-oriented ethic that applies to preserving their kind. This mixed community is justified because the striving for preservation has taken on the aspects of a battle against global adversity, with attendant loss of freedom and even of life, involuntarily. It is these contextually relevant values that zoo and aquarium professionals readily invoke to justify ex situ conservation efforts.

Along these lines, and with some modification to allow for the special circumstance of the captive exotic, Callicott (1989) articulated a vision that has potential for reconciliation of the different ethics that today foster conflict among people everywhere concerned about the well being of our planet's inhabitants:

> If the case for animal rights would be theoretically restructured to divide animal rights holders from non-holders along the domestic/wild axis rather than subject-/non-subject-of-a-life axis, then its reconciliation with environmental ethics could be envisioned. Both would rest upon a common concept—the community concept. And the very different ethical implications of either would be governed by the different kinds of communities humans and animals comprise—the "mixed" human-domestic community, on the one hand, and the natural, wild biotic community, on the other.

(p. 47)

Reconciliation may also advance from the proposition that no animal lives wholly unto itself but is the "subject-of-a-group-life" or a "community-life," a concept introduced by Livingston (1994, as described by Noske, 1998) to counter the individual or self-centered focus of the rights view. Livingston's thesis asserts the participatory consciousness of wild animals flowing from everyday membership in entities greater than their individual selves and overcomes the problem of redefining animals in the human terms that attend the "subject-of-a-life" construct.

It is fair to presume that zoo professionals are strongly committed to animal welfare but less so to animal rights. Theirs is a profession that, by its very nature, shares the holistic ethic, viz., that preservationist goals can only be achieved by unfailingly giving highest priority to collections of individuals. Zoo professionals frequently find individual welfare and species preservation to be in conflict and in such cases will give higher priority to the preservation of species. It does not follow, as is often claimed, that there is indifference to the interests of individuals or lack of respect for them. In fact, goals of species preservation are more likely to be realized where the lives of individuals are given the highest respect (McManamon, 1993; Lindburg and Lindburg, 1995; Maple *et al.*, 1995), and where every effort is made to safeguard their interests. These dual concerns indicate that those who toil in zoos readily embrace the ethical pluralism that offers a basis for reconciliation with any who question the morality of their acts.

References

Bekoff, M. 1995. Naturalizing and individualizing animal well-being and animal minds; an ethologist's naiveté exposed? In: Rowan A.N., editor. *Wildlife Conservation, Zoos and Animal Protection*. Philadelphia: Tufts Center for Animals and Public Policy. pp. 63–115.

Bostock, S. St C. 1993. *Zoos and Animal Rights: the Ethics of Keeping Animals*. London: Routledge. 227 p.

Callicott J.B. 1989. *In Defense of the Land Ethic*. Albany, NY: State University of New York Press. 325 p.

Cavalieri P., Singer P. (eds). 1993. *The Great Ape Project*. New York: St Martin's Press. 312 p.

Ehrenfeld D. 1991. Conservation and the rights of animals. *Conserv. Biol.* 5:1–3.

Eudey A. 1995. To procure or not to procure. In: Norton B.G., Hutchins M., Stevens E.F., Maple T.L. (eds). *Ethics on the Ark: Zoos, Animal Welfare, and Wildlife Conservation*. Washington, DC: Smithsonian Institution Press, pp. 146–52.

Fox M. 1986. *Laboratory Animal Husbandry: Ethology, Welfare, and Experimental Variables*. Albany, NY: State University of New York Press, 267 p.

Geist V. 1992. Opening statement, panel discussion on "Wildlife conservation and animal rights: are they compatible?" In: *Proceedings of the American Association of Zoological Parks and Aquariums Annual Meeting*, Toronto, Canada. Wheeling, W.V.: American Association of Zoological Parks and Aquariums. pp. 10–2.

Gibbons E.F. Jr, Durrant B.S. Demarest J. 1995. *Conservation of Endangered Species in Captivity: an Interdisciplinary Approach*. Albany, NY: State University of New York Press, 810 p.

Grandy J.W. 1989. Captive breeding in zoos: destructive programs in need of change. *Humane Soc. News* summer: 8–11.

Herzog H.A. 1993. Animal rights and wrongs. *Science* 262:1906–8.

Hutchins M., Fascione N. 1991. Ethical issues facing modern zoos. In: *Proceedings of the American Association of Zoo Veterinarians*, Calgary, Canada, 1991. Philadelphia: American Association of Zoo Veterinarians. pp. 56–64.

Hutchins M., Wemmer C. 1987. Wildlife conservation and animal rights: are they compatible? In: Fox, M.W., Mickley, L.D. (eds). *Advances in Animal Welfare Science 1986–1987*. Washington, DC: Humane Society of the United States. pp. 111–37.

Hutchins M., Dresser B., Wemmer C. 1995. Ethical considerations in zoo and aquarium research. In: Norton B.G., Hutchins M., Stevens E.F., Maple T.L. (eds). *Ethics on the Ark: Zoos, Animal Welfare, and Wildlife Conservation*. Washington, DC: Smithsonian Institution Press. pp. 253–76.

Jamieson D. 1985. Against zoos. In: Singer P., (ed.). *In Defense of Animals*. New York: Harper and Row. pp. 108–17.

Jamieson D. 1995. Zoos revisited. In: Norton B.G., Hutchins M., Stevens R.F., Maple T.L. (eds). *Ethics on the Ark: Zoos, Animal Welfare, and Wildlife Conservation*. Washington, DC: Smithsonian Institution Press. pp. 52–66.

Jamieson D. 1998. Animal liberation is an environmental ethic. *Environ. Values* 7:41–57.

Koontz F. 1995. Wild animal acquisition ethics for zoo biologists. In: Norton B.G., Hutchins M., Stevens E.F., Maple T.L. (eds). *Ethics on the Ark: Zoos, Animal Welfare, and Wildlife Conservation*. Washington, DC: Smithsonian Institution Press. pp. 127–45.

Lacy R.C. 1991. Zoos and the surplus problem: an alternate solution. *Zoo Biol.* 10:293–7.

Lacy R.C. 1995. Culling surplus animals for population management. In: Norton B.G., Hutchins M., Stevens E.F., Maple T.L. (eds). *Ethics on the Ark: Zoos, Animal Welfare, and Wildlife Conservation*. Washington, DC: Smithsonian Institution Press. pp. 187–94.

Lindburg D.G., Lindburg L.L. 1995. Success breeds a quandry: to cull or not to cull. In: Norton B.G., Hutchins M., Stevens E.F., Maple T.L. (eds). *Ethics on the Ark: Zoos, Animal Welfare, and Wildlife Conservation*. Washington, DC: Smithsonian Institution Press, pp. 195–208.

Livingston J.A. 1994. *Rogue Primate: an Exploration of Human Domestication*. Toronto: Key Porter. 278 p.

Loftin R. 1995. Captive breeding of endangered species. In: Norton B.G., Hutchins M., Stevens E.F., Maple T.L. (eds). *Ethics on the Ark: Zoos, Animal Welfare, and Wildlife Conservation*. Washington, DC: Smithsonian Institution Press. pp. 164–80.

Maple T., McManamon R., Stevens E. 1995. Defining the good zoo: animal care, maintenance, and welfare. In: Norton B.G., Hutchins M., Stevens E.F., Maple T.L. (eds). *Ethics on the Ark: Zoos, Animal Welfare, and Wildlife Conservation*. Washington, DC: Smithsonian Institution Press. pp. 219–34.

McManamon R. 1993. The humane care of captive wild animals. In: Fowler M.E. (ed.). *Zoo and Wild Animal Medicine: Current Therapy*. Philadelphia: Saunders, pp. 61–3.

Morrison A.R. 1994. Animal rights and animal politics. *Science* 263:1073–4.

Norton B.G. 1995. A broader look at animal stewardship. In: Norton B.G., Hutchins M., Stevens E.F., Maple T.L. (eds). *Ethics on the Ark: Zoos, Animal Welfare, and Wildlife Conservation*, Washington, DC: Smithsonian Institution Press. pp. 102–21.

Norton B.G., Hutchins M., Stevens E.F., Maple T.L. (eds). 1995. *Ethics on the Ark: Zoos, Animal Welfare, and Wildlife Conservation*, Washington, DC: Smithsonian Institution Press. 330 p.

Noske B. 1993. Great apes as anthropological subjects—deconstructing anthropocentrism. In: Cavalieri P., Singer P. (eds). *The Great Ape Project*. New York: St Martin's Press, pp. 258–68.

Noske B. 1998. Animals as subjects-of-a-group-life. In: Beckoff M. (ed.). *Encyclopedia of Animal Rights and Animal Welfare*. Westport, CT: Greenwood Press, pp. 69–70.

Regan T. 1983. *The Case for Animal Rights*. Berkeley, CA: The University of California Press. 425 p.

Regan T. 1995 Are zoos morally defensible? In: Norton B.G., Hutchins M., Stevens E.F., Maple T.L. (eds). *Ethics on the Ark: Zoos, Animal Welfare, and Wildlife Conservation*. Washington, DC: Smithsonian Institution Press. pp. 38–51.

Rowan A.N. 1992. Opening statement, panel discussion on "Wildlife conservation and animal rights: are they compatible?" In: *Proceedings of the American Association of Zoological Parks and Aquariums Annual Meeting*, Toronto, Canada. Wheeling, W.V.: American Association of Zoological Parks and Aquariums. pp. 12–15.

Shepherdson D.J., Mellen J.D., Hutchins M. (eds). 1998. *Second Nature: Environmental Enrichment for Captive Animals*. Washington, DC: Smithsonian Institution Press. 350 p.

Singer P. 1975. *Animal Liberation*. New York: Avon Books. 320 p.

Singer P., Regan T. (eds). 1976. *Animal Rights and Human Obligations*. Englewood Clifts, NJ: Prentice-Hall. 250 p.

Soulé M.E., Gilpin M., Conway W., Foose T. 1986. The millennium ark: how long a voyage, how many staterooms, how many passengers? *Zoo Biol.* 5:101–13.

Toone W.D., Wallace M.P. 1994. The extinction in the wild and reintroduction of the California condor (*Gymnogyps californianus*). In: Olney P.J.S., Mace G.M., Feistner A.T.C. (eds). *Creative Conservation: Interactive Management of Wild and Captive Animals*. London: Chapman and Hall. pp. 411–9.

Varner G.E. 1994. The prospects for consensus and convergence in the animal rights debate. *Hastings Center Rep.* 24;1:24–8.

Varner G.E., Monroe M.C. 1991. Ethical perspectives on captive breeding: is it for the birds? *Endangered Species Update* 8:27–9.

Zak S. 1989. Ethics and animals. *Atlantic Monthly* March: 69–74.

Chapter 69

Chris Wemmer

OPPORTUNITIES LOST: ZOOS AND THE MARSUPIAL THAT TRIED TO BE A WOLF

Wemmer assesses the responsibilities and directions of zoos and aquariums following identification of the global diversity crisis. He contrasts the conflicting pressures between providing recreational opportunities for the public, providing education to the visiting public, and providing a greater service to society through science and conservation activities; he advocates greater emphasis on using zoos to support science and conservation efforts.

I**N THE ARCHIVES** of the National Zoo there is a story of an opportunity lost. As zoo stories go, it is not unique. There are many others like it. Such stories sometimes tell us about ourselves.

It started sometime in early 1902. Zoo director William Hornaday wanted to exhibit a thylacine: *Thylacinus cynocephalus*—the pouched beast with a dog's head. Depicted by Patterson as "a species perfectly distinct from any of the animal creation hitherto known . . ." (Quammen, 1997:281), the thylacine had been described almost 100 years earlier. Though sometimes called the Tasmanian tiger because of its striped coat, this strange marsupial was actually a "wannabe" wolf. The long-muzzled head with its short ears, the deep chest, and the feet and legs were distinctively dog-like, but the rear end and long tail hinted of marsupial ancestry. True dogs can wag their tails. This one could not. All the same, the thylacine remains a remarkable example of convergent evolution, and the largest carnivorous marsupial to survive into the twentieth century.

[. . .]

In due course, a Tasmanian trapper caught a female, which was shipped to the states. [. . .]

Over a period of about 90 years some 13 zoos on three continents exhibited about 55 thylacines (Guiler, 1986) (Jones, personal communication). Farmers killed nearly 2,200 for bounties during a 21-year period starting in 1888. The last recorded shooting of a thylacine was in 1930. Six years later the last captive animal died in the Hobart Zoo (Beresford and Bailey, 1981). Even in recent times footprints allegedly have been sighted, but irrefutable evidence of the thylacine's survival is lacking. In reality, the thylacine seems to be gone forever (Quammen, 1997).

What did we learn from the thylacines that lived in zoos? Almost nothing. Guiler (1986:66) commented that "[t]here was an extraordinary apathy shown by the various zoos for the fate of the thylacine." String their lives together and you have more than 100 thylacine years in captivity—ample opportunity for some keen observer to note a few details. [. . .] But the zoo legacy to knowledge and conservation of this species is scant. It is recorded in some amateur movie footage, and a few photographs. The rest is stored in a few museum cabinets.

I feel a nostalgic longing when I think of thylacines. But I feel the same way when I visit a zoo and look at any mysterious creature or endangered species. Will they too become opportunities lost to the institutions that celebrate their uniqueness? How many species we now exhibit will share the planet with us in 25 years, when our numbers reach 10 billion? I don't believe zoos are apathetic about the fate of their charges, but I am concerned about their ability to have a lasting and meaningful impact in a rapidly changing world. The biodiversity crisis is on our lips, but our actions send another message. We know zoos can't change the world, but many of us believe we can have a far greater impact than we do at present.

Zoological institutions have clearly acted upon the calls of their visionary leaders to heed the global biodiversity crisis. In the 1980s, the conservation movement added a challenging new dimension to our profession. We saw a remarkable convergence of purpose among the rank and file of our association. Directors, curators, and keepers from different zoos found themselves working together on American Zoo and Aquarium Association (AZA) Species Survival Plan (SSP) committees. Talented keepers and curators discovered latent skills. For many curators, humdrum jobs suddenly became more interesting. New friendships emerged based on a shared vision. The movement grew into a groundswell. The AZA's conservation movement, embodied in the SSP, Taxon Advisory Groups, Scientific Advisory Groups, and Conservation Action Partnerships are extraordinary examples of planning and cooperation among institutions (Hutchins and Conway, 1995). The IUCN/Species Survival Commission's Conservation Breeding Specialist Group was born as a parallel movement in the international realm.

But not everyone was ready to ride the new wave. More midlevel zoo personnel were committed to the movement than directors, and some of the latter believed that "the tail was wagging the dog." When the AZA examined its mandate in the late 1980s, the board of directors consulted with institutional directors, and determined that the association's highest purpose was to provide members with services. While these services were seen clearly by the directors as serving the conservation mandate, the decision was disappointing for those who had been lifted by the surge of the new wave. Many midlevel members of the AZA had hoped for a declaration of commitment to a higher cause. They acknowledged that the AZA had made great advances in developing a conservation ethic, but their perception was that the organization's leaders were unable to agree that, as a unifying principle, conservation transcended the need for services.

[. . .]

Until we adopt a unifying philosophy for zoos and aquariums, our collective potential will not be achieved. We have all said it: "The public goes to the zoo to have a good time. Sure we 'do education,' but the hook is recreation." It's that familiar notion of service. We serve the public what it wants (entertainment) and at the same time we give it what it needs (education). But the word "entertainment" somehow doesn't do justice as a reason for keeping wild animals in captivity. Think about it. Isn't education the highest service zoos and aquariums can offer the visiting public? Surely, as a means of achieving conservation, it deserves to be our highest institutional mandate.

But there is another defect in what many perceive to be mainstream thinking about zoos and aquariums, and that is the notion that our visitors represent the ultimate target audience. Looking back, we can honestly say that the 18 zoos that exhibited thylacines certainly served their visitors, but did they serve society as a whole? They might have, had they been able to work together to prevent the thylacine's extinction. Serving society is a lot different from entertaining the public. Here is where science, captive breeding, reintroduction, education, and in situ conservation play a role. Unfortunately, the public doesn't always understand the benefits to society from zoos and aquariums. That's our responsibility, and that is what zoo and aquarium education should be all about.

Zoos and aquariums of the past didn't have the resources to study and conserve every species in their collections. The biodiversity crisis didn't loom darkly on the horizon. Nevertheless, people like Hornaday knew what was happening in the world, and took decisive action to save the American bison from extinction (Rorabacher, 1970). A lot has happened since then. Time is of the essence, and if we don't act soon, the world will lose much of its biota, including many of the most charismatic and engaging life forms we exhibit. Conway (2000) recently cited a prevailing excuse for inaction voiced by some of our colleagues: "Zoos and aquariums were not designed to be conservation organizations." Zoological institutions have unique and rich resources, staff with diverse skills and talents, and prominence in society. But do the leaders of our profession have the foresight and will to retrofit their organizations for a higher cause, and to make conservation and science their primary reasons for being? Let us think deeply about it, and resolve not to witness another opportunity lost.

References

Beresford Q., Bailey G. 1981. *Search for the Tasmanian Tiger*. Hobart: Blubber Head Press. 81 p.

Conway W.G. 2000. *The Changing Role of Zoos in the 21st Century*. AZA Communique, January: 11–12.

Guiler E.R. 1986. *Thylacine: the Tragedy of the Tasmanian Tiger*. Melbourne, Australia: Oxford University Press. 207 p.

Hutchins M., Conway W.G. 1995. Beyond Noah's ark: the evolving role of modern zoological parks and aquariums in field conservation. *Int. Zoo Year b.* 34:117–130.

IUDZG/CBSG (IUCN/SSC). 1993. *The World Zoo Conservation Strategy. The Role of the Zoos and Aquaria of the World in Global Conservation*. Brookfield, IL: Chicago Zoological Society. 75 p.

Quammen D. 1997. *The Song of the Dodo. Island Biogeography in an Age of Extinctions*. New York: Simon and Schuster. 702 p.

Rorabacher J.A. 1970. *The American Buffalo in Transition: an Historical and Economic Survey of the Bison in America*. St Cloud, MN: North Star Press. 142 p.

FURTHER READING

Bostock, Stephen St. C. (1993) *Zoos and Animal Rights: The Ethics of Keeping Animals*, London: Routledge.

Cohn, J.P. (1992) "Decisions at the zoo," *BioScience* 42(9): 654.

Conway, W. (1995) "Wild and zoo animal interactive management and habitat conservation," *Biodiversity and Conservation* 4(6): 573–594.

Fiore, W.J. and Brunk, G.G. (1992) "Norms of professional behavior in highly specialized organizations: The case of American zoos and aquariums," *Administration and Society* 24(1): 81.

Hancocks, D. (2001) *A Different Nature: The Paradoxical World of Zoos and Their Uncertain Future*, Berkeley: University of California Press.

Hardy, Donna Fitzroy (~1999) The role of domestic animals in the zoo. Online at: http://www.quantum-conservation.org.

Hargrove, E. (1995) "The role of zoos in the twenty-first century," in *Ethics of the Ark: Zoos, Animal Welfare and Wildlife Conservation*, B.G. Norton, M. Hutchins, E.F. Stevens, and T.L. Maple (eds.), Washington D. C.: Smithsonian Institution Press.

Hosey, G.R. (2000) "Zoo animals and their human audiences: What is the visitor effect?" *Animal Welfare* 9: 343–357.

Hutchins, M. (2001) "Animal welfare: What is AZA doing to enhance the lives of captive animals?" *AZA Conference Proceedings* 1996: 77–86.

Hutchins, M. and Conway, W.G. (1995) "Beyond Noah's Ark: The evolving role of modern zoos and aquariums in field conservation," *International Zoo Yearbook* 34: 84–87.

Hutchins, M, Smith, B., Fulk, R., Perkins, L., Reinartz, G., and Wharton, D. (2001) "Rights or welfare: A response to the Great Ape Project. Pp. 329–366, in *Great Apes and Humans: Ethics of Coexistence*, B.B. Beck, T. Stoinski, M. Hutchins, T.L. Maple, B. Norton, A. Rowan, E.F. Stevens, and A. Arluke (eds.), Washington, D.C.: Smithsonian Institution Press.

Hutchins, M., Wiese, R., and Willis, K. (1996) "Why we need captive breeding," *AZA Annual Conference Proceedings* 1996: 77–86.

Jamieson, Dale (1995) "Zoos revisited." Pp. 52–66, in *Ethics of the Ark: Zoos, Animal Welfare and Wildlife Conservation*, B.G. Norton, M. Hutchins, E.F. Stevens, and T.L. Maple (eds.), Washington, D.C.: Smithsonian Institution Press.

Maple, T.L., McManamon, R., and Stevens, E.F. (1995) "Defining the good zoo: Animal care, maintenance, and welfare." Pp. 219–234, in *Ethics of the Ark: Zoos, Animal Welfare and Wildlife Conservation*, Washington, D.C.: Smithsonian Institution Press.

Masci, David (2000) "Zoos in the 21st Century." CQ Researcher, CQ on the Web: www.cq.com. 28 April 2000, pp. 355–364.

Midgley, Mary (1999) "Should we let them go?" Chapter 11, pp. 152–163, in *Attitudes to Animals: Views in Animal Welfare*, F.L. Dolins (ed.), Cambridge, U.K.: Cambridge University Press.

Smith, B. and Hutchins, M. (2000) "The value of captive breeding programmes to field conservation: Elephants as an example." *Pachyderm* 28: 101–9.

Stoinski, Tara S., Ogden, Jacqueline, Gold, Kenneth C., and Maple, Terry L. (2001) "Captive apes and zoo education." Chapter 5, pp. 113–132, in *Great Apes and Humans: The Ethics of Coexistence*, B. B. Beck, T. S. Stoinski, M. Hutchins, T.L. Maple, B. Norton, A. Rowan, E.F. Stevens, and A. Arluke (eds.), Washington, D.C.: Smithsonian Institution Press.

Weichert, John and Norton, Bryan (1995) "Differing conceptions of animal welfare." Pp. 235–250, in *Ethics of the Ark: Zoos, Animal Welfare and Wildlife Conservation*, B.G. Norton, M. Hutchins, E.F. Stevens, and T.L. Maple (eds.), Washington D.C.: Smithsonian Institution Press.

STUDY QUESTIONS

1   In light of Eaton's descriptions, what would be your response to a proposal to prohibit any future retention of marine mammals in captivity? Give your reasoning.

2   How do you respond to Acampora's analogy between zoos and pornography? How does the work of Hutchins *et al.* influence your perception of that analogy? To what degree, if any, do the arguments of Jamieson influence this issue?

3   Lindburg argues that the rights of individual animals should be secondary to the care for populations and species, in contrast to an animal rights view. What is your perspective? Give your reasoning.

4   Wemmer believes that zoo professionals, in contrast to continuing to focus a major emphasis on public recreation and education, should place greater emphasis on supporting science and conservation efforts. Explain your position.

Animal companions

INTRODUCTION TO PART NINE

WHAT MORAL RESPONSIBILITIES DO WE have to our animal companions? In the essay "Affection's Claim" Konrad Lorenz relates some wonderful stories of friendships between dogs and human beings, and asserts that a dog's fidelity imposes a responsibility upon us which is as morally important as our responsibilities to a human friend. Bernard Rollin and Michael Rollin address our responsibilities to our animal companions in a comprehensive way, arguing that we have obligations to all domestic animals because we have built a world in which they have no room to live on their own.

Paul Shepard describes the sequence leading from the sacredness of wild animal life in early human societies to our current situation, in which wild animals are confined in zoos and seen as equivalent to pets and stuffed toys. Pets were created by selective breeding and cannot restore us to wholeness with the natural world. They are "deficient animals," "monsters," "biological slaves." Wild animals, on the other hand, are the last remaining riches of the planet.

Sometimes the bond with a wild animal can approach that experienced with our domesticated animal companions. Anna Merz relates her remarkable experience of raising the wild rhino Samia in a rhino sanctuary in Africa. Merz and Samia experienced a bond of deep love, trust, and friendship over ten years, illustrating that beings of two wholly different species can reach out to each other for understanding.

Freya Mathews asserts that the company of both wild and domesticated nonhuman animals is a necessary part of human life, important for us and for our relationship with the environment. She defends domestication of animals and suggests that we need to find new ways to increase urban habitat for wildlife. Mathews describes her experience of how human psychological intimacy with the "unknowable subjectivity" of other animals helps open us to the world "astir with presence" vastly exceeding just human experience.

In "Protecting Children and Animals from Abuse" James Garbarino argues that child welfare and animal welfare ought to be natural collaborators, even though there have sometimes been divisions between these two caring communities in the past. There are empirical connections between cruelty to animals and cruelty to children. Garbarino points out that the persistent problem is not having too much empathy but having too little. In the next article James Serpell, Raymond Coppinger, and Aubrey Fine point out several important sources of stress or suffering experienced by assistance and therapy animals.

Clare Palmer discusses the complex issues involved in killing healthy animals in animal shelters. She considers three common claims about humane killing based on minimizing pain, as well as Tom Regan's rejection of painless killing. Palmer finds both approaches troubling, and recommends a relational approach. According to this approach the relations of dependence and independence between humans and animals should be taken into account. In the final reading Diane Leigh and Marilee Geyer, former shelter workers, provide their recommendations based on their long experience with homeless animals. They discuss companion animal overpopulation as well as the pressing need to reaffirm the preciousness of life itself.

Chapter 70

Konrad Lorenz

AFFECTION'S CLAIM

Konrad Lorenz describes several memorable dogs and affirms that he has always taken very seriously the responsibility imposed by a dog's fidelity and love. He believes that all love rises from instinctive feeling and that we have obligations to our dogs which are "no less binding" than those to our human friends.

> Knowing me in my soul the very same—
> One who would die to spare you touch of ill!—
> Will you not grant to old affection's claim
> The hand of friendship down Life's sunless hill?
>
> Thomas Hardy

I ONCE POSSESSED a fascinating little book of crazy tales called 'Snowshoe Al's Bedtime Stories'. It concealed behind a mask of ridiculous nonsense that penetrating and somewhat cruel satire which is one of the characteristic features of American humour, and which is not always easily intelligible to many Europeans. In one of these stories Snowshoe Al relates with romantic sentimentality the heroic deeds of his best friend. Incidents of incredible courage, exaggerated manliness and complete altruism are piled up in a comical parody of Western American romanticism culminating in the touching scenes where the hero saves his friend's life from wolves, grizzly bears, hunger, cold and all the manifold dangers which beset him. The story ends with the laconic statement, 'In so doing, his feet became so badly frozen that I unfortunately had to shoot him.'

If I ask a man who has just been boasting of the prowess and other wonderful properties of one of his dogs, I always ask him whether he has still got the animal. The answer, then, is all too often strongly reminiscent of Snowshoe Al's story, 'No, I had to get rid of him—I moved to another town—or into a smaller house—I got another job and it was awkward for me to keep a dog,' or some other similar excuse. It is to me amazing that many people who are otherwise morally sound feel no disgrace in admitting such an action. They do not realize that there is no difference between their behaviour and that of the satirized egoist in the story. The animal is deprived of rights, not only by the letter of the law, but also by many people's insensitivity.

The fidelity of a dog is a precious gift demanding no less binding moral responsibilities than the friendship of a human being. The bond with a true dog is as lasting as the ties of this earth can ever be, a fact which should be noted by anyone who decides to acquire a canine friend. It may of course happen that the love of a dog is thrust upon one involuntarily, a circumstance which occurred to me when I met the Hanoverian Schweisshund, 'Hirschmann', on a skiing tour. He was at the time about a year old and a typical masterless dog; for his owner the head forester only loved his old Deutscher Rauhaar (German Pointer) and had no time for the clumsy stripling which showed few signs of ever becoming a gun-dog. Hirschmann was soft and sensitive and a little shy of his master, a fact which did not speak highly for the training ability of the forester. On the other hand I did not think any the better of the dog for coming out with us as early as the second day of our stay. I took him for a sycophant, quite wrongly as it turned out, for he was following not us but me alone. When one morning I found him sleeping outside my bedroom door, I began to reconsider my first opinion and to suspect that a great canine love was germinating. I realized it too late: the oath of allegiance had been sworn nor would the dog recant on the day of my departure. I tried to catch him in order to shut him up and prevent him from following us, but he refused to come near me. Quivering with consternation and with his tail between his legs he stood at a safe distance saying with his eyes, 'I'll do anything at all for you—except leave you!' I capitulated. 'Forester, what's the price of your dog?' The forester, from whose point of view the dog's conduct was sheer desertion, replied without a moment's consideration, 'Ten shillings.' It sounded like an expletive and was meant as such. Before he could think of a better one, the ten shillings were in his hand and two pairs of skis and two pairs of dog's paws were under way. I knew that Hirschmann would follow us but surmised erroneously that, plagued by his conscience, he would slink after us at a distance, thinking that he was not allowed to come with us. What really did happen was entirely unexpected. The full weight of the huge dog hit me broadsides on like a cannon ball and I was precipitated hip foremost on to the icy road. A skier's equilibrium is not proof against the impact of an enormous dog, hurled in a delirium of excitement against him. I had quite underestimated his grasp of the situation. As for Hirschmann, he danced for joy over my extended corpse.

I have always taken very seriously the responsibility imposed by a dog's fidelity, and I am proud that I once risked my life, though inadvertently, to save a dog which had fallen into the Danube at a temperature of $-28°C$. My Alsatian, Bingo, was running along the frozen edge of the river when he slipped and fell into the water. His claws were unable to grip the sides of the ice so he could not get out. Dogs become exhausted very quickly when attempting to get up too steep a bank. They get into an awkward, more and more upright swimming position until they are soon in imminent danger of drowning. I therefore ran a few yards ahead of the dog which was being swept downstream; then I lay down and, in order to distribute my weight, crept on my belly to the edge of the ice. As Bingo came within my reach, I seized him by the scruff of the neck and pulled him with a jerk towards me on to the ice, but our joint weight was too much for it— it broke, and I slid silently, head first into the freezing cold water. The dog, which, unlike myself, had its head shorewards, managed to reach firmer ice. Now the situation was reversed; Bingo ran apprehensively along the ice and I floated downstream in the current. Finally, because the human hand is better adapted than the paw of the dog for gripping a smooth surface, I managed to escape disaster by my own efforts. I felt ground beneath my feet and threw my upper half upon the ice.

We judge the moral worth of two human friends according to which of them is ready to make the greater sacrifice without thought of recompense. Nietzsche who, unlike most people, wore brutality only as a mask to hide true warmness of heart, said the beautiful words, 'Let it be your aim always to love more than the other, never to be the second.' With human beings, I am sometimes able to fulfil this command-ment, but in my relations with a faithful dog, I am always the second. What a strange and unique social relationship! Have you ever thought how extraordinary it all is? Man, endowed with reason and a highly developed sense of moral responsibility, whose finest and noblest belief is the religion of brotherly love, in this very respect falls short of the carnivores. In saying this I am not indulging in sentimental anthropo-morphization. Even the noblest human love arises, not from reason and the specifically human, rational moral sense, but from the much deeper age-old layers of instinctive feeling. The highest and most selfless moral behaviour loses all value in our estimation when it arises not from such sources but from the reason. Elizabeth Browning said,

> If thou must love me, let it be for nought
> Except for love's sake only.

Even to-day man's heart is still the same as that of the higher social animals, no matter how far the achievements of his reason and his rational moral sense transcend theirs. The plain fact that my dog loves me more than I love him is undeniable and always fills me with a certain feeling of shame. The dog is ever ready to lay down his life for me. If a lion or a tiger threatened me, Ali, Bully, Tito, Stasi, and all the others would, without a moment's hesitation, have plunged into the hopeless fight to protect my life if only for a few seconds. And I?

Chapter 71

Bernard E. Rollin and Michael D.H. Rollin

DOGMATICISMS AND CATECHISMS: ETHICS AND COMPANION ANIMALS

Bernard Rollin and Michael Rollin enumerate the many ways in which companion animals are mistreated. They trace the source of this mistreatment to the invisibility of our treatment of companion animals. The solution is to examine our own behavior and to accept regulation of animal acquisition: a demonstration of knowledge should be required.

Welfare problems in companion animals, and the shortfalls of the social ethic

[. . .]

WE KILL SOMEWHERE between 10 and 20 million healthy dogs and cats a year (or between two and four million). (I am always astounded by the ferocity with which the exact number is debated and I am reminded thereby of a Marxist-Stalinist colleague who, confronted with the accusation that Stalin killed 50 million people, loudly proclaimed that he had killed no more than 20 million!) In addition, we treat them appallingly. We perpetuate dozens of genetic diseases of dogs through aesthetically-based dysfunctional "breed standards." The Bulldog's respiratory problems or the Shar-Pei's skin problems provide clear examples. We ignore the functionality of these animals and treat them as, in the words of one of my veterinary colleagues, "living statues." (Veterinary medicine should take a strong stand against this approach for reasons of preventative medicine alone!)

We acquire these animals while knowing nothing of their needs and natures, then get rid of them because they cannot help those needs and natures. We lavish affection on them—as a child does on a new toy—until familiarity or age takes the edge off cuteness. We adopt them on a whim, and get rid of them when it passes. And, exactly like the profit-motivated confinement agriculturalists most pet owners would profess to abhor, we alter them surgically to fit the truncated environments or hoops to jump we provide. Many trim beaks in chickens, crop ears and dock tails in dogs. Many castrate and sometimes spay, beef cattle without anesthesia, and do the same to companion animals without analgesia and sometimes with "anesthesia" that is in fact little more than chemical restraint—e.g. ketamine alone—for cat spays. Many owners train with shock collars and negative reinforcement, rubbing a puppy's nose in its feces when it does what comes naturally. Many find nothing problematic in crating a dog all day, while we profess to abhor the crating of veal calves. Where it is still legal, many declaw cats, yet let them go outside, robbing them of both defense and escape. Others "devocalize" dogs because they bark. These owners fail to understand and respect companion animal nature as surely as do those animal researchers or intensive agriculturalists who see animals as tools, and keep them in a manner determined by our convenience, not by their needs or comfort. Rhinestone collars (or diamond collars), painted toenails, and birthday parties do not begin to compensate for days of neglect followed erratically by hours of child-substitute attention.

If ever any social use of animals does not warrant abuse, suffering, or death, it is animals as companions. After all, almost all of the pet-owning public will resoundingly declare that they see their animals as "members of the family," more perhaps, a bitter attestation to our growing numbers of dysfunctional families than a glowing tribute to our moral behavior towards our animal friends.

[. . .]

In our urban and suburban society, where *society* not *community* dominates—where we don't know our neighbors, and don't care to know our neighbors; where we stand in an elevator as far away from everyone else as possible; where so many marriages end in divorce; where inaugurating a conversation with a stranger is virtually unthinkable; where, if you fall down, people step over you—a companion animal is kept to give, and to receive, love, probably the ultimate human requirement. And, ironically, it is kept to bring us closer to other humans. In New York City, only people with dogs (or babies) get to talk to strangers without suspicion. Thus, as the phrase human–animal bond suggests, there ought to be an unbreakable contract between both parties, analogous to the one found in the best cases of husbandry agriculture.

[. . .]

I do believe, as I have affirmed for almost 20 years, that we have a contractual relationship with all domestic animals, but most clearly so with those who are totally dependent on us, and for whom we have left no room to subsist, let alone thrive, on their own. If the human animal bond is to be more than a slogan for the very lucrative pet industry, more than a marketing ploy for veterinary services, we must face up to the fact that animals are doing fine holding up their end of the bargain; it is we who should be ashamed.

For many years those who advocate for companion animals have promulgated the same solutions— spay and neuter, early spay and neuter, harvest gonads, or seek high-tech equivalents. Adopt, foster, euthanize. Yet while spay and neuter has reduced our killing of puppies and kittens, so that some humane societies must import litters, it has not stopped the killing of dogs and cats. If stray animals were the issue, the problem would have been resolved a generation ago through efficient animal control. The typical animal trashed is not a stray; but a young adult male dog or cat. Meanwhile, as a veterinarian friend once bitterly remarked, we kill them so nothing bad will happen to them, even though Alan Beck[1] and others have shown that at least some unowned dogs, even urban ones, would survive and thrive, while it is evident that large numbers of feral cats do as well or better. Indeed, it can be argued that feral dogs and particularly cats can be viewed as urban wildlife, and left alone, as Dr. Steve Frantz of the New York State Health Department has asserted to me in conversation. There is some evidence that aggressive destruction of feral cats leads to a rodent outbreak that is far more dangerous to human health than leaving the cats alone.[2]

A secondary tragedy, virtually unnoticed by society, is thereby perpetrated on those who care most about animals—they do society's dirty work at the expense of their physical, mental, and spiritual health. Be these people humane society volunteers, animal control personnel, or veterinarians, they suffer for our sins, as victims of what I have elsewhere called moral stress,[3] resulting from the constant tension arising out of what they believe they *should* be doing, in contrast to what they are doing. It is no wonder that, at the 1981 conference I helped organize with the Animal Medical Center and the Columbia University College of Physicians and Surgeons on client grief over pet loss, veterinarians wanted most to speak of their own grief at the constant assault on their souls occasioned by client requests for convenience euthanasia. It is no wonder that animal control people have told me repeatedly that they would do anything to make their own job obsolete. It is no wonder that humane society people "burn out."

[. . .]

Things can be invisible in two ways—either too remote or too familiar. We as a society are making it our business to ethically illuminate animal use that was historically remote—animal research, agriculture, genetic engineering—but we are not yet ready to criticize what is invisible to us because we take it for granted. We have not yet realized, as the comic-strip character Pogo wisely remarked, that we have "met the enemy, and they is us." Unwittingly, our shelters and humane societies have contributed to the problem—they have swept our dirt under the carpet, and sheltered us in the end from the truth more than they have sheltered the animals.

Extending the social ethic: regulation, education, and policy

[. . .] [All] societies must have a *social consensus ethic*, an ethic encoded in law and rules, and constraining everyone's behavior lest we degenerate into chaos and anarchy. Hence it is universally known that murder, rape, robbery and so on are seen as wrong, and "not in my opinion" does not exonerate you from the social consequences of such actions. On the other hand, much action of ethical significance is left to our individual views of right and wrong, our *personal ethic*. Such ethically significant issues as what we eat, what we read, what charity we contribute to or what religion we profess are all left to our personal ethic in our society, though not, of course, in all societies.

[. . .]

The treatment of animals—with the exception of social forbidding of cruelty—was for most of human history a paradigm case of that which was left to people's personal ethic. However, [. . .] it is ever-increasingly being subsumed by the social ethic. With the coming, for example, of solid empirical evidence that the research community was not doing right by animals in failing to control pain and distress, in failing to provide consistent high quality care, in failing to suit the environments of animals to their needs and natures (thereby both harming the animals and the scientific activity for which they were being used), society felt compelled to regulate something they didn't fully understand, for moral reasons.

As we have sketched, the suffering of companion animals is profoundly troubling morally. Essentially no benefit emerges from it, save for the emotional satisfaction of the owner; there is no claim comparable to that of the morally conscientious scientist who affirms that though there is ultimately no moral justification for harming innocent animals for human benefit, he or she will continue to uneasily do so for the tangible benefit it provides. Our injustice—for such it is—to companion animals cannot even be seen as constituting a moral dilemma, for what is the upside of our behavior? Indeed, there is a demonstrable down side—we treat irresponsibility as acceptable, the sidestepping of moral responsibility as inevitable, the bond to others who depend on us as revocable for convenience. If failing to check cruelty to animals inexorably leads to cruelty to humans, does something similar result from failing to honor our responsibilities to animals?

[. . .]

The only solution then is to shine our new social ethic on ourselves, to illuminate our own backyards. If the agricultural community were openly creating genetically diseased animals for profit (such as the genetically engineered super-pig) society would shut them down. Is doing it to our companion animals anymore justifiable morally? (Dozens of new genetic diseases in companion animals have been identified since I first wrote of this issue 20 years ago).

Recent work by Salman et al.[4] provides solid empirical grounding for what most shelter workers have known anecdotally—people relinquish animals to be trashed because they are cheap; they have no major investment in them (and they can always get another one). People relinquish animals because they have "personal problems," because they are allergic to them, because they cannot deal with their behavior, because they have no knowledge or false knowledge of what it takes to have and care for an animal and, above all, as Salman does not tell us but common sense does, because there are no consequences resulting from being irresponsible—not even social opprobrium or censure. Companion animals—easy come, easy go.

What can be done via the social ethic? Obviously, one cannot legislate responsibility as a character trait. But one can legislate responsible behavior, even as we can and do legislate morality—our whole social ethic embodied in law is in fact legislated morality!

Before discussing strategy, however, let me make a personal disclaimer. Philosophically, I tend to be an anarchist, and loathe regulation. I will not, for example, ride my Harley-Davidson in states with mandatory helmet laws. And I am very uncomfortable in general with being required to do things "for my own good." But just because we are over-regulated in some areas in a paternalistic way does not mean we are sufficiently regulated in others. In general, I believe that we are too paternalistic in dealing with rational adults, yet too lax in dealing with infractions against innocent objects of moral concern—infants, children, animals. I see great moral incongruity in people who batter babies and children to death or blindness or a permanent vegetative state getting their wrists slapped while those who swindle wealthy (and greedy) professionals go to jail for a decade.

The only solution to our widespread, systematic, and unnoticed moral irresponsibility towards animals is to regulate—i.e., encode in the social ethic—the acquisition, management, and relinquishment of companion animals. One cannot get a driver's license or a hunting license without (at least officially) becoming educated about the nature and rules of driving. One cannot own a car without permanently identifying it so that it is always traceable. And one cannot simply abandon a car or even simply park it on the street indefinitely. Creating a similar situation for companion animals seems to me a reasonable way to address the ignorance from whence flows our current irresponsibility. Animal "overpopulation" is not a birth control problem to be solved by high-tech gonad hunting—it is a moral problem, a problem of human behavior and abrogation of responsibility. In a responsible society, nothing more high-tech than a leash is needed for birth control. In fact, I believe that excessive gonad hunting has probably harmed the canine gene pool, with responsible people who acquire the best animals assuring that these animals' genes are not passed on, while clueless people happily breed disasters.

Currently an animal is often an impulse item. I see the Disney film "101 Dalmatians;" I want a Dalmatian. I see the film "Turner and Hooch;" I want a Tibetan Mastiff. Kittens are cute; I want a kitten. I want one, I get one. As Salman's[4] study indicates, most pet owners know very little about their animals. Philosophically, I cannot have a rational desire for a dog if I have no idea what owning a dog entails.

I would therefore argue that people wishing to acquire an animal should at least be compelled to demonstrate that they know what they are getting into. Licensing of owners should be a precondition of acquiring an animal; demonstrated knowledge should be a precondition of licensure. How one best acquires the knowledge is an empirical question. Perhaps a mandatory course in pet husbandry and responsibility (ethics) could become a staple of junior high or high school curricula. There is precedent here in the unparalleled growth of environmental awareness among young people in the late 1960s.

Alternatively, one could provide adult education and counseling for prospective pet owners. Although Americans resist jumping through bureaucratic hoops, they respect education. Many people seeking concealed weapons permits do not oppose mandatory shooting and safety courses—indeed welcome them—realizing that acquiring a gun is a major responsibility. So too is acquiring an animal. If one can't have an animal because of allergies, it would be good to know this *before* one gets an animal!

Such education could be undertaken, as I suggested years ago, by veterinarians, or by other trained animal behavior counselors. They ought to be paid, perhaps from the license fees, and will benefit by being exposed to members of the public they would not otherwise meet.

[. . .]

Obviously one cannot force such a policy upon society without risking the absurdity of Prohibition. Plato said that when dealing with ethics and adults, one must not teach, one must remind. In other words, one must show them that what one is trying to get them to do is implicit in what they already believe, only they don't realize it. So any law must be preceded by public education analogous to what convinced the public that the research community was not meeting its obligations to the animals it uses or that our environmental despoliation was intolerable. The public must be made to realize that "they is us," that often our treatment of companion animals is as egregious, shocking, immoral, and unacceptable—indeed more so—than any animal use in society. And this means telling the truth.

Finally, a system of permanent identification for companion animals must be put into effect, and humane societies and veterinarians positioned to reject convenience euthanasia for morally unacceptable reasons. (For example, pet owners could post a bond that they forfeit if they elect convenience euthanasia.) The technology is becoming increasingly available for trace-back of companion animals, as society demands irrefutable trace-back of food animals for reasons of food safety.

I do not propose legislation lightly, nor am I clear about what form it should take. This must evolve through public discussion informed by an awareness of the moral unacceptability—by society's own lights—of our current treatment of companion animals. As principal architects of 1985 federal law for laboratory animals, my colleagues and I faced a similar challenge—how does one legislate moral use of animals when the community using the animals sees no moral issues therein, and in fact further affirms that one must be agnostic about animal pain and that science is "ethics-free?" By legislating moral deliberation in animal care and use committees and mandating the control of pain and suffering, we were able to elevate the thinking of scientists beyond their ideological denial of the meaningfulness of these issues. Many believe that this has worked, as we raise a generation of young scientists to whom moral discussion and pain control are second nature. A good law, in the end, becomes an educational device, which, if it works properly, eventually vitiates the need for its own existence by creating a new culture in the regulated population.

I would very much like to believe that the society that has developed a new ethic for animals would have the moral courage to turn that ethic on itself. We who advocate for animals must therefore begin an educational campaign to force that dramatic turn. That, in turn, means not allowing people to escape the visible consequences of their own irresponsibility. We must cease to worry about offending the guilty; we must cease to be their sin eaters; we must cease battering the souls of those who care most. If we fail, we risk the moral revulsion of society as a whole, who could conceivably react by eliminating companion animal ownership altogether, as some societies have done. And this would be a great pity, for as both cowboys and Indians can tell you, we are irretrievably and mortally diminished if we must live without animals.

Notes

1   Beck, A. M. 1973. *The Ecology of Stray Dogs: A Study of Free-Ranging Urban Animals*. Baltimore, Maryland: York Press.
2   Personal communication, Dr. David Neil, University of Alberta.
3   Rollin, B. E. 1986. Euthanasia and moral stress. In *Loss, Grief, and Care* 115–26, ed. R. DeBellis. Binghamton, NY: Hawarth Press.
4   Salman, M. D., New, J. C., Scarlett, J., Kass, P., Ruch-Gallie, R. and Hetts, S. 1998. Human and animal factors related to the relinquishment of dogs and cats in 12 selected animal shelters in the U.S. *Journal of Applied Animal Welfare Science* 1: 204–26. See also Scarlett, J. M., Salman, M. D., New, J. C., and Kass, P. H. 1999. Reasons for relinquishment of companion animals in U.S. animal shelters: selected health and personal issues. *Journal of Applied Animal Welfare Science* 2: 41–57; and New, J. C., Salman, M. D., King, M., Scarlett, J. M., Kass, P. H. and Hutchison, J. M. 2000. Characteristics of shelter-relinquished animals and their owners compared with animals and their owners in U.S. pet-owning households. *Journal of Applied Animal Welfare Science* 3: 179–203.

Chapter 72

Paul Shepard

THE PET WORLD

Paul Shepard traces the dramatic change from wild and sacred animal life through domestication, stuffed animal toys for children, pet dogs and cats, and finally to zoos. He describes pets as "civilized paraphernalia," created by selective breeding and hence unable to restore us to wholeness with the Others. Pets only confuse our perception of the wild universe, an outer wilderness which we need to become aware of in our own selves.

[. . .]

AGAINST THE INDIFFERENCE of the wild animals, the impetuous affection of our pets seems like an enormous boon. In a world so full of problems and suffering, only the worst curmudgeonly cynic would sneer at our indulgence, their simple pleasure in us, and our joy in them. Something, however, is profoundly wrong with the human/animal pet relationship at its most basic level. Given the obvious benefits of that affiliation, one has to poke very carefully into its psychology and ecology before its fragile core can be exposed.

[. . .]

During the rise of [the] biological void in urban existence in the industrial world from 1850 to 1950, the middle classes began to have fewer children, for whom the household could be a lonely place. In fiction, such a child who represented childhood without siblings and without easy access to street friends was Christopher Robin, for whom Winnie the Pooh was the substitute. Pooh Bear is an animated and storied teddy bear. In this way the Anglo-American concept of animal friends is prefigured in childhood, with the aid of "bedtime" stories, by pretending that one's stuffed toys are alive. This scenario creates a very different childhood orientation toward the living pets than in earlier times, when household animals like rabbits might be eaten, cats caught mice, and dogs served as guards or hunters. From Pooh Bear it is not very far to the doggy friend and but a step from the doggy friend to an imaginary relationship with or among wild animals—animals which, for the first time in history, are almost completely lacking in the child's experience. This sequence is a drama in five acts.

Act I is an outer circle of wild animal life which was a major focus of human attention, establishing the expectation of a rich, surprising, meaningful, and beautiful diversity of life around us. Some animals were sacred. All were conscious, unique, and different in spiritual power.

In Act II people took certain animals into captivity, manipulated their reproduction, and altered their biological natures to conform to human dominance, reconstructing them as members of the household. These became the domestic animals. The wild forms, reduced in number and diversity, literally receded.

Act III begins not with animals but with a class of things called "transitional objects." These are toted around by anxious three-year-old children who are having difficulty becoming independent from their mothers and who are comforted by a soft object that is subjectively intermediate between themselves and the outside world. The children who do not seem to require the security of such objects are those who are surrounded by abundant other forms of life. The exact reason for this is not entirely clear, but apparently animals in their diversity model a world of likeness and difference which makes the child's impending separation less frightening and also resonates with internal, psychic structures which can best be described metaphorically as a fauna. The stuffed toys are simultaneously huggable, transitional objects and "animals." They appeared in large numbers in the industrial, nuclear-family era, compensating children for their lonesome social and ecological situations and preparing them for lifelong pet keeping. The mode of this preparation is pretend-play, the self-dramatization of all life as a happy playground.

Act IV is the transfer of this affection from effigies to dogs and cats. As the toys had been pets, the pets became toys. Even "wild" animal manikins, such as stuffed bears and lions, are little people in the imagination, who participate in a household society, who have expectations, reasons, worries, expressions, voices, tastes, and complicated affinities and antipathies toward each other and their human companions.

Act V extends the equivalence of the living domestic pet and the stuffed wild toy to living nature. If the domestic forms have all along been substitutes for the wild and the latter have become unavailable and unknown, it is easy to fuse the domestic and wild. The wild are simply those potential pets who do not happen to live with us. They are each other's pets, or perhaps creatures whose friendship we have lost. Zoos seem to affirm this identity. The zoo has "toy verisimilitude," foreshadowing the modern child's menagerie of stuffed animals and friendly pets, each zoo creature enduring in blind lethargy, withdrawn except in moments of hyperactivity when the feeder comes, like the puppets waiting in the closet to be flung into tea parties or wagons by a child.

[. . .]

Pets are not part of human evolution or the biological context out of which our ecology comes. They are civilized paraphernalia whose characteristic combination of accompaniment and accommodation is tangled in an ambiguous tyranny. Constance Perrin, an anthropologist, calls it "attachment theory." The animal triggers nurturant behavior and serves as a kind of intermediate object between the owner and a more or less alien world, but at the same time it is dragged about like a tattered security blanket. Indeed, the domestication of animals has never ensured their tender care. In recent Anglo-American tradition the dog is "man's best friend," but it is abhorred in the Bible. In Muslim tradition the dog's saliva is noxious, and contact between people and dogs requires ritual cleansing. Over most of the planet the dog is a cur and mongrel scavenger, feral, half-starved, the target of the kick and thrown rock, often cruelly exploited as a slave. Although looked upon with affection, even modern pets are property that is bought, sold, "put down," and neutered. Pets are deliberately abandoned by the millions and necessitate city-run slaughter-houses, shelters, and "placement" services. This paradox of frenetic emotion and casual dismissal reveals our deep disappointment in the pet's ability to do something, be something, that we cannot quite identify. Yi-Fu Tuan considers our behavior to be exercises in casual domination that symbolize human control of nature.[1] In an earlier book I argued that pets were unacknowledged surrogates for human companionships or substitutes for the resolution of interpersonal social problems, and therefore impaired normal human sociality by enabling people to avoid mending, maturing, or otherwise dealing with their personal relationships.[2] Pets can cause family conflict, even divorce, and may become bridges of unhealthy transference relationships and regression to infantile human behavior.

Even so, I now see that the pet may be more than a human replacement. "Pet-facilitated therapy," casual or institutionalized, reduces human suffering. It is truly an astonishing solace. The "companion animal" is a medical miracle to which we should be kind and grateful. But like all psychotherapy its presence is not a true healing. It cheers, modulates pain, and helps the owner/patient to cope.

Domestic animals were "created" by humans by empirical genetic engineering over the past ten thousand years. They are vestiges and fragments from a time of deep human respect for animals, whose abundance dazzled us in their many renditions of life, helping us to know ourselves by showing all that we had not become. The pet cannot restore us to that wholeness any more than an artificial limb renews the original; nor can it do more than simulate the Others among whom our ancestors lived for so long, the Others that constituted for them a cosmos. They and all captive animals are like organ transplants: healthy for us but cut out of their own organic fabric.

What is wrong at the heart of the keeping of pets is that they are deficient animals in whom we have invested the momentum of two million years of love of the Others. They are monsters of the order invented by Frankenstein except that they are engineered to conform to our wishes, biological slaves who cringe and fawn or perform or whatever we wish. As embodiments of trust, dependence, companionship, esthetic beauty, vicarious power, innocence, or action by command, they are wholly unlike the wild world. In effect, they are organic machines conforming to our needs.

No one now doubts that pets can be therapeutic. But they are not a glorious bonus on life; rather they are compensations for something desperately missing, minimal replacements for friendship in all of its meanings. Mass society isolates us in ways and degrees that seem to contradict our population density. Pets occupy by default an equally great human need for others who are not part of our personal lives. The diversity that nourishes the mind extends to the whole realm of life and nature. Pets, being our own creations, do not replace that wild universe. But as living animals they confuse our perception and hide the lack of a wild, nonhuman comity of players on a grand scale—a spectacular drama of life to which our human natures commit our need and expectation.

Wild animals are not our friends. They are uncompromisingly not us nor mindful of us, just as they differ among themselves. They are the last undevoured riches of the planet, what novelist Romain Gary called "the roots of heaven." We cannot comprehend the world as it is experienced by a bat, a termite, or a squid; we cannot force them into barnyard conviviality or household banality without destroying them. More than bearded prophets and great goddesses they are the mediators between us and plants, the rock and suns around us, the rest of the universe. Wild animals connote the wildness in us which cannot be equated to our domestic affairs or reconciled with the petty tyrannies of "dwellers in houses," domesticates, from the same root word that gives "constrain" or "subdue." As a fauna only the wild are a mirror of the multifold strangeness of the human self. We know this. It is why we scrutinize and inspect and remark on them, make them the subject of our art and thought, and sometimes kill and eat them with mindful formality, being in place with our own otherness.[3]

Notes

1   Yi-Fu Tuan, *Dominance and Affection: The Making of Pets* (New Haven: Yale University Press, 1984).
2   Paul Shepard, *Thinking Animals* (New York: Viking, 1978).
3   James O. Breeden (ed.), *Advice Among Masters: The Ideal in Slave Management in the Old South* (Westport: Greenwood Press, 1980).

Chapter 73

Anna Merz

HAND-RAISING A RHINO IN THE WILD

Anna Merz describes how she raised Samia, a female black rhino abandoned by her mother. The tiny baby rhino slept in her bed. When Samia matured and integrated with wild rhinos, she protected Merz in dangerous situations and returned to visit with her daily. Merz's story is so evocative that the reader grieves with her at the tragic death of Samia and her baby.

S AMIA, THE FEMALE black rhino who was my pride and my joy, was born ten years ago in the Ngare Sergoi Rhino Sanctuary on the western side of Lewa Downs, a 45,000-acre cattle ranch situated on the northern slopes of Mt. Kenya. I have lived all my life with animals and I have handraised many, but Samia was truly unique. Between us there existed a love, a trust, a reaching out for understanding unlike anything I had known in a relationship before. With her there was none of the usual relationship between man and beast. I never tried to discipline or hold her; she lived as a wild rhino. Yet of her own free will, she kept alive with me the bonds of love, trust, and friendship until her death.

Early in 1984 the sanctuary received its first rhinos, including Samia's mother, Solia. At the present time there are nineteen white and twenty-two black rhinos. Twenty calves have been born here. Not all have survived, but those that died, died of natural causes; none have been poached.

On February 15, 1985, Solia gave birth to a calf, Samia, and promptly deserted her. At that time I knew virtually nothing about rhinos, and certainly nothing about raising rhino babies, not even the proper composition of black rhino milk. Over weeks and months I battled with Samia's unending bouts of diarrhea, dehydration, and abnormal temperatures. As a tiny baby, she slept in my bed, causing matrimonial complications with the amazing messes she produced. Raising her was a series of crises, but at about six months, she started to stabilize.

Each day I walked her over ever-increasing distances to introduce her to the world of which she would be a part and its inhabitants. I remember our first encounter with a group of giraffes; long black eyelashes aflutter, they peered at us with astonishment, this strange combination of old woman, baby rhino, and black dog. Samia didn't see them until they moved and then, in terror at their size, dashed between my legs for safety. This was not a practical proposition and I sat down with a thud. Unable to get under me she compromised by sitting on my prostrate form, snorting her disapproval.

Samia learned quickly that I did not really appreciate being knocked over, even in play, and as her strength grew so her gentleness with me increased. As we walked, she would, of her own accord, offer a helping tail to pull me up the steeper trails. When I weaned her at three and a half years, I expected the bond between us to loosen, as would be only natural, but it never did. For ten years, Samia and I were companions, and even when she was mature and integrated with the wild rhinos, she usually returned to visit with me at least once a day.

During our time together, she taught me so much about the world of the rhino that I could never have learned otherwise. I also tried to teach Samia what I thought she would need to know in order to survive. But I was not always successful. To help Samia develop her sense of smell, I hid, hoping she would put her nose to the ground and search after me. Instead, she went to the garden gate, opened it to let the dogs out, then galloped after them straight to me. By no stretch of the imagination can this be described as instinctive behavior.

Rhinos are not, as reputed, solitary, bad-tempered, stupid animals. I had been warned that after my experience with chimps in Ghana, I would find them dangerous and boring. Rather the opposite. Rhino intelligence is close to that of chimps and their outstanding characteristics are curiosity and nervousness rather than aggression. Through her incredible intelligence, Samia was able to reveal a great deal about the social structure of rhino society and much of the complex methods of communication her species uses, including a wide variety of noises and the regulation of breathing to form a sort of Morse code of sound.

In the beginning of our relationship, I was the teacher and the protector. As she matured our roles reversed, and she showed herself capable of teaching and protecting me. A few weeks before the birth of Samia's own calf, she joined me, which was not unusual, when I was walking the dogs one evening. The thick tropical dusk was falling when three rhinos emerged on the track ahead of us. To avoid them I would have to make a long detour through the thorny bush in the dark. Samia, sensing both my fear and my indecision, realized my predicament and took charge of the situation. She knew these three white rhinos well and would normally have ignored them. Now, she trotted up to them, ears laid flat, huffing and hurrumphing angrily, and they retreated in astonishment at her aggressive behavior. Satisfied that they were routed, she returned to me and the dogs and escorted us safely past where they had been. When she was satisfied that we were safe, she left us to resume her own affairs.

When Samia was mated it was by the wild and violent-tempered bull Kenu. He was a small but immensely powerful rhino and many times he came near my house. On one occasion, Samia saw I was in danger and moved very quickly between us with the intention of stopping his charge. Another day Samia and Kenu visited me together. I went to the gate to greet her not realizing he was there. She stood between us and I could sense his rage and hatred of me, his desire to obliterate both me and that gate that stood between us. For forty long minutes we three stood together and I could both see and hear the breathing patterns by which they were communicating with one another. I could literally see the control that Samia was exercising over his behavior. The first time she protected me, I thought it was chance and good luck, but the second and subsequent times revealed her focus and intention. From running to me for safety, she had come to act as my protector against buffalo and her own kind, but never had I expected her to actually protect me from her own mate.

On the morning of April 11, 1995, I learned, via a radio call, that Samia had had a baby. With both joy and terror, I and a tracker crept to where I could see her, feeding quietly. Deep in the long grass near her flickered the tips of two long ears. There was no sound but that of Samia's munching. I was relieved because I knew from painful experience that baby rhinos cry only if they are in trouble. Half an hour later, the tiny creature staggered to its feet, wobbled round Samia's hind legs, thrust its wee nose into her flank, and started to suckle. Samia stopped feeding and stood quietly while it drank from first one teat and then the other. There was no doubt that she had milk, nor was there any doubt as to the baby's sex—Samia had a son.

Two days later, I was watching her with two trackers and was so absorbed that I did not notice the change in the wind. The trackers moved back but she had got my scent. Now what? These long years of observation have taught me that rhinos are fiercely protective mothers and very solitary for the first year of their baby's life. My knees were shaking so much I had to sit down. Then Samia came to me and, as she had in the past, rested her great head in my lap. While her baby stood a scarce foot away wearing a bewildered expression, I rubbed behind her ears and gently told her how clever she was and how beautiful her son was with his huge ears, blunt nose, big feet, and pearl satin skin. Obviously the bond we had created over the past ten years had withstood his birth.

When Samuel was still a few days old, Samia came to me, leaving him sleeping under a nearby bush. She was standing beside me when he awoke and cried out in fear at finding himself alone. Samia's action was swift and wholly instinctive. She swiped me sideways with her head, knocking me to the ground, and ran to him. Seeing that no harm had befallen him, she returned to me, still sitting where I had fallen. She thrust her nose at me and I assured her that I was unhurt. Then she turned and, as often in days gone by, presented me with her tail for a pull up!

I never attempted to touch her baby, but slowly he got used to my scent and his inborn fear of me lessened. Almost daily at dawn, Samia would come to visit me with him at heel. Each day would start with the knowledge that they were well and safe and that she knew how to raise and protect her child. Frequently, hand-raised animals do not.

I had worried whether Samia would appreciate the dangers surrounding her baby; there was so much I had not been able to teach her. But after some time, I realized that these fears were groundless. Samia had also always been fully aware that I only pretended to eat thornbushes and had not been able to teach her how to manipulate the thorn in her mouth. But at four months, Samuel browsed on these same thornbushes alongside his mother. It was something very beautiful to behold. I watched Samia's affection for her baby, saw how the bond between them became stronger, and felt quite ridiculously proud of her.

Because our April rains virtually failed, I started to supplement Samia's natural browse with a small quantity of alfalfa so her milk wouldn't fail. Almost daily at dawn, she came to my garden fence with her baby. As soon as she heard me open the door, she called to tell me that she was there and hopeful of being fed. The rest of the day she spent in the bush. Seeing her thus was my greatest joy.

Then tragedy struck. Samia did not come to visit me one morning. I went down the valley with Patrick, a tracker, to look for her and found her dead. She was lying on her back below the cliff from which she and her child had fallen. Her death must have been instantaneous. Her baby lay nearby, still alive. I tried to help him rise, but being unable to do so, sent Patrick with the radio to call for help. For two hours, I knelt beside little Samuel, offering what poor comfort I could. Nearby a leopard was grunting, but I could not see it. The valley was beautiful, full of birds and color, and I thought of the many happy hours and days that Samia and I had spent there.

Ian Craig, who came with ropes and other people, realized what I had not, that the baby rhino's back was broken low down near his tail. A merciful shot ended his suffering. Later, after the local Game Warden had come to remove Samia's horns, the trackers laid Samuel beside his mother and I went to say good-bye to them and to cover them with a sackful of flowers.

Samia's death has to me been a tragedy. There was real love and friendship between us and I miss her all the time. Beyond that it was my dearest hope that through her life and that of her child, awareness of and caring for her species could be awakened. In her life, she had proved beyond all doubt that there can be a meeting between two wholly disparate species.

Chapter 74

Freya Mathews

LIVING WITH ANIMALS

Freya Mathews argues that we need to find ways to restore animals to our day-to-day urban reality and suggests ways in which we can increase the amount of urban habitat for wildlife. Mathews also recounts her own childhood, during which she learned to engage with the unknowable subjectivities of animals and found that this experience is "the principal bridge" to communication with the unknowable subjectivity of the wider world beyond human selfhood.

'WITHOUT ANIMALS,' SAYS Peter, a Maasai nomad interviewed in the *New Internationalist*,[1] 'life isn't worth living'.

Sitting here in my inner-city backyard writing this, with a circle of attentive little upturned canine and feline faces surrounding me, and my cranky duck tugging at my shoelaces, I could not be in more heartfelt agreement. But how many people today would share this sentiment? For how many would it be football that makes life worth living, or cars, or opera, or ice-skating? Is there anything to ground the conviction that I want to defend here, that the company of non-human animals is a necessary part of human life, in a way that football, cars, opera and ice-skating manifestly are not, and that we relinquish or forego it at our peril?

There are two parts to this question. The first is, is it important for *us*, for our own well-being or the realization of our human potential, that we live in intimate commensal relations with animals? The second is, is it important for the *environment* that we live in such relations? Does the *world* need us to continue to live in our ancestral communalism with animals?

My view is that our present estrangement, as human beings, from both the natural world (as evidenced in the environmental crisis) and from ourselves (as evidenced in the intense neuroticization of life in contemporary "advanced" societies) is due at least in part to the progressive removal of animals from our day-to-day urban reality; consequently I shall argue that, in order to address both the environmental crisis and our own crisis of consciousness, we need to find ways of restoring animals to the human household.

[. . .]

If it is accepted that companion animals do induce in us a new moral seriousness about animals generally, then a question arises concerning the status of domestic animals used for productive purposes. Does this new moral seriousness condemn the utilization of animals for such purposes?

[. . .]

The short answer to this question is, I think, that such reconciliation of empathy and use is possible to the extent that utilization is of net benefit to the animals concerned.

[. . .]

To reconcile utilization with empathy, we need to be assured that the life that our exploitative intentions bestow on an individual domestic animal affords both the experiential opportunities and the requisite life span to enable it to achieve a significant degree of the form of self-realization appropriate to its particular kind. This implies that the use we may justifiably make of animals will vary according to their species.

[. . .]

In short, I think the fact that domestic utilization affords evolutionary niches for certain species, in a world of disappearing niches, is a prima facie reason for regarding such utilization as compatible with respect. However a full-blown attitude of empathy such as we develop through intimate association with animal companions—requires that the forms of utilization we countenance be compatible with the self-realization of the animals used, where this implies that different forms and degrees of utilization will be appropriate for different species. I would also add that, once we have acknowledged the subjectivity and moral significance of the animals we use, and the moral gravity of our practices of utilization, it becomes incumbent on us to develop cultural expressions of respect, gratitude and indebtedness for the lives we have thus dedicated to our own ends. In this way, our attitude towards domestic animals can develop more affinity with the familial attitudes of hunter-gatherer peoples towards the wild species that constitute their prey.

When domestic utilization of animals is subject to the qualifications I have outlined above, I think it is not only consistent with empathetic concern for the interests of animals: it is actually required by such concern. As environmentalists, committed to the maximal preservation of non-human life on earth, yet facing the cold, hard fact that in the twenty-first century, the processes of urbanization and industrialization that have been synonymous with the disenchantment and tragic devastation of the non-human world are only going to accelerate and intensify, don't we have to admit that one of our best chances for 'saving Nature' is by bringing Nature back into the human domain? We have, for the last few centuries, witnessed the runaway humanization of Nature; now let us inaugurate the wholesale naturalization of human habitat. Our cities are one of the major biological habitats of the future, and our task, as environmentalists, is to ensure that they provide the best opportunities for non-human life that we can devise. We can do this partly by increasing the amount of urban habitat for wildlife. Such habitat can be created by way of indigenous plantings and by permacultural programs of food production in the city. Buildings can also be designed or adapted to create, rather than exclude, habitat opportunities for wild animals (by way of stork-friendly chimneys, for instance, and roofs that accommodate bats and nesting birds). However we can also increase the urban opportunities for non-human life by finding new ways for animals to 'earn their living' in the city.

[. . .]

The possibilities for reintegrating animals productively into urban life are as limitless as our imaginations. However, the principal way in which animals can 'earn their living' in the city is still, I think, via their companionate role. The exclusive reign of the dog and the cat in this connection needs to be challenged, and the adaptability of other species to the human hearth and home investigated.

[. . .]

The 'green' city of the future, then, would be a mixed community rich in habitat opportunities for a great diversity of animal species. This reintegration of animals into human life would also help to expand human imaginative and empathetic horizons, undermining anthropocentrism and reinforcing commitment to the protection of the non-human world. At the same time, the multiple contacts with animals that it would afford would enhance the health and sanity of the human population.

[. . .]

These then are some of the reasons why I think that our living with animals is important both for us and for them. However, this commensality shapes not only our ethical attitudes towards non-human individuals and species, but our very sense of the world. I have not yet brought this larger significance of the relationship fully to light, nor can I hope to do so with any pretence of completeness. In order to capture a little of this cosmological significance however, I would like to recount, in these concluding pages, the experiential origins of my own conviction that 'without animals, life isn't worth living'.

I grew up surrounded by loving animals on what today would be described as a hobby farm, situated on the rural outskirts of Melbourne, Australia. These animals included dogs and cats, ducks, geese, hens, and, at one stage, a turkey. There were brief episodes with sheep and cows. The main focus of my entire childhood, however, was my ponies. My first pony, and the horses that came after her, were my day-long playmates and confidants. It was to them that I recited my earliest poems, and to them that I ran when I was hurt or excited. They nuzzled me in the same soft, considerate way whatever the occasion. I chose their company not for want of family and friends, but for its own sake. The form of intimacy that grew up between us was qualitatively different from anything that could have developed between myself and human persons. It was a kind of uncluttered closeness, or being-with, which existed despite the fact that our subjectivities were, in terms of content, mutually unknowable. We took it for granted, on either side, that this unknowability did not matter, that our psyches could touch and pervade each other, without need for explanations or self-disclosures, such as those conveyable by language. These animals were, for me, 'primary others', in the psychoanalytic sense; they were not substitutes for, but additional to, significant humans, nor could humans substitute for them. My subjectivity—my sense of self and world—was constituted through my 'object relations' with these animals just as fundamentally as it was through my relations with primary human others.[2]

[. . .]

Looking back on my early years now, it seems more plausible to me to assume that the ample opportunities for close communion with animals that were available to me throughout my childhood had opened me to a larger world, a world astir with presence or presences that vastly exceeded the human. It was this direct contact with unknowable but pervasive presence which instilled in me a sense of the sacredness or enchantment of the world, and the potentiality for 'magic' within it. 'Magic' was, in this context, just the possibility of the world's response—the possibility, indeed probability, that the world, when invoked in good faith, *will* respond, though not necessarily in the manner one anticipates or with the results for which one hopes. One should certainly not, in my view, rely on this world to fulfil requests or afford protection, but if one entreats it simply to reveal itself, to engage in an act of communication, then, in my experience, it will generally do so, though in its own ever-unpredictable way. I learned this as a child, through the receptiveness that my animal familiars created in me, and it filled my whole being with a sense of being accompanied, of never being alone, a sense of background love, akin to the background radiation of which physicists speak. This is a 'love' which has nothing to do with saving us from death and suffering, or with making us happy. From the viewpoint of the world, death and suffering are just inevitable concomitants of individual life. The point for individuals, from this perspective, is not to seek to evade these inevitabilities, but to reach beyond them—to call into the silence beyond human selfhood in search of a reply. This is the moment for which the world has been waiting, and in which it will rejoice: the moment when we ask it to speak. To receive its reply is to enter a love far greater than the kind of protection and indulgence that our traditional importunate forms of prayer expect, for that reply signifies that we belong to an animate order, a pattern of meaning, from which death cannot separate us, and to which suffering only summons us.

I offer these concluding reflections, not as argument, but as testimony relating to my own personal sense of the larger import of human-animal commensality, especially when that commensality is established in childhood. To engage with the unknowable subjectivities of animals, and to experience their response to us, is perhaps the principal bridge to communication with the unknowable subjectivity of the wider world. To experience the world thus, as an ensouled or spiritual thing, will not only direct the course of our own self-realization in the most fundamental way; it will also ensure an attitude of profound mutuality and awed protectiveness towards the world itself.

Notes

1   Nikkivan der Gaag, 'The Maasai and the Travellers', *New Internationalist*, 266 (1995), pp. 24–5.
2   The term 'object relations' is deployed in a branch of psychoanalytic theory, known as 'object relations theory', to designate the kinds of relations with primary others that an infant internalizes in the process of developing its individual sense of self. It is associated with the work of D.W. Winnicott, and later feminist theorists, such as Nancy Chodorow.

Chapter 75

James Garbarino

PROTECTING CHILDREN AND ANIMALS FROM ABUSE: A TRANS-SPECIES CONCEPT OF CARING

James Garbarino argues that empathy for animals and empathy for children are natural partners. The correlation between child maltreatment and animal abuse is well established by social science research. We need to expand our empathy so that we treat both children and animals with respect and caring.

ALTHOUGH MY PROFESSIONAL career has been spent seeking to improve the quality of life for children, I come from a family of avowed and unabashed animal lovers. From my childhood, I recall clearly that the greatest outrage arose in my parents and siblings from stories of cruelty to animals. When the cowboys and Indians battled on television or in the movies, it was for the wounded *horses* that the greatest sympathy was reserved. In fact, in the household of my childhood it was accepted practice to root for the animals whenever they were in conflict with humans.

[. . .]

In this I am not alone. Josephine Donovan (1990) dedicated her analysis of "Animal Rights and Feminist Theory" "to my great dog Rooney . . . whose life led me to appreciate the nobility and dignity of animals." This is particularly interesting and important in the present context, because in her article Donovan recounts the fact that one of the contributions of feminist theory to the formulation of animal rights is the assertion that it is from their capacity to *feel* that the rights of animals derive. As outlined by psychologist Carol Gilligan (1982), this orientation to feelings stands in sharp contrast to conventional masculine thinking, which sees the origins of animal rights either in the ability to think or in the use they serve in the human community. I begin my analysis on precisely this issue, that any genuine understanding of the rights of children and animals must arise out of empathy. *We (and they) feel. Therefore we are entitled.*

[. . .]

But how far can we take this kinship? And what does it imply for the coordination of child welfare and animal welfare programs and policies?

[. . .]

Child welfare and animal welfare ought to be natural collaborators, even if in practice there have been historical wedges driven between these two caring communities. Certainly the more we postulate the need for a general ethic of caring the more we can see a natural collaboration. What is more, the repeatedly documented correlation between child maltreatment and the abuse and neglect of animals (Ascione 1993) warrants a synchronicity of effort. The fact is that professionals who uncover one sort of abuse in a household should be on special alert for the other. Thus, child protection investigators should be trained to be on the lookout for animal abuse—both as a condition bolstering their concern for the children and as a step in the direction of cost effectiveness by forwarding their observations to animal protection professionals. The reverse is true for animal protection officers as well, that is, using the occasion of investigating animal abuse as an opportunity to do an assessment of the quality of care for any children cohabiting with the animals in question. This sort of coordination ought to be a matter of elementary human policy at the highest community and state levels. Rather than closing ourselves off to the suffering of beings beyond our professional or institutional mission, we should at the very least conceptualize a generic empathy for the victimized as part of our core missions.

Is a unitary approach to children and animals wise?

Despite the obvious need for a generic approach to protecting the vulnerable, we should consider the possible limits of this approach. Perhaps we can restate this question in the following way. Is it wise to have unbounded empathy? Certainly empathy is one of the foundations upon which to build morality in general, and a morality of child and animal protection in particular. *When we open ourselves to the feelings of abuse we create a prima facie case for protection.* Conceptual discussions of "aggression" or "punishment" may result in an abstract conclusion that children need discipline, that punishment is an acceptable strategy, and that under stress parents may engage in aggression. But look at a child who has been beaten or burned and the feelings create a powerful moral mandate. We reserve a special brand of judgment for those who inflict or profit from such violence to children.

But can we say the same of animals? Who can bear to look at a fox mutilated in a trap? Obviously the fox hunter can. Is he just an insensitive clod or a sadistic maniac? How is he different from the person who can tolerate or even enjoy being witness to or perpetrator of the suffering of an abused child? It is easy enough to see the similarities—unless you have known a hunter who cares for his children with gentleness and compassion.

Popular culture sometimes struggles with this issue. One recent example was to be found in the film *Powder*, in which a rather odd young man possesses the capacity for *imposing* empathy on others. At one point in the film he confronts a deer hunter by transmitting a wounded deer's feelings to the hunter. The hunter—regretfully and with reluctance to abandon a way of life—disposes of his rifle collection and abandons hunting immediately. Who (other than a masochist who actually enjoys pain) could do otherwise? This, of course, is behind the oft repeated insight that if fish could scream there would be far fewer among us who would cast a baited hook into the water. I know that as I have expanded the boundaries of my own empathy there came a point where I could imagine the screaming of fish—and then ceased to be able to cast that baited hook.

Can we accommodate "human rights" and an "ethic of caring"?

In practice, this issue of unlimited empathy is not a matter of much concern in most situations, most of the time. The more common problem, it would seem, is not too much empathy, but too little. Dealing with the most obvious cases of child and animal abuse and neglect already strains our response capacities to, and beyond, breaking point. Some of us, however, recognize that the foundation for *child* protection is *childhood* protection, because child maltreatment is at least in part a social indicator, that is, an indicator of deficiencies in the supportive quality of the social environment. Thus, by examining the values and policies that either support or undermine quality of care for children (childhood protection) we understand better the factors that generate the need for child protection among vulnerable families. This analysis leads to a focus on "social toxicity" in the community and the larger society (Garbarino 1995). Similarly, we can make progress in animal protection by focusing on the foundation for animal protection in the larger issue of the very concept of an ethic of caring for nonhuman life forms. This is where the animal rights movement intersects with animal protection.

Indeed, those of us who have worked with the most victimized among the human population (i.e., the most horribly abused who become perpetrators of heinous violence and end up in prison), see the loss of human dignity as the principal precipitator of "bestial" violence. I find this in my interviews with boys incarcerated for murder (Gabarino 1999). Psychiatrist James Gilligan (1996) worked with men in the Massachusetts prison system for a long period and from his experience learned that shame based upon denial of basic human rights is the engine that drives the violence machine. A rights-based culture is a culture that has a chance of establishing the reservoirs of self-worth and positive identity that promote high standards of care for children—and animals. An ethic of caring is the goal if we are to build the foundation for both child and animal welfare and protection.

[. . .]

We seek an expansion of caring, the progressive application of an ethic of caring that conveys respect within the terms available to us in our culture—both our local culture, and what the cultures of the larger world have to offer.

I believe we would do well to seek an ever-expanding ethic of caring, in part because dignity, respect, and caring knit together a social fabric that clothes all who are dependent upon the powerful. Desmond Morris (1967) observed, "The viciousness with which children are subjected to persecution is a measure of the weight of dominant pressures imposed on their persecutors." This seems true when we examine the socioeconomic and demographic correlates of child maltreatment.

But by the same token, the cruelty with which animals are treated seems a measure of the cultural foundations for cruelty in general. We know there is some empirical connection developmentally—cruelty to animals bears some correlation with subsequent cruelty to children (Ascione 1993). I hear it often in my interviews with boys who have committed acts of lethal violence.

In principle and in fact, when we say that someone is treating a child "like a dog" we tell a great deal about the person and the culture from which they come. Linking our animal protection efforts to a general ethic of caring for nonhuman life forms is, I think, a powerful strategy for elevating the quality of care for both animals and children.

Opening our eyes and hearts to the rights of animals to dignity and caring (even when we accept their use as instrumentalities under carefully controlled and evaluated conditions to meet the needs and improve the welfare of human beings) is one foundation for establishing the minimum standards of care for children. Animal protection and child welfare are natural partners.

References

Ascione, F. 1993. Children who are cruel to animals: A review of research and implications for developmental psychopathology. *Anthozoös* 6:226–47.

Donovan, J. 1990. Animal rights and feminist theory. *Signs: Journal of Women in Culture and Society* 12:350–75.

Garbarino, J. 1999. *Lost boys: Why our sons turn violent and how we can save them*. New York: The Free Press.

—— 1995. *Raising children in a socially toxic environment*. San Francisco: Jossey, Bass.

Gilligan, C. 1982. *In a different voice*. Cambridge, Mass.: Harvard University Press.

Gilligan, J. 1996. *Violence*. New York: G. P. Putnam.

Morris, D. 1967. *The naked ape*. New York: McGraw-Hill.

Chapter 76

James Serpell, Raymond Coppinger, and Aubrey H. Fine

THE WELFARE OF ASSISTANCE
AND THERAPY ANIMALS:
AN ETHICAL COMMENT

James Serpell, Raymond Coppinger, and Aubrey Fine identify the situations in which animals used to assist persons with disabilities or as therapeutic aides may themselves be harmed. Dogs can be harmed when they are kept too long in kennels or subjected to a succession of handlers. Capuchin monkeys may be harmed by the invasive measures needed to render them safe for people with serious disabilities. The authors also note that the assistance dog industry often fails to breed "in" desirable characteristics and that aversive conditioning is used for many assistance dogs.

Introduction

ETHICAL QUESTIONS ABOUT the use of animals as therapeutic aides or for assisting persons with disabilities arise out of a tension between interests. Throughout history, people have used animals—whether for food, fiber, sport, adornment, labor, or companionship—as a means of satisfying human interests. But animals also have interests—in avoiding pain, fear, distress, or physical harm, and in pursuing their own needs, desires, and goals through the performance of species-typical patterns of behavior. Relations between people and animals only become morally problematical where there is a conflict of interests between the two: where the human use either causes pain, fear, or harm to an animal, or it in some way thwarts or prevents the animal from satisfying its own needs and goals.

During the last 10 years, purveyors and proponents of animal-assisted activities and therapy (AAA/T) such as the Delta Society have made concerted efforts to professionalize the "industry," and establish selection and training standards that aim to minimize the risks of harm to all concerned, including the animals (Hines and Fredrickson, 1998). However, AAA/T has experienced explosive growth within the last decade, and in many cases these standards have been set in the absence of any systematic or empirical evaluation of the potential risks to animals imposed by current practices. Indeed, there is a general but unsubstantiated feeling across the industry that these are "good" activities for animals to be engaged in. The fact that a large number of animals fail to respond to the nurturing and training they receive has not generally been taken as evidence that they do not want to, or are unable to, participate. Instead, practitioners tend to respond to failure by changing the selection or the training procedures, as if the animals are theoretically capable of responding positively to any demands made of them.

[. . .]

[I]n this chapter [. . .] our goal is to reexamine the animal–human partnership from the animal's viewpoint to see what the benefits might be for the animal, or to see if the raising, training, and deployment of assistance and therapy animals is causing significant degradation in their welfare.[1] In doing so, however, we recognize that there is a shortage of reliable scientific evidence to reinforce some of our claims. Additionally, the authors want to make an impression for clinicians to examine their ethical responsibility for the welfare of their therapeutic adjuncts. Clinicians must respect the integrity of the animals and recognize that their involvement must be carefully monitored, so that their rights and safety are safeguarded.

The information that follows pertains more to the authors' concerns about the rearing, training, and expected responsibilities of service animals. [T]he term *service animal* is defined in the U.S. civil rights law (Americans with Disabilities Act of 1990), as "any animal individually trained to do work or perform tasks for the benefit of a person with a disability." However, some of the issues covered in this discussion have direct relevance to animals incorporated in AAA/T. When appropriate, the authors will also highlight their specific concerns for clinicians' considerations.

Possible sources of animal welfare problems with service animals and those incorporated in AAA/T

Failure to provide for animals' behavioral and social needs

In addition to having physical requirements for food, water, protection from the elements, etc., most animals have social and behavioral needs that should be provided for whenever possible (Dawkins, 1988). An understanding of these social and behavioral needs by primary caregivers is part of the ethical obligation attending animal ownership and use. Different species tend to have different social and behavioral needs (Mason and Mendl, 1993). Judging the value of a particular behavior or social interaction to an animal may sometimes be difficult. However, in general, if an animal is strongly internally motivated to perform a particular behavior or social interaction, and if its motivation to perform appears to increase following a period of deprivation, it is an indication that the activity or interaction is probably important to the maintenance of that animal's welfare. Common indications of deprivation include animals performing abnormally high frequencies of displacement activities, stereotypies, or self-mutilation (Broom and Johnson, 1993).

All animals need to be safe from any abuse and danger from any client at all times. The animal must be able to find a safe refuge within the working environment to go to if he or she feels exhausted or stressed. Throughout the day, the animal utilized in AAA/T needs to have a break from actual patient contact. Therapy and service animals must be free from pain, injury, or disease. All animals should be kept up to date on their inoculations. If the animal seems ill, stressed, or exhausted, medical attention must be given.

For assistance and therapy animals, welfare problems are most likely to arise in circumstances where animals are either residential within health care settings or spend large amounts of time in holding facilities such as kennels or stables. In the former context, inadequate advance planning, selection, and staff commitment and oversight can lead to animals being improperly cared for (Hines and Fredrickson, 1998). Small mammals, birds, and reptiles that are caged or confined are probably at greater risk of neglect or improper care, and nondomestic species that tend to have more specialized requirements than domestic ones are also likely to be at risk. "Improperly cared for" in these contexts should have the broadest definition. Most often it is defined as animals that are inadequately fed, watered, or cleaned. However, any failure to attend to individual needs should be regarded as improper care. Overfeeding animals to the point of obesity is just as negligent as underfeeding. Giving an animal the opportunity to exercise is not enough without ensuring that the individual takes advantage of the opportunity.

With regard to AAA/T, an additional challenge may arise when an animal begins to age. Naturally, the animal's schedule for therapeutic involvement will have to be curtailed. This may cause some disruption and adjustment to both the clinician as well as the animal. [. . .]

Welfare problems may be particularly severe where animals, such as dogs, have been reared in the enriched environment of a human foster home and then kenneled individually for months as part of their final training (Hubrecht, 1995). Such an abrupt change in social and physical environment appears to be highly stressful for some animals (Coppinger and Zuccotti, 1999) and may not only affect their immediate welfare, but also has the potential to foster obnoxious behaviors that might preclude successful training and placement.

Assistance animals may also be at risk because of the changing nature of their relationships with successive human owners and handlers throughout their lives. Most of these animals are picked because they are innately social—that is, they are internally motivated to seek social interactions with others—and because they form strong bonds of attachment for their human partners. Having to endure a whole succession of different handlers with different characteristics, experience, and motivations for "ownership" is likely to be particularly stressful for these individuals.

[. . .]

Selecting or breeding animals for assistance

Most domestic animals have been selected to show a higher degree of tolerance of stressful situations and stimuli compared with nondomestic species, even those reared entirely in captivity (Hemmer, 1990). Nondomestic species are also harder to train, and their entrained responses extinguish more quickly in the absence of appropriate reinforcement. Some species, such as many nonhuman primates, are also highly intelligent and socially manipulative (Cheney and Seyfarth, 1990), and this tends to make them potentially unreliable or unsafe as social companions for people. All of these factors make nondomestic species less suitable for use in AAA/T programs, and more likely to experience welfare problems if used.

This point is well illustrated by recent efforts to train and use capuchin monkeys to assist people with serious disabilities. In most cases, these programs have found it necessary to neuter and surgically extract the canine teeth from the monkeys before they can be used safely with such vulnerable human partners. Monkeys may also be required to wear remotely controlled, electric shock-collars or harnesses in order to provide the user with a means of controlling the animal's potentially aggressive and unreliable behavior. Clearly, the necessity of using of such extreme and invasive measures raises doubts about the practical value of such programs, as well as serious ethical questions concerning the welfare of the animals involved.

[. . .]

Some service dogs, such as the hearing ear dogs, are almost exclusively obtained from shelters. [. . .] In-house breeding programs are favored by guide dog and wheelchair dog organizations. [. . .] The history of dog breeding until modern times has been to create superior working animals through hybridization. [. . .] In the nineteenth century, a shift toward prezygotic selection began that has intensified ever since. The assumption behind this process is that excellence of form and behavior can be purified and preserved within a breed. Although such breeding practices do tend to produce uniformity of appearance and behavior within breeds, in the absence of periodic outcrossing, they also promote inbreeding depression, and the expression of various recessively inherited "genetic" diseases.

Unfortunately, the assistance dog industry has been slow to recognize these dangers. [. . .] Each generation gets more inbred because of the shrinking genetic variation, creating highly homozygous strains. In theory, dogs generated in these systems are more vulnerable to infectious disease, as well as being more likely to show phenotypic expression of deleterious mutant alleles.

[. . .]

There is another ethical issue buried within this production system. Creating large numbers of animals year after year with hip dysplasia or retinal atrophy is ethically questionable in itself, but ethical questions also attend the disposal of animals diagnosed with disease and dropped from assistance programs. Should these animals be euthanized or should they be put up for adoption? Overall, these kinds of issues raise certain doubts about the wisdom of maintaining purebred strains of dogs for assistance work.

Failure to take account of developmental events and processes

It is well established from research on canid development that early experiences have more profound and longer lasting effects on behavior than those occurring at later stages of the life cycle (Serpell and Jagoe, 1995).

[. . .]

Now consider where most service puppies spend the first 8 weeks of their lives: in a sterilized kennel being protected from any environmental insult that might challenge their little immune systems. The kennel is the equivalent of an orphanage.

[. . .]

These dogs are growing up on a fabricated diet, in a contrived and impoverished environment in which the handlers' motivations are primarily to do with health care and cost effectiveness. As a system, it pays practically no attention to neurologic and cognitive development. And yet the behavioral result of what happens to a pup during this period is largely permanent. Once the brain connections are made, there is no changing them. How and what a pup can learn is virtually fixed by 1 year of age.

[. . .]

Using inappropriate or inhumane training methods

[. . .]

[T]he reason dogs have been so successful as companions is that they are prepared to work for the reward of social interaction with people. Second, because particular dog breeds innately "like" to search for game, or like to herd sheep, it is not essential to reward such performance. Working dog specialists generally consider it impossible to train an animal that does not show the internal motivation to perform the specific task. Most sporting or traditional working dogs, such as sheep dogs or sled dogs, are not aversively conditioned nor are they given food rewards for proper performance.

[. . .]

In contrast, aversive conditioning is the primary method of instruction for many assistance dogs. It may be the only method that is practical because many assistance dog tasks are not discrete, nor is the significance of the task understood by the dog.

[. . .]

The attitude of many assistance dogs in public seems to reflect the aversive training techniques, and the internal confusion as to what is expected (Coppinger, personal observations). This is probably more true of wheelchair than guide dogs. The high failure rate in AAA/T animals may in part be due to inappropriate training procedures. There has recently been some interest in "click and treat" methods using a variation of Pavlovian conditioning. This is a useful approach for "civilizing" assistance dogs and works reasonably well on hearing ear and therapy dogs. As yet it has not been demonstrated to work as a viable system for wheelchair or guide dogs. It may be that there is in fact no appropriate or humane training technique for dogs of this type, which might lead one to the ethical conclusion that animals shouldn't be asked to perform such tasks.

Use of badly designed equipment and facilities

By analyzing the "physics" of some of the tasks that service dogs are asked to perform, Coppinger *et al.* (1998) have recently drawn attention to inherent design flaws in some of the equipment used by persons with disabilities that may result in discomfort or injury to the dogs. Harnesses, for example, suggested that the designers did not understand the basic principles of harness design. Some had pulling webs which crossed moving parts, thus chafing the dog badly as it moved. Trying to get a dog to pull a wheelchair that is designed to be pushed forces the dog into awkward positions, increasing the difficulty of the task. Some of the tasks, such as pulling a wheelchair or pulling open a door with the teeth, reach the limits of what a dog is physically able to perform.

[. . .]

End-user problems

Although there have been no systematic studies of the problem, anecdotal observations suggest that some assistance dog users are insufficiently experienced with handling or training dogs. [. . .] Some agencies provide refresher courses for their clients with disabilities, or can send a trainer to the person's home to correct special problems. However, greater continuing education efforts by agencies would certainly help to ensure improved quality of life for animals used in this way.

[. . .]

Conclusions and recommendations

The concept of using trained and socialized animals to assist people with disabilities, or as therapeutic adjuncts, has great intrinsic appeal, exemplifying as it does for many people the ultimate in mutually beneficial animal–human partnerships. Nevertheless, while the advantages to the humans in these relationships may be obvious, the benefits to the animals are by no means always self-evident. Indeed, the use of animals for animal-assisted activities and therapy imposes a unique set of stresses and strains on them that the "industry" is only just beginning to acknowledge.

[. . .]

Note

1   The concept of welfare or "poor" welfare has been variously defined by animal welfare scientists. Some definitions stress the presence of unpleasant mental or emotional states such as pain, fear, frustration or suffering (Dawkins, 1980); some place the emphasis on impairments to an animal's biological fitness (McGlone, 1993; Broom and Johnson, 1993), while others refer to the extent to which environmental stresses and strains exceed the animal's ability to cope or adapt (Fraser and Broom, 1990). Rather than lend support to any one of these competing definitions, we will consider welfare as comprising elements of all of them.

References

Broom, D. M., and Johson, K. (1993). *Stress and animal welfare.* London: Chapman & Hall.

Cheney, D. L., and Seyfarth, R. M. (1990). *How monkeys see the world.* Chicago: Chicago University Press.

Coppinger, R., and Zuccotti, J. (1999). Kennel enrichment: Exercise and socialization of dogs. *Journal of Applied Animal Welfare Science.*

Coppinger, R., Coppinger, L., and Skillings, E. (1998) Observations on assistance dog training and use. *Journal of Applied Animal Welfare Science,* 1, 133–44.

Dawkins, M. S. (1988). Behavioural deprivation: A central problem in animal welfare. *Applied Animal Behaviour Science,* 20, 209–25.

Hemmer, H. (1990). *Domestication: The decline of environmental appreciation* (trans. Neil Beckhaus). Cambridge, UK: Cambridge University Press.

Hines, L., and Fredrickson, M. (1998). Perspectives on animal-assisted activities and therapy. In C. C. Wilson and D. C. Turner (eds), *Companion animals in human health* (pp. 23–39). Thousand Oaks, CA: Sage Publications.

Hubrecht, R. (1995). The welfare of dogs in human care. In J. A. Serpell (ed.), *The domestic dog: Its evolution, behaviour, and interactions with people* (pp. 179–95). Cambridge, UK: Cambridge University Press.

Mason, G., and Mendl, M. (1993). Why is there no simple way of measuring animal welfare? *Animal Welfare,* 2, 301–20.

McGlone, J. (1993). What is animal welfare? *Journal of Agricultural and Environmental Ethics,* 6 (Supplement 2), 28.

Serpell, J., and Jagoe, J. A. (1995). Early experience and the development of behaviour. In J. A. Serpell (ed.), *The domestic dog its evolution, behaviour, and interactions with people* (pp. 80–102). Cambridge, UK: Cambridge University Press.

Chapter 77

Clare Palmer

KILLING ANIMALS IN ANIMAL SHELTERS

Clare Palmer addresses the important topic of killing healthy, unwanted animals in animal shelters. She notes that a utilitarian approach of "humane killing" finds painless killing acceptable. Regan's rights approach, on the other hand, rejects painless killing as harmful in that the animal experiences the ultimate loss of future satisfaction. Palmer recommends instead a relational approach which both values the duties of care for dependent domesticated animals and respects the independence of feral cats and dogs.

Introduction

[. . .]

I **WANT**, in this essay, to consider the painless killing of healthy animals (primarily cats and dogs) in animal shelters[1]. Although no completely reliable statistics exist, it is estimated that between 6 and 10 million dogs and between 7 and 10 million cats were humanely killed in pet shelters in the United States in 1990.[2] In particular, I will be exploring the ethical debate around this practice, not with the intention of proposing any definitive "solution," but in order to clarify existing arguments and to suggest some new perspectives on the issues raised. It should also be noted that this essay focuses on ethical, rather than economic, issues about killing animals in animal shelters. Clearly, there is a sense in which financial expedience is the primary reason for the killing of such animals. It would be extremely expensive to house indefinitely all the healthy animals that currently come into animal shelters. But that such killing is accepted and tolerated socially is an ethical issue worthy of investigation in its own right.

Animal shelters: context and practices

Animal shelters take several forms. Some are provided and run by local or city authorities, others by animal protection charities. Almost all of the former, and many of the latter, regularly humanely kill healthy animals. A small number of animal charity shelters and adoption organizations have no-kill policies (except in cases where animals are seriously ill and suffering). Organizations of this kind often select "adoptable" animals from local authority pounds and hold them until they can place them in a home. However, the majority of animal shelters do kill. Statistics suggest that on average, six out of ten stray dogs and eight out of ten stray cats never make it out of an animal shelter alive.[3] [. . .]

Several different methods of humane killing are routinely used in animal shelters. The most widely advocated and commonest method is by injection of barbiturates. The Report of the American Veterinary Medical Association (AVMA) Panel on Euthanasia in 2000 recommended this as the preferred method of humanely killing dogs and cats (some animal welfare organizations consider this to be the only acceptable way)[4] on the grounds that it works very quickly with minimal discomfort to the animals and is relatively inexpensive. There are disadvantages: those administering the barbiturate injection must be trained and skilled in doing so; a second member of staff is always required to restrain the animal; the drugs are dangerous to humans; the animal may produce "an aesthetically objectionable terminal gasp"; and the drugs linger in the carcass and may be hazardous if eaten by another animal. The other main alternatives used for humane killing in animal shelters are gases, primarily carbon monoxide and carbon dioxide.[5] Animals may be gassed together in larger numbers in gas chambers (though it is recommended that animals be separated from one another during the process) and no specialist training is required, though correct gas flow levels must be maintained. Carbon monoxide is particularly effective; the AVMA reports that it "induces loss of consciousness without pain and with minimal discernible discomfort" and that at correct levels, death follows rapidly. However, the chambers must be well maintained and sealed, both to get the flow level right and to avoid affecting nearby humans.

The AVMA report—although contested in some quarters—maintains that these methods of killing, if correctly administered, are painless to animals. For the purposes of this essay, I am going to accept this judgment and assume that killing in animal shelters can be carried out without pain or significant distress to the animals. This, obviously, does not mean that no ethical issues are involved; indeed, it is these issues that I will now move on to consider more closely.

Common claims about humane killing

Arguments in support of humane killing in animal shelters tend to maintain that it is the best option for unadopted or unadoptable animals, given the complex of circumstances that brought them there. Specifically, such arguments usually put forward some or all of the following claims (they may be mutually reinforcing):

1   Humane killing is best for the individual animal concerned.
2   Humane killing of such individual animals is required because of animal overpopulation.
3   Humane killing of such individual animals is best for human beings.

Claim 1, that humane killing is best for the individual animal concerned, rests on the judgment that continued life for that animal would be worse than death. Such arguments are commonly found among those who surrender animals to shelters and among shelter workers. Stephanie Frommer and Arnold Arluke report that many who surrender animals to animal shelters "consider euthanization a better solution for their pets than allowing them to live in poor situations. . . . Death was preferable to sacrificing the quality of life that the animal deserved and had come to expect."[6] Similarly, Frommer and Arluke found that shelter workers also used this argument: "By assuming that animals would meet a worse fate as a stray or with uncaring people, shelter workers enable themselves to view euthanasia as merciful."[7] Some shelter workers also maintained that the lives of animals in shelters are of such low quality that humane killing just helps along a process of dying already under way. Although Frommer and Arluke consider these responses only in the context of guilt-displacement strategies, they may be taken as ethical arguments in their own right. That is to say, in terms of the animal's own welfare, humane killing in animal shelters is ethical because it is in the interests of the animal concerned. The alternatives are likely to be poor living conditions that may include abandonment, ferality, hunger, lack of shelter, and ill-health or killing that might be far less humane than that practiced in the animal shelter. Any of these things, so the argument runs, would be worse for the animal than a painless, if premature, death. I will return to this claim later.

Claim 2, that humane killing of individual animals is required because of animal overpopulation, is usually located in the context of a broader discourse about animal overpopulation. The fundamental problem is understood as being the constant production of surplus dogs and cats—more than there can be homes for with human beings. Such surplus animals are likely to be unsterilized and to have a high fecundity rate, thus multiplying the problem.[8] Overpopulation of dogs and cats, it is argued, leads to the creation of feral cat colonies and dog packs (this rests on the assumption that those who take unwanted animals to animal shelters would abandon them if shelters were not available). Alongside poor individual welfare (as in claim 1), diseases and infestations may be carried beyond feral populations into homed populations (though homed populations can at least be vaccinated against some diseases). Even as it is, as fast as animals are killed in animal shelters, new animals are produced to take their place. Without animal shelters, feral populations would rapidly expand, and without killing, animal numbers in animal shelters would quickly grow far beyond the ability of the shelters to deal with them. This view tends to rest on the idea of total animal population welfare rather than on the welfare of specific individuals, as in claim 1. It may thus be argued that even if in the case of any particular individual animal, humane killing may not seem to be in its interests, from the perspective of the total, accumulated welfare of all the individual animals in that population—say, cats in New York—humane killing is required to keep the remaining cats reasonably healthy and with sufficient access to food and shelter. Some individuals must be sacrificed for the welfare of the cat population as a whole.

Claim 3, that humane killing of individual animals is good for human beings, is a further step from claim 2—now the limiting of animal populations is good for humans as well as for animal populations. This is usually explained in terms of hygiene, possible disease, and nuisance. Abandoned and feral animals and colonies of such animals are often seen as health hazards to humans as well as to homed animals. Dog and cat waste, for instance, may harbor parasitic diseases such as toxoplasmosis, which can cause eye or brain damage to infants and the immunosuppressed. The animals may also be considered as the cause of mess and noise and to be of unsightly appearance. [. . .]

These common arguments are consequentialist in nature: that is, they rest on the view that humane killing in animal shelters brings about the *best consequences* for individual humans and animals and/or for human and animal populations. Central to this kind of consequentialist position is the idea of *welfare*, construed with particular attention to the avoidance of pain to individual animals and to the health of populations as a whole. Humane killing is seen as maximizing animal and human welfare. Although not usually couched in philosophical terms, these arguments assume a form similar to classical utilitarianism, sometimes used as a basis for philosophical arguments for "animal liberation." Utilitarian arguments of this kind usually maintain that the ability to feel pain is the basic characteristic that determines whether a being should be taken into account when making moral decisions and that the central principle of moral decision-making should be the minimization of total pain in the world, whether that pain is human or animal.[9] Such arguments, while militating against the painful transportation and killing of animals for food and against pain inflicted in experimentation, have nothing obviously negative to say about painless killing in animal shelters. Indeed, guided by pain-minimization alone, practices involving painless killing with a view to promoting total welfare would seem (at first sight, at least) morally laudable. If no pain is involved, and if the continuing life of the animal would be a painful one or contribute to greater pain in animal or human populations, the killing feeds nothing negative into a decision-making calculus.[10] So the common claims I have outlined above and philosophical utilitarian positions associated with animal liberation can be, paradoxically, quite close to one another.[11]

However, very different ethical perspectives can be taken on humane killing in animal shelters. I want now to move on to consider just one, the animal rights position taken by philosopher Tom Regan.

Regan, rights, and humane killing

Tom Regan's book *The Case for Animal Rights*, published in 1983, is a sustained philosophical defense of the argument that we should think of animals (he focuses primarily on mammals) as bearers of particular kinds of rights, primarily rights to respect and to freedom from harm. These rights, he argues, rest on the inherent value possessed by animals, independent of their usefulness to or relationships with human beings;

this value is equally present in all animals (and humans). Animals possess such value by virtue of being "subjects of a life"—that is, in Regan's words, as beings displaying the following characteristics:

> beliefs and desires; perception, memory and a sense of the future, including their own future; an emotional life together with feelings of pleasure and pain; preference and welfare interests; the ability to initiate actions in pursuit of their desires and goals; a psychophysical unity over time and an individual welfare in the sense that their experiential life fares well or ill for them, logically independently of their utility for others and logically independently of their being the object of anyone else's interests.[12]

Resting on this theoretical basis, Regan's view is thus rather different from the pain-minimizing, consequentialist positions considered above. He argues that an animal's (or, indeed, a human's) welfare can be harmed without causing pain. Harms to welfare may involve deprivations, even where the individual concerned does not know that or of what they are being deprived.[13] One might, for instance, rear a child in a cage from birth while maintaining the child in a pain-free state; the child would still be harmed, even if he or she did not know what he or she was missing (and, Regan points out, part of the harm is actually *that* the child does not know what he or she is missing). Further, Regan goes on to argue, killing painlessly is just such a harm by deprivation. Indeed, it is fundamental and irreversible; it forecloses all possibilities of finding future satisfaction; it is thus "the ultimate harm because it is the ultimate loss" (although it may not be the worst harm there is—living a life of relentless physical agony would be worse).[14] So, he maintains, "to bring about the untimely death of animals will not hurt them if this is done painlessly; but they will be harmed."[15] Thus there is an immediate contrast with the earlier view, where, since pain is all that is to be taken into account, painless killing does not seem to be a harm at all.[16]

Regan's view that painless killing is a harm clearly has a bearing on the killing of animals in animal shelters. He does not explicitly discuss moral decision-making in this context. However, he makes one point about such killing very clear: the killing of healthy animals in animal shelters should not be regarded as euthanasia (a term I have avoided using until now for just this reason). Regan maintains that euthanasia of animals must have the following characteristics: (a) killing must be by the most painless means possible; (b) killing must be believed to be in the animal's interests, and this must be a true belief; and (c) the one who kills must be motivated out of concern for the interest, good, or welfare of the particular animal involved.[17] Even where (a) applies in animal shelters, according to Regan (b) and (c) usually do not. As we have seen, often the reasons offered for painlessly killing animals are based on the consequences for whole populations, not on the interests, good, or welfare of the particular animal being killed. This may, Regan suggests, be called "well-intentioned killing," but it is not appropriately called euthanasia. [. . .]

As a nonconsequentialist, Regan takes the view that some actions are morally unacceptable, even if they are aimed at bringing about a greater good. And killing any being with inherent value and a right to respect in order to further any other purpose at all, including minimizing the pain of other animals, humans, or populations of animals and humans, is just such an unacceptable action. For Regan, the only grounds on which killing an animal is morally acceptable is if it is in the interests of the animal concerned, and that could only be if the animal were to be in acute pain with no prospect of that pain ever ceasing[18] Humane killing of healthy animals in animal shelters does not fall into this category; it is thus an ethically unacceptable practice and should be ceased.

A relational approach

Two conflicting ways of thinking about painless killing in animal shelters have so far been identified. One is the broadly consequentialist view that painless killing is the best solution, in terms of minimizing pain, to the perceived problem of dog and cat overpopulation. The second is that painless killing is an unethical, harmful practice that takes the lives of beings entitled to respect. Yet there seems something troubling about both perspectives, taken alone. On the one hand, looking at the issue from a consequentialist, pain-minimization perspective, painless killing does not seem problematic at all. And yet surely the killing of cats and dogs on such a scale does merit, at least, some ethical unease. The rights view, on the other hand, seems excessively demanding, both philosophically, in terms of human responsibilities for animal lives, and in practice, with its implication that all abandoned cats and dogs should be treated, in terms of the provision of essentials, as members of what is almost an animal welfare state.

As I said at the beginning, the purpose of this essay is not to propose any straightforward "solution" to the problem of killing animals in animal shelters. Rather, I want to suggest another possible perspective that I think is at least worth considering alongside the two I have already outlined. This perspective could be thought of as a "relational approach." That is to say, rather than focusing on the outcomes of particular actions or on the value-giving qualities or abilities possessed by animals in themselves, the focus is on the nature of the relationships *between* humans and animals. While not denying the significance of the pain-minimizing, consequentialist view and the rights view, such a relational approach can highlight other moral questions that arise. It can look broadly at the context of human relationships with domestic cats and dogs, seeing painless killing in animal shelters as emerging from a whole nexus of historical and cultural relationships and practices. [. . .]

Dependence and independence

Dogs and cats kept as pets are domesticated species, bound into historical relationships with human beings. Exactly how such relationships began is contested, and how "domesticated" should be defined is also an area of dispute.[19] But it is undisputed that one key element of domestication is human intervention in animal breeding, in particular in the selection of mates in order to produce offspring that manifest characteristics desired by humans. Domesticated dogs and cats bear witness to these human desires in the shape and form of their bodies and in particular in their neotonization (that is, their retention of infantile characteristics). One consequence of this intervention in breeding is the diminished ability of many domesticated dogs and cats to live independently of humans.

It is, though, important to be careful here. Only some dogs and cats are fully dependent on humans (especially when bred in particular bodily shapes that make hunting, scavenging, or reproducing difficult). If abandoned, they would die, perhaps in painful ways. But other dogs and cats can survive partially, or wholly, independent of human beings. Studies of feral dogs, for instance, have suggested that they can live reasonably well, although they are indirectly dependent on scavenging from human settlements.[20] Colonies of feral cats may also scavenge but can live by hunting for birds and rodents. Certainly, such animals may be more vulnerable to disease and injury than homed animals and do not have access to veterinary care; but nonetheless their lives in general do not seem to be ones of unremitting pain such that they might be considered to be lives not worth living.

Significant issues arise from these relations of dependence/independence. First, where domestic cats and dogs are wholly dependent on humans, a special relationship, created by humans, has been established. By relationship here, I do not mean a relationship of affect, though such a relationship may exist in some cases. Rather, I mean that humans have acted to create animals that are constituted such that they are unable to be independent.

[. . .] At the individual level, one could maintain that along with an individual's decision to produce or adopt pets comes a duty to care and provide for them.[21] This is a commonplace, of course, which often forms one part of an animal welfare organization's educational campaign. The second level, though, follows a broader, social obligation arising out of the social creation of dependent domesticated animals. That there is a population of domestic dogs and cats, whether homed, unwanted, abandoned, or feral, is due to human action and human relations with these animals. On this basis, it can be argued that humans have *acquired* ethical responsibilities toward humanly originating dependent animals that do not exist toward, say, urban rat populations (where the rats are wild in origin).[22] The existence of animal shelters at all may indicate some basic recognition of this (after all, no such shelters exist for urban rat populations, for which painless killing is rarely considered to be of ethical significance). But it is questionable whether painless killing is an appropriate way of discharging responsibilities to unwanted but dependent animals humans have themselves created.

On the other hand, though, some domesticated cats and dogs do manage to live lives that appear to be satisfactory, outside the context of a home with an owner. They may live as individual hunters and scavengers; they may form colonies and packs with others; they may take up residence in abandoned buildings or the grounds of institutions, allotments, cemeteries, and other backwaters of human development. For these animals, either indirectly reliant on human beings or largely independent of them, being taken to an animal shelter for painless killing seems to be a denial of their *lack* of relationship with particular human beings rather than the failure, as in the previous case, to recognize the ethical force of dependence. Animals that have strayed for some time, or which are feral, are regarded as "unadoptable"; they are likely to be quickly dispatched in a shelter.

The question then arises whether it is better to live a life of ferality, provided that it is not one of interminable agony, or to be painlessly killed. How one answers this question depends on a number of factors, including whether cats and dogs are thought of as the kinds of beings that have any sense of themselves as beings that exist over time and whether they have nonmomentary future-oriented desires that entail continued existence in order to be fulfilled.[23] (Regan obviously thinks they do, and Peter Singer, a utilitarian, suggests in recent editions of *Practical Ethics* that dogs and cats may be self-conscious with a sense of themselves as beings that exist over time, such that killing them, however painlessly, is wrong).[24] In any case, it may be that some sort of double-bind is in operation here. Domestic dogs and cats are recognized in Western urban settings, in particular, as properly living in relationship to particular human owners. This relationship is not regarded as so binding that painless killing—often merely for convenience—is thought of as morally unacceptable, not just by the individuals who surrender animals but at a broader social level where the collective and historical responsibility for having created dependent animals is not taken seriously. But, on the other hand, the relationship is regarded as binding enough that individual animals living outside such a relationship are regarded as inevitably unable to cope, out of place, and (perhaps) better off dead.[25] On both counts, this leads to an increase in the number of animals being humanely killed in animal shelters.

So I am suggesting that greater *collective* responsibility needs to be taken for the existence of all domestic animals (rather than the responsibility being regarded as one attaching solely to individual owners). This may mean both that there are duties of provision and care for dependent domesticated animals and obligations to respect the independent lives of those cats and dogs that succeed in surviving outside the context of a human home; their lives should not be regarded as lives not worth living. These domesticated animals are in particular situations substantially as a result of their relationships to humans and human society; having deliberately put animals into these situations, the appropriate ethical response is to do what is best for the animals concerned within the context in which they are located.

Power and instrumentalism

[. . .] Pets are, generally, viewed with what might be called an "attitude of instrumentalism." Of course, this attitude is to be expected in the relations humans have with animals kept for food and experimental purposes. But it is unsettling in a relationship described, as we have seen, in terms of companionship or the familial. Yet this attitude not only seems widespread with respect to pets but also is at least plausible that educational campaigns about responsible pet-ownership can actually promote just such a perspective. At the same time, it is this attitude of instrumentalism that makes the surrender of dogs and cats to animal shelters more, rather than less, likely.

One good example of how this attitude of instrumentalism plays out is with respect to de-sexing. Almost all animal welfare organizations advocate de-sexing; they pay for it, encourage it, and campaign for it. The main arguments presented in favor of it are that it prevents the production of unwanted offspring and reduces roaming and other unwanted behaviors in pets themselves. That is to say, it is better both for animal populations and for human owners if pets are de-sexed. But what of the animal itself? We cannot know whether de-sexing matters to a cat or dog, and if it does, how much and in what ways. But it might be the case that there is a way in which de-sexing harms animals, even if it does not matter to them in the sense of being aware of what they are missing. Perhaps the pursuit of sex and the interactions involved in that pursuit, the practice of sex, and the process of producing young would be rich experiences for cats and dogs, so that once de-sexed their lives are less rich, even though they do not know it.

However one might regard animals' *loss* by de-sexing, it is rarely the case that de-sexing is carried out solely for the *benefit* of the animal concerned. When animals are de-sexed, they are, in most cases, being treated as instruments, as a means to an end, where the end is the good of the whole population or, more frequently, an easier life with the owner. So, animals are anesthetized and made to undergo surgery that will change their lives, a process of human domination—understood here as a power relation that they are unable to resist—for reasons not usually to do with their own welfare but as instrumental to other ends. And while there are occasions in many dependent relationships where dominating behavior toward the dependent being seems ethically appropriate or necessary, such occasions are usually in the interests of the one being dominated; that is to say, they are a form of paternalism. This, however, is rarely the case with pet de-sexing, where domination combines with instrumentalism, not paternalism.[26]

But this description—a process of human domination that they are unable to understand or resist, for reasons not to do with their own welfare but as instrumental to other ends—might equally be used to describe much painless killing in animal shelters. What I am suggesting is that both de-sexing and killing in animal shelters flow from the same underlying attitude toward pets. This attitude is one of willingness to adopt dominating practices that treat animals as means to other ends. If this is right, campaigns to promote de-sexing, while at one level being successful in reducing the number of kittens and puppies born[27] at another level actually promote dominating and instrumentalist underlying attitudes and relationships that make people more likely to surrender animals to animal shelters. Removal of the sex of a domesticated animal (unless that sex can be used for other instrumentalist purposes, such as pedigree breeding) is seen as being good for animal populations and as making the animal into a better, more amenable companion. Precisely the same arguments, as I have already maintained—the need to manage animal populations and problems in "companionship" with animals—lead to the surrender of animals to animal shelters. Rather than seeing the killing of animals in animal shelters as an aberration resulting from overpopulation and some irresponsible owners, it can be viewed instead as the inevitable outcome of a widespread set of human-pet relationships, flowing from an underlying human attitude of instrumentalism, an attitude sometimes promoted by animal welfare organizations themselves.

Conclusion

In this essay, I have considered some of the ethical issues around the practice of painless killing of cats and dogs in animal shelters. I have looked at the most prominent ethical approaches to such killing—that is, a kind of pain-minimizing consequentialism and an animal rights approach. I have suggested that another way of framing the situation would be to explore aspects of the human-animal relations involved, focusing on the relations of dependence/independence between humans and domesticated cats and dogs, and the underlying human relational attitude toward these animals. I have suggested, first, that the ethical responsi-bilities of the creation of dependence where it exists should be taken more seriously; second, that, on the other hand, relative independence where it exists should be respected; and third, that an underlying cause of the high death toll in animal shelters is an attitude toward pet animals of instrumentalism, an attitude that can actually be promoted by some attempts to reduce the number of animals coming into animal shelters.

Only the second of these points constitutes any kind of practical recommendation at all: that cats and dogs leading feral lives that do not seem to be lives of interminable pain should be left alone to live out their lives, even if their presence seems messy and unhygienic to nearby humans.[27] Aside from this, I have merely attempted to think through some of the underlying relationships, attitudes, and responsibilities that lead to the painless killing of so many animals in animal shelters. Such deep-seated relationships and attitudes are not amenable to simple educational campaigns about "snipping and chipping"—indeed, as I have suggested, such campaigns may serve to reinforce, not undercut, existing attitudes. To change the practices of killing in animal shelters will require a substantial cultural change in attitudes toward those animals humans increasingly like to call "companions."

Notes

1   I am, in this essay, interested in the special case of killing healthy animals rather than sick and suffering animals. There is a degree of ambiguity about this, but the broad distinction will suffice here.

2   P. N. Olson and C. Moulton, "Pet (Dog and Cat) Overpopulation in the United States," *Journal of Reproduction and Fertility*, supp. 47 (1993): 434. These statistics, though, are contested. See Bernard Rollin and Michael Rollin, "Dogmatisms and Catechisms: Ethics and Companion Animals," *Anthrozoos* 14, no. 1 (2001): 6. I am using the expression "humanely killed" rather than "euthanized" because, as will be seen later, some object to this name for the practice.

3   SAFE 2003 at http://www.safeanimals.com/euthanasia.

4   See the "2000 Report of the AVMA Panel on Euthanasia," *Journal of the AVMA*, 218, no. 5 (March 2001): 669–96. The US Animal Protection Institute, for instance, maintains barbiturate injection to be the only acceptable method of animal euthanasia in a shelter. See Jean Hofve, "Euthanasia and the Animal Shelter," *Animal Issues* 32, no. 2 (Summer 2001), http://www.api4animals./org.

5   Methods deemed unacceptable by the AVMA still seem to be used in some places: there is, for instance, a report that in Enoch, Utah, stray animals are killed by exhaust fumes from a truck.

6   Stephanie Frommer and Arnold Arluke, "Loving Them to Death: Blame-Displacing Strategies of Animal Shelter Workers and Surrenderers," *Society and Animals* 7, no. 1 (1999): 5.

7   Ibid., 8.

8   Olson and Moulton, "Pet Overpopulation," 434.

9   This view is often associated with Peter Singer in *Animal Liberation* (1975; repr., London: Jonathan Cape, 1984). Although Singer is well known for being a utilitarian (though more recently a preference utilitarian rather than a classical utilitarian), as has been pointed out by Keith Burgess-Jackson, the book *Animal Liberation* is not explicitly utilitarian. It is compatible with utilitarianism but does not presuppose it. See Burgess-Jackson's Web log at http://analphilosopher.blogspot.com/2003_12_01_analphilosopher_archive.html.

10   Of course, this is a somewhat simplified position, since there are a range of other factors involved—for instance, the well-documented distress caused to those working in animal shelters at having to carry out the humane killing. I will discuss other possible consequentialist verdicts later.

11   This, though, is not the only possible utilitarian "take" on the situation. See Peter Singer, "Killing Humans and Killing Animals," *Inquiry* 22 (1979): 145–55, and his more recent discussion in Peter Singer, *Practical Ethics*, 2nd ed. (Cambridge: Cambridge University Press, 1993), 132, where he suggests that dogs and cats may be self-conscious and, if so, should not be killed, however painlessly, as noted on p. 181.

12   Tom Regan, *The Case for Animal Rights* (Berkeley: Univ. of California, 1983), 243. Obviously, very many difficulties exist with this argument at all stages; it is not necessary to go into these difficulties here.

13   Ibid., 98–99. This is a view that could be shared by some utilitarians, since one would expect deprivation to mean that an individual's experiences were less happy or less rich than they would otherwise be.

14   Ibid., 100, 113, 117.

15   Ibid., 103.

16   Painless killing, though, ends the possibility of a particular individual having future happy experiences, which (unless replaced) would matter in some forms of utilitarianism as affecting the total happiness in the world. There isn't space to pursue this issue here; Singer discusses it further in *Practical Ethics*.

17   Regan, *Case for Animal Rights*, 114.

18   Regan, in fact, does make a couple of exceptions to this, in particular in what he calls the "miniride" principle. I do not think that the miniride principle applies in this case, though it would be an interesting study to explore this in more detail. See ibid., 305.

19   See, for instance, Stephen Budiansky's *Covenant of the Wild: Why Animals Chose Domestication* (London: Wiedenfeld and Nicholson, 1992), where it is argued that animals connived in their own domestication, a view that is in contrast with more traditional accounts where domestication is presented as humans capturing or confining animals (that is to say, humans were the only active agents in the process).

20   See Joanna Newby, *The Pact for Survival* (Sydney: Australian Broadcasting Corporation, 1977), 61.

21   Just this case has already been convincingly argued by Keith Burgess-Jackson, and I will not argue for it further here. See Keith Burgess-Jackson, "Doing Right by Our Animal Companions," *Journal of Ethics 2* (1998): 159–85.

22   I recognize that significant philosophical difficulties exist with the idea of collective or social responsibilities and that many philosophers will find this claim unsatisfactory. There is not, however, space to consider expanded senses of responsibility in more detail here.

23   Nel Noddings raises this question as part of her discussion of caring. She asks, "Does one who cares choose swift and merciful death for the object of her care over precarious and perhaps painful life?," and answers that "it depends on our caretaking abilities, on traffic conditions where we live, on the physical condition of the animal." See Nel Noddings, *Caring* (London: University of California Press, 1984), 13.

24   Peter Singer, *Practical Ethics*, 110–34.

25   The idea that feral animals—specifically cats—are often regarded as being "out of place" is explored by H. Griffiths, J. Poulter, and D. Sibley in "Feral Cats in the City," in *Animal Spaces, Beastly Places*, ed. Chris Philo and Chris Wilbert (London: Routledge, 2000), 56–70.

26   A recent study of Web sites advocating spaying and neutering in fact does uncover paternalistic arguments. It is claimed that de-sexed animals are less susceptible to disease (since they are not mating), are less likely to be harmed by fighting, and do not suffer from thwarted sexual urges. See, for instance, http://www.ktvu.com/family/2003733/detail.html. I don't think that the presence of such paternalistic arguments invalidates my claims here, since the same kinds of paternalistic arguments also exist for humane killing, as I have pointed out.

27   Though this may not be achieved: see Olson and Moulton, "Pet Overpopulation," 43.

28   It might be, for instance, that development of the policy implications of ideas in this essay would lead to advocacy of a much more stringent licensing scheme for pet ownership.

Chapter 78

Diane Leigh and Marilee Geyer

THE MIRACLE OF LIFE

Leigh and Geyer highlight unintentional breeding, intentional breeding based on ignorance, and "puppy mills" as important causes of companion animal overpopulation. They commend mandatory spaying and neutering of most dogs and cats. They urge the long-range goal of eliminating the disconnection of humans from other beings so that animals are never considered to be trash. Solving the problem of homeless animals is a step toward expanding our caring to all living beings.

FOR DECADES, SHELTERS have been fighting a battle against companion animal overpopulation, the tragedy of too many puppies and kittens born into a world that cannot provide homes for them all. The statistics, however familiar to many people, are still staggering: a female dog and her puppies are theoretically capable of multiplying to over 67,000 in just six years, and a female cat and her kittens can result in over 400,000 offspring in only seven years.

The reasons for companion animal overpopulation are varied. Unintentional breeding is part of the problem – the mating of animals whose guardians didn't realize they were old enough, or didn't realize they were in heat, or just didn't take any action to prevent it. There are those who don't know about overpopulation and the need to prevent the births of more animals, and those who can't afford to spay or neuter their animal.

Intentional breeding also contributes to overpopulation, by those who let their animal have a litter because they want their children to witness the "miracle of birth," or those who are still under the outdated impression that animals *should* have one litter before being spayed.

The breeders who create and supply a market for a variety of purebred animals, and those who create non-purebred, "designer" dogs and cats, each contribute, as do those who breed their purebred as a way to recoup the purchase price of the animal or just to bring in some extra cash.

The demand in this country for purebred animals has also created a lucrative and horrific trade in living beings. It is estimated that three to five hundred thousand purebred puppies are sold in pet stores each year, and that 90% of those animals come from large-scale commercial breeders commonly referred to as "puppy mills." These mills mass-produce puppies for profit, typically keeping dozens to hundreds of female dogs in crude, cramped cages, or tied, for their entire lives. The dogs are bred incessantly, then disposed of – killed – after four or five years, when their bodies are worn out and they are no longer "productive." Their puppies are sold to brokers who ship them to other parts of the country to be resold in pet stores. The largest concentrations of puppy mills are found in the states of Arkansas, Iowa, Kansas, Missouri, Nebraska, Oklahoma, and Pennsylvania. And while the demand for purebred cats is significantly smaller than for purebred dogs, there are "kitten mills" churning out the most popular breeds: Persians, Himalayans, and Siamese.

Commercial breeders are required to be licensed, although some ignore this requirement, by the United States Department of Agriculture (USDA), and are subject to the provisions of the Animal Welfare

Act, the laws which regulate the care the animals are supposed to receive. But the USDA is notoriously understaffed and inspections of puppy mills are infrequent at best. Fewer than 100 inspectors oversee over 11,000 animal facilities nationwide, which include research laboratories, circuses, zoos, and about 4,100 commercial dog breeders.

Reports of hideous conditions found in puppy mills are shockingly frequent, detailing conditions of unimaginable suffering: wire cages stacked on top of each other, feces and urine from animals on top dripping down on animals in cages below; no shelter from heat or cold; filthy, matted dogs malnourished and near starvation, with open sores and skin worn bare from rubbing against their cages, feet wounded from standing on wire for months, even years; rampant disease and illness.

The puppies born in these abysmal conditions have a high incidence of genetic defects due to careless breeding. Surveys have found that half of the puppies sold in pet stores are sick or incubating a disease. Many of the pups have behavior problems due to lack of socialization and the horrendous conditions they endure during some of the most formative weeks of their lives.

American Kennel Club (AKC) "papers" are no guarantee that a puppy did not come from a puppy mill. Contrary to what many people believe, and according to the AKC itself, it does not guarantee the health or "quality" of a dog, and does not assure that the dog came from humane conditions. The AKC is simply a registry, recording the births and lineages of dogs. The AKC does, however, take in millions of dollars each year from the registrations they process to create the papers that accompany purebred dogs, including puppy mill pups. It also opposes new legislation intended to strengthen the laws regulating puppy mills and protecting puppy mill dogs.

All of this while millions of other dogs are waiting in shelters, and dying there, for simple lack of homes. The answer is simple: when the public no longer buys into the notion that purebred dogs are the "best" dogs, when they refuse to buy puppies from pet stores, the puppy mill industry will no longer be profitable and there will be no incentive to perpetuate this brutality.

At its most basic level, as long as there are not enough homes for them all, any animal added to the existing population, for *whatever* reason, helps feed companion animal overpopulation, with devastating results. Puppies and kittens for whom homes cannot be found are brought to shelters in droves and fill the facilities beyond capacity, contributing to the euthanasia of millions. A secondary impact is borne by the adult animals in the shelter, who are in desperate need of homes but who suffer very reduced chances of getting them when they must compete with adorable puppies and kittens. Disproportionate numbers of adult animals end up as euthanasia statistics because of this disadvantage.

Spay and neuter, the solution to the companion animal overpopulation tragedy, is the impassioned battle cry of shelter workers. These routine surgical procedures sterilize dogs and cats by removing the reproductive organs of female animals (spaying) or the testicles of males (neutering). In addition to helping stop overpopulation, the animals also benefit: studies show spayed and neutered animals live longer, healthier lives with fewer medical and behavioral problems.

Animal advocates have done everything imaginable to make spay/neuter operations inexpensive, easy to obtain and desirable. Millions of flyers have been distributed extolling the many health and behavioral benefits of spaying and neutering. Countless articles have been published, and even more countless media interviews have been given. National campaigns and events have centered around the idea – a U.S. postal stamp promoting sterilization has even been released. Shelters have built low cost and free spay/neuter clinics, and some have even created mobile clinics to bring these services to the streets.

Responsible shelters also work to ensure that the animals they adopt into the community are spayed and neutered. Some collect a monetary deposit from the adopter which is refunded upon proof of sterilization, although this requires diligent and time-consuming follow-up to ensure that every adopted animal does, in fact, get spayed or neutered. Other shelters have their own clinics to perform the surgeries on site, or arrange to have the surgeries done by local veterinarians, to guarantee that adopted animals are spayed and neutered before being released to their new homes.

More recently, a new tool has been added to the arsenal fighting companion animal overpopulation: many communities across the country have adopted ordinances requiring the spaying and neutering of all dogs and cats except in very limited, designated cases.

In some areas of the country this battle has seen some success. Some shelters that once handled seemingly endless litters are finally seeing fewer, as the flood of incoming puppies and kittens has slowed. In those areas, although not completely eliminated, companion animal overpopulation is no longer the primary source of homeless animals. [. . .]

Afterword

[. . .] Shelters should be leaders in the battle to end the homeless animal tragedy, but they cannot end it for us. Shelters should, and must, create programs that reach out beyond their walls to prevent animals from becoming homeless – identification and microchipping programs, low cost spay/neuter, pet parenting classes and animal behavior help, for instance – but we must use these programs. We are the ones who must make the commitment, and take the actions, to ensure we never cause an animal to be in an animal shelter. We must understand: as soon as this country stops filling animal shelters with homeless animals, the killing can stop.

Ultimately, though, we need to transcend sheltering and the current shelter system in this country. The shelter system, as it exists today, and has existed for decades, has as one of its primary functions the processing of living beings – either by recycling them to new homes or destroying them, but disposing of them somehow and relieving people and communities of their responsibility for them. It is a tangible sign of our society's deep disconnection from other beings, a disconnection so profound and damaging that we could legitimately categorize it as a sickness.

We need to acknowledge this sickness and how it plays out in our shelters, and never make excuses for it or believe that it is acceptable. The truth is, there should not be a need in a civilized society for a system that disposes of animals as if they were trash. We need to tell this truth, as an act of respect to the animals, and because the truth cannot be changed until it can be seen.

At the deepest level, the only thing that will heal this sickness, and alleviate the pain we feel over this issue, is to end the killing, by creating communities that no longer have overwhelming homeless animal problems and have, therefore, no need to kill animals. By creating communities that find killing to be an unacceptable answer, and that see animals as having value and beauty, as beings with a sacred spark of life and spirit.

People sometimes ask, in light of the devastating and important issues that face us in our modern times, why the homeless animal issue is important, why we should be concerned about it. The answer to this question is critical, as the underlying societal values that enable the homeless animal problem also enable and are deeply connected to other social issues of our time – issues which exist on a continuum created by our attitudes toward our fellow beings and the planet we share.

The homeless animal problem is a reflection of a society that has lost touch with other living beings, with the natural world, and with the very web of life. It is but one tragic symptom of a culture that does not see its connections to others, does not see others as having inherent value, and instead sees them as put here for our use, as disposable or somehow lesser, as somehow not worthy of reverence, compassion and respect. This same societal thinking, this way of separating ourselves from "others," allows for the possibility of the destruction of ancient forests, damage to our environment and the animals in it, of racism and exploitation of third world peoples, of poverty and human homelessness, of children going hungry in a land of plenty, of devaluing our elders . . . this way of viewing the "others" in our world enables and underlies a continuum of issues.

The systematic mass destruction and disposal of millions of living creatures every year constitutes a kind of violence in our society that is no less violent because it is institutionalized and mostly overlooked. When killing those who are closest to, and most dependent upon us becomes an unquestioned fact of daily life, we have set a very dangerous and damaging precedent as to what is ethically acceptable, what we are willing to tolerate, and what we are capable of doing to others. How much easier is it to deny consideration and compassion to one group when we have learned to accept the mass killing of another – and especially, of beings whom we call our "friends"?

The homeless animal issue is critically important because it is so fundamental: dogs and cats are the closest most people ever get to other species and the natural world. If our concern and compassion are so weak and limited that we are unable to save those animals closest to us, how will we ever be able to save the more distant beings – the endangered species we may never see, the redwoods and mountains and wilderness we may never visit, the suffering people we may never meet and whose misery we may never experience directly?

And yet, there is unique power in this issue. Solving this problem offers us the chance to take a first step toward healing our relationship with the natural world, to reawaken and embrace our connection with other living beings, to reaffirm the preciousness of life itself. It offers us the potent opportunity to become better human beings, to call forward the finest parts of ourselves and express the very best of our humanity. If we are able, as a society, to find the compassion and dedication to save our companion animals, to treat them with the love and respect they deserve, to solve this problem in an ethical way, then perhaps we can extend that compassion and dedication to others in need.

Perhaps this issue can be a stepping stone toward an expanding circle of compassion and action, toward creating a society that is just and caring to all living beings – beginning with the precious ones "right in our own backyards."

The two cats who live with me, Otto and Raphael, walk into the room as I write. They swirl around my feet, nibble at some food, look out the window. One huge black cat, one skinny orange one, each with his own unique, quirky personality, each with his own story.

They are ordinary cats: six years old now, they have lived in my home since their kittenhoods, and are healthy, safe, and happy. They play and pick on each other, follow the sun each day from window to window, sleep in deep peace.

And they are extraordinary cats: they shine into my life their unconditional love, share with me their in-the-moment wisdom, show me how to live with generosity, gentleness, and joy. Their innocent presence is a constant reminder of the preciousness of all life.

Our companion animals live with us in our world, but they bring with them gifts from their animal worlds. It is a privilege to have them near. They are our link to the wild animals we will never see except in books or on television. They are the animal fur we get to stroke, and the paws we get to touch. They are the wild, mysterious eyes we get to gaze into. They give us a glimpse into "other nations." They are messengers, bringing us a critical, sacred message of connection; they are teachers, showing us back to our place in the web of life, showing us the way back home.

Can there be any doubt of what we owe them in return?

FURTHER READING

Beck, Alan and Aaron Kather (1996) *Between Pets and People,* West Lafayette, IN: Purdue University Press.

Fine, A. (ed.) (2006) *Handbook on Animal-Assisted Therapy, Second Edition: Theoretical Foundations and Guidelines for Practice,* San Diego: Academic Press.

Grandin, Temple and Catherine Johnson (2005) *Animals in Translation: Using the Mysteries of Autism to Decode Animal Behavior,* Orlando, FL: Harcourt, Inc.

Podeberscek, A.L., Paul, E.S., and Serpell, J.A., (eds) (2005) *Companion Animals and Us: Exploring the Relationships between People and Pets,* Cambridge: Cambridge University Press.

Sheldrake, R. (1999) *Dogs That Know When Their Owners Are Coming Home and Other Unexplained Powers of Animals,* New York: Crown.

Slater, M.R. (2002) *Community Approaches to Feral Cats,* Washington, D.C.: Humane Society Press.

STUDY QUESTIONS

1   Konrad Lorenz, Bernard Rollin, and Michael Rollin maintain that "having" an animal companion involves serious moral responsibilities. What responsibilities do you believe should be associated with having an animal companion?

2   Do you agree with Paul Shepard that pets cannot connect us to the natural world? Explain why or why not.

3   How does Anna Merz's experience with a wild rhino affect your view of the intelligence or emotional capacity of wild animals?

4   Is Freya Mathews' description of the psychological intimacy she has experienced with animals supported by your own experience of animals? Explain any similarities or differences.

5   Do you believe that we should keep animals as companions? Explain the possible benefits and disadvantages to such animals, as well as to humans.

6   If you live in an urban setting, what are some interactions you have had with wild or feral animals? What recommendations might you suggest for changing urban habitat for the benefit of animals?

7   James Garbarino notes that people often have assumed that concern for animals means less concern for people. To what extent do you believe this is true?

8   Reflect on your experience of observing (or using) animals for assistance and therapy. Have you observed stress or suffering? What suggestions do you have to improve the welfare of animals performing these services?

9   Clare Palmer discusses several approaches to the killing of healthy dogs and cats in animal shelters. To what extent do you agree that relations of dependence/independence are morally relevant to this issue? How do you respond to the assertion that both de-sexing and killing are results of human domination of pets?

10 Leigh and Geyer argue for ordinances requiring the spaying and neutering of dogs and cats, with limited exceptions. Do you agree with their view? In "Afterword" they argue that ultimately we need to transcend the current shelter system in the U.S. What are some of the reasons they provide?

Animal law/animal activism

INTRODUCTION TO PART TEN

SHOULD ANIMALS HAVE LEGAL RIGHTS? How can the situation of animals be improved? Is civil disobedience morally justified? The authors in this Part present widely diverging answers to these questions. In "A Great Shout," attorney Steven Wise notes that we have assigned ourselves the exalted status of legal persons and consider every other animal as merely legal things which can be owned. Wise argues for fundamental legal rights for the great apes based on their possession of autonomy.

In a book review of Wise's book *Rattling the Cage*, Richard Posner critiques Wise's analysis. He points out that Wise does not show that having cognitive capacity is a necessary or sufficient condition of having legal rights. Wise downplays the fact that such legal rights would be a drastic departure from existing law. Posner argues that making wild animals property is the best way to increase animal protection, given that "aggressive implementations" of animal-rights thinking are not likely to prevail.

In "The Dangerous Claims of the Animal Rights Movement," Richard Epstein points out a number of important differences between human beings and animals which support the view that human welfare is more important than animal welfare. He maintains that treating animals as the moral and legal peers of human beings would undermine the liberty and dignity of human beings. It is appropriate that animals remain our property. In contrast to Epstein's views, Kate Douglas describes recent efforts by some animal rights activists to acquire legal protection for animals.

In "Every Sparrow that Falls," Wesley Jamison, Caspar Wenk, and James Parker analyze animal rights activism as a movement which functions like a religion, based on their research in Switzerland and the United States. They identify five components of animal rights activism which fulfill the definition of "functional religion" stated by the U.S. Supreme Court.

The four essays which conclude the Part discuss strategies by which to improve the condition of animals. In "Understanding Animal Rights Violence" Tom Regan explores the split between "immediatists" and "gradualists." The diversity of views within the animal rights movement means that it is accurately characterized neither as nonviolent nor as terrorist. Regan proposes incremental abolitionist change, in which one use of animals at a time is completely stopped.

Courtney Dillard examines the effectiveness of two organized protests and acts of civil disobedience against the largest pigeon shoot in the United States. Her findings suggest that the effectiveness of civil disobedience is increased when it is enacted in nonviolent and nonthreatening ways and when participants demonstrate both a willingness to suffer for their beliefs and an interest in communicating that suffering to onlookers.

Chris DeRose describes his activism on behalf of animals in an excerpt from *In Your Face*. His willingness to be arrested and go to jail when he has broken trespassing laws is part of the process of civil disobedience. He maintains that animal slavery has to be abolished because it is wrong.

In "Ten Ways to Make a Difference," Peter Singer draws on the work of Henry Spira, an activist who has had remarkable successes in reducing animal suffering. He presents Spira's life as an example of finding meaning by living in accord with one's own values. The ten suggestions are the result of Spira's experience in changing public opinion.

Chapter 79

Steven M. Wise

A GREAT SHOUT: LEGAL RIGHTS FOR GREAT APES

Steven Wise argues that legal rules that may have made good sense in the past may make good sense no longer. As the scientific evidence of the capacities of nonhuman animals such as the great apes continues to mount, it is apparent that treating animals as things is unjust. Wise argues on both legal and philosophical grounds that the "practical autonomy" exhibited by many animals is sufficient to justify the attribution of basic legal rights.

THE EARLIEST KNOWN law is preserved in cuneiform on Sumerian clay tablets. These Mesopotamian law codes, 4,000 years old, the Laws of Ur-Nammu, the Lipit-Ishtar Lawcode, the Laws of Eshunna, and the Laws of Hammurabi, assumed that humans could own both nonhuman animals and slaves (Wise 1996). It took most of the next 4,000 years for subjective legal rights to develop. Even in Republican and Imperial Rome, legal rights were understood to exist only in the objective sense of being "the right thing to do" (Wise 1996, 799). Subjective legal rights, claims that one person could make on another, first glimmered in twelfth-century writings. It was only in the fourteenth century that the notion that one's legal rights were one's property began to root (Wise 1996).

Not until the nineteenth century was slavery abolished in the West and every human formally cloaked with the legal personhood that signifies eligibility for fundamental legal rights. So the final brick of a great legal wall, begun millennia ago, was cemented into place. Today, on one side of this legal wall reside all the natural legal persons, all the members of a single species, *Homo sapiens*. We have assigned ourselves, alone among the millions of animal species, the exalted status of legal persons, entitled to all the rights, privileges, powers, and immunities of "legal personhood" (Wise 1996).

On the other side of this wall lies every other animal. They are not legal persons but legal things. During the American Civil War, President Abraham Lincoln was said to have spurned South Carolina's peace commissioners with the statement, "As President, I have no eyes but Constitutional eyes; I cannot see you" (*Oxford Dictionary of Quotations* 1979, 313). In this way, their "legal thinghood" makes nonhuman animals invisible to the civil law. Civil judges have no eyes for anyone but legal persons.

[. . .]

The legal thinghood of nonhuman animals has a unique history. An understanding of this history is instrumental to what Oliver Wendell Holmes Jr. called the "deliberate reconsideration" to which every legal rule must eventually fall subject (Holmes 1897). Alan Watson has concluded from his studies of comparative law that "to a truly astounding degree the law is rooted in the past" (Watson 1993, 95). The most common sources from which we quarry our law are the legal rules of earlier times. But when we borrow past law, we borrow the past. Legal rules that may have made good sense when they were fashioned may make good sense no longer. Raised by age to the status of self-evident truths they may perpetuate ancient ignorance, ancient prejudices, and ancient injustices that may once have been less unjust because we knew no better.

[. . .]

To think about it was to condemn it

The wall's foundations have rotted. Because its intellectual foundations are unprincipled and arbitrary, unfair and unjust, its greatest vulnerability, at least in the English-speaking countries, is to the unceasing tendency of the common law "to work itself pure," to borrow a phrase from Lord Mansfield, the great eighteenth-century English judge.[1] Once a great injustice is brought to their attention, common law judges have the duty to place the legal rules that are its source alongside those great overarching principles that have been integral to Western law and justice for hundreds of years—equality, liberty, fairness, and reasoned judicial decision making—to determine if, in light of what are believed to be true facts and modern values, those rules should be found wanting.

[. . .]

Recall that the abomination of human slavery was finally abolished in the West little more than 100 years ago. It continues in a few countries to this day. The first thinking about the justice of the legal thinghood of nonhuman animals occurred just as slavery was flickering in the West. To date it has resulted mostly in the enactment of pathetically inadequate anticruelty statutes. But as the scientific evidence of the true natures of such nonhuman animals as chimpanzees continues to mount, that thinking will be its undoing. Because to think about the legal thinghood of such creatures as the great apes will be finally to condemn such a notion.

This process has begun. Modern law has begun slowly to disassemble the radical incommensurability said to exist between all human and all nonhuman animals from both the top down and the bottom up. The intrinsic value of human beings is now seen in law as commensurable with other legal values. This was reflected, for example, in the enactment in the English-speaking countries of wrongful death statutes in the middle of the nineteenth century. These statutes were intended to alter the ancient, and unfair, common law rule that the loss of human life, understood to be incommensurable with anything else, could never be compensated by money (Wise 1998b). The lives of at least some nonhuman animals have begun to be infused with a degree of intrinsic and not merely instrumental value. The preamble to the United Nations World Charter for Nature states that "every form of life is unique, warranting respect regardless of its worth to man" (World Charter 1982, 992). Respected international law commentators have argued that the legal right of individual whales to life may be becoming a part of binding international law (D'Amato and Chopra 1991). While interpreting the federal Endangered Species Act, the U.S. Supreme Court was guided in its decision by the declaration of the American Congress that endangered species were of "incalculable value."[2]

[. . .]

Liberty: the supreme value of the Western world

Today liberty "stands unchallenged as the supreme value of the Western world" (Patterson 1991, ix). Out of the more than 200 recorded senses of "liberty," Sir Isaiah Berlin famously identified two central senses: negative and positive (Berlin 1969). One's negative liberty, with which we are concerned, is often described as "freedom from" and depends on being able to do what one wishes without human interference

(Berlin 1998). On the other hand, one's positive liberty may be described as "freedom to" (Berlin 1969, lvi; McPherson 1990, 61).

[. . .]

I refer to these fundamental negative liberty rights as "dignity-rights." International and domestic courts and legislatures around the world recognize that for a human being to have a minimal opportunity to flourish, such dignity-rights as bodily integrity and bodily liberty must be protected by sturdy barriers of negative liberty rights that form a protective legal perimeter around our bodies and personalities (Berlin 1969; Dworkin 1977; Feinberg 1966).

Anglo-American common law recognizes a general negative liberty right. The constitutions of most modern nations protect fundamental negative liberty rights (Allan 1991).[3]

[. . .]

Fundamental rights derive from a practical autonomy

It is true, as the Kansas Supreme Court has said, that "Anglo American law starts with the premise of thorough-going self determination."[4] But what kind of autonomy is required? Philosophers often understand autonomy to mean what the German philosopher Immanuel Kant intended it to mean 200 years ago. We will call Kant's notion of autonomy "full autonomy." Though whole books have been written about what Kant meant, I will try to catch much of his core meaning in a single sentence: I have autonomy if, in determining what I ought to do in any situation, I have the ability to understand what others can and ought to do, I can rationally analyze whether it would be right for me to act in some way or another, keeping in mind that I should act only as I would want others to act and as they can act, and then I can do what I have decided is right. My ability to perform something like this calculus is what makes me autonomous, gives me dignity, and requires that I be treated as a person. If I cannot do this, I lack autonomy and dignity and can justly be treated as a thing, according to Kant.

Whether I have summarized Kant's idea perfectly or not is irrelevant. What is important is that anything that resembles this analysis demands an ability to reason at an almost inhumanly high level. Perhaps our Aristotles, Kants, Freuds, and Einsteins achieved it some of the time. But it is only a glimmering possibility for infants and children, most normal adults never reach it, and the severely mentally limited and the permanently vegetative do not even begin. How did Kant deal with them? Well, he did not, and his "deep silence" on the moral status of children and nonrational adults has not gone unnoticed (Herman 1993). Even Aristotle and company pass significant portions of their lives on automatic pilot or often act out of desire, and not reason, which is precisely how Kant argued nonhuman animals act (Herman 1993; Langer 1997). Were judges to demand full autonomy as a prerequisite for dignity, they would exclude most of us, themselves included, from eligibility for dignity-rights.

Beings may possess a much simpler ability that allows them to act to fulfill their intended purposes. They may have varying capacities for mental flexibility and responsiveness. Autonomy can encompass a range of capacities for consciousness from the most simple awareness of one's present experience to a much broader and deeper self-awareness, self-reflection, and an awareness of the past, present, and future. The full autonomy of, say, Plato might be said to approximate the high end of full Kantian autonomy, whereas the consciousness of a typical preschooler might approximate the low end of a practical autonomy.

A full Kantian autonomy is too narrow a prerequisite for dignity-rights. Not all humans possess it to any degree. Most possess it only in varying degrees. No humans possess it all the time and no one expects them to. Many more humans, though still not anencephalic or even normal infants, the most severely retarded adults, or adults in persistent vegetative comas, possess a practical autonomy than possess full Kantian autonomy (Russell 1996; Wright 1993). A practical autonomy merely recognizes that a being has a somewhat "less than perfect ability to choose appropriate actions" (Cherniak 1985, 5). Any being capable of desires and beliefs has a practical autonomy if she can have beliefs and desires and is able to make "some, but not necessarily all of the sound inferences from the belief set that are apparently appropriate" (Cherniak 1985, 10; Rachels 1990; Regan 1983; Wright 1993). A practical autonomy, therefore, much more closely coincides with the way in which human beings are normally understood to be autonomous.

Perhaps most important for our purposes, fundamental common law and constitutional rights were not designed to protect only the fully autonomous. Courts are exquisitely sensitive to autonomy's practical sense.[5] Once some minimum capacity is attained, courts generally respect the choices made within exceedingly wide parameters, at least with respect to human adults. Practical autonomy acts as a trip wire for dignity-rights. This is because a choice emanating from even a flickering autonomy is more highly valued, regardless of whether the actions are rational, reasonable, or even inimical to one's own best interests, than is any specific choice.[6] That is why the judges of the California Court of Appeals said that "respect for the dignity and autonomy of the individual is a value universally celebrated in free societies. . . . Out of fidelity to that value defendant's choice must be honored even if he opts foolishly to go to hell in a handbasket."[7]

American courts routinely hold that incompetent human beings are entitled to the same dignity-rights as competent human beings. For example, the U.S. Supreme Court held that a man with an I.Q. below 10 and the mental capacity of an 18-month-old child had an inextinguishable liberty right to personal security.[8]

[. . .]

Now comes the exceedingly odd part: Even humans who have always lacked autonomy and self-determination are said to possess the requisite dignity for legal personhood.[9] "Can it be doubted," state the judges of high courts rhetorically, "that the value of human dignity extends to both (competent and incompetent humans)?"[10] Undoubting courts grant competent, incompetent, and never-competent humans the same common law dignity-rights and the rights to protect their powers to use them as well.[11] The result is that humans with minimal, or even no, capacity for autonomy and self-determination, even terminally ill infants who lack all cognition, possess not just protected dignity-rights but the right to use their power to enforce them.[12]

[. . .]

Courts recognize human dignity-rights in the complete absence of autonomy only by using an arbitrary legal fiction that controverts the empirical evidence that no such autonomy exists. Conversely, courts refuse to recognize dignity-rights of the great apes only by using a second arbitrary legal fiction in the teeth of empirical evidence that they possess it (Nino 1993; Rachels 1990). But legal fictions can only be justified when they harmonize with, or at least do not undermine, the overarching values and principles of a legal system. Thus the legal fiction that a human who actually lacks autonomy has it is benign, for at worst it extends legal rights to those who might not need them. At best it protects the bodily integrity of the most helpless humans alive. But the legal fiction that great apes are not autonomous when they actually are undermines every important principle and value of Western justice: liberty, equality, fairness, and reasoned judicial decision making. It is pernicious.

[. . .]

Equality: likes should be treated alike

Equality is the axiom of Western justice that likes be treated alike. [. . .] Equality's logical component requires that dissimilar treatment rests on some relevant and objectively ascertainable difference between a favored and disfavored class with respect to the harm to be avoided or the benefit to be promoted (Simons 1989).[12]

[. . .]

Equality's normative component means that no matter how perfect the relationship between ends and means may be, some means and some ends are unacceptable solely because they are arbitrary, irrelevant, invidious, or are otherwise normatively illegitimate.[13]

Together, the logical and normative elements of equality mean that only qualities that are objectively ascertainable and normatively acceptable should be compared. Actual and relevant likenesses that are examined in light of current knowledge and normative understandings that are not false, assumed, unproveable, or anachronistic assumptions or contain "fixed notions" about likeness should be the measure.[14] These are the teachings of the fundamental value of equality.

Closely related to equality rights are proportionality rights. Proportionality requires that unalikes be treated proportionately to their unalikeness (Simons 1989).

[. . .]

At least three independent equality or proportionality arguments support fundamental legal rights for the great apes (Wise 1998a). First, great apes who possess Kant's full autonomy should be entitled to dignity-rights *if* humans who possess full autonomy are entitled to them. To do otherwise would be to undermine the major principled arguments against racism and sexism.

Second, great apes who possess a practical autonomy should be entitled to dignity-rights in proportion to the degree to which they approach full Kantian autonomy *if* humans who possess a practical autonomy are entitled to dignity-rights in proportion to the degree to which *they* approach full Kantian autonomy. Thus if a human is entitled to fewer, narrower, or partial legal rights as their capabilities approach the quality Q, so should nonhuman animals whose capabilities also approach the quality Q.

Third, in perhaps the clearest argument for equality, great apes who possess either full Kantian autonomy or a practical autonomy should be entitled to the same fundamental rights to which humans who entirely lack autonomy are entitled. Placing the rightless legal thing, the bonobo Kanzi, beside an anencephalic 1-day-old human with the legal right to choose to consent or withhold consent to medical treatment highlights the legal aberration that is Kanzi's legal thinghood.

Probably the strongest argument that just being human is necessary for the possession of fundamental equality rights has been offered by Carl Cohen, who has argued that at least moral rights should be limited to all and only human beings. "The issue," said Cohen, "is one of kind" (Cohen 1986, 866). He acknowledged that some humans lack autonomy and the ability to make moral choices. However, because humans as a "kind" possess this ability, it should be imputed to all humans, regardless of their actual abilities. But Cohen's argument can succeed only if the species, *H. sapiens*, can nonarbitrarily be designated as the boundary of a relevant "kind." That is doubtful. Other classifications, some wider, such as animals, vertebrates, mammals, primates, and apes, and at least one narrower—normal adult humans—also contain every fully autonomous human.

As well as being logically flawed, Cohen's argument for group benefits is normatively flawed. It "assumes that we should determine how an individual is to be treated, not on the basis of *its* qualities but on the basis of *other* individuals' qualities" (Rachels 1990, 187). Rachels calls the opposing moral idea "moral individualism" and defines it to mean that "how an individual may be treated is to be determined, not by considering his group memberships, but by considering his own particular characteristics" (Rachels 1990, 173). It is individualism, and not group benefits, that is more consistent with the overarching principles and values of a liberal democracy and that has the firmer basis in present law.

[. . .]

Will we affirm or undermine our commitment to fundamental human rights?

The destruction of the legal thinghood even of the great apes, our closest cousins, will necessarily involve a long and difficult struggle. It is the nature of great change to stimulate great opposition. But the anachronistic legal thinghood of the great apes so contradicts outright the overarching principles of equality, liberty, fairness, and rationality in judicial decision making that it will eventually be denied only by those in whom a narrow self-interest predominates.

[. . .]

Notes

1   *Omichund v. Barker*, 1 Atk. 21, 33 (K.B. 1744).

2   *Tennessee Valley Authority v. Hill*, 437 U.S. 153, 188 (1978). The Endangered Species Act, 16 U.S.C. §§ 1531–43 (1973).

3   *E.g., Youngberg v. Romeo*, 457 U.S. 307, 317 (1982); *Bowers v. Devito*, 686 F.2d 616, 618 (7th Cir. 1982).

4   *Natanson v. Kline*, 350 P.2d 1093, 1104 (Kan. 1960). *See also Stamford Hospital v. Vega*, 674 A.2d 821, 831 (Conn. 1996).

5   *E.g., Rivers v. Katz*, 495 N.E.2d 337, 341, *reargument denied*, 498 N.E.2d 438 (N.Y. 1986); *Schmidt v. Schmidt*, 450 A.2d 421, 422–23 (Pa. Super. 1983) (a 26-year-old woman with Down's syndrome with the mental ability of a child between 4½ and 8 years can rationally decide whether to choose to visit a parent).

6   *E.g., Thornburgh v. American College of Obstetricians and Gynecologists*, 476 U.S. 747, 778 n.5 (Stevens, J., concurring); *Application of President & Directors of Georgetown College*, 331 F.2d 1010, 1017 (D.C. Cir. 1964); *State v. Wagner*, 752 P.2d 1136, 1178 (Ore. 1988).

7   *People v. Nauton*, 34 Cal. Rptr. 2d 861, 864 (Ct. App. 1994).

8   *Youngberg, supra* note 3, at 315–16.

9   *E.g., Gray v. Romeo*, 697 F. Supp. 580, 587 (D.R.I. 1987); *Conservatorship of Drabick*, 245 Cal. Rptr. 840, 855, *cert. denied sub nom., Drabick v. Drabick*, 488 U.S. 958 (1988); *Superintendent of Belchertown State School v. Saikewicz*, 370 N.E.2d 417, 427, 428 (Mass. 1977); *Eichner v. Dillon*, 426 N.Y.S.2d 517, 542 (App. Div.), *modified* 52 N.Y.2d 363 (1980); *see Conservatorship of Valerie N.*, 707 P.2d 760, 776 (Cal. 1985), citing *Matter of Moe*, 432 N.E.2d 712, 720 (Mass. 1982).

10   *Matter of Guardianship of L.W.*, 482 N.W.2d 60, 69 (Wis. 1992), quoting *Eichner, supra* note 16, at 542. *See also Gray, supra* note 16, at 587; *Matter of Moe, supra* note 16, at 719; *Delio v. Westchester County Medical Center*, 516 N.Y.S.2d 677, 686 (N.Y. App. Div. 1987).

11   *E.g., Gray, supra* note 16, at 587; *Conservatorship of Drabick, supra* note 16, at 855; *Foody v. Manchester Memorial Hospital*, 482 A.2d 713, 718 (Conn. Sup. Ct. 1984); *Matter of Tavel*, 661 A.2d 1061, 1069 (Del. 1995); *Severns v. Wilmington Medical Center, Inc.*, 421 A.2d 1334, 1347 (Del. 1980); *John F. Kennedy Memorial Hospital v. Bludworth*, 452 So.2d 921, 921, 923, 924 (Fla. 1985); *In re Guardianship of Barry*, 445 So.2d 365, 370 (Fla. Dist. Ct. App. 1984); *DeGrella by and through Parrent v. Elston*, 858 S.W.2d, 698, 709 (Ky. 1993); *In re L.H.R.*, 321 S.E.2d 716, 722 (Ga. 1984); *Care and Protection of Beth*, 587 N.E.2d 1377, 1382 (Mass. 1992); *Matter of Conroy*, 486 A.2d 1209, 1229 (N.J. 1985); *In re Grady*, 426 A.2d. 474–75 (N.J. 1981); *In re Quinlan*, 355 A.2d 647, 664 (N.J.), *cert. denied sub nom., Garger v. New Jersey*, 429 U.S. 922 (1976); *Eichner, supra*, note 16, at 546; *Matter of Guardianship of Hamlin*, 689 P.2d 1372, 1376 (Wash. 1984); *In re Colyer*, 660 P.2d 738, 774 (Wash. 1983); *Matter of Guardianship of L.W., supra* note 17, at 67, 68.

12   *E.g., In re L.H.R., supra* note 18 (4-month-old in chronic vegetative state); *Care and Protection of Beth, supra* note 18 (10-month-old in irreversible coma); *Strunk v. Strunk*, 445 S.W.2d 145 (Ky. 1969) (27-year-old with an I.Q. of 35 and a mental age of 6 years); *In re Grady, supra* note 18; *In re Penny N.*, 414 A.2d 541 (N.H. 1980); *Saikewicz, supra* note 16 (67-year-old with an I.Q of 10 and a mental age of 31 months); *Matter of Guardianship of L.W., supra* note 18, at 68; *In re Guardianship of Barry, supra* note 18 (anencephalic 10-month-old with no cognitive brain function).

13   *E.g., Logan v. Zimmerman Brush Co.*, 455 U.S. 422, 442 (1982) (plurality opinion); *Rinaldi v. Yeager*, 384 U.S. 305, 308–309 (1966); *McLaughlin v. Florida*, 379 U.S. 184, 191 (1964).

14   *E.g., Romer v. Evans*, 116 S. Ct. 1620, 1627–29 (1996); *Skinner, supra* note 34. *See Thoreson v. Penthouse International, Ltd.*, 563 N.Y.S.2d 968, 975 (Sup. Ct. 1990).

15   *E.g., United States v. Virginia*, 116 S. Ct. 2264, 2277–78 (1996), quoting *Mississippi University for Women v. Hogan*, 458 U.S. 718, 725 (1985); *Craig v. Boren*, 429 U.S. 190, 197 (1976). *See Romer, supra* note 35, at 1628.

References

Berlin, I. 1969. Two concepts of liberty. In *Four essays on liberty* (pp. 117–72). Oxford: Oxford University Press.

———. 1998. My intellectual path. *New York Review of Books*, May 14, pp. 53–60.

Cherniak, C. 1985. *Minimal rationality*. Cambridge: MIT Press.

Cohen, C. 1986. The case for the use of animals in biomedical research. *New England Journal of Medicine* 317: 867–70.

D'Amato, A., and Chopra, S. K. 1991. Whales: Their emerging right to life. *American Journal of International Law* 85: 21–62.

Dworkin, R. 1977. *Taking rights seriously*. Cambridge, MA: Harvard University Press.

Feinberg, J. 1966. Duties, rights, and claims. *American Philosophy Quarterly* 3: 37.

Herman, B. 1993. *The practice of moral judgment*. Cambridge, MA: Harvard University Press.

Holmes, O. W., Jr. 1897. The path of the law. *Harvard Law Review* 10: 457–78.

Langer, E. 1997. *The power of mindful learning*. Reading, MA: Addison-Wesley.

McPherson, J. M. 1990. *Abraham Lincoln and the second American revolution*. Oxford: Oxford University Press.

Nino, C. S. 1993. *The ethics of human rights*. Oxford: Oxford University Press.

Oxford Dictionary of Quotations. 1979. (3rd ed.). Oxford: Oxford University Press.

Patterson, O. 1991. *Freedom: Freedom in the making of Western culture*. New York: Basic Books.

Rachels, J. 1990. *Created from animals*. Oxford: Oxford University Press.

Regan, T. 1983. *The case for animal rights*. Berkeley: University of California Press.

Russell, J. 1996. *Agency—Its role in mental development*. Hove, UK: Erlbaum.

Simons, K. W. 1989. Overinclusion and underinclusion: A new model. *UCLA Law Review* 36: 447–89.

Watson, A. 1993. *Legal transplants—an approach to comparative law*. Athens: University of Georgia Press.

Wise, S. M. 1996. The legal thinghood of nonhuman animals. *Boston College Environmental Affairs Law Review* 23(3): 471–546.

———. 1998a. Hardly a revolution—The eligibility of nonhuman animals for dignity-rights in a liberal democracy. *Vermont Law Review* 22: 793–915.

Wise, S. M. 1998b. Recovery of common law damages for emotional distress, loss of society, and loss of companionship for the wrongful death of a companion animal. *Animal Law* 4: 33.

World Charter for Nature. 1982. GA Res. 37/7 Annex UNGAOR, 37th Sess. Suppl. No. 51, UNDO A/ 37151 (Oct. 28) (preamble). In H. W. Wood, Jr., The United Nations World Charter for Nature: The developing nations' initiative to establish protections for the environment. *Ecology* 12: 977–92.

Wright, W. A. 1993. Treating animals as ends. *Journal of Value Inquiry* 27: 353–66.

Chapter 80

Richard A. Posner

BOOK REVIEW: *RATTLING THE CAGE: TOWARD LEGAL RIGHTS FOR ANIMALS* BY STEVEN M. WISE

Richard Posner responds to Wise's arguments by pointing out that Wise has not shown that having cognitive capacity is necessary or sufficient for having legal rights. In Posner's view, Wise is not urging judges to develop doctrines already implicit in legal tradition, but rather to "set sail on an uncharted sea without a compass." Posner recommends instead that we build on the liberating potential of legal property, because people tend to protect what they own, and that we extend and more vigorously enforce laws designed to prevent cruelty to animals.

Rattling the Cage: Toward Legal Rights for Animals. By Steven M. Wise. Cambridge, Mass.: Perseus Books, 2000.

T HE "ANIMAL RIGHTS" movement is gathering steam, and Steven Wise is one of the pistons. A lawyer whose practice is the protection of animals, he has now written a book in which he urges courts in the exercise of their common-law powers of legal rulemaking to confer legally enforce-able rights on animals, beginning with chimpanzees and bonobos (the two most intelligent primate species).[1]

[. . .]

If Wise is to persuade his chosen audience, he must show how courts can proceed incrementally, building on existing cases and legal concepts, toward his goal of radically enhanced legal protection for animals. Recall the process by which, starting from the unpromising principle that "separate but equal" was constitutional, the Supreme Court outlawed official segregation. First, certain public facilities were held not to be equal; then segregation of law schools was invalidated as inherently unequal because of the importance of the contacts made in law school to a successful legal practice; then segregation of elementary schools was outlawed on the basis of social scientific evidence that this segregation, too, was inherently unequal; then the "separate but equal" principle itself, having been reduced to a husk, was quietly buried and the no-segregation principle of the education cases extended to all public facilities, including rest rooms and drinking fountains.

That is the process that Wise envisages for the animal-rights movement, although the end point is less clear. We have, Wise points out, a robust conception of human rights, and we apply it even to people who by reason of retardation or other mental disability cannot enforce their own rights but need a guardian to do it for them. The evolution of human-rights law has involved not only expanding the number of rights but also expanding the number of rights-holders, notably by adding women and blacks. (Much of Wise's book is about human rights, and about the methodology by which judges enlarge human rights in response to changed understandings.) We also have a long history of providing legal protections for animals that recognize their sentience, their emotional capacity, and their capacity to suffer pain; these protections have been growing too.

Wise wants to merge these legal streams by showing that the apes that are most like us genetically, namely the chimpanzees and the bonobos, are also very much like us in their mentation, which exceeds that of human infants and profoundly retarded people. He believes that they are enough like us to be in the direct path of rights expansion. So far as deserving to have rights is concerned, he finds no principled difference between the least mentally able people and the most mentally able animals, as the two groups overlap—or at least too little difference to justify interrupting, at the gateway to the animal kingdom, the expansive rights trend that he has discerned. The law's traditional dichotomy between humans and animals is a vestige of bad science and of a hierarchizing tendency that put men over animals just as it put free men over slaves. Wise does not say how many other animal species besides chimpanzees and bonobos he would like to see entitled, but he makes clear that he regards entitling those two species as a milestone, not as the end of the road.

[. . .]

From his principle of equality Wise deduces that chimpanzees should have the same constitutional rights and other legal rights that small children and severely retarded adults have: the rights to life, to bodily integrity, to subsistence, and to some kind of freedom (how much is unclear), but not the right to vote. He does not discuss whether they should have the right to reproduce. But he is emphatic that since we would not permit invasive or dangerous medical experimentation on small children or severely retarded adults, neither can we permit such experimentation on chimpanzees, no matter how great the benefits for human health.

The framework of Wise's analysis, as we have seen, is the history of extending rights to formerly excluded persons. Working within that conventional lawyerly framework, he seeks to convince his readers that chimpanzees have the essential attribute of persons, which he believes is the level of mentation that we call consciousness, but (to avoid a *reductio ad absurdum*) that computers do not have it. In short, anyone who has consciousness should have rights; chimpanzees are conscious; therefore, chimpanzees should have rights.

How convincing is the analysis? [. . .] It is the major premise that presents the immediate difficulty with this syllogistic approach to the question of animal rights. Cognitive capacity is certainly *relevant* to rights; it is a precondition of some rights, such as the right to vote. But most people would not think it either a necessary or a sufficient condition of having legally enforceable rights, and Wise has not attempted to take on their arguments. Many people believe, for example, that a one-day-old human fetus, though it has no cognitive capacity, should have a right to life; and, after the first trimester, the Supreme Court permits the fetus to be accorded a qualified such right, though the cognitive capacity of a second- or even third-trimester fetus is very limited. And Wise is not distressed at the thought of destroying a "conscious" computer,[2] showing that even he does not take completely seriously the notion that rights follow cognitive capacity. Most people would think it distinctly odd to proportion animal rights to animal intelligence, as Wise wishes to do, implying that dolphins, parrots, and ravens are entitled to more legal protection than horses (or most monkeys), and perhaps that the laws forbidding cruelty to animals should be limited to the most intelligent animals, inviting the crack "They don't have syntax, so we can eat them."[3] And most of us would think it downright offensive to give greater rights to monkeys, let alone to computers, than to retarded people, upon a showing that the monkey or the computer has a greater cognitive capacity than a profoundly retarded human being, unless perhaps the human being has no brain function at all above the autonomic level, that is, is in a vegetative state. Cognition and rights-deservedness are not interwoven as tightly as Wise believes, though he is not, of course, the first to believe this.[4]

There is a related objection to his approach. Wise wants judges, in good common-law fashion, to move step by step, and for the first step simply to declare that chimpanzees have legal rights. But judges asked to step onto a new path of doctrinal growth want to have some idea of where the path leads, even if it would be unreasonable to insist that the destination be clearly seen. Wise gives them no idea.

[. . .]

But what is meant by liberating animals and giving them the rights of human beings of the same cognitive capacity? Does an animal's right to life place a duty on human beings to protect animals from being killed by other animals? Is capacity to feel pain sufficient cognitive capacity to entitle an animal to at least the most elementary human rights? What kinds of habitats must we create and maintain for all the rights-bearing animals in the United States? Does human convenience have *any* weight in deciding what rights an animal has? Can common-law courts actually work out a satisfactory regime of animal rights without the aid of legislatures? When human rights and animal rights collide, do human rights have priority, and if so, why? And what is to be done when animal rights collide with each other, as they do with laws that by protecting wolves endanger sheep? Must entire species of animals be "segregated" from each other and from human beings, and, if so, what does "separate but equal" mean in this context? May we "discriminate" against animals, and if so, how much? Do species have "rights," or just individual animals, and if the latter, does this mean that according special legal protection for endangered species is a denial of equal protection? Is domestication a form of enslavement? Wise does not try to answer any of these questions. He is asking judges to set sail on an uncharted sea without a compass.

The underlying problem is the practitioner-oriented framework of Wise's discussion, with its heavy reliance on argument from analogy and on the syllogism described above. Analogy gives him his major premise, and the syllogism takes him from there to his conclusion. Chimpanzees are like human beings; therefore, so far as Wise is concerned,[5] giving animals rights is like giving black people the rights of whites. But chimpanzees are like human beings in some respects but not in others that may be equally or more relevant to the question of whether to give chimpanzees rights, and legal rights have been designed to serve the needs and interests of human beings having the usual human capacities and so make a poor fit with the needs and interests of animals.

Wise's book illustrates the severe limitations of legal reasoning. Because judges (and therefore the lawyers who argue to them) are reluctant for political and professional reasons to acknowledge that they are expanding or otherwise changing the law, rather than just applying it, departures from existing law are treated as applications of it guided by analogy or deduction. Wise either is playing this game, or has been fooled by it. He makes it seem that animal rights in the expansive form that he conceives them are nothing new—they just plug a hole unaccountably left in the existing case law on rights. Animals just got overlooked, as blacks and women had once been overlooked. But correcting a logical error, removing an inconsistency—in short, tidying up doctrine—is not what would be involved in deciding that chimpanzees have the same rights as three-year-old human beings. What Wise's book really does, rather than supplying the reasons for change, is supply the rationalizations that courts persuaded on other grounds to change the law might use to conceal the novelty of their action. Judges are not easily fooled by a lawyer who argues for a change in the law on the basis that it is no change at all but is merely the recognition of a logical entailment of existing law. The value of such an argument lies in giving judges a professionally respectable ground for rationalizing the change, a ground that minimizes its novelty. But judges must have reasons for wanting to make the change, and this is where a lawyer's brief, of which Wise's book is an extension, tends to fall down.

[. . .]

There is a sad poverty of imagination in an approach to animal protection that can think of it only on the model of the civil rights movement. It is a poverty that reflects the blinkered approach of the traditional lawyer, afraid to acknowledge novelty and therefore unable to think clearly about the reasons pro or con a departure from the legal status quo. It reflects also the extent to which liberal lawyers remain in thrall to the constitutional jurisprudence of the Warren Court and insensitive to the "liberating" potential of commodification. One way to protect animals is to make them property, because people tend to protect what they own.

[. . .]

[. . .] Wise has overlooked not only the possibilities of commodification, but also, and less excusably, an approach to the question of animal welfare that is more conservative, methodologically as well as politically, but possibly more efficacious, than rights-mongering. That is simply to extend, and more vigorously to enforce, laws designed to prevent gratuitous cruelty to animals.

[. . .]

No doubt we should want to do more than merely avoid gratuitous cruelty to animals. [. . .] But neither philosophical reflection nor a vocabulary of rights is likely to add anything to the sympathetic emotions that narratives of the mistreatment of animals are likely to engender in most of us.

I close with a recent judicial opinion by one of our ablest federal judges, Michael Boudin, in a heart-rending "animal rights" case.[6] The plaintiff had rescued an orphaned raccoon, whom she named Mia and raised as a pet. Mia lived in a cage attached to the plaintiff's home for seven years until she was seized and destroyed by the state in the episode that provoked the suit. A police officer noticed Mia in her cage and reported her to the local animal control officer, who discovered that the plaintiff did not have a permit for the animal, as required by state law. The police then forcibly seized Mia from her cage after a struggle with the plaintiff, carried her off, and had her killed and tested for rabies. Testing for rabies in a raccoon requires that the animal be killed, and a supposed epidemic of raccoon rabies had led the state (Rhode Island) to require the testing of raccoons to whom humans (in this case the plaintiff) had been exposed.[7] Mia tested negative, but of course it was too late for Mia.

The plaintiff claimed that the state had deprived her of property, namely Mia, without notice and an opportunity for a hearing and thus had violated the Due Process Clause of the Fourteenth Amendment. Property for these purposes depends on state law, and the court found, undoubtedly correctly, that Rhode Island does not recognize property rights in wild animals unless a permit has been granted,[8] and fear of rabies had deterred the authorities from granting permits for raccoons. To be owned is the antithesis of being a rights-holder. But if Rhode Island had a more generous conception of property in wild animals, the police might have been deterred from what appears to have been the high-handed, indeed arbitrary, treatment of Mia. As the court explained, it does not seem that the plaintiff had been "exposed" to Mia in the relevant statutory sense: There was no indication that the raccoon had bitten the plaintiff or that its saliva had otherwise entered the plaintiff's bloodstream.[9] And since Mia had been in a cage for seven years,[10] it was unlikely, to say the least, that she was infected with rabies. Moreover, from the standpoint of controlling the spread of rabies, there was no reason to worry about Mia infecting the plaintiff, since people do not spread rabies. Mia was dangerous, if at all, only to the plaintiff, who was happy to assume the risk. The refusal to allow her to keep Mia made no sense at all, but there was no constitutional issue because Mia was not the plaintiff's "property" within the meaning of the Due Process Clause of the Fourteenth Amendment.

This is just one example, and it does not prove that animals benefit less by having human-type "rights" and thus being "free" than by being "imprisoned" and by being "reduced" to "mere" property. I note in this connection that the average life span of an "alley cat" is only about two years, and that of a well-cared-for pet cat at least twelve years, but that is just another example, and against it may be placed the sad fate of the laboratory animal, who is the laboratory's property. The most aggressive implementations of animal-rights thinking would undoubtedly benefit animals more than commodification and a more determined program of enforcing existing laws against cruelty to animals. But those implementations are unlikely, so the modest alternatives are worth serious consideration. We may overlook this simple point, however much we love animals, if we listen too raptly to the siren song of "animal rights."

Notes

1   These are closely related species, and Wise discusses them more or less interchangeably. For the sake of brevity, I will generally refer only to chimpanzees, but what I say about them applies equally to bonobos.

2   *See* Steven M. Wise. Rattling the Cage: Toward Legal Rights for Animals (2000) p. 268.

3   *See* Richard Sorabji. Animal Minds and Human Morals: The Origins of the Western Debate (1993) note 3, p. 2.

4   E.g., Bruce A. Ackerman, Social Justice in the Liberal State 80 (1980) ("The rights of the talking ape are more secure than those of the human vegetable.") *But cf.* Wise, pp. 262–3.

5   *See* WISE, *supra* note 2 pp. 123–4.

6   Bilida v. McCleod, 211 F.3d 166 (1st Cir. 2000).

7   *Id.* p. 169.

8   *Id.* p. 173–4.

9   *Id.* p. 169 n.2.

10   *Id.* p. 169.

Chapter 81

Richard A. Epstein

THE DANGEROUS CLAIMS OF THE ANIMAL RIGHTS MOVEMENT

Richard Epstein is unconvinced by the arguments of Wise and others for the personhood of great apes. Animals lack the capacity for higher cognitive language and thought that characterizes human beings as a species. Epstein points out a number of unfortunate consequences which would ensue if we accepted the claims of the animal rights movement. He concludes that it is appropriate for animals to be treated as property.

The separation of the species

BEHIND [THE] TRADITIONAL debates lies one key assumption that today's vocal defenders of animal rights brand as "species-ist." Descriptively, they have a point. Sometimes the classical view treated animals as a distinctive form of property; at other times animals became the object of public regulation. In both settings, however, the legal rules were imposed largely for the benefit of human beings, either in their role as owners of animals or as part of that ubiquitous public-at-large that benefitted from their preservation. None of our laws dealing with animals put the animal front and center as the *holder* of property rights in themselves—rights good against the human beings who protect animals in some cases and slaughter them in others.

Our species-ist assumption is savagely attacked by the new generation of animal rights activists, whose clarion call for *person*hood—the choice of terms is telling—is a declaration of independence of animals from their human owners. Their theme generates tremendous resonance, but it is often defended on several misguided grounds.

First, they claim that we now have a greater understanding of the complex behaviors and personalities of animals, especially those in the higher orders. Even though the fields of sociobiology and animal behavior have made enormous strides in recent years, the basic point is an old one. Descartes got it wrong when he said that animals moved about like the ghost in the machine. The older law understood that animals can be provoked or teased; that they are capable of committing deliberate or inadvertent acts. Sure, animals may not be able to talk, but they have extensive powers of anticipation and rationalization; they can form and break alliances; they can show anger, annoyance, and remorse; they can store food for later use; they respond to courtship and aggression; they can engage in acts of rape and acts of love; they respect and violate territories. Indeed, in many ways their repertoire of emotions is quite broad, rivaling that of human beings.

But one difference stands out: through thick and thin, animals do not have the capacity of higher cognitive language and thought that characterizes human beings as a species, even if not shared at all times by all its individual members. We should never pretend that the case against recognizing animal rights is easier than it really is. But by the same token, we cannot accept the facile argument that our *new* understanding of animals leads to a new appreciation of their rights. The fundamentals have long been recognized by the lawyers and writers who fashioned the old legal order.

Second, animal activists such as Wise remind us of the huge overlap in DNA between human beings and chimpanzees. The fact itself is incontrovertible. Yet the implications we should draw from that fact are not. The observed behavioral differences between humans and chimpanzees are still what they have always been; they are neither increased nor decreased by the number of common genes. The evolutionary biologist should use this evidence to determine when the lines of chimps separated from that of human beings, but the genetic revelation does not establish that chimps and bonobos are able to engage in the abstract thought that would enable them to present on their own behalf the claims for personhood that Wise and others make on their behalf. The number of common genes humans have with other primates is also very high, as it is even with other animals that diverged from human beings long before the arrival of primates. The question to answer is not how many genes humans and chimpanzees have in common; it is how many traits they have in common. The large number of common genes helps explain empirically the rapid rate of evolution. It does not narrow the enormous gulf that a few genes are able to create.

Third, Wise and other defenders of personhood for animals have line-drawing problems of their own. If that higher status is offered to chimps and bonobos, then what about orangutans and gorillas? Or horses, dogs, and cows? All of these animals have a substantial level of cognitive capacity, and wide range of emotions, even if they do not have the same advanced cognitive skills of the chimps and bonobos. Does personhood extend this far, and if not, then why does it extend as far as Wise and others would take it? The frequent analogy of chimpanzees to slaves hardly carries the day, given the ability of individuals from different human populations to interbreed with each other and to perform the same set of speech and communicative acts. Nor is it particularly persuasive to note that individuals with serious neurological or physical impairments often have far less cognitive and emotional capacity than normal chimpanzees or dogs. For one, we in fact *do* recognize that different rules apply to individuals in extreme cases, allowing, for example, the withdrawal of feeding tubes from individuals in a permanent vegetative state. In addition, important human relations intrude into the deliberations. These human beings, whatever their impairments, are the fathers, mothers, sisters, and brothers of other human beings in ways that chimpanzees and bonobos are not.

Fourth, the animal rights activists often attack the question from the other side by offering bland assurances that people today do not need to rely on animal labor and products in order to survive as human beings. Typically, animal rights activists put their claims in universalistic terms. But in so doing they argue as though in primitive times animals and agriculture fell into separate compartments, when in truth they were part of a seamless enterprise. Animal power was necessary to clear the woods, to fertilize and plow the fields, and to harvest the crop. Meat and dairy products were an essential part of primitive diets. The early society that did not rely on animals for food, for labor, for warfare was the society that did not survive to yield the heightened moral sensibilities of today. It was the society that perished from its want of food, clothing, and shelter—a high price to pay for a questionable moral principle. And, if this new regime is implemented, the animal rights movement condemns millions of less fortunate people around the globe to death today. Just this past March the *New York Times* ran a painful story about the question of whether the preservation of gorillas in Africa placed at risk the subsistence economies of the nearby tribes.

Today, perhaps people fortunate enough to live in prosperous lands could live without having to use animals for consumption or labor, but the long-term agenda, if not the immediate demands, of the animal rights activists cut far deeper. For activists such as Gary Francione of Rutgers-Newark Law School, the mere ownership of animals is a sin: no pets, no circuses, no milk, no cheese, no horses to ride, no dogs, cats, birds, or fish around the house. These relationships are condemned in good Marxist terms as being based on power differentials, and thus are barred: the animals who seem to like being pandered to suffer from, as it were, a form of false consciousness.

Fifth, more ominously, if pets are out, so too is the use of animals for medical science. In dealing with this issue, Wise is brutally explicit in describing what it is for chimpanzees to suffer in isolation the final effects of the ravages of AIDS. No one could argue that this conduct did not cry out for justification. Yet by the same token, the question is could the conduct itself be justified? To answer that question in human terms, one has to look at the other side of the equation, and ask what has been learned from these experiments, what wonder drugs have been created, what scourges of human (and animal) kind have been eliminated. I do not pretend to be an expert on this subject, but so long as the vaccine for smallpox comes from cows or the insulin for treating diabetes comes from pigs, then I am hard pressed to defend any categorical rule that bans all use of animals in medical experimentation. One has to have an accurate accounting of what is on the other side, and on that issue the silence of the animal rights activists is deafening.

The argument here has its inescapable moral dimension. No matter what one's intellectual orientation, no one would—or should—dispute the proposition that animals should not be used in research if the same (or better) results could be achieved at the same (or lower) cost by test tubes and computer simulations alone. Nor would any one want future surgeons to try out new techniques on animals if they could be risklessly performed on human beings the first time out. But, alas, neither of these happy eventualities come close to being a partial truth. It is easy to identify many situations where human advancement comes only at the price of animal suffering. How to proceed then turns on the balance between these two unquantifiable considerations.

[. . .]

Sixth, medical research is not all that is at stake once the asserted parity between animal rights and human rights is acknowledged. Our entire system of property allows owners to transform the soil and to exclude others. Now if the first human being may exclude subsequent arrivals, what happens when animals are given similar rights? Their dens, burrows, nests, and hives long antedate human arrival. The principle of first possession should therefore block us from clearing the land for farms, homes, and factories unless we can find ways to make just compensation to each individual animal for its own losses. But I fail to see how this system would work, for to transfer animals from one habitat to another only unlawfully displaces animals at the second location. The blunt truth is that the arrival of human beings necessarily results in the death of some earlier animal occupants, even if it increases the welfare of others who learn to live in harmony with us. So if prior in time is higher in right, then we should fold up our tents right now and let the animals fight it out for territory, just as if we had never arrived on the face of the globe.

[. . .]

The current legal scene

Animal owners have recovered large awards for the malpractice of veterinarians. The damages paid are meant to cover not only the market value of the animal, but the loss of companionship to the owner. This is simply solid economics—for what the defenders of animal rights do not tell is that this outcome derives its power from recognizing that the actual losses *to the owner* exceed the market value of the animal, precisely because they include these nonmonetary elements. [. . .] These cases therefore gain their resonance from a traditional property rights conception.

[. . .]

A similar logic also applies to a 1998 decision in the District of Columbia, *Animal Legal Defense Fund, Inc. v. Glickman*. Here a zoo visitor was held to have "standing" to sue under the Animal Welfare Act of 1985, which provided generally that animals' keepers must meet conditions of confinement that ensure "the psychological well being of primates." That objective is certainly laudable in simple human terms, even if the new animal rights activists would shut down all zoos. But allowing a zoo visitor to sue to protect the zoo animals made it crystal clear that the rights vindicated by the action were those of the individual plaintiff, and not those of the animal. And no one doubts that Congress could reverse that decision by a statutory amendment that allows only for public inspection and enforcement of the provisions of the Act.

In sum, no one can deny the enormous political waves created by animal rights activists. [. . .] It is, however, one thing to raise social conscience about the status of animals. It is quite another to raise the status of animals to asserted parity with human beings. That move, if systematically implemented, would pose a mortal threat to human society that few human beings would, or should, accept. We have quite enough difficulty in persuading or coercing human beings to respect the rights of their fellow humans to live in peace with each other. [. . .] We should not undermine, as would surely be the case, the liberty and dignity of human beings by treating animals as their moral equals and legal peers. [. . .] Animals are properly property. It is not, nor has it ever been, immoral for human beings, as a species, to prefer their own kind. What lion would deny it?

Chapter 82

Kate Douglas

JUST LIKE US

Kate Douglas describes campaigns for legal rights for great apes. She reports that the regional parliament in Spain's Balearic Islands has become the first to recognize the individual rights of the great apes, giving them similar status to a child or dependent adult. New Zealand and the United States have taken smaller but significant steps, while research using great apes is now banned in Europe. Douglas briefly explains some of the controversy in this focus on great apes in confinement.

Humans have rights, other animals don't – no matter how human-like they are. Kate Douglas investigates the controversial campaign to get that changed

HIASL IS A gregarious 26-year-old who enjoys painting, watching wildlife documentaries and eating bananas. He's emotional, empathic and self-aware and he shares 98.4 per cent of your DNA. But Hiasl is a chimpanzee, and so has no more rights in law than a car or a television.

A growing number of people want to change all that. Campaigners across the world are attempting to persuade governments to grant great apes rudimentary "human rights". They argue that great apes are enough like us to deserve special treatment over other animals. For Hiasl it's more than a philosophical debate. The sanctuary near Vienna in Austria where he has lived all his life is facing bankruptcy, and unless he is granted "personhood" and allocated a human legal guardian he will be sold to the highest bidder.

This month, a judge rejected Hiasl's case. Unless the Austrian appeal court overturns the decision he and the other chimps at the sanctuary face an uncertain future.

If Hiasl lived in Mallorca or any other of Spain's Balearic Islands the story would be quite different. In February this year, the regional parliament made history by becoming the first to recognise the individual rights of chimps, bonobos, gorillas and orang-utans, giving them similar status to a child or dependent adult. Any apes living in the Balearic Islands are no longer property to be owned but instead are protected by guardians, who must ensure that their rights to freedom from torture, mistreatment and unnecessary death are being respected. The Spanish parliament will decide this summer whether to follow suit for the rest of Spain.

The campaign has gathered momentum over the past few years and is stirring up a good deal of controversy. The Catholic Church and Amnesty International point out that we have a long way to go to secure human rights before we start thinking about animals. Other critics argue that the move is not radical enough and should be extended to other intelligent social animals such as elephants and dolphins, and potentially to all animals. Meanwhile, all species of great ape face extinction in the wild – possibly within your lifetime.

Planet of the apes

By voting for great-ape rights, the Balearics become the first region to adopt the proposals of the Great Ape Project (GAP), an international organisation that has been lobbying for legal rights for apes since 1993. GAP began when philosophers Peter Singer, now at Princeton University, and Paola Cavalieri from Italy brought together a group of academics, including some of the world's leading primatologists, to consider the idea of extending human rights to great apes. The result was a book, *The Great Ape Project: Equity beyond humanity*, which contained 31 essays highlighting the similarities between humans and great apes, challenging readers to reassess their ethical assumptions and calling for an immediate change in laws to recognise the personhood of these other species. After the book came the organisation. GAP now has representatives in seven countries, all working to persuade national governments and international institutions such as the United Nations to change their laws.

The project has had some degree of success. New Zealand considered the possibility of extending human rights to great apes in 1999 as part of its new animal welfare bill. In the end, the bill did not go so far as granting apes individual legal rights, but did give them special status. Testing or teaching involving apes now requires government approval and must demonstrate that any likely benefits are not outweighed by harm to the individual animal. In effect, that means no biomedical testing, only behavioural and physiological studies that increase our understanding of these species.

The US took a smaller, but significant, step in December 2000 when the CHIMP Act (the Chimpanzee Health Improvement Maintenance and Protection Act) was signed into law. The act prohibits routine euthanasia of chimpanzees that are no longer needed for medical research and commits the federal government to funding their lifetime care in sanctuaries. Yet as Michele Stumpe, a lawyer based in Atlanta, Georgia, and president of GAP International, points out, there are still more great apes in captivity in the US than anywhere else. GAP estimates there are at least 3000, with around half of these used in medical research. "As an American, I'm ashamed of that fact," she says.

Rights or wrongs

In Europe, apes have a much better time of it. The UK government banned their use in biomedical research in 1997, Sweden and Austria have done likewise, and after a similar move by the Dutch government in 2002, research using great apes ceased at the Biomedical Primate Research Centre at Rijkswijk, ending the practice in Europe.

So with all this legal protection already in place, what's the big deal about individual rights? GAP campaigners say that these regulations don't go far enough and they still allow people who own great apes to lawfully neglect their needs. Stumpe points out that without rights animals are mere property and their owners have no obligation to consider their best interests. "You can do whatever you want with them." Legally, however, only "persons" can have "rights", which is why the law needs to change to recognise the "personhood" of apes.

Singer has been surprised by the world's reluctance to embrace the GAP message. "We didn't think it was a great leap to ask for great-ape rights," he says. "We saw it as an achievable aim." Having struggled to get the message across for 14 years, though, even he now accepts that the project is controversial.

Stumpe says that one reason for the resistance is the use of terms like "rights" and "personhood". "It seems like an extremist or radical idea and that scares people, but when we talk about rights, it really just means protection in layman's terms," she says. For Singer, the opposition to GAP runs deeper than just semantics. He says great apes are "the victims of arbitrary discrimination", or what he calls "speciesism". He makes an argument on moral grounds for extending the human rights to all beings that show intelligence and awareness – including some level of self-awareness – and have emotional and social needs. That means going beyond the boundaries of our own species – and therein lies the problem. "It's that gulf between humans and animals that people want to maintain," he says. Others take a similar view. "It's the next step in the Darwinian debate – it requires a paradigm shift in people's ideas about themselves," says Ian Redmond, chief consultant for the UN Great Apes Survival Project. Gary Francione, a leading animal-rights lawyer from Rutgers University in Newark, New Jersey, and a member of the original GAP group, calls it "spiritual superiority". "We just think we're special because we're human."

Those less sympathetic to the animal-rights agenda see things rather differently. Some argue that beyond the species barrier lies a slippery slope. "Mice share around 90 per cent of human DNA: should they get 90 per cent of human rights?" asks geneticist Steve Jones from University College London. He is concerned that giving rights to great apes would be the beginning of the end of all research with animals. Singer accepts that there is a question about where you draw the line, but sees no reason for that to stop society from taking the first step. "The strongest and clearest case is with great apes, but we're open to arguments that it could be extended to elephants, dolphins and other mammals," he says. He wants a wide debate about how far we should extend "the community of equals."

Some take it even further. Francione no longer supports the idea of extending rights to great apes on the basis that their minds are like ours. Instead, he argues that all sentient beings should have just one right: the right not to be treated as the property of humans (*New Scientist*, 8 October 2005, p 24). He believes his approach has the advantage of simplicity, because sentience – the ability to feel pain or distress – is an objective quality, and because it would bring an end to captive animals altogether. It would make it illegal to breed any animals – not just great apes, but everything, including farm animals and even pet dogs and cats. His ideas highlight a logical inconsistency at the heart of the GAP agenda: it seeks to give legal rights to animals but does not give them the right to be free. Francione's approach is undoubtedly several steps too far for many people, and whatever they may believe in private, most campaigners for great-ape protection shy away from such an uncompromising stance in public.

In a world where human rights are so often violated, some critics of the GAP agenda see the debate as a luxury we cannot afford. Last year, with the Spanish parliament due to vote on accepting the GAP agenda, the Catholic Church and Amnesty International expressed just such misgivings. The two groups have since made it clear that they are pro human rights rather than anti animal rights. GAP for its part accepts that a bill of rights for apes is not a priority for everyone.

When it comes to wild apes, there are probably more pressing concerns. The primatologist Jane Goodall has recently commented that when she began working in Africa 50 years ago there were at least a million chimps on the continent. "Now there are perhaps only 150,000," she says. There may be as few as 10,000 wild bonobos left. Orang-utan numbers are plummeting, and the last few thousand animals could be killed off within a generation by habitat destruction and poaching. Fewer than 5000 lowland gorillas remain, and their extinction may be hastened by the deadly Ebola virus. Only mountain gorilla numbers are increasing – to just 720 or so at the last count.

It is not clear what GAP's proposals mean for wild apes, however, and even some of the animals' most outspoken defenders are not convinced that giving great apes human rights is the best way to protect them. Primatologist Frans de Waal from the Yerkes Regional Primate Research Center in Atlanta, Georgia, questions the GAP rationale of lobbying for their rights. "The concept of rights applies only to those capable of carrying responsibilities within our society," he says. He believes the emphasis should be on the obligations humans have towards other animals, both for their care and through conservation.

Redmond, on the other hand, suggests that applying GAP to wild populations might lead to increased penalties for killing apes or even give them land rights, though he concedes that the GAP agenda is extremely unlikely to be taken up by any of the countries where these animals live. "One can discuss this academically, but in practice even land rights for people are not recognised in many of these places," he says. He is hopeful, however, that if western countries embrace GAP, they could have influence in Africa and Asia. Spain, for example, might help its former colony Equatorial Guinea to improve the enforcement of wildlife law and the planning of land use. At the very least, an increased regard for the well-being of apes among people in western countries would lead to a decreased demand for animals like Hiasl being kidnapped from the wild.

Whatever the outcome of Hiasl's case, the issue of how best to protect our closest relatives isn't going away. Not everyone agrees that GAP's campaign for rights is the right approach – some say it has alienated more people from the cause of great-ape protection than it has attracted. But if Spain adopts the GAP agenda later this year it will send a clear message to the rest of the world. It's no longer about them and us. We apes have got to stick together.

Worth fighting for?

The Great Ape Project's declaration argues for the legal extension of the "community of equals" to include chimpanzees, bonobos, gorillas and orang-utans and for the legal enforcement of the following rights:

1   THE RIGHT TO LIFE
     The lives of members of the community of equals are to be protected. Members of the community of equals may not be killed except in very strictly defined circumstances, for example, self-defence.
2   THE PROTECTION OF INDIVIDUAL LIBERTY
     Members of the community of equals are not to be arbitrarily deprived of their liberty; if they should be imprisoned without due legal process, they have the right to immediate release. The detention of those who have not been convicted of any crime, or of those who are not criminally liable, should be allowed only where it can be shown to be for their own good, or necessary to protect the public from a member of the community who would clearly be a danger to others if at liberty. In such cases, members of the community of equals must have the right to appeal, either directly or, if they lack the relevant capacity, through an advocate, to a judicial tribunal.
3   THE PROHIBITION OF TORTURE
     The deliberate infliction of severe pain on a member of the community of equals, either wantonly or for an alleged benefit to others, is regarded as torture, and is wrong.

Source: The Great Ape Project

Chapter 83

Wesley V. Jamison, Caspar Wenk, and James V. Parker

EVERY SPARROW THAT FALLS: UNDERSTANDING ANIMAL RIGHTS ACTIVISM AS FUNCTIONAL RELIGION

Wesley Jamison, Caspar Wenk, and James Parker have found that the goals of animal rights activists in Switzerland and the United States often require extremely high levels of commitment and conviction. An analysis of the movement as a functional religion demonstrates some of the sources of this commitment. The analysis uses Yinger's five categories: intense and memorable conversion experiences, newfound communities of meaning, normative creeds, elaborate and well-defined codes of behavior, and cult formation. The authors predict changes within the movement should it evolve into a mainstream political force.

THE [. . .] GOALS OF animal rights activists often require extraordinary levels of personal commitment and conviction (Jasper and Nelkin, 1992; Herzog, 1993; McAllister, 1997). What are the sources of this intensity and commitment? Once mobilized, what keeps an animal rights activist motivated toward the transformation of society's relationship with animals? And what course of action will the movement take should it fail to redeem society? A guide for activists who object in conscience to classroom vivisection and dissection advises that their objection is a constitutionally protected exercise of religious belief (Francione and Charlton, 1992). The authors' claim that such activists are acting out of religious belief may surprise many observers. Social science data indicate that most animal rights activists are not members of traditional churches; indeed, they think of themselves as atheist or agnostic (Richards, 1990).[1] Nonetheless, social scientists have argued that animal rights may serve as a cosmological buttress against anomie and bewilderment in modern society (Sutherland and Nash, 1994; McAllister, 1997; Franklin, 1999).[2]

Francione and Charlton (1992) argue that . . . "The law does not require a belief to be 'theistic' or based on faith in a 'God' or 'Supreme Being' " in order to be protected.

[. . .]

The United States Supreme Court, the authors point out, has adopted a "functional" definition of religion:

> The Court has recognized that in order to determine whether a set of beliefs constitutes a religion, the appropriate focus is not the substance of a person's belief system (i.e., whether a person believes in a personal God of the Jewish, Christian or Muslim traditions), but rather, what function or role the belief systems plays in the person's life.
>
> (Francione and Charlton, 1992, p. 4)

Yinger (1970) articulated the distinction between substantive and functional definitions of religion for social scientists. It is a distinction that allows us to analyze seemingly secular movements as religions because they function as religions; that is, they provide meaning around which individuals coalesce, interpreting life through a system of beliefs, symbols, rituals, and prescriptions for behavior. Indeed, Berger (1992; 1999) has noted the emergence of such functional, secular religiosity as an alternative expression of "repressed transcendence." Berger argues that in response to modernity's cultural delegitimization of traditional religions and objective truth, individuals, rather than ending their quest for religious truth, shift the foci of their quest toward other outlets.

[. . .]

We drew the data for this article from long interviews with informants in both the United States and Switzerland. Although the political manifestations of animal rights ideology are context dependent, social scientists have hypothesized that mass movement activism (e.g. animal rights) may be a reaction to sociological factors that transcend culture and thus share relatively uniform causes (Giddens, 1990; Giddens, 1991; Beck, 1992; Sutherland and Nash, 1994). Switzerland and the United States share similar representative, federal political systems that are highly decentralized and shunt many political issues toward the lowest levels of political participation where, over time, intensity in citizen involvement is emphasized. Likewise, democracy in the United States resembles Swiss democracy in that citizens have the opportunity to pass or amend legislation through direct democracy, and this similarly emphasizes political intensity among political participants. The Swiss and U.S. systems are similar in that multiple checks and balances thwart radical political movements and cause incremental change (Linder, 1994).

[. . .]

The animal rights movements in both countries differ in significant ways. The U.S. movement has diverged into a reformist arm that allows for humane use of animals and a radical arm that seeks to protect them from all human use through the extension of inalienable rights. In Switzerland, the *Tierschutz* movement similarly contains reformist and radical branches, but because of political history the Swiss movement tends to shy away from the language of rights. Another difference is that the U.S. system is intentionally confrontational, pitting interest groups against each other in perpetual conflict, whereas the Swiss system is by intent more consensual and cooperative (Berry, 1994; Linder, 1994). One manifestation of this difference is that in the United States the animal rights movement has sought confrontation outside the boundaries of political legislation both to shock citizens and to bring about strategic legislative change (Francione, 1996), while in Switzerland the animal rights movement has sought redress through primarily political means and has stayed relatively non-confrontational (Linder, 1994).

[. . .]

Results: the elements of functional religion

Conversion

Morally persuasive religious belief often originates in an experience of conversion. Coming from a biblical expression meaning "to be turned around," conversion can reverse a person's life.

[. . .]

Our informants reported having had formative events that sensitized them to movement rhetoric and images and began the process of dissonance. Our informants confirmed Jasper and Poulsen's (1995) hypothesis concerning activist recruitment. For our informants, awareness of incongruence between behavior and feelings remained a vivid but nebulous reality coupled to a vague sense of guilt over not doing more. Their unease grew until it eventually became manifest in a single emotional epiphany. One informant noted:

> I received literature, [that was] doing an exposé on dog-meat markets in Asia; I still remember it vividly. I was reading this mailing postcard while eating a ham sandwich. There was a picture of this dog, his legs tethered, a tin cup over his muzzle; then it hit me! I made the connection between the being in the picture and the being in my mouth. Before, everything seemed to be OK, but now, I realized that treating animals as objects was bad. It was like someone had opened a door. I felt incredible sadness, and at the same time incredible joy. I knew that I would never be the same again, that I was leaving something behind . . . that I would be a better person, that I had been cleansed.

[. . .]

Community

Converts create communities. [. . .] [One] informant experienced separation from her previous relationships: "I had a sense of being 'called out.' I had trouble relating to some people. People would stare when I would order [vegetarian food] in restaurants. It was embarrassing for me, and very uncomfortable." Indeed, some of our informants attributed their divorces to their newfound beliefs. After their conversion, our informants uniformly experienced feelings of social isolation, which in turn led them to seek out others who believed. Our informants often faced ostracism and scorn from family and friends as they tried to relate to their conversion.

[. . .]

Creed

Although most animal rights activists do not recite a formal profession of faith (Richards, 1990), they have beliefs that may be compared to traditional religious doctrines. At first glance, their creed seems obvious and simple: animals either have the right to live their lives without human interference or have the right to be considered equally with humans in the ethical balance that weighs the right and wrong of any action or policy (Singer, 1975; Regan, 1983). Nevertheless, the commitment of our informants to political guarantees of rights for animals is part of a larger system of beliefs about life and the human–nonhuman animal relationship. That system includes several beliefs about nature, suffering, and death and is typified by creedal doctrinaire beliefs. Our informants agreed that active inclusion in the movement carries with it certain proscribed beliefs such as the assertion of the moral righteousness of the movement and the necessity of spreading that revelation. Believing entails spreading the faith, and animal rights activists are proselytizers. Herzog (1993) has found that the involvement of almost all animal rights activists contains an evangelical component.

[. . .]

In our informants' creed, suffering is evil, and its alleviation is good; humans are at once derived from, and unique in, the natural world. In other words, people are related through evolution to animals but ethically constrained from using them because we, alone, are conscious of the suffering such use causes and can exercise free will to end it.

[. . .]

To our informants, nature acquires normative value and is the repository of nobility and virtue, while humans acquire negative and even evil attributes (Dizard, 1999; Chase, 1995). [. . .] Certainly, animals are part of nature, but to our informants their goodness lies in their perceived moral innocence. [. . .] Indeed, for our informants it appeared that people were the problem, that innocence could be found only in animals, and that humans just by existing—are detrimental to animals.

[. . .]

An all-encompassing statement of faith professed by some of our informants demonstrated the codified edicts of animal rights: "Animals are not ours to eat, wear, experiment on, or use in any way!" Finding its ultimate expression in the form of veganism, this lifestyle consciously forgoes the use of materials that have, in any way, caused animal suffering. Our informants defined vegans as "a person who doesn't use, to the greatest extent possible, any products that come from animals . . . it's impossible to get away from animal use . . . but if an alternative is available, they use it."

Unlimited in scope, veganism provides an elaborate superstructure with which activists support their lives. Bordering on asceticism, the constraints placed on personal behavior and the resultant emotional demands of compliance can be extraordinary (Sperling, 1988; Herzog, 1993).

[. . .]

Cult (collective meanings expressed as symbols and rituals)

Substantive religions often organize their worship around the teachings of sacred texts/inspired narrative or the consumption of a holy food. Although nothing so formal as listening to the inspired text or eating a sacred meal characterizes the gatherings of animal rights partisans, elements of those gatherings neverthe-less resemble the ritual behavior of traditional religions. An informant reflected this repetitive reification of belief:

> [I] was shy . . . I don't classify myself as an activist, but I went along with a friend. When we got there, the meeting began with people introducing themselves and talking about the problems [professing the creed and keeping the behavioral code] they had had.

[. . .]

Animal rights activists often share news clippings, letters, and personal stories that tell of recent conversions and encourage participants in their commitment. The introduction and welcoming of new and potential members often are an integral part of animal rights meetings.

[. . .]

During such moments of epistemological challenge, symbols helped to remind and rejuvenate our informants. [. . .] Animal rights activists use pictures of monkeys strapped in chairs, cats wearing elec-trodes and rabbits with eye or flesh ulceration in much the same way: that is, as symbolic representations of human values and the corresponding affronts to those values. Looking on and identifying with those innocent victims, just as Christians look upon and identify a lamb as the propitiatory sacrifice of Jesus, can bring about conversion and redemption (Sperling, 1988; Jasper and Nelkin, 1992). Indeed, most of our informants had such symbols in their social environments.

[. . .]

[T]he thesis may explain how our informants retain enthusiasm and how the movement retains its cohesion in the face of seemingly insurmountable obstacles posited by the incremental U.S. and Swiss political systems. Central to the stories of our informants was a profound sense of guilt at discovering personal complicity in the suffering of animals. The movement places moral culpability squarely upon their shoulders, and its rhetoric exacerbates this. Then, in the tradition of all purposive mass movements, it offers itself as the ultimate form of absolution. With a creed that presents a disheartening picture of their world and a code of behavior that at once is unattainable and noble, believers are drawn into further activism as a source of penance.

[. . .]

Predictive Power

[. . .] We can look to the course run by religious and secular movements to find answers to intriguing questions about the animal rights movement's future.

[. . .]

We might ask how the movement, should it evolve into a mainstream political force, might retain its distinctive redemptive flavor? First, while maintaining its transcendent goal, it could pick and choose its battles, settling for those it can win: not the end of animal use in agriculture, but the end of raising calves for veal; not the end of all animal products, but the end of wearing furs; not the end of using animals in medical research, but the end of research that can be presented as an affront to decency. Second, the movement might develop two distinctive and separable tiers of membership.

[. . .]

An elite would hold out for the original vision of societal transformation, keep themselves from any compromise, and pursue a prophetic course. Others entangled in earning a living, rearing a family, and enjoying friendships do what they can: adopt a dog, write a protest letter to a shampoo manufacturer or buy synthetic clothes.

A parallel with the early Christian church is instructive. The Church moved in this direction during the second, third, and fourth centuries. An elite chose to move into isolation and live by the evangelical counsels. With their vows of poverty, chastity, and obedience, they foreswore personal property and wealth, family responsibilities, and even personal autonomy. The way of these monks was declared the way of perfection. For those who were not able to live so purely a second tier of citizenship developed. Gradually, the word *laos*, which in earliest times referred to all Christians (as in the expression *laos theou* or 'the people of God'), came to refer to those who did not follow the monks—the laity. In other words, the animal rights movement may develop a secularized monastic system as a means to assuage the schismatic tension between pragmatism and purity implicit within an incremental political system.

[. . .]

It is no mistake that the movement has had success—although each of the informants was disheartened by the glacial rate of change. The modern movement to protect animals, whether it be in Switzerland or the United States, has, at the least, sensitized non-believers to the plight of animals and perhaps even continued to sow the seeds of epistemological discontent that led our informants to convert to the cause.

Notes

1   For a relevant discussion of animal rights as a derivative of modernity, see Franklin (1999).
2   It could be argued that cultural differences between the Swiss and Americans confound any useful examination of animal rights activism. On the contrary, a central theme in modernity and the study of pluralization is that 'modern' post-industrial Western nations are buffeted by the same effects of modernity. Our data showed little cultural differences between informants from the two countries.

References

Beck, U. (1992). *Risk society: towards a new modernity*. London: Sage Publishers.

Berger, P. (1992). *A far glory: the quest for faith in an age of credulity*. New York: Basic.

—— (1999). *The desecularization of the world: resurgent religion and world politics*. New York: Eerdmans Publishing Company.

Berry, J. (1994). *The interest group society*. Boston: Scott, Foresman/Little, Brown.

Chase, A. (1995). *In a dark wood: the fight over forests and the rising tyranny of ecology*. New York: Free Press.

Dizard, J. (1999). *Going wild: hunting, animal rights, and the contested meaning of nature*. Amherst: University of Massachusetts Press.

Francione, G. (1996). *Rain without thunder: the ideology of the animal rights movement*. Philadelphia: Temple University Press.

Francione, G., and Charlton, A. (1992). *Vivisection and dissection in the classroom: a guide to conscientious objection*. Jenkintown: The American Anti-Vivisection Society.

Franklin, A. (1999). *Animals in modern culture: a sociology of human–animal relations in modernity*. London: Corwin Publishers.

Giddens, A. (1990). *The consequences of modernity*. Stanford: Stanford University Press.

—— (1991). *Modernity and self-identity: self and society in the late modern age*. Stanford: Stanford University Press.

Herzog, H. (1993). "The movement is my life": The psychology of animal rights activism. *The Journal of Social Issues*, *49*, 103–19.

Jasper, J., and Nelkin, D. (1992). *The animal rights crusade: growth of a moral protest*. New York: Free Press.

Jasper, J., and Poulsen, J. (1995). Recruiting strangers and friends: moral shocks and social networks in animal rights and anti-nuclear protests. *Social Problems*, *42*, 493–512.

Linder, W. (1994). *Swiss Democracy*. London: Sage Publishers.

McAllister, J. (1997). *Hearts and minds: the controversy over laboratory animals*. Philadelphia: Temple University Press.

Regan, T. (1983). *The case for animal rights*. Berkeley: University of California Press.

Richards, R. (1990). *Consensus mobilization through ideology, networks, and grievances: a study of the contemporary animal rights movement*. Ann Arbor: University Microfilms.

Singer, P. (1975) *Animal Liberation*. New York: New York Book Review.

Sperling, Susan. (1988). *Animal liberators: research and morality*. Berkeley: University of California Press.

Sutherland, K., and Nash, W. (1994). Animal rights as new environmental cosmology. *Qualitative Sociology*, *17*, 171–86.

Yinger, M. (1970). *The scientific study of religion*. New York: Macmillan Publishing Company.

Chapter 84

Tom Regan

UNDERSTANDING ANIMAL
RIGHTS VIOLENCE

Tom Regan draws connections between two social justice movements: the nineteenth-century anti-slavery movement in the United States and the contemporary animal rights movement. Both exhibit the split between those who insist on the immediate end to unjust practice (abolitionists) and those who are gradualists or reformists. It is the abolitionists who include those who are willing to commit acts of violence. A second split is between those who work with the government and those who refuse to do so, and a third is between those who condone violence against property in defense of animals and those who do not. Regan recommends "incremental abolitionist change" as a shared agenda.

T HOSE PEOPLE WHO view themselves as advocates of animal rights—and I certainly include myself among them—also see themselves as part of a social justice movement: the animal rights movement. In this respect, animal rights advocates believe that common bonds unite them with those who have worked for justice in other quarters: for example, for women, people of color, the poor, and gays and lesbians. The struggle for equal rights for and among these people is hardly complete; the struggle for the rights of animals has only begun, and this latter struggle promises to be, if anything, more difficult and protracted than any of its social justice relatives. For while demands for equal rights for many historically disfranchised people face formidable obstacles, they have one advantage over the struggle for animal rights. None of the other movements I have mentioned challenges the conception of the moral community that has dominated Western thought and traditions, the one that includes *humans only*; rather, all these struggles work with rather than against this conception, demanding only (and I do not mean to minimize the enormous difficulties such a demand inevitably faces) that the boundaries of the moral community expand to include previously excluded human beings—Native Americans, for example, or humans who suffer from various physical or mental disabilities.

The struggle for animal rights is different; it calls for a deeper, more fundamental change in the way we think about membership in the moral community. It demands not an expansion but a dismantling of the for-humans-only conception, to be replaced by one that includes other-than-human animals.

Not surprisingly, therefore, any obstacle that stands in the way of greater justice for people of color or the poor, for example, also stands in the way of greater justice for chimpanzees and chickens, whereas the struggle for justice for chimpanzees and chickens encounters obstacles at once more fundamental and unique, including the resistance or disdain of people who are among the most enlightened when it comes to injustice done to humans. Any doubt about this can be readily dispelled by gauging the indifference and hostility showered on the very idea of animal rights by both many of the leaders and most of the rank and file in any human rights movement, including, for example, those committed to justice and equality for women and racial minorities.

Despite these differences, those of us involved in the struggle for animal rights need to remember that we share many of the challenges other social justice movements face. [. . .] By way of illustration, I want to explore a few of the similarities between the nineteenth-century antislavery movement in America and today's animal rights movement.

Before doing this, I want to try to defuse a possible misunderstanding. I am not in any way suggesting that the animal rights movement and the antislavery movement are in every respect the same (clearly, they are not), any more than I would be suggesting that all African Americans must be either gay or lesbian because there are similarities between the movement to liberate slaves, on the one hand, and the gay and lesbian movement, on the other. Similarities are just that: similarities. And one thing similarities are not is sameness.

[. . .]

Animal rights versus animal welfare

When it comes to what we humans are morally permitted to do to other animals, it is safe to say that opinion is divided. Some people (abolitionists) believe that we should stop using nonhuman animals, whether as sources of food, as trained performers, or as models of various diseases, for example. Others (welfarists) think such utilization is permissible as long as it is done humanely. Those who accept the former outlook object to such utilization in principle and believe it should end in practice. Those who accept the latter outlook accept such utilization in principle and believe it may continue in practice, provided the welfare of animals is not unduly compromised, in which case these practices will need to be appropriately reformed. Clearly real differences separate these two ways of thinking, one abolitionist at its core, the other not. Anyone who would deny or attempt to minimize these differences would distort rather than describe the truth.

[. . .]

One area where these differences can make a difference is the particular matter before us. For it is among abolitionists, not reformists—among animal rightists, not animal welfarists—that we find those willing to commit acts of violence in the name of animal liberation. Nevertheless—and this is of great importance—not all animal rightists are prepared to go this far. That is, within the animal rights movement one finds deep, protracted, principled disagreements about the limits of protest in general and the permissibility of using violence in particular.

Analogous ideological and tactical themes are to be found in the antislavery movement. That movement was anything but monolithic. True, all abolitionists shared a common goal: slavery in America had to end. Beyond their agreement concerning this unifying goal, however, partisans of emancipation divided over a rich, complex fabric of well-considered, passionately espoused, and irreconcilable disagreements concerning the appropriate means of ending it. For my purposes, reference to just three areas of disagreement will suffice.

Abolition first versus abolition later

Following the lead of William Lloyd Garrison (1831), some abolitionists called for the unconditional emancipation of slaves, insisting as well that former slave owners not receive compensation for their financial losses. "Immediatists" (as they were called) wanted to end slavery first and then go forward with various plans to educate and in other ways prepare the newly freed slaves for the responsibilities of full citizenship. Other abolitionists (Channing 1835) favored a "gradualist" approach: complete emancipation was the eventual goal, but only after various alternatives to slave labor and improvements in the life of the slaves were in place. Thus, some gradualists sought freedom for slaves after (not before) those in bondage had received at least a rudimentary education or acquired a marketable skill or after (not before) a plan of financial compensation to former slave owners, or another plan calling for voluntary recolonization, had been implemented.

[. . .]

This split between slavery's immediatists and gradualists is mirrored in today's animal rights movement. Some people who profess belief in the movement's abolitionist goals also believe that these goals can be achieved by using gradualist means—for example, by supporting protocols that aim to reduce or refine animal use in a scientific setting, with replacement possibly achieved later on, or by decreasing the number of hens raised in cages today as a step along the way to emptying cages tomorrow. In this way, it is believed, we can succeed both in making the lives of some animals better today and in ending all animal exploitation in the future.

Other animal rights abolitionists are cut from more Garrison-like cloth. For these animal rightists, *how* we get to the abolitionist goal, not just *that* we get there, matters morally (Francione and Regan 1992). Following the higher moral law that we are not to do evil that good may come, these activists believe that they should not tacitly support violating the rights of some animals today in the hope of freeing others tomorrow. For these activists, as was true of their counterparts in the antislavery movement, it is not a question of first finding an alternative to the evil being done before deciding whether to stop doing it; instead, one must first decide to end the evil and then look for another way to achieve the goals one seeks. For these animal rights activists, then, our first obligation is to stop using animals as we do; after we have satisfied this obligation, there will be plenty of time to search for alternative ways of doing what it is we want to do. To end evil now rather than later is what conformity to the higher moral law requires.

Working with the government versus working independently

A second common theme concerns the role of government. The antislavery movement once again was sharply divided. Whereas Garrison and his followers refused to cooperate with the government, others insisted on the necessity of working with elected representatives; among this latter group, Frederick Douglass was unquestionably the most illustrious representative (see Douglass 1845).

[. . .]

The Constitution contains no ambiguous language concerning nonhuman animals that might occasion a split among today's animal rights advocates like that between Garrison and Douglass. Cows and pigs, chimpanzees and dolphins, ospreys and squirrels—all are total nonpersons as far as the Constitution is concerned. Even so, what we might term the *political sensibilities* of Garrison and Douglass live on in today's animal rights movement.

Douglass's faith in the role of government is represented by those animal rights advocates who look to the government—laws, enforcement mechanisms, and the courts— as essential elements in realizing the abolitionist goal for which they labor. In contrast, Garrison's disdain for the government is mirrored by today's animal rights activists who have lost faith in the progressive role current or foreseeable laws, enforcement mechanisms, or court proceedings might play in the struggle for animal liberation. For these activists, the government is not only historically rooted in and constitutionally committed to the ideology of speciesism but also daily subject to the influence of powerful special interests that perpetuate speciesist practices as a matter of law. These activists see the government as part of the problem, not part of the solution.

Violence versus nonviolence

Despite his belief in the necessity of working with the government, Douglass was to his dying day a staunch supporter of "agitation," a commitment poignantly captured by Philip Foner's description of a meeting that took place some weeks before Douglass's death. "In the early days of 1895, a young Negro student living in New England journeyed to Providence, Rhode Island, to seek the advice of the aged Frederick Douglass who was visiting that city. As the interview drew to a close the youth said, 'Mr. Douglass, you have lived in both the old and new dispensations. What have you to say to a young Negro just starting out? What should he do?' The patriarch lifted his head and replied, 'Agitate! Agitate! Agitate!'" (Foner 1950:371).

To our ears, Douglass's prescription might sound like a license to lawlessness, but this is not what he meant. For most of his life, Douglass, like the vast majority of abolitionists, favored only nonviolent forms of agitation: peaceful assemblies, rallies, the distribution of pamphlets and other materials depicting the plight of slaves, and petitions—measures that collectively were referred to as "moral suasion." People were to be persuaded that slavery was wrong and ought to be abolished through appeals to their reason, their sense of justice, and their human compassion, not coerced to agree through violence or intimidation.

On this point Garrison and Douglass, who disagreed about much, spoke with one voice. When Garrison said abolitionists were not to do evil that good may come, he meant that they were not to do evil *even to slaveholders, even in pursuit of emancipation*. As he saw it, respect for the higher moral law requires that all efforts made in the name of emancipation, whether immediatist or gradualist and whether in concert with the Union or apart from it, treat all persons respectfully and thus nonviolently.

[. . .]

On this matter, today's animal rightists, if not unanimously then at least solidly, align themselves with Garrison and Douglass. Evil, in the form of violence, should not be done to any human being, even in pursuit of animal liberation, and anyone who would perform such an act, whatever that person might say or believe, would not be acting according to the higher moral law that should guide and inform the animal rights movement.

This prohibition against violence to human and other forms of sentient life, however, does not necessarily carry over to property. Most of slavery's opponents understood this. If the cost of freeing a slave was damaged, destroyed, or in the case of slaves themselves, stolen property, then Garrison, Douglass, and most (but not all) of their abolitionist peers were prepared to accept such violence.

The same is true of many of today's animal rights advocates. Let me be perfectly honest. Some animal rightists obviously believe that violent acts against property carried out in the name of animal liberation, as well as the liberation of animals themselves (the theft of property, given current law), are perfectly justified. Other animal rightists disagree, believing that a principled commitment to the "higher moral law" of nonviolence must be maintained even in the treatment of property.

How many believe the one, how many believe the other, no one, I think, can say. What we can say, and what we should say, is this: it is just as false, just as misleading, and possibly just as dishonest to say that the animal rights movement is a nonviolent movement as it is to say that it is a terrorist movement.

[. . .]

How to lessen animal rights violence

This violence is something that everyone, both friend and foe of animal rights, must lament, something we all wish could be prevented. The question is how to do so.

[. . .]

My own (very) modest proposal is this. Although Garrison-like abolitionists cannot support reformist measures, they can support *incremental abolitionist change*, change that involves stopping the utilization of nonhuman animals for one purpose or another. One goal, for example, might be not fewer animals used in cosmetic or industrial testing but no animals used for this purpose. Other goals might be not fewer dogs "sacrificed" in dog labs, or fewer primates "studied" in maternal deprivation research, or fewer goats shot and killed in weapons testing, but no animals used in each of these (and an indefinite number of other possible) cases.

A shared agenda of this type could set forth objectives that animal rights abolitionists, scientific policy makers, and biomedical researchers, for example, could agree on and work collaboratively to achieve; as such, it would go a long way toward reducing animal rights violence. It would demonstrate that it is possible to achieve incremental abolitionist goals by acting nonviolently within the system. This in turn would help defuse the idea that such goals can be achieved only by acting violently outside the system.

[. . .]

[U]nless we practice preventive ethics in this quarter, animal rights violence will increase in the coming months and years. Indeed, as things stand at present, the wonder of it is not that there is animal rights violence but that there is not more of it.

[. . .]

Works cited

Channing, William Ellery. 1835. "Essay on Slavery." In *The Works of William E. Channing*, 6 vols., 2:123–33. Boston: Anti-Slavery Office.

Douglass, Frederick. 1845. *Narrative of the Life of Frederick Douglass, an American Slave. Written by Himself*. Boston: Anti-Slavery Office.

Foner, Philip S. 1950. *Frederick Douglass: A Biography*. New York: Citadel.

Francione, Gary, and Tom Regan. 1992. "A Movement's Means Create Its Ends." *The Animals' Agenda*, January/February, pp. 40–3.

Garrison, William Lloyd. 1831. "Immediate Emancipation." *The Liberator*, September 3, pp. 1–2.

Chapter 85

Courtney L. Dillard

CIVIL DISOBEDIENCE: A CASE STUDY IN FACTORS OF EFFECTIVENESS

Courtney Dillard presents her observations of two protests against the largest pigeon shoot in the United States. In the second protest activists lay flat on the ground, bound themselves to one another at the neck, remained silent, and remained calm. In being bound together they attempt to represent the helplessness of the birds. The onlookers who were interviewed indicated that this approach was very effective in changing attitudes.

ADVOCATING FOR ANIMALS in this country dates as far back as the colonial period. In 1641, legal arguments were put forth that made cruelty to domestic animals unlawful in the Massachusetts Bay Colony. By the mid-1800s, several social movement organizations, such as the American Society for the Prevention of Cruelty to Animals (ASPCA) and the Philadelphia Society for the Prevention of Cruelty to Animals were created to advocate for animal welfare in the wider courts of public opinion. Over time, the numbers of people and organizations arguing on behalf of animals grew substantially. In addition, the tactics and strategies employed in such advocacy became more varied and creative.

Such changes perhaps are most notable in surveying the activities of social movement organizations in the last two decades. The 1980s witnessed not only major ideological shifts from welfare to rights but also tactical shifts from behind-the-scenes negotiation in the courtroom or legislative bodies to very public acts of protest and civil disobedience. As the media, particularly television, quickly became an essential part of educating and persuading the public on animal issues, tactics that gained media coverage were often employed. Because one of the enduring news values is controversy and conflict (Stephens, 1980), the potential for acts of civil disobedience often ensured media attention. Today, some activists and organizations wholly embrace the use of civil disobedience.

[. . .]

Instead of wrestling with the question of whether civil disobedience is an effective advocacy tool in general, I ask if the effectiveness of civil disobedience may be determined in part by the way it is enacted. To pursue this question, I analyze a specific case study of a long-term animal advocacy campaign—The Fund for Animals' campaign to abolish the Hegins pigeon shoot. In this article, I compare the enactment of civil disobedience in two years of protest that differed considerably from one another.

[. . .]

Hegins: a case analysis

The event

The Fred Coleman Memorial Shoot, the shoot's official name, began more than a half century ago in the early 1930s. Pigeon shooting is a rather common sport in the rural counties of Pennsylvania, but the shoot at Hegins quickly grew to become the largest event of its kind in the country. Each Labor Day weekend, people from a number of surrounding counties and states descended on the town to shoot over 5,000 birds. Funds from the event were used to raise money to continue maintenance on the park and subsidize such local services as the firehouse (B. Tobash, personal communication, February 20, 1997).

The rules surrounding the shoot and the manner in which it is conducted haven't changed since the event's earliest days. Organizers of the shoot purchase pigeons from breeders or those who have trapped the birds in the wild. They then keep the pigeons in cages, often cramped together for days or even weeks before the event. Participants in the shoot, limited to 250 at Hegins, pay an entry fee, typically $75, for a chance to shoot as many pigeons as possible. The shooter with the largest number of hits at the end of the weekend wins the event.

During the shoot, participants stand ready with their guns and then shout "Pull," ordering the strings tied to the cage doors to be pulled and the doors opened, releasing the pigeons one at a time. Pigeons either fly out or, having been weakened by their captivity, walk out of the cages. At that moment, the shooter fires, attempting to kill the pigeon (H. Prescott, personal communication, October 25, 1996). If the shooter misses, the bird may fly out of the park boundaries to safety. If wounded, the pigeon often lands in the shooting field. While the shooters aim to kill, they often only wound the birds. One field estimate suggested that only 30 percent of the birds died instantly (Fund Press Release, 1996). It is the duty of the trapper boys, typically about age 12, to retrieve the wounded birds from the shooting field and kill them by decapitating them over the rim of a barrel or with their bare hands. Although it is not advocated, birds also are killed by being jumped upon, left to suffocate in the barrel of bodies, or occasionally ripped apart. Once the shoot ends, the dead birds are thrown away as trash (Becker, 1996).

[. . .]

The protest in 1992

Before the event in 1992, The Fund encouraged activists to protest the shoot, running advertisements in animal activist magazines and networking through other national and local groups. The organization created a press release promising to stage "what is likely to be the nation's largest ever protest on behalf of animals" (Fund Press Release, 1992). The goal was to have as many people as possible engage in protest activities and willingly be arrested for breaking various laws. Though The Fund had been successful in attracting 1,500 protestors, it did little to organize protest activity before the event. A workshop in civil disobedience was optional, and no specific acts were arranged.

Because there had been no attempt to regulate the behavior of the activists, the overall context for the protest was one of chaos and tension. Several incidents led to a feeling of threat and anger. Videos of the event show the Black Berets, an animal rights militia of sorts, taunting spectators, calling them "pigeon sucking perverts," and trying to elicit a response. All people interviewed, including Prescott, agree that there were obscenities, insults, and screaming matches "breaking out all over the park" (H. Prescott; Media representatives 1–4, personal communications, February 20, 1997). [. . .] Most of the 114 activists were arrested on charges of disorderly conduct, criminal trespass, theft and harassment (Helgeson, 1992).

Period of reconsideration

Following the protests of 1992, leaders at The Fund assessed their situation. It was clear that despite many acts of civil disobedience, they had not been able to gain much public support. The most disturbing trend that Fund leaders noticed was the media's approach to the protest. Only minimal attention was given to the actual plight of the pigeons. Reporters chose to focus on the more controversial conflict between supporters and protesters of the shoot.

[. . .]

In 1996, The Fund decided to reinstate some form of civil disobedience. Leaders at The Fund focused on developing an approach to civil disobedience that would better communicate their objections to the shoot and generally be more effective in persuading both the local and national audience to speak out against the event. In so doing, they tried to better understand their audience and more clearly represent themselves.

[. . .]

Protests 1996

The correspondence with activists before the event in 1996 differs notably from that in 1992. Instead of encouraging large numbers to attend, The Fund solicited only a small group of activists. As "peacekeepers," they were told that their job was to assure that "public attention—including media attention—is not distracted from the cruelty of the event by loud and potentially violent confrontations between activists and shoot supporters" (H. Prescott, personal communication, October 25, 1996).

[. . .]

In the midst of this context, those participating in the civil disobedience followed the plans that were carefully constructed prior to their arrival. Twelve activists in two groups of six entered the shooting fields before the event began. Locking steel bicycle locks together, they bound themselves to one another at the neck and then lay down. Their goal was twofold: (a) to prevent the start of the shoot for as long as possible and (b) to make the argument, with their bodies, that the shoot was unjust and should be discontinued (H. Prescott, personal communication, February 21, 1997).

In conducting the civil disobedience, the activists remained silent and at a distance from the crowd. They lay flat on the ground, putting their "health and safety in jeopardy" (Police representative, personal communication, February 20, 1997). Even when the crowd tried to provoke the disobedients, they remained calm and did not respond in any way. When finally they were cut free from the kryptonite octopus, they did not resist arrest and were quietly removed from the field. The shoot was held up for close to two hours. The disobedients acted totally without violence (physical or verbal). In being bound together, they attempted to represent the captivity and helplessness of the birds. This small act of suffering was put forth as a type of representation for the ultimate suffering of the pigeons who were to be wounded and killed.

[. . .]

Discussion

At the protests of the pigeon shoot in Hegins, leaders of The Fund wanted to communicate a message about the suffering of the birds. Initially, this suffering aroused their anger, and they represented themselves in anger. At the protest in 1992, those involved in the protest often hurled insults at the crowd, which included a number of children. [. . .] In 1992, the protesters and those engaged in civil disobedience were neither nonviolent nor able to demonstrate clearly a willingness to suffer.

[. . .]

The most important aspect of civil disobedience that was recognized and respected by the activists in 1996 was nonviolence. The disobedients realized that their argument could not be put forth in violence, as those who were threatened would be unlikely to acknowledge some common ground and therefore could not be persuaded. Almost everyone interviewed agreed that the protesters were more effective when they engaged in "true" civil disobedience and abandoned the angry and violent tone set early on (Media representative 2, personal communication, February 20, 1997). One representative from the local media even suggested that if "they [the protesters] keep it toned down, at a low level, they can win over a good majority of the solid decent people in the town" (Media representative 2, personal communication, February 20, 1997).

The second key aspect of civil disobedience activists acknowledged in 1996 was a willingness to suffer for their beliefs and to communicate that suffering to onlookers. Instead of showing anger at the treatment of the pigeons during the shoot, the disobedients and other activists tried to represent the suffering of the pigeons through their own suffering.

[. . .]

In many ways, 1996 was the turning point in the battle over pigeon shoots in Hegins, Pennsylvania. In 1997 and 1998, The Fund basically stayed away from the event, choosing to capitalize on growing support for its position. The Fund pursued cruelty cases in court and lobbied for bills in the state legislature. After a series of legal rounds, supporters of the shoot agreed to discontinue the event. In 1999, and for every Labor Day since then, the shooting fields in Hegins have been silent. After 10 years and various approaches to the tactic of civil disobedience, the activists are finally sounding victory.

[. . .]

Civil disobedience can be an empowering activity for both activists and the general public. Activists join together and publicly advocate their position. The general public witnesses commitments and challenges to the system that extend beyond the voting booth and individual consumer choices. When civil disobedience is truly effective, it can change society's relationship to animals and even revitalize our public sphere.

References

Becker, C. (1996). [Videotape] *Gunblast, culture clash*.
Fund Press Release. (September 2, 1992). Silver Spring, MD: Author.
Fund Press Release. (September 6, 1996). Silver Spring, MD: Author.
Glaser, B. and Stauss, A. (1967). *The discovery of grounded theory*. Chicago: Aldine.
Stephens, M. (1980). *Broadcast news*. New York: Holt, Rinehart & Winston.
The Fund. (1996). *Guidelines for animal protection activists at Hegins, 1996*. Unpublished document.

Chapter 86

Chris DeRose

IN YOUR FACE: FROM ACTOR TO ACTIVIST

Chris DeRose has been jailed and staged hunger strikes several times for actions he has taken on behalf of animal rights. He states that he is motivated by a hatred for injustice. He has never injured people in his activities. DeRose believes that animals are screaming for our help, and that most people want to know the truth about how their tax dollars are being used.

MY NAME IS Chris DeRose. By profession, I am a Hollywood actor. Not a superstar earning millions of dollars, but a working actor in films and television. At different times in my life, I've also been an altar boy, a black-belt in martial arts, a cop, an unofficial "big brother" to about two dozen tough street-kids, a private investigator, a pilot, a bouncer in a bar, and a TV reporter.

I still do some acting, but now I spend most of my time as an activist for social change, for justice, for the rights of the most oppressed and exploited of all populations on Earth: animals. I'm part of the growing movement for animal rights.

I've been arrested eleven times and jailed on four of those occasions for actions I've taken on behalf of animal rights. I'm not getting rich or famous by fighting for this cause. It's just what I believe in. Once I got shot in the back by a guy who had told me he believed in the same things.

I'm not talking about the roles I've played on screen. This is reality.

The most important reality for me is helping animals and exposing the people and institutions that profit from exploiting, torturing and killing animals. The group I head—Last Chance for Animals (LCA)—has been responsible for gathering the evidence that put some of the worst of these people out of business, and for sending a few of them off to well-deserved prison terms.

I'm no soft-hearted sentimentalist who just feels sorry for fuzzy, furry creatures. I have never even had a pet. But I hate injustice, and one of the greatest injustices in the world right now is how we treat animals.

A lot of people ask me why I got into this movement. Why did I let my acting career get sidetracked by a cause that has made me look straight at cruelty and suffering, at the most atrocious crimes human beings are capable of committing, at things so awful and ugly that I still sometimes have nightmares about them? Why did I decide to go to jail and stage hunger strikes when I could have stayed out of trouble and just issued a few good sound-bite protests against animal exploitation, from the safety and security of a successful and law-abiding career?

The answer is a principle that was eloquently expressed by Dr. Martin Luther King, Jr.: "If a man hasn't discovered something that he will die for, he isn't fit to live." To me, the fight to save animals from torture and death is worth living for and, if necessary, dying for.

This principle doesn't make me a fanatic. Believing in something and being willing to act on that belief is not fanaticism. To me, fanatics are people who will commit acts of violence to further what they see as a just cause.

I'll tell you right up front that I've done some less-than-legal things on behalf of animals, but never anything violent. I've gone to jail for trespassing and other acts of civil disobedience, but I've never shot anyone or planted bombs or done anything that could endanger anyone's life.

Some people say, "Breaking the law is breaking the law." They don't see any difference between the nonviolent crimes I and some other animal rights activists have committed, and the shootings and bombings committed by fanatics devoted to other causes. What can I say? I *do* see a difference.

Someone once asked me, "Who appointed you God? Who gave you the right to decide which laws you'll obey and which ones you'll break?" Obviously, no one gave me any such right. That's why I willingly went to jail when I broke the law. That's what civil disobedience is all about.

But the most common question people ask me is, "Why animals, when there is so much human suffering in the world? Why not try to help human beings?" That's an easy one to answer. First, the plight of animals is far worse, and there are already a lot of people working for human rights. I feel I can do more good by working for animal rights, which doesn't yet have as much public support. Second, it's not an either-or choice. As Dr. King said, "Injustice anywhere is a threat to justice everywhere." And by showing how animal exploitation also harms humans, I believe I am helping people at the same time.

Some people try to analyze me, looking for some dark secret that would explain why I have chosen this path. Well, I don't need a psychology book to know why I do what I do. I can't not do it. And I don't need an excuse to rationalize fighting against injustice. The only time I'd look for an excuse would be if I *weren't* out there fighting. If you see injustice in the world, do you need to find a special reason to fight it?

There is nothing pleasant about struggling against the entrenched forces that profit from animal exploitation. I wish the fight were over. I'd like to do more acting, maybe get married and lead a normal life. But I can't and won't walk away from this fight. Again, to quote Dr. King: "I don't march because I like it. I march because I must."

How can people turn their backs on injustice and suffering? Saying the problem is too big to solve is bullshit. If enough people are determined to solve a problem, it will get solved. Saying that human concerns outweigh animal concerns is just more bullshit; the same changes that would help animals would also help people.

Look—if you heard someone screaming for help next door, wouldn't you try to do something? Sure you would. You'd come running even if you couldn't actually hear the screams, especially if you knew that the person was being tortured to death and needed your help.

The animals are screaming for our help right now. Each year, four billion animals scream to us from inside factory farms. Sixty to a hundred million a year from research labs. What am I supposed to do, just shrug at their screams? Would feeling indifferent to their needless suffering and death make me "normal"? If so, then I don't want to be normal. If it means not caring enough to try to do something to help, then normal must be another word for *dead*.

[. . .]

What makes the fight especially tough is that so many people have been led to believe that we have to choose between the needs of humans and the rights of animals. But that's false. A few people get rich from exploiting animals, but the rest of us always pay the cost. And we're not even talking about the suffering and death of the animals.

Factory farmers may make bigger profits by keeping cows, pigs and chickens in conditions you wouldn't want your worst enemy to suffer. But society pays the price in environmental devastation and avoidable illness.

Vivisectors get federal grants to do the same experiments hundreds of times, publishing hundreds of scientific reports detailing exactly how animals die under torture ("Canine subjects in restraint were sacrificed through introduction of saline solution into the bronchial passages" means "We took some dogs, strapped them down so they couldn't struggle, and pumped salt water straight into their lungs until they drowned"). But society pays the price—needless sickness and death—as people are misled into relying on high-tech medical salvation instead of learning to take responsibility for their own health.

I've spoken with doctors, scientists and environmentalists, and I've read thousands of articles and reports on how animals are abused and killed in laboratories, factory farms, circuses, rodeos and fur farms. I've gone into animal research labs where scientists are using our tax dollars to do things that anyone else would be arrested for doing. [. . .] I've seen and held animals dying in pain, fear and despair, and I swore that their suffering and death would never be forgiven or forgotten—*never!*

I've seen the horror first-hand, and I've committed my life to stopping it. It has to be stopped. Cruelty and exploitation are wrong, period. We can't justify injustice. We don't ask whether human slavery turns a profit, and we don't try to reform it by passing laws to make sure that slaves are treated humanely. It had to be abolished completely because it's wrong.

Same thing with animal slavery. It has to be abolished because it's wrong. And it doesn't help people, anyway. It's all useless, even if you don't care about animals.

I've written this book to tell you about these issues because the mainstream media won't touch them. But it's not a textbook. There are lots of books with loads of facts and statistics about the use and abuse of animals. To name just a few: On vivisection, a British scientist named Robert Sharpe wrote a great book called *The Cruel Deception*, which explains why animal experimentation doesn't benefit human health. On factory farming, you can read Jim Mason's classic work, *Animal Factories*, or John Robbins' *Diet for a New America*, which shows why vegetarianism is healthier for people and for the planet. On sport hunting (if ever there was a contradiction in terms, this is it), a guy named Ron Baker wrote *The American Hunting Myth*, which debunks the lies told to convince nonhunters which is most of the population that going into the woods to blow Bambi's head off with a high-power rifle is somehow natural and necessary as well as good fun.

This book is about my own experiences as an activist for animals. It is a highly personal account of what I've seen and done. If the language is sometimes rough, too bad. So is what happens to the animals. I won't try to soften it or make it any less ugly than it is. (In reconstructing conversations from years ago, I've tried to convey the content, tone, and actual language as accurately as I can remember, but these dialogues are not necessarily word-for-word transcripts.)

Some people don't want to learn the truth about how humans treat the nonhuman inhabitants of Earth. But I'm hoping that many more people want to know what's going on, how their tax dollars are being used and how their government sanctions cruelty and exploitation. Some people will even join in the fight to end it.

Maybe you will be one of them.

Chapter 87

Peter Singer

TEN WAYS TO MAKE A DIFFERENCE

Peter Singer builds on the work of Henry Spira (1927–98) in suggesting ten effective strategies to use on behalf of animals. To many, Henry Spira was the most effective activist of the modern animal rights movement. He put the issue of cosmetics testing on the political map, and convinced the USDA to abandon a face-branding requirement slated to include all cattle imported from Mexico. His success shows that one person can still make a difference.

1 Try to understand the public's current thinking and where it could be encouraged to go tomorrow. Above all, keep in touch with reality

TOO MANY ACTIVISTS mix only with other activists and imagine that everyone else thinks as they do. They start to believe in their own propaganda and lose their feel for what the average person in the street might think. They no longer know what is achievable and what is a fantasy that has grown out of their own intense conviction of the need for change.

[. . .]

Henry Spira grabs every opportunity to talk to people outside the animal movement. He'll start up a conversation with the person sitting next to him on a bus or train, mention an issue he is concerned about, and listen to their responses. How do they react? Can they feel themselves in the place of the victim? Are they outraged? What in particular do they focus on?

2 Select a target on the basis of vulnerabilities to public opinion, the intensity of suffering, and the opportunities for change

Target selection is crucial. Henry knows that he can run an effective campaign when he feels sure that, as he said about the New York state law allowing laboratories to take dogs and cats from shelters, "it just defies common sense that the average guy in the street would say, 'Hey, that's a real neat thing to do.' "

You know that you have a good target if, by merely stating the issue, you put your adversary on the defensive. During the museum campaign, for example, Henry could ask the public: "Do you want your tax monies spent to mutilate cats in order to observe the sexual performance of crippled felines?" The museum was immediately in a very awkward position. Cosmetic testing made another good target, because you only had to ask, "Is another shampoo worth blinding rabbits?" to put Revlon officials on the defensive.

Keeping in touch with reality is a prerequisite for selecting the right target: If you don't know what the public currently thinks, you won't know what they will find acceptable and what will revolt them.

The other elements of point 2 suggest a balance between the good that the campaign can do and its likelihood of success. When Henry selected the cat experiments at the American Museum of Natural History as his first target, he knew that he would directly affect, at best, about sixty cats a year—a tiny number compared to many other possible targets. But the opportunity for change was great because of the nature of the experiments themselves and the location and vulnerability of the institution carrying out the experiments. In 1976, it was vital for the animal movement to have a victory, no matter how small, to encourage its own supporters to believe in the possibility of change and to gain some credibility with the wider world.

[. . .]

3 Set goals that are achievable. Bring about meaningful change one step at a time. Raising awareness is not enough

When Henry first took an interest in opposing animal experimentation, the antivivisection movement had no goal other than the abolition of vivisection and no strategy for achieving this goal other than "raising awareness"—that is, mailing out literature filled with pictures and descriptions of the horrors of vivisection. This was the strategy of a movement that talked mainly to itself. It had no idea how to get a hold on the levers of change, or even where those levers might be located. It seemed unaware of its own image as a bunch of ineffective cranks and did not know how to make vivisection an issue that would be picked up by the media. Henry's background in the civil rights movement told him that this was not the way to succeed:

> One of the first things that I learned in earlier movements was that nothing is ever an all-or-nothing issue. It's not a one-day process, it's a long process. You need to see the world—including individuals and institutions—as not being static but in constant change, with change occurring one step at a time. It's incremental. It's almost like organic development. You might say, for instance, that a couple of blacks demanding to be seated at a lunch counter really doesn't make a hell of a lot of difference because most of them don't even have the money to buy anything at a lunch counter. But it did make a difference, it was a first step. Once you take that first step and you have that same first step in a number of places, you integrate a number of lunch counters, you set a whole pattern, and it's one of the steps that would generate the least amount of resistance. It's something that's winnable, but it encourages the black struggle and it clearly leads to the next step and the next step. I think that no movement has ever won on the basis of all or none.[1]

Some activists think that accepting less than, say, the total abolition of vivisection is a form of compromise that reduces their chances of a more complete victory. Henry's view is: "I want to abolish the use of animals as much as anybody else, but I say, let's do what we can do today and then do more tomorrow."[2] That is why he was willing to support moves to replace the LD50 with tests like the approximate lethal dose test, which still uses animals, but far fewer of them.

Look for targets that are not only winnable in themselves, but where winning will have expanding ripple effects. Ask yourself if success in one campaign will be a stepping stone toward still-bigger targets and more significant victories. The campaign against Revlon is an example: Because it made research into alternatives respectable, its most important effects have been felt beyond Revlon and even beyond the cosmetics industry as a whole.

While raising awareness is essential if we are to bring about change, Henry does not usually work directly at raising awareness. (His advertisements against meat are an exception.) Awareness follows a successful campaign, and a successful campaign will have achievable goals.

4 Establish credible sources of information and documentation. Never assume anything. Never deceive the media or the public. Maintain credibility, don't exaggerate or hype the issue

Before starting a new campaign, Henry spends several months gathering information. Freedom of information legislation has helped enormously, but a lot of information is already out there, in the public domain. Experimenters report their experiments in scientific journals that are available in major libraries, and valuable data about corporations may also be a matter of public record. Henry is never content simply to quote from the leaflets of animal rights groups, or other opponents of the institution or corporation that he is targeting. He always goes to the source, which is preferably a publication of the target itself, or else a government document. Newspapers like the *New York Times* have been prepared to run Henry's advertisements making very specific allegations of wrongdoing against people like Frank Perdue because every allegation has been meticulously checked.

Some organizations describing experiments will conveniently omit details that make the experiments less shocking than they would otherwise appear. They may, for example, neglect to tell their readers that the animals were anesthetized at the time. But those who do this eventually lose credibility. Henry's credibility is extraordinarily high, both within the animal movement and with its opponents, because he regards it as his most important asset. It is therefore never to be sacrificed for a short-term gain, no matter how tempting that may be at the time.

5 Don't divide the world into saints and sinners

When Henry wants to get someone—a scientist, a corporate executive, a legislator, or a government official—to do something differently, he puts himself in the position of that person:

> [The question to ask yourself is:] If I were that person, what would make me want to change my behavior? If you accuse them of being a bunch of sadistic bastards, these people are not going to figure, "Hey, what is it I could do that's going to be different and make those people happy?" That's not the way the real world works.

Being personally hostile to an opponent may be a good way of letting off steam, but it doesn't win people over. When Henry wanted to persuade scientists working for corporations like Procter & Gamble to develop nonanimal alternatives, he saw their situation as similar to that of people who eat animals:

> How do you change these people's behavior best? By saying you've never made a conscious decision to harm those animals. Basically you've been programmed from being a kid: "Be nice to cat and doggy, and eat meat." And I think some of these researchers, that's how they were taught, that's how they were programmed. And you want to reprogram them, and you're not going to reprogram them by saying we're saints and you're sinners, and we're going to clobber you with a two-by-four in order to educate you.

As Susan Fowler, editor of the trade magazine *Lab Animal* at the time of the Revlon campaign, put it:

> There is no sense in Henry's campaign of: "Well, this is Revlon, and no one in Revlon is going to be interested in what we are doing, they're all the enemy." Rather . . . he looks for—and kind of waits for, I think—someone to step out of the group and say: "Well, I understand what you're saying.[3]

Without this attitude, when Roger Shelley came along ready to listen to what Henry wanted Revlon to do, the opportunity to change the company's approach could easily have been missed.

Not dividing the world into saints and sinners isn't just sound tactics, it is also the way Henry thinks. "People can change," he says. "I used to eat animals and I never considered myself a cannibal."[4]

6 Seek dialogue and attempt to work together to solve problems. Position issues as problems with solutions. This is best done by presenting realistic alternatives

Because he doesn't think of his opponents as evil, Henry has no preconceptions about whether they will or will not work with him to reduce animal suffering. So he opens every campaign with a polite letter to the target organization—whether the American Museum of Natural History, Amnesty International, Revlon, Frank Perdue, or a meatpacker—inviting them to discuss the concerns he has. Sometimes Henry's invitations have been ignored, sometimes they have received an equally polite response from a person skilled in public relations who has no intention of doing anything, and sometimes they have led directly to the change he wanted without any public campaigning at all. But the fact that he suggests sitting down to talk about the problem before he does any public campaigning shows that he isn't just stirring up trouble for the fun of it, or as a way of raising funds for his organization.

Henry puts considerable thought into how the person or organization he is approaching could achieve its goals while eliminating or substantially reducing the suffering now being caused. The classic example of an imaginative solution was Henry's proposal to Revlon and other cosmetics manufacturers that they should fund research into alternatives to the Draize eye test. For more than a year before his campaign went public, Henry had been seeking a collaborative, rather than a confrontational, approach with Revlon. In the end, after the campaign finally did go public, Revlon accepted his proposal and, together with other companies, found that for a very small expenditure, relative to their income, they could develop an alternative that enabled them to have a more precise, cheaper form of product safety testing that did not involve animals at all.

Having a realistic solution to offer means that it is possible to accentuate the positive, instead of running a purely negative campaign. In interviews and leaflets about the Draize test, for example, Henry always emphasized that in vitro testing methods offered the prospect of quicker, cheaper, more reliable, and more elegant ways of testing the safety of new products.

[. . .]

In terms of offering a positive outcome, the difference between the campaigns against the cat experiments and those against the Draize test was one of degree, not kind. If your tube of toothpaste is blocked, whether you will be able to get any toothpaste out of it will depend on how badly blocked the tube is and on how much pressure is exerted on it. So, too, whether an institution or corporation will adopt an alternative will depend on how negatively it views the alternative and how much pressure it is under. The more realistic the alternative is, the less pressure will be needed to see it adopted.

7 Be ready for confrontation if your target remains unresponsive. If accepted channels don't work, prepare an escalating public awareness campaign to place your adversary on the defensive

If point 6 is about making it easy for the toothpaste to come out of the tube, point 7 is about increasing the pressure if it still won't come. A public awareness campaign may take various forms. At the American Museum of Natural History, it started with an article in a local newspaper, then it was kept up by pickets and demonstrations, and finally it spread through the national media and specialist journals like *Science*. The Revlon campaign went public with a dramatic full-page advertisement in the *New York Times*, which itself generated more publicity. The campaign continued with demonstrations outside Revlon's offices. The Perdue and face-branding campaigns relied much more heavily on advertising and the use of the media. Advertising takes money, on which, see point 8.

8 Avoid bureaucracy

Anyone who has been frustrated by lengthy committee meetings that absorb time and energy will sympathize with Henry's desire to get things done rather than spend time on organizational tangles. Worse still, bureaucratic structures all too often divert energy into making the organization grow, rather than getting results for the cause. Then when the organization grows, it needs staff and an office. So you get a situation in which people who want to make a difference for animals (or for street kids, or for rain forests, or for whatever cause) spend 80 percent of their time raising money just to keep the organization going. Most of the time is spent ensuring that everyone in the organization gets along with one another, feels appreciated, and is not upset because he or she expected to be promoted to a more responsible position or given an office with more windows.

Henry has been able to avoid such obstacles by working, essentially, on his own. That isn't a style that will suit everyone, but it has worked well for Henry. Animal Rights International has no members. It has a long list of advisers and its board consists of trusted close friends whom Henry can rely upon for support without hassles. Henry doesn't need a lot of money, but he does need some. He has been fortunate in finding two donors who support him regularly because they like to see their money making a difference.

When Henry needs more clout, he puts a coalition together—as he did on the repeal of the Metcalf-Hatch Act, in fighting against the Draize and LD50 tests, and now, to persuade McDonald's to take a leading role in improving the welfare of farm animals. Since his early success at the American Museum of Natural History, other organizations have been eager to join his coalitions. At their height, these coalitions have included hundreds of organizations, with memberships in the millions. Here, too, though, Henry keeps hassles to a minimum. Organizations are welcome to participate at whatever level they wish. Some get their supporters out to demonstrate or march, while others don't. Some pay for full-page advertisements, and others ask them to write letters to newspapers, where they may reach millions without spending a cent. What no organization can do is dictate policy. Henry consults widely, but in the end, he makes his own decisions, thus avoiding the time-consuming and sometimes divisive process of elections and committee meetings. Clearly, in the case of major disagreements, organizations have the option of leaving; but if the coalition is making progress, organizations will generally swallow the disagreements in order to be part of a successful team.

9 Don't assume that only legislation or legal action can solve the problem

Henry has used elected representatives in his campaigns to put pressure on government agencies and to gain publicity. But the only campaign in which he achieved his aim through legislation was the repeal of the Metcalf-Hatch Act. Here, since bad legislation was the target of the campaign, he had no choice. Otherwise, as far as he can, Henry stays out of conventional political processes and keeps away from the courts: "No congressional bill, no legal gimmickry, by itself, will save the animals." No doubt there are other situations, and other issues, on which legislation will make a difference. But on the whole, Henry sees laws as maintaining the status quo. They will be changed only in order to keep disturbance at a minimum. The danger of getting deeply involved in the political process is that it often deflects struggles into what

Henry calls "political gabbery." There is a lot of talk, but nothing happens. Political lobbying or legal maneuvering becomes a substitute for action.

10 Ask yourself: "Will it work?"

All of the preceding points are directed toward this last one. Before you launch a campaign, or continue with a campaign already begun, ask yourself if it will work. If you can't give a realistic account of the ways in which your plans will achieve your objectives, you need to change your plans. Keeping in touch with what the public is thinking, selecting a target, setting an achievable goal, getting accurate information, maintaining credibility, suggesting alternative solutions, being ready to talk to adversaries or to confront them if they will not talk—all of these are directed toward creating a campaign that is a practical means of making a difference. The overriding question is always: *Will it work?*

[. . .]

Notes

1   "Singer Speaks with Spira," *Animal Liberation*, January–March 1989, p. 5.
2   Ibid., p. 6.
3   Susan Fowler, videotaped interview with author, New York, December 1996.
4   "Singer Speaks with Spira," p. 5.

FURTHER READING

Datta, A. (1998) *Animals and the Law: A Review of Animals and the State*, Chichester, England: Chichester Institute of Higher Education.

Favre, D. (1996) "Legal Rights for Our Fellow Creatures," *Contemporary Philosophy* 28(4–5): 7–10.

Francione, G. (2000) *Introduction to Animal Rights: Your Child or the Dog?* Philadelphia: Temple University Press.

Garner, R. (1998) *Political Animals: Animal Protection Politics in Britain and the United States*, New York: St. Martin's.

Hall, Lee (2006) *Capers in the Churchyard: Animal Rights Advocacy in the Age of Terror*, Darien, CT: Nectar Bat Press.

Jasper, M.C. (1997) *Animal Rights Law*, Dobbs Ferry, N.Y.: Oceana.

Munro, L. (2001) *Compassionate Beasts: The Quest for Animal Rights*, Westport, CT: Praeger.

Singer, P. (1998) *Ethics into Action: Henry Spira and the Animal Rights Movement*, Lanham, MD: Rowman and Littlefield.

—— (ed.) (2006) *In Defense of Animals: The Second Wave*, Malden, MA: Blackwell.

Sunstein, Cass R. and Nussbaum, Martha C. (eds.) (2004) *Animal Rights: Current Debates and New Direction*, New York: Oxford University Press.

Waisman, Sonia S., Frasch, Pamela D., and Wagman, Bruce A. (2006) *Animal Law: Cases and Materials*, Durham, N.C: Carolina Academic Press.

Wise, S.M. (2000) *Rattling the Cage: Toward Legal Rights for Animals*, Cambridge, MA: Perseus Books.

—— (2002) *Drawing the Line: Science and the Case for Animal Rights*, Cambridge, MA: Perseus Books.

STUDY QUESTIONS

1   Steven Wise and Richard Posner disagree concerning the role of an animal's cognitive capacity as a basis for legal rights. Which position do you find more convincing? Justify your position.

2   Wise proposes that we recognize "practical autonomy" as sufficient to justify the attribution of basic legal rights. To what degree do you support Wise's proposal? To what degree do the positions of Gómez and Cavalieri in Part Three support such a concept?

3   Richard Epstein discusses a number of negative consequences which follow from the recognition of animal rights. Do you believe that such consequences are likely? Give your reasoning.

4   What is your evaluation of extending legal rights to great apes as described in the article by Kate Douglas? In your view what disadvantages might there be in doing so?

5   Both Posner and Epstein point out that the current legal situation of treating animals as the property of human beings often has a positive effect on animal welfare. To what extent does your own experience ratify this claim?

6   Which of the five characteristics of a religion discussed by Jamison, Wenk, and Parker are characteristic of the animal rights movement, in your experience? Which do not appear to be characteristic? Justify your positions. Can you cite other social reform movements which also share some or all of these religious characteristics?

7   Tom Regan describes the current abolition/reform split in the animal rights movement. Explain which approach you believe to be more effective and why. Under what circumstances, if any, do you believe that violence against property on behalf of animal welfare is morally acceptable?

8   Tom Regan proposes a solution to the abolition/reform split at the end of his article. Do you believe that his solution is workable? Give your reasons.

9   Courtney Dillard analyzes effective civil disobedience. How might the strategies she describes be used in social reform movements not involving animals?

10 Chris DeRose argues that direct action on behalf of animals with the possibility of arrest and jail time is warranted by the injustices suffered by animals. Under what circumstances (if any) do you agree?

11   Peter Singer recommends ten strategies in working to improve the conditions for animals. Which strategies do you believe to be most effective? Justify your choices. Are there others which Singer does not list?

Index